INTRODUCTION TO PSYCHOLOGY

8561

INTRODUCTION TO PSYCHOLOGY

CLIFFORD T. MORGAN

RICHARD A. KING
University of North Carolina

THIRD EDITION

MCGRAW-HILL BOOK COMPANY

*New York   St. Louis   San Francisco
Toronto   London   Sydney*

Illustrations and line work
by Graphic Arts International, New York City, U.S.A.

THE AIM IN this third edition, which is essentially the same as that in the previous two editions, is twofold: to provide a broad coverage of the more important and representative areas of psychology that concern psychologists in the middle of the twentieth century, and to deal in some depth with each topic selected.

Many decisions about what to include and what to exclude have been difficult. One guide has been an idea of what a student should know when he takes a second course in psychology. Further, most of the students in an introductory course will not major in psychology, and we have tried to include information that such students can apply to their fields of interest and to their lives. We hope we have succeeded in presenting a well-rounded, factual, and nontrivial picture of psychology for any student who is getting his first serious introduction to the subject.

Instructors, as well as students, approach the introductory course from different points of view. Instructors, for instance, have different tastes and habits in presenting their courses, and they must adapt to the time available for the course as well as to the needs of their students.

In order to meet these differing needs of students and instructors, the book has been organized flexibly. It provides the instructor with considerable freedom in planning both the material he will cover and the way in which he will cover it. Suggestions in "To the Instructor" include outlines for two different courses for which this book might be used: a life-oriented course and a science-oriented course. These outlines are merely examples and can be adapted by instructors in a variety of ways. The chapters themselves have been written to accommodate alternate courses, and cross references have been provided to explain terms and concepts as they appear. The organization of this third edition has been changed so that a comprehensive course, one including all chapters, can logically follow the present chapter order. Learning and motivation are stressed early—the more applied aspects of psychology later. The chapters on the biological bases of behavior are last because they draw on the concepts developed in the first half of the text. Finally, the glossary at the end of the book aids in using the text however the course is organized.

In the first edition, other psychologists, each expert in his particular field, prepared first drafts of many of the chapters. In the second edition, with the exception of the chapters on social psychology, the text was revised by Dr. Morgan alone. In this third edition, Drs. Morgan and King have collaborated in the revision.

Other people, many of whom must remain nameless, also contributed to the preparation of this new edition. Mrs. Margaret S. King helped with the revision of the chapters on social psychology. Many instructors who taught from the first and second editions gave the benefit of their experience. Credit is given in the legends of the illustrations, and on the acknowledgment page, to the many individuals and publishers who kindly permitted the use of their material.

CLIFFORD T. MORGAN

RICHARD A. KING

TO THE INSTRUCTOR

THIS BOOK HAS been written and organized with the expectation that instructors may sometimes find it necessary to omit chapters and to assign material in an order different from that in the book. Each instructor must make his selection in the light of the time available to him and the needs of his students. In the hope of simplifying this task, we offer here two possible alternative arrangements.

Life-oriented course

THE SCIENCE OF PSYCHOLOGY *(Chapter 1)*

MATURATION AND DEVELOPMENT *(Chapter 2)*

PRINCIPLES OF LEARNING *(Chapter 3)*

HUMAN LEARNING, REMEMBERING, AND FORGETTING *(Chapter 4)*

THINKING AND LANGUAGE *(Chapter 5)*

MOTIVATION *(Chapter 6)*

EMOTION *(Chapter 7)*

PSYCHOLOGICAL MEASUREMENT *(Chapter 11)*

PSYCHOLOGICAL TESTING *(Chapter 12)*

PERSONALITY *(Chapter 13)*

BEHAVIOR DISORDERS *(Chapter 14)*

MENTAL HEALTH AND PSYCHOTHERAPY *(Chapter 15)*

SOCIAL INFLUENCES ON BEHAVIOR *(Chapter 16)*

ATTITUDES *(Chapter 17)*

PSYCHOLOGY IN INDUSTRY *(Chapter 18)*

Science-oriented course

THE SCIENCE OF PSYCHOLOGY *(Chapter 1)*

MATURATION AND DEVELOPMENT *(Chapter 2)*

PRINCIPLES OF LEARNING *(Chapter 3)*

HUMAN LEARNING, REMEMBERING, AND FORGETTING *(Chapter 4)*

THINKING AND LANGUAGE *(Chapter 5)*

MOTIVATION *(Chapter 6)*

EMOTION *(Chapter 7)*

SENSORY PROCESSES AND VISION *(Chapter 8)*

HEARING AND THE OTHER SENSES *(Chapter 9)*

PERCEPTION *(Chapter 10)*

PSYCHOLOGICAL MEASUREMENT *(Chapter 11)*

PSYCHOLOGICAL TESTING *(Chapter 12)*

PERSONALITY *(Chapter 13)*

NERVOUS SYSTEM AND INTERNAL ENVIRONMENT *(Chapter 19)*

PHYSIOLOGICAL BASIS OF BEHAVIOR *(Chapter 20)*

YOU MAY TAKE it for granted that psychology deals with many of the problems of everyday life and thus with many things that you have already experienced; therefore you are in a position to derive some personal benefits from the study of psychology. In a formal college course, however, it is not possible for the instructor to relate everything that you experience to everything that is taught. Hence, to get the most from the course, you should try to make many of these applications yourself. To do that, you must continually ask yourself, "How does this apply to my experience?" and "How can I put to use what I am learning?" By taking such an attitude, you will profit much more from the course than if you simply learn by rote what is assigned.

Here are some suggestions for the reading of each chapter. You might begin by reading the summary. Obviously it does not cover everything that is in the chapter, but it does hit the high spots. After reading the summary, it will usually prove worthwhile to skim the headings before settling down to a careful reading. In the few minutes that it takes to do this, you can add a few details and get the overall organization in mind.

Many students try to read textbooks the way they read novels; they sit passively, running their eyes over the words and hoping that some information will sink in. But textbooks are packed with facts and explanations. To assimilate them, you must work actively at the task, reading every sentence carefully and turning over in your mind what it says and what it means. You would do well to follow the recommendations made in a section of Chapter 4—Techniques of Study. It might be profitable to look at this section before beginning your more detailed study of the text.

Many students fail to grasp the subject they are studying because they do not give sufficient attention to illustrations and tables. In this book, the illustrations and tables are fully as important as the corresponding discussions in the text. When you encounter a reference to one of them, you should turn to it promptly and study it carefully. In some cases, we have used illustrations to teach something that is not included in the text. At appropriate points in your reading, usually before going on to a new heading, you should scan the illustrations to make certain you have examined them and gleaned all you could from them.

Every technical subject uses terms whose definitions must be learned, and psychology is no exception. Ordinarily a definition is given in the text whenever a new term is introduced. Since chapters will not always be assigned in the order of their arrangement in the book, a glossary is included in the back of the book. You should be especially cautious not to neglect a definition just because the term is already familiar to you. Do not, for example, pass over words like "attitude," "personality," "intelligence," and "motive" because these are words that you use in everyday speech. In psychology these and other common terms often have specialized meanings that differ from those commonly employed. To get the most from your study of psychology, make sure you know the *psychological* definitions of all terms.

Science is produced by scientists, and it is common practice in science to ascribe particular experiments and ideas to the scientists who have contributed them. Sometimes this practice is annoying and distracting; so we have tried not to use too many names. But to give credit where credit is due, we have put the names of the experimenters in brackets where particular studies or ideas are cited. These names refer to the reference section at the back of the book where you can find more details if you are interested in finding more about the topic under question.

Two appendices have been added. One is for those students who might be interested in psychology as a professional career. Here will be found information on the training necessary for certain roles in the field of psychology. The other is for students who wish to find more information about topics in psychology. Here you will find information on How to Look It Up. Suggestions for Further Reading are also given at the end of each chapter.

There is also a *Study Guide* that you may purchase and use as an aid in study and review. This guide contains exercises that not only make the study of psychology more interesting but also permit you to assess for yourself how well you have mastered the material.

CONTENTS

INTRODUCTION

PART ONE

1

THE SCIENCE OF PSYCHOLOGY

ALL LIFE IS AN EXPERIMENT.
OLIVER WENDELL HOLMES

NEARLY EVERYONE FEELS that he would be happier and more successful if he "understood people" a little better. The businessman must manage people, the salesman must sell to people, and the physician contends not only with physical illnesses but also with the behavior of the people who have them. Even the man whose work has little to do with people must get along with his wife, his children, his relatives, his fellow workmen, his friends, and his neighbors. Indeed, dealing with people effectively is vital in many aspects of vocational success and in many facets of personal happiness.

THE FIELD OF PSYCHOLOGY This need to understand people better is both a help and a hindrance in undertaking the study of psychology. It helps because it motivates, and one must have motivation to learn. It helps too because the subject is enjoyable for both the student and the teacher.

A ready-made interest in psychology can also be a hindrance in two ways. One is that it leads some students to think they know more about psychology than they really do, just because they have previously taken a keen interest in observing people. Being amateur observers, such students usually have mistaken ideas about psychological matters that need straightening out. Hence, as you study this book you should be prepared to find that, although many of your observations are correct, some of them will not stand up to analysis and close scrutiny. One job of a psychology course is to provide a sound framework for understanding our own behavior as well as that of others.

An interest in psychology may also lead students to expect the wrong things from a course in psychology. They may expect both too much and too little from it.

They expect too much if they look for a few patent remedies to use in solving their personal problems or in seeking success and happiness. No one learns to be a physician, lawyer, engineer, or musician in a single course. Neither can he quickly become a psychologist. In each case, long years of training in the subject and in many related subjects are necessary to become professionally proficient. So, although you will learn much from this book that can be of value in understanding yourself and other people, you must expect to acquire only the rudiments of the subject. It will be enough, perhaps, if the course enables the student to "step back from himself at least a little distance and look at his behavior as an object of study in the world of nature" [Harvard University Commission, 1947].

It is possible also to underestimate the range of topics covered in psychology. How to deal with people or to cope with personal problems, for example, is only one part of psychology. The subject also encompasses problems of social groups, of intelligence and abilities, of work and efficiency, of learning and perception, of the physiological basis of behavior, and of animal behavior—to name just a few. You should therefore be prepared to study a subject of considerable breadth—one that touches on a wider variety of problems than most people realize.

DEFINITION OF PSYCHOLOGY Now let us see specifically what psychology is. If you ask a psychologist to define his subject, he will probably give you the generally accepted definition: *Psychology is the science of human and animal behavior.* Upon hearing this definition, however, the person untrained in psychology is likely to be surprised at three of the important words: "science," "animal," and "behavior." Is psychology really a science?, he may ask. Why "behavior" rather than "mind" or "thoughts" or "feelings"? And why "animal" behavior? What has animal behavior to do with psychology?

Let us consider separately each of these three words, beginning first with science. A *science* is a body of systematized knowledge. Such knowledge is gathered by carefully observing and measuring events, sometimes, but not necessarily, in experiments set up by the scientist to produce the events he is studying. The things and events observed are systematized in various ways, but principally by classifying them into categories and establishing

general laws or principles that describe and predict them as accurately as possible. Science may be distinguished from art in that *art* is skill or knack in doing something that is acquired by study and practice.

Psychology, by these definitions, is both an art and a science. Since an art is something an individual develops, it is difficult to learn it from books and in classroom study. Moreover, artistry in psychology, as in medicine or engineering, is best developed after mastering the subject matter of the underlying science. The psychological arts, as we see them displayed in politics, diplomacy, salesmanship, and other fields, are as yet woefully ineffective in solving our most serious problems in human relationships. On the other hand, through the valiant efforts of many research workers over the last century, there is now a science of psychology—a large body of systematized knowledge—which can be taught and which is the best foundation for developing an understanding of behavior. It is for these reasons that we stress "science" in our definition of psychology and in this book. We wish that we had more scientific knowledge of human behavior; as it is, in some areas we must rely upon primitive observations and some shrewd guesswork. In other areas, the scientific work which has been done leaves much to be desired with regard to control and generality.

We come now to the word *behavior*. Behavior, rather than mind or thoughts or feelings, is the subject of psychology because it alone can be observed, recorded, and studied. No one ever saw, heard, or touched a mind, but one can see, hear, and touch behavior. He can see and measure what a person does, or hear and record what a person says—which is vocal behavior. Anything else must be inferred. We do, indeed, infer that mental processes take place and that people think and feel, but for systematic knowledge of psychological events we are limited to the observation of behavior.

Now, finally, the word *animal*. Science does not arbitrarily limit itself to any one realm of events or to that knowledge which has immediate practical value. In fact, nearly everyone—even our most practical politicians and businessmen—has now learned that pursuing knowledge for its own sake ultimately has great practical value. And animal behavior can be as fascinating a study as human behavior, if not more so. So, just as the zoologist studies the form and function of all members of the animal kingdom, the psychologist systematically observes animal as well as human behavior. Animal behavior is then a legitimate area of study in its own right (see Figure 1.1).

But there is another, equally important reason for studying animal behavior. Many similarities exist between animal and human behavior. In fact, animals display, or can be taught to display in the laboratory, in more rudimentary forms of course, some of the kinds of behavior which people display. Thus a study of animal behavior is a great aid in understanding human behavior. We are able to do many important experiments with animals that we cannot do with people because human beings cannot be treated like guinea pigs. Psychologists therefore frequently use animals to find the answers to many general questions about behavior. For that reason, this book includes many studies of animal as well as human behavior.

THE BEHAVIORAL SCIENCES Although behavior is the subject of psychology, it is by no means the exclusive property of psychology. Several other disciplines make the study of human and animal behavior their business. These include psychiatry, anthropology, sociology, economics, political science, and history. Taken together, these have recently come to be called the *behavioral sciences*. Each of them focuses its attention upon certain aspects of behavior, although differences among them are not always clear-cut.

Sociology and social anthropology are concerned with the behavior of groups of people. Specialists in these fields study the cultures and social structures of various societies or groups of people living together. The sociologist typically deals with modern, literate cultures, such as our own; the anthropologist, with more primitive cultures. Each science has devised its own methods and acquired its own fund

PSYCHOLOGISTS STUDY ANIMAL BEHAVIOR

FIGURE 1.1 *Rat in a Skinner box. The equipment in the background is for recording and programming the experiment. (Photo by Eliot Elisefon.* Life Magazine, © *1958 by Time, Inc.)*

of information. At the present time, however, the lines between them are becoming fainter as they pool their knowledge and apply each other's methods.

History, of course, is a behavioral science because it attempts to reconstruct and understand the events—mostly events of human behavior—that make history. Economics and political science deal, respectively, with economic and political behavior, which are simply the aspects of behavior one sees institutionalized in trade and government. To a certain extent, both subjects are historical sciences because they make use of records of events that have transpired in the past.

The *natural sciences,* such as physics, chemistry, and biology, are *not* primarily behavioral sciences; yet they sometimes have occasion to study behavior. Some of our most useful knowledge about human perception, for example, has come from physicists and biological scientists who ventured to measure human reactions to different kinds of physical stimuli. The anatomists and physiologists, who are primarily concerned with structures and functions of the body, have also contributed greatly to our knowledge of behavior by studying physiological factors related to behavior. The zoologists, finally, have been interested in the classification of animals and have carried out many studies on the behavior of animals. In this way, they have both improved zoological classification and aided the psychologist in his efforts to understand animal behavior.

It is becoming increasingly difficult to establish boundary lines separating the behavioral sciences. Actually there are no such boundary lines; scientists of different labels work at times side by side in overlapping domains, at times separated by territory as yet unexplored. In the general area of behavioral science, psychology is a kind of meeting ground for the natural sciences, such as physics, biology, and physiology, and the social sciences, such as sociology, economics, and political science. Some psychologists are almost physiologists—for example, the physiological psychologists who study the biological basis of behavior; others are almost sociologists—for example, the social psychologists who study the influence of groups upon individual behavior.

The subfields of psychology

Another way to define psychology is to describe what psychologists actually do. Yet such a practical definition of the whole field would be almost unworkable for the activities of psychologists are varied indeed. We can, however, enumerate and describe certain large categories, or subfields, within psychology, and perhaps that endeavor will bring us closer to an understanding of the field as a whole.

The number of professional psychologists in each of the psychological subfields was derived from the 1962 National Scientific Register [Lockman, 1964]. Some of the results appear in Table 1.1. Although there are actually about 25,000 professional psychologists—members of the American Psychological Association—in the United States, the number participating in the study was 9,348. Incidentally, a population explosion appears to be taking place among psychologists, as elsewhere. It has been estimated that there will be 44,000 members of the American Psychological Association by 1970 [Sanford, 1951; and Albee, 1963]. Facetiously, we hope, it has also been estimated that, at the present rate of growth, there will be 59,000,000 psychologists by 2050 [Sanford, 1951; and Albee, 1963]—truly a chilling thought.

The 11 major subfields of psychology and the relations between them are shown in Figure 1.2 [Lockman, 1964]. The area of the rectangles gives an indication of the relative number of psychologists in each of the subfields; an indication of the relationships between the subfields is given by the thickness of the lines between the rectangles. For in-

TABLE 1.1   *The subfields of psychology and the approximate percentage of psychologists in each subfield*

SUBFIELD	NUMBER	PERCENTAGE OF TOTAL
Clinical	3,441	37
Experimental	1,210	13
Counseling	1,000	11
Industrial	866	9
Educational	731	8
School	633	7
Social	527	6
Engineering	293	3
Psychometric	248	3
Developmental	201	2
Personality	198	2
Total	9,348	

SOURCE: *Based on Lockman, 1964.*

stance, a close relationship exists between metrical psychology (measurement and testing) and industrial and educational psychology. Conversely, the experimental and social psychologists seem to have little to do with the other subfields. In the descriptions which follow, an attempt is made to characterize each of these subfields.

CLINICAL PSYCHOLOGY At the present time, clinical psychology is the largest field of specialization in psychology; it employs about 36 to 38 per cent of all psychologists [Clark, 1957; Lockman, 1964]. When the number of individuals in clinical psychology is added to the number in counseling psychology, which is closely related, the percentage swells to about half of the entire profession.

In order to understand better what clinical psychology is, we should first distinguish among three kinds of specialists who do clinical work: psychiatrists, psychoanalysts, and clinical psychologists.

Both *psychiatrists* and *psychoanalysts* hold an M.D. degree, although there are a few nonmedical psychoanalysts. Usually, they have been trained in medicine and then have had specialized training in the diagnosis and treatment of deviant behavior. Such training consists largely of work in psychiatric wards and hospitals and usually does not include any substantial amount of work in psychology. The psychoanalyst is actually a psychiatrist, but he differs from other psychiatrists in that he subscribes to the general theory of personality and treatment of disorders put forth by Sigmund Freud and his followers.

The *clinical psychologist*, on the other hand, takes his basic training in normal psychology, rather than in medicine. After that, usually in the last 2 or 3 years of postgraduate training, he goes on to specialize in psychological diagnosis, psychotherapy, and research into the causes and alleviation of disturbed behavior. His training in diagnosis emphasizes the administration, scoring, and interpretation of psychological tests. His training in *psychotherapy,* like that of the psychiatrist and psychoanalyst, includes training in psychoanalytic tech-

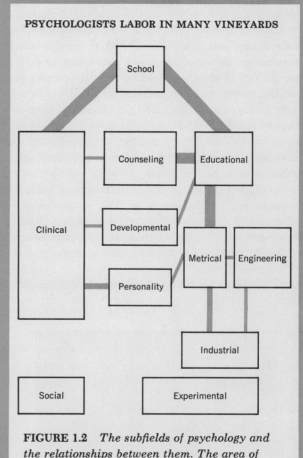

PSYCHOLOGISTS LABOR IN MANY VINEYARDS

FIGURE 1.2 *The subfields of psychology and the relationships between them. The area of each rectangle is an indication of the number of psychologists in a subfield; the degree of relationship between subfields is indicated by the thickness of the lines connecting the rectangles. (Modified from Lockman, 1964.)*

niques and other interview methods of helping patients solve their emotional problems. The term "psychotherapy" refers to psychological methods of treating behavior disorders and maladjustment, as distinguished from shock therapy, drug therapy, and other medical methods of treatment.

The classification and treatment of mental illness

have long been the responsibility of the psychiatrist. He began, however, to enlist the aid of psychologists in his work when he found that intelligence tests helped him estimate what he could accomplish by psychiatric care and treatment. He came to rely on psychologists even more when they developed tests for the assessment of personality. Today he regularly looks to them for aid in *personality diagnosis*. From their tests and professional opinions, as well as from his own interviews and knowledge of case histories, he arrives at a diagnosis and strategy of treatment for mental illness.

For some psychiatrists, aid in diagnosis is all that is expected or accepted from the psychologist. In other cases, the psychologist may also assist in psychotherapy. Certainly most clinical psychologists of recent vintage are trained and equipped to par-

TESTING MAY GIVE VALUABLE INFORMATION

FIGURE 1.3   *Clinical and counseling psychologists use tests of various kinds in measuring abilities and diagnosing personality problems. (New York University Testing and Advisement Center.)*

ticipate in therapeutic work. In many hospitals, especially those of the Veterans' Administration and other public agencies, the need for psychotherapists is unusually great. In such institutions, clinical psychologists frequently undertake considerable psychotherapy. This is less often the case in private practice and private hospitals; here the matter rests with the preferences of the psychiatrist in charge. It should be pointed out, however, that many psychologists, working both in hospitals and in private practice, are currently conducting psychotherapy on their own responsibility. In such cases, they first refer their patients to a physician to determine if any physical complications are present that require medical care.

Although considerable progress has been made in the diagnosis and treatment of mental disorders, we still have a long way to go before we can feel that the problems are reasonably well in hand. There is, therefore, a pressing need for research in this area, as everyone concerned will agree. Since the psychiatrist is trained primarily for *practice* and not for research, whereas the psychologist is typically trained in *research* and its methods, the psychologist has assumed an increasingly responsible role in the field of psychiatric research.

In recent years, the idea has been gaining acceptance that psychiatric diagnosis and care should be in the hands of a psychiatric team consisting of a *psychiatrist*, a *psychologist*, and a *social worker*. In such a team, the psychiatrist has final responsibility for the care of the patient. The psychologist assumes leadership in research and assists in diagnosis and therapy. The social worker provides information about the family and background of the patient.

COUNSELING   The work of the counseling and guidance psychologist is somewhat different from that of the clinical psychologist. The counseling and guidance psychologist works with individuals having less serious problems than those requiring the services of a psychiatric team. He counsels those with emotional or personal problems who need some expert guidance. Thus he serves as a screen to separate those persons who need no more than wise counseling from those who need intensive psychiatric attention (see Figure 1.3).

The counseling and guidance psychologist also helps individuals with vocational and academic problems. Working in schools, in industry, in colleges, and indeed in private practice, he administers tests of intelligence, aptitudes, interests, and personality and gives such guidance as is needed. Often this is a matter of apprising parents of the abilities and limitations of their children, or of helping a student improve his study habits, or of advising him about a vocational choice, or of helping a person work out a minor personal problem. The counseling psychologist may also engage in psychotherapy. When he does, he must always be on the alert for severe emotional problems that should be referred to a psychiatrist or clinical psychologist for a final judgment.

The employment of counseling psychologists has increased substantially in recent years. Many colleges and universities have established psychological clinics or counseling centers. Some of the larger industrial and manufacturing concerns have formal counseling programs to render aid in solving personal problems. Many schools, particularly high schools, are installing counselors whose chief duty is to help students with their vocational and personal problems. Hence this field of psychology is rapidly expanding.

EXPERIMENTAL PSYCHOLOGY Many psychologists (about 13 per cent) are not primarily engaged in work which has a direct application to practical problems. Instead, they are interested in experimental psychology, the aim of which is the understanding of the fundamental causes of behavior—this field tends to be abstract and theoretical. *Sensation and perception, learning and memory, motivation,* and the *physiological basis of behavior* are the primary problems of experimental psychology. In other words, the experimental psychologist would like to know how we are able to experi-

ence our environment and the variables which determine our interpretation of it; he would like to know how behavior is modified and how these modifications are retained; he would like to know what urges us on and gives direction to our behavior; and he would like to know the ways in which the nervous system functions to produce behavioral results. Much of this text is devoted to a consideration of the knowledge which experimental psychologists have obtained about these fundamental problems.

The experimental psychologist is especially fond of controlled experiments. In order to achieve the necessary degree of control, it is often necessary to use animal subjects. Another reason for the use of animal subjects is that it often helps us to understand a process if we can trace its development from simpler to more complex animals. The comparison of the behavior of one species with another and the tracing of the development of processes is the job of the *comparative psychologist. Physiological psychology,* the investigation of the physiological basis of behavior, is another specially named subdivision of experimental psychology (see Figure 1.4).

The use of experimental methods is not unique to experimental psychology; many psychologists who would not be called experimental psychologists use experimental methods. For instance, social and personality psychologists may use experimental designs. Experimental psychology is distinguished as much by its problems as by its methods.

INDUSTRIAL AND ENGINEERING PSYCHOLOGY Some years ago, business and industry made relatively little use of scientific psychology. Recently, though, the situation has been changing. As Table 1.1 shows, an appreciable percentage of psychologists are now employed in industrial and engineering psychology. This field is still growing, and it may well be the next one to undergo the kind of expansion experienced in clinical psychology, counseling, and school psychology.

The first applications of psychology to industrial problems were in the use of intelligence and apti-

THE PHYSIOLOGICAL PSYCHOLOGIST
STUDIES THE RELATIONSHIP OF
BRAIN TO BEHAVIOR

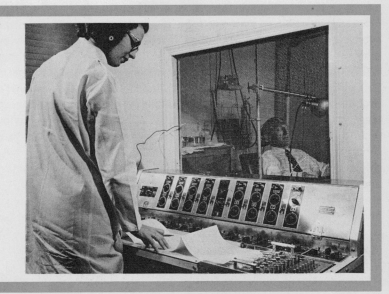

FIGURE 1.4 *An electroencephalogram (EEG) is being recorded so
that the gross electrical activity of the
brain can be studied. (Richard
Saunders, Scope Associates, Inc.)*

tude tests. Today many of the larger business firms have well-established programs of selection and placement that make substantial use of psychological tests. They are also finding other applications of psychology to problems of training, to supervision of personnel, to improving communications, to counseling employees, and to alleviating industrial strife. Psychologists are seldom in managerial positions which would enable them to deal directly with these problems, but they are called upon as consultants. Moreover, an increasing number of businessmen are getting some training in business and industrial psychology.

Firms of industrial psychologists are also growing in number and prestige. They are usually incorporated and sell their services to many different concerns. For one business, they may set up a selection program; for another, they may make recommendations concerning its training program; for another, they may examine the problems of supervision and human relations within the company; and for still another, they may survey consumer attitudes toward products or the effectiveness of the company's advertising. Utilizing the services of nonstaff psychologists seems to appeal to many businesses as being more efficient than employing psy-

chologists on a permanent basis. It has advantages for the psychologists, too, allowing them to become familiar with similar problems in different enterprises and conserving their time for the solution of practical problems rather than enmeshing them in routine nonpsychological duties that are likely to be involved in regular employment. At any rate, the separate firm of psychologists is becoming an established way of putting psychology to work in industry.

World War II opened up another application of psychology to industry, sometimes called *human engineering* or *engineering psychology*. It concerns the *design of equipment,* and the tasks of the individuals who operate such equipment. Thus psychologists have become involved in the design of airplane cockpits, the controls of computers, the design of stoves and refrigerators and many other items. To these design problems, psychologists bring their knowledge of perception, of learning, and of experimental methods of measuring human performance under various conditions. Obviously this application of psychology is of great importance to the military services which are charged with getting the most out of very complex equipment. Human engineers also assist in the design of civilian machines, such as automobiles, stoves, lathes, cranes, locomotives, and printing presses, to name just a few. We are beginning to see more applications in this direction (see Figure 1.5).

SCHOOL AND EDUCATIONAL PSYCHOLOGY

Those counseling psychologists who are involved in the testing and guidance of individual students are usually called *school psychologists*. Testing provides information which can be useful in the diagnosis and disposition of behavior difficulties. A large part of the work of the school psychologist consists of working with students who need some sort of special attention. For instance, the school psychologist may recommend, after a study of the case, that a student with reading difficulties be assigned to a remedial-reading class; students with mild adjustment problems may be counseled by the school psychologist. In some colleges and universities, school psychologists are employed to evaluate and administer the tests used in the selection of new students. Some school psychologists may do a great deal of vocational counseling, but most of this work is done by *school counselors* who have specialized in testing and counseling courses in a department of education. In practice, the difference between school psychologists and school counselors is often not clear.

Educational psychology may include school psychology, but educational psychologists as such are usually concerned with more general, less immediate, problems than the majority of school psychologists or school counselors. Educational psychologists are especially concerned with increasing the efficiency of learning in school through the application of psychological knowledge about learning and motivation.

SOCIAL PSYCHOLOGY

We all belong to many different kinds of groups—our family, our social class, an informal friendship clique, to mention a few. The groups we belong to affect our behavior and shape our attitudes about many things. Social psychologists devote themselves to the study of the effects of group membership upon individual behavior. Social psychology merges into sociology, but a distinction can be made between the two disciplines: the primary interest of the social psychologist is the ways in which individual behavior is influenced by group membership; the sociologist is much more concerned with the group as such—its structure and formal characteristics. In his quest for information concerning group effects on individual behavior, the social psychologist may use various methods of study, experimental and otherwise.

ENGINEERING PSYCHOLOGY HELPS FIT MEN TO MACHINES

FIGURE 1.5 *A personal jet propulsion system. The design of such complex systems often involves engineering psychology. (Aerospace Medical Research Laboratories, Wright-Patterson Air Force Base, Ohio.)*

Techniques of attitude measurement have been developed and perfected by social psychologists.

Social psychology also has its practical side. For instance, many private agencies, such as the National Conference of Christians and Jews, the American Jewish Congress, and the National Association for the Advancement of Colored People, have become acquainted with the facts and principles that psychologists have uncovered concerning matters of prejudice. In some instances, they employ psychologists who have conducted research on prejudice and who advise them concerning strategies for combating it. Municipal and state agencies engaged in dealing with crime and delinquency also make use of social psychologists and their skills in waging their battles for healthier communities.

Aside from such social problems as prejudice, crime, and delinquency, our leaders in government are relying more and more on information collected by polling techniques to find out what people think about important issues. During the Depression, when the government undertook to help the farmers out of their dire economic plight, psychologists made careful surveys of what farmers wanted most, what kinds of controls they were willing to accept as necessary for their own betterment, and their attitudes toward numerous policies designed to improve their lot. Often these surveys made it clear that schemes based on sound economic principles would fail solely because people held negative attitudes toward them. In other cases, campaigns were conducted to educate and inform farmers on important problems. Our Treasury Department, in its efforts to increase wartime savings and to combat inflation, often based its decisions on how to sell government bonds on information about people's savings habits and attitudes collected through polling techniques. These are just a few ways in which survey methods developed by social psychologists are put to work in the interest of the general welfare and the better solution of social problems.

PSYCHOMETRIC PSYCHOLOGY   Tests and other devices for measuring human abilities are the province of the psychometrician. He is concerned with the development of new tests, research on the usefulness and stability of tests, and the development of statistical techniques. Psychometricians supply some of the tools used by psychologists in the applied fields of school, counseling, industrial, and clinical psychology. Those who are primarily responsible for giving and scoring tests are sometimes called *psychometrists* rather than psychometricians.

DEVELOPMENTAL PSYCHOLOGY   Developmental psychologists study and describe behavioral changes which accompany changes in age. Since behavior and abilities change most rapidly during the first few years of life, *child psychology* is used as a synonym for a great deal of developmental psychology. Behavioral changes with age at the other end of life, old age, are also much studied by developmental psychology. Developmental psychology has both research and applied aspects. For instance, a great deal of research has been done on the development of thinking in children. Are progressive and systematic changes taking place in the nature of thought as a child grows older? On the applied side, developmental psychologists may work with disturbed children. The kinds of deviant behavior and the methods of treatment used are quite different from those which would be used with adults by clinical psychologists.

PERSONALITY PSYCHOLOGY   The interests of personality psychologists and clinical psychologists overlap to a great degree. Both are primarily interested in the individual case. Beyond this, there are differences in emphasis. For instance, clinical psychologists typically apply knowledge to the amelioration of deviant behavior; personality psychologists are largely concerned with understanding the nondeviant individual case.

A wide range of techniques and strategies are used by the personality psychologist. In order to find out more about the person under study, he may make carefully recorded observations in naturalistic settings, use interviews, or give psychological tests.

In order to develop general principles which may aid in the understanding of behavior, the personality psychologist may do experiments under carefully controlled conditions—either in the laboratory or in more natural settings. The ways in which a personality psychologist seeks information which may help him in understanding a single case are largely determined by the particular personality theory that he holds. Personality theories are general statements about the factors which determine individual behavior. For instance, the Freudian personality theory states that much behavior is due to the expression of unconscious motives; stimulus-response (S-R) theories stress learning as the prime determiner of individual behavior. The Freudian personality theorist would probably use the special free-association interview technique; the stimulus-response personality theorist would be likely to use controlled experimentation. Whatever the theory or method, the aim of the personality psychologist is the understanding of the causes or dynamics of the behavior of an individual.

Psychology as science

We have said that psychology is both an art and a science, but we have elected to stress its scientific aspects. In support of this emphasis, we can point to the scientific characteristics of psychology, its uses of scientific methods, and its employment of theory as a scientific tool.

SCIENTIFIC CHARACTERISTICS OF PSYCHOLOGY Psychology as a science is, first of all, *empirical.* That is to say, it rests on experiment and observation, rather than on argument, opinion, or belief. The psychologist does experiments which other psychologists can repeat; he obtains data, usually making quantitative measurements, that another can verify. This approach is to be distinguished from forming opinions on the basis of experience, or reporting experiences that few others have had or can have, or arguing from premises that no one can test.

Not that scientists do not have opinions or do not, occasionally, argue with one another. Indeed, scientists often disagree on the interpretation of results. Scientists must also reason by inference: for example, since A = B and B = C, they infer that A = C. If the scientist had only his opinions and inferences, however, he would have no science. What makes his science secure as science are the unarguable facts, the observations which he has made and which others can check, and the instances of A = B and B = C with which no knowledgeable person can argue. Also of crucial importance is his ability to do *research* and through it to establish new observations. Without research his science would become static. He would not be able, as he now is, to erase gradually the areas of ignorance and conflicting opinion. Through research, psychology already has acquired a wealth of facts and is continuing to amass additional ones. In a later section of this chapter, we consider in more detail what psychological research means.

Psychology is also *systematic.* Observations, though essential to science, are by themselves of little use. They can be selected to suit one's purpose, or acquired without any purpose at all, piling up in a disorderly, meaningless array. What is important in science is that observations "make some sense"; they must be capable of being summarized economically by a limited number of principles. The principles may be merely a system of classification, such as we find in zoology, or they may be rather precise laws stating the order or relationship among the phenomena observed, such as we meet, for example, in physics. In any case, we attempt in science to systematize our observations in an orderly and economical way.

The effort to develop a science follows a circular path from observations to principles and back again to observations. The first part of the circle has been called *induction.* We make observations wherever we can, without too much rhyme or reason to them, and then, after careful analysis, we attempt to formulate tentative principles that we think pretty well summarize our observations. Next we trace the part of the circle called *deduction*. We reason that, if our analysis is correct, we should be able to predict observations not yet made. We then set out to collect new observations according to some plan that will test the adequacy of our tentative principles. Sometimes our tentative principles prove to be wholly or partly wrong; at other times, they are correct. If our analysis is wrong, we analyze our results again and test this new deduction. Even if the analysis is correct, our work does not cease. Either we will wish to analyze at a more fundamental level, or the confirmed deduction will suggest other analyses. It is a truism that every confirmed deduction shows up the need for further analysis and research. There are no "final" answers in science. But by systematically following the path from observations to principles to observations, we are continually formulating, modifying, and extending principles to accord with observations.

Another distinguishing feature of science is *measurement*. Almost all of us take it for granted that each science measures things. We rank highest among the sciences the one that has developed the most precise measurements. For that reason, physics is usually credited with being the most "scientific" of the sciences because its measurements are so precise. Actually, measurement is not always essential to science. In a field such as zoology, for example, the important principles may consist of a systematic classification of the members of the animal kingdom. Such a classification is not measurement in the strict sense of the word. In psychology, too, we learn classifications of different kinds of behavior. However, most of our problems are questions of "more than" or "less than." We would like to know, for example, whether children of highly intelligent parents are brighter than those of less intelligent parents. To answer a question such as this, we need measurements that tell us *how intelligent* both parents and children are. Since most psychological problems are quite complex, it has not been easy to devise methods of measurement for studying them. Later in the book we summarize the methods that have been devised. Although we usually do not delve into the details of such measurements, almost every discussion in this book is rooted in the measurement of behavior.

Careful *definition* of terms is essential to clear thinking in science. This is especially true in psychology where we would like to give precise definitions to terms which are used imprecisely in everyday language. For example, can we find some way to give such terms as intelligence, memory, motivation, learning, attention, and emotion definitions that will convey the same meaning from one psychologist to the next? Can we find a way to make sure that psychologist X knows what psychologist Y is referring to when he is using the concept of "intelligence"? The trick in science, and in psychology, is to define concepts by relating them to something observable.

One way of making sure that we are defining concepts in terms of observables is to use *operational definitions* [Bridgman, 1927]. When we define a concept operationally, we define it in terms of measurable and observable operations. For example, the concept of length is defined in terms of observable measuring operations—How many times was the ruler put down when measuring a table? In psychology, such concepts as intelligence may be defined in terms of the observable operations performed to measure them; intelligence might be operationally defined as a score on a certain test. With a definition of this sort, many of the vague and emotional meanings of the concept of intelligence are lost. For purposes of scientific communication, this is exactly what is wanted; what is lost in richness is gained in precision. We are now sure that psychologist X and psychologist Y are talking about the same thing when they are talking about intelligence; they are talking about a score on a test.

Although not related to measuring operations, we have already used another operational definition when defining psychology. We can observe the professional behavior of those who call themselves psychologists. An operational definition of psychology simply consists of a description of the professional behavior of these people. Similarly, memory, motivation, learning, and attention may be described operationally, that is, in terms of observables.

METHODS OF PSYCHOLOGY How can we find out about behavior in a systematic and scientific way? There are many ways of making observations in psychology. The *experimental methods* are used to investigate behavior which can be brought into the laboratory and studied under controlled conditions. The method of *systematic observation* is used to study behavior in situations which cannot be controlled or manipulated by the observer. When using this method, the psychologist observes and analyzes "nature's experiments." Finally, by intensive study of the problems and behaviors of an individual person, it is possible to understand the individual and to arrive at some general principles of behavior. This method of studying the problems and behaviors of a single person is termed the *clinical method.* We shall now examine each of these methods of investigation in a little more detail.

Experimental methods. The essence of the experimental methods is simple. The experimenter: (1) changes or varies something, (2) keeps other conditions constant, and (3) looks for an effect of the change or variation upon the system he has under observation (see Figure 1.6). Since psychology is the science of *behavior,* the experimenter looks for an effect of the changes he has made upon behavior. Simple enough, but let us look at the experimental methods in greater detail.

First of all, the experimental methods involve *variables.* A variable, as the word implies, is something which varies. Ideally, it is a condition which can be measured and varies quantitatively. In Figure 1.7, for example, one variable, altitude, can be varied in feet; the other variable is the amount of light required to make an object just visible to an observer. The amount of light may be varied in standard light units. In many cases, however, a variable may be merely the presence or absence of a condition. Suppose that we wish to do an experiment to determine the effects of a tranquilizing drug

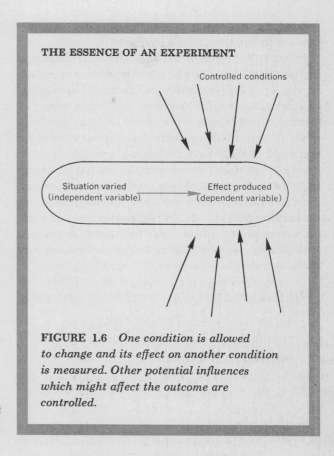

THE ESSENCE OF AN EXPERIMENT

Controlled conditions

Situation varied
(independent variable)

Effect produced
(dependent variable)

FIGURE 1.6 *One condition is allowed to change and its effect on another condition is measured. Other potential influences which might affect the outcome are controlled.*

on memory span as measured by the number of digits which can be repeated after hearing a list of them repeated once. Here we might simply compare the performance of groups of subjects with and without tranquilizers. In this example, the tranquilizer is a variable because one group of subjects gets it whereas the other does not.

Variables may be either independent or dependent. An *independent variable* is a condition set by or selected by the experimenter—a stimulus presented, a drug administered, or so many feet of altitude. The *dependent variable* is the subject's behavior or report—his response to a stimulus, his score on an intelligence test, or his report of seeing or not seeing a light. The dependent variable is called dependent because its value depends, or may depend, on the value of the independent variable, the one independently set by the experimenter.

In every experiment we must have at least one independent variable and one dependent variable. In the preceding example, the tranquilizer was an independent variable because we could vary its amount—in this case all or none—independently of other factors in the experiment. Memory span, on the other hand, was a dependent variable because we were interested in whether or not variations in memory span could depend upon the tranquilizer.

In some experiments, we may have more than one dependent variable. In the tranquilizer experiment, for example, we could have had more dependent variables by measuring other things besides memory span, say, speed of reaction.

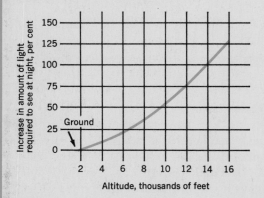

DEPENDENT VARIABLES ARE PLOTTED ON THE VERTICAL AXIS; INDEPENDENT VARIABLES, ON THE HORIZONTAL AXIS

FIGURE 1.7 *In plotting the results of experiments in psychology, the horizontal axis represents the independent variable—in this case, altitude; the vertical axis represents the dependent variable—in this case, the percentage of increase in the amount of light required to see at night (After Millikan, 1948.)*

When the results of an experiment are presented in a graph, it is customary to let the horizontal axis (also called the *abscissa* or *x* axis) represent the independent variable and the vertical axis (also called the *ordinate* or *y* axis) the dependent variable. Figure 1.7, for example, shows the results of an experiment on the effects of high altitude (lack of oxygen) on visual sensitivity [Millikan, 1948]. The experimenter simulated altitude by varying the amount of oxygen in a sealed chamber. Altitude, or oxygen, then, was the independent variable; it is plotted on the horizontal axis. The subjects were tested at different altitudes for the amount of light necessary to see a standard test object. This light, expressed as a percentage of increase in the amount required at ground level, is the dependent variable and is plotted in the vertical axis of the graph. Thus, the convention for plotting graphs permits us to identify at a glance the independent and dependent variables.

Another very important characteristic of the experimental methods is *control*. In an experiment, it is important that only the variables be allowed to change. Factors other than the independent variable, which might possibly affect the dependent variable must be held in check. It would do no good to study the effects of varying an independent variable while other factors, unknown to the experimenter, varied also. In an experiment we must *control* variables or conditions which will give misleading results. Two main strategies are used to control extraneous variables. One strategy uses *control groups;* in the other, each *subject serves as his own control.*

Suppose that we decide to use the control-group method in the experiment on the effects of tranquilizers on memory span. Ideally, we wish to have a control group composed of subjects *matched* with those of the experimental group in every relevant way except one—the experimental subjects receive the tranquilizer whereas the control subjects do not. If the two groups are alike in every respect except the independent variable, we are then able to say with some confidence that any differences in the dependent variable of memory span are due to the tranquilizer.

What are some of the factors which might affect the results and which must be controlled? Obviously we would want the subjects in the control and experimental groups to be equal in memory span before the experiment. To make certain of this, we would probably give all the subjects a preliminary memory-span test and assign them to the control and experimental groups so that individual differences in memory span were equalized in the two groups. Variables such as intelligence, sex of the subject, and so forth, which do not seem to be so immediately relevant, might also be controlled by matching the subjects.

In drug experiments of this kind, another not-so-obvious variable should also be controlled. The subjects might be influenced by the knowledge that they have been given a tranquilizer; they might try to act as they *think* they should under the effect of a tranquilizer. To control this possibility, the control subjects would be given inactive pills, called *placebos*, which appear identical to the tranquilizer pills. Subjects therefore do not know whether they are in the experimental or control group. The technique of not letting subjects know which group they are in is called the *single-blind technique.*

At this point, you will probably feel that things have been well controlled. There is, however, another difficulty. The experimenter knows, when he gives the memory-span test, which subjects are in the experimental and control groups. How can this affect the results? After all, experimenters are supposed to be honest—the unforgivable sin in science is the falsification of results. However, a substantial number of experiments indicate that the experimenter, in good faith, can influence, unconsciously and in subtle ways, the outcomes of experiments [Rosenthal, 1964]. These outcomes tend to be influenced in the direction desired by the experimenter. Human subjects presumably pick up subtle guiding cues from the experimenter.

The obvious way to control for this effect is to keep the experimenter in the dark about which subjects are in which group. A person who never has any contact with the subjects may assist the experimenter by assigning code numbers to the subjects. The experimenter who does not know the code can then run the subjects without knowing whether they are in the experimental or control groups. This technique of disguising group membership from both the subjects and the experimenter is known as the *double-blind technique.*

Perhaps better control can be achieved more easily when *each subject serves as his own control.* The same tranquilizer–memory span experiment will serve as our example. This time we simply select subjects and look at the *difference* in the memory-span behavior of each subject *before* and *after* administration of the drug. Again, we must be careful to make sure that neither the experimenter nor the subject knows when the subject has been given the drug. With this technique, there is no need to control the initial memory-span behavior and certain other relevant variables; they are always the same for the subject because he remains constant while the experiment is taking place.

Unfortunately, the use of this before-and-after technique of using each subject as his own control introduces another problem. Practice effects may obscure the results. For instance, if a series of trials is given in which the subject sometimes receives the tranquilizer and sometimes not, he may get better in memory span as more and more trials are given. Fortunately, there are often ways of controlling these practice effects. When practice effects are not so great as to preclude its use, this before-and-after method probably gives the best control over irrelevant variables.

An especially powerful variant of the method of using every subject as his own control is one in which *baselines* are used [Sidman, 1960]. In baseline technique, the subject is first given training until a stable level of performance is reached. Next, the experimental variable is introduced and changes in the stable baseline are noted. In addition to all the advantages outlined for the before-and-after method, the baseline method provides a constant

baseline—animals

starting point from which the changes in behavior can be measured. Controls of this sort are often used in experiments with animals, and we shall see examples of them later.

Many experiments are described in this book. Control is an important feature in each of them. What is controlled varies with the case. For example, let us say that we want to study the effects of heredity and environment. In order to control the factor of heredity, we try to find twins who have identical heredity; then we put them in different environments and observe how they differ in behavior. In another instance, we may be interested in an area of the brain. One control is to take some animals or human beings who are similar in most respects, but who differ in that some have had an area of the brain damaged while others have not. By comparing the behavior of the two groups, we can ascertain what that brain area has to do with behavior. Another technique of control, of course, could be a comparison of the subjects before and after the damage to the brain area.

It is literally true that an experiment is no better than its controls. The careful student will be critical of the controls in an experiment. He will look for uncontrolled variables which might make the results of an experiment inconclusive. It is a mark of scientific sophistication to be able to spot defects in experimental controls. As you go on into the original literature in psychology or other experimental sciences, you should develop this skill. And keep your sense of humor—you will need it.

Repetition is another important aspect of experimental methods. We can repeat an experiment. In elementary chemistry, for example, we can demonstrate that water is made up of oxygen and hydrogen simply by burning hydrogen (that is, combining it with oxygen) and collecting the water that results. Anyone with the proper equipment can do this experiment, and it has been done repeatedly. In psychology, for example, we can demonstrate that recitation is an aid to study by having two groups of students study something, one with recitation and one without, and later measuring differences in learning. This and other experiments can be repeated.

The advantages of repetition are probably obvious. If we are able to repeat an observation over and over again under controlled conditions, we can be sure of it beyond all reasonable doubt. Then, too, the same experiment can be done by different people. A scientist in England and one in the United States can do the experiment, and though widely separated in time or place, they can agree on the same observations. Agreement between different observers is an important advantage. Indeed, it is a kind of "check-up-ability"—as one distinguished scientist, J. B. Conant, has called it—that is essential to science. Finally, the repeatability of an experiment makes it convenient. We can do it at will, without waiting for the next opportunity to make a casual observation. This convenience lets us create such opportunities at our pleasure; it saves a lot of time that otherwise would be wasted waiting for the right observation.

The experimental method also has *limitations*. In many ways the experiment is the best method the scientist has, and he uses it whenever he can. It is such a good method that scientists often neglect to point out its disadvantages, but knowing them is of some value in appreciating the data it yields.

Perhaps the most obvious shortcoming is that *it cannot always be used.* Physicists, chemists, and other natural scientists do not face this difficulty often, because the lights, sounds, and chemicals that they work with never object to their experiments. People and animals are not so docile; they are not always willing to cooperate. It is hardly possible, for example, to experiment with what makes a happy marriage—for obvious reasons. We dare not experiment with many things in psychology.

A second limitation of the experiment is that *it is artificially arranged by the scientist.* In an attempt to uncover important variables, the psychologist must select particular ones. To do this, he must often be something of a detective and act on hunches or suspicions. In selecting his variables, he may be fortunate enough to pick those which are significant; but he may have bad luck and do an experiment that actually means nothing. Worse yet, he may have an experiment that seems to mean something that it really does not mean. Indeed, the scientist and psychologist must continually stand on guard against false conclusions that come from limited and somewhat artificial experiments. No matter how careful they are, they can make mistakes.

A final limitation of the experiment is that *it sometimes interferes with the very thing it attempts to examine.* Physicists long ago discovered, in the field of quantum mechanics, that their experiments sometimes interfered with the behavior of small particles so that their measurements of this behavior were in error. Psychologists have even more trouble on this account.

Consider, for example, the attempt of the psychologist to find out how people fatigue when they are exposed to loud noises for a long time. He brings people into the laboratory and subjects them to loud noises (the independent variable). Then he measures their performance with all sorts of tests (the dependent variables) only to find—he thinks— no fatigue. It turns out that when people know they are in an experiment they are highly motivated to perform well and will not show the fatigue they might exhibit under normal circumstances. Or, to take another example, if a psychologist brings subjects into an experiment in which they know that their personalities are being studied, they are usually not their normal selves, but may show quite unusual aspects of their personality. Hence the possibility that people or animals may not behave in an experiment as they normally do is something we have to consider seriously in psychological experiments.

Systematic observation. What alternatives to the experimental methods do we have? One alternative has no generally accepted name, but we shall call it the *method of systematic observation.* Others call it the survey method. Whatever the name, it is similar to the experimental method in that variables are measured, but it is different in that one cannot willfully manipulate these variables—nature has already done this for him. The researcher simply makes the most systematic study he can of conditions as he finds them.

Consider the problem of studying marriage. We cannot study it experimentally, but we can look at it scientifically with survey techniques. The following paragraphs describe a famous study of marriage by Professor Terman of Stanford University [1938]:

Terman sought out 792 married couples. He was careful to select them from different income levels (one variable), from different age groups (another variable), from different occupations (another variable), and from different educational groups (still another variable). In fact, he had even more variables than that.

By using many subjects and collecting data from them in a systematic fashion, he was able to reach several conclusions about the causes of successful marriages. One, for example, is that the happiness of a couple depends partly on how well matched they are in strength of sex drive. By giving each couple a standardized questionnaire about their marital relations, then scoring it objectively, he was able to obtain a "happiness score." Also, by asking each spouse to rate his or her own sex drive and that of the partner, he could correlate differences in strength of sex drive with happiness. He found that happiness is greatest when the drive of the two spouses is about the same, and is less when one spouse is considerably more or less passionate than the other.

This study of marriage provides an example of correlating the answers to different questions on a questionnaire given to a large representative group. In other cases, it may be possible to select groups that differ on some objective basis and then, by interviewing, to determine psychological reasons for the group differences. The following example is drawn from an industrial situation [Katz et al., 1950]:

A large insurance company, like many companies, found that it had some groups of clerical workers within its organization that were producing a relatively large amount of work, while other groups were low producers. It wanted to know whether the leadership of the groups had anything to do with productivity. It selected twelve high-producing

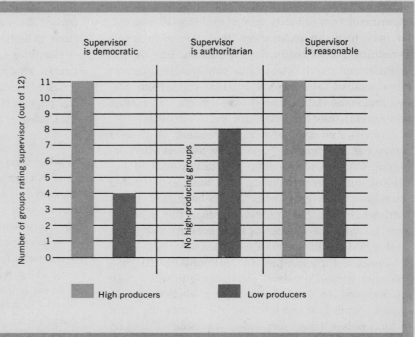

THE METHOD OF SYSTEMATIC OBSERVATION, LIKE THE EXPERIMENTAL METHOD, YIELDS SCIENTIFIC RESULTS

FIGURE 1.8 *In this example of systematic observation, most high-producing groups in the office of a large insurance company regarded their supervisors as democratic and reasonable; several of the low-producing groups considered their supervisors authoritarian. (Based on data from Katz et al., 1950.)*

groups and twelve low-producing groups, matched well for number of workers in the groups, for the ages of the workers, and for the kind of work done. This matching was necessary in order to "control" such variables as size of group, age, and kind of work. The members of the groups were interviewed about their opinions of their supervisors. Did they consider the supervisor to be democratic or authoritarian? Did they consider him reasonable?

The results are summarized in Figure 1.8. Eleven out of twelve of the high-producing groups thought their supervisor was both democratic and reasonable, while none thought him to be authoritarian. Several of the low-producing groups, on the other hand, regarded their supervisor as authoritarian rather than democratic and reasonable. From such results, it could be concluded that the personality of the leader, as perceived by the subordinates, was clearly related to their production.

Survey-type methods are applicable to a large number of problems—the study of public opinion and the factors affecting it, the effects of advertising on consumer purchases, factors involved in success in college, and even such basic questions as the role of heredity and environment in the development of intelligence, to name just a few examples. Today these methods of systematic observation are contributing much to the science of psychology, particularly to our knowledge of personality, social processes, and industrial problems.

Clinical methods. Clinical methods ordinarily are used only when people come to psychologists with problems. Little Alice is doing badly in school, and her parents bring her to the psychologist to find out why. Little Basil is throwing temper tantrums, not eating his meals, crying all night, and generally making life miserable for his parents. Chumly, an otherwise fine young boy in high school, is caught stealing nickels from the Sunday school collection plate. Or young Mr. Squabble, married for 5 years, comes in worried because he and his wife just cannot get along. Such examples could go on endlessly. All are people with problems who come to the clinical psychologist for help.

Not all clinical problems require thorough study, but when they do, the psychologist usually begins by getting a detailed account of the person's past history, and of his family relations. He usually gathers this from interviews with the person and his associates. Very often he may have a specially trained social worker study the social background and environment of the person.

Then the psychologist will use tests of various kinds that have been developed through previous research. He may use intelligence tests, reading tests, interest tests, tests of emotional maturity and personality, or any of a large number he has at his command. From these and the biographical information, he will try to make a diagnosis of the problem—and then he will take steps to try to remedy it. The tests, the diagnosis, and the remedy will vary with the individual cases. We shall study later in more detail some of the problems dealt with by clinical psychologists.

We are concerned here with the clinical method as a tool in science. As a method, it combines features of systematic observation, experiment, and survey. Working with individual cases, the clinician may *observe* some datum he considers to be important. By observation of cases, for example, Sigmund Freud discovered that dreams often reflect strong desires that people have but are unconscious of. In general, however, clinical observation does not provide much scientific information. It is usually too subjective, casual, uncontrolled, and lacking in precise measurement. What appear to be cause and effect in one case may not be in another. Even in a single case it is extremely difficult to sort out with certainty the significant causal factors. Probably the greatest value that clinical observation has is that it suggests fruitful ideas which may be investigated more rigorously by experimental and survey methods.

THEORY IN SCIENTIFIC PSYCHOLOGY Having reviewed methods of collecting observations in psychology, we should complete the picture by indicating the role of theory in psychology.

To the layman the word "theory" sometimes has an unsavory connotation. It may mean simply somebody's unsupported and unfounded notion of how things ought to be done. Or it may mean a set of principles obtained from books or highly artificial situations that do not work out very well in practice. Even in science, we have had some theories that turned out to be wrong or misleading.

Theory, nevertheless, is an important part of science. In fact, it is one of the chief objectives of science, for science makes its greatest advances when it arrives at theories which neatly summarize many observations and predict accurately what can be expected to happen in new situations. Theory in science serves three important functions.

It serves, first, as a sort of *scientific shorthand*. A theory can summarize and generalize a lot of observations. In physics, for example, the law of gravitation is a very simple way of summarizing a host of observations about apples, stones, and feathers falling to the ground and about planets moving in their orbits. Instead of spelling out a great array of physical observations, the law of gravitation very neatly and briefly encompasses them all. In psychology, we have developed a principle—the principle of reinforcement—that the behavior of people and animals is strengthened or weakened by the use of reward or punishment, respectively. This, in a sense, is a theory that may not be entirely correct, but it is useful because it summarizes the essence of literally hundreds of experiments about learning. Hence a theory, to the extent that it states laws or principles, is a useful shorthand way of summarizing observations.

Theory is also a *predictor*. It lets us tell in advance—given certain conditions—what will happen. And the ultimate object of all science is to predict. If science were just the collection of observations, and if one could never predict from one set of observations to another, there would be little point in science. It would do us little good to find out something, because it would never apply to any other situation. A well-developed theory is like a model house or a road map. A map, for example, depicts many of the features of a geographical area, but not all of them. Its main purpose is to tell us how we may travel in the area. Similarly, a theory lays out for us in advance many of the important features of an area of knowledge. A good map must be reasonably accurate, but it cannot tell us everything about an area. Likewise, to be useful, a theory must represent fairly well the observations it encompasses, but it need not be perfectly accurate or predict every possible detail.

Another important use for theory, even if a theory is inaccurate or wrong, is to *guide* us in collecting further observations in research. It was a theory about the nature of the atom that led atomic scientists to the experiments that resulted in the atomic bomb. It was a theory, that reward and punishment are necessary for learning, that led to many experiments whose results eventually changed our methods of education. In these and many other cases, theories have been guides for research, and they have been the basis on which scientists decided how to take their next steps in making observations. When a theory is wrong or inadequate, the discrepancy is soon discovered in the course of the experiments and we discard the theory. When it is correct or largely correct, we keep it and use it as a guide for other experiments that add further details to our knowledge.

Origins of psychology

A description of the field of psychology is one aim of this chapter. Toward that end, we can take another tack—the historical approach. An understanding of the origins of psychology should help us to appreciate psychology as a discipline and science. Two general trends—one concerned with the questions asked, the other with methods—bear our attention.

TREND IN PROBLEMS   Man has been curious about himself ever since he has been able to think abstractly. We have changed the wording, but since the beginning we have wrestled with such questions

as: How do we experience the world around us? What is the relationship, if any, between our experience of the world and the working of our body? Can we measure experience and behavior? Under what conditions do we learn things? What are the roles of environment and heredity, or nurture and nature, in producing behavior? Why do people differ so much in temperament and behavior? Why do some people have severe behavior problems? None of these problems has been satisfactorily resolved; plenty of work is still to be done. One very broad generalization about the approach to these problems is that the major emphasis in psychology has shifted from the study of mental, that is, inner, processes and experience to external, or observable, behavior. This is why we defined psychology as the science of *behavior*. Let us hasten to point out that this shift is only one of emphasis. Early psychologists were relatively more concerned with attempts to measure and understand the mind, while later psychologists are generally more concerned with attempts to measure and understand behavior. However, psychology has not yet lost its mind.

TREND IN METHODS   The history of psychology has been characterized by an increasing use of the empirical method—the appeal to observation as the way of answering questions. Most psychologists prefer to rely upon verifiable observations rather than upon intuition or fiat from prestigious authorities. Such effort has almost invariably met resistance from groups who feel that their beliefs might be upset or their accepted authorities challenged by new observations or by principles based on them. Historically, this resistance was first shattered in settling questions about the physical world; hence physics and chemistry were first established as sciences. It took longer to overcome opposition to probing the world of living things and thus to put biology, psychology, and the social sciences on an empirical basis. Even today a hue and cry is raised when psychological data that run counter to established attitudes are brought forth. Nevertheless, psychology continues to prosper as an empirical science.

Before the dawn of modern science, observation and the interpretation of data were the business of the *philosopher*. Beginning with the ancient Greeks, philosophers learned a great deal about the world around them, attempted to arrange their learning in an orderly way, and speculated on its meaning. Thus philosophy became the parent of our modern departments of knowledge. As philosophers increased their knowledge, they developed specialities within the field of philosophy. Natural philosophy dealt with areas now included under physics, chemistry, and the natural sciences; mental philosophy was concerned with what is now the field of psychology; and moral philosophy considered many of the social problems now encompassed by the social sciences. Thus philosophy is the parent of our modern sciences, both natural and social. This fact is still reflected in the awarding of the Ph.D. (doctor of philosophy) degree to postgraduate students in such diverse subjects as chemistry, psychology, and economics.

Sooner or later, the new sciences, like most children, had to leave the fold. What gave tremendous impetus to the movement, however, was the discovery of a new method, the *experimental* method. As we have seen, the method of systematic observation limits the scientist to observing the events and things that nature has provided for him, and observing them, moreover, under nature's conditions. The experimental method, on the other hand, enables the scientist to make those events happen which he needs to observe in order to develop a science, and to do this under conditions of his own choosing.

Physicists and chemists were the first to discover and exploit the experimental method. With the aid of this method, they formulated many of the principles of physics and chemistry still taught today. In time, physicists and physiologists began to experiment on some of the problems encompassed in psychology, such as color vision, hearing, and brain functions, which we shall study later. As these problems yielded to the experimental method, it became more and more evident that psychology, like the other sciences, could forge ahead only by developing experimental methods suited to its own unique problems.

In 1860, Gustav Fechner (1801–1887) published a book, *Elemente der Psychophysik,* which is taken by some to mark the beginning of experimental psychology. This book was concerned with the measurement of sensory experience. In 1879, Prof. Wilhelm Wundt (1832–1920) founded the first laboratory of psychology at the University of Leipzig in Germany. Perhaps the first laboratory actually came before that, because William James at Harvard was known to be doing experiments too. In any event, experimental laboratories of psychology mushroomed rapidly as the movement got under way. In the United States, the first formal laboratory was set up at the Johns Hopkins University in 1883. Within a few more years, laboratories had been established at most major universities in the country.

A science, like a child, must have time to mature. It takes thousands and thousands of experiments, performed with different methods and under different conditions, to establish a healthy body of scientific observations and principles. In the meantime, especially when observations are scarce and new methods are developing, there is likely to be a period of "isms" characterized by different points of view which are often espoused with considerable zeal. Psychology went through such a period during which different schools of thought occupied the limelight. As psychology has matured, it has become much more eclectic—there has been a good deal of selection of what seems best from all the schools. (This, for instance, is an eclectic textbook.) Because these schools are important in the history of psychology, we shall discuss some of the most important of them. Several of the leaders of these schools of thought are pictured in Figure 1.9.

STRUCTURALISM   The first school, or "ism," owes its character to the ideas prevalent during the time in which experimental psychology got under way. The physical scientists of the time could claim great

success, not only for their experimental method, but also for their atomic theory of matter. This theory, or set of principles, stated that all complex substances could be analyzed into component elements, much as elementary physics or chemistry is explained today.

It was only natural that the first experimental psychologists should follow this example, and they did. They started searching for *mental elements* into which, they hoped, all mental contents could be analyzed. The element, they thought, must be a *sensation,* such as red, cold, sweet, or putrid. To search for these elements and the rules for combining them, they used a special kind of experimental method called *introspection* [Boring, 1953]. A subject was trained to report as objectively as possible what he experienced in connection with a certain stimulus, disregarding the meanings he had come to associate with the particular stimulus. He might, for example, be presented with a colored light, a tone, or an odor and asked to describe it as minutely as possible. It was hoped that in this way the mental content of an experience would be reconstructed from elementary sensations.

Many valuable observations were collected in this way, and some aspects of the method are still being used. The approach, however, proved too narrow, for it was limited to reports of what a person experienced. Moreover, it gradually became apparent that mind cannot be thought of as a structure

made up of elementary sensations [Wertheimer, 1923]. Hence structuralism gave way to other approaches to the study of psychological events.

FUNCTIONALISM One of these new approaches, much influenced by the Darwinian theory of evolution, came to be known as functionalism. Two of its most influential proponents were William James (1842–1910) and John Dewey (1859–1952). James's textbook, *The Principles of Psychology* [James, 1890], is a classic statement of the functionalist point of view. Functionalists were interested in the fact that behavior and mental processes are adaptive—they enable an individual to adjust to a changing environment. Thus they sought to study the adaptive *functions* of behavior and mental processes, not merely their structure.

To study functions, the functionalists extended experimental methods to include not only the method of introspection but also the *observation of behavior*—what a person does. Instead of limiting themselves to the description and analysis of sensory experience and of mental content, they emphasized the total activity of the individual—how he learns, how he is motivated, how he goes about solving problems, how he forgets. So functionalism had two chief characteristics: the study of the total behavior and experience of an individual, and an interest in the adaptive functions served by the things an individual does.

INFLUENTIAL FIGURES IN THE HISTORY OF PSYCHOLOGY

FIGURE 1.9   *Wilhelm Wundt, William James, J. B. Watson, Max Wertheimer, and Sigmund Freud. (Bettmann Archive, Free Lance Photography, Underwood & Underwood, United Press International, Inc., Bettmann Archive.)*

BEHAVIORISM   Functionalism tended to put the emphasis on the observation of behavior, but it still accepted the introspection of mental processes as a legitimate method. Another now famous psychologist, John B. Watson (1878–1958), went a step further. Beginning about 1912, Watson rejected completely the introspective method and insisted that psychological experiments be restricted to the study of behavior [Watson, 1925]. This position characterized the school known as behaviorism.

Behaviorism also had three other important characteristics. One was an emphasis on conditioned reflexes as the elements—the building blocks—of behavior. Behaviorism, in fact, was very much like the structuralism it rejected in that it held that complex processes are built up out of more elementary ones. Its element, however, was the conditioned reflex rather than the sensation. We must leave the detailed explanation of the conditioned reflex to a later chapter, but we can describe it loosely as a relatively simple learned response to a stimulus. Watson felt that man's complex behavior was made up almost entirely of sets of conditioned reflexes.

Another closely related characteristic of behaviorism was its emphasis on learned, rather than unlearned, behavior. It blatantly denied the existence of instinct or of inborn tendencies. To Watson, almost all that a man becomes is a matter of the conditioning of reflexes. One of his most famous statements, in fact, is to the effect that he could take almost any infant and through proper training make him into a beggar, a lawyer, or any other kind of person he desired.

Behaviorism, finally, was also characterized by an emphasis on animal behavior. It held that there is no important difference between man and animals and that we can learn much about man by the study of animals, particularly since animals are easier to experiment with. This emphasis, in the hands of Watson and his students, led to an enormous amount of animal experimentation, which continues to the present day and has helped significantly in the solution of many psychological problems.

These characteristics of behaviorism have left their mark on modern psychology. Although behaviorism often went to extremes, it made an important underlying point that the data of psychology, like those of any science, must be out in the open for all to see. In other words, the observations of psychology must be public observations which others can repeat and check. Behaviorism thus had a lot to do historically with gaining acceptance for the current definition of psychology used throughout this book.

The behaviorist school has left its mark on psychology in still another way. Several newer, neobehaviorist schools have sprung from the original stem. These schools were especially prominent in psychology during the later 1930s and the 1940s and were characterized by attempts to develop general theories of behavior—usually from a few animal experiments. Supporters of the rival theories of Tolman (1932), Hull (1943), and Guthrie (1952) often engaged in rather acrimonious debate and attempted to set up "crucial experiments" to show that the predictions from their theory were correct and those from other theories were wrong. Some useful data were obtained from these experiments, but the idea of doing crucial experiments turned out to be a delusion. The major fault was that the predictions did not follow uniquely from the theories—you could predict almost any result by proper combination of the theoretical terms. Since this flirtation with general theories, behaviorists have turned toward small-scale theories from which unique predictions can be made. Behaviorism, and psychology in general, has also turned toward the collection of "theoretically neutral data" [Koch, 1951]. Some present-day behaviorist circles have a definite bias against explicit theory [Skinner, 1961].

GESTALT PSYCHOLOGY   While behaviorism was displacing introspectionism in the United States, another school of thought, starting about 1912, was gaining ground in Germany. This was gestalt psychology, founded by Max Wertheimer (1880–1943) and his colleagues K. Koffka and W. Köhler [Wertheimer, 1912; Koffka, 1935; Köhler, 1947]. (*Gestalt* is a German word having no exact translation, but meaning something like *form, organization,* or *configuration.*) Gestalt psychology, like structuralism before it, was greatly influenced by concepts developing in physics. Coming along some thirty years later, however, the new concepts were now field concepts of such things as the pattern of lines making up a magnetic field. For that reason, gestalt psychologists, and particularly their modern descendants, are sometimes called *field theorists.*

Gestalt psychologists were characterized, first of all, by an opposition to "atomism." They felt that both structuralism and behaviorism had taken the wrong path in looking for elements such as sensations or conditioned reflexes. Our experiences and our behavior, they held, are not compounded from simple elements. Rather they are patterns, or organizations, somewhat analogous to a magnetic field, in which events in one part of the field are influenced by events in another part. A gray piece of paper, for example, is gray only in relation to its background or to something with which it is compared. On a black background, it appears light; against a white background, it appears dark. A series of dots in any orderly arrangement is perceived as a pattern. When, for instance, you view the dots in Figure 1.10, you do not perceive merely isolated dots. Rather, you see a square and a triangle sitting on a line. The dots are somehow *organized* in perception so that they are seen as a configuration. It will be possible to explain and illustrate the concept of organization better when we come to the subject of perception, but the point made by gestalt psychologists is that the patterns or forms of our experience cannot be explained by compounding elements. As some were fond of saying: "The whole is more than the sum of its parts."

Gestalt psychology was also characterized by the use of a method called *phenomenology.* This is

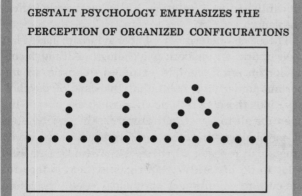

GESTALT PSYCHOLOGY EMPHASIZES THE PERCEPTION OF ORGANIZED CONFIGURATIONS

FIGURE 1.10   *The dots are perceived, not as so many isolated elements, but as a square and a triangle on a line.*

like the structuralists' introspection, with one important difference. The structuralists believed in *trained* introspection for the purpose of dissecting the supposed elements of experience. The gestaltists, on the other hand, believed in naïve introspection. That is to say, they wanted to study what something looked like to an observer. Put another way, they held that the raw phenomena of experience as reported without elaboration or analysis were legitimate observations. Thus phenomenology is a kind of method of natural observation applied to human perceptions.

Emphasis on the phenomenological method led early gestalt psychologists to emphasize the study of human experience and perception, but they were also empirical scientists who studied a wide range of problems. They have, for example, made important contributions to our understanding of learning, thought, and problem solving, which we shall take up at the appropriate time.

PSYCHOANALYSIS   Psychoanalysis is not a major school of psychology, for it originated outside the laboratory in medical practice, but it has had an impact on psychology, particularly in recent years. Moreover, it is so often confused with psychology that its nature and role need to be explained.

As almost everyone knows nowadays, psychoanalysis was founded and developed during the years 1885 to 1939 by Sigmund Freud (1856–1939). Freud, a Viennese psychiatrist, frequently found himself unable to handle the problems with which his patients confronted him within the diagnostic tenets current at the time. Psychiatry was then characterized by an elaborate system of classifying mental disorders, but this system mainly pigeonholed people without providing very convincing explanations of the causes of the disorders or offering very effective methods of treatment.

Freud concerned himself with both the problems of understanding and treatment. Being a physician, he made little use of the techniques and concepts of scientific psychology. He was also limited, so to speak, to the method of natural observation, that is,

to studying whatever he could observe in the course of treating his patients. But he was a keen observer. He developed hypotheses as he went along and tried to test them in his interviewing and treatment of patients. In this sense, he was an empiricist and something of an experimentalist, even though he could not really experiment in a systematic way. Being a prolific writer, he exercised a wide influence on the thinking of psychiatrists, psychologists, modern literature, and even the general public through his books.

Out of his experience, Freud contributed two things. First of all, he developed a method of treatment; the word "psychoanalysis" primarily refers to that method. The emphasis of this treatment is on *free association*—the patient freely associates on his thoughts and experiences—with the objective of having the patient, with the help of the psychiatrist, analyze the causes of his difficulty. Second, he constructed a theory of personality, known as the Freudian, or psychoanalytic, theory. This theory is elaborate, stressing the role of motives, often hidden and repressed from both the individual and society.

Freud's theory of personality, rather than his method of treatment, is of the greater interest to psychology [Dollard and Miller, 1950]. The theory contains many unverified assertions, but it has nevertheless been valuable, for it has been a stimulus to further systematic research. In some cases, research has given support to Freud's notions, whereas in others it has not. Psychologists therefore do not subscribe fully to the theory. They merely regard it as a deductive guide in planning research on the nature of personality.

Psychologists tend to take the same attitude toward other theories of personality which have grown up in the psychoanalytic tradition. The famous split of 1911–1912 between Freud and his adherents Alfred Adler and Carl Jung gave rise to two rival psychoanalytic schools. Jung's school is sometimes called the "analytical school," while Adler's school is sometimes called "individual psychology." The history of the psychoanalytic movement is further complicated by the changing theoretical views held by Freud himself and by a number of neo-Freudian theories developed by others in more recent times. We shall describe the neo-Freudian theories of Horney (1937), Fromm (1941), Sullivan (1953), and others when we discuss personality.

These several schools, or "isms," have been important in the development of modern psychology. Each emphasized a different aspect of psychology or a different method of observation. None was completely right or wrong. All had some beneficial effect on the development of the science of psychology.

Today these major schools have largely disappeared. Few psychologists, if any, identify themselves completely with one school. Some lean more toward one than another, but this bias is very evident only in matters close to the frontiers of psychology where one finds alternative theories about the explanations of events. This is as it should be, for it leads people to do different kinds of experiments. Theoretical differences among psychologists do exist, and there are many unsolved problems in psychology, just as in physics and biology. We shall not stress the theoretical differences or the unsolved problems, though we shall sometimes mention them. Instead we shall focus on the basic, well-established facts and principles of modern scientific psychology.

SYNOPSIS AND SUMMARY

Why have we spent so much time describing the science of psychology? One reason is simply that most people have a very hazy notion of what psychology actually is and what psychologists do. By defining, by describing some of the subfields of psychology, and by providing a capsule history of the field, we have tried to make you aware of psychology as it actually is and not as the Sunday supplements picture it.

Another reason has to do with the word "science." Most of us are not used to thinking of behavior as something which can be described and understood by using the tools of science. It is possible to build up a structure of reliable knowledge about behavior through the use of scientific method. The things that we do, think, and experience have their causes, and these may be sought on many levels—from the physiological to the sociological.

That we may come to understand the causes of behavior has tremendous implications. It is also cause for sober reflection. As we begin to understand more about behavior, the ability of people armed with psychological knowledge to predict and control the behavior of others will grow. The ethics of the use of this power is a potentially serious problem. That such a problem looms in the future is a tribute to the power of the scientific method. Because it is such a powerful tool, this text emphasizes scientific, rather than intuitive, data.

1. Although the beginning course in psychology offers much of practical value, the student should expect to acquire from it only the rudiments, not profound knowledge or skill.
2. Psychology, the science of human and animal behavior, covers a wide range of problems. Not only does it deal with people and understanding them; but it also deals with the problems of social groups, learning and perceiving, intelligence and abilities, working efficiently, and many others.
3. Psychology is one of the behavioral sciences. These disciplines include certain aspects of history, economics, and social and political sciences, and they sometimes overlap the domains of such natural sciences as physiology and physics.
4. Psychology, for the first few years after its establishment as a scientific subject, was mainly a pure academic

science. It began to have practical applications during World War I. Now it is growing at a very fast rate.

5. Psychologists do many things, and psychology has many subfields. Clinical psychology is the largest single subfield. It deals with research, diagnosis, and the therapy of deviant behavior. Other large subfields within psychology are counseling, experimental psychology, industrial and engineering psychology, school and educational psychology, social psychology, psychometric psychology, developmental psychology, and personality psychology.

6. Psychology as a science is (*a*) empirical, (*b*) systematic, (*c*) dependent upon measurement, and (*d*) careful about using operational definitions of terms.

7. The experimental method has been a cornerstone in the emergence of modern psychology. The essence of this method is that an independent variable is changed under controlled conditions and an effect on a dependent variable is sought. Control is often achieved by using special control groups or by arranging it so that subjects can serve as their own controls.

8. The experimental method cannot be used in every case. When it cannot be used, scientific information can be obtained by use of the method of systematic observation. The clinical method is a special method in which information is obtained by an intensive study of an individual—usually one with a behavioral problem.

9. Theory is essential in scientific psychology, as in every science. It serves as (*a*) a scientific shorthand, (*b*) a predictor of facts, and (*c*) a guide to further research.

10. For many years, psychological research was guided by different schools of thought: structuralism, behaviorism, gestalt psychology, funtionalism, and psychoanalysis. These schools, however, have tended to dissolve and merge into one as more and more factual information has accumulated.

RELATED TOPICS IN THE TEXT

APPENDIX 1   CAREERS IN PSYCHOLOGY   The training of a psychologist in graduate school is described here. You will find discussions of the qualifications for graduate study in psychology and of the specialized training necessary in several of the subfields of psychology, as well as an indication of the types and amounts of assistantship and fellowship aid which are available.

CHAPTER 11   PSYCHOLOGICAL MEASUREMENT   Techniques for ordering and describing data are outlined in Chapter 11. The correlation coefficient, a measure of the degree of relationship between two sets of data, and tests of statistical significance are also described.

SUGGESTIONS FOR FURTHER READING

Bachrach, A. J. *Psychological research: An introduction.* New York: Random House, 1962. (Paperback.)
An interesting and informal account of experimental methods in psychology.

Baker, R. A. (Ed.). *Psychology in the wry.* Princeton, N.J.: Van Nostrand, 1963. (Paperback.)
A collection of amusing, satirical articles in which psychologists make fun of their own pomposity and other shortcomings.

Boring, E. G. *A history of experimental psychology* (2d ed.). New York: Appleton-Century-Crofts, 1950.
An authoritative and well-written history of experimental psychology that is a standard work in its field.

Conant, J. B. *On understanding science.* New Haven, Conn.: Yale, 1947. (Paperback available.)
A brief, interesting account of the development of scientific method in the physical sciences, written by a distinguished chemist and educator.

Kimble, G. A., and Garmezy, N. *Principles of general psychology.* (2d ed.). New York: Ronald, 1963.
Chapter 1 is an excellent summary of the logic, aims, and program of science.

King, R. A. (Ed.). *Readings for an introduction to psychology.* New York: McGraw-Hill, 1966. (Paperback.)
A book of readings designed to accompany this text.

Ogg, Elizabeth. *Psychologists in action.* Pamphlet No. 229. New York: Public Affairs Committee, Inc., 1955. (Paperback.)
An interesting, easy-to-read introduction to psychology and its subfields. (This pamphlet is put out on a nonprofit basis by the Public Affairs Committee, Inc.)

Watson, R. I. *Psychology as a profession.* Garden City, N.Y.: Doubleday, 1954. (Paperback.)
A brief résumé of psychology as a profession intended for the beginning student in psychology.

Webb, W. B. (Ed.). *The profession of psychology.* New York: Holt, 1962.
Descriptions of their jobs by psychologists engaged in several of the most prominent fields of psychology.

Woodworth, R. S., and Sheehan, Mary R. *Contemporary schools of psychology* (3d ed.). New York: Ronald, 1964.
A summary of the various schools of psychology, their historical origins, and their important contributions to psychological theory.

2

LOOK AROUND AND you will see vast differences between people in behavior. Some are phlegmatic, while others are easily aroused; some are intelligent, while others are stupid. Some are anxious, while others seem relatively free from anxiety, and so on. What are some of the causes of these individual differences in behavior? Learning is one of the major factors; individuals have different learning histories and, as we see in the next chapter, this produces profound effects. Unlearned causes of individual differences, such as heredity and maturational influences, also strongly affect behavior. So, when we look around, we see that the causes of behavior may be classified into two major types: learned and unlearned. Some of the unlearned causes of behavior are examined in this chapter.

To set the stage, we present first a brief description of the mechanisms of heredity. Next, we discuss some of the behaviors which seem most directly influenced by heredity. For instance, instincts—unlearned behaviors—express the influence of heredity on behavior. Finally, we discuss maturation and development—the unfolding of hereditary potential.

Mechanisms of heredity

Individual differences begin at conception. There is no behavior until 8 weeks after conception, 7 months before birth, but behavior will be greatly affected by the genetic potential received at conception. At conception, two *germ cells,* one a *sperm cell* from the father and the other an *egg cell,* or *ovum,* from the mother, unite to form a new individual, at this stage called a *zygote.* Each of the two germ cells, sperm and ovum, which unite to form the zygote, consists of a dark nucleus surrounded by a light watery substance, the cytoplasm. The whole cell, nucleus and cytoplasm, is enclosed in a membrane. When the two cells form a zygote, they merge their parts into a single cell of the same general structure. The part of the zygote of principal interest to us is the nucleus, for it contains the

MATURATION
AND
DEVELOPMENT

WHERE ARE YOU GOING
MY LITTLE ONE,
LITTLE ONE?
WHERE ARE YOU GOING
MY BABY, MY OWN?
TURN AROUND AND
YOU'RE TWO,
TURN AROUND AND
YOU'RE FOUR,
TURN AROUND AND
YOU'RE A YOUNG GIRL
GOING OUT OF THE
DOOR.
TURN AROUND AND
YOU'RE TINY,
TURN AROUND AND
YOU'RE GROWN,
TURN AROUND AND
YOU'RE A YOUNG WIFE
WITH BABES OF YOUR
OWN.*

genetic material that transmits hereditary characteristics from the parents to the new individual.

CHROMOSOMES   The genetic material consists of *chromosomes* and *genes*. The genes are the real genetic units, but they are carried on chromosomes. Hence both must be considered.

The term *chromosome* means colored body, and it is so called because it stains darkly when treated with special dyes. When thus stained, it can be seen in the microscope as a twisted string of odd-sized and odd-shaped beads in the nucleus of the cell. Chromosomes are visible in most of the cells of the body, but only the chromosomes in the sperm, egg, and zygote have anything to do with inheritance, for the merger of the chromosomes of the egg cell and the sperm cell, when they form the zygote, is the only genetic link between an individual and his parents.

Each species of animal has a characteristic number of chromosomes per cell. In the case of man, the number is 46. The chromosomes occur in pairs: thus human chromosomes are arranged in 23 pairs (see Figure 2.1). The egg and sperm cells, however,

pass through a stage in their production when the pairs of chromosomes split apart, leaving only one of each pair—a set of 23 single chromosomes—for each germ cell. The two single sets from the sperm and egg combine to make new pairs when the sperm and egg unite; therefore, in the zygote we find 23 pairs of chromosomes (see Figure 2.1).

GENES   Genes are contained on the chromosomes, and for our purposes, they may be thought of as the units of heredity. They are complex chemical packets, very probably parts of the large *deoxyribonucleic acid (DNA)* molecules found in the nuclei of cells. Because of their composition and chainlike construction, these DNA molecules can carry the code both for their own reproduction and for the ultimate production of substances, called enzymes, which control the formation of proteins within a cell. The chain of events through which the DNA of genes produces enzymes is a long one in which there is some uncertainty about the individual links. Various types of *ribonucleic acids (RNA)* are almost certainly involved in this chain. For instance, it seems likely that one of these RNAs,

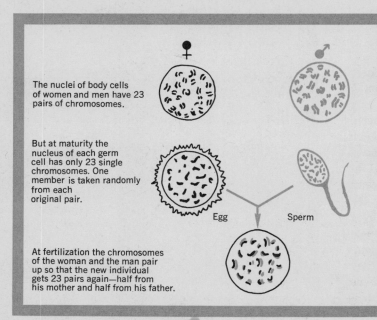

The nuclei of body cells of women and men have 23 pairs of chromosomes.

But at maturity the nucleus of each germ cell has only 23 single chromosomes. One member is taken randomly from each original pair.

Egg   Sperm

At fertilization the chromosomes of the woman and the man pair up so that the new individual gets 23 pairs again—half from his mother and half from his father.

A NEW INDIVIDUAL IS FORMED BY THE UNION OF THE EGG OF THE MOTHER AND THE SPERM OF THE FATHER

FIGURE 2.1   *The mechanism of transmission of chromosomes from the germ cells of the mother and father to the fertilized egg.*

"messenger RNA," may be constructed according to the code in the nucleic DNA; then "messenger RNA" may carry the genetic information from the nucleus of the cell to the microsomes—the areas in the cytoplasm where proteins are synthesized.

We may summarize by saying that the modern concept of a gene is that it is "a functional area required for the formation of an enzyme" [Bonner, 1961]. By controlling enzymes and the production of proteins within a cell, and by somehow influencing the interaction of cells with each other, genes are able to determine the kind of tissues formed to make the various organs and the structure of the body. That is to say, they direct the course of development of the body. This is the basic mechanism of inheritance, for it is in this way that genes duplicate in the new individual the characteristics present, whether visible or not, in his ancestors.

Genes always work in pairs, one member of which comes from the mother and the other from the father. A pair of genes working together directs the development of some particular characteristic of the body or of behavior. Sometimes two genes in a pair are identical even though they come from different parents. Then there is no doubt about the characteristic they will produce. If, for example, each gene of a pair is so constituted that it will produce blue eyes, the new individual will certainly have blue eyes; or if both genes are "brown-eyed," the individual will surely have brown eyes.

Often two genes of a pair are not identical, but govern the same characteristic in slightly different ways. In other words, slightly different genes may be present at the corresponding places on the chromosomes from the mother and father. The different kinds of genes which may be present at a place on a chromosome are called *alleles*. Many different kinds of genes may be present at a location on a chromosome. For instance, there are three alleles which determine human A, B, AB, and O blood types. Usually one gene is dominant over the others, and the outcome which we observe depends upon which gene is dominant and which genes are recessive (see Figure 2.2). A *dominant gene* is one whose characteristic will show up when paired with another gene; it produces the observable characteristic—the *phenotype*. A *recessive gene*, conversely, is one whose characteristic will not be observable when it is paired with a dominant gene.

The actual genetic constitution of an individual—the *genotype*—may contain the recessive gene, but its effect is not expressed. The only way that we can tell that the recessive gene is there is by knowing that one parent possessed the recessive characteristic, or by observing that some of the offspring of the person have the recessive characteristic. The offspring can have the recessive characteristic only when both of the genes governing a particular trait are recessive. This can happen only when both mother and father have the recessive genes which, by chance, may pair to determine a certain characteristic. Brown eyes are a good example of a dominant characteristic, blue eyes of a recessive characteristic. Table 2.1 lists other common characteristics that may be either dominant or recessive.

MULTIPLE DETERMINATION   Traits that are determined by a single pair of genes illustrate nicely

TABLE 2.1 *Some dominant and recessive characteristics*

DOMINANT CHARACTERISTIC	RECESSIVE CHARACTERISTIC
Brown eyes	Blue eyes
Dark or brunette hair	Light, blond, or red hair
Curly hair	Straight hair
Normal hair	Baldness
Normal color vision	Color blindness
Normal sight	Night blindness
Normal hearing	Congenital deafness
Normal coloring	Albinism (lack of pigment)
Immunity to poison ivy	Susceptibility to poison ivy
Normal blood	Hemophilia (lack of blood clotting)

SOURCE: *Modified from Krech and Crutchfield, 1958*

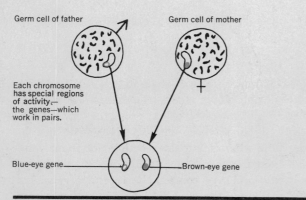

Germ cell of father   Germ cell of mother

Each chromosome
has special regions
of activity—
the genes—which
work in pairs.

Blue-eye gene ————— ————— Brown-eye gene

All genes for a specific characteristic,
in this case, blue eyes, are the same.

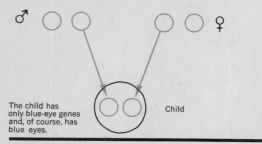

♂   ♀

The child has
only blue-eye genes
and, of course, has
blue eyes.

Child

Different genes are present and
both mother and father have
only one type.

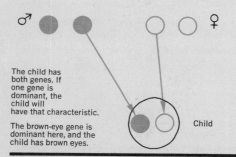

♂   ♀

The child has
both genes. If
one gene is
dominant, the
child will
have that characteristic.

The brown-eye gene is
dominant here, and the
child has brown eyes.

Child

Different genes are present and
both mother and father have both
types.

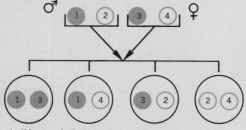

♂ (1) (2) (3) (4) ♀

(1)(3)   (1)(4)   (3)(2)   (2)(4)

In this case, both the mother and father have brown eyes
which were determined by the dominant gene. Both have
recessive blue-eye genes, however. The various possible
combinations are shown; the numbers designate the genes.
On the average, three of the children will have the dominant
gene and brown eyes; one will have two blue-eye genes and
blue eyes.

FIGURE 2.2   *The inheritance of brown and blue eyes.*

the basic principles of genetics. (Some of these
traits are listed in Table 2.1.) In general, these
simply determined traits depend on the presence
or absence of some one thing in a tissue or organ of
the body. Eye color, for example, is a matter of pig-
mentation of the iris. The pigmented iris is brown,
the unpigmented is blue. Color blindness is probably caused by lack of a photosensitive substance
in the eye. Cases even appear in which something
as complex as a particular kind of mental retardation
can be traced to a single pair of genes, and in such
cases, the trouble lies in the lack of a single substance in the brain necessary for its normal functioning. Hence traits that are determined by single
pairs of genes depend on the presence or absence of
some one thing in the body that affects the structure
or appearance of an organ.

Many traits, obviously, depend on more than one
thing. Athletic ability, intelligence, temperament,
and susceptibility to some mental illnesses, or behavior disorders, for example, have a hereditary
basis, although they are not entirely determined by
heredity. Insofar as they are, they are multiply determined by many pairs of genes, not just one. In
some cases of multiple determination, usually where
a small number of genes is involved in establishing
a characteristic, geneticists have been able to work
out the rules of inheritance. In most cases of multiple
determination, however, this has been impossible,
just because the situation has proved too complicated. Without knowing the rules, it is nevertheless
possible to conclude from appropriate studies of
inbreeding and crossbreeding that a particular trait
is multiply determined. A little later we shall give
some examples of psychological interest.

SEX DETERMINATION   Genes also determine
whether the new individual will be male or female.
The genes concerned are found on one particular
pair of chromosomes. If the two chromosomes are
identical, that is, if both are what we call X chromosomes, the result is a female. (see Figure 2.3). If

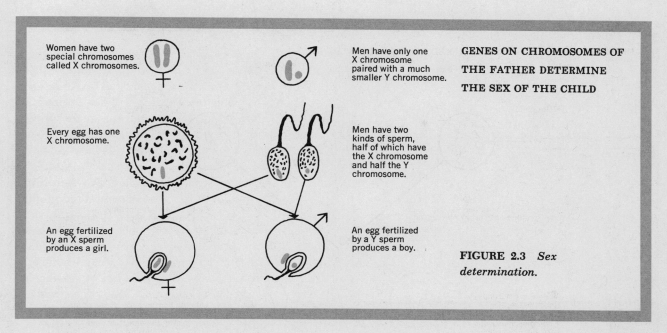

Women have two special chromosomes called X chromosomes.

Every egg has one X chromosome.

An egg fertilized by an X sperm produces a girl.

Men have only one X chromosome paired with a much smaller Y chromosome.

Men have two kinds of sperm, half of which have the X chromosome and half the Y chromosome.

An egg fertilized by a Y sperm produces a boy.

GENES ON CHROMOSOMES OF THE FATHER DETERMINE THE SEX OF THE CHILD

FIGURE 2.3 *Sex determination.*

one of the pair is not an X chromosome but a somewhat smaller chromosome, called a Y chromosome, the result is a male.

The sex of the individual is determined by the sperm of the father, not by the egg of the mother. Since each member of a pair of the mother's chromosomes contains an X, all eggs produced by the mother have only X chromosomes after the cells go through the process, mentioned earlier, in which the pairs of chromosomes split apart. When the sperm of the father goes through the same process, however, half of the resulting sperms contain Y chromosomes, and the other half X chromosomes. Subsequently, the kind of sperm (X or Y) which fertilizes the egg determines whether the offspring will be male or female.

SEX-LINKED CHARACTERISTICS The chromosomes that determine sex also carry on them genes that govern other characteristics. These genes are found only on the X chromosomes, not on the Y. Since the male has only one X chromosome, he consequently always possesses the characteristics produced by these genes, whether they are dominant or recessive. Females, however, have two X chromosomes, and the usual rules for the pairing of the dominant and recessive genes of these X chromosomes hold. As a result, a recessive *sex-linked characteristic* always shows up in the male, but may be hidden in the female if it is paired with a dominant characteristic.

Color blindness is a good example of a sex-linked characteristic (see Figure 2.4). It happens to be recessive, but it is carried on the X chromosome. So whenever a male has a recessive gene for color blindness, he is color-blind, without exception. If he marries a normal woman carrying no genes for color blindness, all his sons will be normal because they will receive their father's Y chromosome and their mother's X chromosome. All his daughters, however, will be *carriers* without displaying any color blindness, for they will receive a dominant X from their mother and a recessive X from their father. When the carrier mother marries, the possibility of her children being color-blind depends upon whether their father is color-blind and upon which of her X chromosomes, the dominant or the recessive one, is passed on to the offspring. The possibilities, includ-

COLOR BLINDNESS IS A SEX-LINKED CHARACTERISTIC

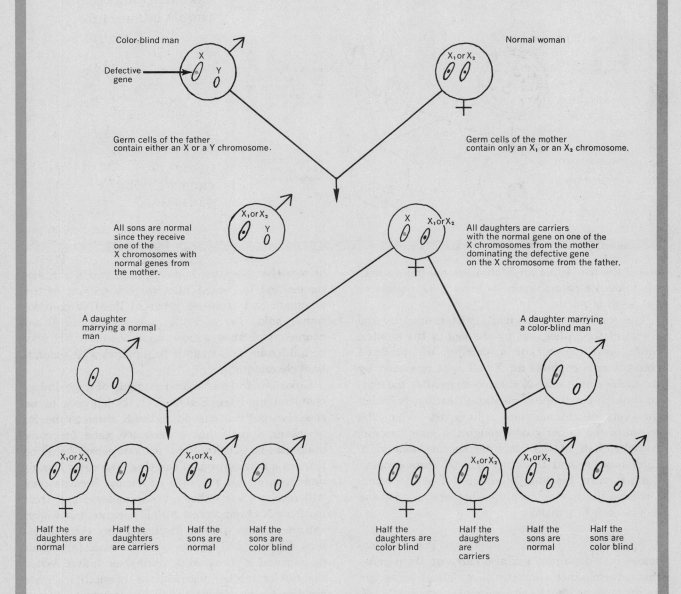

Color-blind man

Defective gene

Normal woman

X_1 or X_2

Germ cells of the father contain either an X or a Y chromosome.

Germ cells of the mother contain only an X_1 or an X_2 chromosome.

X_1 or X_2

X X_1 or X_2

All sons are normal since they receive one of the X chromosomes with normal genes from the mother.

All daughters are carriers with the normal gene on one of the X chromosomes from the mother dominating the defective gene on the X chromosome from the father.

A daughter marrying a normal man

A daughter marrying a color-blind man

X_1 or X_2

X_1 or X_2

X_1 or X_2

X_1 or X_2

Half the daughters are normal

Half the daughters are carriers

Half the sons are normal

Half the sons are color blind

Half the daughters are color blind

Half the daughters are carriers

Half the sons are normal

Half the sons are color blind

FIGURE 2.4   *The inheritance of color blindness as an example of a sex-linked characteristic.*

ing the proportions that may be expected, are given in Figure 2.4.

GENETIC CHANGE Genes, we have seen, are the units of heredity, and a person receives his genes from his parents, who in turn received theirs from their parents, and so on back to the first man and woman. Indeed, an unbroken line of transmission runs through the germ cells of one generation on through all succeeding generations. The other cells of the body are outside this line. Anything that happens to them, through injury, disease, or the acquiring of new characteristics, is irrelevant to heredity, for they never contribute their genes to the next generation.

It follows from this that acquired characteristics cannot be inherited. A person who acquires great athletic or musical skill cannot pass this on *genetically* to his child, because the skill is developed in the use of his muscle and nerve cells but has no way of modifying the genes in his germ cells. A few geneticists have contested this conclusion, notably Lamarck in the nineteenth century, when the science of genetics was still very young, and more recently Lysenko in Russia, who presumably was motivated by ideological considerations. Indeed, it would be very nice if we could improve the quality of the human race by training individuals or by modifying them through drugs or surgery and passing on the new characteristic to their offspring. Unfortunately, the mechanisms of heredity, as we know them, make this seem completely hopeless, and no satisfactory evidence to the contrary has ever been presented.

It also follows from the fact of continuity of germ cells that any changes in heredity can take place only through changes in the genes. This fortunately, but also unfortunately, does sometimes happen. In the long history of the human and animal races, genes and the traits they determine have occasionally changed. By far the majority of such changes have had no lasting or beneficial effect, for they have produced traits that are incompatible with the life of the organism, either causing it to die very

early in its existence or making it unsuitable for survival in its normal environment.

Only a few changes, probably one in many millions, have produced traits compatible with the survival of the organism and the species. Such changes in genes are called *mutations.* Mutations take place spontaneously in the sense that we do not always know what causes them. One cause, however, is known—the irradiation of germ cells by charged particles. Such particles exist in abundance in the cosmic rays of the ionosphere of the earth 20 to 600 miles up. Few ever get through our atmosphere to the earth, but some do, and if they penetrate the body and hit a gene, they may knock something off it or otherwise rearrange its structure. There may be other causes of mutations, but this one has been established. In fact, it has been duplicated in the laboratory by using X rays, which are similar to the particles generated by cosmic rays, to induce genetic mutations in animals. Geneticists figure that there have been enough such spontaneous mutations in the last few hundred million years to account for the creation of all the species in the animal and plant kingdoms.

FAMILY INHERITANCE Each species of animal, man included, has its set of chromosomes and genes that determine the particular characteristics of the species. Within a species, the combination of genes an individual receives is a matter of chance. First, it is chance that determines which member of a pair of genes goes into a sperm or egg when the pairs of chromosomes are divided into single sets. Consequently, no two sperm or egg cells are alike, for each receives a random set of genes. Second, it is purely by chance that a particular sperm fuses with a particular egg to form a zygote. Since the number of genes is very large, the number of possible combinations of genes is astronomical. Hence there is an extremely small chance that any two individuals can have exactly the same genetic makeup. We may therefore expect individuals to differ widely in their heredity and thus in their traits.

Individuals of the same family, however, may be

expected to have similar genes and traits. Each parent contributes half of his genes to his child, and the child in turn contributes half of his to his children. Although each half is unique, it may happen that some of the genes of a brother and sister will be identical. So too will be some of the genes of parent and child. Thus it is to be expected that brothers and sisters will resemble each other, and their parents in some traits. A child may also resemble a grandparent, but to a lesser degree, for a child on the average receives only a quarter (one-half of one-half) of the genes of a particular grandparent.

In only one case can two or more individuals have absolutely identical heredities. This is the case of *identical twins* (or identical triplets, identical quadruplets, and so on). Identical twins develop from the same zygote. If a zygote divides into two cells, each separately goes on to form a new individual. Since each cell has the same genes as the zygote, the heredity of the two individuals will be identical

(see Figure 2.5). It follows from this that identical twins are always of the same sex, for each has the same sex chromosomes as the original zygote.

Not all twins, however, are identical. In fact, most twins are *fraternal twins*. These develop from two separate eggs of the mother, and hence begin as two zygotes formed independently by the union of two different sperms with two different ova. For this reason, fraternal twins are no more alike genetically than ordinary siblings born at different times. For this reason, too, fraternal twins may or may not be of the same sex. Hence when twins are not of the same sex, they are fraternal, not identical. The only unique thing about fraternal twins is that they are born at the same time and thus have more similar environments, both before and after birth, than brothers or sisters born at different times.

Twins are extremely useful in the study of the problems of heredity and environment, the subject we take up next. Since identical twins have identical heredities, any differences between them must

FIGURE 2.5   *Identical twins have the same heredity. The hereditary potentialities bequeathed at birth persist throughout life. (From Kallmann and Jarvik, 1959. By permission of Lucy Jarvik, J. E. Birren, and the publisher.)*

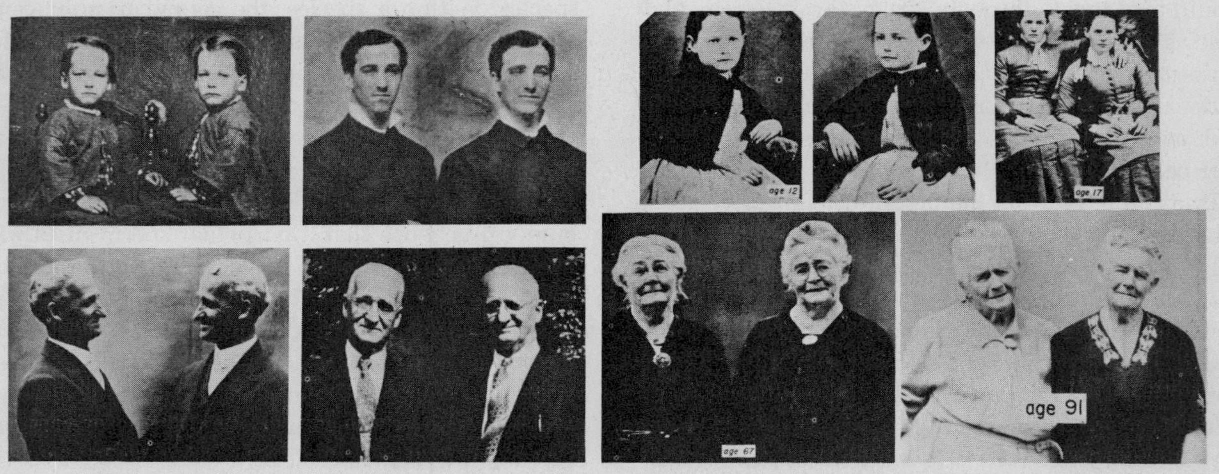

be explained on the basis of different environments. Since, on the other hand, fraternal twins are no more alike genetically than ordinary siblings, differences between fraternal twins would be attributable to genetics only if their environments were identical, and this situation cannot be achieved.

Heredity and environment

With the mechanisms of heredity in mind, we are now prepared to consider a problem that has long interested almost everyone who attempts to understand human behavior. It has been called the problem of heredity *versus* environment or of nature *versus* nurture. The "versus" gets in to these phrases because people often argue for one against the other, taking either the view that a man's hereditary nature determines pretty much what kind of person he can be, or the contrary view that men are more or less equal in heredity and that the environment in which one is nurtured determines what he becomes. Such arguments, however, are quite futile, for in reality both heredity *and* environment, or nature *and* nurture, jointly fashion a person's abilities, skills, and psychological characteristics. The problem is not to choose between them but rather to define precisely how the two interact with each other to determine these characteristics.

ROLE OF HEREDITY   Since no obvious connection exists between genes and what a person does, it is reasonable to ask what connection there might be between them. The link has to be the structure and function of the structures of the body, for nothing else is plausible. The genes control the development of the tissues and organs of the body, such as the brain, the sense organs, and the muscles, all of which participate in behavior. Here, then, is the connection between genes and behavior. By keeping this link in mind, we know when and when not to expect heredity to play a role in behavior.

The link might work in several ways. One is through simple structure. If a person inherits short legs, stubby fingers, or a deaf ear, it is clear that his abilities in some fields must be limited. This accounts for some of the psychological defects that are inherited as well as for hereditary limitations in the skills a person can develop. Another way for the link to work is through chemical functions. Myriad chemical substances are concerned in the body's activities—photosensitive substances take part in vision, other substances are essential to normal functioning of the brain, others for clotting of the blood, and so forth. Genes determine whether such substances are present or absent, and even how adequate they are. Some psychological characteristics such as color blindness and certain kinds of mental retardation are inherited because they depend on such substances.

In the case of psychological characteristics such as intelligence, temperament, and aptitudes, which depend partly on heredity, the link between genes and behavior is complex. The characteristics are multiply determined, we know, and this means that many genes are linked to them. These characteristics probably depend on such things as whether certain pathways are formed in the brain, the sensitivity of sense organs, the general level of activity in the brain, and the secretions of certain glands. Until we fully understand the physiological basis of inherited psychological characteristics, and also know just how genes multiply determine organ structures and functions, we shall not be able to say exactly how genes are linked to behavior patterns. The possibilities, however, are clearly there. Hence we have every reason to expect heredity to play some role in behavior.

THE INSTINCT PROBLEM   We often use the term *instinct*. We say that a mother instinctively cares for her young, that a man has an instinct to fight, or that a father instinctively leaps into the water to save his drowning youngster. Such uses of the term, unfortunately, are loose, unscientific, and incorrect. They tend to confuse behavior that is impulsive or automatic with behavior that is inherited and unlearned. They also imply that an instinct is something that somehow explains behavior.

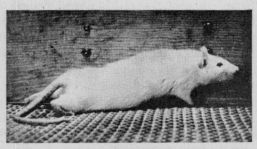

FIGURE 2.6 *Top, the stretching reaction just prior to the delivery of the pups. Middle, after the pups are born, the mother cleans them and eats the placenta. Bottom, the mother has placed the pups together in a nest. (From Farris and Griffiths, 1949.)*

Because of this confusion, instinct was long a controversial word among psychologists. Some, like John B. Watson, denounced the word because they did not believe any behavior, except simple reflexes, was inborn or unlearned. Others defended it because they were convinced that instinctive behavior did exist. Today the controversy has largely died down, partly because of the mounting evidence for the

existence of instinctive patterns of behavior and partly because we define and use the term more precisely.

Instinctive behavior, it now is generally agreed, is an *inherited pattern of behavior*. We still avoid the term instinct, however, because it implies "something" inside the organism that makes him do things, when actually there is no such thing. Often instinctive behavior is related to a drive such as sex, but this is only one of the conditions for eliciting the behavior, not the instinct. To qualify as instinctive behavior, a pattern must meet three conditions:

1. It must be generally characteristic of a species or a breed. In other words, one must have good evidence that the behavior is genetically determined.

2. It must appear full-blown at the first appropriate opportunity without any previous training or practice. This is also a test of its being inherited, rather than learned.

3. It must continue for some time in the absence of the conditions evoking it; that is to say, it may be triggered by some stimulus, but it is not controlled by the stimulus. This distinguishes it from *reflexes*, which are automatic reactions to stimuli, and from *taxes*, which are innate tendencies to orient toward and approach particular external stimuli. Neither the reflex nor the taxis persists for any length of time after the stimulus has been removed.

To say that instinctive behavior is an inherited pattern of behavior is not to say that it is necessarily present at birth. Actually, it may appear at various times in the life cycle up to sexual maturity or even later. The body takes time to develop and mature along the lines laid down by the genes. Hence patterns of behavior that depend on growth and development can be, and are, inherited even though they may not be present at birth.

One example of instinctive behavior is the maternal behavior of the rat (see Figure 2.6). A pregnant rat builds a nest some time before her young are born. When they are born, she cleans them and sees to it that they are safely in the nest. When they wriggle out, she retrieves them. For many long hours a day, she keeps them warm and nurses them.

Although the details of the maternal pattern vary from one species to another, the pattern is relatively consistent within a species. It also appears full-blown, in the absence of any experience or training, at the time of the first litter. Hence, in the rat, at least, it qualifies fully as instinctive behavior.

Patterns of instinctive behavior are found in many species. In general, they are more prevalent in lower animals, such as the insects, fish, and birds, than in mammals. The most characteristic instinctive pattern in mammals is the maternal pattern described above for the rat. Because mammals nurse their young until they are relatively capable of fending for themselves, they probably have less need for instinctive patterns, other than maternal, than many lower animals.

When it comes to human beings, with the possible exception of a few behaviors which mature without practice, we cannot say with certainty that there are any instinctive behavior patterns. Man seems to have become so sophisticated in learning to adapt to his world, and in teaching his young how to adapt, that instinctive behavior is not considered to be a prominent human characteristic.

GENETICS AND BEHAVIOR Instinctive behavior is only one psychological characteristic that is inherited. Differences between individuals, shown in tendencies to react in certain ways and aptitudes for learning certain things, may also be inherited, although they are not instinctive patterns. In fact, such tendencies and aptitudes, rather than complete instinctive behavior patterns, are the principal inherited characteristics in higher animals and man.

Methods of study. There are several ways to test whether particular tendencies are inherited or learned. One is to take individuals of the same or similar heredity and raise them in different environments. The environment may be changed artificially as in the following example:

As we ordinarily see them, dogs respond almost continuously to human behavior. In this case it is possible to . . . separate the dogs from their human environment.

At our laboratory we wished to find out how much of their behavior was native to dogs and how much was the result of the human environment. We placed groups of adult dogs in large fields where they could be watched apart from human beings and found that they reacted towards each other with the same basic behavior patterns with which they responded to people. They wagged their tails at each other, growled and barked, and fawned on any animal which was in possession of food. When all these behavior patterns were written down, they were found to be essentially the same as those exhibited by their wild ancestors, the wolves. Puppies born to these animals and kept out of contact with people showed the same behavior as the adults except that they were extremely wild and fearful toward people. The puppies literally went back to the wild in one generation. They apparently had an inherited tendency to develop fear toward strangers. As we might expect from the lasting nature of learned fears, once the puppies had developed timidity the friendly attitude of their parents had little effect in overcoming it. [Scott, 1958, page 114.]

Another means of changing the environment is by *cross-fostering*—having the young reared by foster parents who have characteristics different from those of the natural parents. This technique has been used in both animal and human studies, and it has been one of the best ways to study the inheritance of intelligence in children. The following is an example of cross-fostering in animal research:

Hungry mice of the C strain eat peacefully side by side off the same pellet of food, whereas mice of the C57/10 strain actively compete for a single pellet. When the two strains were cross-fostered at birth, the young C mice did not take up the active habits of their foster parents and thus remained true to heredity. The mice of the other strain likewise acted in accordance with their heredity and attempted to take food away from their peaceful foster parents. [Scott, 1958, page 117.]

The development of different genetic populations is interesting because it permits analysis of the chromosomes responsible for the behavior under study [Hirsch and Erlenmeyer-Kimling, 1962]:

The animals used in this experiment were fruit flies, the standard animal for chromosome analysis, and the behavior studied was *geotaxis*—the instinctive tendency of animals to go against or with gravitational forces. Negative geotaxis, going against the force of gravity, and positive geotaxis, going with the pull of gravity, could be measured in a special apparatus [Hirsch, 1959]. Figure 2.7 shows this apparatus. The flies were put in the single tube at the left and, after making a series of choices, they arrived at one of the final collecting tubes at the right. The flies flew through the maze because a taxis was at work—they were attracted toward a fluorescent light at the end of the maze. Cones at the choice points prevented retracing. It was a relatively easy matter to make accurate counts of the number of flies entering the final eleven collection

tubes. As might be expected, more flies entered the middle collection tubes, but some found their way to the uppermost and lowermost collection tubes. Those arriving at the uppermost tubes were displaying strong negative geotaxis, while those arriving at the lowermost tubes were showing strong positive geotaxis. Two populations of fruit flies, those with positive and negative geotactic tendencies, were established through many generations of selective breeding. When these populations were compared with each other and with the unselected foundation population, it was found that changes in three chromosomes accounted for a large part of the differences in geotactic behavior.

This last method—comparing strains or individuals of different heredities in similar environments—can

SOMETIMES EVEN FRUIT
FLIES MUST CHOOSE

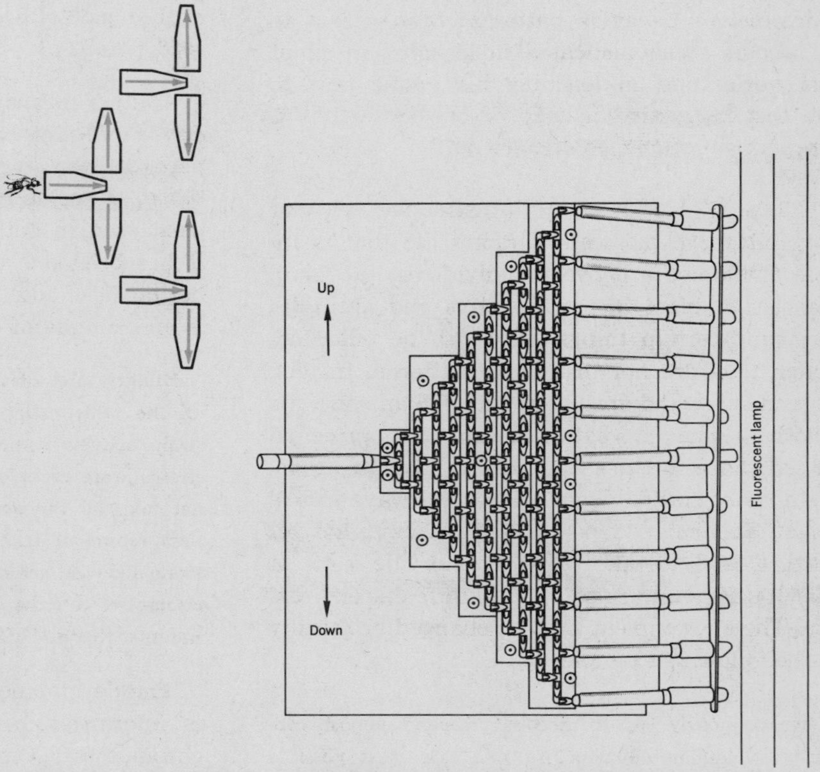

FIGURE 2.7 *Right, multiple-choice maze for fruit flies used in studies of the genetic basis of geotaxis. Flies are put into tube at left and, after making ten choices, are taken out at the right. The maze is oriented vertically; flies with strong positive geotaxis will fly downward and will end in the lowermost tube at the right; flies with strong negative geotaxis will fly upward and end in the uppermost tube at the right; flies with moderately strong geotactic tendencies will end in one of the middle tubes at the right. Above, detail of maze choice points. (After Hirsch, 1959.)*

FIGURE 2.8 *The chimpanzee and the human infant were reared together and treated alike. In many respects, the chimpanzee, Gua, developed more rapidly than Donald, but Donald caught up with and surpassed Gua, especially in the development of language. (Kellogg and Kellogg, 1933.)*

be extended logically to the comparison of different species.

Studies of species differences. The difference between two species of animals is genetic, and by giving them the same opportunities for learning and development, we can assess the role of heredity in their respective behaviors. This has been done for two species very close to home: man and ape. Here is one such study [Kellogg and Kellogg, 1933]:

A nine-month-old boy, named Donald, and a seven-month-old female chimpanzee, named Gua, were brought up together like brother and sister. The experimenters made every effort to treat the ape and their child exactly alike. They treated both with the same affection, dressed them alike, and gave them the same chance to practice different kinds of behavior like standing, walking, opening doors, eating with a spoon, and learning to use the toilet. Of

course, the difference in heredity between a boy and a chimpanzee is tremendous, and the experiment gave us a chance to see how much this difference could be overcome by training.

As we might have expected, Gua, the chimpanzee, developed certain kinds of behavior earlier than Donald, the boy. The chimpanzee has about one-third the life span of man and matures much earlier. In the beginning of the experiment, Gua was better than Donald in such things as standing and walking (see Figure 2.8). Gua also learned to use a spoon sooner than Donald and developed the capacity to respond to verbal instructions earlier. But after 9 months, when the study was ended, Donald had caught up on almost everything except strength, and he was beginning to develop capacities such as language that Gua showed no signs of developing.

The important point in this experiment is that

the ape and the child developed according to their hereditary potentials. Even though the ape's special training allowed it to develop behavior normally seen only in human beings, it very soon reached the limits of its potential and was far outstripped by the child.

The ability to learn to use language provides an interesting example of the study of species differences. It is often said that what sets man off from animals is his ability to use language. This certainly is true in the world as we know it, but we can ask whether it is a matter of heredity or learning. Man might by good fortune have learned language, then perpetuated it by teaching it to his offspring. Some animals may have the capacity to learn a language, but may never have happened to develop it.

Several birds, such as the parrot, obviously inherit the ability to talk and are very good at uttering words distinctly. But there is more to language than just talking; language, as we use it, employs words to refer to objects or situations and combines words in novel and meaningful ways. Parrots, however, just "parrot": they repeat over and over again a few simple phrases they have mimicked. Although many people with pet parrots have spent many hours teaching them language, no one can claim that they use language in a meaningful way. Apparently they lack the hereditary ability to do so.

Since apes are more nearly like man than other animals, especially in body and brain structures, experimenters have tried to teach them language. So far none has succeeded very well. One experimenter taught an orangutan to say "papa" and "cup" and to use these words with some meaning, but the process was laborious [Warden et al., 1936]. More recently, a childless couple took a newborn chimpanzee into their home and reared it as they would a child [Hayes and Hayes, 1951]. Their idea was that an ape might learn to talk if it were treated exactly like a human baby and given all the love and attention possible. After almost 3 years, however, although the chimpanzee could occasionally use the words "mama," "papa," and "cup" meaning-

fully, it had not developed its linguistic skills any more than that.

So far as we know, then, apes can learn to use a few simple words only through painfully slow practice, and we have no evidence that they can ever learn to speak a variety of words or anything like sentences. So the limit of language ability in the ape is very low and can be realized only very gradually and by intensive training. Quite different, of course, is the human infant with his much greater hereditary potential for language behavior.

HUMAN INTELLIGENCE   A great many human studies have been conducted on the inheritance of such things as emotionality, learning aptitude, behavioral disorders, and intelligence. Some of these studies are covered in later chapters. Here we shall consider the genetic basis of intelligence and the interaction of heredity with environment.

Intelligence is a general term covering a person's aptitudes in a wide range of tasks involving vocabulary, numbers, problem solving, concepts, and so on. It is measured by standardized tests, which usually involve several specific aptitudes, often with emphasis on verbal aptitudes. A test score on an intelligence test can be converted into an intelligence quotient, or IQ, which indicates the individual's relative standing in the population independently of his age. Since an intelligence quotient reflects several aptitudes, not just one, and each of these is itself fairly complex, we should expect that the inheritance of intelligence would be multiply determined; that is, it would depend on many genes rather than on one or two pairs.

A natural family, consisting of parents and children all of whom are related by blood, offers us the opportunity to compare individuals who differ in inheritance by various degrees and who have relatively similar environments. To make such a comparison, we use a statistical index called a correlation coefficient which expresses the degree to which pairs of individuals make similar scores. A correlation of 1.00 indicates perfect agreement. (Tests, however, are never perfectly reliable; so we never

TABLE 2.2 *Correlations of intelligence scores (IQs) and heights for individuals related to different degrees*

RELATIONSHIPS		CORRELATION OF INTELLIGENCE	CORRELATION OF HEIGHT	
HEREDITARY SIMILARITY	Identical twins*	.88	.93	ENVIRONMENTAL SIMILARITY
	Fraternal twins (like sex)*	.63	.64	
	Siblings†,‡	.51–.53	.54–.60	ENVIRONMENTAL SIMILARITY
	Parents and children‡	.49	.51	
HEREDITARY SIMILARITY	Grandparents and grandchildren‡	.34	.32	ENVIRONMENTAL SIMILARITY
	Uncles (aunts) and nephews (nieces)‡	.35	.29	
	Cousins	.29	.24	

NOTE: Braces indicate those relationships which, among themselves, have about the same degree—either high or low—of similarity of heredity or environment.
* Newman et al., 1937.
† McNemar, 1942.
‡ Burt and Howard, 1956.

obtain correlations of 1.00.) A correlation of .00 indicates no relation; each pair of scores is no more alike than we would expect from chance. In between, various degrees of correlation are possible.

Some of the relationships in a natural family are shown in Table 2.2. These relationships may be grouped according to either similarity of heredity or similarity of environment. If heredity were the dominant factor in intelligence, we would expect the intelligence scores of those most similar in inheritance to be most highly correlated. If environment were the dominant factor, we would expect the highest correlation coefficients to be among those with the most similar environments.

Actually both expectations are met, as one can see by comparing different groupings in Table 2.2. The highest correlation of .88 is obtained between identical twins, who have identical heredity and almost identical environments. The correlation drops to .63 for fraternal twins of the same sex, who have about the same environments as identical twins but less similarity in heredity. This indicates that heredity is a factor. It drops again, however, from fraternal twins to siblings (brother or sister), who have about the same degree of hereditary similarity as fraternal twins, but less similarity in their environments. This indicates that environment is a factor. Sibling pairs and parent-child pairs have about the same degree of hereditary similarity, and fairly similar, but somewhat different, environments. As one might expect, the correlation coefficients are about the same, but slightly lower for the parent-child pairs. There is another drop in correlation for grandparent-grandchild and uncle-nephew pairs, which have, among themselves, about the same degree of similarity of both heredity and environment, but less of both than do siblings and parent-child pairs. Cousins, who have less similarity of heredity than uncles and nephews or grandparents and grandchildren, have even lower correlations.

Note that the correlations for height are about the same as those for intelligence. They tend to run a little higher for closely related individuals and a little lower for remotely related individuals. The fact, though, that the two sets of correlations closely parallel each other makes us believe that heredity plays about as important a part in the physical characteristic of height as it does in intelligence.

From studies of this kind, we see that when heredity changes, leaving environment relatively constant, the correlation of intelligence test scores between groups of relatives drops. Hence heredity is a factor in intelligence. On the other hand, when the degree of similarity of heredity remains constant and the similarity of environment changes, the correlations also go down. Hence environment is also a factor. Unfortunately, we cannot tell from such data which is the more important factor, if

indeed either is; we can tell only that both are involved.

To evaluate the relative roles of heredity and environment in intelligence, we must refer to another kind of study, one that is more difficult to do. Such a study seeks to compare the intelligence of identical twins reared apart in different environments, thereby holding heredity constant and allowing environment to vary. This has been done in a study of 19 sets of twins [Newman et al., 1937].

Most of the 19 sets of twins were separated at less than two years of age, although one pair parted as late as six years of age. The intelligence of each set of twins was tested later, at ages varying from eleven years to fifty-nine years, but each twin of a pair was tested at the same age. To obtain a measure of the different environments of each twin, judges independently rated their educational advantages on a scale of 1 to 10. From such ratings, the sets of twins could be divided into three general groups: those with very dissimilar environments, those with very similar environments, and those in between (see Table 2.3). Those of nearly similar environments differed hardly at all in intelligence. Those, on the other hand, who had very dissimi-

TABLE 2.3 *Comparison of IQs of identical twins reared apart*

NUMBER OF PAIRS OF TWINS	EDUCATIONAL ADVANTAGE	AGE AT SEPARATION (IN MONTHS)	AVERAGE DIFFERENCE IN IQ BETWEEN TWINS	SUPERIORITY IN IQ POINTS OF TWINS WITH GREATER ADVANTAGES
6	Very unequal (5.1 on 10-point scale)	15	15.2	15.2
7	Somewhat unequal (2.4 on 10-point scale)	9	5.4	4.6
6	Relatively similar (1.6 on 10-point scale)	24	4.5	1.0

SOURCE: *Based on Newman et al., 1937.*

FIGURE 2.9 *Early steps in human development.*

lar environments differed by sizable amounts; on the average, it was 15 points. Those in between differed by about 5 points, which is not a particularly significant difference.

We may therefore conclude that a relatively poor environment handicaps a person's intelligence quotient. It is interesting, however, that the correlation between the IQs of identical twins reared apart was .77. This is somewhat poorer than the .88 for identical twins reared together, but it is still better than that for fraternal twins and siblings reared together. Thus, again, both heredity and environment are important in intelligence.

It is not proper, however, to think of aptitudes such as intelligence as being concocted of so much heredity and so much environment, like a cooking recipe. Rather the relation between heredity and environment is an *interaction*. This means that the two general variables, heredity and environment, jointly determine a trait or aptitude. The importance of one depends on the other. If a person of high hereditary aptitude, for example, is subjected to a very poor environment, his measured ability will probably be low. If on the other hand his hereditary potential is low, his measured aptitude will probably be low even if he has the best of environments. In order, therefore, for him to possess high measured aptitude, he needs both high hereditary potential and a good environment.

Maturation and growth

Heredity, we have seen, plays its role by directing the development of the organism. This development takes time. Indeed, it is not complete until an individual is well along into adulthood. It proceeds in stages throughout life—before birth, during infancy, childhood, adolescence, and adulthood—and different processes are prominent in each of the stages.

FERTILIZATION

At time zero, the sperm penetrates the egg.

CELL DIVISION

In about 24 hours, the fertilized egg divides in two.

In about 48 hours, each new cell divides in two.

DIFFERENTIATION

In about 13 days, three layers of specialized cells appear within the ball.

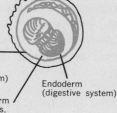

As the new individual grows inside its mother these layers become:

Ectoderm (skin, sense organs, nervous system)

Endoderm (digestive system)

Mesoderm (muscles, bone, blood)

EMBRYO

2 to 8 weeks

FETUS

3 to 9 months

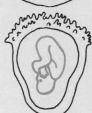

By studying these different processes and stages, we can obtain a better idea of the way in which heredity is linked to behavior. We shall begin by tracing the embryological development of an individual, since this lays the groundwork for behavior, and after that we shall consider the development of behavior.

First, we must get acquainted with the concept of maturation, for this concept embraces the processes going on in development. *Maturation* is the process of bringing the various parts of an organism to full development. Actually it is not one process, but many, for different parts develop at different rates and some reach their full development before others. We may speak, for example, of the maturation of the nervous system, of the sex glands, or of walking ability, referring in each case to the processes through which the organ or the behavioral ability reaches its full development.

ORGAN DEVELOPMENT   The fertilization of an egg by a sperm takes place in one of the fallopian tubes which lead from the mother's ovary, where the egg was produced, to the womb or *uterus*. About 24 hours after fertilization, the zygote begins to divide by reproducing two cells like itself (see Figure 2.9). Each of these cells again divides in two, and the process is repeated until many cells have been produced. While this cell division is going on, the cluster of cells slowly travels down the tube to the mother's uterus. Usually it reaches the uterus in about 9 days, at which time it has become a hollow ball of cells. This ball, still only about $2/100$ inch in diameter, attaches itself to the wall of the uterus.

The first 2 weeks of life, during which these events are taking place, are called the period of the *ovum*. During this period, all the cells being reproduced are much alike. Then a new period, the period of the *embryo*, begins and lasts for about 6 weeks. At the beginning of the period, the cells of the ball differentiate into three layers, each somewhat different, called *endoderm* (inner layer), *mesoderm* (middle layer), and *ectoderm* (outer layer). Each of these layers goes on differentiating

various kinds of cells to form tissues and organs (see Figure 2.9). At the end of the embryonic period, 2 months after conception, the cells and organs have taken the crude form of a human being and the embryo then becomes a *fetus*. The period of the fetus lasts 7 months, from the third to the ninth month of gestation. At birth, the fetus becomes an *infant*.

TIMING OF DEVELOPMENT   When the embryo is about 6 weeks old, its heart begins to beat. About the same time, the organs necessary for behavior begin to function. At first, the *nervous system, muscles, sense organs,* and *glands* develop separately, and without any connection between them. At this stage of development, the muscles can be excited electrically and can be made to contract. At a little later stage, the nervous system sends down nerves to the muscles; then the nervous system can be excited electrically and contractions can be seen in the muscles. Finally, the sense organs connect with the nervous system, thus making a sensory-motor arc. At this stage, a muscular response can be produced by stimulating a sense organ. Such a response is the most rudimentary of all patterns of behavior.

The timing of these developments varies somewhat with different parts of the nervous system, different muscles, and different sense organs. Some connections between muscles and sense organs of the skin are established within 3 months after conception, and thus some reflexes are possible at this time. Connections with the eyes and ears develop more slowly, and reflexes involving these sense organs do not occur until about the seventh month.

MATURATION AND BEHAVIOR   One of the interesting and important things about this development is the large margin of safety that it provides. Organs mature, and connections are made, well in advance of the time they are needed. The human fetus stands practically no chance of surviving, for example, if it is born before the sixth month; yet it can make breathing movements in the fourth month.

The fetus, similarly, makes walking movements with its legs in the fifth month; in the sixth month it will suck if its mouth or cheek is brushed, and it may grasp an object in its palm or even vocalize. The fetus will not need these elements of behavior until it is born; yet they are ready 2, 3, or 4 months ahead of time.

By the time the infant is born, then, most of its reflexes and elementary forms of behavior are ready for use. The breathing reactions, sucking reflexes, crying reactions to cold and discomfort, and the other behavior patterns that infants need to get along in the world are fully developed. Many other patterns that are not needed, however, are not ready; they develop slowly after birth, and may not fully mature until the child is ten or twelve years old or even later.

THE NERVOUS SYSTEM   Of all the organs of the body, the nervous system and the endocrine glands are among the slowest to reach complete maturity. Although the spinal cord, nerves, and lower parts of the brain are relatively mature at birth, the brain and particularly its rind, or *cortex,* go on maturing for some time. Most infants, for example, are unable to follow moving objects with their eyes until several weeks after birth, because the pathways in the brain necessary for this activity are not mature.

The cerebral cortex (see Chapter 19), which is important for learning and more complex behavior, is even slower to mature [Munn, 1955]. Scientists have repeatedly observed in pathological cases that a lack of cortex at birth makes little difference in behavior at the time and for several months afterward; they have concluded, therefore, that the cortex is not functioning at that time [Sherman et al., 1936]. The ability to sit up, to crawl, and to walk all depend on the cortex, and it is not until it matures that infants are able to do these things. Most maturation of the cortex is completed by the time the child reaches the age of one to two years, but electrical records of the brain's activity show that some maturation goes on until a person is ten or fifteen years old [Smith, 1941].

THE ENDOCRINE GLANDS   The term *endocrine* applies to those glands of the body which empty their secretions, called *hormones,* directly into the blood rather than into cavities of the body. The glands that do the latter are called *exocrine* glands. Among the endocrine glands are the sex glands (ovaries and testicles), the pancreas, which secretes the hormone insulin, and the thyroid glands in the neck. The salivary glands are a familiar example of exocrine glands; they secrete saliva into the mouth. Of the two kinds of glands, the endocrines are the more important in psychology, because their hormones, as we shall see in Chapters 7 and 19, affect behavior in a variety of ways.

The endocrine glands mature slowly. This may be explained in part by the fact that the supply of hormones furnished to the fetus by the mother makes it unnecessary for the fetus to secrete its own. Then, too, many of the hormones of the endocrine glands are not needed until later in life. The sex glands are a good example of endocrine glands which mature late. They do not mature until puberty, when boys and girls, at the age of twelve or thirteen, begin taking on the characteristics of men and women. Some of the changes that take place then, such as the growth of the beard and change of voice in boys and the development of the breasts in girls, are brought about by sex hormones. So, too, are changes in sexual motivation and the emergence of patterns of sexual behavior. This connection has been established in experiments with many different kinds of young animals by injecting sex hormones into them and noting the appearance of sexual behavior at a considerably younger age than that at which it would otherwise appear [Beach, 1949]. This is just one kind of evidence that the schedule of maturation of sexual behavior is controlled by the maturation of the sex glands.

MATURATION WITHOUT PRACTICE   The maturation of different organs of the body could conceivably be linked to behavior in several general ways. One is that maturation might bring a certain behavior into play without the aid of any learning or practice. This surely happens in the case of reflexes and instinctive patterns, for these appear without any learning when maturation has proceeded far enough. For such patterns, we can say that the *behavior* itself matures. Second, maturation might merely make a certain kind of behavior possible but leave it to learning or practice to develop the behavior. This, too, surely happens, and we say that it is an ability or *readiness* that matures, not the behavior itself. This concept was implied in our discussion of various abilities, but we shall note specific examples of it in a moment. Between these two possibilities lies an area in which the behavior, it would seem, might almost mature but would require a slight amount of practice at an optimum time in order to perfect it. Indeed, as we shall see, the development of behavior proceeds in *all three* of these ways.

A number of behavior patterns mature with little or no practice required for their perfection. In few cases, if any, can we say flatly that no practice whatever is required, for the behavior almost invariably becomes a little more skilled after some

practice. However the effect of practice can be almost negligible, and when it is, maturation can be given the lion's share of the credit for the emergence of the behavior. The following paragraphs describe a classical study of this question [Carmichael, 1927]:

A psychologist took two groups of salamanders before they had begun to swim. He let one of the groups grow up in a tank of plain water, but he lightly anesthetized the other group by putting chloretone in their water. The chloretone kept the salamanders motionless without interfering with their growth, since salamanders are born with a yolk sac which supplies food for some time. The experimenter waited until the normal salamanders started swimming and had been swimming for 5 days. Then he transferred the anesthetized salamanders to plain water.

Within half an hour, all the salamanders were swimming normally. To see whether this group learned rapidly in the half hour or simply required that long for the anesthetic to wear off, he also anesthetized the control animals which had already been swimming. When he returned this group to plain water, it took them a half-hour to swim normally

IN CHICKS, BOTH MATURATION AND LEARNING PLAY A PART IN PERFECTING THE SWALLOWING OF GRAIN

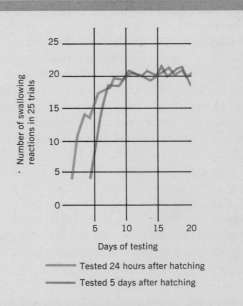

FIGURE 2.10 *Improvement of swallowing reactions in chicks. Chicks were kept in the dark until they were first tested. The first group was tested 24 hours after hatching, the second group 5 days after hatching. Chicks in both groups at first swallowed the grain on only a small proportion of the total number of pecking trials. The chicks in the group tested 24 hours after hatching improved gradually; those tested 5 days after hatching improved rapidly and caught up with the first group in about two days. (After Cruze, 1935.)*

again, just as it had the group that had been under pro-longed anesthesia. Thus he demonstrated that maturation was the important, if not the sole, factor in the emergence of swimming behavior of salamanders. The half-hour delay, during which the anesthesia wore off, involved no learning.

Another study of this subject was done with baby chicks [Cruze, 1935]. Newly hatched chicks peck fairly accurately but fail to hit the grain about 25 per cent of the time. When they hit it, however, they frequently do not seize it, and even when they seize it, they often do not swallow it. The most sensitive measure of the complete eating reaction, consisting of pecking, seizing, and swallowing, is therefore the ratio of the number of swallowing reactions to the number of pecking trials. And swallowing reactions can be studied separately from accuracy of pecking.

The experimenter kept two groups of newly hatched chicks in the dark, to prevent practice in pecking, one group for 24 hours and the other for 5 days, feeding them by hand in the meantime. At the end of the period in the dark, each group was tested for 25 pecking trials daily. On the first testing, both groups were practically perfect in hitting the grain when they pecked at it. Hence pecking, as distinguished from swallowing, depended almost entirely on maturation. Each group, however, did rather poorly when scored on swallowing reactions (see Figure 2.10), making an average of less than 5 swallowing reactions in 25 trials. Each group improved as testing went on, but the second group, kept in the dark for 5 days, progressed much more rapidly than the first group, catching up to it in about 2 days. From this fact, we conclude that the development of swallowing reactions depends upon both maturation and learning.

These studies demonstrate that swimming in sala-manders and pecking in chicks, both simple but essential activities, mature at the appropriate time without practice being necessary, but that swallow-ing in chicks is a skill which improves with practice.

Research on human beings is not so neat or unequivocal, because of the difficulty of doing con-trolled experiments with children, but it confirms the conclusion that basic activities are largely, if not wholly, dependent on maturation.

One study takes advantage of the way Hopi Indians restrict the behavior of their babies during infancy [Dennis, 1940]:

The Hopi Indians bind their infants tightly to a board so that the infants cannot move for most of the day. (Other groups, such as the Shoshone, also do this; see Figure 2.11.). Usually the infant is unbound for only an hour or two a day while he is cleaned. Hence he does not get the same opportunity to practice sitting, creeping, and walking that normal unbound infants do. Yet these bound children de-velop the ability to sit, creep, and walk just as rapidly as children who are never bound. It seems, then, that it takes little or no practice for a human child to develop these capacities.

The following experiment employed the method of co-twin control to study the relationship between maturation and development [Gesell and Thomp-son, 1929]:

Two girls who were identical twins, and who thus had identical heredity and the same maturational schedules, were used in an experiment. One girl, twin T, was trained in special activities such as climbing, while the other twin, C, was given no opportunity to practice these activities. After 6 weeks, twin T progressed from not being able to climb stairs at all to making five stairs in 26 seconds. At this point, control twin C was allowed to try the stairs. On her first attempt and without prior practice, she climbed all five stairs in 45 seconds. With only 2 weeks of training, twin C could make the stairs in 10 seconds. The same results were found in other types of basic activity.

From evidence of this kind, two conclusions can be drawn: (1) Maturation, not learning, is pri-marily responsible for the development of such basic behavior patterns as walking and climbing in human children, swimming in salamanders, or pecking in chicks. (2) To the extent that training or practice helps to perfect such patterns, it develops skill much more rapidly in the more mature individual.

READINESS FOR LEARNING Some things, quite obviously, never are acquired merely by maturation; they have to be learned. A person does not acquire

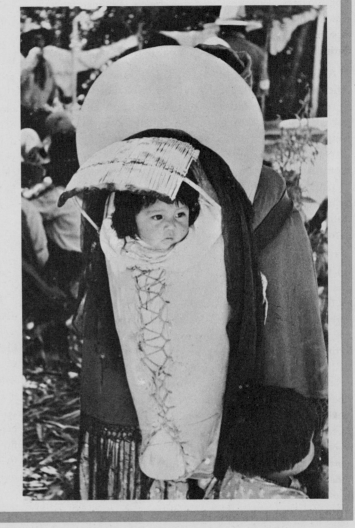

FIGURE 2.11   *A Shoshone Indian baby is carried firmly bound in a cradle board, protected by a sunshade. She is carried wherever the mother goes, and the cradle is hung on a bush while the mother gathers berries or digs roots. The practice of baby bundling, which is common in some Indian and Eskimo groups, restricts the baby's opportunity to practice reaching, sitting, creeping, and walking, but it does not interfere with motor development. (Courtesy of E. A. Hoebel.)*

the ability to talk, to read, or to do arithmetic by maturation alone; he has to learn to do them. In such skills, nevertheless, maturation plays an essential role, for what matures is the *readiness* for learning them. Until the readiness appears in the schedule of maturation, there is no point in attempting to learn them.

The following case dramatically illustrates this point [Davis, 1947]:

A deaf-mute mother hid her young daughter from all outside social contact until she was more than six years old. The child was thus deprived of practically all opportunity to learn spoken language. When neighbors discovered the child at age six, she could not speak; she uttered only incomprehensible sounds. In 2 months of training, however, she learned many words. By that time, too, she started putting sentences together as fast as a child normally does at three years of age. Of course, she had to learn the vocabulary of English and the rules of constructing sentences, but her progress was rapid. Her case demonstrates strikingly that the capacity or readiness for learning language is something that gradually matures without practice, even though learning is required to develop skill.

There are many kinds of readiness. Generally, each appears at a characteristic age. Readiness for learning speech appears typically in a child's second year, that for learning to read at about six years. In each case, the readiness appears rather abruptly, usually over the course of a few weeks. When it appears, the child's progress in learning takes a spurt. Before he is ready, he learns slowly, and training is almost useless. When he is ready, if he has the opportunity to learn, he learns rapidly. From this fact, to be illustrated in a moment, we infer that a characteristic time arrives for the maturation of an ability or readiness to be completed.

All children, however, do not mature at the same rate. Some mature slowly, others rapidly. In general, if one ability matures slowly, others will too, though this is not always so. A child's general rate of maturation of abilities, however, is something that can be measured. It is, in fact, just what intelligence tests for children do measure. Most children's intelligence tests sample several of a child's abilities and supply an overall score called a *mental age (MA)*. The MA is arrived at by comparing the child's score with that of average children at various age levels. If, for example, a child's overall ability is the same as that of the average six-year-old, he is given an MA of 6, regardless of what his *chronological age (CA)* happens to be. Thus the MA is the measure of an individual's general level of maturation of abilities. The IQ is simply MA/CA multiplied by 100.

The point that each readiness comes to maturity rather abruptly can be demonstrated by using the MA to match children on their maturational level and then comparing them on some skill, such as reading. The following study is an example [Morphett and Washburn, 1931]:

One hundred and forty-one children were given an intel-

ligence test when they entered the first grade. The test furnished an MA for each child. About halfway through the year, without knowing the test results, teachers rated each child on his progress in learning to read, giving him either a "satisfactory" or an "unsatisfactory." Figure 2.12 shows that the percentage of children making satisfactory progress in reading rises sharply from zero to about 70 per cent during the 6 months between an MA of 6 years and an MA of 6½ years. We would not have seen this jump, however, if the CA of the children had been used, for they were all about six years old, and slight differences among them in CA were inconsequential.

The practical implication of studies such as these is that we must wait until an ability or readiness is mature before attempting to teach skills that depend on readiness. Our common practice in the United

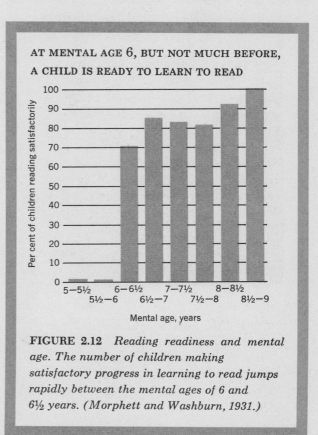

FIGURE 2.12 *Reading readiness and mental age. The number of children making satisfactory progress in learning to read jumps rapidly between the mental ages of 6 and 6½ years. (Morphett and Washburn, 1931.)*

FIGURE 2.13 *Imprinting of goslings. The goslings have been imprinted on the experimenter, Dr. Konrad Lorenz. Though he carries a food bucket, his rhythmic sounds, not hunger, keep them with him. (Life Magazine, © 1955, Time, Inc.)*

States of admitting children to school and programming the education of children on the basis of CA does not recognize this point. Children of six years of age vary in general readiness, that is, in MA. For instance, some children may have MAs of 4½ or 5; others may have MAs of 8 or 9. The child of low MA cannot profit from training until he is considerably older than the child of very high MA. Since the time to start training in reading is at a mental age of 6 to 6½, the common practice of admitting children to school at a CA of 6 is all right for the average child, but not for the duller and brighter ones.

OPTIMUM TIME FOR PRACTICE It does no good, we have seen, to attempt to teach a skill before the readiness for learning it has matured. So as a practical matter we should wait for the maturation of ability or readiness. Having done that, however, another important question arises. Is it possible to wait too long? If a skill is not learned or practiced when maturation makes it possible, is it more difficult to learn or perfect the skill later?

Evidence exists that this is indeed true for some skills and abilities. Often there is an *optimum* time for learning when behavior patterns should be practiced or the ability to perform deteriorates.

Deterioration without practice. Such deterioration without practice probably takes place for many of the behavior patterns that mature with little or no practice.

In one experiment, the flying behavior of birds was studied [Dennis, 1941]:

The experimenter placed two baby turkey buzzards, taken from their nest, in a cage that was barely large enough to permit them to stand up, thus restricting their activity. At intervals he tested their ability to fly, but they regularly failed. Indeed, they were still unable to fly long after wild buzzards judged to be the same age could be seen flying in the vicinity. Eventually, however, they did fly and joined a group of wild buzzards. The restriction, nevertheless, retarded the development of their flying skills.

Experiments of this kind demonstrate that restriction of the opportunity for making responses up to the time when the skill normally matures does not handicap the development of the skill. Beyond this point, however, further restriction retards or prevents the appearance of the skill.

Imprinting. The same conclusion holds for the rather special phenomenon of *imprinting* which takes place most strongly in such birds as ducks, geese, and chickens. Imprinting is characterized by the very rapid development, at a critical period or age, of a response to a stimulus. In many ways imprinting resembles a certain type of learning [Moltz, 1960], but an argument has been made for important differences between imprinting and learning [Hess, 1964]. The response of following a moving stimulus has been investigated extensively. A gosling or chicken, for example, imprints on its moving mother and soon follows her around. The stimuli for this imprinting of the response of following seem to be the movement of the mother and the sounds she makes. If an experimenter substitutes himself or another object for the mother at the critical time when imprinting ordinarily takes place, the young bird will begin to follow the substitute (see Figure 2.13). The following study makes use of this and illustrates imprinting [Ramsay and Hess, 1954]:

The experimenters set up a wooden model of a duck as the object on which to imprint young ducklings. By remote control, they could make the duck move around a track and/or emit sounds of *gock, gock, gock* (recorded on tape) normally made by mother ducks (see Figure 2.14). Using a standard procedure, they gave each of 92 ducklings an opportunity to become imprinted on the model duck. Later in systematic tests, by observing responses to the model, they determined whether the ducklings had in fact become imprinted on the model. Groups of ducklings were given their imprinting experiences at different times, one group at 5 to 8 hours, and so on up to 29 or 32 hours. On later testing, the experimenters obtained the results shown in Figure 2.15. The ducklings exposed within a few hours after birth imprinted fairly well, but the optimum time for imprinting was 13 to 16 hours of age. Ducklings exposed at 30 hours after hatching hardly imprinted at all.

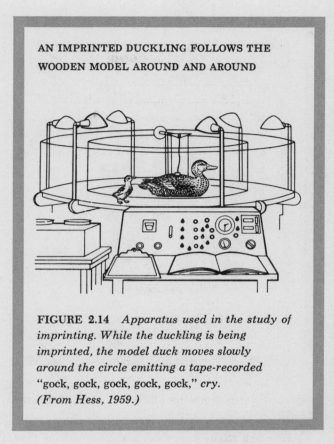

AN IMPRINTED DUCKLING FOLLOWS THE WOODEN MODEL AROUND AND AROUND

FIGURE 2.14 *Apparatus used in the study of imprinting. While the duckling is being imprinted, the model duck moves slowly around the circle emitting a tape-recorded "gock, gock, gock, gock, gock," cry. (From Hess, 1959.)*

Thus, even more important than the mere existence of imprinting is the fact that it takes place at a *critical time.* Not all studies have shown a critical period of imprinting at 13 to 16 hours, but most have shown that some critical time period exists [Moltz, 1960]. Imprinting must take place at the right time in development; otherwise it will not occur in a strong way.

Special training. Does an optimum time occur for human learning of special skills? We suspect that there may be a best time for learning special skills, but the evidence is not very extensive. People who attempt to acquire athletic, artistic, musical, or linguistic skills late in life seldom achieve the proficiency of those who began earlier when the readiness for such learning had just matured. Other

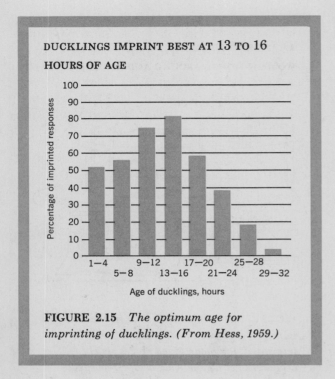

DUCKLINGS IMPRINT BEST AT 13 TO 16 HOURS OF AGE

Percentage of imprinted responses

Age of ducklings, hours

FIGURE 2.15 *The optimum age for imprinting of ducklings. (From Hess, 1959.)*

evidence comes from the following study [McGraw, 1935]:

Johnny and Jimmy were twins who, it turned out later, were fraternal rather than identical. During the first year and a half of infancy, Johnny was given intensive training in a whole series of skills, first in walking, later in such things as swimming, roller skating, and tricycling. Jimmy was left to develop on his own, with even less than the normal amount of practice and training. As soon as Johnny had perfected an activity, Jimmy was tested on it. When the twins were twenty-two months old, Jimmy was trained intensively in the activities in which Johnny was already proficient. After that, both were tested at regular intervals until they were six years old.

In such basic things as walking, Jimmy caught up with Johnny in very short order. Once given the chance, Jimmy showed that he could equal Johnny with little or no practice. In certain activities, however, where special techniques were helpful, Jimmy was at a disadvantage and sometimes failed to catch up with Johnny at any time. At one stage,

for example, Johnny learned to climb down from a pedestal by hanging with his hands and dropping onto the mattress below. Jimmy did not learn this feat. Later, when Jimmy was trained in roller skating, he was unable to do so well as Johnny who had been taught it some months before. In general, Johnny remained superior to Jimmy in nearly every skill involving muscular coordination.

This study seems to indicate that the best time to start teaching athletic skills is during the first two years, and that if the opportunity to begin then is missed, it may be difficult to develop these skills to the fullest later.

Isolation studies. Practice at the right time in the maturational schedule, we have just seen, is needed for the fullest development of some skills. It also seems true that sensory experience at crucial times is a requisite for normal development. An individual must be able to see, hear, and feel objects in his environment in order to acquire appropriate ways of responding to them. As yet we cannot say exactly when it is necessary to have this experience or how it depends on the maturation of any particular ability, but we do have evidence on the general point from isolation experiments, and we discuss it fully in the chapter on perception (see Chapter 10).

Isolation studies also show the role of experience at a crucial time in the development of social and emotional behavior. One study used isolated dogs as subjects [Thompson and Melzack, 1956]:

In this study, puppies were raised singly in closed pens that admitted light from the top but denied them any experience with the outside world or with each other. As controls, litter mates of these puppies were raised as pets. These conditions were maintained for the first 6 to 9 months of life, at which time the isolated puppies were taken out of their pens and treated like the controls. Differences between the two groups were observed and recorded.

The pups reared in isolation were markedly different. They were naïve and immature in many respects. Strange objects, such as an umbrella or a balloon, readily excited them, whereas the control pups showed little interest in the objects. The isolated pups ran around randomly and generally were more excitable than the controls. In tests of learning to solve problems, the isolated pups were greatly inferior to the controls. Even after several years, there were observable differences between the groups.

Isolation studies with monkey subjects are perhaps more relevant to the human condition [Harlow and Harlow, 1962]:

As part of a series of studies on the effects of early isolation on emotional and social behavior, baby monkeys were raised under several different conditions. Control animals were raised with their mothers and allowed to play with other small monkeys. Experimental monkeys were raised under several different types of isolation conditions. Baby monkeys of one group were taken from their mothers soon after birth and raised alone in cages which allowed them to see and hear, but not play with, other baby monkeys. Other experimental monkeys were raised under conditions of true solitary confinement and not allowed to see or hear other monkeys. The social, emotional, and sexual behavior of the experimental monkeys from both groups was markedly abnormal. For instance, although sexual motivation was apparently normally strong, the experimental monkeys tended to be inept and not know the rules of monkey "courtship." So inept were they that very few of the isolated female monkeys became pregnant. In fact, these monkeys could not be used for laboratory breeding stock. The isolated monkeys tended not to develop stable social hierarchies or "pecking orders"; nor did they play so vigorously and maturely when tested in a special monkey "playroom." The totally isolated monkeys also tended to be submissive and fearful in threatening situations. The *crucial period* for the development of social skills in the monkey seems to be during the first year, but after the first 3 months of life; isolation during the first 90 days seems to produce little effect on social and emotional behavior. It was also found that only a few minutes of social experience each day would prevent the consequences of social isolation; but after a monkey had been raised in isolation, social experience itself did little to make behavior more normal.

Observations on the behavior of children who, as normal infants, were reared in rather impersonal institutions until about the age of three, have shown that such children have emotional difficulties and intellectual deficits [Goldfarb, 1945]. Thus an environment which provides opportunity for social contact and "tender loving care" at a crucial time seems to be necessary for the social and emotional development of human beings and other primates.

Sensory and motor development

Having gained some understanding of the roles of heredity, maturation, and learning in development, we may now turn to a description of the major events that take place in development. In this section, we shall consider sensory and motor development. *Motor* means moving or movement and, hence, is used by psychologists and physiologists to refer to human and animal movements, such as walking, swimming, steering, grasping, typing, and so on. It may be distinguished from verbal or intellectual activities that do not involve doing things.

PRENATAL DEVELOPMENT During the prenatal period, the individual exists as an aquatic creature and as a parasite within the body of its mother. Here it is well protected from harmful stimuli and has all its needs supplied. On the whole, the uterine environment is relatively constant, and it is relatively similar from one mother to another.

To the psychologist, the important feature of the fetal period is the unfolding of behavior that takes place. In a few short months—sometimes they seem long to the mother—the nervous system and other parts of the response mechanism mature almost completely. By the seventh month of prenatal life, the individual has fully developed most reflex patterns, such as turning the trunk and head, flexing and extending the limbs when touched, grasping objects that touch the palms of the hands, sucking when a nipple or similar object touches the mouth, and crying when in discomfort.

INFANCY Most of the features of the prenatal environment—a warm, dark, quiet, and watery environment—are relatively constant and require no adjustment on the part of the fetus. Birth changes all that. The infant is suddenly thrust into a highly variable environment where food is available only at intervals, where the temperature changes from time to time, and where lights, sounds, and other stimuli impinge intermittently on him. The newborn, of course, must now breathe to get his own oxygen. He must make his own adjustments and begin to establish some independence of the environment. He must ingest and digest his own food and regulate the temperature of his own body. It usually takes a few days for the infant to make these adjustments well, and in the course of them, he may lose a little of the weight that he had accumulated before birth. The newborn is now in the stage of *infancy,* which lasts for a period of about two years.

SENSORY DEVELOPMENT At birth, the baby has rather well-developed sense organs but some are more functionally mature than others. There is, however, wide variety among very young infants in their ability to use their senses. Some of this variation may be due to very early learning [Lipsitt, 1963]. Sensory development—as most other kinds of development—is due to *interaction* between maturation and learning.

In general, the senses of touch and temperature appear to be relatively well developed at birth or soon afterward, for babies refuse milk that is too hot and are sensitive to environmental temperatures. Pain, however, appears not to be so well developed as it is a few weeks later, as judged by the newborn's relative insensitivity to pinpricks and other noxious stimuli. The senses of taste and smell apparently are functional, but only on a rudimentary level.

Rudimentary hearing and vision are present at birth. It is difficult, but by no means impossible, to test these senses accurately in the very young infant. Several ingenious tests have been devised. Newborn infants can hear, and they give a startle response to

loud sudden noises. They do not seem to respond much to ordinary environmental sounds such as voices, but they are probably able to discriminate pitches, high and low tones, within the first 5 days of life. Studies of tone discrimination in one- to five-day-old infants have been done by using the phenomenon of habituation [Bridger, 1961]. When a loud tone is presented to the infant for a long time, he stops showing restlessness and other responses such as an increased heart rate—he habituates. After habituation, we may then sound another equally intense tone and see whether the infant responds to it. Responses to the new tone would indicate that the infant had perceived it as different from the original one to which he had habituated. This technique has shown that one- to five-day-old infants can discriminate between tones which are about one step apart on the musical scale [Mussen et al., 1963]. By the time the infant is three to four weeks old, he begins to respond to voices, and hearing is probably close to the adult level of acuity.

The visual system is only partially developed at birth. The retina and visual parts of the brain, the muscles controlling the movement of the eyes, and the muscles controlling the shape of the lens are not fully functional. About two weeks after birth, although there is much variation, the infant can follow a bright light with his eyes. However, good coordination of the eyes may take several more months to develop. Many months must elapse before the muscles controlling the shape of the lens—the muscles of accommodation—are working normally. This means that light from objects is not brought to a sharp focus on the retina; near objects must appear especially blurred to the infant—in other words, babies are farsighted. In spite of all this, the visual acuity of the infant is surprisingly good, as is shown by the following study [Fantz, et al, 1962]:

A special testing apparatus such as that shown in Figure 2.16 is used. The infant lies in a crib looking up at the ceiling of the testing chamber. The test stimuli, mounted on cardboard sheets, can be positioned by dowel

APPARATUS FOR A SOPHISTICATED GAME OF
PEEK-A-BOO

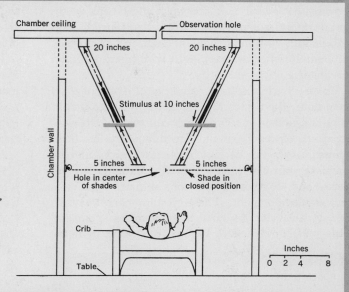

Chamber ceiling — Observation hole

20 inches — 20 inches

Stimulus at 10 inches

Chamber wall

5 inches — 5 inches

Hole in center
of shades — Shade in
closed position

Crib

Table

Inches
0 2 4 8

FIGURE 2.16 *Apparatus used to study visual
acuity in very young infants. As shown in this
cross-section, stimuli can be shown at three
positions, 5 inches, 10 inches, or 20 inches, from
the eyes of the baby. During actual observations,
only one pair of stimuli was used and the shades
were in the open position. The observation
hole is not drawn to scale—it was only ¼ inch
in diameter. (After Fantz, Ordy and
Udelf, 1962.)*

rods at 5, 10, or 20 inches from the infant's eyes. While
the stimuli are being changed, shades are drawn across the
lower part of the test compartment. The observer looks
through a peephole at the top of the apparatus and notes
the visual responses of the baby. In earlier experiments
[Fantz, 1958], it had been shown that infants much prefer
to look at patterned objects; they spent more time looking
at complex figures than at homogeneous fields. In the
present experiment, lines of different width were paired
with blank gray stimulus panels, and the observer noted
the length of time the infant looked at the pattern. The
reflection of the pattern could be seen on the cornea of the
eye when the infant looked at the pattern, and this made
it easy to score responses. A test of visual perception is
thus made possible: the baby would look longer at the
patterned panel only if he could see the pattern; if the
lines were so close together that the pattern looked like a
blur, he would not show the differential looking responses.

Results showed that very young babies have surprisingly
good visual acuity and that it improves rapidly with age.
One-month infants can discriminate stripes as narrow as
⅛ inch at a 10-inch viewing distance; at six months,
infants can discriminate ¹⁄₆₄-inch stripes at 10 inches.

These values may be expressed in the Snellen notation (see
Chapter 8). (This is the familiar "20/20" notation. If you
have 20/20 vision, you can see at 20 feet what the normal
person can see at 20 feet; if you have 20/50 vision, your
vision is impaired and you can see at 20 feet what the
normal person can see at 50 feet.) With this notation, the
one-month-old baby, when compared with the adult, has
approximately 20/800 vision; the six-month-old infant has
approximately 20/100 vision.

Although vision is present at birth, there is plenty
of room for improvement through physical maturation and learning. 20/20 vision is not achieved until
the child is about seven years old [Hughes, 1963].

SEQUENCE OF MOTOR DEVELOPMENT The
most conspicuous events in the early development
of the infant are motor. During the first two years,
the infant gradually gains skills in controlling his
body. In contrast to a newborn infant, for example,
the child of two years is a miracle of muscular precision. He has good postural control in a wide
variety of positions. In fact, he often gets into posi-

tions that seem impossible to adults. He can walk forward, backward, and sideways, and he can go up and down a flight of steps. He has developed a good deal of skill with his hands—enough, in fact, to pick up a small pellet by grasping it with his thumb and forefinger.

If we chart carefully, as several psychologists have done, the things the infant can do from month to month and year to year, we can see that there is a *pattern* of development. The infant lifts his head before he sits up, he sits before he crawls, and he crawls before he walks. Actually, there are many little—and, to the parent, very important—details in this development. These developmental details fit into an orderly sequence; they make a pattern. This pattern is almost exactly the same in every

human infant, and each infant passes through the same steps in his development. As we might expect, the pattern is uniform because it is largely the result of maturation of the response mechanism.

Since there is a pattern to development in infancy, it is possible to construct *norms* for development. We may state, for example, that the infant can pick up a pea-sized object at 7 months and is able to creep at 9½ months. These ages at which the average child displays a particular skill, we call "norms." Many parents buy books that give detailed norms and then watch Junior with bated breath to see whether he progresses on schedule. They should remember, however, that norms are only averages, that some infants will be slower and some faster in acquiring successive stages of skill. They should realize, too, that speed of motor development has very little to do with intelligence [Shirley, 1933], for the child whose motor development is slow, but in the normal range, is as likely to have high or normal intelligence as the one whose motor development is rapid.

Figure 2.17 illustrates norms for the development of skills in the infant as well as variations in the rate of development. The skills named there are selected from a more extensive list for which norms have been obtained. The mark near the center of each bar indicates the median age at which the skill is attained; the median age is the age at which one-half of a typical population of infants attains the skill. The left end of each bar is the age at which the fastest quarter of the infants attain the skill; the right end is the age at which three-quarters acquire it. Note that the fastest quarter and the slowest quarter of infants lie outside the range of the bars. Consider, for example, the skill of standing alone. The median age at which children stand alone is about 62 weeks, but one-quarter of children can stand alone by 56 weeks, and another quarter have not reached this stage of development by 66 weeks. The *full range* of ages at which this skill is attained is considerably greater than that.

We know, then, the order in which skills appear and that each skill sets the stage for the develop-

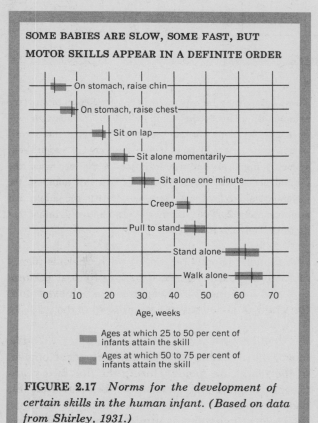

SOME BABIES ARE SLOW, SOME FAST, BUT MOTOR SKILLS APPEAR IN A DEFINITE ORDER

On stomach, raise chin
On stomach, raise chest
Sit on lap
Sit alone momentarily
Sit alone one minute
Creep
Pull to stand
Stand alone
Walk alone

Age, weeks

▬ Ages at which 25 to 50 per cent of infants attain the skill

▬ Ages at which 50 to 75 per cent of infants attain the skill

FIGURE 2.17 *Norms for the development of certain skills in the human infant. (Based on data from Shirley, 1931.)*

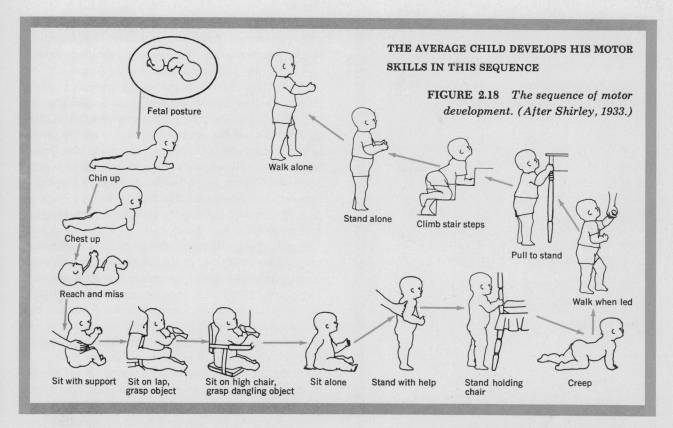

THE AVERAGE CHILD DEVELOPS HIS MOTOR SKILLS IN THIS SEQUENCE

FIGURE 2.18 *The sequence of motor development. (After Shirley, 1933.)*

Fetal posture

Chin up

Chest up

Reach and miss

Walk alone

Stand alone

Climb stair steps

Pull to stand

Walk when led

Sit with support

Sit on lap, grasp object

Sit on high chair, grasp dangling object

Sit alone

Stand with help

Stand holding chair

Creep

ment of succeeding patterns. It is unwise, however, to try to predict the exact age at which any specific skill will appear for any individual child. The series of sketches in Figure 2.18 depicts the general pattern of development for the average infant.

Once the child has mastered the art of getting about, he progresses rapidly to more advanced skills, such as walking up and down stairs, jumping, hopping, skipping, and running. As he develops speed and accuracy, he begins to coordinate all these skills into more complex activities. So the little girl who formerly used her doll carriage to steady herself as she took her first halting steps now casually wheels her "baby" to the store on a "shopping" tour. The boy who at first was content merely to balance himself on his tricycle now hitches a wagon on behind and goes tearing down the road playing fire engine.

PREHENSION *Prehension* is a term denoting the *grasping of objects.* The simplest kind of prehension is palmar grasping: the object is grasped in the palm of the hand, as when a person hangs from the limb of a tree or takes hold of the rungs of a ladder. By using the thumb in apposition to the index finger, a more precise grasp is possible, as when a person picks up a pencil or uses a pair of tweezers. This kind of prehension enables us to manipulate objects with considerable precision.

Prehensile abilities develop rather slowly in the infant. Like locomotion, they grow out of more basic patterns of behavior that must develop beforehand [Halverson, 1931]. (See Figure 2.19 for all the stages of this process.) First, the infant makes more or less random movements involving the whole arm in the general direction of the object, and frequently he misses it altogether. In time, his movements are

A BABY LEARNS TO REACH BEFORE HE CAN GRASP, THEN TO GRASP WITH HIS PALM AND FINGERS BEFORE HE CAN GRASP WITH HIS THUMB AND FINGER TIPS

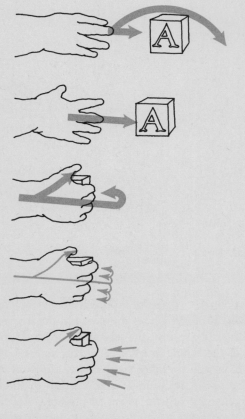

FIGURE 2.19 *Five stages in the development of reaching and grasping. (Modified from Halverson, 1931.)*

independently of the upper arm and, eventually, the wrist separately from the arm. By this time, the reaching movement that was a circular pattern originally has become a straight-line approach.

While the infant is perfecting reaching movements, another important ability is developing, the ability to move the thumb in apposition to the other fingers. We see the emergence of this ability in the infant's grasping of objects. At first, the infant squeezes an object with his fingers, without using his thumb. Later, he curls his fingers over the object and opposes them with his thumb. Finally, he uses only the tips of his fingers and his thumb to grasp and manipulate the object.

A good deal of evidence suggests that maturation, rather than learning, is the important factor in the development of both locomotion and prehension [McGraw, 1946]. All children develop these skills in the same sequence, and we find relatively little variability in how any particular behavior pattern is expressed. After the infant gets the fundamental ability "down pat," there is considerably more variation in the way each infant uses it. Here the influence of environment comes into play, and learning increases in importance. This, of course, is seen most clearly in the different kinds of toys that boys and girls play with, and the kinds of games they play.

Language development

Although language may be written or spoken, or may consist of special signaling systems such as the Morse code or deaf-and-dumb signs, speech is the kind of language that ordinarily is developed and used first. Thus we stress speech development here.

EARLY VOCALIZATION   Although the infant does not use words to communicate to others until after his first year, other means of communication are in evidence as early as the first or second month. The vocalization of the newborn infant is restricted to generalized undifferentiated crying and perhaps

directed at the object, and the arm is used more or less as a rake to sweep in the object with a roundabout motion. Soon, as the infant gains more control of the various arm muscles, he can use the forearm

TABLE 2.4 *The development of language in the infant, based on the results of eight major studies of infant development. The two numbers represent the range of average ages obtained in the different studies.*

LANGUAGE BEHAVIOR	AVERAGE AGE, MONTHS AFTER BIRTH
Cries, grunts, and makes other respirant sounds	0
Makes different sounds for discomfort, hunger, and pain	1
Makes vowel sounds like *ah, uh, ay*	1–2
Looks toward sound of human voice	2–4
Babbles and coos	3–4
Talks to self, using sounds like *ma, mu, do, na*	4–6
Makes sounds of pleasure and displeasure	5–6
"Sounds off" when he hears a familiar voice	6–7
Puts sounds together and repeats them over and over like *mamama-mama, booboo, dadada*	6–9
Imitates sounds made by others	9–10
Understands gestures (can wave bye-bye and often can say it)	9–12
Understands and responds to simple commands ("Hold the spoon," "Look at the doll baby")	11–15
Imitates syllables and simple words (the first word?)	11–15
Says two different words	12
Says three to five different words	13–18
Understands and responds to the "don'ts" ("Don't touch that," "Don't spit it out")	16–20
Names one object or picture in book (cup, ball, doggy, baby, etc.)	17–24
Combines words into phrases ("Go out," "Give me milk," "Where ball")	18–24
Identifies three to five familiar objects or pictures	24
Uses phrases and simple sentences	23–24

SOURCE: *Modified from McCarthy, 1946.*

some sort of grunting noises. Anyone who is around a young baby cannot fail to be impressed with such behavior. By his second month, the infant makes different types of cries for various states of discomfort. One cannot always tell from the cry just what is wrong, but certain cries do communicate distress of some kind. On the other hand, gurgling and other miscellaneous sounds signify contentment and well-being. Thus, by the end of his first month, the child is using sounds to communicate his needs and feelings to those around him.

As he grows older and the relevant muscles and brain structures mature, the child develops a repertory in which many other sounds appear. In Table 2.4 some of these are listed. In time, he enters the so-called "babbling" stage, when he seems to enjoy making these sounds over and over again. Many of the sounds the baby makes defy written representation, even with a phonetic alphabet, but babbling is necessary and important because it provides practice with the vocal muscles and lets the child hear his own sounds. Indeed, feeling how sounds are made and at the same time hearing the sounds help the infant learn to associate spoken words with the objects they refer to [Lewis, 1936]. By his sixth month the baby can produce practically all the vowel and consonant sounds. These are often combined in simple ways and repeated again and again. Without understanding the significance of the sounds, the child may say "mama," or "dada," or "re-re-re." By his ninth or tenth month he can imitate sounds made by others. From this point on, any of these sounds can be associated with a particular object in the environment, especially if the sound and the object are presented together to the child repeatedly. Figure 2.20 indicates how this may happen.

COMPREHENSION   Many studies have shown that the child can respond to sounds long before he can make the sounds himself [McCarthy, 1946]. By his fourth month the infant reacts positively to the sound of a human voice by turning his head toward the direction from which he hears the sound. At six months he can distinguish between different tones of voice. He responds differently to angry and friendly voices and will stop doing something at the sound of a warning tone. By ten months he can respond adequately to commands, especially when they are accompanied by gestures. He can wave bye-bye after having his hand waved for him a few times. If his mother says, "Put the spoon in the cup," and points to these objects, he quickly learns to associate the sound of the word with the object to which it refers.

THE USE OF WORDS   Although it may not seem so, it is relatively difficult to determine the age at which the average child utters his first word. What do we mean by the first word? Our criterion is that the sound made must refer to an object. When the child says "ball" he must mean something remotely resembling a ball; "dada" must refer to a man. The sound must not be made randomly when his father by coincidence happens to be present. Since the development of speech is a gradual process, it is difficult, if not impossible, to pin down the age at which the first word is spoken. Furthermore, two or

A CHILD LEARNS IN STAGES TO
ASSOCIATE A SOUND WITH AN OBJECT

FIGURE 2.20   *Associating a sound with an object. Top left, uttering the sound is associated with hearing it. Top right, an adult makes a similar sound which the child imitates. Bottom left, the sound is often accompanied by the object to which it refers. Bottom right, sight of the object by itself is finally sufficient to produce the sound. (After Allport, 1924.)*

three words may sometimes emerge at about the same time. In combining many observations, however, we find that usually the first word is spoken between the tenth and thirteenth months. Once the first word appears, the vocabulary increases rapidly. Nouns, generally related to things in the immediate environment, come first; then verbs; then adjectives and adverbs; pronouns appear last [McCarthy, 1930]. Children seem to have more difficulty in learning the correct use of pronouns than any other part of speech. Such remarks as "Pick my up" or "Me going outside" are typical. As his vocabulary increases, the child begins to combine the words he has learned into sentences. The first type of sentence he uses consists of a single word. He may say, "Eat," to mean "Give me something to eat," or "Out," meaning "I want to go out." Sometimes people misinterpret this sort of speech, but it is reasonably efficient. Later the child begins to string two or three words together. By the age of two, he may be using the following sentences, which are incomplete but which contain all the essential words: "Where doggy go?" "No night-night!" "Me going on swing." "When baby wake up, me give bottle."

FACTORS IN LANGUAGE DEVELOPMENT We have traced the main steps in language development in the infant. Maturation plays a part in it; so does learning. In addition, other factors enter the picture, and we ought to say a few words about them.

Intelligence. People commonly believe that children who talk the earliest are the most intelligent. They are partly right. One psychologist, for example, who worked with gifted children with IQs above 140[1] found that such children began talking, on the average, 4 months earlier than average children [Terman, et al., 1925]. Children of subnormal intelligence, on the other hand, are several months slower than the average child in beginning to talk. Indeed, severely retarded children may never learn

to talk. There are, however, many reasons why a child may be slow to talk, and if he is slow it does not necessarily mean that he is deficient in intelligence.

Sex. Psychological studies of this factor reveal that on the whole girls are slightly ahead of boys in most measures of language skill. In such studies, the influence of intelligence and socioeconomic background must be controlled, and care must be taken not to use situations which favor one sex over the other. At all ages studied, girls use more words per sentence than boys, they begin to talk earlier, they articulate better, they are more easily understood, and they have larger vocabularies, especially when they are young.

Social environment. Once the child has matured enough to control his speech mechanism, further progress depends to a great extent upon learning. And, at this early stage, how rapidly he learns depends upon the amount and kind of stimulation he gets from the environment around him.

The environment is a complex of many factors and people. The parents make up one important part of it. If the child gets what he wants from his parents by gesturing, he will be more reluctant to give up this form of communication in favor of learning to speak. If the child's parents do not bother to point out objects to him and pronounce their names, he will build his vocabulary more slowly. If they consistently use baby talk or if they are sloppy in their pronunciation and sentence structure, the child will develop bad speech habits which will be extremely difficult to break. It is just as easy for a child to learn to say "thank you" and "train" as it is to learn "ta-ta" or "choo-choo," once he reaches the stage at which he can pronounce the relevant sounds. If he is not ready or able to pronounce a particular word correctly, no great harm will be done by waiting until he is ready.

Many studies have shown that twins are more retarded in speech development than single-birth children. One experimenter reported that five-year-old twins used sentences of about the same length as three-year-old singletons [Day, 1932]. Another study showed, however, that after twins began

---

[1] Less than 2 per cent of the general population are this intelligent. For a more detailed explanation of the IQ and its meaning, see Chapter 12.

school they were not so far behind single children [Davis, 1932]. The likely explanation of these findings is that twins are left alone together in the home more often than single children, and consequently they do not have the advantage of stimulation from older children or adults who are more skilled in language.

Bilingualism is another aspect of the social environment that affects speech development. If two languages are spoken in the home, or if the child is forced to learn a foreign language while he is still learning his mother tongue, he gets confused and his skill in both languages is retarded. In one study it was found that it is better for children in a home where two languages are spoken to hear each one from a different adult, each adult using one language exclusively [Smith, 1935].

One finding which has been consistently reported is the high relationship between the socioeconomic status of the family and the rate of development of language. The following study reports this finding [Young, 1941]:

The language of poor children was compared with that of well-to-do children by taking records of what they said for 6 hours. The well-to-do children, it turned out, did better than the poor children in every aspect of language that was considered. At all early ages, children of well-educated, well-to-do families had a higher level of language ability than did children from poorer, less educated families even when the factor of intelligence was excluded from the picture.

If we consider that a stimulating environment is necessary for rapid development of speech, it is easy to understand the data concerning socioeconomic background. The homes of well-educated people are more likely to have books, pictures, music, and even a wide variety of the more prosaic articles of household furniture. If a family is well-to-do, also, the number of places to go, activities to engage in, and things available all increase proportionately. In fact, it has been found that the greater number of toys a child has and the greater amount of travel he experiences, the faster he acquires vocabulary and learns to use sentences. Then again, well-to-do parents usually have more time to spend specifically teaching a youngster.

We can say in conclusion that the greater the variety of experiences made available to the child and the more time spent in teaching him about the world, the greater his mental development in general and his language development in particular.

Intellectual development

Besides sensory, motor, and language development, three other facets of development should be considered: emotional development, personality development, and intellectual development. Emotional development, however, is more conveniently treated in the chapter on the emotions, and personality development fits better into the chapter on personality. Hence, at this particular point, we shall cover only the topic of intellectual development.

Can we trace stages of development in general ways of adapting to the world? One psychologist, Jean Piaget, has attempted to do this. He regards "intelligence as a specific instance of *adaptive* behavior, of coping with the environment and organizing (and reorganizing) thought and action" [Mussen, 1963, page 52]. He has tried to show that the ability to use thought and action to adapt to the world goes through several stages of development.

SENSORIMOTOR OPERATIONS   The first stage of development (ages 0 to 2) is called the stage of *sensorimotor operations*. Early in this period the infant does not differentiate himself from the environment and simply uses the reflex equipment which he has at birth or shortly after. As he gets older, the baby progresses through substages, and finally, at about eighteen months, begins to be able to use thought and imagination to solve problems. The invention of new ways of dealing with the environment is one characteristic of this final period of the sensorimotor stage; another characteristic is the beginning of foresight—the ability to evaluate the consequences of future actions. Of course, just the bare beginnings of foresight are present at this age.

PRECONCEPTUAL THOUGHT The second stage (ages 2 to 4) of Piaget's outline is called the stage of *preconceptual thought*; the third stage (ages 4 to 7) is termed the age of *intuitive thought*; the fourth stage (ages 7 to 11) is the stage of *concrete operations*; and the fifth stage (beginning at approximately age 11) has been termed the age of *formal operations* [see Mussen et al., 1963].

In the stage of *preconceptual thought*, objects begin to stand for other things—representational thought begins. For instance, toy wooden blocks can stand for building bricks and toy bulldozers may be treated as the real thing. This stage has its beginnings in the first uses of imagination and invention at the end of the sensorimotor period, and it ends in the stage of intuitive thought.

INTUITIVE THOUGHT During this stage of *intuitive thought*, the child begins to group objects and events into classes, but the grouping is based upon some dominant and outstanding perceptual characteristic of the situation. The child in this stage is not able to make general statements; his thought is tied to the immediate perceptual characteristics of the situation. Experiments on *conservation* illustrate the type of thought characteristic of this stage of development [Piaget, 1952]:

Suppose that a child is shown a glass of water which is half full and then the water is poured into a tall thin cylinder while he watches. The level of the water in the cylinder rises much higher than it did in the glass, but the amount has not changed. A child in this stage of intuitive thought would probably say, when asked, that there was more water in the tall thin cylinder. His judgment seems based on the outstanding perceptual characteristic of this situation—the height of the water. In other words, the child does not appreciate that the amount of water has been "conserved" in spite of appearance.

Experiments on the conservation of number also illustrate thought at this stage of intellectual development. Suppose a child is presented with a row of identical pennies on a table. If the experimenter puts down just as many pennies directly opposite the original row, the child will reply, when asked, that the number of pennies is the same in the two rows. A simple manipulation will change this judgment of the child. If the experimenter puts the same number of pennies down in the second row, but with greater spacing between them so that the row looks longer, the child will reply that there are more pennies in the second row. Here again, the dominant perceptual characteristic of the situation, the length of the row, determines the response of the child.

Two other characteristics of the intuitive stage of thought are (1) egocentrism and (2) the emphasis on successive states of a situation, rather than the transformations by which one state grades into another. Egocentrism refers to the inability of the child to take the point of view of another person; he has difficulty describing how a situation would look to someone else. Emphasis on states rather than transformations means that the child in the intuitive stage does not have a grasp of the fact that a situation can change gradually and grade into a new one; he emphasizes the beginning and end states.

CONCRETE OPERATIONS In the next stage, the stage of *concrete operations*, the child becomes less egocentric, begins to be able to deal with transformations rather than end states, and is able to group objects and events on the basis of several concrete observations. He is still bound to concrete situations, but he is not bound to single outstanding perceptual characteristics as he was in the previous stage. Children in this stage are supposed to be able to think about many and different concrete instances of events relating to the problems they are now trying to solve. They are able to bring this thought to bear on the concrete problem at hand. Conservation is present at this stage because children are able to *reverse* concrete operations. In the water-pouring example, they can see that the same amount of water would still be in the two vessels if the operations were reversed and the water were poured from the tall cylinder into the glass. Note that this last example is still a concrete situation and abstract thought is not involved—this is the hallmark of the next, and final, stage.

FORMAL OPERATIONS   In the stage of *formal operations,* children begin to use formal verbal rules of thought and logic; they begin to formulate and test hypotheses. They can think abstractly, and they can generalize, using abstract concepts, from one situation to another.

Intellectual development of this sort involves both physical maturation and learning. Some of the early development in the sensorimotor stage depends upon the physical maturation which we have already described. The later stages seem to depend more upon learning. These later stages are not so regular as our account implies, and one of the criticisms of Piaget's description is that it may give too inflexible a picture of intellectual development. This account of Piaget's description is only a very brief outline; the complete description of intellectual development covers many more facets of childhood thinking.

SYNOPSIS AND SUMMARY

The stress in this chapter has been on the unlearned or instinctive bases of behavior. We are born with a particular genetic heritage transmitted by our parents and, to a lesser degree, by all our progenitors. Our genetic composition, interacting with environmental influences, guides the maturation and development of bodily structures such as brain, muscles, and glands. As these and other structures mature, behavior develops in a rather orderly sequence.

This is the general picture, but what of individual differences in behavior? Always recognizing that the genetic potential interacts with the environment, we have found good evidence that differences in genetic composition can produce large differences in adult behavioral characteristics such as intelligence. Individual differences in the rate of maturation are also controlled to a large degree by genetic factors. Our *nature* is important; but so is our *nurture.*

In the next chapter, and throughout most of the rest of the text, we stress environmental influences, especially learning, which fashion behavior. Given the genetic substrate, human society, first as represented by our parents, and then as represented by our peers and others, is busily molding us. This

molding process takes many idiosyncratic forms, and individual differences in behavior result. However, the genetic nature of the individual is always there setting limits and providing the framework within which learning must operate. It seems fair to say that some individual characteristics are more controlled by genetic factors, others more determined by learning, and that none is completely determined by one or the other. We are mixtures of the fixed interacting with the variable.

1. Chromosomes and the genes carried by them are the transmitters of heredity and govern the biological characteristics of each new individual.

2. Genes always work in pairs. The characteristics they control may be either dominant or recessive. When a dominant gene is paired with a recessive gene, the characteristic of the dominant gene is expressed; a recessive characteristic is expressed only when two recessive genes are paired. Most characteristics, including height, intelligence, and emotionality, are multiply determined; they depend on a combination of genes.

3. The genes form an unbroken line of transmission from one generation through succeeding generations. What is transmitted by inheritance can be changed only by mutations in genes; acquired characteristics cannot be transmitted.

4. Since chromosomes from two parents randomly pair up in the child, each individual is different genetically from every other, except for cases of identical twins, who begin life as a single cell. Other individuals related by blood, however, have varying degrees of common inheritance.

5. Heredity and environment jointly determine the development of behavior in the individual, though some kinds of behavior are determined more by heredity, others more by environment.

6. Instinctive behavior is an inherited pattern of behavior that appears full-blown at the first appropriate opportunity and is triggered by some stimulus situation. In the human case, the principal behavioral characterostics that are inherited, however, are tendencies to react in certain ways and aptitudes for learning certain things.

7. Inherited tendencies and aptitudes may be studied by raising individuals of the same or similar heredity in different environments, or by developing different genetic populations or strains which are studied in the same environment.

8. Differences between species are primarily determined by inheritance. Furthermore, inheritance limits the ability to learn such things as language and complicated skills. For this reason, attempts to teach apes to talk have not succeeded very well.

9. Intelligence is highly correlated in identical twins, less so in brothers and sisters, and even less so in more remotely related individuals. Studies indicate that heredity and environment jointly determine a person's intelligence.

10. During the months immediately before and after birth, various organs within the individual are maturing in preparation for their normal functions. Maturation proceeds on a time schedule that is relatively similar for all normal individuals of a species. Maturation precedes behavior, so that by the time a function is needed the organs for carrying it out have matured.

11. The development of reflexes and motor abilities, such as sitting, standing, and walking, is almost wholly a matter of maturation and requires little or no practice.

12. Ability, or readiness for learning, is also determined by maturation. Practice and learning are required for perfecting the skill, but they must await the maturation of the relevant ability.

13. In the case of some skills, an optimum time for practice and learning occurs. If this time passes without an individual's having an opportunity to learn the skills, he will thereafter find it difficult or impossible to acquire them.

14. Touch sense and temperature sense appear to be well developed at birth. Hearing and vision are less well developed at birth, and it may take some time before visual acuity is near the adult level.

15. Motor skills develop in a pattern that is similar for all children. This makes it possible to set up norms for the ages at which such abilities as grasping, sitting, and walking should appear. Some individuals are slower than others in their development, but they are not necessarily any less intelligent.

16. Prehension is a particularly important aspect of motor development because it is necessary for the acquisition of other skills that involve the manipulation of objects.

17. Infants begin life with no language other than their cries and grunts. As their language mechanism matures, they make more and more sounds. Even before they can use these sounds as language, they begin to comprehend the meanings of words that they hear, and they can also communicate some of their wants with gestures and cries.

18. The first word appears when the child is about one year of age; it carries the meaning of a sentence which usually means, "I want such and such." After that, vocabulary grows by leaps and bounds.

19. Language ability depends in part on maturation, but also on other factors. Those children who talk earliest, on the average, later prove to be the most intelligent. Girls tend to talk a little earlier than boys. Single children also tend to talk earlier than twins. By and large, those with a more stimulating home environment make more rapid progress in language development than those with a poorer environment.

20. General intellectual development, according to one point of view, may go through a series of major stages: the stage of sensorimotor operations (ages 0 to 2), the stage of preconceptual thought (ages 2 to 4), the stage of intuitive thought (ages 4 to 7), the stage of concrete operations (ages 7 to 11), and the final stage of formal operations (beginning at about age 11).

RELATED TOPICS IN THE TEXT

CHAPTER 3 PRINCIPLES OF LEARNING Here we begin to discuss the environmental factors in behavior.

CHAPTER 7 EMOTION The sequence of emotional development is described.

CHAPTERS 8 AND 9 VISION AND HEARING An account of the mechanisms of vision and hearing as they eventually develop is given.

CHAPTER 10 PERCEPTION Here we see that perception—the organization, integration, and interpretation of sensory input—depends upon past experience.

CHAPTER 12 PSYCHOLOGICAL TESTING The measurement of intelligence is discussed at greater length.

SUGGESTIONS FOR FURTHER READING

Birney, R. C., and Teevan, R. C. (Eds.) *Instinct.* Princeton, N.J.: Van Nostrand, 1961. (Paperback.) *An interesting collection of papers on innate factors in behavior.*

Bonner, D. M. *Heredity.* Englewood Cliffs, N.J.: Prentice-Hall, 1961. (Paperback.) *Genetics from the point of view of modern molecular biology.*

Fuller, J. L., and Thompson, W. R. *Behavior genetics.* New York: Wiley, 1960. *The genetic bases of behavioral characteristics, such as intelligence, personality, temperament, and behavior disorders are lucidly discussed.*

Ilg, Frances L., and Ames, Louise B. *The Gesell Institute's child behavior.* New York: Dell, 1955. (Paperback.) *An account of child development with special emphasis on practical problems.*

King, R. A. (Ed.) *Readings for an introduction to psychology* (2d ed.). New York: McGraw-Hill, 1966. (Paperback.) *A book of readings designed to accompany this text.*

Munn, N. L. *Evolution and the growth of human behavior.* Boston: Houghton Mifflin, 1955. *A comprehensive text on psychological development which includes chapters on the evolutionary aspects of animal behavior.*

Mussen, P. H., Conger, J. J., and Kagan, J. *Child development and personality* (2d ed.). New York: Harper & Row, 1963. *A textbook on child development that stresses the role of learning and socialization.*

Stern, C. *Principles of human genetics* (2d ed.). San Francisco: Freeman, 1960. *Genetic principles are applied to human physical and behavioral traits. An authoritative, well-written text.*

U.S. Department of Health, Education, and Welfare. *Infant care.* Washington: Children's Bureau Publication No. 8, U.S. Government Printing Office, 1955. *Practical advice about child rearing, with an account of development in the first year of life.* Available from the Superintendent of Documents, U.S. Government Printing Office, Washington, D.C.

U.S. Department of Health, Education, and Welfare. *Your child from one to six.* Washington: Children's Bureau Publications No. 30, U.S. Government Printing Office, 1956. *Similar in tone to the pamphlet on Infant Care.* Available from the Superintendent of Documents, U.S. Government Printing Office, Washington, D.C.

LEARNING AND THINKING

PART TWO

3

PRINCIPLES OF LEARNING

LEARNING IS A KEY process—some would say *the* key process—in human behavior; it pervades everything we do and think. It influences, in one way or another, the language we speak, our customs, attitudes and beliefs, goals, personality traits, both adaptive and maladaptive, and even our perceptions. In this chapter we cover the fundamental principles of learning in order to be in a better position to understand how learning plays its role.

IMPORTANCE OF LEARNING Consider the changes that take place in a child's behavior during his first few years of life. During this period he is molded, or socialized, to become a functioning member of his society. To be able to do this in any culture, he must learn a staggering number of things. These include: learning appropriate ways of interacting with people, learning appropriate ways of eating and eliminating waste, learning to avoid potentially dangerous situations, learning to think somewhat logically and realistically, learning the values and customs of his group, learning to perceive the world as others perceive it, and learning the many distinctive responses and adjustments that make him different from other people. It is a wonder that he ever learns *all* these things. The fact that he does testifies to the remarkable plasticity of human behavior and the human nervous system.

This plasticity seems to extend throughout the animal kingdom. Although it is still uncertain whether unicellular organisms can learn [Katz and Deterline, 1958], such lowly organisms as the flatworm possess a rudimentary learning capacity [Thompson and McConnell, 1955], and learning has repeatedly been demonstrated in vertebrates, from fishes to man. The number and kinds of things that can be learned increase markedly in the higher mammals, and man is distinguished by his enormously greater capacity.

DEFINITION OF LEARNING *Learning* may be defined as any relatively permanent change in behavior which occurs as a result of experience or

IN LEARNING WE MAY ASSOCIATE A STIMULUS WITH ANOTHER STIMULUS OR WITH A RESPONSE

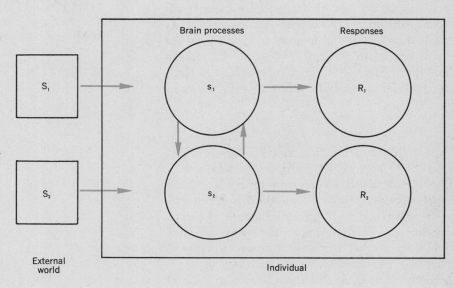

FIGURE 3.1 *Schematic diagram of the associations formed in sensory-sensory (S-S) and stimulus-response (S-R) learning. Events in the external world are represented by sensory brain processes within the individual which may be thought of as being connected in the process of S-S association. Similarly, external events, and the sensory nervous processes aroused by them, may be associated with responses to form S-R connections.*

practice. This definition, it should be noted, has three important elements [Kimble and Garmezy, 1963]: (1) Learning is a *change in behavior,* for better or worse. (2) It is a change that takes place through *experience or practice;* changes due to growth, maturation, or injury are not to be considered as learned. (3) The change, to merit the term learning, must be *relatively permanent,* that is, it must last for a fairly long time. This rules out change due to motivation, fatigue, adaptation, or the sensitivity of the organism.

This last point leads to an important distinction to be made between learning and *performance.* Many factors, both learned and unlearned, affect performance. At the same time, how an organism performs is all that we can measure or study. Hence, we must infer, by appropriate control or knowledge of the conditions affecting performance, when performance has been changed through learning and when it is changed by other factors. Moreover, un-

learned and learned factors interact in complex ways. For example, many kinds of behavior, even learned behavior, depend on motivation. A rat that has learned a maze does not perform well unless it is hungry or motivated in some way. In this case, learning is not manifested in performance until it is brought out through motivation. For this reason, when studying learning processes, psychologists must be very careful to remember the various factors that affect performance.

Factors in learning

There are a great many phenomena of learning. All have technical names, and the conditions under which they occur are in many cases rather complicated. The student can easily become lost in a profusion of terms if he has no framework in which to put them. Many of the phenomena, however, involve the same or similar factors combined in slightly different ways. By first considering the factors that are common to many learning phenomena, it will be easier to understand the phenomena when they are described in detail.

ASSOCIATION   One factor that is common to most situations in which learning takes place is *association.* The term association as used here, means some connection in time and place between two events. The connection usually first exists in the physical world. For example, fires and many other things that light up are hot. Hence the physical events of light and heat are often connected, or *associated,* with one another. Lightning and thunder usually occur in close sequence; so the light and sound may be connected. These connections in the physical world provide opportunities for an organism to form associations from experiencing two events simultaneously or in close succession.

The formation of such associations is a function of the brain. The process involved has not yet been discovered, but it is almost certainly not a simple connection like that formed when two wires are joined [Lashley, 1950]. For purposes of discussion, it may be assumed that the process in the brain representing one event becomes associated with the process representing the other event. This means that once an association has been formed, the initiation of one process tends to arouse the second process in the absence of any physical event which ordinarily sets off the second process. Stated symbolically, if S_1 and S_2 are two events in the physical world, and s_1 and s_2 are the corresponding processes in the brain, the occurrence of S_1 and S_2 together will tend to form an association between processes in the brain so that s_1 can now arouse s_2 or s_2 arouse s_1 (see Figure 3.1).

Sensory associations. The view that learning involves an association between processes in the brain representing stimulus events experienced by a person was formulated by English philosophers during the eighteenth and nineteenth centuries. The conception was called *associationism,* and those who subscribed to it were called *associationists.* They regarded the experience s_1 aroused by the external event S_1 as a *sensation,* and the process s_1 aroused by S_2 in the absence of S_1 as an *idea.* An idea in this sense has also been called an *image.* Within this framework, the associationists then attempted to formulate laws stating the conditions under which ideas were learned by association. In other words, they inquired into how s_1 comes to be aroused by S_2 in the absence of S_1.

Late in the nineteenth century, when experimental work on learning got under way, the language of associationism was revamped because rigorous experimentalists felt they could not experiment with "ideas" or "images." Although the inference that the processes aroused in sensory association are often ideas or images is probably correct, it was all too easy to lapse into loose, untestable speculation about the properties of ideas. For this reason, psychologists stopped talking about the association of ideas and began referring simply to association, sensory association, or to S-S association, meaning association between two stimuli [Spence, 1951].

In the heyday of behaviorism (see Chapter 1) those of the behaviorist persuasion went so far as to argue that there was no association between sensory experiences and that association could exist only between a stimulus and a response. However, there is impressive evidence for sensory association. Some of the evidence for the concept of sensory association will be presented later in this chapter.

Stimulus-response associations. Another kind of association, an S-R or stimulus-response association, is more easily studied. In this case the learner associates a stimulus event with a response. For instance, when you learn a foreign-language vocabulary you are forming S-R associations; the foreign word is a stimulus for your English response, or vice versa. When driving a car we are almost continuously engaged in making learned responses to stimuli: the traffic light turns red and we stop; it turns green and we start; we speed up to pass another car; and so on through the whole range of near-automatic responses (see Figure 3.1).

The example of driving a car also illustrates an-

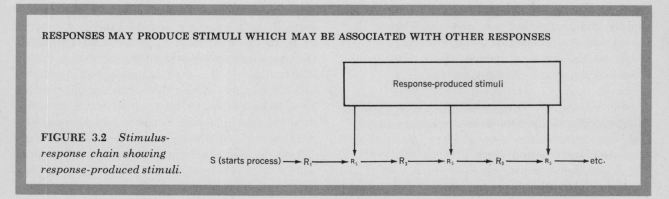

RESPONSES MAY PRODUCE STIMULI WHICH MAY BE ASSOCIATED WITH OTHER RESPONSES

FIGURE 3.2 *Stimulus-response chain showing response-produced stimuli.*

other point about S-R connections: the stimulus may come from the response itself. When we move, the movement causes stimulation to arise in the receptors of our muscles and joints—these are called *kinesthetic* receptors. This stimulation, although little of it ever reaches consciousness, is fed back into the nervous system and can, through learning, form a connection with the next response. This response, like the one before it, feeds back information that can connect with the next response, and so on. In this way, a *chain* of associations between *response-produced stimuli* and responses is formed (see Figure 3.2). Such a chain can be very long and complex.

Some skilled acts, but not all, are chains of the sort just described. Consider the shifting of gears in automobiles equipped with a manual gearshift. When we shift gears, we first step on the clutch and this provides response-produced stimuli which are associated with the response of pushing the gearshift. This in turn provides a cue for letting up on the clutch. On the other hand, some complex acts, particularly those requiring very rapid sequences, are certainly not chained in this way [Lashley, 1951]. A skilled musician, in playing an arpeggio, makes responses far faster than information from the responses can be fed back into the nervous system. Thus, in this instance, a previous response cannot provide the stimulation for the next one. Rather, the chaining must take place entirely in the nervous system. Nevertheless, the concept of

the chaining of response-produced stimuli and responses is important in understanding certain learned sequences of behavior.

S-R associations lend themselves nicely to objective observation, and for this reason they have received the greatest attention in psychological experiments. S-S associations can be studied only in roundabout ways, and therefore, they have been relatively neglected. Indeed, as we have previously said, some psychologists have attempted to explain all association as S-R association, and this is one of the points on which theorists still disagree. An increasing body of evidence, however, shows that both kinds of associations can be formed.

Contiguity. The concept of association implies contiguity. That is to say, for two physical events to be connected, and hence for the corresponding processes in the brain to become associated, they must occur at approximately the same time and place. They must be contiguous, or paired, events. For this reason, contiguity has long been stated as a basic law governing the formation of associations.

What must be contiguous varies with different learning situations. In simple conditioning, as we shall see, it is the contiguity of two stimuli that is essential for learning. In this case, we speak of the pairing of stimuli. In other, somewhat more complex learning situations, it is the contiguity of a response and a reward or punishment that is important for learning. For example, we give a dog a bit of food when he performs a trick, or we slap a child's hand when he reaches for a lighted cigarette. In every case, it is the pairing of events—making them contiguous—that is essential in learning.

Interference. Still another aspect of forming associations deserves emphasis—the possibility of interference among associations. One stimulus may become associated with two different stimuli or with two different responses. If the two associations with one stimulus are incompatible, one tends to block or interfere with the other.

The learning of two languages at the same time is an example. Children who are reared in bilingual homes are slower in language development than those who learn only one language at home. A child learns a good deal of language by associating a word (R) with some stimulus (S). He learns to associate "hot" with the sight of the fire on the stove or a lighted match. But if he must learn to associate *heiss* (German for "hot") or *chaud* (French for "hot") at the same time, he has two different associations (R_1 and R_2) for the same visual stimulus (S). He cannot say them both at the same time. Hence one association interferes with the other and neither association is built up so rapidly as it might be. The principle of mutual interference of associations is a general one which accounts for several of the phenomena of learning and forgetting.

REINFORCEMENT Another important term, one the psychologist repeatedly uses when talking about learning, is *reinforcement.* This term has two meanings, depending on the kind of learning situation one is talking about. In simple conditioning, it refers simply to the second stimulus of the pair being presented. Why the reinforcement is the second rather than the first will become clear later in the chapter. However, here we are concerned with the other meaning of reinforcement. This corresponds to what the layman would call reward or punishment. Examples of the many things which can serve as reinforcement are food for a hungry animal or human being, certain "pleasing" tastes [Pfaffmann, 1964], praise for a child, a "well done" from the boss, or escape from punishment.

Reinforcement is of such obvious importance in learning that it was long ago dignified as the *law of effect* [Thorndike, 1911]. This law states that an act that has a satisfying effect—for instance, satisfaction of a motive state, escape from punishment, or relief from fear—will be learned, but an act that has an unpleasant effect—such as frustration of a motive, punishment, or fear—will not be learned. It is relatively easy to observe that reinforcement does indeed strengthen certain kinds of associations. The simple fact that reinforcement works to strengthen associations has been called the *empirical law of effect* [McGeoch and Irion, 1952].

In contrast to the empirical law of effect is a so-called *theoretical law of effect* [Kimble, 1961]. This refers to the hypothetical mechanism through which reinforcement acts to strengthen associations. Actually, not one, but at least five different mechanisms have been proposed as the key feature of reinforcement. A case can be made for each one, and each appears to be useful, often in combination with others, in some learning situation. For this reason, and because reinforcement is of such crucial importance in most learning situations, we shall consider briefly five theories about the law of effect.

Two closely related theories are the *need-reduction* theory and the *drive-stimulus reduction* theory. The need-reduction theory holds that the satisfaction of bodily needs, for instance hunger and thirst, is the crucial factor in the learning of associations [Hull, 1943]. The term "reward" is sometimes used instead of reinforcement when this theory is discussed. A sister theory, and one that attempts both to broaden and to make more explicit the need-reduction theory, is the *drive-stimulus reduction* theory [Miller and Dollard, 1941]. Reinforcement, according to this view, is due to a reduction in the intensity of stimulation arising from need states. For example, the reduction of hunger pangs or the pain from an electric shock would be reinforcing according to the drive-stimulus reduction theory.

A third theory of reinforcement has been called the *terminal-response* theory [Guthrie, 1952]. In this theory, a reinforcer is regarded as an event that takes the learner out of the learning situation so that the last-made stimulus-response association is preserved. This association is the one that is preserved because it is not followed by other associations that might interfere with it.

A fourth theory, the *stimulus* theory, holds that some stimuli are inherently reinforcing. Sweet tastes are among the stimuli which seem inherently to be reinforcing [Sheffield and Roby, 1950; Guttman, 1953]. Novel stimuli also seem to be reinforcing in some cases [Butler, 1954; Montgomery and Segall, 1955]. For instance, a confined monkey will learn to make a response which permits him to look out of a closed cage; even a mere look at the experimenter may be reinforcing. Of course, in evaluating instances in which a stimulus seems to be inherently reinforcing, we must make certain that the effect is not a learned effect [Smith and Capretta, 1956]. For example, we should make sure that a sweet taste is not reinforcing because it has previously been associated with satisfaction of hunger. Some examples can be criticized on this basis, but there is now good evidence that at least some stimuli are inherently reinforcing [Smith and Kinney, 1956; Pfaffmann, 1964].

A fifth theory is called the *response* theory [Premack, 1959]. This theory states that if a weak response occurring at a low rate is followed by a stronger response occurring at a high rate, the weak response tends to be strengthened. In one experiment, for example, rats were taught by standard procedures to press a bar for a few drops of sugar water [Premack, 1961]. The rate of bar pressing, it was found, depended upon the rate at which the sugar water was licked: the higher the rate of licking, the higher the bar-press rate. This seems to suggest that a high-rate activity, in this case licking, is reinforcing a low-rate activity, bar-pressing in this experiment.

In summary, the following hypotheses or theories have been suggested concerning the mechanism of reinforcement in situations where reward or punishment is used:

1. Need reduction
2. Drive-stimulus reduction
3. The terminal-response, or response-preservation, theory
4. The stimulus theory
5. The response theory

It is possible to ignore or sidestep the theoretical issues just discussed, and some psychologists have done that [Skinner, 1953]. They go back to the empirical law of effect and maintain that a reinforcement is simply any event which, following a response, makes the response more likely. They have supplanted hypothetical mechanisms of reinforcement with a description of what reinforcements actually do to behavior. Reinforcements increase the frequency of responses which produce them, and any event that increases this frequency is, by definition, a reinforcement. According to this view, for example, if we are training a dog to stand up, we simply watch to see whether the incidence of standing increases when it is always followed by a certain event such as giving the dog a piece of food. If the response increases in frequency following the presentation of a certain stimulus, the stimulus is called a *reinforcer*. Reinforcers, such as food, discovered and investigated in one particular situation, can then be used to increase the frequency of responses in other situations.

More about reinforcement comes later. In any case, whatever the mechanism, *reinforcement helps strengthen associations in instrumental learning.* Whether reinforcement is necessary for *all* associations is another question which will be considered in the section of this chapter dealing with perceptual learning.

MOTIVATION   As has already been stated, motivation is an important factor in performance. It is also a factor in learning through its relation to the reinforcement process. If the need-reduction theory of reinforcement is correct, some degree of motivation is obviously essential for reinforcement.

Motivation is also important in controlling the variability of behavior. When learning a new habit, a motivated organism will run through an extensive repertory of actions, one of which may be correct. For example, suppose a mother is interested in teaching her child, who is a little thirsty, to say "milk" when a glass of milk is shown to him. One way of doing this is to show the child a glass of milk while saying "milk" at the same time. If the child says "milk," he will be given a sip as reinforcement. If motivated, the child will quickly run through many behaviors: he may grab for the glass; he may cry; he may shake his head; he may stick his tongue out at his mother; or he may imitate and say "milk"—the "correct" response. If not motivated, this repertory of responses will be less likely to occur. The same point also applies to certain non-physiological motives. Curiosity and exploratory drives bring the individual into wider contact with his environment and thus enlarge the number of associations that can be formed. We may say in summary that motivation is important because of its role in reinforcement and because it controls the variability of behavior.

We have discussed *association, reinforcement,* and *motivation* as common factors in many learning situations. The remainder of this chapter deals with four kinds of learning situations: classical conditioning, instrumental learning, avoidance learning, and perceptual learning. For the most part, the experiments described and the illustrations employed refer to animal learning. Human learning is emphasized in the chapters that follow.

Classical conditioning

Classical conditioning gets its name from the fact that it is the kind of learning originally studied in the "classical" experiments of Ivan P. Pavlov (1849–1936). Beginning in the late 1890s, this famous Russian physiologist introduced the concept of conditioning and established many of its basic principles [Pavlov, 1927]. Much of present-day Russian psychology is based on the conditioned response and theories of its significance in human and animal behavior. Although classical conditioning is sometimes called *respondent conditioning,* the term classical is used here.

SALIVARY CONDITIONING   To present a picture of the phenomena of classical conditioning, which is summarized in Figure 3.3, we shall describe a number of experiments, starting with a typical Pavlovian experiment. But first it is necessary to state some definitions. The essential operation in classical conditioning is a *pairing* of two stimuli. One, initially neutral in that it elicits no response, is called the *conditioned stimulus (CS)*; the other, which is one that consistently elicits a

CS + US = CR

FIGURE 3.3 *Schematic diagram of the classical conditioning process. During conditioning, a neutral stimulus (bell), called the conditioned stimulus (CS), is paired a number of times with an unconditioned stimulus (US)—food—which evokes an unconditioned response (UR)—salivation. As a result of continued pairing, the conditioned stimulus comes to produce salivation, which is now called the conditioned response (CR), in the absence of the unconditioned stimulus (US).*

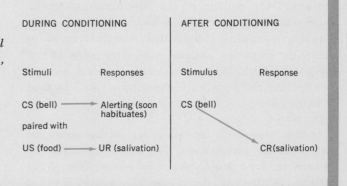

DURING CONDITIONING		AFTER CONDITIONING	
Stimuli	Responses	Stimulus	Response
CS (bell) ⟶	Alerting (soon habituates)	CS (bell)	
paired with			
US (food) ⟶	UR (salivation)		CR (salivation)

PAVLOV CONDITIONED DOGS TO SALIVATE WHEN THEY HEARD A BELL

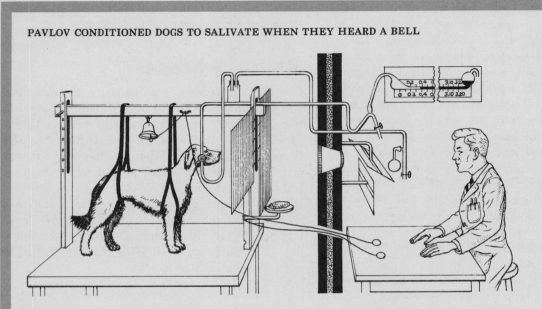

FIGURE 3.4 *Pavlov's apparatus for studying the conditioned salivary response. The amount of saliva is measured by means of a tube attached to a cup placed over one of the salivary glands. The apparatus is in a soundproof room with a one-way vision screen between the experimenter and the dog. The experimenter can sound the bell (CS) and present food (US) by remote control. (After Pavlov, 1928.)*

response, is called the *unconditioned stimulus* (*US*). The response elicited by the unconditioned stimulus is the *unconditioned response* (*UR*). As a result of the pairing of the conditioned stimulus (CS) with the unconditioned stimulus (US), the previously neutral conditioned stimulus comes to elicit the response. Then it is called the *conditioned response* (*CR*). With these terms in mind, we can now describe a typical experiment in classical conditioning.

Pavlov devised an operation and an apparatus for measuring the flow of saliva (see Figure 3.4). The apparatus consisted in part of a tube running from a cup attached to a dog's cheek. This cup was arranged in such a way that it collected drops of saliva flowing from the parotid salivary gland which had been displaced to the outside of the cheek. The saliva replaced air in the tube from the cup, and this in turn displaced a colored fluid in a calibrated instrument which looked somewhat like a thermometer and from which very minute changes could be read. The animal was placed in a soundproof room equipped with a one-way vision screen through which it could be seen. By remote control, Pavlov could swing a food pan out within the dog's reach or, alternatively, puff some food powder into its mouth through a special apparatus. He could also present the dog with several kinds of stimuli, including the sounds of a bell, buzzer, or metronome.

In a typical experiment, Pavlov trained the dog by sounding a bell (the CS), immediately afterward presenting food (the US), and then measuring the amount of saliva secreted (the UR). After pairing the sound of the bell with food a few times, the effects of the training were tested by measuring the amount of saliva which flowed when the bell was presented alone without food. Pavlov then resumed the paired presentation of bell and food a few more times and then tested with the bell alone. He found that as training proceeded, the amount of saliva secreted in response to the bell alone (the CR) gradually increased as test trials proceeded. This increase over test trials could be plotted as a learning curve.

Figure 3.5 presents a learning curve typical of an experiment in salivary conditioning. It is drawn without specifying the number of trials or the amount of saliva—as would be done in an actual experiment. This curve, an *acquisition curve,* shows that the strength of the response on test trials gradually increases with more and more pairings of CS and US. Note that this curve gradually flattens; that is, each increase due to a trial is less than the preceding one. In other words, this curve is negatively accelerated; that is, it is a curve of "diminishing returns."

FLEXION CONDITIONING   Another famous Russian, the neurologist and anatomist Bekhterev (1857–1927), pioneered the school of "reflexology" and another type of classical-conditioning experiment [Bekhterev, 1932]. The principal difference between Pavlov's and Bekhterev's experiments is in the unconditioned stimulus and its response. Instead of food, Bekhterev used shock to the forelimb or hindlimb as his US; this produces an unconditioned response of arm or leg flexion. Other details of these experiments are as follows:

The subjects may be human or animal. In the case of animals, the shock (US) is usually applied to the bottom of a foot. In the case of human subjects, it may be delivered to either the foot or a hand. To take just one case for illustration, let us assume that a human subject is used and the shock is applied to the hand.

Shocking the back of the hand causes a rapid and brisk bending or flexion of the hand. This is the unconditioned response. Just before the shock is delivered, however, another kind of stimulation (CS), a tone for instance, can be presented. After several pairings of the tone followed

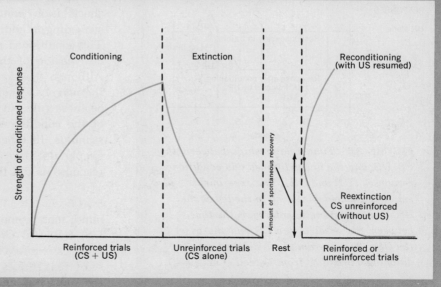

THE UPS AND DOWNS OF CLASSICAL CONDITIONING

FIGURE 3.5 *Schematic diagram of the course of conditioning, extinction, reconditioning, and reextinction. Spontaneous recovery after a rest period is shown by the vertical arrow. (After McGeoch and Irion, 1952; adapted from Gregory A. Kimble and Norman Garmezy,* Principles of General Psychology, *2d ed. Copyright © 1963 The Ronald Press Company.)*

by shock, that is, of the conditioned and unconditioned stimuli, the subject promptly flexes his hand when the tone is presented. This flexion response to a previously neutral stimulus is the *conditioned response* in this type of experiment.

A learning curve similar to that for the Pavlovian experiment can be plotted. In this situation, however, the measure on the ordinate (vertical axis) is not the amplitude of the conditioned response; it usually is the percentage of times that a conditioned response is given to the conditioned stimulus. For instance, the percentage of conditioned responses on each block of 10 trials may be plotted.

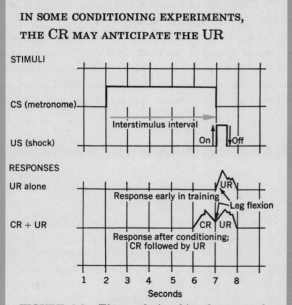

IN SOME CONDITIONING EXPERIMENTS, THE CR MAY ANTICIPATE THE UR

STIMULI

CS (metronome)

Interstimulus interval

US (shock)   On   Off

RESPONSES

UR alone   UR

Response early in training

Leg flexion

CR + UR   CR   UR

Response after conditioning; CR followed by UR

1 2 3 4 5 6 7 8
Seconds

FIGURE 3.6 *Time relationships between the CS, US, and the unconditioned and conditioned responses (UR and CR). The experiment employs unavoidable shock to the leg as the US. The interstimulus interval is the time between the onset of the CS and the onset of the US. This diagram shows delayed conditioning. (Modified from Liddell et al., 1934.)*

Two important features of this type of experiment should be noted. One is that the subject cannot escape the shock. He always receives it following the presentation of the conditioned stimulus. In this respect, it is like the Pavlovian experiment in which food always follows the CS; it is unlike experiments discussed later in this chapter in which the subject can escape or avoid shock. A second feature, and one in which it is unlike the Pavlovian experiment, is that no test trials are employed. In salivary conditioning, test trials consist of presenting the CS without the US to see whether salivation occurs with the CS alone. In Bekhterev's experiment, this is unnecessary because the conditioned response anticipates, that is, occurs prior to, the presentation of the shock (see Figure 3.6). For this reason, CRs in such an experiment are sometimes called "anticipatory" CRs. These are a distinct advantage for they permit the experimenter to assess the progress of conditioning trial by trial rather than to check it only on interspersed test trials.

Another important point which can be demonstrated in this type of experiment is that the conditioned response is usually not exactly the same as the unconditioned response. In experiments with sheep, for example, the unconditioned response to shock is a complex one which includes much struggling in addition to leg flexion [Liddell, 1954]. The conditioned response, however, is a rather precise flexion of the leg with very little struggling. Although the exact nature of associations made in the nervous system is not known, observations such as these rule out the idea of a simple substitution of the conditioned stimulus for the unconditioned stimulus. In other words, the conditioned stimulus simply does not come to elicit exactly the same response as did the unconditioned stimulus.

SOME DEFINITIONS With these examples in mind, more complete and formal definitions of *CS, US, UR,* and *CR* may now be given. The *conditioned stimulus (CS)* is one which is neutral in the sense that it does not produce a marked response at the outset of an experiment. It may produce an

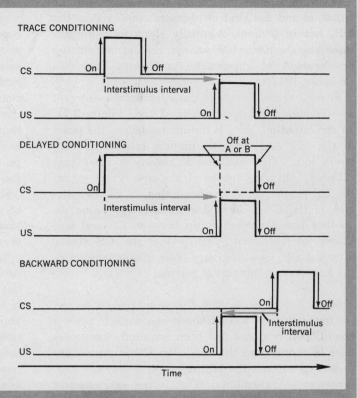

THE CS MAY GO OFF BEFORE THE US,
IT MAY LAST THROUGH THE US,
OR IT MAY COME AFTER THE US

TRACE CONDITIONING

CS — On — Off
Interstimulus interval

US — On — Off

DELAYED CONDITIONING

Off at
A or B

CS — On — Off
Interstimulus interval

US — On — Off

BACKWARD CONDITIONING

CS — On — Off
Interstimulus interval

US — On — Off

Time

FIGURE 3.7 *Time relationships between CS and US in trace, delayed, and backward conditioning. The interstimulus interval is shown in each case. Note that the CS comes after the US in backward conditioning.*

alerting response, for example, the human or animal being conditioned may turn his head toward the source of the stimulation, but this response soon adapts or *habituates*. The *unconditioned stimulus (US)* is one which always elicits or produces a reflex-like response. The response produced by the unconditioned stimulus is termed the *unconditioned response (UR)*. After *pairing* of the CS and US, the conditioned stimulus will come to elicit a response which is similar to, but usually not identical with, the unconditioned response. When, after pairing, the conditioned stimulus elicits such a response, the response is then called the *conditioned response (CR)*.

CONTIGUITY IN CONDITIONING Several points can be made concerning the pairing operation, that is, the contiguity of CS and US, in classical conditioning. One concerns reinforcement. In classical conditioning, the conditioned stimulus is said to be "reinforced" by the unconditioned stimulus. Hence, the operation of pairing itself is the reinforcement in classical conditioning. This is the other meaning of reinforcement alluded to in the discussion of reinforcement and the law of effect.

Another point is that there is an *interstimulus* interval in the pairing that is optimal for conditioning to take place. The interstimulus interval is the time between the onset of the CS and the onset of the US. The pairing of CS and US may be such that they occur simultaneously, but it is more usual for the US to follow the CS by a definite interval (Figure 3.7). This produces better conditioning and also permits the use of "anticipatory" responses.

The optimal interstimulus interval varies with the situation and the kind of response employed as the UR, but in general, relatively short interstimulus intervals, about one-half second, are optimal for the development of classically conditioned responses [Kimble, 1947].

Several arrangements of the interstimulus interval are possible and have been tried (see Figure 3.7). In one situation, the CS terminates before the onset of the US, and the interstimulus interval is relatively long. This situation is known as *trace conditioning*. On the other hand, the situation in which the CS persists until the beginning, or through the end, of the US is termed *delayed conditioning*. In another possible relationship between CS and US, known as *backward conditioning*, the CS comes *after* the US. However, very little, if any, conditioning results from this sort of pairing.

EXTINCTION   So far the discussion has concerned the *acquisition* of a conditioned response. If, after a conditioned response has been acquired, the procedure is changed so that only the CS is repeatedly presented without the US following it, another phenomenon is encountered. This is the *extinction* of the conditioned response—a gradual weakening of the strength of the response, salivation in Pavlov's experiment, or a decrease in the frequency of responses, flexion in Bekhterev's experiment. Extinction may be illustrated as follows:

In another of Pavlov's experiments, a conditioned dog was placed in the apparatus in the usual way. The bell was presented without food as it was in the test trials of the conditioning procedure. In this case, however, the bell was never accompanied by food. On trial after trial, the dog heard only the bell and never saw or received food. The amount of saliva was measured in the usual way. As the procedure was continued, the amount of saliva secreted when the bell was presented gradually diminished until it reached a level little different from that at which it had been at the beginning of the experiment (see Figure 3.5).

SPONTANEOUS RECOVERY   Another phenome-non, called *spontaneous recovery*, may be demonstrated in conditioning experiments. Spontaneous recovery refers to the fact that a conditioned response which has been extinguished may spontaneously recover some of the strength lost in extinction after an interval of rest following extinction (see Figure 3.5). If, for example, a dog whose conditioned response has been extinguished is brought back into the experimental situation and the presentation of the bell is resumed, the amount he salivates is considerably greater than it was at the end of the previous series of extinction trials. This shows that even after extinction some degree of association remains between the bell and salivation and that the conditioning has not been entirely erased.

It is possible, as indicated in Figure 3.5, to re-*extinguish* the conditioned response by giving the dog another series of extinction trials, again bringing the response down almost to zero. After this, another intermission may be followed by some spontaneous recovery, although not to such a degree as before. By repeated reextinctions, the conditioned response may eventually be extinguished more or less completely and permanently.

This process raises the question of what is happening in extinction. Are the associations that were formed by conditioning weakened? The answer depends on what is meant by "weakened." Two factors seem to be at work in extinction. One is *interference*—the learning of a new association which interferes with the original one. This involves learning *not* to respond—at least not in a particular series of trials. Such an association, of course, is the opposite of the original one and, hence, competes with it. Another factor is *inhibition*—a tendency not to respond. This performance factor is probably also at work during original conditioning, diminishing the observed strength of the conditioned response, but there is usually no way of disentangling it from the strengthening effects of the conditioning procedure.

If the inhibition built up in extinction decays with time, spontaneous recovery would be expected. Interference might also produce spontaneous recovery. When, after an intermission, the animal is brought back into the experimental apparatus, the situation is ambiguous to it. The subject has learned competing responses to the same set of stimuli, that is, to respond and not to respond. After a few reextinction trials, the situation is no longer ambiguous. Initially, then, a few conditioned responses would occur before it became clear to the animal that this is, as in the last series of trials, still an extinction situation. If we put ourselves in the subject's place for a minute, we can readily see that it would take a few trials before it became apparent that this was an extinction situation. Before this was obvious, we might respond to these same stimuli as we had during the conditioning trials.

All this tends to show that extinction does not merely weaken the association formed in conditioning. This is also brought out if we attempt to *recondition* the animal, to provide again the reinforcement, or pairing, given in the original conditioning. Pavlov did this, and the general results he obtained are shown in Figure 3.5. If a conditioning procedure follows an extinction procedure, reconditioning takes place at a faster rate than it did in the original conditioning. Indeed, an experimenter can condition, extinguish, condition, and extinguish alternately, and each time, up to a certain point, the animal will condition a little faster and extinguish a little faster than the time before. Thus the original conditioning is not erased by extinction; instead, learning both to respond and not to respond is taking place. The animal is learning *when* to do one or the other.

STIMULUS GENERALIZATION Pavlov discovered very early that if he conditioned an animal to salivate at the sound of a bell, it would also salivate at the sound of a buzzer or the beat of a metronome, though to a lesser degree. Thus the animal tended to *generalize* the conditioned response to stimuli that were different from, but somewhat similar to, the one to which it was specifically conditioned. Although Pavlov described generalization of con-

ditioned responses, the example of generalization we shall use comes from a study of the galvanic skin response (GSR) in man [Hovland, 1937]. The galvanic skin response is usually measured as a decrease in the resistance of the skin to the flow of a minute electrical current. The mechanisms responsible for it are quite complex. Such decreased resistance of the skin is characteristic of alertness and aroused emotional states, and it is one of the responses measured by the lie detector or polygraph. For our present purposes, it is enough to state that the GSR can be manipulated in the laboratory and can be used as an unconditioned response to the unconditioned stimulus of a strong, painful shock. The following experiment shows stimulus generalization in connection with GSR conditioning [Hovland, 1937]:

In this experiment, an electric shock was the unconditioned stimulus for the GSR. The experimenter began by conditioning the subject's GSR to the sound of a pure tone of a particular frequency. This was done by presenting the shock and tone (the CS) simultaneously, or nearly so. After the GSR had been conditioned to this tone, Hovland measured the strength of the conditioned GSR given to tones that were of frequencies different from that of the original tone (the conditioned stimulus). Figure 3.8 indicates the results of this experiment. As we would expect, the tone used in the original conditioning evoked the largest GSR; tones closer to the original tone in frequency evoked the next largest GSRs; tones furthest in frequency from the original CS evoked the weakest responses. Thus, a rough rule of thumb can be formulated: the *greater the similarity between stimuli, the greater the generalization between them.*

Many responses and characteristics of people seem to be acquired through the processes of conditioning and generalization illustrated in the experiment with the GSR. There the shock served as an unconditioned stimulus eliciting pain in the subject and the conditioned stimulus elicited a fear of pain. This simple experiment serves as a model for the development of people's irrational fears. Such

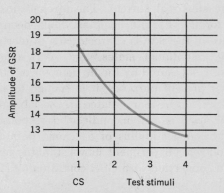

WE TEND TO RESPOND TO STIMULI
THAT ARE SIMILAR TO STIMULI
TO WHICH WE HAVE BEEN CONDITIONED

FIGURE 3.8 *Generalization of a conditioned galvanic skin response. Stimulus 1 (CS) was the tone to which the GSR was originally conditioned. Stimuli 2, 3, and 4, respectively, were tones of increasingly different frequency. Note that there is less generalization as the difference in frequency between the CS and the other tones increases. (After Hovland, 1937.)*

fears or phobias are irrational because they are acquired through accidental conditioning to some stimulus, then generalized to situations that otherwise would not be frightening.

HIGHER-ORDER CONDITIONING   Pavlov did something else in his experiments that helps us understand more complicated behavior. He discovered that he could use one conditioned response to build up another conditioned response, thus producing what is called *higher-order conditioning.* The following is a typical experiment in higher-order conditioning:

In the first stage of the experiment, a dog was conditioned in the usual way to salivate to the sound of a metronome. After the dog was well conditioned, the second stage, the "higher-order" stage, of the experiment was begun. In this second stage, a card with a black square on it was thrust into the dog's view just before the metronome was sounded. No food was given during this second stage. In effect, then, the card was being paired with the sound of the metronome. A diagram of this experiment is shown in Figure 3.9. After several pairings of the card and metronome, the dog started to salivate when the card with the black square on it was presented. Thus, although the card with the black square on it was never paired with food, it nevertheless came to elicit salivation.

The higher-order stage of this experiment is not really different from any classical conditioning if we remember that an unconditioned stimulus was defined as one which consistently elicits a reflex-like response. In this experiment, as a result of conditioning in the first stage, the salivation is conditioned to the sound of the metronome, that is, the metronome now consistently elicits the response of salivation. In the second higher-order stage, the card with the black square is the conditioned stimulus while the metronome, which consistently elicits the response, acts as an unconditioned stimulus, as shown in Figure 3.9.

Higher-order conditioning is difficult to do in the laboratory, and it cannot be carried too far from the original conditioning. The reason should be obvious. Successful higher-order conditioning depends upon conditioning of the primary response—salivation to the metronome in this case. However, while the secondary conditioned stimulus, the card with the black square, is being paired with the metronome, the conditioned response to the metronome is being extinguished because the metronome sound is not being paired with food. If the conditioned response to the metronome sound becomes extinguished, the sound of the metronome can no longer act as an unconditioned stimulus in the higher-order stage. Because of extinction of the primary conditioned response, experiments on higher-order conditioning usually require a few trials in which the primary CS and US are repaired during the attempt at higher-order conditioning. By pairing another stimulus with the card, Pavlov was able, with great difficulty, to carry higher-order conditioning one more stage—to a third-order stimulus.

SIGNIFICANCE OF CLASSICAL CONDITIONING

It seems probable that many of our subjective emotional feelings, from violent emotions to subtle nuances of mood, are conditioned responses. A face, a scene, or a voice may be the conditioned stimulus for an emotional response. It is little wonder that we are not always able to identify the origins of such emotional responses. Generalization, higher-order conditioning, and the fact that many such responses have been learned before we could talk and label them, all make it difficult to trace such feelings back to their conditioned beginnings. According to some, much of what is called the "unconscious" consists of just such unknown conditionings [Dollard and Miller, 1950]. At least this is one way of looking at it.

Although the origins of conditioned emotional responses often remain obscure, it is sometimes possible to discover the roots of such responses in ourselves and others. In the following quotation, the author describes the origin of the development and elimination of a conditioned fear response in a young boy. He also describes the origins of some of his own conditioned emotional responses. Perhaps you can discover such responses and some of their origins in your own experience.

Before and after tonsillectomy a boy was given examination and treatment by a white-coated, shiny-instrument-wielding physician. For a year and more thereafter he was terrorized by the very sight of a barber wearing his white coat and manipulating his nickeled clippers and scissors. . . . This fear reaction was eventually overcome by a barber who set a bowl of goldfish near the child, directing his highly interested attention to them, and saying "fish," meanwhile working upon the boy's hair unobtrusively and casually. . . . Later the child, upon hearing the word "fish" or "haircut" or "Dayton's" (the barber's shop) spoken aloud would smile, and with a hand describe circular gestures accompanied by rising and falling vocal inflection (mimetic of the swimming of the goldfish).

A college student relates that once he greatly enjoyed Chopin's Marche Funèbre, but that ever since he heard it played in a certain naval hospital whenever the body of an unfortunate sailor was being removed for burial, he has been unable to react to it with anything but extreme depression. . . . And who does not still react with a touch of dread to the mere words "Lidice" or "Dachau" or

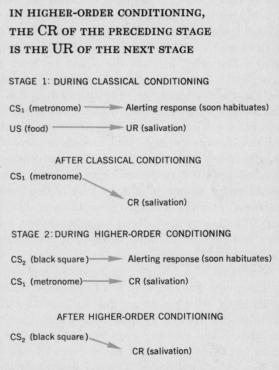

IN HIGHER-ORDER CONDITIONING,
THE CR OF THE PRECEDING STAGE
IS THE UR OF THE NEXT STAGE

STAGE 1: DURING CLASSICAL CONDITIONING

CS_1 (metronome) ——▶ Alerting response (soon habituates)

US (food) ——▶ UR (salivation)

AFTER CLASSICAL CONDITIONING

CS_1 (metronome)

    ↘ CR (salivation)

STAGE 2: DURING HIGHER-ORDER CONDITIONING

CS_2 (black square) ——▶ Alerting response (soon habituates)

CS_1 (metronome) ——▶ CR (salivation)

AFTER HIGHER-ORDER CONDITIONING

CS_2 (black square)

    ↘ CR (salivation)

FIGURE 3.9 *Diagram of higher-order conditioning. Stage 1 is simply classical conditioning. In Stage 2, a second conditioned stimulus (CS_2) is paired with the first conditioned stimulus (CS_1) and the conditioned response (CR) which follows this stimulus (CS_1). As a result of this pairing, CS_2 now produces the CR.*

"March of Death" or "Iwo Jima"? . . . The writer acknowledges a strangely warm, almost affectionate liking for pink willow-pattern dinnerware, which he can trace back to childhood lunches eaten from a pink plate. . . . In good contrast is the case of Arnold Bennett, who once wrote of a sudden dejection that came upon him whenever he saw anything pink; eventually he was able to trace it to the pink-colored almshouses of the English countryside. [Modified slightly from Dashiell, 1949, page 433.]

Perhaps many of the symbols we use are the result of conditioning. A *symbol* is simply something which stands for something else. One theory of symbol formation traces these steps [Allport, 1924]: A child is shown a doll and an adult says the word "doll." The child imitates the sound he hears and says "doll." In this example, the sight of the doll is the CS, the saying of "doll" by the adult is the US, and the imitative response by the child is the UR. According to simple classical conditioning, the child will soon come to say "doll" when he sees that object, or a similar one, because of the pairing of sight of the doll with the saying of the word. Saying "doll" when shown a doll is thus a conditioned response. Perhaps classical conditioning plays a part in giving us the tools of thought—words. However, instrumental learning, or operant conditioning, undoubtedly plays a part also.

Numerous physiological preparations and adjustments to the environment are probably classically conditioned. Hunger pangs due to gastrointestinal mobility conditioned to time cues are an excellent example. Some evidence even suggests that the ongoing electrical activity of the nervous system can be classically conditioned. The so-called brain waves (see Chapter 20) can be classically conditioned [Jasper and Shagass, 1941]. The Russians, who experiment and theorize liberally with classical conditioning, have done a great deal of work on the conditioning of physiological adjustment, such as breathing and gastrointestinal activity. They believe that many psychosomatic disorders (see Chapter 7) are caused, or at least aggravated, by classically conditioned responses inside the body [Razran, 1961].

Instrumental learning

Let us now turn to another kind of learning called *instrumental learning*. Although not precisely synonymous, the term *operant conditioning* is sometimes used in place of instrumental learning. We shall use the term instrumental learning. Whatever this type of learning is called, its important feature is that a response by the learner is *instrumental* in producing a reinforcing stimulus. The response which produces the reinforcement becomes stronger, that is, more likely or probable, whereas that which is not reinforced becomes weaker. Instrumental learning is therefore quite different from classical conditioning. In the first place, the learner is active and *emits* responses instead of having responses elicited from him by a US. Second, instrumental learning differs from classical conditioning in that the reinforcement is *contingent* upon only certain responses. The response either may obtain something which the organism needs—positive reinforcement—or it may allow the learner to escape from a painful or fear-producing situation—negative reinforcement. After an example, which should make things clearer, we shall return to these two main differences between classical and instrumental learning.

The apparatus for this demonstration is a simple box with a lever at one end. The lever is a switch which may operate a food-delivery or water-delivery mechanism. Alternatively, the lever may be wired so that it turns off a shock given to a rat through the grid floor of the box. In other words, reinforcement is contingent upon operation of the lever. Such a box, now called a "Skinner box," was first used by B. F. Skinner to study instrumental learning.

Suppose a hungry rat is placed in this box (see Figure 3.10). After an initial period of inactivity, the rat, being hungry, begins to explore the box and eventually presses the lever. A pellet of food is released, that is, reinforcement is contingent upon the lever press, but the rat does not eat the pellet at first. The animal continues exploring, stopping to wash itself from time to time. After a while it presses the lever again, and again a pellet is released. The third time the rat presses the lever, it still fails

REINFORCEMENT MAKES PRESSING THE BAR A HIGHLY PROBABLE RESPONSE

FIGURE 3.10 *A rat in a Skinner box. When the rat pushes the bar, a pellet is delivered from the feeder. The delivery of the pellet constitutes the reinforcement in this Skinner box. The box can also be arranged so that not every response produces a pellet* (partial reinforcement). *(Modified from Charles Pfizer and Co., Inc.)*

to eat the food immediately, but eventually finds and eats it. On the fourth lever response, however, the rat immediately seizes the pellet of food and eats it. Now the rat presses the lever rapidly and eats every pellet which is delivered.

Each depression of the lever is recorded on a device called a cumulative recorder. On such a recorder, each response causes a pen to make a very small movement on a piece of paper which moves at a constant speed (see Figure 3.11). Thus a cumulative and continuous record of responses is plotted against time, and the rat "draws" a record of his responses with this device. The slope of the curve is the measure of response rate: High rates of re-

sponse give steep slopes, while low rates of response result in shallow slopes. When no responses are being emitted, the line drawn on the cumulative recorder has no slope.[1] In the demonstration we have been describing, the rate of response was very low initially—the first response occurring after 15 minutes, the second response about 35 minutes

[1] In order to understand the cumulative recorder thoroughly, skip ahead to the section "Programmed Learning" at the end of the next chapter. There you will find a set on the cumulative recorder from a programmed textbook [Holland and Skinner, 1961]. It will take you about 11 minutes to work through this set.

THE LEARNER "DRAWS" A RECORD OF HIS
RESPONSES WITH A CUMULATIVE RECORDER

FIGURE 3.11 *A cumulative recorder. Each response causes the pen to move a very small distance to the left. Time is represented by the moving paper; as the paper moves at a constant rate under the pen, the learner traces a cumulative record of his responses. A high steady rate of response is shown by the slope of the lines in the foreground. (Ralph Gerbrands Co.)*

later. After about 30 more minutes, the response rate increased and the slope on the cumulative recorder increased correspondingly (see Figure 3.12).

This simple demonstration illustrates the basic features of instrumental learning. Although a rat was the subject in that instance, much human learning is also the result of reinforcement for particular responses. The learner, first of all, is motivated toward some goal, and general exploratory activity ensues. In the course of such activity, a response

happens to be made, or emitted, which is instrumental in achieving the appropriate goal. This response becomes more probable and becomes the learned response.

Instrumental learning does not require elaborate apparatus; it goes on around us all the time. Its essential feature is that reinforcement follows a response. Experiments have shown that we can change the verbal responses of other people by judicious use of reinforcement. One experimenter reinforced subjects by saying "hm-mmm" when they said plural nouns [Greenspoon, 1955]. A large increase in the number of plural nouns occurred as a result of this reinforcement. In another experiment, subjects were reinforced for expressing attitudes toward a particular topic—the Harvard University philosophy of general education—during an interview over the telephone [Hildum and Brown, 1956]. In one condition, with "good" as the reinforcer, the subjects who were reinforced for endorsing general education shifted toward a more favorable attitude, whereas those reinforced for anti- opinions shifted toward a less favorable attitude. Apparently attitudes as well as particular responses, giving plural nouns for example, can be learned through the use of reinforcement.

SHAPING We have seen that one of the differences between instrumental and classical conditioning is the freedom of the learner to emit responses. This makes it possible, in instrumental learning, to *shape* behavior through the appropriate use of reinforcement. For instance, instead of waiting for the first response to be emitted by the rat in the demonstration, the experimenter would probably shape behavior through reinforcement. First, the hungry rat would have been allowed to habituate to the Skinner box. Next, the animal would be given pellets from the food magazine until it ate promptly, that is, it would be "magazine trained." Finally, shaping of the pressing response would begin. Whenever the rat wandered into the front part of the box near the bar, the experimenter would press a switch releasing a food pellet, thus reinforcing this behavior. The rat would then be required to get a little closer to the desired response of pressing the lever. Perhaps it would be reinforced for putting its paws on the bar, and then for only actually pressing the bar. A skillful experimenter can shape such behavior with a very few reinforcements in a relatively short time. Note that the essential thing about shaping is that the learner is led to the final response through the learning of a chain of simpler responses leading to the final response. In other words, the learner comes to approximate the final response through a series of successive steps. The technique of shaping is sometimes called the method of *successive approximations*.

It should be obvious that the principle of shaping is a general one, applying to human instrumental conditioning as well as to lower animals. As an example, let us take a report of shaping the behavior of a seriously disturbed child [Wolf, Mees, and Risley, 1964].

In addition to numerous other difficulties, this boy was practically blind after a series of operations for cataracts when he was two years old. It was extremely important for him to wear glasses, and this behavior was shaped by successive approximations to the desired final response of continuously wearing the glasses. The child was placed in a room where several empty glasses frames were lying around. Whenever he picked up one of these, he was reinforced with small pieces of candy or fruit. Soon he touched the frames quite often, but it was extremely difficult to shape the next step in the chain, putting the glasses on in the proper way. The therapists then arranged to use more powerful reinforcers by making bites of lunch contingent upon having the glasses closer and closer to the proper wearing position. In a very short time, with this more powerful reinforcer, it was possible to shape both the behavior of putting on the glasses and the behavior of looking through them after they had been put on properly. The boy was soon wearing his glasses for 12 hours each day. A cumulative response curve for this behavior is shown in Figure 3.13. Although the curve does not show the frequency of a discrete event such as lever pressing, it may be interpreted in the same way as any cumulative

response curve. Note that the slope of the curve becomes steeper and finally stabilizes with a steep slope.

With a little thought we can probably all think of responses which are shaped—if not deliberately shaped—in the process of child rearing. Many attitudes and beliefs, customs, learned goals, and certain aspects of the use of language, for example, result from such shaping by means of reinforcement.

EXTINCTION In instrumental learning, just as in classical conditioning, it is possible to remove or *extinguish* a learned response *by withholding rein-*

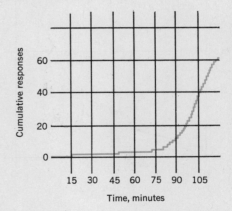

LOW RATES OF RESPONSE PRODUCE SHALLOW SLOPES; HIGH RATES PRODUCE STEEP SLOPES

FIGURE 3.12 *A cumulative record from a rat in the demonstration Skinner box. The rat did not make its first response until about 15 minutes after being placed in the box; it did not make its second response until about 35 minutes later. The effect of food reinforcement becomes apparent and strong after about 80 minutes; the rate of response then becomes high and fairly steady. Every response was reinforced when this record was made.*

forcement. If, for example, a rat in a Skinner box no longer gets food when it presses the lever, its rate of responding gradually slows down until it makes no more responses than it did before it was trained. When the number of responses is no greater than it was before any training, that is, at the *operant level* of responding, the behavior is said to be *extinguished.* A sample cumulative extinction curve resulting from the withholding of reinforcement is shown in Figure 3.14.

PRIMARY AND SECONDARY REINFORCEMENT

A reinforcing stimulus or event of some sort is necessary, by definition, in instrumental learning. We have seen that reinforcement refers to quite different processes in classical conditioning and instrumental learning. We have also seen that the mechanisms of reinforcement can be viewed several ways, for example, as need reduction or drive-stimulus reduction.

A distinction is sometimes made between primary and secondary reinforcers. From the point of view of need reduction, *primary reinforcers* are those which reduce some innate, vital physiological need of the organism, such as the need for food or water, or to escape pain. *Secondary reinforcers,* on the other hand, do not meet such innate needs, but come to be effective through a learning process. From the descriptive point of view, a *primary reinforcer* is simply one which is effective without any prior training, whereas a *secondary reinforcer,* sometimes called a *conditioned reinforcer,* requires prior association with a primary reinforcer to be effective. More formally, a *secondary reinforcer* may be defined as a stimulus which, after it has been paired with a primary reinforcer, will itself begin to act as a reinforcer. That is, it will increase the probability of a response. Secondary reinforcement may be illustrated by the following example [Fox and King, 1961]:

The sound of a buzzer, in itself, is not reinforcing to a rat. If, however, the buzzer is paired with a *primary reinforcer,* it will acquire the ability to reinforce. The experiment begins by sounding a buzzer every time a rat is given a sip of sugar water. Then the rat is put in a Skinner box and allowed to learn, for the first time, to press the lever. Instead of reinforcing the rat with sugar water, however, the experimenters reinforce it with the buzzer that had been paired with sipping sugar water. The buzzer now works very well as a *secondary* reinforcer to increase the rate of lever pressing.

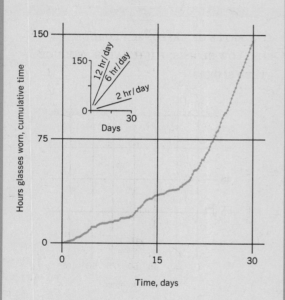

INSTRUMENTAL LEARNING IS NOT RESTRICTED TO ANIMALS

FIGURE 3.13   *A cumulative response curve for the behavior of glasses-wearing in an autistic child. This response was* shaped. *Note that the final rate of response is quite high— approximating a rate of 12 hours per day. The inset graph shows the slopes which correspond to three rates of response—2 hours per day, 6 hours per day, and 12 hours per day. This sort of key often appears in cumulative response curves. (After Wolf et al., 1964.)*

In addition to serving as reinforcement for the learning of *new* responses, secondary reinforcers can also act to *maintain* behavior when no primary reinforcement is forthcoming after a response—as in extinction. This is shown in the following experiment [Bugelski, 1938]:

In this study, rats were trained to press a bar in a Skinner box with a click accompanying the presentation of primary reinforcement. After the animals had learned the response, two groups were formed. Neither group received primary reinforcement for bar presses, but in one group bar presses were followed by the click. In the other group, no stimulus followed bar presses. The results showed that responding was maintained far longer in the "click group" than in the "nonclick group."

As always, these examples merely illustrate a principle which seems important in human behavior. The instance of a child learning to behave in the way demanded by his culture, that is, becoming socialized, comes to mind. Parents rarely use primary reinforcers, except for escape from punishment, to shape behavior. Instead, secondary reinforcers, such as praise, encouragement, and threat of punishment, are used to shape new learning and to maintain learned behavior.

PARTIAL REINFORCEMENT   So far we have been discussing the situation in which every response is reinforced. A far more common everyday life situation, and one which can easily be studied in the laboratory, is one in which only a certain proportion of the responses are reinforced, that is, *partial* instead of *continuous reinforcement* is involved. In other words, only some, but not all, responses are reinforced.

Partial reinforcement is ordinarily administered according to some plan or schedule—at least it is in experiments on partial reinforcement. For that reason the term *schedule of reinforcement* is sometimes used more or less synonymously with the term partial reinforcement. The schedule may consist of reinforcing, say, every fourth response; in that case, it would be a *ratio schedule*. Or it might be a

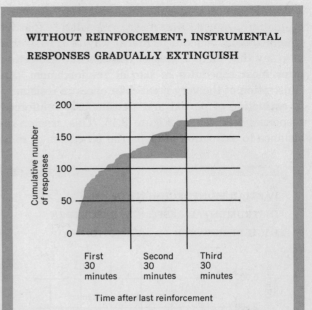

WITHOUT REINFORCEMENT, INSTRUMENTAL RESPONSES GRADUALLY EXTINGUISH

FIGURE 3.14 *An extinction curve for a rat in a Skinner box. When no food is given for presses of the lever, the rate of pressing gradually slows down. The dark areas indicate the relative numbers of responses added in each 30-minute interval. (After Skinner, 1938.)*

schedule of reinforcing once every minute, provided that the subject made a response in that interval; in this case, the schedule would be an *interval schedule*. More complicated arrangements are possible, and some of these will be described. At the extremes, we have situations in which either all or no responses are reinforced. The first of these is *continuous reinforcement* (*crf*); the second, *extinction* (*ext*). But both are instances of a schedule of reinforcement.

As a general rule, where comparisons of partial and continuous schedules of reinforcement have been made, learning is usually found to be slower under partial schedules, especially in classical conditioning [Reynolds, 1958]. However, after comparable degrees of learning have been reached, behavior is maintained far longer in the absence of any reinforcement after most schedules of partial reinforcement. A more technical way of stating this is to say that there is greater resistance to extinction after most schedules of partial reinforcement. An illustration of the very great differences in resistance to extinction of partial and continuously reinforced responses is given in Figure 3.15. This greater resistance to extinction after partial schedules of rein-

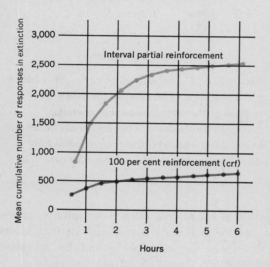

PARTIAL REINFORCEMENT OF INSTRUMENTAL RESPONSES RESULTS IN HIGH RESISTANCE TO EXTINCTION

FIGURE 3.15 *Resistance to extinction after 100 per cent and partial reinforcement. Responding is much more resistant to extinction after partial reinforcement; almost five times more responses were made after partial reinforcement. Note also that this is a cumulative graph: the number of responses made in any period is added to the number made in the preceding periods. (Modified from Jenkins et al., 1950.)*

forcement is one reason why human beings and animals tend to persist in responding long after reinforcement has ceased. Although some responses may be maintained by secondary reinforcement, others, learned early in life, may persist simply because they were strongly learned during the course of many partially reinforced trials. Parents and others simply are not, and cannot be, consistent in meting out reinforcements.

Partial reinforcement schedules can be arranged in several ways. The delivery of reinforcement may be made contingent upon the *number, rate,* or *pattern* of responses. Delivery of reinforcement may also depend upon *time,* independent of the number, rate, or pattern of response.

The *fixed-ratio schedule (FR)* is an example of a partial schedule in which the number of responses determines when reinforcement occurs. A certain number of responses must be made before a reinforcement is produced, that is, there is a fixed ratio of nonreinforced responses to reinforced responses. For example, every third (ratio of 3:1), fourth (4:1), or hundredth (100:1) response might be reinforced. Under the FR schedule, the rate of response tends to be quite high and relatively steady, as indicated in Figure 3.16.

The *fixed-interval schedule (FI)* is one in which reinforcement is given after a fixed interval of time. No reinforcements are forthcoming, no matter how many responses are made, until a certain interval of time has gone by. Behavior under this schedule tends to vary in rate during the interval. Immediately after a reinforcement the rate is low, but it increases steadily during the interval until the next reinforcement is given. In a cumulative record, this tends to produce a "scalloped" record, as in Figure 3.16, which shows typical behavior under a fixed-interval schedule.

Schedules can also be made variable, for example, *variable-ratio (VR)* and *variable-interval schedules (VI)* can be set up. In the *variable-ratio schedule,* subjects are paid off after a variable number of responses. For instance, reinforcement might come once after two responses, again after ten responses,

FIXED RATIO, FIXED INTERVAL, VARIABLE INTERVAL, AND VARIABLE RATIO CUMULATIVE RECORDS

Development of behavior on FR schedule

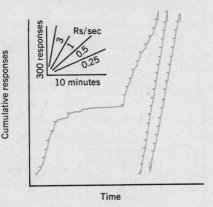

Development of behavior on VR schedule

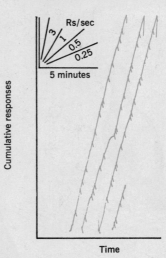

Development of behavior on FI schedule

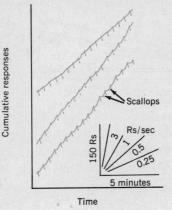

Development of behavior on VI schedule

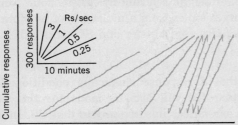

FIGURE 3.16 *Characteristic cumulative response records for four partial schedules of reinforcement. Note two things about these records: (1) The horizontal or vertical slashes on the response curves show when reinforcements were given. (2) Although the record for each schedule is in several sections, the response curves are really continuous; the long, continuous response records have been cut and displaced on the paper to save space. Top left, the development of characteristic responding on a* fixed-ratio *schedule of partial reinforcement; the rate of response increases to a steady rate of about 3 responses per second. Middle left, the development of characteristic responding on a* fixed-interval *schedule of reinforcement; note the "scallops" in the final portion of the record. Bottom left, the development of characteristic responding on a* variable-interval *schedule of reinforcement; note that the reinforcement marks come at variable intervals; note the high, steady rate of response—especially in the 5th to 8th segments. Top right, the high, steady rate of responding characteristic of* variable-ratio *schedules of reinforcement. (Modified from Ferster and Skinner, 1957.)*

EVEN PIGEONS MUST WORK TO EAT

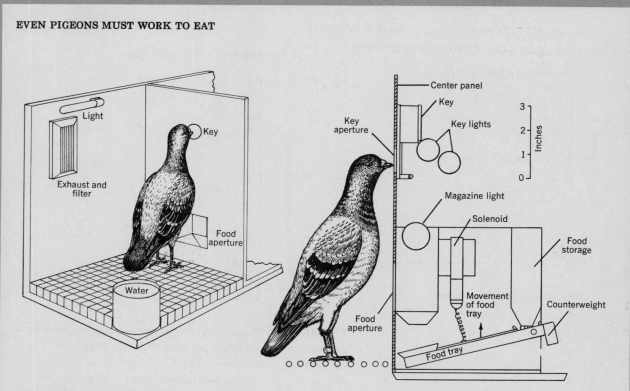

FIGURE 3.17 *Left, a Skinner box for pigeons. Key-pecking is the response which is reinforced. Reinforcement (food) is given when the food dipper comes up to the floor of the box where the pigeon can reach it. Right, a side view of the front part of the Skinner box for pigeons. Note the key and food tray especially. The key is a translucent panel which can be illuminated by the key lights. (Modified from Ferster and Skinner, 1957.)*

again after six responses, and so on after different numbers of responses. A variable-ratio schedule can be specified in terms of the *average number* of responses needed for reinforcement. Under *variable-interval schedules,* the individual is reinforced first after one interval of time, then after another interval, and so on, the schedule being specified by the *average interval.* Both of these variable schedules produce especially great resistance to extinction and steady rates of responding. (See Figure 3.16 for examples of behavior under variable-ratio and

variable-interval schedules.) These four examples are only samples from a multitude of possible types of schedules [see Ferster and Skinner, 1957].

STIMULUS GENERALIZATION We have already seen that a response classically conditioned to a particular CS will also be made to other stimuli which are similar in some way to that CS. In instrumental conditioning, stimulus generalization also takes place. The response in instrumental conditioning is made in a particular stimulus situation, in a Skinner box with a certain type of light, for example. If the stimulus situation is changed, the response still occurs, but at a lower rate than in the original stimulus situation. The rate will further depend upon the degree of similarity between the original training situation and the changed stimulus situation. The following experiment will illustrate stimulus generalization in instrumental conditioning [Olson and King, 1962]:

Instead of rats, pigeons, another standby in studies of instrumental learning, were used. The pigeon was required to learn to peck a translucent disk which was a switch and was mounted on the wall of a Skinner box for pigeons, shown in Figure 3.17. In the original learning, a moderately bright light illuminated the disk. After the instrumental pecking response to this stimulus had been well learned and the rate of response was high and steady, the animals were tested with six other light intensities on the key. These test stimuli were spaced in steps of equal intensity from low to high through the test stimulus. In the graph of Figure 3.18, the original stimulus is called 8; the more intense stimuli are 2, 4, and 6; and the less intense stimuli are 10, 12, and 14. The graph shows that there is a tendency to respond to these new stimuli and that this tendency depends upon the degree of separation between the original and test stimuli.

DISCRIMINATION LEARNING In a sense, discrimination is the opposite of stimulus generalization. In stimulus generalization the response spreads to similar stimuli, whereas in *discrimination learning* the response comes to be made to one stimulus, but not to others. The method of achieving discrimination is simply to reinforce responses to one stimulus, called the *positive stimulus,* or S^D, and not to reinforce or to extinguish responses to all other stimuli, called the *negative stimuli,* or S^Δ. The following experiment illustrates discrimination learning in a pigeon Skinner box [Hanson, 1959]:

The bird was reinforced only for responses when the translucent disk was illuminated by a light which appeared yellow-green to human observers. The pigeon received reinforcements during the intervals of yellow-green illumina-

tion on a variable-interval schedule; this was done to ensure a rather high and steady rate of response. If another light, say a red one, illuminated the disk, the pigeon received no reinforcement. Under these conditions the pigeon learned to respond during the yellow-green, but not the red, periods. After a discrimination has been learned in a situation of this kind, the change in behavior when the stimuli are

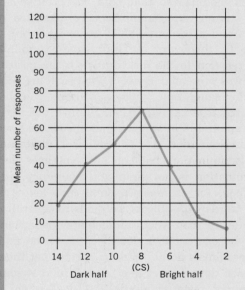

RESPONDING FALLS OFF AS STIMULI BECOME MORE AND MORE DIFFERENT FROM THE ORIGINAL

FIGURE 3.18 *A generalization gradient for instrumental learning. Note that the greatest number of responses was made to the original stimulus—somewhat loosely called the CS in this graph. As the stimuli become more and more different from the original stimulus, the number of responses diminishes; this is the case for both the brighter and dimmer stimuli. (Modified from Olson and King, 1962.)*

shifted is dramatic—almost like turning a faucet on or off. The ability of a stimulus to control behavior, the turning on and off of responses in this case, is sometimes referred to as the *stimulus control of behavior.*

This demonstration experiment illustrates *successive discrimination learning,* that is, the positive (S^D) and negative (S^Δ) stimuli are presented one after another. This type of successive discrimination is sometimes called *go no-go* discrimination; when the S^D is on, the correct response is to "go" or respond, while with the S^Δ, the correct response is "no-go" or not to respond. The experiment might have been modified so that both the positive and negative stimuli were simultaneously presented on two disks and a response could be made to either stimulus. In this case, the bird would gradually learn to respond to the disk on which the positive stimulus was presented. Since both stimuli are present at the same time, this is sometimes called *simultaneous discrimination.* The Skinner box is not the only apparatus in which simultaneous and successive discrimination may be studied. T mazes and special discrimination chambers are sometimes used.

Discrimination is not simply a laboratory curiosity. When, for example, a child first learns to associate words with objects, he tends to generalize. All animals are "bow-wow," all men are "dada," and anything he can eat is a "cookie." When he finds that some animals do not bark or let him pet them, that all men do not react like "dada," or that some things do not taste at all like cookies—when he finds, in other words, that some objects are not reinforcing—his generalized responses to them extinguish. Thus through differential reinforcement and extinction he comes to discriminate properly. In fact, we might suggest that skill in almost anything is largely a matter of the extent to which behavior is under stimulus control. The expert detects and responds appropriately to stimuli which the novice may not even notice.

SIGNIFICANCE OF INSTRUMENTAL LEARNING

Beliefs, customs, and goals may be learned through the operation of instrumental learning. This learning is especially evident during the period when young children are being taught the ways of their group—that is, when they are being socialized. The importance of instrumental learning in the socialization process has been pointed out by B. F. Skinner in a book entitled *Science and Human Behavior* (1953). Skinner has also pointed out some of the ways in which agencies of human society—for example, government and the schools—often use reinforcement to shape behavior.

In addition to such everyday and immediately practical uses, instrumental learning has become a very powerful and useful experimental technique. For instance, it has been used to study sensory processes in lower animals. Instrumental learning makes it possible to get information which could not previously be obtained; it gives the animal a kind of reliable "language" by which he can tell us what he experiences [Blough, 1958]. We can then begin to find the factors, such as physiological variables, which are related to the changes in experience.

The major advantage of instrumental learning as an experimental technique is that it provides a stable baseline upon which changes can be imposed (see Chapter 1). For instance, in studies of the effects of drugs on behavior, a stable rate of responding is first obtained without the drug; changes upon this stable rate may then be seen after the drug is administered [see Dews, 1958]. In this way, the effectiveness of the drug on behavior is immediately obvious. Since the behavior in instrumental learning can be made very stable and reliable, effects can be seen in a single subject. When properly done, this may eliminate the need for statistical evaluation of experimental results.

Avoidance learning

Up until now we have been examining instrumental conditioning with positive reinforcement. We may now turn to learning that is based on negative reinforcement—something painful, uncomfortable, or fearful that is to be escaped or avoided. Learning of this kind falls into two categories: escape learning and avoidance learning. *Escape learning* is learning to get away from or to eliminate an unpleasant situation, once the organism is in it. *Avoidance learning* is learning to avoid or to prevent the unpleasant situation *before* it occurs. Usually, these two kinds of learning are linked together; one must first learn to escape before he learns to avoid the situation another time. For this reason, the two kinds of learning will be treated together under avoidance learning. An experiment on dogs will serve as an illustration [Solomon and Wynne, 1953].

A dog was placed in a compartment which was divided into two halves by a low fence—one that the dog could easily jump over. The floor of the compartment was an electric grill through which shock could be administered to the dog. In each training trial, a buzzer was first turned on, and this was followed in 10 seconds by a shock on the side of the compartment where the dog was. The dog was supposed to jump over the fence to the other side of the compartment some time within this 10-second interval between the onset of the buzzer and the shock. If he did, the buzzer was turned off and no shock was given; if he did

not, he got a shock which was continued until he jumped over the fence. Since the jumping is instrumental in escaping from shock or in avoiding shock, it may be said to be a response of the same kind as lever pressing.

A curve for this kind of learning is shown in Figure 3.19. In this figure, the time to make a response after the onset of the buzzer—the *latency* of response—is plotted for each trial. If the latency was more than 10 seconds, the response might be classed as an escape response because the shock had come on and the dog was escaping from it. If the latency was less than 10 seconds, the response might be called an avoidance response because the dog jumped the fence *before* the shock came on and thus avoided it. As can be seen in Figure 3.19, the dog in this experiment went for a number of trials without making any avoidance responses. Then relatively suddenly the dog began to learn, and within a few more trials, he was avoiding quite consistently.

TWO-FACTOR THEORY Considerably more is involved in such avoidance learning than can be expressed in a single graph or experiment. One point is suggested by the relatively long period during which no apparent learning takes place and by the relatively sudden onset of correct responses. If we were watching the dog during this period, we might get a hint of what is going on in this kind of

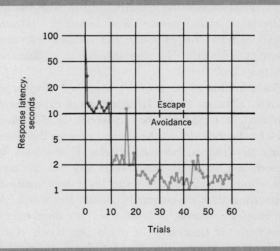

LEARNING TO AVOID PUNISHMENT TAKES PLACE RATHER ABRUPTLY AFTER A PERIOD OF LEARNING TO ESCAPE PUNISHMENT

FIGURE 3.19 *Acquisition of an avoidance response to a buzzer. Note the rather abrupt transition from escape to avoidance. Note, too, that the time scale is not linear— the times on the ordinate are plotted on a logarithmic scale. (Modified from Solomon and Wynne, 1953.)*

avoidance learning. The dog really learns two things in what seems to be a two-stage process.

The first stage, or factor, in avoidance learning is the classical conditioning of an emotional fear response to the buzzer. All that happens is that the buzzer, sounded before the shock, becomes associated with the emotional reactions to shock. One sees this association building up in the early trials of learning. When the buzzer is turned on, the dog alerts, squirms, yelps, and shows various other signs of fear.

The second stage of avoidance learning, the instrumental stage, builds upon the first. At first the animal simply learns to escape from shock as rapidly as possible. In Figure 3.19 this learning is shown by a drop in the curve to a point just above the line representing correct avoidance responses. Later the animal makes a response or two before the shock comes on and the buzzer is turned off. The cessation of the buzzer after these correct or preshock responses is reinforcing because the conditioned stimulus for fear, the buzzer, is turned off. This reinforcement through fear reduction is sufficient to maintain these correct avoidance responses.

Our analysis, then, of avoidance learning is that it consists of two types of learning, classical and instrumental conditioning. This has been called the *two-factor theory* of avoidance learning [Mowrer, 1947]. First comes the conditioning of fear to the buzzer, and second comes the learning of the particular instrumental response that reduces fear and also avoids shock. (See the discussion of learned fear, page 247).

The stimulus to be avoided need not always be explicit [Sidman, 1953]. In this type of experiment with rats in a Skinner box, a shock is delivered every 20 seconds unless the animal presses the lever during the interval between shocks. If the lever is pressed, the shock is postponed—say for 20 seconds—from the time when the lever was pushed. Responding thus momentarily avoids the shock. A high rate of response, at least one lever press every 20 seconds, is necessary to avoid the shock completely. If we assume that fear builds up during the interval between the shocks, the results of this

experiment can be explained by the two-factor theory.

EXTINCTION In some experiments, dogs have been known to jump at the sound of the buzzer for *thousands* of trials after the shock has been turned off completely. Some dogs appear never to extinguish. Such a result undoubtedly varies somewhat from one species to another, and with the experimental procedures used, but resistance to extinction, when an intense, painful event is to be avoided, is very great.

A combination of reasons, all related to the two-factor analysis of avoidance learning, helps to explain this very great resistance to extinction. One is that fear responses are slow to extinguish even under the best of conditions for extinction training. However, these conditions are not met in avoidance conditioning. In making avoidance responses, the learner leaves the original fear-producing situation—a signal paired with shock—*before* receiving shock. He therefore has no chance to experience the pairing of *no* shock with the fear-producing stimulus, which is the condition required for extinction training of fear. Finally, the instrumental part of the avoidance response is being reinforced by fear reduction throughout the period when no shock is being given. Hence, on the one hand, conditioned fear is not extinguished because the avoidance response prevents the possibility of extinction training, and on the other hand, the avoidance response is reinforced by the reduction of fear.

This resistance to extinction is very reminiscent of avoidance behavior in human beings. A person who once learned to avoid snakes or mice frequently goes on avoiding them all his life. So it is too with the avoidance of water, high places, airplanes, and many other things. People do not easily get over habits of avoiding things. Getting rid of *unwanted* avoidance behavior—some is very useful—can be quite a problem (see Chapter 13).

PUNISHMENT Avoidance learning is learning motivated by punishment, that is, by the application of a noxious, or unpleasant, stimulus. Such punishment seems to be effective if we simply want to teach an individual to respond to a signal to avoid punishment. The situations in which parents, policemen, and society use punishment are not always so simple. Yet punishment is widely used by society in an effort to eliminate undesirable behavior and to teach approved behavior. We punish dogs for chewing on rugs; we punish children for running into the street, lying, fighting with one another, not doing their homework, and so on through a long list of undesirable behaviors. Society punishes people for driving too fast or holding up banks. The use of punishment to control behavior is indeed widespread. The question is: How well does it work? When does it work?

Looking back at the experiments on avoidance learning in dogs, we may note some features of the learning situation in which punishment was effective:

1. What was punished was failure to make a response, not some already established habit. Had we punished the dog for something it had previously learned to do, the results would probably have been different.

2. No motivation existed other than the avoidance of shock. For instance, the dog was not hungry and there was no conflict between trying to get food and avoiding shock.

3. A response for avoiding the punishment was readily available. All the dog had to do was to move around a little, and the chances were good that it would hit upon the jumping response as the avoidance response.

4. There was a definite cue, the buzzer, for impending punishment. If the dog learned to react to the cue, it successfully avoided the punishment at the appropriate time.

5. The punishment was *consistently* administered for failure to make the correct response. Until the animal made the desired response, the buzzer was always paired with shock.

6. The punishment was a strong one. The shock, though not harmful to the dog, was still strong enough to be painful and to evoke very strong fear reactions.

Each of these features of the avoidance-learning experiment is important in the use of punishment to control behavior. When any one of them, or any combination of them, is altered, different results are obtained. In many cases, punishment can be completely ineffective in teaching new behavior. It may also cause neurotic emotional disturbances. (See the discussion of conflict in Chapter 13.)

Punishment during extinction. In a situation in which nearly all the above conditions are reversed, let us consider the use of punishment to eliminate a habitual response made under conditions of high motivation [Skinner, 1938].

Two rats were trained in the usual way in a Skinner box by reinforcing them with pellets of food for pressing the lever. Then they were placed on an extinction schedule. One of the rats, however, was slapped on the paws for the *first few responses* made during extinction. This was done by a device connected to the lever. The responses of the other rat, a control rat, were extinguished in the usual way.

The results of the experiment are given in Figure 3.20. The two curves in this figure are extinction curves obtained from the two rats after an equal amount of conditioning. The initial effect of the punishment, slapping, was to reduce the rate of responding. At least for a time, the punished rat responded much more slowly after the slapping than did the unpunished rat. The amazing thing, though, is that the punished rat later responded at a fairly high rate even after the unpunished rat had slowed down, and that in the end, the two rats made just about the same total number of extinction responses.

This experiment has been repeated in other ways, with electric shock instead of slapping, for example, and it nearly always gets the same results [Estes, 1944]. Punishment temporarily depresses the rate of responding but does not lessen the total number of responses required for extinction. In the long run, therefore, nothing is gained by punishment. Extinction, rather than punishment, is required to eliminate a habit.

One must be careful, however, not to overgeneralize from such experiments. The punishment was a mild one, and it was not administered regularly,

PUNISHMENT MAY SUPPRESS A RESPONSE
TEMPORARILY RATHER THAN ELIMINATE IT

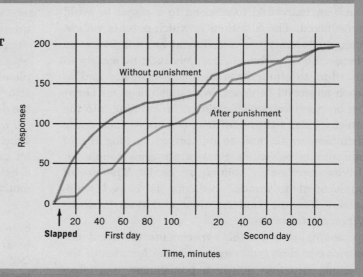

FIGURE 3.20 *The effect of punishment on extinction. Punishment at first depresses the extinction curve, but in the long run the punished rat makes just as many responses as the unpunished animal. (After Skinner, 1938.)*

so that it did not build up fear to the point of completely suppressing the habit. By giving a strong shock *every time* the rat pushes the lever, it is possible to suppress completely and permanently all lever-pressing behavior. If this is done, however, one may have a fear-ridden neurotic animal on his hands [Masserman, 1943]. The animal is strongly motivated to press the lever, yet is overcome with fear. Thus it experiences the kind of conflict which may produce neurosis (see Chapter 13).

We can conclude, however, from experiments like the one described above that *mild punishment,* administered *intermittently,* for a *well-learned habit,* when there is no obvious *alternative* to making the response, will in the long run be *ineffective.* These conditions are frequently encountered in human behavior. An occasional slap on the fingers, for example, will not keep a child out of the cookie jar permanently; the only thing that will do this is to keep the jar empty. An occasional light traffic fine will probably not improve a person's driving habits, though it might bring money into the city treasury.

Punishment with alternatives. Punishment, we have just seen, will temporarily suppress a response. In doing this, it also makes behavior more variable; it increases the likelihood that some other response will be made. If things are so arranged that one of these alternatives will satisfy any existing motives, and at the same time avoid punishment, then punishment can be very effective in eliminating undesirable habits and teaching desirable ones.

We regularly use punishment in this way in psychological experiments. We can, for example, provide a Skinner box with two levers. If we shock a rat on one lever, it will try the other lever, and if this never gives a shock, the rat quickly learns to use the no-shock lever. Or in a simple T-shaped maze, we can put shock in the left arm and food in the right arm; the animal will quickly learn to go right at the T intersection.

Sometimes there are no obvious alternative behaviors when responses have been suppressed by punishment. For instance, a child punished for some action might not know what is required of it. Then it is possible to take advantage of the period when undesirable behavior is temporarily suppressed to teach other more desirable behaviors by instrumental or perceptual learning. Most parents probably do something like this when they direct behavior into substitute channels after suppression by punishment. For example, a child who is pulling things from shelves in a grocery store as he and his mother shop might be punished for this and given a "job" to do for mother, such as taking care of an unbreakable box of cereal for the rest of the shopping trip. An occasional "good boy" from mother will probably help to reinforce such desirable behavior. A balance needs to be struck, however. The new habit might become too strong and therefore objectionable. To say the least, the control of children's behavior through combinations of punishment and reinforcement will often tax a parent's ingenuity and resourcefulness.

Cue functions of punishment. In sophisticated organisms that have acquired a large repertory of alternative responses, it is not necessary to learn a new alternative response when punishment for one response is encountered. In this case, punishment, especially if it is mild, merely serves as a cue for selecting the correct response from among the repertory. The punishment, or some sign that punishment is coming, merely tells the individual what is "right" and "wrong." It tells him how he is doing.

Many of the little punishments used in society serve as such cues. A low grade in an hour examination is a kind of punishment that tells a student where he stands in his mastery of the subject. Critical remarks made about a person's clothes or behavior may induce him to change his ways. In fact, all words of reproof come to have cue functions, since reproof or "wrong" stands for potential punishment. So long as the person has something else he can do when he runs into a punishment cue, he can quickly learn to do the "right" thing.

Conclusions about punishment. Punishment, first of all, does not permanently weaken a habit that has been learned under strong motivation. If the punishment is strong enough, it may completely suppress the habit, but this leaves the individual in a conflict between fear and other motives. If the punishment is mild, it temporarily suppresses the habit and gives an opportunity for other responses to be learned. Without such alternative responses,

mild punishment does little good. When an individual has already learned many alternative responses, mild punishment may serve as a cue for what is "wrong" and thus indirectly encourage him to do what is "right."

Perceptual learning

In the preceding sections dealing with classical conditioning, instrumental learning, and avoidance learning, the emphasis has been on the learning of *responses*. In each case, the learner acquires a response to a situation—an S-R association is formed—that he did not make in that situation prior to learning. In addition to responses, however, changes can and do take place in the way a learner perceives his world. We shall see what these changes are, but for the moment let us simply say that the learner comes to know something about the stimulus situation that he did not know before. Such changes in perception are called *perceptual learning*.

THEORETICAL APPROACHES Two general theoretical approaches to perceptual learning may be distinguished. One is *association* theory. According to this theory, perceptual learning consists of the formation of S-S associations. Because two stimuli are repeatedly paired, the presentation of one stimulus comes to arouse in the learner an image, idea, or some process representing the second stimulus, even when it is not present. Of course, almost any stimulus situation contains many stimuli, not just two, and hence whole complexes of stimuli may become associated. When this happens, the descriptive term *cognitive map* has been used [Tolman, 1948]. This is a technical way of saying what the layman means when he speaks of a "mental picture" of something. The term cognitive map is especially applicable to the learning of spatial relationships of objects in the environment. For instance, a dog learns its way about the neighborhood, that is, learns the spatial relationships between its house and other objects in the neighborhood. You form a cognitive map of the way you go to the college library, your classrooms, the dining hall, and so on.

Another view of perceptual learning is presented by the *gestalt* psychologists or, more generally, the *field* theorists (see Chapter 1). To the field theorist, the term *association* is anathema because it implies a mechanical formation of connections that they believe does not occur. Rather, they view perceptual learning as a reorganization of the perceptual field. Otherwise said, they view such learning as coming to perceive the world in a different way [Adams, 1931]. To them perceptual learning is akin to *insight*, which is a relatively sudden and rather radical change in the way a situation is perceived.

There is merit, as we shall see, in each point of view. Some perceptual learning, particularly of a routine sort, is best described as the formation of associations or cognitive maps. Other perceptual learning involving more complex problems sometimes seems to consist of a sudden perceptual reorganization.

Dozens of experiments on perceptual learning have been performed. We shall cover a representative sample of them. Some of the experiments relate to the theoretical issue just presented and attempt to determine what sort of perceptual change takes place. Others are concerned with the question of whether any sort of reinforcement or need reduction is necessary for perceptual learning to occur. Others, and the ones we shall begin with, are simply attempts to demonstrate the existence of perceptual learning in the absence of any specific stimulus-response associations.

PLACE LEARNING   One kind of perceptual learning is learning the place at which some event occurs, and the routes to and from this place. This is like learning where the post office is, or learning any set of spatial relationships. It is called place learning and can be illustrated by the following experiment [Gleitman, 1955]:

The basic purpose of the experiment was to give rats two contiguous experiences, without requiring them or permitting them to make any responses, and then to deter-

mine by further tests whether the two stimulus situations had become associated. In this case, one stimulus situation was a shock and the other consisted of the places in the apparatus at which the shock was turned on and off. In order to eliminate the possibility of the rat forming any stimulus-response associations, the rats were carried through the apparatus in small Plexiglas cars.

Figure 3.21 gives the experimental arrangement. As this figure shows, there were three possible tracks, A to B, B to C, or A to C, over which the rat could be carried. The ends of the track were marked by distinctively painted panels and a buzzer. Each animal was drawn over one of the tracks 18 times. The shock was turned on as soon as the animal had been placed in the car and was turned off at the end of the ride, which took about 20 seconds. If S-S associations were formed during the course of this experience, the rat should associate the stimuli at the beginning of the ride with the beginning of shock and the stimuli at the end of the ride with a relief from shock.

To determine whether such associations had been formed, it was necessary to have a test situation in which the rat could make a choice between the two stimulus situations, that is, the beginning and end of the track. To provide such a situation, the track was removed from the apparatus, and a T maze was put in its place with the cross bar of the T being where the track had been (see Figures 3.21 and 3.22). Now the rat was placed in the stem of the T and observed to see which way it turned. Of a total of 35 animals tested in this way, 26 turned in the shock-off direction at the end of the track, while only 9 turned in the shock-on direction at the starting point. This result showed that S-S associations had been formed in the absence of any response by the rat during the training trials.

BLOCKED-RESPONSE EXPERIMENTS   Another way of determining whether S-S associations are formed in the absence of any response is to set up situations in which responses are somehow blocked. There are, it happens, physiological means of doing this. One is to use a drug such as bulbocapnine hydrochloride which produces a cataleptic, or stuporous, state in which little if any movement occurs. Another is to sever motor nerves necessary for response. Both conditions are reversible, for the drug effects wear off in time and, since peripheral nerves regenerate, motor function is eventually restored after nerve section. Details of an experiment, in which responses were blocked in these ways, are as follows [Beck and Doty, 1957]:

Cats were the subjects in a classical conditioning experiment. A flash of light was the CS, and an unavoidable shock to the leg was the US. Normally, a leg flexion would have been the UR. In this case, however, the conditioning sessions were conducted while the animal was under the influence of bulbocapnine or after sectioning of the motor nerves. Hence, during training, no response was made. The cats were simply subjected to the paired presentation of light and shock for as many trials as is ordinarily required for conditioning to take place in normal cats. Tests of whether conditioning had occurred were made on the bulbocapnine animals 5 days after the conditioning trials; on the nerve-sectioned animals tests were made about 10 weeks later, the time required for regeneration. The tests were positive and thus indicated that an association between the light and shock had been formed in the absence of a response at the time of conditioning.

Other experiments, similar in principle to this one, but differing in the conditioning task, or the means used to block responses, have been done. They usually give positive results, that is, they show that associations are formed when responses cannot be made; these must be S-S, rather than S-R, associations.

CHANGED-RESPONSE EXPERIMENTS Another way of demonstrating the formation of S-S associations is the so-called "changed-response" experiment. The rationale of the changed-response experiment is as follows: A task is learned with one set of responses, and then something is done so that these original responses can no longer be utilized; new responses must be used. If the subject still shows that he has learned the problem with the new responses, the original learning probably did not consist of S-R associations. If S-R associations formed the basis of the original learning, great disruption should take place when the subject is forced to change to other responses which had never

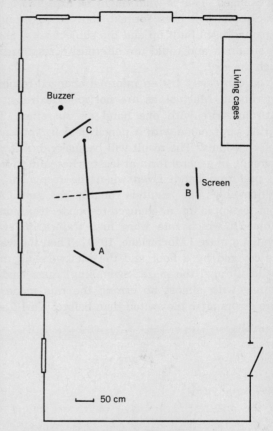

ANIMALS CAN LEARN TO FIND THEIR WAY FROM PLACE TO PLACE

FIGURE 3.21 *The experimental room in Gleitman's study of place learning. Screens were placed directly behind points marked A, B, and C. Vertical stripes were painted on the screen at A; horizontal stripes were on the screen at B; the panel at C was unpainted. In addition, a buzzer was located behind C, and the animal could always see the windows and other objects in the room. The tracks ran between A and B, A and C, or B and C. They are not shown in this figure. Two positions of the T maze for testing choices between A and C are shown. (After Gleitman, 1955.)*

been associated with the stimuli of the learning situation. In most changed-response experiments, very little disruption takes place when the responses are changed. This is what might be expected if S-S associations had been formed, that is, if cognitive maps had been built up and the subject knew about the situation and could use alternative responses to reach the goal.

You can easily try an informal changed-response experiment. Most of us are not ambidextrous; we learn to write with one hand or the other. Try writing your name with a pencil held in your non-preferred hand. The result will be shaky, but it will resemble, in general form at least, what you do with the preferred hand. Even when the responses are nothing alike, the result is roughly the same. Another example of a changed-response experiment is one in which rats were first trained to swim through a maze [Macfarlane, 1930]. Then the water was covered by a floor and the rats were required to run through the maze. Swimming transferred to running with almost no errors; the rats made no more errors after the switch than before. Karl Lash-

ley (1890–1958) performed several of these changed-response experiments [Lashley, 1924].

In one experiment, monkeys were first trained to open boxes to get food. Rather precise sequences of response were required to open the boxes. One of the boxes, the hasp box, was secured by an ordinary gate hasp and staple with a wooden pin through the staple (see Figure 3.23). The monkey needed to pull the wooden pin, lift the hasp, and then hold up the lid of the box before it could reach the food. After this sequence of responses had been well learned, an area of the cerebral cortex (and probably some underlying fibers) which regulates movement of the hand and arm muscles was removed (see Chapter 20). This operation at first made the hand and arm spastically, or "stiffly," paralyzed. But, with time, there was gradual and almost complete recovery of motor function, although some residual spasticity and weakness often remained. This residual paralysis forced the monkeys to solve the problem with different hand and arm movements after the operation. Even though different movements were now employed, they retained the learned sequence of steps needed to solve the problem.

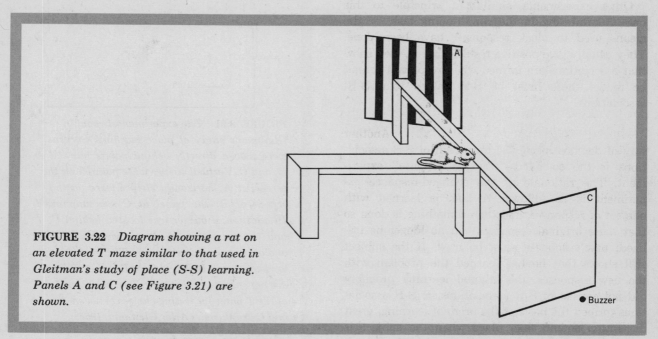

FIGURE 3.22 *Diagram showing a rat on an elevated T maze similar to that used in Gleitman's study of place (S-S) learning. Panels A and C (see Figure 3.21) are shown.*

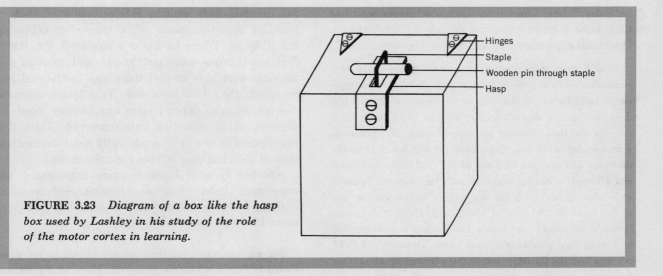

Hinges
Staple
Wooden pin through staple
Hasp

FIGURE 3.23 *Diagram of a box like the hasp box used by Lashley in his study of the role of the motor cortex in learning.*

The case of one monkey was especially clear. This animal was right-handed before the operation. As a result of the operation, paralysis was more pronounced in the right hand than in the left hand. Postoperatively, the much-weakened right hand was used at first, but when this proved ineffective the monkey switched to the left hand. Performance transferred from the right to the left hand even though completely different sets of muscles were being used.

The monkeys apparently had not learned a chain of stimulus-response connections, but had learned the *relationship* between the hasp, the pin, and the opening of the box. To put this in human terms for a minute, the monkeys had simply learned "what led to what," or "how to open the box."

In studies on the sequence of responses necessary for maze learning, Lashley reached conclusions similar to those we have just considered.

Observations on the behavior of animals with pronounced motor disturbances following spinal or cerebellar injuries emphasize the relative unimportance of the movement system. Animals which have learned the maze before the development of the motor inco-ordinations continue to traverse it, although the manner of progression may be almost completely altered. One drags himself through with his forepaws; another falls at every step but gets through by a series of lunges; a third rolls over completely in making each turn, yet manages to avoid rolling into a cul-de-sac and makes an errorless run. . . . If the customary sequence of movements employed in reaching the food is rendered impossible, another set, not previously used in the habit, and constituting an entirely different motor pattern, may be directly and efficiently substituted without any random activity. [Lashley, 1929, pages 136–137.]

LATENT LEARNING The experiments just described make it quite clear that S-S associations can be formed and that such S-S associations may include the learning of spatial relationships or cognitive maps. Now we turn to another question that has been given considerable experimental study. This is the question of whether any need reduction, or more generally, any reinforcement is necessary in perceptual learning. The experiment in which rats were carried through an apparatus in a car does not appear to involve need reduction, but other experiments are directed more specifically to the question. They are called *latent-learning* experiments. In general, these experiments permit subjects, usually rats, to explore an apparatus when they are fully fed and unmotivated, at least physiologically. Then, later, they are tested to see whether they have learned anything during the exploration. One such experiment is as follows [Seward, 1949]:

After 6 days of adaptation in a straight-alley maze, rats were allowed to explore a T maze with distinctive compartments (end boxes) at the ends of the crossarm. On the test day, each animal *was allowed to explore the T maze* for 3 minutes and then detained for approximately 25 minutes in a remote detention box. Next, each rat was taken from the detention box and put into one of the distinctive end boxes and allowed to eat for approximately one minute. Immediately after eating, each rat was placed in the starting box at the base of the stem of the T and allowed to choose between the empty goal boxes. Food odors were controlled by having food outside both goal boxes. Twenty-eight (87.5 per cent) of the 32 rats went to the end box in which they had been fed. One control experiment, in which no exploration was allowed before feeding in the end box, indicated that prior exploration of the T maze was necessary for this result: 27 of the 55 rats (49 per cent) chose the end box in which they had been fed in this control experiment. This is very close to the chance expectation—50 per cent. Other control experiments strengthened the case for latent learning and learning without reinforcement.

One interpretation of these results is simply that

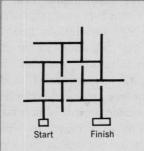

FIGURE 3.24   *Diagram of the multiple T maze used by Tolman and Honzik in their study of latent learning in the rat. (Modified from Tolman and Honzik, 1930.)*

the animals were making S-S associations, that is, building cognitive maps, while they were exploring the T maze. When food was introduced, the latent S-S associations were put to use and most of the animals were able to find their way to the end box in which they had been fed. This latent learning did not seem to depend upon any obvious need- or drive-stimulus reduction reinforcement. Thus this experiment seems to be a relatively clear demonstration of S-S learning without reinforcement.

Another type of latent-learning experiment has sometimes been cited as showing S-S learning without need- or drive-stimulus reduction reinforcement [Tolman and Honzik, 1930].

The experimenters ran three groups of rats in the maze shown in Figure 3.24. One group was given food reinforcement at the end of each trial. As might be expected, they made steady progress in learning the correct path through the maze. A second group was run without any reinforcement; they simply wandered around the maze for a given period on each trial. A third group was treated the same as the second group for the first 10 days. After that, however, the experimenter began rewarding them when they reached the end of the maze.

The results of this experiment are shown in Figure 3.25. All groups of rats evidently learned something because they made fewer errors as they were given more and more trials. The unreinforced groups, however, did not improve so much as the reinforced group. But when the experimenter began to reinforce the third group, their error scores suddenly dropped to about the same level as those of the first reinforced group. Apparently the unreinforced rats had learned a great deal about the maze in their early trials. They merely did not give evidence of their learning—it was latent, or hidden—until they were reinforced for performing well.

This experiment has been criticized, however, on the ground that the rats were put into the maze at its starting position and that they were taken out at the goal box. Since the maze was a strange, fear-producing situation, the rats probably were being reinforced by being removed to their home cages at

LEARNING MAY OCCUR WITHOUT OBVIOUS REINFORCEMENT

FIGURE 3.25 *Latent learning of a maze. One group of rats was never given food in the maze and learned very little. Another group received food in the maze after every trial and made steady progress in learning the maze. A third group was not given food reinforcement for the first 10 days of maze running, but did receive food in the maze after that. Upon introduction of the food reinforcement (shown by an arrow), this group quickly caught up with the group which had received food reinforcement from the beginning. (After Tolman and Honzik, 1930.)*

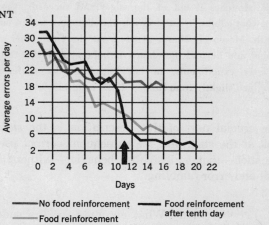

the end of each period of exploration. The decrease in the number of errors before the introduction of a reinforcer seems to indicate that such fear-reduction reinforcement may have been operating. From this we get an indication of the problems involved in designing an unambiguous experiment.

Even though the Tolman-Honzik experiment does not give clear evidence of S-S learning without reinforcement, it does make clear the distinction between *learning* and *performance*. The animals in the third group, which were given food in the goal box after 10 days without food, apparently *learned* something about the maze in the first 10 days. The animals made use of this learning—they *performed* well—only after reinforcement had been introduced.

INSIGHT Experiments in which the solution to a problem appears to come by a sudden insight have been cited as showing perceptual learning. Here again, as in some latent-learning experiments, the situation is not completely clear. In a typical insight experiment, a problem is posed and a period follows during which no apparent progress is made. Suddenly the solution comes; a learning curve of insight learning would show no evidence of learning followed *suddenly* by evidence of almost complete

learning. Another characteristic of insight learning is that it generalizes widely to similar problems.

Many experiments performed on chimpanzees seem to show insight. One of the simplest ones requires the animal to reach for food with a stick when it cannot be reached by hand. The following quotation describes one such experiment on a chimpanzee named Nueva:

Nueva was tested three days after her arrival. . . . She had not yet made the acquaintance of the other animals but remained isolated in a cage. A little stick is introduced into her cage; she scrapes the ground with it, pushes the banana skins together into a heap, and then carelessly drops the stick at a distance of about three-quarters of a metre from the bars. Ten minutes later, fruit is placed outside the cage beyond her reach. She grasps at it, vainly of course, and then begins the characteristic complaint of the chimpanzee: she thrusts both lips—especially the lower—forward, for a couple of inches, gazes imploringly at the observer, utters whimpering sounds, and finally flings herself on to the ground on her back—a gesture most eloquent of despair, which may be observed on other occasions as well. Thus, between lamentations and entreaties, some time passes, until—about seven minutes after the fruit has been exhibited to her—she suddenly casts a look at the stick, ceases her moaning, seizes the stick, stretches it out of the cage, and succeeds, though somewhat clumsily, in drawing the bananas within arm's length. Moreover, Nueva at once put the end of her stick behind and beyond the objective, holding it in this test, as in later experiments, in her left hand by preference. [Modified slightly from Köhler, 1925, pages 32–33.]

The crucial part of this description is the *sudden* look at the stick and the subsequent correct use of the stick—that is, insightful behavior—without any trial-and-error fumbling.

LEARNING SETS　What accounts for the sudden solution that is the hallmark of insight learning? It may be sudden perceptual reorganization, or it may depend upon previous learning. We usually see such sudden solutions in organisms that have had considerable opportunity—and capacity—for previous learning. How may insight learning depend on what has been learned previously? The period before the sudden solution might simply be the time necessary to remember and reconstruct what was previously learned. According to this point of view, insight learning is nothing more than the carry-over, or *transfer,* of previously learned habits, with some rearrangement, to a new situation.

That transfer from previous problems to a new problem can result in sudden solutions has been shown in a series of experiments by Harlow (1949). Whereas the usual experiment stops after one problem, or at most two or three, the same subjects here continued to new ones, finally completing as many as 344 problems. Some of the later problems were similar to earlier ones, but others required the subject to *reverse* his response to the same cues—a type of learning called discrimination-reversal learning. The apparatus used in these two-choice (correct versus incorrect) discrimination problems, the Wisconsin General Test Apparatus (WGTA), is shown in Figure 3.26.

What did the subjects learn here? Only a specific problem? Or did they learn something that trans-

ferred to the next problem and then the next? The answer is given in Figure 3.27 which is based on reversal learning. The percentage of correct responses on the *second* trial of each problem is the dependent variable. The first trial acts as an "instruction" to the subject, telling him that the problem has been changed. What he learns on the first new trial is measured by his performance on the *second* trial. If he had learned nothing, his *second* trial score would be chance—in this case, 50 per cent correct. If he had learned to transfer from previous problems, the second-trial score should approach perfection—100 per cent correct. The first "instruction" trial tells the subject who has learned to transfer from previous problems to stick with a correct solution, but to switch to the other alternative if the choice on the first problem is incorrect. The sophisticated subject has learned a rule: correct, stick with the same response; incorrect, switch to the other response.

In the reversal problems used to obtain the results of Figure 3.27, the subjects were given a few trials (6 to 11) on a problem and then the problem was reversed so that the correct alternative was incorrect for the next group of 6 to 11 trials. Then the correct alternative was reversed again, and so forth through approximately 98 problems.

In Figure 3.27, results are presented from such a series of reversal problems for both monkeys and children. Note that the monkeys initially performed at a chance level. But they gradually improved until in later problems they approached very near perfection on the *second* trials of each group of problems. The children started at a higher performance level, indicating greater initial sophistication with this type of problem, but the trend was the same.

From these results we may conclude that: (1) the amount by which a subject can profit from a single experience can, through learning, increase from nothing to a great amount; (2) inter-problem improvement is a transfer effect from one problem to another. This transfer process is called *learning set,* or sometimes, *learning to learn.* Since performance in later problems reached near per-

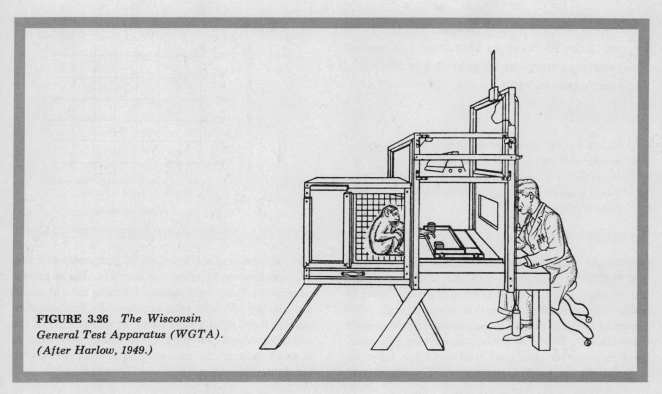

FIGURE 3.26 *The Wisconsin General Test Apparatus (WGTA). (After Harlow, 1949.)*

fection, that is, there was one-trial learning or complete transfer, it is clear that sudden solutions were regularly made on problems near the end of the series. If we did not know the past history of these subjects, their performance would be truly astonishing. In most insight experiments, the past reinforcement history of the subjects is not known and they may be transferring from previously reinforced learning. There is much evidence that sudden solutions—the indicators of insight learning—grow out of specific conditioning and learning. In short, in learning to learn, we may learn to produce insights. For this reason, insight experiments may not give clear evidence for perceptual learning.

PERCEPTUAL REORGANIZATION Insight experiments are also sometimes cited as giving evidence for learning as perceptual reorganization in the face of an obstructed need. In one of Köhler's (1925) experiments with apes, he describes the behavior of

an ape which was familiar with the use of sticks as a rake. This animal needed a stick to rake in food from outside the cage. No sticks were available (the need for the stick was obstructed), but there was a tree near the cage. After some unsuccessful attempts to reach the food, the animal suddenly went to the tree, broke off a branch, and used this to rake in the food. This has been interpreted by saying that the tree was perceived as a "treasury of sticks" when the need for a stick was obstructed [Adams, 1931]. We must, however, be cautious before accepting this interpretation of perceptual reorganization; the problem of past experience arises here. Since Köhler's animals had lived in the wild before captivity, we have no assurance that this particular individual had not previously learned this use of tree branches in a reinforced trial-and-error fashion.

The perceptual reorganization view of perceptual learning is significant because much human problem solving seems to be of this sort. A problem (an

WE LEARN TO LEARN BY REPEATEDLY LEARNING PROBLEMS THAT ARE DIFFERENT BUT OF THE SAME GENERAL KIND

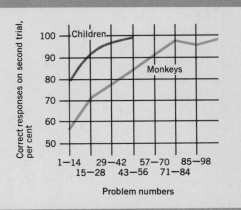

FIGURE 3.27 *Learning to learn in children and monkeys. Note that this is not the usual type of learning curve; per cent correct on the second trial of a problem set is plotted against problems. (Modified from Harlow, 1949.)*

obstructed need) arises; we try new symbolic and perceptual arrangements until one of them satisfies the blocked need. We often have the experience of suddenly seeing that a solution is appropriate after a period of more or less unsuccessful rearrangement (see Chapter 5). It is difficult to explain this away as a carry-over from past trial-and-error learning.

It would be hard to overemphasize the significance of perceptual learning in our everyday life. We are forever learning our way about new places, associating faces with names, learning new ideas, or associating one idea with another. We are also constantly faced with problems to be solved. One of the ways in which we may solve these problems is through perceptual reorganization—one variety of perceptual learning.

SYNOPSIS AND SUMMARY

We have emphasized three different processes by which changes in behavior may come about. These three processes are classical conditioning, instrumental learning, and perceptual learning. Avoidance learning is not listed here because it seems to be dependent upon classical and instrumental conditioning. Rather than attempt to bring all learning under one process, as was done in the heyday of learning theory, we have emphasized that learning occurs by different processes. Much of the knowledge about these processes has come from studies with lower animals. The exact results cannot be applied to human beings; rather, the *processes* uncovered by animal research can be applied to human learning. We have attempted to show when, and in what areas, classical conditioning, instrumental learning, and perceptual learning are important in human life.

1. Learning is any relatively permanent change in behavior which occurs as a result of experience or practice.

2. Certain factors are common to many situations in which learning takes place. These common factors are: association of stimuli or stimulus-response events, reinforcement, and motivation.

3. In classical conditioning, a neutral conditioned stimulus (e.g., a bell) is paired with an unconditioned stimulus (e.g., food) that evokes an unconditioned response (e.g., salivation). After repeated pairings of the two stimuli, the conditioned stimulus will elicit a response similar to the unconditioned response. This elicited response is called the conditioned response (CR).

4. The phenomena of extinction, spontaneous recovery, stimulus generalization, and higher-order conditioning are typical of classical conditioning. Extinction—the weakening of the conditioned response—is obtained by presenting the conditioned stimulus (CS) without pair-

ing it with the unconditioned stimulus (US). In spontaneous recovery, a conditioned response (CR) which has been extinguished recovers (spontaneously) some of the strength lost in extinction after an interval of rest. Stimulus generalization is the tendency to give conditioned responses to stimuli which are similar to the conditioned stimulus (CS). In higher-order conditioning, the conditioned response of a first conditioning is paired with a new neutral stimulus. As a result, this new neutral stimulus will call forth the conditioned response (CR).

5. In instrumental learning, a response is instrumental in producing reinforcement; the response which produces the reinforcement becomes stronger—more likely or probable. Complex responses can be shaped by reinforcing each step in a chain of steps leading to the final complex set of responses.

6. In instrumental learning, a primary reinforcer is simply one which is effective without prior training; a secondary reinforcer is one which becomes effective after it has been paired with a primary reinforcer. Both primary and secondary reinforcers may be given on every trial (continuous reinforcement) or on a certain proportion of the trials (partial reinforcement). Schedules of partial reinforcement include the fixed-ratio, fixed-interval, variable-interval, and variable-ratio schedules.

7. Stimulus generalization in instrumental learning is similar to that in classical conditioning. The operation for producing discrimination is to give reinforcement in the presence of one stimulus while withholding it when others are present.

8. Avoidance learning can be considered to be two-stage learning. The first stage is the classical conditioning of a fear response to cues paired with punishing stimulation. The second is instrumental learning that relieves the fear.

9. Punishment, in general, only temporarily eliminates learned responses. When a response is strongly motivated and there is no alternative response, punishment is relatively ineffective in eliminating undesirable behavior. Punishment may be effective, however, when it serves as a cue for making alternative responses.

10. Perceptual learning refers to cases in which we learn something about a stimulus situation which we did not know before. One view of perceptual learning is that it consists of the association of stimuli (S-S learning). An alternative point of view is that perceptual learning is the reorganization of the perceptual field under the influence of an obstructed need.

11. Place learning, or learning the routes to and from a place at which some event occurs, blocked-response experiments, and changed-response experiments show that perceptual learning of the S-S type occurs.

12. Some latent-learning experiments show that perceptual learning may occur without any obvious reinforcement. However, subtle reinforcement makes many latent-learning experiments difficult to interpret. Some insight experiments seem to give evidence supporting the view that perceptual learning consists of reorganization of the perceptual field. However, the past experience of the learner must be known before definite statements to this effect can be made. The way in which past experience can produce results which mimic those of true insight learning is shown by experiments on learning sets.

RELATED TOPICS IN THE TEXT

CHAPTER 5 THINKING Insight learning is related to problem solving. A discussion of problem solving is given in this chapter on thinking.

CHAPTER 10 PERCEPTION We have seen that perceptual learning consists of learning to associate stimuli. Learning also enters into perception because it seems necessary for the organization of sensory input into the worlds we experience.

CHAPTER 13 PERSONALITY We have said that learning is a key concept in the development of personality traits. A more detailed treatment of the application of learning principles to the origin of personality traits in childhood is given in this chapter.

CHAPTER 20 PHYSIOLOGICAL BASIS OF BEHAVIOR Some of what we know about the fascinating problem of the physiological basis of learning and memory is presented in this chapter. Unfortunately, the present state of knowledge in this area is unsatisfying. The clarification of the role of the nervous system in learning and memory is one of the great challenges in psychology and great advances should be made in the next fifty years. This chapter, together with Chapter 19, might also be of interest to those who wish to know more about the anatomy of the nervous system which was mentioned cursorily here in Chapter 3.

SUGGESTIONS FOR FURTHER READING

Birney, R. G., and Teevan, R. C. (Eds.) *Reinforcement*. Princeton, N. J.: Van Nostrand, 1961. (Paperback.) *A book of readings which attempts to give several sides of this many-faceted problem. The need-reduction, drive-stimulus reduction, and terminal-response reinforcement theories are all represented by important papers.*

Deese, J. *The psychology of learning* (2d ed.). New York: McGraw-Hill, 1958. *An introductory textbook on the psychology of learning.*

Hilgard, E. R. *Theories of learning* (2d ed.). New York: Appleton-Century-Crofts, 1956. *A scholarly, but readable, summary and evaluation of the major theories of learning.*

Hill, W. F. *Learning: A survey of psychological interpretations*. San Francisco: Chandler, 1963. (Paperback.) *Some of the major psychological theories of learning are discussed.*

Holland, J. G., and Skinner, B. F. *The analysis of behavior: A program for self-instruction*. New York: McGraw-Hill, 1961. (Paperback.) *This programmed text on operant conditioning is not a book to be read casually; a thorough grounding in the terminology and techniques of operant conditioning can be obtained by working through it. It is also a good example of the art of programming.*

Kimble, G. A. *Hilgard and Marquis' conditioning and learning*. New York: Appleton-Century-Crofts, 1961. *A complete revision of one of the standard texts on classical and instrumental conditioning. This revision includes an account of most of the significant experiments in classical and instrumental conditioning; it also shows the relationships of these experiments to many of the major theoretical issues which divide learning theorists.*

King, R. A. (Ed.) *Readings for an introduction to psychology* (2d ed.). New York: McGraw-Hill, 1966. (Paperback.) *A book of readings designed to accompany this text.*

Pavlov, I. P. *Conditioned reflexes*. New York: Dover, 1960. A reprint of: Pavlov, I. P. *Conditioned reflexes*. (Trans. by G. V. Anrep) London: Oxford, 1927. (Paperback.) *Not a difficult book to read after the fundamentals have been mastered. The first few chapters describe the technique and some of the basic results.*

Thorpe, W. H. *Learning and instinct in animals* (2d ed.). London: Methuen, 1963. *A description of the instinctive and learned response repertories of animals throughout the phylogenetic scale. Contains especially interesting accounts of insect behavior, bird migration, and perceptual learning in nonmammalian animals.*

Skinner, B. F. *Science and human behavior*. New York: Macmillan, 1953. *A description of the operant analysis of behavior and its application to many human problems.*

4

THIS CHAPTER STRESSES learning that is characteristically human—especially the learning of verbal and symbolic materials. Such learning is particularly important to you, the student: you have learned such materials throughout all your school days, and you will continue to for the rest of your academic and professional careers. Although verbal learning is our main concern here, something is said also about the learning of manual skills—driving a car, using a typewriter, repairing radios, and so on. In this chapter, too, we consider the problem of forgetting—the problem raised in the quotation from William James. Finally, we discuss techniques of study and programmed learning, applying some of the principles derived from laboratory experiments to the problems of studying that the student faces, and providing some hints to the skill of successful studying.

In Chapter 3, we covered three basic types of learning—classical conditioning, instrumental learning, and perceptual learning—and certain principles of learning such as reinforcement. Although the examples were mostly from animal learning, the points made are also applicable to human learning. For example, rote verbal learning has been regarded as a special form of classical conditioning [Hull et al., 1940], and much of human verbal learning falls into the category of instrumental learning. Reinforcement for instrumental learning in the early stages is similar to that in animal learning in that it may consist of the satisfaction of some bodily need. But in the later stages it is often a "self reward"—the pleasing knowledge that "I got it right that time." We shall also see that perceptual learning, the third type of learning discussed in Chapter 3, is important in human verbal learning.

Measurement of human learning

Let us begin with the learning of skills. If we were to study carefully the way in which a person learned such a skill as driving a car, probably one of the first things we would decide to measure would be

HUMAN LEARNING, REMEMBERING, AND FORGETTING

THE STREAM OF THOUGHT FLOWS ON; BUT MOST OF ITS SEGMENTS FALL INTO THE BOTTOMLESS ABYSS OF OBLIVION. OF SOME, NO MEMORY SURVIVES THE INSTANT OF THEIR PASSAGE. OF OTHERS, IT IS CONFINED TO A FEW MOMENTS, HOURS, OR DAYS. OTHERS, AGAIN, LEAVE VESTIGES WHICH ARE INDESTRUCTIBLE, AND BY MEANS OF WHICH THEY MAY BE RECALLED AS LONG AS LIFE ENDURES. CAN WE EXPLAIN THESE DIFFERENCES?
WILLIAM JAMES

SUCH MEASURES OF LEARNING AS SPEED, TIME ON TARGET, AND ERRORS
MAY BE USED AS DEPENDENT VARIABLES IN PLOTTING LEARNING CURVES

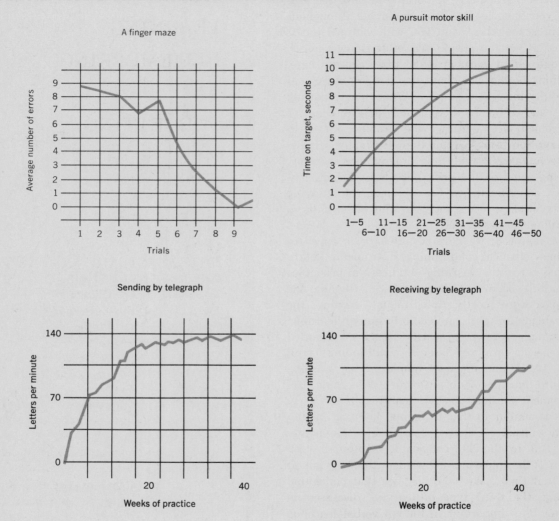

FIGURE 4.1 *Four examples of learning curves. The curve at top left shows errors in learning a finger maze; the curve at top right, time on target in learning a pursuit motor skill; the curve at bottom left, learning to send by telegraph; the curve at bottom right, learning to receive by telegraph. (Curves at bottom left and right after Bryan and Harter, 1899.)*

MANY METHODS AND DEVICES ARE USED TO STUDY HUMAN LEARNING

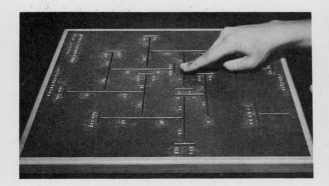

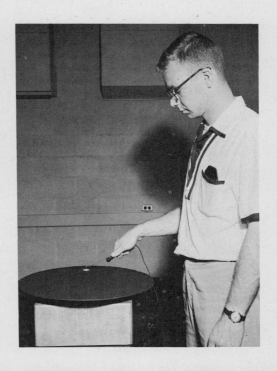

FIGURE 4.2   *Two devices used in studying human learning. At left, a finger maze (see top left curve in Figure 4.1); at right, a rotary pursuitmeter (see top right curve in Figure 4.1).*

how quickly the person's skill improved—the rate of his improvement. Such measures of the rate of learning with practice make up what psychologists call a *learning curve*. Strictly speaking, such a curve is a *performance curve*, not a learning curve, for what is measured is performance, and this performance may be complicated by factors other than learning, such as motivation or fatigue. But since learning is the factor we are most interested in, and most of the changes reflected in such curves are the consequence of learning, we shall call them learning curves.

LEARNING CURVES   The four curves in Figure 4.1 are all learning curves. In the first one (upper left), errors or mistakes are the measure of learning

and improvement is indicated by the *elimination of errors*. The curve happens to be one showing the performance of college students working on a finger maze. In Figure 4.2 (left), the hand of a student is shown in such a finger maze. The student's task is to learn to find his way from one end of the maze to the other by following the "true path." Learning the correct path through the maze is shown either by the number of errors the subject makes or by the length of time it takes him to get through the maze. The upper left curve in Figure 4.1 is a chart of the elimination of errors in learning the maze.

Another way to measure performance related to learning is to plot the *accuracy* or *correctness* of performance as a function of practice. There are many ways to do this. The upper right curve in

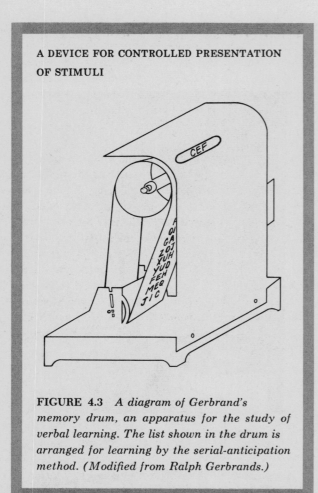

A DEVICE FOR CONTROLLED PRESENTATION OF STIMULI

FIGURE 4.3 *A diagram of Gerbrand's memory drum, an apparatus for the study of verbal learning. The list shown in the drum is arranged for learning by the serial-anticipation method. (Modified from Ralph Gerbrands.)*

Figure 4.1 shows the percentage of time a learner is able to keep a small metal stylus in contact with a moving disk. A subject working at this problem is shown in Figure 4.2 (right). This apparatus, which is used in studies of motor learning, is known as a rotary pursuitmeter or pursuit rotor. The curve of performance for the rotary pursuitmeter is, of course, an increasing-score curve.

The lower two curves in Figure 4.1 are curves of learning for verbal material. These curves are taken from a famous study—one of the earliest experimental studies of human learning—in which the ability to send and receive telegraphic code was measured as a function of practice [Bryan and Harter, 1899].

VERBAL LEARNING TECHNIQUES   Obviously, much that we learn, especially in a world of buttons, gadgets, and machinery, is motor learning. Much of human learning, on the other hand, is verbal; that is, it consists of learning new associations between and among words. By the time a person enters college, the great majority of his learning is done in terms of words. Having learned what words stand for in the world of objects and events, he learns new things about the world by learning to relate words in new ways. Although this learning is supplemented by diagrams, demonstrations, and laboratory work, the brunt of learning still falls on words.

The way in which verbal associations are formed has been the subject of considerable experimental study. Various experiments employ different *materials* and different *methods* of presentation. The material used may vary from highly meaningful stories, on the one hand, to almost meaningless *nonsense syllables,* at the other extreme. Nonsense syllables usually consist of three-letter combinations in one or another of two forms: (1) One common type begins and ends with a consonant, having a vowel in the middle (the CVC type); *zeb, cor, muv,* and *dib* are examples. (2) Another type, the consonant trigram, consists of three consonants [Winter, 1935]; *zqj* and *xfg* are examples. Such nonsense syllables are used because their association value can be evaluated more easily than that of words.

Nonsense materials, or indeed more meaningful words or phrases, may be presented to subjects by different methods. Two of the most common methods, *serial anticipation* and *paired-associate* learning, are described here briefly.

Serial anticipation. One of the common methods of studying verbal learning is known as serial anticipation [see Ebbinghaus, 1885]. A list of the syllables to be learned is constructed. The words are then presented one at a time for a standard time interval in the window of a device called, somewhat inappropriately, a *memory drum* (see Figure 4.3). The first time the list is presented (see Figure 4.4), the subject has no chance of getting any of the syllables correct because he has not seen the list before. Beginning, however, with the second run, he is asked to *anticipate* the syllable that follows the one which he is looking at in the window. If the list consisted of *cef, dax, vuq, sij,* and so on, he would first be shown *cef* and expected to say *dax*. A moment later—a standard interval is 2 seconds—*dax* would appear in the window, telling the subject whether or not he was correct and also giving him the cue for anticipating *vuq*. This would go on until the end of the list; then the list would be repeated until the subject reached a certain *criterion of learning*—for example, all correct on one run through the list—on a trial.

Paired-associate learning. In the paired-associate method, pairs of nonsense syllables, words, numbers, or other symbols are shown to the subject. The subject must learn to associate the first member of a pair, the stimulus (S) member, with the second, or response (R) member. In other words, he must learn a series of S-R associations; given the stimulus member, he must be able to respond with the response member. This kind of learning is similar to the learning of a foreign-language vocabulary list in which the stimuli are the foreign words and the responses are the English words.

Experiments on this type of learning are often done with the aid of a memory drum. The tape for this drum is usually prepared so that the stimulus term of the stimulus-response pair precedes the paired stimulus and response members (see Figure 4.5). The subject must learn to give the response that goes with the stimulus term when it is shown alone in the window. After a short interval, the drum advances to the stimulus-response pair and the subject sees whether or not he has made a correct response. If the response was not correct, the presentation of the stimulus-response pair gives the subject a chance to learn the association. Then the drum moves to the stimulus term of the next S-R pair, and the process is repeated until the end of the

list. In order to prevent the learner from simply memorizing the order of the correct responses, it is important that the order of the items be changed from trial to trial. In practice, therefore, several lists containing the same stimulus-response pairs in different order are used in an experiment.

ONE-TRIAL VERSUS INCREMENTAL LEARNING

A problem that has both methodological and theoretical interest in the measurement of human learning, particularly verbal learning, is the question of how much is learned on a single trial. Is each association strengthened a little bit on a single trial, or is an association completely formed on a single trial? Two theories, one giving a yes to the first alternative, and the other giving a yes to the second alternative, have been formulated to account for the progress of verbal learning. The first theory is known as the *incremental* or *continuity* theory; the second is called the *one-trial, noncontinuity,* or *all-or-none* theory.

X
CEF
DAX
VUQ
SIJ
QAP
GAH
ZOJ
XUH
YUD
FEH
MEQ
JIC

FIGURE 4.4   *A list of CVC non-sense syllables of low association value arranged for serial-anticipation learning. The X at the beginning of the list is the cue for the anticipation of the first syllable in the list; thereafter each syllable serves as the cue for the anticipation of the next one. (Syllables taken from Glaze, 1928.)*

FIGURE 4.5 *Nonsense syllables arranged for paired-associate learning. The stimulus member of each pair is presented first and the task of the subject is to learn the response which goes with each stimulus. Thus, when* qew *appears, the correct response is* zaj. *After the stimulus item has appeared, the stimulus-response (S-R) pair appears. The appearance of the S-R pair confirms correct associations and serves as a learning trial after incorrect responses.*

Stimulus (S)	Response (R)
QEW	
QEW —	ZAJ
KEZ	
KEZ —	FUH
QOS	
QOS —	MIF
XAJ	
XAJ —	NUX
GUX	
GUX —	PIW
WUJ	
WUJ —	BOF
DAQ	
DAQ —	ZUY
CEJ	
CEJ —	KOJ

According to the *one-trial theory,* each association is formed either full strength, or not at all, on a single trial [Estes et al., 1960]. One or more associations may be learned on a single trial, but any association is learned either not at all or completely. According to the *incremental* theory, which is probably the most favored one, associations are gradually strengthened from trial to trial. Some are strengthened more than others, but all are strengthened to some degree. Some threshold of associative strength is assumed so that when the associative strength builds up to a certain level, the person gets the item "correct."

The following example illustrates the difference between one-trial and incremental theories as applied to verbal learning [Underwood and Keppel, 1962]:

Suppose a subject is presented with a list of paired associates, one member of which is *zak-xof.* On the first test trial he does not get this pair correct, that is, when presented with *zak* alone he does not respond with *xof.* On the second and third test trials he still does not get this item correct, but on the fourth test trial he says *xof* when he sees *zak.* The one-trial theory says that the subject did not learn anything about this particular paired associate until the fourth trial; thereafter, except for some forgetting, the subject will always respond correctly to the stimulus term *zak.* The dashed line of Figure 4.6 shows the period of no learning and the quantal jump in associative strength predicted by one-trial learning theory.

One form of the incremental theory [especially Hull, 1943, 1951, 1952] says that the association of *zak* with *xof* is strengthened a little bit on each trial, but that the correct response will not be made until associative strength has exceeded a certain value—the *threshold value,* shown by the horizontal dotted line in Figure 4.6. This figure also shows the increments of associative strength which the incremental theory would predict would be added on each trial. The threshold has been drawn so that the associative strength predicted by incremental theory is crossed on the fourth trial. When associative strength for an item has crossed the threshold, there is a high probability that it will remain above the threshold and be correct on succeeding trials. For instance, on the fourth test trial (and following ones), the stimulus *zak* will produce the response *xof.* Before the associative strength for an item has crossed the threshold, correct responses will not be made.

This example shows how the one-trial and incremental theories may be formulated to predict the same behavior. For that reason, it has been extremely difficult to make a crucial test of the theories. There have, however, been numerous attempts at such a test in both human and animal learning. The results have been divided, with many experiments favoring the incremental theory and somewhat fewer favoring the one-trial theory—but experimentation continues, and the balance may change in the course of time. It seems rather likely that the final answer, when it is in, will be "both." In other words, some learning, particularly that which is akin to conditioning and which involves relatively meaningless material, may follow the incremental rule; other learning, particularly that which involves meaningful material, may follow the one-trial or all-or-none formula.

Individual differences in verbal and motor learning

Both the *method* a person uses to learn and the *material* he learns, as we shall see, make a difference in his rate of learning. But before considering these in more detail, we should keep in mind that certain characteristics of the learner also make a difference. In speaking of these characteristics, we use the term *individual differences*. There are all sorts of individual differences, such as differences in speed, strength, sensory acuity, and personality traits, but here we are concerned with individual differences that affect human learning [McGeoch and Irion, 1952]. Four will be mentioned: (1) intelligence, (2) chronological age, (3) motivation, and (4) learning sophistication.

Intelligence, in the sense of an IQ score on an intelligence test, is, as might be expected, positively related to learning. Generally, those with higher IQs learn new material more rapidly. However, in a number of instances learning is not related to intelligence [Woodrow, 1946]. One implication of this is that intelligence cannot be defined solely in terms of learning ability.

Verbal learning ability depends, in part, upon chronological age [Thorndike et al., 1928]. From approximately five years of age, when the first accurate measurements on verbal learning are possible, verbal learning ability steadily increases until approximately seventeen to twenty years of age; thereafter verbal learning ability remains fairly constant, dropping only very slightly, until approximately fifty years of age (see Figure 4.7). Beyond fifty there is a fairly sharp drop in the ability to learn new material. Data of this sort have been used in the construction of intelligence tests for adults.

Motivation, the learner's "intent to learn," is important, and is gone into further in the section on study habits later in this chapter. It is a commonplace that we learn more efficiently when we are trying to learn. For instance, although we handle 1-dollar and 5-dollar bills almost every day, most of us cannot describe the pictures on the backs of these bills. *Incidental learning*, learning without explicit

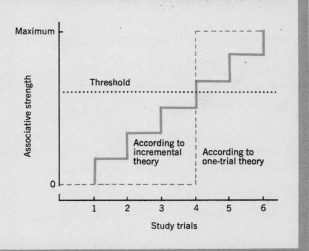

ARE ASSOCIATIONS FORMED GRADUALLY OR ALL-OR-NONE?

FIGURE 4.6 *The difference between the incremental and one-trial theories of verbal learning. The learning of a single paired associate,* zak-xof, *is shown. According to the incremental theory, the association between* zak *and* xof *is strengthened a little on each trial; eventually this association becomes strong enough to exceed the threshold and the correct response is made. According to one-trial theory, the strength of the* zak-xof *association increases from zero to full strength on a single trial, in this case, the fourth one. (Modified from Underwood and Keppel, 1962.)*

instructions or intent to learn, is possible [Postman and Senders, 1946]; but only under rather special laboratory conditions does the degree of incidental learning approach that of intentional learning [Postman and Adams, 1956].

Another important individual variable is the learning sophistication of the individual: How much does the person bring with him from previous learnings? In other words, the amount of transfer from previous learning will partially determine the rate of learning here and now. Both positive and negative transfer effects are possible, as we shall see later in the section on Transfer of Training. Has the individual "learned how to learn"—one kind of positive transfer—or has he learned habits which interfere with new learning—negative transfer?

Methods of learning

So far we have distinguished between motor (skill) and verbal learning, considered curves of learning, and described two principal methods of studying verbal learning, namely, serial anticipation and paired-associate learning. We have also discussed one-trial versus incremental learning and individual differences in human learning. Now, in this section and the two that follow, we shall cover the highlights of what is known about other factors influencing the rate of learning. In other words, we shall study the efficiency of learning. The factors that affect rate of learning fall into three main groups: the methods of learning, the material learned, and transfer from previous learning. A major section is devoted to each.

DISTRIBUTION OF PRACTICE One of the most important factors determining how rapidly a person learns is the rate at which he practices the task. For an amazingly wide variety of situations, short periods of practice interspersed with periods of rest permit more efficient learning than does continuous practice [McGeoch and Irion, 1952]. This statement is true for motor habits, for example, learning to use a typewriter. It is also true for many verbal habits, such as learning a list of paired associates. Some possible exceptions to this rule are: (1) tasks which involve problem solving or inductive thinking [Cook, 1934; Ericksen, 1942] and (2) certain verbal learning tasks [Underwood, 1961; Underwood and Schultz, 1961]. Even so, the rule of facilitation of learning by the distribution of practice is one of the most general in human learning. To discuss and illustrate this point further, we shall take up motor learning and verbal learning separately.

Motor learning. Figure 4.8 illustrates the effect of distributed practice upon some curves of motor learning [Lorge, 1930]. It represents progress on a mirror-drawing task.

LEARNING ABILITY REACHES A PEAK
NEAR TWENTY YEARS OF AGE

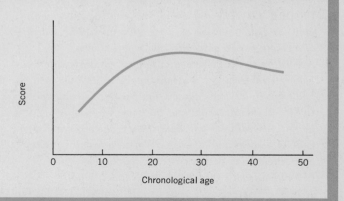

FIGURE 4.7 *Idealized diagram of learning ability as a function of chronological age. (After Thorndike et al., 1928.)*

The subject's task was to trace a complex pattern with a pencil, viewing the pattern and his pencil in a mirror that reversed the apparent direction of movement. Thus everything the subject did appeared to be reversed. One group of subjects learned the task with massed practice; as soon as they completed one tracing of the pattern, they began another. Another group was allowed 1 minute of rest between trials. A third group did only one trial a day and therefore had 24 hours of rest between trials. Notice the large and consistent difference between the learning curves for continuous, or massed, practice and those for distributed practice. Even an interval of 1 minute between trials gave considerably better results than massed practice.

For most motor tasks, the difference between massed and distributed practice is usually not so great as it was in this experiment: Moreover, there is some optimal way in which to intersperse practice and rest to obtain the most rapid learning. Three features can be varied: (1) the length of the practice period, (2) the length of the rest period, and (3) the location of the rest periods in the course of learning.

Practice periods should, in general, be short. For, within limits, the longer they are, the more they tend toward continuous practice and thus slow the rate of learning [Kimble and Bilodeau, 1949]. On the other hand, practice periods should not be so short as to break up the task into artificial or meaningless units.

In general, the longer the rest, the more effective a given amount of practice; improvement tends to increase with the length of the rest period. However, very long rest periods, say 24 hours, do not make learning much more rapid [Lorge, 1930]. In other words, the optimal length of a rest period is probably quite short for most tasks, and increasing it beyond a relatively brief optimal time will not materially increase the rate of learning a task.

No clear-cut recommendations can be made about the location of rest periods because experiments with different kinds of tasks give different results [Cook and Hilgard, 1949]. The best general summary we can make concerning distribution of prac-

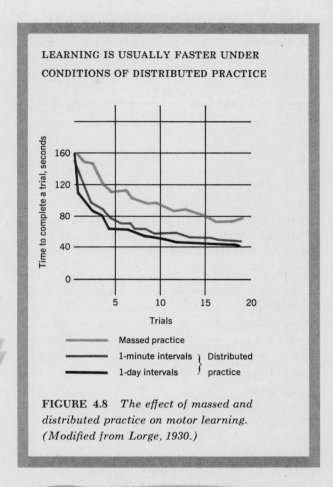

LEARNING IS USUALLY FASTER UNDER CONDITIONS OF DISTRIBUTED PRACTICE

FIGURE 4.8 *The effect of massed and distributed practice on motor learning. (Modified from Lorge, 1930.)*

tice is this: It is much more important to have short practice periods interspersed with frequent short rest periods than to have only one or two long rest periods and one or two long practice periods.

The facilitation of learning produced by distribution of practice has applications both to college study and to work in business or industry. Although learning a task and working at a task that we can already do well are not comparable in every respect, the facts about distribution of practice apply to the distribution of periods of rest and work in vocational situations as well.

Verbal learning. Distribution of practice usually facilitates verbal learning. For instance, a faster rate of learning was obtained under conditions of dis-

TABLE 4.1 *Average number of trials required to reach successive criteria of learning under massed and distributed practice*

	CRITERIA OF LEARNING (SYLLABLES CORRECT)					
	2	4	6	8	10	12
Massed practice	1.55	3.04	5.27	7.20	10.38	14.89
Distributed practice	1.48	2.83	4.41	6.47	8.73	11.18

SOURCE: Modified from Hovland, 1938.

tributed practice in an experiment in which lists of 12 nonsense syllables were learned by the serial-anticipation method [Hovland, 1938].

In this experiment the trials—complete runs through the 12 nonsense syllables—either followed each other with a 6-second pause (massed condition) or with a 126-second interval (distributed condition). As shown in Table 4.1, learning was faster in the distributed condition. In order to reach a criterion of 12 correct anticipations, an average of 11.18 trials was required under distributed conditions; 14.89 trials were required under massed conditions. The number of errors was smaller in the distributed condition, and this was especially true for nonsense syllables in the middle of the list. Figure 4.9 shows this, as well as the *serial-position effect*—the number of errors made in the middle of the list in serial-anticipation learning is greater than at the ends. Such an effect is very common in serial-anticipation learning.

The facilitating effect of distributed practice on verbal learning is not nearly so great as on motor learning. In fact, an analysis of the variables producing the distributed-practice effect, based on several verbal learning experiments, shows that distributed practice often *retarded* or had *no effect* on learning [Underwood, 1961]. The variables that are probably responsible for the presence or lack of the distributed-practice effect in these experiments have been identified and are understood by psychologists, but we shall not detail them here. The lesson of these exceptions to the distributed-

practice effect is that even such a simple bit of behavior as the learning of paired-associate lists is influenced by the operation of many variables. In general, however, the best rule for verbal and motor learning is that distributed practice is facilitating.

KNOWLEDGE OF RESULTS Another factor of importance in motor and verbal learning is *knowledge of results*. Ideally, a person should know on each trial exactly how well he has done. If, for example, he is shooting at targets, he should know after each shot just how close he came to the target and in what direction he was off. In learning golf, a person should be able to see exactly where his ball goes. If it is not possible to supply this kind of information, the next best thing is knowledge of "hit or miss," that is, whether the person was correct or incorrect. This is not so helpful as information about the extent and direction of an error, but it does let him know which trials are correct, and thus provides some guidance.

An experiment [Baker and Young, 1960], which repeats with some modifications an old experiment [Thorndike, 1932], illustrates the value of knowledge of results in learning a simple skill. For convenience in describing the experiment, let us speak of knowledge of results as "feedback" of information.

The task of the subjects was to reproduce as accurately as possible the length of a 4-inch piece of wood. The subjects were blindfolded throughout the experiment and never saw the piece of wood. They could, however, feel it with their hands whenever they wanted to. To reproduce its length, they inserted a pencil in a slot running from left to right and drew a line on graph paper. They were scored as correct when the line drawn was within ± 0.20 inch of 4 inches. Each subject drew 200 lines a day in blocks of 20 at a time; about a half-minute of rest was given between each block.

Two groups of subjects participated in this experiment. Both groups began with a pretraining day in which they drew 200 lines and received no knowledge of the results. This was to allow the experimenters to find out whether the subjects were roughly equal at the outset. On the average, subjects were accurate about 12 per cent of the time. Then one group, the feedback group, had 7 days during which the subjects were told whether they were right or wrong, that is, within ± 0.20 inch of the correct length, but they were not told the direction of their errors. The other group, the no-feedback group, was run for 9 days with no knowledge of results. At the end of its 7 days of knowledge of results, the feedback group was switched over to no-feedback for 7 days.

The outcome of the experiment is shown in Figure 4.10. The curves are somewhat bumpy because the number of

subjects (12) was not large, but they nevertheless show clear-cut differences. The no-feedback group made no consistent progress throughout the experiment. At the end, it was performing accurately on about 12 per cent of the trials. The feedback group, on the other hand, improved rather steadily while receiving knowledge of results, finally reaching about 60 per cent accuracy. As soon, however, as the feedback was stopped, the group's accuracy dropped abruptly to about 30 per cent. Still the feedback group performed better than the no-feedback group.

The experiment therefore shows that learning is aided by knowledge of results—indeed knowledge of results in some kinds of learning, gunnery, for example, is essential. It also shows that, even if one has to perform without feedback, he is better off if he has had feedback during the learning process. It is also important that knowledge of results be timely. If a gunner fires a group of shots without seeing after each shot the hole that he has made in a target, he will not progress so rapidly as he will if he does see (or know) immediately the result of each shot. The reason is probably obvious; the learner needs to associate what he is doing correctly or incorrectly on each trial with the outcome of the trial. He can do this best if he learns the details of

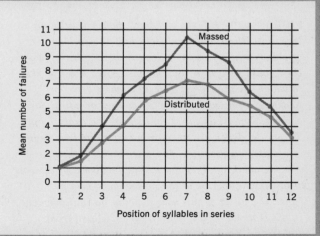

THE MIDDLE ITEMS IN A SERIES
ARE THE HARDEST ONES TO LEARN

FIGURE 4.9 *Serial-position curves for distributed and massed practice. In a serial-position curve, a measure of learning (errors in this case) is plotted against the position of the syllables in a serial-anticipation list. The inverted-U shape of these serial-position curves is typical. Note that more errors are made in the massed condition. (Modified from Hovland, 1938.)*

the outcome immediately. Otherwise all he knows is that he has generally been missing the mark.

Knowledge of results, then, aids learning because it permits the learner to associate the things he is doing with the outcome. The more immediately the knowledge is given, and the more accurate and detailed it is, the faster the learning.

Knowledge of results also aids learning by being an incentive. A person who knows how he is doing is much more interested in learning than one who is not. Especially on tedious tasks where he is likely to get bored, supplying him with some kind of record of his accomplishment helps to maintain his interest in the task. Thus knowledge of results aids learning by improving motivation for learning. A practical application of knowledge of results in verbal learning is described in the section on Teaching Machines.

READING VERSUS RECITATION Many other variations in methods of practice affect the rate of learning. One of particular interest to the student concerns the difference between reading and active recitation in the memorizing of verbal material. We also discuss this problem in the section of this chapter called Techniques of Study.

We point out there that simply reading the material is vastly inferior to reading plus active recitation. In other words, if one only reads something without reciting what he has read, his learning is much less effective than if he reads and also actively recites it. As a matter of fact, if as much as 80 per cent of study time is spent in active recitation, the result is better learning than if all the time is spent reading [Gates, 1917]. This is particularly true for disconnected material, such as a foreign-language vocabulary, but it is also true of highly organized, meaningful material.

We cannot make such clear statements about other modes of practice. We cannot, for example, say unequivocally that it is better to learn by reading than by listening. Many investigators have done experiments on this problem, with no clear-cut results. The answer probably lies in individual dif-

KNOWLEDGE OF RESULTS AIDS LEARNING;
WITHOUT IT THERE MAY BE NO LEARNING AT ALL

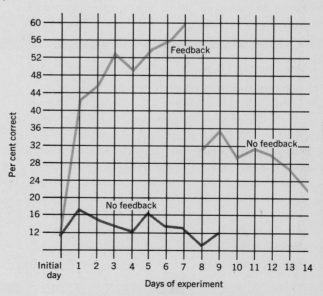

FIGURE 4.10 *Effects of knowledge of results on learning. Blindfolded subjects had the task of drawing a line the same length as a piece of wood they could feel with their hands. After the first day, in which no knowledge of results was given, the feedback group was then told whether or not it was correct, that is, within ±.20 inch of the exact length. The no-feedback group continued with no knowledge of results. On the ninth day, the feedback group was switched to no feedback. The feedback group was at all times superior to the no-feedback group. Since the latter group was showing no improvement, it was stopped on the tenth day. (Modified from Baker and Young, 1960.)*

ferences between people. Some individuals may learn better by ear than by eye, but for others the reverse may be true.

WHOLE VERSUS PART LEARNING   One of the questions facing the student, the actor, or anyone who must memorize or master a large amount of material is whether to study the material as a whole or to learn it in parts. In memorizing a poem or a part in a play, for example, should one go over the whole thing several times or take one part at a time and memorize it piecemeal? In studying a vocabulary list in a foreign language, should one keep going through the whole vocabulary list or take it in small groups? Should one master the sections of a chapter one at a time or work through the whole chapter several times?

The issue of *whole versus part learning* has been extensively studied. Some of the early experiments on memorizing poetry seemed to indicate that the whole method was superior to the part method. Later studies have not been so clear-cut. Each method has its advantages and disadvantages [McGeoch and Irion, 1952].

Part methods are advantageous when a part is easily separable from a whole, as putting and driving are in golf. When the whole is so large that one cannot go through it without running into the disadvantages of massed practice, as in rehearsing a long part in a play, the part method is preferred. The part method also has the advantage of maintaining more interest, because it gives knowledge of results and a sense of achievement more quickly. The part method, on the other hand, has the disadvantage that one must do considerably more memorizing to link the parts together after they have been learned individually. A person is also likely to mix up the parts or get them in the wrong order.

The whole method tends to be more effective under the following conditions: when the learner is intelligent enough to learn things quickly, when practice on the whole can be distributed over a number of sessions, and when the material is so meaningful that it easily hangs together. In general, the whole method of learning is more effective than one might expect, especially for meaningful material that is not too long. And though we cannot positively say that either method is always better or even usually better, the whole method is probably slightly better than the part method for most learning situations.

In the practical situation faced by the student, the best recommendation is to follow a flexible plan that combines both methods. The student should probably start with the whole method, watching out for difficult parts that need particular effort, then shift to the part method, and finally go back to the whole method again. In studying a chapter in a textbook, for example, he should read it over once, then study carefully its individual parts, and finally read it over again as a whole. The specific recommendations made later in Techniques of Study are based on experiments that bear out this general strategy.

The learning material

The kind of material to be learned makes a considerable difference in the rate of learning it. Some tasks are hard, others easy. In the case of motor learning, it is difficult to lay down any rules for saying in advance what is difficult and what is easy. For the present purposes, it is more instructive to confine ourselves to verbal learning. In this kind of learning, two aspects of the learning material are especially significant: meaningfulness of the material and perceptual distinctiveness.

MEANINGFULNESS   As people grow up, they acquire a large repertory of learned behavior. And as they are presented with new tasks to learn, they find that some of them are very much like tasks they have learned before. Or they find that what they have already learned helps in learning the new task. *Meaningful tasks* are new tasks or materials that are more easily learned because they involve old learning. Meaningfulness, defined in this way, is a special case of transfer which will be discussed in the next section.

Once it is understood what is meant by meaningfulness, the next question to consider is how it can be measured; that is, how we can state with accuracy how meaningful a task is. In the case of learning lists of words or nonsense syllables by the method of serial anticipation, meaningfulness can be measured by counting the number of associations which can be given to the word or nonsense syllable [Noble, 1952a]. The greater the number of associations, the greater the meaningfulness. And in general, the greater the meaningfulness, the faster the rate of learning. Both points may be illustrated by the following experiments [Noble, 1952a, 1952b]:

A long list of two-syllable words was constructed. Some were ordinary English words; others were nonsense words, or "paralogs." An index of meaning was obtained for each word by counting the average number of associations given by a group of subjects to each word in a 60-second period. Indices ranged from a low of 0.99 associations for the nonsense paralog *gojey* to 9.61 associations for the word *kitchen*. Incidentally, in measuring meaning this way, it turned out that some English words had lower indices of meaning than some nonsense words. The nonsense word *rompin*, for example, had a higher index than the real, but rare, English words *icon*, *matrix*, and *bodkin*. On the basis of these indices, three lists of words were selected. One list had an average index of meaning of 1.28, a second had an index of 4.42, and the third an index of 7.85.

Subjects were then compared on their rate of learning the lists by the method of serial anticipation. The list with the low index of meaning took almost three times as many trials to learn as the list with the high index. The list with the intermediate index was between the extremes.

It is notable that all the words in these lists were two-syllable words, and the number of words in each list was the same. The only difference between the three sets was meaningfulness as measured by the number of associations given to them. Meaningfulness made one list easy to learn, another list relatively difficult, and a third list very difficult. These results on meaningfulness show that it is easier to learn those things which are associated with earlier established sets of associations, a phenomenon similar to the positive-transfer effect which we discuss later. Retention of meaningful material is also better than that of meaningless material.

PERCEPTUAL DISTINCTIVENESS   Suppose that you are presented with the following list to learn: *gub, kev, 406, dac, rul, hof*. The number stands out and will probably be learned more readily than any of the nonsense syllables [Postman and Phillips, 1954]. You can probably think of other examples. In fact, if you think of the things you remember best in your personal experiences or even in your formal college studies, many of them will be the experiences that were most different, or in some way stood out most, from the experiences that went before or followed them. Such "standing out" is what we mean by distinctiveness. And the fact that distinctiveness aids learning is so clear that it needs no further proof or illustration.

The interpretation to be made of the fact is sometimes argued among psychologists. In general, two interpretations have been made, one by gestalt psychologists and the other by association, or behavioristic, psychologists. The former have proposed that the superior learning of such isolated items is due to lawful changes in the memory trace over a passage of time [von Restorff, 1933]. They theorize that the traces of similar items tend to become assimilated and blend together, whereas the trace of the isolated item is not blurred by other similar traces.

The alternative interpretation of the importance of distinctiveness, and the one most favored, is that similarities among items of a list tend to produce interference and interference among similar items tends to retard learning. Stated another way, items that are similar to each other are learned less rapidly because they interfere with each other, but the odd item is learned most rapidly because nothing in the list produces interference with it [Postman and Phillips, 1954]. This view puts the emphasis on learning rather than on memory as the important factor.

Transfer of training

One of the most important problems in the whole psychology of learning is that of the *transfer of training*. The fact that we are engaged in a program of academic study indicates society's implicit faith in transfer of training. The principal value that comes from formal learning in the school situation lies in the application of what we learn to problems outside the academic world. Because so much of our time is spent in the formal learning of things which are intended to be useful outside the classroom, transfer of training is one of the most important applied problems in learning.

PRINCIPLES OF TRANSFER   Two fundamentally different types of transfer of training need to be understood clearly. Suppose I have learned that in order to keep the attention of my class in introductory psychology I must tell a joke every 10 minutes or so. This seems to be a reasonably successful device; so I try it in my class in physiological psychology, and it works there too. This is an example of *positive transfer*. What I have learned to do in one situation applies equally well in another situation. Suppose, however, that I try to carry this one step further and use the technique in a talk that I give at the faculty club. Here I discover that my jokes fall flat and the technique fails miserably. This is an example of *negative transfer*. What worked in one situation is not applicable to another situation.

Therefore, positive transfer occurs when something previously learned benefits performance or learning in a new situation. Likewise, negative transfer occurs when something previously learned hinders performance or learning in a new situation.

This informal exposition of transfer can be made more rigorous by experimentation; we can investigate some of the conditions which will determine whether transfer will be positive or negative. Since the term transfer refers to the effect of previous learning upon subsequent learning, the following type of experimental design is appropriate [modified from McGeoch and Irion, 1952]:

Experimental group:	Learn task 1	Learn task 2
Control group:	Rest	Learn task 2

If there has been positive transfer from task 1 to task 2, the experimental group will do better, by taking fewer trials to learn to a criterion, than the control group in learning task 2; if there has been negative transfer from task 1 to task 2, the experimental group will not do so well as the control group in learning task 2.

SIMILARITY OF STIMULI AND RESPONSES   One of the most important variables determining whether transfer will be positive or negative is the degree of similarity of the stimuli and responses in the two tasks. Paired-associate learning in the two tasks has been used to investigate this variable [Bruce, 1933].

The paired-associate lists for the two tasks were made up of stimulus-response pairs of nonsense syllables. Several different types of paired-associate lists were prepared (see Table 4.2). In one experimental condition, the stimuli were different in the lists of tasks 1 and 2, but the responses were identical; in a second pair of lists, the stimuli were identical but the responses were dissimilar; in other lists, either the stimuli or the responses in task 2 were similar to those in task 1. Other control lists were used in this experiment, but the most important ones have been enumerated above. The direction of transfer and the position of each list on the Osgood transfer surface are also shown.

The results of this and many other experiments have been summarized by Osgood (1949). A diagram of his *transfer surface* is shown in Figure 4.11. In this three-dimensional figure, the degree and direction of transfer are shown along the vertical axis. Stimulus similarity between tasks 1 and 2 is shown along the axis which runs obliquely from lower left to upper right. Response similarity between tasks 1 and 2 is shown along the axis which runs obliquely from upper left to lower right. The line across the transfer surface between R_i and R_s indicates the points where the transfer surface crosses through the zero transfer plane.

Let us consider point A of Figure 4.11. At this

TABLE 4.2 *Sample stimulus-response items from the Bruce experiment on transfer*

CONDITION	RELATION OF STIMULUS AND RESPONSE ITEMS IN THE TWO TASKS	TASK 1		TASK 2		LETTER ON TRANSFER SURFACE	DIRECTION OF TRANSFER
		STIMULUS	RESPONSE	STIMULUS	RESPONSE		
1	Stimuli dissimilar—responses identical	LAN	QIP	FIS	QIP	A	Slightly positive
2	Stimuli identical—responses dissimilar	REQ	KIV	REQ	ZAM	B	Negative
3	Stimuli similar—responses identical	BES	YOR	BEF	YOR	C	Very strongly positive
4	Stimuli identical—responses similar	TEC	ZOX	TEC	ZOP	D	Slightly positive

SOURCE: Modified from Bruce, 1933.

point, the stimuli are dissimilar and the responses are identical in tasks 1 and 2; there is slight positive transfer (see condition 1 of the Bruce experiment). Point B corresponds to condition 2 of the Bruce experiment: The stimuli are identical, the responses are dissimilar, and negative transfer results. Note that opposite or antagonistic responses would produce much greater negative transfer (see below). Point C corresponds to condition 3 of the Bruce experiment: The stimuli are similar, the responses are identical, and very strong positive transfer results. Notice that the transfer surface shows the strongest positive transfer when both stimuli and responses are identical—task 1 is the same as task 2. Task 2 is then just more of task 1, and a very strong positive transfer should occur if task 1 is simply being continued. Point D corresponds to condition 4 of the Bruce experiment: The stimuli are identical, the responses are similar, and slight negative transfer results. Note that Bruce obtained slight positive transfer with these conditions. This seeming discrepancy occurs because we have not defined "simi-

larity" adequately. There is a wide range between the identical and similar responses on the transfer surface. The Bruce "similar" responses are very close to identical responses. The transfer surface shows that slight positive transfer would be expected if the responses were actually nearly identical.

Some of the major points, as illustrated by the transfer surface, concerning stimulus-response similarity and transfer may be summarized as follows:

1. Learning to make identical responses to new stimuli results in *positive transfer* (conditions 1 and 3 of the Bruce experiment).

2. Learning to make new (dissimilar, opposite, or antagonistic) responses to similar or identical stimuli results in *negative transfer* (condition 2 of the Bruce experiment).

3. The amount of transfer, regardless of whether positive or negative, is a function of stimulus similarity. The greater the stimulus similarity between tasks 1 and 2, the greater the amount of transfer.

4. Whether transfer is positive or negative is largely dependent upon response similarity.

THE AMOUNT AND DIRECTION OF TRANSFER DEPENDS UPON THE SIMILARITY OF STIMULI AND RESPONSES IN THE LEARNING AND TRANSFER TASKS

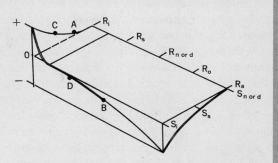

FIGURE 4.11   *The Osgood transfer surface. Decreasing response similarity is shown along the axis which runs obliquely from upper left to lower right. (R_i stands for identical responses, R_s for similar responses, $R_{n\ or\ d}$ for neutral or dissimilar responses, R_o for opposite responses, R_a for antagonistic responses.) Decreasing stimulus similarity is shown along the axis which runs obliquely from lower left to upper right. (S_i stands for identical stimuli, S_s for similar stimuli, $S_{n\ or\ d}$ for neutral or dissimilar stimuli.) The amount of transfer is shown along the vertical axis, positive in the upward direction, negative in the downward direction. The points labeled A–D show the amount and direction of transfer to be expected from representative stimulus-response combinations in the Bruce (1933) experiment. (Modified from Osgood, 1949.)*

The Osgood surface is an attempt to summarize previous work and to predict future results. Attempts to test the surface have shown that some revision may be necessary. For instance, in one experiment, predictions from the Osgood surface were only partially confirmed [Bugelski and Cadwallader, 1956]. However, another attempt to test the surface has given more complete confirmation of the Osgood predictions [Dallett, 1962].

In spite of some problems, the transfer surface is still a good summary. An understanding of the Bruce experiment and the Osgood transfer surface is the first step in appreciating the role of stimulus and response similarity in transfer. Let us now see how similarity of stimuli and responses operates in everyday situations.

Similarity of stimuli. We have seen that very strong positive transfer results when the stimuli are similar and the responses are identical. Positive transfer increases with increasing similarity of the stimuli in previous and subsequent learning. This same fact was expressed in different terms in Chapter 3 under the heading of Stimulus Generalization. In that case, a galvanic skin response (GSR) conditioned to a tone of one frequency was also evoked when tones of similar frequency were presented. The strength of the response varied with the closeness of the test frequency to the original training frequency. Such stimulus generalization is a case of positive transfer. In verbal learning, but probably not in stimulus generalization, there is some positive transfer even when the stimuli are dissimilar but the response is the same.

Let us cite two further examples. After a person has learned to drive one make and model of car, he usually has little difficulty in transferring what he has learned to another car. Instruments on the new dashboard may be arranged somewhat differently, the windshield may be a little higher or larger, and many minor features of the two cars may be different. In general, however, the stimulus situations presented by the two cars are similar; hence, positive transfer is high. In learning languages, if a person has studied Greek, his progress in Latin is faster; if he has studied Latin, his learning of French is made easier; and Latin is also helpful in mastering Italian or Spanish. In each case, the two languages have many similarities, and similar stimulus situations produce positive transfer of training.

Similarity of responses. Positive transfer may increase with increasing similarity of responses in the original and new situations (see condition 4, Table 4.2). Here, however, two responses may be so dissimilar that they are opposites, or near opposites. In that case, the result is negative transfer (see condition 2). Again, in the example of driving two cars, positive transfer from one to the other usually occurs, not only because the stimulus situations are similar, but also because nearly identical responses are required. In both cases, one uses his right foot to brake the car, his right foot to accelerate it, and his left foot to operate the clutch, if there is a clutch. To take another example, if a person has learned to play tennis, he finds it easier to learn ping-pong or badminton because similar responses and skills are involved in all three games.

In some cases, opposite responses are required in two situations with resulting negative transfer. If one is used to steering a sled and then tries to learn to pilot a plane, he will have difficulty because extending a right foot makes a sled go to the left and a plane to the right. Many people have trouble learning to steer with an outboard motor because it requires that one push the stick to the left in order to make the boat turn right, and this seems unnatural.

Negative transfer can be a matter of life and death in airplanes when a pilot changes from one type of plane he has flown for a long time to a plane with rather different controls. In the new plane, he may have to do exactly the opposite of what he has been accustomed to. Airplane accidents are occa-

sionally caused in this way [Chapanis et al., 1949]. In one incident, a pilot who was undershooting the field in attempting to land tried to correct his approach by pulling back on the throttle and pushed the stick forward. This was the reverse of what he should have done, and the plane nosed into the ground. Afterward—he was fortunate enough to survive to tell the tale—he explained that he was accustomed to flying planes in which the throttle was operated with the right hand and the stick with the left hand. In this plane, the positions of the controls were different, so that he used his left hand on the throttle and his right hand on the stick. In an emergency, he had reverted to his old habits, with almost fatal consequences.

In summary, we may say that similarity of stimuli and of responses accounts for positive transfer. A dissimilarity of responses, in which opposite or competing responses are required, accounts for negative transfer. It should be noted that virtually all learning in human beings involves transfer.

Transfer of training in formal education. The whole of our formal educational program assumes that a certain degree of positive transfer takes place between what is learned in school and what is needed in daily life. It is not surprising, therefore, that psychological studies of transfer of training have had a profound influence upon our contemporary notions of education.

Most authorities agree that there is rather direct transfer of the sort which we have been discussing— the so-called "transfer of elements." A more general theory of transfer—formal-discipline theory—has been questioned, however. At one time the notion was fairly widespread that only a limited number of mental faculties needed to be trained, and that once these had been trained they could be used in a wide variety of situations. Thus schoolboys used to study Greek, Latin, Euclid, and Aristotle, not so much because of their intrinsic value but because they were supposed to train the mind. At one time, too, there was widespread belief in the notion that one could train school children to be neat in their appearance and in the care of their belongings by teaching them to be neat in their arithmetic and spelling papers. This general notion has been called the *mental-faculty* theory of transfer or, on occasion, the *formal-discipline* theory of transfer. It has been almost completely abandoned today, largely because of the results of experimental studies on transfer of training.

Some years ago, educational psychologists studied the transfer of Latin grammar to English grammar, of Euclidean geometry to the ability to solve reasoning problems, and of classical physics to the ability to understand the mechanical problems of daily life [Stroud, 1940]. The results were rather discouraging. In nearly every case some positive transfer occurred, but it was disappointingly small. Educators have gradually relinquished the notion that one can instill a general ability through sheer exercise of a particular faculty or habit.

Nowadays educators are concerned, not with "mental discipline," but with producing the greatest amount of positive transfer of elements from school subjects to everyday life. Part of the technique for accomplishing this is to make school problems as realistic as possible. Hence the modern arithmetic book attempts to cast its problems in a form that makes them like the real-life experience of the child. At the higher levels of education, positive transfer can best be increased by making it clear to the learner that what he is learning can be transferred to other situations. Even the old subjects of special delight to the adherents of formal discipline can be made useful by bringing this point home. A study of Euclidean geometry *can* aid one in improving his ability to reason if he has a good and patient teacher with a flair for pointing out the elements that can be transferred from the formal subject to our daily experiences.

Remembering

One of the most interesting problems to the student of learning is that of retention. How much of what we learn do we retain? Why do we forget? Why do we find it difficult to remember certain common things? What produces the distortions of memory that are the common experience of everyone? These questions are all basic, and in the next few pages we consider some of the answers to them.

Remembering and forgetting are but opposite sides of the same coin (see Figure 4.12). What we have forgotten is simply the difference between what we have learned and what we have retained. We can measure directly only what has been retained, of

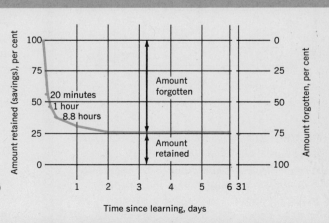

THE LARGEST AMOUNT OF FORGETTING TAKES PLACE RIGHT AFTER LEARNING

FIGURE 4.12 *A long-term forgetting (retention) curve. (Data from Ebbinghaus, 1885.)*

course, but sometimes, especially when we are concerned with theories of why we forget, our emphasis is upon forgetting rather than upon remembering.

SHORT-TERM MEMORY   The term *short-term,* or immediate, *memory* refers to the temporary storage of information for a few seconds. In *long-term memory,* material is stored for days, years, or a lifetime. An interesting experiment illustrates the great amount of forgetting which can take place in a very short time after a single exposure to a stimulus [Peterson and Peterson, 1959].

The subject in this experiment heard the experimenter say a consonant trigram followed by a number, for example,

CHJ 506. When he heard the number, the subject was instructed to count backward from it by threes until he was given a signal. The counting was done to prevent rehearsal by the subject. At the signal, the subject attempted to recall the syllable. The intervals between presentation and the signal for recall were 3, 6, 9, 12, 15, or 18 *seconds;* the frequency of correct recalls for each of these intervals is shown in Figure 4.13. Perhaps the most interesting thing about this figure is the surprising amount of forgetting after 18 seconds: The syllable is almost completely out of storage by that time. (No wonder it sometimes seems as if we cannot learn anything!) Further analysis has shown that this rapid forgetting does not occur on the first few trials and it is only after several trials that the effect becomes prominent. This points to interference by previous activity—called proactive interference—as being important in this experiment.

The limited storage capacity of short-term memory is also shown by the fact that the memory span for a single repetition is only about seven items long [Miller, 1956]. Without processing the information as we receive it, most of us cannot retain more than about seven items, for example, digits, after one exposure to them. However, most of us have learned to recode the information into "chunks" [Miller, 1956]; several items are grouped together in a single chunk by using a single symbol to stand for the whole chunk. In this way a string of 20 items may be broken into five chunks of four items each. Now we need only remember five sequences of four items—a task most of us can manage. The trick is in being able to recode the information as we receive it; with practice and a good recoding scheme, it is possible to remember as many as 40 binary digits, for example, 10100010. . . , after a single exposure to them [Miller, 1956]. The seven-digit telephone numbers come close to the span of immediate memory. Some of us have trouble remembering them because we are not good at recoding them.

Some important differences exist between short- and long-term memory [Melton, 1963]. In the first place, short-term memory is supposed to be carried

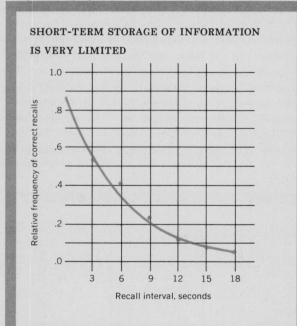

SHORT-TERM STORAGE OF INFORMATION IS VERY LIMITED

Relative frequency of correct recalls

1.0
.8
.6
.4
.2
.0

3   6   9   12   15   18

Recall interval, seconds

FIGURE 4.13   *A short-term forgetting (retention) curve. Note that the frequency of correct responses has dropped to practically zero after 18 seconds. (From Peterson and Peterson, 1959.)*

by active neural processes, while long-term memory is carried by permanent structural changes in the nervous system. Second, the short-term memory traces are supposed to decay spontaneously, while the long-term memory traces are supposed to be much more resistant to spontaneous decay. Finally, short-term memory storage capacity is supposed to be very limited and quite subject to interference. A question occurs as to whether completely different processes are involved in short- and long-term memory. Melton (1963) has argued that some of the processes operating in the forgetting of long-term memories, especially interference, are operating in the forgetting of short-term memories.

Neural processes. The first and second of these supposed differences between short- and long-term memory processes—active versus structural processes and much versus little spontaneous decay—refer to the neural basis for memory. Although we shall see that memory can be studied without worrying about the nervous system, we would all like to know what processes in the nervous system are responsible for short- and long-term memory. This is one of the most ancient, significant, enduring, and still unanswered problems of psychology. The topic, however, is discussed in more detail in Chapter 20.

Disruption of short-term memory. The third difference between short- and long-term memory, the susceptibility of short-term memory to disruption by competing demands for attention, has received much study [Broadbent, 1955]. Most of us have had the experience of being interrupted by someone in the middle of dialing a telephone number; when this happens, we usually end with a wrong number or an incomplete number. The amount of disruption of short-term memory by another competing demand for attention depends upon the amount of information being held in short-term storage [Brown, 1958]. With only a little information in short-term memory, as in dialing a telephone number, a considerable amount of interfering activity is needed; with much information in short-term memory, a little interfering activity will be effective in disrupting memory.

Two hypotheses have been proposed to account for the effects of disruptive tasks on short-term memory. These have been described as follows:

One might think of a trace which fades as fast as it is established and requires to be strengthened at intervals by rehearsal; or one might think of the stored information as passing round a recurrent circuit which periodically runs through a channel used in the perception of fresh information [Broadbent and Heron, 1962, page 190.]

According to the first of these hypotheses, interruption would interfere with the telephone dialing because there was no time for rehearsal when the interruption occurred immediately after a response. According to the second hypothesis, the memory of the last number dialed would be disrupted as it passed through the part of the circuit which was processing the new incoming, interfering information.

Regardless of whether short-term and long-term memory processes are basically different, a single exposure to stimuli in human verbal learning does not usually produce long-term retention. Exceptions to this rule may include exposures to particularly vivid or threatening stimuli, but a considerable amount of exposure to the material and many learning trials are usually required to obtain long-term retention. We now turn to a consideration of long-term retention.

MEASURING LONG-TERM RETENTION Of the several ways of measuring long-term retention, we shall describe three: *recall, recognition,* and *savings.*

Recall. The method of recall is especially suitable for studying the retention of verbal material such as a poem or a section of a textbook. In the recall method, the subject must reproduce, with a minimum of cues, something that has been learned in the past. Of the different methods, recall yields the smallest amount of measurable retention because it is always harder to recall something "cold" than it is to relearn or to recognize something. The essay examination, for example, utilizes the recall method of measuring retention.

Recognition. A second method, the method of recognition, is most frequently used in objective examinations consisting of multiple-choice questions. The subject must simply recognize whether or not he has been exposed to the information before. The amount of retention measured is inflated by a factor of chance, however, and for this reason the recognition method is the least useful for experimental purposes.

Savings. The method most frequently used by psychologists in experimental studies of retention is the method of savings. The subject learns again a task that he learned some time before. The measure of retention is the *difference* in time or number of trials required for original mastery and for the second learning—the savings from the first learning. Suppose, for example, that it took 20 repetitions to learn to repeat a certain poem without making any errors; after a period of a month it took only 10 repetitions to relearn the poem. The savings would be 50 per cent. Such a method has the advantage of being very sensitive and, at the same time, reliable. Furthermore it can show negative values. For example, suppose that for some reason it took 30 trials to relearn the poem; this would represent a negative savings of 50 per cent. A general formula for computing a percentage savings score is:

$$\frac{\text{Number of trials (or time) to learn originally } minus \text{ number of trials (or time) to relearn}}{\text{Number of trials (or time) to learn originally}} \times 100$$

The concept of savings is not new; it is simply an application of positive and negative transfer to the measurement of retention.

Another important point about the savings method is that it may show retention long after the other methods have ceased to show that there is anything retained. A rather dramatic story illustrates this point [Burtt, 1941].

Some years ago a psychologist undertook to read to his son passages in Greek from Sophocles's *Oedipus Tyrannus*. This may not be such a remarkable thing for a professor to do, except for the fact that the son was only fifteen months old. Each day for three months the professor read the same three selections of 20 lines each to the boy. When the boy was eight years old, he was required to learn by rote these selections plus some others of equal difficulty with which he had had no experience. It took the boy an average of 435 repetitions per selection to master the new selections; only 317 repetitions, on the average, were required to master the three old selections. Thus, even in infancy, exposure to complex nonsense material—since that is surely what it was to the subject of this experiment—results in savings at a later date.

Here is the moral: Do not be too upset about the precipitous decline in *recall* of the material that you learn in school; you will probably find considerable *savings* whenever you have an opportunity to use that material again or need to relearn it.

RETENTION CURVES FOR LONG-TERM MEMORY How much of what we learn stays with us after a period of time? Of course the answer depends upon the method used to measure retention, savings producing the longest lasting retention, recall generally giving less evidence of retention, and the recognition method giving the greatest retention score immediately after learning. The first attempt to answer this question was made by the German psychologist Ebbinghaus (1885). Using the method of savings and himself as a subject, Ebbinghaus did many experiments on memory. In a typical experiment, he would memorize a list of nonsense syllables such as *zeb, bep, cex, rab,* and so on; he then waited for varying periods of time, 20 minutes to 31 days; then he relearned the same syllables. In this way he was able to measure retention by the savings method for different intervals between original learning and relearning.

Ebbinghaus's results are shown in Figure 4.12. The savings are great for short intervals, but they decline rapidly during the first day after original learning. Thereafter the decline is much less abrupt. This kind of curve is *negatively accelerated*—it changes more rapidly at the beginning than at the end. Such a negatively accelerated curve of retention is the rule; practically all retention curves are of this general shape.

In some studies of verbal and motor learning, however, the retention curve does not drop during the first few minutes after learning. In fact, the subject, early in the retention period, may do better than he did at the end of learning [Ward, 1937]. This improvement in retention over that at the end of learning is called *reminiscence.*

AMOUNT RETAINED   The variables which may influence amount of retention are manifold. These seem to be among the most significant: (1) *meaningfulness of the material which was learned,* (2) *degree to which the original material was learned,* (3) *amount of interference.* Interference may come from activities preceding learning, or it may come from activities intervening between the original learning and the test of memory.

Meaningfulness and long-term retention. Many investigators have contrasted the retention of meaningful material with that of nonsense material [Kingsley and Garry, 1957]. Educational psychologists, for example, have studied the ability of students to remember material learned in school after periods of rest away from formal education. In general, they have observed a negatively accelerated curve similar to that in Figure 4.12. The curve, however, usually does not fall so fast or so far as the curve for nonsense syllables, which means that meaningful material is more likely to be retained. Such studies make quite clear the relative difficulty of remembering simple isolated facts and the relative ease of retaining meaningful and organized material. This ties in with what we found earlier—that it was much easier to learn sense than nonsense. Here we see that it is also easier to retain sense than nonsense. Actually, one is the consequence of the other; the reason we do not remember nonsense or difficult material is that we never learned it very well in the first place. When the meaningful and meaningless materials are learned *equally well,* there is no difference between them in the rate of forgetting [Underwood, 1964].

Degree of learning and long-term retention. As we

might expect, more complete mastery of the original material leads to greater memory of the material. This is illustrated by the following experiment [Krueger, 1929]:

Subjects in this experiment learned lists of single-syllable nouns to three different degrees: 100 per cent learning, 150 per cent learning, and 200 per cent learning. The 100 per cent learning means that the materials were learned to a criterion of a single correct repetition. In the 150 per cent learning, subjects practiced for half again as many trials as were needed in the original learning; in the 200 per cent condition, twice as many trials were given—in other words, the materials were *overlearned.* Memory for the nouns was tested by both the savings and recall methods after varying numbers of days—1 to 28. The results are shown in Figure 4.14. The results indicate that the amount of retention depended upon the amount of overlearning: greater

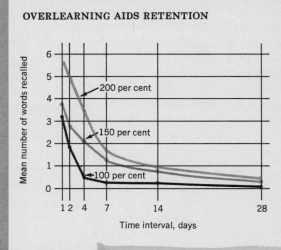

OVERLEARNING AIDS RETENTION

FIGURE 4.14   *Retention curves after different amounts of practice. One-hundred per cent means that learning proceeded to a criterion of one perfect repetition; 150 per cent means that half again as many trials as were needed to reach criterion were given; 200 per cent means that twice as many trials as were needed to reach criterion were given. (Data from Krueger, 1929; figure from Hilgard, 1951.)*

amounts of overlearning led to better retention. These results also show that a moderate amount of overlearning was effective in promoting retention—the difference between the 100 per cent and the 150 per cent groups was great—especially at relatively long intervals after the original learning. Notice also that the difference between the 150 per cent and 200 per cent groups was less, after long intervals, than that between the 150 per cent and 100 per cent groups. This suggests that some overlearning is very effective, but that a great deal of overlearning may not do much more—a point of diminishing returns is reached. For good retention there is probably an optimum degree of overlearning; this optimum, of course, depends upon the type of material and how well the material needs to be retained.

Interference effects. We have already seen that short-term memory can be interfered with by preceding and subsequent activity. Similarly, there are two kinds of interference in long-term memory. One kind is caused by subsequent or *interpolated activity*, and is sometimes called *retroactive inhibition* because the interpolated activity interferes with something learned before. Another kind of interference is referred to as *proactive inhibition*. In this, an antecedent activity interferes with ability to remember materials that come after the activity.

To illustrate retroactive and proactive interference, suppose that you go to a large party where you are introduced to many new people. By the time the evening is over, you will probably have forgotten, or at least mixed up, the names of many people to whom you were introduced. The retention of names heard early in the evening will be interfered with because you heard so many names later; this is retroactive inhibition. On the other hand, you have probably also experienced difficulty in remembering the names of those to whom you were introduced later in the evening, for it is more and more difficult to remember names as you are introduced to more and more people. Here a previous or antecedant activity interferes with the memory of the subsequent one, and this is an instance of proactive inhibition.

The interfering effect of interpolated activity, or retroactive inhibition, is often studied in experiments which use the following design [McGeoch and Irion, 1952]:

Control condition:
Learn 1   Rest   Measure retention of 1

Experimental condition:
Learn 1   Learn 2   Measure retention of 1

If retroactive interference has occurred, a comparison of the retention curves for the control and experimental conditions will show less retention in the experimental condition. The important thing about this design is that *interfering interpolated activity* occurs in one condition, but not in the other. As a rather extreme example, suppose that, in the control condition, sleep followed the learning of 1, whereas, in the experimental condition, normal waking activity followed the learning of 1. If interfering interpolated activity is really a variable in retention, we would expect to find much greater retention when sleep followed the initial learning. Such an experiment with just these results has been done [Jenkins and Dallenbach, 1924].

The two subjects of this experiment learned lists of 10 nonsense syllables just before going to bed in the laboratory. At various times after going to sleep (1, 2, 4, and 8 hours), they were awakened and retention was tested by the recall method. The same subjects learned similar lists, and retention was tested after 1, 2, 4, and 8 hours of normal daily waking activity. The curves shown in Figure 4.15 illustrate that retention was much greater after sleep than after daily waking activity. If we may reverse the beast-to-man line of reasoning customary in psychology to a man-to-beast one, similar differences have been found when cockroaches were used as subjects [Minami and Dallenbach, 1946]. Flattering, is it not?

The interfering effects of antecedent activity, or proactive inhibition, are often studied by using the following experimental design [modified from McGeoch and Irion, 1952]:

Control condition:

Rest   Learn 2   Measure of retention of 2

Experimental condition:

Learn 1   Learn 2   Measure of retention of 2

If proactive interference has occurred, subjects in the experimental group will retain less than those in the control group.

Similarity and interference. Sleep, it was noted above, is an extreme case; it represents a minimum of interpolated activity. In the waking state, various kinds of interpolated activity are possible, and the kind of activity determines the degree of interference with retention. More specifically, the *similarity* of interpolated material and original material is important, but the relationship is not simple.

An early and relatively simple statement of the relationship is known as the Skaggs-Robinson hypothesis [Skaggs, 1925; Robinson, 1927]. This states (1) that when the interpolated and original material are quite similar, interference will be minimal; (2) that when the two materials are very dissimilar, interference will be small, but greater than when they are very similar; and (3) that an intermediate degree of similarity causes the greatest interference. In the first case, interference is minimal because the interpolated material is like having more learning trials on the original material. In the second case, because there is little similarity, there is little transfer, either positive or negative. But in the third case, when there is an intermediate degree of similarity, there is a greater tendency to confuse what was learned in the interpolated period with what was learned originally. Figure 4.16 is a diagram of the predictions to be made from the Skaggs-Robinson hypothesis. Experimental support for this hypothesis has been mixed; some experiments support it; some do not. It serves, however, as a first approximation to the actual state of affairs.

A more complete analysis, in terms of stimulus and response similarities, of the effects of interpolated activity has been made with the aid of the Osgood diagram. The transfer surface of Figure 4.11 also shows the amount of retroactive interference

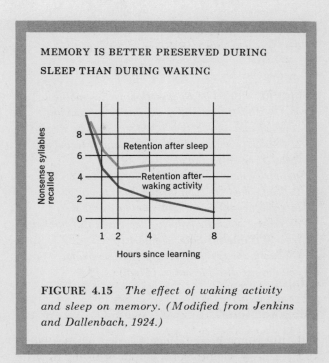

MEMORY IS BETTER PRESERVED DURING SLEEP THAN DURING WAKING

FIGURE 4.15   *The effect of waking activity and sleep on memory. (Modified from Jenkins and Dallenbach, 1924.)*

which might be expected with different degrees of similarity between stimuli and responses in tasks 1 and 2. The portion of Figure 4.11 below the zero plane shows the expected amount of interference; facilitation, or a minimum of inhibition, is shown above the zero plane. For instance, in learning 1 and 2 with similarity of stimuli held constant, increasing the similarity of responses in 1 and 2 results in decreased interference, that is, better performance. The maximum amount of interference is produced when the stimuli in learning 1 and 2 are identical (S_r) and the responses are antagonistic (R_a). For other than identical responses, a minimum amount of interference is produced when the stimuli are rather dissimilar, as is shown by the back line of the diagram. Facilitation, or a minimum of inhibition, is shown when the stimuli and responses are identical, or nearly so.

Obviously, the predictions and conclusions from the Osgood diagram differ, in some respects, from those of the Skaggs-Robinson hypothesis. Some experiments have obtained results more in keeping

THE AMOUNT OF RETROACTIVE INTERFERENCE DEPENDS UPON SIMILARITY

FIGURE 4.16   *The Skaggs-Robinson hypothesis on the effect of stimulus similarity on amount recalled and retroactive interference. The degree of similarity between the original and interpolated tasks is shown on the abscissa. As this similarity decreases from A (high similarity) to B ("intermediate" similarity), the amount of interference increases and amount recalled decreases; as this similarity decreases still farther from B ("intermediate" similarity) to C (dissimilarity), interference decreases and amount recalled increases. (Modified from Robinson, 1927.)*

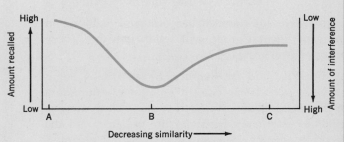

with this hypothesis [Bugelski and Cadwallader, 1956]. One of the problems is that of trying to write rules to cover all types of tasks; another is the specification of "similar" or "neutral" stimuli and responses. So long as these problems remain, differences are to be expected. Perhaps the best course is to remember both the Skaggs-Robinson and Osgood analyses—there is some support for them both.

So far in this section, we have been talking about retroactive inhibition or interference from interpolated activity. As noted, retention is also affected by antecedent activity, or proactive inhibition. In everyday life, as well as in experimental situations, retention is undoubtedly affected by both types of interference. However, interpolated activity certainly does not seem to be sufficient to account for the amount of forgetting. A substantial amount of it must be caused by proactive interference [Underwood, 1957].

Suppose that a person learns a single list of nonsense syllables and is then tested for recall 24 hours later. Usually, in this case, about 65 per cent of the list is forgotten after 24 hours (see Figure 4.12). This is a great deal of forgetting to be explained by

subsequent interpolated activity outside the laboratory, especially when extralaboratory activities are likely to be quite dissimilar to the laboratory-learned lists (see Skaggs-Robinson hypothesis). On the other hand, it seems possible that the subject's prior experience with words and syllables may have a proactive interfering effect on retention of the list learned.

This hypothesis has been tested in the laboratory by having subjects learn more than one list. In fact, in most laboratory experiments, the subject learns not just one list, but many, in the course of the experiment. So it is possible to make an analysis of many experiments in which subjects have learned two or more lists [Underwood, 1957]. Such an analysis shows that retention after 24 hours is very much a function of the number of lists learned in an experiment prior to the one under test (see Figure 4.17). In addition, when no prior lists are learned, retention is much better than when they are. Retention, then, depends very much on the existence of prior learning that interferes proactively with material learned. Extrapolating this general result to learning outside the laboratory, we may conclude that prior learning, and particularly strongly ingrained habits, are sources of interference in the retention of verbal materials.

"FAST" AND "SLOW" LEARNERS   In the previous section, we discussed meaningfulness, degree of learning, and interference as factors affecting amount of retention. Here we consider the influence of the rate of learning on retention. With the first three factors equated, the rate of learning a task depends on individual differences among learners, some being slower or faster than others. Hence the question of how rate of learning affects retention becomes one of how the learning rate *of the learner* affects retention.

In order to answer this question, we must somehow arrange the learning situation so that the *amount* learned by slow and fast learners is the same. Unfortunately, this is not easy to do. One method that has been attempted is to equate learners according to some criterion of learning. This, for example, can be done by continuing trials until each subject has given one perfect set of answers. Of course, in this case, slow learners will receive more trials than fast learners, and this does not, in

fact, equate amount of learning. Slow learners have trouble with particular parts of the material being learned, whereas other parts are learned rather rapidly. Hence the slow learner is overlearning the easy parts, and we have seen that overlearning aids retention. With this experimental design, the slow learner appears to have better retention than the fast learner, but this is probably because he has had more overlearning on some of the material.

Another experimental design, sometimes used to attack this problem and to circumvent the difficulties of the first design, is to allow fast and slow learners equal times to study the material. But this does not equate amount of learning either. With such an equation, fast learners have learned more in the time allotted than slow learners. Hence, in this case, they appear to have better retention than slow learners.

An experimental design that gets around these problems is one in which each item is practiced to the same degree of mastery. For example, it may be practiced until it has been remembered correctly on two successive trials. Then it is dropped, while practice continues on other items that have not yet been learned. With this, or some

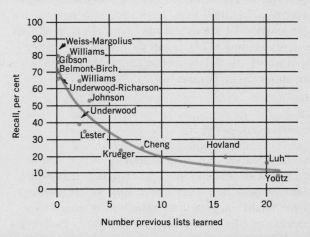

PRIOR LEARNING CAN INTERFERE WITH LATER LEARNING AND RECALL

FIGURE 4.17   *Recall depends upon the number of lists learned prior to the list which is under test. This curve is a summary of the results obtained by the many experimenters whose names appear on the graph. (From Underwood, 1961.)*

equivalent method of bringing each item to the same level of mastery without disparities in the overlearning or underlearning of items by slow and fast learners, there is *no difference* between fast and slow learners in the rate of forgetting associations. In other words, everything hinges on the degree of original learning, and whether this has been achieved rapidly or slowly makes no difference [Underwood, 1954]. This conclusion is similar to the one reached for the degree of meaningfulness and the retention of material.

Some implications for the student can be drawn from this conclusion. Slow learners, naturally, must spend more time than fast learners on their studies if they are to achieve the same mastery of their material. This means fewer parties and more work— a hard fact of life. However, after spending enough time on their studies to achieve the same degree of learning as the fast learner, retention is no worse for the slow learner than the fast one. This, at least, is a slight blessing.

One of the major causes of slow learning in college is lack of positive transfer from previous learning situations. Either specific elements are not there to transfer, because of poor preparation, or the student has not learned to learn. We can supply a few hints such as those included in the section on Techniques of Study, but there is no way, save sheer hard work, to overcome the burden imposed by lack of transfer. In time, with work, one can become a faster learner. In the meantime, more effort must be spent on studies. This is simple "common sense," but most of us fail to act appropriately, and we often suffer the consequences.

Theories of forgetting

Why is retention not better than it is? Of course, the amount of information that the central nervous system gathers in a very short time is staggering, and we might suppose that retention of more than a fraction of this information is inefficient. Perhaps it would be better to restrict the question and ask

about learned material. Why, then, is retention of learned material not better than it is? In this section we discuss several psychological theories of forgetting in some detail; and we discuss briefly one physiological, or brain, theory of forgetting called the *trace* theory. The psychological theories are: the *interference* theory, the *qualitative-change* theory, and the theories of *motivated* forgetting— especially the theory of *repression*.

PHYSIOLOGICAL-TRACE THEORY If you were to ask a reasonably intelligent and well-informed person what caused forgetting, you might get the off-hand reply, "Oh, just the passage of time, I guess." If pressed a little harder he might say, "Well, as time passes, the impressions of what we learn just get weaker and weaker and finally fade away." In other words the trace in the brain, sometimes called the *engram* [Semon, 1921], gradually fades away with time. This is one theory of forgetting.

If there is any truth at all in this notion, it cannot be the whole truth. For instance, older people often seem to remember the remote happenings of their early lives better than more recent events. In any case, a very large number of experiments have now demonstrated that it is not just the passage of time that determines how much we forget, but *what happens in time.*

INTERFERENCE THEORY As we have seen in discussing interference, what we do in between the time that we learn something and the time that we attempt to remember it influences how much we remember. Prior learning can also produce interference. The *interference theory* of forgetting is simply the application of the principles of interference to all forgetting. We have discussed this at length and have seen how important interference is in forgetting.

QUALITATIVE-CHANGE THEORY This theory holds that what we remember is not simply lost, but distorted, as time passes. If the distortion is severe enough, what is recalled will be so different from what was learned that it will seem as if an actual loss of the original material has taken place. In other words, a qualitative change would seem to produce a quantitative change.

You may have played the game of Gossip. A group of individuals arrange themselves in some order. The first individual tells a narrative to the second individual, the second individual passes it on from memory to the third individual, and so on. The last version is compared with the original narrative. The results are usually astonishing and sometimes amusing. The "message" undergoes many changes. It is usually shortened and very much distorted in meaning. This simple game serves as a useful model of certain kinds of social communication. Similar results have been found for visual memory (see Figure 4.18).

Gossip is also interesting because the changes in the narrative as it passes from one player to another parallel the changes in memory which can take place within one individual. If we ask a person to reproduce something after various intervals of time,

we see that his memory of the thing undergoes similar losses and distortions. A British psychologist has studied these qualitative changes very closely [Bartlett, 1932]. He finds that details are forgotten in verbal narrative; the story loses much of its richness and becomes a threadbare structure. Certain phrases and words become stereotyped and appear in each repetition.

Similar changes occur in memory for perceptual objects. If subjects are shown visual forms and are asked later to reproduce them, retention often suffers from a loss of detail. There is a tendency, moreover, for the forms to become more general, more symmetrical, or "normalized," and more similar to familiar objects, or "assimilated" (see Figure 4.19).

Such qualitative changes do occur; the explanation of them is another matter. One hypothesis, proposed by those adhering to the gestalt view (see Chapter 1), states that memory traces undergo spontaneous, inherent, and systematic changes [Wulf, 1922; Koffka, 1935]. According to this view, the memory trace changes toward either "normaliza-

SMALL DISTORTIONS ACCUMULATE TO PRODUCE A CHANGE IN KIND

Original drawing

Reproductions

FIGURE 4.18 *Marked changes are evident in the successive reproductions of a figure. The original drawing was seen by one subject, and he was asked to reproduce it. Second subject looked at this reproduction and then copied it from memory. This same procedure was repeated throughout the series. Note how the distortions of memory change the figure from the conventionalized Egyptian symbol for the owl to a picture of a cat. (Modified from Bartlett, 1932.)*

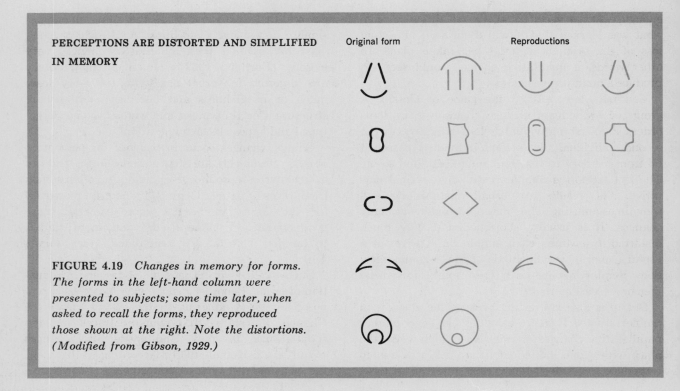

PERCEPTIONS ARE DISTORTED AND SIMPLIFIED
IN MEMORY

Original form   Reproductions

FIGURE 4.19   *Changes in memory for forms.*
The forms in the left-hand column were
presented to subjects; some time later, when
asked to recall the forms, they reproduced
those shown at the right. Note the distortions.
(Modified from Gibson, 1929.)

tion" or "emphasis." In *normalization,* sometimes called *leveling,* irregularities in the trace are smoothed over and the trace tends to become more regular. *Emphasis,* sometimes called *sharpening,* refers to the accentuation of a detail in the memory trace. Both these changes are supposed to be inherent and spontaneous. This idea of spontaneous, inherent, and systematic changes has been tested experimentally [Hebb and Foord, 1945; Lovibond, 1958]. The results were consistently negative. As we have seen, normalization and emphasizing seem to occur, but they probably cannot be explained by the inherent tendencies postulated by the gestalt hypothesis.

Perhaps the observed qualitative changes can be explained more simply by saying that external, not inherent, influences may act upon the trace. For instance, it has been shown that the verbal label given to a visually perceived form may influence memory in a very marked way [Carmichael et al., 1932]. In this experiment, rather ambiguous stimulus figures were presented with two lists of words (see Figure 4.20). When the figure in the top row was presented with the word "bottle," the reproduced figure tended to look like a bottle; when the same figure was presented with the word "stirrup," the reproduced figure tended to look like a stirrup. The external influence of the word seemed to influence what the subject remembered. This tendency for remembered figures, as well as verbal materials, to become more like some ideal or standard has been called *assimilation* [see Hilgard, 1962]. A great deal of forgetting may be due to the use of words to condense complex perceptions. We tend to remember the words and not what has actually been experienced.

Another reason for qualitative changes in retention is that the person may not perceive the original figure accurately. The first time the figure or story is reproduced, the original error in perception will still be there. In the next reproduction, the person may remember what was reproduced the first time and the error will persist. Furthermore, he may make an error in the perception of the reproduction. Thus another error, which can become cumulative, gets started at each reproduction. These repeated errors in perception, together with the tendency to assimilate, should be more than enough to produce qualitative memory changes.

MOTIVATED FORGETTING   One type of motivated forgetting involves the process of *repression*. Repression is a key concept of psychoanalytic the-

ory, and we discuss it at greater length in Chapter 13 where this theory is presented. In brief, it holds that people tend to avoid thoughts and to forget particularly unpleasant or threatening things; thoughts and memories *associated* with unpleasant or threatening events are also avoided or forgotten. *Repression* may be described, then, as the avoidance of thought and the loss of memory for unpleasant events and their associations.

Many trivial examples of forgetting in daily life may be interpreted as due to repression. For example, because I do not like liver, I may forget that my wife has asked me to buy some at the grocery store. We have probably all noticed that people tend to forget the names of people they do not like.

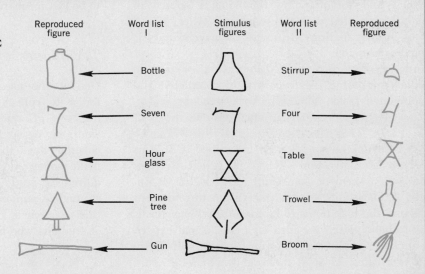

SOMETIMES WE REMEMBER THE LABEL RATHER THAN THE OBJECT OR EVENT ITSELF

Reproduced figure	Word list I	Stimulus figures	Word list II	Reproduced figure
	Bottle		Stirrup	
	Seven		Four	
	Hour glass		Table	
	Pine tree		Trowel	
	Gun		Broom	

FIGURE 4.20   *Materials used in an experiment on assimilation. Subjects were shown the stimulus figures in the middle column; at the same time the label in one of the word lists was presented to the subject. At a later time, the subjects were asked to reproduce the figures they had seen. Typical reproduced figures for subjects given the labels in word list I are shown to the left; for subjects given words from word list II, the reproduced figures are shown on the right. Note the assimilation. (Modified from Carmichael et al., 1932.)*

As we shall see in Chapter 13, however, the more important instances of repression are to be found when powerful motives or strong conflicts have not been relieved. For example, an individual may forget his early childhood sexual experiences because he has an intense anxiety about them.

As one might expect, repression is difficult to produce in laboratory experiments because it is difficult—and undesirable—to create anxieties that are strong enough to cause repression. Some experimenters, however, have discovered that people tend to forget unpleasant things more rapidly than pleasant ones [Sharp, 1938]. It is also clear that people tend to remember better what they like and what fits in with their prejudices [Edwards, 1942]. One investigator, moreover, was able to get people to remember material that they had learned and forgotten by removing a source of anxiety connected with the memory [Zeller, 1950]. These various findings fit in with the psychoanalytic idea of repression.

Another type of motivated forgetting is based on studies comparing the forgetting of completed and incomplete tasks; completed tasks tend to be forgotten more rapidly than incompleted ones [Zeigarnik, 1927]. This tendency is called the *Zeigarnik effect* after the person who first described it. It is as if there is motivation—Zeigarnik called it "tension"—to remember something until we have finished it. Once finished, the motivation to remember goes and the task tends to be forgotten. Zeigarnik is said to have gotten the idea for more formal experiments by observing the behavior of waiters in Berlin sidewalk cafes. Most of them, at least in 1927, did not write the orders down; they remembered who got what and added the total bill accurately in their heads. If they were asked to recall the individual orders after the bill had been paid and their task was complete, however, forgetting was the rule. When "tension" was lost, forgetting took place.

SUMMARY OF THEORIES OF FORGETTING This abundance of theories probably makes you ask, "Well, O.K., but which is right?" One answer is

that, for restricted areas of the broad field of forgetting, they are all probably useful. Conversely, none of the theories covers all the facts of forgetting. For instance, the *physiological-trace theory* may be quite useful in interpreting the data from experiments on short-term memory, but it is not very helpful in interpreting experiments on the effects of interpolated intervening activity. *Interference theory* is most useful in this case. When interpreting the distortions which take place in memory, interference theory is less useful than the *qualitative-change theory*. Finally, the forgetting of disturbing, traumatic, unpleasant material, let us say certain dreams, is best accounted for by a theory of *motivated forgetting*, especially the theory of *repression*. This need for many theories suggests that forgetting is not a single process; the results of learning seem to be lost for many reasons.

Techniques of study

One of the uses of psychology of particular interest to college students is the improvement of methods of study. Psychologists have done considerable research on this problem and have discovered ways in which almost every student can make some improvements, either in the time required for study or in the mastery of the material studied. A summary of the practical applications of this research is given in this section for the benefit of students who may find it helpful in college study.

MOTIVATION TO STUDY The main thing that keeps many students from developing effective study habits is lack of motivation. Many students who would like to do well in college cannot muster the fortitude to study when they should, and even when they settle down to study they cannot really concentrate on the job. We know of no ready remedy for this malady, and can only offer a few good reasons for studying well.

First of all, the grades one makes in college are much more important than most students realize.

To enter a graduate school or professional school of his choice, a student usually needs to have grades well above average. Even business employers pay attention to grades, and some take only students with high scholastic performance. Evidence shows that those with the highest grades in college are also the ones who, on the average, succeed best in the business world [Gifford, 1928]. This may be partly a matter of ambition and ability, but it is also a result of the knowledge and good work habits acquired in college.

Second, being successful gives a student many satisfactions. Aside from the pleasure both a student and his parents take in a student's high grades, the good student can be a happy student because he is free of the worry that goes along with poor performance in courses. He also gets a lot of satisfaction out of knowing how to go about the job of studying and from knowing that he is doing his work well.

Third, once a student gets involved in a subject deeply enough to have some mastery of it, he may discover that it is fascinating in its own right. Studying is then no longer a chore. He can take pleasure in knowing more and more about the subject, and in trying to unravel some of its unsolved problems. Teachers, professors, and creative thinkers in a field usually regard their subject matter in this way. To be sure, not every subject can have a strong appeal for everyone because individual aptitudes and interests vary, but the chances are good that some subjects will prove most appealing, once a person has learned how to study well enough to learn something about them.

ORGANIZING A STUDY ROUTINE   Besides motivation, what many students lack is a routine for study. They do not have certain times and places for study, and they do not apportion their time well among their various subjects. Yet these are essential. Every student should make up a definite schedule for study, based on the difficulty and amount of work to be expected in each course, and then follow it reasonably well. And by all means, he should make sure that he is really studying when he is supposed to, rather than daydreaming, listening to the radio, or talking with dormitory companions. The student should take every possible step to ensure that he studies when he studies, plays when he plays, and does not mix the two.

STUDY METHODS   Probably the two most important things that a student can do to improve his college work are to develop strong motivation for study and a well-organized routine. Here are some specific methods a student can use when he studies. Their value will depend on the individual—different techniques are suited to different students—and on the particular subject being studied. There are, however, some good general rules that it is usually advantageous to follow.

Perhaps the best set of rules is to be found in the *Survey Q3R Method* [Robinson, 1946]. This grew out of an elaborate program at the Ohio State University designed to analyze and treat students' academic problems, and we can rely on it as a soundly tested system. It consists of five specific steps which are labeled *Survey, Question, Read, Recite,* and *Review*—hence, the name Survey Q3R Method.

Survey. When authors write textbooks, they go to some pains to organize their material under various headings so that the headings tell readers what to expect to find in each section. If you leaf through this book, for example, you will find scarcely a page without a heading. Many students, however, ignore the headings and try to read textbooks in the same way they read novels. When they do that, they ignore much of the author's careful work and flounder in a morass of information.

One important precept, then, is *use the headings.* They reveal the author's organization, they tell you how the material is put together, and they make it clear how topics relate to each other. Most important, they make the main subject of each section clear. When you finish reading a section, you should have located a few points that bear on the heading. Anything else in the section will be of secondary importance. The student should also pay attention to the *value* of headings. Most textbooks use two or three orders of headings. This one, for example, has three.

At this point, the student who has noticed the heading of this section, Survey, will realize that we have not yet come to the main idea. We mentioned headings in order to lead up to that point.

The first thing to do when you pick up a textbook is to run through the headings of the various chapters, in other words, *survey* the book in general. In starting on a chapter, begin by surveying the various headings of sections within the chapter. In this way, you learn generally what the chapter is about and know what to expect. It is also a good idea to skim some of the sentences here and there in the chapter and to look at some of the pictures and graphs. In addition, if there is a summary, read it as part of your survey, for it will give you the most important points of the chapter before details begin to clutter up the picture.

Question. Some textbooks contain lists of review questions at the end of each chapter. (We have provided questions in a separate Study Guide designed to accompany this text.) These questions are usually the most neglected parts of the book, for students do not realize their value in studying. If a book has them, read them and try to answer them. It is also valuable to *ask your own questions.* Try to turn the headings of sections into questions, and read the sections with the idea of finding the answers to your questions.

Questions have several benefits. For one thing, they maintain interest in what is being read. For another, they make you participate actively in the learning process, rather than read passively. Psychological research clearly shows that active participation is a great aid in learning. Finally, questions are ways of testing yourself to see what you are learning or have learned. If you test yourself before the instructor does, you will do much better when faced with a formal examination.

Read. The next step, of course, is to read—and to read carefully. Read to answer the questions you

have asked yourself. Do not read passively, as you would read a novel, but continually challenge yourself as you go along to make sure that you understand what you read. And, of course, *read to remember.* Every once in a while, remind yourself of your task—to understand and remember what you read. If you do, you will no longer voice the familiar complaint, "I forget what I read as soon as I'm through." Notice especially any italicized words or phrases. Authors use italics to emphasize important terms, concepts, and principles.

Also, make sure to read everything, and that means tables, graphs, and other illustrations, as well as the main text. Illustrations emphasize important points in the text and clarify them. Sometimes, in fact, a mere glance at an illustration will tell vividly what a whole page of the book is about. In other cases, illustrations convey information that cannot be expressed easily in words.

Recite. Recitation is one of the most important techniques of effective study; yet it is very much neglected—because it takes effort. When one just reads, he has the comfort of thinking that what is read is understood and remembered, but this is generally not true. To make certain that one understands and remembers, he should stop periodically and try to recall to himself what he has read. In other words, he should recite. At this point, for example, you might ask yourself what you have read so far in this section. Try to recall the main headings and the principal ideas under each heading. Can you give a synopsis of your reading without looking at the pages? Try to do it; then check yourself. See whether you have covered everything. If not, note your omissions and errors. Then a little later, recite again. As you read, stop at intervals to recite the substance of each major section of a chapter. When you review for examinations, again make recitation a substantial part of your preparation.

There are at least two good reasons for this emphasis on recitation. One is that recitation serves to keep your *attention* on the task, for you obviously cannot daydream while you are trying to recall something. Another is that it lets you *correct mistakes;* it shows you where you are weakest and where, in a second reading, you can profitably spend the most time.

Recitation is more useful for some subjects than for others. In general, it helps most when what you have to learn is disconnected and not too meaningful. If, for example, you have to memorize a number of rules, items, names, laws, or formulas, recitation is of great help. On the other hand, for meaningful, storylike material such as one finds in history or philosophy, recitation is somewhat less useful— though never useless. Hence you should vary the amount of time or the proportion of study time that you use for recitation according to the subject you are studying. Because this book contains considerable factual information, probably one-third to one-half the time spent in studying it should be spent in recitation.

Review. If you learn something perfectly but do not review it, you will find that a few days or even hours later you will remember only a small part of it.

Here are some pointers for the best way of reviewing. *The best times for review are immediately after first studying and again just before an examination,* but it will also pay to have one or two reviews in between. The first review may be fairly brief because there has been little time for forgetting, and it should be mainly one of recitation. The review just before the examination should also emphasize recitation, but it should be much more intensive—and usually is. Intervening reviews that are relatively brief help, and these may emphasize rereading somewhat more than recitation. Perhaps it could go without saying that reviewing should not be crammed into the last few hours before an examination. This practice makes the final task too hard, and it does not give you, at the time of examination, the mastery that you could have with a few well-spaced reviews.

TAKING LECTURE NOTES The Survey Q3R Method applies to lectures as well as to textbooks, but not in every detail. Obviously, it is difficult or impossible to survey a lecture in advance unless the instructor does it for you—and few do that. The student must therefore provide his own organization and headings as he goes. It is important, however, to *organize.* Do this by trying to identify the lecturer's main points. *Condense his paragraphs into simple phrases or sentences, and do this in words of your own phrasing.* Sometimes this is difficult to do, and you are forced to take copious, unorganized notes to keep up with the lecture. In such circumstances, do not spend so much time trying to take neat, well-organized notes that you lose the point of the lecture; almost any notes are better than none at all. Still the more organized your notes are, the better they will be.

It is hard to say how many notes you should take. This will vary with the lecture, the lecturer, and the temperament of the student. Some students do their best by taking many notes, and others do best by taking relatively few. If you write easily, it is probably best to err on the side of too many.

Review is even more important for lecture notes than it is for reading. Because lecture notes are incomplete, a brief review after class usually is necessary to fill in omitted essentials and correct minor errors. Waiting too long to do that makes one forget, and he may easily wind up saying, "My lecture notes just don't make sense." It will often pay to rewrite lecture notes completely shortly after each lecture, both to provide a good review with recitation and to make it possible to understand your notes later.

Finally, let us remind you that it is important to keep lecture notes well organized. Use the same kind of paper for all notes in one subject, keep them in a notebook, not lying around in various places, and number the pages to keep them in order. In any event, make sure that you have a system that is good enough to let you find all your material quickly and to study it easily.

TAKING EXAMINATIONS Having read this heading, you may say, "Ah, that's what I want to know—how to take an examination." Many of us would like to know how to pass examinations without studying, but that is a bit of magic no psychologist has yet produced. In fact, the only good general rule for taking examinations is, "Be prepared." And in preparation, do not bank too much on guessing what the instructor will ask. Sometimes this works, but sometimes it fails. It is a far better policy to be prepared for any reasonable question that the instructor might possibly ask.

Examinations divide themselves roughly into two classes, the *objective* and the *essay,* though there are several shades in between. You will probably want to prepare for the two types somewhat differently, and you should take them with somewhat different attitudes.

Objective examinations are usually *recognition tests*. They simply require that you recognize the right answer when you see it. It is important, however, to read and answer each question carefully. Sometimes the correct answer may hang on an all-important "not" or "always," and you may miss it if you read carelessly. It is usually best first to go straight through the examination, answering all the questions you are sure of and checking those you cannot answer immediately. When you are through, go back to the harder questions. It is usually a good idea to answer all items in an objective test. Unless there is some special penalty for guessing (find out from the instructor if there is), it is wise to make an intelligent guess for every item of which you are not sure. Remember that in an objective examination it is a mistake to concentrate too much on a few difficult questions, for they usually count no more than the others. If you do that, you will not have time to finish, or you will have to rush through the other questions and will make needless mistakes. If you have time at the end, review your answers carefully and correct your mistakes.

Essay examinations emphasize the ability to understand, organize, and *recall* information. To prepare well for them, you should especially emphasize the active parts of studying—surveying and recitation. In taking the examination, remember that the instructor will usually think better of a paper if the information is well organized rather than rambling and discursive. So take time to organize your thoughts before you begin to write; a thumbnail outline is good for a long essay question. Make sure to answer the question that the instructor asks, not a slightly different one on which you may be better prepared. Keep your answers to the point, and avoid digressions and irrelevant information, for they do not impress most instructors. Try to leave time to reread your answers at the end of the examination so that you can add important points you forgot or correct any mistakes.

Programmed learning

Can verbal learning be made more efficient? The lecture and the textbook have been the standard tools for years, but there has always been some dissatisfaction with these methods because they emphasize presentation rather than doing and they do not provide immediate knowledge of results. Both the making of responses and knowledge of results are important, as we have seen, for efficient verbal learning. Teaching machines and programmed textbooks circumvent these objections, but may possibly add some difficulties of their own.

TEACHING MACHINES AND PROGRAMMED TEXTBOOKS Proposals for devices to serve as "teachers" were made more than forty years ago [Pressey, 1926]. These plans made little headway, however, until the late 1950s. At that time, interest in them was aroused largely through the efforts of B. F. Skinner of Harvard University who designed, built, and tried out a series of machines programmed for different subjects of study [Skinner, 1958]. Now dozens of such devices are either on the market or in an experimental stage of development. They have been called teaching machines, though this is something of a misnomer since they neither teach nor take the place of the teacher. They supplement teachers and textbooks in helping students to learn. To explain what teaching machines are, we shall discuss two prototypes designed by Skinner.

One of the principal purposes of teaching machines is to provide continuous knowledge of results, to let the individual know whether he is making the correct responses or not. Exactly how the machine does this depends on the subject being taught. It is relatively easy to provide continuous knowledge of results in a subject like arithmetic. Hence, one of the first machines Skinner built was to help children learn arithmetic. His machine presents problems to the student one at a time. The student simply records his answer to each problem by pressing keys on the machine. If his answer is correct, the machine immediately rings a bell, flashes a light, or otherwise indicates that the answer is right.

For the kind of material learned in psychology, the social sciences, and the humanities, Skinner designed a different kind of machine. For these sub-

jects, both the question and the answer are put on a tape or a disk (see Figure 4.21). The answer, however, remains covered when the question is first put to the student. The student writes his answer down at the appropriate place on the tape; then he pushes a control that uncovers the answer, and thus he can compare his answer with the correct one. By operating another control, he can move the tape or disk into position for presentation of the next problem.

Teaching machines such as these clearly have the advantage of telling the student exactly how he is doing, as textbooks and teachers cannot. By providing a knowledge of results, teaching machines promote effective learning. Furthermore, the student can spend time learning what he does not know rather than wasting time going over material he already knows. The machine can present problems that have not been answered before and eliminate problems the student has answered correctly. In addition, the tape or disk can be made to repeat

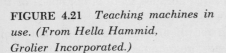

FIGURE 4.21 *Teaching machines in use. (From Hella Hammid, Grolier Incorporated.)*

a problem the student has gotten wrong, and to continue to do so until he has answered every problem correctly. Such perfect learning is seldom achieved with conventional methods.

Teaching machines, then, seem to provide two important conditions for learning which are otherwise difficult to obtain. They get the learner to respond, and they let him know where he stands in the learning process.

Machines have their limitations, however. For one thing, they are relatively expensive. Even the simplest machines cost several times as much as a textbook, and the more complicated ones can run into hundreds of dollars. For this reason, and also because they are bulky and not really portable, one machine must serve a good many students, and the use of machines must be supervised, for example, in a library. Hence a student cannot study on his own schedule. Finally, machines require specially made programmed materials such as tapes, disks, or films. All these limitations restrict their usefulness.

Textbooks, of course, do not have these limitations. A learning program can be printed in textbook form as well as in the form required by a teaching machine. (A sample program is shown at the end of this section.) In such a form, the program can pose problems for the student to solve and thus motivate him to make responses. Knowledge of results is provided by having the answers on a separate page or by moving a cardboard shield down the page to expose the correct answer after each response. However, programmed textbooks have the disadvantage that they do not provide a means of repeating only the questions which elicited incorrect responses from the learner. Both teaching machines and programmed textbooks, with their special advantages and disadvantages, have a place in making learning more pleasant and efficient.

LEARNING PRINCIPLES IN PROGRAMMED INSTRUCTION One strength of both teaching machines and programmed textbooks is that they involve the learner in tasks—they give him something to *respond* to and thus *motivate* him to be an active participant in learning. The basic principle here is that if you give someone a puzzle, or merely ask him a question, he will usually rise to the occasion—he will respond. If, as soon as he has answered one question or completed one task you give him another, he will respond again. If the problems you put to the person are reasonable and interesting and are problems he knows he ought to be doing, he will tend to keep working for a long period of time—usually much longer than he will keep his attention focused on a textbook or a lecture. A properly designed learning program puts questions or problems to a student in such a way that he is motivated to make responses.

A second feature of programmed-learning methods is that they permit the student to *proceed at his own pace*. Lectures certainly do not do this, for they require the same amount of time and attention from everybody. They are too slow for the fast learner and too fast for the slow learner. This is true also of recitation techniques. Learning programs, on the other hand, can be given to students individually, and each student can work away at the program as rapidly or as slowly as his abilities and work habits permit.

A third feature of most learning programs is that the *steps* in learning are made reasonably *small*. From what is known of animal and human learning, as well as from teaching experience, it may be concluded that almost every student can progress in small steps, relatively few in large ones. Small steps ensure that what a person has learned he has learned well and that he is really ready to take the next steps. Small steps also ensure that relatively few wrong responses—responses which may impede the shaping of the final product—are made. With textbooks and lectures the steps taken are frequently too large because there is not space or time to spell out every little step.

Finally, a fourth principle is that both teaching machines and programmed textbooks provide *immediate knowledge of results* (reinforcement). The learner receives immediate information about the correctness of his responses.

THE LEARNING PROGRAM   The series of statements and questions used in a teaching machine or a programmed textbook is called its *program*. How well the method teaches depends on the program. This in turn depends on whether the programmer, the person making up the program, knows what steps the program should take and how to set up the statements and questions. Preparing the program, like most teaching and textbook writing, is still an art rather than a science. The best program for any type of teaching has simply not been discovered. Programmed-learning methods, however, offer the opportunity for experimenting with different programs and finding out through research what kinds of programs are most efficient in guiding the learner to mastery of a subject—something seldom accomplished with conventional lectures and textbooks.

MACHINES AND THE TEACHER   Both students and teachers, when they first hear of teaching machines and programmed textbooks, often ask whether programmers are "trying to do away with the teacher." After all, machines and books lack the personal touch, and the interaction between teacher and student supplies something a book or machine cannot. Moreover, mechanical programs are not, for the present anyway, suited to "explaining things" or to teaching complicated concepts. Programmed-learning methods will probably never do away with teachers.

If programming can be successfully developed, however, it will serve as an important adjunct to the teacher. It may motivate the student to do his homework, a hard thing for teachers to do. It may get him to master the facts that require memorization or simply hard work, so that he will know these when he comes to class. It may relieve the teacher of having to present facts, rules, formulas, and the like, which the students, with proper self-instruction, can learn more efficiently for themselves. If these things can be accomplished by programming methods, then class discussions and interpretative lectures will be much more fruitful learning experiences than they are now. Programmed learning may also make the whole teaching process more economical.

EXAMPLE FROM A PROGRAMMED TEXTBOOK The following set of exercises has been slightly modified from *The Analysis of Behavior* by Holland and Skinner. This programmed textbook, published in 1961, was written to teach the principles of operant conditioning (see Chapter 3). In the original presentation of this program, the items of a set were presented on every other page of the book. This means that the page had to be turned before the answer to an item could be seen. No paper strips were needed to cover the answers in the original programmed text; this is merely a device needed here in a more conventionally printed text.

FIGURE 4.22.   *The program which appears on the following pages is also available in a form suitable for use with a machine such as the one shown here. Answers are covered while the student writes his own answers on the strip of paper at the right. With a turn of the knob, the answer is uncovered and the next question appears. (Koncept-o-graph.)*

THE CUMULATIVE RECORDER

Instructions. Cover the answers when you can see the item and its answer on facing pages of the text. A long, thin strip of folded paper will work well for this. Read the first item and write your answer on a separate piece of paper or on the covering strip itself. Then lift the covering strip of paper or turn the page to compare your answer with the correct one. Continue in this way to the end of the set (30 items). Turn to the next page and begin.

Do not study exhibit in advance; use exhibit as needed in answering items.

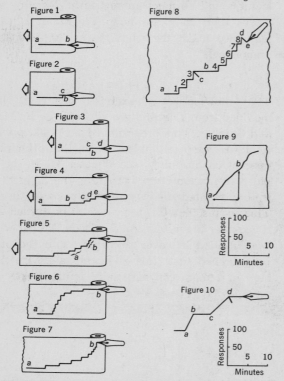

Figure 1
Figure 2
Figure 3
Figure 4
Figure 5
Figure 6
Figure 7
Figure 8
Figure 9
Figure 10

1

NOTE 1. As these pages are presently arranged, questions and answers may be visible on the same spread. In working through the program, you should cover these answers.
NOTE 2. The sequence of items runs across the pages, not down each page.

THE CUMULATIVE RECORDER

See exhibit on preceding page.
Turn to next page and begin. ▶

Estimated time, 11 minutes.

(1) *a* (2) *d* 4	In Figure 3, the time which elapsed between *a* and *b* is _____ than the time which elapsed between *c* and *d*. 5
(1) shorter (2) shorter 9	In Figure 5, the higher the rate of responding, the (1) _____ the slope of the steplike line. We can determine the rate of responding from the (2) _____ of the steplike line. 10
7 14	Negative acceleration refers to a(n) (1) _____ in rate. Negative acceleration is shown in either Figure 6 or Figure 7. Which? Figure (2) _____. 15
3 (and) 8 19	In Figure 10, a response was reinforced at _____. 20
(approximately) 5 24	In Figure 10, the animal emitted about _____ responses between *a* and *d*. 25
(1) vertical (2) horizontal	In a cumulative curve, the *slope* is a record of the animal's ° ° ° 30

2

In Figure 1, a broad strip of paper is unwinding from a roll. The end of the paper is moving slowly toward the left. A pen held against the paper in a fixed position has drawn a line beginning at (1) _____ and ending at (2) _____.

1

longer
(greater,
more)

5

In recording the behavior of an organism, the pen moves upward and draws one short vertical line each time a response is made. In Figure 4, an experiment began when the pen was at a. The first response was made at _____.

6

(1) steeper
(higher,
greater)
(2) slope

10

In Figure 6, responding begins at a relatively high rate at a. The time between successive responses grows progressively _____.

11

(1) decrease
(2) 6

15

An increase in rate is called (1) _____ _____, and a decrease in rate is called (2) _____ _____.

16

d

20

If the paper moves slowly and if each vertical step is small, we cannot see the steplike record of a single response. The _____ of the curve at any point is still a valid indicator of rate of responding.

21

(about) 100

25

In Figure 10, the animal paused about (1) _____ minutes between positions (2) _____ and _____.

26

rate of
responding
(response rate)

END OF SET

3

---

(1) a
(2) b

1

In Figure 2, the slow movement of the paper under the fixed pen has drawn the horizontal line (1) _____-_____. At the end of a–b, the pen suddenly moved a short vertical distance to (2) _____.

2

b

6

In Figure 4, three responses were made fairly quickly (closely together) at _____, _____, and _____.

7

longer
(greater)

11

In Figure 6, the slope of the curve drawn by the pen near a indicates a(n) _____ initial rate of responding.

12

(1) positive
acceleration
(2) negative
acceleration

16

To record other events, the pen moves quickly "to the southeast" and back again. In Figure 8, the pen is shown in the process of drawing a line from (1) _____ to _____. The point of the pen will immediately return to (2) _____.

17

slope

21

In Figure 10, the rate was highest between (1) _____ and _____, zero between (2) _____ and _____, and intermediate between (3) _____ and _____.

22

(1) (about) 5
(2) b (and) c

26

In the cumulative curves shown in the figures, time is shown by the (1) _____ distance traversed by the pen, and the number of responses by the (2) _____ distance.

27

4

(1) a (–) b (2) c 2	In Figure 3, the paper has moved on from the position shown in Figure 2. The fixed pen has drawn a second horizontal line _____–_____. 3	c (–) d 3	In Figure 3, the pen has been in the four lettered positions a, b, c, and d. It occupied position (1) _____ first, and (2) _____ last. 4
c, d, (and) e 7	In Figure 5, the three responses recorded at a were emitted _____ rapidly than the three at b. 8	less 8	The more rapid the responding, the (1) _____ the pauses between two responses and the (2) _____ the horizontal lines drawn by the pen. 9
high (rapid) 12	In Figure 7, the rate increases fairly steadily from a low value near (1) _____ to a high value near (2) _____. 13	(1) a (2) b 13	An increase in rate is called positive acceleration. Positive acceleration is shown in either Figure 6 or Figure 7. (Which?) Figure _____. 14
(1) d (to) e (2) d 17	In Figure 8, the short mark ("hatch" or "pip") at _____ was made by a movement of the pen like the one shown at e. 18	c 18	The "southeast" mark or hatch is most often used to indicate that a response has been reinforced. In Figure 8, the responses numbered _____ and _____ were reinforced. 19
(1) a (and) b (2) b (and) c (3) c (and) d 22	When the steps are small, we cannot count responses. But in Figure 9, the scale at the right tells us that approximately _____ responses were made between a and b. 23	(approximately) 100 23	If paper speed is very slow, we may not be able to accurately measure the time between any two responses; but in Figure 9, the scale tells us that responses at a and b were approximately _____ minutes apart. 24
(1) horizontal (2) vertical 27	The rate of responding is indicated by the _____ of the cumulative record. 28	slope 28	Rate of responding means responses/time (responses ÷ time). The slope of a cumulative record is (1) _____ distance/(2) _____ distance. 29

5

6

NOTE 3. For answers to questions on this page, turn back to program page 2.

SYNOPSIS AND SUMMARY

We have tried to discuss some of what is known about human learning, remembering, and forgetting. Certain variables affecting human learning and some of the reasons for forgetting are fairly well known. But more fundamental and interesting questions of human learning remain. For instance, no one can really describe the processes which take place when a child learns to associate an object with a word. It is done, of course, and we know some of the variables which will speed the process or slow it down, but this is only part of the story. Perhaps, when we know more about how the variables affect the learning of associations, we will feel more satisfied with our knowledge of human learning. Some, with a rather different philosophy of scientific explanation, will not be satisfied until the physiological mechanism of association is known.

We know now that distribution of practice, knowledge of results, recitation, meaningfulness, and perceptual distinctiveness of the material will usually increase the rate of learning. And the influence of prior learning on present learning, or transfer of training, is an exceedingly important factor in human learning.

This chapter began with a question from *Principles of Psychology*, written by William James in 1890. In more modern language, we might ask: What are the variables that control long-term memory? We have seen that the degree to which the material was learned and the amount of interference with the original material are the most important variables controlling the rate of forgetting. Now, years later, James's question has a partial answer.

1. Human learning may be charted as a curve of decreasing errors or increasing accuracy—the so-called learning or performance curve.
2. Experimental studies of human learning often use nonsense syllables and the serial-anticipation or paired-associate learning methods. In the serial-anticipation method, the subject learns a list in which preceding items serve as cues for responding with the succeeding items; in the paired-associate method, the subject learns a list of S-R associations.

3. The one-trial theory of human learning states that associations are formed all-or-none on a single trial; the incremental theory states that the associations are strengthened a little bit on each trial. The evidence to help us decide between these hypotheses is equivocal.
4. Individual differences in intelligence, age, motivation, and learning sophistication affect the rate of learning.
5. Of the many variables that affect rate of learning, three of the most important are: (*a*) distribution of practice over a period of time; (*b*) provision for immediate and accurate knowledge of results; and (*c*) time spent in recitation *and* reading or merely reading alone.
6. The characteristics of the material are important in determining the ease of learning. Meaningfulness is extremely important. Familiar words are easily associated; nonsense words difficultly. The perceptual distinctiveness of the material is also important.
7. Transfer of training refers to the effect of learning one task on the subsequent learning of another. Transfer may be either positive or negative, and the amount and kind of transfer depend upon the similarities of responses and stimuli in the original and subsequent tasks.
8. In formal education, school subjects that have little in common have little or no transfer value. Except for learning to learn, the degree of transfer from one school subject to another depends upon elements which the two subjects have in common.
9. Two memory processes, short term and long term, have been distinguished. Short-term memory is supposed to depend upon active processes in the nervous system; long-term memory is supposed to depend upon structural changes in the nervous system.
10. The three basic methods of measuring retention are: recall, recognition, and savings. Of these, recall is the least sensitive, and savings (in relearning of the same material) the most sensitive measure of retention. Even when there is little retention as measured by recall, there may be considerable retention as measured by the time required to relearn (savings). Whether measured by recall, recognition, or savings, the retention curve is usually negatively accelerated.
11. Variables which influence the amount retained in long-term memory are: (*a*) meaningfulness of the material, (*b*) degree of learning of the material, and (*c*) interference with the learned material. Greater meaningfulness and overlearning enhance retention.

Interference is especially important in producing forgetting. The interference can be produced by previously learned material, proactive inhibition, or by material learned subsequent to the original learning, interference due to interpolated activity, or retroactive inhibition. The amount of interference is a function of the similarities between the interfering material and test material.

12. A number of theories of forgetting have been proposed. The physiological-trace theory, the interference theory, the qualitative-change theory, and theories of motivated forgetting are the most common. In its present form the physiological-trace theory does not explain many of the psychological facts of forgetting. The interference theory simply states that all forgetting is due to interference. The qualitative-change theory states that the memory trace undergoes distortion with time; the end result of this distortion can be so great as to produce memories with very little relationship to the original. The major theory of motivated forgetting is the Freudian theory; the process acting to produce forgetting of threatening events, or things associated with those events, is called repression.

13. The most important problem in studying effectively is the development of motivation to study, but the student must somehow supply this himself. Organizing a study routine helps many students.

14. Through systematic research on techniques of study, a program of study, called the Survey Q3R Method, has been developed. It consists of five steps: survey, question, read, recite, and review.

15. Programmed-learning methods give the student something to respond to, let him proceed at his own pace, and make the learning steps reasonably small.

16. Teaching machines and programmed textbooks have different advantages and limitations. The effectiveness of both depends upon their programs, which must be developed through trial and error and through research. Programmed machines and textbooks are designed to supplement the teacher, not replace him.

RELATED TOPICS IN THE TEXT

CHAPTER 3   PRINCIPLES OF LEARNING   General principles and types of learning are described in this chapter.

CHAPTER 13   PERSONALITY   A more complete account of repression, and its role in the formation of the "unconscious," is given in the sections of this chapter dealing with defense mechanisms and psychoanalytic theory.

CHAPTER 20   PHYSIOLOGICAL BASIS OF BEHAVIOR   Experiments and speculation about physiological events underlying memory—that is, those taking place in the nervous system—are described. No solution to even the most elementary aspects of this very important problem has been accepted.

SUGGESTIONS FOR FURTHER READING

Green, D. R. *Educational psychology*. Englewood Cliffs, N.J.: Prentice-Hall, 1964. (Paperback.)
Contains discussions of transfer, the law of effect, and motivation as they apply to education.

Hughes, J. L. *Programed instruction for schools and industry*. Chicago: Science Research Associates, 1962.
Gives guidance on the construction of programs and discusses the principles of programmed instruction.

Hunter, I. M. L. *Memory: Facts and fallacies*. London: Penguin, 1957. (Paperback.)
A discussion of the major facts and psychological theories of memory is presented.

King, R. A. (Ed.). *Readings for an introduction to psychology* (2d ed.). New York: McGraw-Hill, 1966. (Paperback.)
A book of readings designed to accompany this text.

McGeoch, J. A. and Irion, A. L. *The psychology of human learning* (2d ed.). New York: Longmans, 1952.
A comprehensive text and reference work on human learning.

Morgan, C. T., and Deese, J. *How to study*. New York: McGraw-Hill, 1957. (Paperback.)
A booklet describing techniques of study.

Woodworth, R. S., and Schlosberg, H. *Experimental psychology* (rev. ed.). New York: Holt, 1954.
A comprehensive text on experimental psychology containing chapters on learning, remembering, and forgetting.

5

ASK A MAN on the street, or even a college sophomore, what sets man apart from animals and he is likely to say, "People can talk and think; animals can't." That answer is just about right. Animals have some semblance of the capacities to reason and to communicate, but they are separated from man by a very wide gap. Not so obvious to the man on the street is another respect in which man vastly overshadows the animals—the ability to form concepts. Man can think of and react to certain general properties of objects, redness or goodness, for example, which he has abstracted from his previous experience.

Symbols and meaning

The three abilities just mentioned—reasoning, using language, and conceptualizing—are interlinked. Because symbols are used in all three to convey meaning, to others in communication and to ourselves in thinking, we shall start with a discussion of symbols and the way they acquire meaning. Then we shall be in a position to consider thinking, concept formation, and language in more detail.

SYMBOLS AND SIGNALS[1] A *symbol* is a stimulus used to stand for, or represent, something else. Many words in languages, nouns for example, are symbols; the word "house" is a symbol because it stands for the object house. A *signal* is a stimulus used to indicate that the time and place for something to happen is at hand. Of course, since most signals stand for something else they are also symbols, and the distinction between symbol and signal is not always clear-cut. The red light we encounter at a traffic intersection is both a signal and a symbol: it signals the time to do something—stop—but it is also a symbol representing the word "stop" and the expected action of stopping. But when the emphasis is on the indication of action at a particular

MAN BEGAN TO THINK IN ORDER THAT HE MIGHT EAT, NOW HE HAS EVOLVED TO THE POINT WHERE HE EATS IN ORDER THAT HE MAY THINK.
W. P. MONTAGUE

OUT OF CHAOS THE IMAGINATION FRAMES A THING OF BEAUTY.
J. L. LOWES

[1] Sometimes the term *sign* is used in a general manner to include both symbols and signals.

159

time and place, we may choose to identify the stimulus as a signal rather than a symbol.

Stimuli become symbols and signals when we learn to respond to them in a particular way. When Pavlov conditioned a dog to salivate to a bell (see page 79), he was converting a stimulus into a symbol and a signal indicating that food was coming. When the dog salivated to the bell, it responded *in part* as it would to food.

The conditioning of salivation to a bell is the simplest kind of symbol-signal formation. It conveys only one message, that food is to come. Pavlov, of course, taught his dogs more complicated signals. His next step was to use one kind of bell to signal "food" and another to signal "no food," thereby setting up a conditioned discrimination. This is comparable to the red light and green light signaling "stop" and "go" at our traffic intersections. Sometimes animals have been taught more complex sets of signals in the laboratory or in circus training, but for sophisticated systems of symbols and signals we must look to man.

NATURAL SYMBOLS AND SIGNALS In general, then, learning to respond to stimuli involves the learning of symbols and signals. The thing that the symbol stands for is the meaning of the symbol. Symbols and signals, however, may acquire meaning in at least two different ways. One is by the *natural relation* of events encountered in nature. We learn, for example, that the growl of a dog may be followed by a bite, that thunder is often a prelude to rain, that where there is smoke there is fire. In each case, the meaning perceived depends upon our having learned previously that certain stimuli belong together.

Animals and people learn to adapt to their environment and to survive by learning the meaning of these natural symbols and signals. The number of such symbols and signals, however, is limited, and all kinds of events occur for which there are no natural warnings.

WORDS AS SYMBOLS AND SIGNALS A second class of symbols and signals includes those which

have been *invented* by man and assigned to events. The bell in Pavlov's experiment, of course, is such an invented symbol or signal. It was "assigned" meaning by Pavlov's conditioning procedure. The red light at a traffic intersection is another invented symbol or signal. In each case, the symbol has no natural relation to the event for which it stands. Since such symbols are invented, we can devise any number of them we like and arrange them in a system to stand for a corresponding pattern of events.

Many different kinds of symbols have been devised. In some parts of the world, including some American street corners, a certain whistle is a well-understood symbol; in others, particular drumming patterns are extensively used. Almost all societies use gestures of the hands and face as symbols and signals. Societies which speak different languages, but are in close contact with each other—as was the case with the American Indians—may use hundreds of gestures as symbols and signals to surmount the language barrier (see Figure 5.1). More highly developed systems of symbols, however, are found in the natural languages in which words are spoken and written in different combinations. Certain artificially created languages, computer languages, for example, illustrate the symbolic nature of language to a striking degree. In these computer languages, the symbols are instructions to the machine and stand for operations to be performed.

A language, as we shall see, is more than a set of words, but for the moment let us think of it as that. Each word is a stimulus that can, by conditioning or association, come to symbolize or signal some event in our experience. The distinctive thing about language, as contrasted with naturally occurring symbols and signals, is its enormous capacity for providing discriminably different symbols and signals. A language makes available tens or hundreds of thousands of potential symbols, whereas the symbols and signals afforded by nature are far less numerous.

Another important thing about language is that each individual carries around with him the equipment both for generating and for receiving words as

SYMBOLS ARE NOT ALL VERBAL

FIGURE 5.1. *Some manual signs in Indian sign language. See if you can tell which sign is used to represent each of the following: fast, fight, fish, food, house, hot, hungry, snake, and snow. Correct answers are given in the footnote on page 162. (After Tomkins, 1931.)*

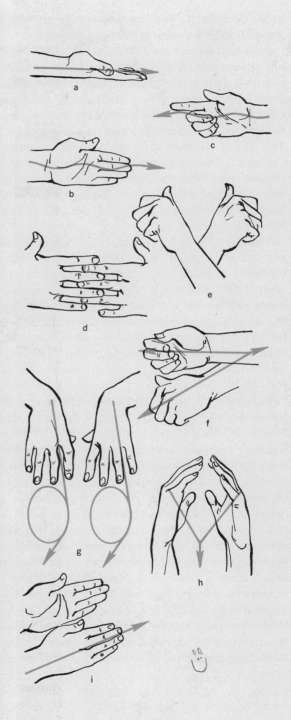

stimuli. No heavy or expensive hardware is required. Our built-in equipment provides many years of trouble-free operation with a minimum of cost in weight, size, and energy expenditure. It is no wonder then that words have become such a highly developed system of communication.

More than mere equipment, however, is required. An enormously large number of discriminations must be learned. Without these, our words would be useless. An organism cannot utilize symbols unless it can distinguish among the different things being symbolized. If the symbols "house" and "tree" are to mean something, for example, an organism must be able to discriminate between such physical objects as houses and trees.

Though many animals are capable of learning such a simple discrimination, none seems able to learn so many fine discriminations as man. Consider, for example, all the different objects contained within each category designated by a single symbol, such as "house," "tree," "plant," "car," or "street." Most human beings have learned to discriminate among literally thousands of such objects. And, of course, we discriminate among many things besides objects, including the words in language itself. The process of learning all these discriminations requires a prodigious amount of effort and time. This process is greatly aided by language itself. In the end, though, man is able to use language effectively only because he can learn to make so many discriminations.

THE MEANING OF MEANING We saw in Chapter 3 that an association is formed whenever any two events, stimuli or responses, are repeatedly paired. The meaningfulness of stimuli was referred to in Chapter 4. We are now ready to see how association and meaningfulness are related.

Associative processes. First, let us recall the Pavlovian experiment of conditioning a dog to salivate to a bell. In our paradigm of this conditioning, we represent the bell (the conditioned stimulus, or CS) as forming an association with the response of salivation (the unconditioned response, or UR). This seems clear enough. However, as we noted in Chapter 3, the dog's *unconditioned response* to food (the unconditioned stimulus, or US) is more than mere salivation. The dog *eats* the food. On the other hand, in the presence of the CS, the bell, it merely *salivates.*

The point here is that the CS calls forth only *part* of the response to the US. Apparently it takes the sight of food, and perhaps other conditions as well, to get a dog to eat. This may seem obvious, for a dog can hardly eat food that is not there. Yet if the conditioning process simply substituted the CS for the US in evoking the response, it might be expected that the dog would make some of the motions of eating food. Obviously, association is no such mechanical process.

This example from Pavlovian conditioning illustrates the general result of many different experiments. Experimenters have often compared the conditioned response with the original unconditioned response. The two are almost invariably different in some respect. Hence the association formed in such learning is between the conditioning stimulus and only a part or *fraction* of the original response.

Salivation in bell-food conditioning is a response we can see and measure. In some circumstances, however, the associated "response" is not observable at all. This is the case in "sensory association" or in perceptual learning in which two different stimuli are paired in the absence of any response (see page 103). We can ascertain the presence of such an association by seeing whether the organism can do something that could be done only if the particular

Correct answers for signs in Figure 5.1 are: (*a*) hungry, (*b*) food, (*c*) fast, (*d*) fight, (*e*) house, (*f*) snake, (*g*) snow, (*h*) hot, and (*i*) fish.

association had been formed. So the association formed in learning is often not even an observable part of an original unconditioned response.

We therefore conclude (1) that an association is a process within the person which occurs between a stimulus and some fraction of the original unlearned (or previously learned) response or sensory event and (2) that the process, or association, may be so small a fraction of the original one that it is not observable. Further, and more important, this process, or association, *is* the meaning of the stimulus that arouses it. In other words, we say that *a stimulus is meaningful* when it arouses some of the same responses or sensory events that are aroused by another stimulus. Thus the word "house" is meaningful because it arouses a response and sensory events which are aroused by the object, the house, itself.

Mediating processes. Meanings can be meanings and nothing more. A symbol can evoke a meaning without anything else happening. I say "house" and that arouses a meaning, or process, in you, but without further instructions or without your having some problem to solve, the matter may end there.

In other cases, particularly in thinking or problem solving, a meaning leads to something further. It is a link to something else. It may be linked either (1) to a response of some kind or (2) to other meanings. If I instructed you to start out with "house" and freely associate to it, you might say "home," "mother," "father," "children," "school," and so on. Here the meaning of the word would be a link both to a response and to another meaning. The important point is that meanings serve as intervening links connecting psychological events.

When we regard meaning as a link, we say that it is a "mediating process." The verb "to mediate" is defined as "to be a go-between," or "to be a connecting link between." Hence to say that meanings may serve as mediating processes is to say that they may link other processes or responses [Osgood, 1952].

To illustrate the mediation of a response, we may cite an experiment in animal learning [Tolman,

1939]. In this experiment, the experimenter observed vicarious trial-and-error (VTE) behavior. This behavior has been described as "turning back and forth," or "crouching to jump at one door and then crouching before the other door, before finally jumping." The nice thing about VTE behavior is that it gives observable evidence of a fractional associative process taking the place of an overt response. It also shows how this process can mediate other responses.

Hunger-motivated rats were observed during their learning of a discrimination in a jumping apparatus. The apparatus consisted of a platform separated by a gap from two doors containing two stimulus cards. In this case, the stimuli to be discriminated were a white card and a black card. When a rat jumped to the white card, it was rewarded; the card fell under the weight of the rat so that the animal landed on a platform where it obtained a morsel of food. When the rat jumped to the black card, it was punished; the animal bashed its nose against a door, and then fell a couple of feet into a net below.

This apparatus and procedure allowed the experimenter to observe the behavior of the rats prior to their jumping. At first, when the animals were making chance scores, indicative of no learning, they simply oriented toward a card, got set, and jumped. After some trials at this, however, they began to show VTE. This behavior, similar to that described above, was clear-cut and could be scored.

Figure 5.2 shows the results of the experiment for a single rat. One chart shows the number of correct jumps; the other shows the number of VTEs. Six trials a day were run; hence a score of three correct choices a day is chance and a score of six is perfect learning. VTE behavior appeared after 7 days (42 trials) when the animal was still performing by chance. VTE behavior increased rapidly until the animal rather suddenly showed evidence of learning. Thereafter it stayed at a high level for a few days, then diminished while the animal continued to perform the discrimination well.

VTE behavior in this experiment is evidence of a mediating process. It is interesting that VTE behavior *decreases* after the discrimination has been learned. This means that the mediating process

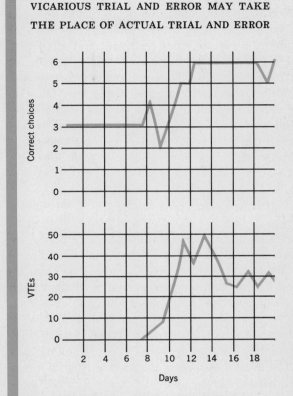

VICARIOUS TRIAL AND ERROR MAY TAKE
THE PLACE OF ACTUAL TRIAL AND ERROR

FIGURE 5.2. *Correct choices and VTE behavior for a rat learning a white-black discrimination. Note that the number of VTEs increases with correct choices, and then declines after the discrimination is mastered. (After Tolman, 1939.)*

gradually becomes a smaller and less observable fraction of the original jumping response. The behavior tends to "go inside" the organism. In many situations, though not in this one, the VTE response becomes either too small to see or a process entirely within the nervous system.

To recapitulate briefly, associations are formed in the course of learning to discriminate among various stimuli and responses. The associations are formed between stimuli and parts or fractions of the original responses or sensory events that were paired. Such fractional processes are what we mean by "meanings." And these meanings are links, or mediators, between other responses and other sensory events. Human beings, of course, acquire so many meanings for stimuli, especially when we consider the meanings of all the words they learn to use and to respond to, that meanings, and the behavior mediated by them, are of enormous importance in understanding human "mental processes" and thought.

The thinking process

A well-known sign in certain business offices commands us to THINK. What does such a command tell us to *do?* Do we really know how thinking differs from other experiences and reactions? Such questions suggest even more difficult questions: Can we tell when another person is thinking? What is thought? How does it start? When does it stop?

Actually, the word "think," or "thinking," as used in everyday speech, covers a very wide range of activities. At one extreme, it means little more than "remember" or "recall." For example, we often see road signs saying, "Think—speed kills." Used this way, "think" merely tells us to remember, or to keep in mind, a connection between fast driving and fatal accidents. Similarly, when somebody asks you to think of who played Rhett Butler in *Gone with the Wind,* he is asking you only to recall or remember a name you may have once learned. The process of recall under these circumstances may actually involve some thinking, but not to any very great extent. At the other extreme, the word "think" refers to the highly rigorous and reflective activity a scientist engages in when he attempts to solve a complex problem. He may spend hours or days juggling mathematical formulas, drawing diagrams, or merely imagining various ways in which the problem might be solved.

But whether the thinking is simple or compli-

cated, it always seems to involve one thing: *a mediating process.* When we think, something links past learning with our present responses. Mediating processes fill in the gaps between the stimulus situation and the responses we make to it. When we are solving problems, these processes substitute for things we might otherwise do overtly in a trial-and-error manner. To illustrate, let us take a common example.

Suppose that you have a jigsaw puzzle to put together. The hard way to work out the puzzle would be to try to fit the pieces together by actually trying each piece to see whether it fitted another piece. This would be solving the puzzle by plain trial and error. If there were many pieces in the puzzle, such a process would take an interminable amount of time and millions of trial-and-error fittings. You would probably do some of this, but only to choose between two or three possibilities that were very close to the correct one. Mostly you would think. The steps in your thinking would represent what you might otherwise do by trial and error. You would often think of putting the pieces together in a certain way without actually doing it. You would try putting them together in your head, and decide whether they would or would not go together before trying with your hands. Thus, by thinking, you would do much more economically and quickly what you might do by trying all the pieces in all their possible places.

Your thinking *represents,* stands for, or takes the place of observable behavior and the physical rearrangement of stimuli. The thinking process is a mediating process. To say this is to indicate how the thinking process functions—it connects—but it does not tell us what thinking is. What goes on inside a person when he thinks? What is the thinking process? This is the question we deal with next.

TRACE PROCESSES The simplest kind of thinking, or mediating, process is a memory trace that lasts for some period of time and can serve in place of a stimulus cue for the solution of a simple problem. This kind of process has been demonstrated in animals in the *delayed-reaction* test. Such a test has been used with a number of different animals, and the experimental situation and procedure with a particular animal, the raccoon, are described below. [Hunter, 1913]:

The raccoon was placed in the starting box of the apparatus drawn in Figure 5.3. The box was made of wire mesh so that the animal could see out of it while being restrained. Facing the raccoon in the apparatus were three openings, each provided with a light bulb. The experiment was begun by training the animal to make the simple discrimination of going to the opening in which the bulb was lighted. The light was turned on and the screen was raised to permit the animal to walk around the box; if it went to the correct opening, it found food in the alley leading from the light. On successive trials, the light appeared at random in one of the three possible positions, and food was presented in the lighted alley. After the raccoon learned to go to the lighted doorway, the procedure was changed. Now the light was turned on briefly as before, but the animal was restrained in the starting cage until after it had gone off. Then, some prescribed number of seconds after the light had gone off, the raccoon was released so that it could go to the doorway that was last lighted. The raccoons were able to solve this problem when delay was introduced.

Such an experiment tests for the existence of a mediating process because the stimulus is no longer present and the animal must use some process representing it in order to solve the problem. The length of time the animal can delay after the cessation of the stimulus serves as a measure of the rate at which the process—the "trace" of the previous stimulus—disappears.

The length of time various animals and children can delay in this kind of test and still solve the problem has been measured. In the earliest experiments with the method, rats were able to delay only 1 to 10 seconds; raccoons, 10 to 15 seconds; cats, 16 to 18 seconds; dogs, 1 to 3 minutes; a two-and-a-half-year-old child, 50 seconds; and a five-year-old child, at least 20 minutes. These figures have been revised and extended somewhat by later experi-

ments, for much depends on how the apparatus is set up, whether or not any distractions occur during the period of delay, and other factors. The essential point, however, is that a simple mediating process is demonstrable. In order to infer from the method that such a process is taking part in the solution of the problem, the test must meet the following criteria: (1) there must be some stimulus which is known to produce a characteristic, differential response; (2) the stimulus must be presented, and then withdrawn during the delay interval; and (3) no other stimulus outside the body should indicate the correct response.

In some of the experiments on delayed reaction, the mediating process could readily be identified as a posture that oriented the head or body toward the proper box during the delay period. This was not a subtle or high-order process, but it was an effective cue-producing process. Was it necessary? Tests by other experimenters showed that raccoons, dogs, monkeys, and children could delay successfully even when posture was radically disturbed during

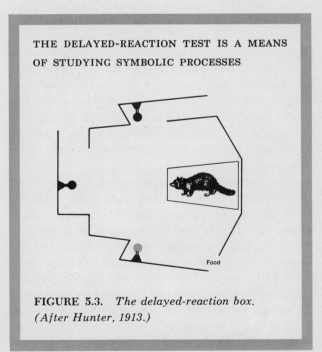

THE DELAYED-REACTION TEST IS A MEANS OF STUDYING SYMBOLIC PROCESSES

Food

FIGURE 5.3. *The delayed-reaction box. (After Hunter, 1913.)*

the delay. Later tests on rats showed that they, too, could delay longer, possibly up to 4 minutes, when the stimuli were made more discriminable or the job of responding was made a little easier. So these animals, under the proper circumstances, can use mediating processes other than postural cues. We can only guess that the process may be some kind of memory image of the correct stimulus, that is, a "visualizing" process.

THE ROLE OF IMAGES   Visual images may be involved in the delayed-reaction experiment, and these may be similar to other memory images. Perhaps the extreme in the ability to image the world is experienced by those people who have *eidetic imagery*. Some people have "photographic memories" for things they have seen and have almost perfect images of visual material. To test yourself, look at the picture in Figure 5.4 on page 168. *Do not read further until you have inspected the picture for 35 seconds.* Now, without looking at the picture, can you spell the German word in it? In one experiment, 3 out of 30 English schoolchildren, unfamiliar with German, could spell the word forward and backward; 7 spelled it with only two mistakes. They, and other "eidetikers," often hesitate a moment before recall. During this time they seem to "project" their image on a "mental screen," to inspect it, and then to read it as if it were actually there. Some people can recall a page of print so accurately that they can repeat any word or line on demand, shifting to different parts of the page as requested.

Most people do not have eidetic imagery, but they usually report that they have images. Hence, even though we cannot observe another person's images objectively, we believe that they exist. In some individuals, visual images apparently predominate. Auditory imagery occurs frequently, but images of muscular sensations, of pain, hunger, and other organic sensations are relatively rare. Even odors and tastes can be imagined by some individuals. Some people, on the other hand, report an almost total lack of imagery.

So far as human thinking is concerned, the question about images is not whether they exist, but what function they have in thinking. Are they the mediating process in thinking? This issue was once hotly debated; some answered with a resounding "yes," others with a vehement "no." To answer the question scientifically, psychologists have conducted rigorous experiments on the role of images in thinking.[2]

The simplest kind of experiment is to ask a person to report on his experiences [Galton, 1907]. One can instruct him, for example, to recall his breakfast table, and ask, "What kind of images do you have?" Most people will give a fairly detailed description, thus proving that they have images. This kind of experiment, however, tells us only what images, and how many relatively, a person may have, but it tells us little about their mediating function in thinking.

Another kind of experiment requires a person to solve some manipulative problem, such as tracing his way blindfolded through a maze with his finger or a pencil [Davis, 1932, 1933]. After he has done this, he is quizzed about his imagery. Many people in such an experiment report truly functional visual imagery; they solve the maze only by building up a "mental map" of it as they go along. Consequently they can draw the maze afterward, sometimes including the blind alleys as well as the true path. Other persons solve the maze by a purely verbal method; they count or name correct turns but do not "see" the maze as a whole in their mind's eye.

IMAGELESS THOUGHT   Experiments of the sort just described indicate that images may promote learning and that they may at times have a mediating function in thinking. But there are other kinds of experiments on the role of images in thinking. One of these, the "thought experiment,"

[2] For a detailed treatment of classical experiments on thinking, see G. Humphrey, *Thinking: an introduction to its experimental psychology.* London: Methuen, 1951. (Paperback available.)

was first carried out about 1900. At that time, a group of psychologists at Würzburg, Germany, who were much interested in understanding thought and consciousness, did the experiment many times. They gave their subject a rather simple intellectual problem, such as "name a fruit," and then asked him to describe the images he had in arriving at the answer.

The Würzburg psychologists were surprised to discover that very few images were uncovered in this way. Moreover, images did not seem to be necessary to solve this kind of problem. If the problem were to "name a fruit," the subject could often say "apple" immediately, but yet be unable to detect any image of a fruit or apple. Apparently the thinking involved in making the appropriate response did not necessarily involve any images. Hence the possibility of *imageless thought* was conceived, a notion that was quite controversial 65 years ago.

Two products of the imageless-thought hypothesis have proved to be of importance. One is the discovery that many of the important events in thinking may not be conscious. We cannot catch and inspect an idea or a thought as we can a bird or a butterfly. This suggests that an idea is more like a process than an object. The other product of the hypothesis is that thought often seems to be governed by a *set* that is formed before it occurs. A *set* is a readiness to think or respond in a predetermined way. If one is given a stimulus word, a thought seems to run off automatically, just as if one has already done his thinking before he starts! And what the thought is depends on the set. You see, for example:

$$\frac{\begin{array}{r} 6 \\ 4 \end{array}}{}$$

You can give a quick answer, but whether it is 2, 10, or 24 depends on whether you are set to subtract, add, or multiply. Of course, with the appropriate instructions, any one of these sets could have been established. Set, as a theoretical concept, has become a most important term in the psychol-ogist's vocabulary. We cannot observe it objectively; yet in order to explain thinking, we must assume that it exists.

Having gotten this far but no further, the early experimental psychologists faced a predicament. They conceived of psychology as the science of conscious experience (see page 22); yet they had established the fact that thinking could take place with no conscious content. The "higher mental processes" had eluded their search. To be sure, images did sometimes accompany thoughts, but the important thing was that images were not essential to thought. The introspective method (see page 24) had come up against a blank wall, for one could not very well introspect if one had nothing to introspect about.

We may conclude, then, that images may sometimes be the mediating processes of thinking, but since thinking can go on without them, other kinds of mediating processes must also exist.

IMPLICIT RESPONSES When this conclusion had been reached by the early psychologists, it occurred to those of a behavioristic bent (see page 25) that some of the content of thinking might consist of small muscle movements.

Perhaps, they suggested, *implicit muscle responses,* not seen by the naked eye but sufficient in size to send back impulses to the nervous system, could be essential elements in the flow of thinking processes. This hypothesis was set forth some fifty years ago by John B. Watson as the explanation of thought.

Two steps are necessary to test the hypothesis. One is to confirm or deny the existence of implicit muscle responses during thinking. The second step is to demonstrate that such implicit responses serve as symbols or cues in the flow of thinking. This is difficult to prove, but it is a more reasonable possibility than it might at first appear.

The idea that implicit muscle responses take part in thinking is made plausible by the relationship between thinking and learning. Thinking begins in learning, and a good deal of learning, as we have

FIGURE 5.4.   *A picture for a test of eidetic imagery. (G. W. Allport.)*

seen, is acquired by doing. One can suppose that learned responses become smaller and smaller as they are practiced and that thinking consists of these reduced movements, differentiated out of the larger movements of original learning. This is the idea of the fractional response.

One experiment used subjects who had been taught to relax their muscles and who were lying relaxed in a darkened room [Jacobson, 1932]:

On a signal, the subject thought of *bending his right arm*. By means of electrodes attached to the arm and connected to a galvanometer, electrical signs of implicit muscular activity were seen to increase at this time. Control tests showed that the action currents varied consistently with the particular instructions. They died out when the subject was told to relax; they did not occur in the right arm when he was instructed to think of *bending his left arm or foot* or to think of *extending the right arm*. Furthermore, a subject could not simultaneously relax his arm and think of

bending it. Similar records were obtained while subjects thought of other activities, such as throwing a ball, turning an ice-cream freezer, and climbing a rope. In order to test the possibility that the action currents came only from the nerves and not the muscles, control experiments were run. In these experiments lightweight levers were placed directly on the muscles; when the levers moved, their action was optically magnified eightyfold. The levers told the same story as the electrodes; the muscles actually were shortening.

A similar experiment employed 19 deaf-mutes who talked with their hands [Max, 1937]:

Electrodes were placed on the subjects' hands, and records were taken during both sleep and waking. The records were especially watched for possible dream activity during sleep. Action currents decreased as the subjects went to sleep and stayed at a low level except for occasional bursts of activity. Were these bursts dreams? To find out, the experimenter tried awakening the subjects during bursts and asking them if they had just been dreaming. In 30 out of 33 instances, the subjects answered "yes." As a control test, they were awakened 62 times during periods of electrical quiet. In 53 instances there were no dreams, but in 9 there were. Thus, in general, the bursts of activity tended to be associated with dreaming. In the waking state, deaf-mute subjects were compared with normal subjects. While solving problems in arithmetic, 84 per cent of the deaf subjects and 31 per cent of normal hearing subjects showed action currents in the hands.

Results such as these indicate that implicit movements may occur during thinking and they may help answer the question, which we raised earlier, of what goes on in imageless thought.

CUE-PRODUCING RESPONSES   What purpose do such implicit muscle responses serve? Are they just a coincidence, or do they have a mediating function in thinking? Some implicit movements are undoubtedly coincidental. They simply represent an "overflow" or "leaking" of activities in the brain. Some of them, however, are probably links in the associative chains of thinking and thus are mediating processes. When they are, their function seems to be one of stimulation, that is, of providing a cue for the next element or response in the chain.

Which way, for example, do you turn your key to unlock your front door at home? The chances are that, when you think out the answer to this question, you imagine yourself putting your key in the lock and turning it. From this you get the cue to answer "right" or "left." In thinking of the event, you probably make some implicit muscle responses, so that receptors in the muscles can signal the presence of muscle tension. In this case, the stimulus or cue produced by the implicit response might, because of previous conditioning, give you the answer.

Cue production from implicit responses is especially important in linguistic thinking—the thinking that is done with words. Much human behavior involves talking, reading, or writing, and we solve many of our problems in terms of language. Words are among the best possible cue-producing responses because almost every word is distinctively different from other words. Except for homonyms, such as "pair" and "pear," spoken words can provide many more discriminable cues than movements of arms, legs, fingers, and so on. Reduced to a subvocal level—to talking that is inaudible to others but sufficiently stimulating to oneself to permit an internal conversation—words can serve in thinking as cue-producing responses. *Words* are probably the major cue-producing and mediating mechanisms in most human thought.

We believe, then, that implicit responses can serve as mediating processes in thinking. Some of the early behaviorists, however, overstated their case when they concluded that thinking was *nothing but* a sequence of implicit responses. The evidence now available does not support such an extreme position. Rather, it indicates that both images and implicit responses play a role in thinking. It also leaves room for other processes.

To explain what these other processes may be, let us point out that the brain is not a simple switchboard between incoming sensory stimulation and outgoing motor impulses. True, some areas are primarily sensory and others are principally motor in function (see Chapter 20). These areas, however, are interlinked in a variety of ways, and certain large areas, especially in the human brain, are not mainly concerned with sensory and motor events. We know little about activity in these regions of the brain, but it is plain that ample opportunity exists for processes occurring in between sensory and motor events. These processes need not be manifested directly in "images," on the one hand, or "implicit muscle responses" on the other.

These considerations, plus the facts we have covered, lead us to the conclusion that some mediating processes may be neither images nor implicit muscle responses. Perhaps at one time, during learning, they were images or responses, but they later diminished to the point of being only connecting processes in the brain. Let us summarize, then, in a very few words: *the mediating processes in thinking may be images, implicit responses, especially words, or other processes taking place in the brain.*

Formation and meaning of concepts

The mediating process, whatever its identity, may represent either something specific or something general. Something specific would be the particular "house I lived in as a little boy." Something general might be "redness," "government," "goodness," or the like. The general mediating processes are often called "concepts."

Concept formation is the process of isolating a common property, or properties, of objects or events. The common properties thus isolated are known as *concepts.* By "common property" we mean some feature that is the same in several otherwise different situations. It may be "redness," "triangularity," "horsiness," or any of thousands of possible characteristics of things, situations, or people.

Concepts enable us to divide things into classes. With a concept of redness, we can sort objects into the classes of "red" and "not red." With a concept of fruit, we can classify things into "fruit" and "not fruit." The common property forms the concept and is the basis for making such classifications.

Since the number of common properties is practically without limit, there is almost no end to the number of classes or of concepts that may be formed. Classes of classes exist, and classes of classes of classes. A concept can exist for any level of grouping. In the class of "dwelling unit" are the subclasses houses, apartments, and caves. In the class of "house" are the subclasses mansions and cottages. Cottages include red ones and white ones. Houses and caves can be big or little, if grouped according to the property of size. And so on and on as far as we wish to go.

TYPES OF CONCEPTS   The term concept, we have seen, refers to properties which objects and events have in common. If only one set of common properties defines the concept, we may call it a

---

CONCEPT FORMATION MAY BE STUDIED EXPERIMENTALLY

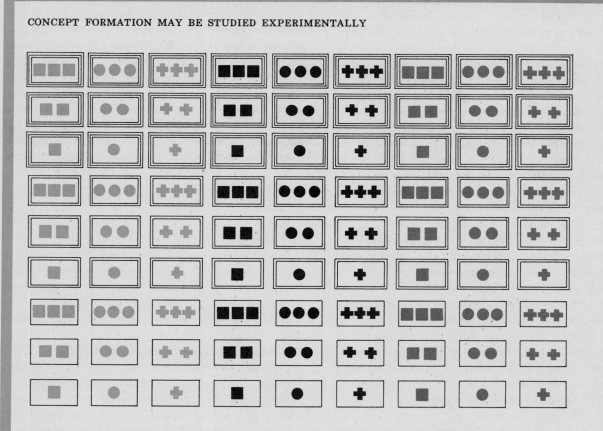

FIGURE 5.5.   *Cards used in a study of concept formation. Note that they differ in four ways: in the number of figures, in the color of the figures, in the shape of the figures, and in the number of borders. Orange stands for red and gray stands for green; the other figures are black. (After Bruner et al., 1956.)*

"simple" concept. "Complex" concepts are also possible, three types of which have been distinguished [Bruner et al., 1956].

Conjunctive concepts. This type of concept is defined by the joint presence of several characteristics. For instance, among the cards in Figure 5.5, which were used in an experimental study of concept formation, all the cards with three green squares comprise a conjunctive concept. The joint presence of three of something, greenness, and squareness defines the concept in this case. Such conjunctive concepts seem to be fairly easy for people to achieve.

Disjunctive concepts. A member of a disjunctive concept class contains at least one element from a larger group of elements. For example, suppose we take three green squares as our group of elements. Any card in Figure 5.5 which has three of anything, *or* contains something green, *or* contains squares, has one element from the larger group and is a member of the concept class. A strike in baseball is an example of a disjunctive concept [Bruner et al., 1956]. A strike is: a missed swing, *or* a pitch at which the batter does not swing but which passes over the plate between the shoulders and knees, *or* a foul ball if there are not already two strikes, *or* a foul bunt if there are already two strikes on the batter. Disjunctive concepts seem to be relatively difficult for people to attain.

Relational concepts. This type of concept is defined in terms of relationships between the elements in a situation. In Figure 5.5, for instance, all the cards with more borders than figures exemplify one such relational concept. Thus, a relational concept does not depend upon the absolute properties of objects or elements; instead, relational concepts are defined in terms of constant relationships between the elements.

WORDS AND CONCEPTS In principle, one does not have to know words or a language in order to have a concept. Indeed, many of our concepts are formed without the benefit of words and are poorly expressed with words. All that is necessary is

that some property of objects be correctly discriminated. For example, by extensive training with all sorts of triangles, it has been possible to teach rats the concept of "triangularity." When trained, they avoid jumping to nontriangles but will jump to almost any kind of triangle, despite differences in detail among the triangles. In this case, the rats signify their concept of triangularity by their discrimination in jumping.

In practice, however, words are very important in concept formation. Language, in fact, is so closely linked to human concept formation that the definition of a concept is almost synonymous with the definition of a word [Osgood et al., 1957]. This is because most words are used as labels to refer to some common property of objects. (The exception is *proper* nouns.) To appreciate this, just select any set of words you want and ask yourself what they mean, or how they are defined. Take "red." "Red" is not the name of any one thing, but rather the name for anything having the property of "redness" regardless of its other characteristics. Hence "red" is the name for a concept, for it arouses in you the concept of redness. Take "wagon," "house," "school," "tree," or any other common noun. In each case, the concept aroused is the property that many different objects have in common.

ABSTRACTION In acquiring word concepts, we learn either simultaneously or successively to do two things. One is to discriminate the property, or properties, that several objects have in common. This is called *abstraction.* The other is to assign a particular *word label* to the abstracted property, or properties. When the label is consistently applied to the property, or properties, abstracted, the concept has been learned. Let us illustrate by taking a case of conjunctive concept formation in children.

First is the process little Charlie goes through in learning the names of things (see Figure 5.6). Suppose that whenever an apple is offered to Charlie, someone says "apple." They say nothing at all or something else whenever they offer him a ball, a cup, or a triangular block. This gives

EARLY CONCEPTS ARE LEARNED THROUGH DISCRIMINATION AND GENERALIZATION

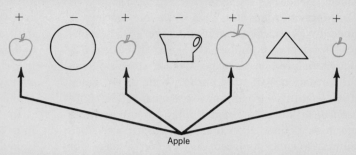

FIGURE 5.6. *Concept formation. A child hears the word "apple" when he sees some objects, but not others. And he is rewarded if he says "apple" when he sees some objects, but not others. In this way, he generalizes the concept of apple and distinguishes it from other concepts. (After Johnson, 1948.)*

Apple

Charlie a chance to associate "apple" with the fruit of that name. In addition, he may be aided by being given an apple whenever he says "apple." The apples he associates with "apple" in this way will vary somewhat in size and shape, but they will all be more or less round, they will be edible, and they will have stems.

Having learned this, Charlie will have the conjunctive concept of apple. But it might not be the concept of apple as we use that concept. In fact, it might turn out to be our conjunctive concept of "fruit," for which he uses "apple," meaning any fruit roughly of apple size that he can eat. This is because his concept of apple is any "round, juicy object he can eat." These are the common properties of apples, but they are also the common properties of many fruits. He will have generalized too much, but quite justifiably. In fact, he will be exhibiting the phenomenon of stimulus generalization which we have previously encountered (see Chapter 3). Such generalization to similar objects, of course, is exactly what is required for concept formation. But to learn the right concept of "apple," he will need more training in distinguishing the properties of apples from those of oranges, plums, and other fruits. In due course, he will certainly get it.

All types of concept formation will go on as rapidly as Charlie can learn to discriminate the differences between objects and at the same time abstract their similarities, thereby forming classes of objects. It will also depend on the *naming responses* available to him. Without appropriate words to label the classes, he will lack the means of responding to them. If appropriate words are available, he can attach a word meaning to each class. Thus, in concept formation, discrimination and abstraction go hand in hand with the naming of classes.

As an illustration, consider our color concepts. Human beings can discriminate several thousand colors, and we have color names for dozens of them. In practice, however, we use only a small number of the color concepts that are possible. A young child usually is taught names for red, green, yellow, and blue, but seldom is he taught crimson, magenta, scarlet, or shocking pink. To him, "red" is first just a name for one property of his red wagon, but he comes to use it for a class of colors of similar properties and hence to use it as a concept. The end points of the class may not be certain; he may wonder whether to call an orange-red "red," "yellow," or "orange," or he may hesitate with purple. Yet the middle points are instantly labeled red, and the class is named for its most frequent elements. On the other hand, lacking names for purple or magenta, he may not build up these color concepts until the time when he has learned the words.

METHODS OF LEARNING CONCEPTS Much of our education, both formal and informal, consists in learning concepts. Partly for this reason, concept formation has been studied extensively. One of the questions frequently asked about it is, How do people learn concepts? That is, what methods do they use? Four may be distinguished.

Discriminative learning. One of the ways of learning concepts, especially simple and conjunctive ones, is the way Charlie learned "apple" and "fruit." The person has the problem of attaching word labels to objects, and in the course of learning to do this abstracts some common properties of objects. A classic experiment illustrating this route to simple concept formation follows [Hull, 1920]:

College students were presented one at a time with cards from a pack of 12. On each card was a different Chinese character. As a card was shown, the experimenter said a nonsense word, like *oo, yer,* or *li.* The first time through the pack, the subject merely repeated the nonsense word after the experimenter. Next, the cards were shuffled and again exposed serially. This time, and on succeeding runs through the pack, the subject attempted to anticipate the correct word. When wrong, he was corrected. Runs were made through the pack until the subject had learned the correct "name" for each Chinese character.

Next a second pack of 12 cards with Chinese characters was presented. The subject was instructed to use the same 12 names he had learned with the first pack, and to start guessing on the first run through the pack. He continued calling until this pack was learned. The same procedure was again followed with four more packs of 12 cards, all containing different characters.

Unbeknown to the subject, the same name was always used when a particular part, or "radical," appeared in the character. Although all characters were different, one part of the "oo" character was the same, and a character containing this common property was in each deck; the same was true of each character given a particular name. The two rows of characters in Figure 5.7 illustrate this. Those in the first row were given the same name, but each character appeared in a different deck. Similarly, each character in the second row was assigned the same name, and each character appeared in a different deck.

The learning of a concept in this experiment was measured by the number of incorrect responses made on the first

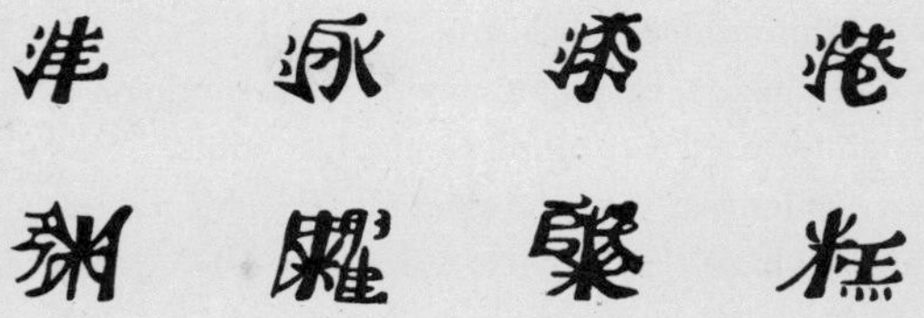

FIGURE 5.7. *Characters used in a study of concept formation by discriminative learning. (After Hull, 1920.)*

trial of the runs through the 12-card packs. The maximum number of errors, of course, is 12. The average numbers of errors made by the subjects were:

Pack number	2	3	4	5	6
Errors on first run through pack	8.7	7.6	6.3	5.5	5.0

Note that the subjects were learning to abstract and label correctly some of the common parts of the characters. The task was so complex, however, that they were, on the average, far from perfect. See if you can pick out the common part or radical in the characters of each row in Figure 5.7.

The learning in this experiment is probably quite analogous to the process young children go through in learning simple and conjunctive concepts, except that it was purposely made complex enough to be difficult for college students.

Context. A second way to learn concepts, especially simple and conjunctive ones, is through context. If we do not know the meaning of a word, but see or hear it used in different contexts, we usually develop a fairly accurate idea of its meaning. The following example is taken from an experiment on conjunctive concept formation [Werner and Kaplan, 1950]. See if you can tell what a "corplum" is:

A corplum may be used for support.

Corplums may be used to close off an open place.

A corplum may be long or short, thick or thin, strong or weak.

A wet corplum does not burn.

You can make a corplum smooth with sandpaper.

The painter used a corplum to mix his paints.

These sentences were presented to subjects one at a time, after which the subjects were asked what "corplum" meant and why they thought so.

You will undoubtedly discover the concept of corplum from the statements made about it. You will find that it expresses the same concept as another word you already know. However, if you did not know the word but were familiar with the properties of corplums, you would still be able to define a corplum. In fact, you would be able to write several more sentences about the properties of corplums.

Definition. A third way of learning new concepts is by definition. In fact, most of the concepts you learn in the later stages of your education are learned in this way. You have, for example, learned many concepts in this book by having them defined for you. Of course, you also use a dictionary for this purpose. In any case, you learn the concept by having it described in other words. Most six-year-old children, for example, have never seen a zebra, but they have a concept of zebra [Osgood et al., 1957]. They have been told that it is an animal that has stripes, that looks and runs like a horse, is about the same size as a horse, and is usually found wild. This definition gives them a fairly accurate concept of zebra.

Classification. Another way of developing concepts is to attempt to form classes of a variety of objects. This method is frequently used by the scientist, especially in the exploratory phases of a problem. The zoologist, for example, has developed conjunctive concepts of "insect," "mammal," and so on, by classifying animals according to their common characteristics. Classification has also been used to study concept formation experimentally [Heidbreder, 1948].

STRATEGIES OF CONJUNCTIVE CONCEPT FORMATION People are not merely passive attainers of conjunctive concepts; they actively strive to learn concepts in as short a time as possible and with as little effort, or "cognitive strain," as possible. To learn conjunctive concepts efficiently, most people devise strategies for concept attainment. In one series of experiments on concept formation, cards like those in Figure 5.5 were used [Bruner et al., 1956]. The experimenter had a concept in mind, and the job of the subject was to sort through the cards in an attempt to find the concept—a sort of "twenty-questions" game. Each time the subject selected a card, the experimenter told him whether or not it was an instance of the concept.

Subjects adopted four different strategies in attempting to attain the concepts. Some subjects hit upon one strategy, others another strategy. These strategies are *simultaneous scanning, successive scanning, conservative focusing,* and *focus gambling* [Bruner et al., 1956].

Simultaneous scanning. Suppose, using the cards in Figure 5.5, that the concept is "red circle." The simultaneous scanner takes a card and is told that it is or is not a member of the concept class. He must deduce what is eliminated and what is not eliminated by this and every other positive or negative instance. Not only must his deductions be correct, he must remember all the previous instances and the deductions made from them—a very difficult task. Simultaneous scanning is not especially efficient because it does not give information about what would be a logical next choice and because it requires that much detail be remembered.

Successive scanning. Using this strategy, the subject chooses a particular hypothesis and tests it; if it turns out to be incorrect, he chooses another hypothesis and tests this. The process of winnowing hypotheses goes on until one of them proves to be correct. This strategy is called "successive" because the hypotheses are taken one at a time, or successively. Although rather inefficient—a person may have to eliminate many hypotheses—this strategy enables the subject to keep track of what he has eliminated and what he has not—it reduces "cognitive strain."

Conservative focusing. A positive card—a positive instance of the concept—serves as a focus for the selection of other cards. The subject focuses on this positive instance and then chooses other cards in which one element at a time is changed. If the card is still an instance of the concept after a single change, the changed element cannot be part of the concept—it is irrelevant. On the other hand, if the card is negative after the change, the changed element is part of the concept. Let us take an example:

If the first positive card encountered contains three red circles with two borders (3R ○ 2b), and if the concept is "red circles," the sequence of choices made would be as follows, each choice changing a *single* attribute value of the focus card:

3R ○ 2b   (Positive) focus card.

2R ○ 2b   (Positive) first choice: eliminate "three figures" as a relevant attribute value.

3G ○ 2b   (Negative) second choice: retain "red" as a relevant attribute value.

3R + 2b   (Negative) third choice: retain "circle" as a relevant attribute value.

3R ○ 1b   (Positive) fourth choice: eliminate "two borders" as a relevant attribute value.

Ergo: concept is "red circles."

[Slightly modified from Bruner et al., 1956, page 87.]

Conservative focusing is a highly efficient strategy in that every choice gives some information.

Focus gambling. This is like conservative focusing except that the subject changes more than one characteristic at a time in an attempt to speed up the attainment of the concept. It works well when the changed instance is still positive; none of the changed characteristics is part of the concept. Negative instances are more troublesome and do not provide much specific information; any of the changed characteristics might have been necessary for the definition of the concept, and we do not

know which of them is part of the concept when several are changed at a time.

The TOTE system. Another description of strategy in concept formation is the test-operate-test-exit (TOTE) system [Miller et al., 1960]. The TOTE system is somewhat similar to the successive scanning strategy outlined above [Hunt, 1962]. The test consists of a comparison of a currently held hypothesis against data and facts about the concept which the person already has discovered. Suppose, when the hypothesis is tested, that a discrepancy between the data and the hypothesis shows up. Now the operate phase will start to generate a new hypothesis which will be tested in the second test phase. Finally, when the hypothesis is confirmed, the person will "exit" from this situation until a new task is proposed.

FACTORS AFFECTING CONCEPT FORMATION

It is of practical, as well as academic, value to know what helps or hinders concept formation, for we would like to improve our methods of teaching concepts to people. We know that a good many factors make a difference, but for our purposes here, a few will be sufficient.

Transfer. One factor, which is also important in other learning, is transfer (see page 129). When a person already knows a concept similar to the one being learned, he can learn it rapidly. This is positive transfer. But similarity can be tricky; it can also produce negative transfer. If a new concept appears to be similar to a known concept, but is also quite different in some important respect, the person may have trouble understanding the new concept. Here, to capitalize on transfer, the teacher must point out both the similarities and the differences.

Distinctiveness. A second factor in concept formation is the degree to which common elements are isolated, grouped, or otherwise made conspicuous. For want of a better term, we shall call this distinctiveness. Anything that is done to make the common property of the concept stand out aids concept formation; whatever obscures it or embeds it in irrelevant details retards concept formation.

Two examples can be presented briefly. In the experiment on Chinese characters cited above, the students were very slow to learn the "concepts" because the common element was embedded in complex characters, and the characters were presented in jumbled order. If all those with the same common property had been grouped together, as they are in Figure 5.7, concept formation would have been much easier.

Another experiment demonstrates the value of isolating the property to be abstracted. In this case, the experimenter used meaningless drawings. When he outlined in red the property to be abstracted, he found that concept formation proceeded much more rapidly than it did otherwise.

Other factors. Worth mentioning in passing are three other factors affecting concept formation [Johnson, 1955]. One is *ability to manipulate materials.* If a person is allowed to rearrange, redraw, or reorganize the materials containing common properties, he is more likely to learn or discover the appropriate concepts. Another is the *instruction* or *general purpose* a person has. If he is told to try to discover a common element, that is, to search for the concept, he does better than if he is given a problem, as in the experiment with Chinese characters, of learning to use the right names. Finally, a person usually learns faster if he has *all the relevant information available at the same time* instead of a piece at a time.

MEANING OF CONCEPTS   Concept learning is like other kinds of learning. The concept can be learned poorly or well, accurately or inaccurately. The concept one person learns may or may not be the same concept another person learns. In fact, it is quite apparent from everyday conversations with people that they often have very different concepts of the same thing. This is especially true in abstract realms such as politics or religion.

A distinction is sometimes made between denotative and connotative meanings of concepts. The *denotative meaning* of a concept is its socially accepted definition; the *connotative meaning* is its emotional and evaluative meaning—its "goodness" or "badness," for instance. Differences in the connotative meanings of concepts are an important source of misunderstanding and failure of communication among people. What, for instance, does "liberal" mean to you? The measurement of connotative meanings of concepts is a significant problem in psychology.

Individual differences in learning concepts and their meanings raise the question of how we can measure the meaning of a concept. How can we tell how well a concept has been learned? How can we measure differences among people in what they understand the meaning of concepts to be? These questions have answers, though the answers vary with the purpose of the question and with the types of concepts. In general, four methods of measuring the meanings of concepts may be distinguished. The first two are most useful with the denotative meanings of concepts we attempt to teach in school, where there is some standard for deciding whether or not a concept is correct. The last two are most useful with connotative meanings of concepts that have no such standard; they are of interest in studying personality and social processes.

Free response. The simplest and most straightforward way of finding out what a concept means to a person is to ask him to *say* what it means. This is the free-response method. The results one gets in this way depend on the instructions given and also upon the concepts tested.

A child's concept of "dog" can be tested by asking him to describe a dog. His description can be scored "accurate," "too general," "abstract," "concrete," "irrelevant," and so forth, with a fair degree of interscorer agreement. In fact, items of this kind are used on intelligence tests and scored with good reliability. When the description avoids irrelevancies and includes only the generally accepted meaning, we call it a *definition.* The description may also be pictorial, as when a child is asked to draw a triangle or a college student is asked to draw a neuron. The descriptions are influenced, of course, by the subject's skill in verbal and pictorial techniques as well as by his mastery of the concept.

Discrimination. The free-response method obviously is subjective, and it is often difficult to score reliably.[3] A more objective method makes use of a set of discriminations. A person is shown a variety of objects, or instances of people or things, and asked to indicate whether each one is or is not an instance of the concept. Alternatively, he may simply be asked to classify objects according to specified common properties. Such a test can yield an objective score, in terms of right and wrong answers, of the accuracy of a person's concept.

One interesting variation of the discrimination method is the *oddity method.* A person is given three or more items and asked to pick out the odd one—the one that does not belong. One of the virtues of this method is that one does not have to specify any particular concept. With one simple question, the experimenter can measure the subject's understanding of several concepts as well as any confusion among concepts. The following is an example [Cofer, 1951]:

skyscraper   temple   cathedral   prayer

The subject is asked to pick out the odd item. Actually, in this case, two odd ones are possible because two concepts are involved. If the subject has a religious concept in mind, he should designate "skyscraper"; if a building concept, "prayer." The concept the subject employs is likely to depend on the order in which the words are presented, and the first word is most important in determining the concept. With the order above, "prayer" is most likely to be considered odd. With the order

prayer   temple   skyscraper   cathedral

the most likely answer is "skyscraper." Of course, people who do not have very accurate concepts of some of these words may choose "temple" or "cathedral," neither of which is ever the correct odd one in this pattern of words.

[3] On intelligence tests, items are carefully selected; the correct answers are standardized; and the scoring is done by trained examiners.

The two methods, free responses and discrimination, do not always give the same results. People frequently can give a dictionary or verbal definition of a concept, but make mistakes in choosing instances of the concept. Conversely, people may be able to identify the common (or uncommon) characteristic in a group of objects and still not be able to give a correct verbal statement of the concept. In the experiment on Chinese characters, for example, some students learned to use the correct names for characters without being able to indicate the common characteristic they named.

Disagreement in results of the two methods is not puzzling. If a person has learned concepts by context or by definition in terms of other concepts, he is more likely to do well with the free-response method. On the other hand, a person who has acquired concepts by simple learning through experience with instances of the concept will probably do better on the discrimination method. This is one of the reasons why strictly formal education, limited to books, can turn out students who do not understand "practical" concepts and why it is a good idea to have, in addition to purely verbal instruction, laboratories and other more concrete methods of teaching concepts.

Word association. Another method of testing the meaning of concepts is particularly suited to studying an individual's idiosyncratic concepts and to finding out whether those concepts are substantially different from the ones held by most people. This is the word-association method. A person is given a word and asked to reply with the first association that comes to mind. Normally he will reply with a word that is in the same class of concepts as the stimulus word. If he replies with something not usually related to the stimulus word, it is an indication that his personal concepts are, in some respects, rather different from those of people in general.

Semantic differential. A more sophisticated method of measuring the connotative meaning of concepts is called the semantic differential [Osgood et al., 1957]. So far, it has been applied primarily as a research tool, but it has many possible uses. Its basic purpose is to analyze concepts in terms of a limited number of dimensions of meaning and to compare these dimensions in various groups of people, including different national and language groups. It also may be used in attitude measurement, in mass communication, and in personality measurement.

To obtain a semantic differential, two things are required: a concept and two or more scales. The concept can be a word such as "father," "sin," "symphony," "Russian," or "America." Each scale consists of two polar words, such as "happy-sad," "hard-soft," "slow-fast." When presented to a subject, each scale has seven spaces placed between the words at each end (see Figure 5.8). The subject is asked to place each concept at some position on each scale. The concept being judged might be "father," for example. If the seven positions from left to right on the scale are given numbers 1 to 7, the subject might judge "father" as a 3 on the happy-sad scale, 2 on the hard-soft scale, 5 on the slow-fast scale, and so forth. The subject does the same thing for "father" on the remainder of the scales, which may number anywhere from 20 to 50. Then he repeats this procedure with the other concepts.

The result of scaling concepts in this way is a semantic differential for each concept. The differential gives the meaning of the concept by showing its position on the scales. If we desire, we can draw a profile for each concept, showing its position on each scale. Then we can compare profiles for different concepts. To the extent that one profile corresponds to another, connotative meaning of those two concepts is similar. To the extent that they differ, their connotative meanings are different.

The semantic differential has also been used in other ways. It has served as a method of analyzing the whole system of concepts used by individuals in a culture. But in obtaining the average result from large groups of people, the meaning of "meaning" becomes distorted. Consider the differences in connotative meaning of the word "army"; a pacifist would scale this one way, a graduate of West Point another way [Carroll, 1964]. Thus the average "meaning" of a concept in a culture cannot be made completely clear.

In any case, factor analysis has been used to analyze the scales for many concepts (see page 406). Analysis of this sort reveals that the many scales can be grouped into three classes, or factors, which have been designated *evaluation, potency,* and *activity*. Scales which measure goodness and badness, fairness and unfairness, or other similar characteristics make up the evaluation factor; scales which measure strength and weakness, heaviness or lightness, or characteristics of this sort, make up the potency factor; scales which measure speed, activity and passivity, or the like, make up the activity factor.

THE SEMANTIC DIFFERENTIAL MEASURES THE CONNOTATIVE MEANING OF A CONCEPT ON SEVERAL SCALES

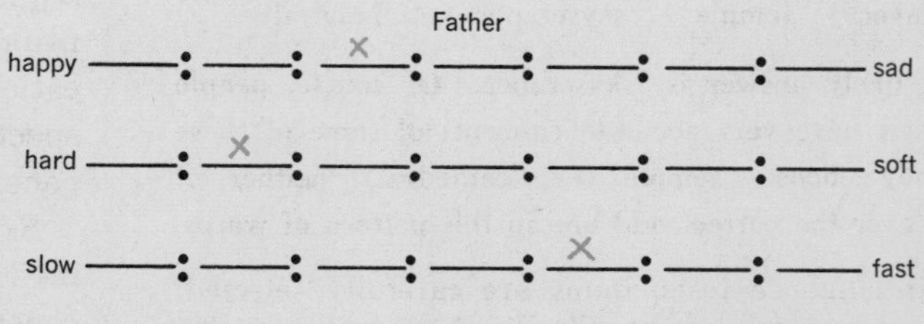

FIGURE 5.8. *Some scales from a semantic differential. A person rates a concept, in this case "father," on 20 to 50 bipolar scales, three of which are illustrated. (After Osgood et al., 1957.)*

Thus, the many scales may be condensed into three "superscales," evaluation, potency, and activity, which appear to be the major dimensions of connotative meaning for a great many of our concepts. An interesting way of depicting the connotative meaning of many different words is shown in Figure 5.9.

Research use of the semantic differential. We have seen that denotative concepts are learned. The semantic differential can be used to show that connotative meanings can also be learned. Consider the following experiment [Staats and Staats, 1957]:

This experiment combines elements of classical conditioning (see Chapter 3) and paired-associate learning (see page 119). Six nonsense syllables were used, and each was paired with several words. Two of the nonsense syllables, YOF and XEH, were crucial: YOF was always paired with words having a pleasant connotation, "healthy," "gift," and so on; XEH was always paired with words having an unpleasant connotation, "sad," "fear," and so on. Most of the subjects did not detect this arrangement because of the other nonsense syllables and words which disguised the crucial relationships. Data from those who did detect it were not used. This experiment contains certain elements of classical conditioning: the nonsense syllable can be considered to be a conditioned stimulus; the pleasant or unpleasant word can be considered the unconditioned stimulus which elicits an unconditioned mediating response—a pleasant or unpleasant meaning. The pleasant and unpleasant meanings are common to all the words which follow YOF or XEH. Is the appropriate connotative meaning attached to the nonsense syllables? The answer seems to be "yes." Changes in the appropriate direction do occur in the semantic differential—the nonsense syllable YOF was evaluated more positively than XEH.

THE USES OF CONCEPTS   Concepts are ways of classifying the diversity of elements in the world around us. As such, they are convenient tools in problem solving and logical reasoning. Whether or not a problem will be solved is, in part, a matter of the appropriateness of the concepts brought to bear on the problem. This has been summarized as follows:

Among the factors that may determine whether an individual will solve a problem are the following:

1. The individual's repertory of relevant concepts.

2. The concepts evoked in the individual by the structure of the problem.

3. The individual's skill in manipulating the concepts evoked, his strategy of solution, his flexibility in changing his mode of attack, and his ability to perceive the relevance of a concept.

[Carroll, 1964, page 85.]

Let us now turn to a discussion of problem solving and logical reasoning.

The solution of problems

Thinking consists of mediating processes, many of which are words and concepts. But a summary statement such as this tells us nothing about what starts thinking, what guides it, or what brings it to a stop. A river is more than water. It springs up somewhere, it changes course, it flows sometimes swiftly and sometimes slowly, and eventually it ends in the ocean. Thinking, too, has beginnings, courses, and ends. What explains them?

MOTIVATION   For one thing, thinking is usually motivated. As one of the leading investigators in this area has said, thinking involves "the desire, the craving to face the true issue . . . , to go from an unclear, inadequate relation to a clear, transparent, direct confrontation" [Wertheimer, 1959]. Thus he stresses the *directedness* of thought processes. Instead of just "happening" by association, each stage in thinking is controlled by motives.

On the basis of all we now know, we ought to differentiate at least two kinds of motives in thinking: (1) a motive for the behavior immediately preceding the problem, which may be love, greed, curiosity, ambition, or a number of other motives, and (2) a motive induced by the problem itself to complete or anticipate the solution of the problem. The former gets thinking started; the latter carries it through to solution.

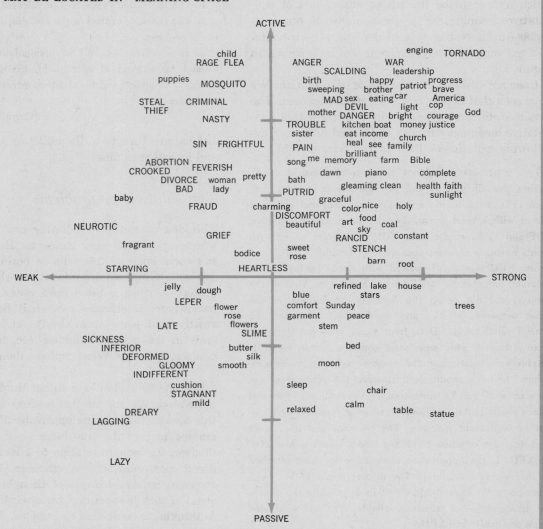

CONCEPTS MAY BE LOCATED IN "MEANING SPACE"

FIGURE 5.9. *Concepts placed with respect to three factors derived from the semantic differential. The three factors are: activity (active-passive), potency (weak-strong), and evaluation (good-bad). The position of the concept with respect to the axes locates it on the activity and potency dimensions. The evaluative factor is represented by the way the words are printed: "Good" concepts are represented in lower-case letters; "bad" concepts by capitals. For instance, ANGER is rated as strongly active, slightly strong, and "bad." (From Carroll, 1964. Based on data from Jenkins et al., 1958.)*

TABLE 5.1 *Practice and test problems used by Luchins. The five practice problems require a roundabout method of solution, but the test problem can be solved easily. Most subjects, however, who acquired a set by solving practice problems first, used the long method of solving the test problem and were blind to the easy method.*

		GIVEN THE FOLLOWING EMPTY JARS AS MEASURES			OBTAIN THIS AMOUNT OF WATER
PROBLEM NUMBER		A	B	C	
1.	Practice	21	127	3	100
2.	Practice	14	163	25	99
3.	Practice	18	43	10	5
4.	Practice	9	42	6	21
5.	Practice	20	59	4	31
6.	Test	23	49	3	20

SOURCE: Luchins, 1954.

In order to account for the thought processes of great thinkers, such as scientists, artists, writers, and inventors, we might have to postulate even a third kind of motivation: a lifelong interest in creative production or in solving challenging problems.

HABIT AND SET Thinking is also guided, and often impeded, by habit and set. Practice in solving problems one way tends to "set" us to solve a new problem in the same way, provided that the new problem situation contains stimuli similar to those in the practiced problems. This is the secret of many trick jokes and puzzles. In one trick, you spell words and ask a person how he pronounces them. You use names beginning with Mac, like MacDonald, MacTavish. Then you slip in "machinery" and see if he pronounces it "MacHinery." With the set for names, he may fall into your trap.

Set may be produced by immediately preceding experiences, by long-established practices, or by instructions which revive old habits (see Transfer of Training, Chapter 4). It biases the thinker at the start of his problem, directing him away from certain families of responses and toward others. It acts as an implied assumption. Like transfer of training, it can be either positive or negative in its effects. If it is helpful, we say, "How clever I am!"; if a hindrance, we say, "How blind I was!"

One investigator did a systematic experiment on habitual set, using the problems in Table 5.1. This experiment is described in part below [Luchins, 1954]:

In the sixth problem, for example, the subject is required to say how he would measure 20 quarts of water when he has only three jars, holding 23, 49, and 3 quarts, respectively. Subjects do it the easy way by filling the 3-quart jar from the 23-quart jar, provided they have no interfering set. However, if they have just solved the previous problems by a longer method—that is, by filling the middle jar, from it filling the jar to the right twice and the jar to the left once, leaving the required amount in the center jar— they usually use the long method and do not notice the short one. Amazingly enough, 75 per cent of a college group were blind to the easy method after having practiced the long method for only five trials.

The frequency of habitual, blind solutions is reduced by (1) warning the subject "Don't be blind! Look sharp now!" just before the critical trial, (2) reducing the number of practice trials, and (3) separating the practice and critical trials by several days or weeks. Comparative data show that habit strength and set, as indicated by number of practice trials, can be much stronger factors than any warning against them.

A special variety of the effect of set is *functional fixedness*. We may be so used to using particular objects in particular ways that we cannot see new ways of using them when new ways are needed to solve a problem. The following experiment shows this effect [Adamson, 1952]:

One of the problems in this experiment was to find a way of mounting three candles on a *vertical* screen. The subjects were provided with the candles, three small pasteboard boxes, five thumbtacks, and five matches. The problem is not a difficult one; the solution is simply to stick the candles on the boxes with melted wax and then to use the thumbtacks to attach the boxes to the screen. Boxes, of course, are usually containers and not platforms. Fixation on this function was established for an experimental group of subjects by placing the tacks, candles, and matches in the three boxes before giving them to the subjects. No attempt was made to establish functional fixedness in the subjects of the control group: the three empty boxes, together with the other materials, were simply placed on the table. Members of the experimental group had difficulty with this problem—only 12 out of 29 (41 per cent)—solved it in the allotted time of 20 minutes. On the other hand, 24 out of 28 (86 per cent) of the people in the control group solved the problem. Similar results were obtained with other problems.

These results seem to provide strong evidence for functional fixedness as a particular kind of set which hinders problem solving. One advantage of

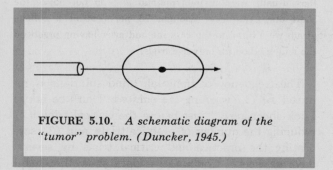

FIGURE 5.10. *A schematic diagram of the "tumor" problem. (Duncker, 1945.)*

quitting a problem which cannot be solved is that you may come back to it with a fresh approach—that is, functional fixedness may be broken.

PROCESSES IN PROBLEM SOLVING　Let us summarize again. Thinking begins with some kind of felt need which cannot be immediately met, a problem, and a motive to solve the problem. It is guided by some set or determining tendency, and it is helped—or hindered—by previously learned habits. Now when we ask about the processes through which the problem gets solved, we can distinguish among mechanical processes, solution through understanding, and insightful solutions.

Mechanical solutions. In attempting to solve a puzzle, you sometimes—but not very often—stumble on the right answer. By trying first one way, then another, you finally hit on the one that works. In the process, you have probably made many "stupid" errors which show that you do not understand the problem. This stumbling is very much like the instrumental learning described in Chapter 3, except that you are using thought processes, or "internal" responses, rather than making overt responses. This method, of course, is not very productive or efficient.

A second kind of mechanical solution may come by rote. If you are given a column of figures to add, you immediately start thinking according to rules which you have learned, and in due time you come up with the answer. Or, if you are asked to spell a word or give the directions for going from one place to another, you do a minimum of thinking and a lot of just plain sequential remembering in order to give the answer. You merely reproduce what you have already learned. To understand this way of solving problems, almost all one needs to know is how the solutions were learned in the first place.

Solving problems by understanding. We usually cannot solve problems by mechanical means. Problems would hardly be problems if we could solve them so automatically. Many problems are solved by working from general principles back to specific means by which the end can be achieved. We may

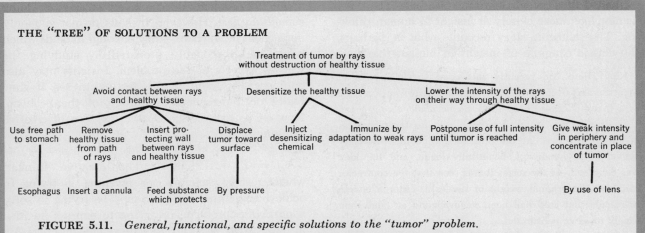

THE "TREE" OF SOLUTIONS TO A PROBLEM

FIGURE 5.11. *General, functional, and specific solutions to the "tumor" problem.*
General solutions are on the second line from the top, functional solutions on the
third line, and specific solutions on the bottom line. (Duncker, 1945.)

go from a general understanding of what constitutes a solution of the problem to a functional solution— the means by which a general solution can be realized [Duncker, 1945; Wertheimer, 1959]. The following example illustrates the search for functional solutions [Duncker, 1945]:

The subjects, who were college students, were given a problem stated thus: "Given a human being with an inoperable stomach tumor, and rays which destroy organic tissue at sufficiently high intensity, by what procedure can one free him of the tumor by these rays and at the same time avoid destroying the healthy tissue that surrounds it." A diagram of the problem is given in Figure 5.10; general and functional solutions produced by one subject are shown in Figure 5.11. The general solutions are on the second line from the top; functional solutions are on the third line. The subject, guided by understanding of the goal, worked from general to functional solutions. At first, subjects often seek impractical functional solutions. For instance, "use a free path to the stomach" is a functional solution because it shows that the subject understands that the problem necessitates getting the rays to the stomach without hitting healthy tissue on the way. It is an impractical solution, however. Gradually, the subject approximates functional solutions which are more practical and finally he hits one

that works. In the case of this problem, a good practical solution might be to cross weak rays at the site of the tumor. Each of the individual rays would be too weak to damage tissue, but the sum of several rays on the tumor would kill it.

This example shows that, when subjects think out loud, it is often possible to trace the steps involved in reaching practical specific functional solutions. Sometimes, however, the solution just seems to come suddenly without the subject or experimenter being able to account for it. In such a case, insight has occurred.

Insightful solutions. Solution by insight may grow out of mechanical processes or the search for functional solutions, but it represents a completely new experience to the thinker. "Aha! I have it" is a characteristic outburst when suddenly he grasps the solution to a baffling problem. He has produced a novel solution—novel to him, at least—through thinking. If the solution is truly novel, he has invented or created something that he can pass on to other members of society for them to use in their "rote-thinking" processes (see the section Creative Thinking, which follows). We have already seen some examples of insight and how they may be explained by previous learning (see page 110). Let us now look more closely at insight in human thinking. The following story recounts what is, perhaps, the classic example of insight in human thinking:

King Hiero had recently succeeded to the throne of Syracuse and decided to place a golden crown in a temple as a thank offering to the gods. So he made a contract at a fixed price, and weighed out the gold for the contractor at the royal scales. At the appointed time the contractor delivered his handiwork beautifully made, and the king was delighted. At the scales it was seen that the contractor had kept the original weight of the gold. Later a charge was made that gold had been removed and an equivalent weight of silver substituted.

Hiero was furious at being fooled, and, not being able to find any way of detecting the theft, asked Archimedes to put his thought to the matter.

While Archimedes was bearing the problem in his mind, he happened to get into a bath and noticed that when he got into the tub exactly the same amount of water flowed over the side as the volume of his body that was under water. Perceiving that this gave him a clue to the problem, he promptly leapt from the tub in a rush of joy and ran home naked, shouting loudly to all the world that he had found the solution. As he ran, he called again and again in Greek, "Eureka, Eureka . . . I have found it, I have found it." [Humphrey, 1948, page 115. As translated from Vitruvius.]

Incidentally, the contractor cheated because the silver in the crown, having a larger volume than an equal weight of gold, made the crown displace more water than it would have had it been made of gold alone.

As we shall see more clearly in the next section, insight seems to be the result of much combination and recombination of mediating processes going on beneath the level of consciousness [Campbell, 1960]. From reports of creative workers, the mathematician Poincaré (1913), for example, it seems that concentrated conscious thinking about a problem may sometimes get one into a symbolic blind alley. When this has happened, insight often comes later, while the person is not consciously thinking

about the problem and is actively engaged in doing something else. However, insights do not suddenly appear out of nowhere—they blossom in fields which have been thoroughly prepared by studying the various aspects of the problem. Insights may also be incorrect—they require testing to see if they really do represent the solution of the problem. Now let us look at the related question of creative thinking.

CREATIVE THINKING   The creative thinker, whether artist, scientist, or inventor, is trying to achieve something new: He may be trying to solve a particular problem, or trying to express an idea in novel ways, or trying to achieve new and pleasing combinations of forms, colors, or word sounds.

Creative thinking in the arts has been the subject of much comment. The ideas often seem to "bubble up" in a seemingly spontaneous manner. This sort of thinking is similar to insight, and it seems likely that the ideas rise to consciousness after much unconscious rearrangement of symbols. The following two examples illustrate the insightful nature of creative thinking in the arts. The first is from the poet A. E. Housman, the second from a critical examination of Coleridge's poetry by John Livingston Lowes. Here is Housman's autobiographical account of his creative thinking.

Having drunk a pint of beer at luncheon—beer is a sedative to the brain, and my afternoons are the least intellectual portion of my life—I would go out for a walk of two or three hours. As I went along, thinking of nothing in particular, only looking at things around me and following the progress of the seasons, there would flow into my mind, with sudden and unaccountable emotion, sometimes a line or two of verse, sometimes whole stanzas at once, accompanied, not preceded, by a vague notion of the poem which they were destined to form part of. . . .

When I got home I wrote them down, leaving gaps, and hoping that further inspiration might be forthcoming another day. Sometimes it was, if I took walks in a receptive and expectant frame of mind; but sometimes the poem had to be taken in hand and completed by the brain, which was apt to be a matter of trouble and anxiety, involving trial and disappointment, and sometimes ending in failure. [Housman, 1933, pages 48–49.]

Many of the ideas contained in Coleridge's poems are related to entries in a notebook in which he kept a record of the materials from which the allusions in the poems were derived. This is what Lowes had to say of Coleridge's notebook:

I have left two-thirds of the mass of entries in the Note Book completely untouched. But the whole could not make clearer one fact of profound significance for us. For there, in those bizarre pages, we catch glimpses of the strange and fantastic shapes which haunted the hinterland of Coleridge's brain. Most of them never escaped from their confines into the light of day. Some did, trailing clouds of glory as they came. But those which did not, like the stars of the old astrology, rained none the less their secret influence on nearly everything that Coleridge wrote in his creative prime. "The Rime of the Ancient Mariner," "Christabel," "Kubla Khan," "The Wanderings of Cain," are what they are because they are all subdued to the hues of that heaving and phosphorescent sea below the verge of consciousness from which they have emerged. No single fragment of concrete reality in the array before us is in itself of such far-reaching import as is the sense of that hovering cloud of shadowy presences. For what the teeming chaos of the Note Book gives us is the charged and electrical atmospheric background of a poet's mind. [Lowes, 1927, pages 30–31.]

In addition to such autobiographical and impressionistic accounts of creative thinking, a great deal of controlled research is being done on creativity. For instance, attempts have been made to obtain objective measures of creativity [Torrance, 1962]. Using such tests, it has been found that creativity is not necessarily highly related to conventional measures of intelligence—that is, to intelligence test scores [Getzels and Jackson, 1962]. Creativity seems to be a dimension of intellect not tapped by conventional intelligence testing. Other studies have been made of the stages of creative thinking and the personality traits of creative peo-

ple. Basically, however, we know little about the causes of creativity.

Stages in creative thinking. The steps involved in the thinking of outstanding creative thinkers have been studied through interviews, questionnaires, and introspection [Wallas, 1926]. Though each has his own way of thinking, and this depends somewhat on the kind of problems to be solved, such thinking seems to have a recurring pattern. It tends to proceed in five stages: *preparation, incubation, illumination, evaluation,* and *revision.*

In stage 1, preparation, the thinker formulates his problem and collects the facts and materials he considers necessary for its solution. Very frequently, he finds, like Poincaré, that he cannot solve the problem, even after hours or days of concentrated effort. Often, he deliberately or involuntarily turns away from the problem; this is stage 2, incubation. During this period, some of the ideas that were interfering with the solution of the problem tend to fade. On the other hand, things he experiences or learns in the meantime may provide the clue to the solution. During incubation, the unconscious processes may be at work. In stage 3, illumination, the thinker often has an "Aha!" insight experience. An idea for the solution may suddenly dawn on him. Next, in stage 4, evaluation, he determines whether the apparent solution is in fact the correct one. Frequently it turns out to be wrong, and the thinker is back where he started. In other cases, it is the right idea, but needs some modification or requires the solution of other relatively minor problems. Thus, stage 5, revision, is reached.

This description of the mental processes of the creative thinker is far from satisfactory. One day, through research, we should be able to understand the pattern better. This description does, however, provide a general picture of the steps that are frequently involved in the solution of problems by our most talented and creative people.

Personality traits of creative thinkers. Is there anything special, in addition to their creativity, about creative persons? Their appearances can certainly vary widely, but do creative people share common personality characteristics? Some evidence, obtained from objective and projective personality tests (see Chapter 12), indicates that original people are especially characterized by the following traits [Barron, 1963]:

1. Original persons prefer complexity and some degree of apparent imbalance in phenomena.

2. Original persons are more complex psychodynamically and have greater personal scope.

3. Original persons are more independent in their judgments.

4. Original persons are more self-assertive and dominant.

5. Original persons reject suppression as a mechanism for the control of impulse. This would imply that they forbid themselves fewer thoughts, that they dislike to police themselves or others, that they are disposed to entertain impulses and ideas that are commonly taboo. . . .

[Slightly modified from Barron, 1963, pages 208–209.]

A knowledge of these important differentiating traits may enable us to find the antecedent conditions in early life which give rise to them as well as the predisposition toward creative thinking. Hopefully, research will uncover some of the characteristics of family life which produce creative thinkers.

Logical reasoning

We have discussed the symbolic and mediating nature of thought processes; we have seen that thought is motivated, that it is guided by habits and sets, that concepts provide useful tools for thought, and that solutions to problems can be obtained in different ways. One feature of thinking, however, has not been discussed. That is reasoning. Perhaps you are accustomed to using the words "reasoning" and "thinking" as though they meant the same thing. We commonly do that in everyday talk. No doubt, however, you can remember many instances of thinking that seem quite lacking in reasoning.

What, then, is reasoning? A little boy was on the right track when he answered, "Putting two and two together." Reasoning certainly is not just any kind of thinking. It involves solving a problem by *following rules* which govern the putting of two or more elements of past experience together to make something new.

VERBAL REASONING   Most human reasoning makes use of symbols—especially verbal symbols. Since we use words so extensively to communicate our thoughts to others, we get in the habit of depending on words for thinking. Yet word meanings often are vague or ambiguous, and we can be led astray by them. Also, when reasoning with verbal symbols alone, we may find it impossible to test whether our conclusion is correct, for we often lack the opportunity to compare the verbal conclusion with actuality.

To help us, society develops standards or norms for checking the results of our reasoning. People have come to believe that certain statements are "reasonable," and some are not. Hence, when a person concludes with an "unreasonable" statement, people tell him so immediately and discourage him from making further foolish statements. The trouble with culturally defined standards of reasonableness is that what is reasonable to one group may be completely unreasonable to another. "It stands to reason that . . . ," a college debater argues; but as an American undergraduate, he completely forgets that the conclusion may not be obvious to, say, an Arabian or a Chinese opponent.

To make the standards for reasoning as rigid as possible, philosophers and mathematicians, over the centuries, have given us rules for reasoning. The systematic organization of these rules is called logic, and it prescribes what kinds of implications statements can have and what kinds of conclusions can be drawn from them. Any reasoning that does not conform to these rules is dubbed "illogical" or "fallacious." Since so much in human affairs hangs on the question of how logical we are in our thinking, we should study some of the psychological factors involved in the logical and illogical thinking of human beings.

LOGICAL THINKING Suppose one conducts a test of reasoning in children and asks them this question: "If all six-year-olds are in school, and if Johnny is six, then where is Johnny?" The psychologist should not be surprised if the answer is, "I hate school," or "He's home sick with a cold," though the logician would be! To the psychologist, the child's answer is "reasonable" because it is a simple association with a stimulus, without regard to logical rules, and this is what people learn long before they learn to reason, let alone reason by the formal rules of logic.

As children grow older they learn to respond according to certain instructions and rules and to keep their associative responses within certain bounds. Suppose I test a high school student: I instruct him that whenever I say a word I want him to respond with a word that is a class name for objects of the same kind. Now I give him the word "table." He will give me back "furniture" or some comparable word, but he will not say "chair" because that would violate the rule that his response must name a class that includes "table." He has learned to follow a rule.

Now for a more complex case. In college, the student may learn syllogisms, one form of which is:

1. All *A* is *B*.
   All men are mortal.
2. All *C* is *A*.
   All farmers are men.
3. Therefore, all *C* is *B*.
   All farmers are mortal. (See Figure 5.12, top.)

This syllogism follows one of the rules of logic and the student may learn it, perhaps by rote. He will immediately encounter difficulty, however, in applying the rule to his thinking about situations in daily life because it is not easy to distinguish validity and truth from fallacy. The form of the syllogism above, for example, *looks* suspiciously like the following:

SIMPLE DIAGRAMS SOMETIMES AID LOGICAL THINKING

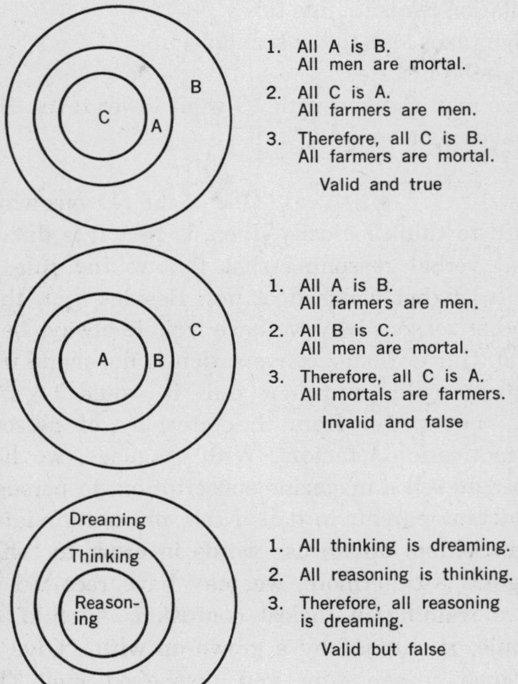

1. All A is B.
   All men are mortal.
2. All C is A.
   All farmers are men.
3. Therefore, all C is B.
   All farmers are mortal.
   Valid and true

1. All A is B.
   All farmers are men.
2. All B is C.
   All men are mortal.
3. Therefore, all C is A.
   All mortals are farmers.
   Invalid and false

1. All thinking is dreaming.
2. All reasoning is thinking.
3. Therefore, all reasoning is dreaming.
   Valid but false

FIGURE 5.12. *Circles for the representation of simple logic problems.*

1. All *A* is *B*.
   All farmers are men.
2. All *B* is *C*.
   All men are mortal.
3. Therefore, all *C* is *A*.
   All mortals are farmers. (See Figure 5.12, middle.)

The conclusion is unsound because it does not follow from 1 and 2. These are very difficult verbal discriminations even in symbol form. They become harder when put in word form. Many of the statements made in politics, business, and everyday life seem to belong in valid syllogisms when the syllogisms are really fallacious. A political candidate, for example, may say:

Inflation leads to high taxes.
High taxes lead to tax scandals.
So, let's cut taxes!

and we may respond with, "I want lower taxes. Say, he makes good sense!"

ILLOGICAL THINKING   One of the reasons why it is hard to think logically, then, is that it is difficult to tell verbal reasoning that follows the rules of logic from that which does not. Besides that, there are other reasons why we have trouble always being logical. Our ordinary conversation is not made from a logical mold—and how dull it would be if it were!—but rather from the interplay of personal and motivational factors. With language, we have learned to sell a magazine subscription, to persuade a reluctant parent, to hail a cab, or to stimulate a mood. Seldom do we use words in order to "think straight." Furthermore, we may have received excessive training in logical confusion. A child, for example, is charged by a grown-up with, "Give me one good reason why you disobeyed me!" The frightened child cannot do so; so he lies or rationalizes until the adult is satisfied with his answer.

Then, too, life itself has a way of confronting us with illogical coincidences, such as the thunderstorm on the only day we play hooky from school. Here an *animistic* fallacy, that is, that our truancy *caused* the thunderstorm, is fostered by nature and often exploited by a moralistic parent. Society's encouragement of such fallacious reasoning is religiously systematic in some cultures and is widespread in our own, especially where cause-and-effect relationships are concerned. It not only can lead to a wrong theory of thunderstorms, it also can lead to wrong habits of reasoning which interfere with the practice of logic.

DISTORTIONS IN REASONING   Ordinarily, then, we have a strong tendency to respond to "logic"

stimuli with free, associative responses, even when we may be trying our level best to be logical. And such responses tend to distort our reasoning. Some circumstances, however, are more likely than others to evoke free associations and thus distortions in reasoning. Since logical thinking is important to all of us, we shall take a moment to look at some common distortions.

One factor is the complexity of the stimulus situation. If a logical fallacy is presented to people in a complicated way or along with a mass of complex facts and statements, they are less likely to detect it.

Another related source of distortion in reasoning is the language in which premises are expressed. An important factor in such distortion is what has been called the *atmosphere effect* [Sells, 1936]. This refers to the impression that a statement may make on a person, inclining him to give a yes or no answer quite apart from the logical implications of the statement. If, for example, the premises of a syllogism are presented in the affirmative, "All p's are q's, and all q's are t's," people tend to reject any negative conclusions containing "no" or "are not." When the premises are split, however, that is, when one is stated affirmatively and the other negatively, they tend to accept negative conclusions. Such atmosphere effects are apparently rather common; college students, at least, are amazingly subject to them.

Another important factor is what we may call the opinion effect on reasoning. As might be expected, numerous experiments have shown that emotion-producing material and words that evoke strong prejudices, beliefs, or opinions may effectively prevent discriminative, logical deductions. One of the most interesting of these is illustrated by a syllogistic test in two multiple-choice forms [Morgan and Morton, 1944]:

The first form was *symbolic;* it used neutral terms like x, y, and z. The second form was "emotionally toned"; it contained phrases that in 1942 evoked strong personal opinions about air power; for example, "Battleships are not as effective as certain other machines of destruction, since the British battleships *Prince of Wales* and *Repulse* were sunk by airplanes." Conclusions drawn by subjects in this experiment are given in Table 5.2. Conclusion 5 is the only correct answer, for the two premises are so stated as to imply jointly nothing whatever beyond what they say as separate sentences. Yet 90 per cent of the subjects accepted either conclusion 1 or 2, apparently because they already believed in air power. When opinions were lacking, as they were in the symbolic *x, y, z* form, the students favored conclusions 3 and 4 (probably because of atmosphere effect; that is, they drew negative conclusions from split negative-affirmative premises).

You would be wise to test yourself with some homemade syllogisms. See if you can distinguish the factual truth or falseness of a conclusion from the soundness or unsoundness of its logical dependence on its premises. For example:

1. All thinking is dreaming.
2. All reasoning is thinking.
3. Therefore, all reasoning is dreaming. (See Figure 5.12, bottom.)

The conclusion is false, since the basic premise is false, but the deduction from the premises is logically valid.

All too often, belief conquers logic when both contend in the same man. The causes are psychological. We know that they lie in the learning history of the individual. People are primarily "psycho-logical," not logical, even when they "reason."

REASONING BY COMPUTER High-speed computers are routinely employed to do tasks which would be tedious and time consuming for human clerks. Most jobs that such machines do are not particularly creative; machines simply work on routine problems far faster and more accurately than people can. Computers are machines which manipulate symbols, however, and it is possible to give them instructions, or programs, which will enable them to solve certain kinds of reasoning problems which involve the manipulation of symbolic mate-

TABLE 5.2. *Conclusions accepted by subjects in a test of syllogistic reasoning. One group of subjects was given two premises stated in neutral symbolic terms. Another group was given the same premises stated in emotionally toned sentences. They were then asked to check on a multiple-choice question the conclusions that could be drawn from these premises. See text for correct answer.*

	PER CENT OF SUBJECTS ACCEPTING CONCLUSION	
CONCLUSIONS	SYMBOLIC FORM	SENTENCE FORM
1. Airplanes are more effective than battleships	0	44
2. Airplanes may be more effective than battleships	11	46
3. Airplanes are not more effective than battleships	47	1
4. Airplanes may not be more effective than battleships	32	0
5. None of the above conclusions seems to follow logically	10	9

SOURCE: Modified from Morgan and Morton, 1944.

rial according to specifiable rules. For example, problems of logic and certain mathematical proofs may be solved by such programs.

The General Problem Solver (GPS) is one such problem-solving program [Newell et al., 1959]. This program has some general features similar to those of the problem-solving analysis proposed by Duncker (1945). We have seen that one of Duncker's major ideas is that a goal determines the search for functional solutions. This might be called a *means-end analysis* [Feigenbaum and Feldman, 1963]. In general terms, the General Problem Solver attempts to reach goals such as the transformation of one object or statement into another and the reduction of differences between objects or statements. If the goal cannot be reached in a few steps, the program sets up subgoals which can be solved. For very complex problems, the program has been arranged so that it will solve simpler problems and use the information gained in the solution of these problems for the solution of the more complex problem [Newell et al., 1959].

Such a creative use of the computer will, in time, probably be put to practical use. It may also serve as a model of human problem-solving processes [Newell and Simon, 1963]. We know what the computer program is designed to do and how it does it—after all, it was written by human beings—and we can analyze the behavior of a computer with a particular problem-solving program. Suppose that we give a human problem solver a problem which a computer can solve. We ask the person to think out loud about his reasoning processes as he solves the problem. If the computer and human processes are similar at a number of points, the computer can be said to be a model for certain kinds of human reasoning. Such a model is advantageous because the processes in it are known and its behavior with certain kinds of problems can be discovered and predicted. If it does serve as a model for human reasoning, we may then be able to predict the way a human being will reason out other kinds of problems.

Language and communication

We have seen that the words of our language are labels for things and concepts and that they may be incorporated into our thinking in subvocal form. Language, of course, is also employed to communicate our thinking to others. Let us see what language is made of, how it is structured, and how it is used.

We should note that several groups of students and scientists make it their business to study language. Some are interested in the sounds of speech, how they are made, how they are related to written symbols, and how speech may be improved; these are the *phoneticians*. Some are interested most in the meaning of words; these are the *semanticists*. Others are concerned with the rules of word form

and order and with habits for speaking and writing words; these are the *grammarians*. Finally, there are specialists who compare different languages and who study the history of words and languages; these are the *philologists* and *comparative linguists*.

Psychologists can profit from the knowledge supplied by these disciplines, but their interest is somewhat different. They are not concerned with the history or grammar of language, but rather with its use as a means of communication—that is, as one of the ways in which people behave, a stimulus people perceive and respond to, and something used in learning and thinking.

LANGUAGE UNITS　Language is composed of units combined in a multitude of ways. The basic units of spoken language are called *phonemes*. These are the sounds that must be distinguished in the everyday use of language. Actually, a skilled phonetician can distinguish many more sounds than those that are called phonemes, but whenever he finds sounds that are similar and are never followed by the same sound, he groups them together into one phoneme because people do not need to distinguish sounds that are always followed by different sounds.

An example will make this point clear. Consider the sound of *k* in the two words "key" and "cool." If you say these words to yourself, you will realize that the *k* sound is different in the two words. Simply notice the position of your lips when you say them. No confusion results, however, by considering these two sounds the same, for the *k* in key is never followed by the *oo* and the *k* in cool is never followed by the *e*. Consequently, though the phonetician can distinguish these two *k*'s, we do not need to pay any attention to differences between them, for the *oo* and the *e* that follow them are our cues. For that reason, the phonetician considers the two *k*'s to be one and the same phoneme.

VERBAL CONTEXT　Phonemes, then, are the essential units of spoken language. About 40 are required to transcribe accurately any variety of

English. Thus, all the sentences we speak and the thousands of words we use in making these sentences can be analyzed into about 40 units. Conversely, these units are combined into syllables, the syllables into words, words into sentences, and so on.

Frequency of units. If someone were given 40 units and told to construct a new oral language, one of the first decisions he would face would be how often to use each of the various units. He could, on the one hand, use each unit just as often as any other unit. In this way he could make the greatest use of the available units. He might, on the other hand, throw away all the units except one and use just that one unit. The result would not be a language—even the animals use more units than that—for it could convey one and only one message. Or he might take some middle course and use some units a good many times and other units only a few times.

It is this middle course that characterizes the languages that people use: some units are used much more frequently than others. Of the 40 English phonemes, 9 are used to make up more than half the sounds we produce. The most frequent sound (*i* as in "bit") is used, on the average, more than 100 times as often as the least frequent sound (*z* as in "azure"). And as you probably have observed yourself, consonant sounds occur more often than vowel sounds. Indeed, only 12 consonant sounds make up about 60 per cent of all sounds produced in speech.

If we study the way in which units are combined into words, we note the same thing. Some units tend to be used more in one part of a word than another. English words end and begin more often with consonants than with vowels. Moreover, of the consonants that begin words, more than one-half are from a group of five sounds, and of those which end words, more than one-half come from a group of eight different sounds. We use some words much more than others. It has been estimated that only 121 words make up about 60 per cent of the typical person's speech and about 45 per cent of his writing.

TABLE 5.3 *Samples of pseudo words constructed according to the statistical properties of English.*

Zero order	First order	Second order	Fourth order
yrulpzoc	stanugop	wallyoff	ricaning
ozhgpmti	vtyehulo	therares	vernalit
dlegqmnw	eincaase	chevadne	mossiant
gfujxzaq	iydewakn	nermblim	bittlers
wxpaujvb	rpitcqet	onesteva	oneticul

SOURCE: Selected from Miller, 1951.

The fact that some units and some combinations of units (words) are used more frequently than others is not simply a statistical matter. It is related to our ability to perceive and comprehend speech. Since we hear or read some units and words much more than others, we expect and anticipate them. Thus we find it easier to perceive these units than others [Howes and Solomon, 1951].

Sequence of units. Certain units not only appear more often than others, they are also more likely than others to follow certain units. That is, certain sounds tend to follow other sounds, and certain letters tend to follow other letters. Thus some *sequences* of units are more likely to occur than others. This fact helps us considerably in our perception of language. It can be illustrated by the following experiment [Miller et al., 1951]:

Subjects were shown words for very brief periods of time. The words were not those of English, but were pseudo words made up for the experiment (Table 5.3). The experimenter first constructed a list of "words" in which the letters were drawn completely at random, and presented this list to his subjects. He measured the length of visual exposure necessary for the subjects to identify the words. This list of words was called a "zero-order" list. He also used another list composed of "words" in which the letters were used as frequently as they occur in English. The letter *e*, for example, occurred as often in these words as it does in ordinary prose, and this was true of every other letter he used.

These words were "first-order" words. Another set of "second-order" words was formed in the same way as the first-order list, but in addition, each letter in these words was preceded by a given letter as often as it is preceded by that letter in English. "Third-order" and "fourth-order" words were formed by the same rules except that each letter was preceded by the combination of two letters and three letters, respectively, as often as it is in English. Examples of these words are given in Table 5.3. The words begin to look more and more like English as they progress from zero order to fourth order. But they are all nonsense words.

You can probably guess what the result of the experiment was. As the pseudo words more closely approximated the sequences of letters found in English, the subjects found it easier to perceive them correctly, and the length of exposure required became shorter and shorter. You can see exactly how the results came out in Figure 5.13. Thus the fact that English uses certain sequences of units more

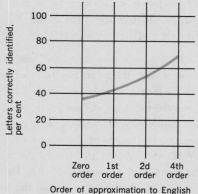

THE FACT THAT SOME SEQUENCES OF LETTERS ARE MORE COMMON IN ENGLISH THAN OTHERS HELPS US TO UNDERSTAND THE LANGUAGE

FIGURE 5.13. *The recognition of letters in pseudo words. More letters were correctly identified as the words approximated English. (Data from Miller et al., 1951.)*

than others and that we learn these over the years helps us in perceiving language.

We are now in a position to understand the term *verbal context.* To perceive speech and written language, people need to perceive not merely the isolated phonemes or letters of the language, but also the frequencies and sequences in which they appear. The fact that one sound or one sequence of sounds is more likely to occur than another gives language a verbal context that makes a difference in our perception of the units of the language. Thus, while phonemes are the units of language, they also form the context in which they themselves appear.

VOCABULARY   Earlier in the chapter we stressed the enormous number of symbols and signals made available by a language. Actually, the English language contains well over a half-million words. Probably no one knows all these words, even if the thousands of technical words used only by scholars to denote their materials and concepts are omitted. In fact, most people have a surprisingly small vocabulary—considering the number of words available—and can expand this vocabulary only under special conditions.

The number of words a person knows is usually considered to be his vocabulary; but to be more accurate, we must recognize that each person has not just one, but rather several vocabularies. First of all is the vocabulary he can *recognize.* This is almost always considerably larger than the one he can speak or write. In Chapter 2, when we traced the development of language in the child, we pointed out that children can understand and recognize words before they can use them—at least in a way that others can understand—and a similar difference continues throughout life between what is recognizable and what is usable.

A difference also exists between the vocabulary that a person *can* use and that which he ordinarily uses. This difference varies from one person to another, but we can make some estimate of it by comparing the words we use in writing a theme or an examination paper with the words we use in everyday speech. When we try hard, which we usually do if we want to impress someone with our vocabulary, we use many more words than we do when we are speaking casually.

VERBAL DIVERSIFICATION   Language offers not only a large reservoir of words to use, but a number of variations in the way these words can be put together. Students of language have worked out several indices for analyzing the structure of language as it is used by people. Two of these may be mentioned briefly.

Type-token ratio. One is the type-token ratio. It is obtained by making two counts of the words a person produces in some sample of his speech or writing. One is simply the number of words; this is the number of *tokens* produced. The second is the number of different words he produces; this is the number of *types* produced. Dividing the number of types by the number of tokens gives the type-token ratio.

This ratio tends to go along with vocabulary size, for those who have limited vocabularies use a few words more often than do people who have a larger number of words at their command. It also partly describes some of the difference between written and spoken language. Written language usually has a higher ratio than spoken language. When we write, we generally try to choose our words with greater care and thus use different words to express shades of meaning.

Verb-adjective ratio. Another index of verbal diversification which has some interesting applications is the verb-adjective ratio. As its name implies, it is formed by taking the number of verbs in a sample of speech and dividing it by the number of words which qualify the action of the verb, including both adverbs and adjectives. Consequently, the higher this ratio for a sample of speech, the more "active" it is.

As one might expect, the verb-adjective ratio varies considerably with different language samples. Scientific writing makes relatively little use of verbs and has a low ratio of about 1.3 verbs for each adjective. Writing which contains dialogue or has more human interest yields a higher ratio. A play, for example, contains about nine verbs per adjective.

THE MEANING OF LANGUAGE   We have covered a few basic points concerning the way language is structured. Now we proceed to consider its meaning when it is used to communicate messages from one person to another. The primary purpose of language, of course, is to communicate meaning. How is this done?

The meaning of a message seems to be carried in two ways. One is by common experiences with words as they have been associated with things and events. The child comes to know the meaning of such words as "chair," "doll," "food," and "bed" because these words are spoken when he is perceiving these objects directly with his senses. In this way we build up a large number of words whose meanings we think we know and understand when we communicate with each other. This kind of meaning, which can be verified by pointing to objects or events, has been called *extensional meaning*.

A second kind of meaning is derived from the first by using dictionaries or verbal equivalents. Most of us have never seen a platypus and therefore have no extensional meaning for the word, but if we look it up in the dictionary we shall find it described in terms of words, such as "small aquatic mammal" and "bill like that of a duck," for which we have extensional meanings. This kind of derived meaning has been called *intentional meaning*, and it covers the learning of concepts through definition (see page 174).

You probably take it for granted that people have somewhat different meanings in mind when they use words. That is to be expected, both because many words do not have precise meanings, and because some words have many different meanings. You might also guess that the intentional, or derived, meanings of words are not so fully agreed upon as are the extensional, or demonstrable, meanings. That is also true. You probably would not suspect, however, how much the meaning of a word varies from one person to another, even for words which most of us think we understand. Students of language have, nevertheless, demonstrated this in a quantitative way, as we shall see.

Since language serves as communication between people, and since people manage to communicate only when the listener or reader has roughly the same meaning for a word as the speaker or writer, the only practicable way to measure the meaning of a word is through agreement among people. We can devise an index of meaning, then, by determining the extent to which people agree. We can let .00 stand for no agreement at all and 1.00 stand for the maximum agreement. To obtain the index of a particular word, we establish the extent of agreement and divide that number by the maximum number of possible agreements.

One research worker who devised this kind of index asked subjects to define words extensionally by accepting or rejecting the names of persons, objects, or phenomena which were offered as examples of the class of things symbolized by a word [Johnson, 1944]. Suppose that in a study of this kind we asked 100 subjects whether or not they considered Franklin D. Roosevelt an example of the class of things covered by the word "liberal." We would then count the number of yes responses and divide by the total possible, 100. If 100 yes responses were given, or 100 no responses, we would have complete agreement among the subjects about this particular extensional definition of liberal. If only 50 yes responses were given to the question, then we would have complete disagreement, since as many subjects rejected the example as accepted it. As a matter of fact, a study conducted in this manner produced an index of agreement of only .24 in the case of Roosevelt. This represents considerable disagreement. In the case of Herbert Hoover, there was considerable agreement that he was not an example of the class of things covered by the word "liberal." The index for his name was .90.

Other methods of measuring the meaning of words, including those for measuring the meaning of concepts mentioned earlier, have been tried. In general, when words are considered one at a time, agreement about meaning is not very high.

MEANING IN CONTEXT We might thus conclude that we are not very successful in communicating meaning. Actually, we are not, but things are not so bad as they seem. Part of the reason for poor agreement on the meaning of single words is that the meaning of a word depends somewhat on the context in which it is used. Put another way, context supplies meaning. Since language is spoken and written according to certain rules, words occur in certain sequences more than in others. These sequences provide the context, and this context makes the meaning of words much more precise than it would otherwise be. How often have you heard someone exclaim, "You have quoted me out of context"? He is trying to say that you cannot tell precisely the meaning of one set of words without knowing the other words with which it is used.

Just as we were able to illustrate verbal context by building up sequences of letters and sounds, we can show the context of meaning by choosing words according to their *order* within a context. This has been done in Table 5.4. In that table, the zero-order list was constructed by choosing words at random. In the first-order sentence, words occur with about the same frequency as we expect them to occur in English. This is also true of sentences of a higher order, but in the second-order sentence, one word is preceded by another as often as we might expect it to be in English. In the third-order sentence, they are preceded by pairs of words as often as we might expect them in sequences in ordinary English, in the fourth-order sentence by triplets, and so on up to the seventh order. Finally a sample of prose is given.

The method used in constructing these sentences is an interesting one, and one which you can try at home or with your friends [Miller and Selfridge, 1950]. To obtain the second-order list, a common word, such as "he," "it," or "the," is presented to a person who is asked to use the word in a sentence. The word he uses directly after the one given him is noted and then presented to another person who is asked to use that word in a sentence. This method is repeated, using a different person each time, until a sentence as long as is desired is obtained. The assumption which is made here is that the persons asked to form sentences will use one word following another about as frequently as the two words occur together in the English language.

In the case of the third-order sentences, persons are given two words, such as "he is," "it became," "the world," and asked to use them, as presented, in a sentence. Then the word used directly after the sequence is added to it, the first word of the sequence is dropped, and the new sequence is presented to the next person to be used in a sentence. The same technique is used for fourth-order sentences, using three-word sequences; for fifth-order sentences, using four-word sequences; and so on. First-order sentences are obtained by drawing words at random from all the higher-order sentences. The resulting sentences contain words occurring with about the same frequency with which they occur in common usage. The zero-order sentences can be obtained by choosing words at random from a dictionary.

When sentences constructed in this way are examined, it is easy to see that from the low to higher orders the sentences gradually begin to convey what we ordinarily accept as meaning. The higher-order sentences look meaningful in spite of the fact that they were not said by any one person intending to say something to somebody.

We should be careful to notice here, however, that the meaning of our language is not all carried by verbal context as defined by the sequence in which words occur. By using the method we have described, we could construct sentences to the fifteenth order, to the twentieth order, and beyond, without ever producing sentences equivalent in real meaning to sentences taken from a prose text. That is, sentences which are constructed by faithfully following the statistical rules governing a language are never so meaningful as naturally constructed sentences. The reason is that, although we are accustomed to using words in certain sequences, we still have a good deal of freedom in choosing a next word even after lengthy sequences of previous words. This flexibility is useful, of course, since in order to communicate something new to another person we must be able to say something which he cannot predict with complete accuracy in advance.

TABLE 5.4. *Samples of pseudo sentences constructed according to the statistical properties of English.*

Zero order
> Betwixt trumpeter pebbly complication vigorous tipple careen obscure attractive consequence expedition pene unpunished prominence chest sweetly basin awoke photographer ungrateful

First order
> Tea realizing most so the together home and for were wanted to concert I posted he her it the walked.

Second order
> Sun was nice dormitory is I like chocolate cake but I think that book is he wants to school there.

Third order
> Family was large dark animal came roaring down the middle of my friends love books passionately very kiss is fine.

Fourth order
> Went to the movies with a man I used to go toward Harvard Square in Cambridge is mad fun for.

Fifth order
> Road in the country was insane especially in dreary rooms where they have some books to buy for studying Greek.

Seventh order
> Easy if you know how to crochet you can make a simple scarf if they knew the color that it.

Prose text
> More attention has been paid to diet but mostly in relation to disease and to the growth of young children.

SOURCE: Miller and Selfridge, 1950.

LANGUAGE AND THE WORLD VIEW We have seen that language symbols are the major mediating process used in thought. According to some, language is more than just a mediator—it is a shaper of thought [Whorf, 1956]. The theory, sometimes called the "linguistic relativity hypothesis," states that the structure of the language determines the way we are able to think about the world. In short, our world view and the relative importance given to things around us are determined by the language structure and the availability of labels for objects. For instance, Eskimo language is supposed to have three words for snow, each designating a particular type of snow. The idea of the linguistic relativity hypothesis is that the Eskimo actually thinks differently about the world of snow than a person without these labels for different kinds of snow. Some American Indian languages use nouns to designate concepts or classes of objects in ways which seem strange to us. In Hopi language, for instance, a single word suffices for all flying objects except birds [Whorf, 1956; Brown, 1958]. The hypothesis is that people using Hopi language think differently about the world of flying objects than people using other languages.

This theory has never been established convincingly. An alternative idea is simply that those discriminations and objects which are important to a group of people speaking the same language are differentiated and named. If a person speaking another language is taught the words which represent discriminations made in the new language, he can also make them [Brown, 1958].

DEFECTIVE LANGUAGE The perceptions and skills involved in producing and understanding language are rather complex, and it takes an individual many years and an almost incalculable amount of learning to acquire them. It is therefore not surprising that such a delicate and complex function should at times result in language defects. A person may be defective in one or in several of the aspects of languages: ability to read it or to comprehend it when it is spoken, ability to produce elementary phonemes or to combine them in the sequences necessary to be intelligible, or ability to use the language with a meaning that can be understood.

Some defects in a person's language ability are the result of injury or disease of the brain. These are called *aphasias,* and they are discussed in Chapter 20. Others are due to some kind of personal maladjustment. Stuttering and stammering, for example, have long been considered as stemming from emotional difficulties, although defects in functioning of the nervous system may play a part. Defects of language often appear in psychoneurotic disorders, and they are almost always prominent in the psychoses (see Chapter 14). One can, in fact, use some of the indices and relations we have described to help in the diagnosis of the psychoses, for in some forms of mental illness there is usually a distortion in the way words are connected with each other and the way they are used.

Consider the case of a female schizophrenic patient presented with a block-sorting test. The examiner asked her the question, "What is the difference between this group and that?" She replied:

Dividing by feeling your hand and calculating the rim. If I wrote on the blackboard by hand wouldn't give out anything at all, no chalk-mark. It's a certain light they leave careless with their work. It's light slatiness; and when I went out there to walk I found lots like that. Like those men working on the roof, keep slipping off. There's somebody copying that light all the time. How in God's name can a man keep spending money on a child and buy her clothes? And that's the way with Constance, and she going to school. They'll be going to fertilize her mind through our farm and get that light. My family took that up great. A woman in Missouri she worked on those children, boiled them and picked them and finished them. I like to do a work there. [Cameron and Magaret, 1951, page 510.]

This example of schizophrenic language is characteristically lacking in connectives and in precise meaning and it is filled with intrusive fragments of

THINKING AND LANGUAGE 197

unrelated topics. In brief, it does not follow very closely the rules which govern the understandable use of language. However, as in the case of all languages, the patient is usually following some rules. If one understands these rules, one can understand the speech.

SYNOPSIS AND SUMMARY

Thinking and using language, the two awesome achievements of man, are very closely linked. The symbols of language are the major mediating responses used in thinking in general and in such specific types of thought as concept formation, problem solving, creative thinking, and reasoning. When the symbols of language and thought stand for common properties of objects or events, they form the concepts which are essential to the solution of problems. Problem solving consists of manipulating the symbols of language and thought in an attempt to reach a particular goal. Creative thinking is also loosely goal directed, but the rearrangement of symbols is more difficult to follow than in problem solving. Perhaps this is because the symbols in creative thinking are not usually entirely language symbols—imagery is important—and because the rearrangement of symbols in creative thinking may be largely unconscious. In reasoning, the language symbols of thought are combined according to definite rules.

In discussing thought and language, we made the following specific points:

1. Symbols and signals are signs used in communication. Their meanings are learned by association. Words and language form a highly developed symbol system.
2. The meaning of a word or symbol is a process within the individual representing the object or thing for which the symbol stands. Such a meaning may serve as a mediating process, or connecting link, between psychological events. For instance, meaning may serve to link a series of responses or sensory events together into a unit.
3. Thinking is a sequence of symbolizing processes that represent past learning and experience. These processes consist in part of images and implicit muscle responses and also of central processes within the nervous system, but implicit language responses are the major symbolic processes.
4. Most, if not all, people experience images, and images often help thinking. Some individuals have such vivid imagery that they can recall things almost perfectly; this is called eidetic imagery. Considerable thinking, however, takes place without the benefit of images.
5. Also involved in thinking are implicit muscle movements that can be recorded with the appropriate instruments. These may be coincidental to thinking, but they may also serve as cue-producing responses that set off the next event in the thinking process.
6. A concept is a process representing a common property of objects or events. In man, language is used extensively for labeling concepts.
7. Children initially learn concepts by learning at the same time to discriminate differences and common properties among objects and to use word labels for the common properties. Once some concepts are acquired in this way, concepts may also be learned (a) by gleaning meanings from the contexts in which words are used, (b) by definition in terms of other words, and (c) by classifying objects and events.
8. Concepts may be of several sorts: simple, conjunctive, disjunctive, or relational. Several strategies of conjunctive concept formation are: simultaneous scanning, successive scanning, conservative focusing, and focus gambling.
9. Several factors affect the ease with which concepts are learned. Among them are: (a) transfer from other concepts, (b) the distinctiveness of the common elements, (c) opportunity to manipulate materials, (d) type of instructions given, and (e) simultaneous presentation of relevant information.
10. The meaning of a concept may be measured in dif-

ferent ways: (*a*) by free response, which is similar to giving a word definition of it, (*b*) by discrimination and classification of words and objects, (*c*) by word associations, and (*d*) by means of a semantic differential, which is obtained by rating the position of a concept on several scales.

11. Concepts provide the tools for problem solving.

12. Thinking is often directed; it solves or attempts to solve problems. Such problem solving requires motivation and especially a goal toward which thinking is directed. Thinking is also aided or impeded by habits previously formed, and by sets. One type of set is called functional fixedness.

13. Problems may be solved by a number of processes. Among these are: mechanical processes, understanding processes, and insight.

14. Creative thinking is frequently characterized by five stages between perception of a problem and obtaining a solution to it: (*a*) preparation, (*b*) incubation, (*c*) illumination, (*d*) evaluation, and (*e*) revision. In addition, it probably involves unconscious rearrangement of symbols.

15. Reasoning involves thinking in which elements of previous learning are combined according to well-defined rules. Most reasoning in people involves the use of words.

16. Because words tend to have equivocal or imprecise meanings, because it is often not possible to check the results of reasoning, and because various groups and societies differ in what they consider "reasonable," reasoning is often fallacious.

17. The rules of logic have been developed to avoid such incorrect reasoning. These are seldom followed, however, in everyday reasoning because (*a*) it is very difficult to discriminate logical from fallacious lines of reasoning, (*b*) our past experiences are often illogical, and (*c*) such factors as the atmosphere effect and prejudice can easily distort reasoning.

18. Computers have been programmed to solve problems, and some programs are designed as models of human problem-solving processes.

19. The spoken English language is composed of about 40 basic units called phonemes. Some of these units are used much more frequently than others. Moreover, certain sequences of units are more likely than others. The expected sequences of units aid us in the perception of language.

20. The way in which people use language can be quantified. Size of vocabulary is one measure, but the vocabulary a person recognizes is usually much larger than the one he uses. Verbal diversification is another measure; this indicates the ratio of the number of different words used to the total number used.

21. Words have two kinds of meanings, extensional and intentional. Neither kind of meaning is very clear when words are used one at a time. Meanings, however, are clarified by context, that is, by the fact that some words occur more often than others and that words tend to come in expected sequences.

22. The linguistic relativity hypothesis states that a person's perception of the world, or world view, is influenced by the language he speaks.

23. Defects in the use and understanding of language which are the result of brain injury or disease are called aphasias. In addition, emotional problems may cause disorders in the use of language.

RELATED TOPICS IN THE TEXT

CHAPTER 2 MATURATION AND DEVELOPMENT A discussion of Piaget's view of the stages of cognitive development and some facts about the development of language use are cited in this chapter.

CHAPTER 3 PRINCIPLES OF LEARNING Symbolic processes are primarily learned responses. In addition, learning can take place through thinking—that is, through the manipulation of symbolic processes. Perceptual learning shares many of the aspects of thinking.

SUGGESTIONS FOR FURTHER READING

Bartlett, F. C. *Thinking: an experimental and social study*. London: G. Allen, 1958.
A description of some recent experiments on thinking.

Brown, R. *Words and things*. New York: Free Press, 1958.
A well-written and lively account of the role of language in psychology.

Bruner, J. S., Goodnow, J. J., and Austin, G. A. *A study of thinking*. New York: Wiley, 1956. (Paperback available.)
A description and synthesis of experiments on concept formation in which strategies of concept formation are discussed.

Carroll, J. B. *Language and thought*. Englewood Cliffs, N.J.: Prentice-Hall, 1964. (Paperback.)
An introduction to thinking and language which stresses the role of language as the vehicle of thought.

Ghiselin, B. (Ed.). *The creative process: a symposium*. New York: Mentor, 1955. (Paperback.)
Selections from creative artists and scientists who talk about their own creative processes.

Johnson, D. M. *The psychology of thought and judgment*. New York: Harper & Row, 1955.
A text covering thinking and problem solving.

McKellar, P. *Imagination and thinking*. London: Cohen and West, 1957.
A discussion of various types of nondirected and creative thinking.

Miller, G. A. *Language and communication*. New York: McGraw-Hill, 1951. (Paperback available.)
A psychological textbook on language.

Thomson, R. *The psychology of thinking*. Baltimore, Md.: Penguin, 1959. (Paperback.)
An elementary textbook which covers most of the important problems in thinking.

Vinacke, W. E. *The psychology of thinking*. New York: McGraw-Hill, 1952.
A text covering experimental results on thinking and problem solving.

Wertheimer, M. *Productive thinking* (rev. ed.). New York: Harper & Row, 1959.
Contains a theoretical analysis of thinking as well as many ideas and experiments on how to solve problems.

MOTIVATION AND EMOTION

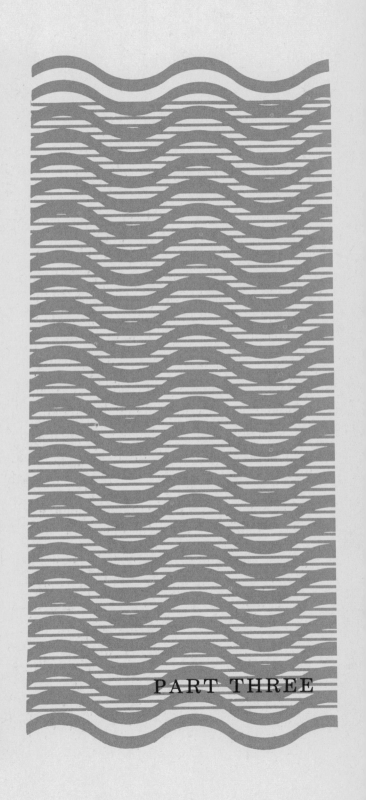

PART THREE

6

ONE MAN WANTS to be a doctor. Another strives for power in the political world. Here is a person who is ravenously hungry and, at the moment, wants nothing more than to eat. A girl is lonely; she wants friends. A man has just committed murder, and we say that his motive was revenge. These are just a few examples of the motives that play so large a part in human behavior. They run the gamut from basic wants, such as hunger and sex, to complicated long-term motives, such as political ambition or the desire to get married. We never see these wants directly, but we know they exist from the way we feel, from what people do and say, and from the common observation that people seem to work for things. In other words, we infer that a motive exists from behavior—what people and animals do.

The nature of motivation

Several hundred words in our everyday vocabulary refer to people's motives. Some of the more common synonyms are wants, striving, desire, need, motive, goal, aspiration, drive, wish, aim, ambition, hunger, thirst, love, and revenge. Each has its own connotation and is used in a certain context. Many can be defined with reasonable precision, and thus can prove useful in the scientific study of motivation. The problem of terminology is nevertheless difficult, and the student should pay special attention to the way in which terms are defined and used here.

THE MOTIVATIONAL CYCLE *Motivation* is a general term referring to states that motivate behavior, to the behavior motivated by these states, and to the goals or ends of such behavior. In other words, motivation has three aspects: motivating states, motivated behavior, and the conditions that satisfy or alleviate the motivating conditions. Each of these aspects may be regarded as a state in a cycle, for the first leads to the second, the second to the third, and the third to the first (see Figure 6.1).

The terms *motive, drive,* and *need* are most com-

MOTIVATION

TO UNDERSTAND HUMAN BEHAVIOR BETTER, TO GAIN INSIGHT INTO AND TO EXPLAIN THE ACTIONS OF PEOPLE (INCLUDING ONE'S SELF), THE STUDENT TURNS TO PSYCHOLOGY AND, ESPECIALLY, TO THE STUDY OF MOTIVATION. PRACTICAL CONSIDERATIONS ALSO LEAD TO THIS STUDY. WE DESIRE TO UNDERSTAND, TO INFLUENCE, AND TO CONTROL OUR OWN BEHAVIOR AND THAT OF OTHERS.

P. T. YOUNG

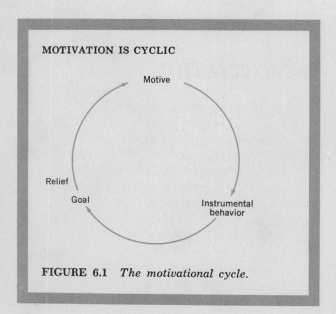

MOTIVATION IS CYCLIC

Motive

Relief

Goal

Instrumental behavior

FIGURE 6.1 *The motivational cycle.*

in part on the presence of certain hormones. The hormones seem to activate regions of the nervous system and thus are not stimuli of the sort that activate sense organs. They nevertheless constitute motivating conditions.

The second stage of the motivational cycle is the *behavior that is instigated by the motive or drive.* This behavior is usually instrumental, sooner or later, in reducing the motive or drive (see page 88). A hunger drive, for example, motivates an individual to explore for food. His exploratory behavior, therefore, is instrumental in satisfying or reducing the drive, but it is only a means toward the goal of satisfaction. Several kinds of instrumental behavior are described later in the chapter.

The third stage of the motivational cycle is the reduction or satisfaction of the drive or motive. This is ordinarily achieved by reaching some *goal.* In the thirst drive, for example, lack of water in the body is a need (first stage) motivating the individual. This need arouses exploratory behavior (second stage) to find water. The goal of drinking water when it is found (third stage) satisfies the thirst and terminates the motivational cycle until the need for water builds up again.

Goals, naturally, depend on the drive that is active. If a person is motivated by hunger, his goal is food; if he is motivated by the sex drive, his goal is sexual satisfaction; if he needs affection or companionship, his goal may be marriage, joining a club, or going to the local poolroom. These goals are *positive goals*—goals the individual approaches or attempts to reach. *Negative goals* are those which the person tries to escape from or avoid, such as dangerous or unpleasant situations.

In everyday speech, the term *incentive* is frequently used for the third stage of the motivational cycle. However, the term also implies that something is being deliberately used by someone to control motivated behavior, or to exploit motives already in existence. An experimental psychologist who wishes to have a rat learn a maze uses food as an incentive for motivating the hungry rat to learn the shortest route through the maze. An employer,

monly used to refer to the first stage. *Motive* is the most general term. It is derived from the same French and Latin roots that give us the word "motion." Motion means movement, and motive means to move in the sense of inciting, impelling, or supplying the power for movement. A motive, then, is whatever moves or incites to action. *Drive* is sometimes used in place of motive, for it has a similar connotation of being an *impetus* to behavior.

A motive or drive may arise from several causes. First, it may arise from a *need* caused by a lack of something required for the survival, health, or well-being of the individual. *Physiological needs* are due to lacks in the tissues of the body of such things as food and water. There are also needs for other things, such as companionship, prestige, and achievement. A motive or drive, secondly, may arise from a stimulus either inside or outside the organism. Hunger pangs, environmental temperatures that are too hot or too cold, painful stimulation, or even novel stimuli that attract attention—all are instances of stimuli which may be motivating. In some physiological drives, hormones in the blood may also be motivating (see page 688). The sex drive and maternal drives in animals, for example, depend

recognizing an employee's motive for money, may offer a bonus as an incentive to spur the employee to additional effort, that is, to increase the employee's motivation for doing good work.

In the basic physiological drives, goals are relatively fixed and unchangeable. If one is thirsty, for example, water is about the only goal that will do, although there are many forms in which the water may be consumed; if one is hungry, nothing but food will do. For more complex motives, however, any of several alternative goals may do. One may satisfy a need for recognition, for example, by becoming a pillar of the church, rising to eminence in politics, or becoming the best golf player in town. So, though goals must be appropriate to one's motives, the study of goals is itself a complex aspect of the study of motivation.

These three stages in motivation are illustrated strikingly by this incident which occurred in a hospital several years ago [Wilkins and Richter, 1940].

A three-year-old boy was brought to the hospital for observation because he showed certain abnormalities of physical development. After 7 days on the regular hospital diet, the boy suddenly died. Autopsy showed that the child's adrenal glands, which are located on the top of the kidneys, were abnormal. Normally the secretions of the adrenal glands keep the salt in the body from flowing out in the urine. But in this abnormal case, the boy had lost salt faster than he could replace it on the standard hospital diet. It seemed clear that the boy died of a salt deficiency.

After the boy's death, his parents reported that he had never eaten properly. Unlike most children, he hated anything sweet, but seemed to crave salty things. He eagerly licked the salt off bacon and crackers, and although he would not eat them, he would always ask for more. One day when he was about eighteen months old, he got the salt shaker off the table and began to eat the salt voraciously. From then on, whenever he came into the kitchen, he would point to the cupboard where the salt shaker was kept and scream until someone let him have the salt. By this time his parents had discovered that he would eat fairly well if they put three or four times the normal amount of salt on his food and, in addition, let him eat about a teaspoonful of plain table salt a day.

This unfortunate case illustrates well the stages of motivation as they apply to physiological drives: (1) the boy's body had a physiological need for salt; (2) this need brought about several kinds of instrumental behavior, including the attempts to get the salt shaker from the table and the cupboard; (3) the goal was salt, and once he got it his need was relieved and the craving temporarily disappeared. All motivation, of course, does not have an immediate physiological basis, and many needs, especially complex social needs, can go unsatisfied without resulting in death. Nevertheless, these three stages form the typical pattern of both simple and complex motivated behavior.

CLASSIFICATION OF MOTIVES It is convenient to divide motives into two general classes. One class consists of unlearned drives that emerge in the course of maturation. Unlearned drives, sometimes called primary drives, may be *physiological* or *general*. Physiological drives have their origin in some internal need or in a physiological condition within the body. General drives, although they are not rooted in any specific physiological need, also appear not to be learned.

The other class consists of *learned motives*, sometimes called secondary motives. Strictly speaking, motives themselves are probably never learned. Rather, through learning, previously neutral stimuli can come to arouse motive states, and the goals which satisfy motives can be modified. Learned fears, for example, involve the arousal of motive states by previously neutral stimuli. Social motives, which are especially typical of human behavior, are examples of motives involving the learning of new goals.

Physiological drives

Physiological drives may arise from any one of three causes: (1) external stimuli, (2) tissue needs, and (3) hormonal substances in the blood. In some cases, a drive may arise from a combination of these causes; in other cases, we are not yet sure of the causes. The drives we are about to consider, however, fall roughly into these three classes in the order named.

HOMEOSTASIS In order to understand physiological drives, we should know the meaning of a concept called *homeostasis* [Cannon, 1932]. This is the tendency of the body to maintain a balance among internal physiological conditions. Such a balance is essential for the individual's survival. Body temperature must not get too high or too low. Blood pressure must not rise or fall beyond certain limits. The blood must not get too acidic or alkaline; it must not contain too much carbon dioxide; it must not become too concentrated; it must have a certain amount of sugar in it. If these limits are exceeded, the individual becomes sick and he may die.

Physiologists have discovered that many homeostatic mechanisms are involved in keeping conditions within normal limits [Cannon, 1932]. Consider, for example, the control of body temperature. Normal body temperature in man is 98.6°F. The temperature usually stays near that point because the body can cool or heat itself. If a person's body temperature tends to get too high, he perspires and the resultant evaporation of liquid cools the body. If his temperature threatens to fall, he shivers and steps up his metabolism. Shivering burns the body's fuels faster and thus generates extra heat. In addition, many animals can insulate themselves against heat loss by fluffing their fur and creating a dead-air space around their skin. All that is left of this mechanism in human beings, however, is the goose pimples one gets when he is too cold.

Physiological mechanisms take care of many of the problems of maintaining a homeostatic balance, but the body also makes use of *regulatory behavior* [Richter, 1943]—behavior that has the effect of regulating internal physiological conditions—to maintain or restore the balance. Such regulatory behavior is *instrumental in satisfying physiological*

needs. When the body becomes depleted of water or food, for example, it cannot maintain a balance by calling on its physiological mechanisms. Rather, it must obtain more water and food from the outside. It does this through motivating the behavior that normally succeeds in procuring more water and food; after that, the homeostatic balance is restored. The important point, then, is that physiological drives are part of a more general physiological mechanism for maintaining homeostatic balance within the body. Now let us consider some of the principal physiological drives.

TEMPERATURE REGULATION AND PAIN Warmth, cold, and pain are senses that take part in our perception of the world, and they are treated as such in Chapter 9. They may also be regarded as occasioning drives, for they can serve as powerful motives. First, we shall consider warmth and cold, then pain.

Warmth and cold, as we have indicated, are regulated within limits by the physiological mechanisms of homeostasis. When the body is too hot, it perspires and does other things to reduce the production of heat; when it is too cold, it burns more fuel and keeps its loss of heat to a minimum. In addition, however, the individual may behave in such a way as to achieve a comfortable temperature. When too hot, he takes off clothes; when too cold, he puts them on. He raises or lowers the room temperature, opens or closes windows, and so on. In extreme conditions of hot or cold, he may exert most of his effort trying to obtain relief. Instances of this sort are so familiar that they need not be dwelt on. The important point is that the maintenance of temperature within certain limits is a strong physiological drive.

In a part of the brain known as the *hypothalamus* are areas concerned with the regulation of body temperature. We consider hypothalamic anatomy and function in detail in Chapter 20. The hypothalamus is a relatively small region at the base of the brain immediately above the back part of the mouth. It functions in emotion, thirst, hunger, sleep, and sex—indeed in almost all physiological motivation. This center probably responds directly to the temperature of the blood circulating through it by increasing or decreasing the flow of blood throughout the body.

In addition, *receptors* for warmth and cold are distributed generously over the surfaces of the body (see page 333). These receptors are so adapted to the temperature of the body that they are relatively quiescent under ordinary, comfortable circumstances. When the temperature around them becomes either too hot or too cold, however, the temperature receptors are activated. Impulses from the receptors are conveyed to the brain, which instigates efforts to relieve the discomfort.

The physiological mechanism of *pain* as a drive is similar to that for temperature regulation except that reactions to pain are much more specific. Sense organs for pain, which are probably free nerve endings, are widely distributed throughout the skin, blood vessels, and internal organs (see page 334). These sense organs are usually stimulated by some injury to the tissues of the body. The individual then strives to remove the injurious stimulus. If that cannot be done, or if it does not help, he looks for some way to relieve the pain.

The body is equipped with certain automatic mechanisms for avoiding pain. A sudden pain in a limb, for example, makes a person *reflexly* withdraw his limb from the source of stimulation. He does not have to think about it; he just withdraws, immediately and quickly. Sometimes when the source of pain is deep within the body, there is no way to withdraw from the source of injury. In such cases, the individual tries many techniques to reduce the pain. Modern pain-killing drugs are, of course, the most effective ways of helping such pain. But they can fail, and often they are not available. Then the individual may writhe, tear at his flesh, lie down, try to sleep, try not to move, or try to distract himself. Since none of these techniques is very effective, the individual may become preoccupied with his

pain and continue endlessly his efforts to reduce it. Such pain constitutes a powerful drive that channels tremendous efforts toward one goal, the relief of pain.

Now let us turn to such drives as thirst, hunger, sleep, and sex. These drives depend mainly upon tissue needs *within* the body.

THIRST   We constantly need water because we are losing it by evaporation from the skin and mouth and in the formation of urine. But what is it about the need for water that makes us thirsty and therefore motivated to drink? Thirty years ago some physiologists declared that the throat and mouth get dry when we need water, and therefore we drink to relieve unpleasant sensations in our throats [Cannon, 1934]. Actually the problem is not so simple as that.

Certainly people will report that they drink to wet the mouth, but apparently a dry mouth and thirst are two different things. There was, for example, a man who had no salivary glands [Steggarda, 1941]. His mouth was always dry, and he would often sip water just to wet his mouth. Despite the fact that his dry mouth was never a good sign of how much he needed water, he would from time to time feel thirsty. Furthermore, he was always able to drink the right amount of water to meet his biological needs.

Dryness of the mouth can be a good sign of thirst in normal people, but it is obvious that other factors must also operate to produce thirst and permit the individual to regulate his drinking in accordance with his needs. This point has been made clear by studies done on dogs [Adolph, 1941].

By careful surgery, the esophagus—the tube from the throat to the stomach—of each dog in these experiments was brought out through the skin of the neck. Then it was opened in such a way that everything the dog drank ran out of the upper part of the opening. Still the dog could be maintained by putting food and water directly into the stomach through the lower part of the opening. When the dog was offered water, it drank just about what it needed and then stopped, even though none of the water got into its body. Of course, after a while it drank again and kept repeating the process until water was put into its stomach. One important point is that the dog had some way of metering the water as it passed through the mouth, even though the water never reached the stomach and a biological, or cellular, need was not satisfied.

The next step in the experiment was to put enough water directly into the dog's stomach to satisfy its biological needs and then let it drink. When the dog drank right after its stomach was filled, it drank just about the amount it needed—as judged by the amount of water that had been lost through deprivation (see Figure 6.2). But if it had to

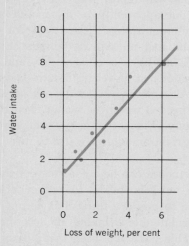

WATER INTAKE IS PROPORTIONAL TO LACK OF WATER IN THE BODY

FIGURE 6.2 *Sham drinking and water deficit. In experiments with fistulated dogs, which can drink water without any of it getting into the stomach, the amount of water lapped up in a standard experimental period is directly proportional to the amount of water that had been lost from the body through water deprivation. (After Adolph, 1941.)*

wait 15 to 30 minutes after its stomach was loaded, then it did not drink at all. So a second important point is that, after water had been in the stomach for a short time, thirst was satisfied.

What happens to make thirst go away when water is put directly into the stomach? The evidence seems to point in this direction. Lack of water makes all the cells in the body give up water. Some cells within a region of the hypothalamus are especially sensitive to loss of water. Through their connections with other parts of the brain, they can regulate thirst according to the relative amount of water in the body.

The existence of such a region has been shown by experiments in which salt solutions have been injected into the hypothalamus [Andersson, 1953]. If the injected solution is more concentrated—a hypertonic solution—than the bodily fluids, the cells in the hypothalamus lose fluid and drinking ensues. It seems as if cells in this region are like *osmoreceptors*—cells sensitive to the concentration of blood plasma—which are known to control the secretion of the antidiuretic hormone which regulates the loss of water through the kidneys [Verney, 1947].

We may conclude, then, that dryness of the mouth and throat serves as a cue telling us when we are thirsty; the cues direct behavior toward an appropriate goal. The thirst drive, however, is probably basically due to the concentration of the blood plasma bathing special regions of the hypothalamus. Mouth-metering—a measure of the amount of water passed through the mouth—and dilution of the blood plasma seem to be the factors which stop drinking when water is obtained. Mouth-metering regulates the length of a drinking session, and cells in the hypothalamus, by sensing the concentration of the blood plasma, cause drinking to stop when this concentration is optimum.

HUNGER The need for food is as obvious as the need for water. The body is always using up materials in growth, in the repair of tissues, and in the

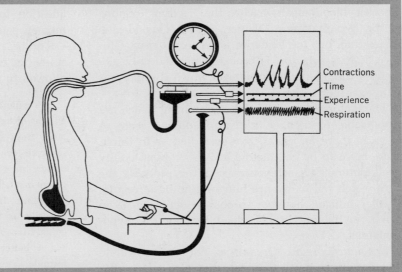

HUNGER PANGS SEEM TO BE DUE TO CONTRACTIONS OF THE STOMACH MUSCLES

FIGURE 6.3 *Hunger pangs and contractions of the stomach. The subject swallows a balloon connected with a marker so that a record is made of stomach contractions. He also presses a key whenever he feels a hunger pang. The record shows that spasms of the stomach are correlated with the subject's experience of hunger. (After Cannon, 1934.)*

storage of reserve supplies. But most important to remember is the fact that every function of our bodies from heartbeat to thinking requires energy, and this energy must ultimately come from the metabolism of food.

When people need food, they usually report that they are hungry. For some, hunger means a feeling of strong contractions in the stomach. But for others, there may be no particular sensation of stomach contractions, just a general feeling of weakness and lightheadedness. Some people have both kinds of feeling at once. Physiologists have shown in some ingenious experiments that hunger and stomach contractions very often are associated [Cannon, 1934].

Cannon and his colleagues trained human subjects to swallow a rubber balloon which was attached to the end of a long thin rubber tube (see Figure 6.3). The experimenter blew up the balloon until it gently filled the stomach. Then to the end of the tube he attached a recording pen that marked a moving tape every time the contracting stomach compressed the air in the balloon. The subject could also make a second pen mark on the paper by pressing a telegraph key every time he felt a pang of hunger. So it was easy to tell whether stomach contractions and hunger sensations occurred at the same time or not. They did. Not only was that so, but the strength of the stomach contractions and the degree of hunger both increased as time elapsed after the last meal.

But stomach contractions are not the whole story. First of all, some people claim they never feel stomach contractions, but still they report the experience of hunger. Second, and perhaps more convincing, are facts obtained from people who have had their entire stomachs removed [Wangensteen and Carlson, 1931]. They have no stomach contractions, of course, but they still get hungry. The same thing shows up in rats whose stomachs are removed [Tsang, 1938]. These animals eat food eagerly, they get restless when it is time to eat, and they learn mazes for food rewards just like normal rats. Hunger therefore exists without the stomach or stomach contractions; so we must look to other factors for the explanation of hunger. Unfortunately, the exact nature of the other factors is not known. Many kinds of chemical changes take place in the body when an individual is in need of food. Some of them undoubtedly are important in hunger too. For instance, it has been proposed that a low level of glucose—blood sugar—excites the "feeding" regions of the hypothalamus [Mayer, 1955]. This idea is interesting, but the evidence is not conclusive. Glucose, if it is a factor, is probably not the only element of the internal environment which is important in hunger motivation.

The factors in the internal environment which are responsible for hunger motivation do not seem so clear as those for thirst. However, just as in thirst, there seem to be cue factors and more basic bodily need factors. Stomach contractions are probably the cues which tell us we are hungry; the basic regulation of hunger, however, probably depends, as in thirst, on factors in the blood bathing the hypothalamus.

Specific hungers. Organisms not only regulate when and how much they eat, they also select what they eat. Given a chance, animals and men balance their diets and eat approximately what they need of proteins, fats, carbohydrates, vitamins, and minerals. Organisms therefore are not motivated merely by a lack of food; rather they are very specifically motivated for many particular foods. As a matter of fact, it has been questioned whether any such thing as general hunger exists apart from the sum total of specific hungers for the various food substances.

But we are still far enough from answering this question to warrant treating hunger and specific hungers separately.

The best way to explain specific hungers is to describe an experiment in which human infants were allowed to select their own diets [Davis, 1928]:

The experimenter took three infants from six to twelve months of age and allowed them to eat all their food from large trays containing from 12 to 20 different foods in separate containers. The babies made quite a mess of things, but they did manage to eat balanced diets. At any given meal, a baby might eat all vegetable or all butter. Sometimes, he would eat the same food for days. But over a period of time, the infants balanced out their diets by going from one food to another so that they grew as well as, or better than, infants fed according to a dietitian's formula.

The same sort of results came out of experiments with rats [Pilgrim and Patton, 1947].

The rats were given each component of the diet in a separate container (see Figure 6.4). Many of them were able to select diets that permitted them to grow as well as, or better than, rats fed on stock diets. But about one-third of the rats failed to select beneficially. In most of these cases, however, the failure was due to the fact that the

FIGURE 6.4 *Apparatus used in the study of specific hungers in rats. Each tube contains a solution of a dietary component. The amount of each component selected by the rat in any particular period can be read from the graduated markings on the tubes. (C. P. Richter.)*

rats would not eat the particular protein offered to them. If another protein was substituted for that one, the animals would often eat balanced diets and grow normally.

Experiments such as these show that animals and human beings possess mechanisms that enable them to select the kinds of food they need.

Need and food preference. In the case of the boy who suffered from salt deficiency, we see an excellent example of how a specific need produces a food preference. The same sort of need can be produced experimentally in rats by surgical removal of the adrenal glands [Richter, 1936]. (These glands are described in Chapter 19.) When the adrenal glands are removed, the rats lose salt constantly, and therefore they must eat extra amounts of it if they are to live. This they do. They will also maintain themselves by drinking large amounts of salt water in place of plain tap water. Increasing their need for salt increases their motivation for salt, and as a result they ingest much more of it than normal, unmotivated rats (see Figure 6.5).

Other specific hungers can be developed by putting the individual into a state of need [Scott and Verney, 1949]. For example, if all vitamin B is left out of the diet, the individual will develop a strong hunger for B vitamins. In pregnancy, the individual needs more fats, proteins, and certain minerals, and thus is strongly motivated to eat foods which provide them. Sometimes the motivation becomes so strong that it assumes the character of a pathological craving, and there have been extraordinary cases of pregnant women who ate plaster off the walls or ate mud, presumably to get some of the minerals they needed but could not, or did not, obtain in their ordinary diets.

In addition to specific hungers for particular foods, needs can produce *specific food aversions.* For example, the parathyroid glands situated on the thyroid glands in the neck secrete a hormone that controls the level of calcium and phosphorus in the body. When the parathyroid glands are removed, calcium levels fall and phosphorus accumulates, so that more calcium and less phosphorus are

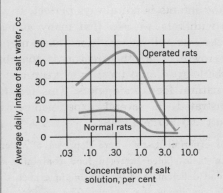

PREFERENCE OR AVERSION FOR SALT DEPENDS UPON THE AMOUNT OF SALT RETAINED IN THE BODY

FIGURE 6.5 *Salt preferences of normal rats and of rats after removal of the adrenal glands. The operated animals drank much larger quantities of salt solution until the salt concentration offered them became quite high. Plain water was available at all times. (After Bare, 1949.)*

needed. It is interesting to note that animals from which the parathyroid glands have been removed eat calcium avidly but avoid phosphorus with equal fervor.

Organisms also avoid foods on which they have just been satiated [Young, 1944]. If an animal's need for protein is satisfied, it will avoid protein, although it may still be quite hungry and highly motivated to eat a fat or carbohydrate (sugar). Thus *specific satiations* exist as well as specific hungers.

Habit and food preference. If organisms tend to select foods that alleviate their needs, why then do people often eat inappropriate foods? We can all think of cases in which this happens. A diabetic patient, whose blood sugar may be dangerously high, may aggravate his condition by eating large amounts of sugar. Other people have been known to eat sweets avidly, neglecting proteins and fats, to the detriment of their health.

There appear to be two reasons for such harmful food preferences. One is that dietary self-selection in animals and infants is not always perfect. In the experiments with rats, we saw that many animals did not select foods well enough to maintain normal health and growth. The other reason is that bad habits may be learned, and these habits can distort or override natural food preferences. This fact has been demonstrated in several experiments with animals [Scott and Verney, 1949].

In one such experiment, rats were deprived of vitamin B_1, then given their choice between food containing the vitamin and food deficient in it. As one might expect, they chose the food containing the vitamin. The experimenter, however, had mixed some licorice with this food. Licorice, which has a strong flavor, is not ordinarily preferred by rats. After considerable training in this situation, the rats were presented with a choice between the vitamin-deficient food with licorice and the vitamin-rich food without licorice. In other words, the licorice was switched from one food to the other. The switch fooled the rats. Now they preferred the food without the vitamin, even though they desperately needed the vitamin. The rats had learned to associate the strong flavor of licorice with the kind of food they needed, and when the licorice was in the wrong food they were misled.

In this particular experiment, the rats eventually learned that a switch had been made and changed their preferences back to the vitamin-containing food. It is important, however, that for a time they were victims of a habit that ran counter to their natural food preferences. Situations in daily living are seldom so simple as they were in this experiment, and people have many opportunities to acquire habitual preferences for food.

SLEEP   Sleep is typical of physiological drives in almost every way except that it involves passive resting of the body rather than an active striving.

We do, however, consider the need for sleep a physiological need comparable to those for water and for food. Occasionally, however, a person who does not believe that sleep is a need tries to get along without it [Katz and Landis, 1935].

One young man, for example, was convinced that sleep was only a bad habit, and resolved to prove he could stay awake indefinitely. He sat by a time clock, punching it every 10 minutes for 7 days, when his vigil had to be terminated because he appeared to be on the verge of a breakdown. Actually, he slept quite a bit the last few days in the 10-minute intervals and often, toward the end, right through some of them. He had reached the point, however, at which he would not believe he had slept and was convinced that his clock was tampered with in some mysterious way.

The need for sleep certainly is real. Yet we cannot put our finger on any accumulation of waste products or special chemicals in the body that helps bring on sleep. Scientists have transfused blood from sleepy to waking dogs, but it did not make them sleepy [Kleitman, 1939]. Siamese twins with joint circulation do not always sleep at the same time (see Figure 6.6). Since, in these cases, sleep occurred independently of the condition of the blood, we are led to believe that sleep is regulated by centers in the brain. Such centers are discussed in Chapter 20. For the present, all we can say is that the physiological conditions that constitute the need for sleep are poorly understood.

SEX   Sexual motivation is unique as a biological motive. It is very powerful; yet the survival of the individual does not depend upon it in any sense. We still have much to learn, particularly about sexual behavior in our own society, but as matters stand now we have excellent information on the sexual behavior of a wide variety of different animals as well as of human beings within a wide variety of societies. Sexual behavior can be understood in terms of two main factors: sex hormones and habits acquired through learning.

The sex hormones. The testis of the male and the ovary of the female secrete *hormones* that are re-

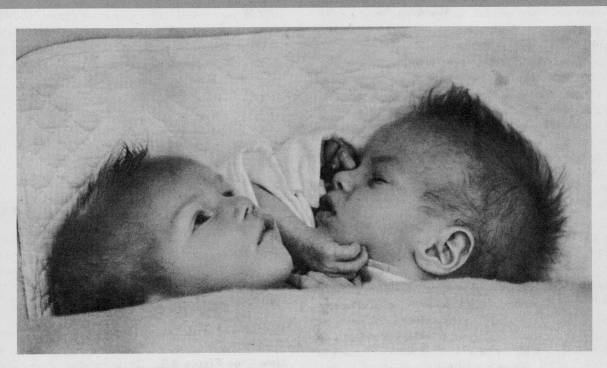

FIGURE 6.6 *A two-headed baby. One head sleeps while the other is awake, indicating that sleep is controlled by the brain rather than by factors in the blood.* (Life Magazine, © 1955 Time, Inc.)

sponsible for the development of the secondary sex characteristics of the body as well as for much of the sexual behavior of the two sexes. When the sex glands mature at puberty, the masculine and feminine body forms, hair distribution, vocal characteristics, and adult sex organs also develop. At the same time, in animals as well as in human beings, interest in the opposite sex typically develops in a sharp spurt. If the sex glands fail to develop properly or are removed in experimental animals, very few of the typical sex characteristics will show up in the individual.

One point should be clear. The sex hormones work no magic, especially in the case of human beings. They are not solely responsible for sexual

behavior—they only help. When sexual motivation is low, extra sex hormones are not likely to help. Neither is it true that homosexuality occurs because an individual has the wrong sex hormones. Giving a homosexual an extra amount of hormone appropriate to his or her own biological sex will more likely increase the homosexuality than reverse it, if it does anything at all [Beach, 1949].

Among lower animals, such as the rat, the sex hormones are more crucial than among the higher animals, such as chimpanzees and men [Beach, 1947a]. The spayed female rat will never mate again unless given hormones artificially. The male may continue to mate for a short while after castration, but he then becomes incapable of sexual motivation unless restored with sex hormones. The comparable story for human beings is not so clear. In some cases among both sexes, removal of the sex glands makes sexual motivation disappear; but in equal numbers of cases, sexual motivation is unaffected by castration or ovariectomy. The picture is all the more complicated by the fact that men and women who are sexually impotent or frigid may still have perfectly normal supplies of sex hormones. The information we have on monkeys and chimpanzees, however, indicates that the higher animals really do not depend crucially on sex hormones. The males in these species can be castrated without noticeable effect on sexual motivation. And it is clear that female monkeys and chimpanzees show sexual motivation at times when their hormonal supply is very low. This is not true among the lower female animals.

So the sex hormones are important in the development of physical sexual characteristics and sexual motivation. Their importance in sexual behavior, however, is much greater among the lower animals than among the higher animals.

Habits and sexual motivation. While the sex hormones are relatively less important in the sexual behavior of higher animals, *habit* and *experience* are relatively more important than in lower animals [Beach, 1947b]. This may be illustrated by comparing the rat and the monkey. Rats raised in isolation, for example, mate normally the first time they are tested. The male rat may be inhibited by emotional situations, but the female resists all but the most severe disturbances to a remarkable degree.

In monkeys and chimpanzees, the story is quite different [Yerkes, 1943; Harlow, 1962]. The male has to learn to mate, usually at the hands of an experienced female. The female chimpanzee, on the other hand, learns to use sexual behavior for nonsexual purposes. For example, she will often win out against a much larger male in competition for food by presenting herself sexually to the male and then making off with the food as the male focuses his attention on her.

Many studies have established that among human beings sexual habits vary widely according to the level of society an individual comes from, and that such habits are quite different in widely differing societies. It has been shown, for example, that premarital intercourse is practiced more among the lower socioeconomic classes than among the higher ones [Kinsey et al., 1948]. The reverse is true of masturbation. Studies of different cultures have shown also that some societies strongly encourage homosexual practices among adolescents, whereas other cultures are even more severe than our own in the restrictions they place on homosexuality [Ford and Beach, 1951].

Habit, then, is much more important in the sexual behavior of man and higher animals than it is among the lower animals. Habit can cause sexuality to persist even when sex hormones are absent. And, of course, habit frequently determines the way in which human beings express their sexual motivation and the kinds of sexual outlets they prefer.

MATERNAL DRIVE   In Chapter 2 we described the maternal behavior of some animals, such as the rat, as instinctive behavior. In these animals, but not in human beings, such behavior is an unlearned pattern that is characteristic of the species. Maternal behavior is motivated behavior arising, like sex behavior, from a physiological drive. Indeed, instinctive behavior is characteristically motivated behavior (see Figure 6.7).

The maternal drive has its basis in a combination of hormones secreted during pregnancy and shortly thereafter. One of the important hormones in the combination is *prolactin,* a product of the pituitary gland. The secretion of prolactin is stimulated by the presence of a fetus in the uterus. Prolactin in turn stimulates the mammary glands, which supply milk for nursing the young, but it is also important in maternal behavior in lower animals. When it is injected into a virgin female rat that has been given the young of another rat, the injected rat will accept the young and care for them in much the same way that the natural mother would [Riddle et al., 1935].

General drives

If we look about us at the everyday behavior of adults, children, and animals, we can hardly escape the conclusion that relatively little of such behavior is directly motivated by physiological drives. True, people say they work to provide food and shelter for themselves, which may be a way of saying they are working to satisfy physiological drives. Yet a great deal that they do cannot be explained at all on this basis.

Think of the amount of time people spend just looking at things—at newspapers, books, television, plays, sports, canyons, mountains, and "points of interest." Think of the amount of activity that goes into playing games, skiing, boating, hiking, hunting, and touring. Most of this looking and moving about is not connected in any obvious way with the physiological drives. Neither is the play of kittens, nor the romping and whooping of children.

Despite the lack of any obvious physiological basis for such drives, some psychologists have tried to find a connection. In some cases, they have suc-

ceeded, as we shall see. Moreover, they have been able to show that a number of complex social motives are indeed derived from more basic drives, including the physiological drives. Increasing evidence, however, points to the existence of some basic unlearned drives which are not physiological drives in the sense we have used. As yet, no satisfactory term for these drives has been coined, so we are calling them "general drives," just to have a name for them. They include drives for activity, for perceiving the world, for exploring and manipulating things, for contact with other people and things; they also include some aspects of the fear drive. In some cases, they have a connection with physiological drives; in others, they do not. All of them, however, seem to be basic, unlearned drives that play an important part in normal behavior.

Many of the general motives are included in the concept of *competence*. As used here, competence refers to "the process whereby the animal or child learns to interact effectively with his environment" [White, 1959]. Exploration, activity, curiosity, and manipulative motives are ways in which a person

FIGURE 6.7 *Instinctive maternal behavior. A white-footed mouse hovers over her young of only a few hours, protecting them instinctively. Instinct, too, has dictated to her the necessity for and the intricacies of the feather and straw nest she has built. (Tom McHugh, Photo Researchers, Inc.)*

comes to be effective in interacting with the environment. Perhaps the term *effectance motivation* might serve for motives in this section [White, 1959].

ACTIVITY   One of the drives that is generally characteristic of all species is the drive for bodily activity. Both human beings and animals spend a good deal of time moving about for no apparent reason except that it satisfies a drive for activity. Appearances, however, may be deceiving, for activity sometimes can be explained by the presence of a physiological drive.

In animals, the presence of a physiological drive causes an increase of activity. Generally, whenever an animal (or human being) is hungry, thirsty, or in physiological need, it becomes more active. It runs, paces, sniffs, or explores its environment. Such changes in activity accompanying a physiological drive have been studied extensively [Reed, 1947].

One technique is to put an animal in a cage so con-

structed that it revolves when the animal walks. A counter mounted on the side of the cage counts the number of revolutions made in any particular period of time. Figure 6.8 shows the record of running activity of a female rat during, between, and after periods of high sexual need (heat). At the peak of heat, the rat ran hundreds or even thousands of revolutions a day, but between periods of heat, activity greatly diminished. The sex glands were removed by spaying when the rat was about 122 days of age, and the sex cycle was thus abolished. Thereafter, activity was permanently reduced to a low level.

Similar records have been obtained in the presence of other drives such as thirst and hunger. So long as the organism remains in good health, activity increases with the presence of a physiological drive.

Activity may also have its origin in sensory stimulation [Hall, 1956]. Lights, horns, or any other strong stimulus will generally rouse an organism and make it more active. To a certain extent, the reason for this is obvious: the stimulation is annoying or disturbing. On the other hand, the stimulation

FEMALE RATS IN SEXUAL HEAT ARE USUALLY VERY ACTIVE

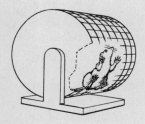

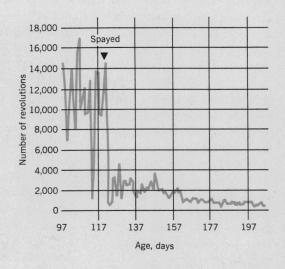

FIGURE 6.8   *Activity and sexual motivation. The normal female rat shows peaks of activity when in sexual heat, which occurs about every fourth day. After the sex glands are removed by spaying, activity drops to a low level. (Richter, 1927.)*

does not need to be disturbing: it may merely be novel and arouse the interest or curiosity of the individual. Such curiosity is itself a drive.

Finally, we come to the question of whether or not activity as such, with no physiological drive or sensory stimulation present, is a drive. The evidence shows that it is. One piece of evidence for this conclusion is that activity can be pent up by deprivation [Hill, 1956].

Groups of rats were confined in small cages where they had enough room to stand up or lie down, but not enough to walk around. One group was confined for 5 hours, another for 24 hours, and a third for 46½ hours. A control group was not confined at all. After confinement, the experimental animals were placed in activity wheels, and their activity was measured for a period of an hour and a half. The amount of activity measured in this time varied with the duration of the period of confinement. Those confined for the longest time were the most active; the control group was least active.

A second kind of evidence for concluding that activity is a drive shows that activity itself can act as a reinforcer for learning a habit [Kagan and Berkun, 1954].

Two rats, an experimental subject and a control, were placed in running wheels and studied simultaneously. Each rat was provided with a lever which it could freely press throughout the period of observation. The control animal's lever, when pressed, did nothing but provide a record of lever pressing. The experimental animal's lever, on the other hand, released the brakes on both wheels so that both animals could run. By pushing the lever, the experimental animal released these brakes for a period of 30 seconds. At the end of the 30-second period, the brakes were reapplied until the experimental animal again pushed its lever.

With this experimental design, both animals had the same opportunity for running in their respective wheels. For the experimental animal, however, the opportunity to run could be a reinforcement for its lever pressing. Was it? The experimental animal pushed the lever significantly more —in some cases two or three times more—than the control animal. It appears then that running in the wheel was itself a reinforcement which satisfied an activity drive.

FEAR Fear as a reaction to environmental situations is discussed in Chapter 7. Here, however, we should pause to note that fear must be considered a drive simply because it motivates behavior. It motivates one to try to escape a fear-producing situation or object, in other words, a negative goal. Fear is so powerful a drive that it may, as we shall see, interfere with the satisfaction of other drives.

We cannot always tell when fear is present, especially in sophisticated organisms that have learned to disguise it. Two general signs, however, may be taken as an indication of fear. One is some kind of withdrawal response—some attempt to escape or to avoid a situation. The other is some overt emotional response, such as defecation, urination, or crying. Hence these may be used as objective measures of emotional behavior.

Many fears are learned, but some appear as unlearned reactions to situations in which the individual finds himself. In general, the situations that provoke unlearned fears in animals and children involve strange noises, strange sights, and strange objects. Infants less than two years of age tend to show fear when they are presented with a strange object or a loud noise (see page 244). Young chimpanzees similarly show fear when they first see certain strange objects, even the face of a human being. Rats also are fearful, as indicated by copious defecation and urination, when first placed in a strange enclosure, especially if it is relatively large. Hence we can say with reasonable assurance that strange or novel situations are the principal causes of fear in young or naïve organisms. This point should be kept in mind as we consider curiosity and exploratory drives.

CURIOSITY Several years ago it was found that a bright light has drive properties for a rat in a box. If things were so arranged that a light shining overhead could be turned off by pushing a lever in the box, the rat quickly learned to push the lever. It was thought, therefore, that light was somehow annoying to the rat—perhaps fear-producing. However, it has been shown that animals—in this case mice, but we

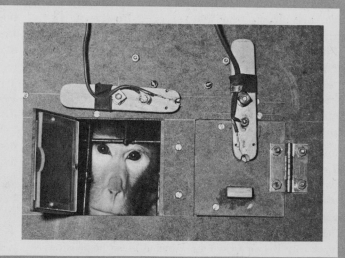

FIGURE 6.9 *Monkey peeping out of the apparatus used to measure curiosity motivation. Monkeys were reinforced for pushing one panel with a look out of the experimental chamber. The reinforced response increased in strength, while the nonreinforced response declined in frequency. (H. F. Harlow, Primate Laboratory, University of Wisconsin, 1953.)*

have no reason to believe it makes a difference—can just as easily be trained to turn a light on [Kish, 1955]. In fact, they can be taught to push a lever to produce almost any kind of novel stimulation, such as clicks of a switch, noises from a relay, or movement of a platform. Sometimes a period of habituation is required—a period in which the subjects get used to the situation, possibly to get over their fear—but after that, the novel stimulation is reinforcing.

This interest in novel stimulation has been called a *curiosity drive*. It has been demonstrated in a variety of experiments with animals as well as in casual observations of children and adults. Rats, after habituation of fear, will explore new mazes or areas in which they are placed, as well as strange objects in their environment. Dogs, monkeys, and children often approach and explore certain new things around them. For animals, the opportunity to explore is often reinforcing; they readily learn to operate levers, run down alleys, or do other things merely for the sake of exploration, as shown in the following experiments [Butler, 1953, 1954].

Monkeys were confined in a closed box which had two small opaque doors on one side (see Figure 6.9); different

stimulus cards were attached to the inside of the doors. One of the stimulus cards was positive, and when the monkey pushed this one, the door opened and he was allowed to look out of the enclosed box. The other stimulus card, the negative one, was on a locked door. If being allowed to look out is reinforcing—if it satisfies a motive—the correct response should increase in strength and the other response should decrease in strength. This simple discrimination, with looking as reinforcement, was readily learned. Furthermore, the type of scene which the monkey saw when he looked out was important. If another monkey, or a moving object, such as a toy train, was seen, high rates of response resulted. Looking out at an empty room resulted in responding, but the rate was lower.

A curiosity drive, like other drives, can be satisfied. Interest in a novel object or situation tends to diminish after some time has been spent with it. The following experiment demonstrates this satiation of the curiosity drive [Welker, 1956]:

Chimpanzees were presented successively with different novel objects, such as pieces of wood of different shapes, sticks that could be moved, lights that could be switched on and off, a chain, and so on. The number of times each chimp manipulated the object or made other observable responses to it was recorded for successive 5-second periods. Each set of objects was presented for 6 minutes each day, and again on successive days. When the experiment was over, the number of 5-second periods in which the chimp made some response to each set of objects was counted. It was clear that interest was highest at the beginning of the period and waned steadily during the succeeding minutes (see Figure 6.10). When the object was presented again the next day, interest was rearoused, though not quite so much as on the preceding day, and then it gradually waned.

This sort of thing, of course, is exactly what happens when we provide children with toys. The novelty of the toy at first arouses great interest, but the novelty soon wears off. It is interesting that experiments with animals permit the conclusion that such a curiosity drive, like physiological drives, is an unlearned drive that increases with deprivation and decreases with satisfaction.

MANIPULATIVE DRIVES It is quite difficult, if not impossible, to separate what is done in exploring a novel situation from what is experienced. That is to say, we have not as yet determined whether different drives are involved, on the one hand, in just looking at or experiencing one's environment and, on the other hand, in manipulating it. So it is not possible to say whether there is a manipulative drive distinct from a curiosity or exploratory drive. We do have experiments, however, which show that a drive to manipulate objects is a relatively strong one which can serve to motivate learning. Here is an example [Harlow and McClearn, 1954]:

Three monkeys were given seven problems to learn. In each problem two screw eyes were placed on a board in front of the monkey. One of the eyes could be removed from the board; the other could not. Each member of the pair was of a different color. For example, in the first problem a red screw was removable and a green one was not. Other color pairs in successive problems were brown-yellow, pink-blue, black-orange, white-orchid, maple-cream, and light green–dark blue. In each case, the first-named color was removable. The monkey was scored correct if he removed the removable eye without attempting to remove the other one. Removal of the screw eye was the only

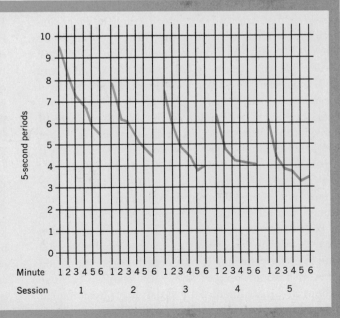

CHIMPANZEES LIKE TO PLAY WITH NOVEL OBJECTS, BUT SOON LOSE INTEREST IN THEM

FIGURE 6.10 *Curiosity drive in chimpanzees. The number of 5-second periods out of 6 minutes each day during which a chimpanzee made some response to a novel set of objects. Note that interest is highest at the beginning of the period and then wanes. (Welker, 1956.)*

reinforcement the monkey got. The monkeys learned to make the discrimination reasonably well, thereby demonstrating that this simple discrimination could be learned without any motivation or reinforcement except the manipulation of the screw eyes.

These few, among many experiments, show the existence of a drive or drives variously called curiosity drive, exploratory drive, or manipulatory drive. The experiments have been done on animals because an experimenter can know the conditions under which animals have been raised and can control precisely the conditions of experimentation; this cannot be done with children. From these experiments, however, we can be reasonably sure that the comparable drives we have all casually observed in human beings are unlearned and are of considerable importance in accounting for the motivation of behavior.

AFFECTIONAL DRIVE We would all agree, without much argument, that love is a powerful motive in human affairs. We love our parents, our brothers and sisters, our wives and husbands, our children, our friends, and our pets. And we love them to such a degree that almost every story, play, or magazine article intended to portray the things people do or work for has love as a major theme.

What is this thing called love? Where members of the opposite sex are concerned, it often has a large sexual component. Leaving this aside, however, love or affection for others is still a drive of considerable importance. And the question is, What is this affectional drive? How does it originate? Is it innate or learned? Toward what is it directed?

Origin of affectional drive. As in the case of other drives not rooted in physiological needs or hormones, the affectional drive may develop from one or both of two sources. It may be an unlearned drive that, given the opportunity, emerges in the normal course of maturation. It may, on the other hand, be learned through experience with people, because people are instrumental in satisfying physiological drives for food, drink, and so forth. These two alternatives, of course, do not need to be mutually exclusive, just as maturation and learning are not mutually exclusive. It is possible that the drive is unlearned, but that the particular objects of affection are largely learned. Indeed, so far as we know now, this is the correct view. But to see how we arrive at this conclusion, let us consider the scientific evidence.

To study the origin of the affectional drive, it would be logical to observe the development of the drive in the human infant from birth onward. As in the study of many similar problems, however, we do not have sufficient opportunity to control the experience of the human infant. In addition, the human infant is so slow to develop its motor abilities that it is not capable at an early age of giving us measurable responses to various situations. As one investigator put it, "By the time the human infant's motor responses can be precisely measured, the antecedent determining conditions cannot be defined, having been lost in a jumble and jungle of confounded variables" [Harlow, 1958].

For these reasons, we turn again to animal subjects. The baby monkey is a very suitable subject, not only because it resembles the human infant in its form and response to other members of its species, but because its motor capabilities develop quite early. Within 2 to 10 days after birth, the baby monkey moves around on its own and manipulates objects; we are thus able to obtain a measure of what it does and does not respond to. The baby monkey can be suckled on the bottle, and thus can be brought up without any contact with other monkeys or with human beings. The following summarizes briefly a series of experiments on the development of affectional drive in baby monkeys [Harlow, 1958]:

The monkeys were raised singly in cages designed to provide a comfortable environment and to take adequate care of bodily needs. In one experiment, each cage was equipped with two mother surrogates. One mother surrogate was a cylindrical wire-mesh tube with a block of wood at the head (see Figure 6.11). This was called the "wire

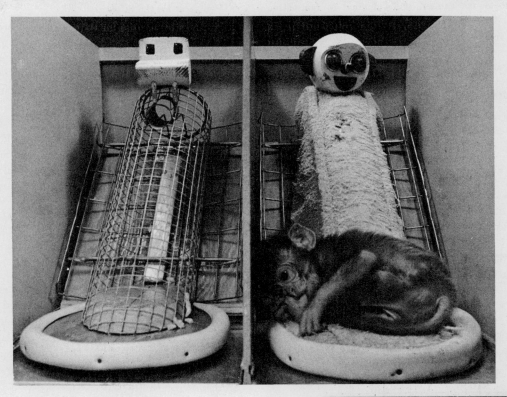

FIGURE 6.11 *Mother surrogates made of wire and of cloth used in experiments on the affectional motive in monkeys. Above, a baby monkey clings to a cloth surrogate mother on which it is not fed; at right, the baby monkey maintains contact with the cloth surrogate mother while feeding from the wire mother's bottle. (H. F. Harlow, Primate Laboratory, University of Wisconsin.)*

mother." The other "was made from a block of wood, covered with sponge rubber, and sheathed in tan cotton terry cloth." This was called the "cloth mother," and it resembled a real mother much more than the wire mother

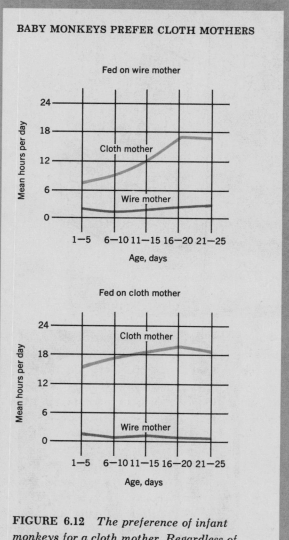

FIGURE 6.12 *The preference of infant monkeys for a cloth mother. Regardless of whether they are fed on cloth or wire mothers, infant monkeys prefer to cling to cloth mothers. (After Harlow, 1958.)*

did. Behind each mother was a light bulb that provided radiant heat for the infant.

Either "mother" could be outfitted with a nursing bottle placed in the center of its "breast." For one group of monkeys the bottles were placed on the cloth mothers, and for another group the bottles were placed on the wire mothers. Measurements were made of the amount of time spent with each mother. Figure 6.12 shows the results. As might be expected, those nursing on cloth mothers spent most of their time with the cloth mother and very little time with the wire mother. Those nursing on wire mothers spent *relatively* more time with the wire mother than did the first group, but from the very beginning they spent *more* time with the cloth mother than they did with the wire mother, and as the experiment progressed, they spent more and more time with the cloth mother. Hence babies in both groups showed a strong preference for the cloth mother surrogate.

This experiment brings out two interesting points. The first is that the monkeys seemed to have a drive to have contact with, or to be near, a mother. This was beyond any physiological drive for food and water, for they spent 15 hours or more a day with a "mother" when only an hour or so was sufficient for feeding. The second point is that the choice of a mother was not associated with feeding. If the affectional drive for a mother were learned through association with feeding, one would expect those nursing on wire mothers to prefer the wire mother; yet they spent more time with the cloth mother. Apparently, there was an unlearned tendency to seek "contact comfort" with something resembling a natural mother.

Fear, curiosity, and affectional drives. Other experiments tell us how fear, curiosity, and affectional drives may conflict with one another [Harlow, 1958].

In a series of tests on the monkeys raised with mother surrogates, an infant monkey was placed in an open-field situation, a room 6 feet square, with a 6-foot ceiling, designed to evoke both fear and exploratory drives (see Figure 6.13). The room had in it a number of strange objects that usually elicit exploration and manipulation in the

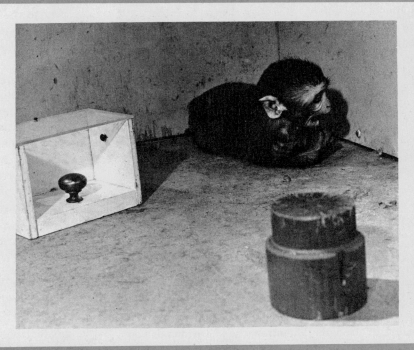

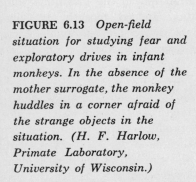

FIGURE 6.13 *Open-field situation for studying fear and exploratory drives in infant monkeys. In the absence of the mother surrogate, the monkey huddles in a corner afraid of the strange objects in the situation. (H. F. Harlow, Primate Laboratory, University of Wisconsin.)*

infant monkey. The size of the room and the strangeness of the objects could also be expected to make the animal somewhat fearful. In some tests in this situation, there was a mother surrogate; in others, there was not.

The presence or absence of a "mother" made a great difference. In her presence, indices of emotionality, based on vocalization, crouching, rocking, and sucking, were cut in half. The infant also came to use the mother as a base of operations. The infant would alternately cling to or manipulate the mother and venture out to explore the room and the objects in it, then return to the mother. The mother was a haven of safety that helped to allay fear in the strange situation, thus freeing the infant from a conflict between fear and curiosity drives.

This experiment illustrates the interplay of affectional, fear, and exploratory drives. Fear and curiosity, we saw earlier, are conflicting drives in a novel situation. When fear is the stronger drive, it reduces curiosity and exploration. Conversely, if fear is somehow reduced, curiosity drives can take over and dominate behavior. Fear may be reduced by habituation, or becoming accustomed to the fear-provoking situation. It may be reduced, too, by the presence of an affectional object. Such an object seems to provide a "feeling of security" that speeds the habituation of fear and permits curiosity to prevail over fear. The object thus provides support for the satisfaction of curiosity drives.

This picture, derived from experiments, fits in well with casual observation. Kittens venture out from their mother to play, but they usually remain in her vicinity and return to her periodically. The human infant, after being with the mother for a while, plays happily in her vicinity, but returns frequently to tug at her apron strings. Left alone, especially in a strange situation, the infant is likely to stop playing and become afraid.

In summary, present evidence leads us to the following conclusions about the affectional drive.

The drive makes its appearance relatively early in the life of an infant. It is not learned; rather, it appears in the normal course of maturation. It is not necessarily associated with feeding or with the satisfaction of physiological needs. It is a drive to have contact with, or to be near, some object that provides "contact comfort." How much the object must resemble another individual we do not know; perhaps it need only be soft and warm. The affectional object allays fear in strange situations, providing a "feeling of security," and it supports the curiosity drive.

Deprivation

At any given moment in an individual's life, some drives are quiescent or at a low ebb, while others are relatively strong. Those which are strong usually produce behavior that satisfies them; in the meantime, other drives are being deprived and are increasing in strength. The strengths of various drives are thus in a state of flux, some waxing because they have been deprived, others waning because they have been satisfied.

Several factors enter into this constantly changing pattern. In the first place, after a drive such as hunger or thirst has been temporarily satisfied, it takes time for the drive again to build up enough strength to dominate behavior. This sequence is established in the physiological economy of the body and results in natural cycles or rhythms. Second, both man and nature impose schedules on the satisfaction of drives. Food, water, and other means of satisfying drives are available only at certain times and places, and we must therefore wait for these opportunities to satisfy our drives. In an abundant economy, these times and places are reasonably convenient, so that drives are not deprived for any lengthy period; hence they do not become excessively strong before they can be satisfied. Third, there is a natural conflict between certain drives. We cannot eat and sleep at the same time; one must wait for the other. In novel situations, fear

and curiosity are in conflict, and one drive must give way to the other. Finally, economic and social conditions often conspire to defeat the satisfaction of certain drives and cause them to grow more and more intense.

All these conditions of deprivation, except the last, are of little practical consequence. It may take a child some time to learn that he must wait for his meals, that he must go to the bathroom, or that he cannot immediately have whatever he wants. But he eventually learns, and in the meantime suffers no great deprivation. Indeed, most of us manage mild deprivation of drives for reasonable periods without important consequences.

DEPRIVATION, MOTIVATION, AND BEHAVIOR

Deprivation is one of the most common ways of inducing motive states. Lack of food, water, or sleep, for instance, will produce drives toward achieving these ends. The degree of deprivation is, within limits, related to the strength of the motive state—the greater the deprivation, the greater the drive.

Up to a point, increasing amounts of deprivation, and hence increasing drive states, produce increases in the strength and effectiveness of performance; in other words, some drives—sleep is an obvious exception—energize behavior. This general rule has been stated in several theories of behavior, and one well-known expression of the relationship between drive and performance states that drive strength multiplies with the strength of habits to produce increased performance strength (drive × habit = performance strength) [Hull, 1943].

Beyond a certain point, however, increasing amounts of deprivation and motive strength produce a decrease in the effectiveness of performance (see Figure 6.14). Such a thing as too much motivation does seem to exist. The decrease in the effectiveness of performance may come about for several reasons. In complex situations which require a shift of response and a sorting out of responses, the dominant response may be so increased in strength by motivation that the person cannot shift to a more appropriate response—he becomes fixated. In other situations, high degrees of deprivation and motivation may increase the strength of competing or interfering responses—emotional responses such as temper tantrums, for example. Both effects of very high degrees of deprivation have been illustrated in experiments with problem solving by chimpanzees [Birch, 1945]. Any solution to the problem of raking in food from outside the cage with a stick was interfered with by high degrees of deprivation. The highly deprived chimpanzees could not shift to responses which were appropriate, and they had many emotional outbursts. Studies of semistarvation in man also illustrate these effects of very high levels of deprivation. Food dominates the thoughts of semistarved people; if they are asked to solve abstract problems, their performance is likely to suffer.

Thus mild deprivations usually improve behavior, whereas severe deprivations can have deleterious effects upon performance. Let us see, in more detail, some of the effects of severe deprivation in man.

SEMISTARVATION IN MAN One study of extreme deprivation in man was conducted during World War II on a group of conscientious objectors who volunteered to submit to 6 months of semistarvation [Keys et al., 1950].

The subjects were placed on a diet so restricted that they lost, on the average, more than 20 per cent of their weight during the 6-month period. They were intensely hungry all the time. They were not on this regimen long before food, and the thought of food, came to dominate their lives and to submerge all other drives. They became relatively inactive, giving up almost all their former recreational activities. Their sex drives were weakened; their romances broke up. They became silent and relatively unsociable, regarding outsiders with hostility and suspicion. They lost their sense of humor, no longer finding anything very funny. In short, they lost interest in everything except food. They talked mostly about eating, and they loved to read anything about food, including cookbooks. They dreamed of food and of breaking their diets. One subject went so far as to steal some food.

We may conclude then that when a drive such as hunger is exceedingly strong, it pervades all behavior, dominating the life of the person and overriding all other drives. This confirms the anecdotal reports from societies where food is chronically short and from areas that have suffered famine. In

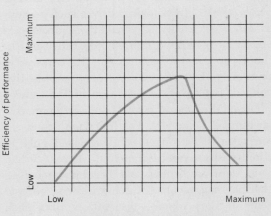

AN OPTIMUM LEVEL OF MOTIVATION SEEMS TO MAKE FOR PEAK EFFICIENCY OF PERFORMANCE

FIGURE 6.14 *The relationship between the amount of motivation (deprivation) and the efficiency of performance. Note that this is a very general relationship and will vary from task to task and motive to motive. (Modified from P. T. Young,* Motivation and emotion. Wiley, 1961.)

Western societies, we do not see such effects of hunger because few people ever suffer severe deprivation of the hunger drive. In our society, however, certain drives are for one reason or another unsatisfied over a long period of time in a substantial number of individuals. These drives, which include the sex drive, the curiosity drive, the drive for novel stimulation and exploration, and the affectional drive can, therefore, be expected to have some practical importance in influencing behavior.

COMPARATIVE STRENGTH OF DRIVES In attempting to understand human behavior, we should like to know which drives are most important in controlling behavior. Are men motivated most by fear, by hunger, by affection, or by what? If there were a simple answer to this question, what a person would do in a situation would be relatively easy to predict, and such an answer would be of great practical value. Unfortunately, the answer depends on several factors.

One is individual differences among people. Some people never get so hungry as others; some do not have the same curiosity, fear, or affectional drive as others. So there is no one answer for everybody.

Another variable, and probably most important, is the degree of deprivation of a drive. Naturally, if a drive is fairly well satisfied, it is not very strong. In a society where physiological drives such as hunger and thirst are easily satisfied, these drives are not going to be very important, simply because they never build up any great strength. In a poverty-stricken society, however, where many people live in prolonged and severe deprivation of the hunger drive, hunger can be the most powerful motive shaping human behavior. The question, then, of which drive is the strongest can be asked only in connection with severely deprived drives. When drives are deprived, then, and become almost as strong as they can become, which are the strongest?

We know from casual observation that such drives as exploration, curiosity, or affection can sometimes be stronger than the drives of hunger or fear. Otherwise men would not risk their lives to scale unclimbed mountains, to explore new territory, or to protect those they love. This sort of casual observation, however, is not very satisfactory to the scientist. Unfortunately, there is no experimental evidence on human beings, and again we must turn to animals. Several years ago, the strengths of the maternal drive, thirst, hunger, sex (female), sex (male), and exploratory drive were compared in rats when each was at its peak strength [Warden, 1931]. The results were exactly in the order named above; that is, the maternal drive was the strongest, and the exploratory drive was the weakest.

Perhaps the most interesting thing about this comparison is that the maternal drive was found to be stronger than hunger or thirst, even when these latter drives were, through deprivation, extremely strong. Whether this result would hold for human beings or not, we have no way of knowing, but it shows that even in an animal as lowly as the rat, such an "unselfish" drive as the maternal drive can be stronger than the so-called "self-preservation" drives of hunger and thirst.

Learned motives

A world of difference exists between the motives of a monkey and those of a man, or between those of a child and those of an adult. The drives we have been discussing, such as hunger, thirst, curiosity, and affection, are all present in the human adult, but there are others as well. Adults seem to be motivated by such things as power, status, money, achievement, and social approval—to name just a few. What is the difference, we may ask, between the drives that emerge through normal maturation and the motives that prevail in the conduct of human affairs? A large part of the difference, surely, is due to learning.

In addition to its effect in modifying the expression of physiological or primary drives, learning has a hand in motivation in several ways. First, through one type of learning—classical conditioning—previously neutral stimuli can come to arouse drive states. This happens when a motive state is paired with a neutral stimulus. For instance, neutral stimuli which are paired with fear-producing situations become capable of arousing fear. The motive state aroused by the neutral stimulus is often called a *learned* or *secondary drive.*

Second, through learning, new goals which satisfy a motive can be acquired. Such new learned goals are often called *secondary goals,* a concept that is related to secondary reinforcement which emphasizes the reinforcement of learned responses rather than the learning of new goals (see Chapter 3). If we look at a situation from a learning point of view, rather than from a motivational point of view, secondary goals, when attained, may reinforce responses and are then called "secondary reinforcers."

Secondary goals may be acquired by classical conditioning when some condition regularly precedes a primary goal. This preceding condition may then itself become a goal. Put another way, a stimulus or situation which is regularly connected with a primary goal can become a secondary goal. If, for example, a mother picks up her baby in order to feed him each time he cries because of hunger, the baby in time acquires the goal of being picked up and may cry to be picked up even when he is not hungry. Thus, *secondary goals* may be acquired when neutral stimuli are paired with incentives; *learned* or *secondary drives* are acquired when neutral stimuli are paired with drive states.

Secondary goals may also be acquired by instrumental learning (see Chapter 3). If a person is consistently reinforced for certain actions and verbalized thoughts, these actions and thoughts will become strong. Suppose that reinforcement is given for actions and verbalized thoughts which are examples of a theme. For instance, achievement motivation, and certain other complex human motives, may develop this way; a child is reinforced for making "achievement" statements—"I want to go to college"—or for achievement actions—getting good grades. Thus a general theme is reinforced and

a secondary goal, achievement in this case, is learned.

LEARNED OR SECONDARY DRIVES As we have seen in Chapter 3, there are several kinds of learning. One of these is called *classical conditioning.* Three elements are involved in the conditioning process: an unconditioned response, an unconditioned stimulus, and a conditioned stimulus. The unconditioned response is ordinarily an unlearned response to the unconditioned stimulus. The conditioned stimulus is some stimulus that has little or no effect on the individual prior to conditioning. During conditioning, however, it is paired, that is, presented along with, the unconditioned stimulus. When the two stimuli are presented together—it may be once or dozens of times—the conditioned stimulus acquires the ability to elicit a response that is much like the unconditioned response.

The conditioning process may be illustrated by the conditioning of a fear response (see Chapter 7). An electrical shock, which is slightly painful, produces an unlearned fear response in both man and animals. The shock serves as an unconditioned stimulus for the unconditioned response, fear in this case. By pairing the shock with some otherwise harmless stimulus—a bell, a light, or even the sight of a box—we can soon obtain a conditioned fear response to the previously innocuous stimulus, as shown by the following experiment [Miller, 1948a]:

White rats, one at a time, were placed in a white box separated from a black box by a door (see Figure 6.15). In the floor of the white compartment was a grill through which shock could be applied. First, each rat was placed in the white box for a 60-second period, during which no stimulus was applied. Then, for a period of 60 seconds, brief shocks were given every 5 seconds. At the end of this period, the door between the compartments was opened, and the shock turned on steadily. By running into the black box, the rat could escape the shock. This sequence was repeated on 10 different occasions; *after that the shock was not used again.*

On five subsequent occasions, rats were placed in the

AN ACQUIRED FEAR OF A WHITE BOX
MOTIVATES LEARNING TO
ESCAPE INTO A BLACK BOX

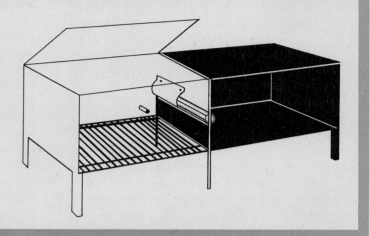

FIGURE 6.15 *Apparatus for studying acquired fears in rats. (After Miller, 1948a.)*

white box with the door open. As one might expect, fear conditioning to the white box was strong enough to motivate them to run immediately to the black box. Following these five trials, the door was closed, but it could be opened if the rat turned a wheel just over the door. In trying to escape, rats turned this wheel accidentally and thus discovered the means of escape. This general procedure was repeated for 16 trials. During the course of these trials, the rats learned to turn the wheel more and more promptly. After they had learned the wheel-turning response well, the wheel was adjusted so that it no longer opened the door. Instead, a lever could be depressed to open the door. The rats quickly learned this response too.

The experiment demonstrates that the fear drive can be conditioned to other stimuli, in this case, to the white box. The conditioned stimulus then becomes an incentive—a negative incentive—motivating the organism to learn habits for getting away from the incentive. In other words, this experiment had two stages: classical conditioning of fear and a test for fear based on instrumental learning.

The result of shocking the rat in the white box has been called a *learned* or *secondary drive*, which is a convenient shorthand for describing the phenomenon, but it is not literally correct. The drive involved, fear, was not learned; it was the unlearned response to the shock. What was new, and hence learned, was the significance of the white box. This now evoked the fear drive, though it did not do so before conditioning. The fear drive is thus evoked by a previously neutral stimulus, and it motivates the learning of new responses—wheel turning and lever pressing.

The process is typical. Most of the things we now fear as adults we did not fear as infants. We learned to fear them by a conditioning process. These learned fears, in many cases, are highly motivating and cause us to learn new habits. In Chapter 7, we shall see other examples of learned fears and consider in more detail the ways in which fear may be motivating.

The essence of the learning of a secondary drive is that a stimulus which has been paired with a primary drive state will come to elicit the drive. Fear is one example; some aspects of hunger motivation constitute another. In an experiment with hunger, satiated rats would eat when they were placed in a cage in which they had been fed when hungry [Danziger, 1951]. Ordinarily, they would not eat in the satiated state, but stimuli which had been paired with the hunger drive evoked eating.

SECONDARY GOALS   The learning of secondary goals by classical conditioning can be illustrated by some experiments performed on chimpanzees [Wolfe, 1936].

The animals were taught how to get a grape or a raisin by putting a poker chip in a small vending machine, called a Chimpomat (see Figure 6.16). The experimenter simply showed a hungry chimpanzee how to insert the chip into the slot of the Chimpomat and collect his reward at the bottom. The chimpanzees learned this operation very quickly. What is more important for our purposes is the fact that after this initial learning, the chimpanzees clearly came to *value* the chips if they could be traded in for food treats. In one part of the study, the experimenter had the chimpanzees pull a heavily weighted box into their cages in order to get a poker chip hidden in it. As a matter of fact, the chimpanzees would pull in the weighted boxes to get chips even when they could not spend them immediately. They simply hoarded large numbers of chips and waited patiently for the chance to spend their hoard.

Later, the experimenter complicated the lives of the chimpanzees even more by teaching them to use a red chip to get food, a blue one to get water, and a white one to get out of their cages and have the freedom to run around. Then the chimpanzees would work hardest for the particular chip that would satisfy their dominant need at the moment.

The parallel between the poker chips and money is obvious, for the chimpanzees were working for poker chips in almost the same way people work for money. Money, indeed, is a secondary goal which we learn to value because it can be used to satisfy simple drives, at first for candy, a bottle of pop, or admission to the movies, and later for other things which themselves are learned as secondary goals. The principle, however, is not limited to money. Almost any thing or situation that is consistently associated with the satisfaction of primary drives will be learned as a secondary goal. The principle applies not only to money and things, but also to somewhat fuzzier goals, such as status, achievement, and values.

Some of the values one acquires by learning involve other people, and some do not. Those which do involve other people are called *social values*. The chimpanzees in the preceding experiment learned to value poker chips. A carpenter comes to value his tools, a sailor his ship and the sea, a child its toys, a soldier his gun, and a farmer his land. One can readily multiply this list of *things* people come to value. With little trouble, however, one can also think of many social values: law observance, cleanliness, proper dress, success in school, honesty, courtesy, sexual morality, respect for one's superiors, and so on. Such social values govern relations between people, what they strive for, what

FIGURE 6.16 *A chimpanzee using tokens to obtain food. The chimpanzee has learned to place poker chips in the machine to obtain food—in this case, fruit. (Yerkes Laboratories of Primate Biology, Inc., Henry W. Nissen, photographer.)*

they fight for, and many of the complex details of human affairs.

A person tends to acquire social values because, from the moment of his birth, other people have so much to do with the satisfaction of his needs to eat, to be warm, to be dry, or to be in a comfortable position. Thus the mother becomes an important and valued person for the child. A little later, when the child no longer needs so much physical care, he still must depend upon parents, brothers and sisters, playmates, and others for many of his needs. These people determine where and when he shall play, where he shall go, what clothes he shall wear, what toys he shall have, when he shall sleep, whether he shall get some candy, and so on. It is no wonder that he rapidly learns a host of social values and goals.

GENERALIZATION AND FIXATION In the classical conditioning that goes on in the development of secondary drives and goals, two processes are sometimes important.

One is *generalization*, which we have dealt with in detail in Chapter 3. Here let us simply redefine it and point out its significance in the modification of motives. Generalization is the tendency to respond in the same way to all situations that are in some degree similar. This is a bit circular, because in practice we are forced to consider situations similar that are responded to in the same way. But let us take the example of the rat that has been conditioned to fear a white box. If, as a result of that conditioning, the rat now displays fear when placed in a gray box, or a larger box, or a box of a different shape, we say that generalization has taken place. The rat is giving the same fear response to situations that are somewhat similar, even though different. Or suppose that the chimpanzee taught to operate the Chimpomat keeps on working the apparatus just the same when it is delivering marbles as when it vends poker chips. Again we would say that the learned response has generalized to objects that are somewhat similar to, but different from, those in the original learning.

The process of generalization accounts for some of the things observed in complex motivated behavior. A person who is desperately afraid of going near the ocean may have generalized from a childhood experience of nearly drowning in a bathtub. Or a person who is highly motivated to please people, whether they are teachers, strangers on a bus, or anybody else, may merely be generalizing from his experience with his father, who was difficult to please and who regularly resorted to punishment whenever he was displeased. It is not difficult to think of other examples from one's own experience.

Generalization is characteristic of most learned responses. Once a response has been learned, it will be made to other objects or situations that are not exactly like the original one. Generalization is particularly characteristic of learned fears. A fear acquired in one situation usually generalizes to many others. Only through additional learning, in which an individual learns to discriminate one situation from another, is it possible to restrict generalization to things that are very similar to the one involved in original learning. The phenomenon of generalization thus accounts for many of our responses to situations and goals when no good reason for them is otherwise apparent.

Fixation is a second process to consider. In some respects, it is the opposite of generalization. As we use the term, it refers to the tendency to value certain goals, when alternative ones might do just as well. When an organism, in learning to satisfy a drive, has repeatedly found one particular object to be satisfying, it may come to prefer that object and to refuse others that might satisfy it just as well. Again let us take some examples.

Food is our general goal when we are hungry; yet many varieties of food can satisfy hunger. If a rat, for example, is fed for a long time on pellets, it will not usually want to change to powdered food, even though the powder is exactly the same food in a slightly different form. Children who have been brought up on vegetables usually do not care for hamburger, though some of us have learned exactly the reverse preference. Examples of this kind can be found in our preferences for companions, for weather, for entertainment, for housing, and so on. Several goals may be equally useful in satisfying a drive, but because certain ones have been attained in the past, we come to prefer them to the others.

SUBSTITUTION OF DRIVES Psychologists who have experimented with secondary goals in animals and children have noted that such goals do not continue to be goals very long unless they are backed up by the satisfaction of primary drives. If, for example, we do not pay off a chimpanzee's poker chips with food at regular intervals, the chimpanzee soon loses interest in working for poker chips. Similarly, if the rat conditioned to fear in the white box does not get a shock once in a while, it gradually loses its drive to escape from the box. This is not strange, of course. We are all familiar with similar cases in human affairs. Interest in money or other things is soon dissipated if these goods become worthless and do not satisfy a motive.

On the other hand, organisms often continue to work for some goals after they have lost any significance in satisfying the more conspicuous drives of hunger, thirst, and the like. The poor boy who earned his first pennies to ward off hunger and discomfort often continues to work day and night at amassing a large fortune long after he has acquired enough money to meet his physical needs. A businessman who approaches retirement age with ample reserves may insist on staying on the job even though he does not need to work any more. Indeed, in a society such as ours, where most physiological needs are met, a great deal of almost everyone's effort is devoted to goals that have little to do with the satisfaction of primary drives. Why?

We can as yet give no sure answer to the question. One proposal is that some secondary goals, once acquired, become *functionally autonomous,* which is to say, they simply go on functioning on their own without being reinforced by the satisfaction of physiological drives [Allport, 1937]. This proposal, however, probably begs the question, and it was offered before we learned of the great power

of the so-called "general drives." What seems more plausible now is that one drive can support or substitute for another. A goal originally learned because it was associated with the satisfaction of one drive may later satisfy another, less conspicuous drive.

An example should make this point clear. A penniless boy who becomes a millionaire starts out with a bundle of drives, both physiological and general. To stave off hunger, he starts working, and money becomes a secondary goal. In his work, however, he finds some satisfaction for his activity drive, and since the work provides all sorts of novel situations, he also indulges his curiosity drive. The work brings him in close relationship with men who become his friends, and thus it may also satisfy his affectional drive. Other factors may be operating, too, but these are most illustrative. After he has made his million, he is still motivated to work simply because the work now satisfies other drives that are strong and not so easily satisfied as the need for food and shelter. Thus the things he learned to do originally to satisfy one drive now satisfy others. Of course, he may keep on saying to himself, out of habit, that he is still motivated to make money, but he may simply be unaware of his true motives. This points to the complex nature of human motivation.

Complex motives

Having studied the physiological and general drives, and some of the ways in which learning plays a part in motivation, we are now in a position to consider the complex motives encountered in people every day as they go about their work and play. We can expect to see many secondary goals acquired in the course of learning how to attain primary goals. We can also expect to find drives and goals connected in diverse ways so that several secondary goals are related to a single primary drive and, conversely, several drives may be satisfied by a single goal. Finally, we can expect to see that instrumental learning plays a part in the development of some complex motives.

This interlacing of drives and goals makes the problem of classifying complex motives difficult if not impossible. It would be nice if we could simply list and classify all the motives found in man. Indeed, psychologists have devised a number of different classifications, one of which is described in Chapter 13 (see page 466). Such classifications are useful for particular purposes—for making up personality tests, for counseling people with personal or vocational problems, and so on—but they are largely arbitrary. Drives and goals may be connected in too many ways, and each individual combines them uniquely. Two individuals with the same goal, for example, may be satisfying quite different drives; those with the same drive may satisfy it with different goals.

For this reason it is best not to attempt here to classify complex human motives. Instead, we shall consider a limited number of representative motives and see how they are derived from primary drives and learned goals. Even the items on this limited list are not mutually exclusive, for each has something in common with one or more of the others. The list, however, gives us a general picture of some of the common human motives.

AFFILIATION By and large, human beings are gregarious creatures. Most of their waking hours are spent with other individuals—parents, family, friends, neighbors, club members, and so on. Modern society, of course, throws people together in work, entertainment, and living, but that condition does not cause these affiliative tendencies. People in primitive societies are also gregarious. And almost all human beings seek the company of others even when there is no particular pressure to do so.

The basis of one kind of affiliation, marriage, is not hard to understand, for the sex drive plays an important part in it. Marriage is partly a means of satisfying the sex drive, but it helps satisfy many other needs as well, including both physiological and general drives. One of these is the affectional drive, which enters into many kinds of affiliation. To affiliate with clubs, churches, or certain prestigious organizations may also satisfy other complex motives, such as the status motive. In any case, affiliation with other people is a goal that satisfies, or can satisfy, many different drives. The motive to affiliate is therefore found almost universally in human cultures. (It is also characteristic of many animals.)

Closely related to affiliation, and probably a subvariety of it, is the *dependency* need—that is, the need or motive to depend on others, to have someone to look up to, someone to turn to for help, someone to be accepted and loved by. Almost everyone has it in some degree. Others, a few, have it to such a degree that they can hardly do anything without depending on someone else for help or support.

The dependency motive arises in part from training in infancy and childhood. We all come into the world helpless and must depend upon our parents throughout the years of infancy, childhood, and adolescence for the satisfaction of many of our primary drives, for decisions about right and wrong, and for control of much of our behavior. Thus their presence, support, and help become secondary goals for us. When we eventually leave home and parents, we do not easily shed this dependency. We remain dependent on them, or find someone else to represent them. Adults, of course, seldom have the extreme dependency of a child, but few, if any, are able to rid themselves completely of the need to depend upon others.

SOCIAL APPROVAL Another common motive is to seek social approval for the things we do and to avoid doing things that evoke social disapproval. In the extreme, this motive becomes one of compulsive conformity to the norms set by the group a person is in. He tries all the time to determine what is approved and what is not, and does his best to act accordingly.

This motive, too, has its roots in childhood training when parents establish what is right and wrong for the child to do. A child learns to please his parents out of hope for the satisfaction of other drives, and perhaps also out of fear of punishment. This desire to please generalizes easily to other people. Indeed, when the child goes to school and moves into adolescence, he finds again that he can be punished and ostracized if he fails to please teachers and associates; or conversely, he finds that he can more easily get the things he wants if he wins his associates' approval. Social approval thus is learned as a generalized secondary goal.

STATUS   Most people are motivated to achieve some status among their fellowmen. At its minimum, this is a motive to be thought well of, to have a respectable standing among the people one knows, and not to be considered inferior. At its extreme, it can be a desire to achieve the highest possible status in one's community, one's profession, or within some other frame of reference. In between, it is a desire to know just where one stands in the status system, to know who is up and who is down, and to behave accordingly. Status systems vary from one group to another. A person's particular status motives depend not only on his own makeup but also on the group he happens to be in.

Status motives may take several different forms. One is to achieve a *rank* in the hierarchy of the group. Efforts to achieve such a rank can be observed not only among members of the rigidly stratified military profession but also in most human societies. It has also been observed in groups of animals living together [Schjelderup-Ebbe, 1935]. Common barnyard hens, for example, quickly establish a "pecking order" among themselves. The most dominant hen may peck most of the other hens. The least dominant hen, on the other hand, is pecked by all other hens but has no pecking rights of her own. In between, in relatively fixed rank, are hens which can peck those below them but not those above.

Such a pattern of pecking and ranking is almost universal in human relationships. We see it in groups of children playing together, in the size of offices and desks of businessmen, in the seating of guests at a formal luncheon, and in numerous little details of everyday life.

Other closely related examples of status motives are those for *prestige* and for *power*. The need for prestige is the need to feel better than other persons with whom one compares oneself. In daily life there are many ways in which prestige is sought and achieved. Children of five or six may consider a pair of roller skates, a new dress, or a cowboy suit a symbol of prestige. A little later, athletic prowess enters the picture as a way of achieving prestige. Among adults such symbols as dress, money, automobiles, homes, and the like are regarded as ways of feeling better than the other fellow.

The need for *power* is similar to, but not quite the same thing as, the need for prestige. Some people shun or ignore prestige, yet aspire to power over their fellowmen. Think, for example, of the businessman who quietly and inconspicuously builds up control of an industrial empire; or consider the professional politician who holds no public office but "pulls the strings" that move the officeholder. Such individuals are displaying a desire for status, but in a different way from those who aspire to achieve prestige.

Each group, community, and society, whether primitive or modern, has its own status system. How such a system arises and what function it serves are discussed in Chapter 16. So far as the individual is concerned, status is a secondary goal that stands for the satisfaction of many primary drives. Persons of a particular status can expect to make a certain amount of money, live in a certain style, and be treated in certain ways. Thus status more or less guarantees that an individual may be able to satisfy other drives. It also frees a person from the fear that he might lose some of the satisfactions that go along with his status.

SECURITY   A feeling of security, or lack of it, is also an important motive, especially in modern, complex societies. The feeling involves being able to hold on to what one has, being sure that one will be able to fare as well in the future as in the past. Conversely, insecurity is a haunting fear that "things may not last," that one may lose what he now has. Insecurity is thus based on fear and especially fear of not being able to satisfy one's other motives. A person may be insecure about almost anything—his status, his wife's affections, his money, social approval for what he does, or his ability to earn a living and hence his ability to satisfy his primary drives.

In a society as highly organized as Western culture, a person depends upon many other people and upon conditions in general for his security. This means, of course, that a person's security may often be threatened or lost through no fault of his own or without any opportunity to regain it. For that reason, security takes on a special importance in people's lives—more so, in many cases, than any of the other motives we have discussed—and it is responsible for much personal unhappiness as well as social unrest. In Chapter 18, we shall see that the security motive is uppermost in the minds of employed workers and may be more important than wages, status, and other motives for working.

ACHIEVEMENT   In some cultures, particularly that of the middle class in the United States, achievement is a powerful motive. This is the motive to accomplish something, to succeed at what one undertakes, and to avoid failure. We are taught that in the land of opportunity everyone can succeed at something, whether it is making money, becoming a professional person, or going into politics, if only he works hard at it. And success is highly prized. Parents prod their children to make good marks in school, then to go on to college, and finally to make good at some business or profession. The picture is very different in many other cultures and in non-middle-class groups within our culture.

The strength of the achievement motive, like that of other complex motives, varies from individual to individual. In some people, the drive to be success-

ful at what they undertake is tremendously strong—they have a *very high level* of aspiration—whereas in others, it is relatively weak. On the whole, though, it is a pervasive motive in middle-class American youths and adults.

The strength of the motive depends, in part, on how successful one has been. A person usually cannot aspire to success as an athlete, scholar, or musician unless he has already had some success along the way. If he has had only modest success, he is likely to set a lower goal for himself than if he has had outstanding success.

In general, people set their goals just a little higher than the level they are sure of attaining, and this is healthy. In some people, however, there is a large discrepancy between the *level of aspiration* and the *level of performance,* probably because they have learned to set goals that gain for them the approval of their parents and associates. In others, the level of aspiration falls considerably below the capacity to achieve. This discrepancy often occurs because individuals have learned to fear failure. They do not set their goals high for fear of not attaining them.

The achievement motive has been studied intensively [McClelland et al., 1953]. As a result, we now have ways of measuring it and of distinguishing those individuals who have strong achievement motives from those who have weak ones. The origin of strong achievement motives has, as one might expect, been traced back to childhood and the kind of training the child received. The person who has a strong achievement motive is, in general, a person who was reared in a home that put strong emphasis on independence [Winterbottom, 1958]. The parents tended to be people who expected their child to solve his own problems at an early age. Thus high achievement motivation springs from the child's early training in independence.

ASSESSING COMPLEX MOTIVES   Motive states are, among other things, inferences from behavior. How can we discover and measure the strength of complex motives? Perhaps by watching a person in many situations and by intensive interviews with him and his associates we might be able to find a common theme, a motive state, running through many seemingly different behaviors. Such a task would be quite time-consuming, however, and other techniques for assessing complex motive states are often used. One common technique is the evaluation of imaginary stories and an individual's fantasies [Atkinson, 1958].

Stories are elicited by pictures similar to those used on a projective test of personality, the Thematic Apperception Test or TAT (see Chapter 12). For instance, one picture shows a boy seated at a desk with a book open in front of him. A person is shown this picture and asked to discuss what is happening, what led up to the situation depicted, what the people in the picture are thinking, and what will happen in the future. Examples of stories told about this picture by two individuals are quoted here.

Person 1[1]

1. This brings to mind T. Edison who is dreaming of possible inventions rather than turning to his studies. A poor student, Edison is probably worried about his future.

2. Probably he is doing poorly in school or is thinking of his girl or perhaps he is being reprimanded by the teacher for inferior work.

3. I think he is dreaming of some childhood invention that he would much rather be working on than studying the boring subjects of grammar school.

4. He is destined to become one of the greatest of American inventors devoting his entire life to things such as the light bulb, phonograph.

Person 2

1. The boy in a classroom who is day dreaming about something.

2. He is recalling a previously experienced incident that struck his mind to be more appealing than being in the classroom.

3. He is thinking about the experience and is now imagining himself in the situation. He hopes to be there.

[1] The spelling and grammar have not been corrected.

4. He will probably get called on by the instructor to recite and will be embarrassed. [Smith and Feld, 1958, pages 698–699.]

These stories and others given in response to other cards by the same two people were scored for achievement imagery. The scoring was done according to a standard system. Which story shows greater achievement imagery?

Similar tests have been devised for other complex motives such as affiliation and power. This technique provides a sample of behavior, or a test, from which other behavioral tendencies, motive states in this case, can be inferred.

UNCONSCIOUS MOTIVES One more point may well be brought out here: *human motives are sometimes unconscious.* We mean simply that a person often does not know what his real motive is or what his goal is. He will probably be able to give some good reasons for his behavior, but often he will not be able to tell you the real motivating factor.

One explanation of this has probably been made obvious. Since several drives and goals may be intertwined in any given bit of behavior, it is difficult for anyone, even a skilled observer who knows the person's life history, always to identify correctly the motive or motives behind an act.

Another explanation is that motives are, in a sense, habits. We all acquire habits of which we are largely unaware. A person, for example, may bite his nails, pull on his ears, tap on the table, or pace back and forth in front of a classroom and not be aware of any of these habits until they are called to his attention. Complex motives may function in the same way. Moreover, motives are not so easily observed as habits, and hence the person is less likely to be reminded of them.

A third explanation is that motives are often fashioned under unpleasant circumstances that we would like to forget. In other words, we may not want to recognize certain of our motives. Consequently, we actively forget them through a process called *repression,* which we take up at other points in the book (see Chapter 13). In brief, repression is a process that enables us to fool ourselves about our motives because we are not willing to admit what they really are. As a result, we disguise them by perceiving them as different from what they really are, or by refusing to recognize them at all.

SYNOPSIS AND SUMMARY

Perhaps you have been impressed by the number of references to other chapters in this chapter on motivation. The central nature of motivation as a concept in psychology should thus be amply clear. Motives develop through maturation; so we need to know something about the principles of growth and maturation. Motives are learned; so we need to know about learning and some of the phenomena of learning. Motives and emotions are very closely related because emotional states are motivating— they energize behavior and direct it toward or away from situations.

Motives are extremely important in personality. In the first place, the strengths of complex motives differ from person to person. The description of these differences comprises a large part of the characterization of personality. In the second place, motives conflict with each other to produce frustration, and the reactions of an individual to frustration—his defenses, for example—are an important part of the description of personality.

Motives are learned in a cultural setting, and different cultural groups stress different motives; so an appreciation of cultural differences is important in the study of motivation. Some motives are the result of activity in rather specific parts of the central nervous system—the hypothalamus, for example—so knowledge of the anatomy and physiology of the central nervous system is necessary for the understanding of some physiological motives.

It should be apparent that an introductory textbook like this could be organized around the topic of motivation. References to motivation occur again and again throughout the book. We have introduced the topic in this chapter with the points which follow.

1. Motivation may be represented as a cycle consisting of three parts: (a) a drive that arouses (b) instrumental behavior, which leads in turn to (c) a goal that satisfies the drive.

2. Drives may be divided into unlearned or primary drives and learned or secondary motives. The primary drives, in turn, may be subdivided into physiological drives, which arise because of physiological conditions in the body, and general drives, such as activity, fear, curiosity, and affection.

3. Physiological processes within the body tend to maintain a balance called homeostasis. When this balance is disturbed, the resulting physiological need arouses regulatory behavior, such as seeking food, water, or a mate, which eventually restores the balance.

4. Drives such as hunger and thirst appear to depend upon chemical conditions in the body. These conditions often produce very specific needs or hungers, for infants and animals can select particular kinds of food that are appropriate to their needs.

5. In lower animals, sexual drives depend on sex hormones, but in human beings, learning is very important and these drives can exist in the absence of such hormones.

6. General bodily activity increases when a drive, such as hunger or sex, is present. Activity is also a drive in its own right; it is satisfied by opportunities for exercise and serves as the basis for learning new responses.

7. Interest in novel stimulation has been called the curiosity drive. The manipulative drive can be aroused by the opportunity to manipulate objects. Both drives can serve as motivation for learning new responses.

8. An affectional drive for "contact comfort" with a motherlike object appears to be an unlearned drive. Its satisfaction can alleviate fear and support the expression of curiosity.

9. Motivation energizes behavior. Performance is optimal with intermediate degrees of motivation.

10. When a drive is severely deprived, it dominates

other drives, and activity is directed toward its satisfaction.

11. In the comparison of primary drives at maximum strength in rats, the maternal drive is stronger than the thirst, hunger, and sex drives; these in turn are stronger than curiosity or exploratory drives.

12. Learning plays a role in motivation in several ways. Secondary drives are acquired by classical conditioning when neutral stimuli are paired with drive states. Secondary goals are acquired by classical conditioning when neutral stimuli are paired with incentives; secondary goals are also acquired by instrumental learning.

13. Through learning, new situations may come to arouse fear and other motive states.

14. Through learning, many new goals or values are acquired. Because people, particularly parents, are so intimately a part of human learning, many of the goals acquired by human beings are social.

15. Drives learned in one situation may generalize to other situations. In addition, activities that are learned for satisfying one drive may also serve later to satisfy other drives. Hence, in the human adult, drives and goals are interlaced in a complex way.

16. Some of the more common complex motives in man are drives for affiliation, social approval, status, security, and achievement. Instrumental learning seems important in the development of some complex motives. One way to measure these motives is to analyze a person's imaginative productions. Complex motives often operate without the individual's awareness of them.

RELATED TOPICS IN THE TEXT

CHAPTER 3 PRINCIPLES OF LEARNING The principles of classical conditioning are especially important in the learning of secondary drives. The distinction between secondary reinforcement and secondary goals should be reviewed.

CHAPTER 7 EMOTION Since emotions can serve as motivation, this is a logical chapter to read next.

CHAPTER 13 PERSONALITY Conflicts between motives may result in frustration. The reactions to frustration—defense mechanisms—are thus directly tied to motivation. Many theories of personality, Freudian theory, for example, are basically motivational theories, and the aspects of motivation related to such theories are discussed in this chapter. Further description of complex motives is also included.

CHAPTERS 19 AND 20 BIOLOGY OF BEHAVIOR The roles of the internal environment and hypothalamus in motivation are detailed.

SUGGESTIONS FOR FURTHER READING

Atkinson, J. W. (Ed.). *Motives in fantasy, action, and society*. Princeton, N.J.: Van Nostrand, 1958.
Readings on the use of imaginative productions for the assessment of human motivation.

Berlyne, D. E. *Conflict, arousal, and curiosity*. New York: McGraw-Hill, 1960.
A compendium and systematic treatment of curiosity and exploration as motives.

Bindra, D. *Motivation: A systematic reinterpretation*. New York: Ronald, 1958.
A textbook on motivation and theoretical analysis of the problems of motivation.

Cannon, W. B. *Bodily changes in pain, hunger, fear and rage* (2d ed.). New York: Appleton-Century-Crofts, 1929.
An account of classical experiments on some of the physiological factors in hunger and thirst.

Cofer, C. N., and Appley, M. H. *Motivation: Theory and research*. New York: Wiley, 1964.
A thorough summary of experiments in motivation from many areas of psychology.

Ford, C. S., and Beach, F. A. *Patterns of sexual behavior*. New York: Hoeber-Harper, 1951. (Paperback available.)
A good account of sexual motives and practices in animals and in different human societies.

Fuller, J. L. *Motivation: A biological perspective.* New York: Random House, 1962. (Paperback.)
An easily read account of motivation with special emphasis on the physiological motives.

Hall, J. F. *Psychology of motivation.* Philadelphia: Lippincott, 1961.
A textbook on motivation which stresses material from experimental studies.

Jones, M. R. (Ed.). *Nebraska symposium on motivation.* Lincoln, Nebr.: University of Nebraska Press, 1953 to present. (Paperbacks.)
Papers delivered at the Nebraska symposium on motivation have been collected into volumes each year since 1953. The papers cover most topics in the field of motivation—from physiological motivation to motivation in human personality.

Miller, N. E. Learnable drives and rewards. In S. S. Stevens (Ed.), *Handbook of experimental psychology.* New York: Wiley, 1951.
A summary of experiments on the acquisition of motives.

Morgan, C. T. *Physiological psychology* (3d ed.). New York: McGraw-Hill, 1965. Chaps. 12, 13, 14.
A textbook summary of the physiological factors in motivation.

Murray, E. J. *Motivation and emotion.* Englewood Cliffs, N.J.: Prentice-Hall, 1964. (Paperback.)
An elementary textbook on motivation which covers most of the important aspects of the subject.

Rethlingshafer, D. *Motivation as related to personality.* New York: McGraw-Hill, 1963.
A summary of the experimental work on motivation.

Stacey, C. L., and DeMartino, M. F. (Eds.). *Understanding human motivation.* Cleveland: Allen, 1958.
A compilation of papers on human motivation which stresses the personality and clinical aspects of the subject.

Young, P. T. *Motivation and emotion: A survey of the determinants of human and animal activity.* New York: Wiley, 1961.
A textbook covering various aspects of the topic of motivation.

7

WE HIGHLY CIVILIZED members of Western culture like to think of ourselves as rational beings who go about satisfying our motives in an intelligent way. To a certain extent we do satisfy them that way. But we are also emotional beings—more emotional than we realize. Indeed, most of the affairs of everyday life are tinged with feeling and emotion. Joy and sorrow, excitement and disappointment, love and fear, hope and dismay—all these and many more are feelings we experience in the course of a day or a week.

Without such feelings and emotions life would be pretty dreary. Our feelings add color and spice to living; they are the sauce without which life would be dull fare. We anticipate with pleasure our Saturday night dates, we remember with a warm glow the satisfaction we got from giving a good speech, and we even recall with amusement the bitter disappointments of childhood. On the other hand, when our emotions are too intense and too easily aroused, they can get us into a good deal of trouble. They can warp our judgment, turn friends into enemies, and make us as miserable as if we were sick with fever.

Despite its practical significance, emotion is not easy to investigate scientifically. We cannot readily control or reproduce emotional situations. Nor can we always observe it objectively, for its many subtle shades are often hard to distinguish. Moreover, people are taught to hide their emotions; so we cannot know, just by seeing a person, what emotion he is experiencing. For these reasons, scientific knowledge of emotion has grown slowly, and we are still far from a complete understanding of it.

Just as emotion is difficult to investigate scientifically, it is also difficult to define. The word *emotion* is derived from Latin roots meaning "to move out." This conveys the idea of an outward expression of something inside, which is one aspect of emotion. "To move out" also implies a second aspect of emotion—its motivational quality. Emotion supplies the motive power for a great deal of our behavior. In addition, however, emotion is an experience; it is something we feel. Finally, it is a

EMOTION

EMOTION CAN BE BOTH ORGANIZING (MAKING ADAPTATION TO THE ENVIRONMENT MORE EFFECTIVE) AND DISORGANIZING, BOTH ENERGIZING AND DEBILITATING, BOTH SOUGHT AFTER AND AVOIDED.

D. O. HEBB

physiological state that can be observed with the appropriate recording equipment. We shall study all these aspects. We usually cannot rely on a general dictionary for the definition of technical psychological terms, but these aspects of emotion have been nicely summarized in the third edition of Webster's unabridged dictionary. Here, emotion is defined as "a physiological departure from homeostasis that is subjectively experienced in strong feeling (as of love, hate, desire, or fear) and manifests itself in neuromuscular, respiratory, cardiovascular, hormonal, and other bodily changes preparatory to overt acts which may or may not be performed." [By permission. From *Webster's Third New International Dictionary,* copyright 1961 by G. & C. Merriam Company, publishers of the Merriam-Webster Dictionaries.]

This chapter introduces what is now known about emotion. We shall discuss emotional development, the motivational aspects of emotion, its physiological basis, its expression, and some theories of emotion. Some of these topics are treated more fully elsewhere in the book.

Emotional development

In each individual, emotions have a history much like that of other responses and abilities. This history begins with the hereditary differences that determine emotional tendencies. It proceeds through a period of maturation during which the individual's emotional patterns of behavior gradually mature in the same sense that his basic motor abilities do. Then, interlaced with this maturation is a good deal of learning. As the individual grows up, he learns to react emotionally to new situations and to modify his emotional behavior. In this section, we shall trace the influence of these factors in emotional development.

INHERITANCE It is fairly obvious that emotionality has some hereditary basis. As we all know, marked species differences in savageness occur among wild and domesticated animals. Gray rats,

wolves, and lions, for example, are savagely emotional, whereas their domesticated counterparts, white rats, dogs, and cats, are relatively less prone to savage emotional outbursts. It is true, of course, that wild animals can be tamed to some degree if the process is started early enough. But they seldom, if ever, become as placid as the commonly domesticated animals. Even when they are raised entirely in human company, many species of wild animals, such as the chimpanzee, still may be potentially dangerous by the time they reach adulthood. Conversely, if normally tame animals, such as the cat and dog, are allowed to grow up away from human beings, they become relatively wild. But they are still more tamable than animals whose ancestors have always been wild.

The case for emotional inheritance does not rest on such uncontrolled observation, however. Hereditary factors in emotion have been studied experimentally. Some years ago, savageness and tameness were compared in the wild gray rat and the laboratory white rat [Stone, 1932].

The white rat, gently handled in the first few months of life, easily becomes tame enough to pose no threat to the experimenter. The wild gray rat, on the other hand, improves somewhat with taming procedures, but always remains a tense, emotional animal, ready to attack and bite at the least provocation. When the two are crossbred, some of the young inherit the relatively tame disposition of the white parent, and others the savageness of the gray parent. Savageness, moreover, is linked to hair color, but to the tan pigment factor rather than to gray. The hair of the wild rat appears to be gray because it consists of two colors of hair intermixed; one is a light tan, the other a brown so dark that it is practically black. These two pigment factors are separable genetically. In the crossing of white and wild gray rats, if the young inherits the tan pigment, it will be savage; if it inherits the black pigment or no pigment at all (white hair color), it will be tame. Thus it has been possible to develop a strain of black rats, which are almost as tame or tamable as the white rat and which are now frequently used in laboratories; but no such strain of tan rats has been developed.

In another experiment, rats selected from various laboratory colonies were tested in an open-field situation [Hall, 1938].

The "open field" is a large compartment that usually elicits fear, as evidenced by copious urination and defecation, when rats are first placed in it. The amount of such emotional behavior in 145 rats was objectively measured in a 2-minute test given each day for a number of days. On succeeding days, the rats habituated to the situation and showed less and less fear.

Of the original 145 rats, 7 of the most emotional females were mated with 7 of the most emotional males. Similarly, 7 of the least emotional males were mated with 7 unemotional females. This kind of inbreeding was continued for several generations. The results were striking in the first generation. The offspring of emotional animals were considerably more emotional than those of unemotional animals. In fact, the scores of one group were seven times those of the other group.

Such experiments as these leave no doubt that savageness and fear in the rat are greatly determined by heredity. This conclusion has been confirmed in other animals, particularly in the dog [Scott, 1958]. Unfortunately, the problem has not been studied very extensively in human beings, partly because, as usual, it is difficult to do genetic experiments on man, but partly through neglect. There is one study, however, that has some bearing on the question [Jost and Sontag, 1944].

Children between six and twelve years of age were studied over a 3-year period. Various bodily states known to be associated with emotion were measured. These included skin resistance, pulse and respiration rates, and salivation. Although the measurements were not of emotionality itself, they presumably are part of emotional expression. Pairs of identical twins, pairs of siblings, and pairs of unrelated children were studied. The idea was to see whether the twins, with identical heredity, were more alike in bodily states associated with emotion than were siblings or unrelated children. Correlation coefficients were used to express the degree of similarity in bodily reactions between pairs of twins, pairs of siblings, and pairs of unre-

lated children (see page 395). Relatively high correlation coefficients indicate that there is a great deal of similarity between members of a pair; low correlation coefficients indicate little similarity. When the correlations of the scores on the different measures were combined, the results over the three years of the study were:

	Year 1	Year 2	Year 3
Identical twins	.434	.470	.489
Siblings	.255	.406	.288
Unrelated	.164	.017	.080

The correlations are not high, probably because measures of bodily states vary considerably from time to time. But the correlations between identical twins are consistently higher than those for siblings; these, in turn, are higher than those for unrelated individuals. On the whole, these relationships indicate that heredity has a role in the bodily states concerned in emotion.

All indications are that emotionality is at least in part an inherited characteristic in both human beings and animals. More research on the inheritance of emotionality in human beings is sorely needed, however, in order to determine to what degree it is inherited and in what respects it is learned.

DIFFERENTIATION OF EMOTIONS Everyone who has systematically studied the development of emotional reactions in infants agrees that this development has a fairly characteristic pattern. Different observers disagree only slightly on the details. The exact age at which different emotions appear varies, of course, with the population studied. But the general pattern of development is clear. It is depicted by the diagram in Figure 7.1 which summarizes one of the early systematic studies of emotional development [Bridges, 1932].

Infants come into the world crying, and they continue to cry periodically whenever they are hungry or uncomfortable. This is an inborn response to internal physiological needs or to discomfort. If we consider the responses to *external situations*, however, we find that almost the only emotional response that can be distinguished in the newborn

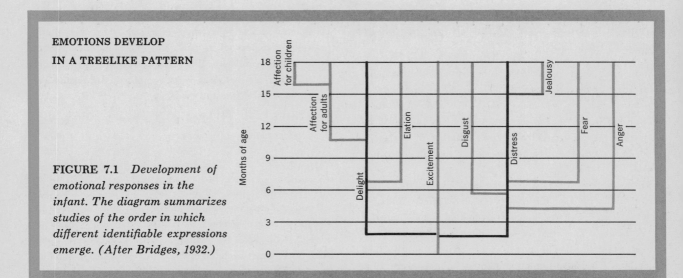

EMOTIONS DEVELOP IN A TREELIKE PATTERN

FIGURE 7.1 *Development of emotional responses in the infant. The diagram summarizes studies of the order in which different identifiable expressions emerge. (After Bridges, 1932.)*

infant is general *excitement*. This response consists of uncoordinated squirming, arm waving, and kicking. It is not a specific response to any particular stimulus, but occurs whenever the external environment changes.

Some time within the infant's first month or six weeks of life, this diffuse excitement, although continuing, begins to differentiate into more specific emotional reactions. The first reaction to appear has been called *distress*. This may or may not include the crying that has been going on since birth, but it is characterized by muscular tension and checked breath. Shortly afterward, something called *delight* is distinguishable. It is evidenced by smiling, gurgling, and muscular relaxation. Thus by the time the infant is six weeks to two months old, the two general emotions—distress and delight, or call them what you wish—that will be felt and expressed throughout life have made their appearance. Such development is almost wholly, if not entirely, a matter of maturation.

As the infant grows older, he develops an increasing variety of emotional responses. At three months of age, for example, he responds to unpleasant situations with general signs of distress, but responds

to nursing, fondling, tickling, and rocking with smiles and general signs of delight. After that, emotions rapidly differentiate, and by the age of two years, the child has a repertory of specific reactions to different situations. This development may be regarded as a differentiation or refinement of the general states of distress and delight. Even though the exact order and ages vary from child to child, the approximate order and the approximate ages at which the different patterns appear are given in Figure 7.1.

FACTORS IN EMOTIONAL DEVELOPMENT Both maturation and learning, undoubtedly, play a part in this differentiation of emotions. From our knowledge of motor development, we may assume that maturation is relatively more important in the early stages and learning more so in the later stages. Also we can believe that the time at which an emotion appears is limited mainly by maturation and cannot be hastened much by learning or training. As yet, however, we do not have sufficient data on human beings to prove these conclusions. The later stages of emotional development in childhood and adolescence are, we can be sure, governed primarily by learning. A number of factors are involved in the modification of emotional behavior throughout this period.

The child's capabilities, especially in motor activities and language, are increasing. At first, the child is frustrated by things he cannot do. He cannot reach the toy he wants, he cannot climb where he wants to, and often he cannot make his wants known. As he grows older and can do more and more things for himself, physical frustration becomes a less frequent cause of emotional behavior.

The child also becomes increasingly familiar with the people and objects in his world. At first, his environment is limited. He sees only the face of his mother and other members of the family. Since he does not see many other people, objects, or animals, a great number of things are strange to him, and he reacts to this strangeness with fear. As he grows up and as his experience broadens, fewer and fewer things are strange to him. So this source of emotional behavior—a limited environment—also becomes less important with age.

On the other hand, the child has increasing opportunities to learn emotional reactions. He usually has the opportunity to learn unnatural fears, both by direct conditioning and by copying the fears of his parents and siblings. He also has the chance to learn emotional techniques for getting what he wants; he may, for example, learn to throw a temper tantrum whenever his wishes are frustrated. These opportunities for learning increase his repertory of emotional reactions; they alter and expand the situations that give rise to emotions.

The growing child is learning new motives and new goals. These enlarge the possibilities of his becoming frustrated and thus emotional. He learns to want all sorts of things—bicycles, clothes, money, social approval. By the time the child reaches adolescence, two general classes of goals, those connected with financial independence and those connected with social approval, have become especially important. Another thing the child learns is to restrain and control his emotions. Parents tend to be annoyed by a child's noisy emotional outbursts;

they think he ought to learn to control his emotions. They therefore start teaching control early by punishing the child and by disapproving his expression of emotion. Teachers and other adults do the same thing. As a consequence of this treatment, the child learns to avoid, or to try to avoid, displaying his emotions.

CHANGES IN EMOTIONAL EXPRESSION These various pressures on the child alter both the situations that give rise to emotion and the way in which emotion is expressed. Over the span from infancy to adolescence, many changes in expression take place.

Displays of emotion are much more frequent in children than in adolescents and adults. If you are around children very long, you will hear some kind of outburst every few minutes. First you may hear loud shouts of joy or gales of laughter; a little later, screams of anger or crying. The air is pierced periodically with some obvious expression of emotion. These outbursts, however, become less frequent as children grow up, partly because the children are maturing, but partly too because adults disapprove the outbursts, especially when they involve crying and fighting.

Emotional reactions are brief in children, but in adolescents and adults they are more prolonged. A small child who is upset usually gets over it in a hurry. As soon as the situation causing fear or anger is done with, he is no longer afraid or angry. Later on, and especially in adolescence, this is not the case. Anger tends to be replaced by sulkiness that can go on for some time; fears are expressed as increased shyness, timidity, and jumpiness. This change occurs in part because the adolescent has been taught to restrain and contain his emotions. It occurs also because his growing intellectual ability enables him to think and brood about emotional problems.

A child's emotions characteristically lack any gradation of intensity. Emotional reactions tend to be all or none. A trivial situation evokes the same screams of laughter or misery as a situation of some importance. In the growing-up process, though, emotions become graded. A small irritation is met with little signs of annoyance but no major outburst. The big scenes are saved for situations of greater perceived import. Even then, what is important to the child may not seem important to the parent, but the older child nevertheless grades his reactions to the seeming significance of the situation.

EMOTIONAL SITUATIONS The situations giving rise to emotional reactions change over the course of emotional development. To describe the changes that take place, we must distinguish between three general categories of emotion: pleasure, fear, and anger. Pleasure is another name for the delight seen early in infancy. Fear and anger are patterns that differentiate from distress when the infant is four to seven months of age.

Pleasure-producing situations. Many different things give us pleasure, but they are all covered by one general principle: Pleasure is a reaction to the satisfaction of a drive or the achievement of a goal. This principle applies to both unlearned or primary drives, including curiosity and exploration, and learned or secondary motives, those concerned with social approval, status, and so on.

Early in life, the child shows signs of pleasure when he is physically comfortable. If an infant is well fed, dry, warm, and if there are no pins sticking in him, he is usually relaxed, smiling, and cooing. By the second or third month, he shows signs of pleasure when he sees a human face or hears a friendly voice. Still later he expresses pleasure when he exercises a new skill, such as reaching out and shaking a rattle, or when somebody plays peekaboo with him. In general, as children develop, they find pleasure in situations that are novel but not frightening and that keep them entertained and offer them some success in what they try to do.

Smiling and laughing are specific expressions of pleasure that occur, just as fear and anger do, in different situations at different ages [Washburn, 1929]. Apparently the nervous system of the infant must mature somewhat before he can smile, for smiling does not occur until the infant is about two months of age. After that, for a time, smiling is a response to being tickled or stroked. Then, smiling begins to occur when there is an interesting noise or some unusual movement—as when parents wave their arms, dance, stand on their heads, or pull toys around the floor to entertain their children.

As the affectional drive matures, the child takes pleasure in having physical contact with adults—clinging to them, riding piggyback, climbing all over them, and so on. When curiosity and exploratory drives develop, the child takes pleasure in pulling things apart, playing with toys, exploring, and doing similar things. By the time adolescence arrives, and many secondary goals have been established, the boy or girl derives pleasure from social activities of various sorts and from achievement in athletics or school.

Fear-producing situations. Unlearned fears are caused primarily by situations that are strange to the child. This statement, however, now needs a little qualification. Fear in infants is caused not so much by strangeness itself as by suddenness or unexpectedness. A loud noise, for example, does not necessarily elicit fear, but one that comes *suddenly* usually does. Similarly, strange objects, like stuffed animals or false faces, produce fear mainly when they appear unexpectedly. Thus the natural stimulus for fear is a strange situation encountered by the child suddenly and unexpectedly.

As children grow older, they may be afraid of imaginary creatures, of being left alone, of the dark, and of potential bodily harm—in other words, of threats. Some of these fear-producing situations are compared at different ages in Figure 7.2. Late in childhood, children become especially fearful of social humiliation and ridicule—social threats—and are much less bothered by the noises and strange things that scared them in infancy.

Several factors are involved in this development of fear behavior. One, of course, is the conditioning of fear (see page 227), but others are important too. In order to learn fear, a child need not be conditioned; he can acquire fear symbolically through the example of his parents or through their stories. This can happen whenever the child's memory and imagination are developed to the point where he is able to imagine the fearful things his parents tell him about.

Another factor is the developing perception of the world. The baby is not very discriminating, for example, about faces or animals. He cannot tell one face from another or one animal from another. If he is used to one face or one animal, another is not going to appear strange. As he learns and matures, however, he comes to discriminate one face from another and becomes aware of the fact that a face is connected with a head. At that point, the face of a stranger or a disembodied face is something unexpected, and he begins to show fear of it. Hence the fear appears only when the perception of what is familiar and what is strange makes it possible. This conclusion is illustrated by the following quotation summarizing some studies of fear in chimpanzees:

Some of the chimpanzees of the Yerkes colony might have a paroxysm of terror at being shown a model of a human or chimpanzee head detached from the body; young infants showed no fear, increasing excitement was evident in the older (half-grown) animals, and those adults that were not frankly terrified were still considerably excited. These individual differences among adults, and the difference of response at different ages, are quite like the human differences in attitude toward snakes, the frequency and strength of fear increasing with age. . . . The increase fits in with the conception that many fears depend on some degree of perceptual development. [Modified from Hebb, 1949, page 243.]

When the individual reaches adolescence and early adulthood, social situations take on increased importance as sources of fear [Wake, 1950]. In

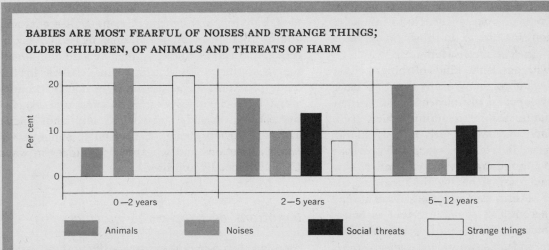

BABIES ARE MOST FEARFUL OF NOISES AND STRANGE THINGS; OLDER CHILDREN, OF ANIMALS AND THREATS OF HARM

FIGURE 7.2 *Situations evoking fear in infants and children. Groups of youngsters were exposed to four different classes of stimuli: animals, noises, or things that made noises, threats of illness, injury, or death, and strange things or people. The bar graphs show the percentage of each group giving a fear response to the four classes of stimuli. (After Jersild et al., 1933.)*

early adolescence (between eleven and sixteen years of age), the individual may still fear animals and potential injury or threats, but social fears are more important—fears of being left out of a group, of making a *faux pas,* of being ridiculed, or of talking to certain people. In early adulthood (eighteen to twenty-four years), at least among university students, the individual attaches even more importance to social fears. Fears of animals and threats have diminished considerably and have been replaced by fears of parental criticism or disappointment and by sexual fears pertaining to pregnancy, venereal disease, or disapproval of sexual conduct.

Perhaps the best way of summarizing the causes of fear in the later stages of growing up is to say that most fears are fears of failure or punishment— fears of failing to achieve various secondary goals that have been learned, such as success in school or social approval.

Anger-producing situations. The situations that make children and adults angry have one thing in common: interference with goal-directed activity. Put another way, frustration of any want or ongoing activity is likely to provoke anger. Restraining the individual or requiring him to do things he does not want to do may provoke anger at any age.

What varies with age is the kinds of things people do and do not want to do. We are thus led back again to the development of unlearned and learned motives. In infants, simple restraint, which frustrates activity and exploratory drives, is regularly a cause for anger. In children, common provocations include: being required to sit on a toilet seat, having things taken away, having the face washed, being left alone, losing the attention of an adult, and failing to accomplish something that is being attempted. In older children and adolescents, the causes of anger shift, as we might expect, from physical constraints and frustrations to social frustrations and disappointments. Sarcasm, bossiness, shunning, or thwarting of social ambitions become frequent occasions for anger.

Social frustrations are likewise common causes of anger in adults. Most adults have learned to contain their anger, however, and hence we seldom observe outright displays of anger. More common are the mild feelings of anger that we call annoyance. One psychologist studied common annoyances and irritations by asking people to list their own annoyances for him [Cason, 1930].

From the replies of over 600 people, ranging in age from ten to ninety, he listed almost 18,000 annoyances. When account was taken of duplications, the number was reduced to about 2,600 separate annoyances. Tabulating these into various categories, he found that more than half the common annoyances are things that other people do, such as blowing their noses without handkerchiefs, coughing in one's face, smelling dirty, or treating others unkindly (see Table 7.1). Almost all these annoyances are socially disapproved behaviors or things that we just do not want other people to do. Only a small minority of common annoyances have to do with *things*—for example, a late bus or train— but even these were mostly frustrations of a motive.

The particular way of expressing anger changes with age. Among preschool children, anger is more likely to take the form of temper tantrums, surliness, bullying, and fighting; among adolescents and adults, these expressions become more subtle, indirect, and verbal, and they include sarcasm, swearing, gossiping, and plotting. This change in the mode of expression of anger is obviously brought about by social pressures. Such pressures, exerted by parents, friends, associates, and the official agents of society, teach the person to suppress his natural reactions and to express his anger in ways which are socially approved.

Emotions as habits and motives

Emotions can function in human life both as habits, which are learned reactions, and as motives [Leeper, 1948]. Learned emotional habits can be reactions not only to physical things and the actions of other people, but also to one's own thoughts and expectations. Emotions are also motives when they impart an impetus to behavior and

TABLE 7.1 *Sources of annoyance. 659 individuals of both sexes, ranging from ten to ninety years of age, were asked to indicate the things that annoyed them.*

CLASS OF ANNOYANCE	PER CENT OF DIFFERENT ANNOYANCES
Human behavior	59.0
Things and activities not connected with people (other than clothes)	18.8
Clothes and manner of dress	12.4
Physical characteristics of people that could be altered	5.3
Physical characteristics of people that are unalterable	4.4

MOST COMMON ANNOYANCES
ASSOCIATED WITH HUMAN BEHAVIOR

A person blowing his nose without a handkerchief
A person coughing in one's face
A person cheating in a game
A woman spitting in public
The odor of dirty feet
A child being treated harshly

SOURCE: After Cason, 1930.

give it direction toward certain goals. Let us consider in detail how emotional habits are acquired and the role of these habits in motivation. The discussion revolves around the three basic emotional patterns: pleasure, fear, and anger.

PLEASURE Pleasure, we have already seen, accompanies the satisfaction of a drive. Hence the achievement of any goal, whether it is a primary goal, such as eating or drinking, or a secondary goal, such as social approval or academic achievement, is experienced as pleasant. This general principle can be extended to the relief of any tension, and indeed to relief from such emotions as fear and anger. The goal of fear is to escape a fear-producing situation or fear itself; the goal of anger is to attack, hurt, or annihilate somehow the thing provoking anger. Hence the achievement of these goals is also regarded as pleasant in some way.

In Chapter 6 we saw that any situation regularly associated with a goal becomes a secondary goal. This principle applies to the pleasure we take in the achievement of goals. Anything connected with the satisfaction of drives may itself become a goal and, when achieved, give pleasure. Thus we like to be around people with whom we have shared satisfying experiences. We like to make money because it satisfies other needs. We like to go back to places where we formerly had a good time. In short, we derive pleasure from those situations which were associated with the satisfaction of goals.

FEARS We have seen that some fears, especially in animals and human infants, may be innate. In addition, fears are learned by both humans and animals. The *conditioned emotional response (CER)*, as it can be studied using the Skinner box, provides an objective index by means of which to investigate learned fears in animals. The following is a typical experiment involving the conditioned emotional response [Hunt and Brady, 1951]:

Rats first learned to press a bar in a Skinner box for water reinforcement (see Chapter 3). The reinforcement was given on a variable-interval schedule and a high and steady rate of response, which could serve as a baseline, was established. Next, the rats were given "fear trials" which consisted of the presentation of a short clicking sound and a mildly painful electric shock when the clicking sound was turned off. In a sense, the clicking sound served as a cue for the coming electric shock. As more and more fear trials were given, the conditioned emotional response of crouching and failing to press the bar increased in strength. The development of the conditioned emotional response is shown by the flat places, or plateaus, in the steady curve of responding (see Figure 7.3). The particular experiment from which these records were taken used the CER technique to study the effect of electroconvulsive shock (ECS) on learned fear, that is, the conditioned emotional response. It was found that electroconvulsive shocks abolished the conditioned emotional response.

THE CONDITIONED EMOTIONAL
RESPONSE (CER) IS SHOWN BY A
"PLATEAU" ON THE CUMULATIVE CURVE

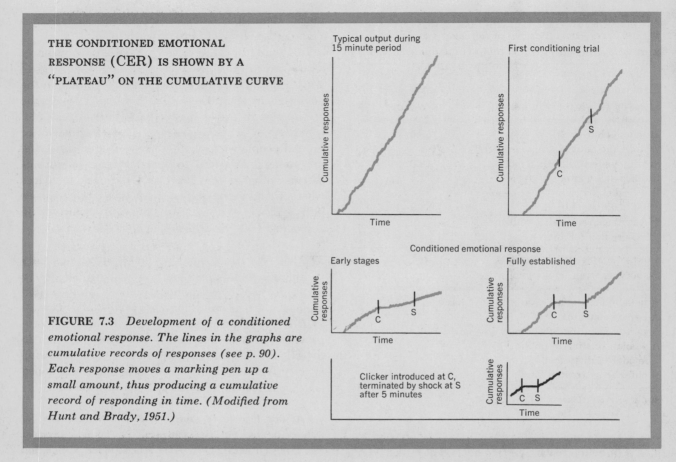

FIGURE 7.3   *Development of a conditioned emotional response. The lines in the graphs are cumulative records of responses (see p. 90). Each response moves a marking pen up a small amount, thus producing a cumulative record of responding in time. (Modified from Hunt and Brady, 1951.)*

Animal experiments are important because of the variables which can be investigated and because of the control which can be exercised, but experiments on the development of fear can sometimes be done with human beings. The way in which we may learn to fear certain things is illustrated in this description of a famous experiment with an infant named Albert [Watson and Rayner, 1920].

Albert was an eleven-month-old boy who displayed no fear of animals. When shown a rabbit (see upper left sketch in Figure 7.4), he expressed delight and made no effort to get away. Later, however, he was shown a white rat (upper right sketch), and at the same time heard a loud and sudden noise. This natural stimulus for fear had the expected effect; he shrank back. The procedure was repeated several times on different occasions. He was then presented with the white rabbit (lower left sketch) which formerly had caused no fear. Now, however, he was frightened by the sight of the rabbit and attempted to get away from it. He was then tested with a number of other white furry objects, including a white beard on a man (lower right sketch). All these provoked fear.

This experiment demonstrates two points. One is the *conditioning* of fear. Any stimulus regularly present when a fear response is made can itself become a stimulus for fear. The other is the phenomenon of *generalization*. The fear that is learned is not necessarily restricted to the conditioning stimulus (see page 85), but generalizes to similar objects—in this case to all white furry objects. Both conditioning and generalization are important factors in building up our repertoire of learned fears.

The way in which a learned fear functions as a motive has already been illustrated in an experiment described in Chapter 6. In that experiment, rats were conditioned to fear a white box by being subjected to shock while in it [Miller, 1948a]. Later, with no shock present, the rats learned to turn a wheel or press a lever to escape from the box, motivated only by their acquired fear.

In a similar way, people acquire many different sorts of fears which can motivate behavior. If a person has a bad fall from a height, he may go through life fearing high places. A child who is lost and terrified in a crowd of people may, even as an adult, fear being in a crowd. If at some time he is locked up in a dark closet, he may thereafter be afraid of being in a room with all the doors closed. Since people may have varied experiences of this kind, a very large number of specific fears may be found in any one person.

Parents and society deliberately use fear of punishment to enforce their demands and to teach approved ways of behaving. The punishment may be something painful, such as a whipping. But most often it is the frustration of other drives—loss of money, such as fines (see Figure 7.5); loss of freedom, or imprisonment, which frustrates a number of drives; or loss of social approval, status, and related social goals.

Fears become important motives in life because we have so many opportunities to acquire them. In childhood, physical hazards, such as falling down the steps or getting burned in a fire, cause the child to fear those situations in which he has been harmed. Soon the parent starts using fear deliberately. By punishing and at the same time saying "no," a parent soon teaches an infant to fear

A BABY LEARNS FEAR OF AN OBJECT BY ASSOCIATING IT WITH AN EVENT HE IS AFRAID OF; THEN HE GENERALIZES THE FEAR TO OTHER SIMILAR OBJECTS

Loud noise

FIGURE 7.4 *Conditioning and generalization of fear in the infant. Upper left, before conditioning, the child approaches a white rabbit without fear. Upper right, a loud noise, which startles and scares the infant, is paired with the presentation of a white rat. Lower left, the child, after conditioning, appears to be afraid of the rabbit. Lower right, he is afraid of the other white furry objects. (After Watson and Rayner, 1920.)*

FIGURE 7.5 *Threat of punishment is often used to motivate behavior. (Jeffrey Norton.)*

punishment, and the signal for evoking this fear is the word "no." Later on, the teaching of fear becomes more complicated. To motivate the child, the parent may put him to bed without his supper, deny him his ice cream or popsicle, or not allow him to go out and play. Thus the child is taught to fear loss or denial of the things he wants.

Governments use fear of fine or imprisonment to enforce their laws, and people use fear of loss of friends, privileges, and social prestige to control each other's behavior. Fear of loss of freedom appears to be a most potent motive for getting nations to fight. Indeed, everywhere we look, we see fear profoundly influencing what people do and what they work for.

ANGER Anger, we have said, is provoked by restraints, including any interference with goal-directed activity. This means that anger is produced by frustration—by not having or not getting what one wants. Frustration may not always elicit anger, but anger is usually caused by frustration or by circumstances that have previously caused frustration. Keeping this in mind, we can note the follow-ing points about anger as a habit and as a motive.

Anger can be learned as a social technique for achieving goals. The persistence of temper tantrums in children is a good example. In many children, the temper tantrum is a natural reaction to frustration. If the baby wants something he cannot have, he gets angry and throws a tantrum. If this does not work, he will probably try other, more reasonable approaches, and the temper reaction to frustration will tend to die out. Thus he learns not to get mad, but to find other means of relieving his frustration. If, on the other hand, the temper tantrum does get him what he wants—as it often will when parents give in because they cannot stand the annoyance of the tantrum—then the baby learns to throw tantrums whenever he is frustrated. If the tantrums continue to be successful, he will habitually get angry whenever he is frustrated, using anger as a device for getting what he wants.

As a corollary to this, if fighting generally is successful, it too tends to be learned. If it is not successful, it tends to drop out. This point is demonstrated in laboratory experiments with fighting mice [Scott, 1958]. When strange mice are paired up, they tend to fight. One usually wins and the other loses. The mouse that wins is more likely to fight again; the one that loses is more likely to retreat and give up without a fight. The same general principle probably applies to fighting in children. The boy who usually wins his battles is likely to become a bully who is always picking fights, but the boy who has lost a few times learns to avoid fighting and replaces it with some other aggressive technique.

Parents and society try in various ways to suppress angry behavior. Children are usually punished for outbursts of anger. In adults, even the slightest display of anger may be frowned upon as socially disapproved behavior. So, both by failing to reinforce anger and by punishing its expression, society attempts to teach us not to get angry.

This raises an interesting problem. The punishment of anger is itself frustrating and hence anger-provoking. First, inability to express anger—to blow off steam—is frustrating because it prevents achievement of one's goal, namely, to attack or destroy whatever is doing the frustrating. Second, since any sort of punishment can be frustrating, the threat of punishment can thus be anger-provoking. Society, therefore, in its effort to suppress anger actually provokes anger. The result then is not so much to teach people not to be angry as it is to teach them not to express anger. Anger smolders inside instead of coming out into the open.

Anger can be conditioned and generalized in the same way as fear. We get angry at whatever keeps us from achieving our ends, and if the same thing frequently frustrates us, we acquire a conditioned hostility toward the obstacle and other things similar to it. A harsh father, for example, who frequently makes his son angry by restricting the son's activities, may become such a stimulus for anger that the boy becomes generally hostile toward him even when he is doing nothing to frustrate the boy. When the boy grows up, he may be hostile to all superiors if he generalizes to them the feelings he has toward his father. Such conditioned hostility is fairly common among older children and adults.

ATTITUDES   The tendency to react emotionally to people and things formerly associated with emotional behavior helps to account for our preferences and aversions. We prefer the kinds of things which formerly gave us pleasure, and we are averse to those which made us fearful or angry. This is also true of our attitudes. An *attitude* is a tendency to respond positively (favorably) or negatively (unfavorably) to certain persons, objects, or situations. In other words, it is a tendency to react emotionally in one direction or another. Whichever it is depends on our previously conditioned emotional reactions to certain kinds of people or things and then the generalization of these reactions to similar people or things.

Attitudes are discussed at length in Chapter 17. Here we simply want to point out that they are emotionally toned tendencies learned through conditioning and generalization.

CONFLICT AND FRUSTRATION   Frustration, we have just seen, is a key to understanding anger and hostility. We have seen too that fear of punishment is frustrating and hence a source of anger. For that reason, we need to consider more carefully the common sources of frustration. Although a section of Chapter 13 is devoted to it, at this point we should introduce a few of the main ideas. Generally speaking, sources of frustration may be classified into the three categories described below.

Environmental frustration. By making it difficult or impossible for a person to attain his goal, *environmental obstacles* frustrate the satisfaction of motives. These environmental obstacles may be something physical, such as a locked door or lack of money. They may be people—parents, teachers, or policemen—who prevent us from achieving our goals. In general, environmental obstacles are the most important sources of frustration for children; what usually prevents children from doing the thing they want to do is some restraint or obstacle imposed by their parents or teachers.

Personal frustration. As children grow up and move toward adulthood, *unattainable goals* loom increasingly more important as sources of frustration. These goals are largely learned goals that cannot be achieved because they are out of reach of the person's abilities. A child, for example, may learn to aspire to high academic achievement, but lack the ability to make better than a mediocre record. He may want to make the school band, the football team, to be admitted to a certain club, or to have the lead in a play, but may be frustrated because he does not have the necessary talents. The trouble here is that one may learn goals—levels of aspiration—that are too high for one's level of performance.

Conflict frustration. The adult, as well as the child, has his share of environmental obstacles and unattainable goals, but his most important source of frustration is likely to be *motivational conflict,* that is, a conflict of motives. In expressing anger, for example, a person is usually caught in such a conflict. On the one hand, he would like to vent his anger; on the other hand, he fears the social disapproval that would result if he did. The anger motive is thus in conflict with the motive for social approval. In Western societies, sexual motivation is often in conflict with society's standards of approved sexual behavior. Motivational conflicts are quite numerous, and more are described later. The important point is that frustration takes place because two motives are in conflict, and it is not possible to satisfy one without frustrating the other. For this reason, many adults are forever being frustrated and hence have almost continual occasion to feel angry or hostile.

ANXIETY AND HOSTILITY Our society, then, gives us plenty of cause to feel anger, but forces us to suppress it. The consequence is a kind of smoldering anger—an unspecific hostility toward numerous things and people, depending on the particular sources of frustration in an individual's life.

There is also plenty of cause for *anxiety*—the general state of apprehension or uneasiness that occurs in many different situations. Fear, as we have seen, is a reaction to a specific thing or situation. Anxiety is a rather vague fear—an "objectless" fear, as it is sometimes called. The person usually is not quite sure what he is afraid of, and that may, in fact, be rather difficult for anyone to ascertain. Anxiety is like a mosquito in the dark. You know it is near, but you do not know quite where, and you somehow cannot locate it to make the final slap that rids you of it. Anxiety is usually less intense but more persistent than fear, although some individuals suffer brief or prolonged attacks of anxiety that are agonizingly severe (see Chapter 14).

Several sources of anxiety may be distinguished. One is linked to hostility. Since society teaches us, through threats of punishment or loss of social approval, that we should not be angry or hostile, feelings of hostility become associated with vague fears of what might happen if we expressed our feelings. Second, through simple conditioning of fear, we may learn to be anxious. If we have many

fear-provoking experiences with parents, teachers, and associates, these can generalize to almost everyone so that we become anxious in the presence of people generally. Human beings, in the third place, are particularly prone to anxiety because they have the ability to recall and imagine experiences. By thinking of fear-provoking situations that have happened or might happen, people elicit in themselves the same fear or anxiety that they would have if they were in the real situation. Finally, anxiety may come from situations which a person perceives to be a threat to the integrity of his personality [May, 1950]. For these reasons, then, people are often anxious, and some people are anxious much of the time. Chapter 14, Behavior Disorders, discusses anxiety and its consequences in greater detail.

Bodily states in emotion

From the development of emotions and the way emotions function as habits and motives, we turn now to another aspect of the subject, the bodily changes that take place in emotion. Almost anyone who has been excited, terrified, or angry has experienced some of them, but he is probably not aware of all that is happening within.

These changes, being objective ones, have been extensively studied, and we probably know more about them than any other aspect of emotion. They can be studied in two ways: by direct measurements with physiological recording devices, or by surveys of what people feel when they are stirred up. A study utilizing the survey approach was done with 4,000 airmen who flew in combat in World War II [Shaffer, 1947]. The airmen had, at various times, been exposed to great danger, and they were asked to report on how they felt. As can be seen in Table 7.2, they were asked to say whether they "often" or "sometimes" experienced certain symptoms while flying combat missions. A wide variety of bodily changes were included in the list of symptoms: pounding of the heart, tenseness of the muscles, dryness of the mouth, "cold sweat," need

TABLE 7.2. *Bodily symptoms of fear in combat flying.*
Over 4,000 fliers in World War II were asked
how often they experienced different symptoms
in combat flying.

SYMPTOM	PERCENTAGE ANSWERING		
	"OFTEN"	"SOME-TIMES"	TOTAL
Pounding heart and rapid pulse	30	56	86
Muscles very tense	30	53	83
Easily irritated, angry, or "sore"	22	58	80
Dryness of the throat or mouth	30	50	80
"Nervous perspiration" or "cold sweat"	26	53	79
"Butterflies" in the stomach	23	53	76
Sense of unreality, that this couldn't be happening	20	49	69
Need to urinate very frequently	25	40	65
Trembling	11	53	64
Confused or rattled	3	50	53
Weak or faint	4	37	41
After mission, not being able to remember details of what happened	5	34	39
Sick to the stomach	5	33	38
Not being able to concentrate	3	32	35

SOURCE: After Shaffer, 1947.

to urinate, and sickness in the stomach. If one were to take the trouble to attach various measuring instruments to fliers so that their physiological reactions could be recorded while they were in combat, one could detect an even wider variety of bodily changes and record them in detail.

AUTONOMIC CHANGES   From physiological studies of the nervous system and of bodily changes in emotion, we know that the changes that occur are initiated by a part of the nervous system called the *autonomic system* (see Figure 7.6). The changes are therefore called autonomic changes [Cannon, 1929].

The autonomic system consists of many nerves leading from the brain and spinal cord out to the various organs of the body (see Chapter 19), including particularly the blood vessels serving both the interior and exterior muscles. The autonomic system has two parts which often, but by no means always, work in opposition to each other. One part, the *sympathetic system,* increases the heart rate and blood pressure and distributes blood to the exterior muscles. It is this part which comes into play when we become emotional—or at least when we become fearful or angry. The other part of the system is called the *parasympathetic system.* It tends to be active when we are calm and relaxed. It does many things that, taken together, build up and conserve the body's stores of energy. For example, it decreases the heart rate, reduces the blood pressure, and diverts blood to the digestive tract.

This is an oversimplified account of the functions of the two systems. The parasympathetic system can, in certain instances, be active in emotion. Indeed, it usually increases in activity whenever the sympathetic system does.

When the sympathetic part of the autonomic system steps up its discharges, as it does in some emotional states, it produces several symptoms that are worth noting. One set of effects concerns the circulation of the blood. In fear, for instance, the blood vessels serving the stomach, intestines, and interior of the body tend to contract, while those serving the exterior muscles of the trunk and limbs tend to become larger. In this way, blood is diverted from digestive functions to muscular functions, and the body is prepared for action that may involve great muscular activity. At the same time, nervous impulses to the heart make it beat harder and faster, the blood pressure goes up, and the pulse rate is quickened. Thus more blood is pumped through the circulatory system to the muscles.

Besides producing changes in circulation, the sympathetic system produces several other bodily changes in fear. Perhaps you have noticed some of them yourself. One is a change in the size of the pupil of the eye, which is ordinarily regulated

THE AUTONOMIC NERVOUS SYSTEM, ESPECIALLY
ITS SYMPATHETIC DIVISION, BECOMES MORE ACTIVE
IN EXCITEMENT, FEAR, AND ANGER

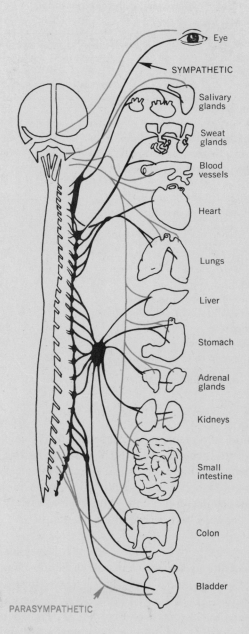

FIGURE 7.6 *Schematic diagram of the autonomic nervous
system. The autonomic nervous system consists of nerves
and ganglia, or collections of nerve cells, that serve blood
vessels, glands, and other internal organs of the body.
It has two main divisions: the parasympathetic system.
shown in color, and the sympathetic system.*

by the amount of light entering the eye. In fear, the pupil gets larger. Perhaps you have seen this if you have observed a fearful cat or person. Another change is a drying of the mouth. This occurs because the sympathetic system stops the secretion from the salivary glands, which ordinarily keeps the mouth moist. Still another is the change in the movements of the stomach and intestines. As can be seen in X-ray pictures or with the balloon technique (see Figure 6.3), contractions of the stomach and intestines are stopped or reversed in strong emotion. Also the principal sphincters may involuntarily relax, causing a person to defecate or to urinate.

Another response of the sympathetic system in emotion is the discharge of the hormones *epinephrine* (adrenaline) and *norepinephrine* (noradrenaline). Nerve impulses in the sympathetic system which reach the adrenal glands, located on top of the kidneys, cause the secretion of these hormones. From this point, the hormones go into the blood and circulate around the body. Epinephrine affects many structures of the body. In the liver, it helps mobilize sugar into the blood and thus makes more energy available to the brain and muscles. Epinephrine also stimulates the heart to beat harder. (Surgeons use epinephrine to stimulate heart action when the heart has weakened or stopped.) In the skeletal muscles, epinephrine helps mobilize sugar resources so that the muscles can use them more rapidly. Thus epinephrine duplicates and strengthens many of the actions of the sympathetic system on various internal organs. The major effect of norepinephrine is to constrict peripheral blood vessels and thus raise blood pressure.

One other bodily change in emotion has been used extensively by psychologists in experiments on learning and personality—the change in the galvanic skin response (GSR). There are two varieties of this response. One type of GSR shows up as a change in the resistance of the skin when a very small electrical current is passed through the skin. In emotional states, the GSR is a decrease in the resistance of the skin to the passage of electrical

current. It seems possible that this decrease in resistance is due to increased perspiration—so-called "nervous perspiration." The second variety of GSR seems to come from the activity of skin structures themselves. This type of GSR can be recorded without passing current through the skin. Electrical activity is present when cells are active, and the voltage changes measured as this type of GSR may represent activity of the sweat glands themselves. Note that it is the cellular activity itself, not the sweat, which is responsible for the electrical manifestations of this type of GSR. Other ideas about the origin of this type of GSR postulate chemical reactions involving perspiration and resulting in electrical responses. Whatever its origin, the GSR is a sensitive indicator of emotional response.

PATTERNS OF AUTONOMIC CHANGE   It is clear that a state of activation occurs in emotion [Lindsley, 1951; Duffy, 1962]. The question immediately arises as to whether there are differences in the pattern of activity of the autonomic nervous system in the different emotional states. Some investigators have been able to find some evidence for different autonomic patterns in fear and anger [Wolf and Wolff, 1947; Ax, 1953; Funkenstein, 1955].

One study of the difference of autonomic activity in fear and anger was done with a patient who had a fistula, or hole, in his abdominal wall; this made direct observation of the lining of the stomach possible [Wolf and Wolff, 1947]. When this patient was fearful or apprehensive, the stomach lining looked pale; when he was angry or resentful, the stomach lining looked red and inflamed.

Only one index of autonomic response, the color of the stomach lining which showed the amount of blood circulating in the stomach wall, was used in this study, but several measures have been obtained in other studies [Ax, 1953]. In these studies, fear and anger resulted in different patterns of autonomic responses. The results obtained were compatible with the idea that the autonomic responses in fear or anxiety are due to the epinephrine which is released into the blood stream; the autonomic responses in anger seem to be due to norepinephrine circulating in the blood. Further evidence bearing on this idea has been summarized by Funkenstein [1955].

Several experiments are involved. In the first experiment, subjects were given epinephrine and norepinephrine, both of which increased blood pressure. Then, after the blood pressure had increased, the subjects were given a drug, Mecholyl, which decreased the blood pressure. In the subjects who had received norepinephrine injections, Mecholyl produced a rapid drop in blood pressure and then a rapid return to the high blood pressure levels which were present before Mecholyl (see Figure 7.7). In the subjects who had received epinephrine injections, Mecholyl also reduced blood pressure, but it stayed down for a long time. Thus, norepinephrine and epinephrine cause two different patterns of physiological response. After it had been estab-

lished that there were different patterns, the next experiment tested subjects under stress in the laboratory, and physiological measurements—blood pressure, for example—were made. The subjects who responded with anger to the stress showed the norepinephrine pattern, while those who responded to the stress with depression or anxiety showed the epinephrine pattern. This may indicate that the patterns of bodily response, and the hormones responsible, are different in these two emotional states—sometimes called the "anger-out" and the "anger-in" states.

Thus it seems likely that different patterns of autonomic response accompany such widely different emotions as fear and anger. The role of these changes in producing the felt emotion is another question, however. For one thing, it seems unlikely that all the subtle variations of mood and emotion are accompanied by differences in bodily states

NOREPINEPHRINE AND EPINEPHRINE HAVE DIFFERENT EFFECTS ON BLOOD PRESSURE

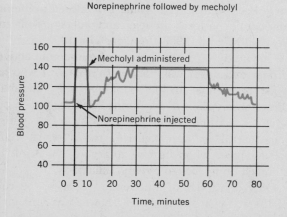

Norepinephrine followed by mecholyl

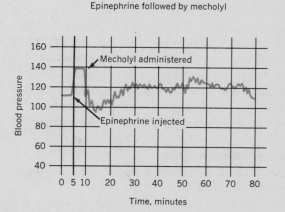

Epinephrine followed by mecholyl

FIGURE 7.7 *Blood pressure changes following injections of norepinephrine, epinephrine, and mecholyl. Injections of norepinephrine and epinephrine both produced sharp increases in blood pressure. Mecholyl, injected about five minutes after the first injections, produced a sharp drop in blood pressure. Blood pressure rose again in the norepinephrine condition; it stayed down in the epinephrine condition. (Modified from Funkenstein, 1955; courtesy* Scientific American.)

which can be detected by the person experiencing the emotion. Second, the pattern in different emotions varies markedly from individual to individual. Each person has a rather specific pattern of bodily responses in emotional states. An individual will show rather similar patterns of autonomic response to a wide variety of stressing situations [Lacey et al., 1953]. Thus, the relationship between bodily states and emotions is not clear, and various theories have been proposed concerning the relationship that exists between felt emotions and bodily states.

THEORIES OF EMOTION   As we have said, the aim of these theories is to relate the felt emotion to bodily states. A description of three such theories follows.

James-Lange theory. This theory proposes the following sequence of events in emotional states. First, we perceive the situation which will produce the emotion; next, we react to this situation; and finally, we notice our reaction, and the perception of the reaction is the basis of emotional experience. Note that the emotional experience occurs *after* the bodily change—the bodily states, internal changes or overt movements, precede the emotion which is felt. As William James has succinctly put it: ". . . we feel sorry because we cry, angry because we strike, afraid because we tremble" [James, 1890].

Emergency theory. In contrast with the James-Lange theory, the emergency theory holds that the bodily states in emotion are simultaneous with emotional feeling and do not cause the felt emotion—the emotional feeling and the felt emotion occur together [Cannon, 1927, 1929]. Cannon's emergency theory states that sensory input initiated by the emotion-producing external situation triggers nerve cells in certain lower parts of the brain. Activity from these areas of the brain is then fed in two directions: to the cerebral cortex where the activity of the lower brain centers is received and felt as emotion; and to the body structures where the changes characteristic of emotion occur. In this theory, then, the bodily states are not the cause of the felt emotion; they are the bodily expression of the activity of the lower brain centers and they prepare the person or animal for emergency reactions—"flight" or "fight." Some of the lower centers of the brain which are important in emotion are discussed in Chapters 19 and 20.

A cognitive theory of emotions. This theory, which has some affinities with the James-Lange theory, states that the emotion which we feel is an interpretation of the stirred-up bodily states [Schachter and Singer, 1962]. The basic idea is that the bodily state of emotional arousal is much the same for many different emotions, and that even when there are physiological differences, they cannot be sensed. This means that the state of bodily arousal is ambiguous and any number of emotional feelings might be felt from very similar bodily states. However, we interpret and label—or have cognitions about—the physiological state, and we experience the emotion which seems appropriate to the situation in which we find ourselves. The sequence of events in the production of emotional feeling, according to this theory, is: perception of the emotion-producing situation, a stirred-up bodily state which is ambiguous, and interpretation and labeling of the bodily state so that it fits the perceived situation.

An example will make this theory of emotional feeling a little clearer.

Imagine a man walking alone down a dark alley, a figure with a gun suddenly appears. The perception-cognition "figure-with-a-gun" in some fashion initiates a state of physiological arousal; this state of arousal is interpreted in terms of knowledge about dark alleys and guns and the state of arousal is labeled "fear." Similarly a student who unexpectedly learns that he has made Phi Beta Kappa may experience a state of arousal which he will label "joy." [Schachter and Singer, 1962, page 380.]

This theory has led to some interesting experiments. Suppose that a physiological state could be induced by drugs and the situation changed so that subjects would have different interpretations of the same physiological state. We would then have different thoughts—cognitions—about the same physiological state, and emotional feelings should be different if the theory is correct. This sort of experiment is done informally every day with a common drug—ethyl alcohol or, to be plainer, booze. The emotional feeling of a person who has had a few drinks varies markedly with the situation in which he finds himself. Presumably, the physiological state is about the same, but the interpretation can be very different. If he is at a gay party, he may feel elated; if he is in a gloomy bar, he may feel depressed. A similar phenomenon has also been noted with some of the experimental drugs which affect mood. Lysergic acid (LSD-25), for instance, produces different moods in the same individual. These may range from euphoria to fear and hostility. The most important determiner of the differences in mood is the situation in which the drug is taken.

More pertinent evidence for this type of theory comes from controlled experiments. The following is an account of one of them [Schachter and Singer, 1962]:

Male college students were the subjects, and the experimenters attempted, with the permission of the subjects, to induce a state of physiological arousal by giving injections of epinephrine (adrenaline). As we have seen, such an injection produces a state of physiological arousal. The subjects were told, however, that they were receiving a vitamin compound. In one condition of the experiment, the subjects were not given any information about the effects which the injection would have; they were left free to interpret the mild state of physiological arousal as best they could. The next part of the experiment consisted of putting the subjects into two different situations: one designed to be a happy situation, the other designed to be perceived as one which might give rise to anger. These situations were produced by having a confederate of the experimenter act in different ways. In the happy situation, the stooge skylarked and fooled around according to a definite script; in the angry situation the confederate and the subject were given a questionnaire with many personal questions on it and the stooge showed increasing irrita-

tion—again following a script—with the experiment and the experimenters as he answered the questions. The subjects, then, had the same states of physiological arousal, but they were exposed to situations about which they might be expected to have different cognitions. The main question was whether they would have different emotional feelings. These feelings were measured by having the subjects fill out rating scales of their moods. Those subjects who were not informed about the reason for their state of physiological arousal tended to feel the emotion and behave in ways appropriate to the situation in which they were placed. Subjects who had been informed that the injection would produce physiological effects interpreted the bodily state as due to the injection and did not tend to experience emotions appropriate to the perceived situation.

This type of theory seems to be supported by both informal and experimental evidence. At least, it provides a way of accounting for the many emotional moods which may accompany very similar physiological states.

THE "LIE DETECTOR".   For the past few years, the public has heard a good deal about a "lie detector" that sometimes can be used to detect a person's guilt in crime. This device makes use of several of the autonomic changes we have just described. Although there are several versions of the lie detector, it almost always affords measurements of blood pressure, respiration, and GSR. The use of such measurements to detect lying rests on the assumption that autonomic changes are not under voluntary control—that a person can lie and hide the overt expression of emotion, but cannot control the autonomic changes that accompany fear and anxiety.

In a lie-detection test, the subject is presented with words and questions carefully chosen to arouse emotion if he is guilty of lying, but not to bother him if he is not. The subject is usually asked a series of questions while a record is made of his physiological responses. Some of the questions are "neutral"; they are routine items such as, What is your name? Where do you work? Where did you go to school? and so on. Others are "critical"; they have to do with the crime the person may have committed. Such questions are designed to evoke fear of detection or feelings of guilt about the crime. After the questions have been asked, the examiner compares the record for neutral questions with that for critical ones. If he finds that emotional responses are distinctly higher for the critical ones than for the neutral ones, he has reason to feel that the person is guilty. If there is no systematic difference, he concludes otherwise.

A skilled operator who has specialized in lie detection must frame the questions, administer the test, and interpret the records if the results are to have any validity. Even so, such a test often fails to reach a conclusion. Some individuals are so emotional about being investigated for a crime that they give very strong reactions to many of the neutral questions. On the other hand, some individuals, particularly hardened criminals, may be so unafraid generally that their autonomic changes are no greater for critical questions than for neutral ones. Consequently, the lie detector does not always detect the lie. In competent hands, however, it often does, and it has never been known to "convict" an innocent person [Inbau, 1942].

PSYCHOSOMATIC REACTIONS   The bodily changes that take place in anger and fear mobilize the body's energy and strength to deal with an emergency—the fear- or anger-producing situation. As we have seen, emotion has frequently been called an emergency reaction of the body [Cannon, 1929]. Stepped-up circulation makes energy available to the brain and muscles faster than it otherwise would be. Slowing of digestion and shunting of blood to the muscles does the same thing. In brief, each of the changes in some way makes it possible for the organism to react more quickly, exert more strength, run faster, or fight harder. Thus bodily changes help the body react more effectively in emotional emergencies.

If, on the other hand, a person is plagued with chronic anxiety or hostility that smolders on day

after day and month after month, the accompanying autonomic changes also go on without any letup and the effects are not desirable ones. In time the high heart rate and blood pressure, the increased secretion of hormones, and the alteration of digestive function can bring about actual damage to tissues and organs of the body. Or if the chronic autonomic effects do not themselves cause harm, they can make the individual more susceptible to infection or make him less able to recover from any diseases he may contract. In this way, chronic tension and anxiety bring about disorders of the body. These disorders are called psychosomatic—"psycho" meaning mind, and "soma" meaning body—because they are induced by psychological stresses [Dunbar, 1954].

It has been demonstrated that many disorders have a psychosomatic basis in some people: peptic ulcers, high blood pressure, asthma, dermatitis, obesity, and others. Ulcers have been produced experimentally in animals merely by subjecting the animals to a regimen in which they suffer chronic fear. Experiments have been done with rats and dogs, but perhaps those with monkeys are the most dramatic [Brady, 1958].

Although we have convincing proof that anxiety and chronic fear can induce such disorders as ulcers, we cannot conclude that all ulcers are psychosomatic. Indeed, ulcers occur in people who are not under any obvious psychological stress, and other factors besides chronic anxiety can produce them. The same is true of other diseases that may be psychosomatic. For this reason, it is often difficult to determine whether a disease is wholly or partly psychosomatic. In a great many cases, probably a combination of causes exists, and the psychological stress only aggravates a disorder or predisposes a person to it. Emotional stress, nonetheless, is the precipitating cause of a great many physical complaints.

GENERAL-ADAPTATION SYNDROME   Some of the bodily changes that take place in emotion also occur under other kinds of stress: overwork, prolonged exposure to cold or heat, severe burns or pain, or the ravages of disease. Therefore, we call any condition that makes the body mobilize its resources and burn more energy than it normally does a *stress*.

Three stages appear to occur in the body's reaction to stress (see Figure 7.8). Taken together, they are called the *general-adaptation syndrome*. The first stage, called the *alarm reaction*, consists of the typical bodily changes in emotion that we have reviewed. If the stress continues for some time, however, a person enters a second stage called *resistance to stress*. In this stage, the person recovers from his first burst of emotion and tries to endure the situation as best he can. Such endurance, however, puts considerable strain on his re-

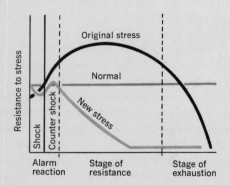

A PERSON DEVELOPS SOME RESISTANCE TO A CONTINUED STRESS; AT THE SAME TIME, HE HAS LESS RESISTANCE TO A NEW STRESS

FIGURE 7.8 *The general-adaptation syndrome. Responses to stress are divided into three stages: the alarm reaction, resistance, and exhaustion. The black line represents resistance to a continuous, original stress; the colored line, resistance to a new stress imposed in different stages of the adaptation syndrome. (After Selye, 1950.)*

sources. Then he may eventually reach a third stage, the stage of *exhaustion*. When he arrives at this point, he has exhausted his internal resources for dealing with continued stress. We do not see this stage too frequently in emotional stresses, but in instances of exposure to severe heat or cold, the person may finally weaken and die.

The first stages of the adaptation syndrome represent an attempt by the body to protect the person from stress. Unfortunately, however, an individual often pays a great price for this adaptation. It may result in such diseases as hypertension, rheumatism, arthritis, ulcers, allergies, and a host of related physical disorders. These disorders are seldom caused by psychological stress alone; yet the stress may be crucial; it may so aggravate ordinary physical causes of disorder as to produce a disorder that would not otherwise occur.

The particular diseases, whether behavioral or physical, that develop in reaction to stress depend upon the person's weak spots and upon the kind of stress he suffers. In any case, they are apparently caused by changes in the metabolism of the body that are produced by stress. There are many such changes, but they are not yet fully understood. The most general one is a reaction of the *adrenal gland*, the organ that seems to react most promptly and most vigorously to stress.

Two substances secreted by the adrenal gland are especially important. As we have seen, epinephrine mimics the action of the sympathetic nervous system by increasing heart rate and blood pressure and by making sugar available to the brain and muscles. *Cortin* includes many hormones that control sodium, water, and other chemicals in the internal environment. One of the components of cortin is *cortisone*. Cortisone and the *adrenocorticotropic hormone* (ACTH) have both received wide publicity as remedies for rheumatism, arthritis, and kindred disorders. ACTH stimulates the adrenal gland to secrete cortin and, hence, cortisone.

To understand how these facts relate to the general-adaptation syndrome of reaction to stress, refer again to Figure 7.8. Note that in the second stage of the adaptation syndrome, resistance to continued stress is increased. This means that *too much* adrenal secretion is being produced. In this stage, therefore, such diseases as hypertension (high blood pressure) and heart disease are prevalent. In fact, the symptoms of these diseases can be duplicated in animals by injecting an excess of adrenal hormones. On the other hand, in the later stages of adaptation to prolonged stress, the person's resources become exhausted. This is accompanied by—and in part, caused by—an exhaustion of adrenal hormones. Then such diseases as rheumatism and arthritis can result. It is for this reason that such drugs as ACTH, which gives added stimulation to the adrenal gland, and cortisone, which takes the place of insufficient cortical hormone, have helped in the treatment of these diseases. These drugs compensate for the exhaustion of adrenal activity resulting from prolonged stress.

TRANQUILIZING DRUGS Other kinds of drugs are required for the treatment of extreme states of anxiety and emotional upset. For many years, only general sedatives—that is, sleeping pills—were available. If an individual was greatly upset and needed calming down, he was given a sedative just as if he were tense and anxious and could not go to sleep. Sedatives will calm a person, but they often incapacitate him temporarily. Sedatives act rather generally on the nervous system to slow it down and do not specifically calm the bodily states in emotion.

In the last few years, however, medical research has developed drugs that are relatively specific for emotional behavior. A number of such drugs are available, and each has somewhat different effects. In general, they act selectively on the parts of the nervous system concerned in emotion. They are "emotional sedatives," rather than general sedatives. They make the person tranquil without making him sleepy or greatly reducing his ability to function. Hence they are called *tranquilizers* or *tranquilizing drugs* (see Chapter 15).

By acting on the nervous system, they can save wear and tear on the body. They reduce heart rate, blood pressure, muscular tension, and other autonomic states in emotion. Thus they make the individual more comfortable and mitigate his feelings of misery. Usually, however, they do not rid the person of his fears or the causes of anxiety. In fact, persons taking tranquilizing drugs generally report that they still worry; the tranquilizer merely keeps them from feeling so badly.

The tranquilizers developed thus far have their limitations [Wikler, 1957]. In the first place, they do not cure anything. They provide temporary relief which often makes it possible for the physician to proceed with other forms of treatment. Second, some individuals seem quite resistant to the tranquilizing effects of the drugs. And finally, they may have undesirable side effects; especially when used for a long period, they may induce muscular tremor, high blood pressure, and other harmful conditions. One must therefore be cautious in using such drugs and take them only under proper medical supervision.

Emotional expression

When a person is very angry, or very much afraid, or very joyous, we usually can tell what his emotion is by the way he behaves. But which patterns of behavior distinguish one emotion from another? And how accurate are we in telling one emotion from another?

In addressing ourselves to these questions, let us first consider a fundamental and universal pattern of emotional response, the *startle pattern*. *Facial and vocal expression* and *postures and gestures* are also ways of expressing emotion. But it is difficult to judge emotional expression correctly unless we also know the emotional situations giving rise to emotion.

THE STARTLE RESPONSE Perhaps the most primitive of all emotional patterns is the startle response. At least, in very careful studies of many

FIGURE 7.9 *Differences in emotional expression. These people are watching the same spectacle, but what varieties of emotion are being expressed? (George Zimbel, from Monkmeyer.)*

individuals, it has been found that this response is more consistent among most people than any other emotional pattern. You can easily observe this response by tiptoeing up to a person who is deep in thought and suddenly yelling "boo" or by clapping your hands loudly when he does not expect it. The reaction you get is what psychologists call the *startle pattern* [Landis and Hunt, 1939].

The whole thing takes place very rapidly but in a consistent pattern. The first part of the reaction is a rapid closing of the eyes. The mouth widens in a suggestion of a grin. Then the head and neck are thrust forward, often with the chin tilting up, and the muscles of the neck stand out. The uniformity of this emotional reaction from one person to another makes us believe that it is an inborn reaction that is modified very little by learning and experience. The startle response is, however, the only emotional reaction of which this is true.

FACIAL AND VOCAL EXPRESSION Emotional patterns other than the startle pattern differ from one person to another and from one culture to another. It should be clear then that each individual develops somewhat unique ways of expressing emotion. Look, for example, at Figure 7.9 which shows some students looking at a spectacle. Whatever the particular situation, it is the same for all of them. Yet notice the great differences in facial expression among the people. If you look at each of these faces separately, you will find it difficult in many cases to say what emotion is being expressed.

If, however, emotions are classified into two general groups, those which seem pleasant and those which seem unpleasant, one can observe some consistent differences in the expression of the mouth. In general, in the unpleasant emotions, the mouth turns down; in the pleasant ones, the mouth turns up. The same thing is true of the eyes; they slant up in mirth, and droop down in sadness. Leonardo da Vinci knew this and stated it as a principle to be used in depicting emotional expression.

In order to study patterns of facial expression, psychologists have presented pictures of faces expressing various spontaneously aroused emotions and have asked people to judge what emotions were expressed. In this kind of experiment, where the judges see only the face, agreement is far from perfect. There is usually rather good agreement upon whether the emotion is pleasant or unpleasant; but it is much more difficult to agree upon whether the emotion is sorrow, fear, anger, distress, or the like. The same result obtains, in general, for posed expressions. When professional actors portray certain emotions and judges rate them on facial expression alone, agreement about the kind of emotion portrayed is not very good.

Some work on this problem indicates that three dimensions of emotional expression can be judged with reasonable reliability [Engen et al., 1957, 1958] (see Figure 7.10). These are *pleasantness-unpleasantness, attention-rejection,* and *sleep-tension.* The dimension of pleasantness-unpleasantness is exactly what its name implies; it is the degree to which a facial expression represents feelings of pleasantness or unpleasantness. On the attention-rejection dimension, attention is characterized by wide-open eyes, and often by flared nostrils and open mouth, as if to bring the sense organ to bear on the object. At the other extreme, rejection, the

EMOTIONAL EXPRESSION CAN BE JUDGED FAIRLY ACCURATELY ON THREE DIMENSIONS: SLEEP-TENSION, ATTENTION-REJECTION, AND PLEASANTNESS-UNPLEASANTNESS

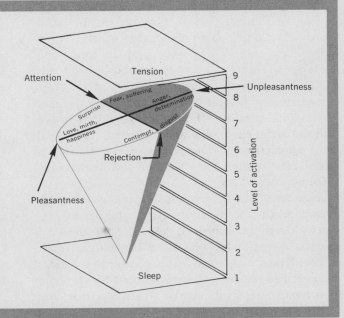

FIGURE 7.10 *A solid representing three dimensions of facial expression in emotion. The top surface is sloped to show that unpleasant emotions, such as anger and fear, can reach higher levels of activation than the more pleasant emotions. (After Schlosberg, 1954.)*

eyes, nostrils, and lips are tightly shut as if to keep out stimulation. The third dimension, sleep-tension, refers to the level of tenseness or excitement portrayed. At one extreme is the relaxation of sleep, and at the other is the expression of extreme emotional arousal.

People ordinarily express a good deal of emotion with their voices. Screams denote fear or surprise; groans, pain or unhappiness; sobs, sorrow; and laughter, enjoyment. A tremor or break in the voice may denote deep sorrow; a loud, sharp, high-pitched voice usually expresses anger. Vocal expressions as well as facial expressions are extremely helpful cues in distinguishing one emotion from another.

POSTURE AND GESTURES Emotions are expressed by means of posture and gestures as well as with the face and voice. In fear, a person flees or is "rooted to the spot." In anger, he usually makes aggressive gestures and may even clench his fists and move to attack. In sorrow, a person tends to slump with face downward, and in joy, he holds his head high and his chest out. Such signs of emotion are all taken for granted in this society.

The question of how consistently emotion is expressed in this way arises, however. As in facial expressions, individuals differ rather widely. When judges have only the expressions of the hands and forearms to observe, they agree fairly well for highly conventional expressions, such as worship, but agreement becomes more difficult for the less conventional gestures. If they are permitted to see both the facial expression and the gesture, however, their agreement improves considerably, though it is still far from perfect [Kline and Johannsen, 1935].

When one studies emotional expression in different societies, it becomes clear that such expression is largely learned. Indeed, a "language of emotion" seems more or less to characterize each culture. The Chinese may express surprise by sticking out their tongues, disappointment by clapping their hands, and happiness by scratching their ears

and cheeks. In our society, sticking out one's tongue is more likely to be a sign of defiance, clapping one's hands a sign of happiness, and scratching one's ears a sign of worry. Then, too, cultures vary in the degree of emotional expression that they encourage. The American Indian, for example, is relatively taciturn and expressionless, whereas the Frenchman characteristically gesticulates vehemently for even the mild emotions.

EMOTIONAL SITUATIONS Any single aspect of emotional expression—facial, vocal, postural, or gestural—is not a very reliable sign of the type of emotion involved. In other words, these components of expression are not uniform from one person to the next. When judges are given all of them together, however, they agree much better than when considering the components singly. Even so, they make a fair number of mistakes and may confuse such different emotions as anger and fear.

We need to see not only the pattern of expression, but the situation in which the emotion occurs in order to judge emotional expression most accurately. When both the situation and the expression are known, we can do quite well at naming the emotion [Klineberg, 1954]. All of us know fairly well what our individual emotions are in different situations, and thus we know what the other person's should be, or are likely to be, in a similar situation. So it is by situation, more than by expression, that we are able to distinguish different emotions. The kinds of situations that give rise to different emotions have already been described in the section on emotional development.

HUMOR AND LAUGHTER Smiling and laughing are distinctive expressions of emotion. In infants, smiling is a response to tickling and stroking or to an interesting noise or unusual movement. In older children and adults, smiling and laughter occur in an increasing variety of situations which appear to fall into two general categories.

One is a situation in which a person can express

his superiority, hostility, sexuality, or other usually unacceptable behavior in a socially acceptable manner. Children laugh when they see a playmate in a silly or sorry predicament, or when by teasing they manage to annoy the other fellow. Thus they express superiority or hostility without the risk of being punished for it. Some adults laugh at "dirty" stories, thereby expressing sexual preoccupations that are otherwise socially unacceptable.

The other situation involves incongruity. A person laughs when there is some contrast or incongruity between what a situation is perceived to be and what it is supposed to be. If a person falls into the water with his bathing suit on, we do not laugh, for nothing is incongruous about that. We do laugh, however, if he falls in with his street clothes on, for this is incongruous. Such incongruity usually makes us laugh only when it occurs at someone else's expense; it is funny only when it happens to the other fellow.

Funny stories usually have elements of the first situation—an expression of superiority, hostility, or sexuality—but they rely primarily on the development of an incongruity. The good storyteller manages to build up an expectation of one thing, but in his punch line he always delivers a surprise. Something happens that we did not expect. This provides the incongruity. The more intense the initial expectation, and the quicker the switch to a different outcome, the better the joke. The surprise, however, must be reasonable; it must be something that could be the outcome of the story had we not been led to expect something else. Thus the incongruity must make sense. Something that is just different or completely implausible usually falls flat.

SYNOPSIS AND SUMMARY

We have not tried to give a psychological account of all the moods and shades of emotion to which man is subject; nobody could do this. Our aim, instead, has been to concentrate on some of the stronger emotions such as fear and anxiety, anger, and pleasure. Perhaps the two most important points can be stated thus: (1) Emotional feelings and expressions are modified by learning; (2) emotions have a motivational function—behavior is directed toward or away from situations which will produce the emotion. The motivational aspect of emotions, especially of fear and anxiety, is stressed again in the chapters on personality, behavior disorders, and psychotherapy. The discussion in this chapter has tried to establish the following specific points.

1. An emotion is any departure from the normal state of an organism; it includes feelings, impulses toward action, and certain internal physical reactions.
2. Emotional tendencies are inherited in animals and probably also in human beings. By selective inbreeding, it is possible to develop strains in which animals are very emotional and others in which they are relatively unemotional.
3. The general pattern of emotional development in infants is one of successive differentiation of emotion. At first, there is only excitement. Out of this, distress and delight become distinct, and these in turn are elaborated into such emotions as anger, fear, elation, and affection for people.
4. Both maturation and learning participate in emotional development. In the later stages when learning is of greater importance, the following factors are involved: increasing capabilities in motor activities and language, increasing familiarity with people and objects, increasing opportunities for learning emotional reactions, the learning of new motives and goals, and learning to control emotions.
5. Emotional expression changes during development. Displays of emotion are more frequent in children than adults, and children's emotional outbursts are briefer. As increasing control of emotions is learned, emotional reactions also become more finely graded in intensity.
6. In general, the satisfaction of a drive or the achievement of a goal gives rise to pleasure. Fear at first is aroused by any strange stimulus suddenly presented.

Later, fear comes from threats of harm; and in adolescence, it is primarily connected with social situations. Anger is aroused by any frustration or interference with goal-directed activity.

7. Emotional habits are acquired because a situation regularly associated with an emotion through conditioning comes to give rise to that emotion. Many fears are acquired in this way. Habitual expressions of anger and hostility may also be acquired as social techniques for achieving goals.

8. Society attempts to suppress the expression of anger, but in so doing, it actually provokes anger and hostility. Both fear and anger are easily generalized.

9. In children, the frustration of motives is primarily caused by environmental obstacles. Later, frustration may be caused by goals that are so far above a person's level of performance that he cannot attain them. In adults, much frustration comes from a conflict between motives in which one motive cannot be satisfied without frustrating another.

10. When an individual experiences rather intense emotion, numerous changes occur within the body. These changes are the result of impulses from the autonomic nervous system and, particularly, the sympathetic part of this system. In addition, the hormones epinephrine and norepinephrine are secreted; these secretions by themselves can cause many bodily changes.

11. Bodily changes in emotional situations can be measured with appropriate instruments. There is evidence that the physiological patterns are different in anger and anxiety. Anxiety, or "anger-in," patterns seem to be similar to the changes resulting from epinephrine, while anger, or "anger-out," patterns seem to be similar to the changes produced by norepinephrine.

12. Several theories of emotion have been proposed in an attempt to relate the bodily changes in emotion to emotional feelings. Among these are: the James-Lange theory, which stresses the causative role of the perception of bodily changes in the production of emotional feelings; the Cannon emergency theory, which states that both the emotional feelings and bodily changes are simultaneously triggered by an emotion-producing situation, but that the bodily changes do not cause the emotional experience; and the cognitive theory, which states that emotional feelings are produced by interpretation and labeling of the stirred-up bodily state.

13. Chronic emotional reactions can cause psychosomatic illness through continued fast heart rate, high blood pressure, increased secretions of hormones, and other reactions. Disorders sometimes caused or aggravated in this way include peptic ulcers, high blood pressure, asthma, dermatitis, and obesity.

14. Three stages in the body's reaction to severe stress may be distinguished: the alarm reaction, consisting of typical emotional reactions; a second stage of increased resistance to stress; and finally a stage of exhaustion in which internal resources for dealing with the stress are totally depleted. The three stages taken together constitute the general-adaptation syndrome.

15. Tranquilizing drugs are sedatives of the emotions; they specifically calm anxieties and emotional reactions. They do not, by themselves, however, cure emotional illnesses, and they often have undesirable side effects.

16. Attempts to judge the kind of emotion portrayed by expressions of the face, voice, and hands alone meet with only moderate success. Best results are obtained when the observer not only sees the entire behavioral pattern but also knows the situation giving rise to the emotion.

RELATED TOPICS IN THE TEXT

CHAPTER 3 PRINCIPLES OF LEARNING Classical conditioning, as discussed in Chapter 3, seems to be especially important in the association of emotional states with particular situations.

CHAPTER 6 MOTIVATION Since emotions can function as motives, a review of the definition and principles of motivation may be helpful at this point.

CHAPTER 13 PERSONALITY Conflicts between motives often result in emotional states. The anxiety and anger which arise from motivational conflict are treated at some length in this chapter.

CHAPTER 14 BEHAVIOR DISORDERS The crippling effects of severe fear and anxiety, as well as other extreme emotional responses, are detailed in this chapter.

CHAPTER 15 MENTAL HEALTH AND PSYCHOTHERAPY
There are many techniques for the alleviation of severe
anrd crippling emotional states, such as anxiety, and
some of the more important ones are elaborated here.

CHAPTERS 19 AND 20 BIOLOGY OF BEHAVIOR Some of
the lower brain structures which are important in producing the bodily states characteristic of emotion are
described in these chapters.

SUGGESTIONS FOR FURTHER READING

Arnold, M. *Emotion and personality.* New York: Columbia University Press, 1960. (2 vols.).
*A two-volume work in which much of the psycho-
logical and physiological work on the emotions is
reviewed. Volume I deals with psychological studies;
Volume II with the physiological aspects of emotion.*

Candland, D. K. (Ed.). *Emotion: Bodily change.* Princeton, N.J.: Van Nostrand, 1962. (Paperback.)
*A set of readings consisting of original papers on
emotion, with special attention given to the physiological changes in emotion.*

Dunbar, F. *Mind and body: Psychosomatic medicine*
(enlarged ed.). New York: Random House, 1955.
*A popular account, written by a physician, of the role
of emotions in health and disease.*

Inbau, F. E. *Lie detection and criminal investigation.*
Baltimore: Williams & Wilkins, 1942.

*An authoritative source on the practical use of lie-
detection methods.*

King, R. A. (Ed.). *Readings for an introduction to
psychology* (2d ed.). New York: McGraw-Hill, 1966.
(Paperback.)
A book of readings designed to accompany this text.

Rapaport, D. *Emotions and memory.* New York: International Universities Press, 1950.
*An analysis of the effects of emotion and emotional
conflicts on memory.*

Reymert, M. L. (Ed.). *Feelings and emotion.* New
York: McGraw-Hill, 1950.
*A symposium of authorities summarizing modern
knowledge of emotion.*

KNOWING THE WORLD

PART FOUR

8

FOR THERE IS NO
CONCEPTION IN A MAN'S
MIND, WHICH HATH
NOT AT FIRST, TOTALLY,
OR BY PARTS, BEEN
BEGOTTEN UPON THE
ORGANS OF SENSE.
THOMAS HOBBES

BEHAVIOR AS WE know it, our own private experience, and the reported experience of others, would be impossible without information about the world around us. The senses are the channels through which we can know about the world. Through the action of the senses, we are able to adapt to and appreciate the world around us: Vision enables us to find our way through crowded streets, to appreciate the riches of an art museum or the delicate freshness of a spring day; hearing makes possible the use of speech for communication between people—the lover's tender words, the bigot's venom, the professor's wry humor would all be lost without hearing; through the skin senses we feel the pain of a bruise or we appreciate the tingle of a cold day and the warmth of a fire; through taste and smell we avoid spoiled foods and we savor the delights of French cooking. These are the so-called "five senses" of man: vision, hearing, skin sense, taste, and smell. But this does not exhaust the list.

THE SENSES OF MAN   The number of senses man possesses is closer to ten or eleven than five. The skin sense is not a single sense; there are at least four skin senses: *cold, warmth, pain,* and *touch.* Other senses give information about pressure, pain, and temperature deep within the body. These may be called the *organic senses.* Sense organs in the muscles, tendons, and joints give us information, most of it utilized without our awareness, about the position of our limbs in space and the state of tension in our muscles. These are the kinesthetic sense organs—they serve the sense called *kinesthesis.* The *vestibular sense* gives information about the movement and stationary position of the head and is the key sense in maintaining balance. In summary, a minimal list of man's senses includes: *vision, hearing, cold, warmth, pain, touch, organic sensibility, smell, taste, kinesthesis,* and the *vestibular sense.* These sensory systems may be classified in various ways, other terms may sometimes be used, and other senses may be added by subdivision of the basic ones; but we shall be content with these.

Each sensory system is a kind of channel which, if stimulated, will result in a particular type of experience. The visual channel, for instance, is usually stimulated by light, but it may also be stimulated by such things as gentle pressure applied to the eyeball. The point is simply that, regardless of the source of stimulation, activity produced in a sensory channel will result in a certain type of experience. In other words, what we experience is the activity in the nervous system [Müller, 1838]; we do not experience the stimulating world directly. Thus it is not quite accurate to say, as we often do, that we sense objects; we experience the pattern of activity in the nervous system corresponding to the object.

Usually, activity in a sensory channel results from a particular kind of stimulation—light in vision, for instance—because the channel is more sensitive to this kind of stimulation than any other. The kind of stimulation which usually excites a sensory channel is called the *adequate stimulus* [Sherrington, 1906].

Each sensory channel consists of a sensitive element, called the *receptor,* nerve fibers leading from this receptor to the central nervous system, and the various relay stations and places of termination within the central nervous system. Although the central processes are mentioned from time to time in this chapter, we shall be concerned largely with the receptor processes. A *receptor* is a cell, or group of cells, specialized to respond to relatively small changes in a particular kind of energy.

Some receptors, those for sight and smell, for example, are really nerve cells that migrated out from the brain in the course of evolution and have become specialized for their particular function. Other receptors, such as those for pain, are merely the relatively unspecialized ends of nerve fibers. In other cases, such as taste, hearing, kinesthesis, and the vestibular sense, the receptor has developed from the same sort of cells that produce skin.

Each of these receptors responds primarily to a certain kind of physical energy. Chemical receptors for smell and taste respond to chemical substances. Warmth and cold are thermal senses—they respond to thermal energy. Five senses—touch, pain, kinesthesis, the vestibular sense, and hearing—are mechanical senses, for some kind of mechanical movement is required to activate them. The pain sense may also be stimulated by extremes of chemical and thermal energy. The remaining sense, sight, responds to a certain range of electromagnetic energy.

The range of stimuli to which each kind of receptor responds is relatively restricted. Electromagnetic energy, for example, covers a tremendous spectrum from gamma rays, through X rays, ultraviolet rays, infrared rays, radar, radio waves, and the alternating current in house wiring (see Figure 8.1). Yet our visual receptors respond only to energy lying in the spectrum between the ultraviolet and infrared waves. Our hearing receptors, similarly, respond to vibrations of matter between about 20 and 20,000 cycles per second, even though ultrasonic energies go up into the millions of cycles per second. Our chemical senses also respond only to certain chemical molecules, and we cannot smell or taste others. Later, we shall specify more exactly the energies to which different receptors respond. The important point here is that they respond to only a very small portion of the energy changes taking place in the world around us. Much goes on that they miss. Consequently, most of the energy changes taking place in the external world are never perceived by human beings without the aid of special instruments, which are basically extensions of the senses.

SENSATION AND PERCEPTION Historically, the simple experiences that arise from the stimulation of sense organs have been called *sensations.* Our experiences of "red," "white," "sound," or "pain," for example, are said to be sensations. On the other hand, more complex experiences, such as "house," "whistle," or "warning," have been distinguished as *perceptions.* In other words, the rather simple ingredients of experience, according to such a distinction, are regarded as sensations, and the experiences that involve several sensations and their interpretation are considered to be perceptions.

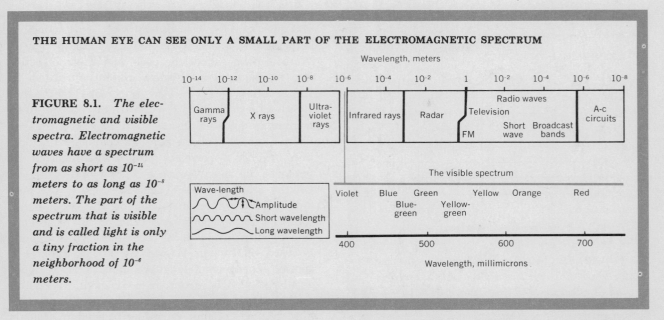

THE HUMAN EYE CAN SEE ONLY A SMALL PART OF THE ELECTROMAGNETIC SPECTRUM

FIGURE 8.1. The electromagnetic and visible spectra. Electromagnetic waves have a spectrum from as short as 10^{-14} meters to as long as 10^{-8} meters. The part of the spectrum that is visible and is called light is only a tiny fraction in the neighborhood of 10^{-6} meters.

The distinction is a useful one even though it is not a rigid one. In any refined analysis of experience, as experimental psychologists discovered many years ago, it is impossible to draw any fine line between sensation and perception. Consequently, they frequently refuse to do so or they avoid the problem as best they can. On the other hand, the rough distinction is useful in classifying various kinds of sensory experiences. And it provides a basis in this text for the organization of material on the senses into three chapters. This chapter, after an introduction to sensory systems and methods of measurement, deals with vision largely at the level of sensation. The phenomena of hearing and the lower senses are treated in the next chapter. Finally, a third chapter considers the phenomena loosely described as perceptual.

Sensory mechanisms

The study of the senses is a natural meeting ground for many sciences, especially psychology, neurophysiology, and physics. As such, it has had a long history. For instance, both Kepler (1571–1630) and Descartes (1596–1650) attempted to answer some of the questions concerning the working of vision. These men were completely mechanistic, Kepler trying to answer the question of how images are formed in the eye, Descartes trying to show the relationship between sensory input and response. Descartes "allowed only one kind of question: What physical motions follow each preceding physical motion?" [Crombie, 1964]. This mechanistic conception of the senses, in the hands of men such as Helmholtz (1821–1894), has been fruitful in later centuries. We can do no better than to be mechanistic also. Our basic question will always be: What are the mechanics of sensory experience? The answer to this question is, of course, very complex, and many of its aspects are imperfectly understood. We shall begin by considering three preliminary questions. Then we shall analyze the mechanisms of sensory experience for the specific senses, with special emphasis on vision and hearing.

TRANSDUCTION Our first question is: What is the process by which physical energy is converted into

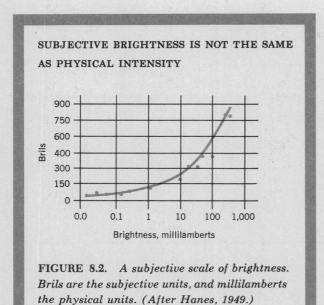

SUBJECTIVE BRIGHTNESS IS NOT THE SAME
AS PHYSICAL INTENSITY

FIGURE 8.2. *A subjective scale of brightness.*
Brils are the subjective units, and millilamberts
the physical units. (After Hanes, 1949.)

information which can be used by the nervous system? We have already said that it is not physical energy which is sensed—it is activity in the nervous system. This process of converting physical energy into activity in the nervous system is known in sensory psychology as *transduction*. Transduction takes place at the receptors—structures which we have already seen are specialized for best conversion of one particular type of energy, the adequate stimulus. The transduction process itself seems to involve several steps. In general, the specialized cells of the receptor act to convert physical energy into a slowly changing electrical potential, the *generator potential*. The generator potential, in turn, acts upon nerve cells and fibers to produce the nerve impulses which travel through the central portions of the channel and eventually result in an experience. In some sensory systems, especially vision, the idea of such a general process is supported by a mass of evidence; in other systems, such as hearing, the idea is attractive but less directly supported by evidence.

THE NERVOUS SYSTEM AND EXPERIENCE   Let us now suppose that certain nerve impulses have

been generated by the transduction process. A second question is now in order: What is the relationship between the nervous activity and experience? We are asking about the code, or pattern of activity, in the nervous system which is related to the experience reported by a person [Pfaffmann, 1959]. In order to find the pattern or code, we need techniques for the investigation of single cells or fibers ("units") in the sensory channels. In addition, in order to correlate pattern with reported experience, we need accurate reports of experience. On the one hand, such accurate reports are best obtained from human beings; on the other hand, the recordings from single cells or fibers are obtained with physiological techniques which cannot be used on human beings. By giving animals a special experimental language, it is possible to get accurate "reports" from them [Blough, 1958; and see below]. In the future it may be possible to combine methods of unit recording from alert animals with methods of obtaining accurate reports from animal subjects. The technical problems are, however, enormous, and as yet unresolved.

PHYSICAL ENERGY AND EXPERIENCE   Suppose we pass over the relationship between neural activity and experience for a while. Instead, we may ask a third type of question: What is the relationship between the characteristics of physical energy and reported experience?

Psychophysics studies this relationship between physical energy and experience, and the methods used in this study are the *psychophysical methods*. Psychophysics is such an important subject that we must devote a section to it.

Psychophysics

Although sensory experience and physical energy are by no means identical, they are related, and the relationship must be discovered. On the one hand is the physical energy which is referred to in physical terms; on the other hand is the experience which is referred to in psychological terms. For

TABLE 8.1. *Some approximate detection threshold values.*

SENSE MODALITY	DETECTION THRESHOLD
Vision	Candle flame seen at 30 miles on a dark clear night (about 10 quanta)
Hearing	Tick of a watch under quiet conditions at 20 feet (about 0.0002 dyne/cm²)
Taste	Teaspoon of sugar in 2 gallons of water
Smell	Drop of perfume diffused into the entire volume of a three-room apartment
Touch	Wing of a bee falling on your cheek from a distance of 1 centimeter

SOURCE: Modified from Galanter, 1962.

instance, the relationship between perceived brightness and the amount of energy in the physical stimulus appears in Figure 8.2. Here the scale of perceived brightness is labeled "brils," and the amount of physical energy is measured in millilamberts. In the middle of the curve, a stimulus that is ten times as intense as another is not perceived as ten times greater, but more like two times greater. Furthermore, the exact relationship between perceived brightness and physical energy varies with the intensity of the physical stimulus. In any case, perception of a change in intensity does not correspond in a one-to-one fashion with the physical change in intensity. Similar types of relationships between perception and physical energy are also present in other sensory modalities.

THRESHOLD SENSITIVITY At very low energy levels, a special relationship between energy and experience occurs. Even though receptors are extremely effective transducers, each requires some minimum level of activating physical energy before detection is possible (see Table 8.1). In our attempt to relate physical energy and experience, we want to know the answer to the question: What is the least amount of physical energy which can be experienced? Or, put in more rigorous terms: What is the least amount of physical energy which can be responded to differentially? The question has turned out to be much more complicated than it might seem at first glance. The classical answer to this question is that there is an *absolute threshold* for each sense. When physical energy levels are below certain values, that is, the threshold, the stimuli are not detected; when they are above this value, detection and differential response are possible. There are difficulties with this view, however, and doubts have been raised about the possibility of measuring absolute threshold points [Swets, 1961].

First, a look at the traditional ways of measuring the absolute threshold is in order. One method, called the *method of constant stimuli,* is to present a stimulus of a given intensity to an observer and ask him to indicate whether he detects it or not. On the next trial, a somewhat different intensity is presented; again, the observer merely signals yes or no. The procedure is usually continued for several hundred trials until the observer piles up one hundred or so responses to each of several intensities of the stimulus. For example, in vision, a typical result is a "frequency-of-seeing" curve (see Figure 8.3). This shows the number of times an observer saw a flash of light at each of several intensities. The threshold is then placed at the intensity at which the observer reports seeing and not seeing the light equally often.

Another method, the *method of adjustment,* allows the observer to adjust the intensity of a stimulus until he just barely detects it. He is provided with a dial with which he can turn the intensity up or down. He turns it down until he cannot see or hear the stimulus, then up a little until he can, and back and forth until he is satisfied that he has the setting at which he can just detect the presence of the stimulus. This is then the threshold intensity. In order to minimize error, he usually is asked to repeat the measurement a number of times, and the

ONE WAY OF FINDING AN ABSOLUTE
THRESHOLD IS TO FIND THE INTENSITY
AT WHICH A PERSON DETECTS THE
PRESENCE OF A STIMULUS 50 PER CENT
OF THE TIME

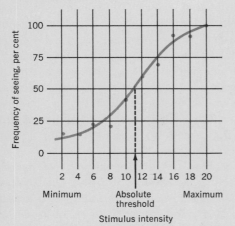

FIGURE 8.3. *A frequency-of-seeing curve obtained by the method of constant stimuli. We might also have such curves for many other sensory modalities.*

average of his various readings is taken as the absolute threshold.

A modified method of adjustment has proved to be a very powerful tool in the study of threshold sensitivity in animals. This is of more than academic curiosity because accurate measures are necessary as a first step in investigating psychophysical relationships in animals. We can obtain records of neural activity from animals in ways which we cannot use for human beings. Thus, in addition to psychophysical relationships between characteristics of the stimulus and behavior, it may be possible to study the relationships between the activity of the nervous system and differential sensitivity. A method which uses instrumental learning to provide the animal with a "language" for reporting has been used by Blough (1958):

An animal, a pigeon, for instance, is placed in an apparatus facing two disks and a lighted stimulus patch (see Figure 8.4). Pecks on the two disks, A and B, activate the apparatus. The box containing the disks is light-tight and is illuminated only by the light on the stimulus patch. The job of the pigeon is to learn to peck key A when the stimulus patch is visible to him and to peck key B when the stimulus patch is not visible. After the animal has been trained to respond appropriately to the two disks by the use of reinforcement and the principles of instrumental learning (see Chapter 3), responses on key A will indicate that he sees that the stimulus patch is illuminated, while

A MODIFIED METHOD OF ADJUSTMENT
MAY BE USED WITH ANIMALS

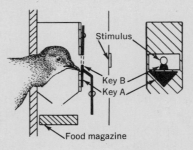

FIGURE 8.4. *Diagram of an apparatus used for psychophysical studies with pigeons. The diagram on the left is a side view; that on the right shows what the pigeon faces. The pigeon has been taught to peck key A when he can see that the stimulus patch is illuminated, and to peck key B when he cannot see that the stimulus patch is illuminated. Pecks on key A reduce the illumination of the stimulus patch, while pecks on key B increase illumination of the patch. The pigeon thus adjusts the illumination around his absolute threshold, and by recording the amount of light on the stimulus patch, we can obtain a direct measure of his absolute threshold. Reinforcement to maintain responding is delivered by the food magazine. (From Blough, 1956.)*

THE VISUAL ABSOLUTE THRESHOLD OF A PIGEON

FIGURE 8.5. *A psychophysical function obtained from a pigeon. This dark adaptation curve (see page 302) shows how the absolute threshold changes as a function of time in the dark. The eye becomes more sensitive in the dark. Note the very low intensity of physical energy which is effective. The ordinate units are micro-microlamberts, millionths of a millionth of a lambert (a definition of a millilambert, or a thousandth of a lambert, is given on page 281). The curve also shows the cone-rod break typical of dark adaptation curves from animals, including humans, which have both cone and rod elements in their retinas (see page 284). (From Blough, 1956.)*

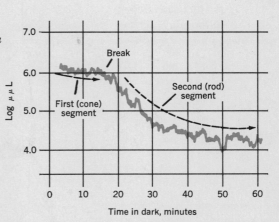

pecks on key B will be given only when he cannot see that the stimulus patch is illuminated.

This technique involves a variation on the psychophysical method of adjustment because pecks made on key A which indicate that the stimulus patch is visible also reduce the illumination on key A. After a few responses have been made on this disk, the pigeon will have driven the illumination to a point where he can no longer detect it and he switches to key B. Pecks on key B, however, increase the illumination of the stimulus patch which eventually brightens to a point where it can be detected by the animal. At this point it switches to key A, which drives the illumination down until he again switches to key B. The illumination on the panel is thus adjusted by the pigeon to a value close to his threshold.

By plotting the illumination of the stimulus panel as the pigeon adjusts it over time, we can obtain a continuous record of threshold (see Figure 8.5). This technique can be used with other senses; for instance, it has been extended to hearing. [Gourevitch et al., 1960.]

A third classical method for the measurement of sensory thresholds is called the *method of limits.* The experimenter usually starts by presenting the subject with stimulus intensities which are well above threshold, gradually decreasing the intensity of the stimulation until the subject does not report detection of the stimulus. Then the experimenter starts with stimulus intensities which are well below threshold and increases intensity until the subject reports that stimulation is present. Several such descending and ascending series of stimulus presentations are usually run (see Table 8.2). The results obtained from descending and ascending series are often a little different. In order to express the threshold as a number, the stimulus intensities at the last consistent reports of failure of detection are found; the mean of these values is called the threshold in the method of limits.

The thresholds determined by these traditional methods are obviously not fixed, absolute numbers. The thresholds are, as the methods of determination make clear, statistical concepts. In addition, so-called *response factors* markedly influence the value of the threshold as determined by traditional methods. It is easy to see that the expectations of the subject concerning the presence or absence of stimuli and the motivation of the subject to be correct are

TABLE 8.2. *Results of a short experiment using the method of limits.*
Yes means that the subject says that he detects the signal.
No means that the subject says that he does not detect the signal.

STIMULUS INTENSITY (ARBITRARY UNITS)	SERIES			
	DESCENDING	ASCENDING	DESCENDING	ASCENDING
100	Yes		Yes	
90	Yes		Yes	
80	Yes	Yes	Yes	
70	Yes	No	Yes	Yes
60	No	No	Yes	No
50		No	No	No
40		No		No
30		No		No
20		No		No
10		No		No
Mean intensity of last failure of detection	65	75	55	65

Mean (threshold) = 65

SOURCE: Modified from Titchener, 1905; Woodworth and Schlosberg, 1954.

important factors: It is one thing to report the presence or absence of light in a psychological experiment on a warm afternoon right after lunch; it is quite another thing to be a radar operator on a ship responsible for the detection of blips indicating approaching aircraft. The payoffs are quite different—a mistake in one situation means nothing; in the other, a mistake may be a matter of life or death.

Signal detection in the classical psychophysical methods differs from that of everyday life in another way. In most laboratory situations, the signal to be detected usually appears against a background with a minimum amount of distraction, sometimes called *noise*. However, in the case of the radar operator, the signal he sees appears against a noisy background. For all these reasons, some people have despaired of giving values to thresholds and have attempted, rather, to find out how detection is affected by variations of the experimental situation [Galanter, 1962].

DIFFERENTIAL SENSITIVITY So far we have been considering the least amount of stimulus energy required for detection. Another important question in psychophysics is: What is the smallest difference between two stimuli—two light intensities, for instance—necessary before we can discriminate a difference between them? The smallest difference which can be discriminated is known as the *differential threshold,* or the *just noticeable difference (JND)*. One of the most important things about the differential threshold is that it is not constant. Suppose you are in a room which is illuminated by one 25-watt bulb and another 25-watt bulb is turned on. The addition of this amount of extra light will be immediately detectable—it is well above the differential threshold. If, however, you are in a room which is illuminated by a thousand 25-watt bulbs, the addition of the light from one more 25-watt bulb will not be noticed. The amount of energy added in the brighter room is the same, but that amount is below the differential threshold.

Thus the value of the differential threshold depends upon the intensity of the stimulus to which more energy is added. It has been found, however, that, for relatively moderate intensities, a constant *ratio* exists between the amount of energy which must be added, called $\triangle I$, to reach the differential threshold, and the intensity, called I, of the stimulation. In other words, $\triangle I/I$ is a constant for the middle range of intensities. This has been called *Weber's law,* and it holds fairly well for all but the extreme intensities of stimulation.

The classical psychophysical methods, discussed in connection with absolute thresholds, may also be used to obtain differential thresholds. Two stimuli—a standard stimulus and a comparison stimulus—are needed to obtain differential thresholds with the classical psychophysical methods. For instance, using the method of adjustment, the subject adjusts the value of the comparison stimulus until it is perceived to be equal to the standard. Many such adjustments are made, and the average, or mean, point of perceived equality is obtained. The point of perceived equality is called the *point of subjective equality (PSE)*. From other statistical manipulations of the results, an estimate of the differential threshold can be obtained. Differential thresholds can also be obtained from statistical manipulations of the results from the method of constant stimuli and the method of limits [Woodworth and Schlosberg, 1954].

THE SCALING OF SENSATION We have said that the basic problem in psychophysics is to relate changes in the physical stimulus with reported experience. Fechner (1860) developed the classical methods of psychophysics in an attempt to solve the psychophysical problem. He attempted to show how reported experience varies with the physical stimulation by using Weber's law and by assuming that all JNDs are psychologically equal—the experience of detecting a difference between any two stimuli is the same. It is clear from Weber's law that the intensity necessary to produce an experience of difference increases progressively. When the increase in physical energy needed to produce an experience of difference is plotted against the equal psychological steps, it can be seen that physical energy increases far faster than differences in experience (see Figure 8.6). The relationship between physical energy and experience was thought by

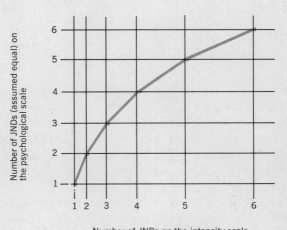

SUBJECTIVE EXPERIENCE IS EQUAL TO $k \log I$

FIGURE 8.6. *The relationship between physical stimulus intensity and subjective experience according to Fechner. In order to obtain this relationship, two assumptions are needed: (1) that Weber's law holds; (2) that the subjective experience in differentiating two stimuli one JND apart is always the same. (From Galanter, 1962.)*

Number of JNDs (assumed equal) on the psychological scale

Number of JNDs on the intensity scale

Fechner to be a logarithmic one; perceived experience equals a constant times the common logarithm of the intensity of the physical stimulus; symbolically stated, perceived experience = $k \log I$.

We have seen that some rather tenuous assumptions underlie this attempt to scale psychological events. As a matter of fact, other techniques and other assumptions yield different relationships. The method of *magnitude estimation* is appealing because of its simplicity and straightforwardness. In this method, the subject estimates the intensity of the physical stimulus directly by assigning numbers to the various intensities—large numbers for the more intense stimuli, smaller numbers for the weaker ones [Stevens, 1956]. When these estimates are plotted against physical intensity, a power function, not a logarithmic function, is the result (see Figure 8.7). The strength of the perceived experience is equal to a constant times the physical stimulus to some power; again symbolically, perceived experience = kI^n [Stevens, 1961].

Here we have two contrasting statements about the relationship between the physical and perceived worlds. No final answer about which is right can be given, but because of serious questions about Fechner's assumption of equal psychological JNDs, the trend seems to be away from the classical logarithmic view and toward the more direct power-function view.

The physical basis of vision

The fact that we experience the world visually is wonderful and amazing, but how can it happen? Certainly, neurophysiologists and psychologists do not know all, or even very many, of the details of the process, but a coherent story for vision, and for some of the other senses as well, is beginning to emerge.

The outline of the story for vision is really fairly simple. The *electromagnetic energy* which we call visible light strikes specialized *receptor cells,* the *rods* and *cones* of the *retina,* and initiates a series of chemical changes in the light-sensitive substances

of these cells. The outcome of this series of reactions is an electrical event, a voltage change, called the *generator potential.* The generator potential is the event which causes barrages of nerve impulses to be triggered, and it is this barrage which constitutes the input into the central nervous system responsible for seeing. What we see depends, of course, on the objects transmitting light to the retina. But, from the point of view of analysis, what we see depends upon the characteristics of the barrage of nerve impulses which reach the central nervous system.

ELECTROMAGNETIC RADIATION If you were asked what you see, you would probably say that you see light. This is true—you do see light. But we must distinguish between the physical stimulus that excites the eye and the psychological sensation of light that you actually experience. Let us consider some of the physical properties of light.

We see objects either because they emit radiant energy or because radiant energy is reflected from them. This energy, which physicists call electromagnetic radiation, may be thought of as consisting of electric charges moving through space at approximately 186,000 miles per second. It is difficult to explain just what these charges or electromagnetic radiations are like, but it is conventional and convenient to talk about them as though they travel in waves. It is also possible to measure and classify radiant energy in terms of the distance from the peak of one wave to the peak of the next, that is to say, in terms of *wavelength.* Some electromagnetic radiations have wavelengths as short as 10 trillionths of an inch (the cosmic rays), some have wavelengths of many miles (radio waves), and all sorts of wavelengths occur in between (see Figure 8.1). The entire range of all possible wavelengths is called the *electromagnetic spectrum.*

VISIBLE RADIANT ENERGY Although all radiant energy—all wavelengths of the electromagnetic spectrum—is very much the same physically, not all of it is visible. Somewhere in the middle of the spectrum, between 16 and 32 millionths of an inch in length (see Figure 8.1), are the wavelengths that we can see. These are known as the *visible spectrum.* Because the word "light" implies seeing, it is only these visible wavelengths that are called light waves. Scientists use the metric scale rather than inches and feet, however, to express length. A micron, for instance, is one millionth of a meter, and a millimicron is one thousandth of a micron. The visible spectrum of wavelengths extends from about 380 to 760 millimicrons (mμ).

As Isaac Newton discovered in 1666, it is possible to break up the visible spectrum into its component wavelengths.[1] The trick for doing this is to pass a beam of white, or mixed, light through a glass prism (see Figure 8.8). Such a prism bends short wavelengths (which appear violet) more than long wavelengths (which appear red). A prism, in fact, spreads all the wavelengths out in a broad band so that we can see and measure each wavelength in a mixed beam of light. Wavelengths in the visible spectrum are related to color experience.

[1] This work was not published in full until Newton presented his *Opticks* in 1704.

UNITS OF LIGHT INTENSITY   The measurement of light intensity is based upon an arbitrary unit, the *international candle.* This is approximately equal to the amount of light emitted by a candle with a flame 1 inch high. *Illumination,* the amount of light falling on a surface, is measured in footcandles, or the amount of light falling upon an area of 1 square foot which is 1 foot from an international candle. In psychology, we are usually interested in the brightness of an object or surface in terms of the amount of light which is reflected back to the retina. This reflected light is called *luminance* and is usually measured in *millilamberts.* A millilambert is the amount of light reflected from a perfectly reflecting and diffusing surface which is 1 foot square and is illuminated by 0.93 footcandle [Morgan, 1965].

Structure of the human eye

Before we discuss the transduction process in vision, we need to set the stage by describing some aspects of the anatomy of the eye and the visual system.

SUBJECTIVE EXPERIENCE IS EQUAL TO $k\,I^n$

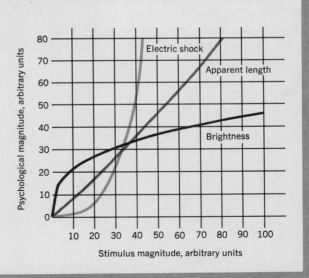

FIGURE 8.7. *The relationship between physical stimulus intensity and subjective experience according to Stevens. These curves were obtained by the method of magnitude estimation. The size of the exponent determines the shape of the curve. The exponent for the brightness curve is less than 1; that for the apparent length curve is 1; that for the electric shock intensity curve is greater than 1. (From Stevens, 1961.)*

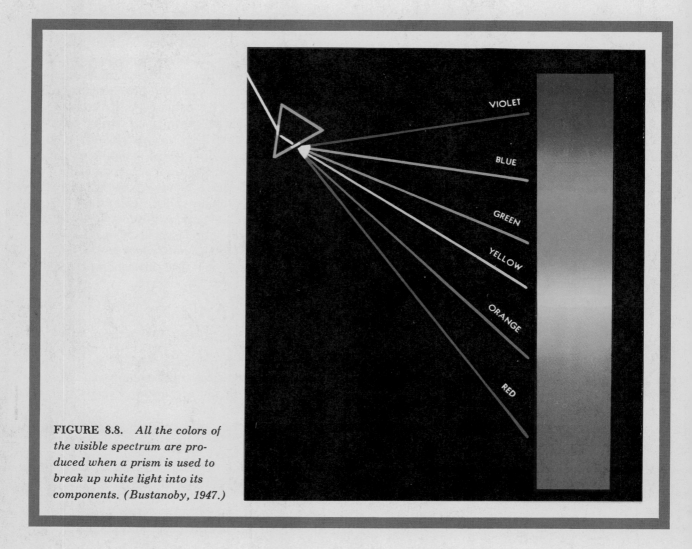

VIOLET

BLUE

GREEN

YELLOW

ORANGE

RED

FIGURE 8.8. *All the colors of the visible spectrum are produced when a prism is used to break up white light into its components. (Bustanoby, 1947.)*

In certain respects, the eye looks and behaves like a camera (see Figure 8.9). Both are essentially dark chambers which admit light through an opening in front. Immediately behind the opening, in each case, is a lens which focuses images of outside objects onto the rear surface. The surface on which the image is projected in the eye is called the *retina;* in the camera, that surface is the photographic film. Just as in a camera, the images falling on the retina are inverted and turned from right to left.

Both the camera and the eye can be adjusted to control the amount of light falling on this surface. To control light entering a camera, the photographer adjusts the diaphragm in front of the lens. When he encounters too much light, he "stops down" the camera diaphragm; when light is relatively dim, he increases the size of the opening in the diaphragm. The eye, however, has its own automatic, or reflex, mechanism for making such adjustment. Its diaphragm is the *iris,* which is the colored part of the eye; the iris controls the size of the opening, known as the *pupil*, which admits light to the eye. In dim light, the iris expands the pupil, thus increasing the amount of light admitted. This adjustment permits a person to see in dimmer and in brighter illuminations than would otherwise be possible. You can easily observe the contraction of the pupil by having a person close his eyelids for a while and then open them. The normal pupil has a maximum range of adjustment of 2 to 8 millimeters in diameter—corresponding to a sixteenfold change in area.

Although it is helpful and instructive to compare the eye to the camera, this comparison must not be pushed too far. The details of the processes are different, and there are other fundamental differences. First, it is misleading to think that we see directly the small images which form on the retina—what we see is the result of a long series of events (see Chapter 10). It is true that the light falling on the retina is patterned, but we do not see this. As we said previously, the activity of the nervous system is what we "see." The neural input is subject to much reorganization on its way through the retina and from the retina to the brain, and the eventual spatial and temporal pattern of nervous activity which underlies visual experience is quite different from the light patterns on the retina. Second, the eye has a double lens system: the *cornea* and the lens itself (see Figure 8.10). As a matter of fact, most light bending, or refraction, in the eye is done by the cornea; the lens simply adds enough bending to the basic corneal refraction to bring near objects into sharp focus on the retina. Finally, the eye is not a passive receiver—it is never at rest. Extremely small tremors of the eye muscles produce small and continual movements of the eyeball. These small movements, which have been called *physiological nystagmus,* are essential to vision. In experiments where special lens systems are used to prevent the play of excitation over the retina, objects disappear from vision [Riggs et al., 1953]. By spreading excitation over a fairly wide area, physiological nystagmus probably prevents fatigue of the receptor elements.

GENERAL STRUCTURE OF THE EYE   A closer look at the eye reveals an organ of enormous complexity—so complex that the drawing in Figure 8.10, which is complicated enough, shows only its essential features. The eye is roughly a sphere and its walls consist of three separate layers: the sclera, the choroid, and the retina.

1. The outer layer, the *sclera layer,* consists of a tough fibrous material that protects the eyeball and maintains its shape. In the front of the eye, this sclera layer becomes transparent and bulges out to form the *cornea.* The *extraocular*

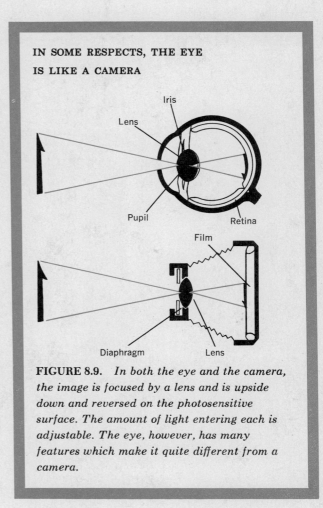

IN SOME RESPECTS, THE EYE IS LIKE A CAMERA

FIGURE 8.9.   *In both the eye and the camera, the image is focused by a lens and is upside down and reversed on the photosensitive surface. The amount of light entering each is adjustable. The eye, however, has many features which make it quite different from a camera.*

muscles which turn the eyeball are attached to this sclera layer.

2. Underneath the sclera layer is the *choroid layer,* which corresponds roughly to the opaque backing on a photographic film or to the blackening on the inside of a camera. This dark layer absorbs stray light in the eyeball and prevents light from entering the eye except through the cornea and lens.

3. The *retina layer,* the innermost layer of the eyeball, is like a photographic film, as we have said; it is the sensitive tissue that enables us to see.

The interior of the eye is divided into two principal chambers: a small one in front of the lens and behind the cornea and a large one behind the lens, the main chamber of the eye. These chambers are filled with gelatinous fluids sometimes called humors. The chambers and the humors are shown in Figure 8.10.

RODS, CONES, AND THE FOVEA   Since the retina is the sensitive element for seeing, it deserves closer attention than the other structures of the eye. Examining it with a microscope, we can see that it is made up of many layers of cells and fibers. Two types of cells—*rods and cones*—are the light-sensitive elements. Figure 8.11 depicts these two types of cells; the rods are cylindrical in shape, and the cones are rather tapered. Our best estimate is

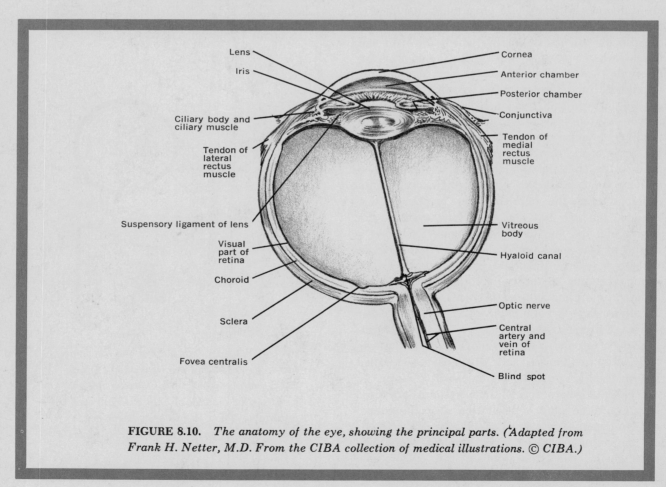

FIGURE 8.10. *The anatomy of the eye, showing the principal parts. (Adapted from Frank H. Netter, M.D. From the CIBA collection of medical illustrations. © CIBA.)*

LIGHT EXCITES THE RODS AND CONES, WHICH SEND MESSAGES VIA THE BIPOLAR AND GANGLION CELLS TO THE BRAIN

FIGURE 8.11. *A schematic diagram of the cells of the retina. At the top are the sensory cells, the rods and cones. These connect with bipolar cells, which connect in turn with the ganglion cells. Fibers of the ganglion cells make up the optic nerve. Note the many interconnections, especially those of the horizontal and ganglion cells. Note also that the retina is inverted with respect to the incoming light: the rods and cones are on the side away from the light. The ganglion cell and bipolar cell layers are quite transparent.*

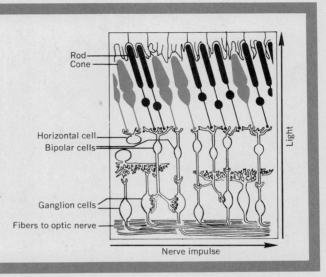

that the eye contains between 110,000,000 and 125,000,000 rods and between 6,300,000 and 6,800,000 cones [Østerberg, 1935]. This tremendous number of rods and cones, however, is not spread uniformly over the entire retina. Rather the cones are most numerous in a highly specialized region of the retina known as the *fovea,* and the rods occur most frequently about 20 degrees away from the fovea. As Figure 8.10 shows, the fovea is a slightly depressed area of the retina. The fovea is the region of most distinct vision and the part that we use most in looking at objects. When we want to see something very clearly, we naturally turn our head and eyes so that an image of the object falls on this part of the retina.

Some special features of this part of the eye should be noted. In the first place, the cones in the fovea are much longer and more slender than those in the periphery of the eye. In fact, foveal cones look something like rods. Since they are smaller, many more of them can be packed into the small foveal area. A second interesting feature of the foveal cones is that they have their own individual nervous connections with the optic nerve—they have "private lines" to the brain [Polyak, 1941].

Outside the fovea, however, several cones, or several rods and cones, are usually linked together into common nerve pathways.

In the *blind spot* of the retina (see Figure 8.10), the fibers of ganglion cells leave the retina and form the optic nerve which connects with the brain. The spot is blind because it lacks both rods and cones (see Figure 8.12).

CONNECTIONS OF THE CONES AND RODS
From the rods and cones, tiny nerve fibers make connections with still other types of cells. Of these, two kinds, the *bipolar* cells and the *ganglion* cells, are in a direct line with the central nervous system (see Figure 8.11). Indeed, the fibers of the ganglion cells make up the optic nerve which conveys impulses from the retina to the brain. Hence the three sets of cells in the retina which transmit information about light are (1) rods and cones, (2) bipolar cells, and (3) ganglion cells. Note that the human retina is an *inverted retina;* the light goes through the almost completely transparent ganglion and bipolar cells before reaching the rods and cones.

The interconnections of the cells in the "direct

FIGURE 8.12.   *Demonstrating the blind spot. Close your left eye, and look at the cross with your right eye. Then move the book toward you or away from you until the sketch of the girl disappears, or largely disappears, from view. At this point, the image of the girl is falling on your blind spot.*

line" are so enormously complex that micro-anatomists have been able to trace only some of the more obvious ones. From the psychologist's standpoint, this network of connections allows a good many possibilities for explaining some of the curious visual phenomena that we discuss later.

FOCUSING AND THE LENS   In most cameras, one adjusts the focus for objects at different distances by moving the lens back and forth. The lens of the human eye does not work this way. The lens changes its shape—that is, it becomes thicker or thinner—to focus at different distances. These changes are termed *accommodation*. The *ciliary muscle*, which is attached to the ligaments that suspend the lens in place, so contracts and relaxes that the lens becomes thin and flat to focus the eye on far objects and becomes thick and curved to focus it on near objects (see Figure 8.13).

One of the common defects for which we wear glasses is the inability to accommodate sufficiently to see objects at all distances, both near and far. Inability to see far objects clearly is called nearsightedness; the opposite is farsightedness. Accommodation normally focuses the eye for different distances. Inability to focus is usually the fault either of the shape of the lens or of the shape of the eye.

Although eyes and their lenses are amazingly constant in shape, it does not take much distortion in shape to make them imperfect as focusing instruments. In some cases, the overall length of the eyeball is a little longer or shorter than it should be. In other cases, the curved surface of the cornea is a little too flat or too curved.

About two-thirds of the people in America see well enough at a distance of 20 feet or more. For that reason it is possible to put blackboards at the front of classrooms in schools, signposts at considerable distances along roads, and seats far back in theaters. Some people, however, are pathologically *farsighted;* that is to say, they cannot see things that are very close (see Figure 8.14). The trouble is usually that the eyeball is too short from front to back. Consequently, when a farsighted person wants to look at an object that is close by, he must accommodate appreciably more than the normal person in order to bring the object to focus on his retina. If his eyeball is markedly shorter than normal, he may be quite unable to produce enough accommodation to obtain a focus. At best, in such extreme cases, the page of a book held 30 inches away always looks fuzzy. If a farsighted person reads for several hours at a time, the prolonged strain of accommodation—that is, of contracting the ciliary

THE LENS CHANGES SHAPE
TO FOCUS OBJECTS ON THE RETINA

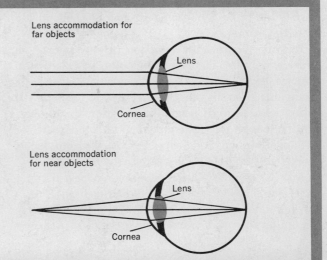

Lens accommodation for far objects

Lens

Cornea

Lens accommodation for near objects

Lens

Cornea

FIGURE 8.13. *The accommodation of the lens. The lens flattens to focus images of objects far away, and it thickens to focus images of nearby objects. Note that much of the refraction, or bending, of the light is done by the cornea. This does not change. The changes due to the lens are added to this constant refraction caused by the cornea.*

WHEN THE EYEBALL IS TOO SHORT, A PERSON
IS FARSIGHTED; WHEN IT IS TOO LONG,
HE IS NEARSIGHTED

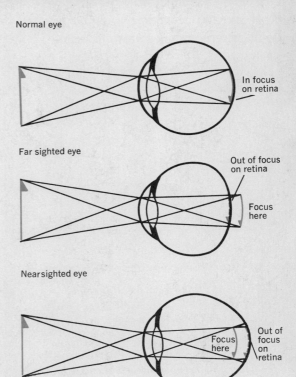

Normal eye

In focus on retina

Far sighted eye

Out of focus on retina

Focus here

Nearsighted eye

Focus here

Out of focus on retina

FIGURE 8.14. *Farsightedness and nearsightedness. In the normal person (top) the image is focused on the retina. The farsighted person (middle) has an eyeball that is too short and focuses images on a plane behind the retina. The nearsighted person (bottom) has an eyeball that is too long and focuses images on a plane in front of the retina. (Modified from Ruch, 1958.)*

muscle—may bring on severe headaches and a variety of other symptoms which are collectively called eyestrain.

Exactly the reverse condition is encountered in *nearsightedness*. Here the difficulty is usually an abnormally long eyeball. For a person suffering from nearsightedness, nearby objects come to focus on the retina with little or no accommodation in the lens, but the lens cannot flatten enough to compensate for the long eyeball and bring far objects into focus. Hence only near objects are clearly focused.

Another condition is called *oldsightedness* because it is characteristic of old people. In short, it is a farsightedness that comes on with advancing age. We often observe older people holding a news-

paper far out in front of them to read. Such farsightedness is due to a hardening of the lens of the eye. This hardening process begins almost at birth, and progresses throughout life. We can, in fact, guess the age of a person rather accurately by simply measuring the maximum accommodation that he can accomplish with his lens.

If you would like to check this, ask someone you know to close one eye and hold this page at arm's length, in front of the other eye. Now have him bring it slowly toward his eye and stop when the print begins to blur. Then measure the distance between his eye and the book; this distance is called the near point of vision, and from it you may estimate your subject's age by using Figure 8.15. Unfortunately, there are two points that we could not get into this figure because they are so far away from the other points: the near point for fifty-year-olds averages 15 inches, and for sixty-year-olds, 39 inches. The scale in Figure 8.15, however, works only for people who have normal eyes to start with; nearsighted or farsighted people get different results.

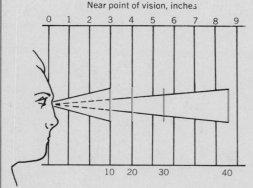

THE OLDER A PERSON IS, THE FARTHER AWAY HE WILL PROBABLY HAVE TO HOLD THINGS TO SEE THEM CLEARLY

Near point of vision, inches

Approximate age, years

FIGURE 8.15.   *The near point of vision depends on age. The near point is the nearest distance one can hold an object, a printed page, for instance, and still see it clearly. This point increases with age. For a person who is fifty years of age, it averages 15 inches; for one who is sixty years of age, it averages 39 inches.*

The transduction process in vision

How do the sensitive rods and cones of the retina change the electromagnetic energy of light into nerve impulses which are necessary for our perceptions? As you might imagine, this is an extremely complex process when all the details are considered. The outline, however, is simple. Three main stages have to be considered. The first of these consists of the chemical events in the light-sensitive pigments found within the rod and cone cells. The second consists of the creation of a generator potential as a result of the photochemical activity, and the third is the generation and propagation of nerve impulses along the fibers of the ganglion cells to the brain.

PHOTOSENSITIVE PIGMENTS   When electromagnetic energy in the visible spectrum strikes photosensitive pigments in the rods and cones, chemical

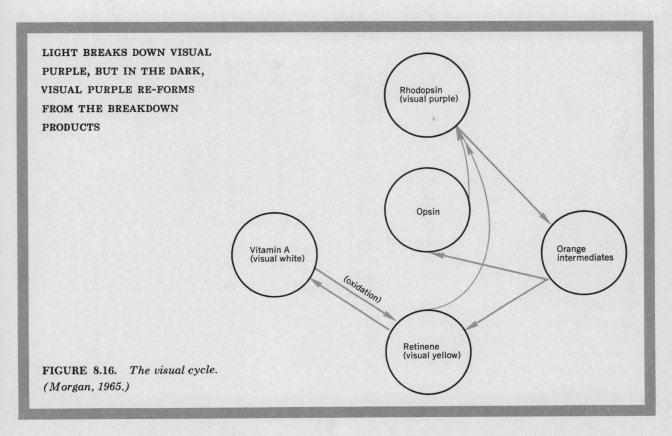

LIGHT BREAKS DOWN VISUAL
PURPLE, BUT IN THE DARK,
VISUAL PURPLE RE-FORMS
FROM THE BREAKDOWN
PRODUCTS

FIGURE 8.16. *The visual cycle.*
(Morgan, 1965.)

changes occur and the chain of processes in seeing is initiated. The fact that photosensitive pigment is involved in vision was first discovered by Franz Boll in 1876. He noticed that the retina of a frog which had been in the dark for some time had a reddish-purple color, but that when the eye was exposed to light, the pigment bleached to a yellowish color. Thus the photosensitive substance was first called "visual purple," and after exposure to light, it was called "visual yellow." Subsequent research has shown that the rods and cones have different photosensitive pigments with different properties. *Rhodopsin* is the major pigment in the rods of the retina; *iodopsin* is the general term which has been applied to the cone pigments of certain animals [Wald, 1959]. It has been shown that three types of cone pigments probably occur in the human retina [MacNichol, 1964]. This fits well with the three-

color theory of color vision which we discuss later.

Rod pigment. Originally called visual purple, rhodopsin is found in the rods of most vertebrate animals. When struck by electromagnetic energy in the visible range, rhodopsin is broken into orange intermediates and then into two substances, *retinene* and *opsin* (see Figure 8.16). Retinene gives the yellowish color which was originally called visual yellow. Retinene and opsin spontaneously change back into rhodopsin, and a cycle of chemical changes, the so-called *visual cycle*, takes place. In this way, an equilibrium is established between the breakdown of rhodopsin and its synthesis from retinene and opsin. The rates of the reactions depend upon the intensity of the illumination. Under dim levels of illumination, the rhodopsin-retinene-rhodopsin reaction is the prominent one, but under intense illumination, some of the retinene is con-

CONES OF THE HUMAN RETINA SEEM TO BE MOST SENSITIVE TO THREE WAVELENGTHS

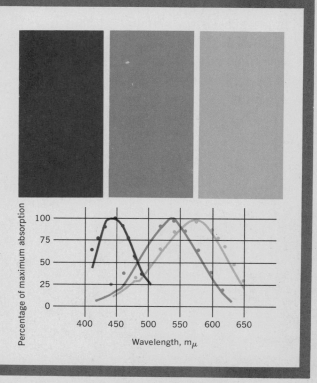

FIGURE 8.17.   *The human retina seems to contain "blue" cones, "green" cones, and "yellow" cones. The lower curves show the absorption of light by the three types of human cones. For instance, the "blue" cones absorb the short wavelengths most effectively; the "green" cones absorb the middle wavelengths; and the "yellow" cones absorb the long wavelengths most effectively. The peak absorptions are at 447 millimicrons, 540 millimicrons, and 577 millimicrons for the "blue," "green," and "yellow" cones respectively. The colors corresponding to the wavelengths of these peak absorptions are shown above. (MacNichol, 1964;* courtesy Scientific American.)

verted to vitamin A. This reaction is also reversible, and after the intense illumination is over, the vitamin A will be converted back into retinene which will then change back into rhodopsin (see Figure 8.16).

Cone pigments. The three human cone pigments have been identified by the study of spectral-absorption curves. Spectral-absorption curves are obtained because the electromagnetic energy which is active in decomposing the visual pigments is absorbed in the process. Some substances absorb some wavelengths best, other substances absorb other wavelengths. For example, in the chicken retina, the general cone substance, iodopsin, has a peak of absorption at wavelengths near 555 millimicrons; rhodopsin, the major rod substance, has an absorption peak near 505 millimicrons.

That three different types of cone substances seem to exist in human and monkey retinas has been discovered by using a device called a microspectrophotometer in which the absorption of light in single cones can be studied [MacNichol, 1964]. The substance in one type of cone seems to have an absorption peak at approximately 447 millimicrons; that in another type, a peak at approximately 540 millimicrons; and that in the third type, a peak at about 577 millimicrons (see Figure 8.17). The cones of the primate retina thus seem to fall into three clusters or populations. Since we see blue when stimulated by wavelengths at 477 millimicrons, green when stimulated at 540 millimicrons, and yellow at 577 millimicrons (see page 297), the different types of cones might be called "blue," "green," and "yellow" cones. Although the peak sensitivity of the yellow cones is in the part of the spectrum perceived as yellow, they are also sensitive to longer wavelengths of light in the part of the spectrum which appears red (see Figure 8.17). These cones with peak sensitivities in the yellow may, therefore, also be called "red" cones.

The next event after light strikes the eye is the production of slow, graded, generator electrical potentials in the retina. They are probably related to the chemical changes in the pigments, but the exact relationship is not clear.

GENERATOR POTENTIALS In the eyes of some animals, *Limulus*, the horseshoe crab, for example, the generator electrical potential following light stimulation is relatively easy to measure [Hartline et al., 1952; Benolken, 1961]. The prolonged deflection of voltage above the baseline shown in Figure 8.18 is the generator potential. The generator potential makes the neural elements more electrically negative—it depolarizes these elements and triggers nerve impulses (see Chapter 19). Generator potentials are characteristic of other sensory systems also [Granit, 1955].

In the eyes of other creatures, similar generator potentials have been discovered. These have been called the S, or slow, potentials [Tomita, 1963]. These slow potentials are like generator potentials in that they are graded—their size depends upon the intensity of the stimulus. The stronger the stimulus, the greater the size of the electrical S potentials. The nerve impulses which arise on top of the slow potentials are not graded—their size does not depend upon the strength of the stimulus (see Chapter 19). The exact site of the generation of these slow potentials is in some doubt. Experiments have shown that they do not originate in rods or cones or at the ganglion cells—they arise between these elements. The current opinion is that they do not originate in the bipolar cells, as one might expect, but in large glial, supporting or nourishing, cells within the retina.

In addition to the generator potentials which seem to be on the direct line of events which result in visual perception, there is another complex potential known as the *electroretinogram* (*ERG*). Since

SLOW VOLTAGE CHANGES, GENERATOR POTENTIALS, AND FAST VOLTAGE CHANGES, NERVE IMPULSES, ARE RECORDED FROM THE EYES OF MANY ANIMALS

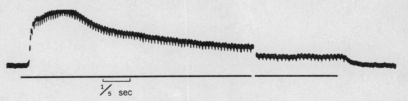

1/5 sec

FIGURE 8.18. *Generator potential and nerve impulses recorded from the eye of the horseshoe crab,* Limulus. *The light is turned on when the lower line starts. Shortly thereafter, a slow and prolonged change of voltage occurs—the generator potential. It seems to be responsible for the production of the fast voltage changes, that is, nerve impulses, which appear as spikes superimposed upon it. The details of this sort of process are discussed at greater length in Chapter 19. (Hartline et al., 1952.)*

this can be recorded from the intact human eye, a great deal is known about it and it is a useful research tool. However, there is some dispute about the origin of the various components of the ERG and about the relationship of these components to the production of nerve impulses which are responsible for visual perception.

NERVE IMPULSES   We have already seen nerve impulses, or *spikes*, arising from the generator potential. These impulses are recorded from the ganglion cells with microelectrodes. A strong relationship exists between the size of the generator potential and the rate at which nerve impulses are produced—the greater the size of the generator potential, the greater the frequency of nerve impulses. This seems to be general, but it has been shown most clearly in the eye of *Limulus*.

It seems clear that nerve impulses arise in ganglion cells when light strikes the retina. However, the picture is more complicated than this. The activity of an individual ganglion cell can be increased or decreased from a wide region of the retina. This brings us to the idea of a receptive field. The *receptive field* of any sensory cell, a ganglion cell in this case, is the area of the receptor surface, the rod and cone layer of the retina in this case, from which its firing can be influenced—either increased or decreased. The receptive fields of many ganglion cells are organized as shown in Figure 8.19. Stimulation of the middle of the field results in an "on" response—the ganglion cell gives nerve impulses, it "fires." Stimulation of the peripheral part of the field results in an "off" response—the same ganglion cell fires when the stimulus goes off. The reverse of this situation is also quite common. A transition zone between the inner and outer "on" and "off" zones gives "on-off" responses.

Thus the message transmitted to the brain from the ganglion cells is not a simple one—it is already highly organized at the ganglion cell level. The information for what we see is in this input, but the code has not yet been cracked. How bright an object appears is probably related in some way to the density of the neural barrage reaching the brain; the color of an object is probably related to the pattern of firing reaching the brain from the three types of cone pigments; but the details are not known, and the situation is certainly not this simple.

In the absence of precise correlations between

GANGLION CELLS OF THE RETINA MAY RESPOND TO LIGHT IN SEVERAL WAYS

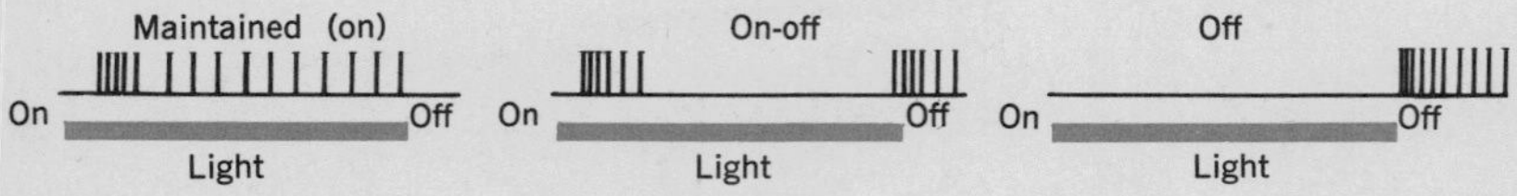

FIGURE 8.19.   *Above, "on," "on-off," and "off" responses from ganglion cells of the retina. Right, types of ganglion cell response from different parts of the receptive field. Stimulation restricted to the center of this receptive field produces "on" responses, indicated by +; stimulation at the periphery of the field produces "off" responses, indicated by ○; stimulation of an intermediate zone produces "on-off" responses, indicated by ⊕. (Above, modified from Hartline, 1938; right, after Kuffler, 1953.)*

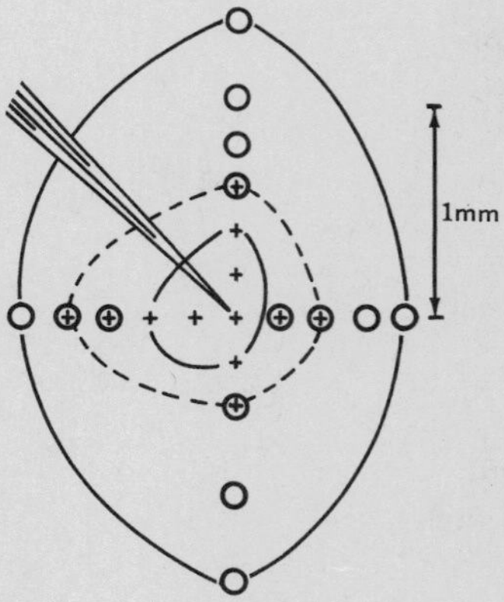

physiological events and reported experience, two strategies have been followed. Theories have been proposed which make use of plausible, but hypothetical, physiological mechanisms. The theories of color vision which we discuss next illustrate this trend. The second strategy is to find correlations between the physical energy and reported experience, neglecting the nervous system. This is, as we have already seen, the psychophysical approach, and we shall return to it later.

Theories of color vision

All theories of color vision have assumed that there are different kinds of cones, and that each kind of cone has its characteristic sensitivity in a certain region of the spectrum. This means, in terms of our modern knowledge of photochemistry, that different cones contain somewhat different photochemical substances, each with its own spectral-absorption curve. For convenience, the theoretical cones have been named according to their assumed peaks of absorption. Hence a "red" cone refers to a cone assumed to be most sensitive in the red region, a "green" cone, one that is supposed to be most sensitive in the green region of the spectrum, and so on.

YOUNG-HELMHOLTZ THEORY The *Young-Helmholtz theory* is named after the two men who formulated it, although they worked on it at different times—Thomas Young (1773–1829) and Hermann Helmholtz (1821–1894). The theory assumes the existence of *three* kinds of cones: "red" cones, "green" cones, and "blue" cones [Helmholtz, 1924]. As we have seen, we now have good evidence for these three types of cones in the primate retina; the theory, however, was formulated long before any of this evidence was available. A further assumption is that the code for color is such that the effects generated in these cones add and combine in a simple way to produce the perceived colors. For instance, an equal amount of activity in all three cones is supposed to produce the experience of "white." It is this assumption of the theory about which we have no direct evidence; we do not know the code for color or white.

The strongest support for a theory based on a minimum of three cones comes from the data on color mixture. We can mix colors by taking three primary wavelengths, one in the blue region of the spectrum, one in the red region, and another in the middle, green and yellow region. It is possible to mix three wavelengths chosen from these regions in various proportions and to reproduce any hue or saturation that human observers see. In the right mixture, they add together to produce white.

The Young-Helmholtz theory has never adequately explained some of the other phenomena of color vision. Certain facts of color blindness have required special modifications of the theory. Many red-green color-blind people can see yellow, for instance. In the Young-Helmholtz theory as originally stated, yellow is supposed to be due to a mixture of activity in the red and green cones. How then can red-green color-blind persons who presumably lack the red and green cones see yellow? The theory thus does quite well in accounting for color mixture, but is quite inadequate, without special assumptions, in accounting for other phenomena. Thus it is not a completely acceptable theory. Some of the difficulty may lie in the particular designation of "red," "green," and "blue" cones.

THE HERING THEORY The *Hering theory,* named for its chief protagonist, Ewald Hering (1834–1918), is another attempt to explain color vision. It is often now called the *opponent-process theory* [Hurvich and Jameson, 1957]. It assumes three sets of cones—white-black, red-green, and yellow-blue—all able to function in opposing ways. Thus the theory states that the cones for brightness are separate from those for color. It further states that the processes for red oppose, or cancel, those for green, and those for yellow oppose those for blue. As originally proposed, the theory held that each pair of processes took place in the same cone. It now seems more plausible to assume that there may be four "color" cones and that these are linked to bipolar and ganglion cells in such a way that they function in opponent pairs. The original Hering theory has always given a better explanation of color blindness than the Young-Helmholtz theory. At the same time, it can handle the laws of color mixture and the laws of complementary colors.

Some of the best physiological evidence for the Hering theory comes from studies of the goldfish retina [Wagner et al., 1960]. In these experiments, measurements of the spike discharge from single ganglion cells were made, and behavior consistent with an opponent-process theory was observed. The evidence is based on the activity of "on" and "off" cells (see page 292). For instance, at the shorter wavelengths many ganglion cells were "on" cells and responded with a burst of impulses; at the longer wavelengths the same cells responded as "off" cells with inhibition during the period of illumination and a burst of firing at the offset of stimulation (see Figure 8.20). This might indicate opponent-process action of a general kind; "on" activity came from one wavelength, "off" activity—an opposite type of activity—came from other wavelengths. It does not fit with specific types of color cones as proposed by Hering, but it does show, in a

WHETHER A GANGLION CELL IS AN "ON" OR "OFF" CELL DEPENDS UPON WAVELENGTH

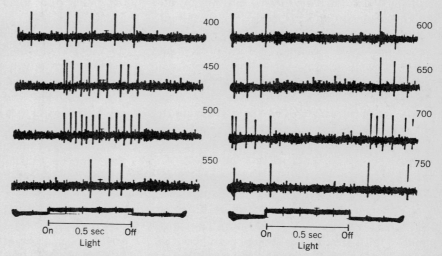

FIGURE 8.20.   *Nerve impulses, or spikes, from a goldfish ganglion cell to different wavelengths of light. The tall spike-like lines are electrical records of single nerve impulses. Wavelength, in millimicrons, is indicated by the numbers to the right of the records. At the shorter wavelengths, the ganglion cell is an "on" cell; at the longer wavelengths, it is an "off" cell and is inhibited during the time the long wavelength light is on. This is shown by the cessation of spontaneous activity when the longer lavelengths are on. Results like these seem to indicate that an opponent-process mechanism may be at work at the ganglion cell level. (Wagner et al., 1960.)*

general way, that there may be an opponent-process mechanism operating at the ganglion cell level. An opponent-process type of activity has also been found further on in the visual system—in the lateral geniculate body [DeValois, 1965].

AFTERIMAGES Both the Young-Helmholtz and Hering theories can account for another phenomenon of color vision, *successive contrast*. If you look steadily at a bright-colored spot for a while and then look away at a gray sheet of paper, you may see two kinds of successive afterimages. The first, the *positive afterimage*, which is the same color as the original stimulation, is very fleeting and may not be seen at all. The second, the *negative afterimage*, develops a little later and is the complement of the original stimulus color. Suppose that the original spot is blue-green; the positive afterimage will also be blue-green, but the negative afterimage will be orange (see Figure 8.21).

Positive afterimages are supposed to be caused by a continuation of the activity after removal of the physical energy. Most of the interest is in the negative afterimages. The Young-Helmholtz theory makes the assumption that the original stimulation fatigues the specific color cones which are excited. A blue-green stimulus, for instance, will fatigue the "blue" and "green" elements and not the "red" elements. Once this has happened, the light of the gray test field, which contains all wavelengths (see Figure 8.8), will not excite the blue and green elements but will excite the red elements which were not fatigued. The laws of color mixture (see page 297) and the absorption characteristics of the red elements account for the fact that the afterimage is orange rather than pure red. The Hering theory also makes assumptions about fatigue of elements. For instance, a blue-green light will fatigue the blue component of the yellow-blue cones and the green component of the red-green cones. The light from the gray test patch will then stimulate the yellow and red components of the Hering elements and the mixture of these will give an experience of orange. If we think of the Hering, or opponent-process, theory as operating at the ganglion cell level, more compli-

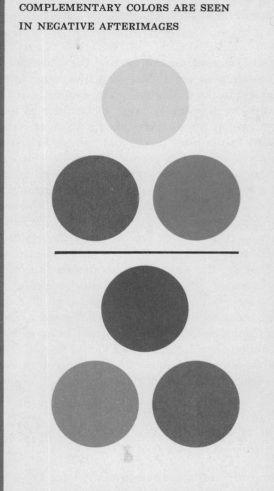

COMPLEMENTARY COLORS ARE SEEN IN NEGATIVE AFTERIMAGES

FIGURE 8.21. *The colors in the lower circles are the complements of those in the upper circles, and vice versa. If you fixate the upper panel at the cross and stare at it for a minute or so under fairly bright illumination, you can expect to see the colors in the lower panel when you look away at a white sheet of paper. Fixation on the lower panel will produce negative afterimages which will look similar to the upper panel.*

cated assumptions involving inhibition and excitation must be made. The point is that both theories can handle negative afterimages.

CONCLUSIONS ABOUT COLOR VISION As we have seen, the information leaving the retina is the final result of a great deal of activity and interaction within the retinal cells. The proposals of the Young-Helmholtz theory seem to be more or less correct in that three cone pigments which are most sensitive in the blue, green, and yellow regions of the spectrum actually seem to be present in the primate retina. Opponent-process principles may be in operation in determining the output of the ganglion cells. It seems possible that both these theories contain the germs of truth, but probably neither of them will be supported by the eventual physiological explanation of color vision. Remember that they are theories—elaborate guesses as to how the system might work. They were designed to make sense out of the accumulation of data on vision, and they are simply plausible guesses as to the physiological processes which may be operating. It would be quite surprising if either of them turned out to be completely supported by the accumulating physiological data.

Some psychophysical relationships in vision

As we come back to psychophysics, or the relationship between the physical stimulus and reported experience, measurement and scaling are now of less concern than the qualitative relationship between the physical energy and reported experience. For example, what characteristics of the physical stimulus are necessary for normal color experience? As we shall see, color experience depends upon the wavelength, the mixture of the wavelength with white light, and the intensity of the stimulation. The perceived experience corresponding to wavelength is called *hue,* that corresponding to the purity of the wavelength is called *saturation,* and the experience corresponding to the intensity of the stimulation is perceived *brightness.* The perceived color, then, is primarily determined by a combination of wavelength, purity, and the intensity of the physical stimulus.

HUE Hue is the perceived dimension of color we refer to when we use common color names such as red, green, yellow, blue, or combinations of them. Thus when we say that something is red, we mean that it has a red hue; greenish-blue, a greenish-blue hue; and so on.

Perceived hue depends primarily on wavelength of light. If several wavelengths are mixed together, as is usually the case with all colors except those made by a prism (see Figure 8.8), hue depends on the wavelength that is dominant in the mixture. The relation between wavelength and hue, however, is not completely stable. The eye is not equally sensitive to all wavelengths, and its relative sensitivity changes with the intensity of the light stimulation. Hue also depends upon *contrast* effects. For instance, two adjacent colored areas may induce what appear as mutual changes in hue in each other near the border between the two areas. This is called *simultaneous contrast.* But under arbitrarily standardized viewing conditions, the hue perceived can be precisely related to wavelength.

The relationship of hue to wavelength is depicted in Table 8.3 and Figure 8.22. The table lists selected wavelengths throughout the spectrum and gives the color name for the hue that the typical observer would apply in viewing these wavelengths. In Figure 8.22, hues and their corresponding wavelengths are arranged in a circle, rather than along a straight scale.

Both illustrations give the wavelengths of the psychologically "pure" or *unique* colors—the hues that observers consider not to be tinged by any other hue. Thus a unique yellow is one judged not to be tinged with green on the one side or red on the other, and it appears on the spectrum somewhat right of center, at 582 millimicrons. Unique blue is located at 477 millimicrons—near the short end—

TABLE 8.3.   *Wavelengths and color names. On the left are hues seen at the shorter wavelengths of the visible spectrum; on the right are their corresponding complementary hues seen at the longer wavelengths. The particular value of wavelength for a given hue varies somewhat with the state of adaptation of the eye. Note that the unique colors are not exactly complementary.*

430 mμ	Violet	571 mμ	Green-yellow
477 mμ	Unique blue	578 mμ	Greenish yellow
482 mμ	Greenish blue	582 mμ	Unique yellow
492 mμ	Green-blue	610 mμ	Orange
495 mμ	Blue-green	660 mμ	Yellowish red
497 mμ	Bluish green		Unique red
515 mμ	Unique green		Purplish red

and unique green somewhat left of center at 515 millimicrons. Unique red is an interesting case because it has no corresponding simple wavelength.

The reddest red in the visible spectrum at 700 to 760 millimicrons—the hue hardly changes at all between these two points—is still not red enough. It requires a little blue from the other end of the spectrum to get rid of a slightly yellowish tinge and to be judged a pure red. For that reason, unique red is said to be "extraspectral," which means that it lies in the hypothetical region between the two ends of the spectrum [Dimmick and Hubbard, 1939].

The extraspectral location of pure red on the color circle provides a clue to one of the basic laws of color vision, the *law of complementary colors*. *Complementary colors* are hues which when mixed together are perceived as gray or white. Gray or white refers to the dimension of brightness, a second dimension of color perception, extending from black at one extreme to white at the other. Complementary hues are hues that when mixed together cancel each other out and produce gray or white. The law of complementary colors states that for

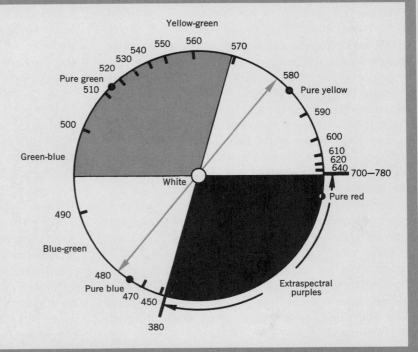

THE HUES OPPOSITE EACH OTHER ON THE COLOR CIRCLE ARE COMPLEMENTARY

FIGURE 8.22.   *The color circle. This diagram shows the arrangement of various hues and their corresponding wavelengths on a circle. Points opposite each other on the unshaded sectors represent complementary hues. Those on the shaded sectors have no complementary wavelengths in the visible spectrum.*

every hue there is a complementary hue, and that complementary hues, when mixed in the appropriate proportions, produce gray or white. As can be seen in Figure 8.22, the yellows and the blues have single complementaries in the visible spectrum, represented by white sectors. Those in the green region have no spectral complementary hues. Their complementaries are extraspectral, which is to say, they are formed out of mixtures of the red and the blue ends of the spectrum. This point is represented by the shaded sectors in Figure 8.22, the dark sector representing the extraspectral hues. It should now be apparent why the hues are arranged in the form of a circle. This way of representing them reflects the law of complementary colors which is operating in all our everyday perceptions of color.

What will happen if, in mixing wavelengths, we do not use wavelengths that are complementaries of each other? We do not ordinarily have lights that are pure enough in wavelength to make complementary matches. Even when we do, they are seldom exactly the right wavelengths to match. The resulting hue will lie in an intermediate position on the color circle.

For hues that are not too far apart, we can find approximately the resulting hue on the color circle by first drawing a line connecting the two hues that are mixed and then making a point on the line that represents the proportions in which they are mixed. Thus if we mix a yellow and a green, in equal parts, we may draw a line between their respective positions on the circle and mark the point halfway between. If we have mixed one part of green with two parts of yellow, we mark off one-third of the distance on that line from yellow to green. A line from this point through the center of the circle intersects the circle at the resulting hue. If we want to know what will happen when we mix any two wavelengths, we can use this procedure to figure it out. The same procedures may be used, though they become more complicated, for predicting the dominant hue when three, four, or even more different hues are mixed.

It will occur to some students who have had occasion to mix paints that the rules for mixing wavelengths do not seem to be the same as those for mixing paints. That is true. The perception of a mixture of yellow and blue wavelengths, for example, is gray or white, but the perception of a mixture of blue and yellow paints is green. Why?

Paints do not emit light; they reflect or absorb it. They never, however, reflect all the light that strikes them. If a substance contains a dye, it absorbs some wavelengths; the remaining reflected wavelengths give it its perceived color. For example, yellow paint generally absorbs violet and blue wavelengths; it reflects some green and red, somewhat more yellow-green and orange, and a lot of the yellow wavelengths. Blue paint, on the other hand, absorbs red, orange, and yellow wavelengths, and reflects the yellow-green, green, blue, and violet ones. When these two paints are mixed, the result is one of subtraction as well as addition. Each of the paints absorbs its part of the spectrum, and what is left to be reflected depends upon both the absorption and the reflectance of the two paints. In the case of a mixture of yellow and blue paints, most of the reflected wavelengths are green. Consequently, the rules for the color mixing of paints do not violate the rules of color mixture. When one mixes paints, the important thing is to figure out what wavelengths finally reach the eye.

SATURATION   So far we have explained the hue dimension of color and mentioned in passing another dimension, brightness, which is treated more fully in the next section. Now we must introduce and explain the other dimension of perceived color— *saturation.*

When hues are mixed, the resulting color is different not only in hue, but also in saturation. Saturation refers to the *purity of color,* and in fact is sometimes called purity. By purity, we do not mean uniqueness of hue or hues. We can have a very pure purple or pure yellow-green, even though these are not unique hues. By purity, or saturation, we refer to the degree to which a hue is diluted or not diluted by grayness or whiteness.

The following example should make this clear. A yellow of 580 millimicrons is the complementary hue of a blue of 480 millimicrons. Each one alone, when produced by a prism, is as pure or highly saturated as it can be. When these two hues are mixed, however, the resulting color lies somewhere along the line joining the two wavelengths in Figure 8.22. When the proportions are right, this color will lie in the center designated as gray or white. At this point, it has no saturation or purity at all, simply because it has no detectable hue. At a point, say, one-third of the way from the center out to the 580 point on the circle, it has some hue—indeed, exactly the same hue as the component 580 wavelength. The saturation of the color, however, is low because the color contains a lot of white. The blue has counterbalanced some, but not all, of the yellow, thus mixing white and yellow.

Saturation, then, may be regarded on the color circle as the position of a color on the spokes of the circle. The farther out it is on a spoke, the higher its saturation, or purity. The closer it is to the gray or white neutral point in the center, the lower its saturation, or purity. Translating this language into more familiar terms, the pastel, or weak, colors are

colors that are relatively unsaturated. To make them, the mixer of paints puts a relatively small amount of dye into a base of white paint. The deep, or strong, colors, on the other hand, are the ones that are highly saturated. To make them, the paint mixer uses a large amount of dye in proportion to the white base paint. In fact, the most highly saturated colors are made by using only color pigments and avoiding any white at all in the mixture.

BRIGHTNESS The third dimension of perceived color is *brightness*. The intensity of the physical stimulus is one of the major determiners of perceived brightness. As we shall see, another major determiner is the state of adaptation of the rods and cones of the retina.

The dimension of brightness extends from black to white through various shades of gray. To represent it along with the dimensions of hue and saturation requires that the color circle be extended into a color solid (see Figure 8.23). To make a color solid, color circle is piled on color circle like so many layers of cake. In this solid, the up-and-down

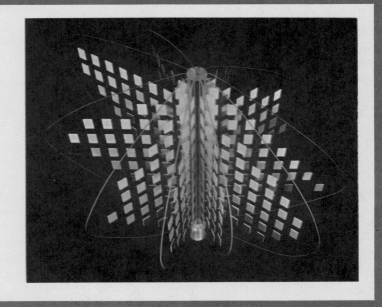

FIGURE 8.23 *The color solid. When all the colors are arranged in three dimensions, they form a color solid. Ten segments from the complete solid are shown. At the top are colors of highest brightness; at the bottom, those of lowest brightness. Around the circle are colors of different hue. The distance out from the center axis of the solid represents saturation. (Courtesy of The National Bureau of Standards, 1965.)*

dimension represents brightness. The colors at the top are bright, those at the bottom dark. The center line of the solid runs through the centers of the various color circles and represents the points at which there is neither hue nor saturation, only varying brightnesses.

The relation of brightness to hue and saturation may be illustrated by referring again to paints. We can vary the grayness of paint by mixing black pigment with white pigment. By using all white pigment and no black, we obtain the brightest paint possible. Conversely, by using all black and no white, we obtain a paint of low brightness. In between, varying mixtures produce different shades of gray. This gives the up-and-down dimension to the solid. Gray can in turn be mixed in varying proportions with pigments of different hues. When the proportion of colored pigment to gray pigment is low, the resulting colors are near the center of the solid and are of low saturation. When the proportion is high, the resulting color is out closer to the periphery of the circle, and its saturation is high. The remaining dimension, hue, of course, determines the position of the color around the circle.

Color blindness

About 1 person in 25 is color-blind, and this defect is likely to influence his everyday behavior in many ways. Some women, for instance, can wear only one particular shade of lipstick; if they use any other shade, they cannot see lipstick smears on their clothes. A color-blind house painter once ruefully reported that he had to repaint half a house because the color he had used on one side of the house did not match that used on the other. Color-blind chemists have to rely on their laboratory assistants to identify colors in flame tests of metallic substances, and some electronic technicians cannot match strands of wire by their color codes.

WHAT IS COLOR BLINDNESS?   Color blindness is certainly not the inability to identify color by a particular name, for that is a question of language. Nor is it actually blindness. Most color-blind people are not really blind to color. They can usually see a great many colors, but they confuse certain critical ones. It was John Dalton, the author of the atomic theory in chemistry, who clearly recognized this fact and presented one of the earliest and best scientific accounts of the defect.

Dalton himself was so color-blind that when Oxford University conferred on him the scarlet gown of a doctor of civil laws, he wore the gown everywhere for several days, not realizing that he presented such a conspicuous appearance. This greatly astonished his friends, who knew he was a Quaker and was supposed to wear the somber garb of that sect. In 1794, at the age of twenty-eight, Dalton described his perception of color to the Manchester Literary and Philosophical Society. Because of this classic description of color blindness, the defect was known for more than a century afterward as *Daltonism*. He said:

All crimsons appear to me to consist chiefly of dark blue: but many of them seem to have a tinge of dark brown. I have seen specimens of *crimson*, *claret*, and *mud*, which were very nearly alike. . . . The colour of a florid complexion appears to me that of a dull, opake, blackish blue, upon a white ground. . . . Blood appears to me . . . not unlike the colour called *bottle-green*. [Boring, 1942, page 184.]

Reduced to essentials, color blindness is a defect that makes a person unable to tell the difference between two or more colors that most other people can easily distinguish. It is not, as is commonly supposed, a single deficiency. On the contrary, several varieties of color blindness exist, and for each kind, the defect exists in varying degrees.

Most kinds of color blindness are inherited, and the defect has been identified as a sex-linked recessive characteristic. The genetic mechanism of color blindness is explained and illustrated in Chapter 2. Because of the genetic relations involved, color blindness is more common among men than among women. Statistics show that about 1 man in 15 is color-blind, while less than 1 woman in 100 is so afflicted.

TYPES OF COLOR BLINDNESS Total color blindness, known more technically as *achromatism,* is extremely rare. Only about a hundred cases have been described in the whole history of visual science. To the totally color-blind person—who usually has other visual defects as well—the world looks like a black and white photograph. He can distinguish among white, black, and grays of various intensities, but he does not see colors as such. By far the most common kind of color blindness is two-color vision, known as *dichromatism* [Geldard, 1953]. For people with this defect, color perception is essentially reduced to two hues: the yellows and the blues. Most of them confuse reds, greens, and yellows of certain shades with one another and are unable to distinguish clearly among bluish-greens, blues, and violets. Dichromats also confuse a particular shade of blue-green with gray. They never, however, confuse the yellows and blues. Besides the people who are indisputably dichromats, there are others who are "color-weak." Their impairment may be so slight that only the most careful tests can reveal it. Such people have little trouble with bright or vivid colors, but their defect appears when they attempt to distinguish among the very pale or light browns, tans, greens, and pinks. We call such color weakness *anomalous color defect.*

AWARENESS OF COLOR DEFECT During World War II, it was a common experience in Air Force and Navy recruiting centers to have color-blind applicants emphatically deny their color blindness. Often they would say, "What do you mean, Doc? I can see colors. I've never had trouble with colors."

To the color-normal person, it seems incomprehensible that a man can go through life unaware that he is failing to see the richness and variety of colors that others see. We must look for the explanation of this puzzling situation in several directions. In the first place, most color-blind persons do see some colors. Second, a person cannot appreciate

a sensation he has never sensed. A man born without taste buds will never understand the saltiness of the ocean or the sweetness of an apple. What is the tone of a 50,000-cycle sound, above the range of human hearing? Or what is the color of infrared light? We cannot answer these questions because they are outside the realm of our experiences. Moreover, since we have never experienced them, we never miss the fact that we cannot experience them. In the same way, color-vision defects often do not reveal themselves in a positive manner.

The last part of the explanation is that the color-deviant person has learned to use correct names for many common objects. He knows that grass is green, lemons are yellow, ripe apples are red, and so on, because he learned these things as a child. From experience he has learned to follow the names used by everyone else, and readily accepts correction. If you correct the mistake of a color-deviant person who says that a light green object is "pink" he will reply, "Oh, yes, it's green, I see it now." All our color names will satisfy him because this is a matter of learning anyway. The difficulty is that he has fewer color sensations than color names, and he is often not sure which names to assign to his sensations.

DETECTING COLOR-VISION DEFECTS Usually it requires special tests to find out whether or not a person has defective color vision. If you ask him to name the colors of common objects, the chances are that he will give you the correct names. But his defect will show up if you take him out on a dark night away from all other means of identification and ask him to pick out yellow, green, and red lights at a distance. These principles underlie many lantern tests in use for testing color vision.

Another, and more satisfactory, way of testing color vision is with special plates (see Figure 8.24). One test, for example, consists of a card with brilliant purplish-red dots arranged in such a way as to form a number. A normal person can see the number immediately because its color contrasts vividly with the background. But individuals with certain

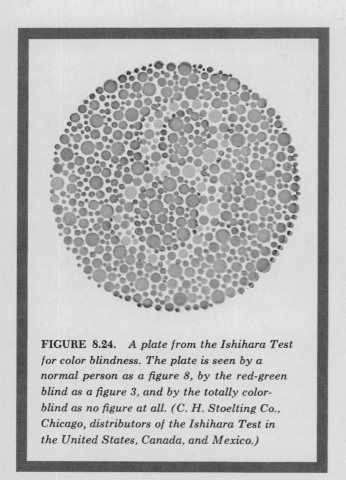

FIGURE 8.24. *A plate from the Ishihara Test for color blindness. The plate is seen by a normal person as a figure 8, by the red-green blind as a figure 3, and by the totally color-blind as no figure at all. (C. H. Stoelting Co., Chicago, distributors of the Ishihara Test in the United States, Canada, and Mexico.)*

types of color deficiency cannot read it because to them the dots all seem to be the same color.

Sensitivity of the eye

We have seen that the brightness of objects is determined by the intensity of the light falling on the retina and the density of the resulting neural barrage. The strength of this barrage also depends upon the state of adaptation and sensitivity of the retina. One of the most remarkable things about the eye is its tremendous range of sensitivity. When the eye is fully dark-adapted, the average person can see the flare of a match 50 miles away on a dark

clear night. In contrast, the eye can also look momentarily at the sun when it is at its zenith in the sky. If we compute the ratio of these two intensities—the flare of the match 50 miles away and the intensity of the sun—we find that the total range of intensities to which the eye is sensitive is something of the order of 100,000,000,000,000 to 1.

DARK ADAPTATION   Everybody knows that the eye becomes more sensitive in the dark. Simply recall the times you have gone to a movie in the afternoon and found yourself unable to see your way down the aisle or into your seat until you had waited a few minutes for your eyes to get accustomed to the dark. Of course, when you come out of the dark and into a bright light again, your eyes light-adapt and lose some of their sensitivity. We can measure the course of dark adaptation by having a person fully adapt his eyes to bright light, then putting him in the dark and measuring his absolute threshold over a period of minutes.

The resulting measurements look something like the curves in Figures 8.5 and 8.25. At first, the threshold is quite high—so high that a candle can be burning in a room and he will not know it unless he sees the flame itself. Sensitivity improves, however, very rapidly at first, and then more slowly. After a half-hour, sensitivity is 1,000 to 100,000 times greater than it was at the beginning of dark adaptation.

Notice that the dark-adaptation curve has two segments: after an initial drop it levels out for a few minutes; then it drops more rapidly again before leveling out for good. These two segments are related to the two different receptors of the eye, the cones and rods, as we can see from measurements of spectral sensitivity.

SPECTRAL SENSITIVITY   The term *spectral sensitivity* refers to sensitivity at different wavelengths of the visible spectrum. To measure it, lights of different wavelengths, instead of a white light, are used to obtain absolute thresholds (see page 275). Then the absolute threshold is plotted against a scale of wavelength.

The particular results depend upon the state of adaptation of the eye. If the eye is kept light-adapted during the measurements by surrounding the test wavelength with a patch of white light, the absolute thresholds are much higher than if the eye is kept dark-adapted. In addition, the lowest thresholds, that is, the greatest sensitivity, for the light-adapted eye are in the region of 555 millimicrons, whereas those for dark-adapted eyes are around 505 millimicrons.

This difference depends upon the kind of receptors which are being stimulated, the rods or the cones [Gibson and Tyndall, 1923]. In dark adaptation, the rods are dominant; in light adaptation, the cones are. This can be demonstrated by picking two different places on the retina for making the measurements. The fovea, we know, contains only cones; so measurements made with a patch of light small enough to stimulate only the fovea provide an index of cone sensitivity. At a point about 20 angular degrees from the fovea, as we have learned from anatomical studies, the rods are most dense. At this position, measurements can be made of rod sensitivity.

The results of these comparisons of the spectral sensitivity of the rods and cones are summarized in Figure 8.26. From such data, we can draw these conclusions. (1) The rods are more sensitive than the cones. This is shown by the fact that the threshold for rod vision is always less than that for cones. (2) Each curve of sensitivity has a central region in which sensitivity is greatest, while the regions to the side are less and less sensitive. (3) The region of greatest cone sensitivity is 555 millimicrons (yellowish-green), while that of the greatest rod sensitivity is approximately 505 millimicrons (bluish-green).

In measuring the thresholds plotted in Figure 8.26, we may ask a subject to report not only whether he sees the test patch of light but in addition, if he does, to indicate its color. We then discover an important difference between the two curves. In the case of the upper curve, when the subject is using his fovea, he can report correctly the color, or hue, of the wavelength used in the tests. In making judgments for the lower curve, however, the subject is totally color-blind. Even though he is presented with single wavelengths, he sees them all as gray. Obviously, this is the basis of the ancient saying, "When all candles bee out, all cats bee gray."

The interval between the rod and cone curves is called the *photochromatic interval*—that is, the interval of intensities in which we can see light but not colors. Let us give an example. Suppose the retina is stimulated by light with a wavelength of

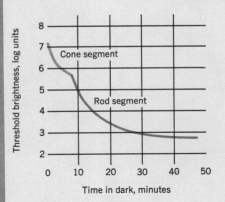

GIVEN ENOUGH TIME, THE EYE BECOMES THOUSANDS OF TIMES MORE SENSITIVE IN THE DARK THAN IN THE LIGHT

FIGURE 8.25. *A typical curve of dark adaptation. After a subject has been in normal or bright illumination for some time, he is placed in the dark and asked to indicate the weakest light (threshold intensity) that he can see. Thresholds are taken repeatedly, minute after minute, and the results are plotted in a curve of dark adaptation. Notice the two limbs of the curve. Compare this curve with the continuously recorded curve for the pigeon in Figure 8.5.*

540 millimicrons, and we measure threshold. At low intensities the subject will report that he sees a light which has brightness but no hue. At these low intensities the rods, but not the cones, are in action. At higher intensities, the cones come into action and hue, greenish-yellow in this case, is seen. It is this interval between the first brightness vision and color vision which is called the photochromatic interval. This is rather convincing proof that the cones are the receptors for color perception and that the rods are not.

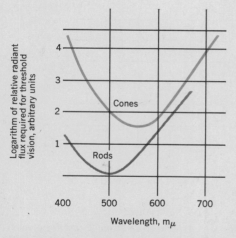

THE RODS ARE MUCH MORE SENSITIVE TO THE SHORT WAVELENGTHS THAN ARE THE CONES

FIGURE 8.26.   *Thresholds for seeing at different wavelengths. The lower curve was obtained while the subject was viewing a patch of light 20 degrees from the fovea, where the rods are most numerous. The upper curve was obtained from a subject who was using his fovea where cones are most numerous. Note also that the rods are generally more sensitive than the cones.*

PURKINJE EFFECT   The sensitivity curve may be plotted in another way (see Figure 8.27). Instead of graphing the absolute thresholds, we may express spectral sensitivity in relative terms. This can be done by taking the point of maximum sensitivity—at 505 millimicrons in the rod curve and 555 millimicrons in the cone curve—and expressing all other sensitivities of each curve as percentages of the maximum sensitivity. This turns the curves upside down, and it also fixes the maximum sensitivity at 100 per cent. In this form, the curves are called *luminosity functions.* From them we can see that for cone vision—that is, for daylight levels of light adaptation—sensitivity is *relatively* better in the red and poorer in the blue. For rod vision—that is, for twilight levels of light adaptation—sensitivity is *relatively* better in the blue and poorer in the red [Hecht and Williams, 1922]. Thus, in daylight, the longer wavelengths are apt to appear brighter; at twilight, the shorter wavelengths may appear brighter.

Such a relative difference in the brightness of colors was discovered more than a century ago by the Bohemian physiologist Purkinje. He noticed what you may observe for yourself if you are sitting outside on a warm summer night just before the sun sets. When the sun is still shining, the reds seem relatively bright as compared with the greens and the blues. As twilight comes on, however, the reddish colors become much darker, whereas the blue colors hardly seem to change at all in brightness. This change in the apparent brightness of colors is called the *Purkinje shift.* The change is accounted for by the fact that the eyes shift from cone functions to rod functions in the course of dark adaptation.

Visual acuity

Objects not only have color and brightness, they also have form. The visual capacity that enables us to see form is called *visual acuity.* Put another way, visual acuity is the ability of a person to perceive fine differences in the details of the visual environment. To measure visual acuity, we always try to find a way of establishing the smallest object a person can recognize when presented with it in some standard situation. The several different ways of measuring visual acuity can be discussed in terms of two general types: one is the type that physicians use for diagnostic purposes, and the other, the type that laboratory scientists use in their research work in the measurement of visual acuity.

EYE CHARTS All of us, having suffered through at least a few physical examinations, are familiar with the physician's eye chart. This chart, called a Snellen chart, compares a person's visual acuity with a standard that has been established as normal.

It may be so designed that letters of different sizes on the chart represent what the normal person sees at various distances. On many charts, for example, the largest letter can be just read at 200 feet, the next largest letters are half that size and so can be read at 100 feet, and so on. If, at 20 feet from the chart, an individual can see what the normal person can see at 100 feet, he has 20/100 vision, which is not so good. If, on the other hand, he can see those letters that the normal person can see only at 10 feet, he has 20/10 vision, which is excellent.

Sometimes physicians prefer to use distance rather than size of letters as an index of visual acuity. For many years, this kind of test was used by the United States Navy. In such examinations, the person starts walking toward the eye chart and continues until he can read the letters on it. The letters are of only one size. The results of the test are expressed in terms of the distance at which a person sees the letters that would be seen by a normal person at 20 feet. In either case, whether distance or size of letters is used as an index, a person's acuity is compared with normal acuity at 20 feet.

It is also possible and, in fact, desirable to use test objects that are not letters. Two such objects are illustrated in Figure 8.28, the *Landolt ring* and the *parallel bars*. Both can be used with people who

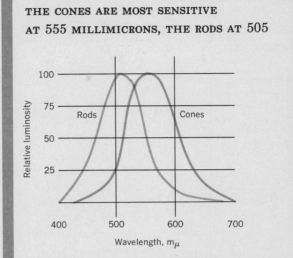

THE CONES ARE MOST SENSITIVE AT 555 MILLIMICRONS, THE RODS AT 505

FIGURE 8.27. *Relative luminosity functions. The curves represent a different way of plotting the data shown in Figure 8.26. Instead of being plotted in logarithms, each threshold is on a relative scale. This is obtained as follows: for the rod and cone data separately, the peak sensitivity is taken as 100. The other points are expressed as percentages of the peak sensitivity.*

cannot read; all the examinee has to do is tell where the gap is in the Landolt ring, or whether he sees white space between the parallel bars. Another advantage of these test objects is that they are always the same in shape, whereas the letters of a test chart differ in size and shape and are not equally easy to recognize. For that reason, visual scientists who are interested in precise laboratory measurements prefer such test objects.

NEAR AND FAR ACUITY In view of what we have already said about nearsightedness and farsightedness, it should not be surprising that visual acuity may vary with different distances. The acuity at 13 inches, for example, may be quite different from

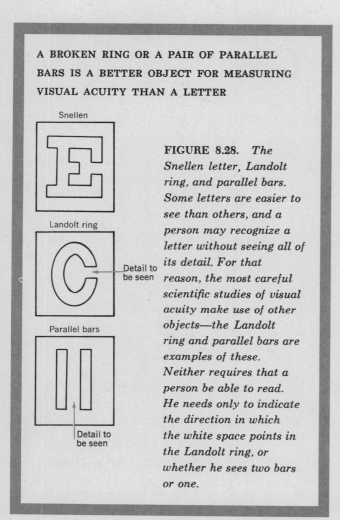

Snellen

Landolt ring

Detail to
be seen

Parallel bars

Detail to
be seen

FIGURE 8.28. *The
Snellen letter, Landolt
ring, and parallel bars.
Some letters are easier to
see than others, and a
person may recognize a
letter without seeing all of
its detail. For that
reason, the most careful
scientific studies of visual
acuity make use of other
objects—the Landolt
ring and parallel bars are
examples of these.
Neither requires that a
person be able to read.
He needs only to indicate
the direction in which
the white space points in
the Landolt ring, or
whether he sees two bars
or one.*

person's visual acuity may be critical in his ability to do his job. Fliers, riflemen, and artillerymen, to mention only a few of the military specialists, must have good far visual acuity. Machinists, needle-workers, many machine operators, and inspectors must have good near acuity. To select people for these positions, employers often require tests of visual acuity as part of a physical examination. If the job calls for good distance acuity, as in the case of truck drivers, it is important that the test be made at 20 feet or more, but if the job calls for good near acuity, as in the case of toolmakers and watchmakers, the test should be made at distances comparable to those important in the job. Otherwise differences between near and far acuity may make the tests invalid.

POSITION ON THE RETINA   We all use our eyes so much that we commonly overlook certain peculiarities about our seeing process and would never notice them if they were not pointed out to us. If, for example, you stare steadily at one letter on this page, it is impossible for you to read letters 2 inches distant from it in any direction; or if you look at the road straight ahead when you are driving, you will not be able to read most signs along the side of the road. From such facts we know that visual acuity is not nearly so good at the side of the retina as it is at the fovea.

In Figure 8.29, you can see more precisely how visual acuity varies with the part of the retina used [Wertheim, 1894]. Acuity is best, of course, when one looks directly at an object, that is, when the image falls directly on the fovea. This is true only under daylight conditions, however, and it is related to the fact that the daylight-sensitive elements, the cones, are most concentrated in the fovea. At night, acuity is greatest at about 20 degrees from the fovea. It is here that the rods, the dark-vision elements, are concentrated. The position of the blind spot, about 15 degrees from the fovea on the side of the retina toward the nose, is also shown in Figure 8.29.

that at 20 feet. Beyond 20 feet, however, acuity appears to be fairly constant. To understand these facts, recall that the lens in the front of the eye has to change shape in order for the eye to focus near and far objects on the retina, and that the ability to do this varies markedly in different individuals. Accommodation remains fairly constant, however, for objects at distances greater than 20 feet.

The fact that people may differ in their near and far acuity is sometimes of practical importance. In some industries and in many military situations, a

AMOUNT OF LIGHT   Visual acuity improves with increasing light [Moon and Spencer, 1944]. We recognize this fact every time we turn on extra lamps to read a book or try to get as much light as we can for visual tasks. In the dark, obviously, visual acuity is zero. As some light is turned on, visual acuity improves very rapidly, but after a certain point, more and more light has diminishing returns, even though almost any increase in light, short of blinding intensities, improves visual acuity somewhat. This means that there is no such thing as the "best amount" of light. Rather, the important problem in everyday life is to get as much light as we need to do the kind of visual work we are going to do.

Because light is so important to visual acuity and because visual acuity is required in almost everything anybody does, the subject has been explored very intensively. There is, in fact, a special branch of engineering called *illumination engineering* that handles practical applications of the subject. Illumination engineers have provided reference handbooks to which we can go for answers to many practical questions. They have given us rules to follow in providing enough light for different visual tasks.

CONTRAST   It has probably become apparent that many factors affect visual acuity. Although we shall not be able to mention all these factors, two are especially interesting and have practical significance. One is contrast, or the difference in brightness between an object and its immediate background. If, for example, we are viewing dark letters on a white background, visual acuity will be better when the letters are coal black than when they are a light gray because the black makes a greater contrast with the white than does the light gray. This means that when we are painting signs or making something we wish people to see as clearly as possible or at as great a distance as possible, we should make the contrast between the dark and the light parts of the display as great as possible. In this way visual acuity is increased (see Figure 8.30).

SURROUND   A final factor to consider is the surround of an object we are viewing. Even though the object itself has high contrast and is illuminated by good light, visual acuity may not be what it could be if the general illumination in the room is poor. Indeed, it is relatively easy to demonstrate in the laboratory that, if the general light in a room is either much greater or much less than the light on the object we are viewing, visual acuity is impaired. The best rule to follow is that the lighting of the surround should be about the same as the lighting of the object.

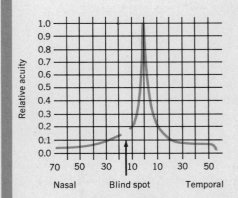

VISUAL ACUITY IS MUCH BETTER FOR THE FOVEA THAN FOR REGIONS OF THE RETINA OUTSIDE IT

FIGURE 8.29.   *Visual acuity varies with the part of the retina used in viewing. It is greatest at the fovea, dropping off quite rapidly toward the periphery of the retina. Note the position of the blind spot on the side of the retina toward the nose.*

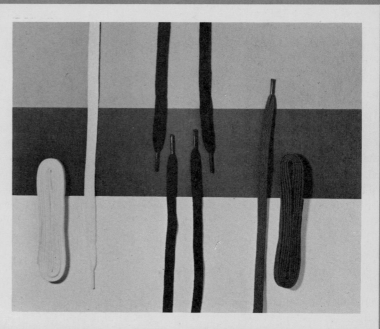

FIGURE 8.30.   *Visual acuity depends upon contrast. It is harder to see dark objects against dark backgrounds than against lighter backgrounds. On the other hand, the light objects are seen best against dark backgrounds. The higher the contrast between an object and its background, the more clearly one can perceive the details of the object. (Fundamental Photographs.)*

SYNOPSIS AND SUMMARY

To a large extent all behavior and experience ultimately depend upon sensory information. For this reason, the study of the senses has had a long history in psychology. The structuralist school of psychologists studied the senses in order to find the elements, or indivisible units, of experience. The endeavor did not prove to be extremely fruitful, and interest in the senses waned, especially after the advent of behaviorism with its emphasis on response processes. It is probably safe to say that interest in the senses has reawakened in modern psychology. Both the practical need of developing efficient sensory displays in complex pieces of apparatus and rapidly accumulating physiological knowledge have given impetus to psychophysics and the physiological study of the senses. Beyond these reasons for increased interest in the senses is an enduring intellectual reason for sensory study. Here psychologists, physiologists, and physicists have be-

gun to find the neural correlates of experience; in the study of sensory processes, reliable answers to the age-old philosophical question of the relationship between neural activity and psychological events—the so-called "mind-body problem"—are to be found.

In this chapter we have discussed sensory processes in general, and we have talked about the physical energy underlying visual experience, transduction in vision, and the perceived visual experience corresponding to various aspects of the physical energy. However, a great deal of our perceived visual experience does not depend upon isolated transduction events at the visual peripheral receptor—the retina. Instead, perceived experience depends upon the selection and reworking of the events set in motion at the periphery. This aspect of perceived visual experience is taken up in Chapter 10—Perception. In describing peripheral sensory processes in general, and the visual process in particular, we made the following general points:

1. Man has eleven or more sensory channels. The eleven most important are: vision, hearing, cold, warmth, pain, touch, organic sensibility, smell, taste, kinesthesis, and the vestibular sense. Each of the sensory systems can be thought of as a channel with the sensitive receptor at the receiving end, conducting nerve fibers in the middle, and nuclei of the central nervous system at the other end.

2. Three questions assist in the analysis of sensory mechanisms. The first is the question of transduction: What is the process by which physical energy is converted into information which can be used by the nervous system? The second question asks: What is the relationship between the nervous activity and experience? The third is the psychophysical question: What is the relationship between the physical energy and reported experience?

3. Psychophysical methods are used for the measurement of absolute and differential thresholds. The classical psychophysical methods are: the method of constant stimuli, the method of adjustment, and the method of limits.

4. Only that electromagnetic energy having wavelengths between about 380 and 760 millimicrons is visible to the eye.

5. The lens of the eye focuses an inverted image on a photosensitive surface, the retina.

6. The sensitive elements in the retina are the rods and cones. These are connected to the brain via an intricate network of cells and nerve fibers. The cones are more concentrated in the fovea of the retina which is used in looking directly at an object. The rods are relatively more numerous in the periphery of the retina.

7. The lens of the eye changes in shape to accommodate for near and far vision. If the eyeball is too long or too short, the person may be nearsighted or farsighted. Farsightedness increases with age as the lens becomes less able to focus light on the retina.

8. The transduction process in vision, as in most of the other sensory modalities, consists of several steps. In vision, the first step is a photochemical one which generates a second process, the generator potential. Finally, as a third step, the generator potential produces nerve impulses in the fibers of the receptor.

9. Rhodopsin, or visual purple, is the photochemical substance of the rods. There seem to be three cone photosensitive pigments. One of these, the "blue" pigment, is most sensitive to wavelengths in the short end of the visual spectrum; a second cone pigment is most sensitive in the "green" region, while a third cone pigment has its peak of sensitivity in the "yellow" region of the visible spectrum.

10. The generator potential has been identified in the eyes of certain animals, but some doubt exists about its precise nature in the mammalian eye. "On," "off," and "on-off" firing patterns of ganglion cells of the retina have been found. Whether a ganglion cell is "on," "off," or "on-off" depends upon the part of its receptive field which is stimulated.

11. In the absence of precise correlations between physiological events and reported experience, several theories have been proposed to account for the physiological mechanisms of some aspects of color vision. The Young-Helmholtz theory postulates three color receptors, each of which is most sensitive in the blue, green, or red region of the spectrum. The Hering opponent-colors theory postulates three pairs of receptors: white-black, blue-yellow, and red-green. Neither of these theories accounts for all the facts of color vision. Physiological evidence indicates that aspects of both may be correct.

12. Three dimensions are necessary to classify all colors into one scheme: (a) hue, (b) saturation, and (c) brightness. Hue is what we commonly mean by color: blue, green, yellow, red, or shades in between. Saturation is the relative amount of color, as distinguished from gray, in a stimulus. Brightness refers to the relative lightness or darkness of the stimulus.

13. Hues can be arranged in a circle with saturations as steps on the radii of the circle. In a color solid, brightness is represented in the vertical dimension.

14. Certain hues are complementary, for example, yellow and greenish-blue, and red and bluish-green. When complementary hues are mixed, gray or white results. When hues which are not complementary are mixed, the result is an intervening hue on the color circle.

15. Total color blindness is very rare, but partial color blindness occurs in 1 out of every 25 people. Partial color blindness shows up as a confusion of certain pairs of colors.

16. The eye can adapt to a wide range of illuminations. In dark adaptation, a shift from cone function to rod function takes place. In the course of this shift, the

eye's best sensitivity to wavelengths changes from about 555 millimicrons to about 505 millimicrons.

17. Visual acuity is important in a number of occupations. It is better in the fovea than in the periphery of the eye. Visual acuity is much better under high illumination than under dim light. It is also better when the contrast between an object and its background is high. Finally, it is better when the surrounding illumination is about the same as that on the object.

RELATED TOPICS IN THE TEXT

CHAPTER 9   HEARING AND THE OTHER SENSES   Sensory processes are further explored here.

CHAPTER 10   PERCEPTION   In this chapter on perception, we deal with the selection and reworking of the sensory input into the world of actual experience.

CHAPTER 20   PHYSIOLOGICAL BASIS OF BEHAVIOR   Visual central nervous system pathways and visual functions of the central nervous system are discussed in this chapter.

SUGGESTIONS FOR FURTHER READING

Boring, E. G. *Sensation and perception in the history of experimental psychology.* New York: Appleton-Century-Crofts, 1942.
An authoritative history of experimental work in sensory perception.

Buddenbrock, W. von. *The senses.* Ann Arbor, Mich.: University of Michigan Press, 1958. (Paperback.)
The sense organs of many animals, including man, are discussed in an interesting fashion.

Galanter, E. Contemporary psychophysics. In *New directions in psychology.* Vol I. New York: Holt, 1962. (Paperback.)
An article which gives an interesting account of some of the recent work in psychophysics, including signal detection and newer concepts of stimulus scaling.

Geldard, F. A. *The human senses.* New York: Wiley, 1953.
An introductory text covering vision and the other senses.

Morgan, C. T. *Physiological psychology* (3d ed.). New York: McGraw-Hill, 1965.
A text containing several chapters on the physiological basis of sensory perception.

Mueller, C. G. *Sensory psychology.* Englewood Cliffs, N. J.: Prentice-Hall, 1965. (Paperback.)
An authoritative text on sensory processes.

Rosenblith, W. A. (Ed.). *Sensory communication.* New York: Wiley, 1961.
A series of articles on recent work in the senses. Some of them are rather technical for the beginner, but they can be mastered with effort.

Scientific American Readings
A number of reprints of articles on vision which originally appeared in the Scientific American *are available.*
A list of the available reprints and reprints themselves may be obtained from: W. H. Freeman and Co., San Francisco, Calif.

Woodworth, R. S., and Schlosberg, H. *Experimental psychology* (rev. ed.). New York: Holt, 1954.
A standard text on experimental psychology which, in addition to discussions of many other topics in experimental psychology, contains chapters on classical psychophysics and visual sensory perception.

Wyburn, G. M., Pickford, R. W., and Hirst, R. J. *Human senses and perception.* Edinburgh: Oliver & Boyd, 1964.
An interesting book because it discusses perception from the physiological, psychological, and philosophical points of view.

9

WE HAVE JUST seen that man is exquisitely sensitive to just that small portion of the electromagnetic spectrum which reaches the surface of the earth most readily. It is, of course, no accident that this should be true. The ability to detect changes in the surrounding flux of energy is necessary for survival. In the billion or so years of their evolution, living organisms have developed receptor structures to deal with the major kinds of energy which they encounter on the earth, in the air, or in the sea. Whenever we look around, we draw on a billion-year heritage from our slimy, scaly, and furry ancestors.

Of course, electromagnetic energy is not the only type of energy which is abundantly present. For instance, pressure changes occur in the gaseous atmosphere and the liquid sea. Devices to detect these pressure changes were soon developed by primitive creatures, and we owe our ability to hear, and therefore to behave adaptively to certain transient changes of pressure in the air, to these primitive pioneers.

Some energies stimulate the skin or move hairs of the body surface; additional energies warm or cool the body surface; still others produce tissue damage. These energies give rise to our experiences of touch, warmth, cold, or pain. As we move around in space, feedback comes from our own movements, allowing us to adjust the position of our limbs for efficient locomotion. Such sensory feedback comes from receptors in the muscles, tendons, and joints, the *kinesthetic receptors,* and from receptors in the inner ear, the *vestibular receptors.* The kinesthetic and vestibular senses are sometimes collectively referred to as the *proprioceptive senses* (Latin: *proprius,* one's own, and *capio,* to take). Sensory input from the deep structures of the body, sometimes called the *organic sense,* gives information about the state of the internal organs—the stomach, for example.

Thus we are truly sensitive creatures, and our sensitivity is the basis of much of our behavior. In this chapter, we shall examine the transduction

HEARING AND THE OTHER SENSES

WITHIN A BONY
LABYRINTHEAN CAVE,
REACHED BY THE PULSE
OF THE AERIAL WAVE,
THIS SIBYL, SWEET, AND
MYSTIC SENSE IS
FOUND . . .
ABRAHAM COLES

and elementary psychophysics (see Chapter 8) of hearing and the remaining human senses.

Hearing

Hearing is probably second only to vision in providing a channel through which we can know, learn about, and appreciate our world. Through hearing, we can understand speech—our chief medium for imparting and acquiring knowledge. Through hearing, too, we receive a great many signals and cues—the warning automobile horn, the chime of the clock, the fire engine's siren, the footsteps of a person approaching from behind, and many other common cues. Through hearing, we also find a great source of aesthetic pleasure in music. Thus hearing is an important sense for operating in our environment.

PHYSICAL BASIS OF HEARING   Before we can understand the sense of hearing, we must study the physical stimulus for hearing because it determines in many ways what we hear. If you were asked what you hear, you probably would say "sound," and you would be right. To say that, however, is not enough. You should distinguish between the physical energy which stimulates the ear and perceived sound, which is the sound you actually experience.

Sound waves. The air, as most people know, is not a vacuum; it is a collection of molecules. These molecules are always moving about at random, colliding with one another and exerting pressure on one another. The more closely packed together they are, the greater the air pressure; the fewer they are, the less the pressure. When there is no sound or wind, the molecules are evenly distributed in the air around us, and thus they have a uniform pressure. When there is a sound, however, changes in pressure occur which move through the air as waves do along the surface of water. It is, in fact, such changes in pressure that constitute the physical basis of sound perception.

Sound waves are ordinarily generated by the vibration of a physical object in the air. When such an object vibrates, the molecules close to the object are pushed together, and thus are put under *positive pressure.* The molecules that are under positive pressure push against the molecules close to them, and these in turn transmit the pressure to neighboring molecules. A wave of positive pressure moves through the air in much the same way that ripples move on the water. Sound-pressure waves, however, travel much faster than waves of water; at sea level, they travel about 760 miles per hour, or approximately 1,130 feet per second at 20°C.

However, most objects, when they are struck, do not move in just one direction. A violin string, for example, vibrates back and forth when it is plucked. As the string moves first in one direction, a positive-pressure wave begins to propagate through the air; but when the string swings back to its original position and beyond, a little vacuum, or *negative pressure,* is created just behind the wave of positive pressure. This vacuum moves with the speed of sound just as the positive-pressure wave does. These alternations in air pressure moving in all directions from the source are called a *sound wave,* and this sound wave is the physical stimulus for everything we hear. Different vibrations produce different sound waves. To understand the physical stimulus for hearing, then, we must understand the characteristics of sound waves.

Sine waves. Common observation tells us that there is an infinite variety of possible sound waves. We regard one kind of wave, called a *sine wave,* as the simplest because this one can be used in different ways to duplicate or analyze any other kind of wave. Figure 9.1 shows a diagram of the sine wave, so called because it may be mathematically expressed by the sine function of trigonometry. It is produced when a single vibrating object moves back and forth *freely* and changes the pressure of the air. The sound that we hear when we listen to a sine wave is called a *pure tone.* Since sine waves can be produced only with special equipment, a pure tone is usually heard only in the laboratory. Some musical instruments, such as the flute, how-

SINE WAVES VARY IN AMPLITUDE AND FREQUENCY

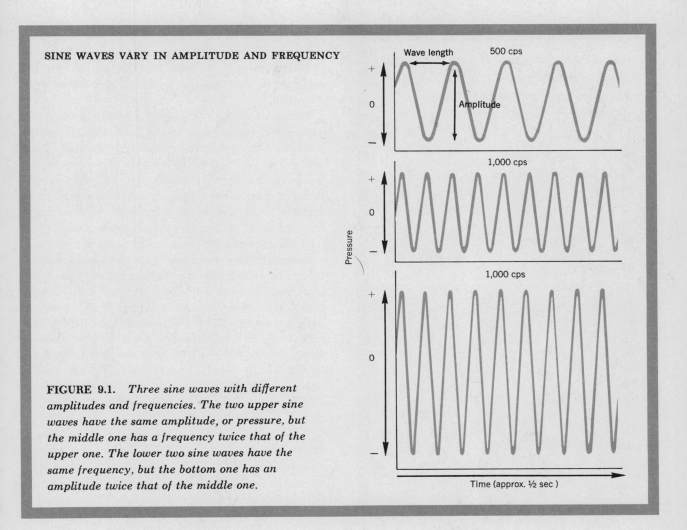

FIGURE 9.1. *Three sine waves with different amplitudes and frequencies. The two upper sine waves have the same amplitude, or pressure, but the middle one has a frequency twice that of the upper one. The lower two sine waves have the same frequency, but the bottom one has an amplitude twice that of the middle one.*

ever, can produce notes that are almost pure tones.

The height or amplitude of the sine wave is an indication of the intensity of the pressure wave. As the peaks of positive pressure pass, the sine waves reach their high points; as the troughs of negative pressure pass, the sine waves reach their low points (see Figure 9.1). The rate of change from peak to trough is defined by the ascending and descending limbs of the sine curves. The distance between the successive peaks of positive pressure, or the distance between the peaks of the sine waves, is the wave-length. In hearing, however, frequency, and not wavelength as such, is used. The frequency of a sine wave is simply the number of cycles—alternations between positive and negative pressure—in a given period of time. We ordinarily use 1 second as the time unit and express frequency as cycles per second (cps). The sound wave at the top of Figure 9.1 alternates fewer times per second than the lower two sine waves—it has a lower frequency. To be more specific, if a sine wave goes to positive pressure, then to negative pressure, and back again 500

NORMAL CONVERSATION IS ABOUT 60
DECIBELS ABOVE THE THRESHOLD OF
HEARING; LOUD THUNDER IS ABOUT
120 DECIBELS ABOVE

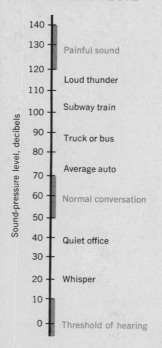

FIGURE 9.2. *The sound-pressure level of familiar sounds. Each of the sounds indicated on the right has a sound-pressure level, or intensity, of approximately the number of decibels shown at the left.*

times in a second, its frequency is 500 cycles per second, for the sine wave has completed that many cycles in 1 second.

If sound waves are changes in the pressure of air, you may wonder how we are able to take pictures of them. There are, in fact, several ways of *seeing*, as well as of hearing, sound waves. The one used most often in the laboratory is a cathode-ray oscilloscope, which has a screen very much like a tele-

vision screen. If we have a microphone, that is, a transducer, with which to convert sound waves into electrical signals, we can lead its wires into the oscilloscope and see the waves on the screen (see Figure 9.1).

Measurement of physical sound intensity. In Figure 9.1, intensity is shown as the height of the wave, and this height represents the pressure of the wave. The two bottom sine waves shown in Figure 9.1 have the same frequency but different amplitudes or intensities. Thus, while frequency gives us a measure of how often the sound wave changes from positive to negative pressure, intensity gives us a measure of how great the pressure changes are.

Scientists have developed a special scale for measuring the intensities of sound energies. The range of sound intensities that people can hear is very great. The loudest sound that people can listen to without experiencing discomfort has a pressure about one million times as great as the weakest sound that is just audible. So if we were to measure intensities in actual sound pressures, we should have to deal with a very large scale of numbers. Consequently, we use the *decibel (db)* as our unit of measurement.

The decibel as a unit for expressing sound, or any other intensity, has two main features. First, it represents a *ratio* of two intensities. When two intensities are expressed in decibels, the numbers tell us that one intensity is so many times the other intensity, but they do not say what either intensity is. Second, a decibel is so defined that 20 decibels represents a ratio of 10 times; 40 decibels, 100 times; and so on up to 100 decibels which represents a ratio of 100,000 times. A person familiar with logarithms can figure out for himself what any number of decibels means if he keeps in mind that the number of decibels is equal to 20 times the logarithm of the ratio of two sound pressures

$$\text{db} = 20 \log \frac{P1}{P2}$$

In order for such a scale to be meaningful, it must have a starting point. Scientists have arbitrarily agreed to use a pressure of 0.0002 dyne per square centimeter—a dyne is a unit of pressure—

as a starting point because this is close to the absolute threshold. In other words, $P2$ in the previous equation is equal to 0.0002 dyne per square centimeter. When this point is used as a reference, we talk about the decibel scale as the scale of *sound-pressure level (SPL)*.

For most practical purposes we can simply regard a decibel scale as a set of numbers, like a scale of temperature, and then learn that certain numbers correspond to certain loudnesses. To give you an idea what the numbers mean, Figure 9.2 shows the scale of sound-pressure levels for some sounds with which you are familiar. If you are not sure what different sound-pressure levels mean, reference to this chart will at least provide a rough idea of the correspondence of SPL and loudness. Remember that loudness is *not* a measure of the physical intensity of a sound; loudness is psychological and is perceived, while pressures and the SPL are measured in terms of the physical energy itself. Figure 9.2 is designed to give an idea of some of the psychophysical relationships between SPL and perception, and we dwell on this in greater detail a little later.

Complex wave forms. Sine waves are extensively used in the laboratory for the study of hearing, but they are seldom encountered outside the laboratory. Rather, the sounds produced by objects in our normal environment are made up of *complex waves*. Three examples of such waves, as seen on an oscilloscope, are shown in Figure 9.3. They may be of almost any conceivable shape, but in general they are either *periodic* or *aperiodic*. This means that either they have a repetitive pattern occurring over and over again, or they consist of waves of various heights and widths in more or less random order. In Figure 9.3, the top two tracings are examples of periodic waves; the lower tracing illustrates an aperiodic wave.

In 1822, a French mathematician named Fourier showed that any periodic function can be expressed as the sum of a number of different sine waves. This fact provides a very simple technique for describing a complex periodic wave. To describe a sine wave, all we need to know is its frequency and intensity.

For a complex wave, we simply need to know the frequency and intensity of each of the sine-wave components of the complex wave. Thus we might describe the tone of a musical instrument by saying that it has a sound-pressure level of 70 decibels at

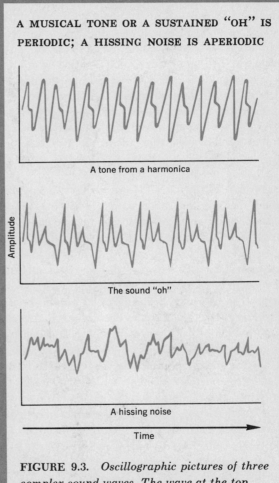

A MUSICAL TONE OR A SUSTAINED "OH" IS PERIODIC; A HISSING NOISE IS APERIODIC

A tone from a harmonica

The sound "oh"

A hissing noise

Time

FIGURE 9.3. *Oscillographic pictures of three complex sound waves. The wave at the top is a musical note played on a harmonica. The middle wave is the sustained vowel "oh." These two sound patterns are periodic because the same pattern repeats itself. The sound wave at the bottom is noise; it is aperiodic because it is completely irregular.*

400 cycles per second, 62 decibels at 800 cycles per second, 43 decibels at 1,200 cycles per second, 29 decibels at 1,600 cycles per second, and so on. This kind of description of a complex tone is known as a *Fourier analysis.*

Notice that in this example each of the frequencies involved is some multiple of the lowest frequency. All musical instruments produce complex tones of this type. The lowest frequency is called the *fundamental,* and all other frequencies are called *harmonics.* The frequency which is twice as great as the fundamental is called the second harmonic; that which is three times as great, the third harmonic; and so forth. The complexity of a tone, then, is a matter of the number and the intensities of the different sine waves that make up the complete tone.

AUDITORY TRANSDUCTION So far we have described the physical energy which impinges upon the ears. Later we shall describe the psychological attributes of pitch, loudness, and timbre to which this gives rise. Now we would like to bridge the psychophysical gap between the physical stimulus and reported experience by discussing the transduction process from physical energy to nerve impulse.

Structure of the auditory receptor. Figure 9.4 shows the major features of the ear. The ear consists of three principal parts: the outer ear, which collects the energy; the middle ear, which transmits the energy; and the inner ear, which transforms the energy into nerve impulses.

The outer ear, or *pinna,* besides being decorative, collects energy which travels through a small air-filled duct, called the *auditory canal,* or *meatus,* to the eardrum. The *eardrum* is a thin membrane stretched tightly across the inner end of the canal. Alternations in the pressure of the sound wave move this small membrane back and forth. The oscillation of the eardrum in turn moves three small bones, the *ossicles,* so that vibration is conducted through the middle ear to the entrance of the *cochlea* in the inner ear. The bones of the middle ear are connected like a series of levers. Hence energy is mechanically transmitted, and amplification takes place through the middle ear.

The inner ear is by far the most complicated of the three major parts of the ear. It consists of two kinds of sense organs, one concerned in the sense of balance and the other in hearing. The organs for balance are called the vestibular sense organs and are discussed later in this chapter. The sense organs for hearing are contained in a bony structure which is spiraled like a snail and thus called the *cochlea,* which means snail shell. The cochlea has three different fluid-filled ducts or canals spiraling around together, separated from each other by membranes. Figure 9.4 shows a side view of these ducts, and Figure 9.5 shows a much enlarged and labeled cross section of them. As the ossicles of the middle ear move back and forth, the foot of one of them, the *stapes,* presses on a membrane, the *oval window,* which is located at the end of the so-called *vestibular canal.* Thus when pressure waves move the ossicles back and forth, this movement is transferred to the fluid of the cochlea. Figure 9.4 shows the direction taken by the wave in the cochlear fluid as it moves from the oval window through the vestibular canal to the *tympanic canal* and the round window.

The important event that takes place in the cochlea is the stimulation of sensitive cells—called *hair cells* because they have hairs on their ends—located in the *organ of Corti* on the *basilar membrane* separating the tympanic canal and cochlear duct. Pressure changes in the fluid of the canals cause a shearing movement of the hairlike processes at the ends of the hair cells. These hairlike processes protrude into the *tectorial membrane* above them, and the structure of the basilar membrane is such that waves in the fluid produce the shearing motion of these hair cells with respect to the overlying tectorial membrane. This movement stimulates the hair cells to produce generator potentials which in turn stimulate the nerve fibers that carry information to the auditory areas of the brain.

Movements of the basilar membrane during artificial stimulation have actually been observed

PRESSURE TRAVELS THROUGH THE EXTERNAL AND THE MIDDLE EAR TO THE INNER EAR

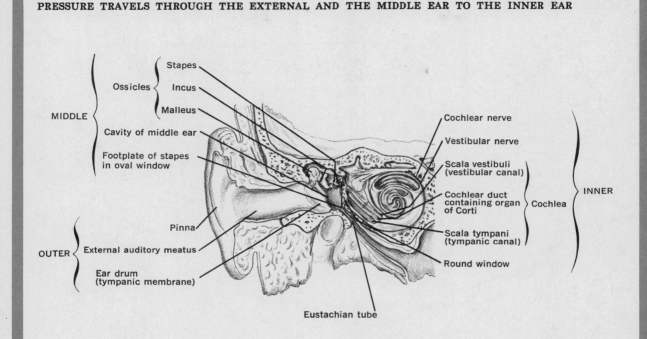

FIGURE 9.4. *The human ear. The ear consists of three principal major parts: the external ear, the middle ear, and the inner ear. The external ear consists of the pinna and a canal that conducts pressure changes to the eardrum. The eardrum, marking the division between the external and middle ears, is set into vibration by the pressure changes. This vibration is transmitted and amplified by the bones of the middle ear— the malleus, the incus, and the stapes. The amplified vibrations push on the oval window and thus the vibrations are transformed into waves of pressure in the fluid-filled cochlea. The direction of the waves in the fluid of the cochlea is shown by the arrows. By distorting the organ of Corti on the basilar membrane, the fluid waves in the cochlea stimulate the hair cells. After the fluid wave has travelled through the cochlea, the pressure is relieved by bulging of the round window. (Adapted from Frank H. Netter, M.D. From the CIBA collection of medical illustrations. © CIBA.)*

[Békésy and Rosenblith, 1951]. These measurements show that the maximum amplitude of displacement of the basilar membrane varies with the frequency of stimulation: the end away from the stapes is stimulated most by low-frequency stimulation; as the frequency increases, the point of maximum stimulation becomes more restricted and moves toward the stapes (see Figure 9.6). This is one of the major bits of evidence for the *place theory* of pitch perception discussed later.

PRESSURE INITIATES NERVE IMPULSES IN THE NERVE FIBERS OF THE COCHLEA

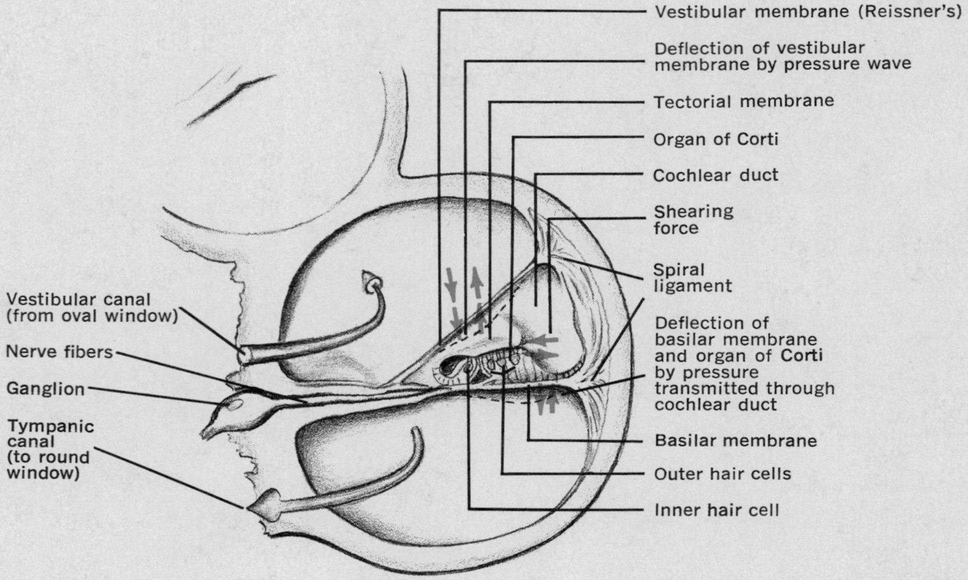

Labels (from top right):
- Vestibular membrane (Reissner's)
- Deflection of vestibular membrane by pressure wave
- Tectorial membrane
- Organ of Corti
- Cochlear duct
- Shearing force
- Spiral ligament
- Deflection of basilar membrane and organ of Corti by pressure transmitted through cochlear duct
- Basilar membrane
- Outer hair cells
- Inner hair cell

Labels (left):
- Vestibular canal (from oval window)
- Nerve fibers
- Ganglion
- Tympanic canal (to round window)

FIGURE 9.5.   *A cross-sectional diagram of the cochlea. The wave of pressure in the vestibular canal causes deflection of the vestibular membrane. Deflection of this membrane causes the fluid in the cochlear duct to be displaced and this, in turn, causes the basilar membrane and the organ of Corti to be displaced. Arrows in the figure show these movements. The hair cells of the organ of Corti are so arranged with respect to the tectorial membrane that the hairs are sheared against the tectorial membrane. Arrows labeled "shearing force" show this movement. All the movements are magnified thousands of times; the actual movements are microscopic. Note that movement is both up and down, corresponding to the positive and negative phases of the pressure wave. (Adapted from Frank H. Netter, M.D. From the CIBA collection of medical illustrations. © CIBA.)*

Generator potential. Several potentials can be distinguished and recorded in the ear [Davis, 1959]. The candidate most likely to be considered the generator potential, however, is the *cochlear microphonic potential.* This potential is recorded as a fluctuating voltage which follows the wave form of the physical stimulus quite closely [Wever and Bray, 1930]. Figure 9.7 shows the microphonic; it also shows that the microphonic tends to occur at the places of maximum displacement of the basilar membrane. The cochlear microphonic is unlike nerve impulses in that it has almost no threshold, occurs almost immediately after stimulation, and follows the frequency of the stimulus at a much higher rate than would be possible for a nerve fiber. The supposition is that the stimulation of the hair cells changes them in such a way that an electric current can flow through them. This current is driven by a steady voltage, the *endocochlear potential*, which exists between the cochlear duct and the other inner ear canals (see Figure 9.8). A flow of current through a resistance will be recorded as a voltage, and this voltage, according to the theory, is the cochlear microphonic. The flow of current across the basilar membrane may excite the ends of nerve fibers which are in very close contact with the hair cells. This theory is still controversial, but at least it does one of the important things expected of a theory—it helps to organize many diverse facts.

Nerve impulses and theories of hearing. When the nerve impulses are finally produced, we need to know which properties of the neural barrage are correlated with reported auditory experience. In other words, what is the neural code for such perceived characteristics as loudness and pitch?

Loudness is not much of a problem. We know that sense organs usually generate more and more nerve impulses as the intensity of a stimulus increases. The number of impulses generated is not usually directly proportional to the intensity of a stimulus, but nevertheless a relationship exists between the two. Hence, it is reasonable to assume that the loudness of a tone is determined by the number of impulses generated and propagated down the auditory nerve to the brain. The evidence we have for hearing supports this conclusion.

The situation is more complicated for pitch perception. We have two major theories to explain the action of the cochlea and the characteristics of the neural barrage in pitch perception. One of these is called the *place theory*; the other is known as the *telephone theory*.

The place theory states that perceived pitch depends upon the fact that a part of the basilar membrane is stimulated maximally by a given frequency. Somehow the central nervous system uses a place

code—that is, nerve impulses arising from a given region of the basilar membrane are perceived as a particular pitch. There is much good evidence for this theory [Békésy, 1960].

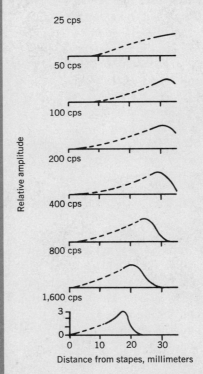

FREQUENCY OF THE PRESSURE WAVE DETERMINES THE PLACE OF MAXIMUM DISPLACEMENT OF THE BASILAR MEMBRANE

FIGURE 9.6. *Measurements of displacement of the basilar membrane with different stimulation frequencies. Note that the point of maximum displacement shifts toward the stapes, or oval window, as the frequency increases. The solid lines represent actual measurements and the dotted parts of the lines represent extrapolations. (Modified from Békésy and Rosenblith, 1951.)*

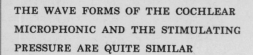

THE WAVE FORMS OF THE COCHLEAR
MICROPHONIC AND THE STIMULATING
PRESSURE ARE QUITE SIMILAR

FIGURE 9.7. *The cochlear microphonic for
different frequencies and places on the
basilar membrane. Note that the wave forms
of the microphonic and stimulating energy
are identical. The higher frequencies do not
produce microphonics in the part of the
basilar membrane at the third turn. This is
at some distance from the stapes and
fits with the data which show that the basilar
membrane is not distorted here when high
frequency stimulation is used (see
Figure 9.6). Such data give strong support for
the place theory of hearing. (After
Tasaki, 1954.)*

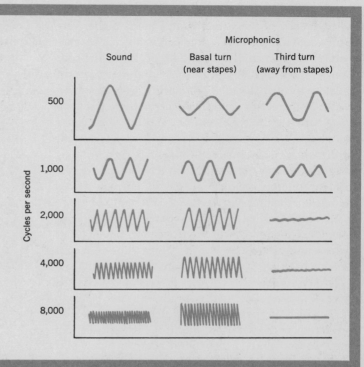

The telephone theory likens the cochlea to a
microphone and the auditory nerve to a telephone
wire. It proposes that the pitch heard by a person
is determined by the frequency of impulses traveling up the auditory nerve. The greater this frequency, the higher the perceived pitch.

With modern methods of recording nerve impulses, the frequency of impulses in the auditory
nerve can be measured while presenting tones of different frequency to an animal (usually a cat or
guinea pig). From such measurements, it is clear
that the telephone theory of pitch could at best be
true only for relatively low frequencies because the
auditory nerve cannot transmit distinctly different
frequencies above a limit of roughly 4,000 cps. At
very low frequencies, up to 500 or possibly 1,000
cps, a group of impulses in the nerve corresponds
to every cycle of the tone, and hence the auditory
nerve behaves in somewhat the same way as a telephone wire. At higher frequencies, however, the

nerve fibers are unable to "follow" every cycle.
They therefore start "skipping" every second or
third cycle of the tone. Since different fibers skip
different cycles, the nerve as a whole still follows
the frequency with volleys of impulses made up of
different combinations of fibers. At still higher frequencies—no one knows exactly where, but probably around 4,000 cps—this system of volleys breaks
down, so that impulses in the nerve no longer correspond to individual cycles of the stimulating tone.
Hence, we conclude that a telephone theory cannot
be true for the perception of pitch above 4,000 cps,
if indeed it applies below that.

In general, experiments support the place theory
much better than they do the telephone theory, and
most scientists concerned with the problem today
take a place theory for granted. We have been able
to demonstrate that different frequencies do indeed
stimulate certain parts of the cochlea more than
others, though the analysis in the cochlea is rela-

tively crude. Any frequency activates a relatively large area of the cochlea, but it activates one region more than another [Békésy, 1960]. Inhibitory processes further on in the auditory pathway are probably at work to sharpen the input. We also know that in the higher centers of the brain, a corresponding "map" represents different parts of the cochlea so that one region responds more to one frequency than to another [Ades, 1959]. However, these maps are not nearly so detailed at low frequencies as they are at higher ones. From this, it seems possible that a telephone-type transmission of impulses plays some role in pitch perception at low frequencies. With this exception, the place theory explains many of the phenomena of pitch perception.

These theories, plausible as they are, deal only with the simplest things about audition. Imagine,

if you can, the movements of the basilar membrane when it is activated by a complex wave of energy. Another puzzle is that very little is known about the ways in which the code from the periphery is interpreted in the central nervous system. All these are problems for future research.

PSYCHOPHYSICAL RELATIONSHIPS IN HEARING

In hearing, as with the other senses, we may again ask the question: What is it in the physical energy that corresponds to the reported experience? In hearing, we are especially concerned with the physical correlates of pitch, loudness, and quality or timbre.

Frequency and pitch of tones. The frequency of stimulation is the major, but not the only, determiner of the experience of pitch. In the earlier sections on psychophysical relationships, we have seen

---

THE "BATTERY" IN THE COCHLEAR DUCT MAY BE A CRUCIAL PART OF THE TRANSDUCTION PROCESS IN HEARING

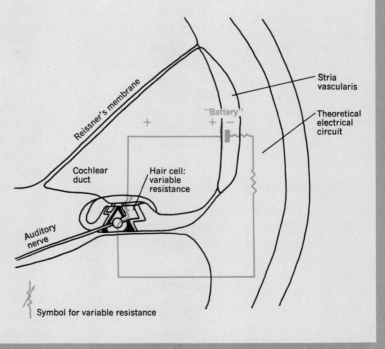

FIGURE 9.8. *A theoretical scheme for the excitation of the auditory nerve fibers. The theory starts with the fact that the fluid of the cochlear duct is positively charged with respect to the other ducts of the inner ear. Positive and negative charges are separated as they are in a battery. The theory goes on to suppose that the pressure wave and shearing movements of the hair cells cause them to lower their electrical resistance. If the resistance of the hair cells decreases, a current will flow between the poles of the cochlear battery. This flow of current through a resistor can be recorded as a voltage and it may be this voltage which is the cochlear microphonic. The current will also excite the nerve fibers which extend into the hair cells. (Modified from Davis, 1959.)*

PITCH IS A PSYCHOLOGICAL EXPERIENCE; FREQUENCY IS A PHYSICAL DIMENSION

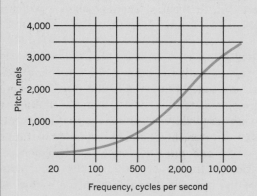

FIGURE 9.9. *The pitch scale. Units of pitch are called mels. The pitch of a 1,000-cycle stimulus is arbitrarily assigned a value of 1,000 mels. Tones that sound twice as high in pitch are assigned 2,000 mels; those that sound half as high, 500 mels. In this way, a pitch scale, relating pitch to frequency, has been constructed. Note, for example, that an experience of "twice as loud," or 2,000 mels, is produced by physical energy of more than twice the starting frequency, 1,000 cycles per second. As frequencies are increased and decreased from the starting frequency, experience does not follow in a one-to-one fashion. (After Stevens and Volkmann, 1940.)*

He is given two switches which he may depress. Pressing one turns on a standard tone of a frequency set by the experimenter. Pressing the other turns on a comparison tone whose frequency can be set by the observer merely by twisting a knob. He is instructed to set the frequency of the comparison tone so that it is perceived by him to be twice the *pitch* of the standard tone. He does this by listening first to the standard tone, then to the comparison tone, in alternation. He then adjusts the comparison tone until he is satisfied that he has set it at twice the pitch of the standard tone. The experimenter notes the frequency chosen.

The procedure is repeated with different standard tones. For example, the first standard tone might be 400 cps, and the observer's choice of a tone that is twice its pitch might be roughly 1,000 cps. This might serve as a standard in the next observation when the observer might choose 3,500 as being twice the pitch of 1,000 cps, and so on. The numbers are only approximate, but they illustrate the point. Observations are repeated until there are many measures of "twice the pitch" throughout the audible range.

From measurements of this kind, a scale can be constructed showing quantitatively the relation between frequency and pitch (see Figure 9.9). Such a scale, called a *pitch scale*, is not a straight line; rather it is curved. Pitch rises slowly between 1,000 cps and above 4,000 cps. Between 1,000 and 4,000 cps, it is more nearly proportional to frequency. Even so, a tone of 4,000 cps has little more than twice the pitch of a 1,000 cps tone. From 4,000 cps to 20,000 cps—a fivefold change in frequency—pitch increases by only 50 per cent. This fact demonstrates conclusively that pitch and frequency are not the same, because pitch does not increase or decrease in exact proportion to frequency.

This conclusion is strengthened by another fact we shall mention only briefly. The pitch of a tone depends not only on frequency, but also on intensity [Morgan et al., 1951]. The relationship between the two is complicated, but in general the pitch of a low frequency falls as it is made more intense, and that of a high frequency rises as its intensity increases. Thus the experience of pitch can be made to vary without changing frequency.

that physical energy and reported experience can be measured separately. Sensory experience is *not* a kind of carbon copy of the physical stimulus; a lawful relationship exists between them, but this relationship must be discovered. The measurement of the relationship between frequency and pitch is illustrated in the following experiment [Stevens and Volkmann, 1940]:

An observer is provided with a set of earphones through which tones of different frequency can be presented to him.

Limits of hearing. There is a limit to the range of frequencies which can be detected by human beings. Generally speaking, we can say that the audible range of frequencies is between 20 and 20,000 cps in man. Other animals have different ranges. The bat, for instance, has an upper limit which extends to the neighborhood of 150,000 cps [Griffin, 1959]. As can be seen from Figure 9.10, the range depends upon the intensity of stimulation. Tones at the extremes of the range of frequencies can be heard only at very high intensities, and at lower intensities the range is considerably smaller.

In order to give a more realistic idea of the frequency limits of hearing, the tones of a piano are also indicated in Figure 9.10. From this we can see that the range of notes is considerably narrower than the range of frequencies we can actually hear, particularly at the higher frequencies. It is, in fact, generally true that we seldom hear frequencies near the higher limits. Tones at these very high frequencies hardly sound like tones at all; rather they sound weak, very thin, and almost without a real pitch. You may have noticed that even the highest notes on a piano have very little tonal character compared with notes in the middle range of frequencies.

At very low frequencies, we can still hear sounds, but they are not tonal. Instead, we actually hear the individual pressure changes rather than a tone corresponding to the frequency of the sound. A tone of 8 or 10 cps, for example, is a throbbing sound. In practice, it is very difficult to measure the frequency at which we no longer hear a tone. A related difficulty is that these very low frequency tones have harmonics, and the harmonics may sound tonal even though the fundamental frequency does not.

Our ears not only limit the range of frequencies we can hear, they also limit the amount of change or difference between two tones that we can detect. To find this limit we sound two tones, one at a time, and ask observers to tell us whether they are the same or different. Then we change the frequency, making the difference larger or smaller, until we have the difference that the observer can just detect. Just as we used the Weber fraction $\Delta I/I$ to express the perception of intensity differ-

ences in vision (see Chapter 8), we can now find the change in frequency Δf which is detectable at a certain starting frequency f. We divide the change in frequency necessary to detect a difference by the frequency of the starting tone to obtain a $\Delta f/f$ fraction. This fraction is not constant over the range of audible frequencies [Shower and Biddulph, 1931]. For example, differential sensitivity tends to be better—the $\Delta f/f$ fraction is smaller—for the middle-range frequencies than for either the highest or lowest ones. To demonstrate this last point, you might strike some keys on the piano and note that it is relatively easy to tell the difference between two adjacent keys in the middle of the keyboard, but relatively hard to do it in the extreme bass or treble.

One should not confuse the ability to detect differences with the ability to identify a single note or tone—which is sometimes called absolute pitch. A very few fortunate people can identify nearly all the notes of the musical scale when they hear them

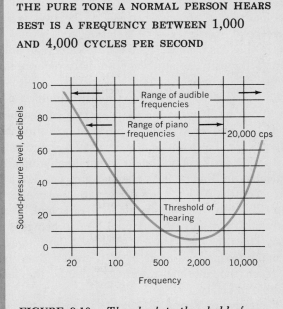

THE PURE TONE A NORMAL PERSON HEARS BEST IS A FREQUENCY BETWEEN 1,000 AND 4,000 CYCLES PER SECOND

FIGURE 9.10. *The absolute threshold of hearing for sine waves of different frequencies.*

played singly. Most of us have a hard time telling the octave in which a note is and can identify accurately no more than 8 or 10 different notes. For most purposes, however, this ability is irrelevant; the important task is usually to perceive the difference between two tones rather than the identity of a single one.

Intensity and loudness. As in the case of frequency, intensity is a physical characteristic; it is not the same as the psychological characteristic of loudness. Loudness, like pitch, is an attribute of auditory experience. Although closely correlated with intensity, loudness does not increase or decrease in exact proportion to changes in intensity. We know this because we have been able to construct loudness scales that are comparable to the pitch scale illustrated in Figure 9.9. The shape of the relationship is different, but the general point is the same: in each case, the attribute can be measured on a psychological scale that is different from the related physical scale.

Just as frequency corresponds most closely to the pitch of tone, intensity corresponds most closely to the loudness of tones. Once again, the two do not correspond perfectly—the relationship is not a linear one. Also, as we shall see, frequency, in addition to intensity, is quite important in determining perceived loudness.

It is probably obvious that intensity limits a person's hearing. If a tone is too weak, we cannot hear it at all, and even though physical measurement might show that a sound wave exists, a sound wave that is too weak cannot be an adequate stimulus. As indicated in Figure 9.2, a sound-pressure level of zero decibels, 0.0002 dyne per square centimeter, is approximately the lowest intensity of sound, at an optimum frequency, that normal human beings ever hear. However, as Figure 9.10 shows, the intensity of many frequencies must be even greater than that to reach the absolute threshold, that is, the just-audible intensity.

The curve of Figure 9.10 depicts absolute thresholds for tones of different frequencies. From it we can see that hearing is best for frequencies between 1,000 and 4,000 cps. At a frequency of 50 cps, for example, a sound pressure about 1,000 times as great is required for a tone to be heard as for a frequency of 2,000 cps. Similarly at higher frequencies, greater intensities are required for hearing.

Now refer again to the curve of Figure 9.10. It suggests that tones in the middle range of frequencies are much louder than those either higher or lower. At low intensities, this is actually true. But at higher intensities, not shown on the graph, all tones tend to sound equally loud. For example, at a sound-pressure level of 110 or 120 decibels, tones of all frequencies are about equally loud.

The detection of differences in intensity is determined by both the frequency and the intensity of tones. Discrimination is poorer for weak tones than it is for loud ones. For most practical purposes, however, one should remember that 1 decibel measures a difference in intensity that we can always detect as long as sounds are reasonably loud. The other point worth noting is that detection of a difference is poorer for the very low and very high frequencies than it is for the middle ones.

Complexity of wave form and timbre. The psychological counterpart of wave complexity is *timbre,* or *tonal quality,* which lets us distinguish rather easily among different musical instruments and different voices. A pure tone, for example, sounds very thin and lacking in tonal quality compared with the complex tone produced by an instrument such as the violin. In contrast, we would describe the violin tone as rich. The difference is that the violin tone has many strong harmonics. It is not just more timbre or less timbre, however, that distinguishes different instruments. Rather, the timbres of different instruments are different, and we learn that each instrument has a characteristic timbre.

There are, of course, other sounds that have little or no tonal quality, and these are called *noises.* Figure 9.3 provides a picture of the noise made by blowing air across a microphone. Notice that the trace of the noise is not periodic: it does not repeat itself in any regular pattern as do the sounds of musical instruments. Such a noise is made up of many different frequencies which are not multiples or harmonics of one another; rather, the frequencies are mixed more or less randomly. When the mixture is really random, we speak of *random noise*. In other instances, such as clicks or tapping sounds, the noises are not completely random—they contain certain dominant frequencies. They are, nevertheless, noises because they contain many frequencies that are not multiples of one another.

Masking. All that we have said so far about the psychophysics of hearing assumes that people are listening in relative quiet. If more than one tone is sounded at a time, or if somebody is making a noise when we are trying to listen to something, the detection of the presence of tones, and difference between tones, is much more difficult. Such changes in the detection thresholds are said to be due to *masking*.

You are all familiar with the masking of sounds by other sounds in everyday life. If you are talking on the telephone and there is a noise around you or in the telephone circuit, you cannot hear so well; if an airplane flies overhead during a lecture, you may not hear what the lecturer is saying. In the light of research which involved measurement of the effects of masking on the limits of hearing in the quiet, masking turns out to be a complex subject. The main points, however, are these. First, tones near together in frequency mask each other well—that is, each tone makes it hard for the other to be heard—but tones far apart in frequency do not mask each other very much. Second, low tones mask high tones better than the other way around. Consequently, if two tones are sounded together, you will be able to hear the tone of lower pitch more easily.

DEAFNESS We should not end this survey of hearing without saying something about deafness. Deafness is a serious problem in a civilization that depends so much on spoken communication. Everything must be written out for the deaf person, or he must "hear" by sign language. Some hard-of-hearing people become quite proficient at reading lips, but this procedure is at best a poor substitute for actually hearing speech.

Deafness is fairly common in our society, and until very recent years any kind of deafness was a serious handicap. It was not until the advent of the modern electronic hearing aid that partially deaf people had a sensory aid almost as good as that provided by eyeglasses. A totally deaf person cannot hear with a hearing aid, however, any more than a totally blind person can see with glasses.

Deafness is a two-way problem; it handicaps a person as a speaker and as a listener. Because he can never hear his own voice, a deaf person eventually loses his ability to speak well. That is why many deaf people speak in a peculiar tone—they have no way of knowing whether or not their voices sound like the voices of other people. In addition, deafness can create serious emotional problems. The deaf person tends to withdraw from people because he cannot, without great difficulty, communicate with them and because of the irritation they show when he cannot understand them.

Kinds of deafness. To measure deafness clinically, one uses an instrument known as the *audiometer*, which is simply a device for testing the intensity and frequency limits of hearing described earlier in this chapter. It produces pure tones at several different frequencies and provides accurate control of the sound pressure at each frequency. The examiner uses it to find the minimum intensity of sound, in decibels, that a person can hear at each frequency. From this data, a special graph, called an *audiogram*, is constructed. This graph shows the hearing loss in decibels relative to average normal hearing. On the average, people with normal hearing will show no hearing loss on the audiogram. The curve for a normal person will be close to zero hearing loss for all frequencies; the curve for a person with deafness will be below the zero line—he will show hearing loss.

The top curve in Figure 9.11 is a typical audiogram for a person with normal hearing. Notice that even the normal person does not hear all tones at exactly the same sound-pressure level as the *average*

IN CONDUCTION DEAFNESS, ALL
FREQUENCIES ARE AFFECTED; IN NERVE
DEAFNESS, THE HIGH FREQUENCIES
ARE MOST SEVERELY AFFECTED

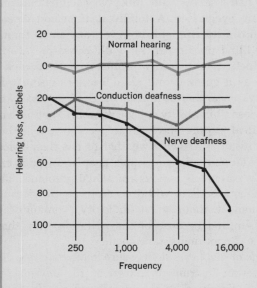

FIGURE 9.11. *Audiograms for normal
hearing and two major kinds of deafness. The
average threshold for normal individuals
at different frequencies is taken as zero. Any
particular individual does not have exactly
this threshold but does not depart from it by
more than a few decibels. The person with
conduction deafness has a rather uniform
hearing loss at all frequencies. The person
with nerve deafness has a greater hearing loss
at high frequencies than at low ones.*

normal person does, for there are always individual
variations from the average. The other two curves
in Figure 9.11 are for two individuals who are partially deaf, that is, who have sizable hearing losses.
The two curves show two kinds of deafness which

result from different causes and are characterized
by different patterns of hearing loss in their respective audiograms.

Conduction deafness involves roughly the same
hearing loss at all frequencies—the person suffering
from it is no more deaf at one frequency than he is
at another. The term "conduction deafness" is used
because the origin of the deafness is to be found
in deficiencies of conduction in the ear. The ear
may be stopped up, the eardrum may be broken, or
the ossicles of the middle ear may be damaged. The
effect of conduction deafness is much the same as
that of stuffing cotton in one's ears.

The lowest curve in Figure 9.11 represents a
second kind of hearing loss, *nerve deafness*. As its
name suggests, in this type of deafness something
is wrong with the auditory nervous system. Either
the nerves themselves have been damaged, or damage has been done in the cochlea, particularly to
the basilar membrane. It is characteristic of nerve
deafness that hearing loss is much greater at high
frequencies, which means that the nerve-deaf person can hear low-pitched sounds reasonably well
but can hear high-pitched sounds very poorly or not
at all. Such a person has a great deal of trouble
understanding speech because the relatively high
frequencies are very important in speech comprehension. He can hear the low tones, but he is not
able to distinguish easily between the word sounds.
For this reason, this kind of deafness has sometimes
also been called *perception deafness*.

Nerve deafness is very common in older people.
In fact, nearly all of us can expect to have at least
mild nerve deafness by the time we are sixty, just as
most of us can expect to be a bit farsighted by that
age. But for most people, the deafness is not serious
enough to require a hearing aid.

The chemical senses

So far, we have covered the two senses, vision and
hearing, that many people consider to be most im-

portant. We can divide the others into four main groups: the chemical senses, the skin senses, the proprioceptive senses, and the organic senses.

SMELL The receptors for smell respond to chemical substances, but only if those substances are volatile. Liquids, for example, do not stimulate the sense of smell. Smell receptors are located high up in the nasal passages leading from the nostrils to the throat (see Figure 9.12). They lie in two small patches, one on the left and one on the right, in the roofs of these passages. They are a little off the main route of air as it moves through the nose in normal breathing, and consequently our sense of smell is relatively dulled when we are breathing quietly. A sudden sniff or vigorous intake of air, however, stirs up the air in the nasal passages and brings it more directly to the receptors, which is why animals and people sniff when they are trying to identify an odor.

Basic odors. Just by recalling the odors that you encounter in one day, you can realize that they have many shades and qualities. This is also true, of course, of color. In both cases, scientists have raised the question of whether or not such a multitude of experiences might not result from mixture of a relatively few primary qualities. Color vision has indeed worked out that way; three hues mixed in various proportions can account for all perceived differences in color (see Chapter 8). Perhaps, in smell, there are similarly a few unique odors which, mixed in different proportions, might account for various discriminable odors.

Attempts have been made to discover or devise such a scheme, but they have not succeeded too well. Although research workers have devoted con-

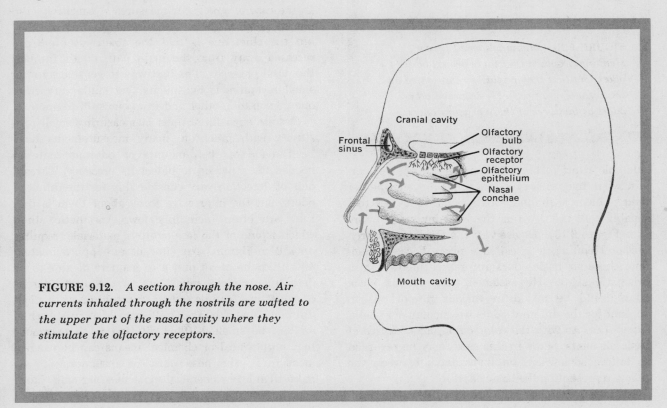

Cranial cavity

Olfactory bulb

Frontal sinus

Olfactory receptor

Olfactory epithelium

Nasal conchae

Mouth cavity

FIGURE 9.12. *A section through the nose. Air currents inhaled through the nostrils are wafted to the upper part of the nasal cavity where they stimulate the olfactory receptors.*

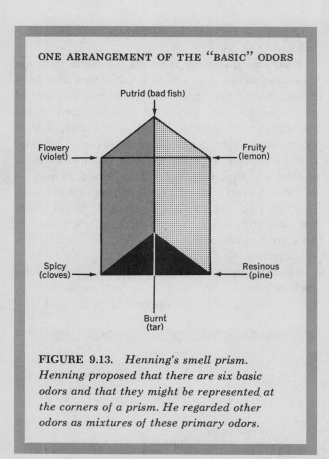

ONE ARRANGEMENT OF THE "BASIC" ODORS

Putrid (bad fish)

Flowery (violet) →

← Fruity (lemon)

Spicy (cloves) →

← Resinous (pine)

Burnt (tar)

FIGURE 9.13. *Henning's smell prism. Henning proposed that there are six basic odors and that they might be represented at the corners of a prism. He regarded other odors as mixtures of these primary odors.*

siderable effort to the problem, we are not yet certain what the primary odors are, or even whether their number is limited. One scheme that does reasonably well is known as the Henning smell prism (see Figure 9.13). Devised by the German research worker Henning, it is called a prism because Henning chose six basic odors and represented them in prismatic shape. He assumed that the six basic odors could be mixed in various proportions to account for the different odors we encounter in daily experience. As with the color circle, all mixtures of basic elements, odors in this case, may be regarded as falling somewhere on its surfaces between the points representing the basic odors.

Industrial chemists, who are faced with the problem of making artificial perfumes and scents, prefer a simpler fourfold classification of odors [Crocker, 1945]. According to this classification, the four basic odors are: fragrant (musk), acid (vinegar), burnt (roast coffee), and caprylic (goaty or sweaty). Still other systems of primary odors have been proposed. Each may serve some particular purpose well, but there is little assurance that in any of them we have found the "real" primaries in the sense that psychological primaries for color have been clearly established. Probably the biggest stumbling block to our accepting any scheme of primary odors as final is the difficulty we commonly encounter of getting individuals to agree consistently, either with themselves or with each other, in classifying different odors.

Smell sensitivity. In hearing and vision, we are able to state precisely how much energy is required for a person to detect, or discriminate, a stimulus. In the case of smell, our measures of sensitivity are not so precise. There are several reasons for this, but the chief one is that the smell receptors are recessed away from the main path of air through the nasal passages. The best way to get odors to the smell receptors is by sniffing; yet sniffs vary from one person to another and from one sniff to another.

Despite such limitations in measuring smell sensitivity with precision, many measurements have been made of the amounts of odorous material needed for a person to detect its presence. Thresholds of detection vary considerably for the different odors, but the impressive thing about them is that they are often incredibly low. Anesthetic ether, which is one of the less odorous materials, requires only 6 milligrams per liter of air—approximately 40 millionths of an ounce to a quart of air—to be detected. Artificial musk, one of the most odorous of substances, can be sensed in extraordinarily small dilutions. Only 0.00004 milligram of it in a liter of air can be smelled. This dilution is so enormous that no physical or chemical means can be used to measure it; the nose must be responding to no more than a few chemical molecules per sniff. However, impressive as this may be, the sense of smell in many animals even surpasses that in man.

Theories of smell. The disagreement concerning the basic types of odors has not impeded the creation of many theories to account for transduction and the psychophysical characteristics of smell. Of the many theories proposed, none has yet met with widespread acceptance. A current one is the stereochemical theory [Amoore et al., 1964].

The basic idea is that certain odors are produced by molecules with particular shapes. It is called a "lock-and-key" theory because these molecules are supposed to fit into "sockets" in the olfactory receptors. For example, the molecules of camphor, and substances which have a camphorlike odor, are supposed to have a spherical shape and fit into a bowl-shaped depression in the olfactory receptor. Five of the odors considered to be basic in this theory—camphoraceous, musky, floral, pepperminty, and ethereal—are supposed to have distinctive shapes. Two other so-called basic odors, pungent and putrid, are supposed to arise from molecules having distinctive patterns of electrical charge allowing them to fit into sockets in the olfactory receptor.

The evidence for this theory is suggestive. For instance, it is possible to synthesize substances with particular molecular shapes and to see whether they would have the odor predicted by the theory. In some tests they do. Thus transduction in smell may depend upon the shape of, and the charges on, the molecule, but the evidence is not yet conclusive.

TASTE   The receptors for taste are specialized cells which are grouped together in little clusters known as *taste buds* (see Figure 9.14). These buds are located for the most part on the top and sides of the tongue, but a few of them are also at the back of the mouth and in the throat. If you examine the tongue closely—you can do it simply by looking at your own tongue in a mirror—you will notice a number of bumps on it, some large and some small. These bumps, called *papillae,* are richly populated with taste buds. To stimulate the taste receptors, substances must be in solutions which wash around the papillae and penetrate to the taste cells within them.

Primary taste qualities. We have said that we are not yet certain of the primary odors. Fortunately we are clearer about the primary taste qualities. Several lines of evidence point to four qualities: *salty, sour, sweet,* and *bitter.* Part of the evidence for these qualities is the fact that the tongue is not uniformly sensitive to all stimuli. If, for example, we apply minute drops of a bitter solution, such as quinine, to different parts of the tongue, we find the bitter taste most pronounced when the drops are put at the back of the tongue. The taste of sweet-

TASTE CELLS ARE LOCATED IN THE TASTE BUDS

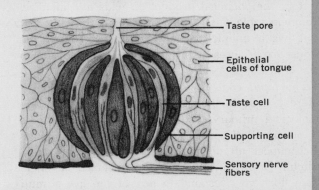

Taste pore

Epithelial cells of tongue

Taste cell

Supporting cell

Sensory nerve fibers

FIGURE 9.14.   *Taste buds are located on the top and sides of the tongue and at the back of the mouth and in the throat. They are especially dense on the bumps, or papillae, of the tongue.*

ness, on the other hand, is most noticeable when sugar solutions are placed on the tip of the tongue. The sides of the tongue respond mainly to sour stimuli, and the tip and part of the sides respond to salty solutions. This as well as other evidence supports the idea that there are four primary taste qualities.

If we now try to state what kinds of solutions give rise to the different qualities, we run into trouble. Sugars, such as common table sugar, taste sweet, but so do many other chemical compounds, such as saccharine, which have little in common, chemically, with sugar. The taste of bitter presents a similar problem. A class of compounds that the organic chemist calls *alkaloids,* which includes quinine and nicotine, tastes bitter, but so do substances such as some of the mineral salts that have little in common with the alkaloids. However, all this may prove only that we have not yet discovered which aspects of a chemical substance are the key ones in determining taste quality. We cannot at present state definite rules for the kinds of chemical substances that produce sweet and bitter qualities of taste.

In the cases of sour and salty tastes, a somewhat better correlation exists between chemical composition and taste. All the stimuli that taste sour are acids. Moreover, the degree of sourness that we taste is fairly proportional to the total number of acid (H^+) ions present. Salty taste, similarly, is usually aroused by what the chemist calls salts— that is, the chemical product of acids and alkalies. Common table salt, however, is about the only salt that has a uniquely salty taste; most other salts arouse experiences of bitter or sweet in addition to that of salt.

The input code in taste. What is the input, or afferent, code in the taste nerves for the four psychological primary tastes? It is clear from studies of electrical responses of single taste nerve fibers that almost all of them respond to several taste stimuli [Pfaffmann, 1964]. For instance, a single taste fiber may respond to any of the five stimuli shown in Figure 9.15 [Erickson, 1963]. Thus the firing of a single fiber is not unique—it may be fired by many stimuli—and a single fiber does not carry reliable information regarding the stimulating agents to the central nervous system. As far as the brain "knows," the fiber could be firing because any of a number of stimuli have come in contact with the tongue. However, several elements together may make a unique combination. Thus it seems that the "neural message for gustatory quality is a *pattern* made up of the amount of neural activity across many neural elements" [Erickson, 1963].

Taste sensitivity. Just as it is difficult to measure accurately a person's threshold for odors, so it is difficult to measure thresholds for taste. All stimuli for taste must be in solution and must reach the taste cells lying beneath the surface of the papillae. For an experimenter to control taste stimuli precisely, he must make sure that all saliva is removed from the surface to be stimulated and also that it is washed free of any solutions which have been used in preceding tests. The temperature of the tongue and the size of the area stimulated must also be carefully controlled.

When an investigator takes all these precautions, he can measure taste sensitivity. From measurements that have been made, it is clear that taste sensitivity is not nearly so good, relatively, as smell sensitivity. It takes, for example, from 4 parts in 100 to 1 part in 1,000 to be easily detected. In general, our sensitivity is greater for acids and bitter substances than it is for sweet and salty substances.

Adaptation. Nearly all our different sense organs adapt to stimuli. That is to say, they gradually become less sensitive during the course of stimulation, and the stronger the stimulation, the greater is such adaptation. Some senses, such as hearing and equilibrium, adapt relatively little. The senses of taste and smell, however, are among those which adapt readily.

We have all noticed such adaptation. Sometimes, upon entering a room, one is taken aback by a strong odor. Yet, after being in the room for a while, one no longer notices the odor and may be unable to detect its presence. Similarly, the full flavor of one's favorite food can be appreciated only upon the first taste. Adaptation soon sets in and some of the strength of the flavor is lost. It is possible to measure such adaptation in the laboratory, and research workers have obtained many curves showing the rate of adaptation for various odors and tastes [Osgood, 1953].

Taste or smell? Although we all believe that we taste with our tongues and smell with our noses, most of us do not realize that we commonly confuse taste and smell. Indeed, we often think that we are identifying a flavor by taste when smell is the more important.

You can prove this by asking a friend to hold his nose while you place drops of familiar beverages on his tongue. If you place a drop of lemon juice on it, the chances are that he will say merely that it is something sour. If you drop a little Coca-Cola on it, he may know only that it is something bittersweet. If you give him a piece of potato, he may be unable to distinguish its taste from that of a piece of apple. If now you repeat the experiment without your

friend holding his nose, he will immediately be able to identify the substances correctly.

Some smells, like tobacco smoke, so mask a flavor that gourmets have been known to refuse to eat in smoke-filled restaurants. The part played by smell explains why food is so "tasteless" when a person has a stuffy head cold that greatly reduces his sensitivity to odors.

The four skin senses

Vision, hearing, and the chemical senses are the sensory channels used most in conscious perception of the world. If these channels are functioning properly, we hardly need any other senses to appreciate what is going on around us. For this reason we tend to ignore what we could do, if we had to, with our skin senses. In general, we rely on our skin senses only for such simple experiences as itches and

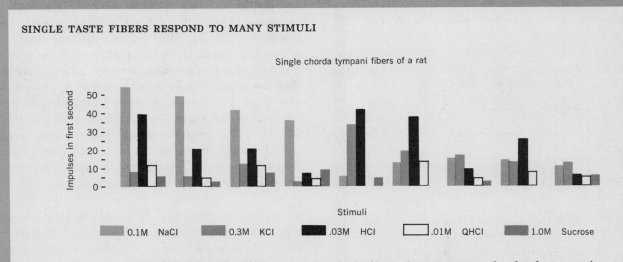

FIGURE 9.15. *Recordings from nine single fibers of a taste nerve, the chorda tympani, of the rat. The stimuli were applied to a spot on the tongue and nerve impulses were recorded from single nerve fibers. The stimuli were: 0.1 molar sodium chloride, 0.3 molar potassium chloride, 0.03 molar hydrochloric acid, 0.01 molar quinine hydrochloride, and 1.0 molar sucrose (common table sugar). Note that the nine fibers fire, in varying amounts, to many of the stimuli. (Modified from Erickson, 1963.)*

tinglings, feelings of hot and cold, and painful sensations of injury. Actually, the skin senses are capable of telling us much more than that. We could, for example, identify many objects by their touch or even read braille, as the blind must do.

Let us begin our account of these senses with an experiment that has now become common in the psychological laboratory [Woodworth and Schlosberg, 1954].

A subject is seated and asked to roll up the sleeve of his shirt, baring his forearm. On the undersurface of the arm, a grid is stamped. The experimenter then takes a hair that

can be applied with known pressure and touches the end of it first to one spot on the grid and then to another. Each time the hair is applied, the blindfolded subject reports whether or not he feels pressure. The experimenter keeps a chart corresponding to the grid stamped on the subject's arm and marks on the chart each position at which the subject reports having felt pressure (see Figure 9.16).

Having plotted all the points on the grid where pressure, or touch, is reported, the experimenter now takes a rod that has been cooled to a temperature, say, of 28°C, and kept at that temperature throughout the experiment. With this rod, he goes again from square to square and charts the points at which the subject reports "cold." He then does the same thing with a rod that has been maintained at a temperature above normal, say 35°C, and he maps all the spots for which "warm" is reported. Finally, with a fine sharp needle applied, with a constant light pressure, he goes over the entire grid again and plots the "pain spots."

Now let us look at the chart on which all these points are plotted (see Figure 9.16). First of all, you can see that not all areas are equally sensitive. In some places, the subject reports "touch," in others he does not. Thus you see that the skin has a *punctate sensitivity*—it is sensitive at some points and not others. (Actually, detailed analysis shows that the skin is simply *more* sensitive or *less* sensitive from one point to another.) Second, you will notice different maps for the different stimulators. The spots of greatest sensitivity of touch, cold, warmth, and pain are, on the whole, different. From data such as these it should be apparent that there is not one skin sense, but four different ones.

PRESSURE OR TOUCH   The experience a subject reports when he is touched lightly with a hair is called either pressure or touch. The amount of pressure required to elicit this experience varies greatly for different parts of the body. The tip of the tongue, the lips, the fingers, and the hands are the most sensitive areas. The arms and legs are less sensitive, whereas the trunk and calloused areas are the least sensitive of all. We experience pressure, it should also be noted, not only when some object

DIFFERENT POINTS ON THE SKIN ARE MOST SENSITIVE TO PAIN, TOUCH, WARMTH, AND COLD

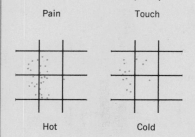

Pain   Touch

Hot   Cold

FIGURE 9.16.   *Mapping the sensitivity of the skin. By marking a grid on an area of the skin and then systematically stimulating different spots, one can construct a map of the sensitive spots. Maps for pain, touch, warmth, and cold stimuli are usually different, indicating that there are four distinct skin senses. (Diagram from Gerard, 1941.)*

THE SKIN IS A COMPLEX ORGAN

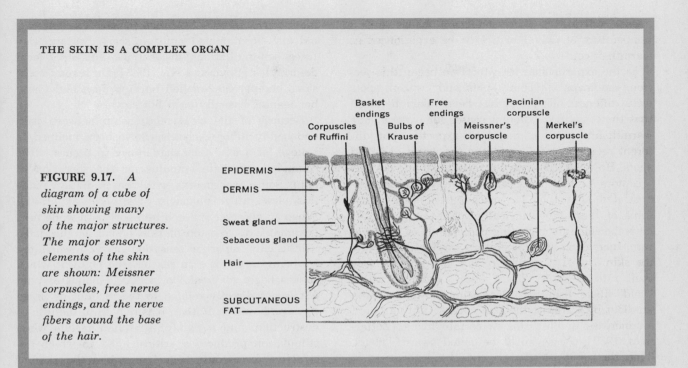

FIGURE 9.17. *A diagram of a cube of skin showing many of the major structures. The major sensory elements of the skin are shown: Meissner corpuscles, free nerve endings, and the nerve fibers around the base of the hair.*

touches the skin but also when hairs on the body are slightly moved.

Psychologists have studied carefully what it is about a stimulus that elicits the experience of pressure. They wanted to know in particular whether it was the weight of an object on the skin or simply a bending of the skin that aroused sensation. They have concluded that it is the latter—the deforming or bending of the skin. A *gradient of pressure,* not uniformly distributed pressure, is the adequate stimulus for touch experience.

For more than fifty years many attempts have been made to determine the receptors for pressure. Seldom have scientists worked so assiduously at a problem with so little success. We think that a fairly complex structure, called the *Meissner corpuscle* (see Figure 9.17), serves the pressure sense in the hairless regions of the body, the palms of the hands for example, and that another structure, the *basket nerve ending,* does it for the roots of hairs. We also have good reason to believe that simple *free nerve endings*—endings not associated with any special structure—also convey touch impulses because we can feel pressure in some areas of the skin where no receptors other than free nerve endings are to be found. A final answer to this problem, however, awaits further more definitive research. In addition to the sense of touch or pressure on the surface of the body, we are sensitive to deep pressure. The receptors for this sense seem to be small capsules called *Pacinian corpuscles.*

TEMPERATURE SENSATION: COLD AND WARMTH Experiences of warmth and cold are elicited by any change in the normal gradient of skin temperature. This gradient, in the case of the forearm, for example, is about 5°C and is the difference between the temperature of circulating blood (37.5°C) and that of the surface of the skin (32 or 33°C). A stimulus of 28 to 30°C, which is definitely felt as cold, increases this gradient a little, whereas a stimulus of 34°C, which can be felt as warm, decreases it a little. Thus it takes a change in skin temperature of only 1 or 2°C to be experienced as warmth or cold.

In the experiment with which we began this section, the maps of "cold" spots and "warm" spots were different. This fact has been taken to mean that there are two different senses for experiencing warmth and cold. It might be expected that different receptors would underlie the warm and cold spots. However, there do not seem to be any obvious receptors for thermal sensitivity which can be demonstrated anatomically. Instead, free nerve fibers, some of them physiologically specialized, seem to be responsible for signaling perceptions of temperature. Increasing the temperature gradient by cooling the skin 5 to 10°C causes certain fibers to increase their rate of firing. These fibers might be called "cold" fibers. Similarly, decreasing the temperature gradient by warming the skin causes, up to a point, an increase in the firing of certain fibers [Zotterman, 1959]. These might be called "warm" fibers. Thus the input, or afferent, code for experiences of cold and warmth appears to be the rate of firing in cold and warm fibers.

It is interesting that some cold fibers show an increase in firing rate when very warm stimuli, say, 45 to 50°C, are applied to the skin. This may be the physiological basis for the psychological phenomenon of *paradoxical cold*—reports by a subject that a small hot stimulus spot feels cold.

PAIN A good many very diverse stimuli produce pain—a needle prick, scalding steam, a hard blow to the skin, or strong acid. One laboratory method of producing pain, which has proved rather precise, is to use a device that radiates heat to a given area of the skin [Wolff and Wolf, 1948]. As the radiant heat is increased in intensity, the person first reports warmth, and then at a particular intensity he reports pain. Other methods which are not quite so precise make use of pinpricks and chemical solutions.

The biological utility of pain is most clearly illustrated in cases of those rare individuals who have no pain sensitivity and who sometimes unknowingly incur grave injuries. One such person, a seven-year-old girl, accumulated multiple scars, bruises, fractures, self-mutilations, dislocations, and other local deformities [Boyd and Nie, 1949]. On several occasions her parents smelled burning flesh and found her leaning casually on a hot stove.

Because of the close relationship between pain and bodily injury, scientists have been inclined to believe for a long time that injury to tissues is the common immediate stimulus for the sensation of pain. Some experiments with heat radiation make this view rather plausible [Hardy et al., 1951]. When an observer is asked to report pain while heat is radiated to a patch of skin on his forehead, he will usually report a sensation of pain when the temperature of his skin reaches the point at which tissues begin to break down. The amount of pain felt is not directly related to the amount of tissue damage, however. Rather, it is related to the rate of destruction, and a painful sensation results when stimulation produces a critical state in which destructive forces just begin to exceed the rate of repair.

The receptors for pain are almost certainly unspecialized free nerve endings that are abundant in most parts of the skin, particularly where sensitivity to pain is greatest.

ADAPTATION Like the chemical senses, the senses of the skin are able to adapt to stimuli within quite wide limits. Pain adapts rather incompletely—if you have ever had a bad toothache, you have discovered how slowly the sensations of pain adapt— but both touch and thermal sensitivity change appreciably during the course of stimulation. Adaptation is especially marked in the senses of warmth and cold. If, for example, one immerses his left hand in warm water and his right hand in cold water, the sensations of warm and cold gradually die out. But then, if both hands are immersed in water at a temperature between those to which the hands are adapted, the left hand now feels cold and the right one feels warm. The pressure sense also adapts readily. For instance, we are not aware, until attention is focused on it, of the pressure of clothes on our body—the pressure receptors, basket nerve endings, free nerve endings, or Meissner corpuscles have an increased threshold.

The proprioceptive senses

Hidden away in our muscles, and in our joints and tendons, are a large variety of sense organs. In addition, there are sensory cells in the semicircular canals and otolith organs of the inner ear. All these sense organs, which give rise to the *proprioceptive senses,* give us information about the position of the body in space.

KINESTHETIC SENSE A bodily sense that physiologists now know a good deal about is one that most people have never heard of: *kinesthesis.* In some ways, it is the most important sense we have because it provides an automatic system for coordinating our muscles in walking and in all our skilled movements. One can see how important it is only by observing a person who has been deprived of it. This sometimes happens in a form of syphilis, known as tabes dorsalis, which attacks the sensory pathways from the kinesthetic sense organs. A patient with this disease gets no information from his muscles about their movement. He is able to walk, balance a ball, or carry out other skills only by watching carefully what his arms and legs are doing. If syphilis invades the brain stem and interrupts kinesthetic impulses from the face and mouth, uncoordinated movements of the face may also occur along with a slurring of speech which, if severe, may make speech unintelligible.

The kinesthetic receptors are found in three distinct places. One is in the muscles, where free nerve endings surround small muscle spindles (see Figure 9.18). These kinesthetic receptors signal the *stretch* of a muscle. A second location of kinesthetic receptors is in the tendons that connect muscles to bones. The receptors here are nerve endings that serve a specialized organ known as the *Golgi tendon organ* (see Figure 9.18). They are stimulated when a muscle contracts and puts tension on the tendon.

Finally, some receptors are to be found in the linings of the joints. These are stimulated whenever a limb moves, changing the relative positions of two bones in the joint. We are still not certain about the receptors in the joints, but it is possible that they are Pacinian corpuscles—the same receptors that yield perception of deep pressure when regions below the skin are stimulated.

THE VESTIBULAR SENSE Just like kinesthesis, the vestibular sense is important in balance and movement, but it does not provide direct experiences of which we are ordinarily aware. The organs of the vestibular sense are well known because they are highly specialized, are reasonably large, and can be studied in detail under the microscope. They are, in fact, part of the inner ear. The inner ear is a series of cavities, only one of which, the cochlea, is concerned with hearing. The rest of

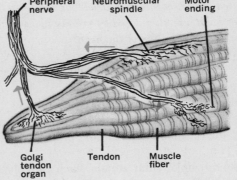

KINESTHETIC RECEPTORS ARE FOUND IN THE MUSCLES, TENDONS, AND JOINTS

Peripheral nerve

Neuromuscular spindle

Motor ending

Golgi tendon organ

Tendon

Muscle fiber

FIGURE 9.18. *Kinesthetic receptors in muscle and tendon. The two kinesthetic receptors shown are the neuromuscular spindle and the Golgi tendon organ. The motor ending is not sensory, but is the ending of nerve fibers which stimulate the muscle fibers to contract.*

THE AMPULLAE OF THE SEMICIRCULAR CANALS RESPOND TO ROTATION; THE OTOLITHS OF THE SACCULE AND UTRICLE RESPOND TO POSITION OF THE HEAD

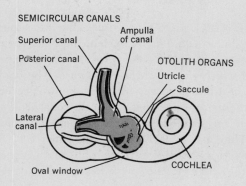

SEMICIRCULAR CANALS

Superior canal

Ampulla of canal

Posterior canal

OTOLITH ORGANS

Utricle

Saccule

Lateral canal

Oval window

COCHLEA

FIGURE 9.19. *The vestibular sense organs. The three semicircular canals are so arranged that one is in each plane. Organs in the ampullae of these canals respond to rotation or movement of the head. The otolith organs located in the saccule and utricle, on the other hand, are stimulated by gravity and hence by the position of the head.*

the cavities constitute the vestibular organs (see Figures 9.19 and 9.20). They divide into two main groups: the *semicircular canals* and the *otolith organs.*

The three semicircular canals, each roughly perpendicular to both the others, are so oriented as to represent three different planes of movement. In an enlarged part of each canal, the *ampulla,* is a set of hair cells similar in general structure to those in the cochlea. These cells are encompassed by the fluid that fills the canal and are stimulated when pressure is exerted on this fluid. Such pressure occurs mainly when the head is rotated, and thus the canals are sense organs for rotation. It appears, however, that the receptors do not respond merely to continuous rotation—continuous pressure—but to changes in rate of rotation, that is, to acceleration or deceleration. So when a person is rotated, or rotates himself as a dancer does, for example, it is only while he is increasing speed or slowing down that the semicircular organs are stimulated.

Dancers and acrobats who do a lot of spinning have learned some tricks which help them overcome the dizziness from prolonged stimulation of the vestibular organs. Watch a ballet dancer spinning, and you will see that he keeps his head as motionless as possible by temporarily fixing his eyes on some object in the environment. The head whips around to pick a new fixation point while the body is still turning.

Two other cavities make up the vestibular organ. On the walls of these cavities are thickenings which contain receptor cells. These protrude into a gelatinous mass that contains small crystals, the *otoliths* (*oto* means "ear"; *lith* means "stone"). These receptors appear to be positional, or static, receptors, for they respond merely to the tilt or position of the head and do not require rotation to be stimulated.

Vestibular reactions. The canals and the otolith organs together provide a sense of balance. Impulses from these organs help a person right himself when he has been thrown off balance. More specifically, they control a number of reflexes that automatically compensate for loss of balance. One such reflex is a movement of the head back to a normal position whenever it has been turned away from it. Another is a reflex twisting of the trunk and body to return the whole body to normal position.

Perhaps the best illustration of these effects of the vestibular sense organs is the righting reaction of the cat, an animal famed for its ability to land right side up when dropped from any height or position. A cat, when turned upside down and dropped, first twists its head around to normal position, then its trunk, and then, through some indirect reflexes, brings its four feet around to orient toward the ground. This series of reactions is controlled primarily by the vestibular receptors.

A special connection exists between the vestibular receptors and the eyes. If one turns his head quickly, his eyes ordinarily move simultaneously in the opposite direction so that they continue to fixate the same point. These compensatory movements of the eyes are controlled in part by the vestibular receptors. When we have been spinning around and then stop, our eyes continue to move back and forth in a movement that is called *rotation nystagmus*. The eyes drift to one side, then move quickly to the other, then drift, then jump, and so on. Such nystagmus is a reflex evoked by the stimulation that the receptors in the semicircular canals have received.

Motion sickness. Motion sickness, which causes some people so much misery, is an effect of vestibular stimulation. We know that the vestibular organs are responsible for motion sickness because the ocasional individual whose vestibular system is not functioning properly does not suffer motion sickness, and also because we cane induce motion sickness experimentally by producing the vestibular impulses that evoke reflex reactions in the alimentary tract [Wendt, 1951]. Other factors such as anxiety can augment such reactions, and they therefore contribute to the direct effects of vestibular stimulation. There are now well-publicized drugs, Dramamine, for instance, which reduce or prevent motion sickness, but it is not known yet whether they work on the vestibular sense, alimentary tract, or some other part of the nervous system involved in the reaction.

Organic senses

We know relatively little about receptors in the internal organs within the body cavity, mainly because these areas are so inaccessible to experimentation. But there must be cold and warm receptors in the esophagus and stomach, for we can experience cold and warmth in these parts. There

THE OTOLITH ORGANS CONTAIN SENSORY HAIRS EMBEDDED IN A GELATINOUS SUBSTANCE

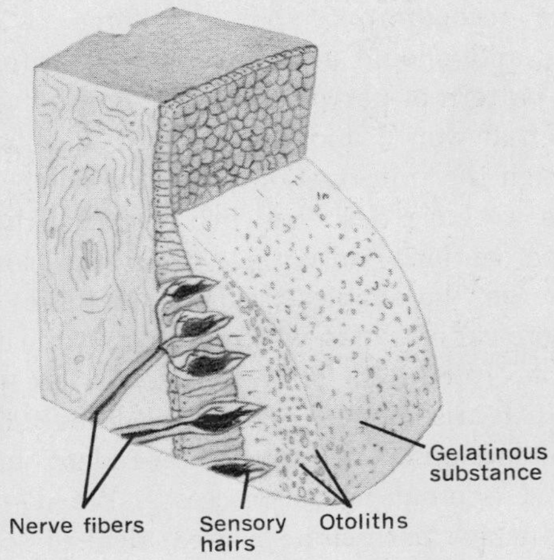

FIGURE 9.20. *Microscopic structure of the otolith organs. The otoliths of the saccule and utricle are embedded in a gelatinous substance and exert pressure on the sensory hairs according to the position of the head. Stimulation of the hairs evokes impulses in sensory nerve fibers which signal the position of the head.*

must also be receptors for pressure and pain. So far as other internal organs are concerned, it is clear that we can feel pressure and pain when they are irritated or put under pressure, but we do not know to what extent these experiences arise from receptors in the organs themselves and to what extent they may arise from other tissues and the abdominal wall, which are indirectly affected by these organs.

SYNOPSIS AND SUMMARY

This chapter completes our survey of the human senses. At this point, a recapitulation of some of the important general points made in this chapter and the preceding one is in order. One point is that all our experience ultimately depends upon sensory processes. Second, the physical energies hitting the receptors are not the same as the experience, and should not be confused with it. Third, the pattern of nervous activity signals events in the external world, and this pattern of activity arises through the transduction process. Fourth, the experiences we have described are best thought of as simple perceptions and not as "basic sensations." In other words, the simple sensory experiences are not like chemical elements which are combined into more complex products. They themselves are perceptions which arise under certain conditions. These sensory perceptions are largely dependent upon receptor and afferent nerve processes. We discuss experiences which necessitate a great deal of selection and reworking of the afferent input by the central nervous system in the next chapter.

Some of the specific points discussed in this chapter are itemized here.

1. Alternations of air pressure, called sound waves, provide the stimulus for hearing. The experience of a pure tone is caused by simple sine waves. Noises, on the other hand, are caused by pressure waves that consist of many frequencies mixed more or less randomly.

2. The pressure waves enter the canal of the outer ear and cause the eardrum to vibrate. This vibration is transmitted via the bones of the middle ear to the inner ear which contains the cochlea and the organ of Corti.

3. The crucial event in auditory transduction takes place in the organ of Corti on the basilar membrane of the cochlea. Here the pressure wave in the fluid of the cochlea causes a shearing motion of the hair cells. One theory states that this shearing motion changes the electrical resistance of the hair cells and allows current to flow across the basilar membrane. This current is recorded as the cochlear microphonic.

4. The two major theories of pitch perception are the place and telephone theories. The place theory states that perceived pitch is a function of the place on the basilar membrane which is maximally stimulated. The telephone theory says that perceived pitch depends upon the frequency of the nerve impulses traveling up the auditory nerve. The place theory is the accepted one for higher frequencies; the telephone theory is accepted by some for the lower frequencies.

5. Pitch, loudness, and timbre are the psychological attributes of sound energy. Pitch is correlated with the frequency of the physical energy; loudness is correlated with the intensity of the physical stimulation; timbre is correlated with the complexity of the wave form. However, intensity also affects pitch, and frequency also affects loudness.

6. Hearing is made more difficult if a sound is masked by another sound.

7. Deafness is fairly common. Two types can be distinguished: conduction deafness involves some loss in the conduction of sounds to the inner ear; nerve deafness involves some defect in the organ of Corti or the auditory nerve. Nerve deafness tends to be greater for high tones than for low tones, and it is common in old age.

8. The number of qualities in the sense of smell is uncertain, although combinations of as few as four or six will account for most odors. Taste seems to have four basic qualities: sweet, salty, sour, and bitter.

9. Smell is much more acute than taste, sometimes requiring only a few molecules per liter of air for detection. Both senses adapt fairly rapidly to continued stimulation.

10. Four basic senses are associated with the skin: warmth, cold, pressure or touch, and pain. Although there seem to be specialized receptors for touch, free nerve endings in the skin can probably serve as the receptors for each of these sensory modalities. It is well established that such free nerve endings are the receptors for warmth, cold, and pain. Pain adapts less readily than the other skin senses.

11. Proprioception consists of the kinesthetic and vestibular senses. The kinesthetic receptors are found in muscles, tendons, and joints. Impulses from these receptors make posture and coordination almost automatic. The vestibular sense organs are located in the inner ear. They respond to the rotation of the head or to changes in its position, thus providing a sense of balance.

12. The organic senses signal pain and changes in temperature and pressure from the body organs.

RELATED TOPICS IN THE TEXT

CHAPTER 8 SENSORY PROCESSES AND VISION Many of the basic principles needed for the study of the senses, as well as a detailed account of vision, are presented.

CHAPTER 10 PERCEPTION This chapter on perception describes the further elaboration of the sensory input.

CHAPTER 20 PHYSIOLOGICAL BASIS OF BEHAVIOR Auditory central nervous system pathways and auditory functions of central nervous system areas are discussed in this chapter. The central nervous system areas devoted to the skin senses and taste are also mentioned.

SUGGESTIONS FOR FURTHER READING

Békésy, G. von. *Experiments in hearing.* New York: McGraw-Hill, 1960.
A well-illustrated account of significant modern experiments in hearing, particularly on the function of the cochlea.

Bergeijk, W. A. van, Pierce, J. R., and David, E. E., Jr. *Waves and the ear.* Garden City, N.Y.: Doubleday, 1960. (Paperback.)
A popular and interesting account of many aspects of hearing and speech sounds.

Boring, E. G. *Sensation and perception in the history of experimental psychology.* New York: Appleton-Century-Crofts, 1942.
An authoritative history of experimental work in sensory perception.

Buddenbrock, W. von. *The senses.* Ann Arbor, Mich.: The University of Michigan Press, 1958. (Paperback).
The sense organs of many animals, including man, are interestingly discussed.

Geldard, F. A. *The human senses.* New York: Wiley, 1953.
An introductory text covering all the senses

Griffin, D. R. *Echoes of bats and men.* Garden City, N.Y.: Anchor Books, 1959. (Paperback.)
The amazing feats of auditory detection performed by the bat are discussed. There is also an excellent discussion of the physical energy which is detected by the auditory receptors.

Morgan, C. T. *Physiological psychology* (3d ed.). New York: McGraw-Hill, 1965.
A text containing several chapters on the physiological basis of sensory perception.

Mueller, C. G. *Sensory psychology.* Englewood Cliffs, N.J.: Prentice-Hall, 1965. (Paperback.)
An authoritative text on sensory processes.

Rosenblith, W. A. (Ed.). *Sensory communication.* New York: Wiley, 1961.
A series of articles on recent work in the senses. Some of them are rather technical for the beginner, but they can be mastered with effort.

Scientific American Readings
A number of reprints of articles on the senses which originally appeared in the Scientific American *are available.*
A list of the reprints and the reprints themselves may be obtained from: W. H. Freeman and Co., San Francisco, California.

Stevens, S. S., and Davis, H. *Hearing.* New York: Wiley, 1938.
A summary of research and some basic facts about the psychology and physiology of hearing.

Wolff, H. G., and Wolf, S. *Pain.* Springfield, Ill.: Charles C Thomas, 1948.
A little book covering various aspects of the topic of pain.

Wright, R. H. *The science of smell.* New York: Basic Books, Inc., 1964.
A readable summary of modern knowledge about the sense of smell.

10

PERCEPTION

WHY DO THINGS LOOK
AS THEY DO?
  KURT KOFFKA

PART OF WHAT WE
PERCEIVE COMES
THROUGH OUR SENSES
FROM THE OBJECT
BEFORE US, ANOTHER
PART . . . ALWAYS
COMES . . . OUT OF
OUR OWN HEAD.
  WILLIAM JAMES

i hate

THE STUDY OF sensory processes and sensory perception in Chapters 8 and 9 has set the stage for the study of other aspects of perception. The term is defined more precisely later, but for now, let us say that it refers to the way the world looks, sounds, feels, smells, or tastes to us. One's perceived world is the world of his immediate experience.

Why should psychologists, especially those interested chiefly in behavior, be interested in how things "seem" to us? The answer is simply that behavior is determined to a large extent by the way in which the world is perceived. Suppose, while talking to a friend, you say something and he changes his expression. Does this new expression signal anger, petulance, or is he merely thinking about his sore big toe? Your behavior in response to your friend will depend upon the way you perceive his expression.

On a more abstract level, we have already established that sensory processes do not produce little copies of the external world. A great deal of coding, transformation, and reordering takes place in the sensory input before the resulting experience is perceived as such. It is also true that most of the physical energy impinging upon the receptors never results in experience—perception is selective; further additions are made to the input from the receptors; and the input from receptors is controlled by feedback from the higher centers of the nervous system. Perception is thus an active process and not the static reception of inputs. How we react to the results of these active processes—perceived experience—helps to explain behavior.

DEFINITION OF PERCEPTION Many different meanings of perception have been suggested [Allport, 1955; Zener and Gaffron, 1962]. Different psychologists use the term to refer to different events, and some prefer not to use it at all. Our best course here is to distinguish between two common meanings of perception and then to give some examples of the sorts of things called "perceptual."

Tough-minded behaviorists, when they use the

term at all, often define perception as the process of discrimination among stimuli. The idea is that if an individual can perceive differences among stimuli, he will be able to make responses which show others that he can discriminate among the stimuli. Perhaps you recognize this as an attempt at an operational definition of perception (see Chapter 1). This definition avoids terms such as experience, and it has a certain appeal because it applies to what one can measure in an experiment. The major problem with this kind of a definition of perception is that it tends to take attention away from perceived experience.

Another definition of perception is that it refers to the world as experienced—as seen, heard, felt, smelled, and tasted. Of course we cannot put ourselves in another's place, but we can accept another person's *verbal reports* of his experience. We can also use our own experience to give us some good clues to the other person's experience. For purposes of this chapter, we shall use this definition: *Perception* refers to the world of experience—the world as seen, heard, felt, smelled, or tasted by a person. To be sure we must rely on verbal reports. What we are essentially interested in, nonetheless, is the person's experience.

CHARACTERISTICS OF PERCEPTION In Chapters 8 and 9 we concentrated on some aspects of experience which could be closely tied to the physical energies which stimulate the receptors. Some might call these "simple" experiences, but as we have seen, they are far from simple. The perceived world is quite different from that which would be expected from an analysis of the physical energies and the transduction processes. The sensory input is drastically reorganized in the receiving areas of the central nervous system (see Chapter 20). In addition to what might be predicted from receptor processes, perception is characterized by: (1) selectivity; (2) organization; (3) constancy of experience in spite of varying inputs; (4) a dimension of depth; (5) movement; (6) the influence of the context within which events or objects are per-

ceived; (7) the importance of relationships and relativity as opposed to absolute differences; and (8) the effects produced by learning and motivation. We shall now proceed to a discussion of each of these major characteristics of perception.

Selectivity of perception

One of the more obvious characteristics of perception is its selective nature. At any given moment our sense organs are bombarded by a multitude of stimuli. Yet only a few of these are perceived clearly at one time. Other stimuli, or events, are perceived less clearly, and the rest form a sort of hazy background of which we are only partially aware. This is another way of saying that, of the various events around us, we attend to only a few. So *attention* is a basic factor in perception.

FOCUS AND MARGIN Attention divides our field of experience, so to speak, into a *focus* and a *margin*. The events that we perceive clearly are in the focus of experience. Because we attend to them, they stand out from the background of our experience. Other items in the margin are dimly perceived. We are aware of their presence, but only vaguely so. Imperceptibly shading off from the margin are other items which are outside our field of attention and of which, for the moment, we are consciously unaware.

To illustrate the nature of attention, let us consider the experience of watching a football game. While we are somewhat dimly aware of the tangle of players at the scrimmage line and of the activity of the blockers, it is the ball carrier and his movements that stand out most clearly. Our attention is focused on the ball carrier. We are at the same time being bombarded by a number of other stimuli. Our feet may be aching with the cold, unpleasant sensations may be coming from our stomach as a result of the last hot dog we ate, and the fellow behind us may be carrying on a conversation with his girl. While the play is going on we are not aware of any of these things in the margin of our attention. Only when the play is finished or time out is called do we perceive how cold our feet are or hear the couple behind us.

SHIFTING OF ATTENTION   The fact that we do at some times hear the conversation behind us and do notice the coldness in our feet illustrates another quality of our field of attention. Attention is constantly shifting. What is at the focus one minute is marginal the next, and still later may have passed completely from conscious awareness. Even when one activity dominates our attention, its dominance usually is not perfectly continuous. Other perceptions come fleetingly into the focus of our awareness and are replaced again by the dominant item.

What does determine what we shall attend to? Although attention shifts, it has a certain orderliness to it. If it were completely chaotic, we should be unable to carry out any extended activity. Actually, as a good advertising man could explain, certain principles determine the direction of our attention—the *principles of attention getting*. These govern what will be most clearly perceived and what may be only dimly perceived or not perceived at all. Two general classes of factors are concerned: external factors in the environment, and internal factors such as motives, set, and expectancy.

EXTERNAL FACTORS IN ATTENTION GETTING External factors governing attention may be considered under four headings: (1) intensity and size, (2) contrast, (3) repetition, and (4) movement. To this list, the factor of novelty might also be added, but this has been discussed earlier in connection with motivation (see page 217).

Intensity and size. The louder a sound, the more likely a person is to attend to it. The brighter a light, the more it tends to capture his attention. By the same token, a full-page advertisement is more likely to be noticed than a half-column one. This factor of intensity or bigness is most pronounced when the person is experiencing something new or unfamiliar; in such a case, the items in the environment that are biggest, loudest, or brightest will attract his attention first. In general, if two stimuli are competing for attention, the one that is most intense will be noticed before the other.

Contrast. As human beings, we tend to adapt or become used to the stimulation around us. The ticking of the clock may be noticeable when we enter a room, but after a while it is not noticed at all. A room may seem hot or cold when we first come in, but after a few minutes we are hardly aware of the temperature. On the other hand, if the clock abruptly stops ticking, we become aware of the sudden silence. As we drive along in a car, we are not aware of the hum of the engine, but if a cylinder misfires, the noise of the engine will occupy the center of our attention.

These examples illustrate the role of contrast in determining attention. Any change in the stimulation to which we have become adapted immediately captures our attention. If we are reading in our room and someone turns on the radio in the adjoining room, we are apt to become acutely aware of it. But after a short while it drops from our awareness as we again become absorbed in our reading. Now when the radio is turned off again, its absence arouses our ATTENTION for a moment. Both the onset and the termination of a stimulus tend to acquire attention because both contrast with what has preceded them.

The word in capital letters in the paragraph above is another illustration of contrast. Most of you noticed the word as soon as you looked at this part of the page. However, if all the text were in capitals, the word would have gone unnoticed. It attracted attention because it contrasts with the words in lower-case letters.

Repetition. At times the repetition of a stimulus is attention getting. A misspelled word is more likely to be noticed if it occurs twice in the same paragraph than if it occurs only once. We are more likely to hear a burst of gunfire than a single shot, or to hear our name if it is called twice. When mother calls Junior in for dinner, she calls his name not once but several times.

The advantage of repetition is twofold. A stimulus that is repeated has a better chance of catching us during one of the periods when our attention to a task is waning. In addition, repetition increases our sensitivity or alertness to the stimulus.

Movement. Human beings, as well as most other animals, are quite sensitive to objects that move within their field of vision. Our eyes are involuntarily attracted to movement in much the same way as the moth is attracted to a flame. Soldiers on a night patrol soon learn this fact and freeze in their tracks when a flare bursts. To fall flat or duck behind shelter makes their detection more likely than if they remain motionless out in the open.

The field of advertising, of course, makes good use of movement as an attention getter. Some of the most effective advertising signs are those which involve movement, either blinking lights or animated figures.

INTERNAL FACTORS IN ATTENTION GETTING

Intensity, contrast, repetition, and movement, all of which attract attention, are external stimulus factors. Of equal importance are internal factors, such as motives, interests, and other states within the person.

Motives. Our needs and interests govern not only what will attract our attention but also what will hold it. Even the sleepiest student in the class can be made to sit on the edge of his chair if the instructor announces that he is going to talk on the topic: "Sex Practices of American Females." Appeal to the sex drive is particularly effective in our culture because the drive is traditionally suppressed. Thus advertisements use shapely girls in bathing suits very effectively to sell items as unrelated as spark plugs and cigars. In a society where food is more scarce than it is in this culture, advertisements showing food objects probably outnumber those which play up sex appeal.

Not only are basic motives such as sex and hunger important in directing attention, but any of the great variety of human motives and interests effectively stimulate attention. If a geologist and a bird fancier take a walk through the same field, the geologist will notice the detailed features of the terrain and the various kinds of rocks, whereas the bird lover will notice the number and variety of birds. If you ask the geologist about the birds, he is very apt to say that he did not notice any, much less how many or what kind. And of course the bird lover is not likely to have noticed any of the geological features that characterize the surrounding terrain.

Set, or expectancy. Besides our interests and motives, set, or expectancy, plays a major role in selecting what we shall perceive. The geologist would have been able to report more about the bird life in the field he traversed had he known beforehand that he would be asked about it. A doctor may hear the phone ring in the night, but not hear the baby crying. His wife, on the other hand, may sleep through the ring of the telephone, but the slightest sound from the child probably will bring her wide awake.

When the drawing in Figure 10.1 is included in a series of two-digit numbers, subjects will report that they have seen the number 13. Another group of subjects who have been exposed to letters of the alphabet will report this drawing as the letter B. In the one case, the subjects have acquired a set, or expectancy, for numbers; in the other case, the set is for letters.

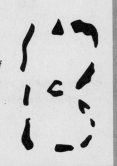

WHAT A PERSON SEES DEPENDS UPON WHAT HE IS SET TO SEE

FIGURE 10.1. *The effect of set on perception. The group of dots and lines can be perceived either as a B or a 13, depending on what a person expects.*

Of the various factors that determine attention, and thus perception, expectancy is probably the most important, for our sets and expectancies largely direct and order the successions of our perceptual experiences. Without them, perceiving would be largely at the mercy of random fluctuations in the environmental stimuli.

THE PHYSIOLOGY OF ATTENTION

Some evidence indicates a possible physiological mechanism for the selectivity of perception [Hernández-Péon et al., 1956]. When one sensory channel is engaged, others may be inhibited or "gated out." The focus of attention is produced by sensory input which reaches the sensory parts of the central nervous system; the input in the margin of attention is gated out. For instance, when watching a ball carrier at a football game, the visual input from the image we see reaches the central nervous system—the visual channel is thus engaged. Other sensory channels are gated out—we do not feel our cold feet.

Evidence for this idea comes from experiments in which recordings are made from the sensory channels themselves [Hernández-Péon et al., 1956].

In one experiment using cats, recordings were made of the electrical activity in the cochlear nucleus of the auditory system. The top row of Figure 10.2 shows the activity in the cochlear nucleus when a click stimulus was sounded and the cat was relaxed. In the middle row, the cat is actively looking at mice in a bottle—the visual channel is engaged. The activity in the cochlear nucleus is much diminished—the auditory input has been gated out to a large extent. The bottom row shows that the response in the relaxed state after the mice have been removed is about the same as it was initially.

Organization in perception

Our perceptual experience is filled with the groups and patterns of stimuli which we call objects. The

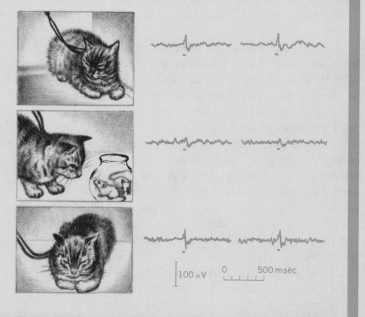

EXTRANEOUS SENSORY INPUT MAY BE "GATED OUT" IN ATTENTION

FIGURE 10.2. *Neural activity of the cochlear nucleus in attention. Top, a click is sounded and the activity of the cochlear nucleus is recorded. The duration of the click is shown by the short line below the record of cochlear nucleus activity. This is a control record. Middle, the click is sounded while the cat is actively looking at mice in a bottle. Note the reduction of cochlear nucleus activity. Bottom, another control record. Cochlear nucleus activity is the same as in the first record. (After Hernández-Péon et al., 1956.)*

100 μV   0   500 msec

AN OBJECT IS PERCEIVED
AS A FIGURE ON A GROUND

FIGURE 10.3.   *A figure-ground involves the simplest kind of perception.*

stimulation that we are constantly perceiving comes into our awareness as shapes and patterns. We do not ordinarily perceive the world around us as patches of color, variations in brightness, and loud or high-pitched sounds. We perceive identifiable patterns or objects. We see tables, floors, walls, and buildings, and we hear automobile horns, footsteps, and words.

Some of this perception of objects is a matter of learning, as mentioned later in this chapter, but much of it is probably an unlearned property of our sense organs and nervous system. These structures tend to organize or modify our perceptions into simple patterns or objects. The measured ticking of a clock, for example, is usually not heard as such. Rather, we tend involuntarily to accent the even tick-tick-tick-tick and perceive it as tick-tock, tick-tock, and so forth. Even when we try very hard, it is difficult to overcome such organizing tendencies in perception. They are somehow built into the functioning of the sense organs and nervous system. Organizing tendencies in perception have been much studied by the gestalt psychologists (see page 26), and the existence of such tendencies has been used to strengthen the argument that the perceived world is not simply the product of the summation of "simple" sensory experiences [Koffka, 1935]. These organizing tendencies take several different forms: (1) figure-ground perception, (2) grouping, (3) contour, and (4) closure.

FIGURE-GROUND PERCEPTION   Perhaps the most fundamental organizational tendency is the perception of figure and ground. The objects that fill our everyday perceptions are seen as standing out as separable from the general background of our experience. Pictures hang *on* a wall, words are *on* a page. In this case, the pictures and words are seen as *figure*, whereas the wall and the page are seen as *ground*. This primitive capacity to distinguish an object from its general sensory background is basic to all object perception.

In glancing at Figure 10.3, you automatically see the dark area as an object. Despite the fact that it may look like no object that you have ever seen, it still is seen as a unitary whole or figure that is distinct from the page. If we examine carefully our general experience of figure-ground relations, we note certain characteristics that distinguish the figure from the ground in our perception. The figure seems to have some sort of shape or object quality, while the ground tends to be formless. The ground seems to extend continuously behind the figure, or in other words, the figure appears to be in front and the ground behind [Rubin, 1921].

Figure 10.4 shows a reversible figure-ground rela-

SOMETIMES A FIGURE BECOMES A GROUND
AND VICE VERSA

FIGURE 10.4.   *A reversible figure-ground. This drawing may be perceived either as a vase or as two profiles.*

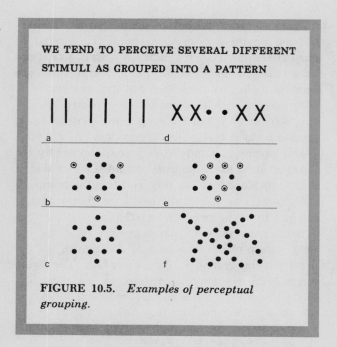

WE TEND TO PERCEIVE SEVERAL DIFFERENT STIMULI AS GROUPED INTO A PATTERN

FIGURE 10.5. *Examples of perceptual grouping.*

The role of *nearness* or *proximity* is illustrated at a. Instead of six vertical lines, we see three pairs of parallel lines. Items which are close together in space or time tend to be perceived as belonging together or constituting a group.

At b and c we can see the importance of *similarity* in grouping. At b most people see one triangle formed by the dots with its apex at the top and another triangle formed by the circles with its apex at the bottom. We see triangles because similar items, the dots and the circles, tend to group together. Otherwise we would see b as a hexagon or a six-pointed star, as is the case at c where the stimuli are all the same. Another illustration of grouping according to similarity is at d. If people are shown this figure and then asked to copy it, most of them will unconsciously draw the two Xs close together and the two circles close together, but the circles will be drawn farther from the Xs than in the figure, thus exhibiting grouping due to similarity.

Grouping according to similarity, however, does not always hold. The figure at e is more easily seen as a hexagon than as one figure composed of dots and another figure composed of circles. In this case, similarity is competing with the principle of *symmetry*, or *good figure*. Neither the circles nor the dots by themselves form a symmetrical organization. In either case, certain members must be left out—a fact which most people find disturbing. In general, the tendency to group is a tendency to form a balanced or symmetrical figure that includes all the parts.

Our last principle of grouping is *continuation*, which is illustrated by the tendency to see a line that starts out as a curve as continuing a smooth course. Conversely, a straight line is seen as continuing straight, or, if it does change direction, as an angle rather than a curve. The figure at f illustrates continuation; we see the dots in that figure as several curves and straight lines. Even though the curves and straight lines cross and have dots in common, it is only with effort that we can see a straight line suddenly becoming curved at one of these junction points.

tion. The figure is perceptible either as a vase or as two profiles. To see the vase, the light area must be perceived as the figure against a dark ground, and conversely, to see the profiles, the dark area must be perceived as a figure upon a light ground. It is seldom possible to see both vase and profiles simultaneously.

The figure-ground relation is also found in senses other than vision. When we listen to a symphony, the melody or theme is perceived as the figure while the chords are perceived as ground. In rock 'n' roll, the guitarist uses repetitive chords as ground against which he sings a more or less varied song, or figure. In observing a person's movements, we might consider the overall posture as the ground for, say, the finer movements of the hands and arms.

GROUPING Another kind of organizing tendency in perception is called *grouping*. Whenever several different stimuli are present, we tend to perceive them as grouped into some pattern. Figure 10.5, for example, gives several illustrations of such grouping, or patterning, which point up different ways in which grouping takes place.

Although all these examples have to do with vision, the same principles of grouping can be observed in the other senses. The rhythm we hear in music also depends upon grouping according to proximity in time and similarity of accents. In the sense of touch, too, grouping occurs. For example, ask a friend to shut his eyes. Mark off three equally distant points on the back of his hand and then touch a pencil to the first two points, pausing slightly before you touch the third point. Your friend will report that the first two points were closer together than were the second and third. This illusion adequately illustrates the grouping of tactile stimuli according to nearness or proximity in time.

The principles of grouping, taken together, partially explain our perception of complex patterns as units or objects. Indeed, we see objects as objects, or units as units, only because grouping processes operate in perception. Were this not so, the various objects we perceive, for instance, a face on the TV screen, a car, a tree, a book, a house, would not "hang together" as objects. They would be merely so many dots, lines, or blotches.

CONTOUR We are able to separate objects from the general ground in our visual perception only because we can perceive contours. Contours are formed whenever a marked change or difference occurs in the degree of brightness or color of the background. If we look at a piece of paper which varies continuously in brightness from white at one border to black at the opposite border, we can perceive no contour. Such a paper appears very uniform to us, and if asked to say where the sheet stops being light and starts to become dark, we can only guess or be arbitrary. On the other hand, if change is marked, rather than gradual—suppose several shades are skipped—we can perceive the paper as divided into two parts, a light and a dark. The distinction occurs quite naturally at the place where the brightness gradient abruptly changes. In perceiving this division, we have perceived a contour.

Contours give shape to the objects in our visual field because they mark off the object from other objects or from the general ground. We must be careful not to conclude, however, that contours *are* shapes. The reversible faces in Figure 10.6 show clearly the differences between contour and shape. Here both faces are formed by the same contour, but it is quite clear that both faces do not have the same shape. Contours *determine* shape, but by themselves they are shapeless.

Contour formation, although it might seem at first glance to be a rather immediate fact of perception, is rather complex. For one thing it takes a surprising amount of time. The following experiment shows this [Werner, 1935]:

Subjects were shown the patterns of Figure 10.7 in a device called a *tachistoscope*—an apparatus for presenting perceptual materials for a very brief time. It was found that a rather long time was necessary for the elaboration of a contour. For instance, if the filled circle is flashed on the tachistoscope screen for 12 to 20 msec (1 msec = 1/1,000 second) and then is followed 150 msec later by the hollow ring, the filled circle will *not* be seen. The inner border of the hollow ring must fall at the place where the outer border of the filled circle had been flashed for this effect

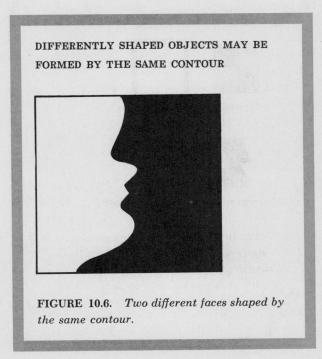

DIFFERENTLY SHAPED OBJECTS MAY BE FORMED BY THE SAME CONTOUR

FIGURE 10.6. *Two different faces shaped by the same contour.*

to appear. It is as if up to 150 msec are required for the elaboration of the border, or contour, surrounding the filled circle, and the presentation of the inner border of the hollow ring interferes. This is quite a long time on the time scale of the central nervous system. Other figures gave similar results.

CLOSURE   Our perception of objects is much more complete than the sensory stimulation we receive from any given object. Perceptual processes tend to organize the world by filling in gaps in stimulation so that we perceive a whole object and not disjointed parts. This filling in is termed *closure,* or the tendency to complete in perception what is

CONTOUR PERCEPTION IS NOT IMMEDIATE— IT TAKES TIME

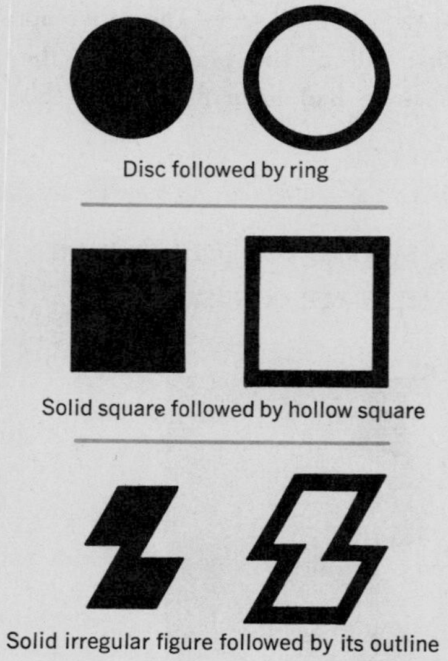

Disc followed by ring

Solid square followed by hollow square

Solid irregular figure followed by its outline

FIGURE 10.7.   *Representative figures used in one study of contour perception. Each figure on the left was first flashed in a tachistoscope and then each was followed by presentation of the paired figure on the right. (After Werner, 1935.)*

physically an incomplete pattern or object. In Figure 10.8, for example, the circle and square with gaps in them are seen as a "circle with gaps in it" and a "square with gaps in it," not as so many disconnected lines. If these incomplete figures were to be presented very rapidly in a tachistoscope, they might even be perceived as complete figures without gaps, which would provide another instance of closure. The same principle applies to the perception of the man on horseback in the lower part of Figure 10.8. There again we fill in the gaps in the stimulus figure and perceive an object, rather than disconnected lines.

The closure process also fills gaps in the visual field which are due to certain characteristics of the receptor or other parts of the sensory channel. The retina, for instance, contains a blind spot where there are no sensitive cells (see page 285). Visual perception extends right across this blind spot and we are not aware of its existence unless we take special pains to focus light on it alone (see page 286). Indeed images falling on either side of the blind spot are seen as continuous. It is also true that people with small blind spots, *scotomas,* due to brain lesions may close the visual field right through these spots [Teuber et al., 1960].

Perceptual constancy

The world as we perceive it is a stable world. The size of a man does not appear to change much as he walks toward us, the dinner plate does not look like a circle when viewed one way and like an ellipse when viewed another, and the location of a sound does not appear to shift when we move our heads. To the layman nothing about this is very surprising. Why shouldn't the world of objects always look the same or remain constant?

Considered more carefully, however, this question raises some interesting problems, for often the physical stimuli from objects are not constant despite the fact that they appear to be. Indeed, as we move about in the world, the stimulation that we receive continually changes. Even the stimuli coming from

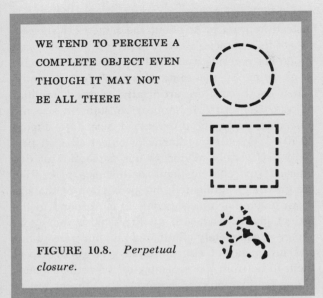

WE TEND TO PERCEIVE A
COMPLETE OBJECT EVEN
THOUGH IT MAY NOT
BE ALL THERE

FIGURE 10.8. *Perpetual closure.*

the same object change markedly as we change our position with respect to it. When we stand directly in front of the window, for example, the retinal image of the window is a rectangle. But when we move to one side of the window, the image becomes a trapezoid. This is simple geometry. Despite this change in the shape of the retinal image, however, we continue to perceive the window as rectangular.

Perceptually, therefore, its shape has not changed, even though its image on the retina has.

The general point is that the perceived shape of objects tends to remain the same irrespective of the positions or conditions under which we view them. This phenomenon is called *shape constancy.* Constancy in perception is not limited to shapes, however. The perceived *sizes* of objects, their *colors,* and their *brightnesses* also show perceptual constancy. We shall now consider these problems in a little more detail for they illustrate not only the general problem of constancy, but also some of the means by which perceptual constancy is achieved.

CONSTANCY OF SIZE   When we recall that the eye works somewhat like a camera, we know that the size of the image on the retina depends upon how far away the object is. The farther away the object, the smaller the image. The geometry of this fact is illustrated in Figure 10.9. This figure also implies an image of constant size can be produced on the retina either by a nearby small object or by a larger object at some distance.

Knowing this much about the size of retinal images, we might expect the perceived size of an object to change as we approach it. At 50 feet, it should appear much larger than it did at 100 feet.

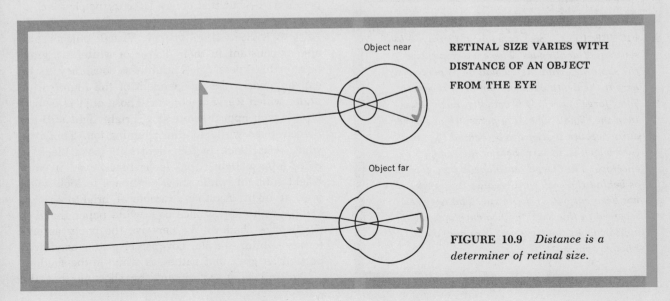

Object near

RETINAL SIZE VARIES WITH
DISTANCE OF AN OBJECT
FROM THE EYE

Object far

FIGURE 10.9 *Distance is a determiner of retinal size.*

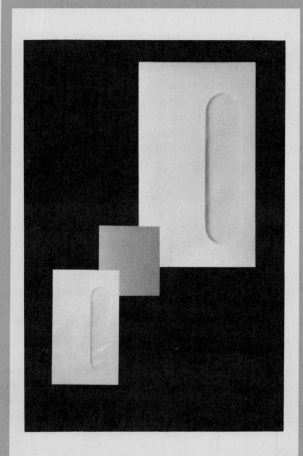

FIGURE 10.10. *Size constancy destroyed by reversal of depth cues. These envelopes are the same size, and they would be so perceived here if the depth cues had not been reversed. The "large" envelope is actually much closer than the "small" one; it is perceived as farther away because it seems to be behind the gray card which is, in turn, behind the "small" envelope. The "large" envelope is perceived as behind the gray card because its corner has been cut out. If depth cues had not been reversed in this way, the two envelopes would appear about the same size. (Fundamental Photographs.)*

But this does not happen. Within limits, the object instead appears to be about the same size irrespective of its distance. When it is perceptibly far away, we do not perceive it as smaller; rather, we perceive it as being of the same size—but farther away. When depth cues are artificially reversed, familiar objects that ordinarily appear constant in size are perceived as vastly different in size (see Figure 10.10). Thus, the constancy of object sizes in perception is closely related to our perception of distance. If the cues to depth or distance perception are gradually eliminated, our perception of the size of an unfamiliar object begins to correspond to the retinal image. And with all depth cues gone, constancy is completely eliminated and our perceptions and judgments of size are what one would expect them to be from the geometry of the retinal image.

For familiar objects, however, the elimination of depth cues does not completely destroy constancy because we know approximately the true sizes of the objects. Under certain conditions, this knowledge gives us some degree of size constancy even in the absence of depth cues. In fact, when comparisons between the relative retinal sizes of familiar objects are possible, the sizes of the retinal images may serve as a cue to distance for familiar objects. Such a cue is one of the monocular depth cues—linear perspective—but that comes later in the chapter.

BRIGHTNESS CONSTANCY Visual objects also appear constant in their degree of whiteness, grayness, or blackness. Such brightness constancy, as we call it, tends to be independent of the illumination under which we view objects. Those objects or surfaces which appear white in a bright light still are perceived as white in dim illumination. Similarly, what looks black in dim light still looks black in more intense light. Coal looks black even in very bright sunlight, while snow continues to look white even at night. Another example of brightness constancy is the appearance of a white paper that lies partly in a shadow. We perceive the paper as uniformly white; we do not perceive the shadowed portion as gray, but rather as white-in-the-shadow.

The following experiment, by showing that the

RATIOS OF INTENSITIES ARE RESPONSIBLE FOR PERCEIVED BRIGHTNESS

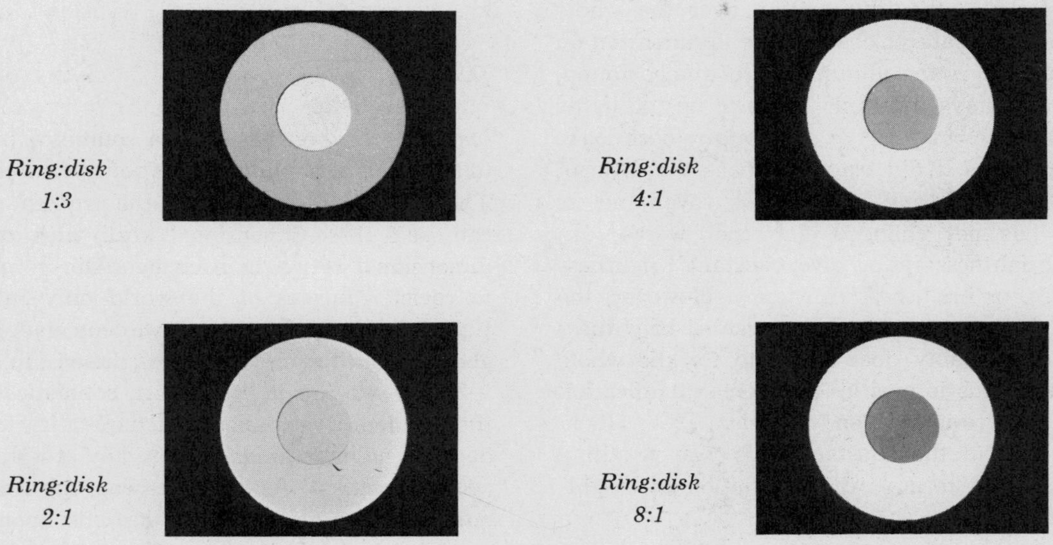

Ring:disk
1:3

Ring:disk
4:1

Ring:disk
2:1

Ring:disk
8:1

FIGURE 10.11.   *Sample stimulus arrangements from an experiment on perceived brightness. Projectors were arranged so that a disk of light could be surrounded by a ring of light and the intensity of light in the ring was varied, but the intensity of light in the disk was kept constant. The perceived brightness of the disk was found to depend upon the ratio of the intensities of ring to disk. For instance, with a ratio of ring intensity to disk intensity of 1:3, the disk was seen as quite bright; with a ratio of ring to disk intensities of 8:1, the same physical intensity of light in the disk was perceived as dim. Note again that the physical intensity of light on the disk does not vary in this experiment; the ratio is manipulated by changing the intensity of the ring illumination. (From Wallach, 1963; courtesy of* Scientific American.*)*

perceived brightness of an object depends upon the ratio between the illumination of the object and its background, helps to explain brightness constancy [Wallach, 1963]:

Light projectors were arranged in a dark room so as to project rings and disks which could be superimposed, with the disk fitting exactly inside the ring (see Figure 10.11).

The intensity of the light in the disks and rings could be varied independently. With the absolute value of the light intensity on the middle disk kept constant, the perception of its brightness changes markedly as the intensity of the surrounding ring is changed (see Figure 10.11). When the ratio of ring intensity to disk intensity is 1:3, the disk is perceived as quite bright; when the ratio of the intensities is 8:1, the disk is perceived as dim.

This experiment shows that a change in the ratios of intensities between an object, the disk in this case, and its surround, the ring in this case, is necessary for a change in perception of object brightness. In most situations outside the laboratory, however, the ratio between an object and its surround stays constant because the illumination over the whole field changes—whatever changes the illumination on the object changes the illumination of the surround, and the ratio stays constant. If I turn up the lights in my room, the cover of the book on my desk looks just as bright as it did before because the ratio of the illumination falling on the book cover and its surround has not changed. In other words, unchanged brightness ratios give constant brightness experiences, or brightness constancy. However, the rule that constant ratios give constant brightness experiences probably does not hold for the whole range of stimulus intensities and some qualification must be made [Jameson and Hurvich, 1964; Hochberg, 1964]. But the constant ratio rule is still a useful first step toward an explanation of brightness constancy.

PERCEPTUAL STABILITY Perceptual constancies are not perfect. Even in the most favorable circumstances, our visual perceptions are a compromise between what we know the object to be and the sensory image on the retina. Objects do appear to become slightly smaller as they move away from us, and white objects do not look quite as white when they are in shadow. In this sense, then, constancies are only relative. Our perceptions of objects correspond more closely to the true object, however, than to the sizes of images on the retina or to the sensory stimulus in general.

As human beings, we enjoy several advantages from perceptual constancy. It would be exceedingly difficult to move about or operate in a world where sounds changed their location when we moved our heads, and where objects changed their shapes and sizes when we viewed them from different positions and distances. Imagine what it would be like if your friends and associates had a multitude of sizes and shapes that depended upon how far away they were

and from what angle you viewed them. Imagine how difficult it would be to live if the colors of things varied markedly with changes in sunlight and weather. The relative constancy of our perceptions of shape, size, brightness, and color gives our world a perceptual stability it otherwise would not have.

Perception of depth

Depth perception has been a source of puzzlement to scientists and philosophers for hundreds of years. They have been bothered by the problem of how we can see a three-dimensional world with only a two-dimensional retina in each eye. Our retina is able to register images of the world only in terms of right-left or up-down; yet we perceive the world about us as having the extra dimension of depth.

Today we are a little more sophisticated about the problem. We realize that the ability to perceive depth is no more amazing than any other perceptual accomplishment. As we have seen, all awareness of ourselves and of the world depends upon physical energy in various forms striking special sense organs. Our brain receives various patterns of neural impulses, not tiny copies of various objects.

The problem of depth perception can be put thus: How do physical stimuli manage to stimulate our sense organs so that our brain is provided with proper cues for a perceptual experience of depth? Part of the answer is that differences in shadows, in clearness, and in the size of the image in the eye provide cues on the retina which are as informative as if the retina were able to register the third dimension directly.

Perhaps this idea can be made clearer by using an analogy. When a mathematician solves a problem involving speed and weight, he may let x stand for miles per hour and y for weight in pounds. Of course neither x nor y has any physical resemblance to what it is representing, but as long as the manipulator of these symbols is consistent in his operations, his results will correspond with the physical world. His symbols will be adequate substitutes for the real objects.

In the case of depth perception, different cues, such as shadow and clearness, are the symbols that represent the physical world. The book lying on our desk or the automobile parked across the street forms an image on the retina. At the same time, senses other than vision are being stimulated, too. When we reach for a book or walk to the car, all these sensory cues or symbols are somehow simultaneously taken account of so that we perceive the distance of the book or car. Visual cues for depth perception are usually classified into monocular and binocular cues, that is to say, those which may be utilized by one eye alone and those which require two eyes.

MONOCULAR CUES   Monocular cues, as the name suggests, are cues for depth that operate when only one eye is looking. These cues were first known to the ancient Greeks; they were exploited by the Renaissance painters who were concerned with the problem of giving depth to their paintings. The problem they had in presenting a three-dimensional world on a two-dimensional canvas is essentially the same problem which must be solved by our retinas. If the artist is able to paint the scene on his canvas so that it looks essentially as the scene looks when its image is focused on the retina, he succeeds in achieving realistic depth in his pictures. Let us examine some of the principles the artist uses to accomplish this.

Linear perspective. Objects which are far away project a smaller image on the retina than do near objects. In addition, the distance separating the images of far objects appears to be smaller. To understand this point, imagine that you are standing between railroad tracks and looking off into the distance. The ties seem to become smaller and the tracks gradually to become closer together until they appear to meet at the horizon. Figure 10.12 owes part of its depth effect to such linear perspective.

Clearness. In general, the more clearly we can see an object, the nearer the object is. The distant mountain seems farther away on a hazy day than on a clear day because the haze in the atmosphere blurs the fine details so that we see only the grosser features. Ordinarily, if we can see the details, we perceive an object as relatively close; if we can see only its general outline, we perceive it as relatively far away.

Interposition. Still another monocular cue is interposition. This occurs when one thing obstructs our view of another thing. When one object is entirely in view, but another is partly covered by it, the first object is perceived as being the nearer. Interposition is illustrated in Figure 10.12.

Shadows. The pattern of shadows or of highlights in an object is very important in giving an impres-

FIGURE 10.12. *Three monocular factors in depth perception. The buildings and the street converge in the distance (linear perspective); some parts of buildings are behind others (interposition); and more distant heights are not so clear as the nearer parts (clearness). (Fundamental Photographs.)*

FIGURE 10.13. *Shadows and the perception of depth. If the picture is turned upside down, the buildings, especially the quonset huts, look like towers. (Wide World Photos.)*

sion of depth. In Figure 10.13, an aerial photograph of a group of quonset huts, we see an example of this cue. When the picture is turned upside down, the quonset huts look like towers. If you note carefully the differences between the quonset huts and the "towers," you will discover that the shadows are responsible for this effect. The reason, briefly, is that we are accustomed to light coming from above. Thus when the picture is turned upside down, we do not perceive the quonset huts as illuminated from below, for we are not used to light coming from this direction. Instead, we see towers because the dark areas are now of such a size and in such a position that they cannot possibly be shadows. They look more like the black-painted tops of buildings, or towers. We do not, of course, reason this out. The perception is immediate and is based on whether or not the dark areas appear to be shadows.

Gradients of texture. A gradient is a continuous change in something—a change without abrupt transitions. In some situations we can use the continuous gradation of texture of the visual field as a cue for depth [Gibson, 1950]. The regions closest to the observer have a coarse texture and many details are seen; as the distance from the observer increases, the texture becomes finer and finer (see Figure 10.14). This continuous transformation of texture provides the central nervous system with information about depth.

Movement. Whenever you move your head, you can observe that the objects in your visual field move relative to you and to one another. If you observe closely, you will find that the objects that are nearest to you appear to move in the opposite direction, whereas distant objects appear to move in the same direction as your head. This, of course, is an obvious cue to the relative distance of objects, and, further, whether we see real movement or move our heads, the relative amount of movement is less for far objects than for near ones. Although movement is an important cue to depth, it cannot be used by artists as can the other monocular cues.

Accommodation. Accommodation is the adjustment of the shape of the lens of the eye in order to bring an image into focus on the retina. This adjustment is accomplished by the ciliary muscles, which are so attached to the lens that they make it bulge when they contract, thus accommodating for near objects. Conversely, they let the lens become thinner when they relax, thus accommodating far objects.

Many muscles of the body contain kinesthetic receptors which respond to the stretch and contraction of the muscles (see page 335). It is possible that kinesthetic impulses from the ciliary muscles provide a cue to depth. It has not, however, been proved that they do. Such a cue would be monocular, for it would be operative in each eye and not dependent on seeing with two eyes at once. Such a cue could work only for distances up to about 20 feet, for beyond that further accommodation is negligible.

BINOCULAR CUES Some cues to depth perception depend on the fact that we have two eyes rather than just one. These are called binocular cues.

Retinal disparity. One such cue is retinal disparity—the difference in the images falling on the retinas of the two eyes. The factor of retinal disparity may be explained by considering the geometry of the situations in which the two eyes view an object (see Figure 10.15). The fovea in the center of each retina is much more sensitive than the rest of the retina. When we look at an object, we fixate our eyes—point them, so to speak—so that the image of the object falls mostly on the fovea of the retina of each eye. But since the two eyes are separated from each other by several inches, they get

GRADIENTS OF TEXTURE ARE A FACTOR IN DEPTH PERCEPTION

FIGURE 10.14. *Two examples of texture gradients. Left, an artificial texture gradient; right, a plowed field as an example of a natural texture gradient. Note the impression of depth in both. (Gibson, 1950.)*

slightly different views of an object, and the two images are not exactly the same. Moreover, the images are more dissimilar when the object is very close, say a few inches away, than when it is far in the distance. In other words, a gradient of disparities is established as the point of fixation changes from the horizon to very near objects. From this gradient we get information about depth.

With the pictures in Figure 10.16 and a small mirror, you can demonstrate to yourself how retinal disparity contributes to the solid appearance of objects. The figure shows the same scene photographed by a stereoscopic camera, a camera that has two lenses about as far apart as the two eyes. The picture on the left was photographed by the left lens and the one on the right by the right lens. When you look at the mirror reflection of the right-hand scene, according to the directions, the reflection appears to be physically located on top of the left-hand picture. When you open both eyes, one

BECAUSE OUR EYES ARE SEPARATED FROM EACH OTHER, THE IMAGE OF AN OBJECT IS NOT EXACTLY THE SAME ON BOTH RETINAS

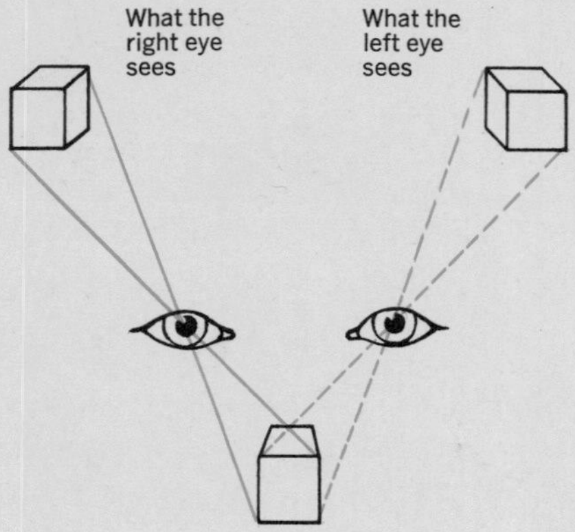

What the right eye sees

What the left eye sees

FIGURE 10.15. *When we look at a cube, each eye has a different view of it.*

eye sees one picture and the other eye sees the other picture. Thus you achieve the illusion of depth. Although the right-left orientation of the objects in the right-hand scene has been reversed for the demonstration, close scrutiny of the pictures shows that they also differ in other details—those which result from retinal disparity.

Convergence. We know that retinal disparity serves very effectively as a binocular cue to depth, but we are not so sure about another possible binocular cue. This is a kinesthetic cue from the muscles concerned in turning and pointing the eyes. For objects farther away than 70 feet, the lines of sight of the eyes are essentially parallel. For nearer objects, however, the eyes turn more and more toward each other, that is, they converge. If such convergence aids in depth perception, the cue is probably kinesthetic impulses from sense organs in those muscles which make the eyes converge.

CONFLICTING CUES   In general, the various cues to depth and distance perception work together and are mutually supporting. In cases where they conflict, one cannot see depth so clearly. When looking at a photograph, for example, most of the monocular depth cues are present; yet one does not perceive all the depth of the real scene. In this case, cues conflict. The monocular cues give the impression of depth, but the binocular cues make the photograph look flat. One's perception, then, is a compromise. It is possible, however, to eliminate the conflicting binocular cues, and thus to see more depth in a photograph.

To do that, roll a piece of paper into a tube. Now close one eye and look with the other eye through the tube at the photograph in Figure 10.12. You will find that the picture seems to have much greater depth. By closing one eye, you eliminate the conflicting binocular cues, and by using the tube, you avoid seeing the edge or frame of the picture. The frame, of course, is a conflicting cue since real scenes do not have frames around them. You can increase the apparent depth even further by having someone else hold the picture for you. In this case, you elimi-

RETINAL DISPARITY IS THE CUE EMPLOYED IN STEREOSCOPES
TO PROVIDE DEPTH PERCEPTION

FIGURE 10.16. *Looking into the third dimension. Select a small mirror whose shortest edge is at least as long as the height of the pictures. Put the mirror's edge in the space between the two pictures at right angles to the page and with its reflecting side to the right. Put your nose on or near the top edge of the mirror. Close your left eye. Look at the mirror with your right eye and adjust the mirror so that the real picture and its mirror image are aligned in the same plane. Now open the left eye. With both eyes open, focus your attention on the left-hand image. The two pictures should now appear as one three-dimensional picture. (Realist, Inc.)*

nate conflicting cues coming from your arms and body.

AUDITORY SPACE PERCEPTION   Our discussion of depth perception has, up until now, centered on vision because man is a "visual animal" who relies more on vision than other senses for perceiving depth and distance in his environment. At times, however, he perceives depth through his other senses. The most important of these is hearing. Indeed, we habitually use auditory cues in the perception of the distance of various objects. The rumble of traffic, the sound of an automobile horn, a boat whistle, the scream of a siren, or the sound of a footstep are all perceived as taking place in some direction and at some distance from us.

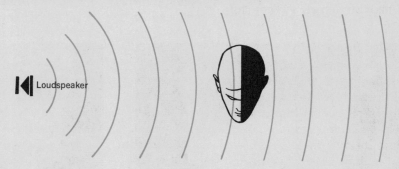

THE DIRECTION OF A SOUND CAN BE PERCEIVED BECAUSE WE HAVE TWO EARS

Loudspeaker

FIGURE 10.17. *How we perceive the direction of a sound. Each arc represents successive crests of an energy wave as it travels from the source. Note that the energy wave reaches the nearer ear first when the head is turned away from the source. In addition, the ear that is farther away receives a lower energy intensity because of the shadow cast by the head. If the head faces the source, of course, the time difference is zero and there is no sound shadow.*

Cues to direction. In visual perception, the fact that we have two eyes usually helps us considerably in perceiving the depth of an object, but one does just as well as two for judging the direction of an object. In hearing, however, the rules are essentially reversed. To tell direction from auditory cues, we must have two ears, although one ear is just about as good as two for judging depth, or distance.

There are three types of *binaural cues* for perceiving the direction of a sound. (The term *binaural* refers to the use of two ears.) The first and most important is *time difference.* If a click is sounded off to one side of your head, the sound travels through the air at a speed of approximately 1,130 feet per second and arrives at the nearer ear before it arrives at the farther one. This effect is shown diagrammatically in Figure 10.17. When the source of the sound is directly opposite one ear, the difference in time of arrival at the two ears is at a maximum and is about $\frac{1}{2}$ millisecond (or $\frac{1}{2000}$ second).

When the source of sound is directly ahead, the sound wave reaches both ears at the same time. At positions in between, the differences in time of arrival at the two ears will naturally be more than zero and less than the maximum value. Thus the time difference serves as a cue to the direction of the sound. The time differences are, of course, extremely slight, and it is remarkable that people can use them as such effective cues to the direction of sound.

A second binaural cue is *intensity difference.* It works because intensity decreases as the square of the distance and because the head casts a sound shadow; the ear opposite to any sound source lies in this shadow. As you can see from Figure 10.17, the head makes a shadow because a sound coming from one side must go around the head to get to the other side, and before it gets there, a great deal of it is absorbed. As a consequence, the sound reaching the farther ear is much weaker than that striking the nearer ear. Once again, as in the case of time difference, the amount of this shadow depends on the direction of the sound source. The shadow is greatest when the sound source is off to the side, zero when it is directly in front, and at intermediate values when the sound source lies at other angles.

A third cue is *phase difference*. This term refers to the difference in the pressure of sound waves at any particular place and moment. Two waves of the same frequency composition are in phase when their peaks of positive pressure, and hence all other aspects of the two waves, coincide exactly. This can be seen in an oscilloscopic record of the waves (see Figure 9.1, page 313). Waves are in opposite phases when the negative peak of one corresponds to the positive peak of the other. Between these extremes, all degrees of phase differences are possible.

A difference in phase of a sine wave at the two ears can come about in the same way as a difference in time of arrival. The sine wave is simply a succession of positive and negative pressures. The maximum positive pressure of the sine wave reaches one ear sooner than the other if the sound source is to one side of the head. Thus at any one time the waves at the two ears may be out of phase, but the amount by which they will be out of phase once again depends on the exact direction of the sound source. Ordinarily, however, the phase cue is useful only at relatively low frequencies because the distance between the ears is so large relative to the wavelength of high-frequency tones that phase differences are unreliable at high frequencies.

Taken together, these three cues enable people to judge the direction of a sound rather well. When both the head and the source of sound are stationary, persons usually can tell where a sound comes from with an accuracy of at least 20 degrees of the circle around the head. When either the head or the sound source is allowed to move, they can do quite a bit better because then they can perceive how the cues change with changes in the relative position of the head or the source. For this reason, people learn to move their heads automatically when they are trying to determine the direction of a sound.

The fact that two ears are necessary for the perception of sound direction explains the difficulty which some hard-of-hearing people have in perceiving direction when they use a hearing aid which has only one earpiece. Such deaf people hear with only the one aided ear and must move their heads a great deal to localize the direction of sounds.

Cues to distance. Only one ear is needed, however, to perceive distance, because the cues to distance are *intensity* and *frequency composition,* and one ear can use them as well as two. The first of these cues depends on the fact that distant sounds are usually much weaker than near sounds. If we have not heard a sound before, we usually judge it to be farther away if it is a weak sound than if it is a loud sound. We cannot usually judge the distance on the basis of intensity, however, unless we know what the sound is. To use this cue effectively, therefore, we must be familiar with the sound. A train whistle in the distance may sound as loud as the chime of a clock nearby, and yet we know that the train is far away and the clock is close at hand. We know this, however, only because we are familiar with the two sounds and know that a train whistle would be much louder than the chime of the clock if both were at the same distance.

The other cue to distance is *frequency composition,* or complexity of a sound. As we pointed out in Chapter 9, this refers to the number of frequencies that make up a sound and to the relative sound pressures of each of these frequencies. We can use frequency composition, or complexity, as a cue because the air and objects in the path of a sound absorb high frequencies much more than they do low frequencies. Thus a low-frequency sound can be heard much farther away than can a high-frequency sound. Foghorns, for example, are always low-pitched so that they can be heard over many miles of the sea.

Since the high frequencies in sound are absorbed more than the low frequencies, the farther away one

LIGHT OF DARKNESS

FIGURE 10.18.   *Perceived motion in a stationary pattern. (Reproduction of a painting, "Light of Darkness" by Julian Stanczak, 1960. Collection of Mr. and Mrs. Robert B. Mayer. Courtesy of the Martha Jackson Gallery.)*

is from the source of sound the more the sound will appear low-pitched. For example, when you listen to a band at a distance, you cannot hear the high notes very well. Thus when you hear music being played, but can hear the low notes much better than the high notes, you perceive the sound as far away.

Perception of motion

It may not seem that movement is a perceptual problem. After all, objects moving through the visual field, or along the skin, stimulate different parts of the receptor. Cannot motion perception be due to this changing stimulation? The answer is that, although such movement of energies across the receptor surface is important in the perception of some

movements, it is neither necessary nor sufficient to explain the perceived phenomenon. It is not necessary because perceived motion often occurs without any movement of energy flux across the receptor surface. This type of motion is called *apparent motion*. Further, it is not sufficient to explain our perception of motion because there are many evidences that higher centers in the nervous system contribute to the reworking of the sensory input. Thus *real motion* is a perceived event involving perceptual organizing processes.

APPARENT MOTION   Many kinds of apparent motion, in which no actual movement of the stimulus pattern over the receptor occurs, have been studied. These include stroboscopic movement, the autokinetic effect, induced movement, movement in stationary patterns, and movement afterimages. Let us begin with stroboscopic movement.

Stroboscopic movement. If you have been to the movies, you have seen this kind of apparent movement. As you know, the movie projector simply presents successive pictures of a moving scene on a screen. Each frame is slightly different from the preceding one, and if you looked at each separately, you would see this. However, when the frames are presented at the right speed, continuous and smooth motion is perceived. Movies made with time-lapse photography illustrate this very nicely. A slow event, such as the growth of a plant, can be made to seem like a continuous movement by taking separate pictures at different stages in the growth of the plant. Then they are put together and shown in a movie projector. You have probably seen such movies, and the apparent motion is quite impressive—sometimes grotesque. The important thing, for our purposes, is that here is movement without any real movement of the energies over the receptor.

A variety of stroboscopic movement, sometimes called *optimal movement* or *beta movement,* is that seen in experiments carried out in a more controlled and simplified situation. The following illustrates optimal, or beta, movement [Wertheimer, 1912]:

Two vertical bars of light are arranged in a dark room at a certain distance apart and alternately turned on and off. The time interval between the flashes is the crucial thing. When the time interval is too short (less than approximately 30 milliseconds), the lights are seen as simultaneous; when the interval is too long (more than approximately 200 milliseconds), they are seen as successive. But when the time interval is right, 60 milliseconds, for example, optimal movement is obtained and a light is seen to move across the open space between the two stimulus lights. At slightly greater intervals, *pure movement,* or *phi movement,* is obtained. Phi movement is movement without an object, if it is possible to imagine such a thing. In other words, phi movement is an experience of movement without the experience that an object is moving.

In addition to the time interval, beta movement is strongly influenced by the intensity of the stimulating lights and the distance between them [Korte, 1915]. It might be expected that such findings would lead to an accepted physiological theory of stroboscopic motion, but in spite of efforts in that direction [Wertheimer, 1912], no theory of brain events in stroboscopic motion has been generally accepted.

Autokinetic effect. A small stationary spot of light in a completely dark room will appear to move if a person fixates on it. The movement can be quite dramatic and large and can be influenced by suggestion [Sherif, 1958]. Movements of the eyes affect, but do not seem to account for, the phenomenon. The important point for us to note is that here, again, is perception of movement without real movement.

Induced movement. A stationary spot may be perceived as moving when the background or frame of reference for the spot moves. For example, the moon is often seen as racing through the sky when it is seen through moving, thin clouds. Of course, the moon is not "racing." The movement of the framework of clouds "induces" movement in the relatively stationary object. Induced movement may be demonstrated in the laboratory. For instance, in a dark room, a fixed luminous spot in a luminous rectangle may be seen to move if the rectangle is moved. As the framework is moved, the motion is induced in the stationary object [Duncker, 1929].

Movement in stationary patterns. Look at Figure 10.18 for a minute or so. The perceived undulation of the lines, although quite intriguing, is so strong as to be annoying for most people. Perhaps this mild conflict is part of the appeal of this picture, but in any case, here is another example of apparent motion without movement of an image over the retina. The movement seems to be the result of complex and shifting patterns of negative afterimages (see Chapter 8).

Movement in afterimages. One such afterimage of apparent movement is produced by the "waterfall apparatus" shown in Figure 10.19. When the subject looks at Figure 10.19 as the center panel is moving down, induced upward movement is seen in the stationary part of the display at the sides. When the center movement is stopped, the after-movement is seen—the panels are seen as moving in the directions opposite to the initial movement. Thus, if the initial movement were down, the afterimage would be an upward movement of the center panel. Again we have perceived movement without real movement. One theory about the origin of this effect held that eye movements were responsible for the perceived movement, but a recent experiment which

cancels the effect of eye movements by using a stabilized image technique (see page 283) has shown that the effect is still there [Sekuler and Ganz, 1963]. The explanation of these effects still needs to be worked out, but it is likely to be found in interactions between excitation and inhibition in the central nervous system.

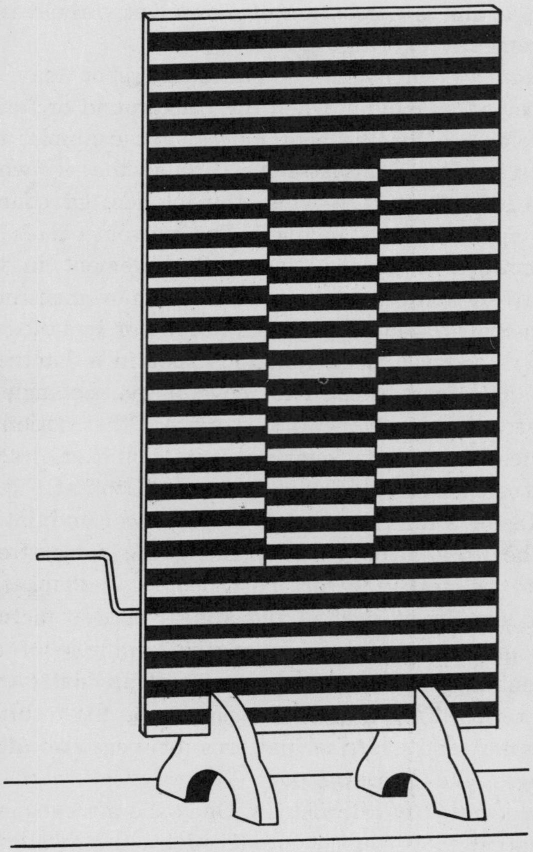

REAL MOVEMENT We have said that movement of the stimulus pattern over the sensory surface will not account for all the phenomena of real motion. For instance, real motion is not simply there or not there—perceived real motion varies as the speed of the moving object varies [Teuber, 1960; Brown, 1931]. The perceived speed of an object depends upon the context in which it is seen [Teuber, 1960], and finally, constancy of velocity must be considered [Wallach, 1939; Teuber, 1960].

In experimental studies of real motion, several kinds of movement are seen as the velocity of the moving object, black squares on an endless belt in this case, is increased [Brown, 1931; Teuber, 1960]. As the threshold for movement is passed, there is first a stage in which the test objects appear to move backward; then, with further increases in the speed of the test objects, an apparent multiplication of the test objects takes place; finally, at higher speeds, the objects fuse into a blur. Thus real movement is perceptually complex.

The background within which a test object moves, that is, the context, influences the perceived speed. Movement through a complex, structured field seems faster than that through a homogeneous field; movement seems faster when the object which is moving is small—this is called the "scurrying mouse effect" [Teuber, 1960].

Finally, when two identical displays, with objects moving at the same velocity, are arranged so that one is at some distance behind the other, the velocity of the two will seem to be about the same [Wallach, 1939; Teuber, 1960]. This is true in spite of the fact that the velocity of movement over the retina from the near and far displays is quite different. Constancy, of the sort already described, must be at work here.

FIGURE 10.19.   *Apparatus for producing the "waterfall illusion." (James, 1890.)*

Context and relational determinants

How we experience an object or event and then react to it depends upon the context in which the object or event appears. The event is perceived against a background of other events. For instance, it has been reported that punishment used to suppress the undesirable behavior of children is much more effective when it comes from loving parents [Sears et al., 1957]. The punishment received from loving parents is perceived and reacted to differently from that given by callous, indifferent parents. This should give the general idea of the effect of context, but other experiments and concepts show the role of context more explicitly.

SIMULTANEOUS CONTRAST One of the best examples of the effect of context on perception is *simultaneous color contrast*. If we take a large piece of colored paper and place a small gray square at its center, the complement of the color of the paper will be induced at the edges of the gray square (see Chapter 8). A red will produce a relatively unsaturated green; a green will induce a relatively unsaturated red, and so on. Simultaneous color contrast is more easily seen, and is really quite striking, when the colored and colorless areas are produced by lights from slide projectors [Walls, 1960]. For instance, a disk of white light projected inside a ring of blue will be seen as a relatively saturated yellow. Obviously these induction effects are due to context.

Contrast effects such as these, and other more subtle ones, are thought to be the cause of Land's observations on color [Walls, 1960]. Land has shown that many realistic colors can be produced by superimposing two projected images on a screen [Land, 1959]. One of the pictures to be projected is taken with a filter which allows only the longer wavelengths to expose the black and white film; the other picture is taken with a filter which allows only the shorter wavelengths to expose the film. The longer wavelength positive transparency is then projected through a red filter, and the shorter wavelength positive transparency is projected without any filter at all. These two transparencies are exactly in register.

Many perceived colors, greens, oranges, yellows, and so on, can be obtained from this situation which contains nothing but red and white light. The obtained colors of the objects in the pictures depend upon interactions between the darker areas of the objects and their lighter backgrounds—the color of the objects depends upon context. When the projected scene is viewed through a long, narrow tube so that only parts of the objects are seen, they look pink, red, or white as would be expected simply from the stimulation presented [Walls, 1960]. Simultaneous contrast, the combination of induced colors, and other contrast phenomena may be responsible for the obtained colors.

ADAPTATION LEVEL The concept of *adaptation level* has been developed to quantify and provide a general theory concerning context effects [Helson, 1948, 1964]. The central idea of the adaptation-level theory is that the context or background acts to set a standard against which events or objects are perceived. For instance, although a rather mediocre student will look like a poor one when in a class of good students, he may seem quite a good student in a class of dolts. The following experiment shows the way perception may be affected by the distribution of stimuli, or the context, to which a subject is exposed [Helson, 1964]:

The perceived or judged size of squares was investigated under several different context conditions, of which we shall describe three. The subjects judged squares on a scale extending from very, very small to very, very large. The context was manipulated by using *anchors*—extreme stimuli which bias a distribution of stimuli in one direction or another. The seven sizes of squares to be judged ranged from 1.0 to 3.82 inches on a side, and the two extreme anchors were squares of 0.30 and 9.00 inches on a side. These anchors were used to distort the distribution of square sizes and to provide a particular background or context against which the stimuli were perceived and judged. With the large 9.00-inch square, the other stimuli might be expected to look small by contrast; with the small anchor, we might expect the stimuli to look relatively large. This is what happened. The background with the large anchor resulted in a reduction of judged size; that with the small anchor increased the judged size of the other stimuli.

The concept of adaptation level is a general one which has been extended from its initial base in sensory perception to social stimuli [Helson, 1964]. An example is shown in Figure 10.20. There is a fine line, as the experiment shows, between perception and judgment. Is it immediate experience —that is, perception—which is changed? Or is it merely the judgment of where stimuli should be placed in a series which is changed? When we attempt to extend the adaptation-level theory, this type of question becomes more and more troublesome.

FIGURAL AFTEREFFECTS The idea of relational determinism has been put forward most strongly by the gestalt psychologists, and studies of the phenomena of *figural after-effects* are used as demonstrations. The following experiment is typical [Köhler and Wallach, 1944]:

The subject first fixates an inspection object (I) for several minutes (see Figure 10.21). After this, the inspection object is removed, the test objects (T) are presented with the same fixation point, and the subject reports how they look to him. The test object on the left of Figure 10.21 will be reported as displaced downward relative to the one on the right. The left test object may also appear paler and farther back in space. The idea is that the previous fixation of the inspection figure has altered the relations in the perceptual field so that the test object on the left appears different. A theory of brain function has been proposed to account for, and make concrete, these relational effects. This theory, in brief, states that there is a long-lasting "satiation" effect of a portion of the visual brain due to the inspection of the I object. When the test object is presented, activity from it is projected to the visual region of the cerebral cortex which is close to that which was satiated by the I object. This is supposed to cause distortions in the brain processes corresponding to the T object and to perceived experience of the T object.

This brief account hardly does justice to the theory, but the important point for us is that events in one part of the perceptual field may affect perception in another part.

FIGURE 10.20. *Adaptation level in everyday life. (By special permission of* The Saturday Evening Post © *1964 by The Curtis Publishing Company. Also by permission of Charles Rodrigues.)*

"*Well, which is it? Was he very tall or very short?*"

RELATIONAL DETERMINISM IN PERCEPTION

FIGURE 10.21. *Figures used for the production of visual figural after-effects. The experiment is done in two parts. First, the subject fixates the X while the inspection object (I) is present; next, the inspection object is removed and, with the same fixation point, the subject reports the appearance of the test objects (T). After inspection, the figural after-effects are present and the T object on the left appears paler, farther back in space, and displaced downward when compared with the T object on the right. (Modified from Köhler and Wallach, 1944.)*

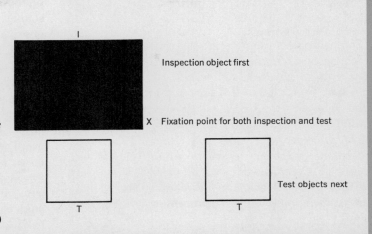

I

Inspection object first

X   Fixation point for both inspection and test

Test objects next

T   T

TRANSPOSITION   The importance of the perception of relations is shown in certain discrimination learning experiments. Suppose we teach a child a discrimination, using the stimuli in Figure 10.22. If we reinforce responses to the larger of the two circles, and never reinforce responses to the smaller circle, he will soon learn to choose the larger circle. Now suppose we present him with two stimuli, one of which is the old positive stimulus and the other of which is a new larger one (see Figure 10.22). Now if we ask him which is the correct one, he will probably respond by saying that the new larger stimulus is the correct one, this despite the fact that the smaller stimulus in the new pair was the one which was reinforced in the first learning period. In other words, the child is responding in terms of a perceived relationship—"larger." This responding in terms of relationships is what is known as *transposition*.

The nature of transposition has been much argued. Some theorists have downgraded the explanation in terms of perceived relationships and have substituted explanations in terms of complex conditioning processes [Spence, 1937]. However, in the light of certain animal experiments, the perceptual explanation seems to be the most plausible one [Lawrence and De Rivera, 1954].

Learning and motivation

The world of perception is, within limits, quite plastic and modifiable: perception is, in part, a learned attainment. The perceptual world, of course, is not infinitely modifiable—some of our perceptual experience is set by our innate structure and our tendencies to function in certain ways.

Motivations, learned and unlearned, also affect the perception of situations. It is common knowledge that we seldom convince people in an argument. Where people are emotionally involved, they tend to see what they want to see, hear what they want to hear, and believe what they want to believe. Love is blind, and the man in love is notoriously poor at perceiving his sweetheart's faults. On the other hand, these faults are only too painfully evident to more neutral observers, such as his parents who "for the life of them can't understand what he

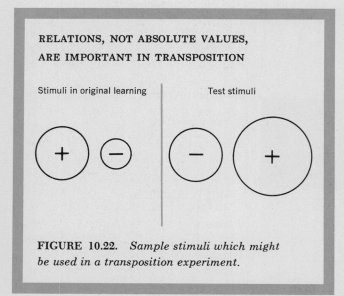

RELATIONS, NOT ABSOLUTE VALUES,
ARE IMPORTANT IN TRANSPOSITION

Stimuli in original learning   Test stimuli

FIGURE 10.22. *Sample stimuli which might be used in a transposition experiment.*

sees in that bleached blonde." Such examples are simply instances of personal motives and values influencing perception.

LEARNING   In discussing perceptual learning in Chapter 3, we were concerned with the learning of new associations between already established perceptions of objects and events. For instance, a gun is perceived quite differently by a lady whose husband has been killed in a hunting accident and a child who is fascinated by cowboys. To the child, the perception of the gun is associated with pleasurable excitement, with fantasies of range wars and galloping horses. To the bereaved person, the perception of the gun is associated with sadness and fear. We can think of many other examples. The sound I hear, for instance, is not just a sound; it is the creaking of the stairway which signals my wife's return from the store. The scent of freshly cut grass may recall memories of languid summer afternoons, childhood baseball games, golf, and other experiences.

In contrast to associations among already established perceptions, we might review some of the

evidence for the influence of learning on the way sensory input is organized into the perceptual world of immediate experience. Can learning affect such organization so that the world actually looks, sounds, or feels differently? Consider the following observations [Kohler, 1962]:

For these observations the subjects wore goggles with prisms in them which distorted the input in various ways. The question was whether people can learn to organize the world differently so that they see it as they usually do in spite of the distortions. One of the first things that happened when the prism goggles were put on was that the prisms broke up the light into its components and colored fringes were seen in the visual field. These fringes went away within a few weeks. This should not surprise us too much because the lens of the eye also tends to refract light in such a way as to produce colored fringes—*chromatic aberration.* We must learn not to see the aberration colors produced by our own lens.

The prisms also bent light in such a way that straight lines were curved and right angles were obtuse or acute. When the prism goggles were first donned, lines and angles were indeed perceived in accordance with the geometry of the situation. But in time the distortions disappeared. Eye and head movements produced curious effects when the prisms were on: The world expanded, contracted, and looked "rubbery" as the eyes swept over the visual field. These effects also disappeared in time.

If a person wore the goggles until the distortions disappeared in the perceived world and then removed them, colored fringes reappeared, lines and angles were again distorted, and the world once again looked "rubbery" as the eyes roved over it. The colored fringes, distortions of lines and angles, and the expansion and contraction of the perceived world were now *opposite* in direction from the original distortions. It was as if the subject had canceled the original distortions with counterdistortions. Now he had to readapt and learn to reorganize without any counterdistortions.

Reversed worlds. The "reversed-world" experiments, in which goggles are worn with lenses that interchange up and down or right and left, are among the most famous experimental attempts to show the modifiability of perceptual input by experience [Stratton, 1897]. Reports of what happens vary a little from one subject to another, but a general picture can be described.

When the lenses are first put on, the effect is quite bewildering. The individual is severely disoriented, and his eye-body coordination is badly disrupted. Every time the subject moves his head, the entire world appears to swim around him. Walking and moving about are difficult. When the subject tries to avoid walking into a chair that appears to him to be on the left, he steps to the right and thus bumps directly into it. To pick up an object that appears to be on his left, he must learn to reach to his right.

After a period of some time, however, the world begins to stabilize itself. Walking about and locating objects in the upside-down world becomes easier and more automatic. The subject's head can be turned without the world seeming to move. Sounds now seem to come from the place where the object is seen to be and not from the opposite direction. One subject, an Austrian professor, rode his bicycle as usual to classes and carried on his duties quite satisfactorily [Kohler, 1951; English edition, 1964].

In most of the experiments, subjects report that they gradually get accustomed to a reversed world, but that it never looks entirely normal to them. Whether this is because they only wear the lenses a few days or weeks after using normal vision all their lives, whether it is because they must always be conscious of wearing the lenses and that they are seeing things differently from other people, or whether it is because an innate tendency to normal perception can be only partially overcome by experience with the lenses, we do not know.

One of the subjects described the situation rather well when asked whether a particular scene looked upside down to him:

I wish you hadn't asked me. Things were all right until you popped the question at me. Now, when I recall how

PEOPLE CAN ADJUST TO AN UPSIDE DOWN WORLD

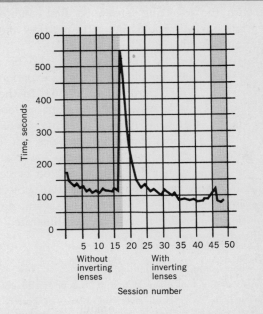

FIGURE 10.23   *Effect on a psychomotor task of inverting the visual world. The graph shows the average time required for sorting packs of cards into boxes. (After Snyder and Pronko, 1952.)*

they *did* look *before* I put on these lenses, I must answer that they do look upside down *now*. But until the moment that you asked me, I was absolutely unaware of it and hadn't given a thought to the question of whether things were right side up or upside down. [Snyder and Pronko, 1952, page 113.]

Thus motor adjustment to the reversed world may be quite complete. Perceptual adjustment, in the sense of seeing the world as it was, is less complete and may be "unreasonable" in that only some parts of the perceived world are seen in their normal orientation; other parts are still seen in reversed orientation [Köhler, 1951; Teuber, 1960]. For instance, with spectacles which reverse the up and down dimension, subjects may report that snow is seen as falling down past trees which are upside down.

Experiments in which the auditory world is reversed have also been conducted, using a device called a *pseudophone* instead of lenses. It consists of a pair of tubes that carry sounds from one side of the head to the ear on the opposite side. The results with the pseudophone are comparable to those with the inverting lenses. At first, auditory perceptions are disrupted, but within a few days, adaptation takes place.

Sensory deprivation. Perception can also be altered by depriving people of sensory experience [Bexton et al., 1954; Heron et al., 1956]. In these experiments, subjects were isolated from as much sensory input as possible, lying in a partially sound-proof cubicle wearing translucent goggles, gloves, and cardboard cuffs which covered the lower arm and hand. Some rather dramatic effects on perceptual organization were reported after the subjects, college students, had been exposed to several days of isolation. Apparent movement, as illustrated in the following report, was a result:

The whole room is undulating, swirling. . . . You were going all over the fool place at first. The floor is still doing it. The wall is waving all over the place—a horrifying sight, as a matter of fact. . . . The centre of that curtain over there—it just swirls downward, undulates and waves

inside. . . . I find it difficult to keep my eyes open for any length of time, the visual field is in such a state of chaos. . . . Everything will settle down for a moment, then it will start to go all over the place. [Heron et al., 1956, page 15.]

In addition, there were distortions of shape and color: vertical and horizontal edges, when not directly fixated, were reported to be seen as curved. Colors were reported to be glowing and luminescent and to be especially bright and saturated.

In addition to these changes in perceptual organization, there were vivid reports of visual imagery in the absence of well-defined sensory input—in other words, hallucinations. One subject, for instance, reported that, with his eyes closed, he saw "a procession of squirrels with sacks over their shoulders marching 'purposely' across a snow field and out of the field of 'vision' " [Bexton et al., 1954]. Other experimenters have failed to find such dramatic effects of sensory deprivation. But these experiments, taken as a whole, show once again the plasticity of perception.

PERCEPTUAL DEVELOPMENT These examples showing the effects of learning on perception are only samples from a voluminous literature. Can it be that all perceptual organization is the result of learning during development? The answer, which is far from complete, seems to be no; some, if not most, perceptual organization seems to be innate.

Psychologists have puzzled about, and at times argued about, the roles of heredity and environment in perception. "How much," they have asked, "is the way we perceive the world due to learning and how much to the way our brain and nervous system are put together?" The general answer to this question is the same as we earlier found it to be for other psychological abilities (see Chapter 2). For some aspects of perception, important limitations arise from the nervous system and the maturing of its structures. For others, learning is important. In the middle ground is an interaction between learning processes and the perceptual abilities developed through maturation. More specifically, however, the

FIGURE 10.24. *The "visual cliff." This test of depth perception can be used with almost any organism, human or animal, as soon as it can crawl or walk. At this stage, most organisms tested have good visual depth perception. (Gibson and Walk, 1960; William Vandivert,* Scientific American.*)*

question is: Which perceptual abilities are to be accounted for in these various ways?

Maturation. Almost certainly the limits of sensory discrimination are established by neural and sensory structures. We cannot learn to see better in the dark or to improve our eyesight. All we can do is use our sensory capacities to the best advantage. The attention value of an intense stimulus, the figure-ground relation, the grouping of stimuli according to nearness and similarity, the perceiving of certain types of illusions—all these are phenomena that seem to depend upon the way our nervous system is

structured. We say "seem" because we cannot prove conclusively that they do. We can only argue from the evidence that small children, primitive peoples, and even many of the lower animals show signs of having perceptions similar to ours in these respects.

Experiments on the maturation of depth perception have been done with the aid of an apparatus called a "visual cliff" [Walk and Gibson, 1961].

The visual cliff is a drop-off from a platform to the floor (see Figure 10.24). In one version of the cliff, the shelf of the platform and the floor are covered with a checkered

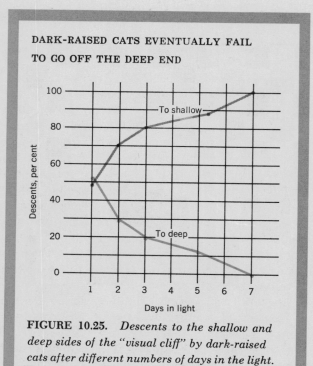

DARK-RAISED CATS EVENTUALLY FAIL
TO GO OFF THE DEEP END

FIGURE 10.25. *Descents to the shallow and deep sides of the "visual cliff" by dark-raised cats after different numbers of days in the light. (Modified from Walk and Gibson, 1961.)*

pattern which enhances the perception of depth. A sheet of heavy glass, from which reflections have been reduced to a minimum, is placed over the shelf, and it extends out over the deep area. This creates a shallow side, the shelf, and a deep side. To a person with depth perception, there seems to be a sharp drop-off at the edge of the shelf. Between the shallow and deep sides is a starting strip on which the subject is placed at the beginning of a test. A test simply consists of putting the subject on the center strip and seeing whether he moves to the shallow or deep side. If he perceives depth, he will avoid the drop-off on the deep side. The test can thus be given to any animal as soon as it is capable of crawling or walking; it has been used with babies, kittens, monkeys, rats, lambs, kids (goats), and several other animals. The results of these experiments are fairly consistent. Any animal mature enough to test is able to perceive depth, as indicated by its unwillingness to cross the glass when the well beneath it looks deep. It is interesting that babies and other organisms tested refuse to cross the "high cliff" even though they can touch the glass and can tell by touch that it can support them. Apparently they trust their eyes rather than their sense of touch.

From experiments such as these we conclude that depth perception matures in time to be useful at about the earliest time that the organism can use it—almost as soon as it can move about. For instance, in animals, such as lambs, which can move around on the first day after birth, depth perception is present on this first day. This perceptual development is probably largely innate and the result of maturation since there is little opportunity to learn much about space during the first few hours of life before crawling and walking are possible.

In animals in which locomotion is delayed, the situation is a little more complicated. They do have an opportunity for some learning, and the effects of learning and maturation become entangled. One way to separate the effects of learning and maturation is to raise animals in the dark and then test them when they are mature enough to locomote. Rats raised in the dark show depth perception immediately after being brought out into the light [Nealey and Edwards, 1960]; no visual experience seems necessary for depth perception in these animals. For cats, however, the situation is different. Dark-raised cats require several days to develop an avoidance response to the deep side of the visual-cliff apparatus (see Figure 10.25).

At least two explanations are possible. It is known that light deprivation produces some degeneration of the retina in the cat—more than in the rat where almost none occurs. It may be that some light experience is necessary before the retinal cells of the cat mature and begin to function normally [Walk and Gibson, 1961]. The other explanation involves learning. It may take several days for the animal to learn about visual space through experience in its home environment. This learning may then transfer or generalize to the visual-cliff tests. It seems likely that the first of these explanations is the correct one and that maturation is the major factor in the normal development of depth perception.

Sensory experience. We have seen that the contribution of sensory experience to the development of perception can be studied experimentally by restricting the sensory environments of developing animals. When carefully done, these experiments show that, in some species at least, exposure to the world through the senses is necessary for the development of some aspects of perceptual experience. The following experiment illustrates this type of experimentation [Nissen et al., 1951]:

A chimpanzee was restricted by having cardboard mailing tubes attached to his arms and legs at 15 weeks of age (see Figure 10.26). When the chimpanzee was 23 months old, training began on a tactual-discrimination problem. The experimenters attempted to teach the subject to turn his head to the left or right depending on whether the left or right index finger had been squeezed lightly. For instance, if the left index finger was squeezed, he was rewarded for turning his head to the left and punished for turning it to the right. After more than 2,000 trials the chimpanzee had failed to learn this response. An unrestricted chimpanzee learned to do this reliably in slightly more than 200 trials. As a check to see whether the tactual restriction had impaired the subject's general ability to learn, visual discrimination learning was studied and found to be normal.

Most of the deprivation experiments on the role of sensory experience have been done with vision. In such visual experiments, young animals are raised from birth in the dark or with occluding lenses over their eyes. One of the problems with these methods is that the ganglion cells of the retina degenerate if not exposed to light [Chow et al., 1957]. This seems to be especially true of the chimpanzee subjects which have been used in visual-deprivation experiments, but to a lesser degree, it is also true of the cat. By using translucent occluders which allow diffuse light to enter the eye, but which preclude pattern vision, this problem is overcome. The results from animals raised with translucent diffusing lenses tend to show that experience with patterned light is necessary for the organization of sensory input which underlies form perception [Riesen, 1961].

Species differ in the necessity of patterned light experience for the development of form perception. Rats, for instance, even though raised in the dark

FIGURE 10.26. *The subject in one experiment on the effect of restriction of sensory input on perception. Note the cardboard tubes taped to the arms and legs and the strange sitting position. (After Nissen Clow, and Semmes, 1951. Yerkes Regional Primate Research Center of Emory University.)*

and possibly subject to a slight amount of retinal degeneration, show unimpaired form discrimination when tested [Hebb, 1937]. Cats and chimpanzees, on the other hand, show impairment.

As might be expected, man also seems to require experience with patterned light stimulation for form perception [Senden, 1932; English edition, 1960]. Observations which seem to confirm this were made on people who were seeing for the first time after operations which removed cataracts that were present from birth. The cataracts sometimes allowed a little diffuse light to reach the retina, and this prevented retinal degeneration. In a sense, these patients were wearing translucent occluding lenses from birth. Other patients, however, were probably completely blind from birth. Although some retinal degeneration occurred, it is generally believed that this was not nearly severe enough to account for the observed effects [Riesen, 1960]. What are the perceptual worlds of these newly seeing people like? One of the physicians who studied his patient after the operation had this to report:

It would be an error to suppose that a patient whose sight has been restored to him by surgical intervention can thereafter see the external world. The eyes have certainly obtained the power to see, but the employment of this power, which as a whole constitutes the act of seeing, still has to be acquired from the very beginning. The operation itself has no more value than that of preparing the eyes to see; education is the most important factor. . . . [Moreau, 1910. Case cited in Senden, 1960, page 160.]

More specific accounts of perception after the removal of cataracts show that the patient is first overwhelmed by the flood of visual input. At first, such patients are able to perceive vague figures against ground; they can see colors and follow moving figures with their eyes. Thus they perceive that something is there, and they can scan it with their eyes, but form perception is almost nonexistent. For instance, it is reported that these patients cannot, before they have had visual experience, distinguish shapes. They can eventually learn to distinguish a triangle from a square, for example, by scanning the figures with their eyes and counting the corners, but the visual recognition of shape takes weeks or months of such scanning to develop. Perceptual organization gradually improves, and vision becomes more nearly normal.

Thus sensory experience, in addition to maturation, contributes to the development of perception. This should come as no surprise since we have seen that the nature-nurture question has no all-or-none answer.

Cell assemblies and phase sequences. The physiological basis for the learning of perceptual organization is obscure, but a theory has been proposed [Hebb, 1949; Milner, 1957]. Based in part upon data from cataract patients, this theory proposes that the perceptual organization corresponds to acquired organization of cells in the brain. For instance, as an infant, or a patient seeing for the first time after a cataract operation, scans a simple figure with his eyes, certain cells in the brain fire in sequence. The main idea of the theory is that such sequential firing may lead to a functional connection being formed between the cells. Thus, if cell A fires and this is followed by the firing of cell B as the person scans the figure, cells A and B will become linked together functionally so that the firing of one will initiate the firing of the other.

Such a functional organization of cells has been called a *cell assembly*. Cell assemblies might be the neural representation of simple parts of figures such as corners or angles. Cell assemblies themselves may be organized into larger units by the same process of sequential firing—first one cell assembly, then another, and so on. For instance, as a person scans a figure, the cell assemblies of the corners and lines may be sequentially activated and organized into a larger functional unit called a *phase sequence*. These may be the neural representation of whole figures, a triangle, for example. Note that the theory proposes that the cell assemblies and phase sequences are developed through learning.

This theory involves more than this simple account would imply, but cell assemblies and phase sequences are two of the main ideas. When this theory was proposed, there was no direct evidence for it. Now, as more direct evidence about the functioning of the central nervous system is becoming available, we find evidence that some of the perceptual organization which was thought to be due to learned cell assemblies may actually be innate [Hubel and Wiesel, 1963]. Whatever the outcome of future attempts to obtain direct evidence for learned cell assemblies and phase sequences, the theory has done its job; many ideas for valuable experiments and the organization of diverse data have come from it.

MOTIVATION It seems reasonable to believe that our needs and motives will influence perception. We see and hear what we want to see and hear. Many experiments have attempted to show that this common-sense notion is correct. Unfortunately, some of these experiments have had serious inherent faults which have made them questionable demonstrations of the effect of motivation on perceptual organization. One of the clearest demonstrations of the effects of motivation on perception follows [Lambert et al., 1949]:

Nursery school children, aged three to five, were presented with a machine which had a crank on it. They received a poker chip for turning the crank 18 turns. By putting this poker chip into a slot, they could obtain candy. Before the experiment began, each child estimated the size of the poker chip by comparing it with a spot of light whose size could be varied by the experimenter, until the child said the two objects matched. Again, after the children had been rewarded with candy for cranking out poker chips, estimates of size were made. The poker chips now seemed significantly larger to the children. The experimenters then instituted an extinction procedure during which the children got no candy for their efforts in cranking. Estimates of size were again made. The chips had shrunk back to their former apparent size. After that, the children were again rewarded with candy, and the chips again increased in apparent size.

This experiment, which is only one of several that

might have been described, indicates that as the poker chip acquired value—that is, as it came to represent something the child wanted—it was perceived as larger than when it had no value. The experiment supports the general conclusion that a person's motivation affects his perception of even such physical characteristics as size.

Generally speaking, however, it is in the perceiving of such complex things as social and interpersonal relationships that our own internal needs and biases have their greatest effect. The concrete objects in our world do not allow us too much freedom in perception. Everyone perceives them in much the same way. The table, the chair, the bookcase—all are seen as such. The occasional atypical individual who sees them differently winds up in a psychiatrist's office. On the other hand, such social situations as parties, conversations, and contacts with friends or associates are often indefinite and ambiguous. Our perceptions of them are less stable and definite than are our perceptions of physical objects. How many times, for example, have we pondered over just what a friend "meant by that remark"? We all remember cases in which a remark was perceived as an insult or slight by one person but was regarded as a compliment by another. Most of us, at one time or another, have suffered from the misperception or misinterpretation of our remarks and behavior by others.

Physiological evidence for perceptual organization

We have said that perception involves the reworking and organization of the input from receptors. In vision there is direct physiological evidence for organization of the input. The evidence which has been obtained does not give a physiological answer to many of the classical problems of perception which have been discussed in this chapter, but it does show the direction in which such physiological answers may be found. Let us look at some experiments and then discuss their significance for

face which will influence its activity. Most units in the visual cortex are not particularly responsive to large spots of light; instead, it has been found that slits of light, edges, and dark bars, in particular orientations, for instance, horizontal or vertical, and in particular parts of the retina, are

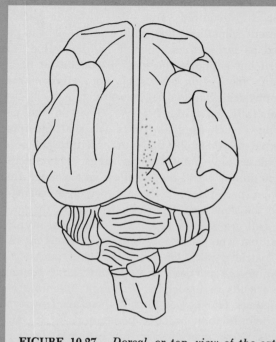

FIGURE 10.27. *Dorsal, or top, view of the cat brain. The right and left hemispheres are shown. The dark lines on each hemisphere are grooves (sulci). The dots show the sites from which single cell recordings were made. (Modified from Hubel and Wiesel, 1962.)*

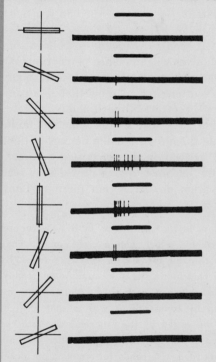

ORIENTATION IN A PARTICULAR PART OF THE VISUAL FIELD IS CRUCIAL FOR THE FIRING OF "SIMPLE" CORTICAL UNITS

FIGURE 10.28 *Left, the orientation of a bar of light in the visual field of a cat; right, responses from a single cortical unit, or cell. The period during which the stimulus is present is shown by the black line above the records. The spike-like records are made with microelectrodes and show the electrical activity or firing of single cortical cells. (After Hubel and Wiesel, 1959.)*

some of the problems of perception [Hubel and Wiesel, 1962, 1963, 1965]:

The experiments were done on the visual cerebral cortex of cats. The cerebral cortex is the layer of nerve cells and fibers covering the brain (see Figure 10.27 and Chapter 19). Records of the firing of single cells or units of the cortex are obtained from microelectrodes which are pushed down through the brain. When the retina is stimulated by patterns of light and dark, a slit of light, for instance, some cells in the cortex respond.

The experiments are designed to measure the receptive fields of the cortical units. As we have seen (see page 292) the receptive field of a cell is the region of the receptor sur-

effective in firing a cell. If the energy on the retina varies from the crucial orientation, the cell will not fire.

Figure 10.28 shows a unit that responds to a slit of light with vertical orientation on the retina. Units which are fired by such highly specific types of stimulation are called "simple" units. Other units, called "complex units," are less specific in the patterns which will fire them. A record from a complex unit is shown in Figure 10.29. On the left of this record, a black bar is shown projecting on different parts of the retina. The firing of the complex unit is shown in the records at the right. Note that the unit fires when the bar is presented in a horizontal orientation and slight tilting of the bar abolishes its effectiveness. The bar is effective over a large area of the retina. Movement of the bar up and down over a wide region of the retina is also quite effective in firing the unit (see Figure 10.30). Horizontal movement is not effective.

The visual cortex is supposed to be organized so that simple cells fire the complex cells. Several simple cells which fire to stimuli with a particular orientation may, for instance, feed into a complex cell. This means that the firing of the complex cell will be influenced by stimulation over a wide region of the retina. "Hypercomplex" cells have also been found; these are supposed to be fired by complex cells. Corners of figures and other discontinuous stimuli are effective in firing hypercomplex units.

This type of experimentation shows that functional organization does take place in the cortex, and it also points toward a "code" for perceived experience. The firing of simple, complex, and hypercomplex cells may provide the basis for perception. For instance, the firing of simple and complex cells, which respond to a particular orientation of stimulation, may be the basis for the perception of straight contours. The fact that complex cells fire from stimulation which moves over a wide region of the retina may give a basis for the perception of real movement. Finally, activity of hypercomplex cells may be the cortical basis for the perception of figure contours which are discontinuous, such as corners. Thus we are beginning to discover information about the way the brain reorganizes input from the receptors.

"COMPLEX" UNITS FIRE TO STIMULI WITH A PARTICULAR ORIENTATION OVER WIDE REGIONS OF THE VISUAL FIELD

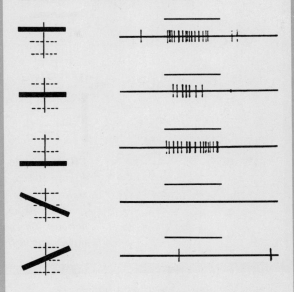

FIGURE 10.29. *Left, position of a black bar in the visual field; right, records of activity of a single cortical cell. The period during which the stimulus is present is indicated by the black line above each of the records. Note that the unit fires when the bar is horizontal, but that deviations from horizontal produce no firing. In contrast with "simple" units, this unit fires from wide regions of the visual field. "Complex" units are thought to be influenced by the activity of several "simple" units. "Simple" units fire at each of the positions of the stimulus in the visual field and their activity feeds into a "complex" unit to fire it. Thus, while "simple" units respond only to stimuli at a particular place in the visual field, "complex" units fire to stimuli in wide regions of the visual field. (Modified from Hubel and Wiesel, 1962.)*

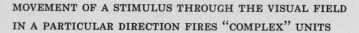

MOVEMENT OF A STIMULUS THROUGH THE VISUAL FIELD
IN A PARTICULAR DIRECTION FIRES "COMPLEX" UNITS

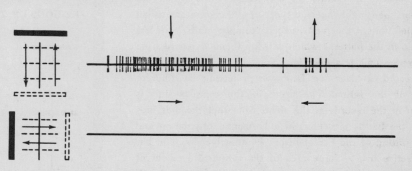

FIGURE 10.30. *Another record from the same "complex" unit (see Figure 10.29). Left, movement of the black bar through the visual field; right, records from the unit. Vertical movement of a horizontal bar produces firing; horizontal movement of a vertical bar does not produce activity. The point is that this unit is sensitive to a particular direction of movement in the visual field. (Modified from Hubel and Wiesel, 1962.)*

SYNOPSIS AND SUMMARY

Because everyone behaves in accordance with the way he perceives the world, perception provides one key for unlocking the riddle of behavior. We have seen that the perceived world is a construction and an achievement. Information comes in through the sensory channels, and the perceptual processes act upon it to form it into the world of experience.

Selectivity of input, organization of input, constancy of experience in spite of varying inputs, a dimension of depth, movement, the influence of context, the importance of relationships, and the importance of learning and motivation are all characteristics of perception. Examining these aspects of perception, we made the following specific points:

1. Perception refers to the world of immediate experience—the world as seen, heard, felt, smelled, or tasted by a person.

2. Attention, or selection of input, is an important determinant of what is perceived. It has a focus in which events are clearly perceived and a margin in which things are less clearly perceived, and it is constantly shifting from one stimulus to another.

3. External factors controlling attention are (a) intensity and size of stimuli, (b) contrast between a stimulus and its background, (c) the repetition of stimuli, and (d) movement. Internal factors controlling attention are (a) motives, needs, or interests and (b) a set, or expectancy, for a particular kind of stimulus.

4. Objects are usually seen as figures on a ground. It is, in fact, almost impossible to "see" them any other way. Such figure-ground perception depends, in turn, on the perception of contours marking off an object from its background.

5. Perceptual processes organize the world around a person into objects and groups of objects. Thus he tends to perceive as a group (a) those objects that are close together, (b) those that are similar to each other, (c) those that are symmetrically arranged, and (d) those that form some continuous line or pattern.

6. Perception also tends to close gaps, so that a person perceives an object even when some of its parts are missing.

7. One of the most adaptive things about perception is that it tends to be relatively constant despite a considerable change in the stimulation of the sense organs. For example, shapes usually appear about the same, whether we view them from an angle or head on; further, sizes tend to appear relatively constant, whether objects are near or far away; finally, brightness similarly remains comparatively constant even under rather different illuminations.

8. Even though the retina of the eye is flat and receives a two-dimensional picture, people perceive three-dimensional depth by using several cues for depth. Most of these cues are monocular, but some are binocular.

9. The principal monocular cues are (a) linear perspective, (b) clearness, (c) interposition, (d) shadows, (e) gradients of texture, and (f) movement.

10. The chief binocular cue to depth is retinal disparity, that is, the slight difference in the images projected on the two eyes when they view the same situation.

11. Two aspects of auditory space perception are direction and distance. The cues to direction are binaural and involve time differences in the reception of sound at the two ears, intensity differences at the ears, and phase difference. Two ears are not needed, however, for the perception of the distance of sound. The cues for auditory distance perception are intensity and the frequency composition of the stimulating energy.

12. Both apparent and real motion are matters of perception. The major types of apparent motion—motion without a moving flux of energy across a receptor—are (a) stroboscopic motion, (b) optimal, or beta, movement, (c) pure, or phi, movement, (d) autokinetic movement, (e) induced movement, (f) movement in stationary patterns, and (g) movement of afterimages. The perception of real movement cannot be attributed only to the movement of energy across a receptor.

13. Simultaneous contrast, adaptation level, figural after-effects, and transposition are examples which show that the context surrounding an object or event is important in determining perception.

14. Perception is modified by experience. New perceptions, or perceptual learning, comes about when we learn to make new associations between already established perceptions. Learning can also influence the organization of the basic sensory data into the perceptual world of immediate experience.

15. Experiments with goggles, "reversed-world" experiments, and experiments in sensory deprivation illustrate the importance of experience in the organization of sensory input.

16. Both innate and experiential factors are important in the development of perception. The importance of sensory experience has been studied by raising animals under conditions of reduced sensory input and by studying cases of patients seeing for the first time after removal of cataracts.

17. Perception is influenced by motivation. To a very considerable extent, we perceive what we want to perceive.

18. Some physiological evidence for organization in perception has been found. Single cells in the brain have been discovered which may provide the neural basis for some of the phenomena of perception.

RELATED TOPICS IN THE TEXT

CHAPTER 3 PRINCIPLES OF LEARNING Perceptual learning—the learning of new ways of perceiving the world through the association of already existing perceptions—is considered at length here.

CHAPTERS 8 AND 9 VISION AND HEARING Perceptions which are largely dependent upon receptor processes and the origin of the sensory input which is organized into perceived experience are discussed in these chapters.

CHAPTER 16 SOCIAL INFLUENCES ON BEHAVIOR Our perceptions of social situations determine our responses to them. When reading the section on conformity in this chapter, try to see the experimental situations as the subjects might see them and project your own responses.

CHAPTER 20 PHYSIOLOGICAL BASIS OF BEHAVIOR Some of the evidence for the physiological basis of perception has been discussed in Chapter 10. The anatomical regions of the cerebral cortex which are involved in perception are described in Chapter 20.

SUGGESTIONS FOR FURTHER READING

Bartley, S. H. *Principles of perception.* New York: Harper & Row, 1958.
A basic textbook on perception.

Beardslee, D. C., and Wertheimer, M. (Eds.). *Readings in perception.* Princeton, N.J.: Van Nostrand, 1958.
Selected articles from the literature on perception.

Dember, W. N. *The psychology of perception.* New York: Holt, 1960.
A description and review of many of the basic topics in perception written from a psychological, not a physiological, point of view.

Gibson, J. J. *The perception of the visual world.* Boston: Houghton Mifflin, 1950.
An account of a point of view about visual perception with many illustrations of experiments in visual perception.

Hochberg, J. E. *Perception.* Englewood Cliffs, N.J.: Prentice-Hall, 1964. (Paperback.)
An interesting and well-illustrated introduction to perceptual phenomena.

King, R. A. (Ed.). *Readings for an introduction to psychology* (2d ed.). New York: McGraw-Hill, 1966. (Paperback.)
A book of readings designed to accompany this text.

Krech, D., and Crutchfield, R. S. *Elements of psychology.* New York: Knopf, 1958.
An introductory textbook which stresses perception in Chapters 2 to 7.

Scientific American Readings
A number of reprints of articles on perception which originally appeared in the Scientific American *are available.*
A list of the reprints and the reprints themselves may be obtained from: W. H. Freeman and Co., San Francisco, Calif.

Solley, C. M., and Murphy, G. *Development of the perceptual world.* New York: Basic Books, 1960.
An interesting book which stresses perceptual learning and perception as a process involving expectancy, attending, reception, trial-and-check, and final perceptual organization.

Teuber, H-L. Perception. In J. Field, H. W. Magoun, and V. E. Hall (Eds.), *Handbook of physiology.* Vol. 3. Washington, D.C.: American Physiological Society, 1960.
Perception discussed from the physiological point of view. Not easy reading, but the beginner will find it understandable by dint of effort.

Vernon, M. D. *A further study of visual perception.* London: Cambridge, 1952.
An excellent and understandable coverage of the main topics of perception.

INDIVIDUAL DIFFERENCES

PART FIVE

PROGRESS IN SCIENCE often depends upon the development of quantitative methods. Without such methods, science is limited to crude observation and classification. With them, it can greatly extend and refine the conclusions it can draw from its data. To take a simple example, people have always known that stones fall when they are dropped, but physics made little progress as a science until its early scientists began to measure how fast stones fall, how far they fall in a given period of time, and whether stones fall as fast as apples or feathers.

The situation is much the same in psychology. Even the ancients recognized that some people were slow-witted and others nimble-witted, some courageous and others timid. Psychology, however, began to be a science only when it found ways of measuring such differences, attaching meaningful numbers to them, and then making useful predictions about them.

The problems of measurement are much the same in all sciences, but psychologists and behavioral scientists are probably more concerned about the logic of measurement than most physical scientists. The reason is that many of the things they want to measure are quite complex and cannot be measured on physical scales. Courage, for example, is not the same sort of thing as the length of a table; there is no simple yardstick for measuring a man's courage. Not everything psychological is so difficult to measure as courage, but much of it is. Psychologists and behavioral scientists have therefore found it necessary to invent new methods of measurement and new ways of describing the results of measurement.

The specific techniques developed for measuring things such as personality, intelligence, and attitudes are described in Chapter 12. This chapter covers the general rules of psychological measurement and presents statistical methods and concepts for describing and interpreting psychological data.

Many students taking introductory psychology are not well prepared to study statistical concepts. In some cases there is no need for them to learn or understand the mathematical formulas involved. For that reason, this chapter relies mainly on words and

PSYCHOLOGICAL MEASUREMENT

I OFTEN SAY THAT WHEN YOU CAN MEASURE WHAT YOU ARE SPEAKING ABOUT, AND EXPRESS IT IN NUMBERS, YOU KNOW SOMETHING ABOUT IT; BUT WHEN YOU CANNOT EXPRESS IT IN NUMBERS, YOUR KNOWLEDGE IS OF A MEAGRE AND UNSATISFACTORY KIND. . . .

LORD KELVIN

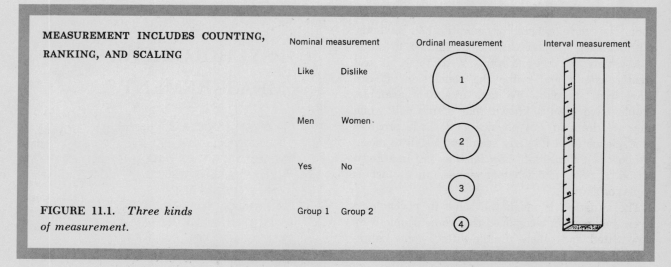

MEASUREMENT INCLUDES COUNTING, RANKING, AND SCALING

Nominal measurement   Ordinal measurement   Interval measurement

Like   Dislike

Men   Women

Yes   No

Group 1   Group 2

FIGURE 11.1. *Three kinds of measurement.*

charts to explain the basic points. At the end of the chapter, however, is a section containing formulas and methods of calculation for the benefit of those who prefer formulas to words or who may have occasion to use the statistics described.

Kinds of measurement

The following definition of measurement is generally accepted: *Measurement* is the assignment of numerals (numbers) to objects or events according to rules [Guilford, 1954]. In less formal terms, this means that in measuring a thing we compare it with some measuring stick—a ruler, a scale, a clock—and give that measurement a number. The number assigned depends on the rules we adopt for making the comparison. These rules vary with the purpose of our measurement or with the measuring sticks available. Many sets of rules are possible, but we need to distinguish only three, and hence only three kinds of measurement (see Figure 11.1). Some writers distinguish four [Stevens, 1951], but the fourth, which is mentioned below, may be regarded as a refinement of the third.

NOMINAL MEASUREMENT   A *nominal measurement* is nothing more than a classification of things

into mutually exclusive categories so that all the things in one category are alike in some particular respect. If we took a basket of mixed fruit and sorted it into separate piles of bananas, oranges, or apples, we would be making the kind of classification involved in nominal measurement. All that would be necessary to complete the measurement, so to speak, would be to assign arbitrarily certain numbers to each kind of fruit. Thus bananas might be category 1; oranges, category 2; and apples, category 3. Using numbers instead of names would have little value for scientific purposes, but it nevertheless illustrates the steps in nominal measurement.

In scientific use, nominal measurements are often employed to designate groups. Group 1 may be the experimental group that is given some particular treatment not given to group 2, a control group. In making comparisons of sex differences, men would constitute one category and women another. Or in comparing achievement of the graduates of different colleges, the categories might be College 1, College 2, College 3, and so on. Nominal measurements may be employed to designate dependent variables (see page 15). Simple categories such as "pass-fail," "for-against," or "like-dislike," which are often dependent variables in a study, are also essentially nominal measurements.

Probably the most important use of nominal

measurements in psychology and the social sciences is in tests from which more sophisticated measurements are compounded. For example, the items on almost any objective examination, or on psychological tests of intelligence and personality, involve nominal measurements. Each item calls for the choice of a simple category, such as *a, b, c,* or *d,* or "like" or "dislike," or "worry" or "don't worry." By making a choice, the individual places himself in one category or another on that particular item. In the typical test, of course, he makes a good many such choices. These can be counted according to some scoring system, and his score can be compared with another person's score. In this case, the outcome belongs to one of the following kinds of measurement.

ORDINAL MEASUREMENT As its name implies, *ordinal measurement* is the ranking of things according to some attribute they possess. I can ask you, for example, to rank order your preference for apples, oranges, bananas, pears, apricots, and prunes. If you assign oranges your number 1 preference, bananas your number 2, pears your number 3, and so on, you have made an ordinal measurement of your preferences for this particular list of fruits. Because of its simplicity, this method of making ordinal measurements is commonly used in psychology and the social sciences.

In general, however, it is not so reliable as another method, the method of *paired comparisons.* This is primarily because a person in making each ranking cannot pay equal attention, and hence cannot do justice, to all other members of the list. The paired-comparisons method has the virtue of requiring that an objective judgment be made of only two things at a time. It also has, for reasons that are pointed out below, the virtue of allowing the scientist to convert ordinal measurements into a third kind of measurement.

In making paired comparisons, the first step is similar to the categorization described above. Things are compared two at a time, and some judgment is made of "greater" or "less," "like" or "dislike," "agree" or "disagree." Having done this for

TABLE 11.1 *Paired comparisons of preferences for vegetables. One hundred individuals were asked to express their preference between pairs of vegetables. All possible combinations of pairs were presented. The number in each column is the proportion of the choices in which the vegetable named at the top was preferred over the one named at the side.*

	CARROTS	SPINACH	STRING BEANS	PEAS	CORN
Carrots	.50	.49	.57	.71	.76
Spinach	.51	.50	.63	.68	.63
String beans	.43	.37	.50	.53	.64
Peas	.29	.32	.47	.50	.63
Corn	.24	.37	.36	.37	.50
Total preference	1.97	2.05	2.53	2.79	3.16

SOURCE: Based on Guilford, 1954.

one pair, a person can make a similar comparison between one member of the pair and a third item. This process can be continued for all the items to be considered (see Table 11.1). When it has been completed, the number of times each item has been ranked above or below another item can be counted, and all the items can be ranked. This particular method has often been used by psychologists for the construction of attitude scales and other tests.

INTERVAL MEASUREMENT An *interval measurement* is a measurement of the magnitude of the difference between one thing and another.

A familiar illustration of interval measurement is to be found in the reading of temperature. For this purpose, two scales are available: the Fahrenheit scale, used in households and commerce, and the Celsius (centigrade) scale, used in scientific measurements (see Figure 11.2). The Fahrenheit thermometer is marked off so that 32°F represents the freezing point of water and 212°F corresponds to the boiling point. The numbers between arbitrarily indicate a given expansion or contraction of the indicator liquid. A change of a particular amount in the liquid, say 1.2 millimeters, always means a change of 1° in temperature, no matter whether the difference is between 0 and 1°, between 53 and 54°, or between 154 and 155°. Equal differences along the scale represent equal differences in the behavior of the temperature-indicating liquid. The same reasoning holds for the Celsius thermometer.

What is lacking in temperature measurements, but not in many physical measurements, is the knowledge of where *true zero* is—that is, where the indicator liquid does not expand at all, rather than the point zero on the thermometer which is considerably above absolute, or true, zero. As it happens, we have discovered that the zero of temperature is about −273°C or −460°F, but neither Fahrenheit nor Celsius thermometers show this. All they do is give the true difference between any two temperatures. A ruler or a balance or a stop watch, however, is a scale which has a true zero. Such scales have been called *ratio scales,* as distinguished from interval scales, for when a scale is calibrated to true zero, different ratios that are equal actually refer to equal ratios.

For example, on a scale of weight, the ratio of 100 pounds to 75 pounds is equal to a ratio of 160 pounds to 120 pounds. This is not true of interval scales, such as the thermometer. On a thermometer, 100°F is not twice as much heat as 50°F. If you are tempted to think so, note the inconsistency as soon as you convert into the Celsius scale. Since 100°F equals 38°C, and 50°F equals 10°C, you can see that 38°C is not twice 10°C. In making this conversion, you do not change the temperatures; you change only your measurement of them.

To a physicist it is of great importance whether he is making interval or ratio measurements. To psychologists, it usually is not. The only difference is whether measurements are anchored to absolute zero, but in psychological or behavioral matters zero is seldom of any consequence. We are primarily interested in *differences* between people or in the *correlation* of differences of one kind with differences of another. Furthermore, any statistical method that is applicable to ratio measurements is usually also applicable to interval measurements. Interval measurements, then, are adequate for almost any psychological measurement.

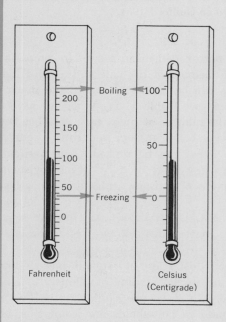

ON AN INTERVAL SCALE, EQUAL
DIFFERENCES ARE EQUAL

FIGURE 11.2.   *The Fahrenheit and Celsius (centigrade) temperature scales provide examples of interval scales. On these scales, equal differences between numbers represent equal differences in temperature, but one cannot say that 60° is twice as hot as 30°.*

USES OF MEASUREMENTS   These kinds of measurement clearly differ in the amount of information they convey. A nominal measurement merely tells us in what qualitative category a thing belongs. Ordinal measurements tell us more; they indicate that one thing possesses more or less of a characteristic than other things, but not how much more or how much less. Interval measurement, on the other hand, does exactly that: It gives the magnitude of the difference between things.

At times we want as much information as we can get in order to describe a person or to make a prediction precisely. In those cases, we like to use interval scales. We automatically have them, or something even better, when we measure human behavior in physical units such as time. On the other hand, strictly *psychological* measurements made with such instruments as intelligence tests or attitude scales do not automatically give us interval measurements.

If we want interval measurements, we must start off with nominal measurements, which is what the individual items on most psychological tests give us, or with ordinal measurements, which are used in rating scales. Then through the compounding of such measurements, and sometimes through special statistical techniques, we convert nominal or ordinal measurements into interval scales. Two of the ways in which this may be done have already been indicated (see page 383).

Two other points should be made about the use of measurements. One is that nominal or ordinal measurements alone may be quite sufficient for some purposes. If one wants to know, for example, whether individuals of high aptitude are more apt to succeed than those of low aptitude in a particular course of training, nominal or ordinal measurements may be as good as more precise interval measurements. In fact, in order to simplify computations, research workers sometimes reduce what was originally a set of interval measurements to ordinal ones, and get about the same result.

The other point is that the kinds of statistics we can use to summarize results, or to indicate a particular person's performance, depend on the kinds of measurements made. Some statistical measures, such as the arithmetic average, are simply not appropriate for ordinal measurements. This is brought out later when we describe ways of summarizing groups of measurements.

Distribution of measurements

For most purposes, one lone measurement is of little value. It may do for reading a thermometer, but only because we have read thermometers a good many times and know how a particular reading compares with other possible readings. We already have a frame of reference for interpreting a reading. In psychology, however, one measurement by itself usually does us little good. Rather, we often need a fair number of measurements of some kind. For instance, if we are trying to describe personality characteristics of a person, we must first have enough measurements to provide a frame of reference for comparing any one measurement with a group of measurements. In doing research, we may need a relatively large number of measurements, if for no other reason than to avoid getting results that are a matter of chance or that are biased in one way or another. This is especially the case when the method of systematic observation is used (see page 19). When the experimental method is used and when the control is good—especially when a prior baseline has been established (see page 17)— a few measurements may be enough and elaborate statistical manipulation may not be required.

If we have obtained a large number of measurements of any given type, the problem of what to do with them arises. Indeed, it frequently happens that a person untrained in statistics collects a lot of measurements, and then comes to a psychologist or statistician and asks, "What do I do with them?" It is a little late to be asking the question at that point, because the kind of measurements one makes hinges on what he expects to do with them. They can be processed in several different ways, depending on the kind of measurements they are. The rest of this chapter is concerned with the processing, that is, the statistical treatment, of psychological measurements.

COUNTING OF FREQUENCIES The first step, usually, is to find some way of organizing measurements so that one can see what they are like. To do this, one *counts frequencies*. This means that he determines how many measurements of a given kind he has. For nominal measurements, this step is easy. All he needs to do is count the cases falling into each of the categories used in making the

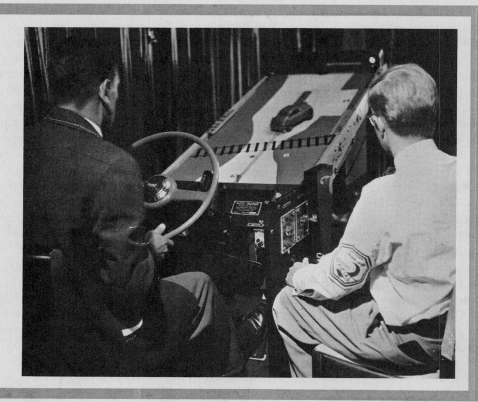

FIGURE 11.3. *An apparatus for measuring braking reaction time. (American Automobile Association.)*

measurements. Such counting is the common way of handling and presenting many measurements of popular interest: the number of automobiles purchased in March, the number of people who say they will vote Republican in the next election, the number of people who prefer Aroma soap, and so on.

The question often arises whether one should use absolute numbers, that is, the actual counts, or express the counts in percentages. In many cases, especially those involving nominal measurements with only a few categories, one does not care about the total number of cases in each category. What is of interest or importance is the *relative proportion* of people or things in each category. If this is the case, it is perfectly legitimate to divide the number in each category by the total number and thereby obtain the answer as a percentage rather than as a count or frequency. In doing this, though, one thing must be remembered: *Per cent means per hundred,* and a percentage should ordinarily be used only when the total number of cases is close to a hundred or, of course, over a hundred. Percentages used on a small number of cases, say 30, can be very misleading, for a change of one case may make a difference of over 3 per cent.

One can make counts of ordinal and interval measurements, but this involves another step that we come to in a moment. After making a count of nominal measurements, the investigator usually finds it desirable to present his figures in some kind of chart so that others can immediately grasp the results. There are as many kinds of charts as there are artists to invent them, but two basic forms are commonly employed. First, the *pie chart* is suitable for depicting counts converted to percentages. One merely takes a circle, slices "pieces of pie" that correspond to the percentage of cases falling into a given category, and then labels the categories.

From a pie chart, a reader can quickly perceive the relative proportions of cases, dollars, or whatever in each category. Another common form is the bar graph, or, more technically, the *histogram*. It can be used either for raw counts or for percentages. It simply represents the counts or percentages by relative heights of bars.

FREQUENCY DISTRIBUTIONS The method of counting frequencies, and then of representing them with a histogram, is also the simplest way of handling interval measurements. This requires, as we indicated, an additional step: The scale on which the measurements were made must be marked off into a reasonable number of equal *intervals*. In order to illustrate this step, let us take as an example a study of the reaction time of automobile drivers. The measurements in this case were all made in terms of time, which for our purposes may be treated as an interval scale.

The study was conducted in a mock-up of an automobile, consisting of a seat, steering wheel, accelerator, and brake pedal (see Figure 11.3). In front of the driver was a panel on which a red light could be made to appear without warning. The subject was instructed to place his foot on the brake the moment the red light appeared. An electrical circuit connected the red light and the brake, and an electric clock recorded the exact time—the *reaction time*—between the moment the light turned red and the moment at which the brake pedal was depressed by 1 centimeter. One braking reaction-time measurement was made on each of 200 men. The 200 measurements obtained are listed in Table 11.2.

One can look over the data in Table 11.2 and guess that the average reaction time was between 0.55 and 0.65 and estimate that the reaction times varied from about 0.45 to 0.75 second. Looking over the "raw figures," however, is not a very satisfactory way, and certainly not a precise way, of finding out what the data are like. A better way is to construct a frequency distribution of the measurements.

There are two steps in forming a frequency distribution from "raw data" such as those in Table 11.2. The first is to choose class intervals into which

TABLE 11.2 *Braking reaction time, in seconds, of 200 normal young men on a test of automobile driving. The scores are arbitrarily presented in blocks of five for convenience. The following measures of central tendency were computed from this set of scores: arithmetic mean, 0.60; median, 0.60; mode, 0.61 from the frequency distribution in Table 11.3, or 0.62 from table below. The standard deviation is 0.10.*

0.65	0.42	0.66	0.77	0.61	0.82	0.44	0.68	0.48	0.60
0.61	0.48	0.64	0.58	0.43	0.55	0.71	0.62	0.54	0.62
0.75	0.67	0.46	0.66	0.57	0.54	0.72	0.43	0.76	0.53
0.70	0.77	0.58	0.51	0.55	0.73	0.41	0.56	0.53	0.48
0.74	0.46	0.57	0.48	0.90	0.60	0.63	0.64	0.75	0.55
0.69	0.62	0.64	0.57	0.73	0.56	0.49	0.66	0.70	0.59
0.72	0.62	0.66	0.56	0.59	0.60	0.57	0.49	0.64	0.66
0.45	0.83	0.69	0.78	0.51	0.58	0.66	0.61	0.64	0.56
0.53	0.60	0.62	0.65	0.62	0.44	0.61	0.60	0.74	0.64
0.85	0.49	0.51	0.39	0.58	0.64	0.69	0.68	0.52	0.74
0.55	0.68	0.61	0.40	0.56	0.59	0.45	0.59	0.65	0.62
0.46	0.64	0.36	0.72	0.41	0.74	0.51	0.58	0.69	0.55
0.50	0.55	0.56	0.49	0.65	0.51	0.62	0.67	0.48	0.48
0.60	0.63	0.61	0.64	0.58	0.60	0.73	0.95	0.69	0.52
0.78	0.70	0.54	0.58	0.65	0.51	0.72	0.63	0.54	0.45
0.42	0.47	0.55	0.65	0.56	0.74	0.54	0.66	0.58	0.70
0.59	0.57	0.49	0.63	0.66	0.46	0.57	0.88	0.61	0.46
0.47	0.62	0.55	0.66	0.51	0.53	0.52	0.59	0.53	0.56
0.70	0.47	0.68	0.57	0.54	0.67	0.48	0.57	0.68	0.58
0.63	0.72	0.62	0.39	0.63	0.67	0.57	0.68	0.61	0.52

the scale of measurement may be divided (see Table 11.3). Such class intervals may be chosen quite arbitrarily so long as (1) the number of intervals is sufficiently large to permit one to see the general distribution of the measurements, and (2) all the class intervals are equal in extent from the beginning of one interval to the beginning of the next; that is, as shown in Table 11.3 each interval spans 0.03 second. Usually 15 to 20 intervals is a good number to take. In this case, exactly 20 class intervals covered the distance from 0.36 to 0.95. These are shown under the column marked "class limits, seconds" in Table 11.3.

The second step in constructing a frequency distribution is to tabulate or count the number of cases falling into each of the class intervals. This may be done, as illustrated in Table 11.3, by making a tally alongside each class interval for each score falling within that interval. The result is a *frequency distribution*. It is so called because it gives the frequency or count of measurements in each interval and shows how the frequencies are distributed along the scale of measurement, which in this case is a time scale. Once the counts have

TABLE 11.3 *Frequency distribution of the data in Table 11.2. A large number of scores may be summarized by grouping them into classes, then counting the frequency (f) of scores falling in each class.*

CLASS LIMITS, SECONDS	TALLIES	FREQUENCY (f) [NUMBER OF MEN]
0.93–0.95	I	1
0.90–0.92	I	1
0.87–0.89	I	1
0.84–0.86	I	1
0.81–0.83	II	2
0.78–0.80	II	2
0.75–0.77	JHT	5
0.72–0.74	JHT JHT III	13
0.69–0.71	JHT JHT I	11
0.66–0.68	JHT JHT JHT IIII	19
0.63–0.65	JHT JHT JHT JHT I	21
0.60–0.62	etc.	25
0.57–0.59		24
0.54–0.56		22
0.51–0.53		16
0.48–0.50		13
0.45–0.47		11
0.42–0.44		6
0.39–0.41		5
0.36–0.38		1

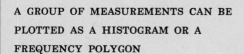

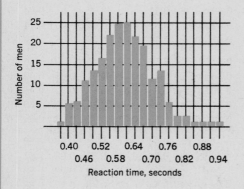

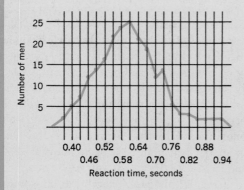

FIGURE 11.4. *A histogram (top) and a frequency polygon (bottom) of the data in Tables 11.2 and 11.3.*

been made, they can be represented graphically in a histogram (see Figure 11.4).

As far as the information shown is concerned, a frequency distribution both loses something and gains something: (1) It loses the identity of each individual measurement. We cannot identify from the distribution the score of the twenty-seventh man who took this test. A particular score, however, may always be recovered from our original record of measurements. (2) It also loses the precise value of any individual measurement. We cannot, for example, specify exactly the five measurements falling in the seventh class interval. Such specific knowledge is seldom of any consequence, however, for the class interval is precise enough for most practical purposes.

The frequency distribution gains for us much more than it loses. It so organizes the information in the measurements that we can immediately grasp important features. We can see, for example, that more scores fall within the interval from 0.60 to 0.62 second than in any other interval, and that with only scattered exceptions, the scores fall between 0.39 and 0.83. Then, by doing a little counting, we can see that nearly half the men (46 per cent) had scores between 0.54 and 0.65. Thus the construction of a frequency distribution has helped us to appreciate quickly the general nature of our measurements.

In passing, we may note that a bar graph or histogram is not the only way to depict a frequency distribution. A simpler way is to plot a point, instead of a bar, at the midpoint of each class interval for the frequency of measurements in the class; then each of these points is connected by a line. The graph which results is called a *frequency polygon* (see Figure 11.4), because it still depicts frequencies, but does so with a many-sided figure. The frequency polygon, then, gives exactly the same information as the bar graph or histogram; it simply uses a set of lines instead of bars.

The distribution of scores in most frequency distributions of psychological traits is such that most of the scores fall in the middle of the distribution; and fewer and fewer scores are found toward the high and low extremes of the distribution (see Figure 11.4). The distribution tends to be symmetrical also; about as many scores are found at the high end—called the "positive end"—as at the low—or "negative"—end. If for some reason scores tend to pile up at one end or the other of the distribution, it is called a *skewed distribution* (see Figure 11.5). Skews are termed *positive* or *negative* depending upon the direction of the longer "tail" of the distribution. Thus, if scores pile up at the low end of a frequency polygon, the tail is toward the high, or positive, end, and the distribution is said to be positively skewed. With an accumulation of scores at the high end, the frequency polygon is negatively skewed. Distributions are often skewed when a particular subsample of a larger population is tested. For instance, the frequency polygon for intelligence test scores from college students is negatively skewed.

NORMAL CURVE   All frequency polygons constructed from real measurements will show some unevenness. In general, the more measurements we take, the smoother the graph becomes because many of the irregularities are the result of chance variations in the population measured. It can be shown both mathematically and by experiments in probability that many frequency polygons eventually approach, as the number of measurements increases and as other conditions of measurements are controlled, a shape known as the *normal curve*. The outline of this curve is shown in Figure 11.6. It is no longer a polygon, but rather a smooth and symmetrical bell-shaped affair. This curve depicts exactly the same thing as the frequency polygon.

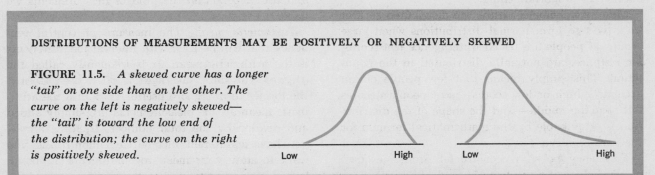

DISTRIBUTIONS OF MEASUREMENTS MAY BE POSITIVELY OR NEGATIVELY SKEWED

FIGURE 11.5.   *A skewed curve has a longer "tail" on one side than on the other. The curve on the left is negatively skewed— the "tail" is toward the low end of the distribution; the curve on the right is positively skewed.*

Low   High   Low   High

FREQUENCY DISTRIBUTIONS OF PSYCHO-
LOGICAL MEASUREMENTS OFTEN
APPROXIMATE THE NORMAL
BELL-SHAPED CURVE

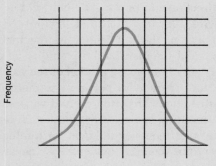

Scale of measurement

FIGURE 11.6. *An idealized frequency distribution known as the normal-probability curve. The height of the curve at any point represents the relative frequency of measurements having the particular value indicated on the horizontal axis.*

Any point along the curve represents the relative frequency of measurements occurring within an interval along the scale. Scale intervals are not depicted, for they are arbitrary; the exact frequencies are not given, because they depend on the number of measurements taken. The *shape* of the curve is the important thing.

Many psychological traits are distributed so that they tend to form normal distributions when large groups of people are tested. Intelligence test scores, for instance, are normally distributed in the population. This simply means that few people obtain extremely high or low scores—most people's scores fall near the middle—and the shape of the distribution is describable by the mathematical formula for the normal curve.

Frequency polygons constructed from measures of psychological traits usually tend to become more

and more like the normal curve as more and more measures are obtained. Since we thus know the shape that the distribution would have if all measurements could be made—for example, if all people could be tested—the normal curve provides a model distribution against which other distributions may be compared.

Measures of frequency distributions

In the preceding section, we described ways of organizing measurements into frequency distributions so that we can "get a good look at them." For some purposes, such as writing popular magazine articles or inspecting someone else's data, this may be enough. For other purposes, especially any sophisticated use of measurements, it is not. A more precise measure of the characteristics of the distribution is then needed. Such a measure, sometimes called a *statistic*, may be derived mathematically from the distribution and used to characterize it in an exact way. There are two general kinds of measures of frequency distributions: (1) measures of central tendency and (2) measures of variability.

MEASURES OF CENTRAL TENDENCY Measures of *central tendency*, sometimes called measures of central value, are numbers that fix the center of the distribution. The center, of course, must be a place on the scale, and hence is a measurement, not necessarily of any one individual, but at least of a hypothetical individual. To measure the center of the distribution, we must know how to define the center, and this depends on the kind of measurements we have.

Arithmetic mean. The measure of central tendency that can be used with interval measurements is the arithmetic mean. It is frequently called the *average,* but since "average" is often used loosely, the former term is more useful. To obtain the arithmetic mean all the measurements are simply added and divided by the total number. If, for example, you have a different income each month and you want to state your mean income over a 12-month period, you add the income received for each of the

12 months, divide by 12, and thus compute your average monthly income. In the same way, you can obtain the arithmetic mean of a group of interval measurements. For instance, the arithmetic mean of the reaction times in Table 11.2 is 0.60. This result can be obtained without making any use of the frequency distribution, but special formulas do exist for computing the arithmetic mean from such a distribution.

The arithmetic mean can be used meaningfully only with interval measurements because it gives every measurement in the distribution equal weight. Hence it implies that all magnitudes of the differences between measurements are to be trusted, and that is not the case for nominal or ordinal measurements. For these kinds of measurements, one of the following measures of central tendency must be used.

Median. The median, very simply, is the *middle score in a group of measurements* when they have been rank-ordered from largest to smallest. If the number of measurements is even, there is no one real middle measurement. In this case, the median is the average of the two middle measurements. The median of the reaction times in Table 11.2 also happens to be 0.60.

The median is the proper and ideal measure of central tendency for ordinal measurements because the middle score is the middle rank. It may also be used, if one wishes, with interval measurements. In fact, with data that are normally distributed, it makes little difference whether one uses the median or the mean. They are identical in the ideal normal curve. The median, on the other hand, is the preferred measure for skewed distributions because it is not influenced so much by extreme measurements.

Mode. The term mode means "most." As a measure of central tendency, it is the *most frequent score.* In a frequency distribution, it is the midpoint of the interval with the most cases in it. The mode is the only measure one can use with nominal measurements, for there is no proper way to calculate the mean or the median. The mode can be used with other kinds of measurement, if there is any point to it—that is, if one really wants to know

what the most frequent score is. Since, however, the mode can shift around quite a bit with chance differences in scores, especially when cases are few, the median or mean, whichever is appropriate, is almost always a better measure of central tendency. The mode of the data in Table 11.2 is 0.62; that in Table 11.3 is 0.61. In the ideal normal distribution, the mode will be exactly the same as the median or mean.

MEASURES OF VARIABILITY Measures of central tendency summarize only one feature of a distribution, namely, where its center is. Distributions also differ from one another in their variability—the spread of scores around the central point. In Figure 11.7 two hypothetical distributions are shown, one fat and the other slender. They both have the same means and medians; they are both based on the same number of measurements. To measure the

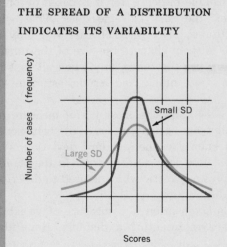

THE SPREAD OF A DISTRIBUTION
INDICATES ITS VARIABILITY

FIGURE 11.7. *Distributions differing in variability. Both distributions have the same central tendency, but one is narrow and the other is wide. Consequently they have different variability. Variability is measured by the standard deviation.*

difference between them, we need a measure of their relative "fatness" or "leanness." Though hypothetical, they depict situations often encountered. Waitresses, for example, have about the same mean intelligence as the general population; yet the general population includes more highly intelligent persons and more mentally retarded persons than does a representative sampling of waitresses. Students in one school may, on the average, have the same aptitude as those in another, but there may be more students with both higher aptitude and lower aptitude in the second school. In each case, the means are the same, but the *variability* of the measurements is different. Hence we need measures of variability.

Range. Of the several possible measures we might use, the simplest, but not the best, is the range. This is the difference between the highest and lowest scores. For ordinal measurements, the range is of little value since differences in scores do not of themselves mean anything; only ranks are important. For interval measurements, the range is a very crude and unstable measure, for it is based on only two measures, the very extreme ones. These, in most distributions, are rather erratic, and only a small change in them changes the size of the range. So statisticians use the range only when all that is needed is a very quick and crude estimate of variability.

Standard deviation. The most useful measure of variability, the one generally used by behavioral scientists, is known as the standard deviation. We shall use the abbreviation SD to refer to the standard deviation as a statistic which is used to describe an obtained distribution.[1]

The standard deviation is a measure of variability—a number representing a distance along the

[1] In some books the standard deviation is symbolized by the small Greek letter sigma (σ); in others, a capital S is used [McNemar, 1962]. If you look at other books on statistics, you may also see s used for another type of standard deviation which is calculated and interpreted differently. Sigma (σ) may also be used for a standard deviation which is not a descriptive statistic— that is, one used to characterize, or describe, an obtained frequency distribution.

scale or baseline of a frequency distribution. This number is proportional to the spread of the distribution—the greater the spread, the larger the standard deviation; the less the spread, the smaller the standard deviation.

In order to understand the standard deviation, suppose we first discuss another measure of variability—the average deviation. The average deviation is based on the mean of the differences (deviations) between each score and the arithmetic mean of the distribution. For instance, in Table 11.2 the first score is 0.65 and the mean is 0.60. The absolute deviation, the number of units of deviation regardless of direction of the deviation, of this first score is 0.05. If we find these absolute deviations for each individual's score in Table 11.2, we will have 200 absolute differences. We next add these absolute deviations and divide by their number (200) to find the mean or average deviation.

It should be clear that the value of the average deviation will depend upon the variability of the distribution. For instance, extreme scores in the distribution will produce large absolute deviations and a larger average deviation; little spread around the arithmetic mean of the distribution will result in small absolute deviations and a small average deviation.

The step from the average deviation to the standard deviation is a short one, and the standard deviation may be thought of and interpreted as a special kind of average deviation. To compute a standard deviation, one squares each of the deviations, adds these squared deviations, divides by the number of deviations, and finally takes the square root of the resulting number. The standard deviation is thus the root-mean-square of the deviations of measurements from their arithmetic mean. The standard deviation of the distribution of the reaction times in Table 11.2 is 0.10. A more precise algebraic definition, as well as more on the procedure for calculating the SD, is given in the last section of this chapter. Here we stress some of its properties and uses.

The reason for performing additional operations on the average deviation to get the standard deviation is that this latter statistic has important mathematical properties in normal curves. The SD is such a good measure of variability that, if the frequency distribution is reasonably normal, the distribution can be reconstructed by knowing only two numbers, the mean and the SD. This is true because mathematicians have a precise formula for the normal curve, and the only two unknowns in it are the mean and the SD. Given these, one can draw the normal curve that best fits a particular frequency distribution. Thus, insofar as a distribution is normal, the mean and the SD completely describe and specify it.

This mathematical nicety has important uses. In the normal-probability curve, the SD can be used as a measuring rod to lay off distances along the scale of the distribution. The exact number of cases (the frequencies) that will be included in any given number of standard deviations is known from tables that have been constructed from the formula for the normal curve. The information supplied by the tables is summarized in Figure 11.8. It shows that 68.3 per cent of the cases in a normal frequency distribution lie between 1 SD above and 1 SD below the mean. About 95 per cent lie in the range between 2 SD above and 2 SD below the mean. And 99.7 per cent fall between 3 SD above and 3 SD below the mean. It is possible to determine from the tables the percentage of cases to be expected between any other two measurements given in terms of standard deviation units along the scale.

STANDARD SCORES   One other use of the standard deviation merits special attention. It may be employed to state individual measurements in a "universal language." All that is necessary for this is that a particular score be expressed in standard deviation units. Scores expressed in terms of standard deviation units are called *standard scores;* the basic standard score is called the *z* score. In order to compute a *z* score, we take the difference between a particular score and the arithmetic mean of the distribution and then divide this difference by the standard deviation of the distribution. The follow-

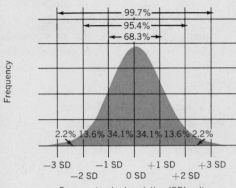

GIVEN THE MEAN AND STANDARD DEVIATION, THE COMPLETE DISTRIBUTION OF SCORES IN A NORMAL DISTRIBUTION CAN BE KNOWN

FIGURE 11.8. *The distribution of scores in a normal curve. Since the normal curve has a known shape, it is possible to state the percentage of scores that lie between +1 and −1 standard deviation, or between any other two points expressed in SD units. This normal curve might represent the distribution of IQ scores in the United States; in this case, the mean would be 100 and the standard deviation would be approximately 15.*

ing is a formula for the computation of *z* scores:

$$z \text{ score} = \frac{\text{score} - \text{arithmetic mean}}{\text{standard deviation}}$$

The principle involved in this conversion of a score into standard deviation units is illustrated in Figure 11.13 (see page 405). The distribution in this figure has an arithmetic mean of 45 and a standard deviation of 11. A score of 56, for instance, is 11 units above the mean and corresponds to a *z* score of +1; a score of 34 is 11 units below the mean and corresponds to a *z* score of −1. Similarly, any other score may be converted into a *z* score.

Other standard scores may be formed from the basic z score. Since half the z scores will be negative in a normal distribution, we may add a constant to the z scores to get rid of these. For convenience, we may also multiply the z score by a constant. The addition of 50 and multiplication of the z score by 10 is a common practice. When this is done to the scores of a normal distribution, the new standard scores are called T scores.[2] The correspondence between z scores and T scores in a normal distribution is as follows:

z SCORE	T SCORE
−3	20
−2	30
−1	40
0	50
+1	60
+2	70
+3	80

Both kinds of scores constitute a sort of universal language for expressing scores because they fall at the same place in all reasonably normal distributions, irrespective of the particular scale on which the measurements were made. From them we can quickly see where the individual stands in the distribution and can compare two or more measurements for one individual drawn from distributions having different means and different standard deviations. In other words, we can see how many standard deviation units above or below the mean a person's score falls in each of several distributions.

As an example, suppose you have taken some tests and have obtained the following raw scores: 71 on a test of mechanical aptitude, 98 on a test of artistic ability, and 23 on a test of anxiety. By themselves, these scores tell us nothing; we need to know your relative standing on each of these tests, and standard scores will help us make comparisons between the tests. Suppose, when we compare each of these scores with the data from normative groups (see Chapter 12), the mechanical apti-

tude score of 71 corresponds here to a z score of +2.0, the artistic ability test score of 98 to a z score of −1.5, and the anxiety test score of 23 to a z score of +0.2. In the light of these z scores it is apparent that you fall at the high end of the distribution in mechanical aptitude, at the low end in artistic ability, and at about the average anxiety level. It would have been impossible to make these comparisons from the raw scores alone.

CENTILE SCORES   Comparisons among individuals and tests may also be made by means of centile scores. A *centile score* is the percentage of scores falling at or below a particular person's score in the distribution. Put another way, it is a person's rank in 100, obtained by dividing his rank by the total number of measurements in the distribution, and multiplying by 100.

A centile score (sometimes called the percentile score) has several uses. If distributions are badly skewed or there is no justification for assuming that they are distributions of interval measurements, then a centile score is a better way of indicating a person's standing in the distribution than a z score. At other times, one may have to present a score to people who do not understand the standard score or standard deviation and who do not have the time or willingness to learn. In such cases, it is better to use the centile score, since in a normal distribution one is easily converted into the other (see Figure 11.9). Notice, incidentally, that the median (z score = 0) is the 50th centile score, the −1 SD point the 16th centile, the +1 SD point the 84th centile, and so on.

We shall not describe in detail the measures of variability that are appropriate for ordinal measurements, because such measures are seldom used. The easiest way to indicate the variability of ordinal measurements, or of distributions of interval scores that are not symmetrical, is to state the 25th, 50th (median), and 75th percentile points. The greater the skewness of the distribution, the greater the difference between the 25th and 50th centiles and the 50th and 75th centiles. In a normal distribution, these differences are equal.

[2] These should not be confused with T-scale scores which are used to normalize skewed distributions.

Correlation

Up until now we have been concerned with the statistical treatment of frequency distributions considered one at a time. Now we come to the topic of *correlation*. This almost defines itself if spelled "co-relation," for it refers to the "co-relation" between two or more distributions of measurements. In one way or another, most of science is concerned with co-relations. In physical science, however, these are usually called "functions"; the behavior of one variable, that is, one set of measurements, is related to the behavior of another variable, that is, of another set of measurements. Usually, the relationship is precise enough to permit the drawing of a line through or near all the points joining the two variables and even to summarize the relationship neatly in a mathematical formula.

Psychology sometimes has this precision too. Examples of it are to be found here and there throughout this book, particularly in the chapters on the senses. More often, however, we are unable to define a function. Our job is, then, to determine whether or not there is a correlation between two variables, and if so, how much of a correlation there is.

To make clear what it is we are trying to do in the statistics of correlation, let us take a common example of heights and weights. We know from casual observation that people differ a lot in both weight and height. If we wish, we can take any particular group of people and find their average heights and average weights. We can also measure the variability of their heights and the variability of their weights. But we know also that there must be a relationship, or correlation, between height and weight. In general, people who are tall weigh more than those who are short. Obviously, however, the correlation is not perfect, for some people only 5 feet tall weigh more than some who are 6 feet tall. So the correlation is one of degree—a statistical matter—and we therefore need a measure that expresses that degree.

For mathematical convenience, the degree of a correlation is expressed by a number between 0.00 and 1.00. Zero represents no correlation at all; 1.00

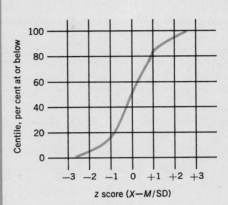

FIGURE 11.9. *The relationship of z scores and centile scores in a normal distribution. From the curve above, or from a table of the normal probability curve, one can determine the percentage of cases falling at or below any particular z score. This percentage is often called the centile score.*

represents a perfect correlation—one comparable to the very precise functions often encountered in the physical sciences.

It is possible to obtain a measure of correlation for any two sets of measurements of the same kind, whether they are two nominal, ordinal, or interval sets. It is also possible to obtain such a measure with any combination of sets, for instance, one nominal and the other interval, and so on. Each combination requires its own particular formula for calculating the answer, however. For simplicity, we shall discuss only the pure cases of nominal-nominal, ordinal-ordinal, and interval-interval.

CONTINGENCY When the measurements being correlated are all in the nominal class, one measure of correlation that may be used is the *coefficient of contingency*. To illustrate this, we shall take an

TABLE 11.4   *The curriculum taken by high school students of different social classes in one town.*

| | SOCIAL CLASS | | | | |
CURRICULUM	I–II	III	IV	V	TOTAL
College preparatory	23	40	16	2	81
General	11	75	107	14	207
Commercial	1	31	60	10	102
Total	35	146	183	26	390

SOURCE: From Siegel, 1956; after Hollingshead, 1949.

example from a study of social classes [Siegel, 1956].

Of all the families in a community called Elmtown, 360 having children in high school were classified into one of five social classes. Various criteria were employed in the classification. There were too few families in each of the two upper classes (I and II) for statistical purposes; so these were lumped together, leaving only four categories of social class. Each child in high school was enrolled in one of three designated courses: college preparatory, general, or commercial. To obtain a correlation, counts were made of each child according to his social class and his high school course. Since there were four social classes and three high school curricula, 12 combinations were possible.

Table 11.4 shows the number (frequency) of individuals in each combination—statisticians call them "cells." It is clear from the table that there is some correlation between social class and type of high school course. The overwhelming proportion of those in the college-preparatory curriculum came from classes I-II and III, and the great majority of those in classes III, IV, and V were not in college preparatory. The greatest proportion of those in the commercial curriculum were in classes III and IV. Computation of one particular index of correlation, the coefficient of contingency, gave a value of .39, a number which expresses the degree of correlation.

The contingency method of measuring correlation, then, makes use of data in nominal categories. A formula for the computation of contingency coefficients is given in the last section of this chapter.

RANK-DIFFERENCE CORRELATION   Where ordinal measurements are the data for determining a correlation, the procedure is different. In this case, a formula has been devised that makes use of the differences in ranks on the two sets of measurements. An example is given in Table 11.5 and Figure 11.10 and may be described as follows [Guilford, 1956]:

Fifteen individuals were shown at different times a series of 15 cartoons and a series of 15 limericks. When shown a cartoon, the subject was asked to rate its humor on a 5-point scale, giving 5 for "very humorous" and 1 for "not funny at all." He did the same thing for the limericks. When all the responses had been recorded, the points given by each individual on cartoons were added up to find a "cartoon score." Similarly each individual received a "limerick score." The question was, How well did these scores correlate? Or what was the relationship between seeing humor in cartoons and seeing it in limericks? Since there was no reason to believe these scores met the criteria of interval measurements, the scores were transmuted to ranks. The subject scoring highest received a rank of 1,

TABLE 11.5   *Humor scores on a cartoon test and a limerick test for 15 individuals. At the right are the rank orders of these two sets of scores.*

INDI-VIDUAL	CARTOON SCORE	LIMERICK SCORE	CARTOON RANK	LIMERICK RANK	D (PAGE 410)
A	47	75	11	8	3
B	71	79	4	6	2
C	52	85	9	5	4
D	48	50	10	14	4
E	35	49	14.5	15	0.5
F	35	59	14.5	12	2.5
G	41	75	12.5	8	4.5
H	82	91	1	3	2
I	72	102	3	1	2
J	56	87	7	4	3
K	59	70	6	10	4
L	73	92	2	2	0
M	60	54	5	13	8
N	55	75	8	8	0
O	41	68	12.5	11	1.5

SOURCE: After Guilford, 1956.

the one scoring next highest a rank of 2, and so on down through 15. Each individual's rank on the other set of scores was determined in the same way. Then the correlation coefficient, known as *rho,* was computed from the differences in ranks. It was found to be .70, which is fairly high as correlations on psychological measurements go.

One can see in Figure 11.10 that the correlation is reasonably good. Although there are some inversions, those who ranked high on one index of humor tended also to rank high on the other measurement. The conclusion is that people show some consistency in how funny they find things in two different situations, cartoons and limericks. Although not earthshaking, the experiment was of some value in research on the development of tests of humor.

The way, then, to measure the correlation between two sets of ordinal measurements is to run a rank-difference correlation, a procedure devised to make use of the ranking afforded by ordinal measurements. A formula for computing rho, the rank-difference correlation, is given on page 410.

PRODUCT-MOMENT CORRELATION COEFFICIENT For measurements made on an interval scale, another method of computation is used. In this case, the index of correlation is called the *product-moment correlation coefficient.* Its symbol is *r,* sometimes called *Pearson's r* after the English statistical psychologist who devised it. An illustration of data yielding a high product-moment correlation is given in Figure 11.11.

This example is drawn from the field of intelligence testing [Terman and Merrill, 1937]. The 1937 Stanford-Binet test of intelligence has two forms: Form L and Form M. A group of children was given the two forms of this test on two different occasions. Hence, two scores or measurements of intelligence were available for each child. These scores were plotted on the graph in Figure 11.11 by letting each point represent a pair of scores. They are all plotted in class intervals, just as were the data for reaction time in Figure 11.4. Here, with the two scales, one for Form L and the other for Form M, at right angles to each other, the two sets of class intervals form boxes or cells. A child scoring

87 on Form L and 90 on Form M has a single point entered in the cell made by the intersection of the class interval 85–89 on Form L and the class interval 90–94 on Form M. This procedure continues until all pairs of scores are plotted.

The Stanford-Binet test was so constructed that the same person would, ideally, make the same score on each form. If it turned out this way, the correlation between the two forms would be perfect and the correlation coefficient would be 1.00. Moreover, on the diagram one would see a perfectly straight line running from the lower left-hand corner toward the upper right-hand corner. In Figure 11.11, the scores

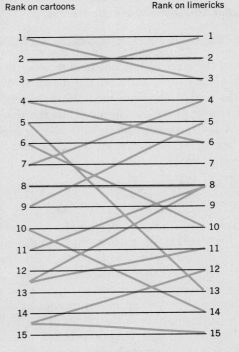

A RANK-DIFFERENCE CORRELATION CAN BE DEPICTED THUS

Rank on cartoons   Rank on limericks

FIGURE 11.10. *Each line connects the two scores made by one individual. (Data from Table 11.5.)*

THE SCATTERGRAM, IN WHICH EACH PERSON'S
SCORE ON TWO TESTS IS PLOTTED AS A
SINGLE POINT, IS ONE WAY OF PRESENTING
A CORRELATION VISUALLY

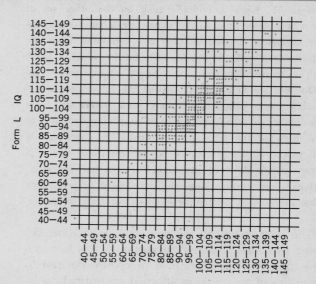

FIGURE 11.11. *A scattergram of IQs obtained on
Forms L and M of the 1937 Stanford-Binet
Intelligence Scale. A high degree of correlation
exists between scores on the two tests—children
scoring high on Form L also score high on Form M;
those scoring low on Form L also score low on
Form M. High correlations between equivalent
forms of a test indicate that the reliability of the test
is high. (After Terman and Merrill, 1937.)*

fall around the straight line but tend to stray in one
direction or another a little off the diagonal. What
this means is that a person tends to make slightly
different scores on the two forms. Thus the correlation is not quite perfect, but is, in fact, very high—
actually about .90. Formulas for the computation of
r, the product-moment correlation are given in the
last section of this chapter.

Plots such as the one shown in Figure 11.11 are
called *scatter diagrams* or *scattergrams.* They provide a visual picture of the degree of a correlation,
because the amount of scatter, and its direction,
varies with the correlation. This point is illustrated
in Figure 11.12. When a correlation is zero, the
points on the scatter diagram are randomly distributed and do not line up in any particular direction. More points appear in the center of the scatter
than around its fringes simply because measurements of each of the contributing frequency distributions pile up more in the center than on the
"tails." If the correlation is moderate, say .50, the
scatter narrows in one direction or another, and as

indicated earlier, the scatter diagram of a perfect
correlation of 1.00 is a straight line.

Another way to say this is to describe the shape
of the scatter diagram. It is circular when the correlation is zero. It becomes more and more elliptical
as the correlation increases and narrows down to a
straight line when the correlation is perfect.

Note, too, in Figure 11.12, that the direction of
the ellipse or line of the scatter diagram indicates
the sign of the correlation, that is, whether it is
positive or negative. Assuming that the scales of the
diagram have been arranged in the conventional
way, so that high scores are at the top of the vertical scale and on the right of the horizontal scale,
positive (+) correlations are indicated by a direction from the lower left-hand corner to the upper
right-hand corner. Negative correlations (−) are
indicated by ellipses or lines running from the upper
left-hand corner to the lower right-hand corner.

All degrees of negative correlation from 0.00 to
−1.00 can occur, just as degrees of positive correlation can run from 0.00 to +1.00. Minus signs and

plus signs in front of a correlation coefficient of a particular size represent equally close relationships. It is the number, not the sign, which indicates the degree of correlation. The sign merely tells us the direction of the relationship. In negative correlations, high scores on one measure are associated with low scores on the other measure, and low scores with high scores. In positive correlations, high scores on one measure are associated with high scores on the other measure, and low scores with low scores.

CAUSATION AND CORRELATION It is easy to think that a high correlation between two sets of measurements means that one of the factors measured causes the other. This, however, is usually not so. When there is a high correlation, both sets of individual differences are usually caused by some common factors. In the case of height and weight, for example, we cannot say that a person's height causes his weight, for both height and weight are caused by individual differences in genetic inheritance, nutrition, and disease. A correlation, in short, simply tells us that individual differences in two sets of measurements tend to vary together, not necessarily that one causes the other.

The need for care in the interpretation of correlation coefficients is amply shown by the following examples:

There is reported to be a positive correlation between the number of storks' nests and the number of births in northwestern Europe. Only the most romantic would contend that this indicates that the stork legend is true. A more prosaic interpretation is this: as population and hence the number of buildings increases, the number of places for storks to nest increases.

During the Italian campaign of World War II, it was found that there was a positive correlation between the number of propaganda leaflets dropped on the Germans and the amount of territory captured from them. While this is consistent with the hypothesis that the leaflets were effective, it is also consistent with other hypotheses, for example, that leaflets were dropped when major offensives were about to begin. [Wallis and Roberts, 1956, page 79.]

This is not to say that we never can tell anything about causation from correlation. We can. To decide what causes what, however, requires a great number of correlations and a careful logical analysis of which variables may be the basic ones.

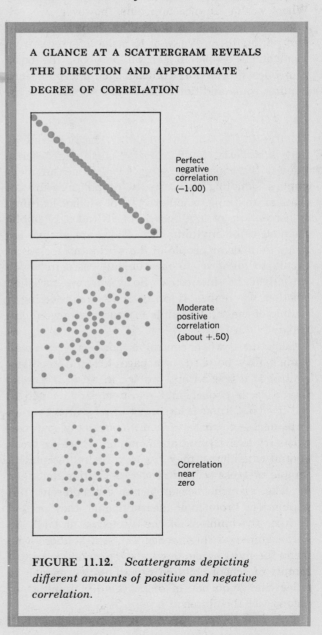

A GLANCE AT A SCATTERGRAM REVEALS THE DIRECTION AND APPROXIMATE DEGREE OF CORRELATION

Perfect negative correlation (−1.00)

Moderate positive correlation (about +.50)

Correlation near zero

FIGURE 11.12. *Scattergrams depicting different amounts of positive and negative correlation.*

Sampling

The measures we have just described may be called *descriptive statistics* because they describe accurately the characteristics of a set of measurements. When we make measurements, however, we are interested not only in describing them but also in *interpreting* them. We want to make inferences from them about people in general or about the basic principles of behavior. To make such interpretations requires some additional statistics—*sampling statistics.*

REPRESENTATIVE SAMPLING The first concept that is essential to interpreting statistical descriptions is the concept of *sampling*. All measurement implies sampling. We usually cannot measure all cases of anything, whether it be of animal learning, of perception, of intelligence, of attitudes, of public opinion, or of anything else. There are always too many animals or people in the world and too many events to allow us to measure all cases in which we might be interested. So when we measure, whether we realize it or not, we are selecting a sample of the total possible measurements we might make.

Sometimes, when control is good, a very small sample may be used (see page 402). More often, control is less good and we try to select a sample that is large enough and representative enough to tell us about a much larger set of measurements we were unable to make. When, for example, psychologists try to measure public opinion regarding presidential candidates, they try to get a representative sample or cross section of the population and then to take enough measurements to represent this population. From their measurements, they predict or infer the opinions of the electorate at large. In our example of intelligence-test scores, those who made the measurements were interested in getting a sample of school children representative enough to reflect the frequency of distribution of intelligence among school children at large.

Biases of samples. It is not always an easy task to get representative samples. In fact, the most frequent fault with a set of measurements is that it is not representative and that we therefore cannot properly make the inferences from it that we would like. We run into this difficulty because so many "biasing" factors are always at work. It may happen that, because of factors we are not aware of, the school children in one geographical area seem to be brighter or duller than school children in general. If we try to sample political opinion by calling people on the telephone, it may happen that people who own telephones are more often of one political opinion than another. If, as many psychologists are forced to do, we use college students for a set of measurements, it may be that they are not representative of the population in general. So various kinds of biases make it difficult to get a representative sample.

Methods of sampling. We have developed a number of different methods to try to ensure representative sampling, and some of these methods are described in detail in Chapter 17. In general, they take two different forms. One we may call *random sampling.* We use this when we know little or nothing about biasing factors in our measurement. To sample randomly, we try to see that only chance determines what is included in our sample. In making surveys of radio listening, for example, we may select every two-hundredth name in the telephone directory. Or, to measure intelligence, we may draw at random 2 out of every 100 names of children in each of the schools of a state. Or to study learning in rats, we select 1 out of every 10 rats in the laboratory.

The other general method of obtaining a representative sample is to do *controlled sampling*. In this case we select certain factors, such as age, sex, economic status, educational level, or type of employment, and deliberately balance these factors in making up our sample. In sampling public opinion, for example, we may try to see that people are selected from small towns and large towns, from poor people and rich people, from the West and East, from labor and from management—all in proportion to their numbers in the population at large. This kind of sampling, if it is done correctly, makes reasonably certain that biasing factors are controlled. Thus controlled sampling is the most economical sampling method because it is usually possible to make correct inferences from a smaller number of cases selected by controlled sampling than by random sampling.

SAMPLING ERROR   Even when we have done our best to obtain a representative sample, we are still left with a *sampling error*. This, as its name implies, is an error due to the fact that we have measurements from only a sample of a population rather than measurements from an entire population. The error is due to chance differences in the selection of individuals from the total population. When our sample is relatively small, the error tends to be relatively large; as the sample size increases in proportion to the population, the error decreases. As a rough general rule, the sampling error is inversely proportional to the square root of the number of measurements. In other words, the error of sampling 10 cases is about ten times as large as the error of sampling 1,000 cases.

The mean, median, standard deviation, indices of correlation, and other measures we have described always have some error, depending on the size of the sample used. By error, we mean that the measure differs somewhat from the value we would get if we had the "true" measure of the population sampled. This fact is easy to demonstrate in practice by taking more than one sample of measurements. If, in our example of measuring braking reaction time, we had taken a second set of 200 measurements on different people, the two frequency distributions would have been somewhat different. Hence their means and standard deviations would also have been different.

Mathematicians have worked out formulas for establishing sampling errors. A formula for the sampling error of the mean is given on page 410. By using these formulas, we obtain numbers indicating the amount by which different samples might be expected to differ simply by chance. Whether or not we know and use such formulas, however, it must always be kept in mind that any measure we use

has an error. This means that if we made the measurements over again on a new sample, each measure would have a slightly different value. That is why we should never put very much stock in small differences in means, percentages, or other measures of a distribution.

STATISTICAL DECISIONS   This brings us to statistical decisions and the concept of *significance*. If we are comparing two groups of measurements in an experiment, we will almost always obtain a difference between their means. Similarly, in correlating any two sets of measurements, we seldom get a correlation of zero. The question is, When is a difference or a correlation significant? By this we mean, When is the difference from zero greater than we would expect by chance?

This question must always be answered in terms of probabilities. There are no absolute certainties in statistics. If, for example, we flip 10 pennies and get 10 heads, we may ask whether this result can be expected by chance or whether it means that the coins are biased. From tables of probability, we know that 10 heads on 10 flips can be expected once in every 1,024 times, 20 heads in 20 flips once in about a million times. This may be very unlikely, but if we flip pennies several million times, we can expect this sequence to occur some time by chance. So the question of whether something is significantly different from chance must be answered in terms of chance.

In practice, we arbitrarily select two different levels of significance. One is a loose criterion of $P = 0.05$; another is a stricter criterion of $P = 0.01$, P meaning the probability, expressed as a number between 0.00 and 1.00, that a result occurs by chance. These probability values may help us to make decisions about the outcome of an experiment. Suppose we make observations and we find that there is a difference between the means of the control and experimental groups. How do we interpret this difference? For instance, in making observations of children from culturally impoverished homes, we might obtain a mean score of 150 (a score, not an IQ) on a test of general intelligence.

A matched control group of children from homes which were not culturally impoverished might obtain a mean score of 200. Is this difference between means of 200 and 150 a real one? Or is it simply the result of chance variation in the samples of children we have chosen for our groups?

We can answer these questions by the use of techniques which help us to interpret the difference which was obtained. When these techniques are applied to this example we might, depending upon the size of the samples and the variability of scores within each sample, obtain a P value of 0.01. This would mean that there was 1 chance out of every 100 that the difference between the means of 200 and 150 was due to chance alone. Looked at from the other side, we can be rather certain that a real difference does exist between the intelligence test scores of children from the two types of homes.

What if the P value had been 0.05? Here there is 1 chance in 20 that the difference between means is due to chance, and we face a difficult decision. Our strategy will be dictated by the immediate importance of being right or wrong. If it is important that we know here and now whether or not there is a real difference between the two types of homes, we would probably repeat the observation with better control; we would hope to bring out the difference more clearly. If the cost of being wrong is not very great, we would probably accept the 1 out of 20 chance of being wrong. Then we would proceed to other experiments as if there were a real difference between the two groups. If the obtained difference were really due to chance, that is, if it were that 1 time out of 20, we would probably find it out in the course of future experiments. In the meantime, nothing much has been lost. Finally, if the probability of the difference being due to chance is greater than 1 out of 20, say 0.10 or 1 out of 10, we would most likely decide that the difference is really a chance one. However, good experimenters will still worry about the differences, and they may try to refine their controls in further experiments so that any real differences will come out clearly. We can never be sure from probability figures that there is no difference; we can say only that we have

not been able to demonstrate beyond a reasonable doubt that there is a difference.

Thus the purpose of these techniques is not to substitute for judgment, but to aid the experimenter in planning his strategy for future research. They aid in the interpretation of results by allowing the experimenter to make inferences about the state of affairs in a large population from small samples from that population. For this reason, these methods are termed *inferential techniques;* the statistics, such as the standard error of the mean, used in the application of these techniques, are termed *inferential statistics.*

Differences which might look large to the unsophisticated may not be statistically significant. A difference of 5 IQ points, or a difference of 20 percentage points, for instance, may fall far short of statistical significance. A correlation of .25, although it seems large, is unlikely to be significantly different from zero. Not much importance will be attached to these results by the statistically sophisticated person. Most of the results reported in this book, when evaluated statistically, were significant at the .01 level or better.

NONSTATISTICAL DECISIONS   Sometimes, when the experimental control is very tight, we may make inferences about populations and the effects of variables from quite small samples. Animal experiments in Skinner boxes are often done under such strictly controlled conditions that statistical analysis is not necessary (see Chapters 1 and 3). Suppose we have established a very stable baseline of responding and we give the animal a drug which changes the rate of responding. Eventually the effect of the drug will wear off and the rate of responding will return to its initial level. We give the drug again with the same effect as before; the drug effect wears off and we give it again with the same effect. We may repeat this over and over again with the same result each time. Just to make sure, we might try the drug on another animal. Suppose we obtain the same regular and reliable results with this second animal. We can then, without any statistical manipulation, be rather certain that the drug has a particular effect upon the rate of responding. The reliability, regularity, and lack of variability in the results allow us to reach this conclusion with only a few experimental subjects. The essence of this approach to experimentation is very strict control and lack of variability in the behavior resulting from the experimental manipulations. Unfortunately, such control is impossible in most psychological investigations.

Characteristics of "good" psychological tests

If we wish to measure the dimensions of a room or how much weight we have gained, we are accustomed to look for whatever ruler, scales, or appropriate measuring device is handy and to make our measurements without more ado. We do not ask any questions about the instrument; we assume that it is all right. Unfortunately, this attitude tends to carry over into things psychological. The public has heard a great deal in recent years about psychological tests and is inclined to "run to the nearest test" for the measurement of intelligence, personality, vocational aptitude, or what have you. Such an attitude has been cultivated by the unwarranted use of tests of unknown value in popular periodicals.

Tests of any kind, psychological or physical, must be used intelligently. They are invented to do a particular job. Some succeed in doing it; some do not. Even tape measures and bathroom scales often prove unreliable. In more sophisticated measurement, many tests prove to be worthless. Others are exceedingly valuable, but only when they satisfy certain requirements and are used for the purposes for which they were intended. This is especially true of psychological tests. For that reason, it is worthwhile knowing just what the characteristics of a good test are.

RELIABILITY A good test, first of all, must be *reliable*. It must, in other words, be consistent in the answers it gives. If you cannot measure some-

thing twice with it and get about the same answer each time, its measurements are not worth very much. This is quite aside from the problem of sampling error discussed above. In sampling, we measure two different things, or people, from the same population. The sampling error is due to chance differences in the things or people measured. Here we are talking about measuring the same thing, or person, twice and having the two measurements agree fairly well.

The concept of reliability can be illustrated by considering an example that, we hope, is quite unrealistic. A professor has given his class an examination, and now his somewhat odious task is to grade it. In this case he has no sampling problems because he has obtained papers from all members of the class. All he has to do is choose a measuring stick, that is, a method of scoring them. One possible method is to throw them down the stairs and, assigning a number to each step, grade each paper according to the step on which it falls. If he does this, he will obtain a frequency distribution for which a mean and a standard deviation can be calculated.

Two obvious faults are inherent in this method of grading: it is invalid, and it is unreliable. The method would be unreliable simply because it would not give the same answer twice. If the professor gathered up the papers and threw them down the stairs a second time, he would not get the same score for the same paper. Assuming that the papers landed randomly on the steps, the score a person got on the second grading would bear no relation to the score on the first grading.

The statistical method for inferring quite precisely the relative reliability or unreliability of a set of measurements is the correlational method which we have already described. By correlating one set of scores with another set obtained by the same method, we obtain a measure of the reliability of the measurements. Suppose we give the same psychological test to the same people at two different times which are far enough apart so that the people being tested do not remember specific questions from the test. If people get about the same score both times, the correlation will be high and positive, as it is in the case of intelligence tests. In such cases, we can assume that our measuring instrument is measuring something reliably. If results do not correlate well, our measurements are unreliable—we might as well be throwing papers down the stairs.

Reliability is a *sine qua non* of psychological measurement. If measurement is not reliable, it cannot be much of anything else. If, in other words, we cannot get the same set of scores, or almost the same set of scores, for people on two successive, independent measurements, we are not really measuring. Flipping pennies, rolling dice, or spinning roulette wheels would be just about as good. To put the matter another way, if a measuring instrument cannot be correlated rather well with itself, it is useless for making inferences about anything else.

VALIDITY   A good test or measurement must also be *valid*. It must correlate with something in addition to itself so that it is measuring something meaningful. In the simplest case, validity refers to how well a test measures what it is intended to measure. If we are trying to measure intelligence, our test should measure intelligence, not reaction time, cultural background, or something else. If it does not measure intelligence, we say that it is not a valid test of intelligence. More generally speaking, however, a test is valid to the extent that it correlates with something else. A test that correlates highly with reaction time would be a good test of reaction time, but if it does not correlate with intelligence, it is not a valid test of intelligence.

This problem of validity of measurement is a very serious one for psychologists. It is relatively easy, although not so easy as one might suppose, to devise measuring instruments that are reliable. It is much harder to devise valid measures. To determine the validity of measurements, once their reliability has been established, we must use the correlational method. In this case, however, we must have some standard, or *criterion*, against which the test may be correlated.

One of the major criteria of intelligence, for example, is ability to learn and to solve problems, or

to put it more generally, the ability to profit by education. The criterion, then, of an intelligence test *might* be success in school. To assess the validity of an intelligence test, we might therefore correlate a person's scores on intelligence tests with his educational progress—his grades or how far he has progressed for his age. If the correlation is high, we may say that the intelligence test is valid; if it is low, the test is not so valid.

To take another example, if our purpose is to select pilots, our criterion would be whether they succeed or fail in their training for flying. When we have tests that correlate well with such success or failure, we say they are valid. If they do not correlate with the criterion, no matter how reliable they may be—no matter how well they correlate with themselves—they are invalid.

Although other types of validity exist, validity typically is an index of the degree to which a test correlates with a criterion [Cronbach, 1960]. Usually the criterion is what we say we want to measure. Sometimes it turns out that a test is not valid for that, but is valid for some other criterion. To be valid, however, it must correlate with the criterion that it is used to measure. Hence it can be used properly to measure or predict only that criterion.

SAMPLING OF TASKS   Good tests are samples of the many tasks that go to make up the criterion. A lot of things, for example, go into intelligence. Hence many different measurements correlate with intelligence: speed in problem solving, ability to memorize, size of vocabulary, and so on. A test of any one of these things has validity as a test of intelligence. To stick to one of them, however, is to limit the validity to a very low level. The highest validity is obtained by having in the test a fair sample of all the behaviors involved in the criterion.

Ideally, then, to develop the most valid test, we should have to measure an almost infinite number of things. This, however, would be far too expensive and impractical to do, and after it was done, it would take so much time to give a test that we seldom would be able to administer it properly to those who should have it. In practice, then, we must

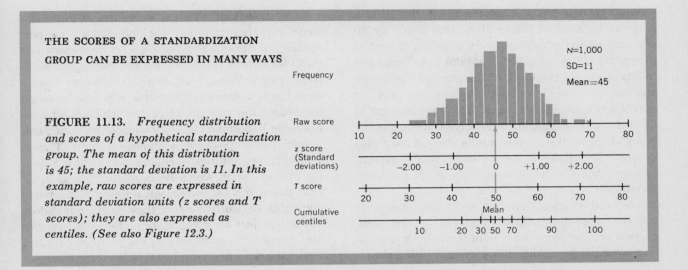

THE SCORES OF A STANDARDIZATION
GROUP CAN BE EXPRESSED IN MANY WAYS

FIGURE 11.13. *Frequency distribution
and scores of a hypothetical standardization
group. The mean of this distribution
is 45; the standard deviation is 11. In this
example, raw scores are expressed in
standard deviation units (z scores and T
scores); they are also expressed as
centiles. (See also Figure 12.3.)*

devise tests with a reasonable number of items, sometimes compromising the highest validity we might obtain ideally in order to have a usable test. Nevertheless, the good test—the valid test—is one that includes as fair a sample as possible of the tasks that make up the criterion.

STANDARDIZATION GROUP   Finally, a good test for general use as a measuring instrument should be based on a large and well-defined standardization group. The *standardization group* is a large and representative sample of people to whom the test has been given. The various scores made by people in this group are called *test norms*. For research purposes, standardization groups and norms may not be necessary, but for tests used in counseling, guidance, and making general predictions about people, they are essential.

The reason for having a standardization group and test norms is that in psychological measurement we are primarily interested in comparing people. We are interested in the differences between them or in their rank order (see the sections on interval and ordinal measurements). A psychological trait is not like pounds and inches; it is a relative thing. It does us no good to know that John completed 83 questions on an intelligence test un-

less we are also told that the average number completed by other people was 60 and that fewer than 10 per cent of them completed more than 83 questions. With this information, we have a rather good picture of how John rates in comparison with other people. Without it, we simply have a meaningless fact.

The test norms tell us what the average score is and also how much variability there is among scores. They allow us to compare a particular score with scores obtained by the standardization group. There are various ways of reporting such norms. It is often possible to convert from one way of reporting norms to another. This can be seen in Figures 11.13 and 12.3 (see page 425), which show the relationships among several different ways of reporting norms. Figure 11.13 gives a distribution of scores made by a standardization group on a hypothetical test of ability. The scores range from 25 to 70. Below the scores are three scales. One shows the scores corresponding to different standard deviation units above and below the mean. The next scale shows *T* scores. The last scale shows the percentage of persons scoring below any particular score.

To illustrate these scales, let us suppose that a person made a score of 59 on our hypothetical test. By consulting the test norms, we discover that his score is about 1.3 SD above the mean, that it is a score as high as, or higher than, that made by 90 per cent of the standardization group, and that it represents a *T* score of 63. Test norms are expressed in any, and sometimes all, of these ways. Age norms are usually given when the test is to be used for people of heterogeneous ages. They are omitted if the test is to be used for a relatively homogeneous group, for instance, young adults. Norms may also be given for grades in school, occupational groups, or any other classification of individuals that may be relevant.

One further point, however, is of importance. It concerns the standardization group. If our comparison of a person's score with test norms is to be fair, we must know the characteristics of the standardization group. Not any group will do. If John is ten years old and we give him an intelligence test, it is not fair to use test norms from a standardization group of adults. The group should be children of John's own age. If we give an intelligence test to a person who grew up on a farm in the South, it is not proper to use norms obtained from people living in Northern cities. So to interpret test results accurately, we must make sure that our test norms represent the kind of people with whom it is proper to compare a person's score.

One should also bear in mind that the standardization group should be reasonably large—at least several hundred and preferably a few thousand. If the group is too small, norms may be too high or too low just as a matter of chance in the selection of people for the group. Norms must also be obtained, and the tests must be given, under standard conditions. For example, instructions and time limits, if allowed to vary, may affect performance. Therefore, these aspects, and others, of test administration must be standardized.

FACTOR ANALYSIS In using tests for both practical and research purposes, we often raise the question, What does the test measure? The glib answer might be intelligence, personality, scholastic aptitude, or whatever the tester *thinks* it measures. The answer might be essentially correct if validity studies show that the test correlates highly with some accepted criterion for intelligence or personality, for example. Even so, such a question can mean something much deeper and more precise. It could mean, What psychological factor or factors does the test measure? Put this way, the question introduces the concept of *factor,* which is of considerable importance in psychological measurement.

Each person possesses a number of traits. That is to say, he has abilities, aptitudes, and ways of thinking and acting in which he is relatively consistent from day to day. A psychological test, if it is reliable and valid, measures some of these traits, but it does not tell us just what traits are being measured. We may guess at them by naming the particular traits a test appears to measure, but this is not a precise or scientific answer. Moreover, literally thousands of trait names are given in the dictionary, many of them so similar that we cannot easily distinguish one from another. As students of human behavior, we should like to know, not merely to guess at, the traits that are being measured by psychological tests.

A scientific approach to the problem has been devised; it is known as *factor analysis.* The details of this method are beyond the scope of this book, but the principle of it can be explained by considering a hypothetical example.

Suppose we administer six tests to a group of people. Let us call the tests A, B, C, D, E, and F. When the tests have been scored, we can calculate correlation coefficients between every possible pair of tests. There are 15 such pairs. To make the case extremely simple, let us assume that all correlations turn out to be either 1.00 or 0.00—something that would never happen in practice—and that they are as shown in this table.

TEST	A	B	C	D	E
B	1.00				
C	1.00	1.00			
D	.00	.00	.00		
E	.00	.00	.00	1.00	
F	.00	.00	.00	1.00	1.00

What would such a set of correlations mean? Notice that there are two clusters of coefficients. One cluster is formed by tests A, B, and C; the other by tests D, E, and F. The tests in each cluster correlate perfectly with each other but not at all with the tests in the other cluster. Consequently, we have isolated two factors in the tests. Since there are only two factors, there is no need in the future to use six tests. Tests B and C measure exactly the same thing as test A, and tests E and F measure exactly the same thing as D. We can select any one test in each cluster and measure a factor. What at the outset might have seemed to be six characteristics or traits can be reduced to two.

In actual practice, we never find things so simple as we assumed them to be in the hypothetical example. Correlations making up a cluster are almost never as high as 1.00, and correlations between clusters, or tests in different clusters, are usually greater than zero. And the correlations within a cluster vary somewhat in value. Consequently, we usually cannot test a factor simply by selecting one test within a cluster. Nevertheless, our hypothetical example illustrates the principle of factor analysis. In such an analysis, a few common factors in a large number of tests may be isolated by discovering those tests which correlate highly with each other but not with other clusters of tests.

Factor analysis enables one to get "deadwood" out of tests—to eliminate tests or parts of tests that contribute nothing or add little to measuring the factors in which the tester is interested. In some cases, tests have been so constructed through factor analysis that each test measures predominantly one factor [Thurstone, 1938; Thurstone and Thurstone, 1941]. In other cases this is not desirable, for several factors are often involved in a criterion and hence need to be measured by a test designed to predict the criterion. In other instances, factor analysis has served as a powerful research tool to single out, and reduce in number, the factors being measured by a particular test. Thus it has helped greatly in the construction of good tests. Factor analysis, thought a complicated technique, is a valuable tool and concept in psychology.

PREDICTION FROM MEASUREMENTS It should be pointed out, finally, that the purpose of a good test is to make successful predictions. We would not go to the trouble of constructing or administering tests if they were not supposed to predict something we did not know or could not easily measure in the first place. Sometimes the prediction is for research or scientific purposes. Very often it has important practical advantages. Several cases of such prediction are described in later chapters, but one example here illustrates the point.

During World War II, the Army was faced with the general problem of selecting men for specialized training—in this particular case, training in a tank-mechanics course. Naturally it wanted to pick men who were most likely to succeed in such training. As can be seen in Figure 11.14, there was some correlation between the number of grades a man had completed in school and his success in the tank-mechanics course. Those who had completed 14 grades of school had 6 chances in 10 of doing above-average work in the course. Those, however, who had only 6 grades of school had less than 3 chances in 10 of doing this well. Consequently, the correlation between grades completed and success in the course provided some basis for prediction.

But a somewhat higher correlation existed between the Army General Classification Test and success in the tank-mechanics course. This test is a test of intelligence especially designed for the purposes of the Armed Forces. The upper part of Figure 11.14 shows that men in the highest-scoring group (I) on this test had 8 chances in 10 of doing above-average work in the course. Those in the lowest-scoring group (V) had hardly any chance of doing well. This prediction was considerably better than that afforded by number of grades completed.

The figure illustrates the predictions one can make from reliable and valid measurements. Give a statistician a correlation coefficient between a test and a criterion, and he can make up a diagram like that in Figure 11.14 which predicts a person's chances of success from any particular score on the test. He can do this because he has the appropriate formulas that have been proved both mathematically and in practical experience to predict from one set of measurements to another. The use one makes of such predictions depends upon many practical considerations, such as the cost of training people with a low chance of success, or how much choice one has in selecting people. The important point is that valid measurements lead to useful predictions.

Formulas and calculations

For a list of the symbols used in this section and their respective definitions see the left-hand column on page 409.

MEASURES OF FREQUENCY DISTRIBUTIONS The formula for the *arithmetic mean* is:

$$M = \frac{\Sigma X}{N} \qquad (1)$$

The formula for the *standard deviation* may be written in several ways. Among them are:

$$SD = \sqrt{\frac{\Sigma x^2}{N}} \qquad (2)$$

and

$$SD = \sqrt{\frac{\Sigma X^2}{N} - M^2} \qquad (3)$$

Computation of the mean by formula (1) and the standard deviation by formula (2) is illustrated in Table 11.6. The work proceeds by first obtaining the sum of the measurements (ΣX) and then calculating the mean (M). Next the column of xs can be filled in by subtracting the mean from each measurement $(X - M)$, and from that the column of x^2 values can be obtained. From the sum of the deviations squared (x^2), one can then obtain the standard deviation by dividing by the number of cases (N) and taking the square root.

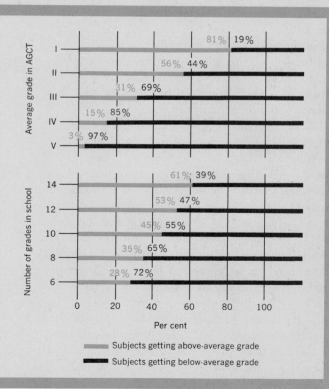

SPECIFIC PREDICTIONS CAN BE MADE
FROM VALID TESTS

FIGURE 11.14. *Predicting success in tank-mechanics school from scores on the Army General Classification Test (AGCT) and from number of grades completed in school. In this case, the AGCT predicts success in tank-mechanics school better than the number of grades completed in school. (After Boring, 1945.)*

If a desk calculator is available, the computation of the mean is the same as just described in formula (1), but that of the standard deviation is faster by formula (3), which eliminates the step of converting each measurement into a deviation.

The formula for a *z score* is:

$$z = \frac{x}{\text{SD}} \tag{4}$$

DEFINITION OF SYMBOLS

X or Y The numerical value of a measurement

M Arithmetic mean

Σ Greek capital sigma used to mean "sum of"

N Number of cases in a distribution or set of measurements

SD Standard deviation of a distribution—a descriptive statistic

x or y The deviation score, that is, a measurement expressed as a deviation from the arithmetic mean, $(X - M)$ or $(Y - M)$

z The result of the deviation score divided by the standard deviation, x/SD or y/SD

O Obtained frequency, or the number of cases counted, in the cell of a contingency table

E Expected frequency, or the number most likely to fall in the cell if the frequencies in all cells were determined by chance and hence if there were no correlation

ρ Rho, the rank-difference coefficient of correlation, a measure of correlation when measurements have been made on an ordinal scale or are expressed as ranks

r Pearson product-moment coefficient of correlation, a measure of correlation when measurements have been made on an interval scale

SE_M Standard error of a mean, a measure of the variability that may be expected among the means of different samples of the same size drawn from the same population

MEASURES OF CORRELATION   To calculate the *coefficient of contingency*, it is first necessary to obtain the quantity known as chi-square (χ^2). This calculation can be illustrated by Table 11.7 which

TABLE 11.6.   *Computation of the arithmetic mean and standard deviation. The computation proceeds by getting first the sum of* X; *next the mean is obtained from the sum of* X. *Then the column of* xs *can be filled in and the* x² *values computed. From the sum of* x², *one can then obtain the standard deviation (SD). For large samples, desk calculators are usually used and convenient formulas are available.*

X	$X - M = x$	$(X - M)^2 = x^2$
40	22.5	506.25
35	17.5	306.25
33	15.5	240.25
20	2.5	6.25
19	1.5	2.25
19	1.5	2.25
19	1.5	2.25
16	−1.5	2.25
14	−3.5	12.25
11	−6.5	42.25
10	−7.5	56.25
9	−8.5	72.25
7	−10.5	110.25
7	−10.5	110.25
4	−13.5	182.25

$\Sigma X = 263$ $\qquad\qquad\qquad$ $\Sigma x^2 = 1{,}653.75$
$N = 15$

$$M = \frac{263}{15} = 17.5$$

$$\text{SD} = \sqrt{\frac{1653.75}{15}} = \sqrt{110.25} = 10.5$$

is based on the data in Table 11.4. The first step is to determine the number that would be expected in each cell if there were no correlation between (in this instance) class and high school curriculum. This is done by multiplying the totals of the row and column intersecting on the cell and dividing by the grand total. Thus, the expected number, by chance, in the cell formed by "college preparatory" versus "class I–II" is $\frac{35 \times 81}{390} = 7.3$. For the next cell to the right, $\frac{81 \times 146}{390} = 30.3$, and so on. When

TABLE 11.7 *The computation of chi-square (χ^2) and the contingency coefficient. (Note: Numbers in boldface are those expected by chance; other numbers are those obtained. See text for explanation.)*

| CURRICULUM | SOCIAL CLASS | | | | TOTAL |
	I–II	III	IV	V	
College	7.3	30.3	38.0	5.4	
preparatory	23	40	16	2	81
General	18.6	77.5	97.1	13.8	
	11	75	107	14	207
Commercial	9.1	38.2	47.9	6.8	
	1	31	60	10	102
Total	35	146	183	26	390

SOURCE: From Siegel, 1956, p. 177.

all the expected values—expected by chance if there were really no correlation—have been computed in this way, the following formula is used to complete the computation of chi-square:

$$\chi^2 = \Sigma \, \frac{(O - E)^2}{E} \tag{5}$$

where O is the observed value—the one actually obtained in the study—and E is the expected value just computed. Chi-square turns out to be 69.2. To find the contingency coefficient, one then uses the formula:

$$C = \sqrt{\frac{\chi^2}{N + \chi^2}} \tag{6}$$

The formula for the *rank-difference coefficient* (*rho*) is:

$$\rho = 1 - \frac{6\Sigma D^2}{N(N^2 - 1)} \tag{7}$$

The D in the formula refers to a difference in ranks (see Table 11.5). Hence to compute ρ, one squares each rank difference, sums the squares, multiplies by 6, and divides by $N(N^2 - 1)$, subtracting the result from 1.

The coefficient of correlation r, called the *product-moment correlation coefficient* because of the way

it is obtained, has a formula that may be written in any one of several ways, depending on what other measures are also being calculated and whether a calculator is available. The general formulas are:

$$r_{xy} = \frac{\Sigma xy}{N SD_x SD_y} \quad \text{or} \quad \frac{\Sigma z_x z_y}{N} \quad \text{or} \quad \frac{\Sigma xy}{\sqrt{\Sigma x^2 \Sigma y^2}} \tag{8}$$

Written this way it makes clear that the coefficient is essentially the average of the products of z scores. If a person's z score on one measurement is randomly related to his z score on another, that is, is uncorrelated, the average product moment will be zero because negative z scores will tend to cancel out positive ones. On the other hand, if the correlation is positive, the products of negative z scores being positive, they tend to add to the products of positive scores and hence give a positive correlation.

When a good calculating machine is available, the best formula to use is one that looks forbidding, but is nevertheless easy to solve:

$$r_{xy} = \frac{N\Sigma XY - (\Sigma X)(\Sigma Y)}{\sqrt{[N\Sigma X^2 - (\Sigma X)^2][N\Sigma Y^2 - (\Sigma Y)^2]}} \tag{9}$$

If one has previously computed the standard deviations of the two distributions by formula (3), the only additional quantity to be obtained from the measurements themselves is the sum of the products of X and Y. The rest is simple arithmetic.

It should be noted that the different coefficients C, ρ, and r are not exactly equivalent. In other words, a C of .50 does not have exactly the same meaning, for mathematical reasons, as an r of .50. The differences, however, are usually not very large, and methods of correction are available for determining the r that is equivalent to, say, a particular C or ρ.

SAMPLING *Sampling error of a mean* may be estimated by the formula:

$$SE_M = \frac{SD}{\sqrt{N - 1}} \tag{10}$$

where the result is the standard deviation of a distribution of means that one could expect to obtain by chance if successive samples of measurements of the same number of cases were drawn from the same population. This is the basic measure involved in methods for determining whether an obtained

difference in the means of two groups of measurements is significant in the sense of being greater than one would expect to obtain by chance.

SYNOPSIS AND SUMMARY

Most of us are consumers of statistics and statistical arguments. For example, many, if not most, of the psychological facts and principles in this text are based upon statistical arguments. The major purpose of this chapter has been to help make you a more sophisticated consumer of statistics.

Carefully formulated statistical arguments allow us to draw sound conclusions. For instance, the conclusions of the Surgeon General's report on smoking were based on statistical data [Advisory Committee to the Surgeon General, 1964]. It was found that the number of men in a given age range dying of lung cancer was far greater in the group of heavy cigarette smokers than in the group of light smokers or nonsmokers. Of course, the individual case is lost in the statistics, but the odds are that a heavy smoker will more likely die of lung cancer than a light smoker. You will recognize that this is a correlational argument and that some other factor may be causative. As sophisticated statistics consumers, we conclude that a relationship does exist between cigarette smoking and lung cancer, but that further studies are necessary before it may be concluded with assurance that cigarette smoking actually causes lung cancer. However, the high relationship between cigarette smoking and lung cancer is enough for practical decisions.

Unfortunately, it is also possible to mislead with statistics [Huff, 1954].[3] A common trick is the presentation of graphs which magnify very small differences. Suppose your product is very slightly better than that of a competitor on a particular characteristic. You might tell a statistical fib by magnifying the top part of a bar diagram which

shows only the difference. The use of arbitrary values on the ordinate often helps. Another trick is to make statistically meaningless statements such as "product X is 10 times more powerful."

Some of you may go on in psychology or other fields where you will become users of statistics. So, another purpose of this chapter has been to present some of their uses. For instance, in describing groups, scores may be spread over a wide range. This is often the case in the biological and behavioral sciences, and descriptive statistics are needed to characterize the distribution of scores. In comparing control and experimental groups, distributions of scores will also be obtained. Descriptive statistics may be computed and then inferential statistics used to obtain the probability that the difference between the control and experimental group means is due to chance. Inferential statistics allow us to feel more or less confident about the reality of an obtained difference between means. They also provide a basis for making decisions about the next experiment which should be done.

In many situations, then, statistics cannot be avoided; but as a user of statistics, you should never substitute statistical arguments for experimental control. When such control is possible, it should be exercised. In situations in which a great deal of control over extraneous variables is possible, variability, and consequently the need for statistical arguments, may be reduced.

The use of tests is another area in which some of the points in this chapter may be helpful. If, as a teacher or business person, you have occasion to use tests, make sure that they are well standardized and that adequate norms are available. Since tests are useless if they are not reliable, make sure that reliability is high. In addition, since tests are not

---

[3] "There are three kinds of lies: lies, damned lies, and statistics." Disraeli.

likely to do you much good if they do not predict—that is, if they are not correlated with the ability, trait, or aptitude for which you are testing—they should be valid. Possible exceptions to these strictures are certain so-called projective tests used by clinical psychologists. However, these are more like standardized interviews than tests.

In addition, the following specific points are important to potential consumers and users of statistics.

1. Three kinds of measurements are commonly used in psychology: (a) nominal measurements, in which numbers are used to identify different categories; (b) ordinal measurements, in which numbers designate rank order among the things being measured; and (c) interval measurements, in which numbers represent differences in magnitude.

2. The first step in organizing a set of measurements is usually to count the frequencies of measurements in each category or interval. The resulting counts may be represented graphically in a bar diagram or histogram; they constitute a frequency distribution.

3. To make a frequency distribution of interval measurements, the scale is divided into 15 or 20 intervals of equal size, and the measurements falling in each interval are tallied.

4. Frequency distributions of many psychological and biological characteristics approximate an ideal distribution known as the normal-probability curve. This is bell-shaped, being perfectly symmetrical and having more measurements near the center of the distribution than in the "tails."

5. Asymmetrical distributions are called skewed distributions. These have more of a tail on one side than on the other and are not perfectly centered.

6. A number or statistic derived mathematically from a frequency distribution and used to characterize it in an exact way is called a measure or descriptive statistic. Two general kinds of measures are commonly employed: measures of central tendency and measures of variability.

7. Three kinds of measures of central tendency are the arithmetic mean, the median, and the mode. The arithmetic mean is the sum total of the measurements divided by the number of cases. The median is the middle score when measurements have been ranked.

And the mode is the measurement that is most frequent.

8. Two measures of variability of a distribution are the range and the standard deviation. The range is the difference between the highest and lowest scores; it is a very crude measure. The standard deviation is the root-mean-square deviation of measurements from the arithmetic mean; it is a more useful measure of variability.

9. A measurement may be converted into a z score by dividing its deviation from the mean by the standard deviation. This is one type of standard score and is a way of stating measurements in "universal" terms, independently of the particular scale of measurement or scoring used. Other standard scores may be derived from the z score.

10. A score may be expressed as a centile by dividing the rank of a score in a distribution by the total number of measurements and multiplying by 100, thus reducing all scores to a rank in 100. Since this is readily understood by nearly everyone, it is a popular way of expressing scores on psychological tests.

11. A correlation coefficient states quantitatively the degree to which pairs of scores in two distributions are related. If the correlation is perfect, which it almost never is, the coefficient is 1.00. If there is no relation between the scores in the two distributions, which there almost never is, the coefficient is 0.00. Between these values, any correlation coefficient is possible. The sign of the coefficient, which may be + or −, merely indicates whether the correlation is high-high and low-low, or high-low and low-high, respectively.

12. Different methods of computing correlations are appropriate for different kinds of measurement: a contingency coefficient (C) for nominal measurements, a rank-difference correlation ρ (rho) for ordinal measurements, and the product-moment correlation coefficient (r) for interval measurements.

13. In many cases of psychological measurements, one wants a measure that is representative of a much larger population. To achieve this, one must be careful either to take a completely random sample or to use one of several methods that have been devised for controlling possible biases in the sample.

14. Any set of measurements is subject, by the laws of chance, to a sampling error that makes the sample depart somewhat from the true population. For this reason, measures may differ from sample to sample. Inferential statistics allow us to state the probability

that a difference between measures is statistically significant.

15. In order to be a worthwhile measuring instrument, a psychological test should have certain characteristics. Foremost are reliability and validity. To be reliable, a test must be able to give essentially the same results on repeated measurements of the same person or thing; to be valid, it must measure what is intended to measure, that is, correlate well with some criterion.

16. In addition, psychological tests should be administered under standardized conditions and should have norms based on a large, representative standardization group.

17. By intercorrelating a group of tests, it is possible to isolate the basic factors being measured by the tests, and if desirable, to construct tests that measure well a limited number of identifiable factors.

RELATED TOPICS IN THE TEXT

CHAPTER 1   THE SCIENCE OF PSYCHOLOGY   Both the decision to use statistics and the type of statistics used in an experiment depend upon the experimental design. For instance, correlation is much more common in studies done by the method of systematic observation; inferential statistics are much more common in experimental studies.

CHAPTER 12   PSYCHOLOGICAL TESTING   An understanding of statistics is essential for further study of intelligence, aptitude, and personality testing.

SUGGESTIONS FOR FURTHER READING

Adkins, D. C. *Statistics*. Columbus, Ohio: Charles E. Merrill, 1964. (Paperback.)
Introductory textbook with emphasis on statistical techniques used in the behavioral sciences.

Edwards, A. L. *Experimental design in psychological research* (rev. ed.). New York: Holt, 1960.
Special emphasis is given to the testing of the significance of differences by the techniques of analysis of variance.

Gourevitch, V. *Statistical methods: A problem-solving approach*. Boston: Allyn and Bacon, 1965. *Problems of the sort encountered by the psychologist in doing research are used to teach statistical methods.*

Guilford, J. P. *Fundamental statistics in psychology and education* (4th ed.). New York: McGraw-Hill, 1965.
A comprehensive textbook on psychological statistics.

Hammond, K. R., and Householder, J. E. *Introduction to the statistical method*. New York: Knopf, 1962.
Standard statistical topics are soundly presented.

McCollough, C., and Van Atta, L. *Statistical concepts: A program for self-instruction*. New York: McGraw-Hill, 1963. (Paperback.)
A programmed textbook for learning elementary psychological statistics.

McNemar, Q. *Psychological statistics* (3d ed.). New York: Wiley, 1962.
A thorough and authoritative treatment of psychological statistics.

Wallis, W. A., and Roberts, H. V. *Statistics—a new approach*. New York: Free Press, 1956.
Some very interesting examples are given from many fields. The examples make this a very interesting way to learn statistics.

12

PSYCHOLOGICAL TESTING

A PSYCHOLOGICAL TEST
IS ESSENTIALLY AN
OBJECTIVE AND
STANDARDIZED MEASURE
OF A SAMPLE OF
BEHAVIOR.
ANNE ANASTASI

INTELLIGENCE,
OPERATIONALLY
DEFINED, IS THE
AGGREGATE OR GLOBAL
CAPACITY OF THE
INDIVIDUAL TO ACT
PURPOSEFULLY, TO
THINK RATIONALLY AND
TO DEAL EFFECTIVELY
WITH HIS ENVIRONMENT.
DAVID WECHSLER

PEOPLE OBVIOUSLY DIFFER from one another in a great many ways—in aptitudes, attitudes, achievements, interests, motivations, personality traits, and skills. Some of these characteristics can be measured, and this is the aim of psychological testing. The measurement of human traits is not done out of idle curiosity—it is a highly practical business. In assigning people to training programs, in hiring people for specialized jobs, in the measurement of school achievement, in counseling, and in the psychological clinic, tests are being relied upon more and more. Tests are primarily used in the study of a particular individual. This study of the characteristics of one person has been called the *idiographic* approach. Tests are also used in *nomothetic* psychology—the attempt to discover general laws of behavior. For instance, scores on psychological tests might be used as the dependent variable after control and experimental groups have been put through an experimental procedure. In the light of our increasing reliance upon them, psychological tests bear a thorough examination.

The uses of psychological tests

Tests, while providing scores, are only aids to decision making. Trained persons must be available to interpret the scores and make recommendations on the basis of their interpretations. Although the general public can scarcely be expected to be familiar with the standards set up by the American Psychological Association (1959) for the proper use of psychological tests, remarks such as those which follow register an astonishing degree of naïveté or misunderstanding; yet such are people's notions.

"May I have a Stanford-Binet blank? I'd like to find my little sister's IQ. The family think she's precocious."

"I'd like to borrow the Ishihara color-blindness test to show to my brother. He's applying for a Navy commission and would like some practice so he can pass that test."

"My roommate is studying psych. She gave me a personality test and I came out neurotic. I've been too upset to go to class ever since."

"I represent the school paper. We'd like a list of the

IQ's of the entering freshmen to publish in our first Fall issue." [Anastasi, 1961, page 44.]

When used by trained people, tests can be quite useful. Often, several types of tests are given, and from these, a counselor can obtain a picture of an individual's strengths and weaknesses. In the following example, the centile standings on the different types of tests show how this is done.

The case of Thomas Stiles:[1]
When is an engineer an engineer?

Tom was 17 years old, in good health, of average height and weight, a high school senior when he came to the counselor. He was enrolled in the academic course, in which he liked the work in mathematics and science better than anything else, and cared least for English and history. His leisure-time activities consisted largely of spectator sports; he liked also to read popular scientific and adventure story magazines. As a younger boy he had done odd jobs at home, and since then had had part-time and summer jobs working as a helper on a truck, operating machines in a shoe factory, helping in a garage, and working in a machine shop. Some of these jobs had been for no pay; others, the more recent, had been paid work.

The student's father was an operative in a shoe factory; the mother kept house, and several siblings, all younger than Tom, were still in school.

Tom stated that he was interested in machines, having lived among various types of machinery all his life; his junior high school ambition had been to be a diesel engineer or marine engineer, an ambition which had broadened to include work with almost any type of engine: steam, diesel, or airplane, especially the last-named type, as "it is the coming field." He thought he would like engineering training, but was not certain of his choice. Asked what he would like to be ten years hence he replied: "Foreman or superintendent in an airplane factory."

The cumulative record in the school office showed that Tom's high school work was mediocre (see table of grades). As shown in the accompanying chart, he had failed junior English, did poorly in physics, had made only C's in mathematics after the tenth grade, and was doing no better in chemistry. His IQ on the Henmon-Nelson Test of Mental Ability, administered at the beginning of his junior year

[1] Source note appears on page 416.

and recorded on the school record, was 106. The profile of test results obtained by the counselor during the first semester of Tom's senior year in high school is shown on the following page.

Tom's questions were: "Should I go into engineering? I am interested in engines. Should I continue my education in order to prepare for such work? What about engineering college?"

The Counselor's appraisal. Tom's intellectual level, as shown by his Otis IQ of 101 and confirmed by an A.C.E. score which put him at the 14th percentile point of a typical college freshmen class, was about average when compared with the general population. Occupational intelligence norms from both World Wars indicate that this is the ability level typical of skilled tradesmen and of the most routine clerical workers, [an] observation confirmed by various studies made with the Otis test in industry. His mastery of school skills and subjects as shown by his scores on the achievement tests was about that to be expected from one of his mental ability level, and decidedly below that of the college freshmen with whom he was compared, except for a superior score on the mathematics achievement test—his favorite subject. This suggested that he might have abilities useful in technical occupations at the skilled level which seemed appropriate to his mental ability. His school marks, however, were not so encouraging, being only B's in mathematics prior to his junior year, and C's since then. The explanation may have lain in his being in the more abstract college preparatory course.

On the special aptitude tests Tom appeared to lack speed in recognizing numerical and verbal symbols such as is required of even routine clerical workers. Combined with his marginal intellectual ability for office work, this strengthened the basis for questioning the choice of a clerical occupation. On the other hand, Tom's scores on the tests of spatial visualization and mechanical aptitude seemed to confirm the implications of the mathematics achievement test. His inventoried interests, too, were in the physical science and subprofessional technical fields; the latter field seemed more in keeping with his intellectual level and with his poor achievement scores and fair grades in the natural sciences.

Tom's family background, leisure activities, and expressed vocational ambitions were all congruent with the implications of the test results. His father was a semiskilled

TABLE A *Grades: Thomas Stiles*

SUBJECTS	9TH GRADE	10TH GRADE	11TH GRADE	(1ST SEM.) 12TH GRADE
English	C	D	E	III-G IV-C
Latin I		C		
Civics	B			
World History	B			
Prob. of Democracy			C	
U.S. History				C
Algebra I		B		
Plane Geometry		B		
Review Math.			C	
Math. (Gen.)	B			
Solid Geometry				C
Physics			D	
General Chem.				C
Phys. Education		D		

TABLE B *Test profile: Thomas Stiles*

	TEST USED	NORMS	PERCENTILE	VOCATIONAL INTERESTS	
Scholastic aptitude	A.C.E. Psych. Exam.	College freshmen	14	1. Biological sciences	B+
				2. Physical sciences	A
	Otis S.A. IQ 101	Students	19	3. Technical:	
Reading	Nelson Denny: Vocabulary	Freshmen	1	Carpenter	A
	Paragraph	Freshmen	30	Policeman	A
Achievement	Coop. Social Studies	Freshmen	11	Farmer	B+
	Coop. Mathematics	Freshmen	74	4. Social sciences	C
	Coop. Natural Sciences	Freshmen	5	5. Business detail	B−
Clerical aptitude	Minn. Clerical: Numbers	General clerks	6	6. Business contact	B
		General clerks		7. Literary	B
	Names		6		
Mechanical ability	O'Rourke Mechanical Aptitude	Men in general	67		
Spatial relations	Minn. Paper Form Board, Rev.	College freshmen	65		
Personality	Calif. Pers.:				
	Social	Freshmen	35		
	Total	Freshmen	40		

NOTES: The percentiles give the percentage of people in the normative group who get scores which are the same or lower than the person being tested. For instance, Thomas Stiles earned a score on the A.C.E. Psychological Examination which was as high as that earned by 14 percent of college freshmen. The letter scores on the test of vocational interest are to be interpreted as follows: An A rating means that Tom's interests are essentially like those of people in a particular occupation; a C rating means that Tom's interest pattern does not correspond to that of people in an occupation.

SOURCE: Extract on pages 415–417 is from *Appraising Vocational Fitness by Means of Psychological Tests* (rev. ed.) by Donald E. Super and John D. Crites, pp. 643–645, including Figs. 12 and 13 (retitled Table A and Table B, with slight changes). Copyright 1949 by Harper & Brothers; copyright © 1962 by Donald Super and reprinted by permission of Harper & Row, Publishers.

worker, indicating that work at the skilled level might well be accepted by the family as a step upward. There were no older siblings who might have established a higher record for him to compete with. His leisure activities were nonintellectual, but they did show interest and achievement in mechanical and manual activities, as well as familiarity with work at those levels. He stated that he wanted to work with engines. It was true that, under the influence of a college preparatory course in the academic high school of a substantial middle-class community, he raised the question of going to college to study engineering, but in most contexts his discussions of work with engines were pitched at the skilled level.

The counselor who worked with Tom therefore felt that Tom would be wise to aim at a skilled trade, either by means of a technical school of less than college level, through apprenticeship, or through obtaining employment as a helper in an automotive maintenance shop and taking night school courses.

This example is informative because it shows one of the most important uses of tests—the test as an aid to the counseling and the decision-making processes. First of all, note that the tests are not used alone: information about Tom's home life and his school work are important bits of data used in the counselor's appraisal. Tests are often used to confirm impressions formed from interviews and other sources of information. Second, several tests of the same characteristic are often used. In this example, a rough estimate of general intellectual ability was obtained from a previously given test and from two tests given in conjunction with the present evaluation. Third, the counselor did not seize upon a single test result, or set of results, but instead looked for consistencies within the total battery of tests. The idea is not so much to obtain a score as it is to make sense from patterns of scores from tests of different abilities and tests of personality traits.

Measurement of human characteristics

Having considered one use of tests in some detail, let us now turn to a closer look at the general nature of tests. Many characteristics are appraised by particular psychological tests—intelligence, special aptitudes, interests, achievements, motivations, attitudes, personality characteristics—but certain general attributes of psychological tests can be described. First of all, what is the definition of a test? Second, what are some of the characteristics of "good" psychological tests? Finally, what are some of the general ways in which psychological tests may be classified?

DEFINITION OF A TEST We all make subjective and informal ratings of the characteristics of a person from samples of the other person's behavior. Often this sample is very inadequate; for instance, first impressions are often quite inaccurate. The informal sample of behavior has another shortcoming: we are usually able to sample another person's behavior only in rather special situations, such as at work. Tests, in one way or another, attempt to provide more objective and more representative samples of behavior than we can obtain without them. One definition of a psychological test, then, is that it is "an objective and standardized measure of a sample of behavior" [Anastasi, 1961].

CHARACTERISTICS OF A GOOD TEST In the last chapter we discussed at length the characteristics a test should have to be considered a "good" test—that is, one that can be used with confidence to make decisions about particular individuals in a group, or about differences between groups. Let us review these characteristics briefly.

1. A test should be *reliable*. Different forms of the same test, or repeated measurements made with the test on the same individual, should give substantially the same results.

2. A test should be *valid*. It should correlate with the criterion which the test is used to measure. This means that it should measure what it is intended, or alleged, to measure.

3. A test should be administered according to *standardized procedure*. If it is not, both the reliability and the validity of the test may be in question.

4. A test should have norms based on a *standardization group,* and the standardization group should be relatively large. It should be similar in character to the group of individuals with whom the test is subsequently used. The norms of the standardization group provide a frame of reference for interpreting the results obtained on any particular individual or group.

5. Under some circumstances, it is desirable to know the *factors* measured by the test. Such knowledge refines the interpretation to be made of any particular test result. It also enables the test constructor to improve the efficiency of his tests for different purposes.

Many of the tests described in this chapter possess these characteristics, especially the first four. However, some of the personality tests are weak in one or more of these characteristics, and the perceptive student will mark the flaws as well as the virtues of personality tests.

KINDS OF TESTS   Tests may differ in many general ways. The following are a few of the more significant ways in which they may differ.

Aptitude versus achievement. Aptitude refers to the potentiality that a person has to profit from a certain type of training. It refers to something which a person can do after training, not what he has done or will necessarily do. *Achievement,* on the other hand, refers to what a person has done. These terms are used to distinguish two different kinds of tests: *aptitude tests* and *achievement tests.*

Note, however, that any test, by definition, measures what a person actually does, for there is no other way of testing him. Put another way, we test a person only by asking him to do something, and what he does is an achievement. Hence aptitude tests and achievement tests are both, in a sense, tests of achievement. The difference between them, however, depends on how we use the results.

An aptitude test is used to predict future achievement or achievement in another situation. Such a test given to a student before he goes to college, for example, is used to predict how well he will do in college—his future college achievement. This aptitude test itself is a measure of achievement. It con-

tains questions of knowledge or problems to solve, just as examinations in courses do. But a score on such a test has little merit by itself; the test is not used to assign a grade or to "pass" a person. Its value lies in its power to predict achievement in college or a similar situation, in other words, to measure aptitude. On the other hand, an examination given to a student in a course is designed to measure the knowledge gained in a course. It is therefore an achievement test, even though its results might otherwise be used to make reasonably good predictions about future achievement.

Sometimes we use the word *ability* as a general term referring either to a potential for the acquisition of a skill or to an already acquired skill [Super and Crites, 1962]. Thus the term ability includes both aptitude—the potential—and achievement—the developed skill. For instance, if a general term is needed, intelligence tests might be called tests of *intellectual ability;* or if the emphasis is on intelligence as a characteristic enabling a person to benefit from training, intelligence tests might be called tests of *intellectual aptitude.*

Group versus individual. Some tests must be given by a trained tester to one person at a time; these are *individual tests.* Some may be given to groups of individuals by almost anyone who can follow directions and has a stopwatch; these are *group tests.* The interpretation of both kinds of tests, however, must be made by properly trained psychologists.

Verbal versus performance. Most tests involve the use of written language in the instructions and in the questions to be answered by the examinees. Such tests are called *verbal tests,* because they use words. On the other hand, some tests have been devised for use with preschool children, illiterates, or foreign-born people who cannot read English. These tests are called *performance tests.* Instructions may be given verbally by the tester, but the test itself does not employ words or handicap a person who cannot read (see Figure 12.1).

Speed versus power. Speed tests are limited in time, and the time is so set that the person who can do things quickly makes the best score. *Power tests* are designed to test the ability of a person to

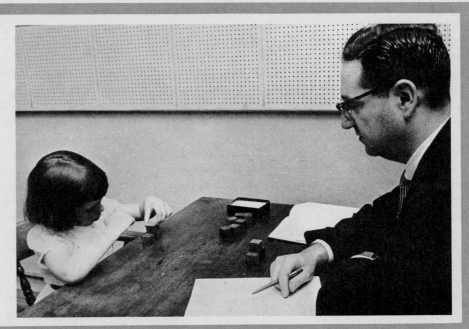

FIGURE 12.1. *The Stanford-Binet Intelligence Scale, Form L-M, year III. The child is asked to build a bridge of three blocks. (New York University Testing and Advisement Center.)*

solve difficult problems irrespective of the time required. Sometimes power tests have time limits, but if so, they are only for administrative convenience and have been established so that the time limit makes no significant difference in a person's performance.

Tests of maximum performance versus tests of typical performance. In many tests we are interested in the best a person can do. For instance: How fast can he cross out all the e's in a line of prose? How many items can he get right on an achievement test? These are the aptitude, achievement, and ability tests. In personality tests, we are interested in what a person typically does [Cronbach, 1960]. For instance: Does a person display hostility toward his supervisor? Does he think people are picking on him? Is he habitually anxious?

Tests may differ in other ways. For instance, we may note that some tests give one overall score, whereas others provide separate scores for different abilities or traits. Some are designed for certain age groups, and some for other age groups. Some are designed for the mentally retarded, others for the especially intelligent. Today there are literally hundreds of tests, and the testing business is a multi-million-dollar industry.

Intelligence tests

Tests that measure general ability or aptitude for intellectual performance are called *intelligence tests*. Actually intelligence tests measure several abilities or aptitudes, not just one. These are the abilities or aptitudes that predict achievement in a wide variety of real situations; for convenience we lump these aptitudes together as "intelligence." These general aptitude tests may be contrasted with tests of the *special aptitudes* required in specific occupations or activities—mechanical, clerical, arithmetic, musical, and artistic aptitudes, to name just a few.

The wide variety of tests that exist for the measurement of intelligence may be confusing to a person who is accustomed to think of intelligence as a single "real" ability, as many people do. Why, he may ask, should we not have just one test of intelligence that "really" measures intelligence?

Most tests of intelligence do, in fact, correlate

reasonably well with one another, which means that they do tend to measure the same thing. Psychological research has made it clear, on the other hand, that there is more than one kind of intelligence—or that intelligence includes more than one ability or aptitude. For this reason, the particular test of intelligence we use depends on what we want to find out. If we want to measure the kind of intelligence involved in doing schoolwork, we use one test; if we are interested in the kind involved in military life, we use another; and if it is intelligence useful in general business life that we want to measure, we use still other tests. Before going further into the nature of intelligence, let us become familiar with some intelligence tests that are commonly used.

THE STANFORD-BINET INTELLIGENCE SCALE

The first test of intelligence to be devised was intended for use in school situations and thus stressed the aptitudes involved in primary education. It was published in 1905 by Alfred Binet, a French psychologist, who designed the test at the request of the Paris school authorities to enable them to pick out children of low intelligence who could not profit from attending school. The test served its purpose and immediately caught the attention of American psychologists. In 1916, Terman [1877–1956] of Stanford University brought out a revision of Binet's test intended for school children in the United States, and his revision came to be known as the Stanford-Binet test [Terman and Merrill, 1937]. It became the model for many intelligence tests developed since then, including its own revision in 1960 [Terman and Merrill, 1960].

Mental age. The 1960 Stanford-Binet Scale is an individual test which is used primarily with children. It consists of a series of subtests arranged according to age levels—for two-year-olds, three-year-olds, and so on, up to fourteen years of age. In addition, there are four adult subtests. The items on the subtests at each age level are chosen so that the children of that age, or older, can pass them, but younger children cannot. For instance, an ideal item for the three-year-old subtest would be one which no child could pass until he was three; after three, all children should be able to pass the item. Of course, the items only approximate this ideal. Figure 12.2 shows the percentage of children passing the three-year-old block bridge item (see Table 12.1) at different chronological ages [Terman and Merrill, 1960].

When a child is being tested, the examiner first finds the age at which all the items of a subtest are passed; this is called the *basal age.* The examiner then continues to give, in order, subtests appropriate to older and older ages. This continues until the child cannot pass any of the items on a particular subtest; this age level is called the *ceiling age.* When the results are tallied, the score the child obtains

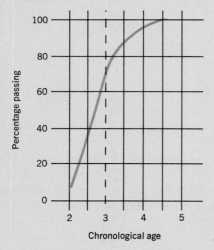

ITEMS FOR THE AGE LEVELS OF THE STANFORD-BINET SCALE ARE CHOSEN BY INSPECTION OF PERCENTAGE-PASSING CURVES

FIGURE 12.2. *The percentage of children passing the block bridge-building item of the Stanford-Binet Intelligence Scale at different ages. This item is at the three-year-old level. Before three years of age few children pass the item; at, and after, three years of age most children pass the item. (Modified from Terman and Merrill, 1960.)*

tells his *mental age* (MA). For example, if a child passed all tests for age 4, half those for age 5, and none of those for age 6, his mental age would be 4½ (54 months). In other words, although only 4, he would have the intellectual ability of a 4½-year-old. Thus mental ages are a type of norm. Usually the computation is not so simple as in this example, but it illustrates the principle.

Table 12.1 presents some of the items from the Stanford-Binet Scale. Notice the kinds of abilities that are tested at various age levels. In the lower age levels, the tests stress information about objects and pictures, as well as perception of forms. In the higher age brackets, the tests stress more the use of words, numbers, and relationships in reasoning problems. At all age levels, there are tests of vocabulary, correct use of words, and span of memory, because these represent the more general aspects of intellectual ability.

A child's mental ability obviously increases as he grows older. When we test him at a certain age and obtain a mental-age score, we know merely the level of his ability at that age. On the average, we would expect a child's mental age to increase at the same rate as his chronological age (CA). Indeed, the test norms were established so that it could hardly be otherwise. The bright child, on the other hand, should show a more rapid increase in mental ability, so that his mental age would be greater than his chronological age. The reverse would be true of the dull child.

Intelligence quotient. This brings us to the idea that relative intelligence is a ratio between mental age and chronological age. If two children both score an MA of 5 years on the intelligence test, but one is only 4 years old and the other is 5, obviously the younger child is the brighter—in fact, much the brighter—of the two. To express this kind of difference and to do it precisely with numbers, we have the concept of the intelligence quotient (IQ). The *IQ* is a ratio of mental age (MA) to chronological age (CA) multiplied by 100 to avoid the inconvenience of decimals. The formula is:

$$IQ = \frac{MA}{CA} \times 100$$

Looked at in this way, the IQ shows how fast a child's abilities are growing in relation to his chronological age. Applying the IQ formula to the two children mentioned above, we find that the brighter one has an IQ of 125 and the other an IQ of 100.

This definition of IQ was used in the interpretation of scores obtained on the 1937 Stanford-Binet Scale, and it gives the basic idea. But other definitions of IQ are possible, and in the 1960 version of this scale, *standard score,* or *deviation, IQs* are used (see the following section on the Wechsler Adult Intelligence Scale for a discussion of deviation IQs). The IQ is a convenient yardstick of mental ability relative to age because it enables one to compare children of different chronological ages even though they have different mental ages and pass subtests that are quite different in difficulty. Great care had to be taken in selecting test items and in establishing age norms. In fact, the test was so constructed that the distribution of IQs is about the same for all age groups. Hence it is possible to say that a child of thirteen who has an IQ of 125 and a child of five who has the same IQ are equally bright. Both, in fact, are rather bright, for only about 5 per cent of children have an IQ that high or higher.

Limitations of the Stanford-Binet Scale. The Stanford-Binet Scale is an excellent instrument for doing what it was designed to do. It has many practical uses, some of which we shall examine. However, it also has some limitations. First, it puts heavy stress upon verbal ability. The directions are given orally for the most part, and many of the subtests require the use of words. If the test were given to a person who for some reason had language difficulties, we would not get an accurate picture of his mental development. Second, the test must be administered to one individual at a time and by testers who are highly trained in its use, because, among other things, many props go along with the test. This makes for inconvenience in testing large groups quickly or when trained testers are not available. Third, the Stanford-Binet Scale gives a score which is indicative of overall or general mental development, but it does not provide an adequate picture of differential development of various kinds

TABLE 12.1 *Some illustrative items from the Stanford-Binet Intelligence Scale. The sample items should be passed, on the average, at the ages indicated.*

AGE	TYPE OF ITEM	EXAMPLE OR DESCRIPTION
2	Three-hole form board	Places form (e.g., circle) in correct hole.
	Block building: tower	Builds a four-block tower from model after demonstration.
3	Block building: bridge	Builds a bridge consisting of the side blocks and one top block from model after demonstration.
4	Identifying parts of the body	Points out hair, mouth, etc., on large paper doll.
	Naming objects from memory	One of three objects (e.g., toys, dog, or shoe) is covered after child has seen them; child then names object from memory.
	Picture identification	Points to correct pictures of objects on a card when asked, "Show me what we cook on," or "What do we carry when it is raining?"
7	Similarities	Answers such questions as, "In what way are coal and wood alike? Ship and automobile?"
	Copying a diamond	Copies a diamond in the record booklet.
8	Vocabulary	Defines eight words from a list.
	Memory for stories	Listens to a story, then repeats the gist of it.
9	Verbal absurdities	Must say what is foolish about stories similar to: "I saw a well-dressed young man who was walking down the street with his hands in his pockets and twirling a brand new cane."
	Digit reversal	Must repeat four digits backward.
Average adult	Vocabulary	Defines 20 words from a list.
	Proverbs	Explains in own words the meaning of two or more common proverbs.
	Orientation	Must answer questions similar to: "Which direction would you have to face so your left hand would be toward the south?"

SOURCE: From Terman and Merrill, 1960.

of intellectual abilities. This problem is important in research on basic mental abilities.

Besides the limitations we have just mentioned, the Stanford-Binet is not a good test to use for testing older adolescents or adults. The kind of intellectual performance represented by the concept of mental age grows very slowly beyond the ages of sixteen or seventeen. So far as the Stanford-Binet is concerned, mental age reaches a plateau at that point. You can see that this causes trouble in figuring the IQ of a person over sixteen years of age although there is an arithmetic device for getting around this difficulty—in Stanford-Binet scoring, the scores on the adult subtests are simply added to the score on the highest age subscale.

WECHSLER ADULT INTELLIGENCE SCALE   The most widely used test for adults is one developed by Dr. David Wechsler (1958) of the Bellevue Psychiatric Hospital. It is called the Wechsler Adult Intelligence Scale (WAIS). The WAIS, like the Stanford-Binet, is an individual test requiring many props and expert testers for its use. Like the Stanford-Binet, it is also made up of a wide variety of subtests. However, the WAIS is not scaled according to age. Instead, the subtests are grouped into two sets of categories, *verbal* and *performance*. There are six verbal subtests and five performance subtests.

VERBAL SUBTESTS	PERFORMANCE SUBTESTS
Information	Picture arrangement
General comprehension	Picture completion
Memory span	Block design
Arithmetic reasoning	Object assembly
Similarities	Digit symbol
Vocabulary	

The subtests can be separately scored so that a person's abilities in the various categories can be compared. Moreover, the verbal and performance sections of the test may be independently scored to give separate IQs on each. This feature is often helpful in testing people of foreign background or of poor education who have not had a fair oppor-

TABLE 12.2 *Age subgroups and proportions of people (in per cent) in the four major geographic regions of the United States in the standardization sample of the WAIS.*

AGE GROUP	SEX	NORTHEAST U.S. POPULATION	NORTHEAST WAIS SAMPLE	NORTH CENTRAL U.S. POPULATION	NORTH CENTRAL WAIS SAMPLE	SOUTH U.S. POPULATION	SOUTH WAIS SAMPLE	WEST U.S. POPULATION	WEST WAIS SAMPLE
16–17	M	24	26	28	26	36	36	12	12
	F	24	24	28	28	36	36	12	12
18–19	M	24	25	27	28	36	35	13	12
	F	25	25	29	31	35	33	11	11
20–24	M	25	26	29	28	33	34	13	12
	F	26	26	29	30	33	31	12	13
25–34	M	26	28	29	27	31	31	14	14
	F	27	27	29	27	31	33	13	13
35–44	M	27	27	29	29	30	30	14	14
	F	28	28	29	29	30	30	13	13
45–54	M	29	29	30	30	28	29	13	12
	F	29	28	30	31	29	29	12	12
55–64	M	29	27	32	33	26	26	13	14
	F	30	29	31	31	26	26	13	14

SOURCE: From Wechsler, 1955.

tunity to develop their verbal abilities. Such individuals frequently do better on performance tests than on verbal tests. It is also helpful in testing brain-injured persons or the mentally ill, because it sometimes makes clearer just where a person's trouble lies.

The method of computing IQs for the WAIS is different from the method we described for the 1937 Stanford-Binet. Instead of using MA and dividing that by CA, which at best is appropriate only for children, a WAIS IQ is obtained by a standard-score method (see page 393). This method, it will be recalled, requires that the mean and standard deviation of a distribution of scores be obtained and that standard-score equivalents be established. In this case, the standard scores are called IQs. Wechsler proceeded in the following way to obtain standard scores and IQs [Wechsler, 1955].

First, he secured distributions of scores on his test from a representative standardization group of 1,700 people. This standardization group was chosen so that: (1) it contained equal numbers of men and women; (2) the major geographic regions of the United States, Northeast, North Central, South, and West, were proportionately represented (see Table 12.2); (3) people from urban and rural areas were included in proportion to their numbers in the population; (4) white and nonwhite people were included in proportion to their numbers in the

population; (5) the proportion of people in different census occupational categories was close to that in the population; and (6) levels of education were represented proportionately.

The standardization group was also divided into seven age subgroups (see Table 12.2). Several age subgroups were used because intellectual ability is not constant with age even in adulthood. The total scores, not computed IQs, on such tests as the WAIS tend to drop with increasing age beyond twenty or thirty (see Table 12.3 and Figure 12.7). Therefore it would not be fair to compare the scores of a twenty-year-old and a sixty-year-old person. Adults are compared with their own age group, for instance, 16–17 or 55–64, in the Wechsler Adult Intelligence Scale.

After the total scores had been obtained, the means and standard deviations for each age subgroup were computed (see Table 12.3). These scores are the number of points obtained on the test, and they served as the basis for assigning equivalent *standard-score,* or *deviation, IQs.* Wechsler set the mean of the scores equal to an IQ of 100; he also set one standard deviation in score points equal to 15 IQ points. In other words, a simple transformation was made. The typical, or average, score—the mean—was given an IQ value corresponding to a typical, or average, IQ—100. One standard deviation in the scores was given an IQ

TABLE 12.3 *Means and standard deviations of verbal, performance, and total scores of age subgroups in the WAIS standardization group.*

AGE GROUP	NUMBER	VERBAL		PERFORMANCE		TOTAL	
		MEAN	SD	MEAN	SD	MEAN	SD
16–17	200	54.59	13.85	48.78	11.25	103.37	23.61
18–19	200	57.31	14.88	49.43	11.83	106.74	25.16
20–24	200	59.47	15.21	50.64	11.97	110.10	25.69
25–34	300	60.82	14.61	49.54	11.75	110.36	24.81
35–44	300	60.24	14.85	46.06	11.33	106.30	24.77
45–54	300	58.03	16.23	41.05	11.27	99.07	26.19
55–64	200	55.79	16.37	37.11	10.75	92.90	25.77

SOURCE: From Wechsler, 1955.

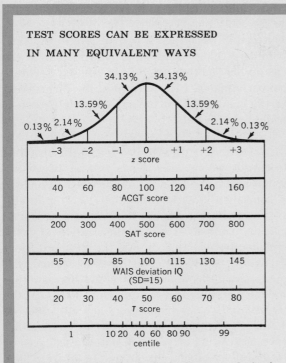

TEST SCORES CAN BE EXPRESSED
IN MANY EQUIVALENT WAYS

FIGURE 12.3. *Equivalence between derived test scores and the percentage of cases falling at or above a particular score. From the normal curve at the top of the figure the percentage of cases falling at or above a particular derived score can be found. This can be done by reading up to the normal curve along a vertical line through the derived score. For instance, a WAIS deviation IQ of 115 is at or above 84.13 per cent of cases. (Modified from Anastasi, 1961.)*

value close to the value of the standard deviations which had been obtained from other earlier IQ tests—namely, 15. Thus, a person having a score one standard deviation below the mean would obtain an equivalent IQ score of 85; an individual having a score one standard deviation above the mean would be assigned an IQ of 115 (see Figure 12.3).

For example, the total, or full-scale, mean score

of the 18–19-year-old subgroup was 106.74 and the standard deviation was 25.16 (see Table 12.3); thus, if you are 18 or 19 and obtain a score of approximately 106–107 on the WAIS, your IQ would be 100; if you obtain a score of approximately 131–132, your IQ would be 115; if you obtain a score of 157–158, your IQ would be 130. Of course, fractional values of a standard deviation correspond to fractions of 15.

All this is just another way of saying that each raw score has an equivalent IQ value. By defining IQs in this way, the distribution of IQs is tied directly to the normal curve. And the percentages of individuals having IQs above, below, or between any particular IQ values are readily predicted from the normal curve (see Figure 12.3). The resulting distribution of adult IQs and the descriptive terms applied to the IQs within different ranges is given in Table 12.4.

It may be of interest to the college student to have a more detailed breakdown of the distribution of above-average IQs. The percentage of the population having IQs of 110 and higher is as follows:

Wechsler IQ	110	113	119	125	128	135
Per cent higher	25	20	10	5	3	1

These figures mean that about 1 per cent of people have IQs above 135, 10 per cent above 119, and so on.

In the latest revision of the Stanford-Binet Scale, published in 1960, data have been provided for

TABLE 12.4 *Distribution of intelligence quotients on the Wechsler Adult Intelligence Scale.*

IQ	VERBAL DESCRIPTION	PER CENT OF ADULTS
Above 130	Very superior	2.2
120–129	Superior	6.7
110–119	Bright normal	16.1
90–109	Average	50.0
80– 89	Dull normal	16.1
70– 79	Borderline	6.7
Below 70	Mentally retarded	2.2

SOURCE: Modified from Wechsler, 1958.

using the same type of computation of the IQ as Wechsler used in the WAIS. As compared with the MA/CA method, the Wechsler method has the advantage of providing exactly the same mean (100) and standard deviation (15) for any standardization group used. Actually, the MA/CA does not quite do this; the mean quotient, as well as the standard deviation of 1937 Stanford-Binet IQs, varies somewhat from one age group to another.

It should be noted in passing that Wechsler (1949) also developed an individual intelligence test for children called the Wechsler Intelligence Scale for Children (WISC). The WISC has been widely used in recent years, perhaps even more than the Stanford-Binet Scale. It is quite similar to the WAIS in its subtests and in providing separate verbal-performance IQs. Naturally, the difficulty of the items is adjusted for the age and intelligence of the child being tested.

GROUP TESTS OF INTELLIGENCE   In hospitals and schools, where intelligence testing is usually only part of the handling of an individual's problem, it is convenient to use individual tests of intelligence. In these situations, too, expert personnel, specifically trained in the administration of tests, are frequently available to give the Stanford-Binet Scale, WAIS, WISC, or some other individual test. In many situations, however, a group test is either desirable or absolutely essential. One of these is the military situation, in which large groups, hundreds of thousands each year, need to be tested. Another is the mass testing of students entering colleges or other schools of higher education. Group tests have been devised to meet such needs.

World War I furnished the impetus for the first large-scale effort to develop group tests. Hundreds of thousands of young men were inducted into the service. We needed some quick method for weeding out the mentally unfit and for selecting the most able for officer training. Finally, to utilize manpower effectively, it was desirable to assign people to different battalions and technical training schools according to their abilities.

Psychologists met these needs in World War I by devising the Army Alpha Test and the Army Beta Test. The Army Alpha Test, designed for the typical individual who can read and write, yielded scores for classifying men roughly according to intelligence. Table 12.5 shows some examples of the problems on this test. Between the two wars, the Army Alpha was frequently revised for use with both servicemen and civilians. The Army Beta was designed as a test that could be given to illiterates and immigrants not proficient in English. It emphasized nonverbal problems for which simple in-

NONVERBAL PERFORMANCE TESTS ARE USED WITH ILLITERATES AND OTHERS HANDICAPPED IN THE USE OF ENGLISH

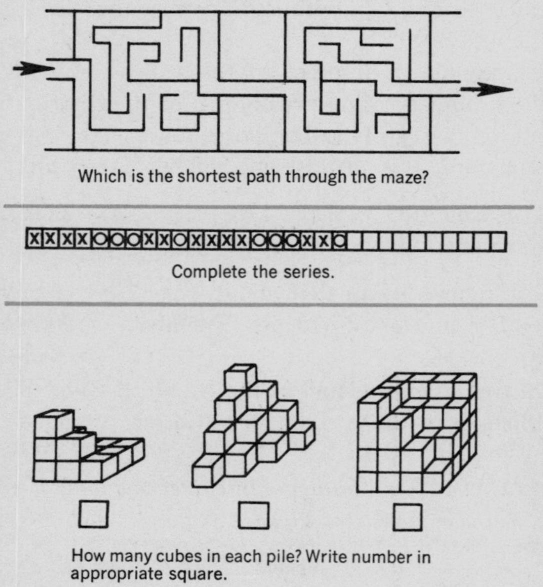

Which is the shortest path through the maze?

Complete the series.

How many cubes in each pile? Write number in appropriate square.

FIGURE 12.4.   *Items from the Army Beta Test used during World War I. The Beta test was used with illiterates and others for whom the verbal Alpha test was unfair. The instructions in the figure were given orally by the examiner. (National Academy of Science.)*

TABLE 12.5 *Some sample items from the Army Alpha Test.*

A. If 5½ tons of bark cost $33, what will 3½ cost? (   )

B. A train is harder to stop than an automobile because
    ( ) it is longer,   ( ) it is heavier,
    ( ) the brakes are not so good

C. If the two words of a pair mean the same or nearly the same thing, draw a line
    under *same*. If they mean the opposite or nearly the opposite, draw a line under
    opposite.

comprehensive	restricted	same	opposite
allure	attract	same	opposite
latent	hidden	same	opposite
deride	ridicule	same	opposite

D. If, when you have arranged the following words to make a sentence, the sentence
    is true, underline *true;* if it is false, underline *false.*

people enemies arrogant many make	true	false
never who heedless those stumble are	true	false
never man the show the deeds	true	false

E. *Underline which*
    The pitcher has an important place in
    tennis   football   baseball   handball

F. *Underline which*
    Dismal is to dark as cheerful is to
    laugh   bright   house   gloomy

structions could be given orally. Examples of items from the Army Beta are given in Figure 12.4.

When World War II came along, Army psychologists took advantage of extensive research in mental testing to make a more drastic revision which they named the Army General Classification Test (AGCT). This was given to several million servicemen upon induction into the Armed Forces. It was prepared in four different interchangeable forms, each form requiring about an hour to give. In addition, longer forms of the test were devised to break down a person's performance into four different categories: (1) verbal ability, (2) spatial comprehension, (3) arithmetic computation, and (4) arithmetic reasoning.

The AGCT, like the Stanford-Binet, is so scored that the average person is assigned 100. The standard deviation, however, is 20 (see Figure 12.3). For purposes of rough classification, the Army divided people into five groups according to score. The spread or distribution is much like that on individual tests of intelligence, but the AGCT score and the IQ are not exactly comparable. The Navy developed and used a similar NGCT, with this difference: Navy tests have an average score of 50. In recent years, one test, the Armed Forces Qualification Test (AFQT), has replaced the AGCT and the NGCT.

After World War I, several group tests were devised for use with civilians—primarily to help in selecting people for jobs in business and industry (see Chapter 18). One of the best known of these is the Otis Self-Administering Test of Mental Ability (Otis SA). This is a short four-page pencil-and-paper test that can be administered simply with a stopwatch and under testing conditions that are relatively easy to keep standard. It can be taken and scored with either a 20-minute or a 30-minute time limit. Scores on the test have been correlated with those on the Stanford-Binet so that it is possible, if one wishes, to convert them to equivalent IQs. The test is so constructed that it emphasizes verbal and reasoning factors but does not sample performance factors very well.

A number of other tests, used in connection with higher education, follow the general pattern of the group tests of intelligence. One series, the School and College Ability Tests (SCAT), is taken by many college students upon entering college. Another group test of ability for college students has been used by Selective Service as a basis for deferment. The Scholastic Aptitude Test (SAT) of the College Entrance Examination Board is used in the selection of college students. The mean of this test is standardized at 500, and the standard deviation is 100 (see Figure 12.3). Other tests are for use at a more advanced level for students seeking entrance to medical and graduate schools. Since these latter are designed for the fairly specific purpose of predicting success in a particular kind of education, they have many of the earmarks of special aptitude tests, and are discussed later under the heading of special aptitudes.

THE NATURE OF INTELLIGENCE   It seems natural to think of intelligence as a single ability or attribute. When we think of Mary as being "bright" and John as being "dumb," we are applying unitary labels to a person. Seldom do we think of Mary as being bright in school, but very dumb in other ways—that is, there are different kinds of intelligence. The fact that most of our tests of intelligence produce one overall score, or IQ, further determines our thinking about intelligence as a unitary thing. Is there a general intelligence as distinguished from specific abilities, or is there just a collection of abilities? What is intelligence actually?

The method of factor analysis furnishes a way of answering this question (see Chapter 11). To perform a factor analysis, research workers give a good many different tests to the same people to see how well the tests correlate with each other. For this purpose, they compute correlations between subtests, not just the overall scores, in order to isolate, as best they can, the elements of intelligence. Having a lot of correlations, they then proceed, by statistical analysis, to see which items form clusters and which ones are independent of each other. It may turn out, for example, that all sorts of subtests that have to do with words may correlate with one another but not with other subtests involving numbers. In this way, they isolate *factors* in a number of tests, and in the example just cited they would conclude that a verbal factor is relatively separate from a numerical factor.

A great deal of research of this kind has been done. Each investigator obtains somewhat different results, depending on the tests he uses and the sample of people he gives them to. Various studies agree, however, in yielding a number of different factors in intelligence [see Guilford, 1959]. Some of the most extensive studies in the United States were carried out by Thurstone [Thurstone and Thurstone, 1941]. After finishing an elaborate factor analysis of dozens of tests given to school children, he emerged with seven factors. Each factor represents a cluster of correlations between subtests and thus what is common to them. His seven factors are named and described as follows:

1. *Verbal comprehension (V)* Ability to define and understand words

2. *Word fluency (W)* Ability to think rapidly of words, as in extemporaneous speech or solving crossword puzzles

3. *Number (N)* Ability to do arithmetic problems

4. *Space (S)* Ability to draw a design from memory or to visualize relationships

5. *Memory (M)*   Ability to memorize and recall

6. *Perceptual (P)* Ability to grasp visual details and to see differences and similarities among objects

7. *Reasoning (R)* Ability to find rules, principles, or concepts for understanding or solving problems

In the course of discovering these factors, Thurstone could identify the subtests that represented each factor, for he knew which subtests were correlated and which were not. This fact enabled him to devise tests that would measure each factor as independently as possible. To do this, he rearranged his subtests, grouping together those which represented the same factor. Actually, in many instances, he tried to improve on this technique by devising new subtests that seemed to be good measures of the factors he had discovered. Now, with a new set of tests of *primary mental abilities* (PMA), he could come to grips with the question of whether or not such a thing as general intelligence exists. Because he had obtained seven factors, he concluded that intelligence is partly made up of separate abilities. The question was: Is there a general factor, apart from the specific ones?

To settle this problem, he obtained scores on each of the tests of primary mental abilities from a large group of children and intercorrelated these scores with one another. If there were no such thing as general intelligence, each factor measured by a test should be independent of every other, and there should be no, or very low, correlations among them. The different tests *are correlated,* in fact, some relatively highly and some not so much. The correlations indicate that some general ability is common to all the tests of primary ability. He therefore came to the conclusion that "each of the primary factors can be regarded as a composite of an independent primary factor and a general factor which it shares with other primary factors." The answer then to our original question—What is intelligence? —is that it is both some general ability and a number of specific abilities.

INTERPRETATION OF TESTS   This conclusion must have considerable bearing on the interpretation of intelligence tests. Though each intelligence test may measure "general intelligence" in some degree and thus measure in part what other intelligence tests are measuring, it also reflects its own particular sample of specific abilities. None of the individual or group tests of intelligence now in common use measures these specific abilities in equal degree. Some weight several abilities more heavily than they weight others.

Actually most intelligence tests, particularly the Stanford-Binet and the Otis, are heavily weighted with verbal content. In the case of the Stanford-Binet, this came about because achievement in school, which is a rather verbal matter, was used as a criterion for selecting many of the items on the test. Group tests such as the Otis are weighted by verbal and numerical ability partly because it is much easier to make up tests of these abilities than it is of other abilities. In any event, the fact is that such abilities are given greater weight. In making interpretations about individuals' abilities from an intelligence test, this fact must be kept in mind.

Another important thing to remember about intelligence tests is that they measure present ability, not native capacity. People have different opportunities to acquire abilities. Poor people, for instance, do not have the same cultural and educational opportunities as those who are financially more fortunate. Moreover, many of the problems used in intelligence tests presuppose a cultural background. If problems concern such things as apples, organs, automobiles, baseball, and trains, then a person who grew up in a culture without these things is certainly going to be handicapped on the test, even if his native capacity is better than average. Growing up in one culture or country thus handicaps a person on tests devised for people in other culture.

Those who devise tests try to make their items as free of such influences as possible, but no one has yet succeeded in making a completely culture-free test of intelligence. Thus tests assume a relatively common background of culture and education. Whenever a person has not had this background or is deficient in it, it is not sensible to regard his results on an intelligence test as comparable to those of other persons who are steeped in the common background. Consequently, intelligence tests are usually not suitable instruments for comparing the abilities of different races and cultural groups.

Individual differences in intelligence

Differences in intelligence make a difference in the occupational and educational achievements which can be expected from people. This is one aspect of the problem of individual differences in intelligence, and we shall look at the educational and occupational achievements to be expected from the IQ groups shown in Table 12.4.

In Table 12.4, where the distribution of WAIS IQs in the United States is presented, the scores were arbitrarily grouped into seven categories: below 70, 70–79, 80–89, 90–109, 110–119, 120–129, and over 130. For convenience, each of these arbitrary categories was given a characteristic name, such as average, superior, and so on. On the basis of intelligence test scores, what occupational and educational achievements can be expected from members of these different groups? The clearest predictions can be made for members of the two extreme groups of "exceptional" people—namely, those with IQs below 70 and above 130.

MENTAL RETARDATION Many terms have been used to refer to those with IQs below 70. In addition to *mental retardation,* the terms *mental deficiency* and *mental subnormality* are commonly used. The term "feebleminded," once much used, has now gone out of favor [Robinson and Robinson, 1965]. On the basis of intelligence tests, between 2 and 3 per cent of the population are in this category (see Table 12.4). In the past, the mentally retarded group was subdivided into three categories: morons, IQ 50–69; imbeciles, IQ 20–49; and idiots, IQ below 20. This classification is no longer used, and more descriptive terms have been substituted for these labels which had acquired unfortunate connotations. There are many newer classifications, but they all

TABLE 12.6 *Classification and developmental characteristics of the mentally retarded.*

DEGREES OF MENTAL RETARDATION	PRESCHOOL AGE (0–5) MATURATION AND DEVELOPMENT	SCHOOL AGE (6–20) TRAINING AND EDUCATION	ADULT (21 AND OVER) SOCIAL AND VOCATIONAL CAPABILITIES
Profound (IQ below 20)	Gross retardation; minimal capacity for functioning in sensorimotor areas; needs nursing care.	Some motor development present; cannot profit from training in self-help; needs total care.	Some motor and speech development; totally incapable of self-maintenance, must have complete care and supervision.
Severe (IQ 20–35)	Poor motor development; speech is minimal; generally unable to profit from training in self-help; little or no communication skill.	Can talk or learn to communicate; can be trained in elemental health habits; cannot learn functional academic skills; profits from systematic habit training.	Can contribute partially to self-support under complete supervision; can develop self-protection skills to a minimal useful level in controlled environment.
Moderate (IQ 36–52)	Can talk or learn to communicate; poor social awareness; fair motor development; may profit from self-help; can be managed with moderate supervision.	Can learn functional academic skills to approximately 4th grade level by late teens if given special education.	Capable of maintaining himself in unskilled or semiskilled occupations; needs supervision or guidance when under mild social or economic stress.
Mild (IQ 53–69)	Can develop social and communication skills; minimal retardation in the sensorimotor areas; is rarely distinguished from normal until later age.	Can learn academic skills to approximately 6th grade level by late teens. Cannot learn general high school subjects; needs special education, particularly at secondary school age levels.	Capable of social and vocational adequacy with proper education and training; frequently needs supervision and guidance under serious social or economic stress.

SOURCE: Modified from Kisker, 1964.

use terms such as *mild, moderate, severe,* and *profound mental retardation.* One such classification, shown in Table 12.6, indicates what may be expected from the mentally retarded at different ages.

The intellectual, but not the social, potentialities of mentally retarded people may be appreciated in another way. If you remember that the IQ may be thought of as a ratio of mental age to chronological age and that mental growth, as measured by the Stanford-Binet Scale, comes to a stop at about sixteen years of age, you can readily figure out the limits of mental age for these four groups. The mildly retarded person's ultimate mental age is approximately 8 to 12 years; that of the moderately retarded, 6 to 8 years; that of the severely retarded, 3 to 6 years; and that of the profoundly retarded, below 3 years.

Knowing these limits of mental growth for the mentally deficient, you can fill in for yourself what we know to be the capacities of the deficient. The profoundly retarded will, at best, be much like a three-year-old all through life. He will never talk very well. The chances are that he will be unable to master some aspects of dressing such as buttoning his clothes or tying his shoes. He can never be trusted to keep himself out of danger. He will not be able to master the simplest tasks at school or at work. The severely retarded, even as an adult, will be something like the first- or second-grade child. He will be able to talk fairly well, clothe himself, and learn simple skills, but he will not profit very much from training in the higher school grades. The moderately and mildly retarded will do somewhat better and may eventually finish four to six school grades. He will be able to learn to read and write, but with difficulty. He may be able to learn a simple occupation and to look after his personal needs. The capabilities of the mentally retarded are summarized in Table 12.6.

Social maturity. These descriptions of the intellectual level of the mentally deficient, however, are not a fair account of their abilities. We must remember that the IQ tests tend to weight verbal factors that are especially important in educational success but not always so important in other, more mundane, daily affairs. If one studies closely the behavior of the mildly retarded, one can see rather wide individual differences among them. Some can take care of themselves much better than others. In work and social situations, some seem much more intelligent than others.

For this reason one psychologist has gone to the trouble of devising another scale, the Vineland Social Maturity Scale, which weights *social* and *vocational* intelligence somewhat more than it does *verbal* intelligence [Doll, 1936]. This scale yields a *social age* (SA) which is comparable to the mental age (MA) of the Stanford-Binet test. As its name implies, this scale takes various social abilities as its standard of comparison: eating with a spoon, washing one's face unaided, being trusted with money, being able to find one's way home, and so on. By checking a child on such items, the psychologist can assign a social age to each child in much the same way that a mental age is assigned.

Since the Stanford-Binet and the Vineland scales measure different things, it is not surprising that they do not correlate perfectly. In general, the ultimate social age of the mentally deficient is somewhat higher than the comparable mental age. For the mildly and moderately retarded, it is 10 to 18 years; for the severely retarded, 4 to 9; and for the profoundly retarded, something below 4. Moreover, social development usually continues for a somewhat longer period than does mental growth as tested by the Stanford-Binet.

Causes of mental retardation. What is known about the causes of mental retardation? If we are to "cure" or prevent this tragic disorder, we must know its causes. Two general classes of mental deficiency can be distinguished and, presumably, two general classes of causes. In one type, *primary* or *familial mental retardation,* there is no obvious organic defect, no evidence of injury or disease that might have caused the mental retardation. The person seems quite sound in every respect except for his intellectual deficit. In such cases, we often find some record of mental deficiency occurring in other members of the family, which is why it is called familial. Intelligence is partly inherited (see Chapter 2 as well as the following section), and it would be expected that those with low intelligence would tend to have offspring of low intelligence.

Another kind of mental retardation is caused by a biological abnormality; this has been called *secondary mental retardation*. The cause in these cases is "secondary" because interference with brain functioning is the outcome of other known, observed, or "primary," conditions. For instance, certain infections of the mother during gestation may produce anomalies in the development of brain functioning. Syphilis is one such infection; *rubella*, or German measles, if contracted within the first three months of pregnancy, is another. Brain injury at birth may produce mental retardation; toxemia of the mother during pregnancy may result in mental retardation of the infant if proper medical care is not received.

In addition, other secondary causes of mental deficiency are to be found in disorders of metabolism and endocrine gland functioning. For instance, mental retardation is an almost certain consequence of the disorder of metabolism known as *phenylketonuria*. Normally, the amino acid phenylalanine is converted to tyrosine in metabolism, but in phenylketonuria the phenylalanine is not converted. It is possible to test newborn babies for this disorder and, since the secondary development of this type of mental retardation is rather slow, to prevent its onset by feeding a low phenylalanine diet. The incidence of this disorder is very low, but the relatively simple test, when applied routinely to all newborn infants, would save the parents of the infant much needless suffering; this, in addition to saving the considerable cost to the state and parents of caring for the retarded child.

An example of mental deficiency which may be associated with malfunctioning of an endocrine gland is *cretinism*. Hypothyroidism, insufficient secretion of thyroid hormone, is the primary cause of the secondary mental retardation in cretinism. Fortunately, mental retardation associated with hypothyroidism has become rather rare because the thyroid hormone can be replaced artificially.

Finally, genetic and chromosomal abnormalities may be the primary cause of secondary mental retardation. For instance, phenylketonuria is a recessive hereditary trait. Other recessively transmitted disorders of metabolism also result in mental retardation. For instance, one such disorder of fat metabolism causes fats to accumulate within the cells of the brain. Mental retardation, blindness, and muscular weakness result. Because this disorder of metabolism produces both blindness and profound mental deficiency as secondary symptoms, it is sometimes called *amaurotic* (blind) *familial idiocy*. *Mongolism*, a syndrome, or collection of symptoms, characterized by moderate mental retardation, obliquely oriented eyes, a round face, short stature, abnormalities of the skull bones and jaw, short little fingers, and other anomalies of the hands and feet, is thought to be related to an abnormality in the chromosomal arrangement (see Chapter 2). Mongoloids seem to have an extra chromosome—instead of 46, there are 47 chromosomes. Usually, the 46 chromosomes are arranged in 23 pairs, but in the mongoloid individual, there seems to be an extra chromosome in one of these pairs. Thus three chromosomes are present where a pair would be expected [Lejeune et al., 1959]. Somehow—nobody is sure quite how—this extra chromosome may produce the syndrome of mongolism.

Treatment of mental retardation. The treatment of mental retardation is a problem of some proportions in our society—some five to six million are afflicted in the United States. All these people are handicapped in the kind of lives they can lead and in the kind of work they can do. What can be done about mental retardation?

Well-educated parents who are confronted with the fact that their child is mentally deficient are likely to think that something can be done to raise the child's IQ. Dramatic stories in the newspapers or magazines sometimes give this impression because they seem to show that it is possible to do much with a mentally retarded child. This possibility has been carefully investigated in several psychological studies, and the evidence unfortunately is against it [Goodenough, 1949]. Special training produces slight changes in IQ and in social intelligence, but seldom does any very dramatic change occur. Mental retardation in most cases is probably a matter of capacity, and one can do little to alter the intelligence of the defective child. People usually deceive themselves if they think otherwise.

However, much can be done to make the most of the limited capacity of the mentally retarded. Most mentally deficient persons are only mildly or moderately retarded; a minority are severely or profoundly retarded. Whatever the degree of deficiency, the training may be long and tedious, but it is worth the effort. Gradually the individual can be taught some of the social skills, such as washing himself, helping with duties around the house, and doing many minor tasks that keep him from being such a burden to others. If his defect is not too severe, he can be taught some vocational skills, such as woodworking, printing, and weaving (see Table 12.6). The better institutions for the mentally deficient have facilities and teachers for training in these social and occupational skills, and each year they return to society many individuals who are capable of earning a living and looking after themselves reasonably well.

Prevention of mental retardation. Prevention is another matter, however. Mental retardation cannot be cured dramatically, but it can be prevented in many instances. We have already seen that the mental retardation associated with phenylketonuria may be prevented if proper tests are given and therapeutic measures are taken. The incidence of mental retardation in cretinism has been markedly reduced by preventive treatment with thyroid hormones. Premarital blood tests have been a large factor in the reduction of mental retardation caused by syphilitic infection of the fetus during gestation; mental retardation due to maternal toxemia has been reduced by the increasing sophistication and standards of medical care. Other preventive measures may be expected from the expanded research into the causes of mental deficiency.

THE MENTALLY GIFTED   At the top end of the distribution of IQs are the very superior (130–140)

and the "near genius" (above 140). It is interesting to see what role persons in these categories play in society and what their problems are—and they do have unique problems. Psychologists have studied the very gifted in three ways: (1) by estimating the intelligence of gifted people who lived years ago, (2) by following the accomplishments of gifted children into adulthood, and (3) by studying the problems of very bright children in school.

Gifted leaders and writers. Enough is recorded about the lives of some of the people who have been prominent in history to make fairly reliable estimates of what their IQs would have been if they had lived in a day when they could have taken the Stanford-Binet Scale. If we know at what age a child began to read, when he used certain words in his vocabulary or mastered certain problems in arithmetic, and so on, we can match these accomplishments with the standards of the Stanford-Binet Scale.

This sort of thing has been done for a long list of people. Table 12.7 names some of these men and gives their estimated IQs. Not all the great men of history are in this list, for we do not have enough biographical data. Still, it is quite plain that men

TABLE 12.7 *The IQs of some eminent men estimated from biographical data*

John Quincy Adams	165
Francis Bacon	145
Samuel Taylor Coleridge	175
René Descartes	150
Charles Dickens	145
Benjamin Franklin	145
Johann Wolfgang von Goethe	185
George Frederick Handel	145
David Hume	155
Thomas Jefferson	145
Gottfried Wilhelm von Leibniz	185
John Stuart Mill	190
John Milton	145
Wolfgang Amadeus Mozart	150
Alfred Tennyson	155
Daniel Webster	145
William Wordsworth	150

SOURCE: From Cox, 1926.

who have contributed much to our literature and to our civilization are also generally endowed with very high intelligence.

Gifted children. Even more information was obtained in a monumental study conducted over a period of 35 years by Terman, the author of the Stanford-Binet Scale [Terman et al., 1925; Terman and Oden, 1947, 1959]. Terman and his associates, having tested many thousands of children, picked out for further study a large group who had IQs of 140 or more, the highest 1 per cent of children.

Terman was able to follow most of these children into their adulthood, and many of them are now in middle life. Periodically he sent them questionnaires or otherwise found out what they were doing, and thus he built up a very detailed picture of their achievements. Some of Terman's associates are continuing to follow up these gifted "children."

One interesting thing about them is the homes they came from. About a third were the children of professional people, about half came from homes of the higher business classes, and only a small proportion (7 per cent) came from the working classes. This is quite out of proportion to the numbers of people in each of these classes, and indicates that relatively more gifted children come from the higher socioeconomic classes. This fact is undoubtedly accounted for by both heredity and environment. These classes can provide a better environment for the development of intellectual abilities, and because the more successful people tend to be the more gifted, they also pass on such gifts to their children through heredity.

The later success of Terman's gifted children is a second striking discovery of his studies. About 700 people of the original study could be contacted 25 years later. Of these, about 150 were very successful as judged by such criteria as (1) being listed in *Who's Who* or *American Men of Science,* (2) holding responsible managerial positions, or (3) receiving recognition for outstanding intellectual or professional achievement. Most of the others were less outstanding but still much more successful than people of average intelligence. On the other hand, some were certainly not very successful—some had

committed crimes, some had dropped out of school early, and some were distinctly vocational misfits and had been unsuccessful at a number of jobs. Careful comparisons of those who were very successful with those who were least successful showed that factors in personality made the difference. The least successful were more poorly adjusted emotionally and more poorly motivated to succeed. Despite the exceptions, the fact was that children of superior ability generally made an outstanding record of social and intellectual achievement.

Contrary to some popular misconceptions about the very bright, Terman's gifted children were above average in height, weight, and physical appearance. In other studies it has been shown that the gifted are not physically superior to their intellectually normal brothers and sisters—they are only superior to the average [Laycock and Caylor, 1964]. This suggests that above-average physical attributes of the superior children are not so much a reflection of general superiority as a reflection of the good care they and their siblings receive at home. The very bright also are generally better adjusted and more socially adaptable, and they have more capacity for leadership than average children. Thus Terman disproved the notion that the "genius" is likely to be peculiar, maladjusted, and socially backward. Some very intelligent people, of course, are like that—and so are some average people—but in general the very bright are less so.

Problems of the gifted. What we have said is true despite the many problems that a gifted child faces. Because he is brighter, he is more likely to be bored by children of his own age, more likely to seek the company of older children and adults and to pester them with questions. In public schools, most of which have been designed for the average child, his problem is acute because his intellectual ability and achievement usually far exceed those of other children of the same age in the same classroom. Moreover, he usually is being taught by a teacher who is far from a genius and often is unable to match either the child's drive for knowledge or his problem-solving ability.

Teachers faced with a child of extremely high

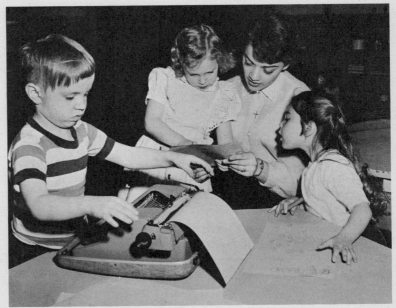

FIGURE 12.5. *Gifted children may be encouraged to participate in special education projects. In some school systems, children are relieved of the boredom of regular education and develop their special talents by working on special projects, such as musical composition and conducting, and typewriting. (Lucien Aigner, from Monkmeyer, and Hunter College Elementary School.)*

ability are likely to consider him fresh, smart-alecky, and a show-off and hence often treat him harshly. The very bright child often finds the pace of normal education so slow and easy that he becomes bored and loses interest in the activities of the classroom. Then he may become a personality problem and a real annoyance for the schoolteacher. Some public schools, of course, are sophisticated about the problems of the gifted child, and others are becoming more so. The better ones find out early what a child's IQ is and try to include an appropriate program for gifted children (see Figure 12.5). In some instances, the gifted children are put in special classes by themselves in which they can achieve more and be given tasks commensurate with their abilities. In other instances, special additional activities are planned for the gifted child.

THE MIDDLE GROUPS   Predictions can be made about the achievements of people with IQs between 70 and 130. The occupational achievements of these people provide a good idea of what might be expected from members of this middle group with low, medium, and high intelligence-test scores.

As might be expected, people in some occupations are, on the whole, more intelligent than those in others. We have a good many studies that show this, but the one that is largest in scope comes from data obtained during World War II [Harrell and Harrell, 1945]. Accountants and teachers are quite high on the AGCT test (see Figure 12.6). Figure 12.6 also gives a rough idea of the correspondence between AGCT scores and deviation IQs. Lawyers and engineers, although their data are not shown in this figure, also had high AGCT scores. At the bottom of the list are farmhands, miners, and teamsters (not shown), with scores in the neighborhood of 90. The variability, however, is large. Some people in

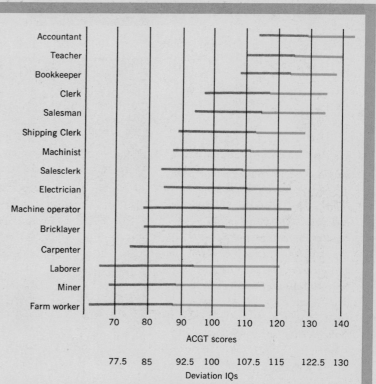

OCCUPATIONAL GROUPS DIFFER IN INTELLIGENCE, BUT A GREAT DEAL OF OVERLAP OCCURS

FIGURE 12.6.   *The ranges of AGCT scores for selected occupations. Each bar shows the range between the 10th and 90th centiles for a sample of hundreds of men selected randomly from each occupation. Scores below the median are shown in gray; those above the median in orange. (Modified from Anastasi and Foley, 1958.)*

every occupation scored over 130 and some scored 100 or below. Again, though there is an average difference in intelligence between occupational groups, there is a great deal of overlap.

It is not hard to understand how these occupational differences come about. In general, the higher-ranking occupations require considerably more schooling than the lower-ranking ones. The child with low intelligence tends not to finish as many years of school, and when he does, he usually makes a poor grade record. The latter fact also partly explains the outcome, because the colleges and professional schools tend to admit those with higher grades and to screen out those with poorer ones. We should consider also the use of special tests of intelligence by these schools for deciding whom they will admit. This introduces a *spurious correlation;* if intelligence is used to admit a person to certain occupations, persons in these occupations will average higher in intelligence, even if there is no necessary relation between occupation and intelligence.

A more interesting and not so easily explained difference in intelligence is among the children of parents of different occupational groupings. The children of those in the higher occupational classes tend to have higher IQs than children of parents at lower occupational levels. The data in Table 12.8 taken from one study of this question illustrate that the IQs of children of professional people average about 115, while those of children of day laborers average about 95. Perhaps part of the explanation for these differences lies in the relatively enriched home and cultural environments of the children of professional parents.

Group differences in intelligence

Everyday thinking is colored by notions about the abilities of different *groups* of people. Many think that Negroes and foreigners are not so intelligent as white Americans. We regard older people as much wiser than, if not so quick as, younger people. Employers think women and young people more suit-able for certain positions, men and older people for other jobs.

Psychological research, indeed, indicates that differences among various groups of people do exist, but these differences are often not the same ones that the layman imagines, or so great as he may think. Let us see here what the facts are about differences in intellectual abilities.

DIFFERENCES BETWEEN MEN AND WOMEN In our society, a division of labor does exist between the sexes. Men are expected to earn a living, and women are expected to care for the home—though that pattern has been changing in the last generation. In other cultures, the economic roles of the sexes are sometimes reversed. This fact alone should make us skeptical of large inherited differences in capacities between men and women. On the other hand, the fact is that most of the leaders in the arts and sciences and in business and industry have been and are men. The eminent woman is the exception rather than the rule. May we assume from this that men are more intelligent than women? Since psychologists have administered thousands of intelligence tests to both men and women, it is easy to answer this question quantitatively. Such testing has shown that the average IQ of men and women is the same. The abilities in which women exceed men are counterbalanced by those in which men surpass women. Differences between the sexes are thus restricted to specific abilities, and not to the composite of specific and general abilities that we call intelligence.

AGE DIFFERENCES IN ABILITY Because people are living to older and older ages, we are in need of an accurate evaluation of the abilities of the elderly. The most general statement we can make about the change in abilities with age is this: As an individual approaches maturity, all his abilities increase to a peak level and then begin to decline. Just where the peak occurs and how rapidly abilities decline depend on what is being tested.

A now classical study was performed by testing substantially all the inhabitants from ages ten to sixty in a group of New England villages. The test employed was the Army Alpha. The various subtests of the Army Alpha were analyzed to sort out different abilities. The test results on two abilities, as well as on the total test, are shown in Figure 12.7. The solid orange line shows that general mental ability, as measured by the Army Alpha, rises to a peak somewhere between the ages of sixteen and twenty, and then declines rather steadily. Subtests, however, show that not all abilities behave in the same way. Tests of vocabulary, for example, which weight previous verbal learning, show no appreciably significant decline. The subtests on analogies, which weight reasoning, reach a fairly sharp peak, followed first by a rapid decline, then by a slower one.

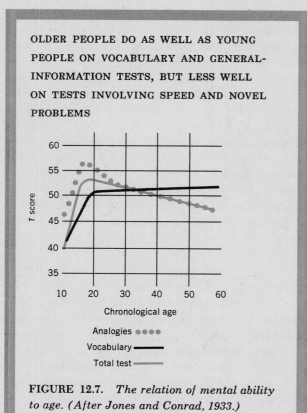

OLDER PEOPLE DO AS WELL AS YOUNG PEOPLE ON VOCABULARY AND GENERAL-INFORMATION TESTS, BUT LESS WELL ON TESTS INVOLVING SPEED AND NOVEL PROBLEMS

Analogies ● ● ● ●
Vocabulary ▬▬▬
Total test ▬▬▬

FIGURE 12.7.   *The relation of mental ability to age. (After Jones and Conrad, 1933.)*

In another more recent study designed to provide norms by age groups for the Wechsler Adult Intelligence Scale, we obtain roughly the same results, though the peak of intelligence is reached at a somewhat later age, in the late twenties (see Table 12.3). Because the WAIS provides separate performance and verbal IQs, it is possible to analyze those two aspects of intelligence separately. It turns out that the peak of "performance intelligence" occurs earliest, in the mid-twenties, and that for "verbal intelligence" comes in the early thirties. And after the peaks, performance intelligence declines more rapidly than verbal intelligence, which fits with the older study.

In all such studies, we have difficulty being sure that the samples are comparable at different ages, because they can be biased, say, by a tendency of younger, brighter people to migrate from one particular area to another. Nevertheless, the general trends seem trustworthy. As a general conclusion, we can say that the peak of intelligence is reached between the teens and the early thirties, depending upon the type of intelligence being tested. Further, older people do as well as younger people in vocabulary and general information tests, but they do more poorly in tests which require the individual to work quickly or to adapt to situations which are different from those he is used to.

Note that the differences we have been discussing are *average* differences between the groups. A great deal of variability occurs within the younger and older groups, and in practically all the studies on aging many individuals in the older group do as well, or better than, the average performance of the best younger group. In other words, the distributions of the two groups overlap each other to a considerable extent.

Overlap is statistically defined as the percentage of people in the lower group who achieve higher scores than the median of the higher group. For instance, a 40 per cent overlap between an older group and a younger group would mean that 40 per cent of the individuals in the older group obtained scores higher than the median of the younger group. Note that a 40 per cent overlap does *not* mean that only 40 per cent of the lower group overlap any portion of the higher group. Sometimes results are reported, especially when controversial issues such as the difference between Negroes and whites are involved, in such a way as to mislead the statistically unwary.

The implication of the great degree of overlap between the older and younger groups is important. Rarely, if ever, must we make social, economic, or political decisions concerning the abilities of whole groups. If such decisions are required, group averages might be appropriate. However, the usual problem is that of selecting a small number of individuals for a particular job. Then the decision of who should be chosen is not determined by sex, race, nationality, age, or other "group" factors but by the *tested abilities of the individuals.*

DIFFERENCES DUE TO HOME ENVIRONMENT

The intellectual environment of children of professional parents is naturally quite different from that of children of day laborers. When we find a difference in intelligence between two such groups of children, the age-old question of heredity versus environment comes to mind. Are children of two groups of parents different in intelligence because they have different inheritance or because they have different intellectual environments? The question is as important as it is difficult, and psychologists have carried out extensive studies in an attempt to answer it. Even so, we do not have as conclusive an answer as we should like. Here are just a few of the most important facts bearing on the question.

Table 12.8 shows the IQs of children tested in different age groups from 2 to 18 and arranged according to seven major paternal occupational groups. The differences in the youngest group (2 to 5½ years) are just about the same as those in the oldest group (15 to 18). From these data, we must conclude either that the differences are hereditary or that they are established very early in life.

In Chapter 2, when we dealt with the general question of heredity and environment, we discussed two other kinds of studies bearing on the point (see page 44). One consisted of correlations of IQs

TABLE 12.8 *IQs of children averaged according to the occupational grouping of their fathers.*

Father's occupation	Age of child			
	2–5½	6–9	10–14	15–18
Professional	115	115	118	116
Semiprofessional & managerial	112	107	112	117
Clerical, skilled, and business	108	105	107	110
Rural owners	98	95	92	94
Semiskilled	104	105	103	107
Slightly skilled	97	100	101	96
Day laborers	94	96	97	98

SOURCE: From McNemar, 1942.

between blood relatives with different degrees of similarity of heredity and environment. The other was a comparison of the IQs of identical twins, all reared apart and separated at different ages after birth. Both studies strongly implicated heredity as a factor in intelligence and gave it a weight equal to, or somewhat greater than, environment.

It is also demonstrable that when children are taken from their true parents and placed in foster homes—as many thousands of children are every year—their intelligence seems more closely related to the intelligence and educational level of the true parents than to those of the foster parents. In one study, the correlation of children's IQs with the intelligence of their true parents was of the order of .30 to .40, while the correlations with the intelligence of their foster parents were in the neighborhood of zero [Hilgard, 1957]. From this we can conclude that relative differences in intelligence are set principally by inheritance rather than by the intellectual influences of the foster home.

In many studies, on the other hand, the intelligence of foster children is considerably higher than one would predict from the IQs of their true parents. In one of the more dramatic studies, children whose true mothers had an average IQ of 91 showed an average intelligence of more than 109 when measured at an average age of thirteen, usually 10 years or more after they had been placed in superior foster homes [Skodak and Skeels, 1949]. Since we are not certain how high their IQs would have been had they been reared by their true parents, we cannot be sure how much of a gain this is, but it is probably fair to say that children may gain as much as 10 IQ points when reared in superior homes. This study, unlike the other ones presented, points to the influence of the intellectual environment. Even so, it appears that the gain is not so much as it would be were it not limited by inheritance.

Facts and researches on the influence of the home environment could fill a book, but these we have cited are typical. What can we make of them? Clearly, both heredity and environment determine measured intelligence. A good environment can improve intelligence; yet poor inheritance limits how much it can be improved. So, even though no amount of favorable influence can fully overcome poor inheritance, such influence can develop what latent intelligence there is to its fullest potentialities and can make a considerable difference in what a person may be able to do.

DIFFERENCES DUE TO CULTURAL ENVIRONMENT If the home environment of a child contributes to his intelligence, we might wonder whether other features of his culture also contribute. After all, the child lives in other environments outside the home, especially as he grows from infancy into childhood. At two or three, he starts to play with other children, and by the age of seven, he is spending a good part of his day in school. In growing up, he experiences intellectual influences from his playmates, his school, and even the community's library facilities. What effect do these influences have on intelligence?

One way of approaching this question is to compare *rural* and *urban* children, since the two kinds of environment differ considerably in the richness of intellectual influences they provide. It is interesting, indeed, that urban children, on the average, score higher on intelligence tests than do rural children; just how much higher depends upon which particular groups are compared, but it is frequently several IQ points. Such differences might be explained in part by the migration of the brighter families to the city, leaving the less intelligent behind. They might also be explained in part by a cultural bias of the intelligence tests which may include items more familiar to city children than to farm children.

Undoubtedly there is something to be said for both these points, and our present data are somewhat inconclusive. On the one hand, it seems rather certain that the stimulating environment of the city, like that of a superior home, can raise substandard intelligence. We have some striking evidence for this view in a study conducted on Negro city boys of twelve years of age [Klineberg, 1935]:

Over 400 boys who had moved to the city were given intelligence tests and compared with 300-odd boys who had been born and reared in the city. The longer the boys had lived in the city, the higher the intelligence scores. Those who had been in the city only 1 to 2 years averaged only 40 (test score, not IQ), whereas those born in the city averaged 75. This is a sizable difference, and it is hard to see how it could be accounted for by selective migration. Apparently city influences affected measured intelligence.

The problem of cultural influences enters into all attempts to determine whether racial differences in intelligence do exist. As you probably realize, it has long been a question whether some "races" are inferior to others in intelligence. When psychologists attempt to settle the question with research—and they have made many studies—they immediately encounter the fact that "races" do not have the same cultural environments. There is also the fact that different groups migrating to this country come from varying socioeconomic and cultural groups in their country of birth. So most studies on this question are inconclusive.

Differences between Negroes and whites. The racial group differences which have been most thoroughly studied are those between American Negroes and American whites. All have the same country of birth and all speak the same language—though the language habits of most whites differ considerably from those of many Negroes. Suppose we test a large group of Negroes and compare their intelligence test scores with those of an equally large group of whites. In most comparisons between unselected groups of Negroes and whites, the mean of the Negro group is lower—often by 10 or 15 IQ points—than that of the white group [see Shuey, 1958]. The question is not whether or not such a difference exists; it lies, rather, in how the difference is interpreted and evaluated.

Some strong evidence for the influence of cultural factors in producing these differences comes from the intelligence tests given during World War I. In general, Negro draftees did more poorly than whites. However, Southern draftees were poorer on the average than Northern draftees. And some Negroes from some Northern states averaged better than whites from some Southern states. Moreover, as we saw above, city Negroes and city whites did better than rural Negroes and rural whites. It is therefore very difficult to separate the factors of race, geography, rural-urban origin, and educational advantages. The latter three factors, however, may all be considered cultural influences, as distinguished from biological differences in the races. From these studies it can be concluded that the difference between Negro and white groups is partially due to the cultural disadvantages suffered by Negroes. Negroes, on the average, still have inferior educational advantages and usually, after centuries of systematic economic exploitation and demoralization, inferior intellectual environments.

However, when attempts are made to equate Negro and white groups with respect to socioeconomic class, the difference between the groups does not disappear [McGurk, 1951]. Also, and this is contrary to what would be expected from a cultural explanation of Negro and white differences, the difference was greater on noncultural test questions than on cultural questions [McGurk, 1953]. Is it likely that this difference represents a true innate difference between the two groups?

Even assuming that an adequate definition of race can be given, this is an unanswerable question at present. The main problem is that Negroes and whites form distinct castes in the United States [Dollard, 1949; Dreger and Miller, 1960]. Even when roughly equal in socioeconomic class, the cultures of Negroes and whites remain markedly different, and there is no way to remove these differences. They are intertwined with the variable, Negro or white, under study. For instance, lower-class Negroes and whites, although similar in some ways, differ in such things as the demands made upon children for achievement [Merbaum, 1961]. It does not seem too farfetched to think that this, and other caste differences, will account for the differences which exist after the groups have been equated on socioeconomic variables.

Fortunately, this unanswerable question on innate racial differences is academic. We are not required to make decisions about groups; instead, the problem is to make decisions about individuals. The question is simply whether an individual has the intellectual aptitude to benefit from a course of training, or whether a person has the intellectual ability to do the job for which he is being considered. This is completely in accord with the philosophy of psychological testing. As we saw in the introductory example, tests are to be used to make decisions about *individuals*.

Special aptitudes and interests

No sharp line exists between intelligence tests and aptitude tests. We use intelligence tests to provide a general assessment of intellectual ability and aptitude tests to measure more specialized abilities required in specific occupations and activities. Having discussed intelligence, we now turn to aptitudes and the tests used to measure them.

We shall also treat interests in this section, not because they are aptitudes, for they definitely are not, but because interests must also be taken into account in making any prediction from aptitude tests. To succeed in a given activity, a person must have both an aptitude for the activity and an interest in it. Hence for any practical use, aptitude and interest tests go hand in hand.

SCHOLASTIC APTITUDES It has become customary to speak of "aptitudes" and "aptitude testing" when we are trying to predict success or failure in specific training or in a line of work. If we are trying to predict success in training, we speak of *scholastic aptitude*. If it is a vocation we have in mind, we refer to the abilities required as *vocational aptitudes*.

Some aptitude tests serve two purposes—as a general intelligence test and as a scholastic-aptitude test. The data in Figure 12.8, for example, are from the Army General Classification Test, which is designed as a test of general intelligence. It also predicts fairly well whether a person is likely to succeed in officer-candidate school. Hence it can be used as a scholastic-aptitude test as well.

Figure 12.8 gives data on this point from World War II. If a person scored 140 or over on the AGCT, his chances of succeeding in officer-candidate school were better than 9 in 10. If his score was less than 110, his chances of succeeding were less than 4 in

10. This illustrates the kind of prediction it is possible to make from a good scholastic-aptitude test, though such predictions depend also on the cultural backgrounds of individuals with whom it is used and on the types of training involved.

A number of scholastic-aptitude tests have been developed for various kinds of training. Probably one of the most widely used is the series known as the School and College Ability Tests (SCAT) which is administered to students entering the liberal arts colleges of the United States. Similar tests are available for schools of medicine, dentistry, nursing, and several other professions. More are being devised each year. Another called the Graduate Record Examination (GRE) has been designed for students who plan to pursue graduate work for the master's or doctor's degree in such specialties as psychology, economics, engineering, and physics, as well as a number of other fields in the arts and sciences. The Miller Analogies Test (MAT) is also used to predict success in graduate school. There is an increasing tendency for graduate and professional schools to require the appropriate aptitude test of all students who apply to them.

VOCATIONAL APTITUDES Scholastic-aptitude tests measure a person's aptitude for success in relatively prolonged training. The great majority of jobs in business and industry, however, do not require such training. Success in these jobs or in training for these jobs can be forecast from a knowledge of specific vocational aptitudes without too much regard for intelligence or scholastic aptitude. Several hundred tests of vocational aptitude are available today. Not all of them are good tests in the sense that they have been proven to be good predictors of vocational success, but some are. Many are slight variations of another test developed to serve some particular purpose. In fact, if time, money, and expert psychological talent are available, it usually is wise to modify existing tests to meet the needs of a particular business or industry. We shall describe the steps that are necessary in selecting a valid test, and then consider briefly some of the many types of tests available.

GENERAL INTELLIGENCE TESTS ARE OFTEN USEFUL IN PREDICTING SUCCESS IN SCHOOL

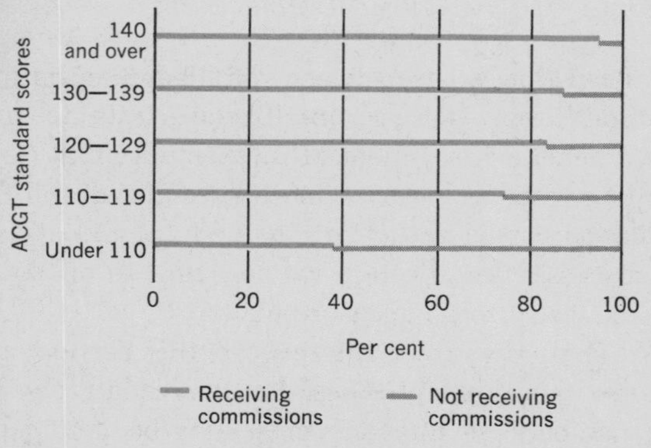

FIGURE 12.8. *The prediction of success in officer-candidate school from AGCT scores. The illustration indicates the chances in 100 that an officer candidate making a certain score on the AGCT would receive a commission. Data are for 5,520 men in 14 schools. (After Boring, 1945.)*

Validation of tests. To evaluate the ability of vocational-aptitude tests to predict success on the job, the following steps are necessary:

1. Give the test to *all* applicants for the kind of job in question until a large number of applicants, preferably several hundred, have been tested.

2. Select applicants for employment *without* considering the test results.

3. After those who are employed have been on the job long enough to be evaluated, divide them according to performance into two or more *criterion groups.* The division may be into satisfactory and unsatisfactory, or it may be into several groups, such as excellent, good, fair, and poor.

4. Compare the tests results of the different groups.

This process, and particularly the last step, is designed to determine the predictive validity of the test for the purposes intended. It is actually a way of obtaining a correlation between the test and the criterion, as described in Chapter 11. If there is such a correlation, the criterion groups will differ on their aptitude scores. And only when there is such a difference, and the difference is considerably more than one could expect by chance, is the test valid and worthy of use for selection purposes. To construct a new test, the steps are essentially the same as for evaluating a test, but the analysis must be made for individual items on the test rather than for the test as a whole. Such an analysis is called an *item analysis.* Items are selected that discriminate between the criterion groups; other items are discarded.

Mechanical-ability tests. Many tests that are intended for mechanics, machine operators, assembly-line workers, repairmen, and similar workers involve mechanical knowledge or ability to manipulate objects. Our experience with such mechanical-ability tests indicates that a relatively unique factor is common to the tests. People who score high on one mechanical-ability test tend to do so on another. On the other hand, different jobs require different combinations of mechanical abilities; hence there are many different tests. Some examples are given in Figures 12.9 and 12.10.

Psychomotor tests. So far there is little evidence of a general motor ability comparable to perceptual or mechanical ability. Rather, a person who has good manual dexterity is not necessarily good at the kind of coordination involved in running a tractor or an airplane. So psychomotor tests must be conceived, developed, and proved for particular jobs and occupations. These tests involve such psychomotor tasks as manual dexterity, steadiness, muscu-

MECHANICAL APTITUDE CAN BE TESTED WITH A PAPER FORM BOARD

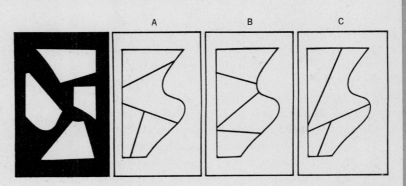

FIGURE 12.9. *A sample from the Minnesota Paper Form Board Test, a mechanical-aptitude test. The examinee looks at the pieces on the left and indicates whether they fit together to make A, B, or C.*

WHICH WOULD BE THE BETTER SHEARS
FOR CUTTING METAL?

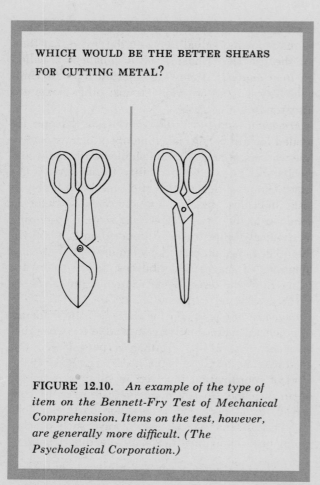

FIGURE 12.10. *An example of the type of
item on the Bennett-Fry Test of Mechanical
Comprehension. Items on the test, however,
are generally more difficult. (The
Psychological Corporation.)*

lar strength, speed of response to a signal, and the
coordination of many movements into a unified
whole.

Aptitudes for logical thinking. The usual aptitude
tests are designed for the conventional occupations
of the industrial world, particularly manufacturing
and office occupations. Modern technology, however,
is bringing to the fore occupations that require primarily logical thinking and problem solving. Complex automatic systems develop malfunctions which
must be diagnosed by technical troubleshooters.
Computers must be programmed by people who can
think through intricate sequences of steps. Development engineers must design machines for all sorts
of purposes.

Until recently, we have not had satisfactory tests
for measuring the aptitudes involved in such jobs.
We still have a long way to go. But research is
being prosecuted vigorously, with some promising
results. One test, for example, is the LAD (Logical
Analysis Device), shown in Figure 12.11. It consists
of an operator's display unit plus a central logic
unit, problem plug-boards, and control and recording units. An examiner can set up various standardized problems of various degrees of complexity for
an operator to solve. The operator's problem is to
discover the rules for responding logically in a
correct sequence.

The LAD has fairly high validity in the selection
of programmers for computers. Research on its

FIGURE 12.11. *Operator's display panel for
LAD, or Logical Analysis Device, which is
designed to measure aptitude for logical
thinking and problem solving. This aptitude
figures in such occupations as computer
programming, engineering development, and
trouble shooting. (The Psychological
Corporation.)*

validity, and that of similar techniques, for assessing problem-solving aptitudes in engineers, technicians, and maintenance men should in time give us suitable aptitude measures for the newer occupations of our modern technology.

The use of aptitude tests. Aptitude tests are used both by the employer to select employees for his jobs and by the vocational counselor in helping a person assess his aptitudes for different types of work. The same tests are usually not suitable for both purposes. The employer, knowing exactly what jobs he has in mind, wants a test that will forecast success in his jobs as accurately as possible. He, therefore, would like a test designed specifically for

---

EIGHT TESTS ARE GIVEN IN THE DIFFERENTIAL APTITUDE TEST BATTERY

Verbal reasoning

Each of the fifty sentences in this test has the first word and the last word left out. You are to pick out words which will fill the blanks so that the sentence will be true and sensible.

Example X: _____ is to water as eat is to _____

A. continue . . . drive
B. foot . . . enemy
C. drink . . . food   C is correct
D. girl . . . industry
E. drink . . . enemy

Numerical ability

This test consists of forty numerical problems. Next to each problem there are five answers. You are to pick out the correct answer.

Examble X: Add 13   A 14
                  12   B 25
                  —   C 16   B is correct
                        D 59
                        E none of these

Abstract reasoning

Each row consists of four figures called problem figures and five called answer figures. The four problem figures make a series. You are to find out which one of the answer figures would be the next, or the fifth one in the series.

Example Y:

PROBLEM FIGURES   ANSWER FIGURES

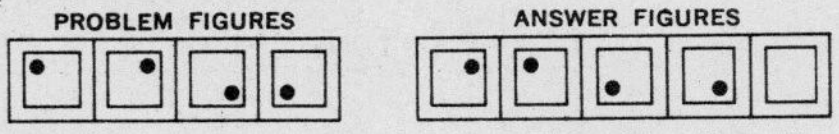

                              A B C D E

B is correct

Space relations

This test consists of 60 patterns which can be folded into figures. For each pattern, four figures are shown. You are to decide which one of these figures can be made from the pattern shown.

Example Y:

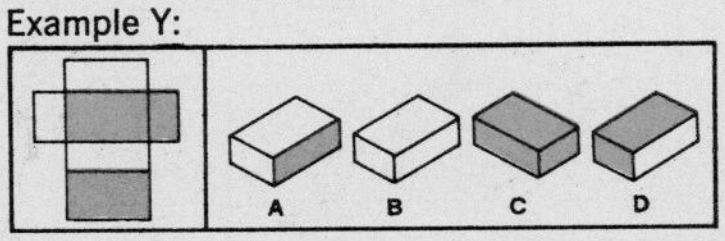

                    A   B   C   D   D is correct

Mechanical reasoning

This test consists of a number of pictures and questions about those pictures.

Example X: Which man has the heavier load? (If equal, mark C.)

B is correct

Clerical speed and accuracy

This is a test to see how quickly and accurately you can compare letter and number combinations. You will notice that in each Test Item one of the five is *underlined*. You are to look at the *one* combination which is underlined, find the *same* one after that item number on the separate answer sheet, and fill in the space under it.

TEST ITEMS   SAMPLE OF ANSWER SHEET

V. AB AC AD AE AF   V. AC AE AF AB AD
W. aA aB BA Ba Bb   W. BA Bb Bb aA aB
X. A7 7A B7 7B AB   X. 7B B7 AB 7A A7
Y. Aa Ba bA BA bB   Y. Aa bA bB Ba bB
Z. 3A 3B 33 B3 BB   Z. BB 3B B3 3A 33

Language usage: Spelling

This test is composed of a series of words. Some of them are correctly spelled; some are incorrectly spelled. You are to indicate whether each word is spelled right or wrong.

EXAMPLES   SAMPLE OF ANSWER SHEET

                              R W   R W
W. man Y. catt   W.   Y.
                              R W   R W
X. gurl Z. dog   X.   Z.

Language usage: Grammar

This test consists of a series of sentences, each divided into four parts lettered A, B, C, and D. You are to look at each sentence and decide which part has an error in grammar, punctuation, or spelling.
    Some sentences have no error in any part. If there is no error in a sentence, fill in the space under the letter E.

Example X: Ain't we / going to / the office / next week?   A B C D E
           A   B   C   D   X.
                                                           A B C D E
                                   SAMPLE OF ANSWER SHEET

FIGURE 12.12. *Sample items from the eight tests of the Differential Aptitude Tests (DAT) battery. These items are generally easier than those on the tests themselves. (The Psychological Corporation.)*

his purposes, for instance, for selecting electronics technicians, electrical welders, or lathe operators. The counselor, on the other hand, is trying to help a person make a choice—usually a fairly general choice—among different lines of work. For this purpose, the counselor wants rather general tests that sample many different aspects of specific aptitudes. He has a large number to choose among.

Vocational-aptitude tests, as well as the vocational-interest tests described below, are frequently available in schools and communities. A psychological clinic or student counseling service, in colleges that have one, is usually prepared to administer such tests. The U.S. Employment Service and the Veterans Administration provide testing services for those who qualify for assistance. In the larger cities, several independent agencies and individuals that offer competent testing facilities for a reasonable fee are usually available.

TEST BATTERIES   For the purposes of counseling, it is often desirable to give several tests measuring different aptitudes. Some of these tests have been combined into batteries which give information about *both* scholastic and vocational aptitudes.

One such battery, designed especially for the counseling of high school students and noncollege adults, is called the Differential Aptitude Tests (DAT). Tests of verbal reasoning, numerical ability, abstract reasoning, space relations, mechanical reasoning, clerical speed and accuracy, spelling, and the use of language in sentences are included in this battery. Sample items are shown in Figure 12.12. The scores on each of these tests are plotted as a *profile of scores* on a special chart (see Figure 12.13).

The sum of the scores on the verbal-reasoning and numerical-ability tests may be used by counselors as an index of scholastic aptitude. The predictive validity of this sum of scores is quite high, that is, high positive correlations with grades are usually obtained. The other scores, either singly, or in various combinations, may be used to predict success in tasks requiring more specific aptitudes. However, since even more specific aptitude tests are available, the specific aptitude tests of this battery are not normally used to predict success on a particular job. Furthermore, these other tests do not predict school success well [McNemar, 1964]. Instead, the counselor typically determines the

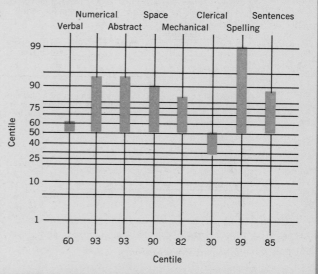

THE RESULTS FROM THE DIFFERENTIAL APTITUDE TESTS ARE PLOTTED AS A PROFILE

FIGURE 12.13.   *A Differential Aptitude Tests (DAT) profile. This profile was obtained from a girl interested in majoring in science in college. If you were a counselor, would you consider this profile consistent with the goal? (Bennett et al., 1951.)*

strengths and weaknesses of an individual from the profile and uses this as a basis for discussion and recommendation [Bennett et al., 1951]. This battery is used much as were the tests given to Thomas Stiles (see page 415).

VOCATIONAL INTERESTS To succeed at a job or a course of training, a person must have not only the aptitudes required for it but also a set of interests that enable him to enjoy its various aspects. Interests, as well as aptitudes, must therefore be taken into account in choosing a vocation and the training to prepare for it. Psychologists have tried two general approaches in developing tests of interest that might serve in vocational guidance. One, developed by Strong, has been called the *empirical approach;* the other, developed by Kuder, has been called the *theoretical approach.* Each approach has its advantages and its limitations.

Strong Vocational Interest Test. The empirical approach to determining the interests required for a vocation involves the measurement of interests that characterize successful people already in the vocation. We find out what the interests of each vocational group are and then choose only those which *distinguish* successful people in this group from successful persons in other groups. We make the assumption that these distinctive interests are actually necessary for success in the vocation. On the basis of this reasoning, Professor Strong went about developing the Strong Vocational Interest Test.

He began by selecting several hundred items that might conceivably distinguish interests in different occupations (see Table 12.9). Items on the test concern preferences for amusements, school subjects, activities, kinds of people, and so forth. Most of the items are presented so that a person taking the pencil-and-paper test can indicate whether he dislikes (D), likes (L), or is indifferent (I) to the item.

Strong had several hundred people, chosen to be as representative as possible of a particular occupation or vocation, take the test so that he could find out what the interests of successful people actually

TABLE 12.9 *Sample items and types of items on the Strong Vocational Interest Test.*

SAMPLE OCCUPATION ITEMS		CHOICES	
1. Actor (not movie)	L	I	D
2. Advertiser	L	I	D
3. Architect	L	I	D
4. Army officer	L	I	D
5. Artist	L	I	D
6. Astronomer	L	I	D
7. Athletic director	L	I	D

TYPES OF ITEMS	NUMBER
Occupations	100
School subjects	36
Amusements	49
Activities	48
Kinds of people	47
Preference for activities	40
Comparison between items	40
Present abilities	40
Total	400

SOURCE: From Strong, 1938.

were. From their responses he was able to discard many items on which there were no substantial differences among occupational groups and to retain those items which successfully discriminated among such groups. Some items, of course, discriminated between certain groups, such as doctors and lawyers, but not between others, such as physicians and chemists. They nevertheless proved useful. In the end, he was able to construct a method of scoring his test for each occupation which summarized how well the examinee's interests corresponded with those of people employed in each of several occupations.

The Strong vocational test, as used in recent years, contains 400 discriminating items. It can be scored for 47 occupations in which men are employed and 28 occupations open to women. Scores are given as grades—A, B+, B, B−, or C. If a person receives an A, his interests correspond quite well with those of successful people in the occupation, and the prognosis of success, so far as interests go, is excellent. On the other hand, a grade of C means that his interests do not correspond at all well with those of people in the occupation and that his chances of success, so far as interests go, are rather poor. Grades of B+, B, and B— are less certain and are interpreted as giving intermediate degrees of correspondence of interest. A sample of some of the occupations for which Strong scales are available is listed in Table 12.10.

Kuder Preference Record. Both an advantage and a limitation of the Strong test is that it provides scores for specific occupations. In order for a person to use its results, he must state the occupations in which he is interested and have the test separately scored for each occupation. Fortunately, machine

scoring has been developed; so the results on several scales can be obtained rather quickly and cheaply. Nevertheless, the Strong test does not give a direct general picture of a person's interests. For this purpose, the Kuder Preference Record is more suitable. It simply divides all interests into nine general categories: mechanical, computational, scientific, persuasive, artistic, literary, musical, social, and clerical.

A person takes the test in much the same way that he does the Strong vocational test. He indicates his likes and dislikes (see Figure 12.14) and receives a score on each of the nine interest categories. Then, in order to see how his interests correspond with those of persons employed in different occupations, the counselor turns to occupational norms which indicate how people in these occupations score in each of the categories. The examinee may, for example, be considering the occupation of engineering. By turning to the appropriate table, his counselor can tell him, for example, that 27 per cent of engineers score as low as he does on "scientific interests," 50 per cent as low as he on "computational interests," and so on. On the other hand, by comparing his scores with those of ministers, teachers, or members of other occupations, he may secure a profile for a different profession. The adviser, by looking at these profiles, may be able to inform the person that his interests correspond more with those of persons in sales, teaching, and social service than they do with those in engineering, science, or medicine.

The use of interest tests. Interest tests, like aptitude tests, are not infallible. People sometimes succeed in an occupation with few, if any, of the interests held by others in the occupation. All a counselor can conclude from interest tests is that the odds are strongly favorable, strongly unfavorable, or perhaps about even. Follow-up studies of people who have taken interest tests show that many more fail to succeed in a profession when their interest test indicates a poor prognosis than when the interest pattern appears highly favorable. The student, or anyone else, who chooses an occupation after receiving strongly unfavorable advice based on in-

TABLE 12.10 *Some of the occupations for which the Strong Vocational Interest Test may be scored. The test is scored separately for each occupation and for men and women. Of the occupations listed below, those accompanied by an asterisk (*) are scored for women only, those accompanied by a dagger (†) are scored for both men and women, and the rest are scored for men only.*

Accountant	Life-insurance sales†
Advertising man	Mathematician
Architect	Minister
Artist†	Musician
Author†	Nurse*
Aviator	Occupational therapist*
Banker	Office worker†
Buyer*	Personnel manager
Carpenter	Pharmacist
Chemist	Physician†
City school superintendent	Policeman
Coast guard	Printer
Dentist†	Production manager
Dietitian*	Psychologist†
Engineer	Public administrator
Farmer	Social-science teacher
Forest service	Social worker*
Housewife*	Stenographer-secretary*
Laboratory technician	Veterinarian
Lawyer†	YMCA-YWCA secretary†
Librarian*	

terest tests is taking a considerable chance and may later regret his choice.

Personality measurement

So far, we have been discussing tests of maximum performance; people try to do the best they can on aptitude and achievement tests. Personality measures, on the other hand, are tests of typical performance [Cronbach, 1960]. There are no right or wrong answers on personality tests; instead, people are asked about what they usually do or what is typical of them.

Personality testing is done for many reasons. For instance, personnel psychologists may want to select people whose personality characteristics make them good salesmen. A military psychologist may want to measure neurotic tendencies that make people unfit for a sensitive assignment. Experimental psychologists may want to measure anxiety in order to control its influence in their experiments on perception or learning. A variety of different methods have been developed to suit these specific purposes.

PENCIL-AND-PAPER TESTS The most convenient type of measure to use for almost any psychological purpose is a pencil-and-paper test which may be given cheaply and quickly to large groups of people at the same time. Hence pencil-and-paper tests are rather popular, and during the last 20 years psychologists have constructed a wide variety of them [Guilford, 1959].

Questionnaires. Pencil-and-paper tests of personality characteristics are usually questionnaires in which the persons being tested must answer questions or say "yes" or "no" to simple statements. Samples of statements are as follows:

I generally prefer to attend movies alone.

I occasionally cross the street to avoid meeting someone I know.

I seldom or never go out on double dates.

The person taking the test must say "yes" or "no," or "true" or "false," to each such statement, thus indicating whether he thinks it applies to him. In some questionnaires a person may also be allowed to answer "doubtful" or "uncertain."

This kind of personality test first gained widespread use during World War I when it was used to weed out emotionally unstable draftees. The statements in the test were chosen to reflect psychiatric symptoms that might predict future emotional breakdown. They included such items as the following:

I consider myself a very nervous person.

I frequently feel moody and depressed.

Do items such as these really test what the examiner

THE KUDER PREFERENCE RECORD GIVES A GENERAL PICTURE OF A PERSON'S INTERESTS

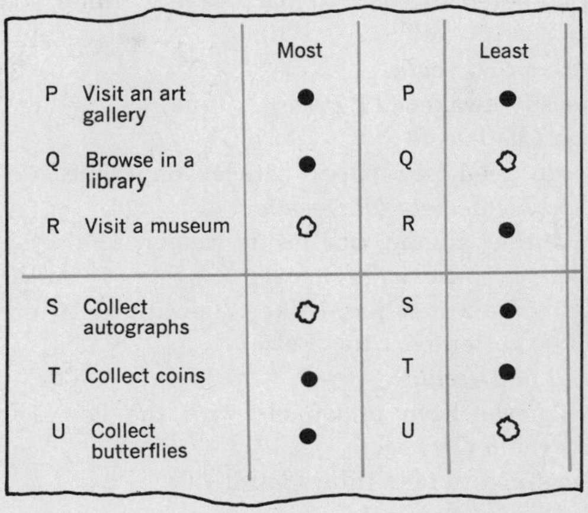

FIGURE 12.14. *Examples of items on the Kuder Preference Record. With a pinprick the subject indicates which of the three alternatives he likes most and which he likes least. In this case, he likes Q least and R most of P, Q, and R, and he likes S most and U least of S, T, and U. (G. F. Kuder and Science Research Associates.)*

TABLE 12.11 *Typical items from the MMPI. The response (true or false) which is scored positively is shown in parentheses. Some of these items are scored on more than one scale.*

Hypochondriasis (Hs) scale
I am bothered by acid stomach several times a week. (True)
Depression (D) scale
I am easily awakened by noise. (True)
Hysteria (Hy) scale
I like to read newspaper articles on crime. (False)
Psychopathic deviate (Pd) scale
I am neither gaining nor losing weight. (False)
*Masculinity-feminity (Mf) scale**
When I take a new job, I like to be tipped off on who should be gotten next to. (False)
Paranoia (Pa) scale
I have never been in trouble with the law. (False)
Psychasthenia (Pt) scale
I am inclined to take things hard. (True)
Schizophrenia (Sc) scale
I get all the sympathy I should. (False)
Hypomania (Ma) scale
I never worry about my looks. (True)
Social introversion (Si) scale
People generally demand more respect for their own rights than they are willing to allow for others. (True)

SOURCE: Items from Dahlstrom and Welsh, 1960.
* High score indicates feminine values.

thinks they test? The validity question is especially acute in personality testing.

The problem of validity. In the case of personality tests, valid measurement means measurement that correlates with one or more personality characteristics. No personality test has perfect validity; the question is whether or not a test has sufficient validity to be useful in drawing any conclusions from its results. In other words: Can we make better decisions with the test than without it?

Since World War I, the use of personality questionnaires has greatly expanded. They are mostly designed to measure emotional maladjustment or such general traits as extroversion-introversion. When constructed by psychologists who are con-

scious of the validity problem, the tests have usually been validated in some way, so that the degree of validity is known.

But many of the questionnaires in popular magazines designed to tell you whether you are a good husband, a happy person, an introvert, and so forth, have not been validated. Neither is there any known validity in some of the tests made up by individuals or "testing agencies" for use in selecting executives or employees in industry. Even though the items on a test may look valid, this is no guarantee that they actually are. Indeed, since validity is so hard to come by, the best assumption is that a personality test is invalid until it is proved otherwise.

Another problem in developing valid personality tests is the possibility of an individual *faking* his answers on the test. A person, for example, who knows that a high score on emotional maladjustment will keep him out of the Army can deliberately get a high score. In World War I, for example, a group of draftees who made abnormal scores on a personality test at the time of induction were able to make quite normal scores on it after the war was over. Conversely, a person who may be quite maladjusted usually can make a low score if that is necessary to get the job he desires.

Minnesota Multiphasic Personality Inventory. Despite instances of this sort, it is possible to construct personality tests with empirical validity. First, the tests must be shown to correlate with a criterion when the people taking the test are being honest in their answers. Second, the test must be so constructed that answers are hard to fake or that faking, when it is done, can be detected. A few such tests are available; a good example is the Minnesota Multiphasic Personality Inventory (MMPI) [Hathaway and McKinley, 1951; Dahlstrom and Welsh, 1960].

The MMPI was constructed by first giving a large number of items to both normal people and abnormal personalities classified into several diagnostic categories. The items, which could be answered "true," "cannot say," or "false," were fairly typical of pencil-and-paper personality questionnaires (see Table 12.11). The scores of the normal group on each item, for instance the number answering it "true," were then compared with those of individuals in each of the diagnostic categories. Items that did not distinguish between normals and abnormals were discarded as invalid; those that did distinguish one or more diagnostic groups from normals were retained. In other words, those that correlated with some criterion of normal-abnormal were retained as valid. In addition, by determining the items which distinguished between men and women, it was possible to construct a scale to differentiate people with masculine and feminine interests, values, and ways of expressing emotion. Some men may have feminine patterns; some women may have masculine patterns. A scale of social introversion has also been constructed from those items which differentiate the socially introverted from the socially nonintroverted. The 10 personality scales which are usually scored on the MMPI are as follows:

1. *Hypochondriasis (Hs)* Exaggerated anxiety about one's health and pessimistic interpretations and exaggerations of minor symptoms

2. *Depression (D)* Feelings of pessimism, worthlessness, hopelessness

3. *Hysteria (Hy)* Various ailments such as headaches and paralyses which have no physical basis

4. *Psychopathic deviation (Pd)* Antisocial and amoral conduct

5. *Masculinity-femininity (Mf)* Measure of masculine and feminine interests; especially a measure of feminine values and emotional expression in men

6. *Paranoia (Pa)* Extreme suspiciousness of other people's motives, frequently resulting in elaborate beliefs that certain people are plotting against one

7. *Psychasthenia (Pt)* Irrational thoughts that recur and/or strong compulsions to repeat seemingly meaningless acts

8. *Schizophrenia (Sc)* Withdrawal into a private world of one's own, often accompanied by hallucinations and bizarre behavior

9. *Hypomania (Ma)* Mild elation and excitement without any clear reason

10. *Social introversion (Si)* Avoidance of other people and removal of oneself from social contacts

The process of empirical validation can be extended to many personality traits and other characteristics of people. In fact, a total of at least 213 scales have been constructed from items of this test [Dahlstrom and Welsh, 1960]. These scales range all the way from a scale for measuring personality patterns similar to those of professional baseball players [LaPlace, 1954] to several for measuring anxiety [Taylor, 1953; Welsh, 1956].

In addition to the 10 personality scales which are usually scored, several "validity" scales are also scored. These are designed to (1) provide a check on the frankness with which individuals answer the items; (2) check on the thoroughness and conscientiousness of the examinee in answering the items; and (3) assess defensiveness, or other sets or attitudes, with which the examinee approaches the test. With these validity scales, malingering and attempts to create an abnormally good or bad impression can be uncovered. The validity scales thus provide a check on faking. Another hindrance to the person who deliberately attempts to fake the test is due to the empirical validation of the test. What an item says does not necessarily mean that it will be on a particular scale; the test has empirical validity, not face validity. Trying to create an impression may backfire. As one writer has expressed it, "This is not a test for the amateur to trifle with" [Whyte, 1956].

The scores on the scales are plotted as T scores—mean of 50 and standard deviation of 10 (see page 394)—on a profile sheet (see Figure 12.15). Scores above 70 and below 30, two standard deviations above and below the mean of the normal reference group, are of interest. The pattern of peaks and the slopes of the profile are also often of diagnostic importance. For example, the first three scales, Hs, D, and Hy, are sometimes called the "neurotic triad," and the pattern of scores on these is diagnostic of neurotic behavioral problems. The profile in Figure 12.15 has elevated scores on the neurotic triad and a particular pattern with the Depression score relatively higher than the Hypochondriasis

A GLANCE AT THE PROFILE SHEET
OF THE MMPI REVEALS
PATTERNS OF SCORES

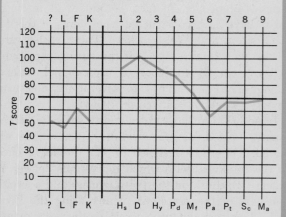

FIGURE 12.15.   *A profile of an individual's scores on the Minnesota Multiphasic Personality Inventory (MMPI). The four "validity" scales are plotted on the left; scores on nine of the scales are* T *scores with a mean of 50 and a standard deviation of 10. Heavy lines are drawn on the chart at scores of 70 and 30, two standard deviations above and below the mean of the normative group. This profile was obtained from a person with a psychosomatic neurotic complaint. Note the marked elevation of the three scales which measure tendencies toward neurotic behavior—Hs, D, Hy. The pattern of scores within this "neurotic triad" is also important; in this case, the D score is higher than the Hs and Hy scores. The Pd score is also elevated. (Modified from Dahlstrom and Welsh, 1960.)*

and Hysteria scores. This profile was of a person with a neurotic psychosomatic illness.

Allport-Vernon-Lindzey scale. The Allport-Vernon-Lindzey Study of Values [Allport et al., 1960] is another pencil-and-paper questionnaire to test personality. It measures a person's major values and interests: theoretical, economic, esthetic, social, political, and religious.

In the first part of the test, the subject must give a yes or no answer to a series of statements, such as, "The main object of scientific research should be the discovery of pure truth rather than its practical applications." If the subject agreed with this statement, his response would help make up a high score on theoretical interests; if he disagreed, his answer would count toward high economic interests. In the second part of the test, the subject must rank four alternatives in the order of his agreement with them. He would, for example, express his agreement with these statements by indicating a rank order for them:

Do you think that a good government should aim chiefly at

(*a*) More aid for the poor, sick, and old?
(*b*) The development of manufacturing and trade?
(*c*) Introducing more ethical principles into its policies and diplomacy?
(*d*) Establishing a position of prestige and respect among nations?

As in the case of the MMPI, it is possible to construct a profile of the results. In this case, the profile is for the six major value areas. An example of such a profile is shown in Figure 12.16.

SITUATIONAL TESTS   At best pencil-and-paper personality questionnaires are somewhat artificial. They attempt to measure personality by asking questions about it. Sampling typical performance by observing people behaving in a fair sample of real-life situations would seem, on the face of it, to be a better measure of personality. Situational tests have been devised which try to meet this need. In these the tester or experimenter constructs some type of real-life situation and observes how personality is expressed in it.

One classical example of this kind of measure is a study of honesty and dishonesty in children [Hartshorne and May, 1928].

Children were put in a number of situations affording an opportunity to cheat without their knowing that the experimenters could catch them. In one situation, children were given a large number of coins to arrange in patterns. When they completed this task, they were asked to put the coins in a cupboard. An inconspicuous code on the coins, however, permitted the experimenters to tell which coins were returned and which were "stolen." Another situation presented the child with a problem so difficult—a complicated finger maze to be traced with the eyes closed—that a child had to peek or "cheat" to obtain a high score on it.

With many situations like these, the investigators exhaustively studied honesty as a personality trait in children. What they found is that honesty is not a unitary trait. Children who are honest in one situation may be dishonest in another situation, and vice versa.

Another example of the use of miniature situations to study personality is to be found in studies by the Office of Strategic Services [Office of Strategic Services Assessment Staff, 1948].

During World War II, the OSS had the task of selecting people to work as agents behind enemy lines. Psychologists developed a wide variety of situations designed to measure important personality traits for this kind of work. Candidates were given such situations as drilling a squad of men, leading a group of candidates in mock-combat conditions, and solving such problems as improvising a bridge to move heavy equipment across a stream. Then, to make the situa-

tions as stressful as possible, the psychologists deliberately made the task more difficult. In one case, for example, a candidate was to construct a tower out of heavy logs within a fairly short period of time and was assigned two helpers to do the job. The helpers, however, were stooges who deliberately failed to carry out orders. They would clumsily knock over parts of the completed structure and argue with the candidate or make insulting remarks about his intelligence, appearance, or race. Faced with such frustrations as these, many candidates broke down in tears or sputtered with rage.

Situational tests have high face validity because they resemble the real thing. Whether they have any real validity or not is usually open to question. In the case of the OSS studies, the exigencies of war made it impractical to validate the tests. In this case and in others, there are several obstacles to achieving high validity. (1) It may not be possible to motivate subjects as they would be motivated in real life. (2) In many cases, it is not possible to disguise the situations well enough to keep the subjects from seeing through them. Then the candidate considers the whole thing a joke. (3) The judgments of observers often do not agree with one another well enough to provide either reliable or valid measurement. For these reasons, the practical usefulness of situational tests largely remains to be demonstrated. Possibly through further research,

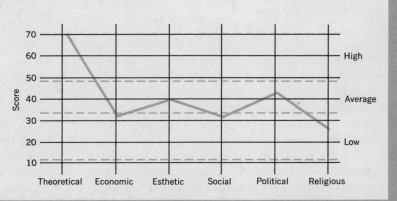

THE RELATIVE STRENGTH OF VALUES IS MEASURED BY THE ALLPORT-VERNON-LINDZEY STUDY OF VALUES TEST

FIGURE 12.16. *A profile of scores from the Allport-Vernon-Lindzey Study of Values. Note the highest and lowest scores. What do you suppose might be some of the other characteristics of this person?*

however, tests of this kind may eventually be developed into valid measuring devices.

EXPERIMENTAL MEASUREMENTS Scientists who are trying to discover basic principles frequently employ experimental measurements that are not practicable on a large scale. This is the case in the study of personality. Of the many kinds of experimental measurements used in research on personality, we shall give one example [Eysenck, 1947].

A subject stands blindfolded, with a hook and thread attached to his collar. The other end of the thread is tied to a pen on a *kymograph*, which is a device that moves recording paper around a drum at some constant speed. Thus it will record any moving or swaying of the subject. Now the experimenter tells the subject that he is falling backward. If the subject is suggestible, he will start to sway. Indeed, some people are so suggestible that they would fall over if the experimenter were not prepared to catch them. In any case, the degree of suggestibility of the person is measured experimentally by the mark on the kymograph record. This measure of suggestibility can be correlated with suggestibility in other situations. In general, the correlations have been small and indicate that suggestibility, like honesty, is not a unitary trait.

As you can see, most experimental measures of personality require an elaborate apparatus and procedure. They are therefore not useful for everyday situations. They are proving helpful, however, in establishing principles of personality and in providing suggestions for designing other, more practicable personality tests.

PERSONAL INTERVIEW The personality measurements discussed thus far are *objective* measurements. A measurement is objective when little or no judgment is required by the measurer; all he has to do is count or read a number. He may count, for example, the number of times a person prefers "theoretical" over "economic" tasks, or the number of times the person cheats in an honesty test. Or he may read the number of inches a subject sways in a suggestibility test. No matter what the test situation is, so long as it can be scored by simple counting or by reading numerical measurements, the measurement is objective. An objective measurement can be made by anyone of normal intelligence who can read and count accurately. However, objective measures, after they have been obtained, require interpretation to the examinee.

Whenever, on the other hand, the measurement itself involves some judgment, rating, or interpretation made by the examiner, it is considered a *subjective* measurement. Perhaps the example most familiar to the college student is the grade given by an instructor on an essay question. The teacher does not count anything; he reads the answer and makes a subjective judgment of its quality. In general, subjective measurement is less reliable than objective measurement; it usually yields less agreement between scorers. Yet the difference is not always large; some scorers skilled in their task can achieve reasonably high reliability in subjective scoring. And when we lack objective means of measurement, as is sometimes the case, we are forced to do the best we can with subjective measurements.

The personal interview is one of the oldest devices for measuring personality. It is obviously subjective. Yet interviewers sometimes make reasonably good measuring instruments. Psychologists and psychiatrists, although they secure all the information they can from objective tests, usually rely on the interview to round out their picture of a personality. The interviewer tries to sample as wide a range as possible of the person's feelings and attitudes by getting him to talk about his personal experiences. In so doing, the interviewer not only notes what he hears but also observes more intangible behavior: the way a person talks about certain topics—the catch in the voice, for example, whenever mother is mentioned, or the tenseness that appears whenever certain other subjects are brought up—and, in many cases, what the person is careful *not* to talk about. From these varied observations, the clinician attempts to reconstruct a picture of a person's major motives, his sources of conflict, his modes of adjustment, and the overall adequacy of his adjustment.

Although the interview is more widely used in the study of personality than any other single method, it has some serious limitations. For one thing, it depends almost entirely on the skill of the interviewer—and skill in interviewing is hard to teach. More serious than that is the difficulty of expressing the results of an interview in quantitative terms. In general, the results can be communicated only in word descriptions, not in objective scores. This makes it difficult to compare people by means of the interview or even to tell whether the interviewer has, in fact, made any valid measurement. There is evidence, however, that interviewing combined with objective tests can provide more valid judgments than either one by itself.

RATING SCALES A partial solution to the problem of expressing interview measurements in objective terms is to be found in the *rating scale*. It may be used to record impressions of personality obtained in interviews or from informal observation. There are several forms of rating scales.

One of the simpler forms lists a number of personality characteristics, such as honesty, reliability, sociability, industriousness, and emotionality, and asks the rater who knows the person being evaluated to give a rating—say, between 1 and 7—on each characteristic (see Figure 12.17). Another method is to provide the rater with a number of alternative descriptions and ask him to check which

alternative applies best to the person being rated. From such checks it is usually possible to convert the results into numerical scores on 5- or 7-point scales. An example of such a scale is one for aggression, which you see in Table 12.12.

Rating scales are so simple that we can use them to record our impressions of almost any aspect of a person's personality. Their simplicity, however, should not fool us. Like any form of personality measurement, they can be unreliable and invalid. In the hands of amateurs they usually are. Rating-scale techniques must be subjected to the same rigorous analysis of validity as other more objective forms of personality measurement.

PROJECTIVE METHODS The last form of personality measurement to be discussed is the *projective method*. It is called projective because the subject is presented with a situation, usually a visual object or picture, which gets him unknowingly to reveal some of his personality characteristics by projecting them into the situation. He is presented with the object or picture and asked to say what he sees or to tell a story about it. In his narration, he ascribes certain characteristics to the things and people he talks about and thus reveals his own characteristics. At least that is the theory of the projective test, and that is why it is called projective. Of the several different projective tests, the Thematic Apperception Test (TAT) and the

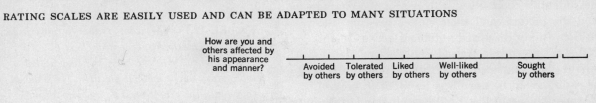

RATING SCALES ARE EASILY USED AND CAN BE ADAPTED TO MANY SITUATIONS

How are you and others affected by his appearance and manner?

Avoided by others   Tolerated by others   Liked by others   Well-liked by others   Sought by others

FIGURE 12.17. *An item on a rating scale. The rater checks a point on the scale to indicate his opinion of the subject. The dash at the end means "no opportunity to observe."*

TABLE 12.12 *An example of a rating scale used to measure aggressive behavior toward other persons.*

INSTRUCTIONS: PLACE A CHECK MARK AFTER THE CATEGORY THAT MOST CLOSELY DESCRIBES THE SUBJECT'S BEHAVIOR.

A. The degree to which the subject displays hostile or aggressive behavior in his relations with others:
  1. Avoids aggression even when it is called for. Never becomes angry or criticizes others.
  2. Seldom becomes angry or critical of others. Will do so, however, if strongly prodded or actually attacked.
  3. Shows normal amount of aggression when the circumstances seem to call for it. Is neither reluctant nor overready to show hostility.
  4. Frequently engages in quarrels or arguments. Is often sarcastic. Tends to be critical of many things.
  5. Almost always aggressive. Has trouble getting along with people because he is ready to argue or fight at the drop of a hat.

Rorschach Test are two that are widely known and frequently used by clinical psychologists.

The Thematic Apperception Test consists of a series of 20 pictures [Murray, 1943]. Each picture is ambiguous enough to permit a variety of interpretations. Figure 12.18 shows an example of the kind of picture used, though it is not one of the test pictures. When presented with a picture, the examinee is asked to make up a story of what is happening in the picture. The story is supposed to begin with events leading up to the scene and end with an outcome. Most people, when they make up such stories, identify themselves with one of the characters in the picture, and their stories may be little more than thinly disguised autobiographies. In this way the examinee may reveal feelings and desires he would otherwise hesitate to discuss openly or, in some cases, would be unwilling to admit to himself.

As generally used, the TAT has no standardized scoring. The tester interprets it by noting recurring themes in the stories—the characteristic needs and frustrations of the hero, the relations of the hero with members of the opposite sex, with parents, or with persons in positions of authority—and the overall emotional tone of the stories, whether depressed or overly optimistic, and so on.

The Rorschach Test is relatively more objective and at the same time more ambiguous than the TAT. The Rorschach consists of 10 ink blots similar to the one in Figure 12.19, although some of the blots have colored parts to them [Rorschach, 1942]. Each card is presented to the subject with the question, "What might this be?" or "What does this

FIGURE 12.18. *An item similar to those used on the Thematic Apperception Test (TAT). The subject is shown a card and instructed to tell a story about what it pictures. He is asked to explain the situation it represents, discuss events that led up to the situation, indicate the feelings and thoughts of the characters in the picture, and describe the outcome of the situation. (After Murray, 1943.)*

remind you of?" After responding for all 10 cards, the subject goes through them again, indicating what parts of the ink blot suggested his responses.

Some of the scoring is done objectively. For instance, the number of times the subject responds to *part* of the blot, compared with the number of times he responds to the blot as a *whole*, can be counted. Counts can also be made of other things, such as the number of responses to color and the number of responses suggesting movement. On the other hand, the clinician interprets not only number of responses in different categories, but also the pattern of the responses, and this can become somewhat subjective. Even more subjective are interpretations based on other cues, such as spontaneous remarks made during the test, signs of emotional upset, and the symbolic meaning of the responses.

Clinicians regularly use projective tests such as the Rorschach and TAT because they believe that they learn about an individual's personality from them. Perhaps they do. After all, the projective test is a subtle kind of interview. Unfortunately, convincing proof of the validity of the tests is lacking. We must therefore withhold judgment about their value as devices for personality measurement.

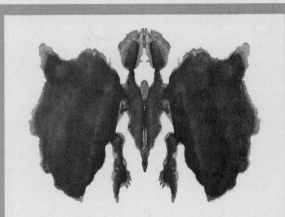

FIGURE 12.19.   *An example of the type of ink-blot figure used on the Rorschach Test. Blots similar to this one are shown to a subject with the instruction to indicate what he sees in them. After all the subject's responses are recorded, the examiner inquires into them more deeply in the attempt to find out what it was about each card that determined the responses.*

SYNOPSIS AND SUMMARY

A test is "an objective and standardized measure of a sample of behavior." In order for these measures to be useful in both practical and experimental situations, they should have the characteristics of reliability, validity, and standardization. Hundreds of more or less reliable, valid, and standardized tests are published [see Buros, 1959]. Some of the most used tests of intelligence, special aptitudes, interests, and personality traits have been presented in this chapter.

Like many other useful devices, tests can be, and have been, abused. Criticism has come from within the psychometric subfield of psychology as well as from journalistic sources [Gross, 1962]. The use of inadequately standardized tests, too much testing, and the inability of some test users to interpret the test results wisely and flexibly are all justified criticisms of psychological testing. Remember that tests are to be used to help make decisions about individuals, and even the objective tests merely give us a score or a set of scores. The use made of these scores is the crucial thing, and this requires a good deal of sophistication in statistics and counseling. As the standard of training and sophistication of test users improves, it is hoped that such abuses of tests will become less frequent.

1. Psychological tests are quite useful in helping others, or the examinee himself, to arrive at decisions. They are intended to be administered and interpreted by trained

people and they are usually used in conjunction with other information available about a person.

2. Ability is a general term which refers either to the potential for acquiring a skill or to an already acquired skill. Aptitude refers to the potentiality that a person has to profit from a certain type of training. Achievement refers to what a person has already learned. Tests can measure each of these aspects of performance. In aptitude tests, the emphasis is on predicting achievement in other situations.

3. Tests also differ in whether they (a) are individual or group tests, (b) emphasize verbal factors or nonverbal performance factors, or (c) measure the speed with which a person can solve problems as compared with the ability to solve difficult problems irrespective of time required.

4. Tests that measure general ability or aptitude for intellectual performance are called intelligence tests. Those which measure special aptitudes for a particular kind of training or for a vocation are called special aptitude tests.

5. The Stanford-Binet Scale is an individual intelligence test devised especially for children of school age. It yields a score called mental age (MA), and from this an IQ may be derived. The Wechsler Adult Intelligence Scale (WAIS) is an individual test for adults.

6. Group tests of intelligence may be used for testing large groups of people at the same time. Two of the best known of these are the Otis and the School and College Ability Tests (SCAT).

7. Intelligence is not only a single general ability. By factor analysis, it has been demonstrated that several abilities are involved in conventional intelligence tests. Some tests weight certain of these abilities more than other tests do. Thus, intelligence is some general ability and a number of specific abilities.

8. Those individuals who have an IQ of less than 70 are regarded as mentally retarded. They are classified into four retardation groups: mild, moderate, severe, and profound. Mental retardation may be brought about by primary or secondary causes. In primary mental retardation, there is no obvious organic defect; in secondary retardation, the mental symptoms are caused by some obvious organic disturbance.

9. At the high end of the distribution of IQs are the mentally gifted. Those with IQs between 130 and 140 are considered very superior; those above 140 are regarded as "near genius." Many of the outstanding leaders of history have been mentally gifted. In general, the gifted are far more successful, more physically fit, and better adjusted than those of average intelligence, though there are notable exceptions.

10. In the middle intelligence groups, a strong relationship exists between tested intelligence and job achievement.

11. Differences in intelligence among various groups in the population can be measured. Although men and women are equal in intelligence, the old do less well than the young on intelligence tests, and Negroes tend to score lower than whites. Group differences in intelligence require careful interpretation and are of little practical significance because of the large amount of overlap between groups and because decisions must be made about individuals, not groups.

12. Both the inheritance of a person and the home and cultural environment play a role in determining the ability called intelligence.

13. Special aptitude tests have been developed to estimate the ability to succeed in college or other advanced training; other special aptitude tests assess the likelihood of success in some particular vocation. Those for training are called scholastic-aptitude tests; those for vocations are called vocational-aptitude tests.

14. Vocational-interest tests serve as additional aids in vocational choice by measuring the degree to which a person's interests coincide with those found most frequently among persons already in a vocation.

15. Special aptitude tests and tests of general intellectual ability are often combined into test batteries.

16. Measurements of typical performance, or personality tests, have been devised both for research on personality and for use in practical situations. Serving both purposes are a great variety of pencil-and-paper tests: the Minnesota Multiphasic Personality Inventory (MMPI) is one which has been empirically validated.

17. Situational tests are tests in which a person is placed in a real-life problem situation with other people and his way of dealing with the problem is observed.

18. Interviews, although often used, are not highly reliable or valid measures of personality. Somewhat more objective and valid are rating scales which require the rating of the presence or degree of particular characteristics.

19. In recent years, projective tests such as the Rorschach and Thematic Apperception Test (TAT) have come into widespread use, particularly in clinical work.

RELATED TOPICS IN THE TEXT

CHAPTER 11 PSYCHOLOGICAL MEASUREMENT An understanding of the statistics discussed in Chapter 11 is essential. Means, standard deviations, standard scores, centiles, and correlation coefficients must be understood before you can make much sense from a chapter on psychological testing.

CHAPTER 13 PERSONALITY Personality tests are ways of measuring some of the traits which make people different. Even the ability, aptitude, and interest tests may be thought of as measuring personality traits; intellectual ability, mechanical aptitude, and patterns of interests are all personality traits. In this chapter on personality we take up the origin and patterning of these traits.

SUGGESTIONS FOR FURTHER READING

Anastasi, A. *Psychological testing* (2d ed.). New York: Macmillan, 1961.
A review of the principles and types of psychological tests.

Cronbach, L. J. *Essentials of psychological testing* (2d ed.). New York: Harper & Row, 1960.
A comprehensive introduction to the field of psychological testing.

Lyman, H. B. *Test scores and what they mean.* Englewood Cliffs, N.J.: Prentice-Hall, 1963. (Paperback).
A very readable presentation of some of the fundamentals involved in using and interpreting psychological tests.

Robinson, H. B., and Robinson, N. M. *The mentally retarded child: A psychological approach.* New York: McGraw-Hill, 1965.
A description of the measurement, treatment, and causes of mental retardation.

Super, D. E., and Crites, J. O. *Appraising vocational fitness by means of psychological tests* (rev. ed.). New York: Harper & Row, 1962.
The use of tests in vocational counseling and selection.

Tyler, L. E. *Tests and measurements.* Englewood Cliffs, N.J.: Prentice-Hall, 1963. (Paperback.)
A lucid primer on tests and the statistics used with them.

Wechsler, D. *The measurement and appraisal of adult intelligence* (4th ed.). Baltimore: Williams & Wilkins, 1958.
Information about the development and use of the Wechsler Adult Intelligence Scale (WAIS).

13

PERSONALITY

PEOPLE IS MOSTLY ALIKE,
BUT WHAT DIFFERENCE
THEY IS CAN BE
POWERFUL IMPORTANT.
VERMONT FARMER,
QUOTED BY
HENRY MURRAY

TO UNDERSTAND other people and himself better is one of the desires of almost everyone, and especially of the student of psychology. Knowledge of many aspects of psychology, including development, motivation, learning, perception, and measurement, furthers this aim. We also learn to understand people better through the study of personality.

The term personality has a wide range of meanings for both the specialist and nonspecialist, and no dogmatic definition can be given. But, for many psychologists, the term *personality* refers to the study of the characteristic and distinctive traits of an individual, the stable and shifting patterns of relationships between these traits, the origins of the traits, and the ways the traits interact to help or hinder the adjustment of a person to other people and situations. This type of definition puts stress on the *structure* and *dynamics* of personality. Structure refers to the description of traits and their relationships; the term dynamics refers to the active influence, especially the motivational influence, of traits upon adjustment. One other fact should be apparent from this definition: In this chapter, the focus of emphasis has shifted somewhat from general laws of behavior to the study of the operation of these laws in a particular person—from the nomothetic to the idiographic (see page 414).

Structure of personality

When we attempt to study an individual in a real-life setting, we are immediately struck by the tremendous number of things we might observe. Every moment in the day he is doing something—sleeping, eating, writing, working, playing, talking, walking. Any attempt to describe and understand every single thing he does involves us in a tremendously complicated, and in the end impossible, task. Once, for example, a group of psychologists attempted to record in detail the activities of a seven-year-old boy for just one day [Barker and Wright, 1951]. The result was a book of 435 pages! Think how voluminous the report would be if we attempted a record such as this for many individuals over a longer period of time.

In attempting to understand personalities, we obviously must make some choices of what to study. To a certain extent, these choices are arbitrary, and they are made according to what we are most interested in knowing about a person. In some circumstances, we may be satisfied with only general traits of behavior. In others, we may want most to characterize a person's attitudes, or his motives, or his way of dealing with personal problems.

No matter what personality characteristics are chosen for study, two requirements must always be met if the selection is to be meaningful and useful. In the first place, a personality characteristic must really be *characteristic*. It does us little good, for example, to know that Mr. A was angry on a certain Tuesday morning. Anyone might have been angry in the situation he faced that particular morning, and he may not have been angry at any other time for a month. What we would rather know about Mr. A is whether he is characteristically an angry or hostile person or whether he is usually of a serene, sunny disposition and is provoked to anger only occasionally or in the most exasperating of situations. If he is usually serene, and only occasionally angry, we characterize him as a serene person.

Second, the aspects of personality that we choose for study should be *distinctive*. Almost all men in the United States work for a living, and almost all of them go to barbershops to get their hair cut. It does us little good to note, therefore, that a person works for a living or gets his hair cut, for these are not characteristics that distinguish him from most other people. On the other hand, some people worker harder than others or let their hair grow longer than others, and these differences do distinguish people one from another. Then we might regard "industriousness" or "an unkempt appearance" as distinguishing personality characteristics. The measurement of some characteristic and distinctive personality traits was described in Chapter 12.

Confining ourselves to those aspects of personality which are characteristic and distinctive simplifies the problem of studying personality considerably. Even so, the possible number of distinctive characteristics is enormous. Moreover, these characteristics are not always easily separated from each other. Is there a clear-cut distinction, for example, between honesty, on the one hand, and conscientiousness, integrity, or dependability, on the other hand? What is the difference between a person's need to depend on others and his need for affection? In these and many other instances, we find that personality characteristics often overlap and are highly correlated with each other. Hence several possible sets of characteristics may not be clearly different from one another. Each set, however, may serve some particular purpose in describing personality.

TRAITS AND TYPES   A *trait* is any aspect of personality that is reasonably characteristic and distinctive. The concept of the trait probably provides our most useful means of characterizing a person. The problem, however, of deciding which traits are useful and which are not is difficult. The unabridged dictionary contains approximately 18,000 adjectives that are used in our language to describe how people act, think, perceive, feel, and behave [Allport and Odbert, 1936]. It also contains about 4,000 words that might be accepted as trait names—such words as humility, sociability, honesty, and forthrightness. Of course, many of these terms are synonyms or near synonyms, and others are so rare and unusual that they are of little value. When these synonyms and rare words are carefully edited, we are left with about 170 words—still an unwieldy number for scientific purposes. It must be further reduced and refined.

This process of reduction should not be carried to the point of setting up personality types, however. We often hear someone say, for instance, that "John is the submissive type," "Harry is the extroverted type," or "Dick is a Don Juan (type)." Such statements may convey more or less correctly *one* of a person's rather distinctive traits, but they overstep the mark in oversimplifying the structure of personality.

Such notions of personality types stem from a

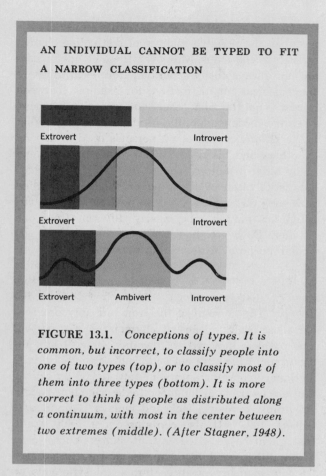

AN INDIVIDUAL CANNOT BE TYPED TO FIT A NARROW CLASSIFICATION

Extrovert   Introvert

Extrovert   Introvert

Extrovert   Ambivert   Introvert

FIGURE 13.1.   *Conceptions of types. It is common, but incorrect, to classify people into one of two types (top), or to classify most of them into three types (bottom). It is more correct to think of people as distributed along a continuum, with most in the center between two extremes (middle). (After Stagner, 1948).*

few dramatic instances of somebody's behavior, from contact with relatively rare personalities, or from exposure to fictional characters who have purposely been overdrawn to make them interesting. We then unthinkingly use these rare instances as models for people in everyday life. The big bully who beats up all the kids in the community becomes a model for an "aggressive type." The relatively rare person who is the "life of the party" may be the model for the "extroverted type." And fictional characters such as Hamlet, Pollyanna, or Scrooge are presented so distinctively that they serve as models for their respective types. Actually, such models are so rare that they are hardly valid in describing real people.

Another objection to typing people is that it lumps together a number of different personality traits. The "introverted type" is supposed to be withdrawn, sensitive to criticism, and inhibited in emotional expression; the "extroverted type" is supposed to be thick-skinned, spontaneous in emotional expression, and little affected by personal failures. It happens more often, though, that one person may be as sensitive as the introvert, yet as sociable as the extrovert, and another person may be as thick-skinned as the extrovert, but as ill-humored and unfriendly as the introvert. A personality is not simple enough to be put into a single basket—the type. People are characterized by a number of traits. Some of these may be introvertive and some extrovertive; seldom do they all fit the pattern of any one type. Even in the rare cases where they appear to fit one pattern, it is very unlikely that all the traits will be so extreme. Most people are not extreme types nor do they exhibit extreme traits; rather, they fall somewhere between the extremes (see Figure 13.1). Thus characterization of people by type tends to be oversimplified, and therefore incorrect.

EXAMPLES OF TRAITS   Although it is usually incorrect to reduce a complex personality to a simple type, it is nevertheless desirable for purposes of study to distinguish certain general, unifying traits from among the welter of human differences.

Factor-analytic studies. Factor analysis is one tool used to reduce the large number of personality traits by finding clusters of related traits (see page 406). For instance, in one study it was found that the more than 170 trait names gathered from a dictionary could be reduced to 12 clusters or factors [Cattell, 1946]. As a first step in this study, 171 traits were reduced by combining under one trait name all the traits that correlated highly with another set of traits. By following this procedure, 35 broad traits or trait clusters were obtained. Then a small group of experienced judges rated a large group of adult men whom they knew reasonably well on each of these 35 broad traits. When all the ratings were made, they were put through a factor analysis. The result was a reduction of the 35 traits to 12 basic traits or factors (see Table 13.1). In other words, 12 basic or primary traits proved to be almost as good as 35 in describing personality, because a person's rating on each of the 35 traits could be predicted from his ratings on the 12 primary traits or factors (see Figure 13.2).

One should not jump to the conclusion that there are just 12 basic personality traits. The study cited is only one example among many studies of the subject. The final number of traits one obtains in such a study depends on several conditions, including the kinds of people observed, the settings or walks of life in which they are studied, the people doing the rating, and the number of possible traits the judges use in making their ratings.

In another study, 128 men, who were graduate students in clinical psychology, were the subjects [Fiske, 1949]. More than 20 trait descriptions were used for rating these subjects. Actually three different sets of ratings were made: one by faculty members who knew the students fairly well, another by fellow graduate students, and a third by the students themselves. Each of these sets of ratings was subjected to a factor analysis. Out of this analysis came five basic traits which are listed and described in Table 13.2. Though the results were slightly different for the three sets of ratings, still the same five traits appeared in all three.

Psychologists have not settled on any one set of traits, nor are they likely to, for just as there is no one "correct" picture to take of a person or a scene, so no one set of traits should be considered final. The important thing is to have a set of traits that is significant for a particular purpose and that can be used for making comparisons among individuals.

Abilities, attitudes, and interests. Any description of personality characteristics is incomplete if it does not include such things as abilities, attitudes, and interests. It may, for example, be characteristic of a person that he is intelligent, conservative, and sports-loving. Such characteristics, in fact, are usually included in the list of traits used for rating personality. In both Tables 13.1 and 13.2, some of the trait names which appear apply to these characteristics.

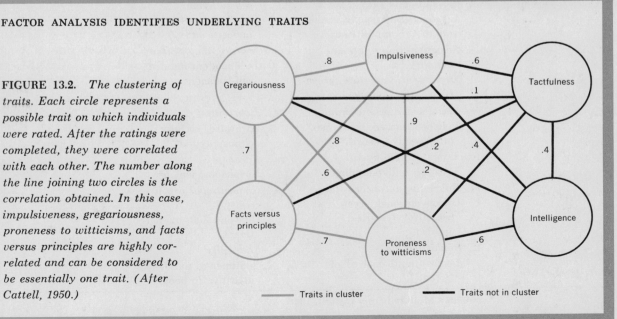

FACTOR ANALYSIS IDENTIFIES UNDERLYING TRAITS

FIGURE 13.2. *The clustering of traits. Each circle represents a possible trait on which individuals were rated. After the ratings were completed, they were correlated with each other. The number along the line joining two circles is the correlation obtained. In this case, impulsiveness, gregariousness, proneness to witticisms, and facts versus principles are highly correlated and can be considered to be essentially one trait. (After Cattell, 1950.)*

TABLE 13.1   *One set of primary traits of personality obtained by the method of factor analysis. A group of experienced judges rated adult men on 35 broad traits. Factor analysis was used on the results to identify the traits that for all practical purposes were duplicates, and the long list of traits was consolidated into 12 primary traits.*

1. *Cyclothymia*
   Emotionally expressive, frank, placid
   vs. *Schizothymia*
   Reserved, close-mouthed, anxious

2. *General mental capacity*
   Intelligent, smart, assertive
   vs. *Mental defect*
   Unintelligent, dull, submissive

3. *Emotionally stable*
   Free of neurotic symptoms, realistic about life
   vs. *Neurotic emotionality*
   Variety of neurotic symptoms, evasive, immature

4. *Dominance*
   Self-assertive, confident, aggressive
   vs. *Submissiveness*
   Submissive, unsure, complaisant

5. *Surgency*
   Cheerful, joyous, humorous, witty
   vs. *Desurgency*
   Depressed, pessimistic, dull, phlegmatic

6. *Positive character*
   Persevering, attentive to people
   vs. *Dependent character*
   Fickle, neglectful of social chores

7. *Adventurous cyclothymia*
   Likes meeting people, strong interest in opposite sex
   vs. *Withdrawn schizothymia*
   Shy, little interest in opposite sex

8. *Sensitive, infantile emotionality*
   Dependent, immature, gregarious, attention-seeking
   vs. *Mature, tough poise*
   Independent-minded, self-sufficient

9. *Socialized, cultured mind*
   Polished, poised, composed, introspective, sensitive
   vs. *Boorishness*
   Awkward, socially clumsy, crude

10. *Trustful cyclothymia*
    Trustful, understanding
    vs. *Paranoia*
    Suspicious, jealous

11. *Bohemian unconcernedness*
    Unconventional, eccentric, fitful hysterical upsets
    vs. *Conventional practicality*
    Conventional, unemotional

12. *Sophistication*
    Logical mind, cool, aloof
    vs. *Simplicity*
    Sentimental mind, attentive to people

SOURCE: Modified from Cattell, 1946.

Abilities, attitudes, and interests, however, are different from other personality traits in two important respects. First, they are more often measured by objective tests, that is, by tests that can be mechanically scored and that make no use of the judgments or ratings of a judge (see Chapter 12). Second, they are often measured for special purposes, such as the selection of students or employees, vocational counseling, or public opinion. Since abilities, interests, and attitudes were discussed in Chapter 12, however, we shall not consider them further here (see also Chapter 17).

Motives. We can also describe a person in terms of his motives and goals—why he does what he does. George, for example, may be quite friendly and attentive, thereby exhibiting desirable traits, but his reason for being this way may be that he wants to sell me a sizable insurance policy. Dave, on the other hand, may show the same traits simply because he likes my company. There is a world of difference. Ferdinand may want very much to be my friend, but he may seem reserved and aloof because he does not have the social skills needed to show his friendship. Consequently, I may mistake his motive entirely if I judge him by his superficial traits alone. We therefore need to have concepts of personality that are cast in terms of general traits, that is, motives, as well as specific traits. Motives and specific traits are not mutually exclusive. On the contrary, many specific traits directly or indirectly describe motives. If we consider a person honest, efficient, and industrious, we certainly are saying or implying something about a general trait—one of his motives. On the other hand, it is possible to focus attention more directly on motives, leaving aside for the moment the precise way these motives may be expressed by particular traits.

As in the case of specific traits, psychologists have not yet agreed on any particular set of motives as the standard for comparing different individuals. The set employed depends on one's theoretical orientation and what one is attempting to find out about a particular individual or group. A set that has been widely used, however, particularly in inter-

TABLE 13.2 *Five general personality traits. More than twenty individual traits, shown on the left, were used in making ratings of 128 men. A factor analysis of the ratings yielded the five general, or more basic, traits listed on the right.*

INDIVIDUAL TRAITS	GENERAL TRAITS
Cheerful vs. depressed; talkative vs. silent, introspective; adventurous vs. cautious; adaptable vs. rigid; placid vs. worrying, anxious	Social adaptability
Unshakable vs. easily upset; self-sufficient vs. dependent; placid vs. worrying, anxious; limited overt emotional expression vs. marked overt emotional expression	Emotional control
Readiness to cooperate vs. obstructiveness; serious vs. frivolous; trustful vs. suspicious; good-natured, easygoing vs. self-centered, selfish; conscientious vs. not conscientious	Conformity
Broad interests vs. narrow interests; independent-minded vs. dependent-minded; imaginative vs. unimaginative	Inquiring intellect
Assertive vs. submissive; talkative vs. silent, introspective; marked overt interest in opposite sex vs. slight overt interest in opposite sex; frank, expressive vs. secretive, reserved	Confident self-expresion

SOURCE: *Modified from* Fiske, 1949.

preting the Thematic Apperception Test (see Chapter 12), is given in Table 13.3.

This set of motives was not chosen by factor analysis or any statistical method [Murray, 1938]. Rather it was arrived at in an extensive investigation of personality conducted at the Harvard Psychological Clinic. A number of young men were thoroughly tested, interviewed, and studied by a group of clinical psychologists. The investigators found that a set of motives such as that shown in

TABLE 13.3 *A classification of major personal motives.*

MOTIVE	GOAL AND EFFECTS	MOTIVE	GOAL AND EFFECTS
Abasement	To submit passively to others. To seek and accept injury, blame, and criticism.	Exhibition	To make an impression. To be seen and heard by others. To show off.
Achievement	To accomplish difficult tasks. To rival and surpass others.	Harmavoidance	To avoid pain, physical injury, illness, and death.
Affiliation	To seek and enjoy cooperation with others. To make friends.	Infavoidance	To avoid humiliation. To refrain from action because of fear of failure.
Aggression	To overcome opposition forcefully. To fight and revenge injury. To belittle, curse, or ridicule others.	Nurturance	To help and take care of sick or defenseless people. To assist others who are in trouble.
Autonomy	To be free of restraints and obligations. To be independent and free to act according to impulse.	Order	To put things in order. To achieve cleanliness, arrangement, and organization.
Counteraction	To master or make up for failure by renewed efforts. To overcome weakness and maintain pride and self-respect on a high level.	Play	To devote one's free time to sports, games, and parties. To laugh and make a joke of everything. To be lighthearted and gay.
Deference	To admire and support a superior person. To yield eagerly to other people.	Rejection	To remain aloof and indifferent to an inferior person. To jilt or snub others.
Defendence	To defend oneself against attack, criticism, or blame. To justify and vindicate oneself.	Sentience	To seek and enjoy sensuous impressions and sensations. To enjoy the arts genuinely.
Dominance	To control and influence the behavior of others. To be a leader.		

SOURCE: After Murray, 1938.

the table provided a satisfactory way of classifying and rating the motives of the young men serving as subjects.

Since the original study was conducted, psychologists skilled in the study of personality have devised techniques for rating the strength of each of the motives, or needs, of a person fairly reliably. For instance, an objective test, the Edwards Personal Preference Schedule (EPPS), has been developed for the assessment of many of these motives [Edwards, 1954].

Modes of adjustment and defense mechanisms. Another way of characterizing people is by their typical modes of adjustment. *Adjustment* refers to the process of accommodating oneself to circum-

stances, and more particularly, to the satisfaction of needs, or motives, under various circumstances. There are a number of characteristic modes or ways of adjusting. Most individuals at one time or another use all the various modes. Yet each person may rely more on some than on others.

For example, we all use *defense mechanisms* to protect ourselves against anxiety and fear, and certain ones are more used by some people than others. In other words, the way a person typically defends himself against fear and anxiety is a characteristic of his personality. Because defense mechanisms are such important personality traits, we devote a special section to them, but that discussion requires a previous consideration of frustration and conflict.

Frustration and conflict

Motivation, that is, goal-directed behavior, is the key concept in understanding the relationship between frustration, conflict, and defense mechanisms. At this point, we may anticipate by saying that a certain sequence of events leads to the need for defense mechanisms. Initially, a strong motive is frustrated, usually as the result of conflict between motives. Fear or anxiety is the frequent product of such conflict-produced frustrations. Finally, defense mechanisms arise to reduce the conflict and, hence, the fear or anxiety resulting from the conflict. This thumbnail sketch is, of course, inadequate, but it should become clear as we develop it subsequently.

FRUSTRATION   A motivated organism is one with a need or drive. If the need goes unsatisfied for very long, we say that the organism is *deprived*. A person, for example, who goes without food all day suffers hunger deprivation. Needs, however, are usually accompanied by a striving to reach a goal that would appear to satisfy the need. A person who is hunger-deprived usually tries to do something about it; he attempts to reach the nearest refrigerator or restaurant. In the naïve organism, striving behavior takes the form of trial-and-error behavior in random searching for the appropriate goal. In more sophisticated organisms, the striving behavior consists of learned patterns of behavior that in the past have led to the goal. All this was spelled out in some detail in Chapter 6.

When the striving behavior of a motivated organism is blocked or thwarted by obstacles, we say that the organism is *frustrated*. That is to say, mere lack of satisfaction of a need is deprivation, but the thwarting of behavior directed toward a goal is frustration. Ordinarily, the stronger the drive, the more intense the striving behavior, and the more severe the frustration. Also, the nearer the goal, or, in the case of human beings, the more clearly the goal is in mind, the greater the frustration.

Human beings have acquired many needs and learned many goals besides the physiological motives with which they are endowed (see Table 13.3).

They have learned many ways of striving toward, or working toward, goals. Hence the possibilities of frustration are much greater in man than in animals. Indeed, human adjustment can be said to be a perpetual battle against frustration. For some, the battle rages more savagely than for others. Some seem to be on the winning side. Others seem to lose more often than they win; these are the ones we call maladjusted, and in the extreme case, mentally ill. Thus the study of frustration and its consequences merits our serious attention.

CONFLICT OF MOTIVES   The obstacle that frustrates the attainment of a goal is the *source of frustration*. In a complex society, the varieties of frustrations are infinite. They may, however, be classified into three main categories according to source: *environmental frustration, personal frustration,* and *conflict frustration*. These have been described in Chapter 7 and need only be recapitulated here.

1. Environmental frustration is caused by environmental obstacles, that is, anything in the environment that blocks the attainment of a goal.

2. Personal frustration grows out of a person's inadequacy for reaching his goals; the person is

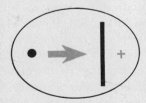

A PERSON ATTRACTED TO A POSITIVE GOAL MAY BE FRUSTRATED BY AN ENVIRONMENTAL BARRIER

FIGURE 13.3.   *Frustration by environmental obstacles. A barrier (vertical line) stands between the person (dot) and the goal (+) that attracts him.*

FRUSTRATION MAY BE CAUSED BY
CONFLICTING ATTRACTIONS TO TWO

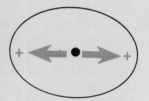

FIGURE 13.4.   *Approach-approach conflict.*
The individual is attracted at the same time
by two goals that are incompatible with
each other.

frustrated because he has unattainable goals. Put another way, personal frustration is due to a discrepancy between the level of aspiration and the level of performance.

3. Conflict frustration is caused by motivational conflict within the person. Because two motives somehow conflict, the satisfaction of one means the frustration of the other.

The nature of frustration may be schematized by a diagram such as that in Figure 13.3. In such a diagram, the ellipse denotes the total *environment* of the person, the dot stands for the *person,* and the vertical line represents the *thwarting* of the motive. Goals are depicted by either a + or a − sign, called a *valence.* A plus sign indicates a goal to which the person is attracted; a minus sign, a goal which repels him—punishment, threat, or something he fears or has learned to avoid. The arrow is used as a vector in physics to indicate the direction of forces acting on an individual who is under the influence of several motives. This particular method of depicting frustrating situations was devised by Lewin [1935] and helps us visualize the sources and effects of frustration. Figure 13.3 describes a situation of environmental frustration.

Of these three general types of frustration, conflict frustration is usually the most important in

determining the adjustment a person makes in life. For that reason, it deserves close study. Actually, on analysis, frustration can arise in three major kinds of conflicts. These have been called approach-approach conflict, avoidance-avoidance conflict, and approach-avoidance conflict.

Approach-approach conflict. As the name implies, approach-approach conflict occurs between two positive goals—goals that are equally attractive at the same time (see Figure 13.4). For instance, a physiological conflict arises when a person is hungry and sleepy at the same time. In the social context, a conflict may arise when one wants to go to both a dance and a swimming party which are scheduled for the same night. The proverbial donkey is supposed to have starved to death because he stood halfway between two piles of hay and could not decide which to choose. Actually, neither donkeys nor people often "starve themselves to death" merely because they are in conflict between two positive goals. A person usually resolves such a conflict by satisfying first one goal, then the other—for example, eating and then going to bed if he is both hungry and sleepy—or by choosing one of the goals and giving up the other.

Avoidance-avoidance conflict. A second type of conflict, avoidance-avoidance conflict, which involves two negative goals, is diagrammed in Figure 13.5. It is a fairly common experience. Little Lewis must do his arithmetic or get a spanking. A student must spend the next two days studying for an examination or face the possibility of failure. A man must work at a job he intensely dislikes or take the chance of losing his income. Such conflicts are capsuled in the common saying, "caught between the devil and the deep blue sea." No doubt you can think of many examples in your own experience of things you do not want to do but must do or face even less desirable alternatives.

Two kinds of behavior are likely to be especially conspicuous in such avoidance-avoidance conflicts. The first is *vacillation.* As we shall see, the strength of a goal increases the closer one is to the goal. As a person approaches a negative goal, he finds it increasingly repelling. Consequently, he tends to retreat or withdraw. When he does this, he comes closer to the other negative goal and finds it, in turn, increasing in negative valence. He is like a baseball player caught in a "run down" between first and second base. He runs first one way, then the other. As he runs toward second base, he comes closer to being tagged out, but when he turns and runs back toward first base, he faces the same danger. Such vacillation is characteristic of avoidance-avoidance conflicts.

A second important feature of this kind of conflict is *an attempt to leave the conflict situation.* Theoretically, a person might escape avoidance-avoidance conflict by running away altogether from the conflict situation. People do, indeed, try to do this. In practice, however, there are additional negative goals in the periphery of the field, and these ordinarily keep a person from taking this alternative. A child, for example, who does not want either to do arithmetic or to get a spanking may think of slipping away from home. This, however, has even more serious consequences than staying in the situation and facing the problem; so he is wiser not to try it. The person in avoidance-avoidance conflict may also try a quite different means of running away. He may rely on his imagination to free him from the uncomfortable situation. He may spend his time in daydreaming instead of facing up to his problem. A student may do this at times when he is supposed to be studying. A person may even conjure up an imaginary world, or recreate in his mind's eye the carefree world of childhood in which no unpleasant tasks have to be performed. In extreme cases, this way of leaving the conflict situation is called *fantasy* or *regression,* depending on the form it takes. These phenomena are taken up later.

Approach-avoidance conflict. The third type of conflict, approach-avoidance conflict, is perhaps the most important of the three because it is often the most difficult to resolve. In approach-avoidance conflict, a person is both repelled and attracted by the same goal object.

A young bride, for example, may have been brought up in an atmosphere where sexual activities were treated as ugly and sinful things. As a conse-

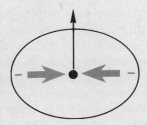

BEING CAUGHT BETWEEN TWO OR MORE NEGATIVE GOALS MAY CAUSE FRUSTRATION

FIGURE 13.5.   *Avoidance-avoidance conflict. The individual is caught between two threats, fears, or situations that repel him. In addition to the negative goals shown, there are usually other barriers or negative goals to restrain the individual. Otherwise, in this type of conflict, he is inclined to "leave the field" (black arrow) in order to escape conflict.*

quence, sexual matters have for her a negative sign (see Figure 13.6). At the same time, her normal sexual drive, as well as other social values involved in marriage, provides the marital situation with a positive sign. Now, as she enters marriage, she is caught between her sexual motives and the attitudes learned in her early environment. She has no alternative except to change her motives, which means erasing or weakening one of the signs shown in the diagram.

The example of the bride's conflict gives us a hint about the way in which approach-avoidance conflicts can develop. Note that the conflict arose because of the social values acquired in early training. These values come to serve as obstacles to the satisfaction of motives. Since they are within the person, the process of acquiring them, which we considered in Chapter 6, is regarded as one of *internalizing obstacles.* Such obstacles frustrate a person in the same way that the environmental obstacles in early childhood do. The fact, however, that they are internal, rather than external, makes them much more difficult for the person to handle. He may find ways of circumventing environmental obstacles, but he can hardly circumvent or get away from something within himself.

This analysis of frustration permits us to reduce frustrating situations to their simplest elements. In everyday life, however, things are seldom this simple. More typical are conflicts in which many different goals, especially negative ones, surround a person with pressures he wishes to avoid. In addition, some complex combinations of the kinds of situations we have described can exist. One such combination is the *double approach-avoidance conflict,* diagrammed in Figure 13.7. Here, two goals have both positive and negative signs. Consider, for example, the student who experiences a conflict between making good grades and making the college football team. Superficially, this conflict appears to be a simple case of approach-approach conflict—conflict between two positive goals. The student, however, may have considerable social pressure from family and associates to achieve both goals. He may incur the disapproval of his parents

MANY FRUSTRATIONS ARE DUE TO CONFLICTS IN WHICH SEVERAL SITUATIONS ARE EACH BOTH ATTRACTIVE AND REPULSIVE

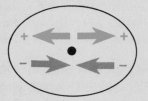

FIGURE 13.7.   *Double approach-avoidance conflict. Many conflicts that appear to be approach-approach or avoidance-avoidance conflicts are really double, or even multiple, approach-avoidance conflicts.*

if he fails to make good grades, and he may lose the esteem of his comrades if he does not make the football team. Thus failure at either one carries with it a threat. Each goal, therefore, has a negative valence as well as a positive one; hence, the student finds himself in a double approach-avoidance conflict.

In concluding this analysis of conflict, one additional point needs to be brought out. As we have indicated, the strength of positive and negative goals varies with psychological distance; the strength of a goal—the amount that it attracts or repels—is stronger the nearer one is to it. This fact is represented by the gradients in Figure 13.8. However, as this figure also illustrates, a difference exists between the *approach gradient* and the *avoidance gradient:* The avoidance gradient is the steeper of the two [Brown, 1948]. This means that, other things being equal in an approach-avoidance conflict, when a person is some distance from a goal having both positive and negative valences, the positive valence seems stronger. On the other hand, when he is near such a goal, the negative valence seems stronger. Where the two gradients cross, some distance from the goal, the valences are equal. In other words, the figure indicates that a person in an

FRUSTRATION MAY BE CAUSED BY THE SAME SITUATION BEING BOTH ATTRACTIVE AND REPULSIVE

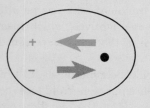

FIGURE 13.6.   *Approach-avoidance conflict. The individual is attracted to a positive goal, but this goal also has a fear or threat (negative goal) associated with it. Such a conflict is difficult to resolve and tends to evoke a good deal of anxiety.*

approach-avoidance conflict will tend to approach the goal, but then, as the tendency to avoid becomes stronger, he will come to a stop some distance from the goal. He is thus trapped and immobile at the point where the two goal strengths are equal. He gives up near the goal without resolving the conflict.

Typical conflicts. When we consider the number of needs that may be distinguished in people and the many ways of satisfying them, we realize that all sorts of frustrations and conflicts are possible. Moreover, we can expect conflict to occur whenever pleasure and pain, or reward and punishment, are associated with the same thing. That is what we mean when we refer to the conflict between positive and negative goals. If we think, then, of the goals with which individuals commonly have experienced both reward and punishment, we can identify the conflicts that are fairly common or typical. Four such conflicts are common in American culture. In foreign cultures, and even at other times in our own culture, other patterns of conflict may be more typical. These, however, are contemporary and illustrative of the point.

1. *Desire to achieve versus fear of failure.* In Western countries, particularly in the United States, achievement is highly valued. Children are expected to make good grades in school, to excel in sports, music, or the like, and generally to "succeed" in life. Individuals are praised, bemedaled, given gifts, and most of all, paid money for superior achievement. It is not surprising, then, that the achievement motive is regarded as one of the individual's strongest motives in our society.

The opposite of achievement is failure, which is punished in one way or another—by lack of approval, by failure to get promoted, sometimes by ridicule and ostracism. Hence the things one does to achieve his goals take on both positive and negative valences. People get caught between the desire to achieve and the fear of failure.

2. *Independence versus affiliation.* We saw in Chapter 6 that children learn to depend on others; they must in order to satisfy their needs. The people they depend on, however, have considerable authority over them, determining what they can and can-

not do. When children reach adolescence, they typically develop a strong drive to be independent—to kick over the traces. This puts them in conflict, because it is difficult to be both independent and dependent. Indeed, independence means standing on one's own feet, and this the adolescent, and all too frequently the adult, may be afraid to do or not know how to do. This conflict between independence and dependence is typical of adolescents. Parents themselves sometimes aggravate such a conflict by being in conflict about it themselves—criticizing the adolescent one moment for being a "baby" and resenting his show of independence a moment later.

Independence also conflicts with more general affiliative needs. One may feel strongly like standing on one's own feet, fending for oneself, and going it

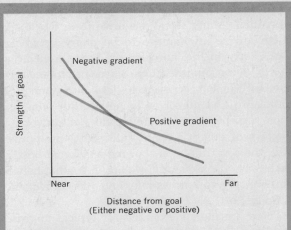

FIGURE 13.8.   *Gradients of goal strength for positive and negative goals. Other things being equal, goals are "stronger" the closer a person is to them. Negative goals, however, are somewhat stronger than positive ones when a person is near the goal, and positive goals are stronger than negative ones when he is far from the goal. This fact accounts for a person's being trapped in approach-avoidance conflict; he approaches the goal, then stops at the point where the gradients intersect, being afraid to go any closer. (After Brown, 1948.)*

alone. At the same time, one may feel equally strongly a need to be approved by his parents, to be accepted by a group, and to have the moral support of others.

3. *Sexual desire versus fear of sex.* Among many mid-Victorians, the conflict that arose between sexual drives, on the one hand, and social or religious scruples on the other hand, was particularly strong. Today, this conflict is not so prevalent, but it is still common. It may be a conflict between religious precepts and sexual interests. It may be a milder conflict between sexual interests and early training. It may concern fears of pregnancy. In any case, sex is frequently the center of an approach-avoidance conflict.

4. *Hostility versus social approval.* Another typical conflict arises between the need to express hostility and the consequent punishment of such expression. Many situations arise from day to day which arouse an impulse to be angry or to fight back. Early in life, however, we have learned, usually by being punished or scolded, not to engage in physical combat or even to lose our temper. As adults, we find ourselves in almost the same situation, except that, generally, all we provoke by displays of anger is some mild social disapproval. Still, the constraints on showing anger and hostility are strong. Consequently, we are in conflict between expressing ourselves and fearing the consequences of doing so.

These are merely examples of typical approach-avoidance conflicts. There are, of course, almost as many sources of conflict as there are situations and people. The kind of conflict and its severity vary from one individual to another and from one culture to another because conflicts are firmly rooted in the training and acquired motives of the individual.

GENERAL REACTIONS TO FRUSTRATION   What does a person do when he is frustrated by conflict or by some other cause? Frustration has many effects, both direct and indirect. The question can be answered in a general way before we progress to an analysis of more specific reactions to frustration.

Learned adjustments. One thing a frustrated person does in response to his frustration is *learn*. He may not learn the "right" thing, the means that would best alleviate his frustration, but he usually learns something in connection with his frustration.

A motivated person usually varies his behavior, trying first one response, then another. Eventually he may hit upon a response that is *reinforced*—something that satisfies his motive (see page 77). If the same response is repeatedly reinforced, it is learned and becomes his regular mode of adjustment whenever he is motivated and in a similar situation. This principle of learning applies not only to simple motivated behavior, but also—and perhaps of even greater significance—to behavior learned under conditions of frustration. It accounts for the habits a person acquires as a means of reducing frustration.

Let us illustrate this principle. A child at an amusement park wants a stick of candy and asks his mother for it. The mother says, "No," explaining that it is too close to suppertime. "Aw, Mom," he pleads, "can't I have one?" She continues to say "No." He pleads some more. Then, frustrated, he accuses his mother of being mean, thus attempting to browbeat her into saying "Yes." Still the answer is "No." At this point, the youngster throws what is commonly called a tantrum. He rolls on the ground screaming, or begins to hold his breath—something that often scares mothers but should not. At this point, from fear, embarrassment, or just the desire to be left alone, the mother relents and gives the child the money to buy the candy.

Thus ends one trial of a learning situation which, in less extreme form perhaps, is typical of many in life. In response to the frustration of a motive, the desire for candy, the youngster first tries one approach and then another. All of them fail until he hits upon the tantrum. Since this succeeds, it is reinforced, and the chances are that he will use the tantrum the next time he is similarly frustrated. It takes only one or two repetitions to learn this particular mode of adjustment. It may then become the person's habitual method of dealing with frustration (see Instrumental Learning, page 88). In all probability, this child will continue to use this

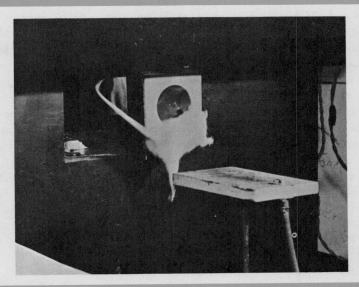

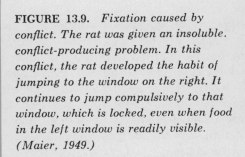

FIGURE 13.9.   *Fixation caused by conflict. The rat was given an insoluble, conflict-producing problem. In this conflict, the rat developed the habit of jumping to the window on the right. It continues to jump compulsively to that window, which is locked, even when food in the left window is readily visible. (Maier, 1949.)*

method of adjustment until it fails. Then he may find some other mode of adjustment. Of course, as he matures, social pressures may make him vary this mode. Even then, it may be only slightly modified, and some form of temper tantrum may continue throughout life as a learned reaction to certain kinds of frustration.

There are many kinds of frustration and many opportunities to learn habitual methods of dealing with them. The opportunities, the frustrations, and the modes adopted will vary with individuals, their families, social groups, and circumstances. The important point is that through learning people tend to adopt typical, habitual responses to frustration. These modes of adjustment are learned according to the principles described in Chapter 3.

Rigidity. Frustrated people, then, learn ways of adjusting to frustration. The way they learn to respond, however, is not likely to be quite the same as that learned by people who are motivated, but not severely frustrated. The severely frustrated person, or animal, is more inclined to *fixations* of response—to rigidity of behavior. His trial-and-error behavior is not so variable and flexible. Instead of trying first one thing and then another to

solve his problem, he keeps on using the same response over and over again. If the fixated response does not happen to be the correct one, or the best one, for relieving a frustration, as it usually is not, he is prevented by his rigidity from discovering the most effective way. Hence the chances of hitting on a response that may eliminate frustration are greatly reduced.

For this reason, the frustrated person often seems stupid to an observer, and the solution to his problem often seems ridiculously simple. "All he has to do is . . . ," the observer may say—and he may be right. But the frustrated person may be so blind to alternatives that he cannot see or try other methods that might prove successful.

This fixation of response as a reaction to frustration is illustrated by the following experiment with rats [Maier, 1949]:

Rats were trained to make a discrimination between two cards in the apparatus shown in Figure 13.9. During the training process, a positive card (for example, a dark circle) was exposed in one window, a negative card (a light circle) in the other. Behind the positive card was food. When an animal jumped from its position on the platform to the positive window, it knocked the card down and found the food. If it jumped to the negative card, it found the window locked, and hence fell into a net below. In time, with the positive card consistently rewarded and the negative one punished, the rats learned to discriminate the two stimuli almost perfectly.

At this point in the experiment, the procedure was changed. In order to produce frustration, the experimenter presented the rats with an insoluble problem. Instead of rewarding the formerly positive card consistently, the experimenter randomly rewarded and punished jumps to both cards. Hence, each card was now rewarded 50 per cent of the time and punished 50 per cent of the time. A rat, therefore, could not escape being punished 50 per cent of the time, as long as it continued jumping. This frustration procedure obviously made the animal emotional, for it squealed and defecated. Soon the animal selected a stereotyped response. It simply adopted a "position habit" of jumping to the same side all the time. Some rats jumped to the left window and some to the right, but for any particular rat, the direction was always the same. In many of the rats, this fixation became so rigid that, even with the other window open and with food in it in plain sight (see Figure 13.9), the rats continued to jump to the side of the fixated response.

Aggression. Most psychologists agree, in a general way at least, with a modified form of the frustration-aggression hypothesis [Dollard et al., 1939]. This hypothesis, as modified, is that frustration tends to lead to aggression. Put another way, one of the most frequent and conspicuous consequences of frustration is some form of aggression, sometimes openly expressed and sometimes felt inwardly but contained. One merely needs to observe his own behavior and that of others through the course of a day to note this link between frustration and aggression. If you drive a car, you may recall some of the choice comments you hurled at another driver who pulled out in front of you when you were in a hurry.

Frustration, however, does not always produce outward aggression. A person may be quite frustrated and display little aggression even though he may be quite angry [Berkowitz, 1962]. In this case, he holds aggressive behavior in check either because

he knows there will be unfortunate consequences of expressing it or because he sees no appropriate object toward which to express it. Suppose, for example, that the driver who pulls out in front of you is quite a tough-looking character who looks angry himself; or suppose that a police car is at the corner. Under these circumstances, although you may be angry, you will not be so liable to express aggressive behavior.

This thwarting of aggressive tendencies may itself produce a conflict. The person is impelled to express aggression, but he is afraid to do it. The closer he comes to doing it, the greater his fear. Hence fear is generated by frustration of aggressive tendencies. There are other more direct ways in which fear results from conflict-produced frustration, and we shall now turn to some of these important consequences of frustration.

Fear and anxiety. Frustrations produced by avoidance-avoidance and approach-avoidance conflicts are especially likely to arouse fear and anxiety as general reactions [Dollard and Miller, 1950]. It is relatively easy to see how this happens in the case of avoidance-avoidance conflicts. We have seen that people in this type of conflict vacillate between two negative, or fear-producing, situations. Fear is produced as a person gets close to one of the situations, and so he moves away from it. But moving away from one situation moves him toward the other fear-producing situation. Back and forth he goes, never escaping from the fear generated by negative goals.

One common way to deal with such an intolerable situation is to stop thinking about the conflicts involved—to *repress* them in other words. Repression, which may start as a more or less conscious attempt to stop thinking about conflicts, soon becomes an automatic habit and a very strong one because it removes the person from awareness of the conflict and hence reduces fear. Thus, in time, although the person is still in the conflict situation, he comes to be no longer aware of it. Moreover, repression is only partially successful in reducing fear. After the conflict is repressed, the person still feels somewhat afraid, but he now does not know exactly what he is afraid of—his fear is diffuse. In other words, he is a victim of *anxiety*—a diffuse feeling of uneasiness (see page 252). Thus, through repression, which is also a defense mechanism (see the section following), fear of something has been converted into objectless dread—or anxiety.

Fear and anxiety may also be generated in frustration produced by approach-avoidance conflicts. In this case, the individual is driven toward a goal which at the same time repells him. The closer he is driven to the goal, the more fearful he becomes that he might actually reach it. Thus, if a person is angry at a policeman, he may be motivated to strike him, but at the same time he fears the punishment that will be forthcoming. Again, the person finds himself in an intolerable situation, especially if the conflict is a basic and long-lasting one. Again, repression will go to work to convert fear into anxiety. This anxiety has two important consequences.

First, anxiety causes *discomfort*. In the extreme, it causes misery. Anxious people, by definition, are unhappy people. At best, they are slightly uncomfortable; at worst, they experience a misery comparable to the pain suffered in severe injury or physical illness. The person who is anxious may not be aware of the frustration or conflict that makes him miserable; he may not be conscious of the peculiarities in his behavior stemming from anxiety; but he is most certainly aware of his discomfort and pain. Very frequently, for example, people come to psychologists or psychiatrists solely to find relief from a feeling of discomfort and misery without being aware of what has caused it.

Second, anxiety *motivates* a person to get rid of it. Anxiety is thus itself a source of avoidance behavior. Like pain, it is something the person tries to avoid or, when it wells up in him, to escape. On this point hangs much of what we have to say about defense mechanisms. Most personality theorists, particularly Freud and Horney, regard anxiety as the key to understanding how a person copes with frustration (see page 493). The frustrated person, as they view him, bends his efforts to ward off anxiety. He attempts to reduce anxiety by using

defense mechanisms. These mechanisms, as we have said, may take many forms, and we all rely on certain ones more than others. Thus they become characteristic traits of personality.

Defense mechanisms

The concept of the defense mechanism comes to us from Sigmund Freud, though others have modified it in various ways [Dollard and Miller, 1950]. A *defense mechanism* is a device—a way of behaving— that a person uses unconsciously to protect himself against ego-involving frustrations. Actually, as we saw earlier, it is not so much the frustration against which he defends himself as it is the fear or anxiety that stems from the frustration. Hence, basically, the defense mechanisms may be regarded as defenses against fear or anxiety. At least, this is a common view.

REPRESSION   Put another way, a defense mechanism is a device, adopted unconsciously by the individual, for fooling himself about his motivational conflicts. A person can be fooled, of course, simply because he has not learned to recognize his own motives and goals. This undoubtedly accounts for some of the confusion people have about their conflicts. More important, however, at least in the Freudian theory of the defense mechanisms, is an active process known as *repression*. We have seen that repression is the process by which fear is converted to anxiety. Now let us emphasize the defensive nature of repression—perhaps the most farreaching and common defense mechanism.

Repression is, in part, a kind of "forgetting" (see page 145). Through repression, a person conveniently forgets the things that might make him uncomfortable. I can easily forget to pay a bill because paying it might bring me uncomfortably close to insolvency. I can forget my appointment with the dentist because I am afraid of his drill. This kind of forgetting, however, is not normal forgetting, for the memories temporarily lost can be recovered when the fear or anxiety connected with them is reduced or eliminated—when I get my next pay check, or after the date with the dentist is past. So, although repression often takes the form of forgetting, it goes deeper than that. It is a process of "pushing down" memories or thoughts that might be expressed openly, or acted upon, if they did not arouse fear or anxiety. Sometimes the repressed memories or thoughts are expressed in disguised fashion in dreams. This idea provides one scheme for the interpretation of dreams and within such a framework dreams may give significant clues to a psychotherapist (see Chapter 15).

The concept may be clarified by referring again to the diagrams in Figures 13.3 to 13.7. Learning, illustrated by the child's learning to have a tantrum, is most effective in environmental frustration (Figure 13.3), when there is merely a barrier to a positive goal. By varying his behavior, a person finds some means of penetrating or circumventing the barrier. Such learning, however, is not likely to be effective in approach-avoidance conflict involving both positive and negative goals, for the thing learned, whatever it may be, does not change the fact that the person has two mutually incompatible motives. Here the solution is to do something to alter the motives or their goals. This cannot really be done, but by fooling oneself about some aspect of the conflict, one can believe that it has been done. This is precisely what is accomplished when repression acts as a defense mechanism.

The thing repressed may be a memory, a motive, a goal, a barrier, a conflict—almost anything connected with a frustration-producing situation. Repression of strong, persistent, deep-seated, and insoluble conflicts is the most significant kind of repression. Through repression, a person fools himself into believing that a conflict, and everything connected with it, does not exist. This, of course, does not really resolve the conflict, but it does partially relieve him of anxiety. The following incident illustrates repression as it may take place in most of us:

A young man who had recently become engaged was walking along the street with his fiancée. Another man greeted him and began to chat in a friendly fashion. The young man realized that he must know this apparent stranger, and that both courtesy and pride required that he introduce the visitor to his fiancée. The name of the other man, however, eluded him completely; indeed, he had not even a fleeting recognition of his identity. When in his confusion he attempted at least to present his fiancée, he found that he had also forgotten her name.

Only a brief behavior analysis was necessary to make this incident comprehensible as an example of normal . . . repression. The apparent stranger was in fact a former friend of the young man; but the friendship had eventually brought frustration and disappointment in a situation identical with the one described. Some years before, our subject had become engaged to another young woman, and in his pride and happiness he had at once sought out this friend and introduced the two. Unfortunately the girl had become strongly attached to the friend and he to her; at length she broke her engagement and married the friend. The two men had not seen each other until this meeting, which repeated exactly the earlier frustrating situation. It is hardly surprising that the newly engaged man repressed all recognition of his former friend, all hints as to his identity, and even the name of the fiancée. [Cameron and Margaret, 1951, pages 367–368.]

Such complete repression serves effectively as a defense mechanism against anxiety. However, repression may be less complete; it may disguise only some aspect of one of the conflicting motives—the nature of the motive, who has the motive, what the goal of the motive is, which motive is behind a particular form of behavior, or ways of circumventing the barrier to a goal. Each one of these ways of dealing with conflict is regarded as a different defense mechanism and has its own name.

REACTION FORMATION   A person may disguise his motivation and conflict by believing that his motive is exactly the opposite of his real motive. This defense mechanism is called *reaction formation*. We may see it in the case of the daughter who unconsciously hates her mother but appears to be oversolicitous of her mother's health and comfort. To admit to herself that she hates her mother may be so abhorrent and may create so many anxieties that she tries to overcome the anxiety by showing excessive affection. The common quotation from Shakespeare, "The lady doth protest too much, methinks," refers to this disguise. When a person is *too* solicitous or *too* modest or *too* affectionate, it is very likely that he harbors aggression or other hostile impulses that are being repressed and disguised by the opposite kind of behavior.

The following example of reaction formation is taken from a letter received from a "kindly, warm-hearted" antivivisectionist by Jules Masserman after his work on alcohol addiction in cats had been publicized.

I read . . . your work on alcoholism. . . . I am surprised that anyone who is as well educated as you must be to hold the position that you do would stoop to such a depth as to torture helpless little cats in the pursuit of a cure for alcoholics. . . . A drunkard does not want to be cured —a drunkard is just a weak-minded idiot who belongs in the gutter and should be left there. Instead of torturing helpless little cats why not torture the drunks or better still exert your would-be noble effort toward getting a bill passed to exterminate drunks. . . . If people are such weaklings, the world is better off without them. . . . If you are an example of what a noted psychiatrist should be I'm glad I am just an ordinary human being without a letter after my name. I'd rather be just myself with a clear conscience, knowing I have not hurt any living creature, and can sleep without seeing frightened, terrified dying cats—because I know they must die after you have finished with them. No punishment is too great for you, and I hope I live to read about your mangled body and long suffering before you finally die—and I'll laugh long and loud. [Masserman, 1946, page 35.]

The person who wrote this letter professed to be interested in the welfare of cats. The love of cats, however, appears to be a reaction formation serving as a disguise for some rather bitter hostility toward people.

PROJECTION   Still another common disguise that protects a person against anxiety-producing impulses is *projection* which disguises the source of conflict by ascribing one's own motives to someone else. If a student, for example, has a strong desire to cheat on an examination but is unwilling to admit it to himself because of his moral code, he may become unduly suspicious of others and accuse them of cheating when they are innocent. Or, if he feels like being nasty to other people and yet knows that this tendency is "wrong," he may accuse other people of being nasty to him when in fact they have not been.

Projection is well illustrated in a study of the attitudes of 97 fraternity members [Sears, 1936].

The students were asked to rate certain of their fraternity brothers on four undesirable traits: stinginess, obstinacy, disorderliness, and bashfulness. After rating others, each student rated himself. Thus it was possible for the investigator to compare a student's rating of himself with other members' ratings of him. Some members seemed to be quite aware of their own traits, for their self-ratings agreed well with the ratings made by other members. From the ratings of the group, however, it appeared that certain students had one or more traits in an undesirable degree. It is interesting that these students assigned a higher degree of their own undesirable traits to other students than they did to themselves. Thus they failed to acknowledge undesirable traits in themselves and assigned them—that is, projected them—to their fraternity brothers.

Examples of projection abound in human behavior. When a person believes incorrectly that other people are out to do him wrong, one can suspect that he is harboring strong aggressive impulses and is projecting them to other people. The unattractive spinster who will not leave her house because she is sure that men are waiting to attack her must be suspected of projecting to others her own thwarted sex desires. Similarly, the white supremacist who eventually reduces all arguments about civil rights to a sexual level must be suspected of projecting his own unacceptable sexual impulses to Negroes. To recognize such desires in himself would make him anxious; so he defends himself by projecting the desires to someone else. In the extreme form, such projection is the mark of the behavior disorder called paranoia.

DISPLACEMENT Displacement is still another kind of defense against anxiety-producing motives. In *displacement,* the object or goal of a motive is disguised by substituting another one in place of it. Again, numerous examples might be cited. The man who gets angry at his boss but is afraid to tell him off comes home and bawls out his wife. Or consider the little girl who finds her baby brother the new center of attention. Her jealousy makes her want to harm the baby. The family, however, forbids that and teaches her that hurting the baby is naughty. Unable to express her aggression against the baby, she substitutes a safer object, a doll, and may succeed in totally destroying it. Thus by displacing her aggression, she finds an acceptable outlet for it. The displacement of aggression has been demon-strated in experiments carried out with rats [Miller, 1948]:

Two rats were placed in a box having a grill for a floor (see Figure 13.10). One rat was the "subject" in the experiment; the other rat was put there merely as an "object of aggression." Periodically the grill floor was electrified. The shock applied in this way made the rat both fearful and angry. As it thrashed around, the subject struck the other rat, whereupon the shock was turned off. This procedure was repeated until the subject had learned to strike the second rat as a means of terminating the shock. Then the second rat was removed, and replaced by a rubber doll. In this situation, the subject turned to the "innocent bystander," the doll, and struck it. Thus aggression was displaced from the unavailable object to an available object.

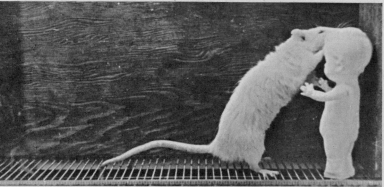

FIGURE 13.10. *The displacement of aggression. A rat that had learned to strike another rat turned to the "innocent bystander," the rubber doll, and struck it when the second rat was no longer present. (Miller, 1948b.)*

Displacement is related to the concept of generalization (see page 85). When it cannot be satisfied directly, the expression of the motive will be directed toward situations which are similar in some way to the ones toward which the motive was originally directed. In other words, the expression generalizes from the original situation. Many factors influence the degree of generalization. For instance, if the drive toward a situation, or goal, is strong, and the negative aspects of the goal are rather weak, the new goal will be rather similar to the original one; if the reverse is true, of course, the new goal will be quite different from the original one.

RATIONALIZATION   Another defense against the anxiety aroused by conflicting motives is known as *rationalization*. In employing this mode of adjustment, an individual explains his behavior in such a way as to conceal the unacceptable motive it expresses and assign the behavior to some other socially approved motive. This mechanism is among the most common, socially accepted ways of reducing anxiety. A student who is motivated to have a good time may rationalize his school failures by attributing them to inadequate teaching, unfairness of the teacher, or too little time to study. A mother whose real motive is to hold onto her son as long as possible may not permit him to go out on dates, rationalizing that his schoolwork will be hampered or that he will fall into unwholesome company. A father may beat his child because—he rationalizes—the child deserves or needs it, but his real motive may be aggression. By rationalizing his behavior, he can gratify his needs without taking the blame.

SUBLIMATION AND COMPENSATION   Two similar forms of defense have been given special names by Freud and others who have observed them to be frequently used as modes of adjustment. One is *sublimation,* or the use of a substitute activity to gratify a motive. For example, when a sexual motive cannot be directly satisfied because of external obstacles or internal conflict, the motive is sometimes said to be satisfied by finding some other outlet which seems to reduce tension. Freud believed that the frustrated urge can be partially gratified by channeling it into art, religion, music, or some aesthetic activity that is socially acceptable. Because of the passionate way in which some people embrace their aesthetic activities, Freud argued that the substitute activity is a means of satisfying sexual drives. This interpretation of sublimation is open to question, for it is doubtful whether physiological motives can be relieved by substitute activities; it is more likely that the motives involved in aesthetic activities are not sexual. On the other hand, the general idea that motives may be gratified by substituting one set of activities for another seems to be sound and acceptable.

Compensation is also a method of adjustment which usually involves a substitute activity for a frustrated motive. However, in compensation, there is usually the implication of failure or loss of self-esteem in one activity which is compensated for by efforts in some other realm of endeavor. The concept of compensation does not carry with it the implication of an outlet for sexual frustration. The unattractive girl may become a bookworm and achieve high scholarship, thereby commanding the respect and prestige that she is unable to win with good looks. The short man may develop his skill in boxing in order to secure the recognition as a "man" that his small stature denies him. An uneducated parent may derive a great deal of substitute satisfaction by having his son well educated. Life is full of compensations through which a person achieves satisfaction that he otherwise cannot obtain. When a person's frustration stems from a feeling of social inferiority, compensation is very likely to be expressed in attempts to gain attention, as in the following example.

One high school girl, Alva B., was notably unattractive because she was overweight and had large, coarse features. Her father was a bartender, an occupation not esteemed in a conservative small town's social scheme. All these circumstances barred her from desired social relationships. In response, Alva took to an excessive use of make-up. She appeared in school well coated with cosmetics, her eyebrows plucked and penciled, and her lips drawn in a most exaggerated manner. The painting did not render her beautiful, but it made her noticed, and this was an effective substitute for social recognition. Later Alva became a cheer leader and was an excellent one, the position being perfectly suited to her need for attention. [Shaffer and Shoben, 1956, pages 171–172.]

FANTASY   Sometimes a frustrated motive can be gratified, at least in part, by a resort to *fantasy* or daydreaming. Fantasy is common among most people, and it is particularly prominent during adolescence. As a form of adjustment, it rarely leads to constructive action, and thus may leave a person's basic conflicts unsolved. On the other hand, if it is not overdone, daydreaming about success, sexual conquests, and the like can produce a certain amount of satisfaction. A person who has been embarrassed in a social situation feels somewhat better if he indulges in a little fantasy about all the things he could have said. If a girl does not get an invitation to the junior prom, she can at least have some fun dreaming about what it would be like. It has been estimated that more than 95 per cent of college students spend some time daydreaming. Their most frequent subjects for daydreaming are academic honors, success with the opposite sex, and a future of fame and fortune.

REGRESSION   Closely related to fantasy is a reaction called *regression*. This is a retreat to early or primitive forms of behavior. We say "early or primitive" because there is some question as to whether regression is one or both of these. On the one hand, regression seems to be a relapse to habits and ways of behaving that the person learned in childhood; on the other, it seems merely to represent a simpler, more primitive, and less intellectual approach to solving a problem. Whatever its interpretation, regression takes the form of a childish, rather than an adult, reaction to frustration. It is a defense mechanism because the person retreats in imagination and behavior to a time before the anxiety-producing conflict was present. It may also help to restore self-esteem and confidence in the face of frustration.

Regression is frequently encountered in children of four or five years of age who are beginning to face an increasing variety of complex frustrations [Barker et al., 1941]. Perhaps the particular occasion that evokes regressive behavior is the birth of another child or the beginning of school adjustments. In any event, the child at this stage frequently reverts to baby talk and acts like a baby of two rather than a child of five.

Regression is by no means limited to children— adults often regress too. Childish fits of anger, or pouting when one fails to get his way, may be regressions to reactions acquired in childhood. A person who goes to bed with the slightest cold or who seems to enjoy being sick may be regressing to behavior which, in childhood, brought him affection and attention.

Extreme frustration of the sort encountered in Nazi concentration camps during World War II can be expected to produce regression in otherwise normal people. At least a more or less general regression to infantile behavior was reported as characteristic of the inmates of the Dachau and Buchenwald camps. The following is a quotation from a psychological study of former prisoners in these camps:

The prisoners lived, like children, only in the immediate present . . . they became unable to plan for the future or to give up immediate pleasure satisfactions to gain greater ones in the near future. . . . They were boastful, telling tales about what they had accomplished in their former lives, or how they succeeded in cheating foremen or guards, and how they sabotaged the work. Like children, they felt not at all set back or ashamed when it became known that they had lied about their prowess. [Bettelheim, 1943, page 443.]

IDENTIFICATION   In addition to the reduction of anxiety, some defense mechanisms are also used to enhance self-esteem. *Identification*, in which we imagine that we are like another person, is a method of doing both. For instance, when we identify with a successful individual or a victorious football team, we feel more worthwhile. Conversely, it is difficult to enhance self-esteem by identifying with a losing team. Perhaps this is one of the reasons for the great stress on winning in college, and other athletics. By identification, we may also satisfy, in fantasy, some of our longings and motives. The unattractive girl who identifies with a glamorous movie star is the classic example.

Identification is a defense because, in some situations, we may reduce anxiety by taking on the characteristics of another person. One example is identification with the aggressor. For example, prisoners in concentration camps not only regressed, some took on the brutal characteristics of their guards. A similar type of identification is supposed to occur, according to Freudian psychoanalysis, in the resolution of the so-called Oedipal conflict (see page 491). In the Oedipal conflict, the son is supposed to be threatened by his father with severe punishment for his attentions to his mother, and the boy removes the threat of punishment by identifying with the father, thus taking on many of his characteristics. The logic of identification with the aggressor is something like this: "If I am the aggressor, I cannot be aggressed against."

USE OF DEFENSE MECHANISMS The student has probably recognized a number of these defense mechanisms in himself. Almost everybody uses them some of the time. Indeed, moderate use of the mechanisms is a harmless and convenient way of disposing of minor conflicts. If defense mechanisms make us feel better and make others more comfortable, as they often do, their value in reducing tension and letting us get on with important problems more than offsets the trivial self-deceptions they entail.

Not all defense mechanisms, however, are so harmless. If they are used excessively to sidestep really persistent and severe sources of conflict, they can get us into a great deal of trouble. Defense mechanisms, when used to excess, have at least two major weaknesses.

First, they fail to solve the underlying conflict of motives. Defense mechanisms are directed mainly at the symptom—anxiety—rather than at the motivational conflicts that give rise to anxiety; thus they merely conceal or disguise the real problem which is still there, ready to produce anxiety again and again. A person harboring homosexual tendencies, for example, may avoid anxiety by repressing such tendencies; yet they may be reawakened by a wide variety of stimuli. Whenever such an individual is confronted with a situation which excites his homosexual tendencies, the latent conflict is reinstated. For that reason, during World War II, many men with latent homosexual impulses developed severe anxieties when thrust into the intimate company of other men, although they could get along in civilian life by avoiding such contact. Hence, if a conflict is serious and persistent, defense mechanisms merely postpone its solution; the conflict is still intact, and it will probably rise again to plague the person.

Second, defense mechanisms may not function to protect the individual in new and unusual situations, when an increase in the severity or salience of the conflict occurs, or when the conflict is quite prolonged. Under these conditions, the defense mechanisms may not be adequate protection against anxiety and they may break down, causing the person to experience a "flood" of anxiety. These breakdowns of defense mechanisms are called *anxiety attacks*, and they can be extremely uncomfortable indeed.

Everyone has conflicts and frustrations; there is nothing abnormal about them, either in ourselves or in others. Nor, as we have said, is there anything abnormal about using defense mechanisms. On the other hand, if the mechanisms are not effective—if the person continues to suffer from a great deal of anxiety—that *is* abnormal. Actually, no sharp line can be drawn between normal and abnormal behavior—it is just a matter of degree. Only when a person suffers from anxiety to an unusual extent or when he becomes a nuisance or a danger to other people can he be considered abnormal. Abnormal behavior is considered in detail in the next chapter. The main point at present is that people differ in their use of defense mechanisms, and the characteristic ones they use constitute important personality traits.

Origins of personality characteristics

We have just seen how one set of personality characteristics, the defense mechanisms, originate in the dynamic interplay and conflict of motives. But can we say anything about the origins of traits in general? We shall see that many theories have been advanced to account for the origins of at least some personality characteristics. Here we examine the origins of traits from an empirical, commonsense viewpoint.

Among the forces molding personality are biological inheritance, social inheritance or culture, and learning. These forces act on each of us in different ways, and to understand a particular person, we need to know how these influences have been at work in his life. On the other hand, we all are subject in varying degrees to these influences, and thus it is possible to describe the principal influences in personality development in a general way.

INHERITED PREDISPOSITIONS Inheritance is one influential factor. As is the case with most things psychological, however, personality is not directly inherited. What is inherited is a *predisposition* to develop in certain ways. This means that an individual inherits tendencies rather than a completely predetermined pattern or trait. Whether he actually develops the kind of personality to which he is predisposed, and the degree to which he does, depend on environmental factors.

You can see some of these predispositions unfolding at an early age in infants before much chance for learning has taken place. Indeed, some striking differences among infants can often be observed. One baby is extremely active, another quite sluggish. One cries and fusses most of the time, whereas another is so placid that its mother calls the pediatrician to see if anything is wrong. It seems obvious that such differences are to some extent innate. These innate personality characteristics are sometimes called *temperamental traits,* and they might have been included in our discussion of personality structure. In addition to activity, or the tempo of actions, characteristic moods and mood changes are often considered to be temperamental traits [Allport, 1937].

Some of the best scientific proof of inherited dispositions to develop certain kinds of personalities comes from studies of so-called "mental diseases," or behavior disorders. These studies cover the inheritance of several kinds of behavior disorders, but this study of schizophrenia will serve as an illustration [Kallmann, 1951].

The general incidence of schizophrenia in the population of the United States is less than 1 in 100. If one parent has the disease, however, the odds increase to 10 in 100 that his child will have it. If one child in the family develops it, the odds increase further to about 15 in 100 that its brother or sister will have it too. In fraternal twins, who differ as much in heredity as ordinary brothers and sisters (see page 38), the odds are still about 15 in 100 that one twin will become schizophrenic if the other one does. For identical twins, however, the odds jump to about 85 in 100 that both twins will develop schizophrenia if one of the pair does. Similar results, with slightly different numbers, have been obtained in studying two other behavior disorders (see Table 13.4).

Figures of this sort argue strongly for the inheritance of a predisposition to develop schizophrenia and certain other behavior disorders. To be sure, members of the same family have somewhat similar environments, but this cannot account for the different odds in fraternal and identical twins— 15 as compared with 85 in 100. Moreover, identical twins *reared apart* have also been studied. They have about the same contingent odds as identical twins reared together. We must conclude, therefore, that something in the inherited biological equipment is a major factor in developing at least certain abnormal personality patterns. Of course, the fact that the odds for identical twins are 85 and not 100 leaves some room for the effects of environment (see page 522).

At present we do not know how such predispositions are inherited. It is possible that the linkage is from genes to enzymes to metabolic processes in the brain (see page 33), but at present that is just a guess.

TABLE 13.4 *The incidence of behavior disorders in the general population and among blood relatives of patients.*

TYPE OF BEHAVIOR DISORDER	INCIDENCE IN GENERAL POPULATION, PER CENT	INCIDENCE AMONG RELATIVES, PER CENT				
		PARENTS	HALF SIBLINGS	FULL SIBLINGS	FRATERNAL TWINS	IDENTICAL TWINS
Schizophrenia	0.9	9.3	7.1	14.2	14.5	86.2
Manic-depressive psychosis	0.4	23.4	16.7	23.0	26.3	95.7
Involutional melancholia	1.0	6.4	4.5	6.0	6.0	60.9

SOURCE: Kallmann, 1951.

ABILITIES Each person is endowed with certain abilities, which are gradually developed through maturation and learning. There can be little doubt that inheritance partly determines these abilities (see Chapter 2). Psychologists refer to the more general abilities to learn, abstract, and solve problems as *intelligence;* they call special abilities, such as talent for music or mechanical things, *aptitudes* (see Chapter 12). These abilities, as we have pointed out, are to a certain extent a part of a person's personality. They are also important influences on personality development. For instance, superior intelligence helps a person make better social adjustments. Since personality may be regarded, in part, as the composite of such adjustments, superior intelligence should be a factor in the development of a "better" personality. The brighter little Nathaniel is, for example, the sooner he can learn to understand that mother may be cross and grouchy because she has a headache rather than because he is a naughty, unlovable child. And the more intelligent child can learn sooner to see into the future, to delay a satisfaction now for one he may achieve a day or two hence.

Intelligence also influences personality by providing a person with a means of gaining recognition. The bright child achieves rewards from parents and teachers for his accomplishments. Another with mechanical ability may become interested in building amateur radio equipment and receive the recognition of adults and friends for his achievements.

Thus intelligence and special abilities permit a child or an adult to develop areas of competence from which he acquires confidence and feelings of self-worth and self-esteem.

Abilities also seem to provide their own motivation. A person with a special talent usually has a strong motive to exercise it. The great musician Handel, for example, had a father who strongly opposed his son's interest in music. Nevertheless, even when faced with severe punishment, Handel as a child would sneak to the garret at night to practice the harpsichord. As a consequence of such strong drives to practice, children with outstanding abilities usually show them at an early age.

CULTURE Now let us shift from the influence of nature to the influence of nurture on personality. One's personality also depends, of course, upon whether he is reared in the United States or in the jungles of New Guinea, whether he lives in the city or on the farm, and whether he is reared in an upper or lower socioeconomic class (see Chapter 16). These circumstances, along with many others, constitute the culture or subculture in which he lives. Culture largely determines the experiences a person has, the frustrations and adjustments he must deal with, and the standards of conduct required of him. Each culture has its distinctive values, morals, and ways of behaving. It lays down the rules for child training and the relationships within a family. Thus culture influences personality because it dictates many of the characteristics a person will acquire [Linton, 1945]. The process of acquiring the personality traits characteristic of members of a particular culture is called *socialization* (see Chapter 16).

Differences in socialization are most convincingly demonstrated in cultures of primitive societies and the characteristic differences in personality associated with them. The Balinese, for example, have been described as an introverted people who seem emotionally blunted. They do not form warm personal attachments; rather, each member seems to live within himself. The Navaho Indians are passive and forbearing in the face of physical discomfort. The Eskimos are rugged individualists. The Arapesh people of New Guinea seem to be without egotism or competitiveness.

In the Balinese people, the lack of emotional response has been attributed to child-rearing practices. Most of the baby tending is done by little girls, and each child may be cared for by a number of little "mothers." Such practices prevent intense family relationships from building up. In addition, the Balinese mother may make things worse by deliberately teasing her child. She will play with him up to the point of evoking love or anger, then lose interest in him or become indifferent. It is small wonder, then, that the Balinese child soon learns to inhibit emotional responses to other people.

FAMILY The family exerts many cultural influences, for it largely determines the environment of children during their early years and decides how cultural standards are to be imposed and adhered to.

Family warmth. One significant influence of the family is the affection it gives or withholds. This is especially important, the evidence indicates, during babyhood. If a child gets fondling and affection during this period, he is more likely to be emotionally responsive later in life. Conversely, if he lacks fondling then, his emotional responsiveness may be blunted. Children, for example, who are reared from birth in orphanages, where they receive every physical care but little personal handling and attention, are less responsive, studies show, than are children who are placed in an orphanage after they are two years of age [Goldfarb, 1947]. Early parental influences are thus important in personality development.

Learning in the family. The training and guidance given by parents also fashion personality. Parents are teachers. By reinforcing some kinds of behavior and discouraging others, they help determine the personality traits, goals, and values of the child. One child may discover that his mother will let him have his own way if he throws a temper tantrum. Another child in another family may find that temper tantrums do not work, but that feigning illness does. The techniques a child develops in dealing with his parents naturally carry over into his contacts with others. The grown man, for example, who sulks because he is angry with his wife probably learned this response in dealing with his mother.

The training given by parents can be seen quite clearly in the process of *sex-typing*—the development of responses and interests appropriate to one's sex [Mussen et al., 1963]. In most families, continuous pressure is directed toward making the little boy or girl behave in ways appropriate to his or her sex role. For instance, little boys are reinforced for rather rough and aggressive play, for inhibiting emotional displays, and for showing an interest in the workings of mechanical things; little girls, on the other hand, are usually reinforced for being more submissive and "sweet," for expressing emotion, and they are discouraged from developing interests in mechanical devices. This pressure is not, of course, usually consciously applied by the parents, but it is nevertheless actively and powerfully present. Later, as the child grows older, much of the socialization of the child, including sex-typing, becomes the province of the peer group, and conformity to its standards carries forward the process of learning the role and traits characteristic of one's sex.

Parental attitudes. Probably parents' attitudes toward their children are as important as anything else in the way personality develops in children. Parents who are well adjusted, who love and respect their child as a person, do much to build up within the child a feeling of self-worth and self-confidence. This in turn gives the child a great advantage in facing his problems. Unfortunately, however, many parents reject their children, enmesh them in the cross-fire of their own emotional problems, or take out on the children the ill-treatment that they may have experienced in their own childhood. In fact, studies have shown that many mothers and fathers unconsciously relive their own childhood problems through their children [Hilgard, 1953]. A mother may unconsciously react to her son with the same emotions and feelings that she herself felt as a child toward her older brother. If she resented and disliked her brother, some of her feelings toward her son may be similar. She may find herself competing with him and thus unable to give him encouragement, love, and praise. It is easy for children in such a situation to feel unwanted and unloved and thus to lack confidence and emotional security that carries over into adulthood.

Parental attitudes also express themselves in the so-called "home atmosphere" [Baldwin, 1948].

Homes were rated as to whether the dominant atmosphere was one of democracy or control. The democratic families were ones in which the children were given explanations of decisions; the children were allowed to participate to some extent in the formation of decisions about policies which would affect them; and a rather high degree of permissiveness prevailed. The controlled atmosphere was one in which permissiveness was low and rather clear-cut sets of "do's" and "do not's" were established. Definite differences in the superficial personality traits of the children from the different atmospheres were observed. The democratic families tended to produce children who were rated as outgoing—they tended to be aggressive, fearless, full of plans, high in leadership, curiosity, and nonconformity. Children from the controlled atmospheres, on the other hand, tended to be much less outgoing—they tended to be socially unaggressive, more fearful, and rather low in planfulness, and tenacity.

In short, they tended to be conforming, well-behaved children.

These results are quite predictable from what we know about learning (see Chapter 3). In the democratic atmosphere, outgoing responses are being reinforced; in the controlled atmosphere, other responses are being reinforced. Although it is difficult to avoid making value judgments about these findings, it should be pointed out that one pattern is not intrinsically better than the other. The outgoing children from the democratic homes were no doubt obnoxious and cruel at times, but they were more socially successful and curious and thus would seem to be more likely to get things done and to be creative. The less outgoing children from the controlled homes were easier to be with and would seem to have developed control over impulsiveness.

Imitation. Parents influence personality development by being *models*. A child learns much by imitation [Bandura and Walters, 1963]. By watch-

LIKE FATHER, LIKE SON

FIGURE 13.11. *Imitation in the family. The boy here is learning to act like his father who was a college and professional football player. Perhaps more important, he is learning to value many of the same things. (Courtesy of Henry Ford.)*

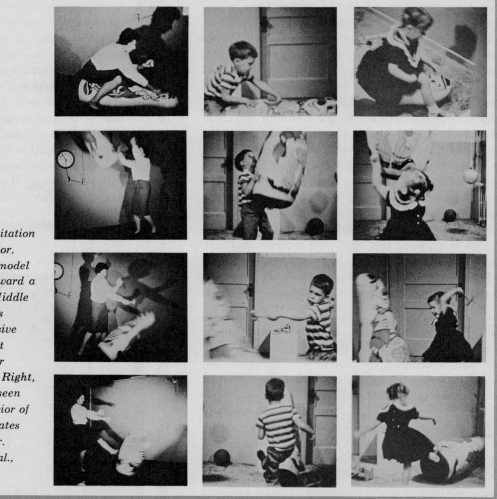

FIGURE 13.12. *Imitation of aggressive behavior. Left row: An adult model acts aggressively toward a large plastic doll. Middle row: A boy, who has watched the aggressive behavior of the adult model, shows similar aggressive behavior. Right, row: A girl, having seen the aggressive behavior of the model, also imitates the model's behavior. (From Bandura et al., 1963.)*

ing his father, a son learns how to act like a man (see Figure 13.11), and by watching her mother, the daughter learns how to play the role of wife and mother. Both general attitudes and specific responses are learned by imitation. An interesting example of the learning of specific aggressive responses through imitation is shown in Figure 13.12 [Bandura et al., 1963]. The photographs in the top row show specific aggressive responses made by an adult model. Children watched the behavior of the model and then were tested. The middle row of pic-

tures shows the imitative aggressive behavior of a little boy after he had seen the model. Note that he displays aggressive responses which are very much like those of the model. The same is true for the little girl in the bottom row of pictures.

Thus children find models, good ones or poor ones, with whom to identify themselves. In so doing, they may copy many of the personality traits of their parents, taking over their moral and cultural standards as well as their mannerisms and typical ways of adjusting to problems. Learning provides one explanation of the way in which such imitation may occur—children are reinforced for making responses similar to those made by the parents. Psychoanalytic theory provides another attempt to explain the dynamics behind some identification (see page 491).

The individual and the self

Now we come to the problem of understanding the *individual personality as a whole*. Each of us tries to do this in dealing with many of the people we know intimately. There is neither a royal road to understanding the individual, nor any set of rules for doing it. There are, however, some important points to consider, and we shall present them under the following headings: (1) individuality, (2) personality syndromes, and (3) the self.

INDIVIDUALITY   A person is not simply a profile of disembodied traits measured by tests or ratings, nor is he a piece of putty molded willy-nilly by environmental circumstances. Personality tests provide only samples of behavior (see page 449), and environmental influences combine in different ways to affect personalities quite differently. The data we do have about personality traits and environmental influences are merely windows through which we catch brief glimpses of the underlying personality. These glimpses must somehow be synthesized into a coherent picture of an individual.

Uniqueness of personality. One thing to realize is that each person is a unique individual. No two people—not even identical twins reared together—can be exactly alike. Each person has his unique set of abilities and habits and, except for identical twins, his unique hereditary endowment. Two individuals with similar rearing are different because their endowments cause them to react differently to environmental influences. Those with similar endowments are different because they have different, or at least slightly different, environmental influences. For this reason, it is not wise in dealing with individuals to generalize glibly from one individual to another. Because Cheryl and Sally have similar backgrounds and even superficially similar personalities, it does not follow that the two girls are to be understood in the same way. An intimate knowledge of their individual motives, traits, and modes of adjustment almost always reveals significant differences between them that make each a unique personality.

Continuity of personality. In understanding any particular person, it should also be borne in mind that personality has a basic continuity. Habits and motives that are learned over a number of years are not easily forgotten or supplanted by new ones. Thousands and thousands of learning trials make up the history of any particular individual. Biological factors, of which the individual is partly a product, do not change greatly, at least not in the adult. In addition to learning and endowment, the roles a person is called upon to play give continuity to his personality. His family, friends, social class, and economic circumstances all are relatively constant. They continue to make demands on him for certain ways of behaving, which we call roles (see Chapter 16). These roles do not change, at least not very rapidly.

Three factors—endowment, learning, and social roles—lead us to expect a certain continuity, consistency, and permanency to personality. We therefore cannot expect a person to change very greatly or very quickly. What he will be tomorrow is an extension of what he is today. If he seems to be a Dr. Jekyll and Mr. Hyde, his appearance is probably deceiving. Beneath the exterior is a person whose motives and habits make sense in terms of the individual's past history. It is therefore best to assume that the future personality will be essentially what it has been in the past.

Personality changes. This is not to say, however, that personality never changes. Over a period of time, it usually does. In some people, it changes more than it does in others. Nearly all people gradually acquire some new habits to supplant old ones. Often they discover ways of satisfying motives that were previously frustrated. Sometimes they change their way of life, and this leads to satisfactions they did not know before or to new roles to be played. Marriage, for example, occasionally produces marked personality changes—although marriage is usually no cure for a personality problem—because it affords a new way of life and exposes a person to a different set of influences. Sometimes, too, personality changes take place as a result of intense religious experience, changing jobs, moving to a new community, achieving success in a line of work, and so on. In these cases, however, the change takes place because something has happened to change motives, satisfy motives, teach new habits, or in a word, change a person's fundamental modes of adjustment.

Most personality changes occur gradually and with no conscious intent. Sometimes, however, a deliberate attempt is made to bring about personality changes. A person may change himself, or someone close to him may effect a change. Psychotherapy and counseling are organized methods for bringing about such changes (see Chapter 15). These methods are employed when a person faces a problem he feels unable to solve, or when he becomes so incapable of making social adjustments that an important personality change is urgently needed. When successful, psychotherapy and counseling techniques effect personality changes by enabling the individual to discard old habits and to learn new ones that reduce his motivational conflicts and provide satisfactions for his needs. Such personality changes may therefore be regarded as cases of relatively rapid learning.

PERSONALITY SYNDROMES   Also of aid in understanding individual persons is the concept of the *syndrome.* This term, from medical terminology, refers to a pattern of causes and symptoms of disease. In the field of personality, it means a pattern of origins and characteristics of the personality. Although each individual's personality is unique, a person may display a syndrome which is similar in many respects to the syndrome found in other individuals.

Several personality syndromes have been described and measured. In fact, one purpose of some personality tests, such as the Minnesota Multiphasic Personality Inventory (MMPI), is to detect such syndromes (see page 450). For example, a *hypochondriacal syndrome,* which may consist of many specific characteristics, is one of abnormal concern over bodily health. A *psychasthenic syndrome* is characterized by excessive doubt, compulsions, obsessions, and unreasonable fears. Both these syndromes are measured on the MMPI. Another syndrome, called the *authoritarian personality,* is marked by highly conventional behavior, desire for power, hostility, prejudice, and intolerance. This kind of personality pattern appears to have its causes in rejection or excessive domination of a child by his parents (see page 603).

Our use of the concept of syndrome does not imply the classification of people into types. Not everyone has a personality syndrome, and hence syndromes cannot be used to classify people. In a syndrome, some personality characteristics tend to be highly correlated and thus to form patterns, and people who display similar syndromes may be compared. If we are aware of a syndrome when it exists, we have a better overall understanding of a person than we would otherwise have.

THE SELF   Each of us has a concept of his *self*— for most of us, this is the real essence of the personality. Unfortunately, the self is rather elusive from the point of view of the scientist, and many problems stand in the way of an objective study. Nevertheless, some conclusions can be drawn about the self which are of benefit in understanding personality.

Origin of the self. From the point of view of psychology, the self represents the individual's awareness or perception of his own personality. We learn to perceive our own body and behavior in much the same way that we learn to perceive other objects and events in the world about us (see Chapter 10). The beginnings of the perceived self can be traced to early infancy when the infant first starts to learn distinctions between his own body and other objects in his environment. At birth, the infant is probably aware only of vague feelings of comfort or discomfort. Then, as his capacity for learning and memory develops and as his experience widens, the child sees that parts of his body are common to all his experiences. Muscular and organic sensations accompany all his activities, and he discovers that pinching objects, such as his doll, does not cause pain, whereas pinching any part of his own body does. By the time the child is two years old, his distinction between his own body and other objects is generally well established.

Self-perception. The perception of the body as a unit distinct from the changing background is probably the core around which all later self-perception takes place, but a number of other influences contribute importantly to the development of self-awareness. Such awareness is fostered by giving the child a name, by holding him responsible for his behavior, and by distinguishing betweeen possessions that are his and possessions that belong to his parents, brothers, and sisters. Since the family and society treat the child as a unit, he comes to perceive himself in this way.

The kinds of experiences that the child has determine to a large degree what his self-perception will be like. The child finds that his behavior and appearance elicit kindness or hostility, respect or rebuke, attention or indifference from parents and fellows. He hears himself described by parents and playmates in terms of various personality traits, and when these traits are consistently applied, he often accepts them as descriptions of himself. Praise and love from parents and respect and attention from playmates will contribute to the development of a picture of himself as a desirable person. On the other hand, rejection and excessive criticism at home and indifference from others can lead to a derogatory self-picture, with resulting inferiority feelings.

Of course the treatment a person receives bears some relation to his traits and abilities. The physically strong child is more apt to receive the admiration of his playmates than is the weak child. The intelligent child will have a greater opportunity for experiences of success and praise in school. Hence we would expect that the individual's perception of his own personality would tend to coincide with the way in which others perceive him. However, this is not always true. We probably never perceive ourselves exactly as others see us. In some cases, the differences between the perceived self and the real or objective personality are quite marked.

Although a child may be intelligent and quite capable physically, he may, if reared by indifferent parents and subjected to constant criticism and belittlement, learn to perceive himself as an inadequate, undesirable person. Most of us have known people who constantly underrate their own performance. By the same token, we have also known people with a grossly exaggerated view of their accomplishments and capabilities. Children surrounded by an admiring and doting family who praise even poor performance excessively are often found to have excessive self-evaluations (see page 501).

The self and emotional adjustment. In many instances, knowing a person's self-picture helps us to understand his behavior. This is particularly true where a marked discrepancy exists between the way the person sees himself and the way others see him. Behavior is largely determined by how the person perceives a situation with reference to himself. From our vantage point, we may think that John should be a popular fellow with the girls—after all, he has good looks and a ready wit—but if John does not perceive himself as having these attributes, he may be just another wallflower.

If the person's self-picture is too different from the true or objective personality, serious adjustment problems may arise. The person is constantly called upon to explain away or ignore evidence which is incompatible with his view of himself. The mediocre student who pictures himself as an intellectual giant is faced with the objective evidence of his poor grades and failures. Often, instead of changing his self-evaluation, he will use rationalizations—bright people are not interested in getting grades because they have broader interests, for example—to explain the evidence away, or he may completely ignore it by repressing his perception of the discrepancy. Thus, defense mechanisms are often used to maintain distorted self-perceptions.

Theories of personality

Having come this far in the study of personality, the student may feel the lack of any overall picture of personality. We have described various facets of personality and some influences bearing on the development of personality. But how do the pieces fit together? What causes what? What is our general theory of personality?

The truth is that psychologists do not agree on any general theory of personality. So far, personality has proved too complex, its manifestations too varied, and its determinants too numerous for us to place the pieces together into one clear picture. Instead, we have many theories. Each represents an attempt to explain the subject. None, however, manages to do it to everyone's satisfaction, for none is complete enough to encompass all that we know about personality. Each stresses certain factors and ignores others.

One day the problem will no doubt be solved through research and new attempts to formulate a general theory. In the meantime, the best we can do is to present several different theories. Actually, the theories that have been proposed are far too numerous to cover completely here. We can only introduce several that have had an important influence on our present conceptions of personality.

PSYCHOANALYTIC THEORY   When we mentioned psychoanalysis in Chapter 1, we pointed out that it involves both a method of psychotherapy and a theory of personality. Psychoanalysis as a method is covered in Chapter 15. As a theory of personality it has been the most influential and, therefore, deserves more space than the others. Psychoanalytic theory has three main themes: a theory of personality structure, a theory of personality development, and a system of personality dynamics [Freud, 1953].

Personality structure. Freud, the founder of psychoanalysis, considered personality to have a three-part structure: the *id*, the *ego*, and the *superego*. The id might be thought of as a sort of storehouse of motives and "instinctual" reactions for satisfying motives. These motives, taken together, are called the *libido*. Left to itself, the id would seek immediate satisfaction for motives as they arose, without regard to the realities of life or to morals of any kind.

The id, however, is usually bridled by the ego. This consists of elaborate ways of behaving and thinking that are learned for dealing effectively with the world. It delays the satisfaction of motives or channels motives into socially acceptable outlets. It keeps a person working for a living, getting along with people, and generally adjusting to the realities of life. Indeed, Freud characterized the ego as working "in the service of the reality principle."

The superego, finally, corresponds closely with what we more commonly call conscience. It consists of restraints, acquired in the course of personality development, on the activity of the ego and the id. The superego may condemn as wrong those things which the ego might do toward the satisfaction of the id's motives. In addition, the superego keeps a person working toward the ideals—the ego ideals—acquired in childhood.

Freud's conception of personality structure very adequately sums up three major aspects of personality. In early chapters, particularly Chapter 6, we described these aspects in different terms. The first aspect, equivalent in some ways to the id, consists of unlearned physiological motives and unlearned reactions for satisfying them. The second, corresponding to the ego, is made up of learned instrumental acts for satisfying motives and also of the perceived self discussed in the last section. The third, represented by the superego, is the set of socially derived motives that affect, and sometimes conflict with, the first two factors. Thus Freud's basic ideas of personality structure, although clothed in different terminology, are in general accord with the conclusions of experimental psychology.

It has been objected that the Freudian view of personality structure divides personality into three compartments, each of which seems to comprise a separate personality in itself. It is indeed easy to slip into this way of viewing the id, ego, and superego, but this was not what Freud intended. The three terms simply represent convenient concepts for summarizing major aspects of personality that have no clear lines separating them. They provide a general picture which, when considered in detail, becomes very complicated.

Two additional points should be kept in mind, although they are more fully treated elsewhere. First, the libido, that is, the motives or instincts of the id, is frequently blocked by the ego and superego. When it is, it may be *displaced* in other directions, and may seek outlets that are acceptable to the ego and superego. Second, because the id is frequently in *conflict* with the ego and superego, *anxiety* is aroused. The person then seeks ways to reduce his anxiety. The methods of reducing anxiety that he learns are the defense mechanisms.

Personality development. Freud conceived of personality as developing from infancy to adulthood through four overlapping stages. The first three stages are the pregenital stages: the oral stage, the anal stage, and the phallic stage. The fourth stage, the genital stage, is entered at puberty. It is possible, according to Freud, for the person to become fixated in any one of the pregenital stages if he experiences unusual frustration, insecurity, or anxiety while in that stage of development. Fixation in a pregenital stage is characterized by certain personality syndromes in the adult.

The *oral stage* occupies much of the first year of life. During this period, the infant receives pleasure from sucking and other activities involving his mouth. If at this time he is prevented from sucking, or made anxious about it, he may acquire an *oral fixation.* Later in life the *oral syndrome* is considered to include excessive oral behavior (see Figure 13.13), greediness, dependence, and passivity.

The *anal stage* is most prominent during the second and third years of life. Largely owing to parental attempts to toilet train the child and to suppress "naughty" behavior connected with excretion, the child is supposed to focus his interest on anal activities. If training is too strict and arouses anxieties about these activities, the adult *anal syndrome* may be one of compulsiveness and excessive conformity or self-control.

After toilet training is mastered, the child focuses his interest on his sexual organs. In this pregenital *phallic stage,* the child typically develops "romantic" feelings toward the parent of the opposite sex—the boy toward his mother, and the girl toward her father. Freud called this the *Oedipus complex,* after the mythical story of Oedipus, who unwittingly killed his father and, upon becoming King of Thebes, just as unwittingly married his mother.

The phallic stage with its concomitant Oedipal complex is perhaps the most crucial one in development according to this theory. In this stage, the child is supposed to be threatened with dire punishment for the romantic attachment to the parent of the opposite sex. For instance, for boys this punishment is supposed to be a direct or symbolic threat of castration by the jealous father. The threat produces anxiety and defenses against this anxiety. In the normal case, the defense which eventually emerges is an *identification* with the threatening parent (see page 480). For example, it is as if the little boy said to himself: "If I become like daddy, I can express my affection toward mother as he does." So the boy begins to become like the father, and in the process of doing so, takes on the behav-

THE ORAL STAGES OF MAN

FIGURE 13.13.   *The expression of orality. Changes occur in the normal expression of oral behavior as a person grows older. Fixation at the oral stage may produce an oral syndrome. (Wattenberg, 1955.)*

ioral patterns and ideas, especially ideas about right and wrong, which are characteristic of his culture. For girls, the situation is a little different and more complicated, but the principles are similar. In other words, identification and, through it, indoctrination into the culture are supposed to be the outcomes of resolution of the Oedipal conflict. In terms of psychoanalytic theory, the superego, or conscience and ego ideal, develop from resolution of the Oedipal situation. On the other hand, if the Oedipal situation is not resolved by the child, the adult may end up with a weak conscience and distorted relations with his friends and members of the opposite sex.

During the pregenital stages, the individual tends to center interest on himself. When he enters the *genital stage* and normal heterosexual interests emerge, his interests focus more and more on others and on playing the normal roles of the adult in society.

Personality dynamics. Psychoanalysis is both a deterministic and a dynamic theory. By this we mean that the theory states that thoughts and behavior are caused by motives. The motives are the id instincts and urges which seek expression. However, many of these impulses would arouse a great deal of anxiety if they were expressed directly because they are in conflict with ego and superego forces. Therefore the id urges are repressed and, if they are expressed at all, they are expressed in disguised form. When disguised, the id instincts may gain expression without causing so much anxiety. Thus, because of repression, although the id motives are there, we are not usually aware of them, and for this reason they are often called *unconscious motives.* Unconscious motivation is, perhaps, the underlying dynamic force in Freudian psychoanalysis.

For example, the Freudian interpretation of dreams is based on the idea of unconscious id urges; dreams are supposed to be the disguised manifestations, sometimes called "wish fulfillments," of id motives (see page 547). In everyday life, the existence of id urges may be revealed by slips of the tongue and selective forgetting. In a book called

The Psychopathology of Everyday Life, Freud analyzed the disguised manifestation of id motives. [Freud, 1914]. The following examples are from the edition of this book translated by A. A. Brill:

A woman wrote to her sister, felicitating her on the occasion of taking possession of a new and spacious residence. A friend who was present noticed that the writer put the wrong address on the letter, and what was still more remarkable was the fact that she did not address it to the previous residence, but to one long ago given up, but which her sister had occupied when she first married. When the friend called her attention to it, the writer remarked, "You are right; but what in the world made me do this?" to which her friend replied: "Perhaps you begrudge her the nice big apartment into which she has just moved because you yourself are cramped for space, and for that reason you put her back into her first residence, where she was no better off than yourself." "Of course I begrudge her the new apartment," she honestly admitted. As an afterthought she added, "It is a pity that one is so mean in such matters."

Ernest Jones reports the following example given to him by Dr. A. A. Brill. In a letter to Dr. Brill, a patient tried to attribute his nervousness to business worries and excitement during the cotton crisis. He went on to say: "My trouble is all due to that d— frigid wave; there isn't even any seed to be obtained for new crops." He referred to a cold wave which had destroyed the cotton crops, but instead of writing "wave" he wrote "wife." In the bottom of his heart, he entertained reproaches against his wife on account of her marital frigidity and childlessness, and he was not far from the cognition that the enforced abstinence played no little part in the causation of his malady. [Freud, 1938, pages 92–93.]

The psychoanalyst is quite adept at interpreting many behaviors and trains of thought in terms of unconscious id motives. In so doing, he assumes that behavior is determined by unconscious motives and that the particular behavior or thought which is expressed is a disguised expression of an id urge.

Psychoanalysis and science. Although some psychoanalysts would disagree, psychoanalytic theory, and for that matter many of the other theories of personality mentioned here, are not scientific theories in the usual sense of the term. Psychoanalytic theory is based on clinical impressions and not on careful measurement under controlled conditions. The theory is intuitive—literary and verbal—a set of seemingly plausible guesses about the structure, origins, and dynamics of personality. The intuitive and literary nature of psychoanalysis is both its strength and its weakness. The guesses of Freud and others about unconscious motives, the development of such motives, their frustrations, and the defense mechanisms which result can all be made to fit almost everyone by appropriate manipulation of the symbols and terms of the theory. But do the terms of the theory describe facts—situations or entities which can be measured and demonstrated under controlled conditions without elaborate interpretation? For instance, is there really a phallic stage in development which has the properties attributed to it by psychoanalytic theory? Evidence on this and similar points is at best moderately convincing.

Thus, most psychologists find themselves in an ambivalent position with regard to psychoanalysis—it cannot be tested the way they would like to see it tested, but at the same time, some aspects of it seem like valid hunches. The ideas of unconscious motivation, repression, and defense mechanisms have found their way into many branches of academic psychology and, for that matter, into much of Western thought. Perhaps the best advice which can be given about psychoanalysis and related theories is that one should proceed with caution.

SUPERIORITY AND COMPENSATION   Freud's theory emphasizes the biological drives—hunger, excretion, and sex, in particular. Most other theories place somewhat greater emphasis on social factors. One of these, put forth by Alfred Adler, an early disciple of Freud who later rejected Freudian theory, emphasizes a drive or striving for *superiority*.

It is to Adler that we owe the concept of the *inferiority complex,* a phrase now part of everyday speech. Because we strive for superiority, argued Adler, we are always seeing ways in which we fall short of our aspirations, and hence ways in which we are inferior. This itself is healthy, for feeling our

weakness in first one respect and then another provides things for us "to work on." We are forever striving to overcome our inferiorities. But an inferiority complex develops when we regularly fail to overcome our weaknesses or when for any reason we come to put too much emphasis on any particular inferiority.

From Adler, too, comes the concept of *compensation* (see page 479). Being aware of a weakness, we may strive especially hard to overcome it. The person who, like Theodore Roosevelt, is fragile and sickly as a child may throw himself into physical activities and *overcompensate* for handicaps or inferiorities. In many instances, because of overcompensation, people ultimately become quite superior in things in which they were originally inferior. In addition, people may compensate for inferiority by achieving distinction in some other area. For example, the homely girl who is a bookworm becomes superior in academic things when she fails in social affairs. This kind of compensation resembles Freud's idea of displacement; the difference lies in the motivation. Freud's displacement is an outlet for libidinal motives; Adler's compensation is a means of satisfying the striving for superiority.

ANXIETY THEORY   Most theories give anxiety an important place in their scheme of things. Freud considered anxiety the outcome of conflict between the id and the ego. Another theorist, Karen Horney, makes *basic anxiety* the central concept of her theory [Horney, 1937]. Moreover, she considers this anxiety to arise from social influences in the development of the child, rather than from the conflict between biological motives and the ego or superego. According to Horney, basic anxiety is first aroused in the child by any social situation which tends to make the child fearful. It can be instigated by threats or domination by the parent, by tension and conflict between the parents, by being required to do too much, by being mistrusted, by criticism, coldness, or indifference, and so on. Once anxiety is aroused, the child attempts to alleviate it by trial-and-error behavior, as any organism might try to solve a problem. In this way, the child learns certain ways of dealing with anxiety; these, in turn, form a pattern of "neurotic needs."

A neurotic need is thus a learned need. If the child learns to cope with anxiety by running to its mother for affection and approval, it may develop a neurotic need for affection and approval. If it managed to cope with some anxiety-producing situations by obtaining prestige or personal admiration, it may have a neurotic need for these things. According to this theory, there could be any number of neurotic needs, depending on the things the child learned to need to reduce anxiety. In any given culture, however, certain patterns of needs can be expected to arise because the sources of anxiety tend to form a repetitive pattern from one family to another and from one child to another. Hence, Horney has formulated a list of 10 needs, which include needs for such things as affection, dependency, power, prestige, achievement, and self-sufficiency.

Horney's theory, like Freud's and most others, has a place in it for *conflict*. To Horney, however, the major conflict is between needs simply because some needs are incompatible. If a person, for example, develops both a need to have someone to depend on and a need to be self-sufficient and independent, these needs will often conflict. Most people possess neurotic needs in some degree, but when they are unable to resolve conflicts between them, some needs tend to dominate their lives. They then become "neurotic" persons.

PSYCHOLOGICAL NEEDS   Another theorist, Henry Murray, has an even longer list of needs than Horney, but he arrived at them in a different way [Murray, 1938]. Although influenced considerably by Freud, he came to feel that one source of motivation, such as Freud's id, Adler's striving for superiority, or Horney's basic anxiety, oversimplified matters. He preferred to determine, as empirically as possible, the needs that could be distinguished in a representative sample of people. From extensive material, consisting of life histories, projective-test data, and interviews, gathered on 51 young men, he formulated a list of 28 needs. Some of these have already been presented in Table 13.3. He felt that a

rather large number of needs was required to account for the strivings observed in people.

According to Murray's theory, the psychological needs he has distinguished can be found in almost everyone, but they vary in strength. In one individual, one pattern of needs may be strong; in another individual, another pattern may predominate. It is the strength of the needs and the pattern they form that characterize any particular individual's personality. The Thematic Apperception Test (TAT) was devised to measure these needs (see page 456).

SELF-ACTUALIZATION   Another theorist, Abraham Maslow, has outlined a theory that for brevity is called the *self-actualization* theory [Maslow, 1954]. At first glance, it might seem to be a single-factor theory like Adler's striving for superiority, but it is not. Rather it is a multiple-factor theory which posits five levels of needs arranged in a hierarchy. Arranged from lower to higher levels, they are:

Physiological needs, such as hunger, thirst and sex

Safety needs, such as security, stability, and order

Belongingness and love needs, such as needs for affection, affiliation, and identification

Esteem needs, such as needs for prestige, success, and self-respect

Need for self-actualization

The order of listing these needs is significant in two ways. This is the order in which such needs tend to appear in the normal development of the person. It is also the order in which they need to be satisfied. And if earlier needs are not satisfied, the person never gets around to doing much about the later needs. It follows then that people in a poor society will be mostly concerned with physiological and safety needs. Those in an "affluent" society, on the other hand, will manage to satisfy the needs lower in the hierarchy and in many cases be preoccupied with the need for self-actualization.

The need for self-actualization refers to the need to develop the full potentialities of the person. Naturally, the meaning of this need varies from person to person, for each has different potentialities. For some, it means achievement in literary or scientific fields; for others, it means leadership in politics or the community; for still others, it means merely living one's own life fully without being unduly restrained by social conventions. One can find "self-actualizers" among professors, businessmen, political leaders, missionaries, artists, or housewives. But not all individuals in any of these categories are able to achieve self-actualization; many have numerous unsatisfied needs, and because their achievements are merely compensations, they are left frustrated and unhappy in other respects.

TRAIT THEORY   Trait theory, which has been espoused by Gordon Allport, gives us no finite list of needs or traits [Allport, 1937]. It assumes a multiplicity of needs that are never quite the same from one individual to the next. It may be distinguished from other theories in two important respects.

One is the concept of the *uniqueness of personality*. Each person, with his unique background of childhood experiences, develops a set of traits that are unique to him.

A second, related feature of the theory is the concept of *functional autonomy of motives*. In the course of development, each person acquires motives as part of satisfying other motives (see Chapter 6). These motives, according to Allport's concept of functional autonomy, continue to function autonomously without further reinforcement of the physiological conditions originally concerned in their acquisition.

Examples of what seems to be the functional autonomy of motives abound in everyday life. The poor boy who earned his first pennies to ward off hunger and discomfort continues to work day and night at amassing a large fortune long after he has acquired enough money to meet his physical needs. A businessman who approaches retirement age with ample reserves insists on staying at his job, probably because he finds that the job now satisfies his needs for companionship and activities, even though his original motivation for working was to earn a living. Even the persistence of sexual interests in

middle age, after hormones are no longer of much importance, has been cited as an example of functional autonomy.

LEARNING THEORY OF PERSONALITY   Certainly learning plays a major role in the development of the characteristics which differentiate personalities. We have seen that complex motives are learned and that such motives are important characteristics of personality. In addition, abilities, attitudes, and interests are shaped by reinforcement (see Chapter 3). Our discussion of the role of the parents as teachers should make this clear.

Not only are many of the characteristics of personality learned, but according to learning theory, many of the modes of adjustment, the defense mechanisms, for example, are learned habits. After all, the defense mechanisms are techniques for reducing anxiety, and the reduction of anxiety is reinforcing. Thus, particular responses, the defense mechanisms, which reduce anxiety are increased in strength [Dollard and Miller, 1950]. In this way, some of the terms and dynamics of Freudian psychoanalysis can be translated into the terms of experimental psychology. The advantage of this is that some experimental rigor may be applied to the intuitions of psychoanalysis.

OTHER PERSONALITY THEORIES   In passing, several other personality theories, the "neoanalytic" theories, which stress social factors in development should be mentioned [see Monroe, 1955]. Erich Fromm, for instance, has stressed that the infant as he grows up eventually becomes free from his parents. However, this new freedom produces a sense of isolation and separateness, and the individual attempts to "escape from freedom" [Fromm, 1941]. Fromm has listed several basic mechanisms of escape by which the person attempts to relate himself to primary groups in order to lose his feeling of separateness. These escape mechanisms are important aspects and themes of personality according to Fromm.

Harry Stack Sullivan has stressed the learning that takes place in crucial interpersonal situations as basic in the development of personality [Sullivan, 1953]. Personality arises in stages as the individual interacts with other significant people in his life. For instance, an infant may develop anxiety if the "mothering one" expresses anxiety when caring for him; there seems to be a kind of empathic communication of anxiety from mother to infant. Such early social learning may form the nucleus for later evaluations of, and reactions in, symbolically similar interpersonal situations.

Erik Erikson has stressed the search for ego integrity as a basic human motive [Erikson, 1950]. The search for integrity involves identification with figures in the culture, and this is supposed to be difficult in modern Western society where models for identification are weak and goals of the society are vague. The development of ego identity procedes through eight stages. At each of the first seven stages, a particular problem must be solved before ego integrity is reached in the eighth stage. Even in this eighth stage, however, ego identity is still threatened. The eight problems and stages are:

(1) trust versus basic mistrust, (2) autonomy versus shame and doubt, (3) initiative versus guilt, (4) industry versus inferiority, (5) identity versus role diffusion, (6) intimacy versus isolation, (7) generativity versus stagnation, (8) ego integrity versus despair [Erikson, 1950].

In recent years, psychoanalytic theory has been concerned more with rational aspects of personality, the ego in other words, than with the expression of id instincts and motives [Hartmann, 1964; Kris, 1950]. Many other variants of psychoanalytic theory might be mentioned, and hopefully the interested student will pursue some of these.

If you go farther in this field, do not lose your skepticism. It is in this area, perhaps more than any other, that psychologists and others depart from the constraints of common sense. Perhaps this is good and "creative," but the careful student will find it valuable to sift and weigh the evidence carefully and to retain his patience, forbearance, and sense of humor.

SYNOPSIS AND SUMMARY

The unique collection of characteristics which comprises the human personality is not an easy thing to study. Some progress, however, has been made. Experimental psychology has contributed knowledge about motivation, learning, and frustration and conflict; child psychology has contributed experimental and observational studies on the development of personality characteristics; psychological testing, or psychometrics, has contributed techniques for the measurement of personality characteristics (see Chapter 12); psychiatry has contributed the insights of psychoanalytic and other theories of personality. In time, we hope, these areas of inquiry will bring us to a more complete understanding of the structure and dynamics of personality.

In this chapter, we have tried to summarize the progress which has been made in this area by making the following points.

1. Characteristics which distinguish individuals from one another are important in the study of personality. One set of characteristics may serve one purpose, another set another purpose.

2. Traits are one means of characterizing personalities. Abilities, attitudes, and interests are also useful. A person's typical motives provide still another means of characterization; so, too, do his typical modes of adjustment.

3. Another class of personality characteristics includes the defense mechanisms which are ways of adjusting to frustration—the thwarting of behavior directed toward a goal—and of reducing the anxiety resulting from conflict-produced frustrations.

4. Conflicts are probably the most important source of frustration in adults. Of the three types of conflict, namely, approach-approach, avoidance-avoidance, and approach-avoidance, the last is probably the most significant.

5. There are a number of general responses to frustration. For instance, a person may learn to modify his responses; he may show a lack of flexibility, or rigidity, in behavior and thought; he may be aggressive; and finally, he may be fearful or anxious.

6. The defense mechanisms are the means that people develop to protect themselves against anxiety and to bolster their self-esteem. The anxiety arising from avoidance-avoidance and approach-avoidance conflicts seems to be especially important in the development of defense mechanisms. A few of the most common defense mechanisms are: repression, reaction formation, projection, displacement, rationalization, sublimation and compensation, fantasy, regression, and identification.

7. The origins of personality characteristics are to be found in inheritance, culture, and learning within the family. In the family, the affection given the child, the training given by the parents, the attitudes of the parents, and imitation of family members are important ways in which personality is influenced.

8. The following points about personality should be kept in mind: (a) each personality is unique; (b) personality is continuous and consistent; (c) personality changes usually occur very slowly; and (d) some individuals display patterns of characteristics, called syndromes.

9. The self develops through the awareness of one's own body and through one's being treated as a single entity during childhood. A person's perception of the self has an important bearing on his relations with others and on his emotional development.

10. Freud conceived of three major aspects of personality structure, (a) the id as a storehouse of motives and instincts, (b) the ego as the conscious part of personality that attempts to cope realistically with the world, and (c) the superego as a conscience that restrains the ego and the id and keeps a person working toward ideals acquired in childhood.

11. Freud also conceived of personality development as proceeding through the following stages: (a) oral, (b) anal, (c) phallic, and (d) genital.

12. Other theories of personality are: (a) Adler's theory based on the drive for superiority, (b) Horney's anxiety theory, (c) Murray's need theory, (d) Maslow's self-actualization theory, (e) learning theory, and (f) various offshoots of psychoanalytic theory which stress social factors.

RELATED TOPICS IN THE TEXT

CHAPTER 3 PRINCIPLES OF LEARNING Since many personality traits, as well as some aspects of adjustment, are learned, a review of the basic principles of learning should be useful.

CHAPTER 6 MOTIVATION Fear and anxiety arise from a conflict of motives. Some important unlearned and learned human motives are named and described here.

CHAPTER 12 PSYCHOLOGICAL TESTING The measurement of personality traits is an important aspect of scientific work on personality. A number of tests used for this purpose are discussed in this chapter.

CHAPTER 14 BEHAVIOR DISORDERS Deviant or abnormal personalities are the result of many causes, biological and environmental. Here we take up types of behavior abnormalities and some of the speculations about their causes.

CHAPTER 15 MENTAL HEALTH AND PSYCHOTHERAPY The treatment of behavior disorders, as well as dreams and hypnosis, are discussed more fully.

CHAPTER 16 SOCIAL INFLUENCES ON BEHAVIOR The influence of culture and social class on personality is elaborated in this chapter.

SUGGESTIONS FOR FURTHER READING

Baughman, E. E., and Welsh, G. S. *Personality: A behavioral science.* Englewood Cliffs, N.J.: Prentice-Hall, 1962.

An introductory textbook on the topic of personality which stresses the study of personality through empirical studies.

Brenner, C. *An elementary textbook of psychoanalysis.* Garden City, N.Y.: Doubleday, 1957. (Paperback.) *A book which is intended, in the words of the author, "to provide a clear and comprehensive exposition of the fundamentals of psychoanalytic theory."*

Dollard, J., and Miller, N. E. *Personality and psychotherapy: An analysis in terms of learning, thinking and culture.* New York: McGraw-Hill, 1950. *Learning theory as applied to the dynamics of personality.*

Freud, S. *New introductory lectures on psychoanalysis.* New York: Norton, 1933. (Paperback available.) *Lectures to a lay audience which illustrate Freud's style of reasoning and some of the most important points of his theory.*

Freud, S. *The basic writings of Sigmund Freud.* (Trans. A. A. Brill.) New York: Random House, 1938. *Selections from some of the most important works of the founder of psychoanalysis.*

Guilford, J. P. *Personality.* New York: McGraw-Hill, 1959. *A text emphasizing the trait approach to personality and its measurement.*

Hall, C. S. *A primer of Freudian psychology.* Cleveland: World, 1954. (Paperback available.) *A clearly written, systematic description of Freudian theory which tries to emphasize his contributions to the psychology of normal people.*

Hall, C. S., and Lindzey, G. *Theories of personality.* New York: Wiley, 1957. *A comprehensive treatment of the major personality theories.*

Lindzey, G., and Hall, C. S., (Eds.). *Theories of personality: Primary sources and research,* New York: Wiley, 1965 *A book of readings on personality theories.*

McCurdy, H. G. *The personal world.* New York: Harcourt, Brace & World, 1961. *A text which covers many unusual topics and treats personality from an interesting point of view.*

Mussen, P. H., Conger, J. J., and Kagan, J. *Child development and personality* (2d ed.). New York: Harper & Row, 1963. *A textbook on child psychology. Chapters 6, 9, and 10 deal with the learning of personality characteristics in infancy and childhood.*

Stagner, R. *Psychology of personality* (3d ed.). New York: McGraw-Hill, 1961. *A widely used textbook on personality.*

White, R. W. *Lives in progress: A study of the natural growth of personality* (2d ed.). New York: Holt, Rinehart & Winston, 1966. *An intensive and interesting study of personality development.*

Yates, A. J. (Ed.). *Frustration and conflict.* Princeton, N.J.: Van Nostrand, 1965. (Paperback.) *Significant papers on the subject of frustration and conflict.*

14

IN THE LAST CHAPTER we considered normal personality development and structure. As we go through life, our natures, or constitutions, interact with our environments. Certain traits develop, certain motives are learned, and normal ways of adjusting to the inevitable conflicts and problems of life are developed. But in some people, nature and nurture interact in ways that produce behaviors which are called "abnormal."

What is abnormal behavior? Actually, in most cases, no sharp line divides normal from abnormal behavior; such a distinction is just a matter of degree. Only when a person is markedly unhappy, or when he fails to use his talents, or when he suffers from anxiety to an unusual extent, or when his behavior becomes a nuisance or a danger to other people is he considered abnormal.

Abnormal behavior is difficult to classify, probably because it grades into normal behavior and because each individual has his unique history and has developed his particular pattern of reacting to the environment. Another problem in classifying abnormal behavior is that what is considered abnormal behavior differs from cultural group to cultural group. The patterns of behavior called "normal" are those which are culturally approved; those called "abnormal" are those which are not culturally approved. Hence abnormal behavior cannot be neatly pigeonholed, as can infectious diseases which are identified by the organism causing the disease. On the other hand, certain general patterns of disordered, or abnormal, behavior which are characteristic of our culture can be named and described in some detail.

In this chapter, several of these general kinds of behavior disorders are described. For instance, many people have relatively mild life adjustment problems. Other people, whose problems are labeled *neuroses*, are usually anxiety-ridden and may develop exaggerated defense mechanisms to reduce their anxieties. People with *personality disorders* may express aggression by pronounced stubbornness, they may be generally withdrawn, they may behave sexually in ways which are considered to be deviant, or they may lack conscience and feeling

BEHAVIOR
DISORDERS

EVERYONE IS QUEER
SAVE THEE AND ME,
AND SOMETIMES I THINK
THEE A BIT QUEER TOO.
QUAKER PROVERB

for the rights of other people. People with another general type of behavior disorder—one or another of the *psychoses*—may experience hallucinations and delusions and act in bizarre ways. Still other people, who are said to be suffering from *chronic brain syndromes*, may have brains so severely damaged that they do not function adequately. These are some of the major types of behavior disorders, but we should not be content with mere categorization. Rather, we must try to find causes and ways of preventing and alleviating these behavior disorders.

The extent and distribution of the more severe behavior problems are discussed in some detail at the beginning of Chapter 15. It should suffice here to indicate that about one person in ten will, at some time in his life, be treated in a mental hospital. This statistic, of course, reveals nothing about the frequency of mild problems of adjustment—problems characterized by symptoms of unhappiness, aimlessness, and unproductiveness. Most of us experience these symptoms during certain periods in our lives, and fortunately, for most of us they are rather transitory. We know that problems of adjustment are very common, but we cannot even guess at their exact frequency. Perhaps we can begin the discussion of behavior disorders most appropriately by presenting the case of a person with a mild adjustment problem.

Mild adjustment problems

The course of life is never smooth. Motives must be satisfied, but situations which frustrate, and competing motives, inevitably arise. Unhappiness, feelings of worthlessness, anxiety, behavior which is unproductive, self-defeating, and contradictory—all are symptoms of the sorts of mild adjustment problems which may come about when learned motives are frustrated. The following case of Joseph Kidd illustrates the symptoms in a typical mild, transient adjustment problem. It also attempts to show how the causes of a disturbance may be analyzed.

JOSEPH KIDD'S CASE   Several general points are noteworthy here. The roots of the problem lie in the frustration of a learned motive. Further, the pattern of frustration involves many particular maladaptive behaviors, but they all seem to be traceable to one motive which is blocked. Finally, Joseph Kidd is seen as a complex individual with certain abilities, habits, personality traits, attitudes, and a particular family background. All these factors interact with the frustration to produce the particular behaviors which are observed. In attempting to understand the disordered behavior of an individual, clinical psychologists and psychiatrists must bring information to bear from any sources. Here is the history of the case.

Present difficulties. At his lowest point, during his junior year at college, Joseph Kidd suffered from acute distress in all relations with people. He was bothered by severe self-consciousness, feeling always a painful uncertainty as to his standing in the opinion of others, and with this went an irresistible submissiveness designed to avoid conflict with people and win their favor. He could neither control this submissiveness nor accept it. If anyone showed him friendliness he immediately, as he put it, "began acting like his son or kid brother," but he was ashamed of this afterwards and wished that he could behave like a man. "I can't make a decision on my own and back it up," he wrote at one point; "it's always guided by some factor outside my own intellect." With his girl he was equally troubled. He was completely dependent on her affection and very jealous if she so much as danced with somebody else. Realizing that he acted toward her "too much like a spoiled child, crying for my own way," he yet could not bring himself to take a more manly and independent attitude. In consequence it became increasingly clear that the girl was bored with him and did not really respect him.

Why did he not take a different attitude? He wanted to, and there was every inducement to do so, but in this respect he was not free. The pattern of his personality was such as to resist this particular change. He expected people to give him a great deal of easy appreciation; when they did not do so, he was worried and hungrily asked for it. Kidd felt that he had no personality of his own, and he tried the following rather desperate expedient:

"I began trying to fit a personality to my make-up. I began acting out personalities, and tried observing people and copying them. But these personalities were all short-lived because they pleased some and not others and because they didn't produce that underlying purpose of making people like me; and every time, unconsciously, I would resort to my childish attitude to make myself noticeable. Examples of these personalities are independence (but I couldn't keep it up); arrogance (but people were arrogant back at me); hatefulness (people paid no attention to me); extreme niceness (people took advantage of it, kidded me about it); humorous nature (but I was only being childish, silly); quiet and studious (but people were only passing me by and I kept feeling I was missing something). I became a daydreamer so intensively that now I find I'm daydreaming almost all the time. I became conscious of a person's approach and would become flustered, would try to make a friend of him no matter who he was, but I overdid it."

Clearly Kidd's problem was not an unusual one. It is a universal problem to develop adult independent attitudes. Everyone learns from experience how to adapt successfully to the people around him; everyone finds out gradually what roles are congenial to himself and others. It is also a universal problem to develop a stable conception of oneself, an enduring sense of personal identity. Kidd's case is peculiar not in kind but in degree. It will be noticed that he was satisfied with a "personality" only if it pleased everybody; he was unwilling that anyone should fail to notice and like him. From his own description we can see that he was making a frantic search for affectionate esteem. His overwhelming motive was to make people like him, and his well-practiced method, when all else failed, was to make himself noticeable. Failure cast him into despondency and alarm. At times he lapsed into passive daydreaming, but at other times he struggled to learn new and more appropriate attitudes. Eventually, as we shall see, his struggle met with success.

Personal history. Whenever it appears that a disorder lies in the sphere of motives and the acquired methods for satisfying them, we must look for enlightenment in the past history. Joseph Kidd was the second son of hard-working, socially ambitious parents. He was a very pretty child with blue eyes and long golden curls, far more attractive than his older and younger brothers. His de-lighted parents showered him with notice and praise. His early memories were crowded with scenes in which he was patted on the head, dressed up, shown off, placed in the center of attention; once the teacher stood him on her desk so that all the pupils might see his new velvet suit with lace collar. He basked happily in this warm light of admiration. The effect on his subsequent development was not so happy. For one thing, his constant exposure to the eyes and praises of other people laid the foundation for that intense self-consciousness which later harassed him. For another thing, he was receiving praise for gratuitous qualities—for good looks and fine clothes, or at best for slight accomplishments—so that he felt little incentive to work for what he got. He formed a habitual expectation of high esteem income received at no no greater cost than making himself noticeable.

In school Kidd progressed well, and through the machinations of his ambitious mother he was given a double promotion from the fourth to the sixth grade. This put him in the same class as his older brother and automatically made him the youngest and smallest of his immediate group. To keep up his popularity he fell into the role of what he called "a clown and a stooge"; he made the other boys laugh and did errands for them. Entering high school in a distant neighborhood, he found these roles no longer productive of esteem. His income in this respect was sharply lowered when he realized that his new companions were contemptuous of his childish ways. Filled with resentment at this turn of events, he began to feel that everyone was against him; so he withdrew from sports and social activities and spent his time at home listening to the radio. He experienced great shame over masturbation, which further increased his feeling of inferiority and unwillingness to mingle with others. Even his interest in studies dwindled, so that he barely passed his examinations for college.

At college he found nothing in the curriculum that awakened enduring interest. His failure to make friends soon cost him the esteem of his parents, who looked upon college as a means of social advancement and compared him unfavorably with his sociable brothers; in addition, he seriously offended his parents by espousing the theory of evolution which they considered at variance with their religious faith. As we have seen, his girl began to withhold her esteem. He sought consolation in promiscuous sexual episodes, which gave him at least a momentary feeling that he was acceptable as a man and could get what he wanted. But when he regaled his fellow students with these proofs of his enterprise and manhood, he got much less admiration than he expected. He who had been rich was now indeed destitute of esteem.

Spontaneous recovery. Under these circumstances it is not surprising that his mediocre academic record went completely to pieces and that he was presently looking for a job. It was at this point that his suffering was most acute and that he fully realized the failure of the various "personalities" he had been trying to assume. After a while, however, things began to go more favorably. He took the step of leaving home to escape the now irksome parental supervision, and he parted with his girl. He found a small business position, acquitted himself well, and enjoyed the company of other young people in the office, most of whom were college graduates. It was a white-collar job which met his parents' social expectations, so that he was somewhat restored in their favor. He resumed his interest in sports and began to read instead of daydreaming. Another girl came upon the scene. Starting the relation on a better footing, he was soon the happy recipient of a fair esteem income from her. His life was again moving forward, and he began to be mildly satisfied with himself.

Having made a good work record for a year, he was permitted to return to college. Ultimately he graduated, but at the cost of a setback in his personal development. Many of the old problems reappeared, particularly his distaste for study and his hunger for the good opinion of his fellow students. When he entered military service it was with a decided sense of relief: at last he could put school behind him and silence his parents' clamor for further professional training. As a private in a health survey unit he was not exposed to the dangers of combat, and he found great satisfaction in the comradeship of the other men in the unit. He resumed the social growth that had been brought to a standstill by his double promotion at school and subsequent estrangement from other boys. He became more assertive, but not to the point of welcoming the role of officer, in which he did so badly that he was at one point demoted. "I like to be *with* other fellows," he said, "not *over* them." Some years later he looked back to his period in the Army as the happiest time in his life.

Returning to the family home, he was at first immersed in some of the old conflicts, but the changes in his personality proved to be enduring. He was no longer at the mercy of parental desires, nor was he enslaved by his hunger for esteem. When an opportunity arose to reorganize his father's dwindling business he took charge of the project and carried it to a successful conclusion. This accomplishment substantially increased his self-respect as well as his income of esteem from others; it also permitted him to feel that he had repaid his parents for their earlier sacrifices on his behalf. Throughout these developments his environment was fairly kind to him, but he displayed initiative and took an active part in overcoming his difficulties. Under moderately favorable circumstances he proved capable of developing new channels for satisfying his needs and promoting his growth. It is this that distinguishes Kidd's maladjustment from the more severe psychological disorders. . . . [Robert W. White, *The Abnormal Personality*, 3rd ed. Copyright © 1964 The Ronald Press Company. Pages 55–58.]

ANALYSIS OF THE CASE   Joseph Kidd was rather lucky because his problems, although a bother to himself and his family, lasted for a relatively brief time and he did make a good adjustment eventually. But why, after so promising a beginning, did he have difficulties?

This case has been analyzed in terms of the interaction between Kidd's learned motives and his abilities [White, 1964]. Need for esteem was especially great because of the learning experiences of childhood. Kidd had come to expect to be appreciated for just being around—not for any particular talent or skill which he had. In high school and college, things changed. No longer was esteem given for being a "cute" little fellow, and Kidd, in whom this complex motive was strong, had no other skills for obtaining esteem. He was not particularly clever, strong, or given to active participation in sports— all talents esteemed in high school and college. He tried various artificial ways of meeting his esteem needs, but through lack of ability, these attempts did not succeed. Kidd also began to develop some hostility toward those who were frustrating his needs for esteem—those whom he would like to have as his friends. This, of course, made it less likely than ever that his esteem motive would be satisfied. In trying to find himself, he was preoccupied with his own problems, and his college work suffered.

Kidd began to lead a happier and more productive life after he had experiences which made him feel valued. His army experience, his better relationship with a new girl friend, and his success with his father's business all satisfied his esteem needs, gave him a feeling of success, and enabled him to find a pattern of life which made esteem possible.

This case illustrates the sort of mild adjustment problems which are due to motivational conflicts and frustration. It also illustrates the sort of spontaneous recovery which often occurs in such cases, and finally, it illustrates the way such a case can be analyzed in terms of basic psychological processes and ideas which we have already discussed—motivation, learning, and abilities.

Psychoneurotic reactions

People suffering from *psychoneuroses,* or *neuroses* as they are more commonly called, are anxious people. Often the anxiety is obvious. The person may be constantly apprehensive, worried, or full of complaints; he may have spells when he is overcome by fear and anxiety. Sometimes the anxiety is not so obvious, the person may appear to be relatively free of anxiety, but his reactions can nevertheless be traced to anxiety and his mechanisms for avoiding it [Fenichel, 1945]. In these cases, the person's unusual symptoms and defense mechanisms provide the clues to his constant battle with anxiety. We shall make no attempt to classify or describe all the variants of neurotic behavior, for they would fill a book. The following descriptions, however, should provide a general idea of some typical neurotic reactions.

ANXIETY REACTIONS   Although anxiety, or the attempt to deal with it, is the mark of neurosis, in many of the neuroses it is concealed by other symptoms. Not so in *anxiety reactions.* In these neuroses, intense and observable anxiety is the principal symptom (see Figure 14.1). The anxiety may be persistent and uncomfortably high most of the time. Or it may come as a sudden attack that lasts from a few hours to several days. An abnormal state of anxiety can make a person thoroughly miserable, force him to the border of panic, and upset his health with gastric disturbances and persistent diarrhea.

Usually neither the person himself nor those around him can assign a cause to the anxiety. The anxiety may become more intense in, or be precipitated by, a stressful situation or a difficult problem. Yet the precise reason for the intense anxiety is not clear—at least not until the patient's history and the situations that make him anxious have been analyzed. The following case illustrates an anxiety attack as well as the analysis of its causes:

A successful business executive developed acute anxiety attacks which occurred about once every two or three months. The patient's wife was eight years older than he, and he was no longer physically attracted to her. He had found himself increasingly interested in younger women and had begun to think how much more enjoyable it would be to have a younger, more companionable wife. During this period, he met a girl with whom he was sure he had fallen in love. It was shortly thereafter that the anxiety attacks began to occur. They were preceded by a period of several days of increased tenseness and anxiety, but the attacks came on suddenly and were very intense.

This man was . . . at a complete loss to explain his attacks. But the explanation was not difficult to find. The patient had had a poverty-stricken and insecure childhood and felt basically inferior, insecure, and threatened by a hard world. These feelings had been intensified when he had failed college courses in his second year, even though the failure had resulted primarily from excessive outside work. He had been able to achieve some security, however, by marrying an older and very strong woman who had instilled considerable self-confidence and initiative in him. The relationship had proved very fruitful financially and the patient was living in a style which as a youth, "I hadn't dared to imagine in my wildest dreams!" His persistent thoughts about divorcing his wife, on whom he felt dependent for his security and style of life, thus repre-

FIGURE 14.1. *The anguish of the anxiety neurotic. (Meade Johnson Laboratories.)*

sented a severe threat to the moderate adjustment he had achieved. The anxiety attacks followed. [James C. Coleman, *Abnormal Psychology in Modern Life.* Copyright © 1964 by Scott, Foresman and Co., Chicago, Ill. Page 199.]

An anxious neurotic may sometimes find a little relief from his anxiety by adopting certain physical symptoms. If he becomes excessively concerned with his physical welfare or constantly complains of minor ailments, he is called a *hypochondriac*. His complaints are either groundless or grossly exaggerated, but by worrying about his health, he manages to take his mind off the feelings of guilt or inadequacy that otherwise cause him to be unbearably anxious. If the person complains of general nervousness, fatigue, and insomnia, he is called a *neurasthenic*. The word literally means "nervous weakness," and it refers to the person's chronic

inability to do anything. The neurasthenic, indeed, frequently claims that he is unable to work because he feels fatigued and worn out all the time. But, of course, the nervous weakness is not due to physical deterioration or disease of the nervous system; instead, the symptoms are psychogenic—they are caused by anxiety. These symptoms, although they incapacitate the person, accomplish some gain for him, for they provide an excuse and a disguise for some underlying source of anxiety. The following case illustrates a persistent anxiety neurosis with physical symptoms:

Thomas R., an eighteen-year-old high school senior . . . was referred to a counselor because he was failing in his studies and had an attitude of apprehension and despair which was readily noticed by his teachers. Interviews showed that the boy's anxieties were not limited to any definite situation, but widely generalized. He was concerned about his academic standing, and especially about his father's reaction to it. Referring to his possible school failure, he said, "It will be the end for me." He felt an acute social incompetence, and said in a vague manner that he did not know much about the world, and that he had many things to learn. Thomas had little association with girls and appeared to be afraid of them, or rather of his inability to impress them as favorably as the other boys. During the preceding year he had had a few dates with a girl a little older than himself, on which he placed a high value, considering himself in love. The girl went away to college, and Thomas felt afraid of "losing" her. He was utterly unable to make decisions. The simplest problem caused him to seek advice or to feel incompetent to face the difficulty.

In addition to his anxiety, Thomas had visceral symptoms, centering around his heart. At times his heart beat very rapidly and his pulse pounded in his ears. Although several physicians examined him carefully and reported that he had no organic disorder, Thomas often rested in bed from early Saturday evening until Sunday noon because of his supposed heart disease. The intensity of Thomas's anxiety was best revealed by notes he scribbled from time to time and gave to the counselor. He wrote, "I can never be at rest and am never satisfied. I fear of not being able to control my mental and physical actions.

Something is always elusive. I am more afraid of life than the basest coward. Why can't I understand people? Why can I remember only my fears, the vacant mental situations and the lonely places in my life? I seem to exist isolated. All the clean wholesome desires which make a man want to live seem to be crushed. Will I snap out of this, or will I never be a man?"

Thomas's anxiety reaction may be interpreted as a nonadjustive response to all the principal problems of late adolescence. He faces the issues of establishing his independence as a sufficient person, of financial self-support, of the choice of a vocation, and of social and sexual adjustment, quite unable to achieve a satisfactory course of action in any of them. Such an inability to adjust must have its roots in his past learning experiences. In Thomas's case, as in most, the basis was found in the attitudes and personalities of his parents. [Shaffer and Shoben, 1956, pages 277–278.]

PHOBIC REACTIONS   An intense and irrational fear of something is a *phobia*. There are many kinds of phobias, depending upon the object of the fear. *Claustrophobia,* for example, is an intense, unreasonable fear of small, enclosed places; *acrophobia,* an intense, unreasonable fear of high places; *nyctophobia,* fear of the dark; *zoophobia,* fear of animals (see Figure 14.2). There are a good many other phobias, of course, and most of them have names; these are among the most common, however.

Some people who are otherwise normal and healthy have phobias. The phobias may be mild or rarely evoked; if so, they cause little difficulty. On the other hand, a phobia may be so powerful and irrational that it alters the whole course of a person's life.

One oft-quoted example of an intense phobia is the case of the poet and professor at the University of Wisconsin, William Ellery Leonard (1927):

Leonard had a phobia of going more than a few blocks away from his home and the university. For years his phobia kept him a virtual prisoner in this small geographical area. Although he knew of his fear, he did not know its underlying cause. During the course of psychoanalysis, he was able to remember a frightening incident in his childhood. He had wandered away from his home and gone over to the railroad tracks, where a passing train had scalded him with steam. His fear, it developed, originated in this incident, and it proved to be the real motive for his staying near home. The phobia was so powerful that it dominated his whole life. It was never completely eradicated even though he recognized its source and could be objective enough to write a book about it—*The Locomotive God.*

Such intense, irrational fears can best be understood by combining the ideas of classical conditioning with concepts from psychoanalytic theory. Most phobias have their origin in fears learned by the association of painful or unpleasant events with particular situations. In Chapter 7, Emotion, we saw how such fears develop through classical conditioning and how such learning may provide the model for the initial development of the fear. The life histories of people with phobias almost always provide examples of especially frightening events, or "traumatic" events, as they are sometimes called. These may, as in Leonard's case, be rather isolated episodes, but more often they are frightening situations which are repeated many times in the early life of the person.

Although the fear was rational when it was initially learned, it diffuses and the actual source of the fear may come to be repressed (see page 475). Thus, the fear seems to be an irrational one. From the point of view of the learning theorist, the spread of the fear to other situations may be considered to be an example of stimulus generalization (see page 85); the psychoanalytic viewpoint provides another explanation. According to psychoanalysis, the spread of fear is due to the operation of the mechanism of displacement together with the use of symbolism. One of Freud's classic cases, the case of little Hans—a five-year-old boy who was afraid of horses—illustrates psychoanalytic ideas rather well. Freud believed that the child was really afraid of his father, but since the recognition of this fear was too threatening to the boy, the father was symbolized by another large, powerful animal—the horse—and the fear was thus displaced from father to horse [Freud, 1955]. When phobic cases are

A PHOBIA IS AN INTENSE IRRATIONAL FEAR OF SOMETHING

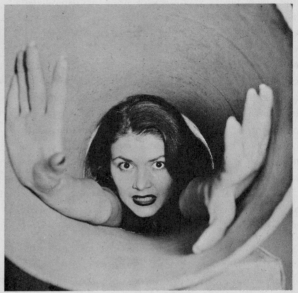

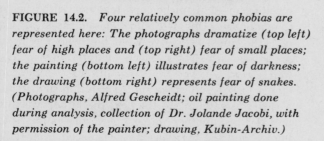

FIGURE 14.2. *Four relatively common phobias are represented here: The photographs dramatize (top left) fear of high places and (top right) fear of small places; the painting (bottom left) illustrates fear of darkness; the drawing (bottom right) represents fear of snakes. (Photographs, Alfred Gescheidt; oil painting done during analysis, collection of Dr. Jolande Jacobi, with permission of the painter; drawing, Kubin-Archiv.)*

analyzed, the symbolic nature of the phobia often becomes obvious. Thus, phobias may get their start in a learning experience, that is, classical conditioning, but the fear may be displaced to objects which symbolize the originally feared object or situation.

No matter what their origin, such phobias serve a purpose—as do most other psychoneurotic symptoms. Although it may seem paradoxical at first, such intense, irrational fears may actually serve to reduce anxiety. They do this by keeping the person away from situations in which he would be overwhelmed by much more intense fear [Dollard and Miller, 1950]. A person with a phobia makes a bargain—he accepts one fear because it keeps him away from situations in which his fear of something else would be much more intense. Leonard, in the case cited earlier, accepted his fear of going away from home because it kept him away from railroads, the real source of his fear.

OBSESSIVE-COMPULSIVE REACTIONS   Another kind of neurotic reaction includes obsessions and compulsions, or both. An *obsession* is an idea that constantly intrudes into a person's thoughts. It is usually foolish and groundless, at least at the time that it is felt. The person may be obsessed with the notion that he has cancer or syphilis, or with the fear that he will kill himself or someone else. In less extreme cases, senseless phrases or ideas may run through his mind over and over again. Current opinion holds that obsessions represent a defense against some motive or anxiety, but it is not always easy to tell exactly what an obsession defends against. Many obsessions defend against anxiety-provoking sexual urges, others against aggressive tendencies, but they may appear in any situation or experience that makes a person very anxious.

Compulsions are similar to obsessions, except that they are *acts*, rather than ideas, that repeatedly intrude into a person's behavior. One compulsive person may wash his hands every few minutes; another must count all the steps he climbs; another assiduously avoids stepping on cracks in the sidewalk. Some people do not have conspicuous, particular compulsions, but are compulsive in a more general way. They find ambiguity and uncertainty extremely uncomfortable, and they strive for orderliness of thought, of dress, or of work. Indeed, any unusual emphasis on "doing things the right way" may be regarded as compulsive. However, these people might better be considered to have *compulsive personality disorders* (see page 512).

The following case illustrates a typical compulsion:

A successful executive who, for various reasons, unconsciously hated the responsibilities of marriage and fatherhood was troubled many times a day with the idea that his two children by his divorced wife were somehow ill or in danger, although he knew them to be safe in a well-run private school to which he himself took them every morning. As a result, he felt impelled to interrupt his office routine thrice daily to make personal calls to the school authorities. After several months the principal began to question the sincerity of the patient's fatherly solicitude and thus intensified his obsessive-compulsive rituals by bringing the issue more nearly into the open. The same patient could not return home at night unless he brought a small present to his second wife and each of his children, although, significantly, it was almost always something they did not want. [Masserman, 1961, page 45.]

Obsessions and compulsions are means of reducing anxieties while they repress the motives that arouse them. In the case just cited, for instance, the symptoms acted in very much the same way as a reaction formation to help the patient deny his real motives (see page 476). His overt solicitousness, his compulsions in other words, served to disguise the basic hostility. In other cases, obsessions and compulsions may be ways of attempting to reduce anxiety and expiate guilt over past acts. If someone, for example, is obsessive about developing cancer, it may be because he has anxieties over some past act or misconduct for which he may fear punishment. Similarly, the compulsive person who washes his hands every few minutes may have anxieties over sexual transgressions, and the hand washing may be an unconscious attempt to cleanse himself of guilt. In this way, obsessive and compulsive individuals find some measure of relief from anxiety. But it is not complete. In fact, a cycle is set up in which mounting anxiety evokes the obsession or compulsion, and this in turn temporarily relieves the anxiety until, in the course of time or circumstances, it returns again. The mechanism, however, is a defense that keeps anxiety from reaching unbearable proportions.

The connection between the obsession or compulsion and the original experience from which the reaction stems is often rather difficult to discover. Occasionally the person has some insight into the connection. More often he rationalizes his obsessions and compulsions to make them appear reasonable and appropriate, and thus he disguises to himself their real basis. In such circumstances, it probably will take an experienced clinician to find, after extensive probing, the source of the anxiety.

CONVERSION REACTIONS Occasionally, when a conflict is unusually severe and repression is relatively complete, the conflict may be converted into a physical symptom. Hence the reaction to conflict is called a *conversion reaction*. The particular symptom that appears varies with the individual, his conflict, and his habits. It may be a paralysis of almost any part of the body, a localized loss of feeling, blindness or deafness, or almost any other sort of incapacity. The symptom is convenient in that it relieves the individual of the necessity to work or otherwise resolves the conflict he would have. It should be emphasized, however, that the symptom does not have a biological cause in the sense that it is not caused by a lesion, germ, or other detectable physical agency. A physician cannot find the cause of this kind of disorder in a physical examination, no matter how thorough. The symptom, which is real enough, however, is a device for coping with conflict and anxiety. Another name for a conversion reaction is *hysteria*. But the student should note that this meaning of hysteria, namely, the conversion of a motivational conflict into a physical symptom, is not the same as the common meaning of hysteria—any outbreak of uncontrolled emotional behavior. The following case illustrates a hysteria or conversion reaction:

A woman was admitted to a hospital with a paralysis of the legs. Her legs were extended rigidly and close together, like two stiff pillars. Neurological examination indicated no physical disorder; so physicians looked into other aspects of her problem. They discovered that she was the mother of several children, that she had reason to fear having any more, that her husband desired frequent intercourse, and that she had strong prohibitions against both birth control and denying her husband's sexual demands. Here were all the elements of a complex conflict situation. After interviewing the woman at length and investigating the case thoroughly, physicians concluded that her paralysis was an unconscious device for eliminating conflict.

Hysterical reactions illustrate well the process of *repression*, for in them repression is complete. In other reactions some, but not all, aspects of a conflict are repressed. In hysteria, however, the entire conflict is repressed. The individual completely rejects any thoughts and motives that may be involved and does this effectively by resorting to physical symptoms that dispose of them all. The woman with the paralyzed legs, for example, no longer had to worry about birth control, resisting her husband's sexual demands, or having more children. With her hysterical symptom, she had completely eliminated any occasion for the conflict.

The particular symptom that the hysteric employs may first occur by accident or as the result of a real physical illness. For example, a person may suffer a temporary paralysis as a result of an automobile accident. Although the injury is a handicap, it may also prove to be a boon in satisfying other wants. It may make the person's wife, husband, or parent become very attentive, thus giving the person the love and care he has lacked. Or the ailment may punish those who have the work and expense of taking care of him; in this way, the ailment indirectly expresses aggression. In still other instances, the ailment may protect the individual from anxiety-producing situations, such as a job, school, or social relations. The point is that the patient may experience a "secondary gain" from the ailment. In other words, what begins as a physical ailment may be prolonged because it reduces conflict and the attendant anxiety. Of course, the patient does not consciously realize he is doing this; he has repressed the conflict and his need to defend himself from anxiety.

An experienced doctor usually can recognize the hysterical personality, even if no full-blown physical symptoms have appeared in his patient. One of the signs is unusual naïveté. The individual is naïve because the anxiety he feels in many situations makes him avoid them, and thus he either misses or represses experiences that are normal for other people. Another sign is that he is easily disturbed emotionally. When confronted with an unpleasant situation, his thoughts become blocked and confused, and he may grow so disturbed that he becomes dizzy or ill, or he faints. On a small scale, this is the kind of symptom that protects the hysteric against anxiety. In addition, the person who is using a conversion reaction as a defense against anxiety may be indifferent to his very real physical symptoms. In marked contrast to the patient with a biologically caused illness, the hysteric does not seem really concerned about his illness. He displays what has come to be called *la belle indifférence*.

DISSOCIATIVE REACTIONS Other reactions which, like conversion reaction, represent a great deal of repression are known as the *dissociative reactions*. They are so called because some personality traits and memories appear to be dissociated from each other. In a mild, relatively harmless form, dissociative reactions may involve no more than a compartmentalization of a person's thinking and way of living. The businessman who is a vigorous competitor and not too scrupulous in his business affairs may be kind to his family, a fervent churchgoer, an upholder of all things righteous, and active in the philanthropic affairs of his community. However, he may see no conflict whatever between these two modes of living. He compartmentalizes his thinking and his activities so that his two personalities do not consciously get in each other's way. In more extreme forms, however, dissociative reactions are bizarre and incapacitating. They furnish the most dramatic instances of neurotic behavior.

Amnesia. One well-publicized type of extreme dissociative reaction is amnesia. The amnesiac is the subject of numerous plays, "psychological" stories, and news items. A person suffering from amnesia usually forgets his own name, where he has come from, who his relatives are, and what he has been doing for some weeks, months, or years. Amnesia can be caused by a blow to the head or an injury to the brain. As a neurotic disorder, however, amnesia represents repression in the extreme. To cope with a painful conflict, the person unconsciously represses the memory of his own identity and things closely connected with it. As in other instances of repression, the memories are not forgotten; they are merely made unavailable to consciousness. Hence, if the source of the conflict can be discovered and if something is done to make the conflict less painful for the person, he frequently can be helped to recover his memory. The following case provides an example of this type of amnesia:

Donald G., twenty-two, attended college at night while working to support his forty-five-year-old mother. He was in love with a girl whom he hoped to marry. Donald's mother, however, did not like the girl and tried to break them up.

The girl could see that Donald would never be able to support both her and his mother. She also knew that the three of them could never get along together under the same roof. She gave Donald a month to decide what to do about it. A week before the deadline, he suddenly disappeared. He was found two weeks later in another state, completely unable to say who he was, where he was, or what he was planning to do. He could not recall, or even recognize, the name of either his mother or his girl friend. Obviously, he had developed a case of amnesia as a solution to his conflict.

This behavior was not inconsistent with his previous history. In his earlier school days, he had frequently forgotten his homework and been absent-minded. Forgetting things was already a convenient habit for him. When a major conflict developed, this mode of adjustment became a full-blown amnesia. [Based on Tiegs and Katz, 1941, page 53.]

Some amnesias are temporary lapses accompanied

by flight. The person suddenly disappears, wanders around aimlessly, or takes a long journey. During the period of flight or wandering, the person suffers from amnesia. Days or perhaps weeks later, he recovers his memory partially or fully. At this point, he may go to the police or someone else for help; or, if he is fully recovered, he may contact his friends or relatives. Temporary amnesia, accompanied by flight, is called a *fugue,* the term being derived from the Latin word meaning "to flee."

Multiple personality. Occasionally, repression works in such a way as to dissociate two or more relatively complete personalities, as in the fictional case of Dr. Jekyll and Mr. Hyde. In this story, one personality is evil, the other good. The transformation is accomplished by drinking a potion. In real cases of multiple personality, however, the transformation is tripped off by stress or emotional trauma, and it stems from a deep-seated conflict of motives. Though often dramatized and talked about, split or multiple personality is relatively rare. Only a few cases have been studied in detail by competent clinical authorities. A recent case is reported in the book *The Three Faces of Eve* [Thigpen and Cleckley, 1957]:

Eve White, age twenty-five, came to a psychiatrist complaining that she suffered painful, blinding headaches, often culminating in blackouts. In obtaining her case history, the doctor learned that she had had trouble with her husband from whom she was separated. She had a four-year-old daughter whom she had been forced by financial circumstances to leave some hundred miles from the city where she was working. The woman seemed unhappy at being separated from her daughter and was very much afraid she would lose the love of the child.

At first, the case looked like one of neurosis with conversion symptoms. One day, however, the doctor received an unsigned note which was obviously from the patient but part of which was in a completely different handwriting from the rest. The next time he saw Eve, the doctor asked about the note. She denied sending it. All through this interview, she was agitated and uncontrolled, although previously she had been reasonably calm. Then,

suddenly, a strange look came over her face; she put her hands on her head briefly, and then took them away. At that moment, her whole manner changed; she cocked her head, smiled, and said, "Hi, there, Doc!" She crossed her legs coquettishly, and took on an entirely new personality. Indeed, she was. This was Eve Black, not Eve White. From then on, in subsequent interviews, the doctor had "two patients." For a while, he could make Eve Black appear only by using hypnotic techniques (see page 543), but in time, he could call out one personality or the other at will.

The two Eves, he learned, had lived side by side for years. Eve Black knew about Eve White, but not vice versa. Eve White only learned about Eve Black from sessions with the therapist. Eve White was a retiring, controlled, well-behaved, though neurotic girl. Eve Black, on the other hand, was a mischievous, "bad" girl—though not so bad as to get into any serious trouble—who frequently played pranks on Eve White. Eve Black once said to the therapist, "When I go out and get drunk, *she* wakes up with the hangover. She wonders what in the hell's made her so sick." As the therapist learned in subsequent interviews, Eve White waged a continuous unconscious struggle against Eve Black. The bouts of headache appeared to represent her attempts to keep Eve Black from emerging and taking control.

Therapy went on for several months, and Eve White seemed to be getting better. Then the painful headaches and the blackouts became more intense. At this time, during a rather stressful interview with the therapist, a new personality, Jane, came forth. Jane's personality was the best of the three; she was more mature, lively, and competent than either of the Eves. She seemed to have healthier attitudes toward herself and others than they had.

For a time, all three personalities were in evidence from time to time; the therapist was able to call any one of them out at will. Jane developed as the dominant personality, but the therapist called on the two Eves to ferret out information from the girl's past that would help her achieve a better adjustment. Several circumstances in her childhood appeared to be connected with her multiple personality. One was the birth of twin sisters when she was about six. She resented them intensely. Four months after their birth, her grandmother died, and her mother apparently had forced her to the grandmother's coffin to kiss her grandmother "goodbye." This painful experience seemed to be the one that tripped off the dissociation of her personality.

The rest of the story, as told in *The Three Faces of Eve*, is that Jane managed to establish a satisfactory adjustment. As Eve White, she divorced her former husband. Then, as Jane, she fell in love with another man, who had proved understanding and helpful throughout her ordeal, and married him. The two established a home and a normal life with her little girl.

Though the psychiatric account ends there, the story does not. Jane did not turn out to be the well-integrated person it appeared she would be at the end of treatment. Under the stresses of her second marriage, she broke down and "destroyed herself," psychologically speaking. This time, though, she was able to resolve the basic conflicts that had dissociated Eve Black and Eve White and was able to establish a final, and fourth, well-adjusted personality—according to her own autobiography *The Final Face of Eve* [Lancaster and Poling, 1958].

DEPRESSIVE REACTIONS   The older term for this disorder, "reactive depression," describes one aspect of this behavior disorder: Neurotic depression is often a reaction to some severe loss that the patient has sustained. Neurotic depression is differentiated from psychotic depression, which we discuss later, by the absence of such symptoms as hallucinations, delusions, and severe thought disturbances. The following paragraph describes the symptoms of the neurotic depressive reaction:

The neurotically depressed individual gives the outward general appearance of being dejected, discouraged, and sad. He may have an extremely sorrowful expression on his face or a dull, masklike one. He seems to see only the dark side of everything, seems uninterested in any pleasurable activities, may stay by himself, may just sit and stare. Although his thinking is not slowed up, he may complain of difficulties in concentrating. He may have trouble sleeping, feelings of restlessness, irritability, and inward tension.

Vague hostile feelings may be detected. [Kutash, 1965, page 967.]

The depressive reaction tends to be of short duration. Suicide is a danger while the patient is in the depths of the depression, but spontaneous recovery is the rule rather than the exception in this type of neurotic disorder.

Persons who suffer from neurotic depression are often found to have feelings of guilt connected with some aspects of the loss which brought on the depression. For instance, the depressed person might have had ambivalent feelings toward a deceased parent or spouse; he sometimes hated them and sometimes loved them. The depression, occasioned, for example, by the death of the person toward whom the ambivalent feelings were directed, may sometimes be looked on as a way in which the depressed person punishes himself for the hostile feelings he may have had.

Personality disorders

Some 17 per cent of people admitted to public mental hospitals in the United States for the first time are diagnosed as suffering from personality disorders [Kisker, 1964]. The deviant behaviors which fall in this class are a little hard to describe because many different kinds of symptoms and symptom syndromes, or collections of symptoms, are shown in the cases that are put into this category. But some general characteristics are typical of this group. In contrast to psychotics (who are discussed in the next section), they show little of the thought disturbance and bizarre behavior so characteristic of many psychotic disorders. The basic problem seems to be the development of deviant lifelong personality-trait patterns. The general characteristics of the personality disorders have been summarized thus:

These disorders are characterized by developmental defects or pathological trends in the personality structure, with minimal subjective anxiety, and little or no sense of distress. In most instances, the disorder is manifested by a lifelong pattern of action and behavior, rather than by mental or emotional symptoms. [American Psychiatric Association, 1952, page 34.]

The general category of personality disorders may be further divided into the following groups: *personality pattern and trait disturbances* and *sociopathic personality disturbances* [American Psychiatric Association, 1952; and Kisker, 1964].

PERSONALITY PATTERN AND TRAIT DISTURB-ANCES Individuals who can be placed in this group manage a marginal adjustment, and most of them stay out of mental hospitals. They seem to most of us to lead rather unrewarding lives, but they themselves generally do not feel this way. Perhaps we can define this class of personality and trait disturbances by a discussion of some of the most common symptom syndromes.

Schizoid personality. The schizoid personality is characterized by withdrawal from other people, eccentric thinking, and a lack of normal aggressiveness in relations with others. As *The Diagnostic and Statistical Manual* of the American Psychiatric Association phrases it, people with schizoid personalities are characterized by:

. . . coldness, aloofness, emotional detachment, fearfulness, avoidance of competition, and day dreams revolving around the need for omnipotence. As children, they were usually quiet, shy, obedient, sensitive, and retiring. At puberty, they frequently become more withdrawn, then manifesting the aggregate of personality traits known as introversion, namely, quietness, seclusiveness, "shut-in-ness," and unsociability, often with eccentricity. [American Psychiatric Association, 1952, page 35.]

The general picture which comes to mind is that of the eccentric fellow who lives down the block in the back room of the big house on the corner. He is rarely seen in the neighborhood, preferring to come and go when other people are not about. If approached, he shies away and flees back to his room.

Another personality pattern is termed the *paranoid* personality. Those in whom it appears have many of the traits of the schizoid personality, but in addition they show a marked suspiciousness of other people and their motives. Note that people who display both the schizoid and paranoid patterns are *not psychotic*—they are not suffering from the psychosis *schizophrenia;* nor are they suffering from a psychotic *paranoid reaction.* Some of the symptoms of these personality pattern disturbances resemble those of psychosis, but contact with reality is maintained far more adequately than in the psychotic behavior disorders.

Passive and aggressive personalities. Three varieties of passive and aggressive personalities are commonly described: the *passive-dependent* variety, the *passive-aggressive* variety, and the *aggressive* type. The passive-dependent person clings to others in the same way that a dependent child clings to adults. Such people are helpless, and they expect, and want, other people to dominate them. The helpless little wisp of a girl who must rely on her big strong boyfriend to do almost everything comes to mind immediately as the exemplification of this disorder. However, passive-dependent personalities are by no means the exclusive domain of the gentle sex.

The passive-aggressive person expresses his feelings of rebellion and resentment by passive means such as "pouting, stubbornness, procrastination, inefficiency, and passive obstruction" [American Psychiatric Association, 1952, page 37]. Here, the picture of the disgruntled, grumbling, petulant salesclerk or the receptionist who cannot seem to be of any assistance comes to mind.

The aggressive personality is just what the term implies—the aggressive person burns with resentment and irritability and is prone to temper tantrums and violent aggressive attacks. These people act out their hostility by striking out at the world, and they can be dangerously aggressive at times. They are especially dangerous because the aggressive attack is often apparently unprovoked.

Compulsive personality. It has been jokingly said, if somewhat incorrectly, that this personality pattern characterizes the successful graduate student or scientist. Here is what the *Diagnostic and Statistical Manual* of the American Psychiatric Association has to say about this disorder:

Such individuals are characterized by chronic, excessive, or obsessive concern with adherence to standards of conscience or of conformity. They may be overinhibited, overconscientious, and may have an inordinate capacity for work. Typically they are rigid and lack a normal capacity for relaxation. [American Psychiatric Association, 1952, page 37.]

Many other types of personality pattern and trait disturbances might be mentioned, but these are some of the major ones, and they should serve to give an idea of the kinds of behavior included in this category.

SOCIOPATHIC PERSONALITY DISTURBANCES

People with sociopathic personality disturbances are not mentally ill in the sense that they experience anxiety or have bizarre thoughts. Rather, they are people who feel little guilt over violations of the rules, regulations, laws, or mores of their culture. Several classes of sociopathic personality disturbance are distinguishable—the *antisocial reaction,* the *dyssocial reaction, sexual deviations,* and *drug addictions.*

Antisocial reaction. Persons diagnosed in this category have little feeling for other people or other people's rights. They display no sense of responsibility and are incapable of loyalty. They are, generally speaking, without conscience, and to use one of the older terms, they might be called "morally insane." They tend to be selfish and are quite good at rationalizing their immoral behavior. Within this framework, several patterns of antisocial behavior can be discerned.

One common pattern is that of the suave "con man." Superficially, these people are quite convincing, their behavior is bland, they are glib talkers, and they are even quite charming. But they do not feel constrained by conscience.

Impulsive behavior is typical of another antisocial pattern. The New York bus driver who became bored with his route one day and drove across the George Washington Bridge and down the East Coast to Florida was manifesting such behavior in a rather impressive way. When apprehended by the police, the driver explained his 1,500-mile trip by saying, "I just wanted to get away from New York." [Kisker, 1964, page 231].

Perhaps more typical of this behavior disorder is a pattern of sordid, irresponsible, impulsive episodes which culminate in arrest after arrest. The following case illustrates this pattern:

Calvin F. was admitted to the psychiatric hospital at the age of eighteen with the diagnosis of antisocial personality. Two months after admission he escaped from an attendant, but was returned by the police. The following month he escaped again by breaking a screen on a porch, and the next day he was arrested while driving a stolen car. He was transferred to a maximum security hospital where he remained for three years. At the end of this time he was returned as "improved." A month later, he escaped by sawing the iron bars on a window. Four months later he was arrested in Montana for wearing the uniform of an Army officer, and was placed on Federal probation for five years. Six months later he was arrested in Spokane, Washington for stealing automobiles. He was hospitalized in Spokane for a short time, and was then returned to the psychiatric hospital. Two months after his return he attacked an attendant with a soft drink bottle, taped his mouth, stole his money, and escaped. [Kisker, 1964, page 232.]

A particularly vivid and terrifying documentary account of the antisocial reaction is to be found in the book *In Cold Blood* [Capote, 1966]—a description of the apparently unmotivated murder of a family of four by two young men with antisocial personalities.

What can be said about the psychological causes, or *psychogenics,* of the antisocial disorder? The lack of concern for others and the lack of conscience may be said to be due to a failure to develop both aspects of the superego—the ego ideal and conscience (see page 490). Since the superego is supposed to arise out of resolution of the Oedipal conflict, the psychoanalyst would say that the antisocial person is an individual who failed to solve his Oedipal conflict (see page 491). In a way, then, we have a theoretical idea about the way in which the disorder may have originated. But it is often very difficult to put this idea into practice with particular cases.

Perhaps the antisocial syndrome may be related to psychological rejection within the family. That is, the child who has not been given affection does not learn how to express affection. On the one hand, this defect in social learning would impede the development of the "family love affair," or the Oedipal situation, discussed by psychoanalysts. If this happened, the child would neither need nor be able to identify with a parent in order to resolve the Oedipal conflict since no one cared enough about him to put him in conflict in the first place. On the other hand, lack of affection may simply mean that the child does not have an opportunity to learn that affectionate relationships and concern for others are accepted and important aspects of interpersonal behavior. In other words, because he is treated as an object to be manipulated, he may learn to deal with other people in this way. Perhaps some of the behavior problems of adolescents who were reared in foundling homes may be related to such failures in social learning (see page 57).

Dyssocial reaction. Individuals with dyssocial reactions have probably grown up in a deviant moral climate. They are at odds with society but not because of any basic failures in social learning. They have established identifications, but they have identified with the wrong people. Thus, they are able to form strong loyalties, and they have attachments within their own criminal group. They tend to be against society because this is the normal pattern of the subgroup within which they were socialized (see page 484).

Sexual deviations. Various types of sexual deviations are considered to be sociopathic behaviors. We shall mention a few of these without going into great detail: *Exhibitionism* involves exposing one's sexual organs to the view of others; *voyeurism* is the compulsion to look at scantily clothed or naked bodies, usually of the opposite sex; *fetishism* occurs when sexual excitement is produced by the sight, touch, or smell of an article of clothing or some part of the body not usually associated with sexual activity; *sadism* and *masochism* are the terms used for sexual pleasure derived from giving pain to another (sadism) or receiving pain from another (masochism); *homosexuality* is the sexual desire for members of the same sex; *pedophilia* involves sexual interest in heterosexual or homosexual activity with a child; *zoophilia* involves sexual relations with animals.

The psychodynamics of these sexual deviations are quite complicated, and we shall not explore them further. It might be mentioned, however, that there is some disagreement as to whether or not some of these sexual deviations are really deviations. For instance, some forms of voyeurism are socially approved and even encouraged, as any glance around the beach in summer will attest. Voyeurism is widespread and most members of the male population have such tendencies. Homosexuality is another example of sexual behavior which is fairly widespread in our culture and which may not be a deviation in the statistical sense. For instance, 37 per cent of all men interviewed in the Kinsey report stated that they had had definite homosexual relations [Kinsey et al., 1948]. This survey is reasonably accurate, and its findings indicate that homosexuality is not rare. Although we might still wish to pass moral judgment on such behavior, it is difficult to apply the term "deviation" to such common behavior. Perhaps we might say that voyeurism and homosexuality are deviations only when they are symptomatic of fundamental problems or when they cause the individual to make a nuisance of himself.

Addictions. Behavior disorders in which a person is dependent upon a drug or alcohol are known as addictions. *Alcohol addiction* is common and troublesome, and it exemplifies the addictions rather well. Addiction to alcohol is somewhat complex because it affects the individual at many points in his life. First, there is the behavioral disorganization due to addiction and drunkenness itself. Later in life, there may be behavior disturbance caused by brain damage which comes from prolonged use of alcohol. The disturbances in behavior consequent to brain damage produced by alcohol are discussed in the section on Chronic Brain Syndromes.

The line between the heavy social drinker and alcohol addiction is not an easy one to draw, but the crucial things appear to be the dependence of the addict on alcohol to solve his basic adjustment problems and his loss of control over drinking [Jellinek, 1952]. Thus, getting drunk does not make a person an addict; it is only when he is almost constantly drunk and craves alcohol that he is an addict.

The behaviors of those addicted to alcohol are quite variable and depend upon situational factors and the personality structure of the addict (see page 257). Just as the behaviors of nonaddicts who have had too much to drink vary considerably, so do the behaviors of alcoholic addicts. The addict may be depressed, hostile, or euphoric; he may act out his aggressive or sexual motives—alcohol is a notorious "solvent of the superego." As this sort of behavior persists, trouble accumulates. The alcoholic probably loses his job, his marriage suffers, and his relationships with other people in general are deranged. He begins to function at lower levels of psychological adjustment; he tends to lack foresight; he becomes slovenly in appearance. As one tie after another with the past is severed, he may end up on "skid row."

The causes of this disorder are a question of considerable debate, and explanations range from the constitutional to the psychogenic. Both probably have some degree of truth in them, and as in so many of the behavior disorders, interaction of nature and nurture is the crucial thing. Among the psychogenic ideas about the cause of this disorder, certain ones enjoy some currency. Psychoanalysts have stressed the oral nature of alcohol addiction, and some regard it as due to a fixation at the oral stage of development (see page 491). Other psychologists stress the ability of alcohol to reduce anxiety. For them, alcoholic addiction is a very special kind of defense mechanism. Finally, others point out that a person under the influence of alcohol often acts out his hostilities and sexual wishes. Thus alcohol may provide a means through which strong aggressive and sexual motives may be gratified [Kisker, 1964]. Obviously, there is little agreement on this problem of the causation of alcohol addiction.

There is also much disagreement about the best method of treating this addiction. The group known as Alcoholics Anonymous relies upon group supportive therapy and religious faith. These techniques have been criticized, but they seem effective in many cases. The surest point, however, is that for this addiction there is no easy cure.

Psychotic reactions

For a long time it was thought that neurosis and psychosis were two completely different kinds of disorders. "Once a neurotic, never a psychotic" was almost an axiom. This meant that neurosis and psychosis were such different reactions that they could not develop in the same person. Today we are not so sure about this. Certainly many patients encountered in clinical practice are difficult to classify—they appear to be somewhere in between. For the present, therefore, we must consider this question unresolved.

In principle, however, we can make a distinction. Whereas the neurotic individual is characterized by anxiety or strenuous defenses against anxiety, the psychotic individual is typically one who has lost considerable contact with reality. He may simply withdraw and fail to respond to things going on around him. Or he may be so excited or depressed that his reactions are quite inappropriate to circumstances. In many instances, his thought processes, and hence his communication with others, may be seriously disturbed by *hallucinations*—reported experiences for which no sensory input exists—or by *delusions*—ideas, sometimes used to explain the presence of hallucinatory experience, which have no foundation in actual happenings. In any case, he tends to live in a world of his own—that is, he is said to be *autistic*—rather than in the real world around him. For this reason, psychosis is more severe than neurosis, and the psychotic person is more likely to require hospitalization and protective care. Most of the inmates of our mental hospitals, particularly those who stay a long time, are psychotic, not neurotic, individuals.

The psychotic reactions were at one time classified into "functional" and "organic" categories on the basis of their causative agents. Functional psychotic reactions were thought to be entirely of psychogenic origin, that is, they were thought to be caused by psychological factors. Such factors as stressful and inconsistent family life in childhood and faulty opportunities for learning accepted modes of emotional expression were thought to be especially important. The brains of people with functional psychotic reactions were almost always found to be normal in appearance. In the organic psychotic reactions, on the other hand, gross, or obvious, brain damage was present and a physical agent responsible for this damage could usually be specified.

It is now becoming clear that some functional psychotic reactions are, in fact, organic in the sense that biochemical disorders are present in the brains of people who suffer from psychotic disorders. The data on the inheritance of psychotic reactions tend to support this idea (see page 482). Consensus is growing around the idea that many of the functional psychoses require a disorder of brain chemistry as a necessary condition which must be present before particular kinds of psychological stress can then bring on the psychotic reaction. Thus, the old distinction between functional psychoses—that is, psychogenic ones—and organic psychoses—that is, those due to gross brain damage—no longer makes much sense. Rather, it seems preferable to use the term *psychotic reaction* for disorders previously considered to be functional and the term *chronic brain disorder* for behavior disorders previously considered to be organic. The psychotic reactions may be described under four main headings: affective reactions, paranoid reactions, schizophrenic reactions, and involutional reactions.

AFFECTIVE REACTIONS The major characteristic of one variety of psychosis is *extremes of mood*. Hence it is called *affective psychosis*—one in which marked disturbances of mood or emotion take place—or sometimes, *manic-depressive psychosis*. Affective reactions often appear as relatively short psychotic episodes in the otherwise normal behavior of a person. The psychotic episodes, which may be either manic or depressed, tend to last about 6 months, the depressed episodes being on the average longer than the manic ones. Most sufferers from this disorder experience several such psychotic episodes in their lives.

Symptoms. As the term manic-depressive implies, the mood of the patient may swing to either extreme —manic, or depressed—or one mood may follow the other in close succession. The manic individual is unduly elated and active. He may sing, dance, run, talk a lot, and generally expend more energy than one would think humanly possible. He may also exhibit obsessions and delusions. Frequently, he is aggressive and obstreperous. He may break chairs, attack people, use vile language, and generally put life and property in jeopardy. Or he may try so hard to be helpful that he becomes extremely troublesome. The following case illustrates some of the typical characteristics of manic excitement:

A thirty-five-year-old biochemist was brought to the clinic by his frightened wife. To his psychiatrist the patient explained: "I discovered that I had been drifting; broke the bonds and suddenly found myself doing things and doing them by telegraph. I was dead tired, and decided to go on a vacation; but even there it wasn't long before I was sending more telegrams. I got into high gear and started to buzz. Then a gentle hint from a friend took effect and I decided to come here and see if the changes in my personality were real. . . ."

When his wife had left, the patient soon demonstrated what he meant by "high gear." He bounded down the hall, threw his medication on the floor, leaped up on a window ledge and dared anyone to get him down. When he was put in a room alone where he could be free, he promptly dismantled the bed, pounded on the walls, yelled and sang. He made a sudden sally into the hall and did a kind of hula-hula dance before he could be returned to his room. His shouting continued throughout the night. . . .

The following morning, after almost no sleep, the patient

was more noisy and energetic than ever. He smashed the overhead light with his shoes and ripped off the window guard. He tore up several hospital gowns, draped himself in a loin cloth made of their fragments, said he was Tarzan, and gave wild jungle cries to prove it. "I've tasted tiger's blood!" he roared. "I'm a success and I'm the man for my boss's job. I've made a killing and this time I will keep going." He made amorous remarks to the nurses, accused them of flirting with him, and announced loudly, "At the present time I am not married; but my body is not for sale, regardless of price." From his talk it could be inferred that, far from being happily relaxed and irresponsible, the patient was in reality deeply disturbed over job competition, sexual conflicts, and his own hospitalization. A study of his personal background confirmed this inference and indicated that, as might be expected, affectional relationships and personal status had presented recurring problems throughout his life. [Cameron and Magaret, 1951, page 332.]

In contrast to the individual who develops the manic variety of affective reaction, the depressed person feels melancholy, worthless, guilty, and hopeless. Some depressed patients cry a good deal of the time, some keep talking about terrible sins they imagine that they have committed, and some are so depressed that they will take no food or water, have to be forcibly fed through a tube, and may refuse to dress or take care of their toilet needs. The extremely depressed patient is often on the verge of suicide and must be watched closely to see that he does not try suicide or otherwise harm himself. The following case is typical:

Pauline B. is a fifty-seven-year-old widow who graduated from high school, attended business school, and had training as a nurse. She has had three commitments to mental hospitals for her depressions. When seen at the hospital on her most recent admission, the patient presented the typical picture of depression. She appeared sad, talked in a somewhat whining voice, and showed psychomotor retardation. She had numerous self-condemnatory ideas, and was preoccupied with thoughts of suicide. Her general attitude was one of hopelessness. She said that life is not worth living, and that she would be better off dead. She had no interest in anything, and there was nothing left to live for. Between her depressive episodes, the patient is regarded as a happy outgoing person, although subject to rather wide swings of mood. [Kisker, 1964, page 374.]

Sometimes a manic-depressive psychosis is cyclical. The patient is manic for a period and then swings into a depression. The cycle may be repeated rapidly, or a period of months may intervene. It may be repeated more than once. On the other hand, manic states may never swing over into depressive ones, and vice versa. Almost any pattern of affective disturbance may be encountered.

Causes and treatment. Such dramatic behavior immediately arouses our curiosity about the *etiology* of the disorder, that is, its causes. Unfortunately, the causes of manic-depressive reactions are not really known; we have only some shrewd guesses about the origins of the disorder. On the one hand, it seems clear that a strong genetic basis, and therefore probably a biochemical basis, exists for the disorder (see page 482). On the other hand, there are several psychogenic theories. Perhaps the most common psychological explanation holds that the basic disorder is depression and that mania is a reaction to the depressed state.

The problem, then, is to explain depression. According to one theory, depressed people are supposed to be very dependent upon some other person and to need the love of that person very much [Rado, 1951; White, 1964]. When the love is withdrawn, the potentially depressed person first feels angry at the other person; next he comes to feel that his anger itself is responsible for the fact that love was lost, and he turns the anger inward upon himself, blaming himself for the loss of love. In other words, the depressed person begins to feel guilty over the loss of love. The behaviors seen in the depressed state are thus considered by some to be ways of lessening this guilt; by punishing himself, the depressed patient lessens this guilt. The manic state is viewed, in some theories, as a flight into activity in order to ward off depression. Whatever the psychogenic basis of manic-depressive psychosis, the biochemical and genetic basis must still be considered, and the relationship between the psychological factors and the physical factors in this disorder is by no means clear.

Without any special treatment, about 70 per cent of manic-depressive patients recover sufficiently within one year to be released from the hospital [Coleman, 1956]. With treatment, nearly 100 per cent of manic-depressive patients can be released within the first year of hospitalization [Coleman, 1964].

Physical treatment is used more commonly than psychotherapy for this type of disorder. Electro-shock therapy (EST) is frequently used with some success (see page 539). The major effect of EST seems to be that the length of time of the psychotic reaction is shortened [Bond, 1954; White, 1964].

Drugs are also used in managing this behavior disorder, but some, iproniazid, for example, although effective in relieving depression, have damaging side effects [Wittenborn, 1965]. The drugs which seem effective are either those which seem to affect brain biochemistry, the monoamine oxidase inhibitors, or those which affect the production of epinephrine—a substance involved in the activity of the sympathetic nervous system (see page 255).

PARANOID REACTIONS Paranoid psychosis is relatively rare. It takes several forms which are considered collectively in the following discussion.

Symptoms. Paranoid reactions, one of the main varieties of which is called *paranoia,* are marked by *delusions*. The delusions may be imaginings of grandeur or persecution. A paranoid patient may tell you that he is Napoleon or George Washington and spin quite a tale to prove it. He also may have the delusion that someone is persecuting him, that someone has invented a machine that is slowly destroying him by a kind of wave, or that someone is hatching a nefarious plot to deprive him of his rights as the President of the United States.

Except for his delusional system, the paranoid psychotic usually shows almost no disorder in thinking; he appears normal until something happens to precipitate the delusional thinking. The delusional

system is usually well worked out, and it often seems quite plausible. The intact thinking and the more or less logical delusions are in marked contrast to the disordered thinking encountered in the variety of schizophrenia which is labeled paranoid. The following letter from a person with a paranoid reaction illustrates the "logical" delusion typical of paranoia:

Washington, D.C.

Dear Dr. —:

I have a neighbor who owns and operates an ultrasonic machine. The transducer is projected toward us, i.e., we are in the direct beam of its energy! This neighbor has tried at various times to kill us but we have always managed to run from the apartment, thereby getting out of its beam before it affects us too much! Most of the time, he has just turned it on us to give us various feelings (not all of them at once, of course) headaches, fever, extreme fatigue or nervousness, tiredness, irritability, dizziness, nausea, sometimes fainting and a feeling of "impending doom."

There is absolutely nothing in the world we can do about it, or at least there hasn't been so far. That is what makes our case so unique! They could murder us, as they did a neighbor of ours, and even a post mortem would only show an ordinary heart attack. No one can even prove it on our neighbor, because it would only show what an ordinary heart attack would show. His widow knows this fact and so do we. She couldn't even tell the authorities because they would think she was crazy or too unbalanced by her grief.

Really, there is no telling how many more of these machines our neighbor owns throughout the country. He certainly wouldn't stop with one since he has long since recognized his strength and secret treachery. No one has caught him yet and no one is able to except for one thing that I shall write later.

Why is this man doing this? He used to be our neighbor and he hated us for what we are and what we have—those are the only things that we have been able to figure out other than that he has a complex he can't outgrow. He just *happened* onto this machine and he has followed us around the country with it, moving in just next door with it wherever we have moved to get away from him.

Since there is no obvious law governing machines of

this sort, there is nothing we can do to stop him. Can you imagine a flat-foot cop having the knowledge of an ultrasonic machine? There aren't any! It doesn't come under the jurisdiction of the F.B.I. since there is no federal offense committed, nor the F.C.C. because they are only interested in radio waves.

To prove all this in a mechanical way, that this neighbor actually has an ultrasonic machine, and that he projects it on our apartment, we would have to order CUSTOM-BUILT (from a reputable electronics firm) a model GA 1007 sound pressure equipment with built-in calibrator, and with a M-123 microphone, cost around $1350. Who has money like that nowadays to spend on such a thing? WHAT WOULD YOU DO?

Sincerely,

P.S. Call me long distance, reverse the charges. I'll be glad to give you any more information, after 5 P.M. [Kisker, 1964, page 368.]

Causes and treatment. Physiological and genetic causes do not seem to be important in this disorder. This psychotic disorder seems entirely psychogenic. Two factors seem to be most important in the paranoid's peculiar mode of adjustment. One is *aggression.* In general, his attitudes, acts, and thoughts are full of aggression, and we may surmise that he has failed to adjust normally because he has been unable to give vent in normal ways to strong aggressive impulses. The other factor is *projection.* His hallucinations and delusions usually represent a projection to others of his own aggressive or sexual impulses, and that is why he believes someone is plotting against him or persecuting him. The paranoid's aggression is so strong and he believes his projection of it so firmly that he is often dangerous. If not kept in custody, he may do someone harm. The treatment of the paranoid reactions is a very difficult matter, and the *prognosis,* or the expected course of the disorder, is not very good.

SCHIZOPHRENIC REACTIONS The word "schizophrenia" is constantly misused. One often discovers this term being applied to people who behave in inconsistent, but by no means psychotic, ways. Newspapers often label the inconsistent behavior of Mayor Stout, for example, as schizophrenic. If he is psychotic they may be correct; more likely, however, they are absolutely wrong. The term is also incorrect when it is used to mean "split," or multiple, personality. We have seen that multiple personality is a relatively rare neurotic disorder characterized by repression and dissociation. Since schizophrenia does not mean these things, what does it mean?

The word schizophrenia literally means "splitting of the mind," a definition which generally describes people who display schizophrenic behavior if it conveys the idea that disorganization of thought, feeling, and relation to the external world comprise the basic symptoms of schizophrenia [Bleuler, 1950]. But this still does not convey much about the specific symptoms and behaviors of persons afflicted with the schizophrenic psychosis. Perhaps the formal medical language of the description given in the *Diagnostic and Statistical Manual* of the American Psychiatric Association will give a more precise idea of the symtomatology of the various syndromes which are lumped together under the term schizophrenia.

[Schizophrenia] represents a group of psychotic reactions characterized by fundamental disturbances in reality relationships and concept formations, with affective, behavioral, and intellectual disturbances in varying degrees and mixtures. The disorders are marked by strong tendency to retreat from reality, by emotional disharmony, unpredictable disturbances in stream of thought, regressive behavior, and in some, by a tendency to "deterioration." [American Psychiatric Association, 1952, page 26.]

In addition to these symptoms, some types of schizophrenia are characterized by the presence of hallucinations and delusions.

Schizophrenia used to be called *dementia praecox,* which means "youthful insanity," because it tends to develop early in life. Although it may develop at any age, the highest rate of admission to mental hospitals for this disease is among people in their late teens and early twenties. Schizophrenia is no rarity: It is the most common of all the psychotic disorders, and it tends to be the most crippling.

Although the situation has improved a good deal in recent years with the introduction of intensive therapeutic techniques, a substantial number of schizophrenic patients steadily "deteriorate" so that they must be taken care of for many years. Approximately 25 per cent of people admitted to mental hospitals in the United States for the first time are diagnosed as schizophrenic, and the average length of stay in the hospital is approximately 13 years [Wolman, 1965; Lemkau and Crocetti, 1958].

A still clearer picture of this disorder may be gained by considering some of the types which have been distinguished. The American Psychiatric Association has listed nine types of schizophrenic reaction, but we shall take up only four of them here: the *simple* type, the *hebephrenic* type, the *catatonic* type, and the *paranoid* type.

The simple type. Simple schizophrenia has been characterized in the *Diagnostic and Statistical Manual* of the American Psychiatric Association as follows:

This type of reaction is characterized chiefly by reduction in external attachments and by impoverishment of human relationships. It often involves adjustment on a lower psychological level of functioning, usually accompanied by apathy and indifference but rarely by conspicuous delusions or hallucinations. The simple type of schizophrenic reaction characteristically manifests an increase in the severity of symptoms over long periods, usually with apparent mental deterioration, in contrast to the schizoid personality, in which there is little if any change. [American Psychiatric Association, 1952 page 26.]

These characteristics are easily seen in the following case.

Dr.: Do you know who I am?

Pt.: A doctor, I suppose.

Dr.: How do you feel?

Pt.: Oh—OK, I guess.

Dr.: Do you know where you are?

Pt.: It's a hospital.

Dr.: Why are you here?

Pt.: I don't know. . . . I don't think I should be here. I'm all right.

Dr.: Where would you rather be?

Pt.: I don't care, just out . . . I don't know. Maybe with some fellows or something. I don't care. There were some guys I used to know.

Dr.: What did you do with those fellows?

Pt.: I don't know—just go around.

Dr.: How do you like it here?

Pt.: I don't know. I don't care. It's all right, I guess. I liked the boys though. I used to know them.

Dr.: And you used to like them?

Pt.: Yes—they were all right, I guess.

Dr.: Who is "they?"

Pt.: Some men. I don't know them by name.

Dr.: Can you think of any reason why you should be here?

Pt.: No, I'm all right. I feel all right. I'd like to be with the fellows I used to know.

Dr.: Are there any fellows here you like?

Pt.: I don't know. They're all right, I guess.

Dr.: Do you think the men who brought you here had it in for you?

Pt.: No. They were nice to me. They were all right. They didn't have it in for me or hate me or anything.

Dr.: Do you ever hear strange noises?

Pt.: No, I never do that. I'm not crazy.

This patient was hospitalized on the complaint of his sister-in-law, who stated that he had tried to force her at the point of a gun to have sexual relations with him. On admission to the hospital the patient appeared rather indifferent about the whole matter and explained that it must have been some "temporary impulse" which overcame him.

Although 30 years of age, the patient had been living with his parents and was completely dependent upon them. His educational background was good. He made an A average in high school, but during his first year of college he lost interest in his studies and refused to attend classes despite his parents' pleadings. His parents then did their best to help him achieve some vocational adjustment, but the patient seemed indifferent to their efforts and hopes for him. After leaving college he did take several part-time jobs, including one in a grocery store, which he lost soon after because of his listless attitude and indifference to his duties. Thereafter he would not either look for nor accept work and was quite content to remain dependent upon his parents. Although rather handsome, he had never gone out with girls. When questioned on this subject he stated that "I'm not interested in girls. All they ever do is get you in trouble." [James C. Coleman, *Abnormal Psychology in Modern Life.* Copyright © 1964 by Scott Foresman and Co., Chicago, Ill. Page 277.]

The withdrawal from the world and lack of appropriate emotional responsivity that is characteristic of simple schizophrenics are easily observed in this patient. It has been noted that "no type of patient is more colorless and more unlike the popular idea of a lunatic" [White, 1964]. Occasionally, however, violent aggressive behavior or episodes of sexual misbehavior occur, and it is usually these that get the patient in sufficient trouble for him to be hospitalized.

The hebephrenic type. In this type of schizophrenic disorder, the individual seems to regress to childish levels of behavior. He may giggle incessantly; in fact, everything may seem funny or foolish to him. It is typical that his mood seems to bear no relation to the situation. He may talk about the death of his mother and laugh in a silly way. Or he may, for no apparent reason, begin to cry. Sometimes, while he is crying, he may report that he has no real feeling of sadness. He may revert to a child's vocabulary and accents. His habits of eating and perhaps his toilet habits may be childishly sloppy. The general pattern in hebephrenic reactions is shown in this interview with a hebephrenic patient:

The patient was a divorcée, 32 years of age, who had come to the hospital with bizarre delusions, hallucinations, and severe personality disintegration, and with a record of alcoholism, promiscuity, and possible incestuous relations with a brother. The following conversation shows typical hebephrenic responses to questioning:

D.: How do you feel today?

P.: Fine.

D.: When did you come here?

P.: 1416, you remember, doctor (silly giggle).

D.: Do you know why you are here?

P.: Well, in 1951 I changed into two men. President Truman was judge at my trial. I was convicted and hung (silly giggle). My brother and I were given back our normal bodies five years ago. I am a policewoman. I keep a dictaphone concealed on my person.

D.: Can you tell me the name of this place?

P.: I have not been a drinker for sixteen years. I am taking a mental rest after a "carter" assignment or "quill." You know, a "penwrap." I had contracts with Warner Brothers Studios and Eugene broke phonograph records but Mike protested. I have been with the police department for thirty-five years. I am made of flesh and blood— see, doctor (pulling up her dress).

D.: Are you married?

P.: No. I am not attracted to men (silly giggle). I have a companionship arrangement with my brother. I am a "looner" . . . a bachelor. [James C. Coleman, *Abnormal Psychology in Modern Life.* Copyright © 1964 by Scott Foresman and Co., Chicago, Ill. Page 278.]

The catatonic type. Perhaps the most dramatic form of schizophrenia is catatonic schizophrenia. It is not so common as the other forms, but when it does occur, it presents a dramatic picture. The catatonic is extremely negativistic, often doing exactly the opposite of what he is asked to do. He may completely ignore people around him and refuse to say anything under any circumstances. Perhaps the most striking thing about him, though, is his *catatonia,* which is a state of muscular rigidity. For many minutes or even hours, he may stay fixed in some strange position, for example, in a crouch or with arms outstretched. In fact, it is hard to see how catatonic positions can be maintained for so long; no normal person could hold such postures for even a short while.

The paranoid type. Like the victim of a paranoid reaction, the paranoid schizophrenic has delusions of grandeur or persecution. Unlike the person with a paranoid state, the paranoid schizophrenic often has hallucinations and *unsystematized* delusions—delusions that are not too coherent and that he does not defend with such elaborate rationalizations. He may shift with little apparent reason from one delusion to another, showing bizarre attitudes and behavior. The following passage describes such a case:

A schizophrenic young man believed that he was destined to become Emperor of the United States. "I could do a lot for the world," he said. "The United States has presidents. Will it ever have an emperor? I'll bet you think

I'm nuts to ask about that. I must have the morning paper to keep track of world affairs. . . . If the people of the United States want me to rule them, I'm willing to do so; but no one has been to see me and tell me. I'll be glad to lead them. "Later he spoke of hearing public announcements that he was to be crowned emperor. "It's been heard all over the country. . . . The world is in chaos. Thousands will be killed. I'm not a god or a devil, but I'm a supernatural being." All nations would come under his rule but Egypt; and Egypt would eventually fall to him through marriage. Along with these delusional convictions, the patient believed that attempts to kill him were repeatedly being made so that he lived, like Damocles, in constant greatness and in constant danger. [Cameron and Magaret, 1951, page 398.]

Causes of schizophrenia. Since schizophrenia in all its forms is such an important mental health problem, much research effort is being expended to find its causes. The causes are sought in genetics, biochemistry, and in psychological stresses [Jackson, 1960]. As yet, none of the answers is really convincing, and the best that can be done is to cite a few of the promising research leads.

Genetics almost certainly plays some role. The *concordance ratio*—the percentage of relatives of a schizophrenic person who also have schizophrenia—is approximately 86 per cent in the case of identical twins (see page 483). Although not absolutely convincing in itself, this and other similar findings point strongly toward a genetic and biochemical basis for schizophrenia.

Psychological stress also seems to play a role in the genesis of schizophrenia. Much attention has been given to the importance of the role of the mother as an agent fostering schizophrenia. These mothers, who are sometimes called "schizophrenogenic mothers," have been described as "cold, perfectionistic, anxious, overcontrolling, restrictive . . . [connoting] a type of person unable to give spontaneous love and acceptance to the child" [Clausen and Kohn, 1960, page 305]. Others have characterized these mothers as self-sacrificing, tyrant-martyrs who control and demand unceasing love from their children to make up for the love they do not get from

their husbands [Wolman, 1965]. It does seem that middle-class mothers of schizophrenics do tend to be the dominant parent [Clausen and Kohn, 1960]. Thus the family pattern is the opposite of the usual middle-class one in which the father is dominant. The important point seems to be that the unusual dominance pattern can create confused social learning situations for the child, boys especially; coupled with this, the particular behavior of the mother can create an almost intolerable situation for any child.

However, the matter is not really this simple, and not all schizophrenics come from families in which such mothers hold sway [Jackson et al., 1958]. For this reason, attention has also been focused on the *pattern of interaction* within the family between the parents and the preschizophrenic. This interaction pattern seems to be marked by schism and inconsistency [Lidz and Fleck, 1960; Bateson et al., 1956]. In a study of 16 families of schizophrenics, the relationship between the mother and father was characterized as follows:

Most of the marriages upon which the families were based were gravely disturbed. The majority were torn by schismatic conflict between the parents that divided the family into two hostile factions, with each spouse seeking to gain the upper hand, defying the wishes of the other, undercutting the worth of the spouse to the children, seeking to win the children to his side and to use them as emotional replacements for the spouse. The remaining families developed a skewed pattern because serious psychopathology of the dominant parent was passively accepted by the other, leading to aberrant ways of living and of child rearing. Their acceptance and masking of the serious problems that existed created a strange emotional environment that was perplexing to the child. [Lidz and Fleck, 1960, page 332.]

In addition to such disordered family interaction patterns, other theories emphasize the inconsistent demands that are supposed to be put on preschizophrenic children by their parents. One theory which discusses these inconsistencies is known as the *double-bind* theory [Bateson et al., 1956]. The psychological stress involved in schizophrenia is, according to this theory, due to the inconsistencies in the communications which the child receives from his parents. The communication process is supposed to go on at two levels—the ordinary verbal one and the level of action. The inconsistency between these two levels of communication creates the stress and the confusing situation that leads to schizophrenia. For instance, a parent may verbally tell a child that he is loved and then, by his action, communicate to the child that just the opposite is true. The family interactions of preschizophrenics and their parents are supposed to be shot through with such inconsistencies which create an extremely confusing situation for the child. Perhaps it is possible to tie together the studies that show parental discord with speculations about the inconsistencies in the double bind. First, it may simply be that family derangement facilitates inconsistent communication; second, the fact that the families are so disharmonious, but are still living together, is itself a confusing inconsistency—perhaps a basic one [Weakland, 1960].

Still other theories attempt to find relationships between the genetic evidence and the psychological evidence. In order to facilitate this, one theorist proposes that we distinguish three terms: *schizotaxia, schizotypy,* and *schizophrenia* [Meehl, 1962]. Schizotaxia is an inherited brain defect. Schizotypy is a syndrome of personality traits. These traits are a tendency toward mild thinking disorder, called "cognitive slippage"; interpersonal aversiveness, that is, a tendency to stay away from other people; anhedonia, a tendency toward being unable to experience pleasure; and ambivalence, a tendency toward liking and disliking the same thing or person to an exaggerated degree. Schizophrenia, of course, is the disorder that we have already described. The relationship between these terms, and between the genetic and psychological roots of schizophrenia, is described as follows:

I hypothesize that the statistical relation between schizotaxia, schizotypy, and schizophrenia is class inclusion: All schizotaxics become, *on all actually existing social learning regimes,* schizotypic in personality organization; but most of these remain compensated. A minority, disad-vantaged by other (largely polygenetically determined) constitutional weaknesses, and put on a bad regime by schizophrenogenic mothers (most of whom are themselves schizotypes) are thereby potentiated into clinical schizophrenia. What makes schizotaxia etiologically specific is its role as a *necessary* condition. I postulate that a non-schizotaxic individual, whatever his other genetic makeup and whatever his learning history, would at most develop a character disorder or a psychoneurosis; but he would not become a schizotype and therefore could never manifest its decompensated form, schizophrenia. [Meehl, 1962, page 831.]

This is only a sample of some of the more prominent ideas concerning the origin of schizophrenia. None is conclusive. Nobody yet knows the causes of schizophrenia—research may one day uncover them.

Treatment and prognosis. In the absence of firm knowledge as to the causes of schizophrenia, a wide variety of treatments has been proposed. These range all the way from physical therapies, such as prefrontal lobotomy and insulin shock, to various forms of psychotherapy (see Chapter 15).

In the bad old days, not so many years ago, little was done for the schizophrenic patient in the mental hospital. Perhaps he was given insulin shock treatment or electroshock therapy, but he was given very little understanding care—to say nothing of psychotherapy. Sometimes these physical treatments help, but they are most effective when used as adjuncts to some type of psychotherapy.

More currently, the tendency is to make the mental hospital a more meaningful therapeutic environment and tranquilizing, or ataractic, drugs are used to produce partial remission of symptoms, reduction of anxiety, and some clearing of thought (see page 539). Perhaps the most important thing about these drugs is that, in common with the other physical therapies, they help the patient reestablish some contact with the external world; thus they also make him able to pay attention to, and perhaps to benefit from, psychotherapy.

The classical kinds of psychoanalysis are not suited for the treatment of schizophrenia—for rather obvious reasons (see page 546). Instead, much of the psychotherapy for schizophrenia consists of the establishment of an understanding relationship with the patient so that he can learn to cope with the family disorganization which may have been one of the causes of his disorder in the first place. These attempts to establish meaningful social relationships between the patient and the psychotherapist take several forms. On the one hand, rather direct and rough interpretation of the schizophrenic's behavior may prove a useful technique [Rosen, 1953]. The schizophrenic is told in no uncertain terms how the therapist sees his behavior. On the other hand, the therapist may use sensitive and solicitous attention to the schizophrenic's needs as a technique to establish contact and to let the schizophrenic know that someone is trying to understand him.

In addition to the development of such specific types of psychotherapy, a concerted effort has been made in recent years to change the underlying philosophies of the mental hospital and its staff and to establish new routines in the care of schizophrenics and other kinds of patients. It is felt that the hospital should be a *milieu*, or environment, in which the patient can establish contact with the world as we know it. Generally, this has been done by shifting from a custodial pattern of care to a pattern which provides for more activities and allows more free choice among them. Thus the formation of friendship groups among the inmates becomes possible. Opportunities for structured social interactions are also provided in sports programs and dances. Sometimes, depending upon the home situation, visits home are arranged. Of course, much of this has been made possible by massive use of the ataractic drugs and, here again, we see how these drugs, although not curative agents in themselves, make successful therapy possible.

The prognosis of schizophrenic disorders depends upon a number of factors. One of the most important of these is the adjustment which the person made before becoming sick enough to be sent to the hospital. If the onset of the schizophrenic symptoms is rapid, if some pronounced shock, or trauma, befalls the patient just before the schizophrenic break, and if the patient was rather well adjusted before the

break, the prognosis is rather good. In other words, the chances of recovery are rather good for what has been called *reactive schizophrenia*. On the other hand, if the onset of the disorder was slow and the symptoms gradually increased in severity, if there was no precipitating trauma, and if the adjustment of the patient before being diagnosed as schizophrenic was marginal, the prognosis is poor. In other words, the chances of recovery are not good for what has been called *process schizophrenia*. Early treatment is another factor which is extremely important in the prognosis of schizophrenia. Rather than being hidden and protected by their families—perhaps because of some ill-formed fears on the family's part, and perhaps because of the general disorganization of the families of schizophrenics—people with schizoid symptoms should receive early treatment.

The treatment of schizophrenia is at best a chancy business—there is no assurance of a cure. As with all health problems, it is better to stay well in the first place. How much better it would be if prevention of schizophrenia, and other behavior disorders, too, were possible! As we learn more about the family conditions which seem to be at the roots of schizophrenia, and as community mental health clinics become more and more acceptable, we shall be on the way toward partial eradication of this most crippling of the psychotic disorders.

INVOLUTIONAL REACTIONS Just as schizophrenia seems to be a psychosis which begins early in life, involutional psychoses begin later in life. Women, during the involutional period—the period of menopause at forty-five to fifty-five years of age—sometimes have psychotic episodes which may be either depressed or paranoid in nature. Men, at a somewhat later age—fifty-five to sixty-five—often undergo involutional changes, and similar psychotic behavior sometimes occurs.

The syndromes of the psychotic episodes which come about during the involutional periods are of two main types—agitated depression or paranoia. We have examined paranoid symptoms, and the symptoms of the paranoid type of involutional disorder are similar. Agitated depression is characterized by crying, moaning, lamentations, wailing, restless pacing, wringing the hands, and attacks on one's own body—hair pulling, for example. The following case illustrates agitated depression:

Laura A. is a 50-year-old woman who was admitted to the psychiatric hospital after complaining at home that she was "losing her mind." For days she made this complaint, spoke of a "visual fog," and said her mind was a "blank." She had involuntary episodes of crying over a period of several months, and was sent to a private hospital where she received treatment which did not alleviate her symptoms.

When seen at the psychiatric hospital, Laura was a short woman who looked many years older than her age. Her eyes were sunken and her long straight hair was disheveled. She had the appearance of a sad and somewhat ghostly person who constantly repeated her symptoms in a flat sing-song voice. She complained that she "had no head," that her mind was gone, and that a nerve in her forehead was making her "holler." She cried out repeatedly, "Help me! Keep me from hollering!" Her moaning and occasional screaming could be stopped temporarily by distracting her, and it was possible with some effort to get her to talk about herself. She was well oriented in all areas, athough her thinking was somewhat rambling and egocentric. While her mood was one of dejection, she was restless and disturbed.

The patient was seen on a number of subsequent occasions, and there appeared to be some degree of deterioration. She did not remember the examiner, and she became increasingly hostile and vicious. At the time of her admission to the hospital she had been a rather gentle person in spite of her agitation. The patient was placed on medication, and two weeks later was sitting quietly on the ward in a rather relaxed state. She did not remember talking previously to the examiner, but she repeated the ideas that her mind was gone, her head was no good, and that she was "crazy." She said that she talks too much, walks up and down too much, and "acts like an animal." She concluded by saying there was no hope for her. While these ideas were similar to those expressed when she was admitted to the hospital, they were now expressed in a relatively calm and unemotional way. Several months later the patient was able to leave the hospital and make a satisfactory adjustment. She returned to work as a secretary, and managed her home efficiently and with growing interest in her activities. [Kisker, 1964, pages 377–378.]

In spite of the fact that these psychoses occur at the time of the involutional period, their causes seem to be mainly psychological. This is a time of crisis for both men and women. For some women, menopause is a sign that life is coming to an end and it signals the end of their sexual attractiveness. By the time of menopause, many of the previous life adjustments are no longer appropriate. For instance, after years of having children in the house, suddenly, it seems, they are grown, and the mother may feel lonely and left out. Worries about such things as financial security in old age, regrets over opportunities lost, and so on, may also be pressing. The depressed patient tends to blame himself for the predicament in which he finds himself, whereas the paranoid patient blames others.

Prognosis is moderately good for the depressed involutional psychosis, but the depressions typically last for several years. Various ataractic drugs and electroshock therapy often help. Prognosis is less good for the paranoid type of involutional psychosis, and these patients often show increasing deterioration as they grow older.

Chronic brain syndromes

Our concern here is with the agents and conditions that produce long-lasting, or chronic, brain damage rather than those which produce acute, or short-lasting, alterations in brain function and behavior. Among the causes of brain damage which can result in behavior disorders are syphilis of the brain, physical blows to the head, disturbances of the blood supply in the brain, brain tumors, disorders of metabolism, physical changes in the brain with old age, and chemical agents, drugs, or alcohol. Behavior disorders due to brain changes with old age, or *senile psychosis,* and those due to the overuse of alcohol are by far the most common types of chronic brain syndromes.

SENILE PSYCHOSIS Old people may develop psychotic behavior that is characterized by delusions, defects of memory, and general disorientation. For example, the person may imagine that he has been talking to someone who really was not there, or he may imagine that people are boring holes in his head. As his memory grows worse, he may forget what he has just said, at the same time insisting that he remembers things that never happened. Very frequently in senile psychosis the person has great difficulty in knowing where he is, where he has been, or what is going on—in other words, he is generally disoriented. The following case points up these symptoms:

A housewife, aged seventy-three years, was brought to the hospital by relatives who found it impossible to give her the care and protection she needed. According to their account, she had been "losing her memory" during the preceding three years. . . .

Up to the age of seventy years, the patient had shown nothing unusual in her behavior. She had gone about her household duties competently, maintained her social contacts reasonably well, and kept her person well groomed and clean. The first change that anyone noticed was a growing tendency to misplace articles at home, to leave packages in the stores, and to forget the purpose of an errand after she had started on it. The patient accepted these lapses good-humoredly as the forgetfulness that was natural to old age; and the family often joked about "grandma's absent-mindedness." After a few months, however, it became apparent that the forgetfulness was becoming a serious problem. The patient spent so much time searching for misplaced articles that she could not get her housework done, and she was unable to retrace her steps for the forgotten packages because she could not remember what they were or where she had been shopping. . . .

Meanwhile, the patient gave further evidence that she was undergoing general behavioral deterioration. She required a great deal of urging before she would bathe, keep her hair combed, or change her clothing. Sometimes she put on two or more of the same articles, one over the other, and sometimes she came to breakfast with her dress on backwards. She began hoarding all kinds of things under her bed—food, newspapers, kitchenware, ornaments,

clothing and toilet articles. When her daughter-in-law or her husband removed these the patient at first resisted and then wept. She became progressively confused with reference to the time of day. For example, she protested at six in the evening that it was "too early for breakfast"; soon after going to bed, she would get up and insist that it was morning. . . . Not long after she had finished a meal she would ask when they were to eat, as though she had not eaten for some time.

The day before her hospitalization, the patient had disappeared from home during the afternoon; and, in spite of their frantic search of the neighborhood, her relatives could not find her. That evening she was returned cold, dirty and dishevelled, by the police, who had observed her crossing streets against traffic. . . . She arrived home cheerful and garrulous, unable to tell where she had been, to appreciate her situation, or to understand her relatives' frightened behavior. While preparing for bed, she was only with difficulty dissuaded from climbing out of the bathroom window, which she insisted was the door. These events led to a family conference, the upshot of which was that further attempts at home care were considered to be out of the question. [Cameron and Margaret, 1951, pages 547–548.]

Such confused states are typical of senile psychosis, but paranoid symptoms and depression are also common.

Some of the brain damage in senile psychosis is due to deficiencies of the blood circulation in the brain. The diameter of some of the small arterioles supplying the brain cells becomes decreased by fatty deposits which accumulate. When the blood flow to a portion of the brain ceases, or is markedly diminished, the cells die and that part of the brain is said to be atrophied. Other brain damage in senile psychosis is due to less specific causes; for instance, it seems that as we grow older we are constantly losing nerve cells which are not replaced. This cell loss seems to be simply a consequence of age.

INTOXICATION PSYCHOSIS (ALCOHOL) The long-term effects of prolonged, large-scale drinking—for example, a pint to a fifth of whiskey a day for 10 to 30 years—can bring about this psychosis which is quite distinct from the marked changes in behavior that take place in acute cases of alcoholic intoxication, *delerium tremens,* for instance.

Chronic alcoholism can result in irreversible damage to brain cells. The alcoholic suffers from a pronounced nutritional imbalance, and apparently a prolonged lack of B vitamins is the important factor in the damage to nerve cells of the brain. Sometimes the damage can be partially reversed by massive doses of vitamin B, but often the damage is irreversible.

The typical pattern of symptoms associated with chronic alcoholism and vitamin-B deficiency is called *Korsakoff's syndrome.* The symptoms of this syndrome are disorientation, confusion, memory disorders, impulsiveness, and some physical symptoms such as inflammation of the peripheral nerves. *Confabulation*—the filling in of gaps in memory with plausible guesses—is characteristic of the memory disorder which forms part of Korsakoff's syndrome. A similar syndrome, but without the nerve inflammation and other specific physical symptoms, tends to occur whenever there is any generalized and widespread damage to the cerebral cortex. After a severe blow to the head, for example, such a syndrome may ensue.

CATASTROPHIC REACTION   In the cases we have been discussing, the major symptoms are easily related to brain damage, but that does not mean that the severity of the symptoms, and the pattern of symptoms, is unrelated to psychological factors. For instance, the severity of senile psychosis, and the form it takes, is very much dependent upon the prepsychotic adjustment of the person.

What has been called the *catastrophic reaction* is another psychological factor in chronic brain syndromes [Goldstein, 1940]. Consider, for a minute, the situation facing a person with chronic brain disorder when he fails on a simple problem that he knows he was once able to do. He is liable to feel frustrated and hopeless—in short, he experiences a catastrophic reaction. Thus, some of the symptoms which are typical of the chronic brain disorders may be secondary to the brain damage. The sequence of events may be something like this: Brain damage causes the person to be reduced to a much lower level of functioning, and this deals a severe blow to his self-esteem. It is easy to see how depression might follow. In paranoid suspiciousness, the patient is, perhaps, attempting to rationalize his deficit by blaming others for his problems. Plots, ray guns, and the like may be invented to give "plausible" explanations for the otherwise inexplicable changes which have taken place in behavior and experience.

SYNOPSIS AND SUMMARY

Here ends our tale of anguish and misery. Sometimes students and authors tend to depersonalize the people who are described in discussions of behavior disorders. But these are real people who, in most cases, are suffering a great deal of misery and anguish. Perhaps the student will object that this accusation of depersonalization does not apply to him. Quite the contrary, he may say. He has found some mild forms of these symptoms in himself; he may, then, have a little insight into some of the feelings of those with behavior disorders. This finding of mild forms of symptoms, where no problem really exists, is sometimes called the "medical student's disease." It is only natural, and perhaps it helps to establish empathy with the sufferers we have been describing.

One of the prerequisites in any discussion of behavior disorders is objectivity. We need not lose appreciation for people and their problems, but we should regard behavior disorders as natural phenomena with causes which are no less real than those of other diseases. Three large problems seem to impede progress in finding causes. In the first place, the causes are complex, and interactions of nature and nurture, although important in all diseases, are perhaps even more complex and confusing in the behavior disorders. In the second place, the causes must be sought in psychological mechanisms—disordered opportunities for learning, disorganized family situations, and so on—and objective investigation of these situations is rather difficult. In the third place, all the ignorance, fear, and superstition about behavior disorders must be overcome.

One of the purposes of this chapter has been to impress upon the reader that behavior disorders have natural and understandable origins. To put it another way, given a certain nature, or constitution, and given particular forces interacting with this nature, a behavioral disorder will be the expected and natural outcome. When we understand the origins, or etiology, of the behavior disorders, and even before we understand them completely, great strides can be made toward preventing these disorders and the anguish that attends them.

Here are some of the specific points that were made in our attempt to provide an objective description of some of the behavior disorders:

1. Mild adjustment problems, which often involve frustration of motives, can produce unhappiness and can interfere with a person's efficiency and strivings toward self-actualization. Such adjustment problems are common, but they tend to be short-lived, and recovery in the course of ordinary living is the rule.

2. The psychoneurotic reactions, or neuroses, are characterized by anxiety and attempts to reduce anxiety. The psychoneurotic symptoms may be thought of, in some cases, as special varieties of defense mechanisms.

3. Some of the major types of psychoneurotic reactions are: (a) anxiety reactions, in which anxiety, chronic or acute, is the prominent symptom; (b) phobic reactions, involving intense irrational fears; (c) obsessive-compulsive reactions, in which ideas or acts involuntarily intrude into the ongoing stream of behavior; (d) conversion reactions, involving the conversion of a motivational conflict into symbolically meaningful physical symptoms; (e) dissociative reactions, in which a person represses many ideas, and which may result in such disorders as amnesia or multiple personality; (f) depressive reactions, in which the major symptom is profound depression, usually after a person has experienced a severe loss.

4. People with personality disorders are characterized by "developmental defects or pathological trends in personality structure." In contrast to the psychoneurotic reactions, anxiety is at a minimum; in contrast to the psychotic reactions, little thought disturbance is present. Two varieties of personality disorder are the personality pattern and trait disturbances and the sociopathic personality disturbances.

5. Among the personality pattern and trait disturbances are: (a) the schizoid personality, in which the major symptoms are withdrawal and autistic thinking; (b) passive and aggressive personalities, in which dependency motives and aggressive tendencies are expressed in various ways; and (c) the compulsive personality, in which the major symptoms are excessive concern with standards of conduct and conscience.

6. People with sociopathic personality disturbances show many symptom patterns. Among these are: (a) the antisocial reaction, in which the major symptoms are little concern over right and wrong, inability to be loyal or responsible, and impulsive criminal acts; (b) the dyssocial reaction, in which people have learned the criminal patterns of behavior that are commonplace in their environments; (c) sexual deviations; and (d) addictions, of which alcoholic addiction is the most common.

7. Psychotic reactions are those in which the individual has, for a time, lost contact with reality. Hallucinations, reported experiences for which no sensory input exists, and delusions, or ideas which have no foundation in actual happenings, often exist. The thinking of many psychotics tends to be private, or autistic, and many bizarre associations are characteristic.

8. Among the major types of psychotic reaction are: (a) affective reactions, involving extreme moods of excitement or depression; (b) paranoid reactions, characterized by systematized delusions of persecution or grandeur; (c) schizophrenic reactions, marked by disorientation, confused thinking, withdrawal, and delusions; and (d) involutional reactions, in which depression or paranoid-like delusions originate in late middle age.

9. Of the nine types of schizophrenia, we have described four of the most dramatic and common ones: (a) the simple type, involving withdrawal from other people and deterioration of behavior with time; (b) the hebephrenic type, in which behavior regresses to a childish level; (c) the catatonic type, involving negativism and the prolonged assumption of postures and

unresponsiveness to surroundings; and (*d*) the paranoid type, characterized by unsystematic delusions of persecution.

10. Because schizophrenia is such a common, tragic, long-lasting, and crippling disorder, research into its causes has been pursued vigorously. Among the ideas advanced concerning the causes of schizophrenia are genetic hypotheses and psychogenic interpretations. The psychogenic interpretations stress faulty social learning in disordered family situations and contradictory patterns of communication within the family.

The trend in theorizing about the origins of schizophrenia is toward a recognition of some pattern of interaction between genetic and psychological causes. 11. The behaviors included under chronic brain syndromes are caused by damage to the brain. The most common syndromes result from brain changes as a result of old age and as a result of chronic alcoholism—the senile and alcoholic psychoses. Psychological factors are also important in determining the strength of symptoms, and in shaping the particular symptom patterns, shown by people with brain damage.

RELATED TOPICS IN THE TEXT

CHAPTER 13 PERSONALITY Some of the reactions to frustration and some defense mechanisms are discussed in this chapter. Since some behavior disorders may be thought of as special defense mechanisms, and since defense mechanisms make up the symptom syndromes of many behavior disorders, a review of the types, origins, and functions served by normal defense mechanisms is well advised.

CHAPTER 15 MENTAL HEALTH AND PSYCHOTHERAPY Some methods of treatment for the psychoneurotic and psychotic reactions are described in this chapter.

SUGGESTIONS FOR FURTHER READING

Coleman, J. C. *Abnormal psychology and modern life* (3d ed.). Chicago: Scott, Foresman, 1964.
A popular textbook on abnormal psychology.

Gorlow, L., and Katkvosky, W. (Eds.). *Readings in the psychology of adjustment.* New York: McGraw-Hill, 1959.
A selection of articles and excerpts from books on the topic of human adjustment.

Kaplan, B. (Ed.). *The inner world of mental illness: A series of first-person accounts of what it was like.* New York: Harper & Row, 1964.

Persons who have suffered from behavior disorders report on their experiences.

Kisker, G. W. *The disorganized personality.* New York: McGraw-Hill, 1964.
A textbook on abnormal psychology stressing the description of the syndromes in the behavior disorders.

White, R. W. *The abnormal personality* (3d ed.). New York: Ronald, 1964.
The origins and dynamics of behavior disorders are stressed in this text.

15

MENTAL
HEALTH
AND
PSYCHOTHERAPY

SOMETIMES I FEEL LIKE
I HAS NO FRIEND
SOMETIMES I FEEL LIKE
I HAS NO FRIEND
SOMETIMES I FEEL LIKE
I HAS NO FRIEND
AND A LONG WAYS
FROM HOME, A LONG
WAYS FROM HOME.
              SPIRITUAL

THE LAST CHAPTER dealt mainly with the *causes* and *nature* of maladjustments in behavior. This chapter deals with *remedies,* or at least with ways and means of treating these maladjustments when they occur, and with steps that can be taken to prevent them. Unfortunately, neither the prevention nor the cure of mental illness is easy, quick, or sure. The problems involved are still largely unsolved, and we are not at all certain of the effectiveness of the methods which are now being used to attack them. Nevertheless, mental health and psychotherapy are of such importance that every intelligent person should know as much about them as he can.

The problem of mental health

The term *behavior disorder,* as used in Chapter 14, is in some ways preferable to the term mental illness for describing maladjustments. However, *mental illness* is the term which is usually used. Other almost synonomous terms are *mental disease* and *mental disorder.* In a way, all these terms are unfortunate, but since they are entrenched in the psychological literature, we shall use them here.

PREVALENCE OF MENTAL ILLNESS IN THE UNITED STATES   Mental health is a problem that concerns everyone. So many people are, have been, or will be mentally ill or seriously maladjusted that none of us can escape some personal contact with it.

Except for the number of people in hospitals, figures for the incidence of various behavior disorders are at best only estimates which are based on studies of certain communities. These estimates vary with the particular criterion used for deciding whether a person is maladjusted enough to be judged mentally ill.

Psychoneurotics undoubtedly make up the largest single group. Those neurotic enough to be severely handicapped in social adjustment probably constitute about 5 per cent of the adult population. Extremely conservative figures give something less than 1 per cent, whereas more liberal estimates run as high as 37 per cent of adults. Another 2 or 3 per cent are addicted to alcohol or are problem drinkers. Roughly a million individuals, or about .5 per cent of adults, can at any one time be classified as psychotic. If we add another 3 million or so individuals who have personality trait disorders or display antisocial reactions, the number of mentally ill and seriously maladjusted persons approximates 10 per cent of the population.

These figures represent only one given point in time. Over a period of years, the incidence of maladjustment is even higher. For some years past, the chances of a person spending some part of his life in a mental hospital have been about 1 in 17, or 6 per cent. And it is primarily psychotics, rather than neurotics, who are admitted to mental hospitals. Now that modern medicine has extended the life span so dramatically, many more individuals will live long enough to become victims of the senile psychoses. In view of that fact, we now estimate that about 1 individual in 10 will at some time or other be admitted to a mental hospital.

The number of patients in mental hospitals gives us another, and quite shocking, idea of the prevalence of mental disease. Almost half of the hospital beds in the United States are occupied by mental patients. In terms of the number of hospital beds required, mental diseases are as numerous as all other diseases combined. Beds in mental hospitals number roughly 1 million. Since most mental hospital facilities are provided by state and local governments, a sizable share of our local taxes must be used to care for the mentally ill.

Of all the patients admitted to mental hospitals for the first time, the largest single group consists of those diagnosed as having brain syndromes—behavior problems secondary to disease or destruction of nervous tissue. Most of the patients with brain syndromes are old people in whom brain damage has been caused by the diseases of old age. The second largest group of first admissions to mental hospitals is made up of those diagnosed as psychotic, with the various schizophrenic types of psychoses making up the majority of the psychotic admissions to mental hospitals. Because the prognosis of recovery for these two groups is poor, their stay in the hospital tends to be long; and because their admission rates are high in the first place, people with brain syndromes and schizophrenic individuals make up the vast majority of hospitalized mental patients. Those with personality disorders—antisocial reactions, sexual deviations, alcoholic and drug addictions, for instance—make up the third largest category of first admissions to mental hospitals. Psychoneurotics constitute the fourth largest group of first admissions, their number being small because they are mostly treated as outpatients or as private patients by psychiatrists. Figure 15.1 summarizes the first admission data on these four categories, as well as several others.

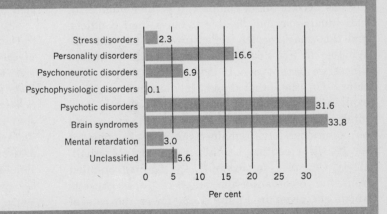

MOST PATIENTS ADMITTED FOR THE FIRST TIME TO MENTAL HOSPITALS HAVE BRAIN SYNDROMES OR PSYCHOTIC DISORDERS

FIGURE 15.1. *Percentages of patients in particular diagnostic categories upon first admission to public mental hospitals. (From Kisker, 1964. Adapted from data furnished by the National Institute of Mental Health, 1963.)*

Stress disorders 2.3
Personality disorders 16.6
Psychoneurotic disorders 6.9
Psychophysiologic disorders 0.1
Psychotic disorders 31.6
Brain syndromes 33.8
Mental retardation 3.0
Unclassified 5.6

Per cent

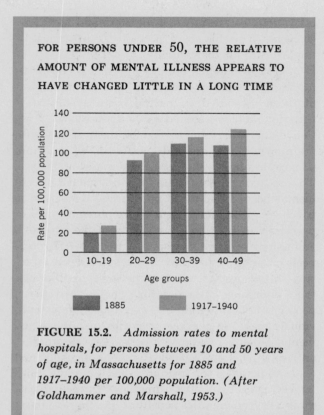

FOR PERSONS UNDER 50, THE RELATIVE AMOUNT OF MENTAL ILLNESS APPEARS TO HAVE CHANGED LITTLE IN A LONG TIME

FIGURE 15.2. *Admission rates to mental hospitals, for persons between 10 and 50 years of age, in Massachusetts for 1885 and 1917–1940 per 100,000 population. (After Goldhammer and Marshall, 1953.)*

Environmental factors. It is frequently assumed that the stress of modern life is an important factor in mental illness. Some observers feel that, since life has become more complex, a greater number of individuals may not be able to solve their conflicts, and thus may become maladjusted or mentally ill. Whether or not this is true for all kinds of mental illness we cannot say. It may be the case for neurotics. On the other hand, it does not seem to explain the number of admissions to mental hospitals. For people under fifty years old, the figures on admissions have remained surprisingly constant for nearly a century [Goldhammer and Marshall, 1953]. Consider, for example, the figures compiled from the records of the state of Massachusetts which are given in Figure 15.2. There the rate of admission, at various age levels below fifty, was

about the same in the period from 1917 to 1940 as it was in 1885. Other data from different sources show almost the same thing. Perhaps this is not surprising in view of the genetic factor in some of the psychoses (see page 522). In any case, the precipitating factors in psychoses apparently have not been altered appreciably by changes in our culture in the last eighty years.

Although the admission rate for patients under fifty does not seem to have increased markedly since 1885, the admission rate for all ages has increased, mainly because of the increasing incidence of senile psychoses as more people live to be older (see Figure 15.3, top). However, the picture is not completely bleak. Another look at the upper part of Figure 15.3 shows that the number of patients per 100,000 population has dropped steadily. The lower part of Figure 15.3 indicates that this drop is due to the fact that the discharge rate has, on the average, gradually increased in recent years. New techniques of therapy and a greater dependence upon out-patient treatment have speeded the discharge of patients from mental hospitals.

Social class. The trend toward a gradually increasing total admission rate and a gradually increasing discharge rate in mental hospitals probably cuts across all social classes. However, marked differences occur between the classes in overall incidence and type of mental illness. A team of research workers at Yale University has gathered the data on this question [Hollingshead and Redlich, 1958].

The researchers classified virtually all the patients under psychiatric care at one particular time in the New Haven area. Patients "under psychiatric care" included not only those in mental hospitals, but those making regular visits to psychiatrists in clinics and private practice. The social class of each patient was determined by using certain well-establshed criteria of social class: income level, occupation, educational level, housing, and so on (see Chapter 16). In this way the patients were classified into one of five groups; Class I included the highest social class, Class V the lowest. There were, however, too few cases in Classes I and II to treat them separately; so these were

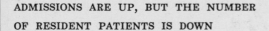

ADMISSIONS ARE UP, BUT THE NUMBER
OF RESIDENT PATIENTS IS DOWN

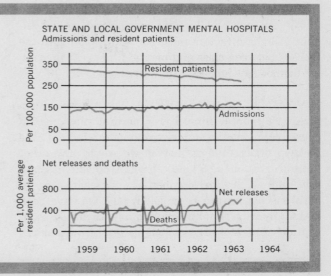

FIGURE 15.3. *Above, rate of admission and numbers of patients in public mental hospitals; below, rate of release and death rate in public mental hospitals (Health, Education and Welfare Indicators, 1963).*

combined. Hence comparisons were made of four groups: Classes I-II, Class III, Class IV, and Class V.

Some of the results of the study were clear cut. The total incidence of cases (rate per 100,000 within a given class) was quite different for each of the four classes (see Figure 15.4). Incidence was relatively low for Classes I-II and III, rose significantly for Class IV, and then rose very sharply for Class V. On the other hand, the incidence of new cases—cases coming under psychiatric care for the first time—was more nearly the same for all four classes, although Class V was definitely higher than the others. Thus the differences among the classes was largely due to the fact that the lower classes accumulated relatively more individuals with protracted illness.

The accumulation of mental illness in the lower classes may be attributed in part to the better facilities for psychiatric treatment enjoyed by the upper classes. That is not the major factor, however. The kinds of illnesses prevalent in the classes are remarkably different (see Figure 15.5). Of the patients in each class, approximately two-thirds in Classes I-II were classified as psychoneurotics, whereas less than 10 per cent in Class V were so classified. Class III and Class IV showed intermediate percentages. Thus people in the lower classes are considerably more prone to develop

psychoses than neuroses; the reverse is true of people in the upper classes. This statement applies to individuals actually under psychiatric care. It must be remembered, however, that low-income groups are less able to afford psychiatric care and are less likely to obtain care for psychoneurotic disorders than the high-income groups. We thus know that the true percentage of neurotic disorders in the lower classes is understated by these statistics, but we have no way of knowing actual figures since we know only the number of *treated* disorders.

Among those classified as psychoneurotic, there are also class differences. The obsessive-compulsive reactions are for the most part concentrated in the upper class (I-II), whereas reactions involving physical complaints are most prevalent in the lower classes. That is to say, psychosomatic anxiety reactions and conversion reactions are found in relatively greater numbers in the lower classes than in the upper classes.

The major facts emerging from this large-scale study of social class and mental disorder are certainly clear. They leave no doubt that mental illness, both in incidence and kind, is linked to social class. The interpretation of the fact, however, is not nearly so clear. Social-class differences include differences in genetic background, in learning experiences, in the types of stress and frustration encountered, and in the amount and kind of psychiatric care available. All these factors must somehow enter into the linkage between class and mental illness. At present, we cannot say just how they interact.

HISTORICAL BACKGROUND Today, we recognize that mental illness is a natural phenomenon caused by genetic and environmental factors. We seek to understand it just as we would any other natural phenomenon and, through objective scientific inquiry, to develop methods for combating it. This has not always been so. In fact, we have been extraordinarily slow in arriving at our present conception of mental illness. The history of the ways in

CHRONIC MENTAL ILLNESS IS MORE FREQUENT IN THE LOWER CLASSES THAN IN THE UPPER CLASSES

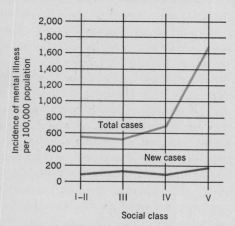

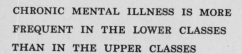

FIGURE 15.4. *Relative prevalence of mental illness in different social classes. The total incidence of cases (rate per 100,000 within a given class) differs according to social class. Much of the difference is due to the accumulation of relatively more individuals with protracted illness in the lower classes. (Hollingshead and Redlich, 1958.)*

MENTAL ILLNESS IN THE UPPER CLASSES IS LIKELY TO BE A PSYCHONEUROSIS; IN THE LOWER CLASSES, A PSYCHOSIS

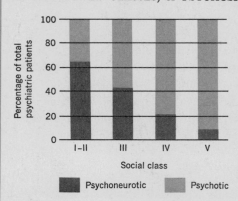

FIGURE 15.5. *Kinds of mental illness prevalent in the different social classes. Neuroses predominate in the upper classes, psychoses in the lower classes. (Hollingshead and Redlich, 1958.)*

which man has viewed mental illness is fascinating, and almost incredible [see Zilboorg and Henry, 1941].

Ancient concepts. Among the ancients, mental disorder was attributed to demon possession. This is clear from the evidence we can put together about the cavemen of the Stone Age, living some half-million years ago, and from early writings of the Chinese, Egyptians, Hebrews, and Greeks. Early man, of course, considered almost every event to be the work of spirits. Naturally he regarded the mentally ill person as one possessed by an evil spirit. Among the Hebrews, demon possession was looked upon as a punishment visited by God—a notion later revived and elaborated in the Christian tradition.

For some of the ancients, the treatment was to let the spirits out; to do this, they frequently *trephined* holes in the possessed person's skull. In Biblical times and later, the prescribed treatment for demon possession was *exorcism*. This involved various rituals and techniques for casting out the demons—prayer, religious rites, weird brews and medicines, whipping, starvation, or torture.

The rays of scientific enlightenment shone through first during the Golden Age of Greece. Hippocrates (460–377 B.C.), the Greek physician regarded as the "father of medicine," repudiated the doctrine of demon possession, asserting that mental illness was a disorder of brain function. He recognized that heredity might predispose a person to mental illness and also that head injuries might cause certain disorders. Not all his ideas were correct—indeed, some of his physiological explanations were far wide of the mark—but his belief in natural causes anticipated our modern conception of mental illness. Later Greek and Roman philosophers and physicians for the most part followed in the Hippocratic tradition.

Age of witchcraft. With the decline of Greco-Roman civilization, however, demonology was revived, modified somewhat by the theology and superstitions of the times. Exorcism also reappeared as the accepted method of treatment. In early medieval times, apparently, treatment was left to the priests, and the mentally ill were not, on the whole, treated badly. But as the idea that they were possessed of devils became more widely held, they were treated with increasing cruelty, which was justified on the ground that not only the individual but the devils inside must be punished.

From the fifteenth through the seventeenth centuries, the age of witchcraft, such misguided beliefs about mental illness saw their heyday. Because of these beliefs, victims, whether really ill or not, were regarded as evil. Demon possession was considered a form of God's punishment or, at worst, a sign of partnership with the devil. The possessed were thought to acquire supernatural powers; these "witches," it was claimed, were able to cause sickness, catastrophe, drought, and even to perform miracles, such as turning people into animals or vice versa. Not only simple and pious people, but also prominent clergymen, both Catholic and Protestant, and other community leaders believed in witches. Martin Luther (1483–1546) wrote:

The greatest punishment God can inflict on the wicked . . . is to deliver them over to Satan, who with God's permission, kills them or makes them to undergo great calamities. Many devils are in woods, water, wildernesses, etc., ready to hurt and prejudice people. When these things happen, then the philosophers and physicians say, it is natural, ascribing it to the planets. . . .

In cases of melancholy . . . I conclude it is merely the work of the devil. Men are possessed by the devil in two ways: corporally or spiritually. Those whom he possesses corporally, as mad people, he has permission from God to vex and agitate, but he has no power over their souls. [Quoted in Coleman, 1964, page 32.]

On the basis of convictions such as these, otherwise good and sensible people harassed and tortured witches and felt that they were doing God's will. This was how they justified burning witches at the stake.

Not everyone believed in witchcraft or in the demonological view of mental illness. Those who did not, including many clergymen, physicians, and scientists, gradually became more vocal. Their influence was increasingly felt, and by the eighteenth century, belief in witchcraft was on its way out.

The insane[1] asylum. In the meantime, the problem of how to care for those with behavior disorders received increasing attention. Many of the disturbed were allowed loose in the community; others were kept in monasteries or prisons. Gradually the idea of a separate asylum for the mentally ill took hold. The first asylums were established in the sixteenth century; by the eighteenth century, they were fairly common both in the United States and abroad.

At first the conditions of treatment in these asylums were little better than the patients were used to outside. The patients had their heads shaved and were crowded together in dark cells, fed poorly,

[1] The term "insane" is a legal term that is generally used to refer to those who cannot be held legally responsible for their actions; it is not a medical or psychological term [English and English, 1958]. Psychosis is the proper medical and psychological term (see Chapter 14). However, this term was in use when asylums were beginning to be established.

and often very little, and frequently placed in strait-jackets. The more violent ones were put in chains. Many were bled, doused in cold water, confined in cribs, and kept in weird contrivances. Such treatment reflected the still widespread influence of demonology and, at best, a lack of understanding of the mentally ill. The following passage describes the treatment of the mentally ill in the United States during colonial times:

. . . the mentally ill were hanged, imprisoned, tortured, and otherwise persecuted as agents of Satan. Regarded as sub-human beings, they were chained in specially devised kennels and cages like wild beasts, and thrown into prisons, bridewells and jails like criminals. They were incarcerated in workhouse dungeons or made to slave as able-bodied paupers, unclassified from the rest. They were left to wander about stark naked, driven from place to place like mad dogs, subjected to whippings as vagrants and rogues. Even the well-to-do were not spared confinement in strong rooms and cellar dungeons, while legislation usually concerned itself more with their property than their persons. . . . Whenever public provision was made—usually for the purpose of safe-guarding the community from "dangerous mad-men"—it generally boded ill for the hapless victim of mental disease. [Deutsch, 1949, pages 53–54.]

The late eighteenth century saw the beginnings of the modern revolution in the care and treatment of the mentally ill. A physician named Philippe Pinel was placed in charge of the Bicêtre and Salpêtrière hospitals for the mentally ill in Paris. As an experiment, he was permitted by the authorities to remove the chains of many of the hospitals' inmates. He took patients out of dungeons and put them into sunny rooms, permitted them to walk around outside the hospital, and instituted a regime of kindly treatment (see Figure 15.6). The results were dramatic. Within weeks or months, some patients were pronounced cured and discharged. Others progressed more slowly, but improved enough to live relatively useful and tranquil lives in the hospital. That was in the 1790s.

Like many revolutions, Pinel's was welcomed in some quarters and distrusted or rejected in others. A few hospitals immediately followed suit. The more extreme medieval cruelties gave way to more humane treatment. Still, for another century, mental

FIGURE 15.6. *Pinel removing the shackles from the inmates of La Salpêtrière Asylum, Paris. This signaled a more humane and understanding approach to mental illness. (From a copy of a painting by Tony Robert-Fleury in the Central State Hospital, Indianapolis, Indiana.)*

hospitals were backward custodial institutions, doing little to help their patients and often making their plight worse.

Mental health movement. This was the situation around 1900, when the modern mental health movement began. This movement got much of its initial impetus when Clifford Beers, after several years as a patient in mental hospitals, regained his mental health and wrote the book *A Mind That Found Itself*. In this book, Beers recounted his experiences in mental hospitals, most of which were grim indeed, and told how he "found himself" in the home of a friendly attendant. He campaigned for better conditions and treatment of the mentally ill and for wider public understanding of mental health. The publication of his book and the founding of the Society for Mental Hygiene, both in 1908, were the opening guns in what has proved to be a successful campaign, although we still have a long way to go in ensuring effective treatment for all the mentally ill. Conditions in mental hospitals have improved greatly over the past sixty years. They are, however, far from ideal, owing to inadequate facilities and budgets and to shortages of trained personnel.

Our primary concern here, however, is with the attempts to treat and prevent mental illness which have grown out of the modern mental health movement. Such attempts were unthinkable so long as the mentally ill were regarded as witches to be punished, or as subhuman beings to be "put away" and left in an asylum. Hence only in the last sixty years has a concerted effort been made to do something about solving the problem of mental illness.

TRENDS IN THERAPY *Therapy* is the general name for any method used in treating an illness. Mental illness, as we have seen, may be a psychoneurosis, a personality disorder, a psychosis, or a chronic brain syndrome due to brain damage. Different forms of therapy must be employed to treat these different varieties of mental illness.

Some therapies aim at eradicating the underlying physical disease. Others involve brain surgery, shock induced by electrical means or drugs, or the use of drugs that restore the patient to a more normal

state. Such therapies, naturally, are administered by medical specialists and are therefore classified as *medical therapy.*

Other therapeutic methods are aimed at the emotional and psychological aspects of the patient's problem. They employ interviews, discussions, play acting, and changes in the patient's environment. Since these methods of treatment involve psychological, rather than medical, techniques, and are often in the hands of psychologists, they are called *psychotherapy.*

Medical therapy is much more drastic than psychotherapy and is ordinarily restricted to severe cases of mental illness, particularly to the psychoses. Psychotherapy, on the other hand, is used not only for psychotics and neurotics, but also for persons with less serious personality problems—delinquents and maladjusted children, and people with marital, scholastic, or occupational problems. Thus it is suitable for a wide range of adjustment problems.

At the beginning of this century, attempts to treat mental illness were confined mainly to severe psychotic disorders requiring hospitalization. Therapeutic methods were largely medical. As the understanding of mental illness grew, more reliance came to be put on psychotherapeutic procedures. Psychotherapy was extended first to severe neuroses, then to milder psychoneurotic reactions encountered in people outside hospitals. The psychoanalytic movement, launched by Freud, had a great deal to do with this trend, for psychoanalysis, as one particular kind of therapy, is aimed largely at the milder psychoneurotic disorders.

This trend toward the use of psychotherapy in treating the milder behavior disorders has occurred for several reasons: (1) The severely and chronically ill cost more to treat, and are less likely to benefit from treatment, than less maladjusted individuals. (2) Psychotherapists have been in short supply, and they therefore have bent their efforts where they might do the most good. (3) The treatment of less neurotic individuals offers the greatest benefit to society, for they are still active in social, economic, and political affairs. Any improvement in their adjustment is quickly reflected in their influence on associates and everyday affairs. (4) The successful treatment of mild disorders *prevents* the development of more serious ones.

Of course, if we were to achieve some dramatic breakthrough in treating severe cases of psychoneurosis or psychosis, this whole trend might be reversed. If we do not, the present trend is likely to continue and to expand into widespread counseling and psychotherapy, with the aim of holding down, as much as possible, the incidence of more severe disorders.

Kinds of therapy

A physician treats many different things when he treats physical diseases. If he can diagnose the underlying cause and has the means of combating it, he may treat that. If he knows, for example, that the patient has scarlet fever, which is caused by a particular microorganism, he fights it with the drug most likely to kill the organism. Often he cannot do this, either because of inability to diagnose the cause or for lack of appropriate weapons. Then he may treat the symptoms by doing something to relieve fever, pain, discomfort, or some other disturbing effect of the disease. The same principle is even more true in the treatment of mental illness. When possible, the therapist attempts to treat the underlying causes, but it is often too difficult or too expensive to discover and to treat the underlying complex causes. Hence the therapist often treats or attempts to alleviate the effects of the illness. The therapist should also have a specific, and often limited, goal toward which he is aiming. In other words, he should have a clear objective in mind.

MEDICAL THERAPY Since medical therapy is not the business of the psychologist, it is described here only briefly. Medical therapies for treating mental illness may be grouped into four main classes: psychosurgery, shock therapy, narcosis, and drug therapy.

Psychosurgery. Ancient man sometimes trephined skulls to let out the "evil spirits" in the brains of the mentally ill. Although the technique was crude, the reasoning incorrect, and the results of little value, the general idea had some merit. In the 1930s, a similiar method was adopted for treating certain cases of mental illness. The method was called *psychosurgery* because it consisted of surgery of the brain for the purpose of treating and relieving mental and behavioral symptoms [Freeman and Watts, 1950].

The most common form of psychosurgery involved the *prefrontal lobes* (see page 712). The neurologists who developed the psychosurgical operation on the prefrontal lobes believed that these lobes were somehow more involved in foresight, planning, and anticipation of the future than were other parts of the brain. The prefrontal lobes were also supposed to have something to do with emotional expression because they are anatomically connected with some of the areas of the lower brain which are important in emotion. Thus it was thought that removal of tissue from the frontal lobes, lobectomy, or the severing of the connections between the frontal lobes and the lower areas of the brain, lobotomy, would make the individual less concerned and worried about future events.

It should be noted that the evidence for these supposed functions of the frontal lobes in man is very flimsy. It is little wonder that the claim has been made that psychosurgery of the prefrontal lobes produces a rate of remission of symptoms which is no higher than the spontaneously occurring rate of symptom remission [Mettler, 1949]. In addition to its questionable efficacy and flimsy rationale, the operation is dangerous. These reasons, together with the development of more effective methods of treatment, the use of "tranquilizers," for instance, have accounted for the nearly total disuse into which prefrontal lobe psychosurgery has fallen.

Shock therapy. Shock therapy includes several different kinds of therapy which put the patient for a time into an unconscious state [Jessner and Ryan, 1941]. In most cases, this state is preceded by convulsions, similar to epileptic convulsions. The usefulness of the method was discovered by accident when a mental patient, who was also a diabetic, received an overdose of the antidiabetic substance insulin and subsequently showed remarkable improvement in mental symptoms. Today, no one is quite sure why or how shock treatment works. All that is known is that some patients are improved after a series of shock treatments.

The first form of shock treatment, used in the 1930s, involved relatively large doses of *insulin*. Although insulin treatment often had beneficial results, it was dangerous; at the very least, it was hard on the patient. After that, the convulsive drug *Metrazol* was employed in place of insulin. Metrazol is also dangerous, sometimes producing convulsions so violent that bones are broken. In addition, patients characteristically experience a terrifying emotional upset just prior to the convulsion. A third form of shock therapy is *electroshock*. A brief, carefully regulated jolt of electrical current is passed through the patient's brain. This, like other shock methods, causes a convulsion followed by a period of unconsciousness. Except for feelings of apprehension before the shock, a patient has little unpleasant experience connected with it, and indeed has little memory of the events immediately preceding the shock session. Because of its safety, its simplicity, and its acceptability to patients, electric shock therapy is now the most widely used form of such therapy.

Shock therapy, and particularly electroshock treatment, is most effective with individuals suffering from depression [Noyes, 1948]. It seems to alleviate their guilt feelings, suicidal tendencies, and self-deprecation. Sometimes, after a series of electroshock treatments, the patient seems entirely normal and can be discharged without further treatment. Often, however, shock treatment is combined with psychotherapy. The effects of the shock treatment may be only temporary, but they make the patient lucid and approachable enough for a therapist to make progress with psychotherapeutic techniques.

Narcosis. Narcotic drugs in sufficient dosage put a person to sleep. They differ in several ways: speed of action, length of effect, and degree of effect. Many years ago, before the days of shock therapy, narcosis was used extensively to keep agitated patients under control. It served this purpose, but it was not safe to use repeatedly and over long periods of time. By itself, moreover, it had little or no therapeutic value. Now that tranquilizers are available, narcosis is almost never used merely to calm or control patients.

Narcosis is currently used, however, for *narcoanalysis,* that is, the analysis of the patient's problems while he is under the effects of certain narcotics. A drug often used for this purpose is *Sodium Amytal.* Injected in small doses, it makes the patient groggy for several minutes before he falls into a deep sleep. During the groggy or twilight state, the patient can reenact traumatic experiences and discuss unpleasant subjects with the physician [Orr, 1949]. Thus the medical therapist can uncover deep-seated problems which have been repressed, and the patient can sometimes relieve his tensions. Narcoanalysis has proved particularly valuable in analyzing disorders caused by a traumatic experience, such as a pilot's terrifying experience in combat. It is also a substitute for hypnosis because it is quicker and more dependable. Sodium Amytal has sometimes been called a "truth serum," for it enables a patient to remember things otherwise deeply buried by repression, but it has little or no value in eliciting confessions in criminal cases.

Chemotherapy. Chemotherapy has been so developed that it might be called a biochemical revolution in the treatment of mental illness. There are three main kinds of chemotherapeutic drugs: the so-called *tranquilizers* or ataractic drugs, the psychological *activators,* and the *psychotomimetic* drugs.

Of the many tranquilizing drugs, each of which has different effects [Brodie and Shore, 1957], three of the most widely used are *reserpine, chlorpromazine,* and *meprobamate.* In general, it is thought that the tranquilizers are therapeutic because they act on parts of the brain controlling activity of the autonomic nervous system, thereby tending to reduce felt anxiety and emotionality (see page 253). They keep the anxious person from feeling so tense and miserable and quiet him down. It should be emphasized, however, that by themselves they do not reduce worry or the basic causes of anxiety. They treat the symptom, not the illness.

However, the quieting effect of the tranquilizers is very valuable in some forms of behavior disturbance. With some patients, the quieting effect is sufficient to enable them to be released from the hospital, for it was their agitated behavior that had brought them there in the first place. As a matter of fact, tranquilizers are probably largely responsible for the increased discharge rate from mental hospitals already noted (see Figure 15.3). In other cases, the quieting effect makes it possible for others to deal with the patient, and hence to establish a relationship between therapist and disturbed patient within which psychotherapy is possible (see page 541).

A good many studies have been made of the value of tranquilizers in the treatment and management of patients in hospitals. Many report that tranquilizers permit the hospital staff to do away with various forms of physical restraint otherwise needed with agitated patients. Many studies, although not controlled so well as they might have been, show that tranquilizers are extremely effective in reducing the violence of symptoms and in making patients more amenable to psychotherapy. The following excerpt from the report of a rather carefully controlled study illustrates the benefits to be expected from tranquilizers:

The double-blind technique [see page 17] was used in short-term studies of the effects of reserpine and chlorpromazine in groups of 24 to 42 patients. Studies were made of the action of reserpine in normal individuals, in patients hospitalized with anxiety, and in patients with chronic schizophrenic reactions. . . .

These drugs were found to have distinct value in the treatment of psychiatric patients. Patients hospitalized with anxiety reactions and mild schizophrenic reactions responded well to reserpine and a combination of reserpine and chlorpromazine. There was no advantage noted from the combined use of these drugs. It was felt that use of these drugs in adequate doses possibly shortened the period of hospitalization of this group of patients. A . . . schedule of reserpine produced improvement in two-thirds of treated patients with chronic schizophrenic reactions. A comparable dosage schedule of chlorpromazine to that of reserpine produced benefit in one-half of the treated patients with chronic schizophrenic reactions. Both drugs produced marked improvement in one-fourth of these patients. This improvement far surpassed that accomplished by previous forms of treatment in these patients.

Experience with these drugs thus far would indicate that they represent a significant advance in psychiatric medicine. Even the most hardened skeptic must admit that sometimes they achieve favorable results in patients who have not responded previously to other treatment. However, on the basis of double-blind studies, the enthusiast must revise downward his judgment concerning the frequency and the degree of beneficial results obtained. There remain many unanswered clinical questions concerning the proper selection of patients, the best dose for individual patients, and the optimal duration of treatment.

Use of these drugs promises to make more patients than ever before amenable to effective psychiatric rehabilitation. The trend toward making mental hospitals therapeutic, rather than custodial, institutions is bound to be accelerated by these agents. [Hollister et al., 1956, pages 72–74.]

The activators are, in a behavioral sense, the opposite of the tranquilizers; they can activate patients who are extremely depressed. The drug *iproniazid* is one activator; in a somewhat indirect way, it is supposed to act to facilitate the transmission of nervous activity in parts of the brain. The major difficulty is that these drugs have very strong and dangerous effects on the body in addition to their therapeutic effect. The so-called "side effects" of iproniazid, for instance, are so strong that it has been superseded by other less dangerous drugs.

The psychotomimetic drugs induce some of the symptoms of psychotic behavior and may therefore help a therapist study his patient's problems. The psychotomimetic drug that has received the most attention is *lysergic acid diethylamide,* more commonly known as LSD-25 or, more briefly, LSD [Ruben, 1957]. Its effects on human beings are described by some as a drug-produced psychosis, but this is probably an overstatement. In any case, the drug does sometimes seem to produce some of the symptoms of schizophrenia.

Descriptions given by those who have taken LSD, or by those who have observed the behavior of others who have taken it, include the following observations: heightened anxiety, feelings of euphoria, changes in mood, silliness and giggling, flights of ideas and fantasy, visual illusions and hallucinations, inability to concentrate, feelings of depersonalization and detachment, and distortion of the sense of time. The particular effects observed vary, of course, with the dosage, but they also vary with the individual, with lighting in the room—more hallucinations are observed in the dark—and even with the personality of the experimenter or the people around the person under the influence of the drug (see page 258). When he is alone, the effects are different from those when he is with other people.

When LSD is given to patients already suffering a psychosis, it is said to increase their psychotic symptoms and often to produce additional bizarre symptoms. Some psychiatrists have been trying it out as an aid in psychotherapy. They report that by making the patient somewhat more anxious and prone to fantasy, LSD helps the individual to talk more freely and to verbalize what otherwise would be repressed. It remains to be seen, though, whether or not the drug will be of value in therapy.

Generally speaking, then, the chemotherapeutic drugs are used either to control the mood of patients or to help the therapist analyze patients' problems and conduct psychotherapy. The effective life of a drug in the body, however, is rather short, and ultimately the lasting value of chemotherapy hinges on the success of the psychotherapy it makes possible.

PSYCHOTHERAPY Psychotherapy can be a simple or a very complex process, depending upon the nature of the individual's problem, how severe it is, the type of therapy, and the goals of the treatment.

The aims and overall strategy of psychotherapy must be decided on jointly by the patient and therapist early in the treatment; they may, however, change during the course of therapy. The therapist uses several sources of information to form his opinion of what may be accomplished in therapy. One source is the *life history* of the person as it is given by the person himself and by his friends and relatives. Another is a *physical* examination. A third consists of *psychological* examinations of the person, including tests of intelligence, personality, and vocational abilities. Finally, the therapist draws upon the picture he forms of the person's problems in the course of the first few interviews.

The patient's problem may be considered to stem from (1) environmental frustrations, (2) personal frustrations, (3) motivational conflicts, or (4) faulty learning. Usually all of the four elements are present, but the psychotherapist must decide on the particular aims of treatment. If environmental frustrations are to be the focus of treatment, then changing the situation of the patient will be a psychotherapeutic aim. If personal frustrations loom largest, then providing support temporarily will be the primary aim. If motivational conflict is at the heart of the problem, as very often it is, then the principal aim will be to help the patient achieve insight and self-understanding. If faulty learning is the problem, extinction and relearning techniques may be tried. Let us consider briefly each of these kinds of therapy.

Changing the situation. This is the simplest goal of treatment. It does not involve an attempt to bring about any major change in the patient; rather, an attempt is made to manipulate his situation in such a way as to relieve the stress on him. A patient may be advised to take a vacation, change his occupation, change his educational goals, and so on. Although this may be the only treatment possible in some instances, it is not likely to be satisfactory for most persons. Major changes in the environment are frequently difficult or impossible, and they sometimes make matters even worse for the patient. When the major difficulty is motivational conflict within the person, manipulating the environment is apt to bring only minor relief—the patient carries the problem with him.

Situational changes, of course, can be important, but they are usually secondary to the treatment of the individual. For children, situational changes are frequently necessary. In simple adjustment problems of adults, too, such changes may provide security for the patient. However, for the great majority of persons who come for treatment, a good deal more is necessary. To begin by changing the situation may completely block progress toward other goals of therapy.

Providing support. When treatment is arranged to give support to the patient but not to bring about permanent personality changes, it is called *supportive therapy.* The aim here is to help the individual through a crisis. Much of what is called *counseling* is supportive psychotherapy [Bordin, 1955]. It helps relatively normal people face specific problems of adjustment. The counselor gives information, listens to the person's problems, suggests courses of action, and reassures him about what he has done or proposes to do. In this way, the counselor may support the person sufficiently to enable him to make a satisfactory adjustment.

Giving support and reassurance, however, requires an expertness that is not easily acquired. The counselor must do it subtly or he will increase rather than decrease the person's anxiety. It is usually wise to use supportive therapy only in certain special cases. One type is the chronic case in which illness is of such long standing, the resources for health so poor, and the environmental blocks so great that the chances of effecting a permanent change in the person are small. In such cases, supportive therapy may strengthen the person's ability to deal with some of his problems. Another type of case is that in which the person has been well adjusted most of his life, but temporarily develops a neurotic disturbance in a crisis. Here, supportive therapy may help reestablish healthy modes of adjustment (see Figure 15.7).

Achieving insight. For deep-seated motivational conflicts, insight or uncovering therapy may be appropriate. Its aim is to uncover the causes of a person's difficulty, to rid the patient of his neurotic defenses, and thereby to free him for flexible adaptive behavior. Insight is not obtained through simple intellectual discovery. Rather, it is a long and painstaking procedure in which the patient exposes himself to various emotional attitudes and situations

[Alexander and French, 1946]. He must bring to the fore the emotional situations he has been unable to face, those which he has repressed and around which he has developed his neurotic defenses.

Learning and extinction. One way of looking at some deviant behaviors is to consider them as bad habits which are the result of unfortunate learning experiences. The therapist with this point of view will use explicit techniques to promote unlearning, or extinction, of the bad habits; or the techniques may aim at replacing deviant habits by learning new adjustments. Most psychotherapy is not directly learning-oriented in this way, but learning is an implicit feature of most all psychotherapeutic techniques.

In actual practice, almost all psychotherapy includes some support, some insight, some unlearning and relearning, and eventually even some situational change. However, when the primary effort is to develop insight and to gain continuous emotional growth, the therapy is called *insight therapy.* When the effort to support the self system is greater than the effort to obtain insight, the treatment is called *supportive,* and when the therapy centers around learning and extinction it is called *behavior therapy.*

Techniques in psychotherapy

Now let us turn to the variety of specific techniques that psychotherapists use. Some are rather specialized and are used only occasionally when the situation seems to demand them. One technique may be used more frequently by some therapists than by others because of differences of opinion about its relative effectiveness. Many of the techniques are difficult to distinguish clearly from one another, and in these cases the differences are those of emphasis rather than method.

DIRECTIVE THERAPIES In the early days of psychotherapy, techniques were primarily *directive.* The therapist was an authoritative prescriber. As the medical practitioner prescribed medicine for physical ailments, so the psychotherapist tended to follow the same practice of prescribing for the alleviation of mental suffering. Since the patient developed his difficulties in a particular environment, the therapist was likely to prescribe a change of environment. He often considered the patient unable to plan his own life and took charge of such planning. He prescribed exercise, rest, a hobby, or certain social activities. In many cases, the therapist tried to direct the patient's thinking and emotional life. Thus, in this kind of treatment, the therapist was dominant and the patient depended upon his reactions.

Reeducation. Much early directive therapy was called reeducation. Austin Riggs [1929], a leader in reeducation therapy, usually prescribed temporary environmental changes for his psychoneurotic patients. He believed the patient should be removed from his home, social, and vocational environments because he had developed his neurotic disturbance within them. Then, in another, neutral environment, the patient went to school, so to speak, to learn the principles of satisfactory life adjustment, and lived on a regimented schedule of activities designed to help him develop habits of social cooperation.

Such strictly organized reeducation of the type sponsored by Riggs is seldom recommended today, but reeducation of a less directive type is frequently used. In fact, it is involved in practically all techniques and consists of developing new insights and habits of thought.

Suggestion and hypnosis. Suggestion is a process in which one person gets another to accept an idea or attitude without citing proof or using coercion. It enters into almost all situations in which one person attempts to influence another (see Chapters 16 and 17), but people are most responsive to suggestions from authority and prestige figures. Thus the therapist is in a good position to use suggestion. He may suggest that the patient has made enough progress in psychotherapy to be relieved of his nervous headaches, his nervous indigestion, or his fear of examinations, and the suggestion may prove effective. In extreme conversion reactions, such as hysterical blindness or paralysis, the patient may undergo surgery, take bad-tasting medicines,

FIGURE 15.7. *The psychotherapeutic situation. The patient talks with the psychotherapist, and together they work to understand certain facts leading up to the illness and to develop ways of working out the underlying problems. (Lee Lockwood, from Black Starr.)*

or suffer other discomfort to alleviate his symptoms. In such cases, the medical treatment, though of no value in itself, may have the effect of suggesting the removal of the symptom.

People are extremely suggestible when they are in a hypnotic state. For that reason early psychotherapists used hypnosis as a therapeutic technique.

They would hypnotize the patient and then give him *posthypnotic suggestions*—suggestions which would be effective after he awakened from the hypnotic sleep. A person suffering from hysterical paralysis of the right arm, for example, might be told under hypnosis, "When you wake up, you will be able to use your right arm. It will be completely normal again." Such suggestions as this would often work; the individual would not be paralyzed when he awoke.

One drawback of hypnosis as an aid in therapy is that many patients are difficult to hypnotize. A more important shortcoming of both suggestion and hypnosis is that the symptom, but not the cause, is removed. Neither insight nor an alleviation of the anxiety underlying the patient's symptom is usually produced. Hence his basic problem is not solved. Consequently, when symptoms are removed through suggestion, they usually appear again in somewhat different forms. If neurotic headaches, for example, are relieved through suggestion, the person is liable to develop some other symptom, such as indigestion or backaches. For this reason, suggestion techniques are useful only in certain situations where it is important to give the patient temporary relief. If a pregnant woman has an intense fear of childbirth, for example, it may be possible through suggestion to get her through the experience without any serious disturbance.

Hypnosis has some diagnostic value in psychotherapy quite apart from the use of suggestion [Dorcus, 1956]. A person in a hypnotic state can often remember events that he has repressed and cannot recall in the normal state. The therapist may, indeed, be able to get the patient, under hypnosis, to relive terrifying experiences of the past that are now causing the patient trouble. In this way, the therapist obtains necessary information to use in other phases of the treatment. Through posthypnotic suggestion, he may also be able to have the memories that have been revived under hypnosis carry over into the normal state. Thus hypnosis is a valuable technique in therapy, even though it usually does not itself effect any basic cure. The following case illustrates the use of hyp-

nosis in the recovery of repressed memories. It is also a somewhat unusual case because of the insight which developed after recall. Note that further therapy was able to build on the insight developed under hypnosis.

A neurotic patient, Betty R., age forty-two, visited a psychiatrist with the complaint that she had to clear her throat every few minutes. She had had this compulsive symptom for many years. Besides being an annoyance and an embarrassment, it had kept her, she said, from becoming a successful singer. As a consequence, she was forced into employment in office work, which she hated.

Under hypnosis, she was able to trace the symptom back about twenty years. She was regressed to a time at about twenty-two years of age when she had had no throat trouble, then instructed to recount any emotional experiences she could recall. She remembered attending a picnic with her fiancé, whom she was soon to marry. The two had gone canoeing on a lake, the canoe had tipped over, and she, being unable to swim, had almost drowned. She was saved when her fiancé pulled her to the canoe, which she held onto until other help arrived. He, however, was a poor swimmer and, exhausted by his efforts, himself drowned.

Reliving this experience under hypnosis, the patient began choking as though she were swallowing water. After that, she started crying and said, "I love him so, I can't stand losing him, I just can't swallow it; it sticks in my throat." Then it dawned on her, "Why, that's the reason I clear my throat!" Whereupon the therapist ended the trance.

The insight achieved through hypnosis in this case greatly aided subsequent therapy. In time the symptom disappeared, and the patient's adjustment greatly improved. [Based on Lecron and Bordeaux, 1947, pages 211–212.]

CLIENT-CENTERED THERAPY   The directive techniques just described involve explanation, direction, and control of the patient's life, and they are very useful in certain situations. Psychotherapists, however, have come gradually to realize that many patients cannot make fundamental changes in their adjustments merely by being told to do so or by having their environments changed. Rather, for psychotherapy to be of deep and lasting benefit, the patient must learn how he can solve his own problems.

Some modern therapies have therefore tended to become more *nondirective*. They establish a more permissive situation in which the patient is given freedom to express his attitudes. The most nondirective of current techniques is known as *client-centered therapy*. This is designed not to solve any particular problem of the patient but to provide an opportunity for him to develop his own improved methods of adjustment. The following statement expresses this attitude:

It has seemed clear . . . that when the counselor perceives and accepts the client as he is, when he lays aside all evaluation and enters into the perceptional frame of reference of the client, he frees the client to explore his life and experience anew, frees him to perceive in that experience new meanings and new goals. But is the therapist willing to give the client full freedom as to outcomes? Is he genuinely willing for the client to organize and direct his life? Is he willing for him to choose goals that are social or antisocial, moral or immoral? If not, it seems doubtful that therapy will be a profound experience for the client. . . . To me it appears that only as the therapist is completely willing that *any* outcome, *any* direction, may be chosen—only then does he realize the vital strength of the capacity and potentiality of the individual for constructive action. [Rogers, 1951, pages 48–49.]

In general, client-centered therapy may be described as a therapy in which (1) the individual, not the problem, is the focus; (2) feelings rather than intellect are attended to; (3) the present gets greater attention than the past; and (4) emotional growth takes place in the therapeutic relationship.

The method begins with some explanation of the roles of the counselor and the client and the indication that they will work out the difficulties together. The therapist takes pains to establish a relationship that is warm and permissive, that is, without pressure to follow any prescribed course and without criticism or judgment of what the patient says. The counselor's main aim is to help the person express his feelings freely. In this process, the client gains the ability to accept his feelings without fear and gradually finds it possible to express feelings that were formerly repressed. He then begins to see new relationships among his emotional attitudes and to react positively to situations to which he formerly responded negatively.

The following interchange between patient and therapist illustrates the emphasis upon emotional attitudes which distinguishes nondirective therapy. The patient is a young man who complained of recurring periods of tension and depression at a time when his imminent induction into the Army threatened his close relationship with his mother.

P. I went home, you know. I think I have, well, a better way of getting along with Mom. I mean, take the V-12 tests, for example. She seems to understand better or something. I mean, she said I could even enlist in the Air Corps if I wanted to, and she used to just cringe when I mentioned it.

T. So it seems as if you have a new understanding with her.

P. Well, I think we've reached a pretty good understanding now. It was funny . . . once around her, I got the same old feeling back I used to have when I was younger. For the past year or so, I just haven't been feeling anything, and now I got the same old feeling of love. I didn't think I could. I thought I was just cynical and hardened or something. With a different attitude you find things easier to take. (Pause) I don't know. (Long pause)

T. Feeling petty tense about it, aren't you?

P. Yes. Is it that obvious?

T. I am aware of it, though I guess you'd rather I weren't.

P. Well . . . of course, maybe it was just because I spent such a short time at home, and Mom thought well, I was going away pretty soon, so she was more willing to hear my side. I don't know, really. I feel I am getting back to the understanding I had as a very small person.

T. Things feel more like they used to.

P. It's just a more pleasant relationship, that's all. Take an example like this. Mom used to scream if she saw me with a cigarette—tell me I couldn't smoke, and give me all sorts of reasons and everything. And this time when I was home she offered me one! I was simply bowled over. I just couldn't understand why. (Pause) I decided maybe she just realized I was growing up or something. Oh, she let me do little things. When I was fifteen, I worked one summer at a stock exchange. She let me do that all right, she let me go, but she didn't direct me to do it. There's never been any encouragement or guidance in getting out on my own—I just went. She let me go with a tear in her eye, you know.

T. When you wanted to do things yourself, get out on your own, there was always a tear. . . .

P. Boy, that's sure the truth! I never thought about that before, but it's sure the truth. You know, a kid doesn't realize how much effect his childhood has on him, does he? You think, well, I don't have those conflicts, I didn't have a tough adolescence, you think you're apart from all that, above it, somehow. . . . (Pause) So many of the other fellows act more, well, more cold toward their folks, I think I'll always need some sort of ties, somebody to come home to that I love. [Cameron and Margaret, 1951, pages 564–565.]

Client-centered therapy has been effective in counseling college students and in treating normal people with problems of adjustment, such as marital and vocational problems, and with mild psychoneuroses. It has not been so successful with dependent people and those with extreme emotional difficulties.

PSYCHOANALYSIS   Psychoanalysis is a system of therapy that is somewhat nondirective, but not so much as is client-centered counseling. Its main objective is to help the patient achieve a deep understanding of his own mechanisms of adjustment and thereby to help him solve his own basic problems. It is designed primarily for the treatment of psychoneuroses, but has been used with a great variety of disorders [Alexander and French, 1946]. Although there are shorter varieties of psychoanalysis, it is usually a long, time-consuming therapy that requires at least an hour per week for many months or years. Therefore, it is usually worthwhile only for patients with extreme, deep-seated problems who can afford the time and expense of long treatment.

The term *psychoanalyst*, you will recall, refers to, and should be reserved for, a psychotherapist who follows certain teachings of Sigmund Freud. The theory properly called *psychoanalysis* includes certain fairly specific ideas about personality and related techniques of therapy. In Chapter 13 we discussed psychoanalysis as a theory of personality which emphasizes structure, development, and dynamics. As for techniques of therapy, psychoanalysis emphasizes the analysis of free associations, resistances, dreams, and the transference situation as it develops.

The basic aim of psychoanalytic therapy is to make the patient aware of the sources of his anxiety. According to psychoanalytic theory, the source of anxiety is basically due to the presence in us all of certain threatening sexual or aggressive id urges, wishes, or motives—call them what you will. These taboo sexual and destructive urges and wishes to destroy are, according to the theory, in conflict with the ego and superego systems of personality. Therefore they cannot be expressed directly; the fear of expected punishment is too great, and the urges and the conflicts are repressed (see page 492). After repression, the id urges are unconscious—we cannot think about them or verbalize them—but they are still there in conflict with the ego and superego and dynamically driving for expression. The fear of expression is still threatening, but after repression the person no longer knows why he feels this fear because the motive and the conflict are unconscious. This fear of "I know not what" is called anxiety, and various normal defense mechanisms and abnormal defense mechanisms, that is, some neurotic symptoms, develop to reduce anxiety (see pages 475 and 503).

The hope of psychoanalytic therapy is that anxiety and the need for exaggerated defense mechanisms may be reduced by self-understanding and knowledge of the sources of anxiety; by making it possible for a neurotic to gain insight into the repressed urges responsible for his anxiety, he may be able to face his conflicts and solve them more rationally. In other words, the attempt is to take someone who is "stupid," because of repression, about the origins of his anxiety and defensive symptoms, and "wise him up" [Dollard and Miller, 1950]. This takes time. The analysis of the motives themselves is time consuming, and the patient usually resists any direct interpretation of his symptoms—that would be too threatening. Rather, the patient must be led gradually to believe in the explanations of his anxiety, symptoms, and behavior as they unfold through his own insights in the course of therapy. This goal is accomplished through the psychoanalytic techniques of therapy.

Free association. Psychoanalysis begins with the therapist's explanation of the general procedure, aims, and purposes of the therapy. The patient is told that he should not expect recovery in a specific period of time, that his behavior and attitudes may depend upon emotional factors of which he is unaware, and that these must be traced back to their unconscious motivations, chiefly through *free association*. He is required to say whatever he thinks of regardless of how irrelevant or objectionable it may be. Since letting thought be free is quite different from ordinary thinking, patients frequently take some time to learn how to free-associate. The following is an example of free association taken verbatim from an interview:

The same thing applies to the fact that they told me some time ago about loss of sleep in the beginning of the night or the last part of the night and I insisted the first was . . . I noticed for two or three nights I began waking up at 2:30 and laying awake most of the night . . . of semi-conscious . . . two—three nights . . . is that done because I'm a creature of habit on account of the suggestion of my mind . . . or am I with a nervous disease. (Pause) Thought about nearly everything . . . in general—can't recall it—nothing relating to sex . . . tried to put it out of my mind and I fight to keep it out. Got the habit of thinking about things and would dream about them . . . tried to keep things out of my mind . . . like fighting on account of the past. My mind traced right on through these lights to the fifth floor and a blond woman . . . shows my mind runs on to sex and injury . . . things like how to avoid going up in high buildings . . . afraid of how high I'd go. Didn't want to tell anybody what my trouble was. Saw it was only a four- or five-story building so I

consented. It didn't bother me . . . didn't seem a real test because it wasn't high. Still no confidence in myself . . . still in the dark as to my conflicts . . . two things, one "yes" and one "no." Decided I'd adopt the good because the bad was lashing me. [Cameron and Magaret, 1951, page 511.]

Resistance. During free association, the patient often shows resistance, that is, the inability to remember important events in his past or to talk about certain anxiety-charged subjects. A great part of the analyst's task is to deal with these resistances. By continuous free association, however, the patient goes beyond his unknown resistances and overcomes them. The situation cannot be forced, but the analyst may provide some interpretations. These interpretations are considered tentative and are revised as the free associations continue. The interpretations are not offered to provide solutions but rather to clear the path of the associations and to provide for the possibility of free flow for further understanding. In this respect, psychoanalysis is sometimes quite directive.

Dreams. At any time, the patient may report dreams for analysis and interpretation. *Dream analysis* is considered important because dreams may provide a short road to the unconscious. The theory holds that the unconscious id motives and conflicts are expressed in disguised and symbolic form in the *manifest content* of the dream—that is, the material of the dream itself. In other words, the manifest content is supposed to be symbolic of unconscious motives and conflicts which are known as the *latent content*. Such motives and conflicts are too threatening to be expressed directly in the dream. Thus dreams are to be interpreted, according to psychoanalytic theory, as disguised urge or wish fulfillments. In certain dreams, that is, nightmares, extreme anxiety may be generated because the disguise has worn a little thin. From the analysis of certain dreams, the psychoanalyst can sometimes come to understand the particular urges which have been repressed in his patient.

Of course, the interpretation of dreams as disguised fulfillments of sexual and aggressive urges is not the only way of analyzing them. For example, another somewhat different method is the analysis of a series of dreams from the same patient [Hall, 1953]. The interpretation of a single dream may often be questionable, but the discovery of themes which run through sequences of dreams is sometimes a more valid approach. These dream themes usually concern problems which are significant for the individual, and they are not necessarily conflicts over sexual or aggressive urges. The symbols in dreams, according to this theory, are to be understood as attempts at clear and economical representation of what the referent *means* to a person. For instance, a person who views motherhood as a life-giving and nurturant process may dream about a cow to symbolize this idea of motherhood. It is often only after many dreams have been analyzed that the person's ideas about a referent, and his symbols for it, can be understood.

The interpretation of dreams in terms of wish-fulfillments or important problems is a difficult art at best, and it is complicated by several facts about dreams. One problem is secondary elaboration of the dream. For instance, certain parts of the dream may not have been clear, and certain parts may have been forgotten—repression may be active enough to wipe out even disguised urge expressions. The reported dream, then, is not the dream which was actually experienced by the person—it is a construction.

Furthermore, several dreams may be compounded into one when we report them upon awakening in the morning. Research on dreams has shown that we often dream as many as five or six times during a single night. It has been found by measurement of the electrical activity of the brain that sleep is cyclical, varying from light to deep and from deep to light several times during the night (see Figure 15.8). After we fall asleep, the level of sleep becomes deeper, and then lighter, until a special stage, the so-called stage of "paradoxical sleep," begins and lasts for several minutes. During this stage, rapid eye movements (REMs) occur, and it is while these rapid eye movements are taking place that dreams

actually occur [Kleitman, 1960]. This can be determined by waking the individual immediately after the stage of paradoxical sleep and asking him to report on his dreams. Almost all the post-REM awakenings result in reports of dreaming; very few of the control awakenings during other stages of sleep result in such reports. After the first stage of paradoxical sleep, the subject is again in a light stage of sleep, and this gradually deepens and then lightens until a second paradoxical stage occurs. This process is repeated five or six times during the night, and the stages of paradoxical sleep gradually lengthen as the night goes on (see Figure 15.8). Note that all the dream periods are long; dreaming is thought which goes on in "real time"; a dream is not an ephemeral thing that is over in a flash.

Transference. Another important phenomenon in psychoanalytic therapy is the transference that gradually develops as the analysis proceeds. Transference involves the transfer of attitudes from one person to another; more specifically, it is a reenactment of previous relationships with people, and principally of the parent-child relationship. It really amounts to a generalization to the therapist of attitudes acquired toward other people (see page 85). It appears when the patient and therapist have established good rapport. The therapist may, for example, become a *father figure* and be regarded emotionally by the patient much as he regarded his father. When the emotions directed toward the therapist are those of affection and dependence, the transference is called *positive*. A hostile attitude may be dominant, however, and this is referred to as *negative* transference.

Transference is significant in two ways. First, if it is positive, it can help the patient overcome his resistances. It gives him a feeling of protection so that he has the courage to uncover repressed thoughts. Second, it helps the analyst understand the patient's problem. The transference substitutes a conflict between the patient and the analyst for the conflict that has gone on within the patient. Thus the analyst gets a better look at the problem.

He analyzes the transference and explains its nature to the patient. The following case illustrates some aspects of the transference relationship:

At one stage in therapy, the patient in this case began to make excessive demands of the therapist, requesting special examinations, medications, extra appointments, and similar types of preferment. When attempts were made to discuss this pattern of behavior, the patient immediately accused the therapist of having no interest in him, of being rejecting, and of not really trying to understand him. In this instance the patient was exhibiting patterns of behavior which he had manifested previously in other life situations. He was relating to the therapist as he had related previously to significant persons in his past life, and was perceiving the therapist as he had perceived other figures in the past who could not comply with his insatiable demands. Part of the therapeutic task was to help the patient understand this behavior and the motivations back of it. [Garfield, 1957, page 258.]

The approach of the termination of the analysis is indicated when the patient gives evidence of insight into the sources of his anxieties. The analysis cannot, however, be terminated until the transference situation has been resolved. This transference must be broken and a normal doctor-patient relationship reestablished, sometimes a very difficult thing to do.

BEHAVIOR THERAPIES   Principles of both classical conditioning and instrumental learning, or operant conditioning, are used in certain therapeutic procedures (see Chapter 3). The rationale behind these techniques is that the symptoms of the behavior disorders were learned in the first place and, with proper training techniques, they can be unlearned, that is, extinguished. Such extinction may involve either the weakening of responses or the learning of new responses that are incompatible with the ones being extinguished. The therapists who use these learning techniques do not believe that the ideas about underlying dynamic mechanisms, for instance, the various psychoanalytic mechanisms, are useful in treatment of behavior

WE DREAM MANY DREAMS IN A NIGHT

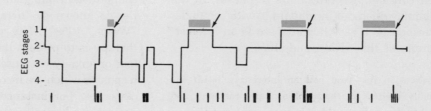

FIGURE 15.8 *The nightly cycle of sleep and dreams. The depth of sleep is shown by the EEG stages on the left—4 indicates deep sleep. Following periods of deep sleep, dream and rapid eye movements (REMs) occur. The length of the dream—REM periods—is indicated by the solid color bars. The lines under the record indicate bodily movement. Arrows show the end of the REM periods. (After Dement and Kleitman, 1957.)*

disorders. Instead, the learning therapists are content to concentrate on the disordered behavior itself in the attempt to alter it [Bandura, 1965]. After all, the argument runs, it is the behavior itself, not some unconscious mechanism, which has gotten the person into the difficulty from which he now seeks relief. Changing the behavior results in improved adjustment so that a person is better able to derive satisfaction from his environment. For instance, a phobic person is uncomfortable in many situations, and his life tends to be dominated by the active avoidance of situations which provoke the phobia; remove the phobic responses and the individual will lead a more satisfying life. Or consider a person whose sexual behavior is deviant, a fetishist, for instance (see page 514). The behavior which centers around the fetish object will get him into trouble with his friends and, perhaps, the police; remove the behavior and the individual has fewer difficulties. Thus behavior therapy is a direct attack on deviant behavior with the aim of eliminating or altering it.

Classical conditioning techniques. One of the major classical conditioning techniques in behavior therapy is *counterconditioning.* The idea here is that disordered behavior is conditioned to a particular set of stimuli or a stimulus situation. Therapy then consists of conditioning responses, to the same stimuli, which are incompatible with the undesirable responses. The following case is an interesting example of this [Raymond, 1956]:

The patient in this case had an interesting fetish—he was sexually excited by the sight of baby carriages and women's handbags. He could only have satisfactory sexual intercourse with his wife when imagining handbags. His fetish was quite a problem because he often attacked baby carriages. Since, in general, other methods of therapy are not successful with this type of disorder, counterconditioning behavior therapy was carried out. Handbags, baby carriages, and a movie which showed baby carriages being pushed were used as the conditioned stimuli. At the same time that the patient was shown these stimuli, he was made nauseous by the injection of a drug; the aim was to condition sight of the sexually exciting objects to nausea. The treatment was successful in removing the fetish: After some days of this treatment, the patient, referring to the handbags and baby carriages, said over and over, "Take them away." A follow-up 19 months later showed that the patient had continued to be free of his fetish.

In this case, nausea was conditioned to the stimuli which triggered the sexually deviant responses. Thus, the sexual response became aversive; generally, this type of counterconditioning therapy is called *aversion therapy.* Similar types of aversion therapy are sometimes used in cases of alcohol addiction as a first step in treatment. The idea is to arrange it so that the alcohol becomes aversive.

Other counterconditioning techniques aim at *desensitization,* that is, making the patient feel comfortable in situations in which he has previously been highly anxious or fearful. For many patients certain situations have been associated with pain, shame, or insecurity, and these situations cannot be approached without fear or anxiety. The counterconditioning therapy in these instances is to have the patient, under special "safe" conditions, face the anxiety- or fear-arousing situations and thus have an opportunity for other responses to be conditioned to the situations.

A special variety of behavior therapy through counterconditioning to desensitize fears and anxieties is known as therapy by *reciprocal inhibition* [Wolpe, 1958]. The main idea in this type of therapy is to present the conditioned stimuli for the fear or anxiety responses when the patient is making responses which are incompatible with fear or anxiety responses. For instance, thorough relaxation of the patient is typically used as an incompatible response. When the patient is relaxed, stimuli which might be expected to produce fear or anxiety are presented in a graded series, that is, those which are likely to arouse little fear or anxiety are presented first and more powerful stimuli are presented only after the patient is desensitized to the weaker stimuli. In other words, the therapist works along the generalization gradient from stimuli which produce weak conditioned responses to stimuli which are close to the conditioned stimulus and which produce strong responses (see page 85). Eventually, even the strongest responses are desensitized through inhibition by incompatible responses. The following case is a very good example of therapy by reciprocal inhibition [Clark, 1963]:

A thirty-one-year-old woman suffered from a phobia of birds and feathers. "She was unable to go for walks out of doors, in parks or go to zoos with her two-year-old boy or to the seaside on holiday with her husband because of the possibility of having birds come near her or, worse still, swoop over her." The reciprocal inhibition therapy consisted of inducing her to relax through suggestion and mild hypnosis. Records of the galvanic skin response (GSR) were also taken as an index of emotional reactivity (see page 255). With the patient relaxed, and the GSR showing responses indicative of this relaxation, the patient was presented with a stimulus far out on the generalization gradient for her fear—a single feather presented 12 feet away. The therapist had a good idea of the relative potencies of stimuli in eliciting the fear because the patient had ranked them before the therapy had begun. Next, the feather was moved closer and closer and the GSR reaction watched for any signs of emotional upset. If such occurred, the feather was immediately moved back. After the patient showed no signs to the single feather when it was only a foot away, the next item in the stimulus hierarchy was presented. The next items, in order from weak to strong, consisted of assorted feathers, bags of feathers, a bundle of feathers, stuffed birds, and finally, live birds. In addition to this therapy at the hospital, the patient, after some desensitization had already taken place, was instructed to visit places where birds or feathers were likely to be found. While in these places, she was instructed to try to remain calm, but to retreat immediately if any fear was felt. By the time the therapy was completed, she "could have handfuls of feathers flung at her, could plunge her hands into a bag of down and no longer feared going out of doors or birds in the garden and hedgerows."

Here, then, is a case in which a specific bit of behavior was altered. It seems to be true that this type of therapy is most successful when the deviant behavior is fear or anxiety which is limited to rather specific situations.

Instrumental learning, operant conditioning, techniques. We know that behavior can be modified, or shaped, through the appropriate use of reinforcers; in discussing this, we have already used an example of behavior therapy (see page 91). Even in cases of psychosis or mental retardation, a therapist with limited goals can accomplish much through reinforcement techniques [Birnbrauer et al., 1965]. The following example makes clear the way in which behavioral changes may be accomplished by instrumental learning, or operant conditioning, techniques [Ayllon, 1963]:

The patient in this case was a woman, diagnosed as a schizophrenic, who had been in the hospital for nine years. Several of her deviant behaviors were selected for treatment by operant techniques. These included overeating and stealing food, hoarding towels, and wearing up to 25 pounds of clothing in the form of extra layers of garments and a peculiar head-dress. All these behaviors were removed by appropriate use of principles of operant conditioning; let us consider the elimination of excessive clothing as an example. The crucial thing is that the therapist had complete control over the patient's environment. For example, he could regulate when and if she were reinforced. In this case, eating was made contingent upon the amount of clothing worn. This was done as follows: The patient was weighed before each meal with all her clothes on, and her actual body weight was subtracted from her clothed weight. In this way, the weight of her clothing could be determined. Whether or not the patient was allowed to eat depended upon the weight of extra clothing she wore. At first, the level was set at 23 pounds or less of clothing— a reduction of 2 pounds over her usual clothing weight. If she had more than this on, she did not eat; of course, she went hungry for a few meals, but this standard was eventually met. Then the limit was set lower and lower until the clothing weight stabilized, after several weeks of this treatment, at 3 pounds. In addition to taking off the excess clothing, the patient began to arrange her clothes more normally and the head-dress was removed. One of the outcomes of this behavioral change, and the removal of the other habits too, was that the patient's family, for the first time in 9 years, asked to have the patient visit home.

Although this type of treatment does not "cure" the disorder, it does ameliorate troublesome symptoms. It is a direct attack on the symptoms, and little if any concern is given to speculations concerning deeper needs met by the disordered symptoms. Therapy with such a limited goal may sometimes be more successful than other types of therapy with certain seemingly intractable psychotic cases. Another difficult behavior to treat is the destructive and disturbing behavior of the antisocial personality. Operant conditioning procedures can successfully modify this behavior in the direction of greater social acceptability [Burchard and Tyler, 1965].

EFFECTIVENESS OF TRADITIONAL PSYCHOTHERAPEUTIC TECHNIQUES It might seem at first glance that this would be an easy problem to investigate. All we need do, it might seem, is go to the records of psychotherapists and find the number of patients treated and compare this with the number of "cures." However, a myriad of problems complicate this simple-sounding program. First is the problem of records; many, if not most, psychotherapists do not keep the kinds of records which lend themselves to scientific evaluation. Second, and far more troublesome, is the criterion problem and its subproblems. For instance, can we decide what constitutes a "cure"? By what standards are the patients to be evaluated? Third is the so-called base-rate problem. What is the number of patients who get better spontaneously? In other words, we need to be able to estimate the rate of spontaneous recovery in order to have a basis for comparison of the effects of psychotherapy. A fourth problem is that of selection. Psychotherapists, especially those in private practice, select the patients with whom they expect to be most successful. Are the figures which we obtain on the rates of "recovery" inflated because of this selection of the most favorable cases? What can be said about all cases if we are looking only at the results with the most favorable cases? After all these questions, perhaps it is easy to see that the problem of the effectiveness of psychotherapeutic techniques is likely to remain just that—a problem. Some brave investigators have done some more or less adequate studies, however.

In one evaluation of many of these "outcome" studies, the effectiveness of psychotherapy was found to be quite low [Eysenck, 1952]:

A careful attempt was made to establish an adequate base rate for spontaneous recovery. One way in which this was done was to find the percentage of neurotics who had been discharged from mental hospitals within one year of admission. These patients received custodial care in the hospital, but very little psychotherapy. Therefore their recovery may be considered to be "spontaneous." Several difficulties with using this as a base rate arise because, for one thing, only the most severe neurotics are admitted to institutions. Because of this, the figure may be biased so that the base rate of recovery is too low—perhaps less disturbed neurotics would show a higher spontaneous recovery rate. In addition to this problem, there are many other difficulties with this estimate of the spontaneous recovery rate. Recognizing the difficulties, and attempting to allow for them, the estimate was made that about 67 per cent of neurotics improved markedly, and spontaneously, in a year. What about improvement in psychotherapy? A study was made of two types of psychotherapy—the psychoanalytic and the eclectic—in which different traditional approaches are used. The results were not encouraging for psychotherapy—44 per cent of those treated by psychoanalytic therapy were "cured," "much improved," or "improved"; 64 per cent of those treated by eclectic methods were "cured," "much improved," or "improved." Since many of the patients in psychoanalytic therapy broke off treatment, the figures may be corrected to exclude these patients. When this is done, approximately 66 per cent of the patients treated in psychoanalytic therapy were "cured," "much improved," or "improved." Summing all this up, we may say that it looks as if no difference exists between the recovery rates of untreated neurotics and those treated by the traditional methods of psychotherapy.

Many would not agree that this study is completely accurate, but it does make clear that the usual kinds of psychotherapy are not panaceas. Prevention would seem to be the most rational course of action.

The overall figures are not encouraging. Perhaps, though, this is not so much a function of the therapeutic technique as of the therapists. Some people, with particular personality traits, seem to make better therapists than others. When we look at average figures, we are lumping the "good" therapists together with the "not-so-good" therapists. It has been pointed out that "the therapist's contribution to the treatment process is a dual one: it is personal *and* technical" [Strupp, 1958, page 66]. It is the personal aspects of the therapist's contribution which we are stressing here. In one study, for instance, the following characteristics were found to be typical of competent, or "good," psychotherapists:

The competent therapists were: (1) "self-confident, outgoing, aggressive persons"; (2) "individualistic, nonconforming, and spontaneous, although they remain within the limits of acceptable social behavior"; (3) "introspective and empathic persons who can admit to personal deficiencies without loss in self-esteem"; (4) "more open and con-

sistent in their relationship to authority figures and tend toward inner control rather than external conformity." [Fox, 1962, page 58.]

Perhaps this set of characteristics would not be the best for every type of psychotherapeutic situation, but the point is that some therapists are more effective than others. Thus, in addition to the many problems inherent in studies of psychotherapeutic effectiveness, the lumping together of "good" and "not-so-good" therapists may make the figures seem a little less encouraging than they should be. No final conclusion can be reached about the effectiveness of traditional methods of psychotherapy—success or failure would seem to depend on the patient, the therapist, and their interaction.

We have now described four general systems of psychotherapy: directive therapies, client-centered therapy, psychoanalysis, and behavior therapies.

FIGURE 15.9. *Psychodrama, a special technique in psychotherapy. Under the guidance of members of the professional staff, patients use psychodrama to work out various problems in human relationships in front of a small audience of other patients. (Moreno Institute, Inc.)*

Other systems of psychotherapy, for the most part, combine or put a different emphasis on various features of these systems.

Special psychotherapies

In addition to the methods we have described, psychotherapy includes many special procedures. Among them are three techniques that deserve at least a brief description here: (1) psychodrama, (2) play and release therapy, and (3) group therapy.

PSYCHODRAMA The drama in some form has been used in mental healing since ancient times. Its therapeutic values were mentioned by many philosophers, and there is evidence that, in the ancient theater, plays were sometimes presented for their therapeutic effects. *Psychodrama,* however, is a specialized technique designed to permit patients to act out roles, situations, and fantasies related to their problems [Moreno, 1946]. It thus affords something not normally provided by therapies in which the patient is treated alone and is able to express his feelings only in words. Psychodrama, by contrast, enables the person to express himself in realistic situations by acts, rather than mere words. It also treats the individual in social situations resembling those which in the past have been a source of his difficulties.

In psychodrama, the patient usually may act out real situations or fantasies freely, spontaneously, and without limitation (see Figure 15.9). Trained therapeutic actors help him get started and play the roles of people significant in his problems. The patient may act out not only those situations he has experienced, but those he has feared and evaded. He may portray himself at times, and at other times he may take the part of someone who is influential in his life. As the therapy proceeds, it may become evident that he avoids certain roles and situations, and it may be necessary to direct him to live through scenes that are painful or undesirable. Psychodrama thus provides some of the same opportunities for free association and reliving of experiences as does psychoanalysis, but psychodrama uses the vehicle of the play to do it. From time to time, the therapist may analyze and interpret the situations that have been acted out.

The therapy may be carried on with or without an audience. In some situations, the audience is allowed to participate in the performance and consequently acts as an aid to the therapy. In other instances, the audience may be made up of patients who may themselves be the object of the therapy, since many of their own problems will be dramatized. Much of the success of this therapy depends upon a very astute chief therapist and a carefully trained staff of assistants. Even under these circumstances, however, many patients find it impossible to participate in such a dramatic procedure.

PLAY AND RELEASE THERAPY Recognizing that play provides unusual opportunities for relieving tension and achieving insight, therapists have devised a variety of techniques known as *play* or *release therapy* [Axline, 1947]. Such techniques are best employed with children. They utilize play with toys, puppet shows, drawing, modeling, and a variety of other activities (see Figure 15.10).

The greatest value of play technique is in the study of personality. The child often cannot or will not explain himself in the first person; yet he may reveal much of his inner life if allowed to play freely with toys. The child who will not tell about his own fears and conflicts may quite easily project these feelings into the dolls with which he plays. Feelings of rejection, insecurity, ambivalent attitudes toward parents, repressed hatreds, fears, and aggressions may all be freely revealed in play. Consequently, the play technique, when properly handled, may offer opportunities for understanding the child that are otherwise difficult to secure.

The play situation may also be therapeutic. In the security and permissiveness of play, the child may release feelings without fear of reprisal and thus may relieve tension. A carefully conducted play situation allows the child's feelings to come to the surface and thus helps him to learn to face them, control them, or abandon them. To the extent that the play situation is a miniature of the real one, desensitization and new learning can take place.

GROUP THERAPY For some years now, the number of trained psychotherapists has not been sufficient for the care of all those who may profit from treatment. Partly for this reason, methods have been devised for the treatment of groups [Klapman, 1946]. *Group therapy*, as this treatment is called, is more, however, than an economy measure; it also has particular values of its own. Since the patient's difficulties are frequently those of interpersonal relationships, the group serves as a therapeutic unit through which patients may be reeducated in the techniques of social adjustment.

Group therapy is sometimes a supplement to individual therapy, sometimes a substitute for it, and sometimes a sequel to it. A patient who has been under individual therapy may begin or continue group therapy when it seems to be doing him more good than individual treatment.

There are many variations of group therapy, but the usual type consists in assembling the group under the guidance of a therapist for meetings of about an hour's duration. The therapist attempts to remain in the background, permitting individuals in the group to talk freely. As the group conversation progresses, certain members of the group may discuss their own problems and symptoms. The perspectives of the other members are presented, and this leads gradually to each one interposing some of his own experiences, attitudes, and feelings. Certain members of the group inevitably profit more than others, but most receive some benefit. Merely learning that their own problems are not unique is of some value. The opportunity to view situations and attitudes from a variety of perspectives is also helpful. It may help the individual to relieve his feelings of isolation and rejection, overcome his self-consciousness, modify a too strict conscience, give vent to aggressions, and obtain substitute gratifications.

Another value of the group method is the support it can provide. In individual therapy, some patients find dependence intolerable and are unable to accept

FIGURE 15.10. *Release therapy. Emotionally disturbed adolescents release some of their feelings in finger painting. (Life Magazine, Time, Inc.)*

the therapist's support. Others accept support too readily and react unfavorably when it is withdrawn. In group therapy, the members of the group support and depend upon one another, without having an obligation to any single person.

Furthermore, in individual therapy the situation is somewhat artificial because the patient expresses himself to one person and is left uncertain of how others will react to him. In the group, his emotional expression takes place in a situation resembling the social environment where the members of the group may represent people who have special meanings for each patient. The situation is thus more real, allowing feelings to be expressed more as they are in everyday life.

Success depends partly upon the wisdom of the therapist. He must for the most part remain in the background, but he must know when to intervene, not only to provide necessary guidance, but also to prevent deleterious verbal attacks by one patient on another. He must also be skillful enough not to take over the situation and kill the spontaneity of the group. The method has been most successful when used to supplement individual therapy or to continue treatment begun in individual therapy.

Personal adjustment

Mental health is probably America's primary health problem. Recognizing this, leaders in many walks of life are bending their efforts to do something about it. Research on mental health has been greatly expanded by hospitals, universities, government, and other agencies. Campaigns have been under way to educate the general public concerning the nature and magnitude of mental health problems. Many states and cities have established clinics to which children and adults can go with their adjustment problems and receive professional aid. The general purpose of the clinics is to detect emotional problems in their early stages and thereby prevent their becoming serious. Many colleges have established psychological clinics to aid students, and courses in mental hygiene, adjustment, and the like, are being offered more widely. These concerted efforts on many fronts should contribute to a general improvement in mental health.

In the end, of course, mental health is an individual problem. It is the individual who has the problem, and it is the individual who must solve the problem. Each person must learn for himself how to achieve and maintain satisfactory adjustments. Clinics, counselors, therapists, friends, and literature can help, but they do so only by helping the person to help himself. The well-informed person should be acquainted, not only with the symptoms of poor mental health and with methods of treating it, but also with the characteristics of good mental health and of the well-adjusted personality—the subject of this last section. We cannot hope to give advice that guarantees a sound personal adjustment, but we can point out some of its characteristics.

REALITY PRINCIPLE   Probably the most general characteristic of the well-adjusted person is that he is "realistic" about himself. He does not fool himself greatly about his own motives, he sets goals for himself that are reasonably attainable, and he avoids unnecessary conflicts. This means that he tries to find out what he can realistically expect to achieve and adjusts his efforts and goals accordingly. He faces his personal problems objectively, much as one would go about solving a problem in arithmetic. He acquaints himself with the relevant facts, makes sure that he understands what the problem is, then proceeds toward its solution.

These, of course, are very general statements. Let us see more specifically how a well-adjusted person manages to deal realistically with his personal problems.

ACHIEVING SELF-UNDERSTANDING   The maladjusted person, we have seen, is typically one who deceives himself about his real motives. He habitually practices self-deceit because he tries, by means of defense mechanisms, to avoid the anxiety arising from conflict and frustration. The picture of the well-adjusted person is just the opposite.

Accepting anxiety. Healthy adjustment requires that we accept, rather than avoid, anxiety. Anxiety, being the natural outcome of experience with fear-provoking situations, can never be completely eliminated. By facing up to it, we accept it, and in the end, we experience less of it.

The problem here is much like that underlying the fear of dentists' drills. Hardly anyone likes to have his teeth drilled, and some people live in mortal fear of it. Individuals, of course, differ in their sensitivity to pain, but it is doubtful that differences of this kind have much to do with attitudes toward dentists. The important difference is one of accepting or avoiding the inevitable discomfort. Those who accept it find that it is not so bad after all. Those who do not accept it find it ten times worse than it actually is. The same thing can be said of other anxiety-provoking situations. It has often been observed that the difference between the courageous soldier and the coward is that the courageous one accepts fear, whereas the coward lets himself be overcome by it. President Roosevelt's famous statement, "We have nothing to fear but fear itself," makes much the same point.

Abandoning defense mechanisms. The well-adjusted person accepts a certain amount of anxiety; therefore, he also avoids using defense mechanisms to excess. These mechanisms are primarily defenses against anxiety; they are also characteristic of the maladjusted person. If one accepts and tolerates anxiety, there is little need for defense mechanisms.

The adjusted person, in fact, can usually recognize, often with humor, his own tendencies toward defense mechanisms. The student who is inclined to blame his instructor for a poor grade can recognize that he is rationalizing for his failure to attend classes, keep good notes, or study. The person tempted to feel that his friends are turning against him can suspect himself of projecting his fears and dislikes to his friends. The practice of looking for such defense mechanisms can be carried too far, that is, to the point of seeing them "under every bush." Nevertheless, recognizing them for what they really are puts one on guard against using them excessively.

Understanding motives. Defense mechanisms disguise one's motives; recognizing them puts one in a better position to unmask and accept his own motives. Motives are not always easy to identify, but the well-adjusted person is better at it than the maladjusted one. When the student is inclined to blame his instructor for a poor grade, he can ask himself, "What do I really want? What are my motives and goals?" An honest answer, at least a very human one, may be that he wants a good grade without doing any work. Admitting this to himself, he can see that such a combination of goals is usually unattainable. He can then decide "Better get to work" or "I'll settle for a lower grade and less work" without the hostility and anxiety aroused by blaming someone else.

ALTERING MOTIVES AND GOALS The well-adjusted person can alter his motives or goals without disguising them with defense mechanisms. Sometimes merely recognizing a motive permits one to discard it with ease. For example, a person who continually rebels against authority, refusing to take directions from superiors and evading the rules of living, may quickly change his attitude if he realizes that his rebellion is really a reaction to an overbearing parent and that he is treating other people as though they were his father. Another person, made aware of his strong prestige-seeking motives, may find this strong interest in prestige dissipating.

Others may change their goals quite abruptly when they discover that they have taken over motives intact from other people. This may be true, for example, of vocational goals, which are often set for a young person by his parents. A boy may come to college with his heart set on being a doctor, only to be frustrated by lack of interest and ability in premedical work. When anxiety has mounted to an acute stage, he may reexamine his goals and recognize that being a doctor is not his own goal at all. He is then in a position to choose another vocational goal better suited to his own interests and abilities.

Understanding one's motives does not, on the other hand, guarantee that undesirable ones will be discarded or that new, appropriate goals will be adopted. Patients in insight psychotherapy often achieve such an understanding without making much improvement. Insight, however, often makes it possible for the person to alter his motives and goals, and thus to improve his adjustment.

Not all changes in goals need to be radical ones. Some are matters of small degree. A student may settle for a B average, which he can attain, rather than be so frustrated and anxious striving for A's that he makes C's. Or he may choose a less prestigeful profession, or a less remunerative job, that is less frustrating because it better suits his abilities and other motives.

REDUCING CONFLICT AND FRUSTRATION Our society is so complex and our goals are so elaborate

that there is little chance, even under the best of circumstances, that we will be completely free of conflict and frustration. The well-adjusted mature person realizes this, just as he learns to accept anxiety, and he tries to keep conflict and frustration to a minimum. Here are some techniques which may serve this purpose.

Postponing satisfactions. One way to resolve a conflict, eventually, is to postpone the satisfaction of one of two competing motives. If an individual is both hungry and sleepy, he can eat first, then sleep.

The student who wants excellent grades in college as well as some fun can study tonight and go out tomorrow night. The principle is simple enough. It means having a plan that postpones, but nevertheless provides for the satisfaction of, one motive until some foreseeable time. This kind of scheduling reduces the conflict between motives and limits it to relatively short periods of time.

Frustration tolerance. Postponing a satisfaction for a time, of course, leaves the person temporarily frustrated. Hence, he must be able to tolerate some

CARE OF THE MENTALLY ILL REQUIRES SEVERAL KINDS OF INFORMATION

FIGURE 15.11. *Patients seeking admission to mental health centers are given comprehensive examinations. Here the prospective patient and her mother confer with a psychiatric social worker. Information on the patient's problem, life history, family background, and physical condition—all of the psychosocial factors which bear on the case—is gathered before a course of therapy can be embarked upon. The psychiatrist examines the prospective patient to explore the nature and severity of her illness. An evaluation unit, composed of the psychiatrist, the social worker, and the psychologist, who has also tested the patient, meets to discuss all aspects of the case. They decide to admit the patient for treatment. A thorough physical examination is part of the admissions procedure. Finally, the patient is settled in her room. (National Institute of Mental Health, Public Health Service, U.S. Department of Health, Education, and Welfare, Bethesda, Maryland.)*

frustration. Indeed, frustration tolerance, like the acceptance of anxiety, is the mark of a well-adjusted person. The healthy person accepts frustration as a normal reality of life. He learns that he cannot always have what he wants when he wants it. He stops fretting about what he cannot have and lets some of his less essential motives go unsatisfied. Once accepted for what it is, frustration is not nearly so frustrating.

Frustration tolerance, like habits and attitudes, can be acquired with practice. The individual starts with little things—the frustration of waiting for an overdue bus, of failure to find a parking place, or of being turned down for a date. When he can accept little frustrations with grace, he is ready to tackle bigger ones. The aim, of course, is not to duck problems that can be solved, but rather to tolerate the frustrations that are inevitable.

Expressing emotions. Some conflicts, we have seen, arise because emotions, particularly hostility, have been repressed. Through previous training, some individuals have become unduly fearful of acting aggressively. The well-adjusted person, on the other hand, can express his feelings somewhat openly without fear of losing friends and alienating people. He realizes that other people expect occasional displays of impatience or anger and can take them in stride. He may even knowingly make others angry, but feel better by releasing his pent-up emotions. He manages to achieve some balance between the excessive and inconsiderate display of emotions, on the one hand, and complete restraint or repression of them, on the other.

The best way of doing this is to develop socially acceptable ways of expressing one's feelings. Without losing his temper, the skillful person can act sternly and state clearly what displeases him. By a joking retort, he can indicate displeasure and at the same time be good humored about it. By expressing emotions in a mature way, he manages not to lose the friendship and respect of others. This requires skill, and skill takes practice, but the well-adjusted person has usually learned to do this.

Useful work. Keeping occupied with useful work or other activities is another mark of the healthy person. Most of the work one does, other than very repetitive activities, is directed toward some goal. It therefore provides the satisfaction of accomplishing something. It also takes one's mind off other things, pushing into the background motives that may cause conflict. Hence useful work is a double-barreled remedy: it satisfies certain motives while weakening others. By itself, of course, work is not a sure cure for conflict; some very maladjusted people work hard. Coupled with other measures, however, it helps a healthy person stay healthy.

SYNOPSIS AND SUMMARY

A few of the major techniques of psychotherapy have been covered in this chapter, and many more might have been added. Some of them may have some effectiveness, but the important point is that none of them, without laborious effort, can relieve the misery of mental illness. It should be apparent that the best public and private course of action is the prevention of behavior disorders. In public terms, prevention rather than treatment and custodial care will result in considerable savings of tax money; in private terms, prevention will save untold and unnecessary misery.

How does one prevent mental illness? The answer is easier stated than applied since the roots of many behavior disorders are to be found in certain maladjustments in the intimacy of the family circle. Somehow, as a start, parents must be made to believe that it is important to take an interest in their children. Many parents, perhaps because it is the accepted cultural pattern in their subgroup, literally abandon their children to the streets; others functionally abandon them by being too busy to spend time with them. After this minimum requirement has been met, parents must not be too inconsistent, too harsh, or too demanding; nor should they give absolute freedom—they should set realistic limits for the child's behavior. It is really not too difficult to rear children who are free from psychoneuroses or personality disorders. In the psychotic disorders, the virulence of the symptoms can probably be lessened by reasonable, understanding, consistent, and loving techniques of child rearing.

Of course, we are caught in a vicious circle when we try to prevent mental illness. Psychoneurotic parents or those with personality disorders are not very likely to set reasonable limits and to provide the kind of love children need to grow to be healthy adults. Perhaps some outside assistance in the form of community mental health clinics can provide help. They can attempt to educate toward the goal of prevention. A sound understanding of the contents of texts such as this one may also educate.

In this chapter we made the following points about mental health and psychotherapy:

1. Mental illness is perhaps the largest and most burdensome of all the health problems in the United States; persons suffering from mental illness occupy more than one-half of all hospital beds.

2. The relative proportion of the population under fifty years old which is admitted to mental hospitals appears to have remained relatively constant over the years; this seems to indicate that the genetic and environmental causes of mental illness are fairly constant.

3. The admission rate to mental hospitals for all ages has risen, but the discharge rate has increased enough to offset the increase in the admission rate. Thus, the proportion of the population in mental hospitals is declining.

4. The doctrine that mental illness resulted from possession by some devil was widely held until about one hundred and seventy-five years ago. During the past century and a half, however, people with behavior disturbances have been treated more rationally and humanely. The modern mental health movement, which stresses understanding and help for the mentally ill, is only some sixty years old.

5. The trend in therapy increasingly stresses psychological, rather than medical, methods of treatment. The trend is also toward the prevention of severe disorders through the treatment of the mildly ill, and more readily treated, individuals.

6. The treatment of an illness is called therapy. Therapy for mental illness is of two kinds: medical therapy and psychotherapy. Medical therapies consist of psychosurgery, shock therapy, narcosis, and chemotherapies. Of the first two, electroshock treatments are now the most widely used; narcosis and chemotherapy are employed more to make the patient available to psychotherapy than to produce long-lasting beneficial results.

7. The aims of psychotherapy consist in some combination of (a) changing the situation, (b) providing support, (c) achieving insight, and (d) learning and extinction.

8. Four major varieties of psychotherapy may be distinguished: directive therapies, client-centered therapy, psychoanalysis, and behavior therapies. Directive therapy emphasizes changing the situation and reeducation of the individual. Client-centered therapy provides a permissive situation for the patient, and attempts to help him talk out and solve his personal problems.

9. Psychoanalysis follows the teachings of Sigmund Freud. As a therapy, psychoanalysis emphasizes the analysis of free associations, resistances, dreams, and transference.

10. The behavior therapies concentrate on the deviant behavior as such and attempt to modify it by use of classical conditioning and instrumental learning techniques.

11. Studies of the effectivenes of psychotherapeutic techniques are very difficult to do, but those which have been done may be interpreted as indicating that psychotherapy is far less effective than we would like it to be. One implication of this is that prevention of behavior disorders must assume greater importance.

12. Psychodrama is a special technique that permits a patient to act out roles, situations, and fantasies in his life. Play and release therapy, used principally with children, encourages patients to exhibit their feelings in play situations. Group therapy, another special technique, permits troubled people to talk over their problems with one another under the guidance of a therapist.

13. Normal individuals may do much to improve their own personal adjustments by (a) attempting to achieve self-understanding, (b) adjusting their goals, and (c) learning various measures to reduce conflict and frustration.

14. Self-understanding is aided by (a) learning to accept and tolerate anxiety, (b) avoiding the excessive use of defense mechanisms, and (c) attempting to understand one's own motives.

15. Goals may often be more easily discarded when a person understands what they really are. Goals may also be set at more realistic and attainable levels, thereby eliminating unnecessary frustration.

16. Conflict and frustration may be minimized by (a) postponing certain satisfactions to a foreseeable time, (b) acquiring greater frustration tolerance, (c) finding socially acceptable ways of venting emotions, and (d) keeping occupied with useful work.

RELATED TOPICS IN THE TEXT

CHAPTER 13 PERSONALITY Some psychotherapies are often thought of as attempting to modify personality characteristics, especially maladaptive ones. This is a difficult job at best because the forces which shaped personality in the first place are extremely powerful. A review of the origins of personality traits in general, and the defense mechanisms in particular, may perhaps be fruitful.

CHAPTER 14 BEHAVIOR DISORDERS The mild adjustment problems, psychoneuroses, personality disorders, and psychoses against which therapy is directed are detailed in Chapter 14.

SUGGESTIONS FOR FURTHER READING

Bordin, E. S. *Psychological counseling.* New York: Appleton-Century-Crofts, 1955.
A textbook on counseling techniques used with individuals having minor personal problems.

Dorcus, R. M. (Ed.). *Hypnosis and its therapeutic applications.* New York: McGraw-Hill, 1956.
A modern authoritative treatment, written by experts, of the nature and uses of hypnosis.

Freud, S. *An outline of psychoanalysis.* New York: Norton, 1949.
A short description of some of the basic ideas of psychoanalysis as a theory and a system of therapy.

Garfield, S. L. *Introductory clinical psychology.* New York: Macmillan, 1957.
An elementary textbook describing methods of appraising personality and mental disorder, as well as psychotherapeutic methods.

Ingham, H. V., and Love, L. R. *The process of psychotherapy.* New York: McGraw-Hill, 1954.
A general summary of the practice of psychotherapy.

Ogg, E. *Psychotherapy: A helping process.* Pamphlet No. 329. New York: Public Affairs Committee, Inc., 1962. (Paperback.)
An interesting, popularly written, nontechnical account of psychotherapeutic techniques and what can be expected from psychotherapy. (This pamphlet is put out on a nonprofit basis by the Public Affairs Committee, Inc.; it may be obtained from Public Affairs Pamphlets, New York.)

Rogers, C. R. *Client-centered therapy.* Boston: Houghton Mifflin, 1951. (Paperback available.)
A description of the methods and results of nondirective, client-centered therapy.

Rotter, J. B. *Clinical psychology.* Englewood Cliffs, N.J.: Prentice-Hall, 1964. (Paperback.)
A description of some methods of clinical psychology and some methods of psychotherapy.

Tussing, L. *Psychology for better living.* New York: Wiley, 1959.
An easily read text in which an attempt is made to apply psychological facts to the problems of living.

Wolpe, J. *Psychotherapy by reciprocal inhibition.* Stanford, Calif.: Stanford University Press, 1958.
A statement of the principles behind one type of behavior therapy.

Zilboorg, G., and Henry, G. W. *A history of medical psychology.* New York: Norton, 1941.
A history of trends and ideas concerning the treatment of behavior disorders.

GROUP
PROCESSES

PART SIX

SURELY YOU HAVE often stopped to consider how much other people have to say about what you do, but perhaps you do not appreciate the extent to which others influence your behavior. Even if you are twenty-one and relatively independent of parental control, you still cannot free yourself from the control of society. Its pressure is brought to bear on all your behavior, prescribing everything from the tie to be worn with a particular suit to the rules for virtuous living. Parents and elders exhort you toward moral behavior, police officers enforce traffic regulations, employers and neighbors gently force you to give to charity drives, and in many subtle and not-so-subtle ways people dictate how you dress, what you drink, and how you enjoy yourself.

Most of the subgroups within a culture also exert influence on the behavior of the individual. The family group is usually the first place a child learns about interpersonal relations and about the behaviors which are appropriate and acceptable in his society. Friends and associates with whom a person has frequent informal contacts also affect how he responds to various situations. Peers are often more important than parents in determining the behavior of teen-agers, whose conformity in type of dress, hair styling, and so on is well known. When an individual associates with a particular group and participates in its activities, he may help to determine the actions of the group. Often, however, in order to be accepted as a group member, he must agree to go along with the plans of the group even if he is not convinced that the group is doing the right thing. A fraternity member may go along with hazing new pledges, although he does not approve of this personally, because he fears criticism. Mob behavior can be an important determiner of individual behavior. The juvenile delinquent conforms to the standards of behavior of his gang and grows up with vastly different social forces shaping his life than does the typical middle-class child. Indeed, practically from the moment each of us is born, society pushes, guides, advises, and constrains us in ways of living which are considered to be correct and appropriate.

SOCIAL INFLUENCES ON BEHAVIOR

CUSTOM AND CONVENTION GOVERN HUMAN ACTION.
PYRRHO

Socialization is the name given to the social learning process through which the infant is trained in the attitudes, beliefs, and behaviors appropriate to his culture. As Ruth Benedict, the social anthropologist, has put it:

The life-history of the individual is first and foremost an accommodation to the patterns and standards traditionally handed down in his community. From the moment of his birth the customs into which he is born shape his life experience and behaviour. By the time he can talk, he is a little creature of his culture, and by the time he is grown and able to take part in its activities, its habits are his habits, its beliefs are his beliefs, its impossibilities are his impossibilities. Every child that is born into his group will share them with him, and no child born into one on the opposite side of the globe can ever achieve the thousandth part. [Benedict, 1959, page 2.]

So steady, so insistent, and so pervasive are cultural influences on our behavior that we rarely stop to perceive or analyze their nature. *Social psychology* studies the behavior of the individual in his society, "as it is influenced by the presence, beliefs, actions, and symbols of other men" [McGrath, 1964]. *Sociology* focuses on the study of the behavior of groups of people, taken as a whole. These fields overlap, but the focus in social psychology is on the social forces which shape and determine individual behavior rather than group behavior.

Culture

The term *culture*, used in a scientific sense, refers to the customs and traditions of a people and to the attitudes and beliefs they have about important aspects of their life. Occasionally culture has been called "social heritage," but this gives the somewhat false impression that culture is inherited unchanged from generation to generation. More accurate, though more imposing, definitions of culture have been provided by anthropologists. One such definition is: "Culture is the configuration of learned behavior and results of behavior whose component elements are shared and transmitted by members of a par-

ticular society" [Linton, 1945, page 32]. As psychologists, our interest focuses on the behaviors, attitudes, and values which are transmitted and shared.

Culture influences behavior through the socialization process. The following passage describes how the culture of a society affects socialization.

The cultural environment (or, more exactly, the members of the community) starts out with a human infant formed and endowed along species lines, but capable of behavioral training in many directions. From this raw material, the culture proceeds to make, in so far as it can, a product acceptable to itself. It does this by training: by reinforcing the behavior it desires and extinguishing others; by making some natural and social stimuli into [discriminative stimuli], and ignoring others; by differentiating out this or that specific response or chain of responses, such as manners and attitudes; by conditioning emotional and anxiety reactions to some stimuli and not others. It teaches the individual what he may and may not do, giving him norms and ranges of social behavior that are permissive or prescriptive or prohibitive. It teaches him the language he is to speak; it gives him his standards of beauty and art, of good and bad conduct; it sets before him a picture of the ideal personality that he is to imitate and strive to be. In all this, the fundamental laws of behavior are to be found. [Keller and Schoenfeld, 1950, page 365.]

Each cultural group has worked out certain ways of handling various universal problems, such as caring for and training children, feeding and sheltering the group members, and so on, and the successful practices are adopted and passed on to successive generations as the culture of that society. Language, traditions, norms, values, and the expectations and sanctions associated with them are taught by the culture through the social learning process. It has been stated that: "Culture influences the person in a massive and pervasive way and thus makes for the stability of a society and the continuity of its culture; the person also influences his culture and thus makes for social change." [Krech et al., 1962, page 341.]

Social anthropologists have taught us most of what we know about culture. Using "field-study" methods and living with the people they study, they have focused their attention on so-called "primitive" societies or "backward" peoples—the American Indians, South Sea Islanders, Africans, and others. They have also applied their methods to more advanced societies, including our own.[1] Thus they have been able to compare different cultures and draw conclusions about the cultural similarities and differences of each.

PATTERNS OF CULTURE Perhaps the most important of their conclusions is that different societies may develop altogether different solutions to the same major and recurrent problems of life. At the same time, despite this diversity, the members of each society believe that *their* way of behaving is natural and best. As an example, consider the respective jobs and duties a society assigns to its men and women. The eminent anthropologist Margaret Mead (1935) compared the roles of males and females in three primitive societies. The Tchambuli of New Guinea assign the economic affairs of the culture to women, instead of to men as is customarily the case in our country. Tchambuli men, furthermore, are the ones concerned with the activities that we in our society expect women to perform, such as ceremonies and beautifying themselves. The beliefs in the Tchambuli culture justify this division of duties. Women are regarded as naturally self-reliant and businesslike, whereas men are supposedly born to be vain and artistic. Many Americans, of course, have just the reverse conception of the "fundamental nature" of men and women. Among the Arapesh, both men and women behave in a relatively passive manner, somewhat as we expect women to behave in our culture. In the Mundugumor, dominant-aggressive behavior is typical in both men and women. These early investigations showed that many differences in male and female behavior are *learned role differences*. We should recognize that the differences in personality characteristics between men and women in our society are not typical of all cultures.

[1] Some examples of famous studies of American society are Lynd and Lynd (1929), Hollingshead (1949), and Barker and Wright (1954).

It is probably true that most, but certainly not all, Tchambuli adults have personalities consistent with their culture's beliefs concerning the basic character of their sex. Similarly, many, but again not all, American adults behave as we generally expect people of their sex to behave. Since most members of a culture are subjected to the same social influences during their lives, they develop characteristics that are similar and appropriate to their society. These widely shared ways of behaving in a society, together with the beliefs that accompany them, have been termed the *cultural pattern*. The cultural pattern, of course, is only generally characteristic of a society, and not everyone conforms to it.

COMPARISONS OF CULTURES The novel ways of living in different cultures are fascinating to study (see Figure 16.1). Students of human behavior, however, have concerned themselves with the comparison of different cultural patterns for other reasons. To them, cultural diversity offers a unique opportunity to study the effects of social influences upon behavior and personality development. Such influences vary more widely among societies than they do within any given society.

The *cross-cultural method* has been used to study similarities and differences in cultural patterns, using a worldwide sample of societies. Information collected about these societies has been recorded and made available at many university libraries so that hypotheses about the relations between certain types of behavior and possible causal, associated, or consequent factors can be investigated without visiting each of the cultures. For instance, this cross-cultural method was used in a study of family, kinship relations, and the regulation of sexual conduct and marriage [Murdock, 1949]. Most of the societies investigated were preliterate. The data indicate considerable diversity in the cultural restrictions placed upon sexual behavior. Only 3 of the 118 societies in the sample appeared to have a general taboo against sexual intercourse outside of marriage, with the others allowing a variety of more permissive sexual behaviors. One of these three societies was a sample of white New Englanders.

FIGURE 16.1.   *Cultural patterns differ. Both of these boys are being formally initiated into full-fledged membership in their groups. Left, a caste ceremony in India. Right, a Bar Mitzvah ceremony. (Left, Margaret Bourke-White, Life Magazine, © Time Inc. Right, Maxwell Coplan, Design Photographers International, Inc.)*

Cultural differences in norms and values among nations may lead to difficulties in international communication and to conflict. For example, in various societies different emphases are placed on time and time perspective, and this has given rise to certain difficulties in the conduct of United Nations' affairs.

Most Anglo-Saxons believe that abiding by regular scheduling is appropriate. Eastern Europeans tend to be more flexible and often would prefer to finish the business at hand before adjourning for lunch. Far Easterners tend to conceptualize life and time as a continuous stream; from their viewpoint, the discussion at hand should continue and those who must leave should be free to do so as the occasion requires, without feeling that this is interrupting the ongoing meeting. When the issue being discussed is an important one, differences in the concept of time perspective can lead to accusations of "insincerity" or "lack of a serious approach to the problem." [Abstracted from Telberg, 1950, as quoted in Krech et al., 1962.]

Societies differ greatly in the extent to which their members compete with one another for cultural goals and rewards. Some societies, such as the Kwakiutl Indians of the Pacific Northwest, compete intensely for social position and the "good things of life." In this respect, the Kwakiutl Indians are not too different from Americans. As is often the case in our society, their rewards are gained through individual initiative. Such a society thus fosters extreme competitiveness among its members. Among the Zuñi Indians of the American Southwest, on the other hand, excessive individual initiative and competition are frowned upon. The Zuñi are therefore characteristically a mild and inoffensive people. Their culture is more preoccupied with ceremony and the proper ways of doing things than with individualism or competition.

Cultural differences may occur in the way situations are defined and in expectations of appropriate behavior. In our culture, two friends may oppose one another in sports or games; in other situations, as on a job or at a party, friends would ordinarily not compete with one another [McGrath, 1964]. Our culture defines certain situations as competitive, and in these situations we expect individuals to try to win, no matter whom they are opposing. In some other cultures, for example, in Samoa, or among the Zuñi Indians, two friends would not want to compete even in games, and an individual would probably refuse to participate in any situation which would tend to build him up at the cost of outdoing a friend.

These comparisons of cultures make it clear that values and many behavioral patterns are shaped by the culture. The culture into which a baby is born inexorably molds his behavior. As he grows up, culture will shape his interpretations of situations and his expectations about appropriate behavior. Thus, knowing about his cultural norms and values will help in predicting his behavior.

DETERMINANTS OF CULTURAL PATTERNS

Differences in culture are affected both by the natural conditions under which a people live—the food available to them, abundance or scarcity of resources, climate, proximity to other peoples, and so on—and by the practices already established in a society that shape the personalities and habit patterns of its members. In other words, the determinants of a culture may lie both outside and inside the culture. Unfortunately, we have not succeeded too well in accounting for the various determinants of culture. We can, however, provide examples of the kinds of determinants that have been studied.

One possible determinant might be a shortage of natural resources in a society. If food and other essentials are scarce, we might expect individuals in a society to be competitive because they have learned to survive by competition for the available resources. In a study to determine the validity of this hypothesis, 13 primitive societies were studied by rank-ordering them on the abundance of food and on the competitiveness of their cultures [Newcomb, 1950]. Contrary to the hypothesis, this study suggests that there is *no* relationship between the competitiveness of a society and the scarcity of its natural resources. Competition is created, apparently, by social or internal cultural influences and is not necessarily developed by natural deprivations.

Let us consider a more specific study of a determinant of a cultural pattern. Some societies have elaborate ceremonies when a boy reaches puberty, while other societies do not have puberty rites. What may be the causes of this cultural pattern? The following summarizes one attempt to find out [Whiting et al., 1958]:

Fifty-six societies, ranging from small tribal groups to complex civilizations, such as the United States, were divided into those which had harsh male initiation rites at approximately the time of puberty, such as circumcision or undergoing severe trials, and those which did not have such punishing ceremonies. The investigators found that certain sex customs were associated with these puberty rites with greater than chance frequency. Analyzing the cultural differences further, they also observed that those societies which had harsh rites of passage for the male also tended to prohibit sexual relations between husband and wife for a long period after the wife gave birth. Furthermore, these societies typically prescribed that a baby son sleep with his mother for a long time after birth. These correlations led the investigators to speculate that the puberty rites are a way of asserting adult male authority over a boy. The rites are an attempt to break the boy's emotional dependence upon his mother. Perhaps they also express a rivalry for the mother characteristically existing between father and son.

Further investigation will be needed before we can begin to specify clearly the probable determinants of many of the behaviors, attitudes, and values characteristic in a given culture. Whether early socialization is basically warm and permissive or strict and rejecting, whether independent or dependent behavior is encouraged, and many other variable factors could be studied in various cultures to see if any basic relationships emerge. The problem might then become a question of what is the cause and what is the effect, that is, does the child-training process affect the culture as it develops, or does the ongoing culture affect the socialization process?

CULTURAL CHANGES Although cultures have definite patterns, these patterns are not handed down like heirlooms for many generations. Rather, they are constantly changing, sometimes slowly and sometimes fairly rapidly. The medieval era was for Western civilization a period of fairly slow change in culture patterns, whereas the modern period, since the Industrial Revolution, has been characterized by rapid and dramatic changes. Other cultures, similarly, have had times when changes were rapid and times when they were slow.

The reasons for cultural change are quite complex. Sometimes cultural changes are forced by *climatic conditions,* by *exhaustion of natural resources,* or especially in modern times, by *technological changes.* Today, technology is stepping up the pace of cultural change, and even the most remote societies have had to yield in some measure to the force of its impact. Finally, cultural changes can be brought about by an *ideology.* Some set of ideas for which there is a general need in the cul-

ture takes hold and brings about major changes in cultural patterns. Christianity and communism are good examples.

On the other hand, it is not correct to assume that cultures change very rapidly or that all aspects of a culture may change, for some continuity always characterizes the cultural pattern. Some patterns may remain virtually unchanged, whereas others are drastically revamped. For example, the Hutterites, a religious sect in the North Central United States and Canada, follow traditional nineteenth-century patterns of dress and weaving, while adopting modern methods of farming and using up-to-date commercial products.

AWARENESS OF CULTURE We have already pointed out that most people are unaware of the enormous power of cultural influences within their societies. Their behavior having been molded by the culture from the moment of birth, they probably take for granted the stereotyped behaviors and attitudes that characterize their culture. They are therefore largely unaware of the extent to which culture shapes their habits and values.

It is also characteristic of cultures that no member of a society ever shares in all elements of his culture. Instead, with very rare exceptions, each member knows only his particular subculture. This is because only certain aspects of a culture ordinarily influence a particular person's behavior, and he is not a part of, or greatly influenced by, other major segments of his culture.

Failure to be aware of certain aspects of culture influences class, or cultural, mobility. To illustrate this point, let us consider caste and class systems in societies in which it is possible to move from one level to a higher one. In such societies, where few legal or economic barriers exist, movement from caste or class may be almost as difficult as in societies where such movement is proscribed by law. The reason is simply that people in a lower stratum of society are ignorant of the cultural ways of the upper class. Even in a society such as our own, where crossing class boundaries is more freely done than in most societies, it is not so easy as it seems.

To cross them, a person must discard the habits and attitudes of his childhood or early adult culture and learn the different ones of the cultural class into which he moves. For example, "upward mobility" as a consequence of children having better education and better jobs than their parents can necessitate learning whole new repertoires of social behavior appropriate to the new way of living.

The immigrant to a new country faces a similar problem—he must learn new cultural patterns. Integration of immigrants into the culture of the new country may not be complete in one generation. Often the transition is most difficult for the second generation, since they can be in conflict between adopting the behavior patterns of the family or those of peers and the new community. This second-generation person may be on the border of two groups, and sociologists have studied the problems faced by the so-called "marginal man" who is caught between conflicting cultures.

Social structure

Each culture, we have said, has its distinctive pattern. Each culture also has its own *social structure*. That is to say, it assigns ranks to people, it expects certain people to do one kind of work and others to do other kinds, it expects its families to be constituted in a certain way, and it expects its members to have certain attitudes and beliefs. In some societies, this social structure is rather rigid; in others, it is more flexible. But no society escapes some degree of structuring.

Much of the structuring arises from differences among people in the goods and services they produce. One person makes trinkets, another makes shoes, another controls the production of a whole factory. The dependence of people upon one another is not equally distributed, and some people are much more important to the society than are others.

Of all the distinctions which can be made in the value of services to a society, those based upon sex and age are most common. These differences, therefore, provide some kind of structure in all societies.

Infants obviously contribute little and demand much, and mothers on the whole are assigned to take care of them. Children may contribute something, but not very much, and thus they are expected to treat adults with the respect befitting their more crucial roles. Young men, in nearly all societies, are expected to be warriors in time of danger. Old men are usually the sources of wisdom and leadership. Thus individual differences in ability to meet society's needs have much to do with the social structure. Technological differences in societies also affect the social structure. Those societies which are more highly industrialized and have more work specialties have more elaborate social structures.

STATUS AND ROLE As we have already implied, divisions of labor help shape social structure. So do positions in the family unit, memberships in social groups, and many other factors, depending upon the particular society. A social structure is established when members of a society categorize people according to differences that are important to their society's needs. Thus they assign to each person in the society what social scientists call a status—or rather, several statuses—age status, sex status, occupational status, social status, and so on. Each *status* is a position representing differences that are important in the exchange of goods and services and in the satisfaction of needs in the society. Status may depend on an individual's occupation, his power to affect others in his everyday relationships with them, his economic resources, or his ascribed rank in the social-class system of the community.

Different people may occupy a particular status at different times, and their statuses may change from time to time. Along with each status goes a *role*. This is a pattern of behavior that a person is expected to exhibit in a particular status. At a very early age, boys and girls in our society learn that different behaviors are expected of them. A father as "head of a household" has a role, or mode of behavior, which he must act out in that status. So does a person in the status of employer, or mother, or teacher. Hence, we must make a clear distinction between status and role: One applies to position in the social structure and the other to the behavior that goes along with that position. Thus status and role are key concepts in understanding social structure (see Figure 16.2).

MULTIPLE STATUS   The system by which statuses are categorized in a social structure usually permits any particular person to be categorized in many ways, for instance, as head of a household, teacher, employee, church member. A person therefore comes to have several statuses in a social structure. For some part of his life, he occupies one status; for another part, another status. In each of these statuses, moreover, he has a role to play that goes along with the particular status. He therefore

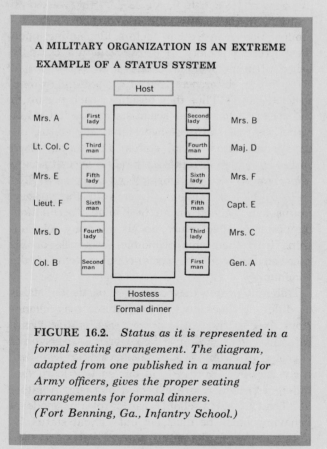

FIGURE 16.2.   *Status as it is represented in a formal seating arrangement. The diagram, adapted from one published in a manual for Army officers, gives the proper seating arrangements for formal dinners.*
(Fort Benning, Ga., Infantry School.)

finds himself in multiple statuses and multiple roles. The following illustration gives a picture of the multiple statuses a person may occupy:

Let us suppose that a man spends the day working as a clerk in a store. While he is behind the counter, his active status is that of a clerk, established by his position in our society's system of specialized occupations. The role associated with this status provides him with patterns for his relations with customers. These patterns will be well known both to him and to the customers and will enable them to transact business with a minimum of delay or misunderstanding. When he retires to the rest room for a smoke and meets other employees there, his clerk status becomes latent and he assumes another active status based upon his position in the association group composed of his store's employees as a whole. In this status his relations with other employees will be governed by a different set of culture patterns from those employed in his relations with customers. Moreover, since he probably knows most of the other employees, his exercise of these culture patterns will be modified by his personal likes and dislikes of certain individuals and by considerations of their and his own relative positions in the prestige series of the store association's members. When closing time comes, he lays aside both his clerk and store association statuses, and while on the way home, operates simply in terms of his status with respect to the society's age-sex system. Thus if he is a young man he will at least feel that he ought to get up and give his seat to a lady, while if he is an old one he will be quite comfortable about keeping it. As soon as he arrives at his house, a new set of statuses will be activated. These statuses derive from the kinship ties which relate him to various members of the family group. In pursuance of the roles associated with these family statuses he will try to be cordial to his mother-in-law, affectionate to his wife and a stern disciplinarian to Junior, whose report card marks a new low. If it happens to be a lodge night, all his familial statuses will become latent at about eight o'clock. As soon as he enters the lodge room and puts on his uniform as Grand Imperial Lizard in the Ancient Order of Dinosaurs he assumes a new status, one which has been latent since the last meeting, and performs in terms of its role until it is time for him to take off his uniform and go home. [Linton, 1945, page 78.]

CONFLICT OF ROLES Serious trouble can arise when a person is caught in a conflict of roles, and this can happen in a society as complex and as mobile as ours. The blustering foreman who drives his men with an iron hand may find his methods quite unsuccessful when he climbs the ladder of executive responsibility. The student leader accustomed to the role of class president in a small-town high school may be unhappy when he becomes just another freshman in a large university. The socialite used to the manners and repartee of cocktail parties may find herself offended and uncomfortable in a gathering of farmers or laborers.

Such changes in status put a person in a conflict of roles. He finds that the role he learned in one status is no longer appropriate in a new status. He becomes uncertain of what role he should play, and when he is forced to decide on one, he may have little confidence in his choice. Thus he may be thrust into motivational conflict of the sort we have previously described (see Chapter 13). The consequences may be frustration, anxiety, hostility, and failure to adjust. Many of the problems of an adolescent in our society are related to difficulties in adjusting to the changing behaviors, or roles, expected of him as he progresses from child to adult [McGrath, 1964].

For many people, conflicts in role are infrequent. This may be because people usually perceive only the particular status that is most appropriate to their immediate situation. An unscrupulous businessman who is also a regular churchgoer probably sees no incompatibility between his business behavior and the beliefs he professes on Sundays in church. During the week, functioning in the status of a businessman, he does not think in terms of his status as a churchgoer. In a sense, he usually does not become aware of other statuses he holds until he is reminded of them by situational demands or other cues [Charters and Newcomb, 1958].

Conflicts of roles may be important problems in the lives of some individuals, however. Recently there has been much discussion of the role-conflict of a well-educated woman who assumes the duties of housewife and mother. Unless she is able to in-ject a bit of intellectual stimulation into her life, she may become bogged down in her multiple roles of maid, babysitter, chauffeur, cook, handyman, and companion. She may experience role-conflict as she adjusts to the changing behaviors expected of her as a consequence of marriage and raising a family.

Negroes in the United States may have especially acute problems with conflict of roles [Kimble and Garmezy, 1963]. In spite of a widely proclaimed "equality" for all, inequities and segregation occur on a nationwide scale—in housing, education, churches, business, and in services available. Expectations of upward mobility, as a result of an education beyond that of his parents, may not be realized in actuality by the Negro youth. For example, many Negro girls in the South who are high school graduates find themselves limited to housekeeping jobs, and their newly learned clerical skills are not used. The probability of a young Negro girl in the South getting a clerical job at other than a Negro business is in reality often very low; yet it is difficult for these young people to accept this "second-rate citizenship." Much more equality of opportunity has been offered in recent years in the North and West, and new Federal civil rights legislation has helped to break traditionally accepted patterns of strict segregation even in the deep South. When actual role possibilities catch up to role expectations, Negroes and other ethnic and racial minorities should experience less role-conflict in their everyday lives.

SOCIAL CLASSES So far we have described social structure in terms of statuses and roles. There is more to social structure, however, than a mere assortment of statuses. In every society, these statuses are arranged on *a scale of prestige*. That is to say, the people in the society regard some statuses more favorably than others, or they rank statuses according to their desirability. Then the awards that the community has to distribute, such as wealth, power, respect, and honors, are parceled out according to this prestige scale. Naturally, there is no one-to-one correlation, say, between wealth and prestige, for those of equal prestige may receive somewhat different shares of the wealth. But taken together, the awards of the community correspond fairly well to status on a prestige scale. Studies have shown that when asked to rank different occupations according to social status, most groups give about the same rankings. For example, occupations such as physician, banker, or manager of a business are highly rated, clerk or salesperson has an intermediate rank, and unskilled factory workers are ranked low [Cattell, 1942].

Thus the prestige scale becomes the basis for forming social classes or strata. Those high on it are largely in one class; those low on it are mainly in another class. In many societies, the class system has become so formalized that it permeates all social organization and behavior. In many ancient kingdoms, for example, the classification of all members into one of three strata—nobility, freemen, and slaves—was unequivocal. Each person belonged to one of the three. Frequently his class membership was indicated by his speech, dress, or some other symbol clear to any observer. Each class was restricted to certain occupations and indeed to certain kinds of social behavior; freemen, for example, behaved in one way toward nobility, in another toward freemen, and in another toward slaves.

Our own society does not formalize classes so rigidly. It is not always easy to pick out a person's social class, and members of a class are certainly not confined so strictly to that class and its particular occupations as are, say, members of a caste in India. In other words, we have more class mobility. There is, nevertheless, a definite class structure in American society.

Social class determines, to a large extent, the social environment of the individual.

The social-class system maintains cultural, economic, and social barriers which prevent intimate social intermixture between the slums, the Gold Coast, and the middle class. We know that human beings can learn their culture only *from other human beings*, who already know and exhibit that culture. Therefore, by setting up barriers to social participation, the American social-class system actually prevents the vast majority of the children of the working classes, or the slums, from learning any culture but that of their own group. *Thus the pivotal meaning of social class to students of human development is that it defines and systematizes different learning environments for children of different classes.* [Davis and Havighurst, 1946, page 699.]

The socioeconomic level of the neighborhood, whether crowded tenement or spacious subdivision, will certainly affect the probability that a young person will ever complete high school or get to college. Social class affects vast aspects of an individual's experiences, for example, how he spends his leisure time, what sorts of things he considers important, what kind of job he will try to get, and even how he will perceive others and be perceived.

The division of society into classes has been scientifically studied. One such study was made in a town pseudonymously called Yankee City, and it revealed the class structure depicted in Figure 16.3 [Warner and Lunt, 1941]. This figure is constructed from a large number of interviews of citizens of Yankee City in which they were asked to rate their fellow townsmen on social status. For the most part, people did not think of social classes by the names used in the illustration. These were furnished by the research workers afterward. Yet it was clear enough that people distinguished three major classes and within each of them a lower and an upper part. With these categories they were able to classify almost everyone in the town. The percentages shown in Figure 16.3, however, would probably vary from one city, state, or section of the country to another.

CHARACTERISTICS OF CLASS In studies of this sort, the question arises, What criteria do the members of a community use when they rate their fellow members in social classes? The answer is never simple. The type of occupation and economic criteria are perhaps the most important, but many other factors enter into the evaluation. In Yankee City, for example, people revealed that they used all the following criteria in making their judgments: kind of income (whether salary, commission, dividend, or the like), moral standing, birth and family geneology, social relationships and organizations, and the kind of residential area in which the person lived.

But whatever the specific criteria employed in defining social-class membership, the classes differ, as we pointed out, in their social prestige. We are all familiar with instances of this broad principle; so it probably is of greater interest to point out the variety of ways in which class differences affect behavior.

The status hierarchy we see in any group represents a small-scale model of the social-class structure in our society as a whole. For that reason, we can study the effects of differences in the hierarchy of statuses by observing them in members of certain groups. This likening of a group to a society is more than a loose analogy. Actually there are a great many parallels between social-class differences and status differences in smaller groups. It has frequently been shown, for example, that people from the higher social classes generally are more attractive to other people than members of the lower classes, even at grade school age [Bonney, 1944]. Essentially the same thing is true of a wide variety of groups, including military units [Masling et al., 1955] and teams of mental-health workers [Hurwitz et al., 1953]. Whatever the basis for the status differentiation, whether it is athletic ability, military rank, or occupation, in many different kinds of groups, high-status people tend to have more social prestige in their group than low-status people do. This tendency to place people on a prestige scale apparently is so strongly learned that it even appears in situations which we like to believe are free of social-class effects. The following study illustrates this point [Strodtbeck et al., 1958]:

A team of investigators studied the deliberations of a mock jury, using jurors drawn by lot from regular jury pools in two large Midwestern cities. The relatively high prestige of the upper socioeconomic classes was revealed in a number of ways. For one thing, a person from a higher occupational level was more likely than others to be chosen jury foreman. For another, practically *all* occupational groups were inclined to say that, if members of

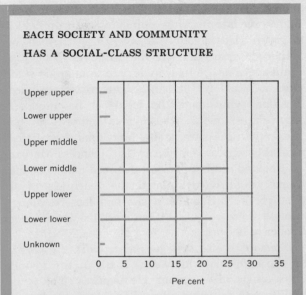

EACH SOCIETY AND COMMUNITY HAS A SOCIAL-CLASS STRUCTURE

FIGURE 16.3   *The class structure of Yankee City. The citizens of Yankee City, a New England community of about fifteen thousand people, were stratified in six classes on the basis of interviews and other information concerning their socioeconomic status and social activities. (Data from Warner and Lunt, 1941.)*

their family were involved in a jury trial, they would prefer the jury to be made up largely of people from the highest occupational ranks.

The high prestige going along with high status means that the high-status individuals often are accorded rights denied to those with lower status. One such right is the freedom to talk! High status seems to give a person the feeling that he can talk a great deal. This conclusion has come out of several studies, among them the studies of juries and mental-health workers mentioned above. In these instances, the higher the individual's status in the group, the more he participated in the group discussion.

High status under some conditions may make a

person feel somewhat freer to violate group mores and to deviate from the opinions generally held by a group [Dittes and Kelley, 1956]. There is one important exception to the principle that high-status persons are freer to deviate from group standards of behavior. If the high-status person occupies a position symbolizing the ideals of his group, he experiences greater pressures to conform to these ideals than the lower-status individual does. This is probably why, several years ago, Princess Margaret of England did not marry a divorced man. The marriage would have violated the teachings of the Church of England, and she had less freedom to violate these teachings than would a British commoner of her faith.

Something else that goes along with the prestige of the high-status individual is the ability to influence others in his group. He acquires some of this ability just by being allowed to talk more. In addition, people are more likely to agree with him and to believe what he says. This is another way of saying that high-status individuals are more likely to be accepted as leaders, a point which is elaborated in the last section of this chapter.

SOCIAL CLASSES AND BEHAVIOR The social classes differ not only in status and the things that go along with status; they also differ in the attitudes and personalities of their members. In regard to attitudes, political scientists, sociologists, and public-opinion pollsters have long known that the social classes differ in their political beliefs and social philosophies. One of the simplest and clearest correlations is that the higher a person is, either on the occupational scale or in the social class he thinks he belongs to, the more likely he is to hold conservative political opinions. This is by no means universally true, however.

One of the "Kinsey reports," an investigation of sexual behavior in the American male, revealed a significant relationship between sexual conduct and social class as measured by occupation [Kinsey et al., 1948]. The semiskilled-labor group showed a relatively frequent incidence of premarital intercourse and relatively infrequent masturbation. This pattern was reversed among professional persons, and the lower-white-collar group showed an intermediate or transitional pattern of sexual behavior. It is interesting to note what happens when an individual moves from one class to another. One of the unexpected findings of the Kinsey study was that "a person born into the skilled-labor class who *ultimately* moves into the professional class shows a youthful sexual pattern congruent with the *class into which he will eventually move!* Similarly, if a person born into the skilled-labor class ultimately locates in the unskilled-labor class, his pattern of sexual conduct closely resembles the pattern of persons born into that class" [Krech et al., page 334]. Thus knowledge of the social environment of the individual facilitates understanding of his sexual attitudes and behavior.

It is not widely recognized that members of the various social classes tend to have somewhat different personalities. Indeed, the kind of home or neighborhood in which one lives, the kind of work, the kind of play, the facilities that are available, and even the minimum necessities for satisfying basic needs all go along with social class and help to determine personality patterns. Even more important, however, the training and education of a child differ according to social class.

Several studies of social-class differences in child-rearing practices provide some interesting information on this point [Bronfenbrenner, 1958]. In the 1930s and 1940s, research studies generally showed that middle-class parents were stricter and more frustrating in their child-rearing practices than working-class parents. Studies conducted during the 1950s, however, have come to the opposite conclusion. Middle-class parents have become more permissive in training their young. The reason for this change, it seems, is that the middle-class parent more often follows the advice of the "experts" in child behavior. When, in the 1930s, these experts prescribed rigid schedules for children, the mother of higher status was more likely to follow the prescription. Similarly, when the experts later advised that children be permitted greater freedom, she followed that advice too. Since most child specialists are now tending to become somewhat more conservative in this matter, advising permissiveness but within definite limits, we can expect middle-class parents to follow this pattern before their counterparts among the working class do so.

Middle- and upper-class parents, then, are more inclined to follow the advice of experts in rearing their children than working-class parents are. But there is another important difference too. The working-class parent is more likely to use physical punishment in disciplining his child than is the middle-class parent. Instead of physical punishment, the middle-class parent more frequently employs "psychological discipline" in which he tries to reason with the youngster and make him feel guilty for doing disapproved things. This technique, the evidence indicates, is more effective in training and controlling the child (see Chapter 3). As one psychologist puts it, "These findings mean that middle-class parents, though in one sense more lenient in their discipline techniques, are using methods that are actually more compelling . . . which are likely to be effective in evoking the behavior desired in the child" [Bronfenbrenner, 1958, page 419].

The social classes also differ, of course, in their occupational goals for their children. The higher classes more often aspire to business and professional occupational status than the lower classes do. This fact is too well known to require proof. The cause is partly economic. If a working-class parent cannot afford to send his children to college and then on to medical school, and in addition must have his boy's income as soon as possible to help support the family, there is little sense in his boy thinking about becoming a doctor. In addition, however, more profound differences in motivation exist among the social classes.

Research with high school students has indicated, for example, that youngsters from the upper and middle social strata tend to have a higher level of achievement motivation (see page 234) than boys from the lower classes [Rosen, 1956]. Teen-agers from the higher classes more often want to do well relative to standards of excellence. The upper- and middle-class youngsters, moreover, are more likely to have some of the personal values and attributes that make for occupational success. More of them, for example, believe that it is possible for an individual to improve his status in life. More of them also think it worthwhile to postpone present pleasures in the interest of attaining future goals.

We see then that a number of important differences occur among individuals from the different social classes: They differ in prestige, in attractiveness to others, in freedom to talk, in a feeling of freedom to deviate from group standards, in ability to influence others, in attitudes and beliefs, in child-rearing practices, in educational goals, and even in certain motivations.

Social groups

We have now seen that every society has a culture and a social structure. Each is also characterized by *social groups*. Each member in a society not only has his statuses, roles, and social class, he is also a member of a large number of groups. For at least part of his life he is a member of a family group. One's peer group changes through the years, but peer groups are important, and the pressures these groups exert are very real determiners of behavior. A college student may belong to a dormitory or other living group, a fraternity, a debating organization, the basketball team, a political group, a bowling league, as well as classroom groups. His behavior affects the group in small or large ways, and the group affects and controls his behavior.

GROUP CHARACTERISTICS Social groups may differ in a number of dimensions, and we are interested in how these may affect the actions of the group. It has been noted that groups may differ in many ways:

1. Size, or the number of members.

2. The degree to which they are organized and operate in a formal manner.

3. The degree to which they are stratified, that is, the extent to which group members are related to one another in a hierarchy.

4. The degree to which they exercise or attempt to exercise control over the behavior of their members.

5. The degree of participation which is permitted, expected, or demanded of members.

6. The ease of access to membership in the group and the ease with which a member can leave or be expelled from the group.

7. The degree of stability of the group over time and the continuity of its membership over time.

8. The degree to which group members relate to one another intimately, on a personal basis and with respect to a wide range of activities and interests, rather than in a formal manner and only with respect to a narrowly defined set of activities.

9. The degree to which the group is subdivided into smaller groups or cliques, and the extent to which such cliques are in conflict with one another. [McGrath, 1964, page 65.]

Although other characteristics descriptive of groups could be mentioned, it is clear that the nature of the interaction between group members will be influenced by how many others are in the group and by the situation as perceived by the group members, as, for example, whether cooperation or competition characterizes the situation. The study of the nature of groups has been given the name *group dynamics* [Lewin, 1951]. This field of investigation seeks to learn more about how groups develop and function and what factors affect the relationships which exist between groups and individuals, or other groups. The discussion remaining in this chapter and much of that in the following chapter on attitudes could be considered to deal with the field of group dynamics.

REWARDS AND COSTS Every day we make decisions about how we shall spend our time and with whom we shall spend it. Although much of each day is routine, in many instances we select one alternative behavior instead of another. Some psychologists have found it useful to discuss interpersonal relations and group functioning in terms of the rewards received by the individual and the costs he incurs [Thibaut and Kelley, 1959; Secord and

Backman, 1964]. A person selects certain people to be his friends, for example, because he enjoys being with them or doing the things they do. *Rewards* are considered pleasures or satisfactions occurring as a result of the behavior chosen. *Costs* refer to anything that would deter or inhibit the behavior, such as great physical or mental effort, or anxiety about the consequences of the action. If an acquaintance has numerous nervous mannerisms which make you uneasy, it is doubtful that you will choose him as a best friend. The individual consciously or unconsciously weighs the various alternatives and decides what he will do in a given situation. He tries to anticipate which course of action will be most rewarding to him, with the least cost, and may compare the attractiveness of the situation or relationship with other possible opportunities. For instance, a college freshman may decide to choose no one "best" friend until he has had an opportunity to get to know many of the others in his dormitory. Once a relationship between two or more persons is begun, each is somewhat interdependent upon the other to receive satisfactory *outcomes*. Generally, each person expects the rewards and outcomes to be proportional to costs in an exchange relationship. A person may be angry if he does not get what he feels is due him; he may feel guilty if he is overrewarded [Homans, 1950].

Social power. Social power depends on the resources or abilities which an individual possesses which permit him to affect the outcomes of another person. Even if one person has more power than another, he is not too likely to use it. The bald exertion of power usually brings some costs to the user, for the other person may still have some control of the goodness of outcomes experienced by the more powerful person. Many relationships are characterized by such *reciprocal control,* where each individual has the "ability to affect another person's outcomes" [Thibaut and Kelley, 1959].

Compromise. Compromise is often necessary to maintain a pleasing relationship so that the outcomes are acceptable to all concerned. For example, if a wife wants to go to a concert which she knows her husband is not too enthusiastic about attending, she may prepare an especially delicious meal before they go out, or even suggest they have a steak dinner before the concert. Much of the theorizing and experimentation dealing with rewards and costs has dealt with two-person groups, called *dyads*. A special closeness exists in a relationship between just two persons, for there are constraints on both to keep the interaction mutually satisfactory [Simmel, 1902–1903]. Many experiments have used various game situations to study how people handle relationships with specific rewards and costs attached to specific behaviors [Mintz, 1951; Hollander, 1958.]

When three persons are in a group, a *triad* is formed. No matter how close these three persons are, there will be some times when two will have an opinion or orientation, the other will differ, and a *coalition* may form. Some of these complications in social relationships are responsible for difficulties that a couple may have in adjusting to their first baby, or they may account for the tendency for less harmonious play of three preschool children as compared with two children.

Each person evaluates the outcomes resulting from a given social relationship by considering available alternatives and the rewards and costs associated with each alternative. As we shall see in the next section, conformity to group norms is one way to reduce costs and increase rewards in many situations.

CONFORMITY TO GROUP NORMS Groups of which we are members influence our behavior in various ways, but probably most powerfully and pervasively through *group norms*. A norm, as the term implies, is a standard of behavior, but it is more than that. To understand its precise nature, we must refer again to the concepts of role and status.

A role, we have seen, is the behavior expected of us in a particular status. The accent should now be placed on the word "expected." A group can *expect* certain behavior from us because it can confer its disapproval on us if we do not do what is expected. Since most of us acquire the need for social approval, and hence do not wish to incur disapproval, we do what is expected of us. In a word, we conform to our group's expectations. For example, as members of many groups—family, university, community, church, and so on—we have many expected roles we must play. We must somehow *conform* to the expectations of the group or suffer the disapproval of the group members. These expectations constitute *group norms* which may be defined more formally as widely shared expectations among most members of a group, class, or culture.

Group norms seem to emerge, like statuses and social structure, whenever a group is formed. A group exists when interaction occurs among individuals. By interaction we mean any conversation, exchange of goods and services, or any joint efforts which could tend to cast group members into any kind of status. The longer people interact, and the more they interact, the more they tend to adopt common ways of interpreting the world and common standards for the behavior of each group member. In other words, group norms to which individuals feel a pressure to conform develop whenever there is any kind of continued interaction among people.

A now classic experiment in social psychology illustrates how expectations about situations, or group norms, may develop with continued social interaction [Sherif, 1935]:

The subjects were placed in a totally dark room and were asked to judge how far a stationary point source of light seemed to move (the autokinetic effect, page 361). Since the walls of the room were not visible, no physical frame of reference was available to aid in making these judgments. In part of the experiment, individuals were shown the light for the first time in a group situation, and each person expressed his opinion aloud for the others to hear. The group members soon began to influence one another. Their judgments at first did not agree very well, but as they listened to one another's opinions, they seemed to agree that the light moved within a certain range. Each group developed its own range of judgments, that is, its own way of perceiving this situation. Later, when each of the group members was asked to make his judgments alone, they still judged the movement to be within the range that had been agreed upon in the group. Thus, in the group, the subjects learned to interpret the ambiguous situation in a given way, and the learning carried over into their judgments when they were alone.

This experiment can serve as a model that helps explain many different kinds of social influences, including the adoption of certain cultural patterns. In their interaction, members of a society develop a common way of perceiving their world and the things in it. Perhaps even the Tchambuli conception of women as naturally businesslike and men as artistic arose in this way.

From shared perceptions, it is only a short step to shared rules or norms governing the behavior of group members in each status position. The difference is that norms have a *demand* quality. Not only does an individual tend to see and act the way other group members do, but he *must* do so. To enforce the demand, the group members devise different degrees of punishment ranging all the way from capital punishment for major crimes to something so innocuous as a social snub. In between are many tangible and effective forms of demanding conformity to group norms. Some years ago, for example, a white physician in Florida was fired from his post as county physician for having lunch with a Negro nurse. The doctor's behavior deviated from the norms then held regarding proper white-Negro relations; so social and economic punishment befell the violator. Women who smoked in public during the nineteenth and early twentieth centuries suffered a less severe punishment. They were simply excluded from "polite society."

FACTORS AFFECTING CONFORMITY People tend to conform to group norms for at least two good reasons. One has already been stressed: Those who go against the norms suffer social disapproval or punishment in varying degrees. This fact is widely known and motivates a good deal of conformity. Pressure to conform, however, is not exerted only by those we know or by those known to have the power to enforce the norms. The desire for

social approval is so ingrained and so generalized to members of the group or community that we may even desire approval from complete strangers. This fact was demonstrated in one of the earliest experiments in social psychology [Allport, 1924]. Subjects in the experiment tended to give less extreme judgments when they were in the presence of other people than when they were alone. We can only surmise that this was because they feared that extreme judgments would bring disapproval from others about them, and they sought to avoid disapproval even though the others were strangers.

A second reason for social conformity is equally obvious. An individual may "go along" with the opinions of his group because he believes these opinions are correct, or at least probably correct. If the situation is somewhat ambiguous and one individual does not know exactly what is expected of him, he is quite likely to seek to compare his behavior with the actions of others who are in the same situation. This sort of *social comparison* does not always lead to conformity, but where objective evaluation of environmental situational cues is difficult, "going along" with someone else is often chosen as the appropriate behavior [Festinger, 1954; Schachter and Singer, 1962].

It is important to distinguish between these two bases for conforming behavior even though it is at times difficult to tell *why* a given person may be conforming. The following experiment seems to suggest conformity due to belief that the majority is correct [Asch, 1951]:

Subjects were asked to make judgments concerning the length of lines. Each experimental session typically employed only one actual subject in a group of people who had been coached to express certain opinions. Hence, the real subject often faced a situation in which his eyes told him one thing while the others in the group agreed that something else was correct. Only a minority of the subjects consistently yielded to the erroneous group opinion. Later interviews with those who conformed to the majority opinion suggested that most of these "conformists" thought something was wrong with their eyesight and that the majority was probably correct.

Several years later, two experimenters repeated this study in its essential details but added some other experimental conditions [Deutsch and Gerard, 1955]:

In one of these conditions, the subjects were led to believe that they could express their opinions anonymously after learning the judgments of others. Under this condition, subjects yielded much less to the erroneous majority than did subjects in the "nonanonymous" condition. Even so, a few of the "anonymous" subjects conformed to the group. Thus most of the subjects who expressed the majority opinion apparently did so in order not to appear different (and hence, in order not to incur disapproval?), rather than because they believed the majority to be correct.

It is not always easy, as these experiments show, to disentangle the two chief reasons for conforming—fear of disapproval and belief that the group is correct. Indeed, both factors are probably at work in most situations in which people conform to group norms.

In addition to these factors, a number of others affect conforming behavior. We shall discuss four: (1) attraction to the group, (2) perceived consensus within the group, (3) orientation to the group, and (4) the need to be liked and accepted. Each of these factors, as we shall see, involves some combination of fear of disapproval and belief in the group's opinion.

Attraction to the group. If a person is strongly attracted to the group, either because he likes it or because he somehow sees it as meeting his needs, he is more inclined to conform to it than if he is not attracted to it. And the greater his attraction, that is, the more he wants to belong to the group, the more likely he is to agree with the opinions of the other members of the group. This conclusion is based on experiments, but it also grows out of daily experience. We usually have a higher regard for the opinions of people we like than for those of people we do not like. This is particularly the case if we have no objective way of determining whether the opinions are correct, as we often do not.

Fear of disapproval is certainly one of the reasons for greater conformity in groups which are attrac-tive to us. The punishment we may suffer by being rejected or disapproved of by a group is obviously more serious if it is meted out by a group to which we would really like to belong. Hence, we tend to conform to the norms of groups that are attractive to us. This point is illustrated in the following experiment [Berkowitz, 1954]:

The situation was so arranged that some subjects developed a great liking for two other people in their group, while other subjects developed less liking for these two people. The subjects were then put to work on a task in a room by themselves. They were then given messages which were supposed to have come from the people they liked or did not like. Thus the subjects believed that the messages came from people in their group, but they were actually standard messages from the experimenter. One set of messages made it known that other group members wanted a high level of productivity on the task, thus establishing a group norm for high productivity. In other instances, the subject was led to believe that the other group members wanted low productivity, thus setting a group norm for low productivity. In other words, the experimental variables were liking versus disliking other group members and high productivity versus low productivity as group norms. How well the subjects did on the tasks yielded a measure of conforming behavior. The results were that the subjects who liked other members of their group conformed more to the group norms, whether these were for high or low productivity, than the subjects who had considerably less liking for their group members.

Perceived consensus within the group. Another important factor affecting conformity is the amount of agreement existing among the group members. If an individual sees that the others about him are unanimously agreed on a certain opinion or course of behavior, he is more likely to conform to their views than if he believes the group members are not in complete accord. This conclusion is borne out by several experiments. In experiments similar to the one just mentioned, in which a subject seated with a group of confederates of the experimenter was asked to express his estimate of the length of certain lines, conformity went up when the other people in his group had been coached to give a unanimous opinion [Asch, 1958]. However, the subject was much less likely to conform to the group judgments when at least one other person also differed from the group. One reason for this result, it seems, is that deviation from a unanimously agreed upon point of view may bring greater disapproval than nonconformity to a less agreed upon opinion.

Orientation to the group. Another factor in conformity is the orientation of the individual to his group. This orientation can vary in a number of ways, of which we shall mention two. One is the degree to which he feels accepted or rejected by the group. The other is orientation to the tasks to be performed by group members.

The first of these, feelings of acceptance or rejection by the group, is of interest because it determines whether a person's conformity is real or only something professed in public. If a person feels rejected by his group, he is probably going to be motivated more by fear of disapproval than by a belief that the group may be correct. And if a person goes along with the views of others because he is afraid of being rejected by them, it stands to reason that he is not likely to adopt their views as his own. He is like a boy who expects to be punished for misbehavior. When threatened with punishment, the boy may accede to his parents' wishes only because he believes he may be caught, not because he believes they are correct. Similarly, the person primarily motivated by the desire to avoid disapproval may conform only publicly just to keep from being caught. Privately, he may continue to hold the disapproved views. On the other hand, an individual who is attracted to his group, or who believes its opinions are correct, will tend to adopt its views as his own.

What we are saying, in brief, is that conformity motivated by fear of disapproval is only superficial. It is not true conformity. This notion can be tested, and has been, by varying the motivation to avoid disapproval. To start with, the individual is made to feel either accepted or rejected by his group. If he feels rejected, he should, according to this theory, have a greater fear of disapproval. The following experiment demonstrates this point [Dittes and Kelley, 1956]:

Some subjects in the experiment were treated in such a way that they felt rejected by the group. Others were made to feel accepted. The degree to which they conformed to group opinion was then measured. The result was that subjects with low acceptance "toed the line" in the group. Feeling that they were on the verge of being outcasts, they went to great lengths to conform to the group. This conformity, however, was only a public, superficial conformity. Privately, they conformed less than those who felt accepted.

We see then that where fear of disapproval is strong, conformity is not likely to be real. Outward conformity, but not inward conformity, is usually the result.

A second way in which orientation to the group affects conformity has to do with whether a person is group-oriented or task-oriented. Some people working in a group are much more concerned with the task the group has to accomplish—with getting things done—than with their personal relations with group members. This may come about because the individual is typically task-oriented rather than group-oriented, because he is seriously interested in the purposes of the group, or because people in the group somehow make him feel this way. In any case, we might expect the task-oriented person to be much less affected by group pressures for conformity than the person who is group-oriented, that is, concerned about his personal relations with the group. This expectation has been borne out by research [Thibaut and Strickland, 1956]:

The investigators manipulated the situation so that some of their subjects were group-oriented and others were task-oriented. The task-oriented subjects were told that their purpose in being there was to find the best answer to an assigned problem. The group-oriented subjects were made conscious of their personal relations with the other group members so that they became more concerned with their acceptability to the other members. All the subjects were then asked to express their opinions about the best solution to the problem. After that, they were placed under varying degrees of pressure to adopt the views of certain other members of the group. The degree to which the two kinds of subjects yielded to this pressure was then measured. The group-oriented subjects, who were concerned about their personal relations with other people in the group, tended to be influenced by this pressure. Indeed, for them, the greater the pressure, the more they conformed. This was not the case, however, for task-oriented subjects.

Need to be liked and accepted. Conformity makes a person more apt to be accepted and liked by others [Walker and Heyns, 1962]. In one experiment where conformity to the opinions of others in the group was represented as being instrumental to the group liking the subject, a high degree of conformity to the group norms was observed when the subject wanted to participate in the group. If an individual wants to be accepted in a certain group, he will learn to conform to the group norms. If a teen-ager wants to be accepted by his peers, he will find it difficult to resist group pressures to conformity. This may take the form of wearing certain types of clothing, adopting certain hair styles, knowing the latest dances, owning a car, or may involve drinking, shoplifting, sex exploration, and experimentation with drugs. Fear of social disapproval of one's peers can provide strong motivation to conform—at least superficially.

A certain sameness is sometimes noted among members of a given fraternity chapter; conformity produces some of these standard behaviors. Even the extreme "nonconformists" who exist on the fringes of many university communities have very identifiable characteristic habits and modes of dress which are norms in their own groups. Though they wish to be considered nonconformists, they often slavishly conform to the behaviors expected of them by their friends.

Thus we may conform because we need to be accepted. Related to this is the use of conformity as a technique to make other people like us. Experiments have shown that conformity is a common "tactic of ingratiation . . . a means of currying favor with a more powerful individual" [Jones, 1965]. By subtly agreeing with the opinions of the more powerful person, we may make him like us more. Research has shown that the ingratiator steers a course between being an obvious "yes man" and outright disagreement [Jones, 1965]. The ingratiator does this by (1) agreeing with the more powerful person, but expressing low confidence in his own opinion; (2) agreeing with the substance but not many of the specific details of the more powerful "target" person's arguments; and (3) agreeing only on those occasions when the "target" person seems open to argument.

We have discussed group norms and conformity behavior at some length because these are concepts basic to understanding group influences on the individual. In fact, the pervasive control that society exercises over our lives—the theme with which we opened this chapter—is exerted very largely through such group norms and our motivation to comply with them.

ANALYSIS OF THE INTERACTION PROCESS Particular attention has been paid by researchers to the patterns of communication and social interaction in small groups, and several category systems have been devised to help in the description and analysis of group behavior. Figure 16.4 shows one such method used in observing social interaction and communication in a systematic way [Bales, 1950]. Ordinarily, an observer is behind a one-way mirror and his task is to classify each verbal statement or relevant communication made by a member of the group into one of 12 categories, recording also who spoke to whom. The categories are: (1) shows solidarity, (2) shows tension release, (3) shows agreement, (4) gives suggestion, (5) gives opinion, (6) gives information, (7) asks for information, (8) asks for opinion, (9) asks for suggestion, (10) shows disagreement, (11) shows tension, (12) shows antagonism. These categories are divided into active task contributions (attempted answers), passive task contributions (questions), and into positive and negative reactions not specifically related to the point under consideration.

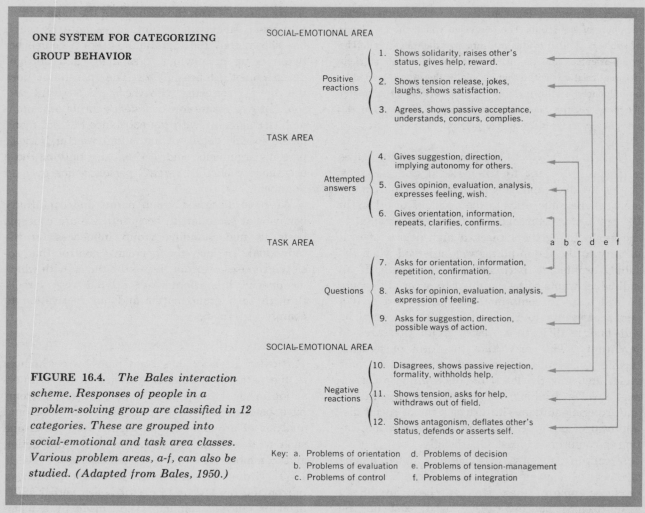

ONE SYSTEM FOR CATEGORIZING
GROUP BEHAVIOR

SOCIAL-EMOTIONAL AREA

Positive
reactions

1. Shows solidarity, raises other's
status, gives help, reward.

2. Shows tension release, jokes,
laughs, shows satisfaction.

3. Agrees, shows passive acceptance,
understands, concurs, complies.

TASK AREA

Attempted
answers

4. Gives suggestion, direction,
implying autonomy for others.

5. Gives opinion, evaluation, analysis,
expresses feeling, wish.

6. Gives orientation, information,
repeats, clarifies, confirms.

TASK AREA

a b c d e f

Questions

7. Asks for orientation, information,
repetition, confirmation.

8. Asks for opinion, evaluation, analysis,
expression of feeling.

9. Asks for suggestion, direction,
possible ways of action.

SOCIAL-EMOTIONAL AREA

Negative
reactions

10. Disagrees, shows passive rejection,
formality, withholds help.

11. Shows tension, asks for help,
withdraws out of field.

12. Shows antagonism, deflates other's
status, defends or asserts self.

Key: a. Problems of orientation   d. Problems of decision
      b. Problems of evaluation   e. Problems of tension-management
      c. Problems of control   f. Problems of integration

FIGURE 16.4. *The Bales interaction scheme. Responses of people in a problem-solving group are classified in 12 categories. These are grouped into social-emotional and task area classes. Various problem areas, a-f, can also be studied. (Adapted from Bales, 1950.)*

The study of changes observed in the frequency of types of communciation in a problem-solving situation, for example, clarifies the nature of the problem-solving process and facilitates comparison of groups. Combining data obtained in observing 22 different groups which had met to deal with various problems yielded information suggesting phases in the problem-solving process [Bales, 1961]. The changes in relative frequency of communications classified in the various categories are shown in Figure 16.5. Problems pertaining to the task—orientation, evaluation, and control—are graphed separately; positive and negative socioemotional reactions are graphed. Discussion tends to begin with emphasis on orientation and clarifying information pertaining to the problem. The middle of the group session emphasizes analysis and evaluation of the task. The final portion of the meeting typically deals most with seeking resolution of the problem. The relative frequency of positive and negative reactions tends to increase from beginning to end of most group sessions, with laughing and joking tending to be highest at the end of meetings.

The Bales analysis tends to show that two types of leaders usually emerge in group problem-solving situations. The conventional leader is the one with the best ideas: the one who usually makes the most contributions toward getting the group to work on the task at hand. The best-liked person provides the "light touch" of humor or encouragement when needed and keeps the group in good spirits. These two roles are seldom held by the same person, as they are somewhat incompatible. Leadership is discussed more completely later in this chapter.

COMMUNICATION STRUCTURES Communications within a group are affected not only by whom the individuals in the group *wish* to talk to, but also by whom they are *permitted* to talk to. Most groups do not allow free-for-all discussions. They have chairmen to govern who may talk and when. They may also have rules about who may talk to whom. The workingman seldom gets a chance to talk to the company president. A junior executive may talk to his boss, but ordinarily cannot go over his boss's head to the boss's boss. Thus the channels of communication are normally limited in certain ways. The pattern of closed- and open-communication channels in a group is known as the *communication structure.*

Let us take as an example two different groups of men, each organized to solve a particular business problem. In one group, each member is free to talk to anyone else in the group. Quite different is a structure in which each group member can communicate with a central person but not with anybody else. If they want to send messages to each other, they must do it through the central person who can relay it on or not as he sees fit. This pattern is usually known as a "star" communication structure. Obviously, there may be many other kinds of structures, but for simplicity we shall discuss only these two (see Figure 16.6).

Behavioral effects of group structure. Is one structure better than another for getting a job done? Unfortunately, there is no simple, clear-cut answer. Many experiments have been done comparing the two structures, and the results seem to depend upon a number of things. Two of the most significant factors are the difficulty or complexity of the job to be done and the work load given to each of the

group members. The thing we can say with assurance, however, is that people feel better in the free communication structure than in the star pattern. People in the free-communication structure generally find their jobs more satisfying and have higher morale than the noncentral members of the star pattern [Shaw, 1955].

The reason usually given for this difference is that the free-communication pattern gives the group members more *independence* [Shaw, 1955]. In this type of group, each person is relatively independent

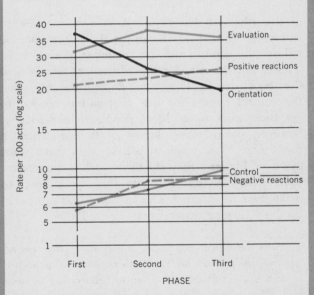

THE BALES TECHNIQUE HELPS TO CHART THE COURSE OF GROUP INTERACTION

FIGURE 16.5 *Changes in the frequency of types of communication in a problem-solving group. The changes were studied with the Bales method. "Control" and "negative reactions" rise from the first to the third phase of the meeting; "evaluation" and "positive reactions" stay about the same, while "orientation" drops sharply. (Adapted from Bales, 1952.)*

THE COMMUNICATION STRUCTURE OF A GROUP IS ITS PATTERN OF OPEN- AND
CLOSED-COMMUNICATION CHANNELS

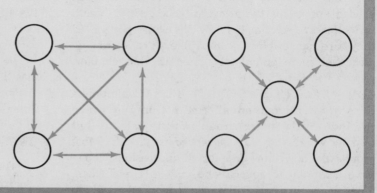

FIGURE 16.6. *Two types of communication structure. On the right, the "star" pattern in which group members may communicate only with a central person; on the left, a completely connected free-communication structure in which each person may communicate with everyone else.*

of the others in his group. A person can talk to whomever he wishes; he can get the information or opinion he wants from any member at any time. This is not the case for the noncentral members of the star structure. They must depend entirely upon the central person for the information needed to get their work done. Most people in our society, however, desire some degree of independence in their jobs. They want to believe they have some say over the way they do their work. Communication structures that frustrate this desire tend to make them dissatisfied. This hypothesis is supported by the following experiment [Trow, 1957]:

Before the experiment began, a personality test was administered to measure each subject's need for independence. In addition, each subject was led to believe that he occupied either a central or a peripheral (noncentral) position in a communication network. Within each of these positions, some people were made to believe that they did not depend upon another group member, while the others were made dependent upon him. The results indicated that job satisfaction was affected by making the subjects either independent of or dependent upon others. It was not affected merely by giving them either the central or peripheral position. Furthermore, it was affected most in those subjects with a relatively strong need for independence. These subjects were happiest when they were independent of other group members in doing their job and unhappiest when they had to rely on others for information.

Superficially, the star-communication structure looks somewhat like an authoritarian group in which the group is dominated by a "dictator" or boss, and the free-communication pattern resembles a democratic group in which individuals have "freedom of speech." Indeed, communication is more restricted in an authoritarian group than in a democratic one. Again, however, the underlying difference is more related to feelings of independence, and the different climate these feelings create, than to the communication structure itself. Individuals in a democratic group can better satisfy their needs for independence. Consequently, they are generally happier. Students of Kurt Lewin have experimentally produced these different climates in children's play groups [Lewin et al., 1939]:

The experimenters created three kinds of groups: autocratic groups, democratic groups, and laissez-faire groups (see Figure 16.7). In the democratic groups, the leader acted as a consultant; he suggested, persuaded, and helped, but refrained from domineering. In the autocratic groups, he ordered and commanded, permitting no suggestions from group members. In the laissez-faire groups, he paid little or no attention to the group members, letting them do whatever they wanted to.

The laissez-faire groups, as one might expect, accomplished relatively little that was constructive; members of these groups were frequently bored, or they broke into horseplay. In the democratic groups, as compared with both the others, and particularly with the autocratic groups, there was less hostility, more enjoyment, and more constructive work, and the group did not fall apart when the leader left it. The experiments point out, however, that some exceptions to the superiority of the democratic climate did occur. For instance, as long as the leader was guiding the group firmly, the autocratic group tended to produce a little more than the democratic group.

Feedback. Feedback is a factor determining the effectiveness of communication. The term feedback refers to information about the state of a system which is "fed back" to guide the control of the system. For instance, knowledge of results in learning can be thought of as feedback. Information about success and failure—the output—is fed back to control the system—the approach the learner takes to a problem. In social communication, feedback can occur in the following manner.

If one person A is presenting information to another person B, A needs some sort of evaluation

THE AUTOCRATIC LEADER ORDERS, THE DEMOCRATIC LEADER CONSULTS,
AND THE LAISSEZ-FAIRE LEADER HELPS ONLY WHEN ASKED

FIGURE 16.7. *Authoritarian, democratic, and laissez-faire groups. In the authoritarian group, above, the leader tells the boys exactly what to do. In the democratic group, right above, he acts as a consultant. In the laissez-faire group, right below, the leader helps only when asked and the children are often bored or break into horseplay. (Ronald Lippitt.)*

of the effectiveness of his presentation. Accurate transmission of the information may require some feedback or communication from B to A, especially if the material is relatively new or complicated. By comparing *free feedback* and *zero feedback* conditions, one experiment confirmed that when the receiver of the communication, B, is free to ask questions, the information is transmitted more accurately [Leavitt and Mueller, 1951]. The questions of B tell A how he is doing. Both persons are also more confident that they have communicated correctly. Feedback does take additional time, but this additional time decreases as A and B learn to communicate more effectively. A sender and receiver can improve their performance without verbal feedback, however, apparently through the sender's gaining experience and confidence, and perhaps through such nonverbal communication as gestures or quizzical expressions indicating a point needing clarification. Zero feedback creates some feelings of doubt by the sender that he is doing a good job of communicating the information. It also creates some hostility in the receiver, if the zero feedback condition seems imposed arbitrarily. Once free feedback has been permitted, additional feedback seems less necessary, as though the common misunderstandings had been clarified.

Leadership

One of the most important characteristics of groups is that they have leaders. One person may get himself out of a burning building, but 500 school children cannot be evacuated without some coordination. Children can play individually as long as they are climbing ropes or riding a bicycle, but in most games they need a leader. You can play football without a captain, but the game is much more fun if someone calls the signals. Anarchists may be efficient individualists when assassinating kings and derailing trains, but anarchism applied to a military organization would result in many dead heroes and few victories. The moral is, of course, that groups need leaders if they are to pull together as a team.

LEADERS AND SOCIAL CHANGE　Although students of human affairs have long tried to evaluate the role of leaders in group behavior, they have not been able to reach agreement on the matter. Writers from Carlyle to Marx have leaned toward one or another of two extreme opinions about leaders. Either leaders are necessary, and history hinges on their actions; or leaders are merely the expression of popular needs, riding the tide of history, but not influencing it.

The first view may be called the "leader principle" or the "great-man theory" of history. It holds that masses of people drift along in aimless confusion until a gifted leader assumes command and tells them what to do. The "man on horseback" is always a dramatic figure. He may accomplish social change, for good or bad, but the truth of the matter is that he *appears* to accomplish much more than he actually does. It is said, for example, that Hitler conquered Poland and that Hitler slaughtered millions of people. Literally speaking, Hitler did not do any of these things. Mostly he just talked. But would these things have happened without Hitler? We do not know, for history is an uncontrolled experiment. Yet under the great-man theory of history, Hitler is credited with *causing* the events.

The second opinion might be called the sociological view. It says that history makes or selects the man, not vice versa. Social and cultural developments are considered to follow their own laws, and the presence of a particular person as leader is purely coincidental. A society is metaphorically regarded as a sprawling organism, adapting slowly to environmental change. Its habits and customs are its culture. If a society finds itself at war, a peaceful leader will not be tolerated; a nation in defeat demands a quisling type of leader. No leader can be at variance with the needs of the group and remain its leader. According to this view, then, it was not Hitler, but the German people who overran Poland and slaughtered the Jews. Extreme adherents of this view will not even admit the temporary influence of the leader. To them, he may be the peoples' voice, but never its brain.

Arguments can be summoned for and against

each of these views of leadership, but neither extreme can be proved or disproved. The truth seems to lie somewhere between the two. Social change is probably a function of *leaders, groups,* and *situations,* all of which interact to determine the outcome. Leaders usually make some difference, sometimes great and sometimes small. On the other hand, the needs and attitudes of groups determine whom they will select and follow as their leaders. And, of course, the behavior of both leaders and groups depends upon the situations they face.

Psychologists have no business playing the role of historian by explaining history. They can, however, conduct experiments on leadership in different kinds of groups and situations. One of these experiments shows how leaders and followers interact to affect each other [Haythorn, 1958]:

Four-man groups were assembled, with one member as the appointed leader. The groups were formed so that the personalities of the leader and his followers differed. First, the subjects were given a personality test designed to measure their "authoritarian" tendencies, that is, the extent to which they desired a clear-cut authority structure in society (see page 602). By using the results of this test, the experimenter established four types of groups: (1) highly authoritarian leaders with highly authoritarian followers; (2) highly authoritarian leaders with less authoritarian followers; (3) less authoritarian leaders with highly authoritarian followers; and (4) less authoritarian leaders with less authoritarian followers. Then the discussions that took place in these groups were studied. The discussions, it turned out, were affected by both the personality of the leader and the personalities of the followers. Groups with authoritarian leaders were more formal in structure and had a more unequal division of the work than the groups whose leaders were less authoritarian in personality, regardless of the followers' personalities. The followers, however, had some influence on the leaders' behavior. Regardless of their own personalities, leaders who had authoritarian followers behaved in a more autocratic manner than leaders with less authoritarian followers. The leader and group clearly affected each other.

PERSONALITIES OF LEADERS   This brings us to the question of what personality traits, if any, characterize leaders. Our libraries are filled with well-meaning books, containing nothing but highly opinionated advice on the subject, usually intended for the young males of our society about to be initiated into the glories of adulthood. Opinions unrelated to facts are next to worthless for a science, and that is what most popular writing on leadership is. In recent years, however, leadership has been studied with scientific techniques.

In many of their studies, scientists have sought to isolate those personality characteristics which are possessed by leaders but not by nonleaders. By and large, the results of the research have been inconsistent [Jenkins, 1947a], partly because too many different kinds of "leaders" have been grouped together, as if there were only one kind of leadership. Clearly, the person who is the leader of an intellectual group concerned with abstract ideas must be different from the individual who leads, say, an athletic club. To get a picture of leaders and leadership, we must consider the situation confronting the group, for the situation in which a leader leads determines to a considerable extent the personal qualities he must have.

This is not to say that leaders of any two groups will necessarily not have any traits in common, or that the person who emerges as the leader of one group is not likely to become the leader of any other group. Indeed, it is possible to list some general qualities that often distinguish people who emerge as leaders. By and large, leaders are more likely to be active participators in their groups, are dependable, persistent, verbally facile, self-confident, and socially popular [Stogdill, 1948]. Having these qualities, however, does not ensure leadership in every group. But if the situation is right, the person who possesses such a combination of traits will probably win a position of leadership.

FORMAL AND INFORMAL LEADERS   Before we can understand why these traits may be important and in what situations they are most effective, we must understand more clearly who a leader is. Basically, of course, a *leader* is a person who influences a group to follow the course of action he advocates, but we generally restrict the term to those who frequently are successful influencers. They must get group members to adopt their proposals more than once or even a few times. Even when another person comes up with an idea that influences the group throughout one of its meetings, the leader's approval is necessary to sanction the idea. Hence in this situation, the leader is really the major influencer; he has influenced the acceptance of the idea.

Formal leaders. The formal leader influences his group primarily because he occupies a formally recognized status. He is the president, chairman, or king. It is his usual role to attempt to influence, and it is the followers' role to follow. Frequently, of course, the followers accept the formal leader's ideas because the leader has authority over them; he dispenses rewards and punishments.

As we have seen, influence based upon the threat of punishment is not likely to be long lasting. The followers will obey orders only so long as they fear getting caught. Such leadership, thus, cannot be very effective, though in some situations, such as in battle, it may of necessity be workable. Generally, a leader is most effective when his followers accept his ideas because they truly believe in them. In any case, the formal leader ultimately derives his authority and influence from the position he occupies.

The following experiment demonstrates how an individual's formal status can affect other group members' acceptance of his proposals [Raven and French, 1958]:

In this study, one person, the investigator's confederate, attempted to influence the real subjects under two different conditions. There were different groups of subjects for each of the conditions. In one condition, the confederate apparently usurped the leadership role when it was not "legally" granted him by the group. In the other, he supposedly was elected to this role. His attempts to influence the group were much more successful when he was elected by the group. From this result, the investigators concluded that, "the election procedure is a formal means for designating the legiti-

mate occupant of an office and for investing him with the legitimate power of that office."

Informal leaders. The informal leader may frequently be quite a successful influencer of his group; yet his influence is not derived from a formal position. More than anything else, the others in the group follow his lead because his personal qualities convince them that they can satisfy their own needs by accepting his ideas. For this to happen, the group members must be unsure of how to attain their goals on their own. Since they cannot cope with the problems facing the group, they turn to the informal leader for ways of achieving their group goals.

But why does a group in this situation turn to one particular person? What are the important personal qualities he must possess? One quality certainly is his proficiency, as the group perceives it, in handling the tasks confronting the group. Of course, it often happens that a group has no sure way of knowing this. Then, in the absence of any objective means for evaluating an individual's task competence, the group frequently relies on the person's past performance. It is as if the group members say, "He has been right before; the chances are he is right now." This is probably one good reason why a person who has done well in the past is more likely to be a successful influencer on subsequent occasions than a person who had not done a good job earlier [Mausner, 1954].

Past performance, however, is not the only basis for accepting an informal leader's ideas. Liking him is another, just as it is in conforming behavior. A person who is well liked has a much better chance of having his ideas accepted, and thus of influencing people, than one who is less popular. Partly for this reason, social skills and personal popularity often characterize the person chosen for a position of leadership. In addition, the leader's job frequently involves promoting and maintaining harmonious relations among the members of his group. Hence, a socially skillful, popular person is better able to achieve these friendly relations within the group than a less socially skillful person.

As one might expect, the person who is highly popular with the members of one group is more likely to be popular with other groups. A person who has social skills and is likable can recruit friends from a wide range of people—but, of course, he may not appeal to or attract everybody. This means, then, that the individual who emerges as leader in one group may well become a leader in other groups, assuming that the tasks and the people involved in these groups are relatively similar [Bell and French, 1950].

Finally, evidence shows that the more assertive individual is more likely to be chosen leader than the less assertive person, at least in the first stages of the group's existence. The assertive person is the individual who talks a great deal and advances a relatively large number of ideas. If he is not arrogant and aggressive in asserting himself, his active participation makes him stand out in the group. This, of course, increases his chances of being chosen as the leader. Talking and participating in the group help it by giving it ideas for coping with its problems. Further, since the assertive person usually presents his ideas with a great deal of confidence in their correctness, the members of the group come to feel that his ideas are indeed correct.

There are dangers, of course, in one's being too assertive. The individual who continues to dominate a group's activities over a number of sessions may well begin to frustrate some of its members' needs for independence. As a group proceeds with its work, many of its original problems are solved and the situation becomes less ambiguous. When this happens, other members want to have more control over their own activities. They no longer need so many ideas as they did at first. At this point, the very assertive person may lose his initial popularity if he continues to assert himself. For this reason, the adroit leader will perceive that it is time to let the other members of the group have more say in what they do.

EFFECTIVENESS OF LEADERS Leadership effectiveness has been studied by investigating relationships between leaders and their coworkers in such diverse groups as basketball teams, steel-mill work crews, student surveying crews, and Air Force bomber crews, as well as in experimentally created groups [Fiedler, 1954]. These experiments suggest that in relatively relaxed situations, a leader who is attuned to the personal feelings of the group members will have a more productive and successful group than a leader who is very much concerned with getting the job done. However, in difficult situations, a more objective and task-oriented leader aids his group to achieve better performance than does a leader who is overly concerned about maintaining good interpersonal relationships with his coworkers or team members at the expense of the task.

SYNOPSIS AND SUMMARY

At the beginning of this chapter, we suggested that behavior is molded to a very large degree by social forces. Now that the force of culture, status, class, and group membership in determining what we do has been discussed, the following exercise should make the truth of our assertion dramatically clear. Think back over all the things you did yesterday and see if anything happened that was not influenced by the social sea in which we all swim—poor fish that we are. Suppose you decided to cut chemistry lab yesterday afternoon to play golf. Leaving aside the cultural determinism which lies behind the fact that you are in school at all, and that you are thinking about playing a particular game, a number of social problems arise. What would the instructor say? Are there rules about this? If there are, are you violating one? If you are violating one, what form of social disapproval will be meted out if you are caught? What are the costs and rewards in this situation? And we have only begun to touch on the social aspects of this fairly simple situation. Even the logical structure of thought about a problem such as this will be culturally determined to some extent. If we add to this the values, beliefs, and attitudes, all social in origin, which are mobilized when you consider this or any course of action, you may agree that behavior is social.

In discussing social influences on behavior, we made the following specific points:

1. Socialization is the process of learning the attitudes, beliefs, and behaviors appropriate to one's culture.

2. Cultures of different societies tend to have characteristic patterns. These are widely shared ways of behaving, together with the beliefs that accompany them.

3. Although cultures tend to resist change, changes do come about. Whether the changes are slow or rapid depends upon such factors as the society's attitudes toward social change, its technological developments, and the intermingling of peoples.

4. Members of a culture are generally unaware of the extent to which culture shapes their habits and values. Each person has his own subculture and is greatly influenced by the smaller groups to which he belongs as well as by the major segments of the larger culture.

5. Individuals in a society tend to be unequal in their ability to satisfy the needs of the group. This fact is largely the reason for the development of social structure.

6. Social structures are made up of different statuses. Individuals occupying a particular status are expected to play an appropriate role. Since a person may have several statuses and roles, conflicts occasionally develop, but often statuses and roles supplement each other or are compartmentalized.

7. Characteristic statuses tend to be arranged on a prestige scale which becomes the basis for a division into social classes. There are several correlates of social class: socioeconomic differences, occupational differences, and social privileges, such as greater freedom to talk, greater freedom to deviate from the standards of the group, and the ability to influence others.

8. Members of social classes also differ in their sexual behavior, in their child-rearing practices, in occupational goals, in their dominant motivations, and in their attractiveness to others.

9. Behavior within groups, the seeking of social power, and compromise among individuals within groups may be analyzed in terms of rewards and costs.

10. Group norms are expected ways of behaving that are widely shared by most members of a group, class, or culture. They have a demand quality; hence most people conform to them. Group norms always seem to emerge whenever continued interaction exists among people.

11. People tend to conform to group norms because (a) they fear disapproval by members of the group, and (b) they are inclined to believe that the group is right.

12. Some of the principal factors affecting degree of conformity to group norms are (a) attraction to the group, (b) the perceived consensus within the group, (c) orientation to the group, and (d) the need to be accepted. The third factor refers to feelings of acceptance or rejection by the group and to whether the individual is task-oriented or group-oriented.

13. Analysis of interaction in groups can be studied by use of the Bales technique. The sequence of changes occurring in group interactions can be studied as the group works toward the solution of a problem.

14. The channels of communication in a group are usually limited in certain ways. How they are limited determines the communication structure. In a star structure, group members may communicate only with one central person; in a free-communication structure, they may communicate with anyone. People in the latter structure usually are more satisfied and have higher morale. Feedback is an important determiner of the effectiveness of communications.

15. Most groups function well in complex situations only when they have leaders. The leader frequently influences other members of the group because he is regarded by them as better able than others to satisfy, or help satisfy, the needs of the group.

16. Since leadership depends on the group and the situation, relatively few qualities universally distinguish leaders from nonleaders. In general, however, leaders tend to be active participators in group activities and to be more dependable, persistent, verbally facile, self-confident, and socially popular than nonleaders. Relaxed situations seem to require a kind of leader different from the kind that is most effective in difficult situations.

RELATED TOPICS IN THE TEXT

CHAPTER 3   PRINCIPLES OF LEARNING   A review of the principles of classical conditioning and instrumental learning, as well as the principles concerning punishment, might be helpful. The reason is, of course, that socialization is a learning process.

CHAPTER 17   ATTITUDES   The social determiners of behavior covered here make up one of the two large concerns of social psychology. The other is the study of attitudes. Social psychologists are interested in these because they are social in origin and often concern social groups and other social matters.

SUGGESTIONS FOR FURTHER READING

Benedict, R. *Patterns of culture* (2d ed.). Boston: Houghton Mifflin, 1959. (Paperback available.)
A classical description and analysis, written by a social anthropologist, of patterns of culture in primitive societies.

Brown R. *Social psychology.* New York: Free Press, 1965.
A text in social psychology which presents basic concepts through discussions of current problem areas.

Cartwright, D., and Zander, A. (Ed.). *Group dynamics* (2d ed.). New York: Harper & Row, 1960.
A collection of recent research reports dealing with the behavior of people in groups, together with some theoretical interpretations of such behavior.

Hollander, E. P., and Hunt, R. G. (Eds.). *Current perspectives in social psychology: Readings with commentary.* Fairlawn, N.J.: Oxford, 1963. (Paperback.)
A carefully selected book of readings presenting an overview of empirical problems, research findings, and current theoretical viewpoints; somewhat more difficult theoretically than Maccoby, Newcomb, and Hartley (see below).

Kluckhohn, C. *Mirror for man.* New York: McGraw-Hill, 1949. (Paperback available.)
A popular survey of cultural differences in behavior and attitudes by an eminent social anthropologist.

Krech, D., Crutchfield, R. S., and Ballachey, E. L. *Individual in society: A textbook of social psychology.* New York: McGraw-Hill, 1962. Chaps. 8–14.
A social psychology textbook containing interesting abstracts of experiments that are used to illustrate points made in the text.

Maccoby, E. E., Newcomb, T. M., and Hartley, E. L. *Readings in social psychology* (3d ed.). New York: Holt, 1958.
A representative sampling of research and viewpoints in all areas of present-day social psychology.

McGrath, J. E. *Social psychology: A brief introduction.* New York: Holt, 1964. (Paperback.)
An overview of the major concepts of the field of social psychology, including a well-written section on society and culture.

Newcomb, T. M., Turner, R. H., and Converse, P. E. *Social psychology: The study of human interaction.* New York: Holt, 1965.
A general introduction to social psychology which attempts to integrate different psychological approaches, with emphasis on the interaction process.

Secord, P. F., and Backman, C. W. *Social psychology.* New York: McGraw-Hill, 1964.
An introductory social psychology text which includes comprehensive coverage of modern research.

17

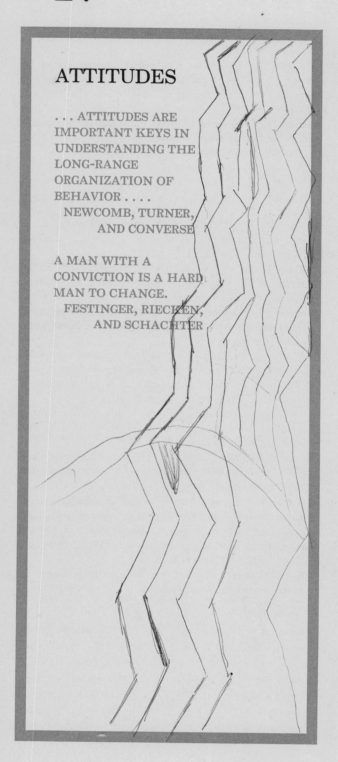

ATTITUDES

... ATTITUDES ARE
IMPORTANT KEYS IN
UNDERSTANDING THE
LONG-RANGE
ORGANIZATION OF
BEHAVIOR ....
   NEWCOMB, TURNER,
     AND CONVERSE

A MAN WITH A
CONVICTION IS A HARD
MAN TO CHANGE.
   FESTINGER, RIECKEN,
     AND SCHACHTER

ALTHOUGH THE ATTITUDES of other people are never seen or felt—they are only inferred—they make a great difference in almost everyone's life. For example, a person may hold specific attitudes toward various groups, such as union members, Negroes, whites, or the mentally ill; or he may hold attitudes toward some event, such as retirement, fluoridation of the local water supply, or an ideal vacation. To the person in business or politics, attitudes may mean the difference between success or failure. The businessman depends upon the favorable attitudes of his customers toward his products and services to keep his business going. The politician needs favorable attitudes from the electorate toward his personality, abilities, and political behavior in order to be assured of reelection. Similarly, each of us strives to create favorable attitudes and to eliminate unfavorable attitudes toward himself among his friends, associates, employers, and others. Indeed, very few acts or decisions in everyday affairs do not somehow take account of the way in which the attitudes of others may be affected.

Nature of attitudes

An *attitude* is usually defined by the psychologist as a tendency to respond positively, that is, favorably, or negatively, that is, unfavorably, to certain objects, persons, or situations. Although this definition is adequate, two other conceptual elements must be kept in mind in order to comprehend the nature of an attitude: *categories* and *goals*. An attitude, like the behavioral response it stands for, tends to involve placement of its stimulus object in one category or another. A kind of discrimination takes place in that the stimulus is reacted to as though it were a member of one class of stimuli, but not a member of other classes of stimuli. This discrimination or categorization of the stimulus object is related to the individual's goals. Hence, to understand attitudes, we must consider the process of categorizing things and the relation of the categories formed to a person's motives and goals.

CATEGORIES AND GOALS

To clarify this analysis of attitudes, let us consider the hypothetical case of a Mr. Smith who has a negative attitude toward Democrats.

One day Mr. Smith finds that he has a new neighbor, Mr. Jones. Very soon after their meeting, Mr. Smith hears Mr. Jones say some kind words about former President Harry Truman. Chances are that one of Smith's first responses will be to classify his neighbor as a Democrat—that is, to put him in the category "Democrat." Unless (or until) he gets to know his neighbor better, he will regard Jones as being fairly similar to other people in the same category. Stimuli placed together in one category are considered essentially equivalent. But more than this, since Smith does not care for Democrats, we may surmise that Democrats represent some sort of threat to his goals. He may believe, for example, that Democrats are trying to bring on socialism (which is threatening to him) and that their taxation program will thwart his ambition to become a wealthy man. Out of this motivation grows mild dislike for Jones. Of course, Smith is not responding to Jones as a person in his own right. He does not know Jones well enough to know what his unique characteristics are. He is reacting to him as a Democrat, as a member of a threatening or potentially punishing category of people.

Now we can see better what it means to say that an attitude is a tendency to respond positively or negatively to something. The hypothetical Mr. Smith has a negative attitude toward his neighbor. But the reason for this attitude is that he has placed his neighbor in a category with other things to which he reacts unfavorably because they threaten his goals. Conversely, if Mr. Jones had done or said something to classify him with Mr. Smith's positive goals and rewards, the attitude toward him would have been positive.

NEGATIVE ATTITUDES AND SOCIAL PREJUDICE

Another way to describe Mr. Smith's behavior is to say that he is "prejudiced." This term today generally means a negative attitude toward a minority group such as Jews or Negroes. But this is a layman's definition, not a psychological one. If we consider only the *operation* of the social prejudice, it does not differ from other negative attitudes. Mr. Smith might have classified Mr. Jones as, say, a Jew if he had seen some sign of "Jewishness"; and if he had been anti-Semitic, he would have disliked his neighbor for being in *this* category. *Psychologically,* in terms of the way the attitude operates, *social prejudice* is but a special instance of negative attitudes.

Etymologically, the word "prejudice" means "prejudgment." In this sense, prejudice means the application of a previously formed judgment to some person, object, or situation. In Mr. Smith's case, he had a preformed judgment about Democrats that he applied to Mr. Jones. This judgment might just as well have been positive, and so might the prejudice. In either case, Mr. Smith's prejudice toward his neighbor stems from the category into which he placed the neighbor. If the prejudgment were favorable, "good things" would be related to the category, instead of "bad things."

CATEGORIES AND STEREOTYPES

Another important consequence of classifying people into categories is that it involves erroneous thinking and beliefs. Since Mr. Smith does not regard Mr. Jones as a unique person, but classifies him as a Democrat, he may be wrong about Mr. Jones. The Democratic party actually has all sorts of people in it. Mr. Jones may be a Democrat, but nevertheless opposed to socialism. If Mr. Smith's notion of the category Democrat includes only people who favor socialism, he will be wrong if he thinks that his neighbor advocates socialism. Consequently, he will be attributing to Mr. Jones characteristics he does not have.

In this particular instance, the error lies in the oversimplified view of the category of Democrat. The category should be composed of subcategories, that is, of different kinds of Democrats. Remember, stimuli included within the same category are considered essentially equivalent. People in one general category are assumed to be all alike. In this case, all Democrats are regarded as sharing the same political beliefs, when actually their opinions vary widely.

TABLE 17.1 *Some of the most common traits supposedly possessed by various national, ethnic, and racial groups.*

GROUP TRAIT	PER CENT OF COLLEGE STUDENTS IN SAMPLE ATTRIBUTING TRAIT TO GROUP
Germans:	
Scientifically minded	78
Industrious	65
Stolid	44
Intelligent	32
Italians:	
Artistic	53
Impulsive	44
Passionate	37
Musical	32
Jews:	
Shrewd	79
Mercenary	49
Industrious	48
Intelligent	29
Ambitious	21
Negroes:	
Superstitious	84
Lazy	75
Happy-go-lucky	38
Irish:	
Pugnacious	45
Quick-tempered	39
Witty	38
Honest	32

SOURCE: Modified from Katz and Braly, 1933.

This kind of thinking often leads to what has been called a stereotype. A *stereotype* is any widespread, oversimplified, and hence erroneous belief [Krech, et al., 1962]. Generally, too, it concerns a category of people. One illustration of such a stereotype is the notion that redheads have fiery tempers. This is a stereotype because it is widespread, at least in some cultural groups, and it is oversimplified. Actually, some redheads are quick-tempered, and some are not. Other stereotypes are prevalent about blonds, scientists, Italians, Jews, Irish, Negroes, and many other groups.

Several years ago, investigators at Princeton University systematically studied the attitudes of their students toward various national, ethnic, and racial groups. They asked the subjects to indicate the traits characterizing each particular group. Some of the results are shown in Table 17.1. In looking over this table, you might judge from your own experience whether the stereotypes revealed there still exist today. A trend away from rigid stereotyping apparently is in progress in the United States [Allport, 1954].

Later, another investigator studied stereotypes in a somewhat different way. This study is described below:

The investigator showed photographs of college girls, selected to be "ethnically nonspecific," to 100 male and female college students and to 50 older male subjects. He asked his subjects to rate the girls on a number of qualities such as beauty, intelligence, character, and ambition. Two months later, the same photographs were shown to the subjects together with other photographs in order to confuse their memories. The subjects were again asked to judge the girls. This time, though, they were given names at random, without regard to the girls' actual ethnic background. Five had Jewish names, five Irish, five Italian, and the remainder, Anglo-Saxon names.

The new ratings were influenced by these names. Judgments of the supposedly Jewish girls, for example, clearly conformed to the stereotype of Jews shown in Table 17.1. In contrast to the way the girls had been rated before they were given names, they were now judged to be less beautiful and to have less character, but as being more intelligent and more ambitious. This pattern of changes did not occur for the supposedly Irish and Italian girls.

Jews, of course, are frequently believed to be intelligent and ambitious. Table 17.1 shows that these traits are often part of the stereotype of Jews. In the experiment just discussed, then, the name given to the girl served to place her in a particular category, Jew. As a result, other qualities were attributed to her that are associated with this category. (Jews are ambitious. She is a Jew. She must be ambitious.)

This phenomenon is not limited to ethnic or racial groups. Whenever we encounter a situation, we tend to place the stimuli present in it, whether they are people, objects, or symbols, into what seem to us to be appropriate categories. Once we classify them this way, we react to them as we would to other stimuli similarly classified (see Stimulus Generalization, Chapter 3, and Formation and Meaning of Concepts, Chapter 5). Such classification simplifies the problem of deciding what to do in each instance when a similar situation presents itself, but oversimplification and distortion may easily occur. A stereotype, then, is just a particular type of category—one that concerns certain groups. The characteristics of the categories are widely agreed upon and are oversimplifications of reality.

ATTITUDES, BELIEFS, AND OPINIONS   In everyday usage, the terms belief, attitude, and opinion are very close together in meaning—so close that they are frequently used almost interchangeably. We can, however, distinguish among them. The nature of an attitude has already been established. A *belief* is the acceptance of a statement or proposition. It does not necessarily imply an attitude of being "for" or "against." For instance, some people believe in flying saucers. Such a belief can be held without the emotional tinge of an attitude. In between belief and attitude is a vague thing called an *opinion.* It usually involves some sort of belief and also some attitude of "pro" or "con," though the attitude may not be strong and the belief may be poorly formulated.

In actual practice, the distinction among these terms is not of very much value. Most beliefs and opinions are closely linked with attitudes. Indeed, they are often rationalizations for attitudes. For this reason, beliefs and opinions also typically involve the classification of things into categories that are related to one's goals.

Development of attitudes

Now that we understand what attitudes are, we can inquire into how they are formed and changed. In the sections which follow, we consider the development of attitudes and beliefs in children and adolescents, some other factors influencing attitudes that are particularly important in adulthood, and the possibilities of attitude change through education and propaganda.

CULTURE   We learned in Chapter 16 that culture consists of the customs and traditions of a people as well as the attitudes and beliefs they hold about important aspects of life. We learned also that these customs, traditions, attitudes, and beliefs influence each individual in diverse ways, through his social class, his social groups, his schools, his family, and so on. Since the individual experiences all these influences simultaneously, or at least within very short periods of time, it is difficult to separate them from one another. *In toto,* however, cultural influences help to shape a person's attitudes.

Cross-cultural comparisons. One of the ways to assess the influence of culture on attitudes is to determine whether societies differ in their patterns of beliefs and attitudes. Obviously there are pitfalls in talking about these differences, for it is easy to indulge in stereotypes and oversimplifications that obscure the outlines of complex realities. If, for example, we were to say that Germany is an "authoritarian society," we would be expressing such a stereotype. Of course, some Germans do prefer authoritarian forms of government and do believe that a few strong leaders generally have the right to tell others what to do. But this does not mean that every German possesses these attitudes or that members of other national groups do not have them.

It is possible, nevertheless, to ask whether or not Germans (or members of any other society) are relatively similar in their beliefs and different *on the average* from people in other societies. Thus, in a statistical sense, we can discuss group differences scientifically. And we can say that one society differs from another on a given characteristic when differences *between* societies are appreciably greater than differences *within* the societies.

Unfortunately, few investigations of differences between nations and societies rest on this statistical footing. Most of them are haphazard observations of relatively few members of a national group without evidence that they are representative of their society. Moreover, the writers ordinarily do not confine their conclusions to the few people studied; instead, they generalize uncritically to the entire society. The dangers of such an uncontrolled and unsystematic approach can be illustrated by the following fictitious, but somewhat typical, case:

Suppose an observer, who had a pet notion that Americans were an extremely hostile people, were to visit two or three classrooms in your school. He might happen to see several incidents in which students were critical of the view advocated by their instructor. Feeling that his theory had been confirmed, he might then go back home and write a paper. In it he might conclude that Americans generally were extremely hostile toward their parents because of their having been subjected to harsh toilet-training practices when they were between one and two years of age. This agressiveness, he might maintain, is generalized to all authority figures, so that Americans have a compulsion to attack, question, and devalue anyone in a position of power over them.

Let us see what this fictitious observer has done. (1) He has interpreted (as aggression) a few incidents entirely from the point of view of this theoretical bias without realizing that other interpretations are possible. (2) He has regarded the behavior he saw as typical of members of our society in general without determining whether this behavior is indeed widespread or common in this country. (3) He has assumed, without the benefit of any scientific evidence, that the behavior pattern has its roots in certain childhood experiences (toilet training). (4) He has assumed that these childhood experiences are common to most Americans, again without any evidence.

Scientific research on national and societal differences is not impossible. The compendium of errors we have just presented highlights the difficulties of such research and indicates some of the things to be wary of when such comparisons are made. Scientific investigations can be conducted, but they are expensive and require a good deal of careful work.

One study carried out shortly after World War II illustrates more adequately controlled procedures, although its results must be interpreted with caution [McGranahan, 1946]:

One hundred and ninety-one German youths between fourteen and eighteen years old from the town of Bad Hamburg were interviewed, and their answers were compared with the responses given by a matched sample of American youngsters from the supposedly comparable town of Oak Park, Illinois. There were differences in the frequency of authoritarian-like beliefs in the two groups. A greater proportion of the Bad Hamburg adolescents felt that people "who unjustly criticized the government of a country" should be thrown in jail (36 per cent of the German youths to 21 per cent of the Oak Park adolescents). A greater proportion also felt that newspapers should report not what they wished, but only what they thought to be "for the good of the people" (43 per cent to 17 per cent).

These and other differences found between the two national groups appear to support a theory that Germans have a greater tendency toward authoritarian social organization than Americans have. By themselves, however, the results of this study do not prove such a theory. We do not know the extent to which the samples were representative of Germans and Americans in general, or even of German and American youngsters. It also is possible that similar differences would not be obtained today. The study does point to average differences of opinion within each sample. All German interviewees are not authoritarian, even though many had the tendency to be, nor was the tendency entirely absent in the American sample.

Even when we assume that national or cultural differences in attitudes and beliefs do exist, we face the important problem of tracing the origin of these differences to their roots. The cross-cultural comparisons of primitive societies described in the last chapter are a start in this direction.

Cultural influences on attitudes. Another way to assess the influence of culture on attitudes is to correlate attitudes with cultural differences within a society. If a certain attitude is held more gen-

TABLE 17.2 *The relationship of education, income, and religion to attitudes toward armed imperialism. Individuals were asked the question: "Some people say we should use our Army and Navy to make other countries do what we think they should. How do you feel about that?"*

RESPONDENTS	GENERAL APPROVAL, PER CENT	GENERAL DISAPPROVAL, PER CENT	NO RESPONSE, PER CENT	NUMBER OF RESPONDENTS
Education:				
Grade school	19	57	24	500
High school	13	77	10	455
College	8	83	9	213
Income:				
Under $2,000	19	58	23	440
$2,000 to $3,999	16	73	11	478
$4,000 and more	8	86	6	216
Religion:				
Protestant	14	70	16	855
Catholic	18	68	14	245

SOURCE: Social Science Research Council, 1947.

erally among individuals in one cultural category than among those in another category, it may be presumed that the culture influences the attitude. An illustration of such a correlation is to be found in a study sponsored some years ago by the Social Science Research Council (1947). It concerned attitudes toward armed imperialism. Individuals were asked this question: "Some people say we should use our Army and Navy to make other countries do what we think they should. How do you feel about that?" As Table 17.2 shows, people generally disapproved of this point of view, but it is interesting that those with a college education and those in the higher economic brackets disapproved more than those of lesser education and income. There was no substantial difference, however, between those of Protestant and those of Catholic religious affiliation. From such a study, it may be concluded that educational and socioeconomic influences probably are important in determining attitudes toward the use of our Armed Forces.

In recent years, a very large number of studies correlating attitudes and culture have been con-

ducted. Almost any public-opinion poll, when analyzed according to the educational status, income level, religious background, and so forth, of the group questioned, yields information about such a relation. On some questions, such as birth control, war, and political issues, religious influences prove to be important: for example, Catholics are usually more conservative than Jews, and those who have had religious training are more conservative than those who have not.

In almost all beliefs and attitudes, socioeconomic position tends to be important. The upper socioeconomic classes tend to be more "liberal" regarding war and the use of force, as the study cited shows, but they tend to be more conservative in political and economic views. Perhaps this means, as other writers have noted, that there are at least two varieties of "liberalism," one in economic affairs, the other in noneconomic matters [Allinsmith and Allinsmith, 1948]. The middle and upper social strata are more conservative than the lower classes in political-economic attitudes, but may be less conservative in other beliefs, such as those dealing with international relations. Other instances of social-class influences on attitudes and beliefs about child rearing and sexual behavior, among others, were cited in Chapter 16 (see page 576).

We should not jump to the conclusion, however, that individuals simply take over the attitudes characteristic of their class or group, for this is not true. We must remember that the correlations are seldom very high (see Chapter 11, page 395); rather, they usually indicate only moderate statistical tendencies. Such an imperfect correlation is to be expected because the individual is exposed to numerous cultural influences and to many different attitudes and beliefs. Though a person may be of one religious training, he ordinarily associates with people of other religious backgrounds. Although he may be of one socioeconomic level, he usually has some contact with members of other socioeconomic groups. In these and other ways, his culture is by no means homogeneous. Even if it were, there are enough differences among members of any particular cultural group to expose him to a variety of attitudes and beliefs.

FAMILY INFLUENCES In the melee of cultural forces continuously playing on an individual, the influences from his parents and associates are especially important because they mediate between the individual and his culture. A child's parents are products of the culture; their attitudes and beliefs have been influenced, and continue to be influenced, by the culture. Because their social contacts, their reading, their entertainment, and their other relations with the culture are considerably wider and more diverse than those of the child, parents are more directly influenced by the culture than the child. Yet they spend a good many hours of the day in contact with the child, all the while controlling his behavior and attempting to instill in him particular attitudes and beliefs. It is not surprising, then, that the attitudes and beliefs of the child tend to correlate with those of his parents.

In one study conducted with 200 college students at Northwestern University, for example, the attitudes of the students toward the New Deal ad-

ministration, toward economic depression, and toward God correlated (see Chapter 11, page 395) with the attitudes of the parents to the extent of .29 to .58 [Hirschberg and Gilliland, 1942].

One eminent student of American political behavior has reviewed a number of investigations of parental influence on political attitudes [Hyman, 1959]. He notes that the studies almost invariably find some degree of similarity between the parents' political beliefs and those of their children, an observation that provides "considerable evidence against the theory that political attitudes are formed generally in terms of rebellion and opposition to parents." Furthermore, this research shows that the similarity between parents and children generally is greater for political-party preference than for political beliefs. As a practical matter, the writer maintains, a man is born into his political party almost to the same extent that he may be regarded as being born into the membership of his church. He adopts his family's political party almost to the degree that he adopts its religion. It is also true that parental indifference to politics is related to indifference on the part of the children of the family.

One major reason for the similarity in attitudes is that children tend to be in the same socioeconomic stratum as their parents. If a person were to enter a different social class from the one occupied by his parents, he might change his party preference. A survey of college graduates in which changes in political orientation were related to social mobility bears on this point [Hyman, 1959]. Among those graduates who came from Democratic, that is, relatively low-income families, the proportion who were Democrats themselves decreased sharply as their own income rose higher. This pattern was not revealed by the graduates who came from Republican families and who were earning less than their parents. For these people, a decline in social class did not alter their preference for the Republican party.

Familial influences, of course, affect more than our political attitudes. They may also determine our attitudes toward other racial and religious groups among other things. In a set of interviews with white grammar school children about their attitudes toward Negroes, one investigator got such responses as these:

First-grade girl: Mamma tells me not to play with black children, keep away from them. Mama tells me, she told me not to play with them. . . .

Second-grade girl: . . . Mother doesn't want me to play with colored children. . . . I play with colored children sometimes but Mamma whips me.

Second-grade boys: . . . mother and daddy tell me. They tell me not to play with colored people or colored persons' things.

Third-grade girl: . . . Mother told me not to play with them because sometimes they have diseases and germs and you get it from them.

[Adapted from Horowitz and Horowitz, 1938, pages 333 and 335.]

PEER INFLUENCES   As the individual grows older he meets more and more people outside his family group and becomes increasingly independent of his parents for the satisfaction of his needs. This does not mean that he now is independent of people generally; rather, he looks to his own efforts and also to people outside the family for gratifications that formerly were provided by members of his family. He relies on peers, friends, and acquaintances for the satisfaction of his desires, for companionship and entertainment. He also may seek them out in order to obtain emotional and social support, wanting their consolation when plans go wrong, their reassurance that his behavior is proper, and their agreement that his opinions are correct. These friends and acquaintances thus become important influences on his attitudes and beliefs.

Two major reasons for this influence were cited in Chapter 16. The individual may express the opinions and do the things advocated by his associates because (1) he believes their opinions and actions probably are correct and/or (2) he fears that his deviation may lead to disapproval and rejection. Whatever the reasons operating in any given case, the outcome is that an individual's peers may shape his views, as well as his behavior, more than his parents do, particularly when he has a great deal of contact with his peers.

One of the most famous investigations in social psychology shows how a young person's peers may influence his political and economic beliefs to such an extent that family influences become secondary [Newcomb, 1943]:

This study was conducted with the girls at Bennington College in Vermont in the mid-thirties. Most of the students entering the college as freshmen came from the upper and middle socioeconomic class and held the conservative political and economic views of their families. The highly self-contained college community to which they came, however, was at that time strongly "New Dealish" and liberal in its political sentiments. What happened to the freshman "conservatives" in this environment? Attitude surveys revealed that the longer the girls remained in college, the more liberal they generally became. Thus, as juniors and seniors they were more liberal than they had been when they were freshmen and sophomores.

Of course, there were individual differences in the degree to which the girls took over the attitudes of their peers. The girls who were regarded by their peers as most closely identified with the community were the ones who developed the most pro-New Deal beliefs. The girls who remained conservative despite the widespread liberalism among their fellow students generally were unable or unwilling to participate fully in college life. Often they were socially withdrawn, either because they were insecure and lacked social skills or because they had met frustrations at Bennington. Some girls did not enter into college life fully because they had strong attachments to other groups, such as their families. Whatever the reason, the girls who did not adopt the prevalent beliefs at Bennington usually participated least in the activities of their peers.

Adult attitudes

So far we have described three sets of influences on the development of attitudes in the child and adolescent—the culture, the family, and peer groups— all of which continue to be important throughout the person's life. In adulthood, however, still other factors assume increasing importance in shaping and maintaining the attitudes of the individual: (1) his personality, (2) the information he receives, (3) the statements and attitudes of authorities to which he is exposed, and (4) the small informal groups, or primary groups, of which he is a member.

PERSONALITY   To recognize that the culture molds attitudes is not to say that the culture simply gives or transmits them to the inert, passive individual. Whether or not attitudes are formed often depends upon the personality structure and receptivity of the individual. At any given time, some individuals are relatively immune to many attitudes and beliefs, but are particularly susceptible to others. Thus, much depends upon the personality of the individual who is exposed to cultural influences. This fact is demonstrated in several studies of the relationship between personality, on the one hand, and attitudes and beliefs on the other.

Personality traits. You will remember from Chapter 12 that traits can be rated by persons who know an individual fairly well or by special tests that have been constructed for the purpose. One test measures a person's relative introversion or extroversion, another his relative dominance or submission in social situations, and still others are available to measure other traits. If we give such tests to a group of people, and at the same time determine their attitudes on a number of issues, we can correlate attitudes with personality traits.

In one study, attitudes on a number of political and social issues were used to divide students into radical, conservative, and more moderate groups [Dexter, 1939]. Correlating these attitudes with personality traits, the investigator found that the women students who were radical in attitudes and beliefs were more introverted, more self-sufficient, and more dominant than other women students in their groups. Such personality traits, it appears, enable a person more easily to adopt less conventional beliefs and attitudes.

Unfortunately, however, few general rules can be applied to personality and attitudes. What may be the "radical" attitudes for one cultural group may be the "conventional" attitudes for another. Thus the personality characteristics which in one group accompany certain attitudes may in another group be correlated with other attitudes. The important point is that the particular attitudes and beliefs a person adopts frequently are related to his personality characteristics.

This last statement does *not* mean that an individual's personality characteristics *always* determine the nature of his beliefs and attitudes. In many cases, a person adopts the attitudes and beliefs of others about him regardless of his own traits. As we indicated in Chapter 16, this is particularly likely if he knows relatively little about the object or issue, if the others about him are in agreement, and if he does not dislike his group.

Personality traits seem to be most strongly related to attitudes when the groups around a person permit him to hold a variety of alternative opinions on a given issue. If a person's associates do not insist that only one course of action is socially proper in a given situation, then his personality traits are more likely to determine his attitudes. When, on the other hand, social pressures are great, the attitudes he expresses may hinge on his desire to conform.

The ethnocentric personality. In many parts of the United States, cultural norms do not define particular minority groups, such as Negroes and Jews, as inferior or threatening. These regions, nevertheless, still contain a fair share of people who are socially prejudiced against these and other minorities. It is not likely that these people developed their dislike for minority groups simply through unpleasant experiences with them, because they tend to be strongly prejudiced against every minority group even though they could not possibly have encountered every one. Why is the pattern of prejudice so frequent and so widely distributed throughout the country in the absence of cultural directives against specific minorities? One plausible explanation for such negative attitudes is that, because of their personality characteristics, socially prejudiced people distrust and dislike others who are different.

Light has been shed on the nature of these personality traits by a famous large-scale study conducted by a team of social scientists at the University of California [Adorno et al., 1950]:

By studying and testing a large sample of people, the investigators found that some people could be described as generally prejudiced because they were biased against a wide variety of groups. These prejudiced people tended to glorify in a very extreme fashion the particular groups to which they belonged (including the United States). At the same time, they were hostile toward the groups in which they had no membership. This pattern of attitudes was termed *ethnocentrism.* Highly ethnocentric individuals then were singled out for further investigation. By administering many psychological tests both to them and to less prejudiced people, it was possible to determine how their personalities differed from those of the less ethnocentric group.

This research and later studies have presented a composite portrait of the highly ethnocentric person:

1. *He is an authoritarian.* Supposedly because he sees the world and most of the people in it as dangerous and unfriendly, he seeks security by submitting uncritically to a powerful authority as if to gather strength from the authority. For this reason, an ethnocentric individual frequently is referred to as having an "authoritarian personality." Such a person is likely to hold beliefs such as these [Adorno et al., 1950; Allport and Kramer, 1946]: "The world is a hazardous place in which men are basically evil and dangerous," and "We do not have enough discipline in our American way of life." The authoritarian person wants people to do whatever the proper authorities tell them to do. He also frequently wants a definite social hierarchy in which everybody has his place and knows who is leader and who is follower.

2. *He is rigidly moralistic.* This ethnocentric individual usually also seeks security in strict adherence to standards of morality and propriety. He feels he is safe as long as he is conventional and shuns the behavior that middle-class people generally regard as socially unacceptable. He also harshly condemns people who violate his moral code.

In one of the California studies, highly prejudiced and less prejudiced women were asked, "What is the most embarrassing experience you've had?" The ethnocentric women usually said that it was some public violation of social rules and regulations. In contrast, the less prejudiced group said that their most embarrassing experiences involved failures in interpersonal relations, such as not living up to a friend's expectations.

3. *He strongly represses socially disapproved tendencies within himself and projects them to others.* Anxiously concerned with being conventional and proper, this person not only tries to avoid doing anything that is socially disapproved, he is uncomfortable at the idea that he might want to do these things. Although less ethnocentric people can readily admit that they have sexual wishes or aggressive inclinations, the highly prejudiced individual frequently denies both to himself and to others that he has such impulses. But more than this, these disapproved tendencies often are attributed—which is to say, projected—to other people, particularly to minority groups. It is as if the highly prejudiced person told himself, "*I* don't have these sexual or aggressive desires, the Negro, or Jew, or Mexican does."

One tendency of ethnocentric individuals, and at the same time one of which they disapprove highly, is hostility toward parents. According to the California investigators, highly prejudiced people often have had harsh and unrealistically demanding parents. Stern treatment by their parents leaves them with aggressive feelings; yet they dare not express such feelings. In the preceding study of prejudiced women, the psychologists found that these women openly expressed great admiration for their parents; nevertheless, through personality tests, they revealed hidden aggressive inclinations toward them. The less prejudiced women, on the other hand, more freely admitted occasionally disliking their parents.

4. *He often places people in oversimplified, black-and-white categories.* The highly ethnocentric per-

son generally does not make fine distinctions among people. He is likely to agree with such statements as: "There are only two kinds of people, the weak and the strong." For him, people fall into only a small number of classes. Thus, members of a minority group are "all alike." Furthermore, these categories are simple and clear-cut; people are all bad or all good. He is not so likely as his less prejudiced peers to believe that both good and bad traits can exist simultaneously in the same person [Steiner, 1954].

5. *He frequently possesses conservative political and economic attitudes.* This conservatism does not seem to be "true" conservatism such as that expressed by some eighteenth-century philosophers or by many present-day advocates of a laissez-faire economy. Rather, it masks a readiness to employ force in order to attain political and economic goals. In extreme cases, the highly ethnocentric person may make patriotic speeches, at the same time acting as an antidemocratic agitator in his attempt to realize his political aims.

This conclusion of one group of investigators in the field sums up the ethnocentric, authoritarian person rather well:

Prejudiced responses are not dissociated from the total pattern of personal life. The person who views the world as a jungle, where the traveler must choose to become "the diner or else the dinner" . . . who is authoritarian in his outlook, who has no disposition to sympathize with the underdog, who rejects legislative attempts to protect minority groups, who feels no shame at his own prejudices— such a person includes prejudices in his style of life. [Allport and Kramer, 1946, page 34.]

INFORMATION A person's attitudes and beliefs are based on what he regards as facts. To understand, then, how he acquires his attitudes, we should consider how he acquires his facts.

It goes almost without saying that the typical individual does not have available to him in his own experience all the facts he needs to form an adequate attitude, opinion, or belief about each of the problems he confronts. In trying to decide whether to vote for a Republican or a Democrat, he has seldom seen the candidates in person or known at first hand how the candidates have behaved or performed in particular situations. In forming an opinion about Negroes, he may not have had very much contact with Negroes. In all kinds of matters he lacks many of the facts that he really ought to have to be able to make his decision intelligently.

Not only are facts relatively scarce, but those that are available are frequently misleading. A person who forms a derogatory opinion about Negroes may have picked up the "fact" that Negroes, when given intelligence tests, tend to score lower than whites. What he may not know is that such Negroes have had inferior schooling and poor socioeconomic circumstances, or that they were much less motivated in taking the tests—all relevant facts in evaluating the statement that their scores were lower. In a good many circumstances, a little knowledge is a dangerous thing because it leads to attitudes and beliefs that are not justified when all the facts are known. Yet we all are regularly called upon to form opinions with only a few of the relevant facts available. Consequently, we all acquire erroneous beliefs and opinions and, indirectly, prejudiced attitudes.

AUTHORITIES Since we have relatively few firsthand facts upon which to base our beliefs, we often find ourselves trusting authorities instead of facts. Indeed, many so-called "facts" are not facts at all in terms of firsthand experience; they are merely statements made by authorities about facts. There is nothing inherently wrong with our relying on authority, for we could hardly manage otherwise. We are forced to rely on the statements of experts, authorities, or "eyewitness" reports. Such specialization of knowledge has been essential in the development of our complex civilization.

Reliance on authority, however, has its disadvantages. For one thing, it is difficult for even the most conscientious person to report facts objectively all the time. The attitudes and beliefs of the authority often affect his perception of a fact and the way he reports it to us. Moreover, the authority may be ignorant of other facts and thus not present them to us—and without them we cannot form a correct opinion. Often authorities disagree among themselves on the facts, and we must choose between two conflicting authorities.

Adding to our difficulties in forming correct opinions is the tendency of authorities to acquire prestige and status outside their special fields of competence. People often regard the successful businessman as the person best qualified to manage in government; actually business and government often require rather different types of knowledge and skill for their successful operation. The man who has acquired a great reputation as a physicist will be listened to when he pronounces on religion and politics; yet he is usually no more qualified in these matters than many persons in other fields of endeavor. All kinds of authorities make this mistake—and it is an easy one to make—with the result that people unwittingly base their beliefs on statements made by persons who are not real authorities on the matters at hand.

Another obstacle to forming correct beliefs and opinions is the tendency of some authorities deliberately to distort the facts in order to have us believe what they want us to believe. The manufacturer may know very well all the facts about his product, but he instructs his advertiser to present us with only certain facts that lead us to form attitudes favorable to his product. The political leader may be intimately aware of corruption among some of his party's members, but he tells only the "good" facts about his administration in order to instill in us an opinion so favorable that he will be reelected next time. In American society, the deliberate selection and distortion of facts is practiced in almost every aspect of life as a means of encouraging erroneous beliefs that are advantageous to the purveyor of the facts.

PRIMARY GROUPS   Sociologists often use the term *primary groups* to identify those small groups with whom we have many frequent and informal contacts, such as family, friends, and associates. They are primary in the sense that they often have an important effect on our attitudes and beliefs. It is usually through these primary-group channels that cultural factors and authorities shape our view of the world about us.

Studies of American voting behavior have documented the influence of an individual's family, friends, and associates upon his political attitudes and actions. The influence seems to stem partly from the fact that a sizable proportion of the American electorate is relatively unconcerned with politics and election campaigns, even during presidential elections. They often do not bother to read newspaper and magazine articles dealing with the issues and the candidates, nor do they want to listen to political speeches on radio or television. Nevertheless, these people do acquire some information about the campaign in informal conversations with friends and associates.

An intensive survey of political opinions in Erie County, Ohio, during the 1940 presidential election showed that politically active and interested people exist in every social stratum [Lazarsfeld et al., 1944]. These people follow the campaign rather avidly, absorb political information from the mass media, and then transmit the information to their friends, neighbors, and coworkers in the course of informal discussions with them. Since these people are so important in shaping the political beliefs of others, particularly if the others are relatively indifferent, neutral, or undecided, the investigators say they function as "opinion leaders."

These informal primary groups do more than serve as a medium for transmitting information. As we saw in Chapter 16, they can influence the opinions of the group members. Naturally, this holds true for political attitudes and opinions as well. A study of the voting process, which was conducted in Elmira, New York, during the 1948 national election, substantiates this [Kitt and Gleicher, 1950]:

In August before the election, citizens of Elmira were asked, among other things, how each of their three closest friends would vote. Most of the people who could identify their friends' opinions reported that their friends were in agreement in preferring one or the other of the candidates.

TABLE 17.3 *August to October shifters in Elmira, New York, during the 1948 election.*

POLITICAL INCLINATION OF THREE CLOSEST FRIENDS IN AUGUST	SHIFTED TOWARD REPUBLICANS BY OCTOBER, PER CENT	SHIFTED TOWARD DEMOCRATS BY OCTOBER, PER CENT
R R R	56	44
R R D ⎫ D D R ⎭	49	51
D D D	39	61

SOURCE: Kitt and Gleicher, 1950.

When asked their own opinion, they tended to support the candidate their friends preferred. Thus, "More than 90 per cent of the respondents with three Republican friends show some degree of Republican vote inclination themselves." This figure declined to only 68 per cent Republican for those people who said one of their three closest friends was a Democrat. Similar tendencies in favor of the Democrats were obtained among those people whose friends preferred the Democratic candidate.

Later on in the campaign, some of the people were interviewed to see whether their opinions had changed. In some cases, of course, they had. In the majority of these cases, the shifts were in the direction of increasing agreement among members of the friendship group. The findings are summarized in Table 17.3.

Thus we tend to form attitudes which agree with those of people we like—our friends. The process also works the other way: "We like those with whom we agree" [McGrath, 1964]. This has been shown in a comprehensive study of the *acquaintance process* [Newcomb, 1961]:

In this study, 17 new men students who did not know one another were invited to live in a house at the university, without charge, where the men were responsible for making their own living and study arrangements. In exchange for the free accommodations, the men were required to participate an hour or so a week in research which was designed to investigate the nature of the acquaintance process. The most lasting friendships which developed were based on similarities of attitudes; early friendships usually did not last if the individuals discovered that they were not actually as similar or compatible as they had thought at first. As part of this study of friendships, attitudes, and interpersonal perception, the students estimated how their preferred associates would respond to various attitude questionnaires. The experimenters compared these estimates of attitudes with the responses made by each person himself and found that all estimates tended to increase in accuracy with increased acquaintance, but that there was a tendency to overestimate agreement with best friends.

Attitude change and propaganda

Now let us consider the question of attitude changes and how they are brought about through education and propaganda. We shall first discuss some of the factors which make attitudes resistant to change—factors in self-preservation of attitudes. After that, we can survey the psychological aspects of deliberate attempts to change attitudes through education, propaganda, and advertising.

PRESERVATION OF ATTITUDES We might expect that as a person's culture changes, as his personality matures, and as he becomes better informed, his attitudes and beliefs would change. They do. On the other hand, they do not change so rapidly as one might expect because they have a way of resisting change and preserving themselves once they have been well formed. The three principal causes of the self-preservation of attitudes are: (1) selective interpretation, (2) avoidance of information that might change attitudes and beliefs, and (3) social pressures for the preservation of attitudes.

Selective interpretation. Attitudes and beliefs tend to be preserved because they alter the perception of new experiences; they emphasize those facts which fit in with existing attitudes and beliefs and deemphasize those which do not. If a person thinks that Negroes are dirty people and he sees a Negro coming home in his work clothes, he may immediately notice the fact that the man's clothes are soiled. A white man in exactly the same state of dress may pass entirely unnoticed, or if he is noticed, he may be perceived as a person coming home from a hard day's work. If an individual who is strongly opposed to government spending sees the newspaper heading, "Congress appropriates 50 billion dollars for Armed Forces," he may perceive the 50 billion dollars as an instance of big government spending while ignoring or forgetting that it is for the defense of the country. If, on the other hand, a person is strongly concerned about adequate defense of the United States, he may perceive this headline as an instance of Congress providing for our defense, but take no note of the amount of money involved. Thus, of the facts presented, a person tends to perceive selectively those which fit in with, or are relevant to, his attitudes and beliefs and to pay little attention to other facts. In this way, his attitudes and beliefs are reinforced and strengthened, rather than changed, by his perceptions.

This concept can be understood readily in terms of the categorization process described earlier in the chapter. A person with anti-Negro attitudes not only associates Negroes with threats and unpleasant events, but also attributes unfavorable qualities to the class of people termed "Negroes." This category is associated with qualities that seem "bad" to him. Seeing a person who belongs to this category, he infers that the person has the unfavorable characteristics which he thinks are generally possessed by other members of that class. So the soiled work clothes are interpreted as meaning "Negroes are dirty." A different interpretation is placed upon the white worker's soiled clothes. "Dirty" and other similar negative traits may not be part of the category "white" for many people. Thus, the soiled work clothes may signify only that, "Here is a fellow who earns his living by honest toil." Similarly, the newspaper headline concerning government spending is interpreted in a manner consistent with the individual's conception of "government." If this category includes the quality "too big," the headline is seen as meaning: "Here is another example of big government."

Most social situations are relatively ambiguous; frequently it is possible to interpret them in a wide variety of ways. This ambiguity increases the likelihood that an attitude or belief will persist, since it enables the individual to interpret the situation in a manner consistent with his attitude. Thus he perceives the situation as supporting his views.

Avoidance of information. For one reason or another, people often are so reluctant to change their attitudes and beliefs that they try to avoid information that is inconsistent with these attitudes and beliefs. Such information appears to make them too uncomfortable. In any case, plenty of situations in everyday life illustrate this widespread tendency to withdraw from everything that conflicts with what one already believes. The person who is a confirmed liberal refuses to read conservative magazines or newspapers. The person who is prejudiced against Jews has nothing to do with them, and thus never gives himself a chance to acquire facts about them that might alter his prejudice. The person who dislikes the views of the Hearst press, or Walter Lippmann, the *Reader's Digest,* or Walter Winchell, refuses to read them or listen to them. Thus he avoids coming into contact with attitudes and beliefs that conflict with his own. On the other hand, he exposes himself only to viewpoints that agree with his own, and this further strengthens the attitudes and beliefs that he already holds.

In the cases we have just mentioned, the person has the opportunity to avoid physically the information that might disturb him. The same resistance, however, is also encountered even when the individual is a member of a "captive audience" and has to listen to or read material opposed to his opinions.

This point was dramatically illustrated in the following experiment [Levine and Murphy, 1943]:

The experiment was conducted with college students. Some of the students were favorable to communist ideas, some were not. All listened to the reading of some passages, part of which were favorable to communism and part of which were not. Later the students were tested to

FIGURE 17.1. *Education or propaganda? A cartoon appearing in a daily newspaper designed to build a favorable attitude toward increasing teachers' salaries. (Walt Partymiller; Gazette and Daily, York, Pa.)*

determine how much they had learned from the passages. The students who were favorable to communism had learned much more of the material that was favorable to their point of view than of the material which was not. On the other hand, the students who were opposed to communism had learned better the passages that supported their opinion.

This experiment demonstrates how people can resist disturbing information even though they are forced to come into contact with it. Paraphrasing an old saying, we might conclude: You can lead a person to information, but you can't make him learn it. If information is opposed to his attitudes or beliefs, he will learn it much more slowly than he will material that is congenial to his attitudes.

Social support. Still another powerful influence for preserving attitudes and beliefs is the social approval of associates. As we have already pointed out, an individual tends to share his attitudes and beliefs with the members of his particular group or culture. The need for social approval is ordinarily a fairly strong motivation (see page 232). So long as a person's attitudes agree with those of his associates, he will tend to secure their approval. On the other hand, if he expresses attitudes and beliefs contrary to theirs, he incurs their displeasure and disapproval. Thus, he punishes himself and thwarts his desire to be approved. Consequently, he consciously or unconsciously wants to believe the same things his friends do in order to have their approval. Since he already tends to have their attitudes and beliefs by virtue of having common cultural influences, the need for social approval lends additional support to his attitudes and makes it much more difficult for him to change them.

PROPAGANDA   This resistance to change, nevertheless, does not wholly prevent attitudes and beliefs from being changed by the impact of daily events and by a constant bombardment of propaganda. Indeed, *propaganda*—now a familiar household word—is the deliberate attempt to influence attitudes and beliefs. Since propaganda is so often used by dictators and others who have ulterior and socially questionable purposes, the term has come to have a rather odious connotation. In principle, however, propaganda is not necessarily either good or bad (see Figure 17.1). It can be used to correct attitudes and beliefs so that they are nearer to the "facts" just as well as it can be used to distort them so that they are further from the facts. Moreover, it is not possible to make any really clear-cut distinction between education and propaganda. In education, we try to emphasize the facts, but these facts nevertheless must always be interpreted. In interpreting them, the teacher has a chance to intrude his own biased attitudes and beliefs, with the result that education changes people's attitudes and beliefs. In practice, though, we regard education as a legitimate attempt to change attitudes and beliefs— as well as to inculcate knowledge—in the direction of the facts, whereas propaganda typically is designed to change them in the direction favorable to the purposes of the propagandist whether these are or are not in accord with the facts (see Figure 17.2).

Many different devices are used by propagandists to influence attitudes and beliefs. We shall discuss only a few of these techniques under the following headings: (1) loaded words, (2) suggestion, and (3) needs.

LOADED WORDS In Chapter 5 we saw that words serve as symbols to represent objects and experiences. Since we experience directly only a few of the facts necessary to form attitudes and beliefs, most of our information about the world is conveyed through words chosen by someone else to symbolize events. The chooser of words—the advertiser, newspaper reporter, magazine writer, radio commentator, or politician—has a very rich language to employ, one which gives him a great deal of latitude in how he may describe a fact or idea to us. A multitude of relatively neutral words accurately describe facts without evoking attitudes one way or another. In addition, many words, through previous attitude formation, can be expected to evoke about the same attitude in most of the people who hear them.

These loaded words are the stock in trade of the propagandist. If he wishes to evoke an unfavorable attitude, he may use such words as "communist," "dictatorship," "regimentation," "agitator," and "egghead," to which the overwhelming majority of Americans react with strongly negative attitudes. If the propagandist wishes to create a favorable attitude, describing exactly the same set of events, he may use such words as "democracy," "freedom," "regulation," "taxpayer," and "advisers," all of which are regarded favorably by the great majority of the people.

You are probably familiar with such loaded words in the newspapers, magazines, and broadcasts to which you regularly attend. If you happen to agree with the point of view being expressed, you probably do not notice the loaded words and you may, indeed, think of them as factually accurate; if you disagree with the point of view, you are more likely to notice the loaded words as propaganda or distortions of the truth. The person who has no strong attitudes or beliefs on the subject can have his attitudes influenced very easily by the loaded words he

FIGURE 17.2. *The people of Peking celebrate May Day, 1965. The people in the parade march with posters and streamers bearing slogans which express their determination to fight shoulder to shoulder with the Vietnamese people. (China Photo Service, from Eastfoto.)*

TABLE 17.4 *Feeling-tone values for terms used by the* Chicago Tribune *and the* New York Times *in describing the same events.*

CHICAGO TRIBUNE		NEW YORK TIMES	
TERM	VALUE	TERM	VALUE
Radical	−53	Progressive	+92
Regimentation	−53	Regulation	+32
Government witch-hunting	−38	Senate investigation	+57
The dole	−35	Home Relief	+27
Alien	−35	Foreign	0

SOURCE: Sargent, 1939.

reads or listens to. Let us give one example from a rather old, but carefully done, psychological study [Sargent, 1939]:

The investigator selected 40 terms from the news columns of the *Chicago Tribune*, 20 of which were used by the newspaper in reporting policies it did not support and 20 of which were used in connection with events or policies it did support. To these 40 terms, the investigator added 10 neutral terms. He presented these terms in a mixed order to several groups of people, including parent-teachers, college students, high school alumni, laborers, and white-collar workers. He asked each person to indicate whether he liked, disliked, or had no feeling about the word. From the results, each word could be assigned a score representing the "feeling tone" for the word: −100 was extremely unfavorable, and +100 extremely favorable. Here are some of the feeling-tone values he obtained in this study:

Czarism	−84	Cooperation	+95
Dictatorship	−84	Freedom	+92
Domination	−79	Reemployment	+88

There was no question but that the *Chicago Tribune* very successfully chose words that evoked the strongly unfavorable or favorable attitudes it wished to evoke in support of its own views.

In a follow-up study, the investigator chose 12 loaded terms from the *Chicago Tribune* and 12 terms from the *New York Times* used in reporting exactly the same events in the two newspapers. As before, he determined feeling-tone values for these words. In Table 17.4 are the feeling-tone values for pairs of words used in describing the same events. Again it was clear that the same news was being slanted one way by one newspaper and another way by the other newspaper. Thus loaded words were being used to create the desired attitudes toward the events being reported.

SUGGESTION Psychologists define *suggestion* as the uncritical acceptance of a statement. This is to say that a person may accept a belief, form an attitude, or be incited to action merely by accepting what someone else says and without requiring facts or other proof. The skilled advertiser, propagandist, and political leader know how powerful suggestion is and employ it to their advantage in changing beliefs and attitudes. They know rather well, moreover, under what circumstances suggestion is likely to work.

One of these is to make use of *prestige*. If an advertiser wishes to sell a certain brand of cigarettes, he tries to use the fact that some famous person smokes these cigarettes. Similarly, politicians make liberal use of the names of George Washington, Abraham Lincoln, and other respected leaders to attempt to gain acceptance of their own ideas. If you watch television for just one hour or motor down nearly any highway in the United States looking at billboards, you will see that prestige is used in many instances to influence people to buy some product, to vote for a political ticket, or to alter their attitudes and behavior in other ways.

To a certain extent, prestige suggestion is merely an instance of our reliance on authorities for the facts behind our beliefs. Since the line between facts and beliefs is often hazy, it is natural that we sometimes accept a belief uncritically simply because we are forced to rely on authorities. To a certain extent, prestige suggestion also involves identification with some leader or idol. The girl who would like to be beautiful may have a fashion model as her beauty ideal, and if fashion models use Beautiface Cold Cream, the girl is likely to use it too as her way of aspiring to the beauty of the model.

Prestige suggestion also plays on already existing negative attitudes and uses them to form new negative attitudes. If people have a generally unfavorable attitude toward Communists, the suggestion may be made that such and such a political belief is "communistic" or endorsed by the Communist press. This is a way of taking an existing attitude and turning it toward another—often innocent—victim. Much of the name calling or "smearing" that occurs in the political arena deliberately or unconsciously makes use of such suggestion.

Another important aspect of prestige suggestion, however, is that it alters a person's perception of an object or situation. When a prestige suggestion is attached to a thing, he views it in a new light. The following study illustrates this point [Asch et al., 1940]:

Students were asked to rank such professions as business, dentistry, journalism, medicine, and politics according to (1) the amount of intelligence they thought the profession required and (2) the social usefulness of the profession. Some students did this without being given any suggestion. Other groups of students were given suggestions by being told that another group of students had, say, ranked politics highest (or lowest). These suggestions were rather effective. The group that was told that politics had been ranked low by others ranked it low, whereas those who were told that others had ranked politics high ranked it high. When these groups were later asked specifically what politicians they had in mind when making their rankings, the group ranking politics low said they had in mind politicians such as "Tammany Hall politicians" and the "usual neighborhood politicians." Those ranking politics high had in mind national politics and named such statesmen as Roosevelt, Hull, and LaGuardia. Thus the effect of the suggestion was to get the students to think of the better or poorer examples of politicians and to express their attitudes accordingly.

"Everybody's doing it," or "More people smoke Nocoff cigarettes than any other cigarette" are examples of *social* suggestion, another kind of suggestion that is often rather effective. It appeals to the general tendency to conform and also to a person's lack of confidence in his own judgment. Advertising aims to evoke interest in trying the product. In many circumstances, we find ourselves uncertain about what we think or should think, and thus we are inclined to go along with the crowd or accept almost any other suggestion made by our peers. Our uncertainty may be due to inexperience or merely to our having no prior attitudes and beliefs. On the other hand, it may be due to the *ambiguity* of the objects or situations to which we are to react. As we have seen before, when a great many interpretations of a situation are possible, the individual frequently adopts the same way of looking at it that others around him have adopted, particularly when they are well agreed or when they are attractive to him (see page 581).

NEEDS Perhaps it goes without saying that suggestion, as well as other methods of altering attitudes and beliefs, must fit in with a person's needs. You will remember that attitudes involve relationships between the category into which the object of an attitude is placed and the individual's goals or values. Thus things we regard favorably are related to pleasant events or to attaining some positive goal, and things we regard unfavorably are associated with threats and unpleasant events. It follows from this that to develop or change an attitude, a category of objects or issues must be associated with an individual's goals or values. If necessary, such goals and values may even be created so that they can be related to the attitude category.

Much of today's advertising attempts to establish such relationships. By associating a particular brand of cold cream with a fashion model, the advertiser is using prestige suggestion and is also playing upon established needs. In essence he tells his audience that the use of this cold cream may lead—that is, it may be related—to the goal of becoming like this model. A girl who develops a positive attitude toward the cold cream because of the advertisement sees some connection between this beauty aid and her goals, either of improving her looks or of being like a fashion model. Obviously, there would be little use in advertising beauty aids in a society where women did not value their looks. Madison Avenue would first have to

create a need in these women for beauty enhance-
ment before it could sell them the product as a
means of satisfying the need.

Need arousal. For this reason, propagandists
often go to some trouble to create needs. Advertisers
also try to do this in order to enlarge the market
for their products. To sell washing machines, they
may emphasize how much washday drudgery is
saved by the washing machine, and then go on to
emphasize the advantages of their particular washing machine. Even in labor-management relations,
where there would seem to be no need to create
problems, management may find it necessary to
foment labor troubles, to fabricate stories of the
dangers of a labor uprising, and so on, in order to get
people to favor legislation designed to restrict labor.
Unions have also gotten quite adept at magnifying
issues in order to convince their members that the
union performs vital functions.

Several investigations have demonstrated that it
is possible to alter attitudes toward an issue by
changing the perceived relationships between the
issue and the audience's goals and values. In one of
these studies, the experimenter changed college students' attitudes toward racially desegregated housing [Carlson, 1956]. He did this by convincing them
that such housing would facilitate the attainment of
certain goals, such as improving American prestige
in the eyes of other nations, and would not interfere
with the attainment of other goals—for example, it
would not necessarily lower property values.

In a later experiment, students who were high in
achievement motivation were given talks on "teaching as a career" [Di Vesta and Merwin, 1960]. A
speech that highlighted the connection between
teaching and the satisfaction of achievement needs
influenced their attitudes more than other speeches
that did not play up this connection, even though
all talks contained favorable assertions about teaching. In other words, the speech that changed attitudes toward teaching most was one that made the
audience aware of the relationship between this
category and their own needs.

Another experiment shows that a similar principal can be applied to negative goals as well as to
positive ones [Weiss and Fine, 1958]:

One group of subjects was exposed to a humiliating and
insulting experience designed to arouse their hostility,
whereas another group was given a nonfrustrating and
satisfying experience. Half of each of these groups then
read a message urging harshly punitive treatment of juvenile delinquents; the other halves of the two groups read a
communication stating that America should be very lenient
in dealing with her allies. The study showed that the
angered people were more likely than the nonangered subjects to accept the idea of treating delinquents harshly. They
were also somewhat less likely to be convinced that the
United States should be lenient toward her allies. People in
the angered group apparently most readily adopted the
opinions congenial to their emotional state.

Defensive avoidance. From the point illustrated
here, it is only a short step to the "common-sense"
notion frequently used in safety campaigns. This is
the idea that you can get people to obey safety
instructions by frightening them about the dangers
of not doing so. This is the reason for such slogans
as "speed kills" and the din of statistics we hear
daily on radio and television about the number of
traffic fatalities. It assumes that frightened people
are more likely to heed appeals to drive safely. Unfortunately, the experimental evidence on this point
is not encouraging. Indeed, the "scare 'em" approach may actually block, rather than aid, the
acceptance of the appeal, as the following study
demonstrates [Janis and Feshbach, 1953]:

High school students listened to lectures on dental
hygiene under one of three conditions: strong fear arousal,
moderate fear arousal, or minimal fear arousal. Under the
strong-fear condition, subjects were made very anxious
about the state of their mouths, whereas under the minimal-
fear conditions no attempt was made to create this anxiety.
In all conditions, the students were urged to adopt certain
dental practices. The results, however, demonstrated that
the higher the level of fear arousal, the *less* likely the
students were to accept the communicator's point of view.

The explanation for the results of this experiment

and others that show about the same thing seems to be that fear arousal produces a "defensive-avoidance" reaction. To defend themselves against the threat created by the message, the audience members avoid accepting the communicator's conclusions. It is as if the listeners believed that these dire predictions would affect other people but not themselves.

Examples of defensive avoidance can be found in everyday life. There is the story of the cigarette smoker who said he was so disturbed by the newspaper articles on how smoking produced lung cancer that he was going to stop reading newspapers. This chap was not only avoiding the disturbing information, he was also tacitly maintaining that other people might come down with lung cancer, but not he.

This is not to say, of course, that people will always avoid accepting fear-arousing messages. Under some conditions they may not resist the communicator's conclusions even though he creates anxiety in them. Whether they do or not undoubtedly depends on the perceived probability of their being hurt. Relatively few people, for example, actually come down with lung cancer, and comparatively few are hurt or killed in automobile accidents. So it is possible for the person to tell himself that the warnings he hears do not really apply to him. If, on the other hand, he knows or feels that he is in real danger, he is not so likely to shrug off or resist the warnings. Tell a seasoned Arctic explorer that he must wear the proper boots or he will be certain to develop frostbite, and he very likely will accept, rather than avoid, the message and act accordingly.

CONSISTENCY OF ATTITUDES AND BEHAVIOR

Attitudes may persist or change in order to preserve consistency between perceptions or actions. Terms such as *balance* [Heider, 1946, 1958], *symmetry* [Newcomb, 1953], *congruity* [Osgood and Tannenbaum, 1955], and *cognitive dissonance* [Festinger, 1957] have been used to represent the tendency of the individual to be consistent, and each of these

several theories is associated with an active research program. The concept basic to each of these formulations involves the tendency of an individual to seek to resolve, or relate, cognitions or attitudes which are out of balance with each other. For example, if two friends support different presidential candidates, and the election is important to each of them, each may attempt to resolve the asymmetry of the situation by trying to persuade the other of the merits of his candidate; or they may decide not to discuss politics for the duration of the election campaign in order not to keep bringing up the sore point; or they may become less good friends, who therefore care less how the other votes. Some attempts to restore a balance to an unbalanced situation can generally be expected. If a married couple or two close friends have an argument, some conciliatory gestures are usually forthcoming in order to restore the relationship to its former basis. The theory of cognitive dissonance is of particular interest because it relates attitude change to actual behavior.

COGNITIVE DISSONANCE Festinger (1957) has noted that ordinarily the attitudes held by an individual are reasonably consistent and that a person's actions are usually consistent with his attitudes. He has developed a theory of *cognitive dissonance* to assist in understanding what happens when inconsistencies between two cognitions do crop up—when, for example, privately held attitudes and overt behavior do not correspond. The theory holds that dissonance is "psychologically uncomfortable," and the resulting tension will motivate the individual to *try* to reduce the dissonance and achieve more consistency between the elements involved. Consistency, or consonance, may be achieved either by changing one's attitude to be closer to the position represented by actual behavior or by devaluing the importance of the dissonant factors. For example, Festinger has noted that those who smoke heavily are less likely to believe the medical evidence linking smoking and lung cancer than are light smokers or nonsmokers. He suggests that smoking enjoyment and believing that smoking is harmful are dissonant perceptions. Accordingly, the individuals who smoke heavily may reject the information that smoking is injurious to the health and try to avoid additional information that increases dissonance. In addition, the smoker may reassure himself that smoking is relaxing and therefore not harmful.

The importance of personal commitment to the decision or action has been elaborated by Brehm and Cohen (1962). For example, if an individual is thinking of buying either a sedan or a station wagon, he is going to consider carefully the relative advantages of each. However, once he has actually made his purchase, he is committed and he will emphasize the strong points of the automobile he chose, overlooking its deficiencies. If the choice was not clear-cut and some features of each car had been quite attractive to him, he will experience a good deal of dissonance. If the rejected alternative was extremely attractive, the person will probably seek to bolster his decision by reducing or eliminating the importance of the factors which contributed to the formation of dissonance. If he actually chose to buy the station wagon, he will emphasize the favorable aspects of owning a station wagon and the undesirable aspects of owning a sedan. He may seek the approval of other persons to confirm that his choice was wise. He might pay particular attention to advertisements for station wagons, particularly those of the brand he chose, to convince himself further that he made the best decision. Thus, in these several ways, dissonance aroused by making a choice between two desirable alternatives will be at least partially reduced, and the buyer will come to have a favorable attitude toward station wagons.

According to this theory, if an individual is induced to do or say something which differs from his personal attitude or belief, he experiences dissonance. Probably the most common way of reducing dissonance in such a situation is to change an attitude to be consistent with behavior. The theory also predicts that *less* attitude change occurs if great pressure is used to obtain the behavior which is inconsistent with the individual's private attitude than if the inducement to act contrary to belief is just barely sufficient to induce the desired behavior. An interesting experiment clarifies these predictions which can be made from dissonance theory [Festinger and Carlsmith, 1959]:

After having students spend an hour working alone at a very boring task, the subjects were asked to tell the next subject that the task was enjoyable and rather interesting, on the pretext that the student helper who usually introduced new subjects to the experimental situation had not arrived. Different groups of students received rewards of $1 or $20 for performing this favor for the experimenter, that is, for passing on a view obviously inconsistent with the subject's private opinion. After serving as helpers, each subject was questioned. The subjects who received the large financial reward for complying with the experimenter's request did not change their attitudes about the dull hour they had spent doing the task but rated the task boring, as did those in the control group who were not asked to serve as helpers. It is probable that the subjects who received $20 felt that the reward was disproportionate to the effort involved and decided that anyone would do such a simple thing for $20. The subjects who were paid only $1 for making the false statement actually changed their attitudes to reduce the dissonance built up by the conflict between their personal belief and their recognition that their actions did not coincide with their convictions. Thus, this attitude change helped reduce the inconsistency which existed following behavior which was discrepant with the attitude originally held concerning the boring experimental task.

During the Korean war, the Chinese Communists made use of techniques of indoctrination, sometimes called "brainwashing," which fit the dissonance formulation [Brehm and Cohen, 1962]. The Communists removed leaders from the main groups of prisoners and then gave the soldiers fairly good treatment, at the same time making good use of favors as rewards for those who accepted the ideas presented by their captors. The pressures toward collaboration were subtle, but ever-present, and not strongly coercive. However, the Chinese demanded constant participation in the indoctrination program.

Once an individual took any part in the group discussions about communism, he could be more easily induced to make some statement which he did not really believe. After an individual committed himself to a stand which was not in agreement with his attitudes or inwardly held beliefs, dissonance might be produced and the prisoners often actually changed their attitudes in the direction of agreement with their overt behavior.

Complete control over the prisoners' environment was especially useful to the Chinese in conducting such an effective indoctrination program. First, they had plenty of time to prepare the soldiers—to create a readiness to change. After the change was effected, they had time also to solidify and reinforce the new attitudes [Schein et al., 1961].

The measurement of attitudes and opinions

Since attitudes, opinions, and beliefs determine so greatly how individuals will react to social situations, it is not strange that there should be considerable interest in the precise measurement of attitudes. Leaders in government and public life like to know people's attitudes and beliefs. Those who conduct business affairs must also know customers' attitudes and beliefs. Then, too, leaders and research workers in the field of education, knowing that much of education is a matter of affecting attitudes as well as knowledge, want to understand the effects of various educational practices and environments on attitudes and beliefs about a topic.

ATTITUDE SCALES The educator and research worker have relatively favorable conditions for investigating attitudes because they usually have access to groups of students who can be studied rather intensively. Their methods, therefore, have been more accurate and detailed than those which, for practical reasons, have been developed for use in the political and commercial fields. Among the methods employed by educators and research workers are some that provide relatively accurate scales for the measurement of attitudes. We shall describe two.

Thurstone scale. One method of measuring attitudes was devised by L. L. Thurstone [Thurstone and Chave, 1929]. It involves the following steps. First, some issue toward which attitudes might be measured must be defined—war is an example. Once the issue has been defined, the next step is to collect as many statements as possible that might be relevant to the issue. In order to be useful in measurement, such statements must be simple and unambiguous, and they must distinguish between the different attitudes people hold. Such statements as "When war is declared, we must enlist," or "Wars are justifiable only when waged in defense of weaker nations" are specific enough and clear enough to evoke approval or disapproval and thus to reveal attitudes toward different aspects of war.

After statements that are thought to bear on the issue have been collected, the next step is to present them to a large number of judges, preferably a hundred or more. Each judge is asked to sort these statements into 11 piles, representing a scale from an extremely favorable attitude toward the issue to an extremely unfavorable attitude toward it. Thus *scale values* for the different statements are established. That is to say, each statement is assigned a number that indicates the degree to which the statement represents an attitude that is favorable or unfavorable to the object or issue. After all the judging is done, a limited number of statements, say 20, are selected that (1) show reasonably good agreement among judges and (2) have scale values that spread out along the continuum from 1 to 11. The median rating assigned by the judges to each of these selected statements is the scale value of the statement (see Table 17.5).

Once constructed, the attitude scale may be administered to any group we desire. The person taking it is instructed to check the statements with which he agrees. One way of scoring the results is to average the scale values of the items checked by an individual. In this way, we get a numerical

TABLE 17.5 *Some illustrative statements from a scale for measuring attitudes toward war.*

SCALE VALUE	STATEMENT
1.3	1. A country cannot amount to much without a national honor, and war is the only means of preserving it.
2.5	2. When war is declared, we must enlist.
5.2	3. Wars are justifiable only when waged in defense of weaker nations.
5.6	4. The most that we can hope to accomplish is the partial elimination of war.
8.4	5. The disrespect for human life and rights involved in a war is a cause of crime waves.
10.6	6. All nations should disarm immediately.

SOURCE: Droba, 1930.

measure of the person's attitudes and beliefs concerning the issue in question.

Likert scale. Several other methods of constructing attitude scales involve starting with a relatively large number of statements that have proven to be the most reliable indicators of a given attitude. One such method was developed by Likert (1932).

A series of statements is presented to subjects with the instruction to indicate their reaction to each in one of the following ways: strongly approve, approve, undecided, disapprove, or strongly disapprove. Their responses are then analyzed to see how they correlate with each other (see Chapter 11). Items that correlate highly with each other—for example, an individual strongly approves of one statement and also strongly approves of another, or vice versa—are considered to be relevant to the attitude being considered. When items do not correlate with other items, they are rejected as not being relevant to the attitude scale. In this way, two things are accomplished: (1) poor statements are discarded, and (2) the statements left in the test involve certain clusters of items.

We can illustrate these steps by describing Likert's construction of an attitude scale on foreign wars. Starting with a large number of items, and giving them to a sample population, he discarded many that did not correlate with the total score. When his analysis was finished, he found that he had two clusters of items; one cluster seemed to concern problems of imperialism in foreign affairs, and the other, internationalism in such affairs. Thus he obtained a scale that could be broken down into two sets of attitudes toward foreign affairs, those toward imperialism and those toward internationalism.

A more detailed consideration of the construction of attitude scales is beyond the scope of this book. We have presented two of the more typical, widely used methods, but there are many variations on these methods and other scaling techniques. The end result of any method is to obtain a "test" which is a reasonably reliable and valid measure of some attitude or attitudes (see Chapter 11). Once such a scale has been developed, it can then be used for a variety of purposes. Most of the facts that were presented in the first two sections of this chapter concerning the effects of culture, socioeconomic status, family, and education on attitudes were obtained by using attitude scales. Many of the conclusions drawn about prejudice are also based on the use of such scales.

PUBLIC OPINION AND MARKET RESEARCH Although relatively few people, other than students of psychology, have heard of attitude scales, most citizens of the United States are now familiar with another kind of attitude measurement, the public-opinion poll. For them such a poll is an attempt to forecast the outcome of political elections. These forecasts, they have learned, may be fairly accurate when the election is not too close. In a close election, however, the polls may be wrong. Since polls are sometimes wrong or do not give good predictions, many people are inclined to distrust them.

Unfortunately, the public's concept of the public-opinion poll is greatly oversimplified. The most notable polling "failure," the 1948 forecast that the Republican presidential candidate, Thomas E. Dewey, would be elected, was not entirely due to inherent shortcomings of the polling method. Some

TABLE 17.6 *The 1960 television debates and electorate opinion.*

POLL TAKEN BEFORE FIRST DEBATE: PRESIDENTIAL PREFERENCE		POLL TAKEN IMMEDIATELY AFTER FIRST DEBATE: "WHICH MAN DID THE BETTER JOB?"		POLL TAKEN IMMEDIATELY AFTER FIRST DEBATE: PRESIDENTIAL PREFERENCE	
Nixon	47	Kennedy	43	Kennedy	49
Kennedy	46	Nixon	23	Nixon	46
Undecided	7	Same	29	Undecided	5
		No opinion	5		

SOURCE: American Institute of Public Opinion, release of Oct. 12, 1960. In H. A. Bone, and A. Ranney, *Politics and voters*. New York: McGraw-Hill, 1963.

of the blame can be attributed to inadequacies in the particular procedures employed by the commercial polling agencies [Mosteller et al., 1949]. Over the years, as several critics have pointed out, these procedures have rather consistently overestimated the Republican vote. The errors in procedure could have been corrected, but only at an increased financial expense to the agencies.

In defense of the pollsters, however, the 1948 election was also an extraordinary one. In the first place, an unusually large number of people did not make up their minds about how they would vote until just before the election. In contrast to previous or subsequent elections, most of these people finally voted for the Democratic candidate. Second, to add to the pollsters' problems, a surprisingly large proportion of voters changed their voting intentions just before the election, particularly in the farm states. In the elections both prior to and since 1948, neither of these things has happened on such a scale. In the meantime, commercial polling agencies have also improved their procedures somewhat. They are now rarely more than a few percentage points off in forecasting the winning candidates' margin of victory in a national election. Consequently, politicians are making increasing use of public-opinion surveys, not only to determine their chances of being elected, but also to guide their campaign strategy.

Here are the results of some recent polls. On the eve of the 1960 election, the Roper poll found 49 per cent of the voters favoring Nixon, 47 per cent

favoring Kennedy, and 4 per cent undecided. The Gallup poll found 49 per cent in favor of Kennedy, 48 per cent favoring Nixon, and 3 per cent undecided. The actual results gave 50.1 per cent of the major party vote to Kennedy, with 49.9 per cent for Nixon. Within the 6 per cent leeway that pollsters ask to be allowed, this election was so close as to be virtually unpredictable. In the 1964 presidential election, an overwhelming Johnson victory over Goldwater was predicted as early as August. Immediately before the 1964 election, both the Gallup and Harris polls predicted 64 per cent of the vote would be for Johnson, 36 per cent for Goldwater. The actual percentages were 61 to 39. Thus the pollsters have shown that they are reasonably accurate in predicting voting behavior and in evaluating public opinion.

Predicting elections is only one—and probably the most difficult—of the uses of a public-opinion poll. But other uses are common. For instance, Table 17.6 shows how polls may be used to measure the effect of mass communication on attitude change. In addition, polls are being used regularly to assess attitudes on many problems, such as acreage allotments for farmers, cost of living, programs of road building, the United Nations, buying of United States government bonds, profits of businessmen, inflation and deflation, unemployment, and a host of other problems of concern to people [Likert, 1947]. Polls are being conducted both by agencies of the government and by groups of psychologists such as the National Opinion Research Center, American Institute of Public

Opinion, and the University of Michigan Survey Research Center. These serve various business groups, as well as advertising and manufacturing groups, and in addition conduct research of their own.

Questions. Unlike attitude scales, polls must be made among people who represent a fair sample of some particular group, such as those who vote in a particular district, those who farm, those who buy mouthwash A, or those who smoke. Such people cannot easily be induced to sit down and fill out a complicated attitude scale. They must be interviewed in a face-to-face situation, their interest and cooperation must be secured without imposing too much on their time or their privacy, and they must be asked questions which are rather simple and quickly covered.

To meet these limitations, the interview is customarily kept brief and each question covers some particular attitude. Thus, in a public-opinion poll, a single question must serve as a measure of an attitude, whereas many statements can be used in the attitude scale. Although more than one question may be used in a poll, the number of questions or items must be greatly restricted. For this reason, the phrasing of a question is a matter of major importance and makes a great difference in the outcome of the poll.

In general, questions developed for use in polls are of two types: the *fixed-alternative question* and the *open-end question.* The first type of question gives the respondent a fixed number of alternatives. For example, "Would you like to see more control over labor unions, less control, or about as much as there is now?" The open-end question allows the respondent to phrase his own answer in his own words. As is readily imaginable, it is sometimes difficult to decide what answers to open-end questions mean. In practice, the interviewer has a number of possible alternatives to the question already coded, and after listening to the respondent, he simply checks one of the possibilities. These alternatives have usually been worked out by making a trial run on a small group of subjects and then classifying their answers into some limited number of categories.

It might seem that the fixed-alternative question is preferable to the open-end question. Certainly it is simpler to use in an interview situation, and interviewers need very little training to be able to present it and to record the answers. One difficulty with this type of question, however, is that it greatly restricts the respondent's answer, often forcing him to answer in a way that does not reflect his true opinion. Given the question about control of labor, the respondent might think that in some respects labor ought to be more controlled and in others less so. Such an attitude is not the same as saying that control ought to remain pretty much as it is; yet he has no way of expressing his real attitude. Another difficulty with the fixed-alternative question is that minor differences in wording can greatly affect the result, often leading to complete misinterpretations of respondents' attitudes.

After World War II, two leading polling agencies asked the following questions at about the same time:

"After the war would you like to see the United States join some kind of world organization, or would you like to see us stay out?" [National Opinion Research Center, January, 1945.]

"Do you think that the United States should join a world organization with police power to maintain world peace?" [American Institute of Public Opinion, April, 1945.]

We have no reason to believe that sentiment changed drastically between January and April, 1945, or that the populations sampled had very different views. However, 64 per cent said yes to the first question and 81 per cent said yes to the second question, while 26 per cent said no to the first and 11 per cent said no to the second. It is quite likely that the phrase "to maintain world peace" greatly increased the affirmative answers, because the pollsters know that inserting any phrase which by itself is generally approved increases the number of approvals of the question as a whole.

Because of the importance of wording, the pollsters do a great deal of research to arrive at their questions. Often they run a preliminary poll on small groups in which they use several different phrasings of a question; they then study the results to see what difference the phrasing makes. From such preliminary studies, they attempt to frame the alternatives that are most likely to give people a chance to express their attitudes. They try to avoid phrasings that are likely to give a spuriously high or spuriously low percentage of any particular answer. They must also try, insofar as time permits, to use different questions either in the same poll or in succeeding polls to be able to interpret the results that they obtain.

Sampling. Once a public-opinion poll has been prepared, the next question concerns the people to whom it should be given. In most polling, an attempt is made to characterize the attitudes of some particular population. Sometimes this population is all the adults in the United States. More often, however, we are interested in some restricted population. Even in political elections we need to know results district by district, because the outcome of elections is determined not by the national result, but rather by congressional districts, electoral districts, and states. In other instances, the population may be farmers, retail-store owners, taxpayers, schoolteachers, and so on.

Whatever the population, it is almost always impractical to poll the whole group, simply because the group is too large. We are therefore faced with the problem of selecting a sample from the total population. Of course, in the end, we wish to draw conclusions about the whole population from the relatively small sample. Statisticians, fortunately, have worked out rather dependable rules for making inferences about a population from a sample. Just how accurate such inferences are depends upon a number of factors. In general, though, it is possible to use a sample of several hundred cases and predict with relative accuracy what the response of the whole population might be. To do this the sample must be so drawn that it is truly representative of the population. Practical people, ignorant of statistical methods, often wonder how one can draw conclusions about a whole population from a small sample. Actually, there is no difficulty at all so long as the sample is truly representative. It is this matter of representative sampling, on which so much stands or falls, that is the major problem of the pollsters.

In general, samples can be constructed in two ways so that they represent the population reasonably well: One is known as probability sampling; the other is known as quota sampling.

In *probability sampling,* each individual in the population has a certain probability of being included in the sample. As a result, the probable degree of error in generalizing the findings from the sample to the population can be computed statistically.

To illustrate this approach, let us suppose that some organization wanted to survey opinions among all the property owners in a large community. This is the population within which they want to generalize the sample's findings, and the sample must be representative of this population. The pollster, then, might go to the tax office, secure complete lists of those who own property, arrange the names randomly, and pick every nth name, for example, every tenth, one-hundredth, or one-thousandth from the list. In this way, each property owner has a one-in-n chance of being included in the sample.

The method of *sampling from lists* is widely used when the target population has been recorded on a list. The great danger in this method is that the list may not represent the population. This was the case in the famed *Literary Digest* poll that so badly predicted the election results in 1936 [Newcomb, 1950]. That poll made use of telephone lists, and its results probably represented fairly well how telephone subscribers were going to vote. The trouble was that only slightly over half the voters in the United States at that time were telephone subscribers. These were the economically favored members of the population who had different political attitudes from the rest of the voters. It usually happens that lists of property owners, telephone subscribers, utility users, and so on, represent the higher socioeconomic strata of society and cannot be taken as representative of the population as a whole.

Another major difficulty in sampling from lists, obviously, is that the population we are interested in may not be on a list. There is no list, for example, of every eligible voter in the United States, and it would be much too expensive to compile one. If the pollster wanted to forecast how the nation would vote in a presidential election, he would have to adopt another procedure. Generally, he must change his technique whenever there is no good list of the population of interest.

A frequent alternative is to sample from areas instead of population lists. The investigation, mentioned earlier in the chapter, of the 1948 presidential campaign, in Elmira, New York, utilized the *area-sampling* procedure. The city was divided into a large number of smaller areas, such as city blocks. Each of these sampling units was then given a number at random. One number, or area, in three was then selected for further study, and a list of dwelling units in each area was prepared. Using this list, the research workers randomly selected a certain number of dwelling units—apartments or houses—to be visited within each of the areas.

In other studies, polling agencies may select addresses so that they are randomly divided among different geographical areas which represent various socioeconomic strata and other demographic factors in the same proportion that they exist in the population. The interviewers are then sent to specified addresses.

This area-sampling method assures about the most representative sample one can expect to get and, therefore, yields very accurate results. However, it is expensive because it means considerable travel for interviewers who often must make many repeated calls before they find their respondents at home. The logic of the procedure demands that a person who has been randomly chosen to be included in the sample must be interviewed even if he is not at home when the first visit is made. People who are at home during the day or who are easily accessible are not necessarily similar in all respects to people who are away from home or who are less accessible to the interviewer. Omission of these not-at-home people introduces a bias into the sample so that it is no longer completely representative of the population [Hilgard and Payner, 1944].

The second of two general methods of sampling, *quota sampling,* is based on the assumption that a sample will be an accurate miniature of a larger population if important sociological groups are represented in the sample in the same proportion that they occur in the population. To achieve this type of representation, the polling agency sets quotas for certain categories such as age, sex, socioeconomic status, and geographical region. Interviewers are then told how many interviews they must conduct with respondents in each category. The interviewers are left some discretion as to how they manage to fill their quota. By establishing quotas in this way, the agency hopes to obtain a fair cross section of the population. Interviewers, however, when given a choice, usually select the person who seems somewhat more cooperative or the house that seems somewhat better kept. Thus biases can creep into the sample. Whenever such biases have anything to do with attitudes, the quota-sampling method gives inaccurate results. This is one reason why attempts to predict national elections encounter a certain amount of unknown error.

From this brief account of public-opinion polling, one can see that constructing and administering a poll is no simple matter. Considerable knowledge and experience with the measurement of attitudes, together with statistical skills, is required to design and carry out a poll. Under the supervision of well-trained persons, public-opinion polls can provide considerable information with relatively little error. In the hands of a novice, they are likely to give only misinformation.

Market research. Closely related to public-opinion polling is a specialized field that has grown greatly in the last 25 years—market research. The principal difference between the two is the kind of attitudes each is attempting to measure. In market research, attitudes concerning specific products, or the advertising of products, are measured rather than attitudes toward public issues. In addition, market research often elicits specific information, such as what brand of mouthwash a housewife last purchased, what advertising she has noticed recently, what magazines she reads regularly, what radio programs she listens to. Such factual information, together with information about people's likes and dislikes of particular products, enables advertisers to devise more acceptable advertising. It also enables manufacturers to design products that will be more favorably received. Aside from these differences, however, the methods and the problems of market research are very much like those of public-opinion polling.

AUDIENCE MEASUREMENT   Advertisers, of course, are interested not only in what they advertise, and how they advertise, but also in the medium through which they advertise—the newspaper, magazine, radio, or television. In fact, these media are wholly or partly financed by the proceeds from advertising. All parties concerned would like to know the extent of the audiences for their advertising. Hence, in recent years, attempts to measure the size, nature, and attitudes of audiences have increased considerably.

Many of the leading magazines, for example, continually conduct surveys to determine how many people are reading their magazines and what kind of people they are—their buying habits, their educational level, their hobbies, and their reading habits. In addition, they may find out just what parts of a magazine are read most often, what kinds of stories are most popular, and what advertising is most noticed, so that they may know better the effectiveness of advertising of different kinds placed in different positions in the magazine.

Radio and television stations have a somewhat different problem. They must first of all find out how many people and what kind of people tune in to them at different times of day and for which types of programs. The most common method of doing this is to call houses by telephone (using the list method) and ask such questions as the following [Hooper, 1946]:

1. Were you listening to the radio (or watching television) just now?
2. To what program were you listening, please?
3. What station, please?
4. What is advertised?
5. How many men, women, and children in your home were actually listening?

From polls of this sort, one can derive a rating that states what percentage of homes have their sets tuned in to a particular station. Such ratings are quite important when an advertiser comes to decide whether or not he is reaching the size and kind of audience he wishes to reach with the program he is sponsoring.

Racial attitudes and conflicts

The word *race,* in ordinary usage, means a group of human beings having common and distinctive innate physical characteristics. Whether any races exist at all and, if so, which they are and how many there are is a much debated issue, and one we shall not examine here [Klineberg, 1954]. However, when we talk of "racial conflict," we refer to social conflict resulting from prejudice against any social group having some distinctive common characteristic, whether that common characteristic is race, religion, or national origin. Most of the illustrations in this section draw upon anti-Negro prejudice in the United States, both because this kind of prejudice is most intense in this country and because it has been well studied by psychologists and others. But the same principles which apply to conflict between Negroes and whites also apply to other "racial" conflicts.

ACQUIRING PREJUDICES   What is a prejudice? We have defined it as an unfavorable attitude toward some person, living thing, or inanimate object. As we use it here, however, *prejudice* refers to a hostile attitude toward some social group. Thus, any attitude of hostility toward whites, Negroes, Germans, politicians, communists, or any other group is a prejudice. In other words, it does not matter whether the prejudice has some objective basis or not. If it is hostility toward a group, it is a prejudice.

Prejudices are attitudes, and just like any other attitudes, they obey the principles of attitude formation and maintenance which were discussed earlier. In particular, prejudices are *learned*, and it is very important to ask how they are learned, since one of the best ways of eradicating them is to prevent their being learned in the first place.

Logically, a prejudice can be learned in two possible ways: (1) from contact with the object of the prejudice or (2) from contact with others who have the prejudice. Prejudices are, in fact, learned in both ways, but various studies indicate that they are more commonly acquired by contact with people who have them.

Contact with prejudiced people. A good many studies have shown that there is a high correlation between the prejudices of parents and those of their children. The correlation exists because parents often train their children to be prejudiced. For example, a study of rural Tennessee children showed that their parents warned them to avoid Negro children and even objects which had been handled by Negro children, and that the parents sometimes punished their children severely for violating these warnings.

The first thing that a child learns about a prejudice is that the object group is "bad." Later he learns more specific things about the group. One study showed, for example, that young Southern white children believed Negroes to be inferior to whites in many traits, including the "trait" of religiousness [Blake and Dennis, 1943]. Older children showed a much more discriminating pattern of beliefs about Negroes; for example, they rated Negroes as more religious than whites.

Parents are not the only teachers of prejudice. Schoolmates, teachers, and general communication media such as newspapers and television are also effective. In addition, most of the people we meet try to influence our attitudes. Hence we are continuously exposed to carriers of prejudice.

A particularly dramatic demonstration of the fact that prejudice is usually learned from contact with the prejudiced rather than from contact with people against whom it is directed is the very strong anti-communist prejudice now held by almost all Americans. Very few Americans have ever met a communist. What they know about communists they have learned from newspapers, television, and other public-information media. If it became desirable—as it was during World War II, when the Russians were our allies—to create a more favorable attitude toward communists, the public-information media would probably be used effectively toward achieving this end.

Contact with object of prejudice. Prejudice may grow out of personal experience with the group against which it is directed, but this source of prejudice is probably rare. In fact, direct contact and shared experience with the group are sometimes a cure for prejudice.

During World War II, the Army experimented with the creation of mixed Negro and white units. Both before and after the whites saw service in such units, their attitudes toward Negroes were measured. In almost all cases, the whites were less prejudiced after their experience in mixed units than they had been before. And the Negroes in mixed units, incidentally, proved to be quite effective in combat, unlike many Negroes in segregated units [Rose, 1946].

In an experimental study of prejudice, two groups of boys at a camp were subjects [Sherif et al., 1961]:

Conditions were arranged so that each group did not know or see any of the other group for the first two days at camp. Thus, each group had an opportunity to become established and to develop group cohesiveness. Next, various frustrating and competitive situations were arranged between the groups, and considerable intergroup rivalry was established. After deliberately encouraging competitive behavior, such as tug-of-war and group games with special prizes for the winning group, the experimenters wanted to change the atmosphere of the camp by reducing the conflict and prejudice that had been built up between the two groups. By creating a series of situations which required cooperation between the groups, such as calling on all the boys to pull on a tow rope to help start a stalled truck, the experimenters led the boys to work toward a common goal, a well-run camp. Increased interaction between the groups removed many barriers to communication so that the previously existing prejudice and hostility between the two groups was changed into more friendly and mutually congenial attitudes.

White housewives' attitudes toward Negroes became much more favorable than they had been after the women had lived in biracial housing projects [Deutsch and Collins, 1951]. Two of the housing areas which were studied were fully integrated and two were relatively segregated, with Negro and white families in the same project but in different buildings or separate parts of the project. Figure 17.3 shows that there was little attitude change toward Negroes in an unfavorable direction; most change in a favorable direction took place in the fully integrated projects where the families had more opportunities for contact and friendship. Interviews with some of the housewives provided additional information about the processes of attitude change.

"I started to cry when my husband told me we were coming to live here. I cried for three weeks . . . I didn't want to come and live here where there were so many colored people. I didn't want to bring my children up with colored children, but we had to come. . . . Well, all that's changed. I've really come to like it. I see they're just as human as we are. They have nice apartments, they keep their children clean, and they're very friendly. I've come to like them a great deal. . . . I'd just as soon live near a colored person as a white, it makes no difference to me."

"I thought I was moving into the heart of Africa. . . . I had always heard about how they were . . . they were dirty, drink a lot . . . were like savages. Living with them, my ideas have changed altogether. They're just people . . . they're not any different."

[Deutsch and Collins, 1961, pages 98–99.]

Thus, the people who lived near Negroes came to feel more favorably toward them. New information that did not fit their prejudiced stereotype of the

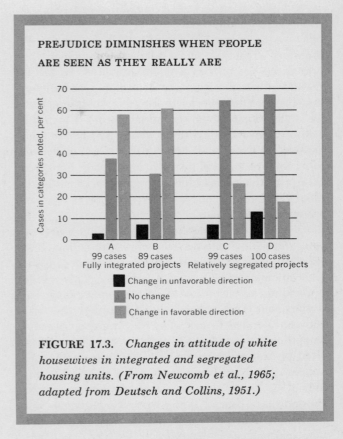

PREJUDICE DIMINISHES WHEN PEOPLE ARE SEEN AS THEY REALLY ARE

A
99 cases
89 cases
Fully integrated projects

C   D
99 cases   100 cases
Relatively segregated projects

Cases in categories noted, per cent

■ Change in unfavorable direction
■ No change
■ Change in favorable direction

FIGURE 17.3.   *Changes in attitude of white housewives in integrated and segregated housing units. (From Newcomb et al., 1965; adapted from Deutsch and Collins, 1951.)*

Negro led to this generally favorable attitude change. Such results might also be explained by dissonance theory (see page 613). Prejudiced people in the integrated housing developments had to cooperate with Negroes and could not indulge their prejudices publicly; thus behavior and attitude were dissonant, and attitudes changed to restore internal harmony.

SUPPORTS FOR PREJUDICE   Once learned, prejudices are not allowed to die out through forgetting or disuse. Rather they continue to serve the purpose of *gratifying an individual's needs*. In addition, they so alter his perception and memory, as we have already indicated, that his everyday experiences tend to support his prejudices. Consequently, between his needs and his perceptions, an individual usually maintains his prejudices at full strength.

Needs. Probably the need best served by prejudice is the need for a feeling of superiority. A prejudice creates a social hierarchy in which the prejudiced person has a superior status. If one is prejudiced against Negroes, for example, he believes that Negroes are inferior to him and, therefore, that he is superior to them. Some people need to think well of themselves—to think themselves better than others (see Chapter 6). The poorest, least-educated, most unimportant white in a backwoods Southern town has the consolation of "knowing" that he is mentally, morally, and socially superior to most of the residents of his area.

Prejudice also serves the need to express *aggression.* Psychologists have good reason to believe that hostility and aggression usually originate in the frustration of needs (see Chapter 13). This notion is certainly consistent with ordinary experience, for we frequently see people irritated or angry because they have failed to get what they want or because something or somebody has obstructed their efforts.

Aggression resulting from frustration can often be vented directly at whatever is doing the frustrating. When a person of superior status or a situation beyond one's control is the frustrator, however, the aggression must be expressed in some other way. The consequence is *displaced aggression* (see Chapter 13).

In an experiment in which psychologists deprived students for a prolonged period of sleep, food, cigarettes, and even permission to talk, one subject vented his aggression in hostile drawings [Sears et al., 1940]. In other instances, the aggression may be expressed in prejudice against some "inferior" group that cannot retaliate. Such displaced aggression is displayed when the lieutenant bawls out the sergeant, the sergeant works it out on the private, and the private kicks the dog. It is illustrated more scientifically in an experiment with boys at a summer camp who were frustrated by not being allowed to go to the movies. Before and after the frustration, their attitudes toward Mexicans and Japanese were measured, and these measurements showed that subjects were considerably more prejudiced after they had experienced frustration than before [Miller and Bugelski, 1948].

Scapegoating. Such displaced aggression is particularly significant in racial conflict. In such cases, it is called scapegoating. The prejudiced person who suffers economic, social, or political frustrations may displace his aggression against some convenient object, and the most convenient object is likely to be the group against whom he already has a prejudice. This is particularly likely if he can so distort the facts that the group seems to be responsible for his frustrations. A most notable example of this sort of displacement is the German persecution of the Jews in the 1930s. Hitler was able to convince his followers—who were presumably anti-Semitic to begin with—that the Jews were responsible for most of Germany's economic and social woes. Thus he made Jews the scapegoats of displaced aggression.

Scapegoating, then, may involve the displacement of hostility onto some minority group, but aggression that cannot be directed against the frustrator is not *necessarily* displaced onto a minority group. Many people would not exhibit the displaced aggression and prejudice displayed by the boys in the summer camp. When that experiment was repeated in other populations, prejudice against minority groups did not always increase.

Some of the factors affecting the likelihood of scapegoating can be discussed here, although a full treatment of them is beyond our scope. One way of understanding scapegoating better is through the concept of *stimulus generalization* (see Chapter 3). A frustrator who arouses hostility in a person can be regarded as an original stimulus giving rise to the response of aggression. As we have seen in our discussion of stimulus generalization in conditioning experiments, once the organism has learned to make this response, then other stimuli can elicit it. The greater the similarity between these other stimuli and the original stimulus, the greater the likelihood that they will produce the response. Thus, people similar to the original frustrator may also arouse hostility within the frustrated person.

This similarity need not be a physical one. Hostility may be generalized when little or no physical resemblance exists between the frustrator and the people it is turned toward. To the angered person, the similarity may be qualitative. For example, the only thing they may have in common is that he dislikes them both. Thus hostility can be generalized from the frustrator to another object because a dislike for both is the quality that makes them similar [Berkowitz and Holmes, 1959]. This analysis suggests that the summer-camp boys may have had some prior dislike for Mexicans and Japanese, and that the same result would not be obtained if subjects had no prior dislike for a particular group.

The main point in this analysis so far is that hostility will be displaced from the frustrator to the person most similar to him when the frustrator is not available for direct attack—because of his absence, for example. A somewhat different prediction must be made when the angered person is afraid to strike at the frustrator because the frustrator might retaliate. In this case, the person may inhibit his aggression both toward the frustrator and toward other people very similar to him. Instead, he will be most likely to attack others who appear to possess some intermediate degree of similarity to the frustrator.

The angered individual's personality traits may also affect the likelihood of his displacing his hostility onto minority groups. In our discussion of the highly ethnocentric individual, we implied that this type of person has a readiness to displace aggression. Perhaps the highly ethnocentric individual has learned to attack others who are relatively powerless, particularly minority groups, as a way of reducing aggressive tensions within himself. Thus, the prejudice may be an outlet for pent-up aggression.

In one experiment among children prejudiced against Negroes, for example, those who were relatively free of repressed aggression learned much more easily not to be prejudiced. The only effect of educational procedures on those with aggressive personality patterns was to make them still more prejudiced, both against their teachers and against society in general [Mussen, 1950]. The value of education as a corrective for prejudiced attitudes is thus limited by the kind of person who is "educated."

Perception and judgment. Prejudice is supported not only by needs but also by changes in perception and judgment. We have discussed this point, but it should be reviewed because it is germane to the preservation of prejudice. Prejudice alters perception so that we tend to see what we want to see or what we believe we are going to see. If we believe that Negroes are dirty and shiftless, we take special note of instances of dirtiness or shiftlessness among Negroes while paying little attention to similar instances among whites, or to outstanding examples of cleanliness or ambitiousness among Negroes. Indeed, with practice, we become quite skilled at perceiving only that which is consistent with our prejudices.

One experiment illustrates the way in which prejudice can distort the judgment and interpretation of situations [Cooper and Jahoda, 1947]. In this study, subjects were shown a series of cartoons involving a character dubbed Mr. Biggott and asked to give their reactions to the cartoons. One subject, known to be prejudiced, interpreted the cartoons in Figure 17.4 in a quite extraordinary way: If Mr. Biggott is only a sixth-generation American, he is a newcomer and is not entitled to put on airs.

Social handicaps. Last but not least in the list of conditions that maintain prejudice are the social effects of prejudice itself. To the extent that prejudice is permitted to operate in social affairs, to that extent it produces a world that is exactly what the prejudiced person expects it to be. People with anti-Negro prejudices, for example, believe that Negroes are less intelligent than whites. Believing that, they prevent Negroes from getting adequate schooling, library facilities, housing, and other cultural opportunities. The result, of course, is a social handicap for Negroes that prevents them from being as educated and as "intelligent" as whites. Thus the prejudice becomes "true." It creates the social conditions that justify the prejudice. This is obviously

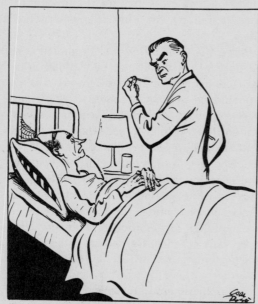

"In case I should need a transfusion, doctor, I want to make certain I don't get anything but blue, sixth-generation American blood!"

Mr. Biggott: "Was it necessary, Reverend, to emphasize the Lord's—er—Jewish background in your sermon?"

FIGURE 17.4. *Examples of Mr. Biggott cartoons used in a study of prejudice. (American Jewish Committee and Carl Rose.)*

a vicious circle in which the effects of prejudice help to maintain the prejudice by providing an observable basis for it.

SOCIAL EFFECTS OF PREJUDICE We have just noted one of the effects of prejudice—the creation of social conditions that confirm the prejudice. Let us now look at the social consequences of prejudice in greater detail.

Perhaps the most significant effect of prejudice is that prejudiced people avoid those against whom they bear a prejudice. This fact applied on a scale affecting thousands or millions of people has a very simple result—*segregation*. In the Middle Ages, and

also in Eastern Europe in recent times, Jews were required to live in ghettos. Nowadays we do not have so many ghettos, but we in America do have large areas in which only Negroes live and much larger ones where Negroes are not permitted to live. Although civil rights legislation has removed many of the official prohibitions against using certain public facilities, such as trains and restaurants, has aided voter registration, and has ended job discrimination in some measure, much progress remains to be made, not only in the South but in the North as well.

Segregation with equal facilities is theoretically possible. The United States Supreme Court in 1896 therefore decided that separate, but equal, facilities were permissible under the law. In practice, however, it does not work. Almost inevitably the segregated minority is forced to use inferior facilities under inconvenient, uncomfortable, or unsanitary conditions, because segregation permits majority groups to "take out" their prejudices on the minority. Having become convinced of this fact, the Supreme Court finally ruled in 1954 against segregation in education. This ruling simply gave legal recognition to the social fact that segregated facilities are seldom equal. In addition to its legal and moral dubiousness, segregation, from a psychological viewpoint, prevents people in the different groups from knowing each other. We have seen that such contact between groups tends to change attitudes in the favorable direction. Without communication, suspicion and ignorance persist, and thus stereotypes and prejudices are perpetuated.

PREVENTING RACIAL CONFLICT We have seen that racial conflict has its roots in racial prejudice. To prevent or alleviate racial conflict requires, then, that we try to combat racial prejudice. From our analysis of prejudice, it is fairly easy to formulate several rules for coping with it. These rules, however, are easier to state than they are to apply.

Prevent parents and teachers from teaching prejudices to children. This is difficult to do, but it has been accomplished more and more in recent years (see Figure 17.5).

Remove the supports for the prejudice and provide prejudiced persons with evidence contrary to the prejudice. This is not likely to be very effective because of the distorting effects of prejudice on perception and judgment.

Make prejudice conflict with other strong needs. The campaigns, extensively used during World War II, which attempted to convince people that it was unpatriotic, irreligious, or undemocratic to be prejudiced, were quite effective. This technique can backfire, though. If a person is propagandized to believe that prejudice is undemocratic, he may react not by rejecting prejudice, but by rejecting the underlying concept of democracy.

Teach people not to be prejudiced. Although such education works fairly well, it is difficult to get adults into a situation which is aimed at changing their prejudices. Consequently, disguised education is likely to be most effective. Television's casual acceptance of Negroes is an excellent example of one way to accomplish this.

Bring potentially conflicting groups together. The success of the Army's mixed units indicates that contact helps to reduce prejudice (see Figure 17.6). However, it is important to make sure that the contact is not with the worst examples of the group against which the prejudice is directed.

FIGURE 17.5. *Teachers can combat prejudice by not teaching it and by ignoring racial differences. (Bob Levin, Black Starr.)*

FIGURE 17.6. *Interaction among members of mixed groups, especially groups of children working together, usually tends to reduce prejudice. (Glenn Mitchell.)*

SYNOPSIS AND SUMMARY

Attitudes tinge practically everything we do. We are continually making evaluations of people and events as good, bad, or in-between. In fact, much of our daily round of activities consists of trying to create favorable attitudes concerning ourselves, in trying to convince other people to change their attitudes, and in justifying our own attitudes. Most differences of opinion can be traced back to differences in attitudes.

We have seen that attitudes are learned in the family and from peers. Once learned, attitudes are quite resistant to change, but we are bombarded with communications which attempt to induce attitude changes in us. The attitude-change business is enormous, encompassing many facets of human communication. Newspapers, radio and television news broadcasts, advertising, and education are all fields in which attempts, some more benign than others, are made to induce attitude change. Some attempts at attitude change are extremely subtle. The popular entertainment business and the creation of "glamorous" personalities, for example, is mainly an exercise in attitude manipulation. Some of it is fun, but we should, perhaps, keep our eyes open and try to realize when we are being shaped. It is often to our advantage; usually someone else gains from our acceptance of propaganda.

Attitudes have a motivational function—they lead us to and away from certain goals. We like many things and we approach these, but we also "can't stand" many other things and these we avoid. Usually the motivational function of attitudes is harmless enough, but when prejudices are involved, it can lead us to do things which can be classed only as wrong.

Many specific points about attitudes were made in this chapter.

1. An attitude is a tendency to respond positively or negatively to certain objects, persons, or situations. It represents a stimulus discrimination in which things are put into categories related to the person's goals.

2. A prejudice is a special case of a negative attitude, the object of which is usually a minority group. When a person harbors a prejudice, he usually holds an over-simplified, and hence erroneous, view of the category into which he has placed the minority group. Widely shared erroneous beliefs are called stereotypes.

3. Although, in principle, one can distinguish between beliefs and attitudes—a belief is the acceptance of a statement or proposition without necessarily being for or against it—in practice, most beliefs are emotionally tinged and they are quite hard to disentangle from attitudes.

4. Culture shapes the development of attitudes and beliefs. Cross-cultural comparisons of attitudes, however, are hazardous, for differences within a culture may be greater than differences between cultures. Attitudes frequently correlate with socioeconomic and other differences.

5. Cultural influences on attitudes are transmitted largely through the family and peer groups. The attitudes of children tend to correlate with those of their parents and the persons with whom they associate.

6. Attitudes tend to be related to personality traits. One personality pattern, called the ethnocentric personality, is prejudiced against most minority groups, is authoritarian in viewpoint, and tends to place people in oversimplified "black-and-white" categories.

7. Since the information a person gets is frequently distorted or inadequate, his attitudes and beliefs are often similarly distorted. They are also influenced by the particular authorities on whom he relies for information.

8. Primary groups, which consist of friends and close associates, help shape a person's attitudes.

9. Once formed, attitudes are relatively resistant to change. They tend to be preserved by (a) selective interpretation and perception of information, (b) avoidance of information conflicting with existing attitudes, and (c) social approval or disapproval from one's associates.

10. Both education and propaganda influence and change attitudes, but propaganda is a deliberate attempt to alter attitudes in a direction favorable to the purposes of the propagandist. Three of the most common devices used by the propagandist are (a) loaded words, (b) suggestion, and (c) appeal to, or creation of, needs.

11. Loaded words, that is, emotionally toned words chosen to create the desired attitude, are the stock-in-trade of the propagandist.

12. Suggestion is the uncritical acceptance of a statement or idea. In prestige suggestion, statements are made about prestigeful people; in social suggestion, the statement that "everybody's doing it" appeals to one's desire to conform in situations where one's own feelings may be ambiguous.

13. Much propaganda and advertising attempt to influence attitudes by appealing to needs. In general, a favorable attitude can be created by arousing a need and relating it to the object of the attitude. Attempts, however, to change attitudes by frightening people, as in safety campaigns, frequently are ineffective.

14. Cognitive dissonance arises when there is a discrepancy between attitudes, or between attitudes and overt behavior. This dissonance is "psychologically uncomfortable," and people often attempt to reduce it by changing their attitudes to bring them in line with overt behavior. This is especially the case when behavior is overt and "on the record" and is difficult to deny or undo.

15. Several methods of measuring attitudes have been developed. An attitude scale provides a precise measure of the degree of an attitude toward an issue, but it can be used only with people who have the time and interest to take it.

16. For many practical purposes, we are limited to the public-opinion poll, which consists of a series of questions answered in a brief personal interview. The phrasing of questions, the context in which they are asked, and representative sampling are all extremely important to the results obtained.

17. Prejudices may be learned either from the object of the prejudice or, more commonly, from contact with others who have the prejudice.

18. Once learned, prejudices are preserved and supported by (a) the needs they help satisfy, (b) the fact that they provide a means of scapegoating, that is, of displacing aggression for which there might otherwise be no outlet, (c) distortion in perception and judgment that make the prejudice seem "true," and (d) creating social handicaps for minority groups which appear to justify the prejudice.

19. The principal social consequences of prejudice are segregation and inferior facilities for minority groups.

RELATED TOPICS IN THE TEXT

CHAPTER 3 PRINCIPLES OF LEARNING Since attitudes are learned, and since stimulus generalization is an important concept in explaining prejudice, a review of these topics might be in order.

CHAPTER 10 PERCEPTION Attitudes seem to result in selective perception—we perceive and interpret those things about which attitudes are favorable in a rather different way from those things toward which attitudes are negative. Some of the basic facts of perception —especially the influence of learning on perception— should be reviewed.

CHAPTER 13 PERSONALITY Information about motivational conflicts, aggression, and projection is presented in this chapter. These phenomena are related to prejudice and scapegoating.

CHAPTER 16 SOCIAL INFLUENCES ON BEHAVIOR The general role of culture and social groups in influencing behavior is discussed here. Conformity to group norms is an important determiner of attitudes, and the section in Chapter 16 on conformity is especially pertinent.

SUGGESTIONS FOR FURTHER READING

Allport, G. W. *The nature of prejudice.* Reading, Mass.: Addison-Wesley, 1954.
A readable summary and analysis of the literature on group prejudice.

Brown, J. A. C. *Techniques of persuasion: From propaganda to brainwashing.* Baltimore, Md.: Penguin, 1963. (Paperback.)
Attitude formation and change are the focus of this survey of various kinds of persuasion, including advertising, political propaganda, and psychological warfare.

Campbell, A., Converse, P. E., Miller, W. E., and Stokes, D. E. *The American voter.* New York: Wiley, 1960.
A discussion of factors affecting voting behavior as discovered by attitude-survey techniques.

Hollander, E. P., and Hunt, R. G. (Eds.). *Current perspectives in social psychology: Readings with commentary.* Fairlawn, N.J. Oxford, 1963 (Paperback.)
A carefully selected book of readings presenting an overview of empirical problems, research findings, and current theoretical viewpoints.

Hovland, C. I. Effects of the mass media of communication. In G. Lindzey (Ed.), *Handbook of social psychology.* Reading, Mass.: Addison-Wesley, 1954.
A useful summary of research on the effectiveness of mass media in changing attitudes, and a review of experiments dealing with procedures for altering beliefs.

Katz, D., Cartwright, D., Eldersveld, S., and Lee, A. M. (Eds.). *Public opinion and propaganda.* New York: Dryden, 1954.
A collection of readings in the areas of communication, propaganda, and public opinion.

Krech, D., Crutchfield, R. S., and Ballachey, E. L. *Individual in society: A textbook of social psychology.* New York: McGraw-Hill, 1962. Chaps. 5–7.
A social psychology text containing a comprehensive section discussing the nature and measurement of attitudes, the formation of attitudes, and the changing of attitudes.

McGrath, J. E. *Social psychology: A brief introduction.* New York: Holt, 1964. (Paperback.)
An overview of the major concepts of the field of social psychology.

Newcomb, T. M., Turner, R. H., and Converse, P. E. *Social psychology: The study of human interaction.* New York: Holt, 1965. Chaps. 2–5.
A general introduction to social psychology which attempts to integrate different psychological approaches, containing a comprehensive section on attitudes.

Secord, P. F., and Backman, C. W. *Social psychology.* New York: McGraw-Hill, 1964. Chaps. 3–6.
A social psychology text containing a comprehensive section discussing social influence processes, with emphasis on attitudes and the communication process.

18

THE PROBLEMS OF business, industry, and the world of work are touched upon by many of the subjects a student may study. Psychology is certainly one of them; almost every facet of vocational life has its psychological aspects.

The history of psychology in industry is characterized by the application of facts and techniques from three major psychological subfields to the problems of industry [Haire, 1959]. These subfields are: psychological testing, social psychology, and experimental psychology. For instance, the selection of employees may involve the application of psychological testing; the study of effective techniques of supervision and factors influencing job satisfaction involves ideas from social psychology; the study of efficiency involves ideas from both social and experimental psychology, and engineering for human use is a part of experimental psychology. In addition to these topics, which we take up here, the discussion of aptitude and interest testing in Chapter 12 has a bearing on vocational adjustment, both in helping the person make the best vocational choice and in helping an employer choose the best person for a particular job.

PSYCHOLOGY IN INDUSTRY

... WE ARE TODAY IN A PERIOD WHEN THE DEVELOPMENT OF THEORY WITHIN THE SOCIAL SCIENCES WILL PERMIT INNOVATIONS WHICH ARE AT PRESENT INCONCEIVABLE. AMONG THESE WILL BE DRAMATIC CHANGES IN THE ORGANIZATION AND MANAGEMENT OF ECONOMIC ENTERPRISE.
DOUGLAS MCGREGOR

Employee selection

An individual has the task of choosing the vocation or job that suits his aptitudes and interests, and the employer has the problem of choosing the right employee for his particular job. The employee, on the one hand, runs the risk of unhappiness and failure if he makes a mistake. The employer, on the other hand, may waste money in lowered efficiency and may disrupt the organization of his work if he picks the wrong people to fill his jobs. Thus both employees and employer are interested in avoiding mistaken choices or at least in keeping them to a minimum.

JOB ANALYSIS In order to know who can do his work best, an employer must first know exactly what work it is he wants done. No one can tell who the best man for a job is without knowing what the job itself is. The process of finding out what a job is has been called *job analysis.* Many people are inclined to think that this is a simple matter, that all one has to do is let a workman or supervisor tell you what the job entails. Experience shows that this is not enough.

In one classical study, for example, secretaries were asked to write down during the course of each day's work exactly everything they did [Charters and Whitley, 1924]. When their notes were collected and tabulated, it turned out that their jobs included over 800 distinguishable duties. Neither the secretaries nor their supervisors could remember beforehand more than a fraction of these duties.

Several different methods may be used for job analyses. Some are better suited than others to a particular job; some are more expensive than others and are undertaken only when the expense is justified by the expected benefits. The following are the principal methods:

1. Employees write down everything they do in the course of a typical day or week. This is the method that was used in the example just cited.

2. An expert job analyst takes over the job for a few days and does it himself to see what it entails.

3. Motion pictures are taken of the work and are later analyzed in detail. This method is especially suitable for repetitive jobs such as those on an assembly line.

4. Some measure of the production or output of the job is used. This may be appropriate for machinists and carpenters, whose efforts are reflected in finished products.

Most job analyses are made in such a way that a complete list of duties can be compiled. These lists, as was the case with the secretarial duties, are often rather long. Then the question arises, What duties are the most important? Many duties do not distinguish one job from another, or if they do, they are not important because almost anyone can do them, and hence they do not spell success or failure in the job. For this reason, psychologists have devised a method called *critical incidents* [Flanagan, 1951]. In applying this method, the analyst attempts to determine those aspects of the job which are critical for its best performance.

The method is especially applicable to jobs where safety is a consideration, such as driving a truck or piloting an airplane. In these jobs, it is not what the person does most of the time that is important but what he does some of the time—in emergencies or especially dangerous situations—that determines whether he is successful, or in fact whether he and his equipment survive. The critical-incidents technique also proves useful in many other jobs, including industrial, secretarial, and managerial jobs.

Once a job analysis is completed, it can be used to write a *job description,* which is a detailed account of all the facts pertinent to a job. Job descriptions may then be compared to see which ones are different and which are essentially the same. All jobs having the same description are considered the same even if they have different names—and they often do, depending upon the region of the country or the particular business or industry. Jobs that are distinguishably different yet have certain similarities are grouped into *occupations.* Occupations, in turn, can be compared and classified into major occupational families.

The U.S. Employment Service has made studies of over 30,000 occupations in industry, business, and government and has classified them in the *Dictionary of Occupational Titles* (1965). This invaluable dictionary shows how nearly all the jobs in the United States are classified into different occupations and gives the names and job specifications for each. It has served during and since World War II as a guide for fitting men to particular jobs and also as a way of finding out what and where our major manpower shortages are.

WORKER CHARACTERISTICS   The job description includes information about the job and about the worker who is needed to fill the job. On the one hand, it gives the kind of work performed, the amount of supervision given and received, the level of difficulty of the work, the standard of work required, the working conditions, and the machines, tools, equipment, and materials that the worker must use. On the other hand, it states the physical and psychological demands of the job, the amount of previous experience considered necessary, the requisite kind and amount of training—in a word, the *worker characteristics* required for a job.

Worker characteristics include a statement of how important each trait and ability is to the job. Each job requires its own particular combination of traits, interests, and abilities. A relatively complete list of the kinds of characteristics that may be included in such a statement are strength of hands, fingers, legs, and arms; dexterity of various kinds; keenness of the senses, such as depth vision or color perception; memory for such things as faces, details, and oral and written instructions; arithmetic computation; intelligence; ability to express oneself orally; and ability to handle people. Figure 18.1 shows a standard War Manpower Commission form used during World War II and since for rating these various characteristics.

SELECTION METHODS   When an employer knows what worker characteristics are required for the jobs he wishes to fill, his next task is to select applicants for the job who meet these requirements, or who best meet them. This process is known as *personnel selection*. Since employers have been selecting employees for centuries and scientific methods have been available for only a few decades, it is natural that present-day methods of selection are a mixture of opinions and facts. Some of the facts are based on long employment experience and some on modern scientific research.

Application blanks. The most generally used source of information about the characteristics of a job applicant is the application blank. This may be made out by the applicant or by someone in an employment office who asks the applicant questions and records the answers on the blank. When used wisely, it is by far the simplest method of obtaining *some* of the desired information about the worker, such as age, sex, education, and most recent employment. Application blanks, however, are frequently loaded with items that have no relevancy to the job concerned, such as birthplace, height, weight, and number of brothers and sisters. Application blanks, moreover, do not allow one to appraise accurately the *quality* of such things as education and previous employment. Some applicants may have had considerable education and employment experience but may not have profited from them as much as they should have. So the application blank has its limitations.

Because the application blank is used so widely in selecting employees, it behooves the student and prospective employee to be prepared to supply the information that it may require. Even the best of memories may not be able to cope with all the questions on such a blank; so it is an excellent idea to make a list in advance of all the items that it may include and to keep available your records of such matters as beginning and ending dates of employment, name of supervisor, name of position held, and salaries received.

For the benefit of the student, Table 18.1 includes many of the items frequently called for on application blanks. It is a composite of many typical blanks.

Interviews.   A second timeworn device used in selection is the employment interview. A survey conducted of personnel-selection practices used in 325 prominent industrial concerns has shown that 96 per cent of these concerns used an interview as part of their employment procedure. [Spriegel and Wallace, 1948].

Despite its widespread use, the interview is very often not so good a selection device as its users might think (see the related discussion in Chapter 12). One classic psychological study, for example, illustrates what can happen under some circumstances [Hollingworth, 1929].

Twelve sales managers interviewed 57 applicants for an actual job under realistic yet controlled conditions. The sales managers were experienced interviewers because their regular positions required frequent interviewing, but they were not necessarily *trained*. They were allowed to conduct the interview as they saw fit. They were required to rank the applicants in order of desirability for the job, and when the interviewing was completed, their rankings

JOB TITLE ENGINE LATHE OPERATOR, FIRST CLASS

Amount O	Amount C	Amount B	Amount A	CHARACTERISTICS REQUIRED	Amount O	Amount C	Amount B	Amount A	CHARACTERISTICS REQUIRED
	√			1. Work rapidly for long periods		√			26. Arithmetic computation
	√			2. Strength of hands		√			27. Intelligence
	√			3. Strength of arms		√			28. Adaptability
	√			4. Strength of back		√			29. Ability to make decisions
	√			5. Strength of legs			√		30. Ability to plan
	√			6. Dexterity of fingers			√		31. Initiative
		√		7. Dexterity of hands and arms			√		32. Understanding mechanical devices
√				8. Dexterity of foot and leg		√			33. Attention to many items
		√		9. Eye-hand coordination		√			34. Oral expression
√				10. Foot-hand-eye coordination	√				35. Skill in written expression
	√			11. Coordination of both hands		√			36. Tact in dealing with people
	√			12. Estimate size of objects		√			37. Memory of names and persons
	√			13. Estimate quantity of objects		√			38. Personal appearance
		√		14. Perceive form of objects		√			39. Concentration amidst distractions
	√			15. Estimate speed of moving objects		√			40. Emotional stability
	√			16. Keenness of vision		√			41. Work under hazardous conditions
	√			17. Keenness of hearing		√			42. Estimate quality of objects
√				18. Sense of smell		√			43. Unpleasant physical conditions
√				19. Sense of taste		√			44. Color discrimination
	√			20. Touch discrimination		√			45. Ability to meet and deal with public
		√		21. Muscular discrimination	√				46. Height
		√		22. Memory for details (things)	√				47. Weight
	√			23. Memory for ideas (abstract)					48. ______
	√			24. Memory for oral directions					49. ______
	√			25. Memory for written directions					50. ______

FIGURE 18.1. *A worker-characteristics form. The letters have the following meanings for satisfactory performance on the job: O, not required; C, a medium or low degree required; B, an above-average degree required; and A, a very high degree required (U. S. Department of Labor).*

were collected and compared. The results are shown in Table 18.2. There is very little agreement. Applicant A, for example, was ranked sixth by one interviewer and fifty-sixth by another. Applicant B was ranked as the best man by one interviewer and as the worst one by another.

These results are fairly typical of many studies of interviewing. Where interviews are conducted under "normal" conditions, there is very often little agreement among interviewers. This fact makes it clear that if the interview is to serve effectively

TABLE 18.1 *Some information often requested on the application blank.*

Name	Dates of employment	Business and evening schools:
Address	Salary	Major course
	Title of your job	College:
Birthplace	Brief description of work	Major course
Age	Supervisor	Degree received
Height		
Weight	Personal references:	Special abilities
	Name	Honors received or offices held
Sex	Address	
Health	How long known and in	Membership in organizations,
	what capacity	societies, etc.
Physical defects	Occupation	Hobbies
Father's occupation		Places traveled
Number of brothers and	Education:	Articles or books written
sisters	Grade school:	
	Name	Reason for wanting a job with
Most recent employment:	Years	company
Employer	High school:	
Address	Major course	Date available for work

as a selection method, certain precautions must be taken.

Three principal factors can make the difference between good interviewing and practically worthless interviewing:

1. The interviewer should know well the job about which he is interviewing.

2. He should acquire good technique. This is usually somewhat nondirective (see Chapter 15); the interviewer must draw out the applicant, rather than ask direct questions. On the other hand, he must be able to keep the interview on the track, and by the time he completes it he must know the answers to a predetermined list of questions.

3. He should be carefully selected for the task. Some people cannot put applicants at ease or establish rapport with them; others are simply poor judges of people under any circumstances.

Many interviews do not meet these important conditions and are therefore unreliable. If the conditions are met, however, the interview can be a valuable aid in selection [Ghiselli and Brown, 1955].

TABLE 18.2 *Sample results of a study of the effectiveness of the interview. Twelve sales managers interviewed 57 applicants, then ranked them for suitability for the job. These are the ranks assigned to three applicants. Agreement among interviewers is clearly not satisfactory.*

	INTERVIEWER											
	1	2	3	4	5	6	7	8	9	10	11	12
APPLICANT												
A	33	46	6	56	26	32	12	38	23	22	22	9
B	53	10	6	21	16	9	20	2	57	28	1	26
C	43	11	13	11	37	40	36	46	25	15	29	1

SOURCE: Hollingworth, 1929.

Letters of recommendation. The letter of recommendation, like the application blank and interview, is widely used in the selection of employees. This is particularly true in selecting students for colleges and professional schools and in selecting clerical, white-collar, and professional personnel.

Though widely used, the letter of recommendation is subject to the same limitations as those of the application and interview and to a few additional ones. Those who write such letters are usually busy people who toss them off as one of many chores in a day's work. The writer may not know very much about the job for which the applicant is applying or about the standards of performance required on the job. He is inclined also to be lenient in his evaluation of the applicant, since the applicant will be working for *someone else*. Furthermore, since the recommender is often chosen because of his high rank in supervision, he may not know very much about the applicant. Finally, the words that are used to describe such traits as honesty, reliability, and initiative are rather vague, meaning different things to different people. It is extremely difficult to use them in a way that discriminates between well-qualified and unqualified applicants.

The users of recommendations have long been aware of their shortcomings and in recent years have taken steps to remedy them. The "letter" now often includes a checklist of traits on which the recommender is asked to rate the applicant. This has the advantage of brevity and of giving ratings that may be compared for different applicants. It has the disadvantages, however, of being rather stereotyped, of permitting the recommender to omit important information, and of encouraging leniency in the rating of the applicant. To offset these limitations, recommendation blanks that call for ratings on traits also often ask the recommender to make comments freely as he would in a letter. Even so, the recommendation is seldom a highly reliable source of information for selecting employees.

Trade tests. Applications, interviews, and recommendations are the three most common sources of information used in selecting employees, especially for the more remunerative occupations. The benefits of scientific tests are not so widely exploited as they might be, but they are being used more and more each year for all sorts of occupations from the semiskilled to the executive classes. Of the many tests which are being used, the two kinds that have

TABLE 18.3 *Distribution of scores made on "Trade Questions for Painters" by expert painters, apprentices, and related workers.*

SCORE GROUP	DISTRIBUTION, PER CENT		
	EXPERTS	APPRENTICES	RELATED WORKERS
9–15	78	17	0
6–8	14	40	0
0–5	8	43	96

SOURCE: Stead et al., 1940.

proved most valid are the trade tests and the aptitude tests.

The trade test is an achievement test; it measures, or attempts to measure, just how good a person is at his trade. It is usually given orally by an employment interviewer, but it may be administered as a pencil-and-paper test. It usually consists of a few items that correlate well with degree of knowledge and experience in a particular job. Of the large number of trade tests available today, many were constructed by expert job analysts in the U.S. Employment Service as part of a program to provide a relatively complete list of tests [Stead et al., 1940].

Some of the questions on a trade test require definitions. A carpenter, for example, may be asked, "What do you mean by a shore?" (Answer: "An upright brace.") Some deal with methods used in the trade. A plumber, for example, may be asked, "What are the most commonly used methods of testing plumbing systems?" (Answer: "Air, water, smoke, peppermint.") Other questions deal with use, procedures, location, names, purpose, and number. An example of number as a basic element in a question is, "How many jaws has a universal chuck?" (Answer: "Three.")

Questions and tests of this type have been prepared, standardized, and validated for most of the common trades. They usually have a high validity in that they distinguish well the different levels of accomplishment within the trade. These, for convenience, are divided into three grades: the expert, who has had long experience in the trade; the apprentice, who is in the process of learning it; and the related worker, who by working with or around experts and apprentices has picked up a limited knowledge of the trade.

In Table 18.3 is evidence of how well a trade test can distinguish among these three grades of training. In this case, the trade is painting. In the highest-scoring category we find that 78 per cent are experts, while no related workers make high scores. On the other hand, few experts make low scores although nearly all related workers do.

Aptitude tests. We have already described aptitude tests in Chapter 12. They can be used both to advise a person about his vocational abilities and to help the employer determine who is best suited for his jobs (see Figure 18.2).

The employer is faced, however, with the problem of deciding which of hundreds of possible aptitude tests is most valid for a particular job. To do that he must first consider, as we have previously explained, the worker characteristics essential for that job. This problem has been met by the construction of *psychographs*.

Two kinds of psychographs are job psychographs and individual psychographs. *Job psychographs*, illustrated in Figure 18.3, show the traits and abilities required in a job or a family of jobs. It is

FIGURE 18.2. *Examples of vocational-aptitude tests. On the peg board, the examinee's job is to put the pegs in the holes in the board as speedily as possible. On the form board, the task is to place the forms correctly in the various spaces, again as rapidly as possible. (Left, New York University Testing and Advisement Center; right, Douglas Grundy, Three Lions.)*

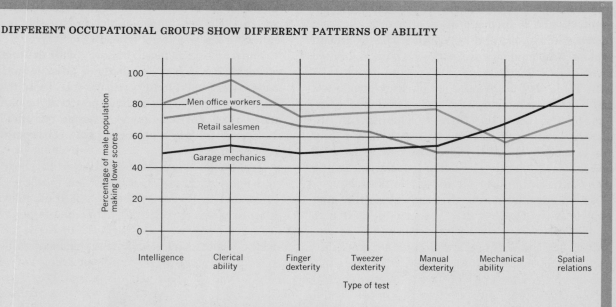

DIFFERENT OCCUPATIONAL GROUPS SHOW DIFFERENT PATTERNS OF ABILITY

FIGURE 18.3. *Profiles of abilities for three occupations. The scale is a centile scale based upon a standard sample of men drawn from all occupational levels. The scores for each occupational group are average scores translated into the general centile scale. Thus, the average male office worker is at the 80th centile of the general population in intelligence, and the average garage mechanic stands at about the 80th centile of the general population in spatial-relations ability. (After Ghiselli and Brown, 1955.)*

drawn up in terms of percentages of the population. The amount of a trait or ability required in a job is defined by the percentage of people in a population who have as much as, or more than, is necessary. To make this kind of representation as simple as possible, the U.S. Employment Service has distinguished three grades of abilities. The A grade is the amount possessed by only the upper 2 per cent of the population; the B grade, the amount possessed by the next 28 per cent; and the C grade, the amount possessed by the remaining 70 per cent. These three grades are close enough for most purposes of weighting the traits or abilities required.

Quite a few occupations have been investigated to determine whether or not a particular pattern of abilities can be distinguished for each one. In Figure

18.3 we see the profiles of three occupations: office clerk, garage mechanic, and retail salesman. The centiles on the psychograph are based upon a standard sample of men drawn from all occupational levels. Clerks seem to score higher than the average person on tests of intelligence, clerical ability, and manual dexterity, but they are about average in mechanical ability. Contrast this score with that of the garage mechanic.

To select an employee, one must know whether an applicant's abilities correspond with those stated on the profile, or job psychograph, of required abilities. This means that some way must be found of constructing an *individual psychograph* for the applicant and matching this with the job psychograph. In some circumstances, this may be done by rating the applicant with information obtained from the application blank, interview, and recommendation. Better yet, it may be done by tests selected to measure the required abilities.

VALIDITY IN SELECTION Whatever method or combination of methods is used to select employees, the validity of the selection procedure is always a problem (see Chapter 11). In the practical world, one cannot always do things as they should be done, and often it may prove too expensive or may require too much research to determine whether one's selection procedures are valid. Nevertheless, it must be recognized that one can be sure of validity only when he has properly followed the necessary procedures for predicting a criterion with a particular population. Anything less is risky. Sometimes one can make a good guess from knowing that the procedures have proven valid in what appears to be a similar set of circumstances. Research experience, however, indicates that procedures are not necessarily valid simply because they look valid to the employer or to a psychologist. It is best, therefore, to be cautious and to make strenuous efforts to measure the actual validity of the procedures one uses in selecting employees.

Supervision

The selection of an employee and his acceptance of a job are just the beginning of the problems of vocational adjustment. After that it remains to be seen whether the employee will succeed in his work and whether the employer will be effective in supervising him. Millions of words—most of them no more than embellished common sense—have been written about "how to succeed." We shall not repeat many of them here. There are, however, certain principles of effective supervision, as well as some scientific information about the satisfactions a person can have in his job.

If you are a college student, the chances are rather good that you will find that your vocation entails the supervision of people. Most college graduates in business and industry are primarily employed in supervisory work. But even doctors, lawyers, teachers, and others in independent work have secretaries, assistants, and students whom they will be called upon to supervise. Despite this fact, relatively few receive any systematic instruction in the art and science of supervision, and many supervisors are consequently poorly prepared for their jobs. The few principles that we sketch here are no substitute for a thorough training in supervision, but if heeded, they may help.

TRAINING The supervisor is, first of all, a teacher. He starts teaching by instructing a new employee in his duties, and he continues to teach as new methods are introduced, as the organization undergoes change, and as day-by-day problems are solved. The most important part of the training, of course, is during the first few weeks that an employee is on the job, but it goes on after that, month in and month out. Whether the employee learns his job slowly or rapidly, correctly or incorrectly, and whether he keeps up as the work changes depend very much on the skill of the supervisor as a teacher.

Perhaps the most important principle a supervisor should keep in mind—and often does not—is that learning proceeds best when a person has knowledge of results. To know what he should be doing and to correct his mistakes, a person should know what he has just done and whether it is right or wrong. This point has been stressed in the chapter on human learning (see Chapter 4). Knowledge of results is primarily a matter of knowing the outcome of one's work, whether it is good or bad, acceptable or unacceptable, accurate or inaccurate. Many illustrations of this principle could be drawn from practical experience in supervision, but one should suffice here [Lindahl, 1945]:

In this case the job involved operating a disk-cutting machine in a highly skilled manner. The operator, in fact, had to learn an intricate pattern of hand and foot movements executed at a certain speed and with a certain form, rhythm, and pattern of pressures. Operators had trouble

KNOWLEDGE OF RESULTS AIDS TRAINING

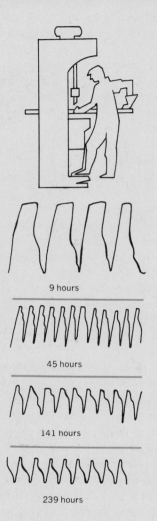

9 hours

45 hours

141 hours

239 hours

FIGURE 18.4. *The records are of foot-action patterns in the operation of a disk-cutting machine. The person being trained has the record of an experienced operator as a guide and attempts to duplicate the record. Notice the great improvement in the course of 239 hours of supervised training. (After Lindahl, 1945.)*

acquiring this skill until supervision stepped in and analyzed the problem. First an apparatus was built to provide a graphic record of the movements of a *skilled* operator. The record was then analyzed and labeled so that the trainee could see what movements were represented in the record. Then the trainees were asked to operate the machine so that they produced a record as much like that of the expert as possible. The results are shown in Figure 18.4. The trainees, once they had knowledge of their own results, learned considerably faster than they had learned before.

Relatively few problems in supervision require the construction of a recording machine to provide knowledge of results. More often the supervisor can supply the necessary knowledge by giving careful directions, pointing out mistakes as a teacher would, and telling the employee as often as possible just what the quality of his work is.

There are several other pointers, drawn from the psychology of learning, that the supervisor, in playing the role of a good teacher, should be aware of and follow:

1. In general, guidance is much more effective early in learning than later; consequently, it is better to show somebody how to do things right in the first place than it is to wait until after he has learned bad habits.

2. People usually master one thing at a time better than they master many things at a time. Therefore, training should be limited to a reasonable number of tasks and to a reasonable degree of complexity at any one time.

3. Transfer of training is a powerful ally. When a person has learned one task, that is the time to show him other tasks similar to it, or other tasks that can involve the same principle. In this way, one can capitalize on positive transfer and avoid negative transfer (see Chapter 4).

These points have been run through hurriedly because they are all applications of principles already presented in detail. The alert supervisor will know well the principles of learning and will continually seek ways to use them in helping his employees work effectively.

COMMUNICATION Closely allied to the supervisor's role as a teacher is his responsibility for communication [Bellows, 1949]. Almost all instructions and information are transmitted to an employee through language, written or spoken. He learns what he is supposed to do and to know from the supervisor's words. Therefore, if the supervisor is to be effective, he must concern himself with language and with ways to use it effectively in communication. Unfortunately, supervisors are all too often unaware of the problem of communication. Here are three general principles to follow.

1. The supervisor makes sure to tell his employees what they need to know. He does not leave it to them to "read his mind" or to "pick up" what they should know. He sees to it that they are promptly and accurately informed of anything relevant to their work.

2. The supervisor dispenses his communications in small doses, for most people can absorb only a limited amount of information at one time. Hence long, involved communications are seldom read or listened to, and if they are, they are rarely digested. Only a few important points should be communicated at a time.

3. The supervisor learns to phrase his communications in simple, direct style. His employees are usually not so well educated or experienced as he. Even if they are, they are more likely to perceive the intended message correctly if it is phrased in the most straightforward manner.

Using simple language. This last point is worth amplifying. Individuals differ widely in their ability to express themselves comprehensibly. Some succeed in making language relatively easy to understand; others make the task unbearably difficult. Research workers in language and psychology have studied this problem in some detail. The results of one study are described in *The Art of Plain Talk* by Rudolf Flesch (1946). Flesch has described those elements of language expression which, in general, make for ease of reading and comprehension. These elements are as follows:

Number of words in a sentence. The shorter the sentence, the more easily it is comprehended.

Number of syllables in a word. The shorter the words—as measured by syllables but not necessarily letters—the easier they are to understand.

Number of personal words and sentences. The greater the percentage of personal words and/or personal sentences, as distinguished from impersonal or abstract constructions, the easier the reading.

Flesch has combined these elements into an index which anyone can compute by following his rules [Flesch, 1946, 1954]. The index is a fairly good measure, although not a perfect one, of the relative difficulty or ease with which a sample of writing or speech can be comprehended. Flesch gives many examples of good versus poor communication as judged by his index; one almost unintelligible sample of legal prose will serve as an illustration of the latter type:

Ultimate consumer means a person or group of persons, generally constituting a domestic household, who purchase eggs generally at the individual stores of retailers or purchase and receive deliveries of eggs at a place of abode of the individual or domestic household from producers or retail route sellers and who use such eggs for their consumption as food.

[Flesch comments:]

That's a lot of words; let's try to cut down on them. Let's say just "people" instead of "a person or group of persons." Then let's leave out all those clauses with the word "generally" in them (they don't belong in a definition anyway); then let's say "eat" instead of "use for consumption as food." Now let's see what we have:

Ultimate consumers are people who buy eggs to eat them. [Flesch, 1946, page 170.]

Note how well Flesch followed his own precepts in explaining how the communication could be made more comprehensible.

EVALUATION Besides being a teacher and a communicator, the supervisor must be an evaluator. He must evaluate the worth of the jobs under his supervision and the worth of the employees holding those jobs.

EMPLOYEE PERFORMANCE AND WORK APPRAISAL FORM

Date............................ 19

Judge the employee on the basis of the work now being done. Be sure that each characteristic is considered separately, regardless of where the appraisal falls on any of the other characteristics. Place a check (√) in the box below the group of words which best describes the individual, but only one check for each line. However, it is essential that every line be checked.

NAME............................ JOB TITLE............................ DEPT............................

How long under your supervision?............................ Date of Employment?............................

Characteristic				
1. Knowledge of Job: Consider knowledge essential to person's job.	Has an exceptionally thorough knowledge of work ☐	Has good knowledge of work ☐	Requires considerable coaching ☐	Has inadequate knowledge of work ☐
2. Quality of Work: Consider the ability to turn out work which meets quality standards.	Highest quality ☐	Well done ☐	Passable ☐	Poor ☐
3. Quantity of Work: Consider the volume of work produced under normal conditions.	Large volume ☐	Good volume ☐	Slightly below average volume ☐	Unsatisfactory volume ☐
4. Attendance & Punctuality: Consider frequency of absences as well as lateness.	Record is excellent ☐	Occasionally absent or late ☐	Frequently absent or late ☐	Undependable; absent or late without notice ☐
5. Attitude: Consider his attitude toward his work, company and associates, and his willingness to work with and for others.	Unusually fine attitude ☐	Good attitude ☐	Passable ☐	Poor attitude ☐
6. Judgment: Consider his ability to make decisions and to utilize working time to best advantage.	Justifies utmost confidence ☐	Applies himself well; needs little supervision ☐	Needs frequent checking ☐	Cannot be relied upon; needs constant supervision ☐
7. Reliability: Consider the ability of the person to get the work out under pressure, and to follow job through to completion.	Can always be counted upon ☐	Generally can be counted on ☐	Unpredictable under pressure ☐	"Cracks up" under pressure ☐
8. Flexibility — Adaptability: Consider the speed with which he learns and the amount of instruction required to teach him new duties.	Learns fast ☐	Learns reasonably fast ☐	Slow to learn ☐	Unable to learn ☐
9. Personal Characteristics: Consider appearance, personality, integrity, "housekeeping."	Decidedly favorable ☐	Good ☐	Passable ☐	Generally unsatisfactory ☐

Appraised by............................ Date............................ Reviewed by............................ Date............................

(See other side)

FIGURE 18.5. *An example of the kind of form commonly used to appraise the performance of employees.*

The first of these evaluations is the *job evaluation*—that is, an assessment of the remuneration to be offered and paid for a particular job. The traditional way of deciding what to pay is to accept the general market evaluation of a job. The supervisor finds out, for example, what secretaries or machinists are currently being paid and offers this when he wishes to employ a person for such a job. This is a relatively unscientific way of evaluating a job, and an employer who uses it as a basis for hiring often fails to get employees who have the necessary abilities. It also neglects the question of what is a fair compensation for the skills and abilities involved in a job. It is gradually being displaced by more systematic methods of evaluation; the evaluations are sometimes done by specialists in these methods.

The general aim of these specialists, called job evaluators, is to assess the worker characteristics required in a job and then to set the pay scale according to the relative availability of these characteristics in the general population. If, for example, the job requires a degree of intelligence that is relatively rare, they set the pay for the job rather high on the scale; if, on the other hand, it requires skills or abilities that almost everyone has, the pay will be relatively low. There are many different systems for arriving at such an evaluation, but, in any case, the aim is to assign a fair value to a job that is well done, not to a worker.

The second aspect of evaluation concerns the worker. Is he doing his job satisfactorily or not? Is he doing it unusually well? Could he do another job better than he is doing his present one? Is he worthy of promotion to another job? These are difficult questions that need to be answered fairly in order to reward the worker for his efforts and to make the most of his abilities in an organization. Again, worker evaluations can be made in several ways.

Production. In industries or businesses where employees produce something that is measurable, the evaluation can be made almost solely in terms of the amount and quality of production. In addition, a good many fringe criteria may be employed, such as seniority on the job, number of times a person is tardy for work, number of accidents, and amount of time required in training for a job. When such criteria are used, a way must be found of weighting each of them into some composite judgment, and several systems for doing this have been developed.

Ratings. In many kinds of work, especially in office operations or work requiring initiative and responsibility, none of the production or fringe criteria may be adequate. Then supervisors must turn to some kind of rating made by the immediate supervisors or associates of the person (see Figure 18.5). For example, one of the common methods used in the civil service system and military establishment is the efficiency report. This usually involves a rating of "excellent," "satisfactory," or "unsatisfactory" for several aspects of a person's work, and it is made out by the immediate supervisor. Because supervisors tend to be lenient, such ratings usually are inflated and therefore yield far too few "unsatisfactories" and far too many "excellents" to be very useful in discriminating the worth of different employees.

To overcome the deficiencies of the simple efficiency report, psychologists have devised more precise methods. One is the *man-to-man rating* in which the supervisor must compare each person with several other persons known to him or under his supervision. This method, although it forces a comparative rating of individuals, is handicapped by the fact that the supervisor is usually not equally familiar with the work of all who are compared.

In a second method, the *forced-choice method,* the rater is presented with a list of phrases describing employees and is asked to check the characteristics most and least typical of a person [Sisson, 1948]. In one example, groups of four statements are presented, two of which are favorable and two of which are unfavorable (see Figure 18.6). One of the favorable phrases describes a characteristic that distinguishes successful people from unsuccessful people, whereas the other favorable phrase is a "screen" that does not distinguish. The same is true of the unfavorable phrases. The person being rated receives a point every time the rater checks the distinguishing favorable phrase as most characteristic of the person. A point is also scored if the rater checks the distinguishing unfavorable characteristic as least descriptive. A supervisor often objects to the forced-choice technique because he does not know whether his ratings will be favorable or unfavorable to the person being rated until they are scored in the front office. Research indicates, however, that the method is a good one if supervisors carefully and honestly make out the forced-choice forms.

These are just a sample of the scientific methods available for evaluating an employee's worth. The good supervisor accepts the responsibility, uses the methods most suitable to his problem, and is always on the alert for any better methods that he might use. In this way he can reward people who are deserving, and he can also maintain the effectiveness and morale of his group.

COUNSELING   We should mention briefly a fourth, and often unrecognized, psychological responsibility of the supervisor—counseling. A man's nagging wife, his personal relations with fellow workmen, his worries about his children's health, and countless other personal problems seriously affect his work and, indirectly, the work of his associates.

This fact was well demonstrated years ago in the famous Hawthorne study of the Western Electric

INSTRUCTIONS: Read carefully each group of four phrases, then check the one that is most descriptive of the person being rated and also the one that is least descriptive of him.

	Most	Least
A. A go-getter who always does a good job	☐	☐
B. Cool under all circumstances	☐	☐
C. Doesn't listen to suggestions	☐	☐
D. Drives instead of leads	☐	☐
A. Always criticizes, never praises	☐	☐
B. Carries out order by "passing the buck"	☐	☐
C. Knows his job and performs it well	☐	☐
D. Plays no favorites	☐	☐
A. Constantly striving for new knowledge and ideas	☐	☐
B. Businesslike	☐	☐
C. Apparently not physically fit	☐	☐
D. Fails to use good judgment	☐	☐

FIGURE 18.6. *These are some forced-choice items formerly used by the United States Army on the job-proficiency section of an officer-efficiency report. (Modified from Sisson, 1948.)*

Company [Roethlisberger and Dickson, 1939]. In this study it was revealed that personal problems had as much to do with factory production as any other single factor. The management discovered, too, after some experimentation, that a counseling system in which they listened to employees' problems and tried to render psychological help made the employees happier and more productive. Many other companies have also instituted and maintained regular counseling services.

We saw in Chapter 15 that counseling is an occupation requiring special skills and trained personnel if it is to be done most effectively. Where feasible, therefore, it is desirable to have members of the staff whose principal function is counseling. On the other hand, every supervisor should be aware of the personal problems of his employees. He should realize, for example, that when a workman starts coming in drunk, when a secretary becomes sulky and disgruntled, or when two men simply do not get along, the problem is one of emotional adjustment. He should try to understand what the problem is and offer some kind of help to alleviate it.

Psychology in management

As industrial organizations have grown in size and complexity, the need for specialized planners and problem solvers has increased immensely. These people are the managers. In earlier, perhaps we might say less sophisticated, times the owner of a company, even a fairly large one, could have expert knowledge of, and close contact with, all the phases of the production and marketing of his product. Now, in large companies, this is no longer so. It has humorously been pointed out, for instance, "that the Ford Motor Co. has grown so that if 'Old Henry' were alive today there would be no place for him in the organization" [Haire, 1959]. The managerial class has grown up between the entrepreneur-owners and the production workers.

Our first concern in this section is with the job

of the manager: What does he do? Next, we consider the training of managerial personnel. Finally, since the psychological theory of human motivation held by the manager influences his decisions, we discuss two contrasting managerial views of motivation.

THE MANAGER'S JOB We have considered supervisors, and although some supervisors may be considered managers, the term "manager" is usually reserved for those who have a large sphere of influence within an organization. The following passage describes in more detail just what a manager does:

We can partially differentiate managerial from other jobs by emphasizing the *change* quality of managerial problems as against the relatively static quality of tasks at lower levels. The manager deals largely with unknowns instead of knowns. He is a solver of *unprogrammed* problems.

We can also differentiate the manager's job from the executive's job. For the word "executive" implies that the executing function is primary. The managerial job should be *more than an executive one*. It should also include information-gathering and problem-defining functions. Once programs have been worked out, the manager is likely either to "execute" them himself or pass them on to other "executives."

The manager ought to do more than search for problems and alternative solutions to them. He must translate his understanding into *decisions for action* and thence into *action* itself. . . .

The factor which differentiates the manager from the rest of us is the *organizational setting* in which he works. Unlike most men (including scientists), the manager operates from a *power position* within a pyramidal structure. [Leavitt, 1964, pages 297–298.]

Furthermore, in addition to technical skill, a manager must be skilled in human relations. Much of what he does is accomplished in group discussions with his superiors, peers, and subordinates.

MANAGER TRAINING It seems useful to distinguish between techniques which are used in training beginning managerial personnel and seasoned managers.

Training beginning managers. Perhaps the most common method in most companies is *job rotation* —the trainee works for a few months in several of the key departments of the company before being assigned to his permanent job. This technique is designed to acquaint the young manager with various aspects of the company's operation, and it probably does this. The big drawback of this training technique is that the manager-to-be does not get practice in solving the sorts of problems which will be coming his way later [Leavitt, 1964]. He is, in many training programs, a rather passive onlooker, without responsibility, in the department to which he is temporarily assigned.

Another training method which may give the responsibility necessary for development of managerial skills is *problem-centered group training* [Leavitt, 1964]. The idea is to set a realistic problem for a group of trainees; the problem may be one with which the senior managers have been grappling. In working on the problem, the management trainees should be allowed to draw on the experiences of, and information available to, the senior managers. A great many things about the company will be learned in this way because motivation to learn is high. In addition to its being a vehicle for learning facts about the company, the problem-centered approach to training provides the fledgling managers with invaluable experience in working with other people in groups. Perhaps a good training program should include some aspects of both job rotation and the problem-solving approach.

Training senior managers. Senior management sometimes comes up against problems which stymie it. One technique for overcoming impasses is the *problem-solving interview* [Maier, 1958]. In such an interview, the interviewer listens to the manager as he talks about his problems and wrestles with solutions to them; he serves as a kind of "active listener" [Anastasi, 1964]. He does not offer solutions to problems, but the hope is that the talking-out of the problem by the manager may facilitate solution in a way similar to that in client-centered counseling (see page 544).

Other training techniques are specifically directed

toward increasing the manager's skill in handling people. The main goal is to make the manager more aware of the feelings, perceptions, and motives of others in the organization which may affect production and harmonious relationships. Of the many "human-relations" techniques, we discuss two: *role-playing methods*, and the *laboratory method of training*, or as it is sometimes called, the *T-group method* [Schein, 1964; Schein and Bennis, 1965].

The role-playing methods are offshoots of the sociodrama or psychodrama techniques pioneered by Moreno (1953). In this technique, a problem is presented to a group and then the members of the group act out the roles of the characters in the problem-solving situation. For instance, a manager might act the role of a union leader or worker. The hope is that the manager will gain some insight into the way the situation is perceived by the person whose role he is taking.

The laboratory method of training also attempts to present people in training groups, called *T groups*, with problems, but the attempt here is to give managers experiences in a controlled setting which will help them to understand, and be able to overcome, some of the forces which impede effective work. Here is a more specific account of the goals of the laboratory method:

The *goals* of the laboratory are to create opportunities for delegates[1] to *learn* about the following kinds of things:

1. *Self.* The delegates' own behavior in groups and the impact which their behavior has on other members.

2. *Others.* The behavior of others in a group and the impact which their behavior has on them.

3. *Groups.* How groups work; what makes them function.

4. *Larger systems.* How organizations and larger social systems work.

5. *The learning process.* How to learn from their own experiences ("learning how to learn").

[Schein and Bennis, 1965, page 13.]

Whatever the training method, it should be stressed that one of the most potent factors in de-

---

[1] The managers are called "delegates" because they come to the laboratory and live together in a convention-like atmosphere.

termining the way a manager acts toward his subordinates is the way his superior acts toward him [Fleishman, 1953]. For instance, it was found that foremen who were considerate of the feelings of the men under them had bosses who were considerate of them. Similarly, foremen whose bosses stressed planning and getting the job done stressed this with their men. Thus there seems to be a kind of communication of basic orientations down the chain of command within a company. The behavior of the manager is determined by the behavior of his superiors, but it is also determined by the philosophy of human motivation which the manager holds.

ASSUMPTIONS OF MANAGEMENT ABOUT HUMAN MOTIVATION　When a manager makes decisions about the people he manages, he is influenced, whether he is aware of it or not, by his philosophy of human motivation [Schein, 1964]. For instance, does he believe that his employees need to be driven, or does he believe that work should be arranged so that the employee can meet some of his deeper needs through employment? As an example, let us look at one formulation of contrasting philosophies about human motivation:

The two contrasting philosophies are labelled "Theory X" and "Theory Y." Those adhering to Theory X believe that:

"The average human being has an inherent dislike of work and will avoid it as he can.

"Because of this human characteristic of dislike of work, most people must be coerced, controlled, directed, threatened with punishment to get them to put forth adequate effort toward the achievement of organization objectives.

"The average human being prefers to be directed, wishes to avoid responsibility, has little ambition, wants security above all."

Those adhering to Theory Y, on the other hand, believe:

"The expenditure of physical and mental effort in work is as natural as play or rest.

"External control and the threat of punishment are not the only means for bringing about effort toward organizational objectives. Man will exercise self-direction and self-control in the service of objectives to which he is committed.

"Commitment to objectives is a function of the rewards associated with their achievement.

"The average human being learns, under proper conditions, not only to accept but to seek responsibility.

"The capacity to exercise a relatively high degree of imagination, ingenuity, and creativity in the solution of organizational problems is widely, not narrowly, distributed in the population.

"Under the conditions of modern industrial life, the intellectual potentialities of the average human being are only partially utilized." [McGregor, 1960, pages 33 and 47.]

A manager who holds with theory X will emphasize wages and security and will fail to understand that most of his employees are really trying to satisfy other motives such as those relating to self-esteem and the realization of potential, or self-actualization (see page 494). His policy will be directed toward manipulating employees through the use of incentives, money, for instance, which are largely ineffective in improving production. After all, most of these incentives can only be used *off the job,* and the job often seems to be a barrier preventing the enjoyment of its own rewards [McGregor, 1960].

The theory Y manager, on the other hand, attempts to arrange it so that the goals of the individual and the organization coincide so that the employee does not need to be coerced into work. This should not be taken to imply that the theory Y manager is a "softy" or a "back slapper"; he simply has a view of human motivation which is potentially a very powerful one.

Perhaps we may best summarize this section on the psychology of management by saying that the manager with technical skill, combined with sound knowledge of human motivation and the problems which arise in groups, will probably be most successful.

Job satisfaction

In Chapter 6, Motivation, we emphasized that people have social as well as physiological needs. In the preceding section, we have also seen that psychological motivation is extremely important in industry. We may expect, consequently, that people's efforts both at work and at play will be directed toward the satisfaction of all their needs, not just those for material things such as food, clothing, and housing. This expectation has been confirmed in many psychological studies of the satisfactions people derive, or fail to derive, from their work. In such studies, employees have been asked what they considered most important to them in their jobs. Although the results vary somewhat from one locality to another and from one kind of work to another, we are justified in drawing some conclusions that generally apply to most people who work.

PAY For those of us who work for a living, pay or income is what enables us to buy the material things we want. Without it, moreover, we could not live. You might think, therefore, that pay would head the list of things people consider important to them in their respective jobs. This is not the case [Smith, 1964]. When asked to rank pay along with several other features of their jobs, most people rank it relatively low, and very few rank it first (see Table 18.4).

Even when they rank pay high, they usually indicate that it is not just high pay that they want. Rather, they want to be paid as well as other people doing the same work, or as well as other people in the same industry. Thus most people are more concerned about being paid fairly than about being paid a large amount. Fair treatment is more important than the amount of money received.

The fact that pay is seldom listed as the most important factor in working should not lead us to think that it is unimportant. Probably most people assume that they will be paid enough to take care of their basic necessities. Above that point, then, pay becomes relatively unimportant. If the pay scale were dropped far below its present level for a particular person, pay would become important again. It is interesting to see, though, how often people decide which job to take or which to keep on grounds other than the pay they receive.

TABLE 18.4 *What industrial workers say they want in a job. A summary of several different surveys. Different language and varying numbers of alternatives were used in the surveys. The factors named at the left have been paraphrased but represent approximately the areas covered. The numbers are rankings of the factors considered in each study.*

	WOMEN FACTORY WORKERS	UNION WORKERS	NONUNION WORKERS	MEN	WOMEN	EMPLOYEES OF FIVE FACTORIES
Steady work	1	1	1	1	3	1
Type of work				3	1	3
Opportunity for advancement	5	4	4	2	2	4
Good working companions	4			4	5	
High pay	6	2½	2	5½	8	2
Good boss	3	5½	5	5½	4	6
Comfortable working conditions	2	2½	3	8½	6	7
Benefits		5½	6	8½	9	5
Opportunity to learn a job	8					
Good hours	9	7½	7	7	7	
Opportunity to use one's ideas	7	7½	8			
Easy work	10					

SECURITY   Probably the factor most often stated as important in work is job security. People want to know that they will have steady work and that the work will continue for many years. They also want security in the personal sense; they want to work on safe jobs. They do not want to run the risk of losing their earning power because of accidents on the job.

The importance of security in job satisfaction partly explains why high pay is not an extremely important problem. Most people prefer a low salary which is guaranteed over a long period of time to a high salary which may not last long. Such concerns are typical of the human species. People are able to look well beyond immediate satisfactions and to anticipate satisfying their needs at some time in the future. They are more concerned about making a guaranteed minimum salary over a long period of time than they are about making the most money right now.

GOOD WORKING CONDITIONS   Good working conditions are frequently listed as important considerations in working. People like to work in a clean and neat working area. If they work in an industrial plant, they want it to be one which makes them feel that they are working in a pleasant environment of which they can be proud. Comfortable jobs are often important, and short hours are frequently preferred over higher pay.

The large class of white-collar workers provides the best example of people to whom working conditions are more important than high pay. Office workers, clerks, and stenographers often earn much less money than they could if they were doing skilled manual labor, and yet they do not often change their job category. In addition, of course, white-collar workers usually have steady work and can look forward to a future of continued employment.

OPPORTUNITY FOR ADVANCEMENT Another illustration of the fact that people are frequently more concerned about the future than about the present is that they usually give opportunity for advancement a high rating. A man often turns down a higher-paying job, for example, to take one which starts at a lower salary but which ensures early advancement. Sometimes the concern about advancement takes the form of wanting a guaranteed rate of promotion after a fixed period of time. In other instances, people simply want to be assured that they will be told about the opportunities for advancement and can compete for them. In still other cases, a person is most interested in the company's providing training opportunities for employees so that he can learn the skills necessary for advancement.

Regardless of the particular form the concern about advancement takes, it is clear that people are as interested in the future as they are in the present. It is also clear that concepts of fair play are important when people ask for equal opportunity for advancement or opportunity to learn. In such cases, people are not asking for a guarantee of advancement, but only for a fair chance. Nobody wants to work where the boss's son-in-law gets promoted regardless of his qualifications.

PERSONNEL RELATIONS Also important to most people are the personnel relations they have in their jobs [McGregor, 1960]. People want to work with companions and coworkers whom they like. They will work for a good boss, and quit when they don't like the boss. They want help from management in their work, and they want to know about how their work is progressing. They want to be sure that they have somebody to whom they can take their grievances and that they will get a fair deal when they have a grievance. For that reason, the organization which provides special means of handling grievances will always have an advantage

in attracting workers. Last, but not least, they want recognition of the importance of their work. They want to be told when they are doing a good job and helped when they are doing a poor one, and they want to feel that their work and their efforts to do better work are appreciated.

This factor of wanting appreciation for work has raised a good many problems for psychologists who have tried to do experiments in industry. In the Hawthorne experiments, several girls were studied over the course of 2 years [Roethlisberger and Dickson, 1939]:

The girls were put in a separate room where many different working conditions could be controlled. First, the illumination was changed, and production immediately went up. Then other factors were changed: The girls were given rest periods, sometimes for 5 minutes and sometimes for 10 minutes. They were given free lunches, and at one time were allowed to go home early. Every time a change was made, production improved. Then all the rest periods, free lunches, and so forth, were taken away, *and production went up still higher.*

What had happened here? The answer, it was learned later, was in the *attention* the girls were getting. Every time a change was made, the girls were reminded that other people were concerned with what they were doing, and this appreciation was what really made production go up.

All this points up the fact that people work for many things besides money. They want security, future opportunity, pleasant working conditions, and good relations with their coworkers and their bosses. We should never forget that people have complex motives that require satisfaction.

Efficiency in work

Having considered job satisfaction and the factors affecting it, we turn now to problems of efficiency in work. Employed adults usually spend half or more of their waking hours in some form of work. Aside from such work, they are also busy in other activities—studying, reading, writing, mowing the

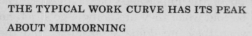

THE TYPICAL WORK CURVE HAS ITS PEAK
ABOUT MIDMORNING

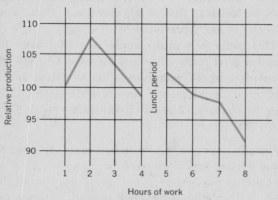

FIGURE 18.7. *A typical work curve for heavy handwork. The curve is rather characteristic of work curves obtained for heavy work. The figures have been adjusted to let 100 stand for the average rate of production for the 8-hour day.*

lawn, repairing the house, or fixing the car. In most such activities, there is the question of efficiency: What is the fastest way of getting work done with a minimum of effort? This question is in part a psychological question, for it concerns the conditions under which we are best able to think and to use our learned skills.

THE WORK CURVE   People seldom work at the same pace over a long period of time. Work has its ups and downs. For example, you probably do not study so effectively at the end of a long period of study as you do at the beginning. Indeed, you may not study so well at the beginning as you do after you have been at it for a little while. So you know that the efficiency of work changes during any considerable period of time.

When we have some measure of the efficiency of work and plot our measurements against the minutes or hours of the work period, the graph that

results is called a *work curve*. Work curves are somewhat different for different types of work, but ones similar to that in Figure 18.7 have been found in many industries and for many tasks.

The typical work curve in Figure 18.7 was obtained several years ago for a job involving heavy handwork. Notice that production was slightly better than average for the first hour of the day, and it improved during the second hour. During the third hour, it was still better than average, but it had dropped considerably from the second hour. It dropped even more during the fourth hour. After the lunch period, production increased again, but then it dropped steadily for the rest of the afternoon.

Work curves of this general description are frequently found in industry and other working situations. The precise shape of the curve, however, depends on a number of factors. By studying the effect of these factors on the work curve, we have been able to analyze the curve into four components, each of which represents a factor in work. These four components are warming up, beginning spurt, end spurt, and fatigue. We shall consider the first three factors in this section and devote the next section to a discussion of fatigue.

Warming up. A warm-up effect may be one of the features that appears in a work curve. It is illustrated in the top line of Figure 18.8. Most of us are familiar with the idea of warming up and deliberately make use of it. A boxer warms up before a fight by dancing around and shadow-boxing. A runner runs back and forth lightly. Football players run a ball before going into a game. In these cases, the warming up is done before the athlete actually enters the game because he knows that he will not be at his top performance if he does not warm up first.

This same type of warming up takes place in other types of activity, even in intellectual activities such as studying for an examination or writing a term paper. When you first start to work, you are poorly organized; you are not really set for the job, and perhaps you fidget or even get up and walk around. The warming-up period may take longer for some people than for others, and it may take longer for some activities than for others. But warming up is of value in almost every type of activity.

Referring now to Figure 18.7, one can see that warming up accounts for the fact that production is greater during the second hour than during the first hour. If the warming up is very slow, the work curve may rise throughout the whole morning period. On the other hand, if it is very fast, it may be over in the first few minutes and not have any appreciable effect on the total productivity for the first hour.

Beginning spurt. The middle curve in Figure 18.8 illustrates another factor in work curves, the beginning spurt. This is exactly the opposite of the warming-up effect and can completely cancel it. We may start off a particular job with a great deal of enthusiasm and put our full effort into it. Then the realization that this job is going on for a long time hits us, and we slow down to a steadier pace— a pace more suitable for the long haul. After people have worked on the same job a good many times, they are less likely to show a beginning spurt. It is characteristic of a new job or activity and does not occur in some jobs.

End spurt. When activity is increased at the end of a job, we call it an end spurt. The end of the day brings with it an increased enthusiasm, and a final burst of energy sends production up. The end spurt commonly occurs in athletic events and probably represents the athlete's willingness to use up all the energy he has left because he knows he need not save it for any later effort. A long-distance runner, for example, usually manages an extra burst of speed at the end of a run, and a boxer frequently fights more vigorously in the last round than he has in any preceding one.

Occasionally the end spurt at the end of a day is so large that it results in a peak of production for the day. When this happens, it is clear that the worker has not really been working at top effort all along. As we shall see in the discussion on fatigue, it is important to recognize the difference between what a man can do and what he is willing to do.

Effects of fatigue

The most important trend in a work curve usually represents fatigue. This is the general downward

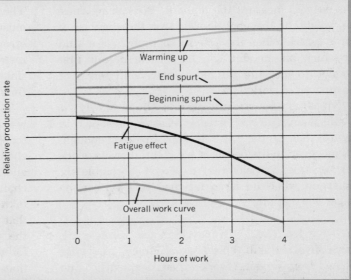

A WORK CURVE CAN BE ANALYZED
INTO FOUR COMPONENTS

FIGURE 18.8. *The components of the work curve. The shape of any particular work curve will depend on the relative importance of the various components.*

trend throughout the whole period of work. It is on this trend that the effects of other factors such as warming up, beginning spurt, and end spurt are superimposed. Fatigue makes the efficiency of work fall far short of what one might expect by looking at the peaks of the work curve.

Because fatigue is a common word, we are inclined to think that we know what it means. Certainly we feel fatigue, and we have many words to describe this feeling—tired, weary, exhausted, spent, worn out, beat, dead. Such subjective reports of fatigue probably make up the best definition of fatigue that can be offered at the present time. *Fatigue* is a feeling of being tired. As we shall see, there is no completely consistent way of measuring fatigue.

OUTPUT   Sometimes fatigue is reflected in a decrement in performance. The decrement may be measured either by a decreased *output* of work, when the work is primarily physical, or by increased *errors*. Decreased output is the usual decrement. If a person is shoveling coal, he shovels less coal when he is fatigued than when he is not. If he is typing, he usually types fewer words per minute when he is fatigued than when he is rested. Here, we are talking about the amount of work accomplished, and it is easy to measure the amount. We can measure the weight of the coal shoveled or the number of words typed. When the activity or work is of a kind for which an amount can be measured, our first attempt to measure fatigue is always in terms of the amount of work done.

Typically, the amount at first drops slowly, if at all. Then it drops faster and faster, as shown in Figure 18.8. If the work is kept up long enough, fatigue eventually becomes so great that no work can be done. We say that a person is completely exhausted when he is so fatigued that he can no longer work at all.

ERRORS IN TIME   In psychomotor work—work which involves skill, speed, or accuracy, as distinguished from physical work—there frequently is no decrement in amount of work done as fatigue increases. Sometimes this is because the work cannot be measured in amounts. Studying for an examination is an activity that can hardly be measured in terms of amount. At other times, the physical effort involved in the work is so slight that no change in amount occurs. In such cases, however, a measurement of errors frequently reveals fatigue when a measurement of amount does not. For example, when a person is receiving telegraphic code, his fatigue is reflected in an increase in the number of errors.

In one study, receivers made between three and four times as many errors in the third hour of receiving code as they did in the first hour [Mackworth, 1950]. In a study of typing errors, the time required to type successive lines was measured, and although the time required per line (a measure of amount of work) went up at first, it later went back down [Robinson and Bills, 1926]. An analysis of the errors made, however, showed that the number of errors per line continued to increase long after the time per line leveled off.

Whether fatigue shows up as increased *time* taken to do a certain amount of work or as increased *errors* depends on the attitude or set of the worker. If he has been instructed to work for perfect accuracy, he can do so over a long period of time. Then as he becomes more and more fatigued, he must slow down in order to keep from making errors. If, on the other hand, the worker has been instructed to work primarily for speed, he may continue to work at the same rate for long periods of time but will make more and more errors.

Thus we see that fatigue can show itself in more ways than one, and we must be careful, in looking for the effects of fatigue, to examine all possible changes in performance. If we measure one thing and neglect another, we may find that there is no change in what we are measuring. The change may take place instead in some aspect of performance that we fail to measure. This is especially true when the worker knows what is going to be measured, for then he strives to keep his performance up in that particular respect. But if he is really fatigued, his work will deteriorate in some other way.

PHYSIOLOGICAL EFFECTS   We should note in passing, without going into details, that fatigue may be reflected in physiological performance. Muscle tension may increase, as may heart rate, blood pressure, and other measures of exertion. The amount of oxygen required to do a given amount of work may also increase. Hence physiological measures of these changes may indicate fatigue when there is little or no evidence in the behavior of the person.

FATIGUE AS A CHANGE IN MOTIVATION   Fatigue can show up in still another way. Suppose that you observe men at work over long periods of time and that their production continues to decline. You then have clear evidence of fatigue. Suppose that you now stop the men at work and give them some tests of ability. The chances are that you will find that their ability to perform on these tests is as good after many hours of work as it was when they were fresh. You might also find that their work was being done with no loss in physiological efficiency. So the men are still able to work as well after many hours as in the first hour, but they are actually not working so well.

What then accounts for the decline in their production? You might be justified in supposing that it is due to a change in *motivation* rather than fatigue—that the men simply are not trying so hard as they might. Alternatively, you might say that to compensate for fatigue more motivation is required [Mackworth, 1948]. Both statements are correct.

The situation is shown schematically in Figure 18.9. The curve of work output continues to drop, but the curve of ability as measured by laboratory tests does not go down. What has changed is the person's feeling of what is necessary, or his willingness to work.

This effect of fatigue is very common in our everyday life. If you have been driving an automobile for several hours and are stopped and given a driving test, you probably will do as well as if you had not been driving for a long time. However, while you are actually driving, you probably change your idea of what is necessary. You are less alert, you do not slow down quite so soon when you approach an intersection, and you take more chances when you pass another car—not because you are unable to do the correct thing, but rather because it no longer seems quite so necessary to do so. The

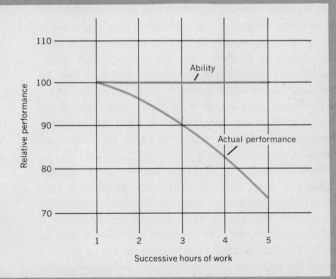

FLAGGING MOTIVATION MAY DECREASE
PERFORMANCE WHILE ABILITY
REMAINS UNCHANGED

FIGURE 18.9.   *Tests may tell us that a worker's ability has not changed, but the fact that actual performance has declined during the course of the working period indicates that motivation has changed.*

term *vigilance* has been used to describe what diminishes, and it is very apt. You can do as well, but you are less vigilant.

The very nature of this effect of fatigue makes it so important. If you have been digging a ditch for several hours, you are fatigued, and you know it. If you are driving a car, however, you do not realize that you are fatigued because the only effect of the fatigue has been to make you relax your standards of what you consider good performance. You do not drive so well because you think you do not have to, and when you have an accident because of carelessness you are sure that you have done everything just as you should. But when you are tired, what you *think* you should do and what you *really* should do are often two different things.

SLEEP One of the obvious ways to make a person tired or fatigued is to deprive him of sleep. By itself, loss of sleep is not the same thing physiologically as fatigue. Nevertheless, the sleep-deprived person, merely by remaining awake and active without the rest afforded by sleep, becomes very fatigued. It is therefore of interest to ask, What are the effects of sleep deprivation?

Dozens of research studies have been done on this question. They have run into the same problems that we have already encountered in other attempts to measure fatigue. If a man goes one night without sleep, it is hard to tell much difference the next day. He may confess that he is somewhat light-headed, his attention may wander a little, and he may have an unusual desire to sit down or lie down. His performance, however, is likely to be about the same, for he can do a fair day's work, take examinations, answer letters, and otherwise function normally.

Suppose we keep the man up for still another night, and then another. In several studies, people have been kept from sleeping for three successive nights. On the fourth day, they have been given tests—psychomotor, intelligence, arithmetic, and so forth. The interesting fact is that they can do just about as well on all these objective tests of efficiency as they could when they were rested. Rather

prolonged loss of sleep, therefore, does not impair efficiency if we use systematic tests to measure it.

Nevertheless, profound effects can be discovered in other ways. People tend to become silly, irritable, and restless. Some may even develop symptoms that resemble mental illness—symptoms such as delusions of grandeur or persecution, or false memories of people and of the passage of time. Their judgment becomes impaired, and if they drive cars, they are more likely to take chances. In general, people who have been deprived of sleep for a long time show all the subtle symptoms of persons who have worked hard for too many hours or who suffer a little oxygen lack. Perhaps the most obvious symptom is that they do not want to work; indeed, all they want to do is lie down and sleep. So loss of sleep, like other effects of fatigue, does not change a person's capacity to perform, but it does change his willingness or motivation to perform.

WORK AND REST We have seen that many factors affect how we work. Fatigue is the most important of these factors, and we can show its effects in many different ways. Since fatigue is so important, we are greatly concerned with ways of preventing it and means of overcoming it after it has occurred.

Recovery from fatigue. Perhaps the best way of learning how to prevent or overcome fatigue is to find out just how fast we recover from it. Figure 18.10 shows the results of an experiment performed with university students [Manzer, 1927].

The students were required to lift a weight with their fingers, and the height to which they lifted the weight was measured on each trial. They were required to continue lifting the weight until they could no longer lift it at all. Then they were given rest periods for various lengths of time, after which they were required to lift the weight again. The height to which they could lift the weight on the first trial after rest was a measure of the relative recovery from fatigue. If they still could not lift it at all, they had not recovered at all. If they could lift it as high as they had on the first trial previously, then the recovery was 100 per cent.

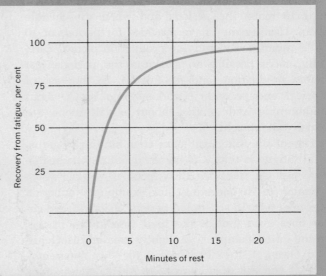

RECOVERY FROM FATIGUE IS MOST RAPID
DURING THE FIRST FEW MINUTES OF REST

FIGURE 18.10. *These are the results of a test for recovery from fatigue. Subjects lifted a weight with their fingers until they could no longer lift it. Then, after various periods of rest, they were required to lift the weight again. The curve shows how high, relative to first lifting, they could lift the weight after rest. (After Manzer, 1927.)*

Figure 18.10 shows that recovery from fatigue is fairly rapid at first but then slows down considerably. Even after 20 minutes of rest, the students had not completely recovered from the fatigue. In fact, at the rate they were recovering, a total of 40 minutes would be required for them to get back to normal.

If the students were stopped before they had reached complete fatigue, and then given rest periods, recovery was much faster. For example, they might have been stopped when they were lifting the weight only 50 per cent as high as they had on the first trial. In this case, recovery would be complete in a much shorter period of time. In fact, recovery from fatigue is so much faster after short periods of work than after long periods that much greater overall efficiency can be obtained with short work periods than with long work periods.

For example, suppose you have a certain amount of snow that has to be shoveled. If you start right in and keep going until you can barely lift the shovel, you will have to stop and take a rest. It will require a long rest, however, for you to recover from your fatigue and get back to work. On the other hand, if you shovel for a little while, then rest for a little while, then shovel, and so on, you never need very long rest periods because recovery from fatigue is rapid when only a little work has been done. In this way, you can shovel steadily for a much longer period of time, and you actually can get the whole job done much sooner than if you keep shoveling until you are completely fatigued.

Rest periods. There is a definite moral to this story: To stave off fatigue and still get work done, one should schedule rest periods often enough to keep from getting very tired. How often they should be and how long they should be depend on the kind of work. Heavy manual labor requires frequent and reasonably long rest periods. For sedentary work, rest periods do not need to be either so frequent or so long. (See the related discussion in Chapter 4 on periods of practice in learning.)

In recent years, industry has been applying these principles more and more by providing for regular rest periods throughout the workday. Industrial concerns have learned by experience as well as experiment that such rest periods allay fatigue and increase productivity. In other words, necessary rest is not time lost but rather work gained. They often face the practical decision, however, of how long to make the periods and when to schedule them. Usually they have provided for periods of 10 to 15 minutes. By studying production records carefully, it is possible to schedule the periods just before production tends to fall off. In the case of clerical and sedentary workers, one break about midmorning and another about midafternoon are usually about right.

One of the things we learn from studies of industrial fatigue is that it is better, usually, to schedule rest periods than to allow people to take them irregularly. In one study, for example, production was greater with scheduled periods than with irregular ones even though the total time taken in rest in the latter instance was slightly greater [McGehee and Owen, 1940]. The reason for this apparently lies in the set of a person for work. Most of us manage to adjust our level of effort to the total amount of work to be accomplished or to the total time we have to work. If, for example, you are starting to run a mile, you do not run as fast as if you are starting to run 100 yards. Likewise, if a person has 10 minutes to work, he is likely to work harder than if he has 2 hours to work. So when a person has a definite time to rest, he is likely to pace himself at a little faster rate than if he works until he gets tired and voluntarily stops.

Length of the workday and workweek. Another factor in work efficiency is the length of the working day. The facts of this matter are very interesting. Many people assume, rather naturally, that if we want to get more from a particular worker, the thing to do is to increase the number of hours per day or per week that he works. In recent years, however, it has become increasingly clear that there is a real limit to the number of hours most people can work in a day or week and still work with reasonable efficiency. Perhaps it is obvious that a man becomes less efficient *per hour* if he works 10 hours a day than if he works 8 hours a day. What was not realized for a long time, however, is that he can become so much less efficient that the total work done in a 10-hour day is less than the total work done in an 8-hour day.

A number of studies demonstrate both points [Ghiselli and Brown, 1955]. If maximum production per hour is what we want, then a workweek between 36 and 44 hours is best. If, however, we want the maximum production per workweek, a workweek between 48 and 54 hours is best. The reason for this difference is that the hourly efficiency drops when the workweek is increased from 40 to 50 hours, but the drop in efficiency is not great enough to offset the greater number of hours. If, however, the workweek is increased beyond this point, then the drop in hourly efficiency is so great that it completely offsets the increased number of hours.

Engineering for human use

In this technological age, still another aspect of the adjustment of people to their work must be considered—their relationship to machines. Machines are taking over countless tasks formerly done by people, as well as doing things that were never before possible. It takes people, however, to run these machines, and the machines in turn control people's behavior. The net result is that people are doing more and more of their work with or through machines. They must somehow "get along" with machines, and do it well, in order to work safely and efficiently and to make machines do what they are intended for.

MAN-MACHINE PROBLEMS   This relationship of man to machines is generating new problems—problems of matching men and machines. One set of problems, which we have already mentioned, concerns selecting and training people for operating machines. Another set of problems concerns the design of machines for human use—designing them so that the man together with the machine gets his job done (see Figure 18.11). The field of knowledge concerned with the solution of these problems has various names. One is *human engineering*, but this is often expanded to *human-factors engineering* in order to make clearer what is meant. Such engineering involves a number of disciplines, but the one of interest here is *engineering psychology*. This is a rapidly growing field of application of psychology, mostly experimental psychology, to problems of engineering design.

Engineering psychology got its start during World War II when wartime demands brought psychologists into contact with engineering problems [Chapanis et al., 1949]. This contact demonstrated that psychology had information which could be useful in engineering design, and it could produce more when necessary through appropriate experiments and tests. Thus engineering psychology began to flourish and has grown rapidly since. Today most of the larger industries concerned with designing complex systems, such as airplanes, missiles, communication systems, computers, and the like, employ engineering psychologists as members of their teams of engineers charged with designing such systems. Although the field now boasts several textbooks and handbooks, we shall give only a bird's-eye view of it here.

The operation of machines may involve various kinds of work—physical, psychomotor, or mental—but it typically falls in the class of psychomotor tasks. Generally speaking, there are two ways to measure performance in such tasks: errors and amount of work. When a man-machine combination fails to perform effectively, the failure may be due to errors made by the operator or to his being overloaded with more work than he can do. These two factors, of course, interact. By slowing down, a man usually can be more accurate; by speeding up, he usually can handle a larger load of work but at the sacrifice of accuracy. Hence, the two factors and their interaction are the general problems of concern to the engineering psychologist. He attempts to design, or redesign, machines in such a way as to minimize errors and to maximize output. The relative importance of each depends on the machine and its purpose.

The work of engineering psychology can also be divided in another way into two general parts: displays and controls. Man may be regarded as a component in a man-machine system. As such, he receives "inputs" from the machine component as well as from his physical environment. In other words, he receives information through his senses. Such information is presented to him through some kind of *display*. On the other hand, his "output" consists of things he does to and with the machine to control its behavior. The "things" he uses for this purpose are *controls*. Thus most of the problems the engineering psychologist works with involve either displays or controls or both.

FIGURE 18.11. *A problem in human engineering. Psychologists specializing in the field of human engineering rearrange and simplify levers, knobs, and dials so that the man who uses them can do his job more easily, more efficiently, and more safely. (American Airlines.)*

MAN COMPARED WITH MACHINES   Before considering some examples of the design and display of controls, a more general question deserves some discussion. How does man compare with machines in ability to do different tasks? Despite the near-miraculous performance of some machines, man can still do many things better than machines. To design the best man-machine system, one must assign to each the tasks it can do best.

Sensing. Some general statements can be made about this comparison [Williams et al., 1956]. Man as a sensor is restricted in the range of the spectrum of light or sound to which he responds, whereas machines can be built to sense signals—infrared energy, for example—of which man is completely unaware. On the other hand, human sensitivity to many forms of physical energy is exceedingly acute and often is better than that of a sensing device. Moreover, man's senses operate through a much wider range of intensities, giving good performance for very weak as well as very strong stimuli, as compared with sensing devices. It is important, however, to realize that one sense may be much better for assimilating a particular kind of information—for example, the eye is much superior to the ear in handling spatial information—and this must be considered in selecting and designing displays.

Data processing. In processing data—remembering and interpreting information—man also has advantages and disadvantages when compared with machines. Man is superior in that he does not need extensive programming, for example, as a computer does. He is more flexible and can deal with unforeseen situations. He can exercise judgment and quickly recall facts and methods of solving problems. However, machines are superior to men in the amount of detailed information they can store or remember, in the speed and accuracy with which they can arrive at answers, in sorting and classifying data, in giving reliable results in routine operations, and in working longer at high speed without being subject to fatigue, prejudice, or other factors that distort judgment and decision.

Controlling. When it comes to controlling things, man is generally inferior to machines, and the controls he uses must be designed to take his limitations into account. He is relatively weak and slow. He is limited in the kind of movements he can make and in the number of controls he can operate either simultaneously or in quick succession. The time he can work without fatigue or wavering of attention is relatively short. For these reasons, the tasks assigned to human control must be carefully chosen and designed.

These statements are only general guides. Specific data of handbook proportions are available for determining how well human beings can perform on various sensing, judging, and control tasks. When available data do not answer specific questions, the engineering psychologist runs tests and experiments to obtain the necessary answers. Then, together with other members of the design team, he draws up an overall design of the man-machine system. This design prescribes, at least roughly, what is expected of the man and of the machine. It serves as a guide to the development of specific components in the system [Morgan et al., 1963].

Knowing at least roughly what the man will be expected to do in a man-machine system, the engineering psychologist can next turn his attention to the design of the displays and controls involved in the man's tasks. In order to proceed with this assignment, he must somehow obtain a complete job description of the man's duties specified in terms of the information needed (for display) and the actions he must take (for control). There are several methods for obtaining a job description; some are like the procedures for preparing a job analysis. Having accomplished that, the engineering psychologist is ready to proceed with the design of the displays and controls of the system.

DESIGN OF DISPLAYS   To design the displays that a man must use in any complicated system, the designer must first consider the chance of overloading one or more of the senses. The sense that is most often overloaded is vision; after that, hearing. Consider, for example, the picture of an airplane cockpit in Figure 18.11. You can readily see that the visual sense is overloaded; there are far too many dials here for a person to attend to. Indeed, studies show that many accidents or near-accidents have occurred for this reason. Since this picture was taken, designers have improved cockpit design, especially in jet aircraft, by utilizing a number of human-engineering principles.

Where one sense is overloaded, the engineering psychologist can devise ways of presenting some of the information through another sense. Simple warning signals, for example, are often better presented as auditory signals, perhaps as buzzers. In some specialized cases, information may be presented as a vibration, say, of a control held continuously by the operator. Tradition and habit often hamper the acceptance of such alternatives, but they are being employed.

When a decision has been made about the mode of presenting information, the next step is to decide on the type of display to be used. Since most displays are visual, let us restrict ourselves to them. Any complicated situation, such as a cockpit, may contain dozens of displays. In designing a group of visual displays, the engineering psychologist must make several decisions.

Pictorial versus symbolic displays. One decision is whether a given display will be pictorial or symbolic. A pictorial display is one that reproduces with some realism the situation it represents. Maps, for example, are pictorial displays. In an aircraft, an artificial horizon indicator may be a pictorial display, for it pictures the position of a plane and its orientation with respect to a horizon. Symbolic displays are instruments that present information indirectly, usually by dials, pointers, or lights. The speedometer on a car is a symbolic display; so is a license plate. One displays speed, the other the identity of an automobile and its owner in numbers that symbolize, but do not picture, the thing represented.

Symbolic displays have the advantages of being simple, versatile, compact, and, above all, accurate. Pictorial displays, on the other hand, can usually be interpreted more quickly than symbolic displays, with little or no training required on the part of the operator. If, for example, you are shown a map with a miniature car marked on it (pictorial display), you can tell quickly where the car is. Given the same information on dials showing longitude and latitude (symbolic display), you would need some training in the use of such a scheme in order to interpret the numbers quickly and correctly. To decide which type of display to use, the engineering psychologist must know what kind of people will be using the display and what will be required of them.

Kinds of indicators. Many interesting problems are involved in the design of pictorial displays, but symbolic displays are most frequently used, primarily because they are compact. Most practical problems, therefore, arise in connection with symbolic displays, particularly dials. In designing symbolic displays, the designer must first ask, What is the purpose of the display? In general, each display serves one of three purposes:

1. *Check-reading indicators.* A check-reading dial tells the operator whether something is on or off, working or not working. The blinker on the dashboard of an automobile that has turn indicators serves this purpose; it merely tells the driver whether the indicator is working. Some automobiles use a red light to indicate whether oil pressure or battery charging is adequate or not. This is a check-reading indicator.

2. *Qualitative indicators.* Some indicators serve the purpose of telling the operator whether things are all right, and if not, in which direction they are off. The temperature indicator on most automobiles is such an indicator. It does not say exactly what the temperature is, for that does not matter, but it does tell whether the car is cold, is warmed up and in the normal range, or is getting too hot.

3. *Quantitative indicators.* Some information needs to be relatively precise. If, for example, we are to obey posted speed limits when driving, we need to know how fast we are going. The customary speedometer gives this information quantitatively.

The automobile has been used as an example because it should be familiar to the reader, but this classification of dials and indicators serves well for all sorts of visual symbolic displays. In order to avoid overloading an operator, it is important to know just what kind of indicator is necessary. If all that is required is check reading, an indicator showing more information than that should not be used. Similarly, a quantitative indicator should not be used when a qualitative one will do. Those who have observed the evolution of the modern automobile panel will realize that these principles are now being utilized more effectively than they were some years ago.

Dial design. Once the type of indicator has been chosen, the problem narrows down to the details of designing each dial for its intended purpose. This is not too much of a problem for check-reading or qualitative indicators, but it may be for quantitative indicators. For one thing, a choice must be made

between a *counter* and a *dial*. (The odometer showing accumulated mileage is a counter; the speedometer is usually a dial.) We have experiments to show that counters usually can be read more quickly and accurately than dials. On the other hand, they may be impossible to use if the operator must set them to a prescribed number or read them while their readings are changing. Hence the choice again depends on the nature of the operator's task.

If the choice is a dial, then there are many types of dials to select from. In Figure 18.12, for example, are five different types of dials: round, semicircular, an open-window dial with the scale moving and the pointer fixed, a vertical dial with moving pointer, and a horizontal dial with moving pointer. This particular set of dials was subjected to extensive experimental comparison in which subjects made over a thousand readings. Their errors were subsequently analyzed [Sleight, 1948]. The results showed that the open-window dial was read with the greatest accuracy, and the vertical moving-pointer dial with the greatest number of errors. This result was obtained under a particular set of experimental conditions, and one cannot therefore generalize it to every situation. It nevertheless shows how one may go about selecting the proper type of dial for a particular task.

Another problem in dial design is how to make the scale divisions on the dial. A dial with relatively few marks on it is obviously difficult to read with any accuracy. On the other hand, a scale that is too finely divided can be confusing, hard to read, and likely to produce errors. Moreover, a human being is rather good at interpolation; he can estimate fairly accurately the position of a pointer between two marks. Psychologists have studied this matter in some detail and have figures available for the design of various dials. In general, for the typical dial used on a cockpit or an automobile panel, the scale markings should be about half an inch apart. This design gives better accuracy than dials that are more or less cluttered with markings.

Many other problems occur in the design of dial displays, especially when the information to be presented is complex and involves a large range of

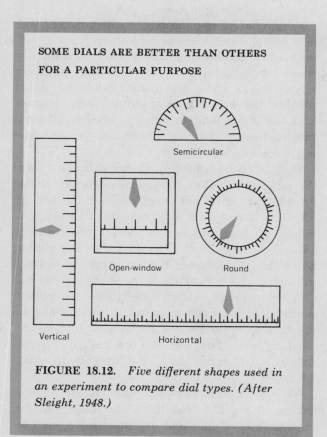

SOME DIALS ARE BETTER THAN OTHERS FOR A PARTICULAR PURPOSE

Semicircular

Open-window   Round

Vertical   Horizontal

FIGURE 18.12.   *Five different shapes used in an experiment to compare dial types. (After Sleight, 1948.)*

numbers. As a final example, however, of the design of displays for human use, let us consider a common problem presented by a large number of dials.

In the upper part of Figure 18.13 is a display of dials as they might appear when arranged on a cockpit panel without regard to their use by people. Indeed such displays can be found in many situations today. Since each dial displays a different sort of information, the normal place of the pointer differs from dial to dial. One can see that it would be difficult and time-consuming for an operator to read each of these dials and determine whether things were all right or, if not, how they differed from what they ought to be.

The task can be greatly simplified by *patterning the dial display* [Woodson, 1954; Woodson and Conover, 1964]. This can be done by orienting each dial so that the normal or usual position of a pointer is the same on every dial. Only when the dial indicates something different or unusual does the pointer move away from the usual position. Thus the task of reading the dials is simplified. At a glance, the operator can see which dials are "out of line" and then read them to find out what the discrepancy means. This principle is being incorporated in airplanes and other systems that involve displays of many dials.

DESIGN OF CONTROLS We have discussed displays, and particularly dials, at some length in order to give a coherent, though still sketchy, picture of one aspect of engineering psychology. Although the design of controls is also a large subject, we shall treat it more briefly, giving only a few points.

Classes of controls. The same distinction among classes of controls can be made as among classes of indicators. *On-off controls* are like check-reading indicators. A toggle switch used in controlling the lights at home is such a control. *Position controls* are like qualitative indicators. They are set at one of three or four positions. The station selector on a television set is an example. *Continuous controls* are like quantitative indicators. Changes in the thing controlled are proportional to the movement

PATTERNING MAKES DIAL CHECKING MUCH EASIER

Unpatterned dial display

Patterned dial display

FIGURE 18.13 *The patterning of dials. Patterning helps the operator to see at a glance which dials are not indicating their normal readings.*

of the control. The foot brake and steering wheel of a car are examples.

Here, as with displays, the tasks of operators must be analyzed and a control selected that is sufficient for the job. In general, the engineering psychologist should not supply a continuous control if an on-off switch or a position control will do.

Placement of controls. The placement of controls often presents a problem, especially where a good many controls are necessary and space is at a premium. One problem is that human beings are limited in the contortions they can make and still operate a control properly. Controls placed too close to the arms are easily knocked accidentally. Those that are too far away cause awkwardness of motion or force the operator to let up or lose contact with other controls being operated by the other hand or the feet. Those that are under seats or panels often cannot be turned or pushed properly.

Another factor in placing controls properly concerns habits the operator has previously acquired. If he is accustomed to finding a certain control in one place and he now finds it in another, he will need time to learn the new position and may make some serious mistakes in the process. He is also likely to revert to old habits in times of emergency.

HABIT INTERFERENCE CAN SOMETIMES BE FATAL

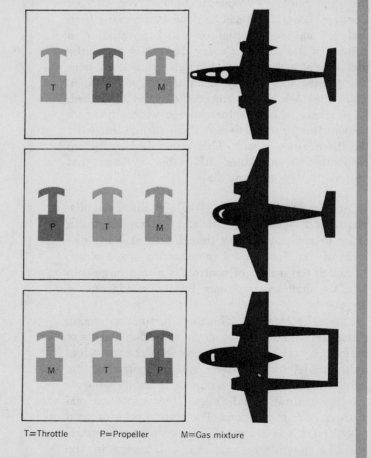

FIGURE 18.14. *Placement of controls on three different airplanes. The controls are for throttle, propeller, and fuel mixtures. Because of the lack of standard arrangement, pilots may make the mistake of operating the wrong control.*

T=Throttle   P=Propeller   M=Gas mixture

SHAPE-CODED CONTROLS ENABLE AN OPERATOR
TO SELECT THE CORRECT CONTROL WITHOUT LOOKING

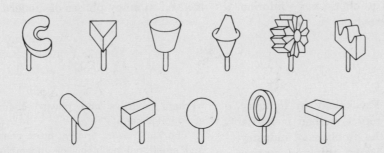

FIGURE 18.15. *Eleven shapes found to be best for shape coding of controls. (After Jenkins, 1947b.)*

This is illustrated by the following account:

Some years ago in tracking down the causes of aircraft accidents, Air Force psychologists noted that a large number of accidents, or near accidents, occurred when pilots switched from one to another of the following planes: B-25, C-47, and C-82. In particular, errors made by the pilots often involved operating the wrong control. The trouble was that different but related controls were arranged in a different sequence on these various planes (see Figure 18.14). The throttle was on the left in the B-25 and in the center on the C-47 and the C-82. The propeller control was in the center on the B-25, on the left in the C-47, and on the right in the C-82. The gas-mixture control was on the right in the B-25 and C-47, but on the left in the C-82.

The student may remember the discussion of negative transfer, or habit interference, in an earlier chapter (see page 129). Here is an example of it. Because of negative transfer, the pilots frequently operated controls as they had been accustomed to operate them in other planes they had flown. Serious efforts are made nowadays in airplane design to standardize the placement of controls.

Coding of controls. When it is not possible to do this or when the operator cannot readily see a control and might mistakenly operate the wrong one, it helps to *code* the controls by shape and/or size. (The coding of displays by color is also a useful device.) By making each of the controls discriminably different, the operator can tell by "feel" whether or not he has the right one.

For the purpose of coding controls used in airplane cockpits, Air Force psychologists investigated a series of 22 possible shapes. This was about as many different ways as anyone could devise of making knobs or controls different from each other. These shapes were then used in a discrimination experiment in which blindfolded subjects attempted to identify each knob by feeling it. The confusions between various shapes were noted, and shapes that were confused more than 1 per cent of the time were eliminated. As a result, the 11 different shapes shown in Figure 18.15 were selected as suitable for use whenever it seemed desirable to use shape coding in the design of controls.

These are just a few of many ways in which psychology is being applied in the design of machines for human use. Sometimes the engineering psychologist does little more than employ common sense. He is, then, a watchdog to see that human factors are not overlooked in meeting engineering objectives. More important, he also draws on a stockpile of knowledge about human capacities and limitations and goes ahead to obtain more information through further experiments.

Comparatively, the number of engineering psychologists is not large. On a liberal count, there are only a few hundred. Several years ago, however, there were only a handful; so growth has been very rapid. Engineering psychology is encountered and utilized in many phases of modern technology.

SYNOPSIS AND SUMMARY

The title of this chapter, Psychology in Industry, implies that many of the topics studied in earlier chapters are applicable to the problems of industry. For instance, aspects of learning, thinking, motivation, sensory processes, perception, psychological testing, psychotherapy, and social psychology can all be useful to industry. Large companies of consulting psychologists use basic discoveries in these branches of psychology in giving advice and assistance to various enterprises. In discussing the applications of basic psychological work to industrial problems, we made the following points:

1. The first step in the scientific selection of employees is to make a job analysis to determine accurately the requirements of the job. Next, the characteristics a worker must have to be able to do the job adequately are assessed.

2. Traditional methods of selecting employees through application blanks, interviews, and letters of recommendation are relatively unreliable unless precautions are taken to obtain the best results from them.

3. Trade tests may be helpful in selecting skilled workers. Aptitude tests also can be valid in selecting many types of employees if the tests are properly chosen and proved through careful research.

4. The duties of a supervisor of employees have several psychological aspects. One is to be a teacher and trainer, not only in breaking in a new employee, but also in day-by-day supervision.

5. The supervisor must also be able to communicate his instructions promptly and intelligibly and to keep employees informed on most matters that they feel concern them in their work.

6. He must also evaluate both the job and the worker on the job so that he can make the fullest use of the

workers' abilities and reward them fairly for their accomplishments.

7. The supervisor, finally, must consider the personal and emotional problems of an employee because these seriously affect performance. He must be able to offer counseling or other aid that may alleviate problems.

8. The psychology of management is a growing field in industrial psychology. It includes the study of how best to train managers and how the ideas that managers hold about human motivation influence performance.

9. Employees do not work for pay alone, but for the satisfaction of all their needs. In fact, once pay is reasonable and fair, other factors, such as job security, good working conditions, opportunity for advancement, and good personnel relations, become extremely important in job satisfaction.

10. Work curves that are typical of the amount of work done during the course of a day have their ups and downs. They can be analyzed, however, into four principal components: (a) a warm-up effect, (b) a beginning spurt, (c) an end spurt, and (d) a fatigue effect.

11. Fatigue can be measured in a number of ways: (a) by amount of work produced, (b) by errors or quality of work, (c) by physiological effects, and (d) by changes in motivation.

12. Often, when there is not a measurable effect of fatigue on production, fatigue shows up as a lowered motivation for work or as a lowered standard of performance.

13. Recovery from fatigue is generally faster when the fatigue is mild than when it has become severe. Thus it is better to take short rests frequently than long rests infrequently.

14. If one attempts to lengthen the workday or the workweek, one finds that beyond a certain point total production declines. Consequently, there is an optimum workday and workweek.

15. Engineering psychology is the field in which psychological methods and research are used to improve the design of machines so that they better fit the capabilities of the human operator.

16. Machines are being designed to take the place of human operators; yet there are several respects in which man is more efficient than any machine. To design the best man-machine system, one must assign to each the things it can do best.

17. Displays for conveying information to the human operator should make use of man's various senses in such a way that no one sense is overloaded. The displays should be designed to enable the operator to comprehend information rapidly, but with minimum error.

18. Similarly, controls should be designed with the operator in mind. The man-machine system can be made to function best by (*a*) choosing the best type of controls, (*b*) placing and arranging controls properly, and (*c*) coding the controls so that they can be identified without having to be seen.

RELATED TOPICS IN THE TEXT

CHAPTER 6 MOTIVATION Learned human motives influence both managers and workers. Chapter 6 thus provides an important background for the points made here.

CHAPTER 12 PSYCHOLOGICAL TESTING Tests are much used in the selection and evaluation of employees, and a review might be fruitful.

CHAPTER 15 MENTAL HEALTH AND PSYCHOTHERAPY Non-directive, or client-centered, therapy is similar to the problem-solving interview used in overcoming managerial problems. The section on nondirective therapy should provide an interesting comparison.

CHAPTER 16 SOCIAL INFLUENCES ON BEHAVIOR The influence of groups on individual behavior is discussed in this chapter, and since managers spend much of their time directing and participating in groups, this discussion is particularly relevant.

SUGGESTIONS FOR FURTHER READING

Anastasi, A. *Fields of applied psychology*. New York: McGraw-Hill, 1964.
All of the topics in this chapter, and some other aspects of applied psychology, are discussed in great detail in this text.

Bingham, W. V. D., Moore, B. V., and Gustad, J. W. *How to interview* (rev. ed.). New York: Harper & Row, 1959.
The revision of a standard text on interviewing.

Chapanis, A. *The design and conduct of human engineering studies*. Baltimore: Johns Hopkins, 1959.
A readable account of the methods used in human engineering.

Ghiselli, E. E., and Brown, C. W. *Personnel and industrial psychology* (2d ed.). New York: McGraw-Hill, 1955.
A widely used text covering the general field of industrial psychology.

Haire, M. *Psychology in management* (2d ed.). New York: McGraw-Hill, 1964.
A brief and interesting psychological analysis of the role of the manager and supervisor.

Leavitt, H. J. *Managerial psychology* (2d ed.). Chicago: Univ. of Chicago Press, 1964.
A very readable book on the principles of psychology in the management of large and small groups.

McCormick, E. J. *Human factors in engineering* (2d ed.). New York: McGraw-Hill, 1964.
An introductory textbook on human engineering.

Schein, E. H. *Organizational psychology*. Englewood Cliffs, N.J.: Prentice-Hall, 1964. (Paperback.)
A readable textbook which presents many of the most important recent developments in the psychology of industry.

Smith, H. C. *Psychology of industrial behavior* (2d ed.). New York: McGraw-Hill, 1964.
A textbook emphasizing the role of motivational and social factors in industry.

Sutermeister, R. A. *People and productivity*. New York: McGraw-Hill, 1963.
A text and set of readings with special emphasis on motivation and social psychology as they apply to individual productivity.

BIOLOGY
OF
BEHAVIOR

PART SEVEN

19

OUR SURVEY of the field of psychology is about finished. It has probably occurred to you that behaviors which are the result of maturation, learning, memory, some aspects of motivation and emotion, sensory perception, and even some of the behavior disorders, have a basis in the structure, function, and biochemistry of the body. This is, of course, true, and some of the biological bases of behavior and experience have already been considered. In this chapter and the next, we shall be more explicit about them. The branch of experimental psychology which studies the relationship between physical structure, function, and biochemistry on the one hand, and behavior and experience on the other, is called *physiological psychology*. The broader term *biological psychology*, however, might be more accurate since the range of topics studied includes structure and biochemistry; its meaning is therefore broader than that which is implied by the term physiology alone.

We wish we knew more about the fascinating relationships between biology and behavior. For instance, we cannot yet say what happens in the nervous system when an individual learns and later recalls something; but we do not need to know this in order to investigate some of the variables which control learning and memory, or to apply our knowledge of learning in a practical way. Still, the understanding of psychological facts in terms of structure, function, and biochemistry—that is, in terms of the data of other sciences—has a great appeal to more analytically minded psychologists. And such knowledge may be potentially very useful.

In order to discover some of the biological correlates of behavior, we proceed in two stages. In this chapter, we take up a little anatomy and physiology —the names, the structures, and some of the functions of the organs that are important in psychological events. Not much is said about the sense organs which have been considered at length in Chapters 8, 9, and 10. However, we do discuss the sensory pathways leading from the sense organs into and through the nervous system. In the next chapter, we consider how the functions of certain organs are related to behavior and experience.

NERVOUS SYSTEM AND INTERNAL ENVIRONMENT

THE THOUGHTS OF WHICH I AM NOW GIVING UTTERANCE AND YOUR THOUGHTS REGARDING THEM ARE THE EXPRESSION OF MOLECULAR CHANGES IN THAT MATTER OF LIFE WHICH IS THE SOURCE OF OUR OTHER VITAL PHENOMENA.
T. H. HUXLEY

A SCHEME OF LINES AND NODAL POINTS, GATHERED TOGETHER AT ONE END INTO A GREAT RAVELLED KNOT, THE BRAIN, AND AT THE OTHER TRAILING OFF TO A SORT OF STALK, THE SPINAL CORD.
C. S. SHERRINGTON

THE NEURON IS THE UNIT
OF THE NERVOUS SYSTEM

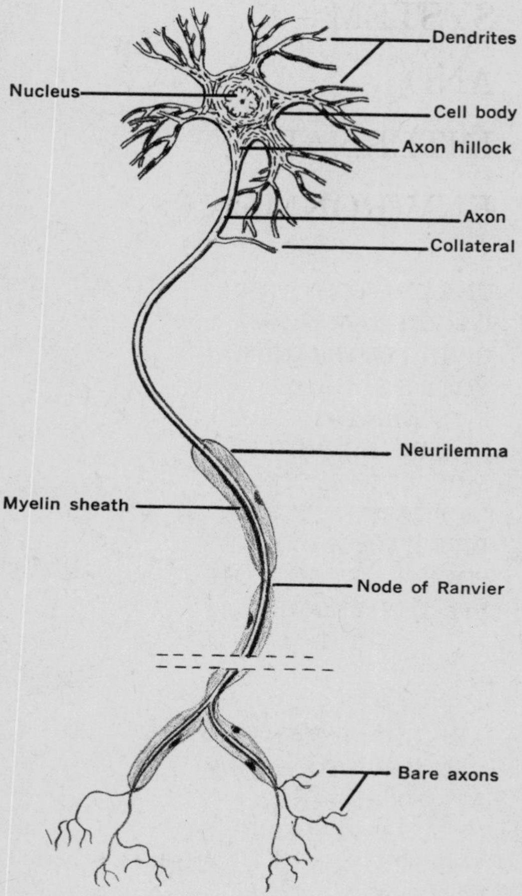

FIGURE 19.1. *An idealized diagram of a neuron. In this motor neuron from the spinal cord, the cell body lies in the ventral horn of the spinal cord and the axon extends to muscles in the periphery of the body. The* collateral *is a branching fiber; the* neurilemma *is an outer covering of the fiber in the peripheral nervous system over the myelin sheath of a myelinated fiber or the axis cylinder of an unmyelinated fiber. (Modified from Brazier, 1960.)*

Neurons and synapses

We have already explained how each individual begins life as a single cell (see Chapter 2). This original cell divides and multiplies over and over again until the various organs of the body take form. In the multiplication, cells differentiate in structure and function, each coming to play a particular role in the body's activities. Although each organ of the body eventually consists of many kinds of cells, one kind of cell usually serves the principal function of the organ. In the case of the nervous system, this kind of cell is the *neuron*—its function is to conduct messages, called nerve impulses. Other cells in the nervous system, the *glial* cells, or *neuroglia,* are considered to be necessary for the structural support and nourishment of neurons.

NEURONS   A schematic drawing of a neuron appears in Figure 19.1. Neurons actually vary a great deal in size and shape, and the one shown is more typical of a motor neuron that extends out from the spinal cord to a muscle than it is of other varieties of neurons. The diagram, however, brings out the essential features of different neurons. They all have two general parts: a *cell body* and *fibers.* The cell body contains structures that keep the neuron alive and functioning normally. Neuron fibers are of two types: *dendrites,* which are stimulated by neighboring neurons or by physical stimuli; and *axons,* which deliver nerve impulses to adjacent neurons or to an effector, such as a muscle. Dendrites and axons may be relatively long or very short, depending on the cells with which they connect. Many of the neurons within the brain that serve as connectors between closely packed neurons have very short fibers (see Figure 19.2). Other neurons within the brain have relatively long dendrites and axons (see Figure 19.2). Still others, such as those motor neurons connected with the muscle fibers of the limbs, toes, or fingers, have very long axons and short dendrites (see Figure 19.1).

From the point of view of its function as a conductor of electrical nerve impulses from one part of the body to another, perhaps the most important part of

NEURONS COME IN MANY VARIETIES

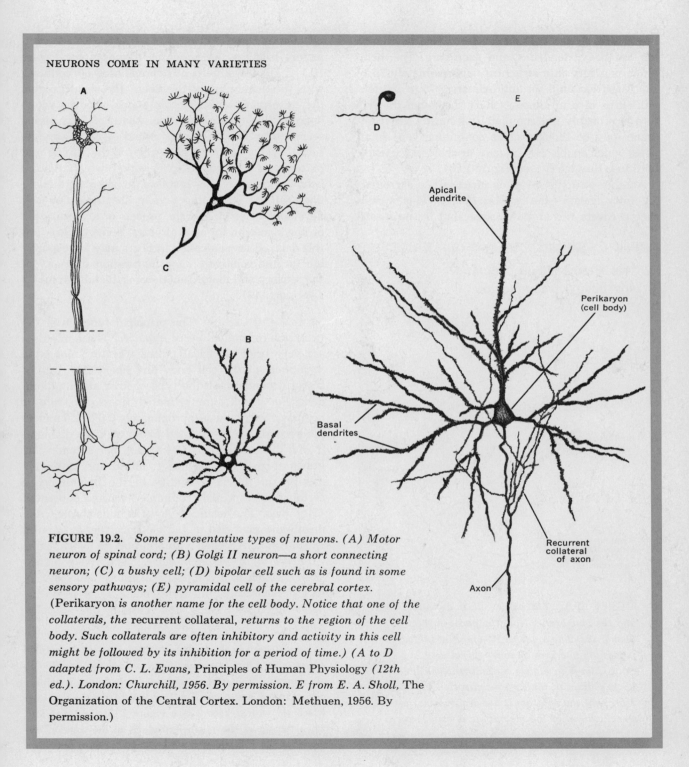

FIGURE 19.2. *Some representative types of neurons. (A) Motor neuron of spinal cord; (B) Golgi II neuron—a short connecting neuron; (C) a bushy cell; (D) bipolar cell such as is found in some sensory pathways; (E) pyramidal cell of the cerebral cortex. (Perikaryon is another name for the cell body. Notice that one of the collaterals, the recurrent collateral, returns to the region of the cell body. Such collaterals are often inhibitory and activity in this cell might be followed by its inhibition for a period of time.) (A to D adapted from C. L. Evans,* Principles of Human Physiology *(12th ed.). London: Churchill, 1956. By permission. E from E. A. Sholl,* The Organization of the Central Cortex. *London: Methuen, 1956. By permission.)*

the neuron is the cell *membrane* which surrounds the cell body, dendrites, and axon core. The membrane is a very thin structure—approximately 75 to 100 Angstrom units, or approximately 75 to 100 ten-millionths of a millimeter, thick. Although the picture is probably not completely accurate, the membrane may be thought of as containing very small pores which enable certain *ions,* or charged particles, to diffuse through it (see Figure 19.3).

Another structure of some neurons is a surrounding fatty sheath—the *myelin sheath.* This myelin sheath covers the axons of some, but by no means

all, neurons, and it is interrupted every 1 or 2 millimeters to form the *nodes of Ranvier* (see Figure 19.1). The myelin sheath should not be confused with the membrane of the fiber—the sheath covers the membrane which is continuous over the whole neuron. The function of this sheath of fatty tissue seems to be to increase the speed of nerve conduction. Myelin may be necessary for the timing and patterns of nervous activity upon which mature behavior depends. For instance, in the case of many fibers of the brain, the myelin sheath is not well developed at birth, and the process of myelinization of fibers goes on for several years. Some believe that this delayed myelinization of fibers may be responsible for the relatively slow maturation of many of the sensory and motor functions of the human infant (see page 49).

NERVE IMPULSES   The principal function of the neuron is to *conduct nerve impulses.* These impulses are very brief electrical pulses traveling along the membrane of the cell body and fibers. The rate of travel depends upon the type of fiber and its diameter. For small, unmyelinated fibers the rate is comparatively slow—approximately 0.6 to 2.0 meters per second; for myelinated fibers of large diameter it may be as much as 120 meters per second. The pulses themselves are due to rapid and reversible changes in the permeability of the membrane to certain ions, especially sodium (Na^+) and potassium (K^+) ions. The resulting flows of ions through the membrane give rise to the electrical nerve impulse which can be recorded with appropriate instruments.

Record of a nerve impulse.   The following example, which is a composite of many neurophysiological recordings, illustrates one way of recording nerve impulses [Ruch and Patton, 1965; Eccles, 1957]:

The first step in the recording is to take a microelectrode —one with a tip approximately 1 micron, or 1 millionth of a meter, in diameter—and gradually lower it with a device called a micromanipulator toward the neuron from which we wish to record (see Figure 19.4, right). At first, when the tip of the microelectrode is in the solution surrounding the cell, the recorded voltage is zero, but when

THE MEMBRANE IS CRUCIAL
FOR IMPULSE CONDUCTION

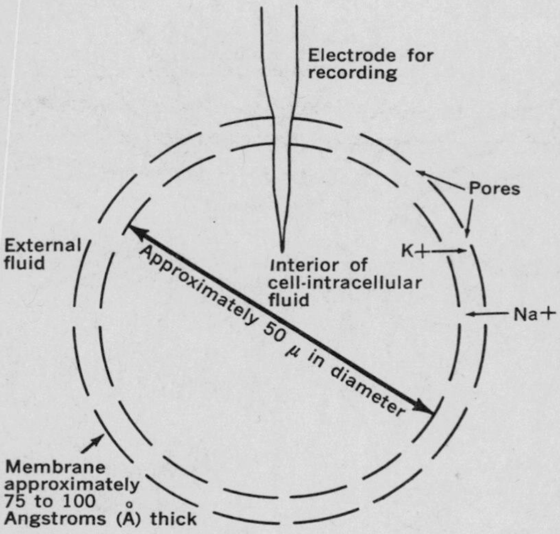

FIGURE 19.3.   *The nerve cell, in cross section, and the membrane. Note the pores in the membrane. The symbols K^+ and Na^+ indicate potassium and sodium ions respectively. Potassium is in higher concentration inside the fiber, sodium in higher concentration outside. Note that the diagram is not drawn to scale— the thickness of the membrane is exaggerated.*

the microelectrode penetrates the cell membrane, the voltage changes abruptly and now reads about −70 millivolts, or thousandths of a volt (see Figure 19.4, bottom). In other words, the inside of the cell is charged negatively, when compared with the outside of the cell membrane, by 70 millivolts. In fact, the nerve cell is like a tiny battery in that it is *polarized*, with the inside of the cell being the negative pole of the battery and the outside of the membrane being the positive pole. This voltage, or potential, of the neuron in the inactive state is called the *resting potential*. Now, suppose we stimulate the cell so that the inside of the cell is made a little less negative, or, from the other point of view, a little more positive. The rate of change of voltage is at first rather slow and depends upon the strength of the stimulus, but then a voltage is reached at which there is suddenly a very rapid voltage change in the positive direction (see Figure 19.4, bottom, C). The voltage level at which this rapid change begins is about 20 millivolts more positive than the resting potential, about −50 millivolts in this case, and is called the *threshold*. After threshold has been reached, the voltage rapidly shoots toward zero and then overshoots zero to become positive by about 20 or 30 millivolts (see Figure 19.4, bottom, C). Thereafter, the voltage declines, somewhat more slowly than it rose, back to the resting potential, or even a little beyond it for a period. The whole sequence of voltage changes is called the *action potential*; the particular part in which the internally recorded voltage rapidly changes toward positivity and then declines is the *spike potential* and it only lasts for approximately 0.5 to 1.0 milli-seconds—or thousandths of a second. The later parts of the action potential are known as the *after potentials*.

If we had recorded from the outside surface of the fiber, instead of from the inside, the voltage changes of the action potential would have been opposite in sign; for example, the spike potential would have been recorded as a rapid negative shift of voltage. The spike potential, which is what we have been calling the nerve impulse, travels down the nerve fiber (see Figure 19.5). Thus the spike potential is seen, from the outside, as a wave of negativity moving along a fiber.

The all-or-none law.   This law states that the size of the nerve impulse does *not* depend on the strength of the stimulus which initiates it; instead, the size of the spike potential and the speed with which it travels down a fiber depend upon characteristics of the fiber itself. It is easy to see that the all-or-none behavior of a neuron is related to the idea of the threshold which was just illustrated. The stimulus either causes threshold to be reached, or it does not; if reached, the voltage changes go to completion. All that is necessary is that threshold be reached; after this, a self-propagating series of events, which cannot be stopped, takes place in the membrane of the fiber. Consider the mousetrap as an analogy. It makes no difference to the trap whether a big mouse or a little mouse steps on the trigger. It is only essential that the weight of the mouse—the stimulus —be sufficient to exceed the threshold of the trigger.

One implication of the all-or-none law is that information in the nervous system is not carried by graded sizes of the voltages of spike potentials. If a particular neuron is stimulated, and if it is in a relatively normal state, its spike potential will always be about the same. Different neurons have different sized spikes—for instance, the spike potential is greater in the fibers with larger diameters— but the size of the spike depends upon the neuron and not on the strength of the stimulus. Thus, information about stimulus strength must be carried by the frequency of firing, and the number of fibers which fire, and not by the sizes of spikes.

Ionic basis of the nerve impulse.   Voltage changes in neurons are caused by flows of charged particles, or ions, through the membrane [Hodgkin, 1957]. The details of this make a fascinating story, but they must be left for courses in physiology or more advanced courses in physiological psychology. Here we can only describe, without explaining fully, some of the ionic changes which give rise to the action potential.

The spike potential is due to a pronounced increase in the permeability of the membrane to sodium (Na^+) ions. This change in permeability seems to depend upon the voltage at which the neuron is polarized, and if this voltage is reduced to threshold, the membrane becomes more permeable to sodium. Although the picture is not completely accurate, it might be useful to think of channels,

FIGURE 19.4. *Right, a spinal motoneuron and microelectrode. Below, records from a microelectrode inside a motoneuron. Oscilloscope A records the strength of the volley of nerve impulses set up by the stimulus. It varies with the strength of the stimulus applied to the afferent nerve. Increasingly stronger stimuli are applied in A, B, C, and D, and the height of the record from oscilloscope A increases. Oscilloscope B is arranged to record from the microelectrode within the motoneuron. (A) Fairly weak stimuli produce relatively slow changes in the potential recorded from the microelectrode—the EPSP. (B) Somewhat stronger stimuli increase the size of the EPSP—it is graded. (C) Stronger stimuli bring the EPSP to threshold and the cell fire— a spike is produced. (D) Still stronger stimuli cause the EPSP to rise to threshold faster, but the height of the spike does not change—it obeys the all-or-none law. (Right, Eccles, 1953; below, modified from Eccles, 1965; courtesy of Scientific American.)*

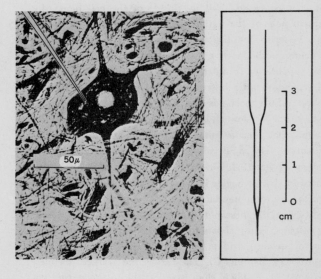

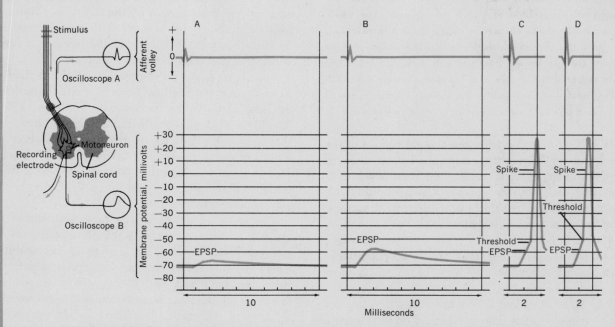

or pores, through the membrane which open up to admit sodium ions when threshold voltage is reached. The flow of sodium ions is from the outside of the fiber to the inside because the concentration of sodium ions is much higher outside the cell than inside it; the sodium ions flow from a region of high concentration to one of low concentration. The difference in concentration of sodium between the inside and the outside is maintained by an active, energy-utilizing process which transports sodium out of the cell. This process is known as the *sodium pump*. The inflow of sodium ions, when the membrane permeability changes, is also enhanced by the resting potential—the polarization of the membrane; since the inside of the cell is negatively charged, the positively charged sodium ions are attracted inward. Only a minute amount of sodium flows in during a nerve impulse, but this is enough to reverse the polarity of the cell for a moment, and the inside of the neuron becomes positive for a brief time. The increased permeability of the membrane to sodium

is but a very transient event and the increased sodium permeability is soon *inactivated*. Now the permeability of the membrane to potassium ions increases, channels for potassium-ion flow are opened, and potassium ions flow through the membrane because the concentration of potassium is relatively greater inside the neuron than outside it. The effect of this outward flow of positive potassium ions after the spike is to reestablish the positive charge on the outside of the fiber—the resting potential. Now the condition of the fiber is back to what it was before the impulse was initiated, and a new impulse may be started down the fiber.

Movement of an impulse down a fiber. The active processes just described travel down the fiber (see Figure 19.5). This movement may be understood in terms of *local flows* of ions around the active region. At the leading edge of the active region, there is a flow from the inactive region, which is just ahead, back into the active region. On the surface of the fiber, positively charged ions flow to the nega-

---

THE ACTIVE REGION OF THE NERVE IMPULSE
TRAVELS DOWN THE FIBER

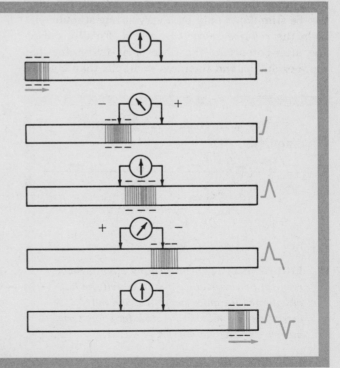

FIGURE 19.5.   *The arrow in the circle represents the needle of a voltmeter making a circuit with the nerve fiber through two electrodes (arrows in contact with membrane). On the right, reading downward, is the record of the swing of the needle as the impulse passes first one electrode, then the other. The active electrode is the one to the left; when it is negative relative to the other one, the record swings upward; when it is positive with respect to the other one, the record swings downward. It is traditional in most neurophysiological recordings to record negative voltages in the upward direction. However, records made from inside cells show positivity with upward swings. (After Gardner, 1958.)*

tively charged active region and depolarize the region ahead of the active segment to threshold. In this way, the next section of the fiber is excited and a spike ensues; this process goes on continuously all the way down the fiber. At the trailing edge of the active region, the neuron is recovering from the spike. Here sodium permeability is inactivated and potassium permeability has increased to restore the resting potential. Thus the impulse, or spike, progresses down the fiber as an active patch, depolarizing the fiber ahead of itself and restoring polarization behind itself.

Excitability of nerve fibers. While a region of a fiber is actively conducting a spike, it cannot be stimulated to fire another impulse—the fiber is said to be in the *absolute refractory period.* Since the nerve impulse lasts for approximately one millisecond, the fiber is absolutely refractory for this long. This limits the rate at which a single nerve fiber can respond to 1,000 impulses per second, and puts a limit on the amount of information which may be carried by the frequency of firing. Immediately after the absolute refractory period, the fiber can be stimulated only by a very strong stimulus—it is in the *relative refractory period.* Finally, during the after-potentials, the fiber is at first somewhat more excitable, and then less excitable, than normal.

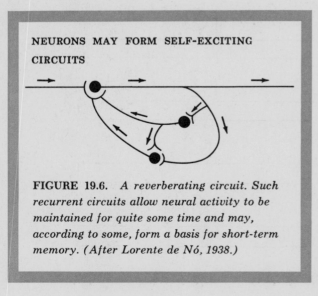

NEURONS MAY FORM SELF-EXCITING CIRCUITS

FIGURE 19.6. *A reverberating circuit. Such recurrent circuits allow neural activity to be maintained for quite some time and may, according to some, form a basis for short-term memory. (After Lorente de Nó, 1938.)*

SYNAPTIC CONNECTIONS Knowing that nerve impulses travel along fibers, we might naturally ask where they come from and where they go. This question has several answers. One is that impulses originate in the receptors of the various senses. Some receptors, such as the free nerve endings in the skin, are themselves fibers of neurons. In such fibers, an external stimulus evokes a response directly. In the receptors for many other senses, neurons are stimulated by the generator potentials produced by the specialized transducer cells of the receptor (see Chapters 8 and 9). In any case, no matter how a neuron from a sensory organ is stimulated, it will carry nerve impulses into the *central nervous system (CNS).*

Fibers carrying information into the central nervous system are called *afferent* fibers. The fibers of some afferent neurons extend all the way from the sense organ—no matter how far away this may be—to the central nervous system, that is, the *spinal cord* and *brain.* When impulses in the afferent fibers reach the central nervous system, they excite other neurons and information is carried further through the nervous system.

Many routes through the central nervous system are possible. For instance, the afferent neuron may pass information directly, or through intervening neurons called *association neurons,* to a motor, or *efferent neuron*—one leading out of the central nervous system to muscle fibers—and movement may occur. Such a simple connection from afferent to efferent, whether through an association neuron or not, is called a *reflex arc,* and it is the simplest complete arrangement for a behavioral response to a stimulus. Of course, the input into the CNS through the afferent fiber may not result in muscle movement. It may, for example, be relayed to excite those cells which, when active, give rise to our experience of the world (see page 274); or the input may excite neurons which loop to form *recurrent nerve circuits,* or *reverberating circuits* (see Figure 19.6), which may be the neural basis for short-term memory storage (see page 727).

Whatever its eventual fate, the information, as it speeds through the CNS, is passed on from neuron

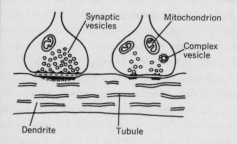

SYNAPSES ARE REGIONS OF FUNCTIONAL
CONNECTION BETWEEN NEURONS

FIGURE 19.7. *Two types of synapses. The synaptic knobs of the presynaptic fibers are shown above; the postsynaptic fiber is below. A type 1 synapse—possibly excitatory—is shown on the left; a type 2 synapse—possibly inhibitory—is shown on the right. (From Eccles, 1964.)*

neuron to which the information is being transmitted is called the *postsynaptic neuron*—its membrane in the synaptic region is the *postsynaptic element.*

A schematic diagram of several types of synapses and synaptic regions is shown in Figure 19.7; Figure 19.8 shows an electron microscopic photograph of a synaptic region. Some important features of synaptic regions are illustrated by such photographs. First, they reveal swellings of the presynaptic fibers—the ends of axons—in the synaptic region; such swellings are often called *synaptic knobs,* or *boutons*—"buttons." Second, two types of structurally different synaptic regions seem to show up—*type 1* and *type 2* synapses [Eccles, 1964]. In type 1 synapses, the

to neuron—typically from the axon of one neuron to the dendrites, or cell bodies, of the next ones. Since each neuron is a separate cell, and there is thus a space, or gap, between the ends of the axon of one neuron and the dendrites or cell bodies of the next neurons, the question of how information is passed from one cell to another is an important one and we shall come to it in a minute. These gaps, or *synapses,* are important because they make it possible for a cell to be subject to fine control by preceding cells. In addition, changes in the activity of the synaptic regions may be the basis for the plasticity of the nervous system which we considered in discussing learning (see Chapter 3) and perception (see Chapter 10).

Synaptic anatomy. As we have seen, the gap between neurons is called a synapse. The whole region, including the end of the axon of one neuron, the gap, and the membrane of the next cell, may be called the *synaptic region.* The neuron along which a nerve impulse comes to the synapse is called the *presynaptic neuron*—its membrane in the synaptic region is called the *presynaptic membrane;* the

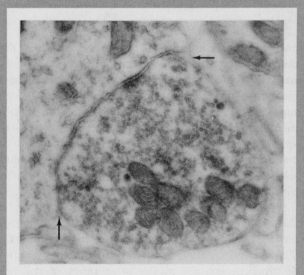

FIGURE 19.8. *A photograph of a synaptic region made by an electron microscope. The presynaptic knob is on the right; the postsynaptic membrane is shown on the left. The arrows show the ends of the synaptic cleft. Note that there is an active region in the presynaptic fiber in which the synaptic vesicles seem to be concentrated. The dark bodies on the right are mitochondria. (Courtesy, Sanford L. Palay and Experimental Cell Research, Suppl. 5, 1958, Academic Press, New York.)*

SOMETIMES CELLS MAY BE
HYPERPOLARIZED

—74mV
(RP)

FIGURE 19.9.   *An inhibitory postsynaptic potential—an IPSP. The resting potential (RP) of this cell was —74 mV. Stimulation through certain fibers making synaptic connection with it made the inside of the cell more negative—it was hyperpolarized. Note that the slow increase in inside negativity drives the potential farther from threshold. (From Eccles, 1957.)*

postsynaptic membrane is thickened and the gap appears to be a little wider than in type 2 synapses. In both types, little hollow spheres may be seen clustering around the presynaptic membrane; no such hollow spheres are seen at the postsynaptic membrane (see Figures 19.7 and 19.8). These little spheres—called *synaptic vesicles*—are thought to contain *transmitter substances* which, as we shall see, are chemicals responsible for carrying the information across the synaptic gap.

Synaptic processes. The events which occur in the synaptic region by which information is passed on from cell to cell are intriguing, to say the least. The synaptic region, as we have seen, is not a region of physical contact of the membranes of the presynaptic and postsynaptic neurons. But it is a region of *functional contact.* Let us first describe some of the electrical events which happen at this region, and then see if we can explain some of the events which have been observed [Eccles, 1957, 1964].

Suppose we combine a number of experiments into one description. First, we impale a postsynaptic cell with a microelectrode and then we stimulate a presynaptic fiber which has synaptic knobs on the cell from which we are recording (see Figure 19.4, bottom). If we stimulate the presynaptic fiber rather gently, we may see the electrical change shown in Figure 19.4, bottom, A. The inside of the

postsynaptic cell from which we are recording becomes slightly less negative—it begins to be depolarized—but threshold is not reached. If the stimulation of the presynaptic fiber is now turned off, the potential of the postsynaptic cell drops back to the resting potential. However, if we stimulate the presynaptic fiber vigorously, we obtain depolarization at a somewhat faster rate, the depolarization reaches threshold, and a nerve impulse is initiated in the postsynaptic cell (see Figure 19.4, bottom, C and D).

The relatively slow depolarization which results from stimulation of the presynaptic fiber is called the *excitatory postsynaptic potential (EPSP).* The EPSP, in contrast with the spike potential, is graded—it can be large or small, and can have a fast or slow rate of rise, depending on the strength of stimulation of the presynaptic fiber (see Figure 19.4, bottom, A and B). EPSPs caused by impulses arriving over several different fibers which synapse on a single postsynaptic cell can sum up to cause threshold to be reached.

In other experiments, we may find that the postsynaptic cell becomes *hyperpolarized*—the inside becomes more negative—when we stimulate certain presynaptic fibers (see Figure 19.9). The result of this hyperpolarization is to drive the potential of the postsynaptic cell farther from threshold and this makes it harder to excite. In other words, the cell is *inhibited.* The potential in this case is called the *inhibitory postsynaptic potential (IPSP).* IPSPs can combine with EPSPs to control the excitability of the postsynaptic cell.

When we look at the types of synapses which depolarize a given postsynaptic cell, we see that they are type 1 synapses. Activity at type 2 synapses seems to hyperpolarize —that is, it is inhibitory.

Any particular neuron is covered by both inhibitory and excitatory synapses. The inhibitory synapses are at the ends of one set of presynaptic fibers, the excitatory synapses at the ends of other presynaptic fibers. Thus inhibitory and excitatory influences from many sources can play upon any given cell. This means that impulses arriving from many parts of the nervous system can impinge upon a postsynaptic cell and, if the timing is right, delicately control its excitability. For this reason, the patterning of the steady pitter-patter of impulses reaching neurons may be important for some aspects of the neural basis of learning and memory.

Now that we know about inhibitory and excitatory electrical events in the postsynaptic element, can we begin to understand them at a more molecular level? In part we can. The sequence of events seems to be something like this: The electrical impulses arriving in the presynaptic knobs cause, in some way, transmitter substances to be released from the vesicles into the synaptic cleft. These substances are then supposed to be received, or to combine with, the postsynaptic membrane so that the permeability of a patch of membrane on the postsynaptic cell is changed.

In excitatory, or type 1 synapses, there are probably several different transmitter substances; one, in particular, is called *acetylcholine*. There is also an enzyme, *acetylcholinesterase*, which destroys acetylcholine. One may think of acetylcholine as being released by presynaptic nerve impulses, having its action on the postsynaptic patch of membrane, and then being destroyed by acetylcholinesterase so that the cycle may be repeated again. Many inhibitory substances are probably released from the vesicles in the synaptic knobs of inhibitory neurons; *gamma-aminobutyric acid (GABA)* has been considered to have such action in the mammalian nervous system, but the evidence remains somewhat inconclusive. The coalition of two lines of research—electrical studies of synapses and chemical studies of transmitters—will, in the future, give us much more information about the basis for learning, memory, motivation, emotion, and the effects of drugs on the nervous system.

REFLEXES   The simplest reflex arc, as we have seen, involves two fibers, afferent and efferent, and one synapse between them (see Figure 19.10). However, most reflex arcs are more complicated than this, containing one or many association neurons—sometimes termed *interneurons*. Reflex pathways of varying complexity are found in many parts of the nervous system. They are responsible for such reactions as the blink of the eyelid when the cornea of the eye is touched, the contraction of the pupil in bright light, salivation when food is placed in the mouth, the pricking of the dog's ears when it hears an unfamiliar sound, and a host of other automatic reactions.

The reflexes just mentioned all involve pathways in the brain. Other reflexes involve only the spinal cord, and these can be classified into two general categories: the *flexion reflexes* and the *extension reflexes*. We have all observed our own flexion reflexes when we have inadvertently touched a hot stove or stepped on a sharp object. The reaction in each case is quickly to flex or bend the limb concerned in order to withdraw it from the painful stimulus. Extension reflexes are even more common than flexion reflexes, but we are less aware of them because they are so "automatic." For example, when one's leg touches the ground, pressure on the foot reflexly extends and stiffens the leg to support one's weight. When one lifts his foot off the ground, the opposite leg reflexly stiffens to support the body. The reflex in this latter case has its stimulus in the kinesthetic receptors of the flexed leg (see Chapter 9). Both are examples of extension reflexes. They aid us in standing, walking, and running, and, although they occur so regularly, we seldom notice them.

These are just a few examples of reflexes. More complex reflexes may involve several association neurons whose fibers extend some distance in the

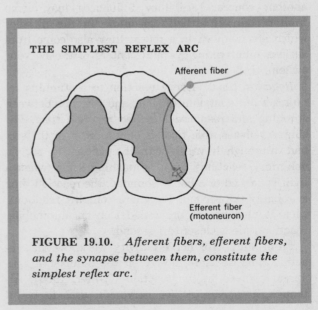

THE SIMPLEST REFLEX ARC

Afferent fiber

Efferent fiber
(motoneuron)

FIGURE 19.10.   *Afferent fibers, efferent fibers, and the synapse between them, constitute the simplest reflex arc.*

nervous system. One example is the scratch reflex which we observe in our pets or even in ourselves. The scratch reflex happens to be a nicely timed alternation of flexion and extension reflexes. Here we see an example of behavior which depends crucially upon the timing and patterning of synaptic activities.

Reciprocal inhibition. The timing and smoothness of reflex action depends on the way in which muscles are arranged and innervated—that is, connected with nerve fibers. The muscles of the body, and particularly those of the limbs, are typically arranged in *antagonistic* pairs. One set of muscles extends the limb; another set, the antagonistic set, flexes it. The two sets of antagonistic muscles, however, seldom contract at the same time. When the extensor muscles contract, the flexor muscles relax, and vice versa. In this way, antagonistic muscles are kept from working against each other, and only one reflex is dominant at a time. This relaxation of antagonistic muscles is called *reciprocal inhibition.*

Reciprocal inhibition is only a special case of inhibition. Inhibition, as we have seen, is a general phenomenon of synaptic function in which impulses from one source can cause a neuron to be less excitable and thus not to respond to impulses from another source. Inhibitory influences may come from certain kinesthetic receptors in the muscles which are involved in a reflex; they also come from various other pathways and centers of the nervous system.

Reaction time. Every reaction to a stimulus requires a finite amount of time, and the time between stimulus and response is called *reaction time.* For simple reflexes, this time is of the order of 0.1 second, although it varies with the reflex. For simple voluntary reactions, such as pushing a key when a light is flashed or a bell is sounded, the reaction time is roughly 0.2 second. For more complex reactions, such as pushing the brake pedal on an automobile, reaction time is closer to 1 second.

From studies of nerve activity we know that reaction time depends mostly on the number of synapses involved in the reaction [Miller, 1965]. Although it takes time for nerve impulses to travel along nerve fibers, the speed of travel is so fast that reaction times would be much less than they are if speed of travel were the crucial factor. Rather, it is probably delay at the synapse that is the important factor, and the more synapses, the more delay. This is what accounts for relatively long reaction times and for greater reaction time for responses that involve many neurons and synapses in the nervous system.

Significance of reflexes. The analysis of reflex action has been very useful in attempting to understand some of the basic processes by which the nervous system functions. Reflexes are also important in some simple, relatively automatic, behaviors. Analysis of them may help us to understand certain types of learning, such as classical conditioning. However, although we do not understand them, the neural basis for most psychological functions probably involves processes other than those implied by a model of the nervous system built on reflexes. In other words, instead of a simple switchboard of connections, other processes must be going on which account for many things we do. We shall mention a guess or two about these processes in Chapter 20.

Structures of the Nervous system

The nervous system may be divided in several ways. One way is to distinguish between a central nervous system and a peripheral nervous system. The *central nervous system (CNS)* is that part of the nervous system—that is, the neurons, or parts of neurons, together with other supporting tissues—which lies within the bony case formed by the skull and spine. Those parts of the nervous system that lie outside this case make up the *peripheral nervous system (PNS).*

PERIPHERAL NERVOUS SYSTEM   The peripheral nervous system consists in part of the fibers of sensory and motor neurons. The sensory, or afferent, fibers run from receptors into the central nervous system; the motor, or efferent, fibers run out from the central nervous system to excite muscles or glands. These fibers are collected together in bundles called *nerves*. For most of the journey to and from the central nervous system, these nerves are both sensory and motor. Some of the nerves entering and leaving the skull, however, are only sensory or only motor. All nerves, moreover, usually divide just outside the central nervous system into two roots, a sensory root and a motor root (see Figure 19.11). They do this because they have different points of origin and departure within the central nervous system.

All of this applies to *fibers* of the peripheral nervous system. This system has two main divisions: the autonomic and the somatic systems. The *autonomic system* was discussed briefly in connection with emotion (see Chapter 7). It is largely a motor system serving the blood vessels, heart, glands, and other internal organs of the body. The *somatic system* is both sensory and motor; it serves the various senses we have described as well as the skeletal muscles of the body involved in standing, walking, writing, and instrumental behavior in general.

Both the autonomic and somatic systems contain cell bodies as well as fibers. The cell bodies are collected together in groups called *ganglia*. Arranged along the spinal column are two series of ganglia: One consists of certain of the *autonomic ganglia*—the sympathetic ganglia—containing cell bodies of the autonomic, sympathetic motor fibers; the other consists of the *sensory ganglia,* or *dorsal root ganglia,* of the somatic system (see Figure 19.11). The cell bodies of somatic motor-nerve fibers,

THE SOMATIC AND AUTONOMIC GANGLIA OF THE PERIPHERAL NERVOUS SYSTEM

FIGURE 19.11. *The relationships between the spinal cord and the somatic and autonomic ganglia. The spinal nerve divides into two roots just before the fibers enter the spinal cord. One of these roots, the dorsal root, is sensory; the other, the ventral root, is motor. The cell bodies of the sensory dorsal root are clustered in a ganglion on the dorsal root, the dorsal root ganglion. In addition, certain fibers from the spinal nerve feed into the sympathetic ganglia where synapses are made. From the sympathetic ganglia, after a synapse, fibers rejoin the spinal nerve to run to the smooth muscles of the organs of the body and blood vessels. The branches connecting the spinal nerve with the autonomic ganglia are called the* rami communicantes. *The coverings of the spinal cord—the* pia mater, *the* arachnoid, *and* dura mater—*are also shown. (From Gardner, 1963; and Morgan, 1965.)*

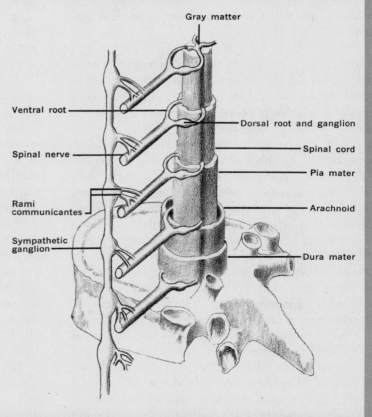

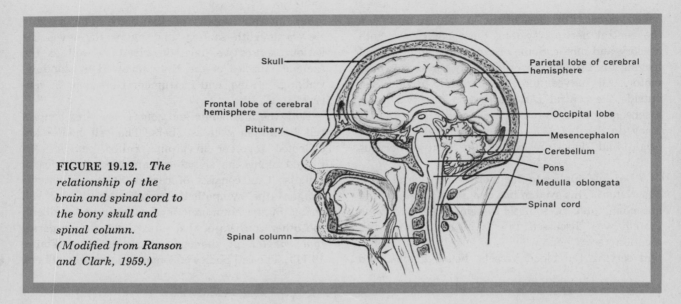

FIGURE 19.12. *The relationship of the brain and spinal cord to the bony skull and spinal column. (Modified from Ranson and Clark, 1959.)*

Labels in figure: Skull; Frontal lobe of cerebral hemisphere; Pituitary; Spinal column; Parietal lobe of cerebral hemisphere; Occipital lobe; Mesencephalon; Cerebellum; Pons; Medulla oblongata; Spinal cord

however, are found inside the central nervous system.

CENTRAL NERVOUS SYSTEM   The neurons within the central nervous system are more or less segregated into centers and pathways. The pathways consist of bundles of fibers, and the centers are made up of cell bodies. Very frequently, however, the cell bodies in the centers have very short fibers that synapse with neighboring neurons within the center. Fibers in the pathways also usually synapse with other neurons in these centers. The center, therefore, is something of a mixture of cell bodies and fibers. Centers have specific names depending on where they are and how they are arranged. Sometimes they are called *nuclei,* in other cases, *ganglia,* and in still others, simply *areas.* We shall have occasion to use all three terms, but it should be remembered that they refer to centers, or collections of cell bodies, where synapses are usually made.

A coincidence of nature makes it relatively easy to distinguish centers and pathways as one looks at the nervous system either with the naked eye or under a microscope. The normal color of a neuron is gray. As we said, however, most of the fibers in the nervous system have a myelin sheath around them and this is white. The cell bodies, on the other hand, do not have this sheath. Consequently, to the observer, pathways appear white and collections of cell bodies appear gray. Thus we often refer to pathways as *white matter* and to centers as *gray matter.*

THE SPINAL CORD   The central nervous system is organized regionally into two principal parts: the *spinal cord* within the spinal column, and the *brain* within the skull (see Figure 19.12). A cross section of a spinal cord is shown in Figure 19.13. Notice that its center is gray and its outside is white. The central gray thus consists of cell bodies of neurons, and the white conducting pathways are outside. Notice that motor pathways bringing impulses down from the brain are toward the front and sides of the cord. The sensory, or ascending, pathways are in several bundles in the white matter; pathways for muscle, or kinesthetic, sensibility and some aspects of touch sensibility are toward the back of the cord; those for temperature, pain, and other aspects of touch sensibility are in two bundles at the side and front.

The spinal cord, generally speaking, has two functions: as a conduction path to and from the brain, and as an organ for effecting reflex action. Hardly any reflex is unaffected by impulses descending from the brain, yet many can be seen as purely spinal affairs when the brain is disconnected from the cord in experimental animals. In fact, the extension, flexion, and scratch reflexes that we mentioned earlier, as well as the basic pattern of alternating steps in walking, are organized at the spinal level.

THE BRAIN   Of the two principal parts of the nervous system, the brain is more interesting than the spinal cord to psychologists because it plays the central role in all complex activities; learning, thinking, perception, and so on. Its part in these processes is the subject of study in the next chapter. In order to understand it, however, we must take time to outline the general structure of the brain. The principal divisions of the brain are diagrammed and labeled in Figure 19.14. They may be considered in three main groups: the hindbrain, midbrain, and forebrain.

1. Within the *hindbrain* are the *cerebellum,* the *pons,* and the *medulla.* The medulla contains vital centers for breathing and heart rate, but it also includes centers that relay sensory impulses upward to the midbrain and forebrain. The cerebellum is one center, but not the only center, for motor coordination; it helps make our movements smooth and accurate. By making use of vestibular and kinesthetic impulses, it also is an organ essential for maintaining posture and balance. The pons consists of fibers connecting the portions, or hemispheres, of the cerebellum on one side with those of the other side. It also contains upward and downward coursing tracts and various nuclei of the central nervous system.

2. The *midbrain* contains a number of tracts which convey impulses upward and downward; it also has important centers in it controlling reflex postural changes of the body in response to visual and auditory stimulation. In addition, the midbrain contains a number of motor nuclei—some of those responsible for eye movement, for example. The two main portions of the midbrain are the upper "roof," or *tectum,* and the lower portion, or *tegmentum* (see Figure 19.14).

3. The *forebrain* is the "highest" part of the brain. Although it was slow to develop in the course of evolution, it has become a very highly developed part of the brain in the higher animals and man. Its mass is considerably greater than that of the midbrain or hindbrain (see Figure 19.14). Many parts of the forebrain are known to take part in complex behavior, but the parts of greatest interest to us fall into three main groups: the *cerebrum,* which is covered by the "bark of the cerebrum," or the *cerebral cortex;* the *thalamus;* and a group of closely related structures forming the *limbic system.* The *hypothalamus, septal area, amygdala,* and *cingulate gyrus* are, for our purposes, the most important structures of the limbic system. The cerebral cortex and thalamus are shown in a different type of section —a frontal section—of the brain in Figure 19.15. Frontal, or coronal, sections are cut at right angles to the medial section shown in Figure 19.14. Outside

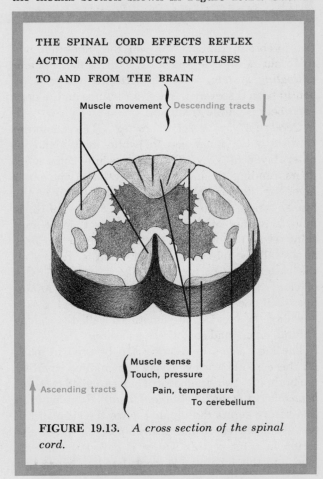

THE SPINAL CORD EFFECTS REFLEX ACTION AND CONDUCTS IMPULSES TO AND FROM THE BRAIN

Muscle movement   Descending tracts

Muscle sense
Touch, pressure
Pain, temperature
To cerebellum

Ascending tracts

FIGURE 19.13.   *A cross section of the spinal cord.*

THE FOREBRAIN IS HIGHLY DEVELOPED IN MAN AND THE HIGHER ANIMALS

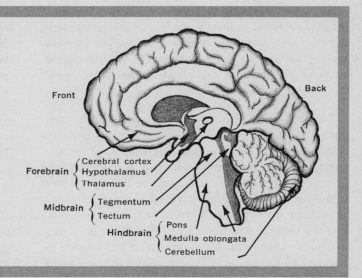

FIGURE 19.14. *Some of the principal parts of the human brain. This is a medial view. In other words, the brain has been cut in half along the longitudinal fissure and we are looking at the medial surface of the right brain. The hindbrain, midbrain, and forebrain, up through the thalamus, form a kind of stalk or stem and for this reason these structures are sometimes collectively referred to as the brain stem.*

the forebrain, running through the hindbrain and midbrain is another set of structures, the *reticular activating system,* whose importance has only recently been discovered. These structures and regions each bear separate treatment.

Cerebrum and cerebral cortex. The cerebrum consists of an inner core of white matter and an outer layer of gray. The inner white consists of fibers running to and from the cells in the outer layer, or the cerebral cortex. A photograph of the human brain, such as the one in Figure 19.16, is more a picture of the cerebral cortex than of anything else, because the cerebrum which encloses almost all the forebrain and midbrain is covered by the cortex. The cortex looks like a rumpled piece of cloth that has many ridges and valleys. Anatomists call one of these ridges a *gyrus* (plural, gyri); a valley, or crevice, is sometimes called a *sulcus* (plural, sulci) and sometimes a *fissure.*

The large sulci, or fissures, can be used to mark off the cerebral cortex. Along the midline dividing the brain into two symmetrical halves, called *cerebral hemispheres,* is the *longitudinal fissure.* Running from this fissure across the top and down the sides of the two hemispheres is the *central fissure.* All of the cortex in front of this fissure is called the *frontal lobe,* and this lobe may be considered an expressive

part of the brain because it contains motor centers for controlling movements and actions. The cortex behind the central sulcus has been called the receptive part of the cortex because it contains the centers at which incoming sensory impulses arrive. (Although there are many exceptions to these statements, they serve as a reasonably good way of dividing the functions of the cerebral cortex.) Finally, along the side of each hemisphere is a crevice known as the *lateral fissure.* The cortex below it and to the side of it makes up the *temporal lobe.* Two other lobes of the cerebral cortex are not set off by any major fissures on the outside cortical surface; these are the *parietal lobe* and *occipital lobe.* The parietal lobe lies immediately behind the central sulcus, and the occipital lobe is the cortex lying under the back of the skull. The functions of these lobes are described in Chapter 20.

Thalamus. The thalamus lies just above the midbrain, well enveloped by the cortex and other structures of the forebrain (see Figure 19.14). It is best thought of as a relay station, although some of its parts have other functions. Impulses from receptors, coming into the spinal cord, hindbrain, and midbrain, make their way, after intervening synapses, to centers in the thalamus. Thalamic centers relay impulses from below to various parts of the cortex—the receptive cortex. These thalamic nuclei are sometimes called the *extrinsic thalamic nuclei*. Other thalamic nuclei do not receive input from the receptors; instead, these centers, known as *intrinsic thalamic nuclei,* receive input from other thalamic nuclei and then send fibers on to the cortex. [Rose and Woolsey, 1949; Pribram, 1958].

The function of another projection system, the *reticular activating system (RAS),* is mentioned here because its function parallels that of the thalamus (see Figure 19.17). It is not properly a part of

the forebrain, but, like the thalamus, it is a sensory relay station on the way to the cerebral cortex [Lindsley, 1958]. The thalamus is a direct relay to the cerebral cortex, and its projection is relatively specific. Visual impulses, for example, arrive at a visual center in the thalamus and are relayed to a visual area of the cortex. Hearing and many of the other senses similarly have their own thalamic nuclei and their respective areas of projection on the cerebral cortex. This is not the case, however, with the RAS which is a relatively diffuse system. It re-

ANOTHER VIEW OF THE BRAIN

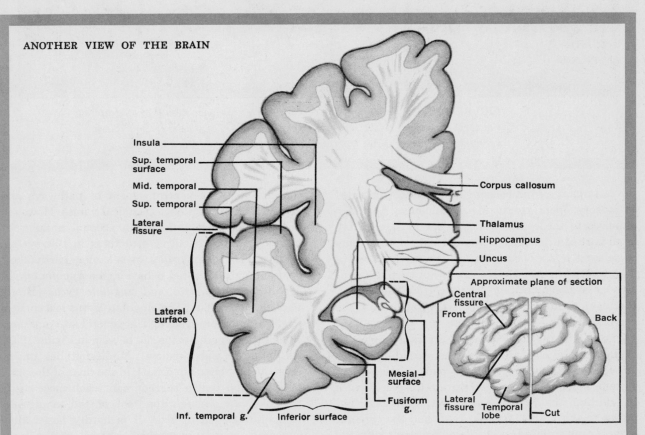

FIGURE 19.15. *A cross section of the brain showing one cerebral hemisphere. The plane of the section is approximately as shown in the inset. Note the temporal lobe under the lateral fissure. Some of the gyri (g) of this lobe are labeled. The shaded area shows depth of the cortex. Other structures—the insula, thalamus, corpus callosum, and hypothalamus—appear. (Modified from Penfield and Roberts, 1959.)*

THE CEREBRAL CORTEX IS LIKE
A RUMPLED PIECE OF CLOTH
THAT HAS MANY RIDGES AND
VALLEYS

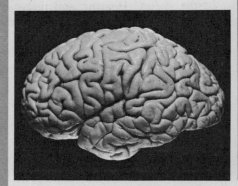

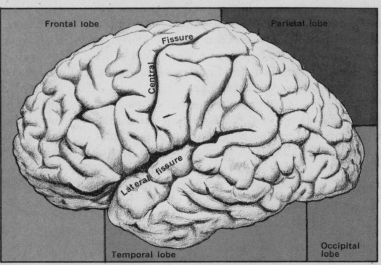

FIGURE 19.16. *The lobes of the cerebral cortex. Left, an actual photograph of the cerebral cortex. Right, a sketch to show the lobes of the cerebrum. These are lateral views, or views from the side. (Modified from Gardner, 1958.)*

ceives impulses from sensory systems "on the side" as sensory fibers ascend to the thalamus. It relays impulses to the cerebral cortex, but to a relatively large part of it. Although more visual impulses may be relayed to the visual area of the cerebral cortex than to other areas, the RAS does not keep different sensory systems entirely separate from each other. Rather it seems to activate wide regions of the cerebral cortex—hence its name.

The part of the RAS that relays sensory impulses to the cerebral cortex is called the ascending reticular activating system. Another part, a descending system, sends impulses downward to the spinal cord. In addition, the cerebral cortex also sends back impulses to the RAS. Thus the RAS and the cerebral cortex form a closed loop in which impulses in the RAS arouse the cerebral cortex, but those in the cortex in turn arouse the RAS. We shall examine later the part that may be played by the RAS in sleep and alertness.

Limbic system. Of particular interest is another region of the forebrain—the limbic system—which

contains a complex arrangement of pathways and centers. All of them have technical names. However, in order not to complicate our account unduly, we need note only the three structures in this system which are most important in behavior, particularly emotion and motivated behavior, the *hypothalamus, septal area, amygdala,* and *cingulate gyrus* [Brady and Bunnell, 1960]. The cingulate gyrus is a cortical part of the limbic system. The general size and position of the hypothalamus can be seen in Figure 19.18. As "hypo" (under, below) implies, it lies underneath the thalamus in a nook in the floor of the skull in a position that a surgeon can reach most easily by going up through the roof of the mouth. Its comparatively small size—it is hardly larger than a peanut—stands in marked contrast to the large number of its very important functions.

The relation of the hypothalamus to the septal area and amygdala is diagrammed in Figure 19.18. The septal area, which is also a relatively small structure, lies in front of and above the hypothalamus in the median plane. The amygdala, or amygdaloid complex, lies somewhat to the side of the hypothalamus. Actually all three structures, like others in the brain, are symmetrically paired. The septal area and hypothalamus, however, lie along the midline so that their two sides are adjacent. The amygdala is not a midline structure, and hence there are two amygdaloid nuclei, one on either side. The fact that all structures have two halves, however, should not be forgotten. Even within the midline structures, the various nuclei are always found in pairs.

The precise connections between these structures are not yet known. They are connected with each other in both direct and roundabout ways, but both the septal area and the amygdala appear to send fibers into the hypothalamus. In a very general way, it may be said that the fibers from the septal area appear to be inhibitory, while those from the amygdala seem to be excitatory—at least, in certain species of animals and under certain conditions. In other words, activity in the septal area sometimes seems to inhibit certain behaviors—the expression of rage, for example—that are organized in part by the hypothalamus. Input from the amygdala apparently excites certain regions of the hypothalamus.

The internal environment

The nervous system is that part of the body most directly tied to behavior, but this system, in common with other organ systems, is itself sensitive to, and to some degree controlled by, the internal environment—*le milieu intérieur* [Bernard, 1859]. The *internal environment* consists of all those chemical, temperature, and stimulus conditions within the body that form an environment for its organs and systems, just as the atmosphere and the external world of stimuli constitute the external environment for the organism.

Many examples of the control which the internal environment exerts on the central nervous system may be noted. For instance, some cells in the hypothalamus are sensitive to the concentration of the blood plasma (see Chapter 6). Other cells in the

hypothalamus seem sensitive to blood temperature. Still other cells in the hypothalamus, the reticular activating system, and portions of the sympathetic division of the autonomic nervous system are sensitized by certain hormones—especially epinephrine and norepinephrine—which circulate in the blood (see Chapter 7). In addition, other hormones may act somewhat less directly to affect the metabolism,

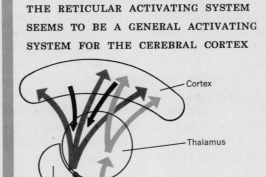

THE RETICULAR ACTIVATING SYSTEM SEEMS TO BE A GENERAL ACTIVATING SYSTEM FOR THE CEREBRAL CORTEX

Cortex

Thalamus

Midbrain

Medulla

Hypothalamus

Spinal cord

Reticular system

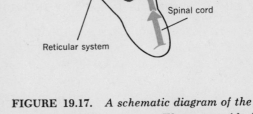

FIGURE 19.17. *A schematic diagram of the reticular activating system. The system (dark region) comprises an indirect sensory pathway (gray arrows) to several areas of the cortex; it receives collaterals from the direct sensory pathway (orange arrows). Pathways also lead back (black arrows) from the cortex to the reticular system, thus forming a loop.*

and hence the excitability, of large masses of neurons in the cerebral cortex. Deficiencies of these hormones may lead to certain types of mental retardation. Further, enzymes affect the nervous system generally, and, when certain of them are deficient, mental retardation can result. Enzymes are also involved in the transmission of nerve impulses at synapses. Finally, when the internal environment is markedly altered by drugs or lack of oxygen, marked changes in behavior occur (see Chapter 15).

Not only does the internal environment affect the nervous system; the nervous system, through neural impulses set up by events in the external environment, affects the internal environment—especially the production of hormones. Thus we have the possibility of a rather complex set of interactions: Neural impulses set off by events in the external environment may cause hormones to be released; these hormones change the internal environment; the alteration of the internal environment, in turn, affects the nervous system to produce behavior.

ENDOCRINE GLANDS   The endocrine glands secrete *hormones*—that is, chemical substances which are poured directly into the blood. A great many hormones are known to exist, although physiologists have not yet identified all of them. Nonetheless, they

do know many of them well, even to the point of being able to synthesize some of them. They also know the functions in metabolism of many of the hormones. Figure 19.19 gives the names and positions in the body of the principal glands that produce hormones. Those that we describe here may have some bearing on behavior.

Thyroid gland.   The thyroid gland, located in the tissue of the neck around the windpipe, produces a hormone known as *thyroxin*. This hormone controls the general rate at which energy is produced in the body. If the amount of thyroxin is low, energy is produced slowly, even though the body may have ample food resources. The individual is sluggish and shows many medical signs of low metabolism. With too much thyroxin, the individual is usually extremely active and shows signs of high metabolism. Thyroxin, then, regulates metabolic rate.

Since the thyroid hormone regulates the rate of metabolism, or the utilization of energy, the brain and other tissues of the body cannot grow or function normally when it is deficient. Children with a lack of thyroxin may suffer from *cretinism,* the symptoms of which are mental retardation, dwarfism, a pot belly, and thick, rough skin. Fortunately, this disease can be recognized reasonably early and thyroid hormones can be administered to alleviate

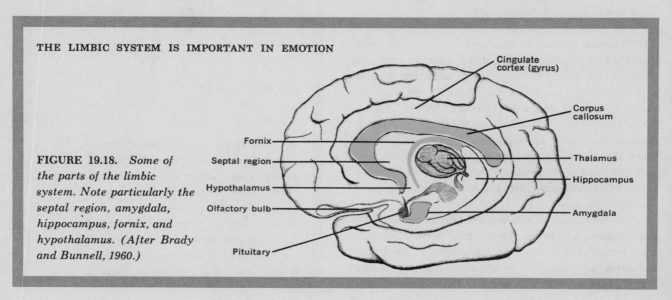

THE LIMBIC SYSTEM IS IMPORTANT IN EMOTION

FIGURE 19.18.   *Some of the parts of the limbic system. Note particularly the septal region, amygdala, hippocampus, fornix, and hypothalamus. (After Brady and Bunnell, 1960.)*

Cingulate cortex (gyrus)

Corpus callosum

Thalamus

Hippocampus

Amygdala

Fornix

Septal region

Hypothalamus

Olfactory bulb

Pituitary

it. Some of the effects of thyroid deficiency on brain function are probably irreversible, especially if the deficiency is severe, but hormone therapy helps the cretin to develop more normally and to have more nearly normal intelligence than he otherwise would. When a thyroid deficiency develops in adults, it is called *myxedema*.

Adrenal glands. We have already mentioned the adrenal glands in describing bodily changes in emotion (see Chapter 7). These glands are located in the back of the body above the kidney. The central part of the adrenal glands secretes the hormones *epinephrine* and *norepinephrine*. These hormones are released in strong emotion. The cortical, or outer, part secretes a number of hormones, collectively known as *cortin,* which govern the level of sodium and amount of water in the internal environment.

Gonads. The sex glands of the male and female are technically known as *gonads*. In the male, the gonads are called the *testes;* in the female, the *ovaries*. In each case, they occur in pairs. They secrete several related hormones, those of the male being somewhat different from those of the female. The sex hormones are not very active in young children. They come into play at puberty, when the child is about twelve years of age, and they are responsible for the marked physical changes that take place in girls and boys at that time—growth of the breasts, the beginning of menstruation, growth of the beard, and changes of the voice—all the secondary sex characteristics that distinguish girls from boys.

Pituitary gland. At first, the sex glands lie dormant under the control of the *pituitary gland*. It is not until the child is about eleven or twelve years old that the pituitary gland stimulates the gonads to secrete actively. The pituitary gland, in fact, secretes a number of hormones that stimulate or inhibit secretion in other glands of the body. For this reason, it is sometimes called the "master gland." In addition, the pituitary secretes other hormones that play a direct role in metabolism. One of these, the *growth hormone,* controls the general rate of growth in a child. If there is too little of it, he becomes a dwarf; if too much, a giant.

Hormonal action. It may be seen from this brief

THE ENDOCRINE GLANDS SECRETE HORMONES THAT CONTROL METABOLISM AND OTHER BODILY FUNCTIONS

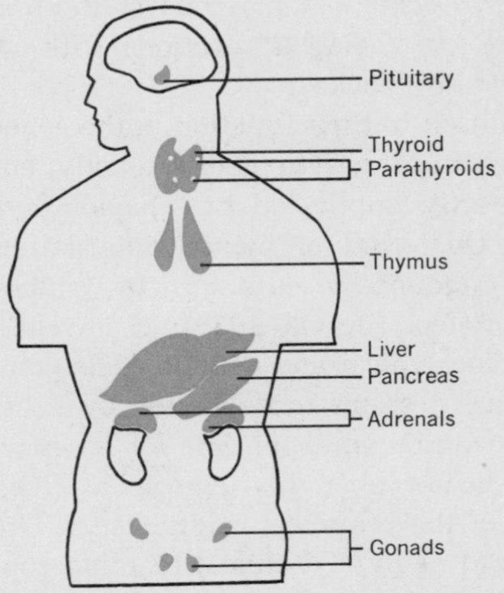

- Pituitary
- Thyroid
- Parathyroids
- Thymus
- Liver
- Pancreas
- Adrenals
- Gonads

FIGURE 19.19. *The names and positions in the body of some of the endocrine, or ductless, glands that secrete hormones.*

survey that the hormones take part in many aspects of the body's metabolism. Biochemists have been conducting intensive research in recent years to find out precisely how hormones participate in the chemical steps of metabolism. They have discovered that rather small amounts of them are required to maintain normal metabolism and that little of them is burned up in the course of metabolism. They conclude, therefore, that hormones are agents that help or hinder certain chemical steps without directly supplying the energy for them [Dempsey, 1946].

ENZYMES   The hormones, however, are not alone in the job of regulating metabolic reactions. In fact, they probably work by increasing or decreasing the supply of other agents known as *enzymes*. Enzymes result from chemical reactions taking place in various cells of the body. These enzymes are the intermediate agents that regulate particular chemical steps in metabolism. Each of the many known enzymes takes part in a particular reaction. For example, in the chemical reactions required to get sugar to the brain or to make use of the by-products of the burning of sugar, several specific enzymes are involved in some steps. If one of these enzymes is deficient, the chemical reactions with which it is concerned are blocked.

In addition to their function in the general regulation of chemical reactions of the body, enzymes are more directly implicated in behavior in certain instances. One kind of mental retardation, *phenylpyruvic oligophrenia,* is known to be due to an enzymatic defect [Jervis, 1939]. It is relatively rare, but its biochemical and genetic causation is reasonably clear. It seems to be caused by a *single defective* gene which is responsible for an enzyme necessary to utilize phenylpyruvic acid. This acid is a product of the brain's burning of fuel. Ordinarily it is disposed of by a chemical reaction controlled by a specific enzyme. If this reaction is blocked and the acid accumulates in the brain, the individual becomes mentally retarded. The diagnostic sign of such mental retardation is excretion of phenylpyruvic acid, for some accumulated acid finds its way to the kidney, and individuals who excrete it are without exception mentally retarded if accumulations have been allowed to build up in the brain. Fortunately, there is a simple test for the presence of phenylpyruvic acid which can be given to infants. If an infant is found to have this metabolic disorder, the symptoms can be much alleviated by restricting his diet to substances which do not contain the building blocks out of which phenylpyruvic acid is synthesized.

The enzyme cholinesterase, as we have seen, inactivates the synaptic transmitter substance acetylcholine and is necessary for proper synaptic conduction. Some evidence exists that changes in the concentration of this enzyme, and probably acetylcholine also, take place in parts of the nervous system when an animal grows up in an enriched and complex environment [Bennett et al., 1964]. It is at least possible that part of the neural basis of behavioral plasticity will be found to be related to changes in enzyme concentrations taking place within nervous tissue.

THE INTERACTION OF THE INTERNAL AND EXTERNAL ENVIRONMENTS   The control which hormones and the external environment, acting jointly, exert over behavior—sexual behavior in this particular case—has been analyzed in detail in a species of pigeon, the ring dove [Lehrman, 1964]. The ring dove goes through a cycle of reproductive behavior which consists of courtship, tending the eggs, and raising the young. Experiments show that both males and females do not show the appropriate nest-building and egg-sitting behavior unless a pigeon of the opposite sex is present and behaves in ways appropriate to its sex. Just the presence of a nest and eggs in a nesting box is not sufficient to induce nesting behavior; the other bird, behaving properly, must be present also.

In other experiments, an ovarian hormone, progesterone, when injected into isolated male or female doves, resulted in nest-sitting. Injection of another ovarian hormone, estrogen, into isolated birds resulted in a period of nest building which was followed by sitting on the eggs. Injections of the pituitary hormone prolactin caused an increase in the growth of the crop, a special pouch in the throat into which a substance called "crop milk" is secreted for feeding the young. Thus these three hormones—two ovarian ones and one from the pituitary gland—affect the nervous systems of these pigeons to produce behaviors and secretions which are part of the reproductive cycle.

In the dove's normal reproductive cycle, stimulation by the behavior of the other pigeon and hormonal effects are combined. In fact, stimuli from behavior and the external environment are thought to trigger the secretion of the hormones which affect the nervous system to produce the reproductive behaviors. For instance, in the case of the female dove, the behavior of the male—bowing and cooing—triggers the hormonal release which, in turn, starts the behavior going. The sight of the behavior in another pigeon is probably the important event because experiments have shown that many of the behaviors of the reproductive cycle will occur when the birds can see each other through a glass partition, even though they cannot touch each other. Thus, through seeing the behavior of the other bird, a complex set of interactions is set in motion: The sight of a dove acting in a special way stimulates the other dove to secrete the appropriate hormone. This hormone causes the dove to act in a certain way; the partner bird is thus stimulated to secrete hormones; its behavior changes, acting as a further stimulus for the other bird—and so on. In addition, the presence of the nest and eggs stimulate the birds. The details of these complex mutual interactions need not concern us here, for the main lesson of this analysis is that hormones usually do not act alone to produce effects upon behavior; instead, hormones produce or alter behavior, in many cases, through a series of interactions with external stimuli.

Methods of study

This bird's-eye view of the organs and functions of greatest importance in behavior is supplemented by additional details in Chapter 20. The general problem of the biological, or physiological, psychologist is to correlate structures and functions of the body with the events of behavior. To do this, he must ordinarily combine a number of methods of study, employing those of the anatomist, the physiologist, and the psychologist. While the methods of the psychologist have been described extensively earlier in the text, those of the biologist have not. Hence, a sketch of these methods may be particularly relevant.

NEUROANATOMICAL METHODS To study the structure of the nervous system, the neuroanatomist must first find ways of distinguishing the fibrous pathways of the nervous system from the centers (nuclei and ganglia) containing cell bodies, and then of tracing the various connections among centers and pathways. In effect, he must attempt to learn the wiring diagram of the nervous system.

The very general features of such a diagram can be seen with the naked eye, once the nervous system

has been exposed to view. Because, as we have said, many of the fibers of the nervous system are clothed in a white myelin sheath while unmyelinated cell bodies are gray, the observer can tell roughly what is a pathway and what is a center merely by its color. This crude method, however, tells us little or nothing about the connections between neurons; it enables us neither to distinguish the "fine-grained" organization of centers and pathways into subdivisions, nor to trace the unmyelinated fiber pathways. Other methods are required.

Staining. One method is to stain the nervous system and then to study it closely under the microscope. Many stains are used. Some are picked up only by the granules in the cell bodies, hence making the cell bodies stand out clearly from the fibers. Other stains are picked up only by fibers—they usually lodge in the myelin sheath—enabling one not only to distinguish fibers from cell bodies but to trace the pathways of fibers from beginning to end.

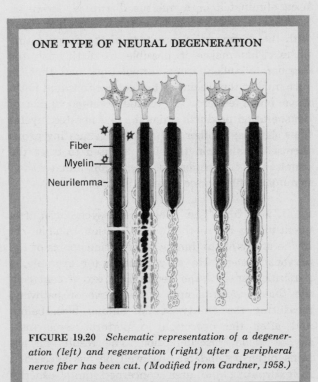

ONE TYPE OF NEURAL DEGENERATION

Fiber

Myelin

Neurilemma

FIGURE 19.20 *Schematic representation of a degeneration (left) and regeneration (right) after a peripheral nerve fiber has been cut. (Modified from Gardner, 1958.)*

Much has been learned about the nervous system with the aid of such stains.

Degeneration. Often staining methods are combined with a method utilizing degeneration. When a fiber is cut, the part away from its cell body degenerates. In the case of some, but by no means all, neurons in the central nervous system, degeneration from a cut fiber also proceeds toward the cell body to affect the whole neuron and to result in its death. This is called *retrograde degeneration.* Thus by cutting a pathway, or part of a pathway, and determining which cell bodies and fibers degenerate and die, one can establish the relation of centers and pathways. Peripheral neurons do not degenerate permanently; given the proper conditions, they can regenerate. This difference between peripheral and central neurons is not fully understood, but it is helpful in the study of the nervous system.

In this degeneration method, stains for fibers and cell bodies may be used to show that a pathway has been eliminated or a nucleus disrupted. However, it is also possible to use special stains which react with the degeneration products of the degenerating fibers. This makes it possible to distinguish the degenerated fibers from normal ones and that, in turn, makes the tracing out of connections and pathways much easier. One of the common stains of degeneration products stains the degenerated myelin fiber sheaths; another stains the degenerating axons themselves and can therefore be used to trace the course and connections of both unmyelinated and myelinated fibers (see Figure 19.21).

EXTIRPATION   The biological psychologist frequently uses the method of extirpation, or ablation, in the study of the functions of various parts of the nervous system. He may remove, for example, a particular area of the cerebral cortex, a center in the thalamus, or simply cut a nerve or pathway, measuring the ability of the animal both before and after the operation to perform some task, say, a visual discrimination. The results he obtains often depend on how well he has succeeded in extirpating the area concerned quite exactly. He frequently cannot determine this when he

is operating. So it is necessary at the end of an experiment to sacrifice the animal, prepare microscopic sections of the nervous system, stain them, and then map exactly the areas that have been destroyed.

Several methods of extirpating or destroying areas of the nervous system have been developed. The oldest one, and the one that is appropriate for relatively large, easily accessible areas, is simple excision, that is, cutting or sucking out with surgical instruments. This does not do, though, when the area is deep in the nervous system and relatively small. For this purpose, *electrolytic lesions,* or injuries, are frequently employed. To make such a lesion, the researcher pushes a fine wire or needle, insulated along its sides but not at its tip, to the desired place, and runs an electric current through the needle and the tissue surrounding its tip. If the current is of sufficient intensity and duration, the tissue around the tip of the needle is destroyed. The size of a lesion made in this way depends upon the size of the needle tip, the amount of current, the length of time it is on, and the type of current—for example, whether it is a direct current or a radio frequency current, and, if direct, its polarity. The needle, being quite fine, usually does not destroy any significant amount of tissue along the path of its insertion.

In making electrolytic lesions, the needle is usually held in a *stereotaxic instrument.* The animal is first anesthetized, his head placed in the instrument, a hole bored in the skull, and the needle lowered to the proper place in the brain. The purpose of the stereotaxic instrument is to allow exact placement of the electrode in the brain. For a particular structure, a nucleus in the hypothalamus, for example, the side-to-side, the front-back, and the vertical coordinates can be found in a special map, or atlas, of the brain. The stereotaxic instrument makes it possible to move the needle in the side-to-side, the front-back, and the vertical planes precisely the number of millimeters called for in the atlas.

ELECTRICAL RECORDING   As we have already noted, it is possible to record nerve impulses in neuron fibers by means of electrodes and a suitable amplifying and recording system. It is also possible to record larger scale activity. These large-scale activities, called *potential changes,* or simply, potentials, may consist of a great many nerve impulses, or spike potentials, firing at about the same time and place summated in one or more waves. Or, more likely, they may be records of more-or-less simultaneous changes in the EPSPs and IPSPs of a great many neurons (see page 678). Some of these potential changes may be thought of as representing relatively slow rhythmic changes in the resting potentials of large groups of neurons. In any case, the recording of potentials has been used to obtain some useful information about the functions of the nervous system. In general, three levels, or degrees of fineness, of recording may be distinguished.

Electroencephalogram. The grossest method of recording, and one which can easily be done with the intact animal or human being, yields what is known as the *electroencephalogram* (EEG). To obtain an EEG, the investigator attaches two or more electrodes firmly to the scalp; the output of the electrodes is suitably amplified and recorded on a tape. The position of the electrodes makes some difference, for some of the potentials recorded in the EEG are much stronger in some areas of the brain than in others. But with a suitable placement, potential changes, sometimes called "brain waves," may be recorded. The frequency and size of these waves change, as we shall see in the next chapter, with a number of conditions and can be correlated to some extent with what the subject is doing (see Figure 20.14, page 721).

Evoked potentials. A more refined method of recording involves placement of electrodes directly on or in the part of the nervous system being studied. In this case, one electrode is usually placed on the part that is of interest, while the second electrode is put at some neutral position in the body. The first, or active, electrode then picks up any potential changes occurring in the region near its placement. The wave that is recorded signals the presence of activity under the active electrode (see Figure 19.22).

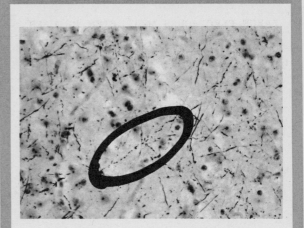

FIGURE 19.21.   *Degeneration as a tool for tracing pathways in the central nervous system. The normal fibers are continuous; the degenerated fibers show as strings of beads which are the remnants of degenerated fibers. A good example of a degenerated fiber is seen in the middle of the photograph; it runs from lower left to upper right. This is an example of the Nauta stain which stains degenerating axis cylinders differentially. In this case, a lesion was made in the lateral geniculate body and degeneration was found, as shown, in the visual cortex (see Chapter 20). (Courtesy of Dr. Mitchell Glickstein.)*

Electrical recording of this sort is valuable in "mapping" the nervous system. One can, for example, place an electrode on the cerebral cortex, and then touch the skin at different spots. By determining which electrode placements show the greatest electrical activity when a particular skin spot is stimulated, one can roughly establish the limits of the skin sensory area of the cortex. Incidentally, there are several such skin "maps" on the cortices of most animals. Such "maps" have also been made for several of the other senses and multiple "maps" seem to be the rule rather than the exception.

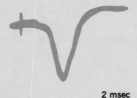

LARGE ELECTRODES MAY OFTEN BE USED
TO RECORD EVOKED POTENTIALS
FROM THE CENTRAL NERVOUS SYSTEM

2 msec

FIGURE 19.22. *An evoked potential from the sensory cortex of a cat. By stimulating the sensory pathway and recording the electrical activity evoked by this at distant points in the nervous system, pathways, and details of pathways, may be discovered. (From Towe, 1965.)*

The use of electrical recording to map areas of response in the nervous system often confirms or corrects conclusions reached from strictly neuroanatomical methods. In addition, however, it has frequently revealed areas and pathways that had escaped detection by neuroanatomical methods. Today, a considerable part of our knowledge of the sensory and motor areas of the brain rests on this method of electrical recording.

Microelectrodes. The most refined of all electrical recording methods is the *microelectrode technique.* As we have seen, this method employs an electrode that has been drawn out so finely that its tip is smaller than the size of a single cell body. Hence, when it is inserted into the nervous system, the experimenter can record spike potentials from inside or just outside individual neurons (see page 373). Often, when the record is obtained from the outside, more than one neuron contributes spike potentials to the record (see Figure 19.23). Because of the all-or-none law, the experimenter knows that spikes of different size must come from different neurons. By recording impulses in this way,

while presenting known stimuli either to the sense organs of the animal or to other specified regions of the nervous system, the extremely "fine grain" of the nervous system can be studied and the responses of particular neurons to particular kinds of stimulation can be determined. The method has been most useful in the study of sensory and perceptual mechanisms (see page 330 and page 373).

STIMULATION METHODS   Electrodes can be used to stimulate, as well as to record from, neural tissue. In fact, the same electrodes may sometimes be used at different times both for stimulation and for recording. More often, one pair is employed in one place for stimulation, and another pair at a different site is used for recording. In this way, activity in the nervous system can be traced from one point to another. The stimulus used is usually an electrical pulse or series of pulses generated by a specially designed stimulator.

One of the first uses of the method of electrical stimulation was in the excitation of the so-called "motor areas" of the cortex (see Figure 20.1, page 700). In fact, these areas were first mapped by means of this method. A neutral, or inactive, electrode is attached to the skull or body and the active electrode is touched to a point on the exposed surface of the cerebral cortex. Because there is a pathway leading from the motor cortex downward to the muscles of the body, stimulation of the motor area of the cortex causes the subject to make various kinds of movements. Stimulation at one point in the cortex causes one movement in a particular part of the body; stimulation at another point causes another movement somewhere else. By keeping track of the movements evoked by stimulation at various points, one can construct a map of the parts of the body controlled by different parts of the motor cortex (see Figure 20.4, page 704).

In recent years, this method has been used in conscious human subjects to explore areas of the cortex concerned in sensation and memory [Penfield and Rasmussen, 1950]. This is done, of course, only when a patient is being operated on for some other reason, usually for the removal of a brain tumor.

The stimulation is done under local anesthesia so that the patient feels no pain but at the same time is fully conscious. Electrodes are then used to stimulate various points on the cortex while the patient reports what he experiences. The method yields considerable information about the functions of the cerebral cortex. It also enables the surgeon to remove a tumor while keeping to a minimum the damage to those areas most concerned in sensory experience and memory.

A method of permanently implanting electrodes for purposes of stimulation has been developed. A fine wire or needle, similar to one used for recording, is inserted in the brain. It is suitably attached to the skull with a socket or connection outside the skin. Then, when the experimenter wishes to stimulate the spot at the tip of the electrode, all he needs to do is to hook up the connector to a stimulator (see Figure 19.24). This method is now commonly used in the study of the functions of the deeper parts of the brain. The stimulus applied through the electrode may be controlled either by the experimenter or by the subject. In certain sites, as we shall see, electrical stimulation is definitely "pleasant"—a subject often closes a switch to deliver stimulation to himself [Olds and Milner, 1954]. Stimulation by elec-

trodes placed in other regions of the brain results in "unpleasant" sensations; at least the subject will respond in order to stop stimulation in these areas [Olds and Olds, 1963].

Although the method of local stimulation usually employs an electrical stimulus, it can also be used with chemical stimuli. In such a case, a small pipette is inserted instead of an electrode. Through the pipette, the experimenter can deliver small amounts of chemical substances in solution and study the response of the particular area to different substances. The method has been employed to advantage in experiments on the mechanism of thirst and hunger motivation [Grossman, 1960].

HORMONAL AND BIOCHEMICAL METHODS   We cannot detail the many biochemical procedures useful in the study of behavior. Instead, mention will be made of two methods used to study the effects of hormones on behavior.

Gland removal. The oldest method of determining the function of an endocrine gland is its surgical removal. By choosing certain measurements to be made on the organism before and after the removal of the gland, the effects of removal can be determined. Some of these measurements may, of course,

THE ACTIVITY OF SINGLE CELLS AND FIBERS MAY BE RECORDED BY MICROELECTRODES

FIGURE 19.23.   *Record of the firing of single cells. Note that two fibers seem to be contributing to the record. Large spikes apparently come from one fiber, while the smaller one apparently comes from other fibers. (Compare with Figures 10.28 to 10.30.) (From Hubel and Wiesel, 1962.)*

WITH CHRONICALLY IMPLANTED ELECTRODES THE BRAIN CAN BE
STIMULATED WHILE THE ANIMAL IS BEHAVING

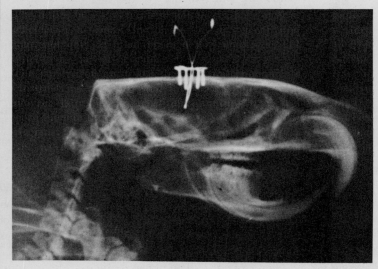 

FIGURE 19.24.   *Left, an X-ray photograph of an electrode chronically
implanted in the brain. Right, the electrode is in a self-stimulating circuit
and the rat is pushing a bar to stimulate his brain. (Olds, 1956; University
of Michigan.)*

be behavioral. In the case of sex behavior, for example, the role of the male and female sex glands, or gonads, has been studied by employing some measure of sexual activity such as number of copulations or number of items of sexual activity displayed in a period of time.

Replacement therapy. The method that complements gland removal and enables an experimenter to check on some of the conclusions drawn from gland removal is the method of replacement therapy.

After a gland has been removed, the hormone of the gland is "replaced," usually by injecting it directly into the blood stream. This method is particularly useful where a gland secretes several different hormones, as many of the glands do, for it permits separation of the effects of the different hormones. It is also convenient because it is reversible; by injecting the hormone or not injecting it, one can repeatedly compare the behavior of the same animal with and without a particular hormone.

SYNOPSIS AND SUMMARY

The correlations between behavior, experience, and events in the body—especially in the nervous system and internal environment—are extremely complex.

Still, people persist in this search for correlation, because, for some, understanding behavior in physical terms is satisfying intellectually. In addition to being satisfying, the "reduction" of behavior to its underlying molecular events would put the explanation of behavioral events into the domains of other sciences—physiology, anatomy, chemistry, and physics, for example. Many of the established laws and principles of those sciences would then have a bearing on behavior. Unfortunately, we are still a long way from understanding even the relatively simple behaviors—classical conditioning, for example—in physiological, anatomical, or chemical terms.

In this introduction to the study of the relationships between body and behavior, we have considered the anatomy and function of neurons and synapses, the gross anatomy of the nervous system, the internal environment, and some of the methods of study in physiological, or biological, psychology. In discussing these topics, we made the following points:

1. The basic unit of the nervous system is the neuron. It consists of a cell body, an axon, and one or more dendrites; the last two taken together are known as nerve fibers.

2. Stimulation of a nerve fiber to threshold generates a nerve impulse which obeys an all-or-none law; it either reaches full size or it does not propagate at all.

3. The nerve impulse, or the spike potential, is due to a rapid influx of sodium (Na^+) ions into the fiber. After the nerve impulse has passed a given point, the flow of potassium ions (K^+) out of the fiber increases to restore the fiber to its resting potential.

4. Impulses move down a fiber as local flows of current ahead of the active region depolarize the inactive region of the fiber to threshold.

5. While the fiber is occupied by the active spike potential, the fiber cannot be excited again and is said to be in the absolute refractory period. Immediately after this period, before the fiber has returned to its resting state, the fiber can only be fired by a very strong stimulus and it is said to be in the relative refractory period.

6. Between the end of one fiber and the fibers or cell body of another neuron is a gap called a synapse. Studies of electron microscope pictures of synapses reveal that the synaptic region contains a number of complex structures.

7. Transmission across synapses in the nervous system of mammals seems to be chemically mediated. When the nerve impulse reaches the end of a nerve fiber, the presynaptic fiber, a chemical transmitter substance is released into the synaptic gap. This transmitter substance crosses the gap and stimulates or inhibits the fiber on the far side of the gap, the postsynaptic fiber.

8. The excitatory and inhibitory synapses have distinct electrical potentials associated with them. The transmitter substance of the excitatory synapses stimulates by partially depolarizing the postsynaptic fiber and produces an excitatory postsynaptic potential (EPSP) in this fiber; the transmitter substance of inhibitory synapses inhibits by hyperpolarizing the postsynaptic fiber. This hyperpolarization is recorded as an inhibitory postsynaptic potential (IPSP).

9. If the synaptic activity depolarizes the cell to threshold, it will fire and an all-or-none spike potential will be propagated down its fibers.

10. Neurons form many different kinds of synaptic connections. One arrangement is the reflex arc, the simplest form of which consists of a sensory neuron, a synapse, and a motor neuron. More complex reflex arcs involve association neurons between the sensory and motor neurons. Reflex arcs are involved in such reflexes as flexion and extension.

11. In most reflexes, muscles are arranged in antagonistic pairs, so that when one antagonist contracts, the other relaxes. This relaxation is brought about by reciprocal inhibition from impulses arriving over sensory fibers which originate in the contracting muscle.

12. The nervous system has two main divisions: (a) a peripheral system, which consists, in turn, of an autonomic system and a somatic system, and (b) the central nervous system contained within the bony cavities of the skull and spine.

13. The peripheral nervous system conveys impulses to and from the central nervous system. The latter system consists of centers and pathways in the brain and spinal cord. The spinal cord, in turn, conveys impulses to and from the brain, but it also is responsible for spinal reflexes.

14. The brain has three principal divisions: hindbrain, midbrain, and forebrain. Within the forebrain, the parts of greatest importance to psychologists are the cerebral cortex, the thalamus, and the limbic system.

15. The internal environment consists of the chemical conditions in the blood and tissues. It is regulated, in part, by hormones and enzymes.

16. Hormones are produced by endocrine glands such

as the thyroid, adrenal, gonadal, and pituitary. Deficiencies in thyroid hormone can lead to the type of mental retardation known as cretinism.

17. Hormones probably do their work by regulating the supply of enzymes—substances manufactured in the body which act somewhat like catalysts to aid or hinder particular chemical reactions. Enzymes are directly related to behavior insofar as they control the activity of neurons and regulate the transmission of activity at synapses.

18. The internal and external environments interact in complex ways to produce behavior. Analysis has re-vealed many aspects of this interaction in the case of the reproductive behavior cycle of the ring dove.

19. The methods of studying neural and glandular functions most often used to establish correlations with behavior are (a) the neuroanatomical methods of making experimental injuries in the nervous system and tracing the degeneration that results, (b) electrical recording of both gross and minute electrical activities of the nervous system, (c) electrical, and sometimes chemical, stimulation of selected regions of the brain, and (d) the surgical removal of endocrine glands coupled with the injection of hormones into the blood stream.

RELATED TOPICS IN THE TEXT

CHAPTER 7   EMOTION   The effects of emotion-producing stimuli and prolonged stress on the adrenal and pituitary glands, and the effects of some of the hormones from these glands on behavior, are discussed. The student may wish to supplement the discussion of the behavioral effects of hormones given in Chapter 19 by referring again to Chapter 7 on emotion.

CHAPTER 8 AND CHAPTER 9   SENSORY PROCESSES AND VISION; HEARING AND THE OTHER SENSES   The transduction processes discussed in these chapters are but special cases of the depolarization of nerve fibers setting off impulses. Perhaps, after absorbing the information in Chapter 19, the statements about the afferent code for experience will also have more meaning.

CHAPTER 10   PERCEPTION   The single-cell recording done in the attempt to discover the nervous system correlates of perceptual organization might be reviewed. It should be much clearer now that we have discussed single-cell recording in Chapter 19. Note that the recording discussed in Chapter 10 is from outside, not inside, the cell.

CHAPTER 15   MENTAL HEALTH AND PSYCHOTHERAPY   The effects of various drugs used in the alleviation of psychoneurotic and psychotic reactions may be understood, broadly, as due to changes in the internal environment which affect the nervous system.

SUGGESTIONS FOR FURTHER READING

Brazier, M. A. B. *The electrical activity of the nervous system: A textbook for students* (2d ed.). London: Pitman, 1960.
   An elementary, but authoritative, treatment of the electrical phenomena of the nervous system.
Gardner, E. *Fundamentals of neurology* (4th ed.). Philadelphia: Saunders, 1963.
   An introductory text on the structure and function of the nervous system.
Morgan, C. T. *Physiological psychology* (3d ed.). New York: McGraw-Hill, 1965.
   A text on the physiological mechanisms of behavior with chapters on the nervous system and internal environment.

Ruch, T. C., and Patton, H. D. (Eds.). *Physiology and biophysics* (19th ed.). Philadelphia: Saunders, 1965. Chaps. 1–26; Chaps. 56–61.
   A text for use in medical school physiology courses. Chapters 1–26 provide an outline of the biophysics of neural processes, current knowledge in neurophysiology, and some aspects of biological psychology. Chapters 56–61 provide a summary of knowledge on the endocrine glands and their hormones. Liable to be difficult reading, but can be mastered with effort.
Stevens, C. F. *Neurophysiology: A primer.* New York: Wiley, 1966.
   A readable and authoritative introduction to neuronal and synaptic physiology.

ALTHOUGH THE PICTURE of the nervous system and internal environment given in Chapter 19 is extremely sketchy, it should have provided a background sufficient for our purposes here. Let us now explore the four areas where connections between brain and behavior have been established: the behavioral functions of the cerebral cortex, motivation, activation and emotion, and the biological basis of learning and memory.

Functions of the cerebral cortex

One of the major concerns of biological psychology has been to analyze the functions of the cortex of the cerebrum—that part of the brain which is most importantly involved in behavior and experience. Careful experimental work on the correlations between areas of the cerebral cortex and behavior has had a short history—about 100 years. During this time, many interesting discoveries have been made, and our speculations about cortical functions are somewhat more advanced than those of the ancients, but we still know comparatively little.

The methods used to investigate the functions of the cortex range from single-cell recordings by physiologists to studies in which whole areas of the cortex are removed, that is, *extirpated,* or *ablated,* and the behavior of the animal observed when it recovers. The experiments of the physiologist are usually *acute*—that is, the animal is anesthetized and not behaving throughout the experiment; ablation experiments are usually *chronic*—that is, after the tissue has been cut out, the behavior of the animal can be observed for as long as necessary. Because our interest is in behavior, we shall concentrate on the results of chronic ablation experiments in cats and monkeys. But first, we should describe, in brief, the general functional organization of the cortex.

FUNCTIONAL ORGANIZATION OF THE CORTEX
The cerebral cortex is composed of variously shaped cells, of which the pyramidal cell is one type (see

20

PHYSIOLOGICAL BASIS OF BEHAVIOR

IMAGINE ACTIVITY . . . SHOWN BY LITTLE POINTS OF LIGHT. . . . THE BRAIN IS WAKING AND WITH IT THE MIND IS RETURNING. IT IS AS IF THE MILKY WAY ENTERED UPON SOME COSMIC DANCE. SWIFTLY THE HEADMASS BECOMES AN ENCHANTED LOOM WHERE MILLIONS OF FLASHING SHUTTLES WEAVE A DISSOLVING PATTERN, ALWAYS A MEANINGFUL PATTERN THOUGH NEVER AN ABIDING ONE; A SHIFTING HARMONY OF SUBPATTERNS.
C. S. SHERRINGTON

THE CEREBRAL CORTEX MAY BE DIVIDED INTO AREAS

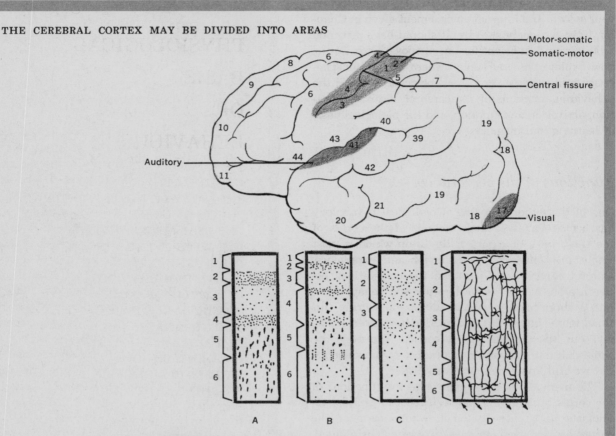

FIGURE 20.1.   *Above, the major sensory and motor regions of the human cerebral cortex are shaded; the other areas constitute the "association" cortex; the numbers are convenient labels for referring to parts of the cortex. Below, the layers of the cortex. Six layers are usually distinguished: the thickness of the layers varies from place to place over the cortex and this is one basis on which the cortex can be anatomically subdivided. In fact, the numbers in the top portion of this figure were assigned to areas with different layer thicknesses. The sketch at the lower right (D) illustrates some of the cells and fibers of the cortex in greater detail. (From Morgan, 1965; as modified from Cobb, 1941.)*

page 671), and fibers which connect these cells with each other and other parts of the brain. In most species of monkey and in man, most of the cortex is said to consist of six layers of cells. The six-layered cortex, or as it is sometimes called, the *neocortex*, is shown in Figure 20.1, bottom. Although, the boundaries between layers are often unclear, differences in the relative thicknesses of the layers make it possible to divide the cortex into several different anatomical regions to which numbers have been assigned (see Figure 20.1, top). Sometimes anatomical differences in regions can be correlated with functional differences, sometimes they cannot. For convenience and for organizational purposes, we may distinguish several major classes of functional cortical regions. One class consists of the so-called motor regions. Fibers leave these regions to play on neurons in the spinal cord and brain stem which are involved, either directly or indirectly, in movement. Stimulation of these motor areas of the cortex will therefore often result in movement.

Another class consists of the primary sensory areas, including the primary visual, auditory, and body-sense receiving areas of the cortex, which receive input from the sensory relay stations of the thalamus. Such a statement should not be taken to mean, however, that the motor and sensory areas of the cortex are sharply separated from each other and from other cortical regions. They are not. For instance, much of the so-called motor region is probably also a sensory receiving area for the body sense, or somesthesis; it is also true that movements can be elicited by stimulation of wide regions of the cortex [Lilly, 1958]; and finally, large regions of the cortex outside the primary sensory regions receive direct sensory input [Buser and Imbert, 1961]. Thus our statements about motor and sensory regions are relative statements: Movements are easier to elicit from the motor area, whereas the density of input through the sensory channels is greatest in the primary receiving areas.

Another major region of the cortex has not classically been considered to receive direct sensory input and it has not been considered to be motor. It has been called the "association" cortex, a term which implies that, in some way, it connects the sensory and motor cortices, or "elaborates" the input to sensory areas. While fiber pathways connect some regions of the cortex with other regions, the association cortex does not seem to link sensory and motor regions together; in fact, much association cortex seems to have special sensory functions of its own, and it seems to be involved, in humans, in the organization and sequencing of speech, and to participate, also, in other complex activities. The major anatomical areas of the "association" cortex in human, monkey, and cat brains are shown in Figure 20.1.

The regions of the "association" cortex may be designated, in terms of the lobes occupied, as parietal-occipital-temporal and frontal association areas. Although the classification of the cortex into motor, sensory, and "association" areas does not give a completely accurate picture, it nevertheless serves as a useful organizational device for discussion.

MOTOR AREAS The area of the cerebral cortex which is of special importance in movement and motor functions lies on both sides of the central fissure (see Figure 20.1). Fibers leave this region to contribute to the two major motor systems—the *pyramidal motor system* and the *extrapyramidal motor system*. The term pyramidal as it is used here refers to the fact that the fibers, as they pass along the lower surface of the medulla of the hindbrain on their way to the spinal cord, form a bundle which is rather cone- or pyramid-shaped. Pyramidal fibers pass into the spinal cord to influence motor neuron, or *motoneuron,* activity. The extrapyramidal system contains motor fibers which do not pass through the pyramids directly to the spinal cord. Fibers in this system leave the cortex and end in motor nuclei of the cerebrum and brain stem. After varying numbers of synapses, the extrapyramidal influence from the cortex—extrapyramidal fibers also arise from other brain regions, such as the cerebellum—reaches the motoneurons of the spinal cord to facilitate or inhibit their activity. In fact, it is useful to think of the motoneuron of the spinal cord or brain stem as the *final common path* which is excited or inhibited by influences from many diverse inputs in addition to the cortical ones we have been discussing [Sherrington, 1906]. Other regions of the cortex also contribute fibers to the pyramidal and extrapyramidal motor systems, but the majority come from this central region.

The motor functions of the cortex have most often been studied by stimulation and ablation methods. Stimulation with lightly anesthetized human patients has been carried out in the course of operations for tumors (see Figure 20.3). These observations, and others on animals, indicate that, although movements can be obtained from other parts of the brain,

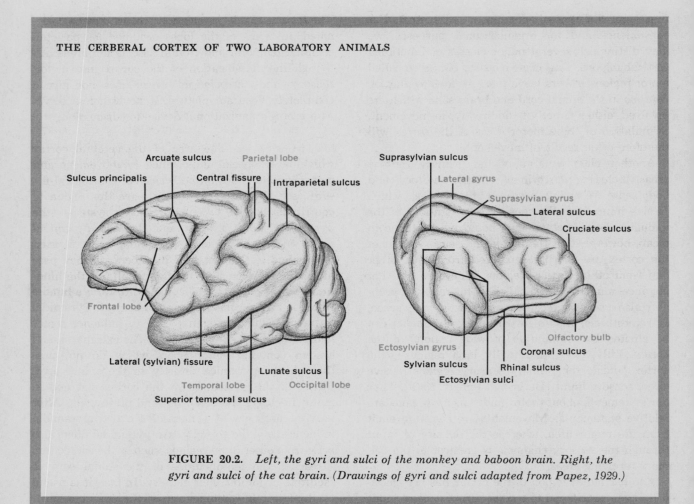

THE CERBERAL CORTEX OF TWO LABORATORY ANIMALS

FIGURE 20.2. *Left, the gyri and sulci of the monkey and baboon brain. Right, the gyri and sulci of the cat brain. (Drawings of gyri and sulci adapted from Papez, 1929.)*

the strip of cortex just in front of the central fissure—the precentral gyrus—is organized so that stimulation produces rather discrete movements of the body—the movement of a thumb or finger, for example. The kind of movement and the place that it occurs depend upon the point stimulated on the precentral gyrus. At the top of the area and around the bend into the longitudinal fissure, between the two halves of the cortex, a stimulus produces movements of the leg. A little to the side of this, a stimulus evokes movements of the trunk. Still more to the side is a region in which stimulation causes movements of the hand and arm. At the side and

bottom of the area, in the direction of the lateral fissure (see Figure 19.16, page 686), movements of the face and mouth are evoked. By carefully plotting each point on the cortex that evokes a movement, an investigator can construct a map of the cortex; one such map is illustrated schematically in Figure 20.4. It shows that the areas concerned with trunk and leg movements are relatively small; those for the hand are somewhat larger; and those for face, mouth, and tongue movements are quite large by comparison.

Another experiment demonstrating the functions of the motor area is one in which the areas are extirpated or otherwise destroyed. If, through surgery, cerebral hemorrhage, or other injury, some of the precentral motor area is destroyed, a paralysis results. Immediately after injury, the paralysis is usually *flaccid*—the muscles of the affected part of the body have little tone; after some time, the paralysis usually becomes *spastic*—muscle tone is increased, and limbs, if affected, may be stiff. If the whole precentral area on one side is damaged, a relatively complete paralysis of the opposite side of the body ensues because most fibers in the pyramidal system of man and many primate species cross over from one side to the other in their descending path through the pyramids. If only a part of the precentral motor area is destroyed, a partial paralysis of the corresponding portion of the opposite side of the body results.

SENSORY AREAS AND PATHWAYS The cortex receives strong inputs from many sensory channels. Among the senses strongly represented in the cortex are vision, hearing, some of the skin senses— warmth, cold, and touch—and taste. In Figure 20.1, the major areas of the cortex devoted to some of these senses are shown; however, as with the motor system, the cortical areas involved are not sharply limited. The sensory inputs go to areas other than those indicated in Figure 20.1. These figures show the major, or *primary*, sensory areas. Let us consider some of these pathways and their projections upon the cortex in greater detail.

Visual areas and pathways. The primary sensory area of the cerebral cortex for vision in man is at the back of the cerebrum on the medial surface along a fissure known as the *calcarine fissure* (see Figure

THE MYSTERIOUS ORGAN

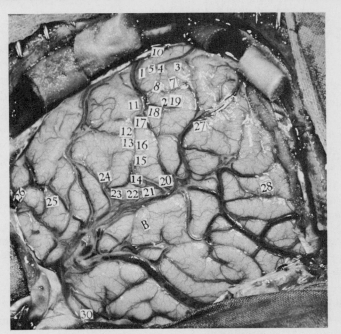

FIGURE 20.3. *Lateral view of human cerebral cortex exposed during an operation. The numbered tickets show points of stimulation and most of them are scattered along the central fissure. The temporal lobe is at the bottom of the picture. (From Penfield and Roberts, 1959.)*

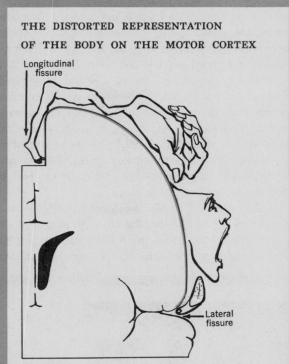

THE DISTORTED REPRESENTATION
OF THE BODY ON THE MOTOR CORTEX

Longitudinal
fissure

Lateral
fissure

FIGURE 20.4. *A depiction of the topographical
organization of the motor area on the
precentral gyrus. Both the motor area in front
of the central fissure and the body sense area
on the postcentral gyrus are so arranged that
the legs are represented near the top of the
area, the arms and hands in the middle, and
the face and mouth near the bottom. (After
Penfield and Rasmussen, 1950.)*

20.5). Figure 20.5 shows the visual pathway from
the retina to the brain. Fibers from the ganglion
cells make up the *optic nerve;* some of them cross to
the other side of the brain at the *optic chiasma,* and
some do not cross. After running through the *optic
tract,* the fibers reach the relay center for vision in
the thalamus, the *lateral geniculate body,* and from
here, after a synapse, fibers project through the *optic
radiations* to the visual sensory area of the cortex
(see Figure 20.5). On their route to the visual area

of the cortex, some fibers in the visual pathway (not
shown in Figure 20.5) go to visual centers in the
midbrain which are involved in reflex actions.

One of the interesting things about the projection
of some of the sensory systems to the brain is the
topographical arrangement which exists. The projection regions are arranged like maps of the sensory
surface. In the case of vision, for instance, the
lateral geniculate body in the thalamus and the
cortical area are arranged so that points on them
represent particular points of the retina. By recording with electrodes and by using degeneration
methods and staining techniques, it can be shown
that for every point on the retina there is a corresponding region in the thalamus and a cortical
area. This arrangement is sometimes called a point-
to-point projection.

The details of this projection are shown in Figure 20.5. First of all, the visual field is represented
as reversed in the right-left and up-down directions
as it is projected on to the retina (see page 283).
Next, the flat surface of the retina is projected,
through fiber connections, back to the brain in the
following manner: The fibers from the halves of the
retina toward the side of the head, or the temporal
regions, do not cross; they are projected back to the
lateral geniculate body of the same side. The fibers
from the halves of the retina toward the nose, or the
nasal regions, cross to the opposite side of the brain.
The point-to-point projection, as indicated by the
shading of Figure 20.5, is maintained in the lateral
geniculate and cortex. Another noticeable fact is
that the areas of both the lateral geniculate body
and the cerebral cortex which receive fibers from the
fovea are disproportionately large. Perhaps this is
part of the anatomical basis for the good visual
acuity of the fovea.

To understand the visual pathway a little better,
we might consider what would happen if a person
had lesions, or damage, in various parts of the visual
system. First of all, if the optic nerve has been
destroyed on the right side (see Figure 20.6, left),
the patient will, of course, be completely blind in his
right eye. Second, if a cut has been made through
the optic chiasma (see Figure 20.6, middle), the

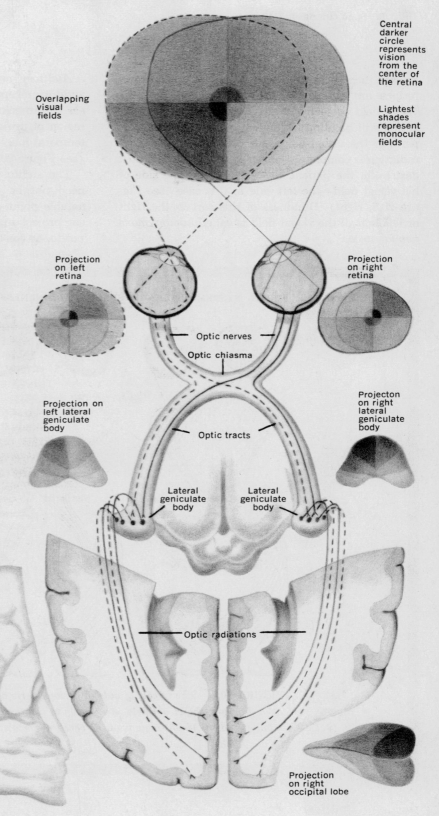

THE VISUAL ROUTE TO THE CEREBRAL CORTEX

FIGURE 20.5. *The projection of the visual fields on the retinas; the projection of the retinas onto the lateral geniculate bodies of the thalamus; and finally, the projection of the lateral geniculate bodies onto the cerebral cortex. Note that a medial view of the cortex is shown at the lower left; the view of the cortex in the lower middle portion is a horizontal one in which the section is parallel to the top of the head. (Modified from Netter, 1962; © Ciba, 1962.)*

Central darker circle represents vision from the center of the retina

Lightest shades represent monocular fields

Overlapping visual fields

Projection on left retina

Projection on right retina

Optic nerves

Optic chiasma

Projection on left lateral geniculate body

Projecton on right lateral geniculate body

Optic tracts

Lateral geniculate body

Lateral geniculate body

Optic radiations

Calcarine fissure

Projection on left occipital lobe

Projection on right occipital lobe

crossed fibers from the nasal halves of the two retinas are cut. Since the temporal parts of the visual field project onto the nasal retinas, the individual will be blind in the two temporal, or outside, parts of the visual fields. Finally, if the right optic radiation is completely cut, or the right visual cortex destroyed, the patient will be blind on one side of his visual field—the left side in this case (see Figure 20.6, right). Blindness of this sort in the right or left half of the visual field is called *homonymous hemianopsia*.

Auditory areas and pathways. Input from the auditory receptors of the organ of Corti in the inner ear is projected to the cerebral cortex. The major region of projection in humans is to the top of the temporal lobe—the lower bank of the lateral fissure (see Figure 20.7).

The auditory pathway is rather complex, and we need not be concerned with all its details. One notable point, however, is that the fibers from each ear project to the same, or ipsilateral, and the opposite, or contralateral, sides of the cerebral cortex.

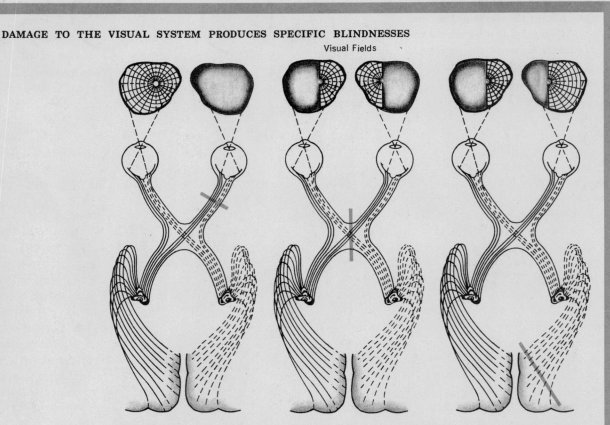

DAMAGE TO THE VISUAL SYSTEM PRODUCES SPECIFIC BLINDNESSES

Visual Fields

FIGURE 20.6. *The effects of cuts in various parts of the visual projection pathway. In each diagram, the visual fields are shown at the top, the retinas and pathways in the middle, and the visual regions of the cerebral cortex at the bottom. (After Teuben et al., 1960.)*

The functional significance of this crossing is that a lesion in the auditory area of one cerebral hemisphere does not produce deafness in either ear.

Topographic organization may also exist in hearing; but the arrangement is not nearly so precise and clear-cut as that for vision. We have already seen that different frequencies of sound waves stimulate different portions of the organ of Corti in the cochlea (see page 319). This co-called *tonotopic* organization may be preserved, in a rough way, in the cortex. For instance, Figure 20.7 shows that the base of the cochlea, which is stimulated by high frequencies, is projected toward the back of the cortex on the floor of the lateral fissure; the apex of the cochlea, which is stimulated most by the lower frequencies, is projected to the front portion of the cortical auditory primary sensory area. The middle range of frequencies is projected to the middle region of the auditory projection area. There is little doubt that the tonotopic organization on the cortex of the human, if it exists at all, is more complex than this, but our knowledge is based on clinical cases and it accumulates slowly. Experimental analyses of lower animals, the cat and monkey especially, have shown that several primary sensory areas seem to exist for audition and that each has its own rough tonotopic organization.

Somatic sensory areas. The skin, or somesthetic, receptors for warmth, cold, and touch also project to the cortex. The cortical primary sensory area for the somesthetic senses is mainly on the strip of cortex just behind the central fissure—the *postcentral gyrus* (see Figure 20.1). The principal of topographic arrangement is present in these projections. The upper part of the somesthetic cortex on the postcentral gyrus receives input from the legs and lower parts of the body, the middle part receives input from the arms and trunk, and the lower part receives input from the head, face, mouth, and tongue. This arrangement parallels quite closely the arrangement for movements in the part of the motor area just across the central fissure (see Figure 20.4).

Taste areas. Information from the taste receptors probably reaches the lower part of the somesthetic sensory region on the postcentral gyrus—the region of somesthetic projections from the face and mouth. In addition, taste sensitivity may be represented in the part of the cortex labelled *insula* in Figure 20.7.

SENSORY EXPERIENCE   Now that the centers and pathways of some of the various senses are known, we may go on to ask how they participate in sensory experience. There are two general methods for studying this question: stimulation and destruction.

The method of stimulation has been used with human subjects who, while under local anesthesia, have had their brains exposed in surgical operations (see Figure 20.3). While an electrical stimulus is applied, the subject is asked to report whatever he experiences [Penfield and Rasmussen, 1950]. The subject reports sensations of warmth or pressure when his somesthetic cortex is stimulated, visual experiences when his visual cortex is stimulated, and various sounds when his auditory cortex is the site of the stimulation. Interestingly enough, however, he never reports pain when his somesthetic areas are stimulated. The experience of pain is complexly determined, and no "center" for pain exists [Melzack and Wall, 1965].

Another method of studying the sensory functions of the brain involves the destruction of a particular area, accompanied by tests of the subject's sensory capacity both before and after the removal. This method, of course, is used ordinarily only with animals. It is occasionally used with human beings when injury or disease requires brain surgery. In general, experiments of this kind show that the cerebral cortex is concerned with the form, spatial, and temporal, or time, aspects of perception. Subcortical centers seem to be more important in mediating the intensity of experience [Morgan, 1965]. However, these are only general statements and therefore not true in every detail.

Visual experience. Vision is probably the best example of the general rule that the cortex is necessary for form perception and that subcortical centers can mediate intensity experiences. In most of the animals that have been studied, the primary visual

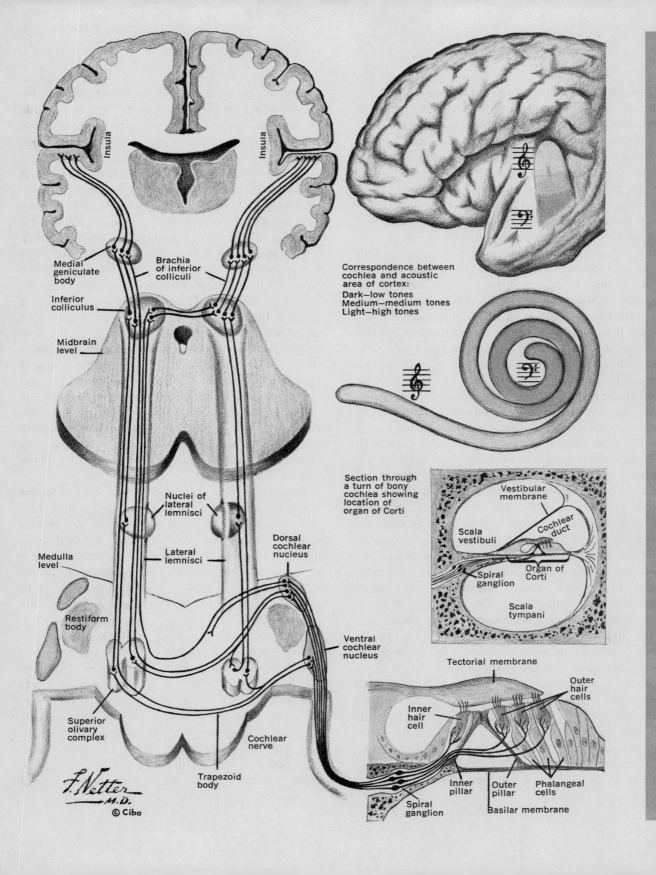

Insula

Insula

Medial
geniculate
body

Brachia
of inferior
colliculi

Inferior
colliculus

Midbrain
level

Nuclei of
lateral
lemnisci

Lateral
lemnisci

Dorsal
cochlear
nucleus

Medulla
level

Restiform
body

Ventral
cochlear
nucleus

Superior
olivary
complex

Cochlear
nerve

Trapezoid
body

Spiral
ganglion

F. Netter
M.D.
© Ciba

Correspondence between
cochlea and acoustic
area of cortex:
Dark—low tones
Medium—medium tones
Light—high tones

Section through
a turn of bony
cochlea showing
location of
organ of Corti

Vestibular
membrane

Scala
vestibuli

Cochlear
duct

Spiral
ganglion

Organ of
Corti

Scala
tympani

Tectorial membrane

Outer
hair
cells

Inner
hair
cell

Inner
pillar

Outer
pillar

Phalangeal
cells

Basilar membrane

sensory cortex is necessary for perception of patterns and visual detail [Klüver, 1942]. Remove this cortical area, and an animal usually cannot distinguish a triangle from a circle or vertical stripes from horizontal ones (See Figure 20.8). The same animal, however, can react to a light going on or off and can distinguish which of two panels is lighted. The ability to experience intensity, or, more accurately, luminous flux, as distinguished from spatial details, is therefore a property of subcortical centers rather than of the visual cortex. Presumably these subcortical nuclei are in the midbrain. We hasten to add, however, that in human beings, the cortex seems to have taken over some of these subcortical functions, for when people lose their visual cortex they are reported to be completely blind, although we are not entirely certain of this.

Auditory experience. If, as seems to be the case, hearing intensity experience, or loudness, is mediated by subcortical nuclei, what aspects of auditory experience are mediated by the auditory sensory areas of the cortex? In animals, good evidence exists that the localization of sounds in space depends upon the auditory cortex [Neff et al., 1956]. But is frequency discrimination, or the ability to distinguish between high and low tones, a cortical function? This may seem a simple question. Analysis, however, reveals that, even if the question is reasonable, it is not simply answered.

Some experiments have shown that discrimination of frequencies seems possible in the absence of the auditory cortex; others have shown that such discriminations are not possible with the auditory cortex removed. It seems clear that partial ablations of the auditory cortex do not result in loss of auditory frequency discrimination. Even with extensive removal of auditory cortex, however, conflicting results have been obtained. Much depends upon the way in which testing of the experimental animals is carried out. Some frequency discrimination seems

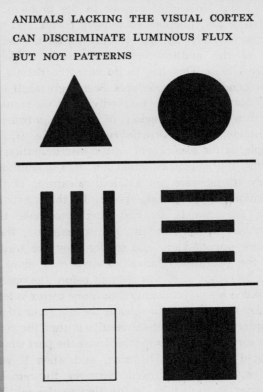

ANIMALS LACKING THE VISUAL CORTEX CAN DISCRIMINATE LUMINOUS FLUX BUT NOT PATTERNS

FIGURE 20.8. *Visual perception in animals lacking the primary visual cortex. In the absence of the visual cortex, rats cannot distinguish between the patterns in top and middle rows. They can, however, distinguish between the elements in the bottom row, for they are able to perceive the differences in brightness—or more correctly in luminous flux.*

THE AUDITORY ROUTE TO THE CEREBRAL CORTEX

FIGURE 20.7. *Input originating in the cochlea eventually reaches the superior surface of the temporal lobe. The sections on the left are cross sections of the medulla, midbrain, and cerebrum (frontal section). The drawing of the brain at the top right shows the temporal lobe pulled down and out to expose the superior surface; the supposed tonotopic organization of the human cortex is also shown. (Modified from Netter, 1962; © Ciba, 1962.)*

possible with all auditory cortex removed [Butler et al., 1957]. However, the discrimination of *frequency patterns* is markedly disturbed by auditory cortex removal [Diamond and Neff, 1957]. The positive and negative stimuli in this discrimination experiment consisted of patterns of tones— high-low-high versus low-high-low, for example. Cats with complete auditory cortex removal lose the discrimination habit if it was learned before the operation and they cannot relearn it with many post operative training trials.

Problems. No simple answer to the problem of correlating the functions of sensory cortex and experience is likely, as the experiments on the functions of the auditory cortex illustrate. Several problems exist. One has to do with the details of training and testing procedures. Seemingly small and insignificant details may markedly affect the results. Second, within many regions of cortex, *equivalence of function,* or *equipotentiality,* is possible. If, for example, in the experiment on the discrimination of patterns of frequencies, small amounts of auditory sensory cortex were not ablated, relearning of the discrimination could take place. In these experiments, the animals are first taught to make the discrimination without any cortex removed, then they are operated on, and finally they are tested after the operation. Almost always they show a failure to retain what was learned before the operation; but if a small amount of auditory cortex is left, they are usually able to relearn the discrimination. One interpretation of these results is that the part of the cortex which was removed was the part which mediated the original learning, and when it was removed forgetting occurred. However, the remaining cortex is equivalent in function to the portion which was removed and may mediate relearning. Thus complete lesions of the part of the cortex involved in any function are necessary before firm conclusions can be drawn. The problem is further complicated, in some cases, by the possibility of equivalence of function between cortical and subcortical areas.

Perhaps the greatest amount of functional equivalence, or plasticity, is seen in the brains of young animals. For instance, in an experiment in which lesions were made in the visual cortex of kittens, no deficit was obtained in visual form discrimination learning [Wetzel et al., 1965]. Adult cats with similar lesions showed great deficit. Similar results have been obtained in various experiments with other lesions and tasks [Benjamin and Thompson, 1959; Scharlock et al., 1963].

"ASSOCIATION" CORTEX   The sensory areas of the cerebral cortex which we have just described receive strong fiber inputs from certain nuclei of the thalamus—the *extrinsic nuclei*—which, in turn, are the central receiving centers for input from sensory receptors (see page 685). Other large areas of the cortex, however, receive input from other thalamic nuclei—the *intrinsic nuclei*—which do not receive input from the receptors [Rose and Woolsey, 1949]. Instead, the intrinsic thalamic nuclei receive input from the extrinsic nuclei and thus are a kind of "secondary" projection system. The functions of the "association" cortex which receives input from the intrinsic nuclei are just beginning to be understood.

The main "association" areas are in the parietal, occipital, temporal, and frontal areas (see Figure 20.1). The speech areas cut across several of these anatomical regions.

Parietal cortex. A portion of the parietal cortex, largely confined to the left hemisphere, is devoted to symbolic speech, as we shall see. In the right hemisphere, the corresponding portion seems to be involved in the recognition and perception of the body; patients with lesions here often fail to perceive and take account of parts of their body [Hécaen et al., 1956].

Other parts of the parietal association cortex seem to be necessary for the recognition of shapes by touch. Such a defect in recognition ability, regardless of the sense modality, is called an *agnosia.* In this case, then, we are considering tactile agnosia. Lesions in one hemisphere of the parietal association cortex probably produce some sensory deficit in touch and the two hemispheres are not exactly equivalent [Semmes et al., 1960]. But, in addition to increased sensory thresholds, lesions in the parietal association cortex interfere with the recognition of shapes by touch [Ruch et al., 1938].

The investigator taught a chimpanzee to discriminate a cone from a pyramid by touch alone. The animal could not see the objects and had to discriminate them by handling them. He also taught the chimpanzee the more difficult discrimination of a wedge from a pyramid. Then he removed the posterior parietal association area. After the operation, the animal lost both habits, but upon retraining, it was able to learn again the discrimination of the pyramid and the cone. No amount of retraining, however, could enable the animal to discriminate the wedge and pyramid—the more complex discrimination. Thus it appears that the touch recognition of subtle distinctions requires intact parietal "association" cortex.

"Association" parietal cortex, then, seems necessary for complex perceptual functions; it does not seem to "associate" motor and sensory inputs. It probably does not "assemble" information from other regions of the cortex, but seems to have its own perceptual functions. Other types of perceptual deficit—difficulties in weight discrimination and roughness discrimination, for example—also occur with lesions in the posterior parietal area.

Occipital cortex. In front of the primary visual area on the lateral surface of the cortex, and above and below the calcarine fissure on the medial surface of the cortex, are the visual "association" areas—sometimes called the preoccipital, or prestriate, areas (see Figure 20.1). It is difficult to assign definite functions to these areas. Their close relation to the visual primary sensory areas would seem to point to a visual perceptual function. There is some evidence that they may be involved in visual perception [Ades, 1946], but other studies have not demonstrated visual deficits after preoccipital removal [Chow, 1952]. Thus, no convincing evidence exists that these areas are necessary for visual perception. However, other regions, in the temporal lobe, are clearly involved in visual perception.

Temporal cortex. The lower portion of the temporal cortex is clearly a region for visual perception in man and monkey [Milner, 1954; Klüver and Bucy, 1939]. Lesions here produce deficits in the ability to recognize and discriminate between forms. The blindess does not seem like that which would occur if the primary visual areas were ablated; monkeys upon which this experiment has been done can be shown to have rather good visual acuity but deficient visual form perception [Wilson and Mishkin, 1959]. The visual problem has been termed "psychic blindness"; it is a kind of visual agnosia in which form or shape recognition seems impaired. While visual form perceptions which were learned before the operation are lost, they can be relearned. Thus other regions of the cortex are equivalent in function with the temporal "association" cortex.

The investigation of the perceptual functions of the temporal cortex is interesting because it illustrates the technique of *double dissociation* in investigating functions of the cortex. In the double dissociation test, lesions of two parts of the cortex and two tasks are involved, and all four comparisons are made between the cortical lesions and the tasks. In testing the functions of the temporal "association" cortex, for example, lesions in this region might be made in one group of animals and lesions in the parietal "association" cortex might be made in another group. The effects on visual and tactile discriminations would then be compared. Double dissociation would show that deficits in visual form perception occur *only* when lesions are made in the temporal lobe, and that deficits in tactile form perception occur *only* with parietal lesions. Lesions in the temporal cortex would be without effect on tactile form perception, and lesions in the parietal cortex would be without effect on visual form perception.

The temporal lobes also seem to have some "memory" functions [Penfield and Roberts, 1959], although it is probably not correct to think of memories as being *localized* in this part of the brain (see page 725). In any case, stimulation of the human temporal cortex during operations on epileptic patients often results in reports of vivid memories of past experiences. The memory is of some fragment of past experience and it is faithfully and vividly recalled.

REMOVAL OF A SMALL AREA OF THE FRONTAL LOBES PRODUCES INABILITY
TO DO CERTAIN TYPES OF DELAYED-RESPONSE PROBLEMS

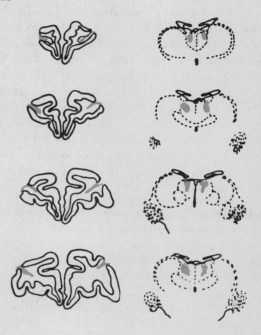

FIGURE 20.9.   *The cortical areas most necessary for the
ability to perform the delayed response correctly. Above,
right, left, and top views of the cerebrum of a monkey; the
blackened areas show the extent of the extirpation. Right,
the left column shows frontal sections through the frontal
lobes; the right column shows the degeneration of the
thalamus which took place after the cortical extirpation.
This is an example of retrograde degeneration—damage
to the fibers from the thalamus causes degeneration of the
thalamic cell bodies. (Modified from Mishkin, 1957.)*

Frontal cortex. The extreme frontal area of the cortex, sometimes called the prefrontal cortex, is a region about which much has been claimed, but little has been proved. Many functions have been proposed for the prefrontal cortical regions of man. For instance, it has been claimed that lesions of the prefrontal lobes result in diminution of drive, lessening of the ability to direct behavior toward goals, and inability to synthesize elements of experience. Others have reported personality changes characterized by loss of social inhibition after prefrontal damage. But the results are variable and most of the statements are based on the study of only a few patients. From studies of this sort, we cannot conclude much about prefrontal lobe function in man.

Furthermore, it has sometimes been claimed that

the prefrontal areas have some special role to play in general intelligence. However, marked intellectual deficits do not usually show up on standard intelligence tests [Teuber, 1964]. But it has been found that certain intellectual abilities seem impaired after prefrontal lesions. One seemingly reliable discovery is that patients with prefrontal lesions *perseverate*—they cannot shift easily from one mode of attack on a problem to another [Milner, 1964]. Others have found that abstract thinking ability seems to be impaired [Goldstein, 1950].

In monkeys, the evidence is clear from a double dissociation analysis of a number of studies that a rather specific ability—the ability to solve certain types of delayed-response problems—is destroyed by lesions of a limited portion of the frontal lobes. The following account is typical of a delayed-response experiment [Jacobsen, 1935]:

A monkey is shown that food is placed in a small well under one of two identical wooden blocks. Then a screen is lowered in front of him so that he cannot stare at the two blocks and solve the problem in this way. (An apparatus similar to that used in this experiment is shown in Figure 3.26, p. 111. In this figure, the monkey is being taught a discrimination problem, not a delayed response problem, and the blocks are not identical.) After an interval of time—say, somewhere between 5 to 50 seconds—the screen is raised and the monkey's task is to select the correct block after the delay. Normal monkeys can do this after delays of up to several minutes. Monkeys with operations in a certain crucial part of the prefrontal lobes cannot solve this problem if the delay is more than second or so. (See Figure 20.9 for a map of the crucial region.)

No doubt exists about the inability of monkeys to make correct delayed responses after restricted prefrontal lesions, but the next question concerns the particular ability which is lost. For example, it cannot be simply a memory deficit because monkeys with frontal lesions can solve go–no-go problems [Mishkin and Pribram, 1956]. In this task, only one block is used and the well is either baited or not while the monkey watches. Then a delay is introduced by dropping a screen in front of the monkey. After the delay, a correct response is to "go" if the well was baited and to "no-go" if the well was not baited. This would seem to be a rather pure "memory" task, but monkeys with prefrontal lesions can solve it with little or no deficit. Another aspect of the deficit after frontal lobe lesions is probably spatial memory. Some evidence exists that the monkey cannot remember, after a delay, whether to go to the right or left. The answer is not this simple, however [Pribram and Mishkin, 1956].

Another effect of frontal lobe lesions is sometimes increased activity, or hyperactivity, characterized by pacing around the cage. Perhaps some of the inability to do the spatial delayed response is due to this hyperactivity. The increased activity may reduce the "attention" which the monkey gives to the baited well, and it may interfere with cues which the monkey may use during the delay period. For instance, the monkey may bridge the delay by orienting his body toward the baited well. Studies have shown that reduction of the hyperactivity through mild sedation sometimes increases the ability to do delayed response [Wade, 1947]. Many other ideas have been proposed, but the problem of what is wrong with the monkey after frontal lobe lesions has not been solved.

Speech areas. The use of symbolic speech for communication is a species-specific characteristic of humans [Beach, 1960]; it constitutes a large part of that which makes us distinctively human. In addition, the symbols manipulated in thought are mainly speech symbols (see Chapter 5). Thus the search for the areas of the cortex which are crucial to the use of human symbolic speech assumes importance.

Several areas of the cortex in the frontal, parietal, and temporal lobes seem to be involved in the symbolic use of speech (see Figure 20.10). Regardless of the handedness of the person, the speech areas are almost always in the left hemisphere of the cortex [Penfield and Roberts, 1959].

These discoveries are the result of much careful sifting of clinical cases by many neurologists. In addition, much of this information comes from the stimulation of the human cortex [Penfield and Roberts, 1959]. These stimulation studies were done on epileptic patients as part of operations to remove foci, or areas, of the brain from which the disturbances causing the epileptic seizures seemed to emanate. The symptoms of epilepsy are caused by abnormal massive discharges of millions of cortical neurons, and sometimes this discharge seems to begin in a particular region—the focus; then the discharge spreads over the cortex. In patients in which the abnormal discharge of the focus cannot be held in check by drugs, surgical excision of the focal zone sometimes helps. But the surgeons do not wish to remove the focal zone if it is involved in significant behavioral functions; hence, careful mapping is done, with patient under local anesthesia, to discover the functions of the focal and adjacent regions before removal of the focus.

Stimulation applied to the anterior speech region

in the frontal lobe, sometimes called Broca's area, or the posterior speech region, which roughly corresponds to Wernicke's area, produces *aphasic* speech —defects in symbolic speech (see page 196). Mild aphasic symptoms are also obtained from a region called the supplementary motor area (see Figure 20.10).

Aphasic symptoms are hard to classify, but they involve speech problems such as the use of inappropriate words, the inability to recall words and the names of things, inability to understand speech,

MUCH OF THE HUMAN BRAIN IS INVOLVED IN SPEECH

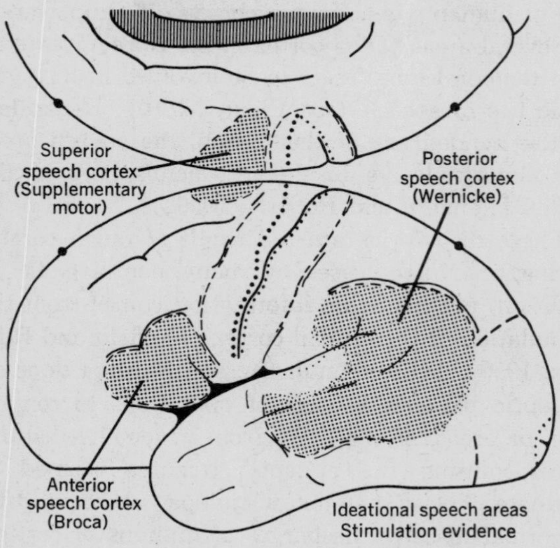

FIGURE 20.10. *The speech areas of the human cortex. Stimulation of these regions in conscious patients produces aphasic disturbances in speech. In addition, lesions in some of these areas also produce aphasic disturbances. The upper part of the drawing shows the medial portion of the cerebrum in an upside-down position; the lower part is a lateral view of the cerebrum. (From Penfield and Roberts, 1959.)*

circumlocutions, and perseveration, or saying the same thing over and over. Some of these aphasic defects are illustrated in the following account of the stimulation of a patient's brain shown in Figure 20.3 (numbers refer to those shown in Figure 20.3):

25—The patient hesitated and then named "butterfly" correctly. Stimulation was carried out then below this point and at a number of points on the two narrow gyri that separate 25 and 24, but the result was negative—no interference with the naming process. . . .

26—The patient said, "Oh, I know what it is. That is what you put in your shoes." After withdrawal of the electrode he said, "foot."

27—Unable to name tree which was being shown to him. Instead he said, "I know what it is." Electrode was withdrawn then and he said, "tree."

28—The patient became unable to name as soon as the electrode was placed here. When asked why he did not name the picture shown, he said "no." He continued to be silent after withdrawal of the stimulating electrode.

[Modified slightly from Penfield and Roberts, 1959, page 117.]

The articulation of speech is largely a function of the lower part of the primary motor area on the precentral gyrus, the adjacent cortex in the frontal lobes, and the cortex of Broca's area. Stimulation of the lower part of the motor area and the anterior adjacent cortex produces a prolonged vowel sound. In addition, the supplementary motor area on the medial surface of the cerebral hemisphere is involved in the production of speech sounds.

Motivation

When we discussed physiological motives in Chapter 6, we explained that they arose from chemical conditions in the body, but we did not explain the mechanism through which they expressed themselves in motivated behavior. Any inquiry into this mechanism leads us to the hypothalamus as a center for controlling and regulating the expression of motivated behavior (see Figure 20.11). Many influ-

THE HYPOTHALAMUS IS A SMALL REGION WITH MANY IMPORTANT FUNCTIONS

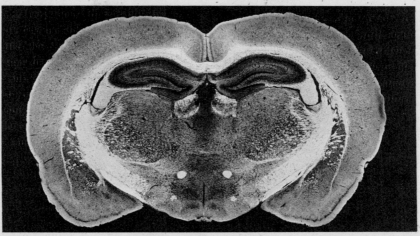

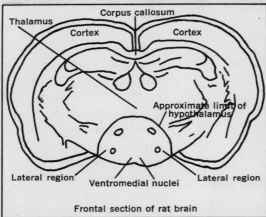

Frontal section of rat brain

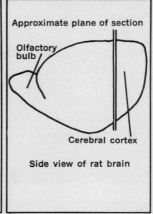

Side view of rat brain

FIGURE 20.11. *A cross section of a rat brain showing the hypothalamus. The plane of the section is shown in the inset. (J. F. R. Konig and R. A. Klippel, The Rat Brain, a Stereotaxic Atlas of the Forebrain and Lower Parts of the Brain Stem. Baltimore: The William and Wilkins Company, 1963. Reproduced by permission of The Williams and Wilkins Company.)*

ences from the internal and external environments impinge upon the hypothalamus, and the outflow from the hypothalamus then influences behavior. Let us examine hypothalamic function more closely before dealing with the details of the hypothalamic control of motivated behavior.

A THEORY OF PHYSIOLOGICAL MOTIVATION
The central place of the hypothalamus in this theory of motivation is shown in Figure 20.12 [Stellar, 1954]. In this schematic diagram, the outflow of nerve impulses from an excitatory nucleus of the hypothalamus controls motivated behavior. The

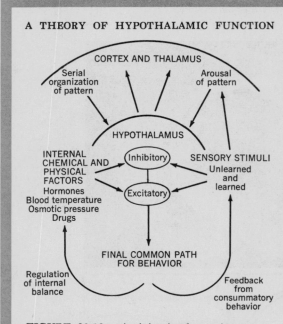

A THEORY OF HYPOTHALAMIC FUNCTION

CORTEX AND THALAMUS

Serial organization of pattern

Arousal of pattern

HYPOTHALAMUS

Inhibitory

Excitatory

INTERNAL CHEMICAL AND PHYSICAL FACTORS
Hormones
Blood temperature
Osmotic pressure
Drugs

SENSORY STIMULI
Unlearned and learned

FINAL COMMON PATH FOR BEHAVIOR

Regulation of internal balance

Feedback from consummatory behavior

FIGURE 20.12. *Activity in the excitatory nuclei of the hypothalamus may determine motivated behavior. The activity of the excitatory areas is controlled by the inhibitory nuclei, the internal environment, sensory stimuli, and cortical influences. (From Stellar, 1954.)*

activity of the excitatory nuclei is, in turn, controlled by activity in other hypothalamic nuclei—the inhibitory nuclei. It is theorized that such pairs of nuclei exist for several of the physiological motives—hunger is perhaps the clearest example. The levels of activity in the inhibitory nuclei and excitatory nuclei are themselves determined by conditions of the internal and external environments. For instance, hormones or other blood factors may act to excite the inhibitory and excitatory nuclei differentially; when a person is hungry, for instance, the blood conditions may act to excite the "hunger" excitatory nucleus. In addition, external stimuli may act directly, or through cortical and thalamic influences, to regulate the degree of excitation in the

hypothalamic nuclei. Finally, after goal objects have been reached or consumed, influences may feed back to regulate excitation of the hypothalamus (see the motivational cycle, Figure 6.1, page 204). This, then, is the general theory and it summarizes a good deal of experimental evidence. The main points are that two hypothalamic centers—an excitatory one and an inhibitory one—exist for many motive states and that the centers are excited by conditions in the internal and external environments. As we discuss physiological motivation, we shall come across considerable evidence for this theory.

HUNGER MOTIVATION We have excellent evidence that hunger is mediated by the hypothalamus. The principal technique used to provide this evidence has been to make relatively small stereotaxic lesions in the hypothalamus and to measure the effect of these lesions on eating.

Hypothalamic centers. One center, the ventromedial, located near the midline of the hypothalamus, restrains hunger and eating; when it is destroyed, animals develop voracious appetites or *hyperphagia* [Brobeck, 1946; Hoebel, 1965]. Such animals, even before they recover completely from the operation, usually attack food ravenously and eat large quantities of it. Their immense appetites continue day after day; they gain weight rapidly and become so obese that they are about three times their normal weight (see Figure 20.13). Then they slack off somewhat and maintain their weight in this state.

Experimenters have studied such animals to see just what has gone wrong with them. Their metabolism is normal, and so is just about everything else in the machinery of the body. Apparently the main disturbance is that their appetites have gotten out of hand. (It may be that this hypothalamic center is deficient in some obese human beings. On the other hand, it is very likely that obesity in human beings is more often a matter of bad eating habits and personality difficulties than of a deranged hypothalamus.)

Is the hyperphagia produced by lesions of the hypothalamus really motivating? One way to test this would be to see whether hyperphagic animals work harder than normals for food; they eat more, but will they work—that is, are they motivated—for what they eat? Experiments differ on this point. Hypothalamic hyperphagic rats did not, in one experiment, press a lever for food so avidly as normal animals [Miller et al., 1950]; but hypothalamic hyperphagic monkeys will work harder at lever pressing than normal hungry monkeys [Hamilton and Brobeck, 1964].

In line with the hypothalamic theory just outlined, a second center exists in the hypothalamus which has quite the opposite function. When experimenters make their lesions just a fraction of an inch to the side of the lesion that produces ravenous appetite, the result is that the animal has no appetite at all [Teitelbaum and Stellar, 1954]. Such animals, unless given special care, never touch food again, and if left alone eventually die of starvation. They suffer from *aphagia*. By maintaining the animals through artificial means, such as stomach tubes, and by offering them water and especially desirable food, such as chocolate bars, experimenters have found that some of them start to eat again. The important point, though, is that two centers controlling hunger exist on each side of the hypothalamus. This is a widely accepted view, but some recent work has tended to indicate that the situation may be more complicated [Reynolds, 1965].

"Start" and "stop" mechanisms. Thus, both "start eating"—that is, excitatory—centers and "stop eating"—that is, inhibitory—centers exist in the hypothalamus. Next, we need to know what controls activity in these regions. Studies seem to indicate that the "start," or facilitating, factors include the sight and smell of food and possibly certain chemical states of the blood—for example, blood sugar level (see Chapter 6). However, little convincing evidence exists as to the nature of the blood chemical factors which start and facilitate hunger.

On the other hand, the "stop" factors in eating, which may be effective because they activate the inhibitory region of the hypothalamus, are fairly well known. For certain fluids, the amount consumed is proportional to the osmotic pressure of the fluid [Shuford, 1959]. That internal factors are

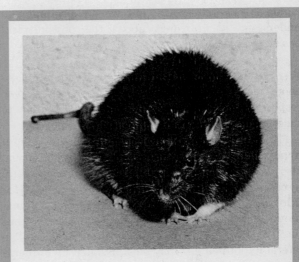

FIGURE 20.13.   *A fat rat. This rat has a ravenous hunger and has almost doubled its weight as a result of a small surgical lesion made in the part of the hypothalamus which normally inhibits eating.*

responsible for the cessation of eating is also shown by studies of intragastric feeding [Epstein and Teitelbaum, 1962]. In these experiments, rats were fed automatically through a tube which led directly to their stomachs; every time they pressed a lever in a Skinner box they received a squirt of liquid food directly into the stomach. Although the food completely bypassed the mouth, these animals were able to regulate their intake so that they consumed just about the same amount as they normally did; when the food was diluted, they ate a greater volume, just as they normally would. Thus, the regulation of intake, and therefore the cessation of eating, is controlled internally, or intragastrically. Of course, this experiment also shows that the control of the beginning of eating is also intragastric and points to internal control of the start of eating—probably by chemical substances in the blood which are not yet known. The way in which the osmotic pressures of fluids and the load in the stomach can affect the inhibitory mechanisms in the hypothalamus is not yet known; but we are beginning to understand some things about the physiological basis of hunger.

THIRST MOTIVATION   We know considerably less about the central mechanisms of thirst, but in some respects they appear to be somewhat similar to those of hunger.

Hypothalamic centers. Lesions of the lateral hypothalamus, in addition to producing aphagia, also produce failure to drink, or *adipsia*. The lateral hypothalamus, then, is the excitatory nucleus for drinking. Eating and drinking centers are not anatomically separated in the lateral hypothalamus, but they may be separated by chemical stimulation. The lateral hypothalamus may be stimulated by implanting a small pipette and then introducing chemicals into it. Acetylcholine stimulates the drinking portion of the lateral hypothalamus, while epinephrine and norepinephrine stimulate the feeding portion of the lateral hypothalamus [Grossman, 1960]. Note the opposed effects of stimulation and lesions in this nucleus—lesions cause a cessation of activity, while stimulation causes activity. This is what might be expected from an excitatory nucleus.

The destruction of another region in the hypothalamus, the supraoptic nucleus, makes animals extremely thirsty. In a way, this nucleus may be considered to be something like the inhibitory nucleus in hunger motivation. It is different, however, because it does not exert its control through inhibitory action on the excitatory nucleus. Instead, it works by secreting a hormone which is stored in, and released from, the posterior part of the pituitary gland. This hormone, the *antidiuretic hormone*, in turn controls the excretion of water by the body. When this hormone is released and in relatively high concentrations in the blood, water is retained by the body and inhibition of water intake results. This set of facts, however, only leads us part of the way toward an explanation of the mechanism of thirst; we must still consider how a water deficit in the body can stimulate the lateral hypothalamus to produce thirst motivation.

"Start" and "stop" mechanisms. One way in which the deficit in body water may be able to "start" the lateral hypothalamus is through an increased concentration of salts in the blood. When the body loses water, by sweating or excretion, it tends to retain the salts normally found in the blood, so that their concentration increases. We do not know whether this increase in osmotic pressure directly stimulates cells known as "osmoreceptors" in the lateral hypothalamus, but we do know that salt solutions applied to the proper point in the lateral hypothalamus cause increased drinking.

In an experiment using chemical stimulation, a goat was outfitted with a pipette whose tip was in the general region of the hypothalamus [Andersson, 1953]. The goat was given its fill of water, and then a tiny amount of salt solution was forced through the pipette. Thereupon the goat resumed drinking water vigorously. A comparable, but opposite effect has been demonstrated with cats. Cats made thirsty by water deprivation stopped drinking when a small amount of plain water was injected into the hypothalamus [Miller, 1958].

Several factors have been found which "stop" drinking behavior. One such factor is the act of drinking itself during which, apparently, a kind of metering of water by the mouth takes place. Possibly stomach distention also plays a part in stopping drinking, but the absorption of water into the blood and the consequent drop in osmotic pressure is undoubtedly an important factor. When the blood is more dilute—when the osmotic pressure has declined—the "osmoreceptors" in the lateral hypothalamus may not be activated so vigorously as when the blood is more concentrated. Therefore less excitatory activity leaving the hypothalamus may occur and drinking behavior ceases.

SEXUAL MOTIVATION   Investigators interested in finding how the nervous system functions in sexual behavior have carried out experiments which attempt to find the hypothalamic areas important in sexual behavior. The following experiment is an example [Dempsey and Rioch, 1939]:

Sections were made at different levels through the forebrain and midbrain of female animals, and attempts were then made to induce typical mating behavior in the animals. Mating behavior was normal so long as the posterior part of the hypothalamus and the mammillary bodies in the posterior hypothalamus were left intact. If, however, the section passed through the midbrain behind these structures, the animals no longer engaged in full-fledged mating behavior.

Following this kind of experiment, the next logical step is to make restricted lesions in the hypothalamus. This has been done in several different animals, both male and female. In several fairly clear-cut experiments, lesions in the hypothalamus abolished sexual behavior in animals, and administration of the hormones which normally induce sexual behavior did not reinstate it [Brookhart and Dey, 1941; Phoenix, 1961]. From experiments such as these, physiologists have been led to believe that hormones excite the hypothalamus and associated structures and that it is from this point that sexual responses are organized.

However, the areas of the hypothalamus regulating sexual behavior are not clearly differentiated. Both exaggerated and decreased sexual behavior have been obtained after hypothalamic lesions, and it seems likely that there are excitatory and inhibitory regions, but they are not so clearly demarcated as in the case of hunger. Electrical stimulation of regions of the hypothalamus has also been shown to cause increased sexual behavior [Vaughan and Fisher, 1962]. All this evidence points to the involvement of the hypothalamus in sexual motivation, but the exact organization is not yet known.

Activation and emotion

Since activation and emotion are related, we shall consider them together. The brain structures involved are similar; furthermore, some psychologists consider activation to be the basic phenomenon in emotionality (see Chapter 7). Modern work in biological psychology has disclosed some of the brain mechanisms seemingly responsible for activation, emotion, and perhaps, awareness of the environment.

ACTIVATION   The level of activation varies continuously from extreme alertness and arousal at one end of the scale to sleep at the other. Sleep has already been described as one of the physiological needs (see Chapter 6). Most animals must sleep in order to stay alive as well as to retain their normal capacities for doing other things. Many animals, including man, the birds, and some domestic animals, take one long period of sleep each day. Other animals, such as the cat, rat, and human babies, sleep more often, alternating a few hours of sleep with a few hours of waking. In any case, whether the periods of sleep be long or short, they always fall into some kind of rhythm or cycle of sleep and waking. We have also seen that even sleep itself is cyclical (see page 548).

The causes of sleep and waking have long puzzled scientists. One possibility—that there are chemical substances in the blood and brain that bring on sleep—has already been discussed (see Chapter 6), but we still know practically nothing about them. Two other possibilities, however, are more firmly established. One is that there may be centers in the brain for sleep and waking; the other is that sensory stimulation from the environment and sense organs in the body may control or influence sleep.

Activating and sleep areas. It was first suggested many years ago, upon encountering patients who were somnolent—that is, who had abnormal tendencies to sleep—that there may be centers for sleep in the brain. Some of these patients had tumors or disease in the posterior hypothalamus. Following this lead, experimental scientists paid particular attention to the posterior hypothalamus, making controlled lesions in animals to duplicate the effects seen in patients. Their efforts were rewarded, for they found a relatively small region in the posterior hypothalamus whose destruction caused pronounced somnolence. Monkeys, for example, sleep almost continuously for 4 to 8 days after destruction of the region and are extremely drowsy for months afterward [Ranson, 1939]. Such monkeys can be aroused briefly by noises or other strong stimulation, but when left alone they quickly fall asleep again. Similar results have been obtained with other animals, and there is little doubt that such an area exists in most animals [Nauta, 1946]. Since the destruction of this center causes somnolence, we may presume that it keeps the animal awake when it is functioning normally; therefore it has been called a *waking*, or *activating, region*. It seems likely that this region is not a special set of hypothalamic nuclei; rather, the effect of lesions in the posterior hypothalamus seems to be to disrupt fibers of the reticular activating system (see page 685).

Other evidence, although not so conclusive as that for an activating region, exists for a *sleep center*, or region [Nauta, 1946]. Lesions of the anterior hypothalamus were found to keep rats from sleeping. The animals seemed relatively normal, but they never slept. They stayed awake for several days, gradually becoming more exhausted; then they fell into a coma and died. Stimulation of this region seems to have an opposite effect. Cats stimulated electrically through chronically implanted electrodes in the anterior hypothalamus go to sleep when the current is turned on [Clemente and Sterman, 1963]. Thus, in the case of sleep, although we do not have clear evidence that the sleep center inhibits the waking center, we do have some evidence for two centers with opposed action.

Reticular activating system. This is by no means the whole story about sleep and waking. The rest of it has to do with the reticular activating system (RAS) (see Figure 19.17, page 687). In order to tell the rest of the story, we must first refer to the electroencephalogram (EEG) recorded from the skull of the intact subject. It has been known for some years now that the EEG pattern correlates with the state of arousal of a person.

As shown in Figure 20.14, the characteristic EEG of a normal, relaxed, but waking person is a rhythmic wave, called an *alpha wave*, of about 10 cycles per second. This pattern is obliterated or "blocked" by the onset of a light or sound. It is also wiped out when a person is apprehensive or anxious. In its place we see a pattern of small fast waves. The alpha rhythm also disappears as a person goes to sleep. At first, when he is drowsy, the waves become slower and larger. As he sleeps more and more

deeply, the waves further increase in size and become very slow.

These changes in wave pattern which are associated with sleep and waking are usually reliable and they have frequently been used in determining objectively whether a person is drowsy or in deep sleep (see page 548). They are also related to activities within the RAS, as the following experiment shows [Moruzzi and Magoun, 1949]:

The investigators were exploring the effects of direct electrical stimulation of the brain by placing electrodes in various positions and noting the effects of stimulation. They were surprised to find that stimulation of the RAS did two things: First of all, it woke up a cat that was sleeping or drowsy, and it alerted one that was already awake. Second, it altered the EEG, producing the same changes in the EEG that accompany waking or arousal. It appeared that the RAS was directly involved in the mechanism of waking and sleeping.

Further research brought out a number of additional facts. One was that sensory impulses traveling toward the cerebral cortex could also be recorder in the RAS (see page 687). This, together with the fact that stimulation of the RAS caused activity in the cerebral cortex, established the RAS as a separate relay station for sensory impulses. The investigators found that stimulation of the cerebral cortex evoked activity in the RAS, and thus demonstrated that a closed loop exists between cortex and RAS. They then went on to do other experiments using extirpation [Lindsley et al., 1950].

The investigators cut the sensory pathways to the cortex, leaving those from the RAS to the cortex intact, and found that this operation had no effect on the sleep and waking pattern of a cat. The EEG pattern, as well as observation of the cat, indicated the typical waking state. On the other hand, when the RAS was severed, the cat fell into a sleeping state and tended to stay in it for long periods of time. How deep and prolonged the somnolence became depended on the level at which the RAS was cut. If the cut was made relatively high, near the junction of the midbrain and hypothalamus, blocking off practically all impulses from the RAS to the cerebral cortex, the somnolence was severe.

If the cut was made lower down, leaving some RAS linked with the cortex, the somnolence was relatively slight.

From studies of this sort, it seems clear that the RAS is a basic arousal mechanism for the brain. Without activation of the cortex by the RAS, an individual remains somnolent, and even though impulses in the sensory systems reach the cortex by the thalamic route, they are not decoded by the cortex. According to this view, then, the RAS determines the general state of arousal of the organism. This conclusion is generally accepted, but other studies have shown that the situation may be more complicated. When the RAS is cut in stages, with time elapsing between each further cut, marked somnolence does not occur; in addition, if the animals are carefully nursed after the RAS has been cut all at once, recovery from coma can occur in the second month after the operation [Adametz, 1959].

EMOTION A number of structures in the brain core are involved in the expression of the stronger emotions—especially rage and fear [Papez, 1937; MacLean, 1958]. These structures are interrelated and are collectively known as the *limbic system* (see Figure 19.18, page 688). Without going into

detail, we shall describe the action of several of the important regions of the limbic system—the *hypothalamus,* the *septal area,* the *amygdala,* and the *cingulate gyrus* of the cerebral cortex.

Hypothalamus. The role of the hypothalamus in emotion was first well established by the now classic experiments of Cannon [1927] and Bard [1928].

Using cats as their experimental animals, they made a series of sections through the forebrain, each time slicing off a little more until they had severed the entire forebrain from its connections with the midbrain and hindbrain. Usually only one level of a section was used in any one subject and experiment. Each animal was tested before and after operation for angry behavior by such procedures as pinching its tail, presenting a dog, blowing a bugle, and so on. The characteristic behavior of angry cats includes growling, hissing, spitting, biting, lashing the tail, thrashing the forelegs, protruding the claws, urinating, and breathing rapidly. The investigators found that the essential pattern of angry behavior was always present as long as the hypothalamus was intact. When the hypothalamus was excluded by the operation, leaving only the midbrain and hindbrain, the pattern of rage response was broken up. The subjects sometimes displayed fragments of emotion, such as growling, hissing, or fur-ruffing, but without the hypothalamus

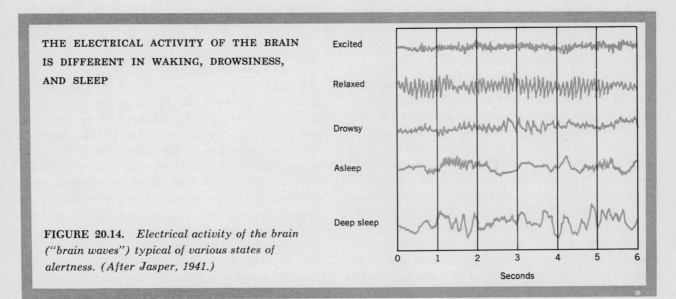

THE ELECTRICAL ACTIVITY OF THE BRAIN IS DIFFERENT IN WAKING, DROWSINESS, AND SLEEP

Excited

Relaxed

Drowsy

Asleep

Deep sleep

0 1 2 3 4 5 6

Seconds

FIGURE 20.14. *Electrical activity of the brain ("brain waves") typical of various states of alertness. (After Jasper, 1941.)*

their characteristic pattern of angry behavior appeared to be lost.

The investigators concluded, then, that the hypothalamus is the area in which the various elements of hostile behavior are organized into a pattern. This conclusion has been strengthened by stimulation studies. If the hypothalamus were an area mediating rage behavior, electrical stimulation of it should produce such behavior. Studies have shown that irritation, rage, and sometimes attack behavior follow stimulation of the hypothalamus [Hess, 1954]. However, the localization of the effective areas within the hypothalamus has proved to be difficult, and the organization of emotional behavior is extremely complex. For instance, lesions of parts of the hypothalamus produce enraged behavior [Wheatley, 1944]. If the area subjected to lesions were an inhibitory area for emotional behavior, the excitatory areas might be released and the emotional behavior would result. Thus, both excitatory and inhibitory emotional effects seem to be obtainable from the hypothalamus.

Septal area and amygdala. Two other areas in the limbic system which are involved in the expression of emotion are the septal area and the amygdala. Their roles in emotion have been studied by making lesions in them and observing the effects on behavior. A number of experiments of this kind have been performed, usually on a rat or cat; they can be summarized as follows [King, 1958]:

A scale for rating the emotionality of a rat was developed. This merely translated into a point system the judgment of skilled raters of the degree of emotionality of the rat when subjected to several standard situations, such as having a pencil thrust at it. Ratings of emotionality were done before and after operation, and on a control group not subjected to any operation. One operative group was subjected to lesions in the septal region; another to lesions in the amygdaloid nuclei. All lesions had to be made bilaterally because of the symmetrical pairing of the structures.

Lesions in the septal region were followed by a great increase in ferocity. Formerly tame animals had to be handled with heavy gloves; they quickly attacked and bit

a pencil thrust into their cage, and they were generally jumpy and ferocious. The effects of such lesions have been found to be relatively temporary, however. Lesions made in the amygdaloid area had just the opposite effect. Animals who were not very wild to begin with nevertheless became unusually placid; they would accept all kinds of irritation and rough handling without showing any rage. Later, in another experiment, some animals were subjected first to a septal operation, which made them ferocious, and then to an amygdaloid operation, which again made them calm and placid. This showed that the two regions oppose each other but that lack of both has about the same effect as lack of the amygdaloid area only.

The destruction of an area, of course, should produce results just the opposite of those produced by the normal function of the area. We may therefore tentatively conclude from the experiments just cited that the septal area normally inhibits ferocious behavior, while the amygdala normally excites it or makes it excitable. It is possible that the two areas exercise their function by acting on the hypothalamic control areas for emotion. However, experiments combining lesions or stimulation of the amygdala, or septal area, with lesions or stimulation of the hypothalamus have not produced the expected results [Kling et al., 1960; Egger and Flynn, 1962]. In summary, then, we may say that we know that these structures are important in emotional expression, but we do not yet know the details and relationships involved.

Cingulate cortex. Some areas of the cerebral cortex are included in the limbic system and one of these is the cortex of the cingulate gyrus (see Figure 19.18, page 688). This cortex seems to exert an inhibiting influence on the expression of the more violent emotions. This effect contrasts markedly with the functions of the rest of the cerebral cortex which seem to be excitatory. These conclusions have been drawn from experiments in which the cerebral cortex was removed in successive stages [Bard and Mountcastle, 1947]. In the first stage, the cortex of the cingulate gyrus was spared, but the rest of the cerebral cortex was removed—the animals were partially decorticated. The animals became more placid after this stage—they were harder to enrage. After the second operation in which the cingulate gyrus was removed, the animals were easily aroused and were ferocious. Thus after the second operation, the animal was nearly completely decorticated and exhibited the behavior known as "decorticate rage" which had been seen in earlier experiments in which nearly complete decortication had been carried out in one step [Bard, 1934].

Despite such experimental evidence, the situation is fairly complicated, as it is with other emotion-controlling regions. For instance, removal of the cingulate gyrus alone, with the rest of the cerebral cortex left intact, is without any marked effect on emotional responsiveness. Apparently the inhibitory functions of the cingulate gyrus are not present when the rest of the cortex is intact. This points to the general principle that the control of emotional expression cannot be understood by studying the action of separate isolated regions; rather, the interactions of many areas of the brain must be studied together—a very difficult task at best.

"PLEASURE" AND "DISPLEASURE" That structures of the limbic system are involved in the expression of the stronger emotions is, as we have just seen, a well-established fact. The brain regions involved in feelings of "well-being" or "pleasure," on the one hand, and "displeasure" and "discomfort," on the other, have been discovered. These terms appear within quotation marks because they represent interpretations of resulting animal behavior. When we use such terms, we read our own feelings into the behavior of the animals tested—in other words, we commit the scientific crime of "anthropomorphizing." We did this when we discussed rage, but perhaps the crime was less reprehensible there, since rage has certain observable physiological manifestations. We could describe experiments on the emotions without anthropomorphizing, and for strictly scientific purposes that is desirable. But let us be a little loose in our terminology for the moment, and, fully warned, plunge ahead.

The technique for investigating the emotions under discussion here involves the electrical stimulation of small areas of the brain through implanted electrodes. The electrodes may be chronically implanted and put into a circuit so that some response of the animal determines whether stimulation will be forthcoming (see page 695). Thus, brain stimulation can be made contingent upon a response and thus may be considered to be a reinforcer (see page 77). Responses such as pressing a bar, turning a wheel, or making a particular turn in a maze may be reinforced by such central stimulation of selected regions of the brain. The reinforcement may be positive or negative, depending upon the part of the brain core which is stimulated. Experiments with stimulation in both positive and negative reinforcing areas have been carried out with rats, cats, monkeys, and, in a few rare cases, man.

"Pleasure." Central stimulation of certain areas of the limbic system, especially parts of the hypothalamus, is positively reinforcing. Animals will repeatedly perform acts which result in stimulation of these areas. This phenomenon is best described in the words of one of its discoverers who gave the following account of the positive reinforcement resulting from brain stimulation:

The result was quite amazing. When the animal was stimulated at a specific place in an open field, he sometimes moved away but he returned and sniffed around that area. More stimulations at that place caused him to spend more of his time there.

Later we found that this same animal could be "pulled" to any spot in the maze by giving a small electrical stimulus *after* each response in the right direction. This was akin to playing the "hot and cold" game with a child. Each correct response brought electrical pulses which seemed to indicate to the animal that it was on the right track.

Still later, the same animal was placed on an elevated T maze. As there was an initial right turn preference, he was forced to the left and stimulated at the end of the left arm. After three such trials, he proceeded to make 10 consecutive runs to the left for electrical stimulation alone, with decreasing running times. Then the stimulus was stopped on the left, and 6 runs were forced to the right with electrical stimulation in the right arm. After this, the animal made 10 runs to electrical stimulation in the right arm. Up to this point, no food had been in the maze at all [Olds, 1955, pages 83–84.]

Following this experiment and other exploratory tests, the phenomenon has been studied more systematically [Olds and Olds, 1963]. The studies were continued by placing rats in a Skinner box (see page 88), which provides for automatic recording of responses and for a very high rate of responding. The lever of the Skinner box actuated a switch that turned on central stimulation for the rat (see Figure 19.24, page 696). Rats were then prepared with several electrode placements, and Skinner-box records were made on each animal. After it was determined whether a particular placement was reinforcing or not, the animal was sacrificed and the exact position of the electrodes was established by staining methods (see page 691). With electrode placement in the hypothalamus, especially in the region of the fiber tract called the medial forebrain bundle, very high rates of response were obtained.

Thus, stimulation of parts of the limbic system seems to be positively reinforcing; it may be reinforcing because it activates the regions of the brain which are active when the usual types of reinforcement—food or water, for example—are received; or it may be effective because it is a fear-reducer [Deutsch and Howarth, 1962]. Finally, such brain stimulation may be effective because it produces in the rat a feeling akin to the "pleasure" felt by humans when they are stimulated in similar limbic regions. As part of operations done for other reasons, patients have been stimulated in the limbic system and, in some cases, these stimulations have been reported to be pleasant [Sem-Jacobsen and Torkildsen, 1960]. Patients have asked for more of the stimulation and have reported that "it felt good."

"Displeasure." Other electrode placements result in the cessation of the behavior which produces brain stimulation. In such cases, we may say that the stimulation is negatively reinforcing (see page 98).

The negative reinforcing effects of limbic system stimulation are illustrated in the following experiment [Miller, 1958]:

The investigator used cats as subjects. Each cat was placed in an apparatus having a grill for a floor and a wheel in the side wall. Shock could be administered through the grill, and the cat could switch it off by turning the wheel. Cats in which brain electrodes had previously been implanted were trained to do this. Thus they learned to escape shock by turning a wheel. After they had learned this, central stimulation was substituted for shock given through the grill, and the central stimulation was continued until the cat turned the wheel. On the first few trials of this procedure, the cat seemed somewhat "surprised" and disorganized, but it quickly transferred the habit of wheel turning from peripheral to central stimulation. Evidently, the central stimulation was painful or unpleasant.

In another experiment, rats prepared with implanted electrodes were placed in a maze. As the rat wandered through the maze, the experimenter turned on a central shock whenever the rat entered an incorrect alley and kept it on until the rat left the alley and got into a correct one, at which time it was turned off. The rats learned the maze in much the same way that they would if electric shock had been administered peripherally at the wrong turn. Here again, central stimulation appeared to be negatively reinforcing.

Many different positions of the electrode have been used in various experiments in order to explore the brain for pathways and centers where stimulation has an aversive effect [Olds and Olds, 1963]. Many such places have been found, especially in the thalamus and tegmentum of the brain stem. Some are near the pathways which carry impulses from pain receptors; in these cases, pain is probably being perceived and the aversive behavior is not particularly surprising. In other cases, the areas from which aversive behavior is obtained are far from the pain pathways, and here we may be dealing with experiences of "unpleasantness" distinct from pain.

So, the brain is complexly organized to mediate "pleasure" and "displeasure." The complexity of organization is further illustrated by the discovery that both positive and negative reinforcement effects can be obtained from the same placement of an electrode [Roberts, 1958]. With certain electrode placements, positively reinforcing brain stimulation seems to become aversive and negatively reinforcing if it persists for a relatively long time. This is a fascinating field of research, and further work will undoubtedly unravel many of the problems.

Learning and memory

We said, in Chapter 3, that an important characteristic of the nervous system is its plasticity. How is the nervous system changed so that new responses can be made to stimuli, so that stimuli can be associated with each other, and so that perceptual organization is changed? What is the physical basis for the retention of learned changes? That these changes take place in the nervous system is agreed, but the nature of the changes is by no means settled.

Two general approaches to these significant problems may be distinguished. One tradition is to study the location of the learned changes in the nervous system and the pathways involved; the other approach is a more molecular one which takes up the problem in finer detail. The molecular approach stresses the changes which may take place within cells, and between cells, in learning and memory. Both approaches are necessary and fruitful [Glickstein, 1965]. Suppose we begin with a consideration of some of the problems involved in the loci of the learned changes.

THE LOCI OF LEARNING AND MEMORY   In discussing the functions of the cerebral cortex, we have already considered many studies on the loci of learning. For instance, we have seen that the "association" portions of the temporal lobes are crucial in the learning of certain visual discriminations. But another aspect of cortical localization should be considered. Mammals have two cerebral hemispheres and we may wonder whether learning is restricted to

ANIMALS WILL WORK ASSIDUOUSLY TO RECEIVE ELECTRIC SHOCKS IN CERTAIN BRAIN AREAS

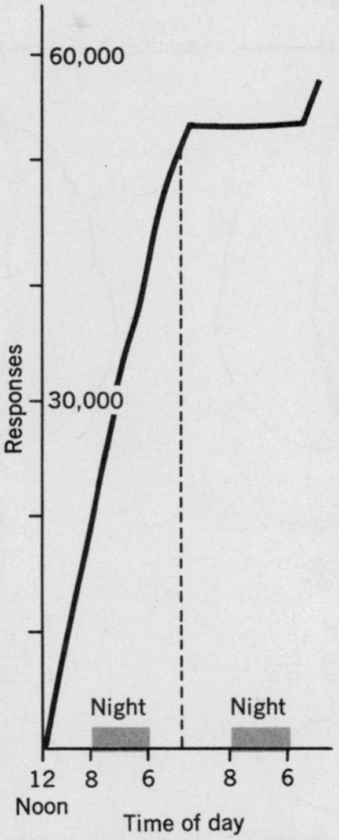

FIGURE 20.15.   *A record of bar-pressing in a Skinner box with the reinforcement being mild electric shock to the hypothalamus. Beginning at noon one day, the rat stimulated itself at a rate of more than 2,000 responses an hour for 26 hours, then slept for about 19 hours, and then resumed self-stimulation at the same rate. (After Olds, 1958.)*

one of them, or whether the changes taking place in learning occur in both hemispheres. In other words, are the changes in learning multiply represented in the cortex? Studies such as the following indicate

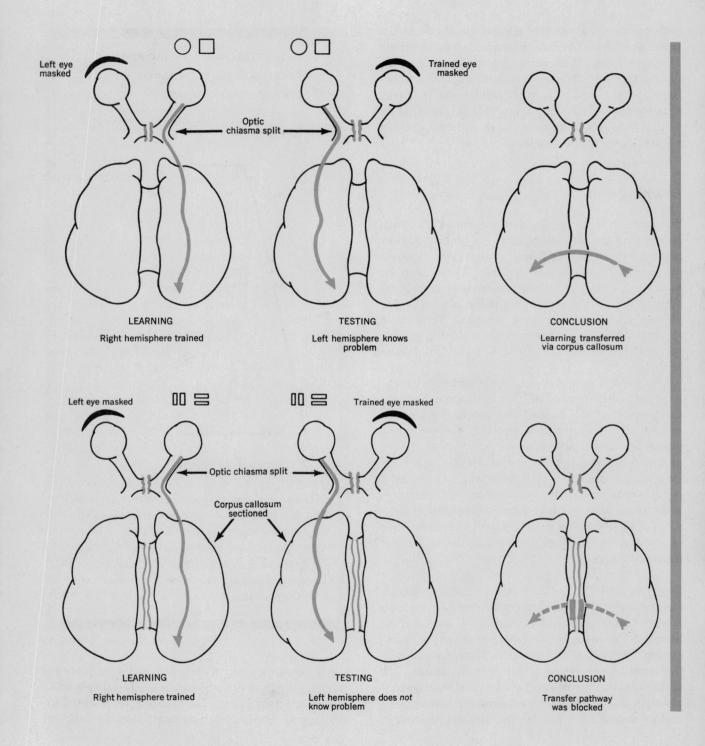

Left eye masked

Optic chiasma split

Trained eye masked

LEARNING

Right hemisphere trained

TESTING

Left hemisphere knows problem

CONCLUSION

Learning transferred via corpus callosum

Left eye masked

Optic chiasma split

Trained eye masked

Corpus callosum sectioned

LEARNING

Right hemisphere trained

TESTING

Left hemisphere does *not* know problem

CONCLUSION

Transfer pathway was blocked

that both hemispheres participate in learning [Myers, 1955, 1956]:

In these experiments, the visual input to the cortex was restricted to one hemisphere by cutting the optic chiasma and covering one eye during learning. Thus, the brain changes in learning a visual discrimination—circle versus square, in this case—were restricted to one hemisphere (see Figure 20.16, top). After the cat had learned the discrimination, the "trained" eye was covered, the "untrained" eye was uncovered, and testing was carried out to see whether, with the input restricted to the opposite hemisphere, the cat would still be able to choose the correct stimulus reliably. It could, and the conclusion was that learning had taken place in both hemispheres even though the input had been restricted to one of them. It was also concluded that the *corpus callosum*, a band of fibers connecting the two hemispheres, was responsible for the transfer of the learned changes from one hemisphere to the other. Thus, in this case, both hemispheres had learned the problem; in the normal case in which the input is not restricted to one hemisphere, both hemispheres probably learn also.

Another experiment was carried out in a similar way to test the conclusion that the transfer was mediated by the corpus callosum. The corpus callosum was cut in this experiment (see Figure 20.16, bottom). If this band of fibers were responsible for the interhemispheric transfer, cats should fail the discrimination problem when tested. This they did, and thus the corpus callosum seems to be necessary for the transfer obtained in the first experiment.

We probably learn with both hemispheres, and this is the reason that the lesions which are used to

ONE HEMISPHERE OF THE CEREBRUM KNOWS WHAT THE OTHER HEMISPHERE HAS LEARNED

FIGURE 20.16. *Diagrams of "split-brain" experiments. Above, visual input was restricted to one hemisphere by a cut of the optic chiasma, but the other hemisphere had also learned the problem. Below, visual input was restricted to one hemisphere, but the other hemisphere had not learned the problem when the corpus callosum was cut. (From Glickstein, 1965. In Ruch and Patton, 1965.)*

investigate cortical functions must be bilateral before any learning deficit is obtained. In other words, these experiments show that the hemispheres are functionally equivalent for some kinds of learning. In discriminations for which the cortex is not necessary, visual brightness discriminations, for example, results of this sort are not obtained [Meikle and Sechzer, 1960]. Presumably midbrain commissures, that is, fiber tracts crossing the midline from one side of the brain to the other, mediate the transfer of brightness discriminations.

MOLECULAR CHANGES IN LEARNING AND MEMORY The general belief, for which little, if any, direct evidence exists, is that the pattern of neuron interconnections is what is altered in learning. These changes are thought by some to be at the synapses where neurons are functionally connected, and such changes are supposed to be relatively permanent. The time scale here is quite different from that in most neurophysiological events—it is a matter of days, months, or years, rather than milliseconds. What is the molecular basis of these long-term changes?

An organizing theory. One of the functions of a theory is to guide research, and the theory we detail here does serve this function: It should not be thought of as a final statement.

The theory states that memory is carried in the nervous system by both short-term and long-term changes [Hebb, 1949]. More than this, the long-term changes depend upon the prior presence of short-term activity. According to this theory, when an organism is first exposed to a learning situation, activity begins in chains, or collections, of neurons in the brain; this short-term activity will not persist unless the learner is repeatedly exposed to the situation. In this short-term stage, the activity is usually considered to be nerve impulses travelling around reverberatory, or self-exciting, circuits (see Figure 19.6, page 676). This activity, if it lasts long enough, changes the synaptic relations between the cells so that they are permanently reorganized. Later, after reorganization has occurred, if one cell

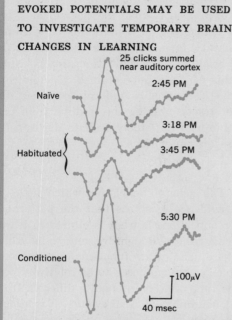

EVOKED POTENTIALS MAY BE USED TO INVESTIGATE TEMPORARY BRAIN CHANGES IN LEARNING

25 clicks summed near auditory cortex

Naïve — 2:45 PM

Habituated — 3:18 PM — 3:45 PM

Conditioned — 5:30 PM

100μV

40 msec

FIGURE 20.17. *The summed auditory evoked potentials recorded from the cerebral cortex of a monkey during three stages of a conditioning experiment. During the first, or naïve, stage, the evoked potentials are relatively large; next, they habituate with repeated presentation of the click stimulus; finally, after the click has been paired with a noxious stimulus, the evoked potential is enhanced. (Modified from Galambos and Sheatz, 1962.)*

clude that several such trace systems are organized in learning new habits. Thus, it should not be surprising if studies show that large masses of brain tissue must be removed before memories are destroyed.

If this theory is more or less correct, we ought to be able to find some evidence for it—after all, a theory is not only a guide to research, it also provides a framework for many rather diverse facts. First, some evidence for temporary changes in the electrical activity of the nervous system during learning should exist to correspond with the short-term phase of trace formation. Next, some studies should show that the memory trace, or engram, is easily disrupted during the time it is consolidating in the short-term phase, but that it cannot be easily disrupted after it has been "fixed." Finally, some studies should tell us something about the actual structural synaptic changes involved in the permanent organization between cells. Studies exist on all these aspects of the problem. What is lacking is any set of experiments showing that the long-term changes actually depend upon the short-term changes. Let us look at the evidence bearing on temporary changes, consolidation and its disruption, and the nature of the permanent change.

Temporary neural changes in learning. Electrical recording techniques provide evidence of temporary neural changes during learning (see page 692). The following experiment illustrates some of the temporary electrical changes which have been seen to occur [Galambos and Sheatz, 1962]:

Recording eelctrodes were implanted in or near the auditory cortex of cats and monkeys. Then the evoked potential in response to a click was recorded (see page 693). At first, the summed evoked potentials were approximately 300 microvolts (μV) in peak-to-peak amplitude; but after the click had been presented alone for a time, the evoked potentials were much smaller (see Figure 20.17). In other words, the evoked response *habituated.* Habituation itself may be evidence of the plasticity of neural tissue. When the habituated response was stable, a conditioning procedure was begun in which the uncondi-

of the circuit is fired, the others organized with it will also fire (see page 372). This relatively permanent reorganization is, according to the theory, the way memories are stored in the brain. The memory trace is rather fragile and can be disrupted while it is in the short-term phase, but after it has passed into the long-term phase it is quite resistant to disruption.

From the evidence on functional equivalence and the fact that both hemispheres learn, we may contioned stimulus was an unpleasantly strong air puff and the conditioned stimulus was the click. Eventually, the animal learned to avoid the air puff, and after it was thus conditioned, the summed evoked response to the click had increased to approximately 550 microvolts peak-to-peak amplitude (see Figure 20.17). With extinction of the conditioned response, the amplitude of the evoked response to the click decreased.

Thus, electrical changes undoubtedly occur in the nervous system during learning, but it is doubtful that these are reflections of the reverberatory activity called for by the theory. In fact, these electrical changes may be more related to mechanisms involved in perception than in learning. When an organism is alert and "paying attention to" a stimulus, the amplitude of the potential evoked by that stimulus tends to be great. When he is not paying attention to the stimulus, or when he is attending to something else, the amplitude of the evoked potential is markedly reduced (see page 344). In conditioning, the animal may be learning to attach significance to the conditioned stimulus—that is, to pay attention to it—and the increase in the evoked potential may simply reflect changes in attention.

Other experiments have shown that prolonged bombardment of the spinal cord along the sensory pathways into the cord reduces the threshold for excitation [Eccles and McIntyre, 1953]. This change in threshold, called *post-tetanic potentiation,* is fairly long lasting, but the bombardment is far greater than any which could reasonably be expected in learning.

Thus, none of these experiments on temporary electrical connection provide evidence for the types of electrical activity crucial to the reverberating trace theory of memory. Perhaps direct evidence will be forthcoming.

Consolidation. According to the theory, a short-term process, electrical, chemical, or otherwise, should occur after exposure to a learning situation if long-term memories are to be "fixed." Experiments have demonstrated the existence of such a *consolidation process* by disrupting it at various times *after* learning trials. Electroconvulsive shock (ECS)—a strong

current passed through the animal's brain which induces a convulsion by stimulating the motor areas—and anesthetic agents given shortly after trials are two of the ways in which the short-term process has been disrupted. The following experiment, one of the first to show the disruption of short-term memory traces, used electroconvulsive shock [Duncan, 1949]:

The rats in this experiment were taught an avoidance response in a two-compartment box. The rats were placed in the black compartment of the box and a foot shock was given if they did not move to the other compartment, a white one, within 10 seconds. The experimenter was interested in the number of these avoidance responses made in 18 trials which were given once a day. Rats in the experimental groups were given electroconvulsive shock (ECS) at various times after the completion of a trial, whether or not they had avoided within 10 seconds; rats in the control group did not receive electroconvulsive shock.

The time between the end of a trial and electroconvulsive shock proved to be crucial: Brain shocks given within an hour after a trial impeded learning, but those given after more than an hour were without effect (see Figure 20.18). This result was interpreted as indicating that the electroconvulsive shock was interfering with a consolidation process which lasted up to one hour. In other words, electroconvulsive shocks given within an hour after a trial interfered with the memory storage of that trial.

More recent experiments, done with better control, have tended to substantiate the general idea of a consolidation period and hence a short-term memory process [Weissman, 1963; King, 1965]. The details of the short-term process are not clear and the time course of the process may not be so long as these experiments would seem to indicate [Chorover and Shiller, 1965]. But something does happen after a trial.

The permanent neural changes in memory. One view of memory traces, as we have seen, holds that the organization of nerve cells is changed in memory so that cells which were not previously excited together react together subsequently. These theories assume that new, and relatively permanent, synaptic connections are made in learning. But what happens

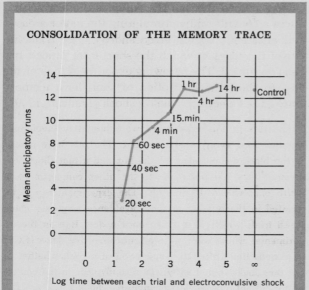

CONSOLIDATION OF THE MEMORY TRACE

Log time between each trial and electroconvulsive shock

FIGURE 20.18. *The number of correct responses depends on the length of time between the end of a trial and the application of electroconvulsive shock. The electroconvulsive shock is considered to be a disrupter of the consolidation of memory traces and the data summarized in this graph are considered to support the idea of a consolidation process. (From Duncan, 1949.)*

to the cells and synapses to make such connections possible? Various chemical theories are among the newer notions of synaptic change. Some of the most popular of these postulate that changes in ribonucleic acid (RNA) molecules in the cell are the ultimate physical basis of memory. RNA controls the formation of proteins and enzymes, especially those involved in the growth of cells and, for our purposes, the elaboration and construction of transmitter substances (see page 679).

These chemical theories propose that stimulation of a neuron, perhaps by repeated activity of the sort postulated to occur in reverberating circuits, changes the RNA and hence the amounts of various types of

proteins and enzymes. Some evidence exists that prolonged stimulation may result in changes in RNA. Studies have shown that the RNA in one of the vestibular nuclei is changed after many trials in which rats were required to balance on a wire when they climbed to a platform to get food [Hydén and Egyházi, 1962]. Other studies have shown an increase in the amount of cellular RNA after prolonged stimulation by other means [Morrell, 1961]. Assuming that the RNA in the cell body can be changed, or increased in amount, by stimulation, the proteins and enzymes whose synthesis is controlled by the altered RNA must somehow affect the synaptic region. No evidence exists for synaptic protein changes due to altered cellular RNA. The idea that the cellular changes in RNA may be important in memory is a tantalizing one, but without further evidence, the chemical theories of memory remain unsubstantiated.

Despite a lack of data supporting a chemical theory in detail, some experiments support the general idea that protein and enzyme synthesis are involved in the permanent changes which take place in memory [Flexner, et al., 1963]:

Mice were taught an avoidance response in a Y maze, and at various times after learning the correct response, they received injections into the brain of a drug which temporarily inhibits protein synthesis—puromycin. The results indicated that injections one to three days after learning, presumably while active protein synthesis was taking place, impaired memory for the learned avoidance response. Injections at later times after learning, unless massive, did not impair memory. Since other drugs did not produce memory loss, these results seem to indicate that protein synthesis is involved in the permanent neural changes in memory. Furthermore, the synthesis of proteins involved in permanent memory seems to take place within several days. However, the time course of this effect does not correspond with that of consolidation experiments.

Finally, if a rather permanent reorganization of synaptic relationships occurs, some evidence for *relatively permanent* electrical changes within the nervous system in learning should exist. Except for the experiments on post-tetanic potentiation, little such evidence exists from studies done under more "normal," or physiological, conditions. However, relatively permanent electrical changes have been shown following classical conditioning, and this may point the way toward a better understanding of the molecular basis of memory [Rutledge, 1965].

In summary, we are still far from a convincing biological, or physiological, theory of memory. About all we have now is a series of guesses and some tantalizing bits of evidence. Further research alone can tell us whether or not these guesses and bits of evidence lead anywhere. The biological explanation of memory, and, for that matter, other behaviors and psychological events, remains one of the most significant problems of psychology.

SYNOPSIS AND SUMMARY

In this chapter, we have been concerned with the relationships between behavior and experience and the nervous system. In other words, we have been concerned with the so-called mind-body problem. Many solutions to this problem have been suggested during the course of intellectual history. The physiological or biological psychologist is not particularly interested in the mind-body relationship as a theoretical philosophical problem; he is interested in it, rather, as an empirical problem. The physiological psychologist usually takes the common-sense view; he uses two languages, the set of terms referring to experience, on the one hand, and the set of terms referring to bodily events on the other. In practice, he is not concerned with the philosophical speculations about the relationship between mind and body. But he *is* concerned with establishing correlations between bodily events and experience and behavior. In studying this correlation, we have made the following points:

1. The cerebral cortex functions in many of the behaviors and experiences of man. Much of our knowledge of man, however, is inferred from acute and chronic experiments on animals.
2. Although considerable overlap exists, three major regions—the motor areas, the sensory areas, and the "association" areas—of the cortex may be distinguished for purposes of discussion. In a very general way, the motor areas lie around the central fissure, the sensory areas behind the central fissure, and the "association" areas in the frontal, parietal, occipital, and temporal lobes.

3. Cells of the cortex contribute fibers to the pyramidal and extrapyramidal motor systems. Although contribution to these systems is fairly widespread over the cortex, movements of the body are most easily elicited by stimulation of the precentral gyrus. The body is topographically represented on this gyrus.
4. Pathways for vision, audition, and certain of the skin and bodily senses, or somesthesis, proceed to the thalamus and from there to the cerebral cortex. Each of these senses seems to have a relatively orderly topographic arrangement on the cortex. The topographic arrangement is best developed in vision, where it is sometimes called a point-to-point projection.
5. If a sensory area of a person's cortex is electrically stimulated, he reports the corresponding sensory experience. The visual cortical areas seem to be necessary for form perception; the auditory cortex seems necessary for tone pattern perception and the localization of sounds in space.
6. The large areas of "association" cortex are involved in many functions. The term "association" is something of a misnomer since this cortex does not "associate" motor and sensory events or "elaborate" sensory input to the sensory areas of the cortex. Instead, the parietal association cortex seems necessary for tactile shape recognition and the recognition of different roughnesses and weights; no functions have definitely been found for the occipital association cortex; the temporal association cortex seems to be involved in visual discrimination; and the frontal association cortex seems to be involved in complex response abilities.
7. The speech areas of the human cortex almost always seem to be on the left hemisphere regardles of handedness. Areas in the frontal, parietal, and temporal lobes on the left hemisphere have been shown to be necessary

for symbolic speech. Lesions in these areas often produce aphasia—disorders of symbolic speech.

8. Centers for the major physiological motives of hunger, thirst, and sex exist in the hypothalamus. Usually they occur in pairs; one member is excitatory, and the other inhibitory. Destruction of one member increases motivated behavior; destruction of the other greatly reduces it. Direct electrical or chemical stimulation of the appropriate centers can "start" or "stop" the motivated behavior. Ordinarily, motivated behavior is "started" and "stopped" by conditions within the internal environment of the body.

9. Mechanisms for activation and sleep are found in the hypothalamus, the reticular activating system, and the cerebral cortex. Regions of the posterior hypothalamus are "waking centers" and there is some evidence for "sleep centers" in the anterior hypothalamus. The reticular activating system receives impulses from sensory systems and activates the cortex.

10. The principal system concerned with emotional behavior is called the limbic system. The hypothalamus, the septal area, the amygdala, the cingulate cortex, and the fiber connections between them are some of the most important components of the limbic system. The septal area and cingulate cortex appear to be inhibitory, the amygdala excitatory, but the balance between these nuclei and regions is complex and the pattern of interaction seems to be the crucial thing controlling emotional expression.

11. Direct electrical stimulation of the limbic system is sometimes "pleasant," sometimes "unpleasant." Stimulation in certain positions can serve as negative reinforcement in avoidance learning; in other positions, stimulation is positively reinforcing, for animals will learn and repeatedly perform habits with electric shock to the brain as the only reinforcement. Stimulation of portions of the hypothalamus achieves this very effectively.

12. The neural basis of learning and memory has been studied by two approaches. One approach is to seek out the areas of the nervous system involved in learning; the other approach attempts to discover the molecular, or cellular and synaptic, changes underlying learning and memory.

13. Studies on the location of the neural changes in learning and memory have shown that learning is multiply represented in the brain. This is clearly demonstrated by experiments showing that both hemispheres of the cerebral cortex participate in learning.

14. It is generally thought that the molecular changes in learning and memory will be found in changes of synaptic organization and in the patterns of neuron interconnections. A theory postulating short-term and long-term memory traces has been advanced, but the evidence supporting this theory is not direct. Evidence bearing on the theory comes from studies of temporary electrical changes in the nervous system in learning, from studies on the disruption of consolidation, and from studies of stimulus-induced changes in the ribonucleic acid of neurons.

RELATED TOPICS IN THE TEXT

CHAPTER 3 PRINCIPLES OF LEARNING Some of the kinds of learning for which a physiological explanation is sought are described here.

CHAPTER 4 HUMAN LEARNING, REMEMBERING, AND FORGETTING Speculations about long-term and short-term processes in human memory are presented. Some similarity may exist between these processes and the long- and short-term processes discussed in the investigation of the physiological basis of memory.

CHAPTER 6 MOTIVATION A review of some of the behavioral facts about physiological motivation may be useful.

CHAPTER 7 EMOTION The changes wrought by the autonomic system in emotion were described in Chapter 7. In this chapter—Chapter 20—some of the central regions controlling autonomic activity are discussed.

CHAPTERS 8, 9, AND 10 KNOWING THE WORLD These chapters describe the peripheral receptors of the central pathways which are discussed here in Chapter 20.

CHAPTER 15 MENTAL HEALTH AND PSYCHOTHERAPY Some of the functions of the frontal lobes, as revealed by human lobotomy cases, are presented in this chapter.

SUGGESTIONS FOR FURTHER READING

Beach, F. A., Hebb, D. O., Morgan, C. T., and Nissen, H. W. (Eds.). *The neuropsychology of Lashley: Selected papers of K. S. Lashley.* New York: McGraw-Hill, 1960.
Some of the most important papers of one of the pioneers in biological psychology are reprinted in this volume.

Diamond, I. T., and Chow, K. L. Biological psychology. In S. Koch (Ed.), *Psychology: A study of a science.* Vol. 4. New York: McGraw-Hill, 1962.
A paper covering the development of the thalamus and relating this to function. It also covers the functions of the cortex and physiological events in learning.

Isaacson, R. I. (Ed.). *Basic readings in neuropsychology.* New York: Harper & Row, 1964. (Paperback.)
A collection of some of the most important papers in the field of physiological psychology.

King, R. A. (Ed.). *Readings for an introduction to psychology* (2d ed.). New York: McGraw-Hill, 1966. (Paperback.)
A book of readings designed to accompany this text.

Morgan, C. T. *Physiological psychology* (3d ed.). New York: McGraw-Hill, 1965.
A standard text on the physiological mechanisms of behavior.

Ranson, S. W., and Clark, S. L. *The anatomy of the nervous system: Its development and function* (10th ed.). Philadelphia: Saunders, 1959.
A standard medical textbook of neuroanatomy. Not particularly difficult reading.

Ruch, T. C., and Patton, H. D. (Eds.). *Physiology and biophysics* (19th ed.). Philadelphia: Saunders, 1965. Chaps. 1–26.
Chapters 22–26 are especially pertinent to the subjects discussed in this chapter.

Teitelbaum, P. *Physiological psychology.* Englewood Cliffs, N.J.: Prentice-Hall, 1966. (Paperback.)
A short, readable introduction to the biological basis of behavior.

Wooldridge, D. E. *The machinery of the brain.* New York: McGraw-Hill, 1963. (Paperback.)
A popularly written book explaining some of the physiological mechanisms of behavior in nontechnical language.

AS A STUDENT you may be taking psychology for many reasons: to satisfy a college requirement, because of an interest developed through high school courses or general reading, or as part of training in a related field—education, social work, nursing, business, and so forth. After this beginning course, you may find your interest satisfied—or perhaps, dissipated; but, more likely, your interest in some aspects of psychology has been whetted. If so, after taking a few more psychology courses to be sure, you may decide to major in psychology.

What can a psychology major do? Two routes are open: He can go to graduate school and become a professional psychologist, or he may go off into the business world after finishing college. Suppose we follow the latter path first.

For the student who does not go into graduate school, psychology offers little or no opportunity for professional employment if one has only a bachelor's degree. There are some positions here and there as assistants, which may be attractive to a girl who plans later to make a career of marriage or to a man who needs temporary employment before going on to other things, but such jobs usually offer little future. Some industrial positions also exist, chiefly in personnel work, which are open to those holding undergraduate degrees in psychology. In general, if one plans to make a career of psychology, he must go to graduate school.

If an undergraduate psychology major does *not* prepare a student for professional work in psychology, what can he do? Actually, he is in practically the same position as any student who has majored in any one of the arts or sciences. A major in English, history, political science, and, for that matter, even chemistry or mathematics does not by itself lead to a professional career—further training is necessary. But industry and government are interested in people who have taken a general education course with a major in any of the arts or sciences. This interest is summed up in the following quotations from employers in government and business: "We look for bright people even though they are not fully trained," or more succinctly, "If you educate them, we will train them."[1]

What of the student whose interests and talents lead him to a career in professional psychology? He has a long but rewarding preparation before him. While still an undergraduate, he should take a broad program in the natural and social sciences. Psychology bridges these groups of sciences and requires some knowledge of each. Hence it is advisable to take some training in mathematics, physics, chemistry, biology, sociology, and anthropology. Students who are most interested in psychology as an experimental science should, of course, emphasize the natural sciences—especially physiology, zoology, chemistry, and mathematics. Those most interested in the clinical, social, educational, and industrial subfields should take further work in the social sciences. In any case, one should not concentrate too much in psychology; specialization can be left to graduate training.

In addition to the training we have been talking about, the psychology major, or anyone for that matter, is probably well advised to develop a skill or interest unrelated to his field. It is fun for most people to be able to do something well, or to know a great deal about some subject. The undergraduate psychology major might develop his skill in music, his interest in some aspect of history, his skill in art, or languages, and so on. This, of course, applies to the psychology majors who are going into the profession as well as those who are not. For the professionally oriented major, skill in languages will be a useful asset in later training because most graduate schools require a reading knowledge of one or two languages for the Ph.D. degree.

[1] For more on this see: King, M. S., and Kimble, G. A. Job opportunities for undergraduate psychology majors. *American Psychologist*, 1958, 13, 23–27. This article has been reprinted in King, R. A., *Readings for an introduction to psychology* (2d ed.). New York: McGraw-Hill, 1966.

Graduate training is a necessary part of the preparation for a professional career in psychology. Standards for admission to graduate school in psychology are quite high. To be admitted, the candidate usually must have aptitudes considerably above those of the average college student—most graduate schools require that the applicant take special tests of aptitude—and his grade record must be good. The majority of those admitted have B to A averages, especially in the junior and senior years of college, and most graduate schools do not admit C or low B students unless something in their records indicates that they can do the quality of work required in graduate school. Such indications might be a marked improvement to the A or B level in the junior and senior years of college and marks of brilliance in the record—for example, excellent grades in the more demanding science courses.

One does not have to be rich, or even able to afford the usual cost of college, to go to graduate school. Numerous fellowships and assistantships are available to graduate students, and it is a very rare student who cannot obtain substantial assistance once he has enrolled and done satisfactory work for a year. Almost all graduate students are self-supporting, although not wealthy, through fellowships or assistantships, by the time they take their doctoral degrees.

Two degrees are available in graduate schools—the master's degree (M.A. or M.S.) and the doctor of philosophy (Ph.D.). The master's degree, which is the only degree offered by some of the smaller graduate schools, requires one to two years of full-time work or its equivalent. The program for this degree usually includes a core curriculum taken by all graduate students in the department; it also provides an opportunity to specialize somewhat in the field in which the person expects to be employed. Sometimes the master's degree is part of the training for the doctor of philosophy degree—that is, the student on the way to this higher degree more or less automatically meets the requirements for the master's degree. Usually, however, students work directly for the Ph.D. which is required for the highest level of professional work in psychology. The Ph.D., whether or not a master's degree is obtained along the way, usually requires a total of three to five years of full-time work or its equivalent. It involves considerably more advanced and specialized work than the master's degree as well as the completion of a significant piece of research. In most graduate schools, the advanced psychology graduate student is treated as an apprentice and works in the laboratory or clinic under the close supervision of a staff member, or a committee of staff members. For those specializing in clinical psychology, one of the years of graduate training, typically the third, is an internship year in which the student works in a clinical setting—for example, a counseling center or hospital—in a professional capacity.

Many employment opportunities exist in public and private schools, in clinical settings, in industry, and in government for those holding the master's degree. The person must expect, however, to receive a substantially lower salary than he could earn if he held a doctor's degree, and his opportunities for promotion are often limited. In some areas, however, particularly in government and industry, he has about the same opportunity to succeed as the person with a doctorate. On the other hand, for most regular teaching positions in colleges and universities and for a position of responsibility in a research organization or clinical setting, the doctorate is now almost mandatory. In general, a person who expects to make a life-long career of psychology in teaching and/or research is well advised to try for the doctor's degree.

The remuneration for positions in psychology varies considerably from one situation to another. In general, it is lowest in teaching positions, somewhat higher in government, and highest in industry. On the whole, the financial rewards in psychology compare reasonably well with those of other professional pursuits, and the positions that are not so lucrative often have the compensation of allowing more freedom for research, writing, and independent work.

For additional information on careers in psychology, the student should consult his professor and the journal *American Psychologist*. This journal publishes an annual list of the fellowships and assistantships available to prospective graduate students. It also contains articles on the income of psychologists working in various settings.

If you do major in psychology, good luck.

SOME OF THE TOPICS mentioned in this text may have aroused interest—we hope so. Many other interesting subjects on the fringes of psychology have been deliberately omitted. But if you want to know more, here are a few general guides.

Perhaps the first place to look is in the *Psychological Abstracts*. Here you will find a list of subjects and authors, together with references to the journals and books in which they appear. The *Psychological Abstracts* are arranged by year so you may have to look through several volumes before you have a fairly complete set of references. Similar index sources are available in other fields related to psychology: *The Sociological Abstracts, Education Index,* and the *Public Affairs Information Service* provide a listing in several of the social-science fields related to psychology. The *Index Medicus* and *Biological Abstracts* list articles in the biologically related fields. Chances are, however, that if the article has any psychological relevance at all, it will be listed in the *Psychological Abstracts*. Incidentally, *Psychological Abstracts* was not started until 1927 and a list of references before that date can be found in the *Psychological Index,* a supplement of the *Psychological Review*. In addition, the *Readers' Guide to Periodical Literature* may help the student find popular articles on many psychological subjects. These are often useful in the first stages of becoming acquainted with a topic, but serious interest should not stop here. Most of these reference sources will be available in any reasonably complete college library. If they are not available, you should complain to the librarian and to your professor.

The general card catalog of the library may be of some help if books have been written about the topic in which you are interested. It often happens, however, that a shorter article is more valuable than a whole book, at least in the initial stages of study. You may also use the Suggestions for Further Reading, which are given at the end of each text chapter, for locating books on a subject.

Finally, when you locate a book or article, look at the list of references at the end of it. These references often prove to be invaluable in calling attention to significant work in an area, for the author has done much of the winnowing for you. For this purpose it is, of course, usually useful to have a recent book or article.

With these hints, and the other resources and techniques you will develop for yourself, you should have no trouble finding information about almost any psychological subject. From here on, it is up to you to select and evaluate the relevance of the articles and books you find. We hope this text and your beginning psychology course have enabled you to begin to do a reasonably good job of this. Always be a little skeptical—there is still a tinge of charlatanism in psychology.

Adametz, J. H. (1959). Rate of recovery of functioning in cats with rostral reticular lesions. *J. Neurosurg.*, 16, 85–98.

Adams, D. K. (1931). A restatement of the problem of learning. *Brit. J. Psychol.*, 22, 150–178.

Adamson, R. E. (1952). Functional fixedness as related to problem solving: A repetition of three experiments. *J. exp. Psychol.*, 44, 288–291.

Ades, H. W. (1946). Effect of extirpation of parastriate cortex on learned visual discrimination in monkeys. *J. Neuropath. exp. Neurol.*, 5, 60–65.

Ades, H. W. (1959). Central auditory mechanisms. In J. Field, H. W. Magoun, and V. E. Hall (Eds.), *Handbook of physiology*. Vol. 1. Washington, D.C.: American Physiological Society. Pp. 585–613.

Adkins, D. C. (1964). *Statistics*. Columbus, Ohio: Charles Merrill.

Adolph, E. F. (1941). The internal environment and behavior. III. Water content. *Amer. J. Psychiat.*, 97, 1365–1373.

Adorno, T. W., Frenkel-Brunswik, E., Levinson, D. J., and Sanford, R. N. (1950). *The authoritarian personality*. New York: Harper & Row.

Advisory Committee to the Surgeon General (1964). *Smoking and health*. Washington, D.C.: U.S. Department of Health, Education, and Welfare.

Albee, G. W. (1963). American psychology in the sixties. *Amer. Psychologist*, 18, 90–95.

Alexander, F., and French, T. M. (Eds.) (1946). *Psychoanalytic therapy*. New York: Ronald.

Allinsmith, W., and Allinsmith, B. (1948). Religious affiliation and politico-economic attitude. *Publ. Opin. Quart.*, 12, 377–389.

Allport, F. H. (1924). *Social psychology*. Boston: Houghton Mifflin.

Allport, F. H. (1955). *Theories of perception and the concept of structure*. New York: Wiley.

Allport, G. W. (1937). *Personality*. New York: Holt, Rinehart and Winston.

Allport, G. W. (1954). *The nature of prejudice*. Cambridge, Mass.: Addison-Wesley.

Allport, G. W., and Kramer, B. (1946). Some roots of prejudice. *J. Psychol.*, 22, 9–39.

Allport, G. W., and Odbert, H. S. (1936). Trait names, a psycholexical study. *Psychol. Monogr.*, 47 (Whole No. 211).

Allport, G. W., Vernon, P. E., and Lindzey, G. (1960). *A study of values: A scale for measuring the dominant interests in personality* (3d ed.). Boston: Houghton Mifflin.

American Institute of Public Opinion, release of April, 1945.

American Institute of Public Opinion, release of October 11, 1960.

American Psychiatric Association (1952). *Diagnostic and statistical manual: Mental disorders*. Washington, D.C.: Amer. Psychiat. Assoc.

American Psychological Association (1959). Ethical standards of psychologists. *Amer. Psychologist*, 14, 279–282.

Amoore, J. E., Johnston, J. W., Jr., and Rubin, M. (1964). The stereochemical theory of odor. *Sci. Amer.*, 210 (2), 42–49.

Anastasi, Anne (1961). *Psychological Testing* (2d ed.). New York: Macmillan.

Anastasi, A. (1964). *Fields of applied psychology*. New York: McGraw-Hill.

Anastasi, A., and Foley, J. P., Jr. (1958). *Differential psychology* (3d ed.). New York: Macmillan.

Andersson, B. (1953). The effect of injections of hypertonic NaCl solutions into different parts of the hypothalamus of goats. *Acta Physiol., Scand.*, 28, 188–201.

Arnold, M. (1960). *Emotion and personality*. Vol. I. *Psychological aspects*. New York: Columbia Univer. Press.

Arnold, M. (1960). *Emotion and personality*. Vol. II. *Neurological and physiological aspects*. New York: Columbia Univer. Press.

Asch, S. E. (1951). Effects of group pressure upon the modification and distortion of judgments. In H. Guetzkow (Ed.), *Groups, leadership and men*. Pittsburgh: Carnegie Press. Pp. 177–190.

Asch, S. E. (1958). Effects of group pressure upon the modification and distortion of judgments. In E. E. Maccoby, T. M. Newcomb, and E. L. Hartley (Eds.), *Readings in social psychology* (3d ed.). New York: Holt, Rinehart and Winston. Pp. 174–183.

Asch, S. E., Block, H., and Hertzman, M. (1940). Studies in the principles of judgments and attitudes. II. Determination of judgments by group and by ego standards. *J. soc. Psychol.*, 12, 433–465.

Atkinson, J. W. (Ed.) (1958). *Motives in fantasy, action, and society*. Princeton, N.J.: Van Nostrand.

Ax, A. F. (1953). The physiological differentiation of fear and anger. *Psychosom. Med.*, 15, 433–442.

Axline, V. M. (1947). *Play therapy*. Boston: Houghton Mifflin.

Ayllon, T. (1963). Intensive treatment of psychotic behaviour by stimulus satiation and food reinforcement. *Behav. Res. Ther.*, 1, 53–61.

Bachrach, A. J. (1962). *Psychological research: An introduction*. New York: Random House.

Baker, C. H., and Young, P. (1960). Feedback during training and retention of motor skills. *Canad. J. Psychol.*, 14, 257–264.

Baker, R. A. (Ed.) (1963). *Psychology in the wry*. Princeton, N.J.: Van Nostrand.

Baldwin, A. L. (1948). Socialization and the parent-child relationship. *Child Developm.*, 19, 127–136.

Bales, R. F. (1950). A set of categories for the analysis of small group interaction. *Amer. Sociol. Rev.*, 15, 257–263.

Bales, R. F. (1952). Some uniformities of behavior in small social systems. In G. E. Swanson, T. M. Newcomb, and E. L. Hartley (Eds.), *Readings in social psychology* (Rev. ed.). New York: Holt, Rinehart and Winston, 1952. Pp. 146–159.

Bandura, A. (1965). Personal Communication.

Bandura, A., Ross, D., and Ross, S. A. (1963). Imitation of film-mediated aggressive models. *J. abnorm. soc. Psychol., 66,* 3–11.

Bandura, A., and Walters, R. H. (1963). *Social learning and personality development.* New York: Holt, Rinehart and Winston.

Bard, P. (1928). A diencephalic mechanism for the expression of rage with special reference to the sympathetic nervous system. *Amer. J. Physiol., 84,* 490–515.

Bard, P. (1934). On emotional expression after decortication with some remarks on certain theoretical views. *Psychol. Rev., 41,* 309–329.

Bard, P., and Mountcastle, V. B. (1947). Some forebrain mechanisms involved in the expression of rage with special reference to suppression of angry behavior. *Res. Publ. Ass. nerv. ment. Dis., 27,* 362–404.

Bare, J. K. (1949). The specific hunger for sodium chloride in normal adrenal ectomized white rats. *Journal comp. physiol. Psychol., 42,* 242–253.

Barker, R., Dembo, T., and Lewin, K. (1941). Frustration and regression, an experiment with young children. *Univer. Iowa Stud. Child Welf., 18,* No. 386.

Barker, R. G., and Wright, H. F. (1951). *One boy's day.* New York: Harper & Row.

Barker, R. G., and Wright, H. F. (1954). *Midwest and its children: The psychological ecology of an American town.* Evanston, Ill.: Row, Peterson.

Barron, F. (1963). *Creativity and psychological health.* Princeton, N.J.: Van Nostrand.

Bartlett, F. C. (1932). *Remembering: An experimental and social study.* London: Cambridge Univer. Press.

Bartlett, F. C. (1958). *Thinking: An experimental and social study.* London: G. Allen.

Bartley, S. H. (1958). *Principles of perception.* New York: Harper & Row.

Bateson, G., Jackson, D. D., Haley, J., and Weakland, J. H. (1956). Toward a theory of schizophrenia. *Behav. Sci., 1,* 251–256.

Baughman, E. E., and Welsh, G. S. (1962). *Personality: A behavioral science.* Englewood Cliffs, N.J.: Prentice-Hall.

Beach, F. A. (1947). Evolutionary changes in the physiological control of mating behavior in mammals. *Psychol. Rev., 54,* 297–315. (*a*)

Beach, F. A. (1947). A review of physiological and psychological studies of sexual behavior in mammals. *Physiol. Rev., 27,* 240–307. (*b*)

Beach, F. A. (1949). *Hormones and behavior.* New York: Hoeber-Harper.

Beach, F. A. (1960). Experimental investigations of species-specific behavior. *Amer. Psychologist, 15,* 1–18.

Beach, F. A., Hebb. D. O., Morgan, C. T., and Nissen, H. W. (Eds.) (1960). *The Neuropsychology of Lashley.* New York: McGraw-Hill.

Beardslee, D. C., and Wertheimer, M. (Eds.) (1958). *Readings in perception.* Princeton, N.J.: Van Nostrand.

Beck, E. C., and Doty, R. W. (1957). Conditioned flexion reflexes acquired during combined catalepsy and de-efferentation. *J. comp. physiol. Psychol., 50,* 211–215.

Békésy, G. von (1960). *Experiments in hearing.* New York: McGraw-Hill.

Békésy, G. von, and Rosenblith, W. A. (1951). The mechanical properties of the ear. In S. S. Stevens (Ed.), *Handbook of experimental psychology.* New York: Wiley. Pp. 1075–1115.

Bekhterev, V. M. (1932). *General Principles of Human Reflexology.* New York: International.

Bell, G., and French, R. (1950). Consistency of individual leadership position in small groups of varying membership. *J. abnorm. soc. Psychol., 45,* 764–767.

Bellows, R. M. (1949). *Psychology of personnel in business and industry.* Englewood Cliffs, N.J.: Prentice-Hall.

Benedict, R. (1959). *Patterns of culture* (2d ed.). Boston: Houghton Mifflin.

Benjamin, R. F., and Thompson, R. F. (1959). Differential effects of cortical lesions in infant and adult cats on roughness discriminations. *Exp. Neurol.,* 305–321.

Bennett, E. L., Diamond, M. C., Krech, D., and Rosenzweig, M. R. (1964). Chemical and anatomical plasticity of brain. *Science, 146,* 610–619.

Bennett, G. K., Seashore, H. G., and Wesman, A. G. (1951). *Counseling from profiles: A casebook for the Differential Aptitude Tests.* New York; Psychol. Corp.

Bennett, G. K., Seashore, H. G., and Wesman, A. G. (1959). *Differential Aptitude Tests.* New York: Psychol. Corp.

Benolken, R. M. (1961). Reversal of photoreceptor polarity recorded during the graded receptor potential response to light in the eye of *Limulus. Biophys. J., 1,* 551–564.

Bergeijk van, W. A., Pierce, J. R., and David, E. E., Jr. (1960). *Waves and the ear.* Garden City, N.Y.: Doubleday.

Berkowitz, L. (1954). Group standards, cohesiveness and productivity. *Hum. Relat., 7,* 509–519.

Berkowitz, L. (1962). *Aggression: A social psychological approach.* New York: McGraw-Hill.

Berkowitz, L., and Holmes, D. S. (1959). The generalization of hostility to disliked objects. *J. Pers., 27,* 565–577.

Berlyne, D. E. (1960). *Conflict, arousal, and curiosity.* New York: McGraw-Hill.

Bernard, C. (1859). *Lecons sur les propriétés physiologiques et les altérations pathologiques des liquides de l'organisme.* Paris: Baillière.

Bettelheim, B. (1943). Individual and mass behavior in extreme situations. *J. abnorm. soc. Psychol., 38,* 417–452.

Bexton, W. H., Heron, W., and Scott, T. H. (1954). Effects of decreased variation in the sensory environment. *Canad. J. Psychol., 8,* 70–76.

Bindra, D. (1958). *Motivation: A systematic reinterpretation.* New York: Ronald.

Bingham, W. V. D., Moore, B. V., and Gustad, J. W. (1959). *How to interview.* (rev. ed.). New York: Harper & Row.

Birch, H. G. (1945). The role of motivational factors in insightful problem-solving. *J. comp. Psychol.,* 43, 159–278.

Birnbrauer, J. S., Wolf, M. M., Kidder, J. D., and Tague, C. E. (1965). Classroom behavior of retarded pupils with token reinforcement. *J. exp. Child Psychol.,* 2, 219–235.

Birney, R. C., and Teevan, R. C. (Eds.) (1961). *Instinct.* Princeton, N.J.: Van Nostrand.

Birney, R. C., and Teevan, R. C. (Eds.) (1961). *Reinforcement.* Princeton, N.J.: Van Nostrand.

Blake, R., and Dennis, W. (1943). The development of stereotypes concerning the Negro. *J. abnorm. soc. Psychol.,* 38, 525–531.

Bleuler, E. (1950). *Dementia praecox or the group of schizophrenias* (trans. J. Zinkin). New York: International Univer. Press.

Blough, D. S. (1956). Dark adaptation in the pigeon. *J. comp. physiol. Psychol.,* 49, 425–430.

Blough, D. S. (1958). A method for obtaining psychophysical thresholds from the pigeon. *J. exp. anal. Behav.,* 1, 31–43.

Bond, E. D. (1954). Results of treatment in psychoses—with a control series. *Amer. J. Psychiat.,* 110, 881–887.

Bone, H. A., and Ranney, A. (1963). *Politics and voters.* New York: McGraw-Hill.

Bonner, D. M. (1961). *Heredity.* Englewood Cliffs, N.J.: Prentice-Hall.

Bonney, M. E. (1944). Relationships between social success, family size, socio-economic home background, and intelligence among school children in grades III and IV. *Sociometry,* 7, 26–39.

Bordin, E. S. (1955). *Psychological counseling.* New York: Appleton-Century-Crofts.

Boring, E. G. (1942). *Sensation and perception in the history of experimental psychology.* New York: Appleton-Century-Crofts.

Boring, E. G. (Ed.) (1945). *Psychology for the armed services.* Washington, D.C.: Combat Forces Press.

Boring, E. G. (1950). *A history of experimental psychology* (2d ed.). New York: Appleton-Century-Crofts.

Boring, E. G. (1953). A history of introspectionism. *Psychol. Bull.,* 50, 169–189.

Boyd, D. A., Jr., and Nie, L. W. (1949). Congenital universal indifference to pain. *Arch. Neurol. Psychiat., Chicago.* 61, 402–412.

Brady, J. V. (1958). Ulcers in "executive" monkeys. *Sci. Amer.,* 199 (4), 95–100.

Brady, J. V., and Bunnell, B. N. (1960). Behavior and the nervous system. In R. H. Waters, D. A. Rethlinshafer, and W. E. Caldwell (Eds.), *Principles of comparative psychology.* New York: McGraw-Hill. Chap. 12.

Brazier, M. A. B. (1960). *The electrical activity of the nervous system: A textbook for students* (2d ed.). London. Pitman.

Brehm, J. W., and Cohen, A. R. (1962). *Explorations in cognitive dissonance.* New York: Wiley.

Brenner, C. (1957). *An elementary textbook of psychoanalysis.* Garden City, N.Y.: Doubleday.

Bridger, W. H. (1961). Sensory habituation and discrimination in the human neonate. *Amer. J. Psychiat.,* 117, 991–996.

Bridges, K. M. B. (1932). Emotional development in early infancy. *Child Developm.,* 3, 324–341.

Bridgman, P. W. (1927). *The logic of modern physics.* New York: Macmillan.

Brindley, G. S. (1963). Afterimages. *Sci. Amer.,* 209, (4), 85–93.

Broadbent, D. E. (1958). *Perception and communication.* New York: Pergamon Press.

Broadbent, D., and Heron, A. (1962). Effects of a subsidiary task on performance involving immediate memory by younger and older men. *Brit. J. Psychol.,* 53, 189–198.

Brobeck, J. R. (1946). Mechanism of the development of obesity in animals with hypothalamic lesions. *Physiol. Rev.,* 26, 541–559.

Brodie, B. B., and Shore, P. A. (1957). A concept for a role of serotonin and norepinephrine as chemical mediators in the brain. *Ann. N.Y. Acad. Sci.,* 66, 631–642.

Bronfenbrenner, W. (1958). Socialization and social class through time and space. In E. E. Maccoby, T. M. Newcomb, and E. L. Hartley (Eds.), *Readings in social psychology* (3d ed.). New York: Holt, Rinehart and Winston.

Brookhart, J. M., and Dey, F. L. (1941). Reduction of sexual behavior in male guinea pigs by hypothalamic lesions. *Amer. J. Physiol.,* 133, 551–554.

Brown, J. (1958). Some tests of the decay theory of immediate memory. *Quart. J. exp. Psychol.,* 10, 12–21.

Brown, J. A. C. (1963). *Techniques of persuasion: From propaganda to brain-washing.* Baltimore, Md.: Penguin.

Brown, J. F. (1931). The visual perception of velocity. *Psychol. Forsch.,* 14, 199–232.

Brown, J. S. (1948). Gradients of approach and avoidance responses and their relation to motivation. *J. comp. physiol. Psychol.,* 41, 450–465.

Brown, R. (1958). *Words and things.* New York: Free Press.

Brown, R. (1965). *Social Psychology.* New York: Free Press.

Bruce, R. W. (1933). Conditions of transfer of training. *J. exp. Psychol.,* 16, 343–361.

Bruner, J. S., Goodnow, J. J., and Austin, G. A. (1956). *A study of thinking.* New York: Wiley.

Bryan, W. L., and Harter, N. (1899). Studies on the telegraphic language: The acquisition of a hierarchy of habits. *Psychol. Rev.,* 6, 345–375.

Buddenbrock, W. von (1958). *The senses.* Ann Arbor, Mich.: Univer. Michigan Press.

Bugelski, B. R. (1938). Extinction with and without subgoal reinforcement. *J. comp. Psychol.*, 26, 121–133.

Bugelski, B. R., and Cadwallader, T. C. (1956). A reappraisal of the transfer and retroaction surface. *J. exp. Psychol.*, 52, 360–366.

Burchard, J., and Tyler, V., Jr. (1965). The modification of delinquent behavior through operant conditioning. *Behav. Res. Ther.*, 245–250.

Buros, O. K. (Ed.) (1959). *The fifth mental measurements yearbook.* Highland Park, N.J.: Gryphon Press.

Burt, C., and Howard, M. (1956). The multiple factorial theory of inheritance and its application to intelligence. *Brit. J. statist. Psychol.*, 9, 95–131.

Burtt, H. E. (1941). An experimental study of early childhood memory. *J. genet. Psychol.*, 58, 435–439.

Buser, P., and Imbert, M. (1961). Sensory projections to the motor cortex in cats: A microelectrode study. In W. A. Rosenblith (Ed.), *Sensory Communication.* New York: Wiley. Pp. 607–626.

Bustanoby, J. H. (1947). *Principles of color and color mixing.* New York: McGraw-Hill.

Butler, R. A. (1953). Discrimination learning by rhesus monkeys to visual-exploration motivation. *J. comp. physiol. Psychol.*, 46, 95–98.

Butler, R. A. (1954). Incentive conditions which influence visual exploration. *J. exp. Psychol.*, 48, 19–23.

Butler, R. A., Diamond, I. T., and Neff, W. D. (1957). Role of auditory cortex in discrimination of changes in frequency. *J. Neurophysiol.*, 20, 108–120.

Cameron, N., and Magaret, A. (1951). *Behavior pathology.* Boston: Houghton Mifflin.

Campbell, A., Converse, P. E., Miller, W. E., Stokes, O. E. (1960). *The American voter.* New York: Wiley.

Campbell, D. T. (1960). Blind variation and selective retention in creative thought as in other knowledge processes. *Psychol. Rev.*, 67, 380–400.

Candland, D. K. (Ed.) (1962). *Emotion: Bodily change.* Princeton, N.J.: Van Nostrand.

Cannon, W. B. (1927). The James-Lange theory of emotions: A critical examination and an alternative theory. *Amer. J. Psychol.*, 39, 106–124.

Cannon, W. B. (1929). *Bodily changes in pain, hunger, fear and rage* (2d ed.). New York: Appleton-Century-Crofts.

Cannon, W. B. (1932). *The wisdom of the body.* New York: Norton.

Cannon, W. B. (1934). Hunger and thirst. In C. Murchison (Ed.), *A handbook of general experimental psychology.* Worcester, Mass.: Clark Univer. Press. Pp. 247–263.

Capote, T. (1966). *In cold blood.* New York: Random House.

Carlson, E. R. (1956). Attitude change and attitude structure. *J. abnorm. soc. Psychol.*, 52, 256–261.

Carmichael, L. (1927). A further study of the development of behavior in vertebrates experimentally removed from the influence of environmental stimulation. *Psychol. Rev.*, 34, 34–47.

Carmichael, L., Hogan, H. P., and Walter, A. A. (1932). An experimental study of the effect of language on the reproduction of visually perceived form. *J. exp. Psychol.*, 15, 73–86.

Carroll, J. B. (1964). *Language and thought.* Englewood Cliffs, N.J.: Prentice-Hall.

Cartwright, D. and Zander, A. (Eds.) (1960). *Group dynamics* (2d ed.). New York: Harper & Row.

Cason, H. (1930). Common annoyances: A psychological study of every-day aversions and irritations. *Psychol. Monogr.*, 40 (Whole No. 182).

Cattell, R. B. (1942). The concept of social status. *J. soc. Psychol.*, 15, 293–308.

Cattell, R. B. (1946). *Description and measurement of personality.* Yonkers, N.Y.: World.

Cattell, R. B. (1950). *Personality.* New York: McGraw-Hill.

Chapanis, A. (1959). *The design and conduct of human engineering studies.* Baltimore: Johns Hopkins.

Chapanis, A., Garner, W. R., and Morgan, C. T. (1949). *Applied experimental psychology.* New York: Wiley.

Charters, W. W., Jr., and Newcomb, T. M. (1958). Some attitudinal effects of experimentally increased salience of a membership group. In E. E. Maccoby, T. M. Newcomb, and E. L. Hartley (Eds.), *Readings in social psychology* (3d ed.). New York: Holt, Rinehart and Winston. Pp. 276–281.

Charters, W. W., and Whitley, I. B. (1924). *Analysis of secretarial duties and traits.* Baltimore: Williams & Wilkins.

Chorover, S. L., and Shiller, P. H. (1965). Short-term retrograde amnesia in rats. *J. comp. physiol. Psychol.*, 59, 73–78.

Chow, K. L. (1952). Further studies on selective ablation of associative cortex in relation to visually mediated behavior. *J. comp. physiol. Psychol.*, 45, 110–118.

Chow, K. L., Riesen, A. H., and Newell, F. W. (1957). Degeneration of retinal ganglion cells in infant chimpanzees reared in darkness. *J. comp. Neurol.*, 107, 27–42.

Clark, D. F. (1963). The treatment of monosymptomatic phobia by systematic desensitization. *Behav. Res. Ther.*, 1, 63–68.

Clark, K. E. (1957). *America's psychologists.* Washington, D.C.: American Psychological Association.

Clausen, J. A., and Kohn, M. L. (1960). Social relations and schizophrenia: A research report and a perspective. In D. Jackson (Ed.), *The etiology of schizophrenia.* New York: Basic Books. Pp. 295–320.

Clemente, C. D., and Sterman, M. B. (1963). Cortical synchronization and sleep patterns in acute restrained and chronic behaving cats induced by basal forebrain stimulation. *EEG clin. Neurophysiol.*, Supplement 24, 172–187.

Cobb, S. (1941). *Foundations of psychiatry.* Baltimore: Williams & Wilkins.

Cofer, C. N. (1951). Verbal behavior in relation to reasoning and values. In H. Guetzkow (Ed.), *Groups, leadership and men.* Pittsburgh: Carnegie Press. Pp. 206–217.

Cofer, C. N., and Appley, M. H. (1964). *Motivation: Theory and research.* New York: Wiley.

Coleman, J. C. (1956). *Abnormal psychology and modern life.* (2d ed.). Chicago: Scott, Foresman.

Coleman, J. C. (1964). *Abnormal psychology and modern life.* (3d ed.). Chicago: Scott, Foresman.

Conant, J. B. (1947). *On understanding science.* New Haven, Conn.: Yale Univer. Press.

Cook, B. S., and Hilgard, E. R. (1949). Distributed practice in motor learning: Progressively increasing and decreasing rests. *J. exp. Psychol.,* 39, 169–172.

Cook, T. W. (1934). Massed and distributed practice in puzzle solving. *Psychol. Rev.,* 41, 330–355.

Cooper, E., and Jahoda, M. (1947). The evasion of propaganda: How prejudiced people respond to antiprejudice propaganda. *J. Psychol.,* 23, 15–25.

Cox, C. M. (1926). *Genetic studies of genius.* Vol. II. Stanford, Calif.: Stanford Univer. Press.

Crocker, E. C. (1945). *Flavor.* New York: McGraw-Hill.

Crombie, A. C. (1964). Early concepts of the senses and the mind. *Sci. Amer.,* 210 (5), 108–116.

Cronbach, L. J. (1960). *Essentials of psychological testing* (2d ed.). New York: Harper & Row.

Cruze, W. W. (1935). Maturation and learning in chicks, *J. comp. Psychol.,* 19, 371–409.

Dahlstrom, W. G. and Welsh, G. S. (1960). *An MMPI Handbook: A guide to use in clinical practice and research.* Minneapolis, Minn.: Univer. Minnesota Press.

Dallett, K. M. (1962). The transfer surface re-examined. *J. verb. Lern. and verb. Behav.,* 1, 91–94.

Danziger, K. (1951). The operation of an acquired drive in satiated rats. *Quart. J. exp. Psychol.,* 3, 119–132.

Dashiell, J. F. (1949). *Fundamentals of General Psychology* (3d ed.). Boston: Houghton Mifflin.

Davis, A., and Havighurst, R. J. (1946). Social class and color differences in child-rearing. *Amer. sociol. Rev.,* 11, 698–710.

Davis, C. M. (1928). Self-selection of diet by newly weaned infants. *Amer. J. dis. Child.,* 36, 651–679.

Davis, E. A. (1932). *The development of linguistic skill in twins, singletons with siblings, and only children from age five to ten years.* Minneapolis, Minn.: Univer. Minnesota Press.

Davis, F. C. (1932). The functional significance of imagery differences. *J. exp. Psychol.,* 15, 630–661.

Davis, F. C. (1933). Effect of maze rotation upon subjects reporting different methods of learning and retention. *Univer. Calif. Los Angeles Publ. Educ., Phil., Psychol.,* 1, 47–63.

Davis, H. (1959). Excitation of auditory receptors. In J. Field, H. W. Magoun, and V. E. Hall (Eds.), *Handbook of physiology,* vol. 1. Washington, D.C.: American Physiological Society, Pp. 565–584.

Davis, K. (1947). Final note on a case of extreme isolation. *Amer. J. Sociol.,* 52, 432–437.

Day, E. J. (1932). The development of language in twins. I. A. comparison of twins and single children. *Child Develpm.,* 3, 179–199.

Deese, J. (1958). *The psychology of learning* (2d ed.). New York: McGraw-Hill.

Dember, W. N. (1960). *The psychology of perception.* New York: Holt, Rinehart and Winston.

Dempsey, E. W. (1946). Metabolic function of the endocrine glands. *Annu. Rev. Physiol.,* 8, 451–466.

Dempsey, E. W., and Rioch, D. McK. (1939). The localization in the brain stem of the oestrous responses of the female guinea pig. *J. Neurophysiol.,* 2, 9–18.

Dennis, W. (1940). The effect of cradling practices upon the onset of walking in Hopi children. *J. genet. Psychol.,* 56, 77–86.

Dennis, W. (1941). Spalding's experiment on the flight of birds repeated with another species. *J. comp. Psychol.,* 31, 337–348.

Deutsch, A. (1949). *The mentally ill in America: A history of the care and treatment from colonial times* (2d ed.). New York: Columbia Univer. Press.

Deutsch, J. A., and Howarth, C. I. (1962). Evocation by fear of a habit learned for electrical stimulation of the brain. *Science,* 136, 1057–1058.

Deutsch, M. and Collins, M. E. (1951). *Interracial housing: A psychological evaluation of a social experiment.* Minneapolis, Minn.: Univer. Minnesota Press.

Deutsch, M., and Gerard, H. (1955). A study of normative and informational social influences upon individual judgment. *J. abnorm. soc. Psychol.,* 51, 629–636.

DeValois, R. L. (1965). Behavioral and electrophysiological studies of primate vision. In W. D. Neff (Ed.), *Contributions to sensory psychology.* Vol. 1. New York: Pergamon. Pp. 137–178.

Dews, P. B. (1958). Effects of chlorpromazine and promazine on performance on a mixed schedule of reinforcement. *J. exp. anal. Behav.,* 1, 73–82.

Dexter, E. S. (1939). Personality traits related to conservatism and radicalism. *Charact. and Pers.,* 7, 230–237.

Diamond, I. T., and Neff, W. D. (1957). Ablation of temporal cortex and discrimination of auditory patterns. *J. Neurophysiol.,* 20, 300–315.

Diamond, I. T. and Chow, K. L. (1962). Biological psychology. In S. Koch (Ed.), *Psychology: A study of a science.* Vol. 4, New York: McGraw-Hill. Pp. 158–241.

Dictionary of Occupational Titles (3d ed.) (1965). Washington, D.C.: U.S. Government Printing Office.

Dingman, W. and Sporn, M. B. (1964). Molecular theories of memory. *Science,* 144, 26–29.

Dimmick, F. L., and Hubbard, M. R. (1939). The spectral components of psychologically unique red. *Amer. J. Psychol.,* 52, 348–353.

Dittes, J., and Kelley, H. (1956). Effects of different conditions of acceptance upon conformity to group norms. *J. abnorm. soc. Psychol.,* 53, 100–107.

DiVesta, F. J., and Merwin, J. C. (1960). The effects of need-oriented communications on attitude change. *J. abnorm. soc. Psychol.,* 60, 80–85.

Doll, E. A. (1936). *The Vineland Social Maturity Scale, revised condensed manual of instructions.* Vineland, N.J.: Smith Printing House.

Dollard, J. (1949). *Caste and class in a southern town* (2d ed.). New York: Harper & Row.

Dollard, J., Doob, L., Miller, N., Mowrer, O., and Sears, R. (1939). *Frustration and aggression.* New Haven, Conn.: Yale Univer. Press.

Dollard, J., and Miller, N. E. (1950). *Personality and psychotherapy.* New York: McGraw-Hill.

Dorcus, R. M. (Ed.). *Hypnosis and its therapeutic applications.* New York: McGraw-Hill.

Dreger, R. M. and Miller, K. S. (1960). Comparative psychological studies of Negroes and whites in the United States. *Psychol. Bull., 57,* 361–402.

Droba, D. D. (1930). *A scale for measuring attitude toward war.* Chicago: Univer. Chicago Press.

Dunbar, Flanders. (1955). *Mind and body: Psychosomatic medicine* (enlarged ed.). New York: Random House.

Duncan, C. P. (1949). The retroactive effect of electroshock on learning. *J. comp. physiol. Psychol., 42,* 32–44.

Duncker, K. (1929). Über induzierte bewegung. *Psychol. Forsch., 12,* 180–259.

Duncker, K. (1945). On problem-solving. *Psychol. Monogr., 58* (Whole No. 270).

Duffy, E. (1962). *Activation and behavior.* New York: Wiley.

Ebbinghaus, H. (1885). *Memory: A contribution to experimental psychology* (trans. H. A. Ruger and Clara E. Bussenius). New York: Teachers College, Columbia Univ., 1913.

Eccles, J. C. (1953). *The neurophysiological basis of mind: The principles of neurophysiology.* Oxford: Univer. Press.

Eccles, J. C. (1957). *The physiology of nerve cells.* Baltimore, Md.: Johns Hopkins Univer. Press.

Eccles, J. C. (1964). *The physiology of synapses.* Berlin: Springer-Verlag.

Eccles, J. C. (1965). The synapse. *Sci. Amer., 213* (1), 56–66.

Eccles, J. C., and McIntyre, A. K. (1953). The effects of disuse and of activity on mammalian spinal reflexes. *J. Physiol., 121,* 492–516.

Edwards, A. L. (1942). Retention of affective experiences: A criticism and restatement of the problem. *Psychol. Rev., 49,* 43–53.

Edwards, A. L. (1954). *The Edwards personal preference schedule manual.* New York: Psychol. Corp.

Edwards, A. L. (1960). *Experimental design in psychological research* (rev. ed). New York: Holt, Rinehart and Winston.

Egger, M. D., and Flynn, J. P. (1962). Amygdaloid suppression of hypothalamically elicited attack behavior. *Science, 136,* 43–44.

Engen, T., Levy, N., and Schlosberg, H. (1957). A new series of facial expressions. *Amer. Psychol., 12,* 264–266.

Engen, T., Levy, N., and Schlosberg, H. (1958). The dimensional analysis of a new series of facial expressions. *J. exp. Psychol., 55,* 455–458.

English, H. B. and English, A. C. (1958). *A comprehensive dictionary of psychological and psychoanalytical terms.* New York: McKay.

Epstein, A. N. and Teitelbaum, P. (1962). Regulation of food intake in the absence of taste, smell, and other oropharyngeal sensations. *J. comp. physiol. Psychol., 55,* 753–759.

Erickson, R. P. (1963). Sensory neural patterns and gustation. In Y. Zotterman (Ed.), *Olfaction and Taste.* Oxford: Pergamon. Pp. 205–213.

Ericksen, S. C. (1942). Variability of attack in massed and distributed practice. *J. exp. Psychol., 31,* 339–358.

Erikson, E. (1950). *Childhood and society.* New York: Norton.

Estes, W. K. (1944). Experimental study of punishment. *Psychol. Monogr., 57* (Whole No. 263).

Estes, W. K., Hopkins, B. L., and Crothers, E. J. (1960). All-or-none and conservation effects in the learning and retention of paired associates. *J. exp. Psychol., 60,* 329–339.

Evans, C. L. (1956). *Principles of human physiology* (12th ed.). London: J. & A. Churchill.

Eysenck, H. J. (1947). *Dimensions of personality.* London: Routledge.

Eysenck, H. J. (1952). The effects of psychotherapy: An evaluation. *J. consult. Psychol., 16,* 319–324.

Fantz, R. L. (1958). Pattern vision in young infants. *Psychol. Rec., 8,* 43–47.

Fantz, R. L., Ordy, J. M., and Udelf, M. S. (1962). Maturation of pattern vision in infants during the first six months. *J. comp. physiol. Psychol., 55,* 907–917.

Farris, E. J., and Griffiths, J. Q., Jr. (Eds.) (1949). *The rat in laboratory investigation* (rev. ed.). Philadelphia: Lippincott.

Fechner, G. T. (1860). *Elemente der Psychophysik.* Leipzig: Breitkopf und Härtel.

Feigenbaum, E. A., and Feldman, J. (Eds.) (1963). *Computers and thought.* New York: McGraw-Hill.

Fenichel, O. (1945). *The psychoanalytic theory of neurosis.* New York: Norton.

Ferster, C. B. and Skinner, B. F. (1957). *Schedules of reinforcement.* New York: Appleton-Century-Crofts.

Festinger, L. (1954). A theory of social comparison process. *Hum. Rel., 7,* 117–140.

Festinger, L. (1957). *A theory of cognitive dissonance.* New York: Harper & Row.

Festinger, L. and Carlsmith, J. M. (1959). Cognitive consequences of forced compliance. *J. abnorm. soc. Psychol., 58,* 203–210.

Fiedler, F. E. (1954). Assumed similarity measures as predictors of team effectiveness. *J. abnorm. soc. Psychol., 49,* 381–388.

Fiske, D. W. (1949). Consistency of factorial structures of personality ratings from different sources. *J. abnorm. soc. Psychol., 44,* 329–344.

Flanagan, J. C. (1951). Defining the requirements of the executive's job. *Personnel, 28,* 28–35.

Fleishman, E. A. (1953). Leadership climate, human relations training, and supervisory behavior. *Personnel Psychol.,* 6, 205–222.

Flesch, R. (1946). *The art of plain talk.* New York: Harper & Row.

Flesch, R. (1954). *How to make sense.* New York: Harper & Row.

Flexner, J. B., Flexner, L. B., and Stellar, E. (1963). Memory in mice as affected by intracerebral puromycin. *Science,* 141, 57–59.

Ford, C. S., and Beach, F. A. (1951). *Patterns of sexual behavior.* New York: Hoeber-Harper.

Fox, R. E. (1962). Personality patterns of resident psychotherapists. Unpublished doctoral dissertation. Univer. North Carolina, Chapel Hill, N.C.

Fox, R. E., and King, R. A. (1961). The effects of reinforcement scheduling on the strength of a secondary reinforcer. *J. comp. physiol. Psychol.,* 54 266–269.

Freeman, W., and Watts, J. W. (1950). *Psychosurgery* (2d ed.). Springfield, Ill.: Charles C Thomas.

Freud, S. (1914). *Psychopathology of everyday life.* New York: Macmillan.

Freud, S. (1933). *New introductory lectures on psychoanalysis.* New York: Norton.

Freud, S. (1938). *The basic writings of Sigmund Freud* (trans. A. A. Brill). New York: Random House, 1938.

Freud, S. (1949). *An outline of psychoanalysis.* New York: Norton.

Freud, S. (1955). *The standard edition of the complete psychological works of Sigmund Freud* (trans. James Strachey). Vol. 10 (1909). London: Hogarth.

Fromm, E. (1941). *Escape from freedom.* New York: Holt, Rinehart and Winston.

Fuller, J. L. (1962). *Motivation: A biological perspective.* New York: Random House.

Fuller, J. L., and Thompson, W. R. (1960). *Behavior genetics.* New York: Wiley.

Funkenstein, D. H. (1955). The physiology of fear and anger. *Sci. Amer.,* 192 (5), 74–80.

Galambos, R., and Sheatz, G. C. (1962). An electroencephalograph study of classical conditioning. *Amer. J. Physiol.,* 203, 173–184.

Galanter, E. (1962). Contemporary psychophysics. In *New directions in psychology.* Vol. 1. New York: Holt, Rinehart and Winston.

Galton, F. (1907). *Inquiries into human faculty and its development* (2d ed.). New York: Dutton.

Gardner, E. (1947). *Fundamentals of neurology.* Philadelphia, Pa.: Saunders.

Gardner, E. (1958). *Fundamentals of neurology* (3d ed). Philadelphia, Pa.: Saunders.

Gardner, E. (1963). *Fundamentals of neurology.* (4th ed.). Philadelphia, Pa.: Saunders.

Garfield, S. L. (1957). *Introductory clinical psychology.* New York: Macmillan.

Gates, A. I. (1917). Recitation as a factor in memorizing. *Arch. Psychol.,* 6 (Whole No. 40).

Geldard, F. A. (1953). *The human senses.* New York: Wiley.

Gerard, R. W. (1941). *The body functions.* New York: Wiley.

Gesell, A., and Thompson, H. (1929). Learning and growth in identical infant twins: An experimental study by the method of co-twin control. *Genet. Psychol. Monogr.,* 6, 1–124.

Getzels, J. W., and Jackson, P. W. (1962). *Creativity and intelligence.* New York: Wiley.

Ghiselin, B. (Ed.) (1955). *The creative process: A symposium.* New York: Mentor.

Ghiselli, E. E., and Brown, C. W. (1955). *Personnel and industrial psychology* (2d ed.). New York: McGraw-Hill.

Gibson, E. J., and Walk, R. D. (1960). The "visual cliff." *Sci. Amer.,* 202 (4), 64–71.

Gibson, J. J. (1929). The reproduction of visually perceived forms. *J. exp. Psychol.* 12, 1–39.

Gibson, J. J. (1950). *The perception of the visual world.* Boston: Houghton Mifflin.

Gibson, K. S., and Tyndall, E. P. T. (1923). Visibility of radiant energy. *Sci. Papers Bur. Standards,* 19 (Whole No. 475).

Gifford, W. S. (1928). Does business want scholars? *Harper's Magazine,* 156, 669–674.

Glaze, J. A. (1928). The association value of nonsense syllables. *J. genet. Psychol.,* 35, 255–269.

Gleitman, H. (1955). Place learning without prior reenforcement. *J. comp. physiol. Psychol.,* 48, 77–79.

Glickstein, M. (1965). Neurophysiology of learning and memory. In T. C. Ruch and H. D. Patton (Eds.), *Medical Physiology and Biophysics* (19th ed.). Philadelphia, Pa.: Saunders. Pp. 480–493.

Goldfarb, W. (1945). Psychological privation in infancy and subsequent adjustment. *Amer. J. Orthopsychiat.,* 15, 247–255.

Goldfarb, W. (1947). Variations in adolescent adjustment of institutionally reared children. *Amer. J. Orthopsychiat.,* 17, 449–457.

Goldhammer, H., and Marshall, A. W. (1953). *Psychosis and civilization.* New York: Free Press.

Goldstein, K. (1940). *Human nature in the light of psychopathology.* Cambridge, Mass.: Harvard Univer. Press.

Goldstein, K. (1950). Prefrontal lobotomy: Analysis and warning. *Sci. Amer.,* 182 (2), 44–47.

Goodenough, F. (1949). *Mental testing: Its history, principles. and applications.* New York: Holt, Rinehart and Winston.

Gordon, D. M. (1962). Diseases of the eye. *Clinical Symposia, CIBA,* 14, 115–142.

Gorlow, L., Katkovsky, W., (Eds.) (1959). *Readings in the psychology of adjustment.* New York: McGraw-Hill.

Gourevitch, V. (1965). *Statistical methods: A problem-solving approach.* Boston: Allyn and Bacon.

Gourevitch, G., Hack, M. H., and Hawkins, J. E., Jr. (1960). Auditory thresholds in the rat measured by an operant technique. *Science,* 131, 1046–1047.

Granit, R. (1955). *Receptors and sensory perception.* New Haven: Yale Univer. Press.

Green, D. R. (1964). *Educational Psychology*. Englewood Cliffs, N.J.: Prentice-Hall.

Greenspoon, J. (1955). The reinforcing effect of two spoken sounds on the frequency of two responses. *Amer. J. Psychol.*, 68, 409–416.

Griffin, D. R. (1959). *Echoes of bats and men*. Garden City, N.Y.: Anchor.

Gross, M. L. (1962). *The brain watchers*. New York: Random House.

Grossman, S. P. (1960). Eating or drinking elicited by direct adrenergic or cholinergic stimulation of the hypothalamus. *Science*, 132, 331–332.

Guilford, J. P. (1954). *Psychometric methods* (rev. ed.). New York: McGraw-Hill.

Guilford, J. P. (1956). *Fundamental statistics in psychology and education* (3d ed.). New York: McGraw-Hill.

Guilford, J. P. (1959). *Personality*. New York: McGraw-Hill.

Guilford, J. P. (1965). *Fundamental statistics in psychology and education* (4th ed.). New York: McGraw-Hill.

Guthrie, E. R. (1952). *The psychology of learning* (rev. ed.). New York: Harper & Row.

Guttman, N. (1953). Operant conditioning, extinction, and periodic reinforcement in relation to concentration of sucrose used as reinforcing agent. *J. exp. Psychol.*, 46, 213–224.

Haire, M. (1959). Psychological problems relevant to business and industry. *Psychol. Bull.*, 56, 169–194.

Haire, M. (1964). *Psychology in management* (2d ed.). New York: McGraw-Hill.

Hall, C. S. (1938). The inheritance of emotionality. *Sigma Xi Quart.*, 26, 17–27.

Hall, C. S. (1953). A cognitive theory of dream symbols. *J. gen. Psychol.*, 48, 186–199.

Hall, C. S. (1954). *A primer of Freudian psychology*. Cleveland: World.

Hall, C. S., and Lindzey, G. (1957). *Theories of personality*. New York: Wiley.

Hall, J. F. (1956). The relationship between external stimulation, food deprivation, and activity. *J. comp. physiol. Psychol.*, 49, 339–341.

Hall, J. F. (1961). *Psychology of motivation*. Philadelphia: Lippincott.

Halverson, H. M. (1931). An experimental study of prehension in infants by means of systematic cinema records. *Genet. Psychol. Monogr.*, 10, 107–286.

Hamilton, C. L., and Brobeck, J. R. (1964). Hypothalamic hyperphagia in the monkey. *J. comp. physiol. Psychol.*, 57, 271–278.

Hammond, K. R., and Householder, J. E. (1962). *Introduction to statistical method*. New York: Knopf.

Hanes, R. M. (1949). The construction of subjective brightness scales from fractionation data: A validation. *J. exp. Psychol.*, 39, 719–728.

Hanson, H. M. (1959). Effects of discrimination training on stimulus generalization. *J. exp. Psychol.*, 58, 321–334.

Hardy, J. D., Goodell, H., and Wolff, H. G. (1951). The influence of skin temperature upon the pain threshold as evoked by thermal radiation. *Science*, 114, 149–150.

Harlow, H. F. (1949). The formation of learning sets. *Psychol. Rev.*, 56, 61–65.

Harlow, H. F. (1958). The nature of love. *Amer. Psychologist*, 13, 673–685.

Harlow, H. F. (1962). The heterosexual affectional system in monkeys. *Amer. Psychologist*, 17, 1–9.

Harlow, H. F., and McClearn, G. E. (1954). Object discrimination learned by monkeys on the basis of manipulation motives. *J. comp. physiol. Psychol.*, 47, 73–76.

Harlow, H. F., and Harlow, M. K. (1962). Social deprivation in monkeys. *Sci. Amer.*, 207 (5), 136–146.

Harrell, T. W., and Harrell, M. S. (1945). Army General Classification Test scores for civilian occupations. *Educ. psychol. Measmt.*, 5, 29–239.

Hartline, H. K. (1938). The response of single optic nerve fibers of the vertebrate eye to illumination of the retina. *Amer. J. Physiol.*, 121, 400–415.

Hartline, H. K., Wagner, H. G., and MacNichol, E. F., Jr. (1952). The peripheral origin of nervous activity in the visual system. *Cold Spring Harbor Symp. Quant. Biol.*, 17, 125–141.

Hartmann, H. (1964). *Essays on ego psychology: Selected problems in psychoanalytic theory*. New York: International Univer. Press.

Hartshorne, H., and May, M. A. (1928). *Studies in deceit*. New York: Macmillan.

Harvard University Commission to Advise on the Future of Psychology at Harvard (1947). (Alan Gregg, Chairman). *The place of psychology in an ideal university*. Cambridge, Mass.: Harvard Univer. Press.

Hathaway, S. R., and McKinley, J. C. (1951). *The Minnesota Multiphasic Personality Inventory manual* (rev. ed.). New York: Psychological Corp.

Hayes, K. J., and Hayes, C. (1951). The intellectual development of a home-raised chimpanzee. *Proc. Amer. phil. Soc.*, 95, 105–109.

Haythorn, W. (1958). The effects of varying combinations of authoritarian and equalitarian leaders and followers. In E. E. Maccoby, T. M. Newcomb, and E. L. Hartley (Eds.), *Readings in social psychology* (3d ed.). New York: Holt, Rinehart and Winston. Pp. 511–522.

Health, Education, and Welfare Indicators (1963). Washington, D.C.: U.S. Dept. Health, Education, and Welfare.

Hebb, D. O. (1937). The innate organization of visual activity. I. Perception of figure by rats reared in total darkness. *J. genet. Psychol.*, 51, 101–126.

Hebb, D. O. (1949). *The Organization of Behavior*. New York: Wiley.

Hebb, D. O., and Foord, E. N. (1945). Errors of visual recognition and the nature of the trace. *J. exp. Psychol.*, 35, 335–348.

Hécaen, H., Penfield, W., Bertrand, C., and Malmo, R. (1956). The syndrome of apractognosia due to lesions of the minor cerebral hemisphere. *Arch. Neurol. Psychiat., Chicago*, 75, 400–434.

Hecht, S., and Williams, R. E. (1922). The visibility of monochromatic radiation and the absorption spectrum of visual purple. *J. gen. Physiol.,* 5, 1–33.

Heidbreder, E. (1948). The attainment of concepts. VI. Exploratory experiments on conceptualization at perceptual levels. *J. Psychol.,* 26, 193–216.

Heider, F. (1946). Attitudes and cognitive organization. *J. Psychol.,* 21, 107–112.

Heider, F. (1958). *The psychology of interpersonal relations.* New York: Wiley.

Helmholtz, H. L. F. von (1924). *Physiological optics* (trans. J. P. C. Southall). Vol. II. Rochester, N.Y.: Optical Soc. Amer.

Helson, H. (1948). Adaptation-level as a basis for a quantitative theory of frames of reference. *Psychol. Rev.,* 55, 297–313.

Helson, H. (1964). Current trends and issues in adaptation-level theory. *Amer. Psychologist,* 19, 26–38.

Hernández-Péon, R., Scherrer, H., and Jouvet, M. (1956). Modification of electric activity in cochlear nucleus during "attention" in unanesthetized cats. *Science.* 123, 331–332.

Heron, W., Doane, B. K., and Scott, T. H. (1956). Visual disturbance after prolonged perceptual isolation. *Canad. J. Psychol.,* 10, 13–16.

Hess, E. H. (1959). Imprinting. *Science,* 130, 133–141.

Hess, E. H. (1964). Imprinting in birds. *Science,* 146, 1128–1139.

Hess, W. R. (1954). *Diencephalon: Autonomic and extrapyramidal functions.* New York: Grune.

Hildum, D. C., and Brown, R. W. (1956). Verbal reinforcement and interviewer bias. *J. abnorm. soc. Psychol.,* 53, 108–111.

Hilgard, E. R. (1951). Methods and procedures in the study of learning. In S. S. Stevens (Ed.), *Handbook of Experimental Psychology.* New York: Wiley. Pp. 517–567.

Hilgard, E. R. (1956). *Theories of learning* (2d ed.). New York: Appleton-Century-Crofts.

Hilgard, E. R. (1957). *Introduction to psychology* (rev. ed.). New York: Harcourt, Brace & World.

Hilgard, E. R. (1962). *Introduction to Psychology* (3d ed.). New York: Harcourt, Brace & World.

Hilgard, E. R., and Payner, S. L. (1944). Those not at home; Riddle for pollsters. *Publ. Opin. Quart.,* 8, 254–261.

Hilgard, J. R. (1953). Anniversary reactions in parents precipitated by children. *Psychiatry,* 16, 73–80.

Hill, W. F. (1956). Activity as an autonomous drive. *J. comp. physiol. Psychol.,* 49, 15–19.

Hill, W. F. (1963). *Learning: A survey of psychological interpretations.* San Francisco: Chandler.

Hirsch, J. (1959). Studies in experimental behavior genetics: II. Individual differences in geotaxis as a function of chromosome variations in synthesized *Drosophila* populations. *J. comp. physiol. Psychol.,* 52, 304–308.

Hirsch, J. and Erlenmeyer-Kimling, L. (1962). Studies in experimental behavior genetics: IV. Chromosome analyses for geotaxis. *J. comp. physiol. Psychol.,* 55, 732–739.

Hirschberg, G., and Gilliland, A. R. (1942). Parent-child relationships in attitudes. *J. abnorm. soc. Psychol.,* 37, 125–130.

Hochberg, J. E. (1964). *Perception.* Englewood Cliffs, N.J.: Prentice-Hall.

Hodgkin, A. L. (1957). Ionic movements and electrical activity in giant nerve fibers. *Proc. Royal Soc., B.,* 148, 1–37.

Hoebel, B. G. (1965). Hypothalamic lesions by electrocauterization: Disinhibition of feeding and self-stimulation. *Science,* 149, 452–453.

Holland, J. G., and Skinner, B. F. (1961). *The analysis of behavior: A program for self-instruction.* New York: McGraw-Hill.

Hollander, E. P. (1958). Conformity, status, and idiosyncrasy credit. *Psychol. Rev.,* 65, 117–127.

Hollander, E. P., and Hunt, R. G. (Eds.) (1963). *Current perspectives in social psychology: Readings with commentary.* New York: Oxford Univer. Press.

Hollingshead, A. B. (1949). *Elmtown's youth: The impact of social classes on adolescents.* New York: Wiley.

Hollingshead, A. B., and Redlich, F. C. (1958). *Social class and mental illness.* New York: Wiley.

Hollingworth, H. L. (1929). *Vocational psychology and character analysis.* New York: Appleton-Century-Crofts.

Hollister, L. E., Traub, L., and Beckman, W. G. (1956). Psychiatric use of reserpine and chlorpromazine: Results of double-blind studies. In N. S. Kline (Ed.), *Psychopharmacology.* Washington, D.C.: American Association for the Advancement of Science. Pp. 65–74.

Homans, G. C. (1950). *The human group.* New York: Harcourt, Brace & World.

Hooper, C. E. (1946). The coincidental method of measuring radio audience size. In A. B. Blankenship (Ed.), *How to conduct consumer and opinion research.* New York: Harper & Row.

Horney, K. (1937). *The neurotic personality of our time.* New York: Norton.

Horowitz, E. L. (1936). The development of attitude toward the Negro. *Arch. Psychol.,* 28 (Whole No. 194).

Horowitz, E. L., and Horowitz, R. E. (1938). Development of social attitudes in children. *Sociometry,* 1, 301–338.

Housman, A. E. (1933). *The name and nature of poetry.* New York: Macmillan.

Hovland, C. I. (1937). The generalization of conditioned responses. I. The sensory generalization of conditioned responses with varying frequencies of tone. *J. gen. Psychol.,* 17, 125–248.

Hovland, C. I. (1938). Experimental studies in rote-learning theory. III. Distribution of practice with varying speeds of syllable presentation. *J. exp. Psychol.,* 23, 172–190.

Hovland, C. I. (1951). Human learning and retention.

In S. S. Stevens (Ed.), *Handbook of experimental psychology.* New York: Wiley. Pp. 613–689.

Hovland, C. I. (1954). Effects of the mass media of communication. In G. Lindzey (Ed.), *Handbook of social psychology.* Reading, Mass.: Addison-Wesley.

Howes, D. H., and Solomon, R. L. (1951). Visual duration threshold as a function of word-probability. *J. exp. Psychol.,* 41, 401–410.

Hubel, D. H. (1963). The visual cortex of the brain. *Sci. Amer.,* 209 (5), 54–62.

Hubel, D. H., and Wiesel, T. N. (1962). Receptive fields, binocular interaction and functional architecture in the cat's visual cortex. *J. Physiol.,* 160, 106–154.

Hubel, D. H., and Wiesel, T. N. (1963). Receptive fields of cells in striate cortex of very young, visually inexperienced kittens. *J. Neurophysiol.,* 26, 994–1002.

Hubel, D. H., and Wiesel, T. N. (1965). Receptive fields and functional architecture in two nonstriate visual areas (18 and 19) of the cat. *J. Neurophysiol.,* 28, 229–289.

Huff, Darrell. (1954). *How to lie with statistics.* New York: Norton.

Hughes, J. G. (1963). *Synopsis of pediatrics.* St. Louis: C. V. Mosby.

Hughes, J. L. (1962). *Programed Instruction for schools and industry.* Chicago: Science Research Associates.

Hull, C. L. (1920). Quantitative aspects of the evolution of concepts. *Psychol. Monogr.,* 28 (Whole No. 123).

Hull, C. L. (1943). *The principles of behavior.* New York: Appleton-Century-Crofts.

Hull, C. L. (1951). *Essentials of behavior.* New Haven: Yale Univer. Press.

Hull, C. L. (1952). *A behavior system.* New Haven: Yale Univer. Press.

Hull, C. L., Hovland, C. I., Ross, R. T., Hall, J., Perkins, D. T., and Fitch, R. B. (1940). *Mathematico-deductive theory of rote learning.* New Haven: Yale Univer. Press.

Humphrey, G. (1948). *Directed thinking.* New York: Dodd, Mead.

Humphrey, G. (1951). *Thinking: An introduction to its experimental psychology.* London: Methuen.

Hunt, E. B. (1962). *Concept learning: An information processing problem.* New York: Wiley.

Hunt, H. F., and Brady, J. V. (1951). Some effects of electro-convulsive shock on conditioned emotional responses ("anxiety"). *J. comp. physiol. Psychol.,* 44, 88–98.

Hunter, I. M. L. (1957). *Memory: Facts and fallacies.* London: Penguin Books.

Hunter, W. S. (1913). The delayed reaction in animals and children. *Behav. Monogr.,* 2 (Whole No. 6).

Hurvich, L. M., and Jameson, D. (1957). An opponent-process theory of color vision. *Psychol. Rev.,* 64, 384–404.

Hurwitz, J. I., Zander, A. F., and Hymovitch, B. (1953). Some effects of power on the relations among group members. In D. Cartwright and A. Zander (Eds.), *Group dynamics.* New York: Harper & Row. Pp. 483–492.

Hydén, H., and Egyházi, E. (1962). Nuclear RNA changes of nerve cells during a learning experiment in rats. *Proc. Natl. Acad. Sci., U.S.,* 48, 1366–1373.

Hyman, H. (1959). *Political socialization: A study in the psychology of political behavior.* New York: Free Press.

Ilg, F. L., and Ames, L. B. (1955). *The Gesell Institute's child behavior.* New York: Dell.

Inbau, F. E. (1942). *Lie detection and criminal investigation.* Baltimore: Williams & Wilkins.

Ingham, H. V., and Love, L. R. (1954). *The process of psychotherapy.* New York: McGraw-Hill.

Isaacson, R. I. (Ed.) (1964). *Basic readings in neuropsychology.* New York: Harper & Row.

Jackson, D. D. (Ed.) (1960). *The etiology of schizophrenia.* New York: Basic Books.

Jackson, D. D., Block, J., Block, Jeanne, and Patterson, V. (1958). Psychiatrists' conceptions of the schizophrenogenic parent. *A. M. A. Arch. Neurol. Psychiat.,* 79, 448–459.

Jacobsen, C. F. (1935). Functions of the frontal association areas in primates. *Arch. Neurol. Psychiat., Chicago,* 33, 558–569.

Jacobson, L. E. (1932). The electrophysiology of mental activities. *Amer. J. Psychol.,* 44, 677–694.

James, W., (1890). *Principles of psychology.* New York: Holt, Rinehart and Winston. 2 vols.

Jameson, D., and Hurvich, L. M. (1964). Theory of brightness and color contrast in human vision. *Vision Res.,* 4, 135–154.

Janis, I., and Feshbach, S. (1953). Effects of fear-arousing communications. *J. abnorm. soc. Psychol.,* 48, 78–92.

Jasper, H. H. (1941). Electroencephalography. In W. Penfield and T. Erickson (Eds.), *Epilepsy and cerebral localization.* Springfield, Ill.: Charles C Thomas.

Jasper, H., and Shagass, C. (1941). Conditioning the occipital alpha rhythm in man. *J. exp. Psychol.,* 28, 373–388.

Jellinek, E. M. (1952). Phases of alcohol addiction. *Quart. J. Stud. Alcohol.,* 13, 673–684.

Jenkins, J. G., and Dallenbach, K. M. (1924). Oblivescence during sleep and waking. *Amer. J. Psychol.,* 35, 605–612.

Jenkins, J. J., Russell, W. A., and Suci, G. J. (1958). An atlas of semantic profiles for 360 words. *Amer. J. Psychol.,* 71, 688–699.

Jenkins, W. O. (1947). A review of leadership studies with particular reference to military problems. *Psychol. Bull.,* 44, 54–79. (a)

Jenkins, W. O. (1947). The tactual discrimination of shapes for coding aircraft-type controls. In P. M. Fitts (Ed.), *Psychological research on equipment design.* Washington, D.C.: U.S. Govt. Printing Office. Pp. 199–205. (b)

Jenkins, W. O., McFann, H., and Clayton, F. L. (1950). A methodological study of extinction following a periodic and continuous reinforcement. *J. comp. physiol. Psychol.*, 43, 155–167.

Jersild, A. T., Markey, F. V., and Jersild, C. L. (1933). Children's fears, dreams, wishes, daydreams, likes, dislikes, pleasant and unpleasant memories. *Child Developm. Monogr.*, No. 12.

Jervis, G. A. (1939). A contribution to the study of the influence of heredity on mental deficiency. The genetics of phenylpyruvic oligophrenia. *Proc. Amer. Ass. Stud. ment. Def.*, 44, 13–24.

Jessner, L., and Ryan, V. (1941). *Shock treatment in psychiatry.* New York: Grune & Stratton.

Johnson, D. M. (1948). *Essentials of psychology.* New York: McGraw-Hill.

Johnson, D. M. (1955). *The psychology of thought and judgment.* New York: Harper & Row.

Johnson, W. (1944). Studies in language behavior. I. A. program of research. *Psychol. Monogr.*, 56, 1–15.

Jones, E. E. (1965). Conformity as a tactic of ingratiation. *Science*, 149, 144–150.

Jones, H. E., and Conrad, H. S. (1933). The growth and decline of intelligence: A study of a homogeneous group between the ages ten and sixty. *Genet. Psychol. Monogr.*, 13, 223–298.

Jones, M. R. (Ed.) (1953–1964). *Nebraska symposium on motivation.* Lincoln, Nebr.: Univer. Nebraska Press.

Jost, H., and Sontag, L. W. (1944). The genetic factor in autonomic nervous system function. *Psychosom. Med.*, 6, 308–310.

Kagan, J., and Berkun, M. (1954). The reward value of running activity. *J. comp. physiol. Psychol.*, 47, 108.

Kallmann, F. J. (1951). Twin studies in relation to adjustive problems of man. *Trans. N. Y. Acad. Sci.*, 13, 270–275.

Kallmann, F. J., and Jarvik, L. F. (1959). Individual differences in constitution and genetic background. In J. E. Birren (Ed.), *Handbook of Aging and the Individual.* Chicago: Univer. Chicago Press. Pp. 216–263.

Kaplan, B. (Ed.) (1964). *The inner world of mental illness: A series of first-person accounts of what it was like.* New York: Harper & Row.

Katz, D., and Braly, K. (1933). Racial stereotypes of one hundred college students. *J. abnorm. soc. Psychol.*, 28, 280–290.

Katz, D., Cartwright, D., Eldersveld, S., and Lee, A. M. (Eds.) (1954). *Public opinion and propaganda.* New York: Dryden.

Katz, D., Maccoby, N., and Morse, N. C. (1950). *Productivity, supervision, and morale in an office situation.* Ann Arbor, Mich.: Survey Research Center. Part I.

Katz, M. S., and Deterline, W. A. (1958). Apparent learning in the paramecium. *J. comp. physiol. Psychol.*, 51, 243–247.

Katz, S. E., and Landis, C. (1935). Psychologic and physiologic phenomena during a prolonged vigil. *Arch. Neurol. Psychiat., Chicago,* 34, 307–316.

Keller, F. S., and Schoenfeld, W. N. (1950). *Principles of psychology.* New York: Appleton-Century-Crofts.

Kellogg, W. N., and Kellogg, L. A. (1933). *The ape and the child.* New York: McGraw-Hill.

Keys, A. B., Brozek, J., Heuschel, A., Mickelson, O., and Taylor, H. L. (1950). *The biology of human starvation.* Minneapolis: Univer. Minnesota Press.

Kimble, G. A. (1947). Conditioning as a function of the time between conditioned and unconditioned stimuli. *J. exp. Psychol.*, 37, 1–15.

Kimble, G. A. (1961). *Hilgard and Marquis' conditioning and learning.* New York: Appleton-Century-Crofts.

Kimble, G. A., and Bilodeau, E. A. (1949). Work and rest as variables in cyclical motor learning. *J. exp. Psychol.*, 39, 150–157.

Kimble, G. A., and Garmezy, N. (1963). *Principles of general psychology* (2d ed.). New York: Ronald.

King, F. A. (1958). Effects of septal and amygdaloid lesions on emotional behavior and conditioned avoidance responses in the rat. *J. nerv. ment. Dis.*, 126, 57–63.

King, M. S., and Kimble, G. A. (1958). Job opportunities for undergraduate psychology majors. *Amer. Psychologist*, 13, 23–27.

King, R. A. (1965). Consolidation of the neural trace in memory: Investigation with one-trial avoidance conditioning and ECS. *J. comp. physiol. Psychol.*, 59, 283–284.

King, R. A. (Ed.) (1966). *Readings for an Introduction to Psychology* (2d ed.). New York: McGraw-Hill.

Kingsley, H. R., and Garry, R. (1957). *The nature and conditions of learning* (2d ed.). Englewood Cliffs, N.J.: Prentice-Hall.

Kinsey, A. C., Pomeroy, W. B., and Martin, C. E. (1948). *Sexual behavior in the human male.* Philadelphia: Saunders.

Kish, G. B. (1955). Learning when the onset of illumination is used as a reinforcing stimulus. *J. comp. physiol. Psychol.*, 48, 261–264.

Kisker, G. W. (1964). *The disorganized personality.* New York: McGraw-Hill.

Kitt, A., and Gleicher, D. B. (1950). Determinants of voting behavior: A progress report on the Elmira election study. *Publ. Opin. Quart.*, 14, 393–412.

Klapman, J. W. (1946). *Group psychotherapy.* New York: Grune & Stratton.

Kleitman, N. (1939). *Sleep and wakefulness.* Chicago: Univer. Chicago Press.

Kleitman, N. (1960). Patterns of dreaming. *Sci. Amer.*, 203 (5), 82–88.

Kline, L. W., and Johannsen, D. E. (1935). Comparative role of the face and of the face-body-hands as aids in identifying emotions. *J. abnorm. soc. Psychol.*, 29, 415–426.

Klineberg, O. (1935). *Negro intelligence and selective migration.* New York: Columbia Univer. Press.

Klineberg, O. (1954). *Social psychology* (rev. ed.). New York: Holt, Rinehart & Winston.

Kling, A., Orbach, J., Schwartz, N. B., and Towne, J. C. (1960). Injury to the limbic system and associated structures in cats. *Arch. gen. Psychiat.*, 3, 391–420.

Kluckhohn, C. (1949). *Mirror for man.* New York: McGraw-Hill.

Klüver, H. (1942). Visual mechanisms. In *Biological Symposia.* Vol. VII. New York: Ronald.

Klüver, H., and Bucy, P. C. (1939). Preliminary analysis of functions of the temporal lobes in monkeys. *Arch. Neurol. Psychiat., Chicago,* 42, 979–1000.

Koch, S. (1951). The current status of motivational psychology. *Psychol. Rev.,* 58, 147–154.

Koffka, K. (1935). *Principles of Gestalt psychology.* New York: Harcourt, Brace & World.

Köhler, W. (1925). *The mentality of apes* (trans. E. Winter). New York: Harcourt, Brace & World.

Köhler, W. (1947). *Gestalt psychology* (rev. ed.). New York: Liveright.

Köhler, W., and Wallach, H. (1944). Figural after-effects: An investigation of visual processes. *Proc. Amer. philos. Soc.,* 88, 269–357.

König, J. F. R., and Klippel, R. A. (1963). *The rat brain: A stereotaxic atlas of the forebrain and lower parts of the brain stem.* Baltimore: Williams & Wilkins.

Kohler, I. (1962). Experiments with goggles. *Sci. Amer.,* 206 (5), 63–72.

Kohler, I. (1951). Über Aufbau und Wandlungen der Wahrnehmungswelt: Insbesondere über "bedingte Empfindungen." *Österreichische Akademie der Wissenschaften, Sitzungsberichte,* 227, No. 1.

Kohler, I. (1964). The formation and transformation of the perceptual world (trans. H. Fiss). *Psychological Issues,* 3, Monograph 12.

Korte, A. (1915). Kinematoskopische untersuchungen. *Z. Psychol.,* 72, 193–206; 271–296.

Krech, D., and Crutchfield, R. S. (1958). *Elements of psychology.* New York: Knopf.

Krech, D., Crutchfield, R. S., and Ballachey, E. L. (1962). *Individual in society: A textbook of social psychology.* New York: McGraw-Hill.

Kris, E. (1950). On preconscious mental processes. *Psychoanal. Quart.,* 19, 540–560.

Krueger, W. C. F. (1929). The effect of overlearning on retention. *J. exp. Psychol.,* 12, 71–78.

Kuffler, S. W. (1953). Discharge patterns and functional organization of mammalian retina. *J. Neurophysiol.,* 16, 37–68.

Kutash, S. B. (1965). Psychoneuroses. In B. B. Wolman (Ed.), *Handbook of Clinical Psychology.* New York: McGraw-Hill. Pp. 948–975.

Lacey, J. I., Bateman, D. E., and VanLehn, R. (1953). Autonomic response specificity: An experimental study. *Psychosom. Med.,* 15, 8–21.

Lambert, W. W., Solomon, R. L., and Watson, P. D. (1949). Reinforcement and extinction as factors in size estimation. *J. exp. Psychol.,* 39, 637–641.

Lancaster, E., with Poling, J. (1958). *The final face of Eve.* New York: McGraw-Hill.

Land, E. H. (1959). Experiments in color vision. *Sci. Amer.,* 200 (5), 84–99.

Landis, C., and Hunt, W. A. (1939). *The startle pattern.* New York: Holt, Rinehart and Winston.

La Place, J. P. (1954). Personality and its relationship to success in professional baseball. *Res. Quart.,* 25, 313–319.

Lashley, K. S. (1924). Studies of cerebral function in learning. V. The retention of motor habits after destruction of the so-called motor area in primates. *Arch. Neurol. Psychiat., Chicago,* 12, 249–276.

Lashley, K. S. (1929). *Brain mechanisms and intelligence.* Chicago: Univer. Chicago Press.

Lashley, K. S. (1950). In search of the engram. *Symp. soc. exp. Biol.* Vol. IV. London: Cambridge Univer. Press. Pp. 454–482.

Lashley, K. S. (1951). The problem of serial order in behavior. In L. A. Jeffress (Ed.), *Cerebral mechanisms in behavior.* New York: Wiley.

Lawrence, D. H., and De Rivera, J. (1954). Evidence for relational transposition. *J. comp. physiol. Psychol.,* 47, 475–481.

Laycock, F., and Caylor, J. S. (1964). Physiques of gifted children and their less gifted siblings. *Child Developm.,* 35, 63–74.

Lazarsfeld, P. F., Berelson, B. R., and Gaudet, H. (1944). *The people's choice.* New York: Duell, Sloan & Pearce.

Leavitt, H. J. (1964). *Managerial psychology.* (2d ed.). Chicago: Univer. Chicago Press.

Leavitt, H. J., and Mueller, R. A. H. (1951). Some effects of feedback on communication. *Hum. Relat.,* 4, 401–410.

Lecron, L. M., and Bordeaux, J. (1947). *Hypnotism today.* New York: Grune & Stratton.

Leeper, R. W. (1948). A motivational theory of emotion to replace "emotion as disorganized response." *Psychol. Rev.,* 55, 5–21.

Lehrman, D. S. (1964). The reproductive behavior of ring doves. *Sci. Amer.,* 211 (5), 48–54.

Lejeune, J., Turpin, R., and Gautier, M. (1959). Le Mongolisme, premier exemple d'aberration autosomique humaine. *Ann. genet. Hum.,* 1, 41–49.

Lemkau, P. V., and Crocetti, G. M. (1958). Vital statistics of schizophrenia. In L. Bellak (Ed.), *Schizophrenia: A review of the syndrome.* New York: Logos.

Leonard, W. E. (1927). *The locomotive god.* New York: Appleton-Century-Crofts.

Levine, J. M., and Murphy, G. (1943). The learning and forgetting of controversial material. *J. abnorm. soc. Psychol.,* 38, 507–517.

Lewin, K. (1935). *A dynamic theory of personality* (trans. D. K. Adams and K. Zener). New York: McGraw-Hill.

Lewin, K. (1951). *Field theory in social science: Selected theoretical papers.* (D. Cartwright, Ed.). New York: Harper & Row, 1951.

Lewin, K., Lippitt, R., and White, R. K. (1939). Patterns of aggressive behavior in experimentally created social climates. *J. soc. Psychol.,* 10, 271–299.

Lewis, M. M. (1936). *Infant speech: A study of the beginnings of language.* New York: Harcourt, Brace & World.

Liddell, H. S. (1954). Conditioning and emotions. *Sci. Amer.,* 190 (1), 48–57.

Liddell, H. S., James, W. T., and Anderson, O. D. (1934). The comparative physiology of the conditioned motor reflex. *Comp. Psychol. Monogr.,* 11 (Whole No. 51).

Lidz, T., and Fleck, S. (1960). Schizophrenia, human integration, and the role of the family. In D. Jackson (Ed.), *The etiology of schizophrenia.* New York: Basic Books.

Likert, R. (1932). A technique for the measurement of attitudes. *Arch. Psychol.,* 22 (Whole No. 140).

Likert, R. (1947). The sample interview survey. In W. Dennis (Ed.), *Current trends in psychology.* Pittsburgh: Univer. Pittsburgh Press.

Lilly, J. C. (1958). Correlations between neurophysiological activity in the cortex and short-term behavior in the monkey. In H. Harlow and C. N. Woolsey (Eds.), *Biological and biochemical bases of behavior.* Madison: Univer. Wisconsin Press. Pp. 83–100.

Lindahl, L. G. (1945). Movement analysis as an industrial training method. *J. appl. Psychol.,* 29, 420–436.

Lindsley, D. B. (1951). Emotion. In S. S. Stevens (Ed.), *Handbook of experimental psychology.* New York: Wiley. Pp. 473–516.

Lindsley, D. B. (1958). The reticular system and perceptual discrimination. In H. Jasper et al. (Eds.), *Reticular formation of the brain.* Boston: Little, Brown.

Lindsley, D. B., Bowden, J. W., and Magoun, H. W. (1950). Behaviorial and EEG changes following chronic brain lesions in the cat. *EEG Clin. Neurophysiol.,* 2, 483–498.

Linton, R. (1945). *The cultural background of personality.* New York: Appleton-Century-Crofts.

Lipsitt, L. P. (1963). Learning in the first year of life. In L. P. Lipsitt and C. C. Spiker (Eds.), *Advances in child development and behavior.* New York: Academic Press. Pp. 147–195.

Lockman, R. F. (1964). An empirical description of the subfields of psychology. *Amer. Psychologist,* 19, 645–653.

Lorente de Nó, R. (1938). Analysis of the activity of the chains of internuncial neurons. *J. Neurophysiol.,* 1, 207–244.

Lorge, I. (1930). Influence of regularly interpolated time intervals upon subsequent learning. *Teach. Coll., Columbia Univer. Contr. Educ.* (Whole No. 438).

Lovibond, S. H. (1958). A further test of the hypothesis of autonomous memory trace change. *J. exp. Psychol.,* 55, 412–415.

Lowes, J. L. (1927). *The road to Xanadu: A Study in the ways of the imagination* (enlarged ed.). Boston: Houghton Mifflin.

Luchins, A. (1954). Mechanization in problem solving: The effect of Einstellung. *Psychol. Monogr.,* 54 (Whole No. 6).

Luckiesh, M. (1944). *Light, vision and seeing.* Princeton, N.J.: Van Nostrand.

Lyman, H. B. (1963). *Test scores and what they mean.* Englewood Cliffs, N.J.: Prentice-Hall.

Lynd, R. S., and Lynd, H. M. (1929). *Middletown.* New York: Harcourt, Brace & World.

McCarthy, D. A. (1930). *The language development of the preschool child.* Minneapolis: Univer. Minnesota Press.

McCarthy, D. A. (1946). Language development in children. In L. Carmichael (Ed.), *Manual of child psychology.* New York: Wiley. Pp. 476–581.

McClelland, D. C., Atkinson, J. W., Clark, R. A., and Lowell, E. L. (1953). *The achievement motive.* New York: Appleton-Century-Crofts.

Maccoby, E. E., Newcomb, T. M., and Hartley, E. L. (1958). *Readings in social psychology* (3d ed.). New York: Holt, Rinehart and Winston.

McCollough, C., and Van Atta, L. (1963). *Statistical concepts: A program for self instruction.* New York: McGraw-Hill.

McCormick, E. J. (1964). *Human engineering* (2d ed.). New York: McGraw-Hill.

McCurdy, H. G. (1961). *The personal world.* New York: Harcourt, Brace & World.

Macfarlane, D. A. (1930). The role of kinesthesis in maze learning. *Calif. Univer. Publ. Psychol.,* 4, 277–305.

McGehee, W., and Owen, E. B. (1940). Authorized and unauthorized rest pauses in clerical work. *J. appl. Psychol.,* 24, 605–614.

McGeoch, J. A. and Irion, A. L. (1952). *The psychology of human learning.* (2d ed.). New York: Longmans, Green.

McGranahan, D. V. (1946). A comparison of social attitudes among American and German youth. *J. abnorm. soc. Psychol.,* 41, 245–257.

McGrath, J. E. (1964). *Social psychology: A brief introduction.* New York: Holt, Rinehart and Winston.

McGraw, M. B. (1935). *Growth: A study of Johnny and Jimmy.* New York: Appleton-Century-Crofts.

McGraw, M. B. (1946). Maturation of behavior. In L. Carmichael (Ed.), *Manual of child psychology.* New York: Wiley. Pp. 332–369.

McGregor, D. (1960). *The human side of enterprise.* New York: McGraw-Hill.

McGurk, F. C. J. (1951). *Comparison of the performance of Negro and white high school seniors on cultural and non-cultural test questions.* Washington, D.C.: Catholic Univer. Amer. Press. (Microcard).

McGurk, F. C. J. (1953). On white and Negro test performance and socioeconomic factors. *J. abnorm. soc. Psychol.,* 48, 448–450.

McKellar, P. (1957). *Imagination and thinking.* London: Cohen & West, (1958).

Mackworth, N. H. (1948). The breakdown of vigilance during prolonged visual search. *Quart. J. exp. Psychol.,* 1, 6–21.

Mackworth, N. H. (1950). *Researches on the measurement of human performance.* London: Medical Research Council Report. No. 268.

MacLean, P. D. (1955). The limbic system with respect to self-preservation and the preservation of the species. *J. nerv. ment. Dis.,* 127, 1–11.

McNemar, Q. (1942). *The revision of the Stanford-Binet scale.* Boston: Houghton Mifflin.

McNemar, Q. (1962). *Psychological statistics* (3d ed.). New York: Wiley.

McNemar, Q. (1964). Lost: Our Intelligence? Why? *Amer. Psychologist,* 19, 871–882.

MacNichol, E. F., Jr. (1964). Three-pigment color vision. *Sci. Amer.,* 211 (6), 48–56.

Maier, N. R. F. (1949). *Frustration.* New York: McGraw-Hill.

Maier, N. R. F. (1958). *The appraisal interview: Objectives, methods, and skills.* New York: Wiley.

Manzer, C. W. (1927). An experimental investigation of rest pauses. *Arch. Psychol.,* 14 (Whole No. 90).

Masling, J., Greer, L., and Gilmore, R. (1955). Status, authoritarianism and sociometric choice. *J. soc. Psychol.,* 41, 297–310.

Maslow, A. H. (1954). *Motivation and personality.* New York: Harper & Row.

Masserman, J. H. (1943). *Behavior and neurosis.* Chicago: Univer. Chicago Press.

Masserman, J. H. (1946). *Principles of dynamic psychiatry.* Philadelphia: Saunders.

Masserman, J. H. (1961). *Principles of dynamic psychiatry.* (2d ed.). Philadelphia: Saunders.

Mausner, B. (1954). The effect of one partner's success in a relevant task on the interaction of observer pairs. *J. abnorm. soc. Psychol.,* 49, 557–560.

Max, L. W. (1937). Experimental study of the motor theory of consciousness. IV. Action-current responses in the deaf during awakening, kinaesthetic imagery and abstract thinking. *J. comp. Psychol.,* 24, 301–344.

May, R. (1950). *The meaning of anxiety.* New York: Ronald.

Mayer, J. (1955). Regulation of energy intake and the body weight: The glucostatic theory and the lipostatic hypothesis. In R. W. Miner (Ed.), *The regulation of hunger and appetite.* New York: *Ann. N.Y. Acad. Sci.,* 63, 15–43.

Mead, M. (1935). *Sex and temperament.* New York: Morrow.

Meehl, P. E. (1962). Schizotaxia, schizotypy, schizophrenia. *Amer. Psychologist,* 17, 827–838.

Meikle, T. H., Jr., and Sechzer, J. A. (1960). Interocular transfer of brightness discrimination in "split brain" cats. *Science,* 132, 734–735.

Melton, A. W. (1963). Implications of short-term memory for a general theory of memory. *J. verb. Learn. and verb. Behav.,* 2, 1–21.

Melzack, R., and Wall, P. D. (1965). Pain mechanisms: A new theory. *Science,* 150, 971–979.

Merbaum, A. D. (1961). Need for achievement in Negro and white children. Unpublished doctoral dissertation, Univer. North Carolina, Chapel Hill, N.C.

Mettler, F. A. (Ed.) (1949). *Selective partial ablation of the frontal cortex.* New York: Hoeber-Harper.

Miller, G. A. (1951). *Language and communication.* New York: McGraw-Hill.

Miller, G. A. (1956). The magical number seven, plus or minus two: Some limits on our capacity for processing information. *Psychol. Rev.,* 63, 81–97.

Miller, G. A., Bruner, J., and Postman, L. (1951). Cited in G. A. Miller, *Language and communication.* New York: McGraw-Hill.

Miller, G. A., Galanter, E., and Pribram, K. H. (1960). *Plans and the structure of behavior.* New York: Holt, Rinehart and Winston.

Miller, G. A., and Selfridge, J. A. (1950). Verbal context and the recall of meaningful material. *Amer. J. Psychol.,* 63, 176–185.

Miller, J. (1965). Neural circuits and reaction time performance in monkeys. Unpublished doctoral dissertation. Univer. Washington, Seattle, Wash.

Miller, N. E. (1948). Studies of fear as an acquirable drive. I. Fear as motivation and fear-reduction as reinforcement in the learning of new responses. *J. exp. Psychol.,* 38, 89–101. (a)

Miller, N. E. (1948). Theory and experiment relating psychoanalytic displacement to stimulus-response generalization. *J. abnorm. soc. Psychol.,* 43, 155–178. (b)

Miller, N. E. (1951). Learnable drives and rewards. In S. S. Stevens (Ed.), *Handbook of experimental psychology.* New York: Wiley. Pp. 435–472.

Miller, N. E. (1958). Central stimulation and other new approaches to motivation and reward. *Amer. Psychologist,* 13, 100–108.

Miller, N. E., Bailey, C. J., and Stevenson, J. A. F. (1950). Decreased "hunger" but increased food intake resulting from hypothalamic lesions. *Science,* 112, 256–259.

Miller, N. E., and Bugelski, R. (1948). Minor studies of aggression: II. The influence of frustration imposed by the in-group on attitudes expressed toward outgroups. *J. Psychol.,* 25, 437–442.

Miller, N. E., and Dollard, J. (1941). *Social learning and imitation.* New Haven: Yale Univer. Press.

Millikan, G. A. (1948). Anoxia and oxygen equipment. In E. C. Andrus (Ed.), *Advances in military medicine,* Vol. I. Boston: Little, Brown. Chap. 24.

Milner, B. (1954). Intellectual function of the temporal lobes. *Psychol. Bull.,* 51, 42–62.

Milner, B. (1964). Some effects of frontal lobectomy in man. In J. M. Warren and K. Akert (Eds.), *The frontal granular cortex and behavior.* New York: McGraw-Hill. Pp. 313–334.

Milner, P. M. (1957). The cell assembly: Mark II. *Psychol. Rev.,* 64, 242–252.

Minami, H., and Dallenbach, K. M. (1946). The effect of activity upon learning and retention in the cockroach. *Amer. J. Psychol.*, 59, 1–58.

Mintz, A. (1951). Nonadaptive group behavior. *J. abnorm. soc. Psychol.*, 46, 150–159.

Mishkin, M. (1957). Effects of small frontal lesions on delayed alternation in monkeys. *J. Neurophysiol.*, 20, 615–622.

Mishkin, M., and Pribram, K. H. (1956). Analysis of the effects of frontal lesions in monkey: II. Variations of delayed response. *J. comp. physiol. Psychol.*, 49, 36–40.

Moltz, H. (1960). Imprinting: Empirical basis and theoretical significance. *Psychol. Bull.*, 57, 291–314.

Monroe, R. L. (1955). *Schools of psychoanalytic thought.* New York: Holt, Rinehart and Winston.

Moon, P., and Spencer, D. E. (1944). Visual data applied to lighting design. *J. opt. Soc. Amer.*, 34, 605–617.

Montagna, W. (1965). The skin. *Sci. Amer.*, 212 (2), 56–66.

Montgomery, K. C., and Segall, M. (1955). Discrimination learning based upon the exploratory drive. *J. comp. physiol. Psychol.*, 48, 225–228.

Moreno, J. L. (1946). *Psychodrama.* New York: Beacon House.

Moreno, J. L. (1953). *Who shall survive? Foundations of sociometry, group psychotherapy, and sociodrama.* (2d ed.) Beacon, N.Y.: Beacon House.

Morgan, C. T. (1965). *Physiological Psychology* (3d ed.). New York: McGraw-Hill.

Morgan, C. T., Garner, W. R., and Galambos, R. (1951). Pitch and intensity. *Acoust. Soc. Amer.*, 23, 658–663.

Morgan, C. T., Cook, J. S., III, Chapanis, A., and Lund, M. W. (Eds.) (1963). *Human engineering guide to equipment design.* New York: McGraw-Hill.

Morgan, C. T., and Deese, J. (1957). *How to Study.* New York: McGraw-Hill.

Morgan, J. J. B., and Morton, J. T. (1944). The distortion of syllogistic reasoning produced by personal convictions. *J. soc. Psychol.*, 20, 39–59.

Morphett, M. V., and Washburn, C. (1931). When should children begin to read? *Elem. Sch. J.*, 31, 496–503.

Morrell, F. (1961). Electrophysiological contribution to the neural basis of learning. *Physiol. Rev.*, 41, 443–494.

Moruzzi, G., and Magoun, H. W. (1949). Brain stem reticular formation and activation of the EEG. *EEG Clin. Neurophysiol.*, 1, 455–473.

Mosteller, F., et al. (1949). The preelection polls of 1948. *Soc. Sci. Res. Council Bull.* No. 60.

Mowrer, O. H. (1947). On the dual nature of learning—A re-interpretation of "conditioning" and "problem-solving." *Harv. educ. Rev.*, 17, 102–148.

Mueller, C. G. (1965). *Sensory psychology.* Englewood Cliffs, N.J.: Prentice-Hall.

Müller, J. (1838). *Handbuch der Physiologie des Menschen*, Coblentz: Hölscher.

Munn, N. L. (1955). *The evolution and growth of human behavior.* Boston: Houghton Mifflin.

Murdock, G. P. (1949). *Social structure.* New York: Macmillan.

Murray, E. J. (1964). *Motivation and emotion.* Englewood Cliffs, N.J.: Prentice-Hall.

Murray, H. A. (1938). *Explorations in personality.* New York: Oxford Univer. Press.

Murray, H. A. (1943). *Thematic apperception test.* Cambridge, Mass.: Harvard Univer. Press.

Mussen, P. H. (1950). Some personality and social factors related to changes in children's attitudes toward Negroes. *J. abnorm. soc. Psychol.*, 45, 423–441.

Mussen, P. H. (1963). *The psychological development of the child.* Englewood Cliffs, N.J.: Prentice-Hall.

Mussen, P. H., Conger, J. J., and Kagan, J. (1963). *Child development and personality* (2d ed.). New York: Harper & Row.

Myers, D., Schlosser, W. D., and Winchester, R. A. (1962). Otologic diagnosis and the treatment of deafness. *Clinical Symposia, CIBA*, 14, 39–73.

Myers, R. E. (1955). Interocular transfer of pattern discrimination in cats following section of crossed optic fibers. *J. comp. physiol. Psychol.*, 48, 470–473.

Myers, R. E. (1956). Function of the corpus callosum in interocular transfer. *Brain.*, 79, 358–363.

National Opinion Research Center, release of Jan., 1945.

Nauta, W. J. H. (1946). Hypothalamic regulation of sleep in rats: An experimental study. *J. Neurophysiol.*, 9, 285–316.

Nealey, S. M., and Edwards, B. J. (1960). "Depth perception" in rats without pattern-vision experience. *J. comp. physiol. Psychol.*, 53, 468–469.

Neff, W. D., Fisher, J. F., Diamond, I. T., and Yela, M. (1956). Role of auditory cortex in discrimination requiring localization of sound in space. *J. Neurophysiol.*, 19, 500–512.

Netter, F. H. *Ciba collection of medical illustrations.* Vol. I. New York: Ciba, 1962.

Newcomb, T. M. (1943). *Personality and social change.* New York: Dryden.

Newcomb, T. M. (1950). *Social psychology.* New York: Dryden.

Newcomb, T. M. (1953). An approach to the study of communicative acts. *Psychol. Rev.*, 60, 393–404.

Newcomb, T. M. (1961). *The acquaintance process.* New York: Holt, Rinehart and Winston.

Newcomb, T. M., Turner, R. H., and Converse, P. E. (1965). *Social Psychology.* New York: Holt, Rinehart and Winston.

Newell, A., Shaw, J. C., and Simon, H. A. (1959). A general problem-solving program for a computer. *Computers and Automation*, 8, 10–16.

Newell, A., and Simon, H. A. (1963). GPS, a program that simulates human thought. In E. A. Feigenbaum and J. Feldman (Eds.), *Computers and thought.* New York: McGraw-Hill. Pp. 279–293.

Newman, H. H., Freeman, F. N., and Holzinger, K. J. (1937). *Twins: A study of heredity and environment.* Chicago: Univer. Chicago Press.

Nissen, H. W., Chow, K. L., and Semmes, J. (1951). Effects of restricted opportunity for tactual, kinesthetic, and manipulative experience on the behavior of a chimpanzee. *Amer. J. Psychol.*, 64, 485–507.

Noble, C. E. (1952). An analysis of meaning. *Psychol. Rev.*, 59, 421–430. (*a*)

Noble, C. E. (1952). The role of stimulus meaning (*m*) in serial verbal learning. *J. exp. Psychol.*, 43, 437–466. (*b*)

Noyes, A. P. (1948). *Modern clinical psychiatry* (3d ed.). Philadelphia: Saunders.

Office of Strategic Services, Assessment Staff (1948). *Assessment of men: Selection of personnel for the Office of Strategic Services.* New York: Holt, Rinehart and Winston.

Ogg, E. (1955). *Psychologists in action.* Pamphlet 229. New York: Public Affairs Committee, Inc.

Ogg, E. (1962). *Psychotherapy: A helping process.* Pamphlet 329. New York: Public Affairs Committee, Inc.

Olds, J. (1955). Physiological mechanisms of reward. In M. Jones (Ed.), *Nebraska symposium on motivation.* Vol. III. Lincoln, Neb.: Univer. Nebraska Press. Pp. 73–139.

Olds, J. (1958). Self-stimulation of the brain. *Science,* 127, 315–323.

Olds, J., and Milner, P. (1954). Positive reinforcement produced by electrical stimulation of septal area and other regions of rat brain. *J. comp. physiol. Psychol.*, 47, 419–427.

Olds, M. E. and Olds, J. (1962). Escape interactions in rat brain. *Amer. J. Physiol.*, 203, 803–810.

Olds, M. E. and Olds, J, (1963). Approach-avoidance analysis of rat diencephalon. *J. Comp. Neurol.*, 120, 259–295.

Olson, G. and King, R. A. (1962). Supplementary report: Stimulus generalization gradients along a luminosity continuum. *J. exp. Psychol.*, 63, 414–415.

Orr, D. W. (1949). Psychiatric uses of sodium pentothal. *U. S. Nav. med. Bull.*, 49, 508–516.

Osgood, C. E. (1949). The similarity paradox in human learning: A resolution. *Psychol. Rev.*, 56, 132–143.

Osgood, C. E. (1952). The nature and measurement of meaning. *Psychol. Bull.*, 49, 197–237.

Osgood, C. E. (1953). *Method and theory in experimental psychology.* Fairlawn, N.J.: Oxford Univer. Press.

Osgood, C. E. and Tannenbaum, P. H. (1955). The principle of congruity in the prediction of attitude change. *Psychol. Rev.*, 62, 42–55.

Osgood, C. E., Suci, G. J., and Tannenbaum, P. H. (1957). *The measurement of meaning.* Urbana, Ill.: Univer. Illinois Press.

Østerberg, G. (1935). Topography of the layer of rods and cones in the human retina. *Acta ophthal., Suppl.* (Whole No. 6).

Palay, S. L. (1958). The morphology of synapses in the central nervous system. *Exp. Cell Res.*, Supplement 5, 275–293.

Papez, J. W. (1929). *Comparative neurology.* New York: Hafner.

Papez, J. W. (1937). A proposed mechanism of emotion. *Arch. Neurol. Psychiat., Chicago,* 38, 725–743.

Patton, H. D. (1965). Special properties of nerve trunks and tracts. In T. C. Ruch and H. D. Patton (Eds.), *Physiology and Biophysics* (19th ed.). Philadelphia: Saunders. Pp. 73–94.

Pavlov, I. P. (1927). *Conditioned reflexes* (trans. G. V. Anrep). London: Oxford Univer. Press.

Pavlov, I. P. (1928). *Lectures on conditioned reflexes* (trans. W. H. Gantt). New York: International.

Pavlov, I. P. (1960). *Conditioned reflexes.* New York: Dover. A reprint of: Pavlov, I. P. *Conditioned Reflexes* (trans. G. V. Anrep). London: Oxford Univer. Press, 1927.

Penfield, W., and Rasmussen, T. (1950). *The cerebral cortex of man.* New York: Macmillan.

Penfield, W. and Roberts, L. (1959). *Speech and Brain-mechanisms.* Princeton, N.J.: Princeton Univer. Press.

Peterson, L. R. and Peterson, M. J. (1959). Short-term retention of individual verbal items. *J. exp. Psychol.*, 58, 193–198.

Pfaffmann, C. (1959). The afferent code for sensory quality. *Amer. Psychologist,* 14, 226–232.

Pfaffmann, C. (1964). Taste, its sensory and motivating properties. *Amer. Sci.,* 52, 187–206.

Phoenix, C. H. (1961). Hypothalamic regulation of sexual behavior in male guinea pigs. *J. comp. physiol. Psychol.*, 54, 72–77.

Piaget, Jean (1952). *The child's conception of number.* New York: Humanities Press.

Pilgrim, F. J., and Patton, R. A. (1947). Patterns of self-selection of purified dietary components by the rat. *J. comp. physiol. Psychol.*, 40, 343–348.

Poincaré, H. (1913). Mathematical creation. In *The foundations of science* (trans. G. H. Halsted). New York: Science Press. Pp. 383–394.

Polyak, S. (1941). *The retina.* Chicago: Univer. Chicago Press.

Postman, L., and Adams, P. A. (1956). Studies in incidental learning. IV. The interaction of orienting tasks and stimulus materials. *J. exp. Psychol.*, 51, 329–333.

Postman, L., and Phillips, L. W. (1954). Studies in incidental learning. I. The effects of crowding and isolation. *J. exp. Psychol.*, 48, 48–56.

Postman, L., and Senders, V. L. (1946). Incidental learning and generality of set. *J. exp. Psychol.*, 36, 153–165.

Premack, D. (1959). Toward empirical behavioral laws: I. Positive reinforcement. *Psychol. Rev.*, 66, 219–233.

Premack, D. (1961). Predicting instrumental performance from the independent rate of the contingent response. *J. exp. Psychol.*, 61, 163–171.

Pressey, S. L. (1926). A simple apparatus which gives tests and scores—and teaches. *School and Society,* 23, 373–376.

Pribram, K. H. (1958). Neocortical function in behavior.

In H. F. Harlow and C. N. Woolsey (Eds.), *Biological and biochemical bases of behavior*. Madison, Wis.: Univer. Wisconsin Press. Pp. 151–172.

Pribram, K. H., and Mishkin, M. (1956). Analysis of the effects of frontal lesions in monkey: III. Object alternation. *J. comp. physiol. Psychol.,* 49, 41–45.

Rado, S. (1951). Psychodynamics of depression from the etiological point of view. *Psychosom. Med.,* 13, 51–55.

Ramsay, A. O., and Hess, E. H. (1954). A laboratory approach to the study of imprinting. *Wilson Bull.,* 66, 196–206.

Ranson, S. W. (1939). Somnolence caused by hypothalamic lesions in the monkey, *Arch. Neurol. Psychiat., Chicago,* 41, 1–23.

Ranson, S. W., and Clark, S. L. (1959). *The anatomy of the nervous system: Its development and function* (10th ed.). Philadelphia, Pa.: Saunders.

Rapaport, D. (1950). *Emotions and memory*. New York: International Univer. Press.

Raven, B., and French, J. R. P. (1958). Group support, legitimate power, and social influence. *J. Pers.,* 26, 400–409.

Raymond, M. J. (1956). Case of fetishism treated by aversion therapy. *Brit. med. J.,* 2, 854–857.

Razran, G. (1961). The observable unconscious and the inferable conscious in current Soviet psychophysiology: Interoceptive conditioning, semantic conditioning, and the orienting reflex. *Psychol. Rev.,* 68, 81–147.

Reed, J. D. (1947). Spontaneous activity of animals. *Psychol. Bull.,* 44, 393–412.

Restorff, H. von (1933). Über die Wirkung von Bereichsbildung im Spurenfeld. *Psychol. Forsch.,* 18, 299–342.

Rethlingshafer, D. (1963). *Motivation as related to personality*. New York: McGraw-Hill.

Reymert, M. L. (Ed.) (1950). *Feelings and emotion*. New York: McGraw-Hill.

Reynolds, W. F. (1958). Acquisition and extinction of the conditioned eyelid response following partial and continuous reinforcement. *J. exp. Psychol.,* 55, 335–341.

Reynolds, R. W. (1965). An irritative hypothesis concerning the hypothalamic regulation of food intake. *Psychol. Rev.,* 72, 105–116.

Richter, C. P. (1936). Increased salt appetite in adrenalectomized rats. *Amer. J. Physiol.,* 115, 155–161.

Richter, C. P. (1942–1943). Total self-regulatory functions in animals and human beings. *Harvey Lect.,* 38, 63–103.

Riddle, O., Bates, R. W., and Lahr, E. L. (1935). Maternal behavior in rats induced by prolactin. *Proc. Soc. exp. Biol., N.Y.,* 32, 730–734.

Riesen, A. H. (1960). Statement in Appendix. In M. Von Senden, *Space and sight* (trans. P. Heath). New York: Free Press. Pp. 313–316.

Riesen, A. H. (1961). Stimulation as a requirement for growth and function in behavioral development. In D. W. Fiske, and S. R. Maddi (Eds.), *Functions of varied experience*. Homewood, Ill.: Dorsey. Pp. 57–80.

Riggs, A. F. (1929). *Intelligent living*. New York: Doubleday.

Riggs, L. A., Ratliff, F., Cornsweet, J. C., and Cornsweet, T. (1953). The disappearance of steadily fixated visual test objects. *J. opt. soc. Amer.,* 43, 495–501.

Roberts, W. W. (1958). Rewarding and punishing effects from stimulation of posterior hypothalamus of cat with same electrode at same intensity. *J. comp. physiol. Psychol.,* 51, 400–407.

Robinson, E. S. (1927). The "similarity" factor in retroaction. *Amer. J. Psychol.,* 39, 297–312.

Robinson, E. S., and Bills, A. G. (1926). Two factors in the work decrement. *J. exp. Psychol.,* 9, 415–443.

Robinson, F. P. (1946). *Effective study* (rev. ed.). New York: Harper & Row.

Robinson, H. B. and Robinson, N. M. (1965). *The mentally retarded child: A psychological approach*. New York: McGraw-Hill.

Roethlisberger, F. J., and Dickson, W. J. (1939). *Management and the worker*. Cambridge, Mass.: Harvard Univer. Press.

Rogers, C. R. (1951). *Client-centered therapy: Its current practice, implications, and theory*. Boston: Houghton Mifflin.

Rorschach, H. (1942). *Psycho-diagnostics*. Berne: Huber.

Rose, A. M. (1946). Army policies toward Negro soldiers. *Ann. Amer. Acad. pol. soc. Sci.,* 244, 90–94.

Rose, J. E., and Woolsey, C. N. (1949). Organization of the mammalian thalamus and its relationships to the cerebral cortex. *EEG Clin. Neurophysiol.,* 1, 391–404.

Rosen, B. (1956). The achievement syndrome: A psychocultural dimension of social stratification. *Amer. soc. Rev.,* 21, 203–211.

Rosen, J. (1953). *Direct analysis: Selected papers*. New York: Grune & Stratton.

Rosenblith, W. A. (Ed.) (1961). *Sensory Communication*. New York: Wiley.

Rosenthal, R. (1964). Experimenter outcome-orientation and the results of the psychological experiment. *Psych. Bull.,* 61, 405–412.

Rotter, J. B. (1964). *Clinical psychology*. Englewood Cliffs, N.J.: Prentice-Hall.

Ruben, L. S. (1957). The psychopharmacology of lysergic acid diethylamide (LSD 25). *Psychol. Bull.,* 54, 479–489.

Rubin, E. (1921). *Visuell wahrgenommene Figuren*. Copenhagen, Gyldendalske.

Ruch, F. L. (1958). *Psychology and life* (5th ed.). Chicago, Ill.: Scott, Foresman.

Ruch, T. C., Fulton, J. F., and German, W. J. (1938). Sensory discrimination in the monkey, chimpanzee, and man after lesions of the parietal lobe. *Arch. Neurol. Psychiat., Chicago,* 39, 919–937.

Ruch, T. C. and Patton, H. D. (Eds.) (1965). *Physiology and Biophysics* (19th ed.). Philadelphia: Saunders.

Rugg, H. (1963). *Imagination*. New York: Harper & Row.

Rushton, W. A. H. (1962). Visual pigments in man. *Sci. Amer.*, 207 (5), 120–132.

Rutledge, L. T. (1965). Facilitation: Electrical response enhanced by conditional excitation of cerebral cortex. *Science*, 148, 1246–1248.

Sanford, F. H. (1951). Notes on the future of psychology as a profession. *Amer. Psychologist*, 6, 74–76.

Sargent, S. S. (1939). Emotional stereotypes in the *Chicago Tribune*. *Sociometry*, 2, 69–75.

Schachter, S., and Singer, J. (1962). Cognitive, social and physiological determinants of emotional state. *Psych. Rev.*, 69, 379–399.

Scharlock, D. P., Tucker, T. J., and Strominger, N. L. (1963). Auditory discrimination by the cat after neonatal ablation of the temporal cortex. *Science*, 141, 1197–1198.

Schein, E. H. (1964). *Organizational psychology*. Englewood Cliffs, N.J.: Prentice-Hall.

Schein, E. H., and Bennis, W. G. (1965). *Personal and organizational change through group methods: The laboratory approach*. New York: Wiley.

Schein, E. H., with Schneier, I., and Barker, G. H. (1961). *Coercive persuasion: A socio-psychological analysis of the "brainwashing" of American prisoners by the Chinese communists*. New York: Norton.

Schjelderup-Ebbe, T. (1935). Social behavior of birds. In C. Murchison (Ed.), *Handbook of social psychology*. Worcester, Mass.: Clark Univer. Press. Pp. 947–972.

Schlosberg, H. (1954). Three dimensions of emotion. *Psychol. Rev.*, 61, 81–88.

Scott, E. M., and Verney, E. L. (1949). Self-selection of diet. IX. The appetite for thiamine. *J. Nutrition*, 37, 81–92.

Scott, J. P. (1958). *Animal behavior*. Chicago: Univer. Chicago Press.

Sears, R. R. (1936). Experimental studies of projection. I. Attribution of traits. *J. soc. Psychol.*, 7, 151–163.

Sears, R. R., Maccoby, E. E., and Levin, H. (1957). *Patterns of child rearing*. New York: Harper & Row.

Secord, P. F., and Backman, C. W. (1964). *Social psychology*. New York: McGraw-Hill.

Sekuler, R. W., and Ganz, L. (1963). Aftereffect of seen motion with a stabilized retinal image. *Science*, 139, 419–420.

Selye, H. (1950). *The physiology and pathology of exposure to stress*. Montreal: ACTA.

Sells, S. B. (1936). The atmosphere effect: An experimental study of reasoning. *Arch. Psychol.*, 29 (Whole No. 200).

Sem-Jacobsen, C. W., and Torkildsen, A. (1960). Depth recording and electrical stimulation in the human brain. In E. R. Ramey and D. S. O'Doherty (Eds.), *Electrical studies on the unanesthetized brain*. New York: Hoeber. Pp. 275–290.

Semmes, J., Weinstein, S., Ghent, L., and Teuber, H.-L. (1960). *Somatosensory changes after penetrating brain wounds in man*. Cambridge, Mass.: Harvard Univer. Press.

Semon, R. (1921). *The Mneme*. London: Allen and Unwin.

Senden, M. von (1932). *Raum- und Gestaltauffassung bei operierten Vlindgeborenen vor und nach Operation*. Leipzig: Barth.

Senden, M. von (1960). *Space and sight: The perception of space and shape in the congenitally blind before and after operation* (trans. P. Heath). New York: Free Press.

Seward, J. P. (1949). An experimental analysis of latent learning. *J. exp. Psychol.*, 39, 177–186.

Shaffer, L. F. (1947). Fear and courage in aerial combat. *J. consult. Psychol.*, 11, 137–143.

Shaffer, L. F., and Shoben, E. J., Jr. (1956). *The psychology of adjustment* (rev. ed.). Boston: Houghton Mifflin.

Sharp, A. A. (1938). An experimental test of Freud's doctrine of the relation of hedonic tone to memory revival. *J. exp. Psychol.*, 22, 395–418.

Shaw, M. E. (1955). A comparison of two types of leadership in various communication nets. *J. abnorm. soc. Psychol.*, 50, 127–134.

Sheffield, F. D., and Roby, T. B. (1950). Reward value of a non-nutritive sweet taste. *J. comp. physiol. Psychol.*, 43, 471–481.

Sherif, M. (1935). A study of some social factors in perception. *Arch. Psychol.*, 27 (Whole No. 187).

Sherif, M. (1958). Group influences upon the formation of norms and attitudes. In E. E. Maccoby, T. M. Newcomb, and E. L. Hartley (Eds.), *Readings in social psychology* (3d ed.). New York: Holt, Rinehart and Winston. Pp. 219–232.

Sherif, M., Harvey, O. J., White, B. J., Hood, W. R., and Sherif, C. (1961). *Intergroup conflict and cooperation*. Norman, Okla.: Univer. Oklahoma Book Exchange.

Sherman, M., Sherman, I., and Flory, C. D. (1936). Infant behavior. *Comp. Psychol. Monogr.* 12 (Whole No. 59).

Sherrington, C. S. (1906). *The integrative action of the nervous system*. London: Constable.

Sherrington, C. S. (1963). *Man on his nature* (2d ed.). Cambridge: Cambridge Univer. Press.

Shirley, M. M. (1931). *The first two years: A study of twenty-five babies*. Vol. I. *Postural and locomotor development*. Minneapolis: Univer. Minnesota Press.

Shirley, M. M. (1933). *The first two years: A study of twenty-five babies*. Vol. II. *Intellectual development*. Minneapolis: Univer. Minnesota Press.

Sholl, D. A. (1956). *The organization of the cerebral cortex*. London: Methuen.

Shower, E. G., and Biddulph, R. (1931). Differential pitch sensitivity of the ear. *J. acoust. Soc. Amer.*, 3, 275–287.

Shuey, A. M. (1958). *The testing of Negro intelligence*. Lynchburg, Va.: J. P. Bell.

Shuford, E. J., Jr. (1959). Palatability and osmotic pressure of glucose and sucrose solutions as determinants of intake. *J. comp. physiol. Psychol.*, 52, 150–153.

Sidman, M. (1953). Avoidance conditioning with brief shock and no exteroceptive warning signal. *Science,* 118, 157–158.

Sidman, M. (1960). *The tactics of scientific research.* New York: Basic Books.

Siegal, S. (1956). *Nonparametric statistics for the behavioral sciences.* New York: McGraw-Hill.

Simmel, G. (1902–1903). The number of members as determining the sociological form of the group. *Amer. J. Sociol.,* 8, 1–46; 158–196.

Sisson, E. D. (1948). Forced choice—the new Army rating. *Personnel Psychol.,* 1, 365–381.

Skaggs, E. B. (1925). Further studies in retroactive inhibition. *Psychol. Monogr.,* 24 (Whole No. 161).

Skinner, B. F. (1938). *The behavior of organisms.* New York: Appleton-Century-Crofts.

Skinner, B. F. (1953). *Science and Human Behavior.* New York: Macmillan.

Skinner, B. F. (1958). Teaching machines. *Science,* 128, 969–977.

Skinner, B. F. (1961). *Cumulative record* (enlarged ed.). New York: Appleton-Century-Crofts.

Skodak, M., and Skeels, H. M. (1949). A final follow-up of one hundred adopted children. *J. genet. Psychol.,* 75, 3–19.

Sleight, R. B. (1948). The effect of instrument dial shape on legibility. *J. appl. Psychol.,* 32, 170–188.

Smith, C. P., and Feld, S. (1958). How to learn the method of content analysis for *n* Achievement, *n* Affiliation, and *n* Power. In J. W. Atkinson (Ed.), *Motives in fantasy, action, and society.* Princeton, N.J.: Van Nostrand. Pp. 685–818.

Smith, H. C. (1964). *Psychology of industrial behavior* (2d ed.). New York: McGraw-Hill.

Smith, J. R. (1941). The frequency growth of the human alpha rhythms during normal infancy and childhood. *J. Psychol.,* 11, 177–198.

Smith, M. E. (1935). A study of the speech of eight bilingual children of the same family. *Child Develpm.,* 6, 19–25.

Smith, M., and Kinney, G. C. (1956). Sugar as a reward for hungry and nonhungry rats. *J. exp. Psychol.,* 51, 348–352.

Smith, M. P., and Capretta, P. J. (1956). Effect of drive level and experience on the reward value of saccharine solutions. *J. comp. physiol. Psychol.,* 49, 553–557.

Snyder, I. W., and Pronko, N. H. (1952). *Vision with spatial inversion.* Wichita, Kan.: Univer. Wichita Press.

Social Science Research Council (1947). *Public reaction to the atomic bomb and world affairs.* Ithaca, N.Y.: Cornell Univer. Press.

Solley, C. M. and Murphy, G. (1960). *Development of the perceptual world.* New York: Basic Books.

Solomon, R. L., and Wynne, L. C. (1953). Traumatic avoidance learning: Acquisition in normal dogs. *Psychol. Monogr.,* 67 (Whole No. 354).

Spence, K. W. (1937). The differential response in animals to stimuli varying within a single dimension. *Psychol. Rev.,* 44, 430–444.

Spence, K. W. (1951). Theoretical interpretations of learning. In C. P. Stone (Ed.), *Comparative Psychology* (3d ed.). Englewood Cliffs, N.J.: Prentice-Hall. Pp. 239–291.

Spielberger, C. D., and Levin, S. M. (1962). What is learned in verbal conditioning? *J. verb. Learn. and verb. Behav.,* 1, 125–132.

Spriegel, W. R., and Wallace, R. F. (1948). Recent trends in personnel selection and induction. *Personnel,* 77–88.

Staats, C. K., and Staats, A. W. (1957). Meaning established by classical conditioning. *J. exp. Psychol.,* 54, 74–80.

Stacey, C. L., and DeMartino, M. F. (Eds.) (1958). *Understanding human motivation.* Cleveland: Allen.

Stagner, R. (1948). *Psychology of personality* (2d ed.). New York: McGraw-Hill.

Stagner, R. (1961). *Psychology of personality.* (3d ed.). New York: McGraw-Hill.

Stead, W. H., et al. (1940). *Occupational counseling techniques.* New York: American Book.

Steggerda, F. R. (1941). Observations on the water intake in an adult man with dysfunctioning salivary glands. *Amer. J. Physiol.,* 132, 517–521.

Stellar, E. (1954). The physiology of motivation. *Psychol. Rev.,* 61, 5–22.

Stern, C. (1960). *Principles of human genetics* (2d ed.). San Francisco: Freeman.

Stevens, C. F. (1966). *Neurophysiology: A primer.* New York: Wiley.

Stevens, S. S. (1951). Mathematics, measurement, and psychophysics. In S. S. Stevens (Ed.), *Handbook of experimental psychology.* New York: Wiley.

Stevens, S. S. (1956). The direct estimation of sensory magnitudes—loudness. *Amer. J. Psychol.,* 69, 1–25.

Stevens, S. S. (1961). The psychophysics of sensory function. In W. A. Rosenblith (Ed.), *Sensory communication.* New York: Wiley. Pp. 1–33.

Stevens, S. S., and Davis, H. (1938). *Hearing.* New York: Wiley.

Stevens, S. S., and Volkmann, J. (1940). The relation of pitch to frequency: A revised scale. *Amer. J. Psychol.,* 53, 329–353.

Stogdill, R. M. (1948). Personal factors associated with leadership: A survey of the literature. *J. Psychol.,* 25, 37–71.

Stone, C. P. (1932). Wildness and savageness in rats of different strains. In K. S. Lashley (Ed.), *Studies in the dynamics of behavior.* Chicago: Univer. Chicago Press. Pp. 3–55.

Stratton, G. M. (1897). Vision without inversion of the retinal image. *Psychol. Rev.,* 4, 341–360; 463–481.

Strodtbeck, F., James, R., and Hawkins, C. (1958). Social status in jury deliberations. In E. E. Maccoby, T. M. Newcomb, and E. L. Hartley (Eds.), *Readings in social psychology* (3d ed.). New York: Holt, Rinehart and Winston. Pp. 379–388.

Strong, E. K., Jr. (1938). *Vocational interest blank for men (revised), Form M.* Stanford, Calif.: Stanford Univer. Press.

Stroud, J. B. (1940). Experiments on learning in school situations. *Psychol. Bull.,* 37, 777–807.

Strupp, H. H. (1958). The psychotherapist's contribution to the treatment process. *Behav. Sci.,* 3, 34–67.

Sullivan, H. S. (1953). *The interpersonal theory of psychiatry.* New York: Norton.

Super, D. E., and Crites, J. O. (1962). *Appraising vocational fitness by means of psychological tests* (rev. ed.). New York: Harper & Row.

Sutermeister, R. A. (1963). *People and productivity.* New York: McGraw-Hill.

Swets, J. A. (1961). Is there a sensory threshold? *Science,* 134, 168–177.

Swift, E. J. (1918). *Psychology and the day's work.* New York: Scribner.

Tasaki, I. (1954). Nerve impulses in individual auditory nerve fibers of guinea pig. *J. Neurophysiol.,* 17, 97–122.

Taylor, J. A. (1953). A personality scale of manifest anxiety. *J. abnorm. soc. Psychol.,* 48, 285–290.

Teitelbaum, P. (1966). *Physiological Psychology.* Englewood Cliffs, N.J.: Prentice-Hall.

Teitelbaum, P., and Stellar, E. (1954). Recovery from the failure to eat produced by hypothalamic lesions. *Science,* 120, 894–895.

Telberg, I. (1950). They don't do it our way. *Courier* (UNESCO), 3, No. 4.

Terman, L. M. (1938). *Psychological factors in marital happiness.* New York: McGraw-Hill.

Terman, L. M., et al. (1925). *Genetic studies of genius.* Vol. I. *Mental and physical traits of a thousand gifted children.* Stanford, Calif.: Stanford Univer. Press.

Terman, L. M., and Merrill, M. A. (1937). *Measuring intelligence.* Boston: Houghton Mifflin.

Terman, L. M., and Merrill, M. A. (1960). *Stanford-Binet Intelligence Scale: Manual for the third revision form L-M.* Boston: Houghton Mifflin.

Terman, L. M., and Oden, M. H. (1947). *Genetic studies of genius.* Vol. IV. *The gifted child grows up.* Stanford: Stanford Univer. Press.

Terman, L. M., and Oden, M. H. (1959). *Genetic studies of genius.* Vol. V. *The gifted group at midlife.* Stanford: Stanford Univer. Press.

Teuber, H.-L. (1960). Perception. In J. Field, H. W. Magoun, and V. H. Hall (Eds.), *Handbook of Physiology.* Vol. 3. Washington, D.C.: Amer. Physiological Society. Pp. 1595–1668.

Teuber, H.-L. (1964). The riddle of frontal lobe function in man. In J. M. Warren and K. Akert (Eds.), *The frontal granular cortex and behavior.* New York: McGraw-Hill. Pp. 410–444.

Teuber, H.-L., Battersby, W. S., and Bender, M. B. (1960). *Visual field defects after penetrating missile wounds of the brain.* Cambridge, Mass.: Harvard Univer. Press.

Thibaut, J. W., and Kelley, H. H. (1959). *The social psychology of groups.* New York: Wiley.

Thibaut, J. W., and Strickland, L. (1956). Psychological set and social conformity. *J. Pers.,* 25, 115–129.

Thigpen, C. H., and Cleckley, H. M. (1957). *The three faces of Eve.* New York: McGraw-Hill.

Thompson, R., and McConnell, J. (1955). Classical conditioning in the planarian, *Dugesia dorotocephala. J. comp. physiol. Psychol.,* 48, 65–68.

Thompson, W. R., and Melzack, R. (1956). Early environment. *Sci. Amer.,* 194 (1), 38–42.

Thomson, R. (1959). *The Psychology of Thinking.* Baltimore, Md.: Penguin Books.

Thorndike, E. L. (1911). *Animal intelligence.* New York: Macmillan.

Thorndike, E. L. (1932). *The fundamentals of learning.* New York: Teachers Coll., Columbia Univer.

Thorndike, E. L., Bregman, E. O., Tilton, J. W., and Woodyard, E. (1928). *Adult learning.* New York: Macmillan.

Thorpe, W. H. (1963). *Learning and instinct in animals.* (2d ed.). London: Methuen.

Thurstone, L. L. (1938). Primary mental abilities. *Psychometr. Monogr.* (Whole No. 1).

Thurstone, L. L., and Chave, E. J. (1929). *The measurement of attitudes.* Chicago: Univer. Chicago Press.

Thurstone, L. L., and Thurstone, T. G. (1941). Factorial studies of intelligence. *Psychometr. Monogr.* (Whole No. 2).

Tiegs, E. W., and Katz, B. (1941). *Mental hygiene in education.* New York: Ronald.

Titchener, E. B. (1905). *Experimental psychology. Quantitative.* New York: Macmillan.

Tolman, E. C. (1932). *Purposive behavior in animals and men.* New York: Appleton-Century-Crofts.

Tolman, E. C. (1939). Prediction of vicarious trial and error by means of the schematic sowbug. *Psychol. Rev.,* 46, 318–336.

Tolman, E. C. (1948). Cognitive maps in rats and men. *Psychol. Rev.,* 55, 189–208.

Tolman, E. C., and Honzik, C. H. (1930). Introduction and removal of reward, and maze performance in rats. *Univer. Calif. Publ. Psychol.,* 4, 257–275.

Tomita, T. (1963). Electrical activity in the vertebrate retina. *J. opt. Soc. Amer.,* 53, 49–57.

Tomkins, W. (1931). *Universal Indian sign language.* San Diego, Calif.: William Tomkins.

Torrance, E. P. (1962). *Guiding creative talent.* Englewood Cliffs, N.J.: Prentice-Hall.

Towe, A. L. (1965). Electrophysiology of the cerebral cortex: Consciousness. In T. C. Ruch and H. D. Pattin (Eds.), *Physiology and biophysics* (19th ed.). Philadelphia, Pa.: Saunders. Pp. 455–464.

Trow, D. (1957). Autonomy and job-satisfaction in task-oriented groups. *J. abnorm. soc. Psychol.,* 54, 204–209.

Tsang, Y. C. (1938). Hunger motivation in gastrectomized rats. *J. comp. Psychol.,* 26, 1–17.

Tussing, L. (1959). *Psychology for better living*. New York: Wiley.

Tyler, L. E. (1963). *Tests and Measurements*. Englewood Cliffs, N.J.: Prentice-Hall.

Underwood, B. J. (1954). Speed of learning and amount retained: A consideration of methodology. *Psychol. Bull.*, 51, 276–282.

Underwood, B. J. (1957). Interference and forgetting. *Psychol. Rev.*, 64, 49–60.

Underwood, B. J. (1961). Ten years of massed practice on distributed practice. *Psychol. Rev.*, 68, 229–247.

Underwood, B. J. (1964). Forgetting. *Sci. Amer.*, 210 (3), 91–99.

Underwood, B. J., and Keppel, G. (1962). One trial learning? *J. verb. Learn. verb. Behav.*, 1, 1–13.

Underwood, B. J., and Postman, L. (1960). Extra-experimental sources of interference in forgetting. *Psychol. Rev.*, 67, 73–95.

Underwood, B. J., and Schulz, R. W. (1961). Studies of distributed practice: XX. Sources of interference associated with differences in learning and retention. *J. exp. Psychol.*, 61, 228–235.

U.S. Dept. of Health, Education, and Welfare (1955). *Infant care*. Washington, D.C.: U.S. Govt. Printing Office.

U.S. Dept. of Health, Education, and Welfare (1956). *Your child from one to six*. Washington, D.C.: U.S. Govt. Printing Office.

Vaughan, E., and Fisher, A. E. (1962). Male sexual behavior induced by intracranial electrical stimulation. *Science*, 137, 758–760.

Verney, E. B. (1947). The antidiuretic hormone and the factors which determine its release. *Proc. roy. Soc., B*, 135, 24–106.

Vernon, M. D. (1952). *A further study of visual perception*. Cambridge: Cambridge Univer. Press.

Vinacke, W. E. (1952). *The psychology of thinking*. New York: McGraw-Hill.

Wade, M. (1947). The effect of sedatives upon delayed responses in monkeys following removal of the prefrontal lobes. *J. Neurophysiol.*, 10, 57–61.

Wagner, H. G., MacNichol, E. F., Jr., and Wolbarsht, M. L. (1960). The response properties of single ganglion cells in the goldfish retina. *J. gen. Physiol.*, 43 (6), Supplement, 45–62.

Wake, F. R. (1950). Changes of fear with age. Unpublished doctoral dissertation, McGill Univer. Cited in J. P. Zubek and P. A. Solberg (1954), *Human development*. New York: McGraw-Hill.

Wald, G. (1959). The photoreceptor process in vision. In J. Field, H. W. Magoun, and V. E. Hall (Eds.), *Handbook of Physiology*. Vol. 1. Washington, D.C.: American Physiological Society. Pp. 671–692.

Walk, R. D., and Gibson, E. J. (1961). A comparative and analytical study of visual depth perception. *Psychol. Monogr.*, 75 (Whole No. 519).

Walker, E. L., and Heyns, R. W. (1962). *An anatomy for conformity*. Englewood Cliffs, N.J.: Prentice-Hall.

Wallach, H. (1939). On constancy of visual speed. *Psychol. Rev.*, 46, 541–552.

Wallach, H. (1963). The perception of neutral colors. *Sci. Amer.*, 208 (1), 107–118.

Wallas, G. (1926). *The art of thought*. New York: Harcourt, Brace & World.

Wallis, W. A., and Roberts, H. V. (1956). *Statistics: A new approach*. New York: Free Press.

Walls, G. L. (1960). Land! Land! *Psychol. Bull.*, 57, 29–48.

Wangensteen, O. H., and Carlson, A. J. (1931). Hunger sensations in a patient after total gastrectomy. *Proc. Soc. exp. Biol., N.Y.*, 28, 545–547.

Ward, L. B. (1937). Reminiscence and rote learning. *Psychol. Monogr.*, 49 (Whole No. 20).

Warden, C. J. (1931). *Animal motivation studies. The albino rat*. New York: Columbia Univer. Press.

Warden, C. J., Jenkins, T. N., and Warner, L. H. (1936). *Comparative psychology*. Vol. III. New York: Ronald.

Warner, W. L., and Lunt, P. S. (1941). *The social life of a modern community*. New Haven, Conn.: Yale Univer. Press.

Washburn, R. W. (1929). A study of smiling and laughing of infants in the first year of life. *Genet. Psychol. Monogr.*, 6, 397–539.

Watson, J. B. (1925). *Behaviorism*. New York: Norton.

Watson, J. B., and Rayner, R. (1920). Conditioned emotional reactions. *J. exp. Psychol.*, 3, 1–14.

Watson, R. I. (1954). *Psychology as a profession*. Garden City, N.Y.: Doubleday.

Wattenberg, W. W. (1955). *The adolescent years*. New York: Harcourt, Brace & World.

Weakland, J. H. (1960). The "double-bind" hypothesis of schizophrenia and three-party interaction. In D. Jackson (Ed.), *The etiology of schizophrenia*. New York: Basic Books. Pp. 373–388.

Webb, W. B. (Ed.) (1962). *The profession of psychology*. New York: Holt, Rinehart and Winston.

Webster's Third New International Dictionary (1961). Springfield, Mass.: G. & C. Merriam.

Wechsler, D. (1949). *Wechsler intelligence scale for children*. New York: Psychological Corp.

Wechsler, D. (1955). *Wechsler adult intelligence scale, manual*. New York: Psychological Corporation.

Wechsler, D. (1958). *Measurement and appraisal of adult intelligence* (4th ed.). Baltimore: Williams & Wilkins.

Weiss, W., and Fine, B. J. (1958). The effect of induced aggressiveness on opinion change. In E. E. Maccoby, T. M. Newcomb, and E. L. Hartley (Eds.), *Readings in social psychology* (3d ed.). New York: Holt, Rinehart and Winston. Pp. 149–156.

Weissman, A. (1963). Effect of electroconvulsive shock intensity and seizure pattern on retrograde amnesia in rats. *J. comp. physiol. Psychol.*, 56, 806–810.

Welker, W. I. (1956). Some determinants of play and

exploration in chimpanzees. *J. comp. psysiol. Psvchol.,* 49, 84–89.

Welsh, G. S. (1956). Factor dimensions A and R. In G. S. Welsh and W. G. Dahlstrom (Eds.), *Basic readings on the MMPI in psychology and medicine.* Minneapolis: Univer. Minn. Press.

Wendt, G. R. (1951). Vestibular function. In S. S. Stevens (Ed.), *Handbook of experimental psychology.* New York: Wiley. Chap. 31.

Werner, H. (1935). Studies on contour. I. Qualitative analyses. *Amer. J. Psychol.,* 47, 40–64.

Werner, H., and Kaplan, E. (1950). Development of word meaning through verbal context: An experimental study. *J. Psychol.,* 29, 251–257.

Wertheim, T. (1894). Über die indirekte Sehschärfe. *Z. Psychol.,* 7, 172–187.

Wertheimer, M. (1912). Experimentelle Studien über das Sehen von Bewegungen. *Z. Psychol.,* 61, 161–265.

Wertheimer, M. (1923). Untersuchungen zur Lehre von der Gestalt. II. *Psychol. Forsch.,* 4, 301–351.

Wertheimer, M. (1959). *Productive thinking* (rev. ed.). New York: Harper & Row.

Wetzel, A. B., Thompson, V. E., Horel, J. A., and Meyer, P. M. (1965). Some consequences of perinatal lesions of the visual cortex in the cat. *Psychon. Sci.,* 3, 381–382.

Wever, E. G., and Bray, C. W. (1930). The nature of acoustic response: The relation between sound frequency and frequency of impulses in the auditory nerve. *J. exp. Psychol.,* 13, 373–387.

Wheatley, M. D. (1944). The hypothalamus and affective behavior in cats: A study of the effects of experimental lesions, with anatomic correlations. *Arch. Neurol. Psychiat., Chicago,* 52, 296–316.

White, R. W. (1959). Motivation reconsidered: The concept of competence. *Psychol. Rev.,* 66, 297–333.

White, R. W. (1964). *The abnormal personality.* (3d ed.). New York: Ronald.

White, R. W. (1966). *Lives in progress: A study of the natural growth of personality* (2d ed.). New York: Holt, Rinehart and Winston.

Whiting, J. W. M., Kluckhohn, R., and Anthony, A. (1958). The function of male initiation ceremonies at puberty. In E. E. Maccoby, T. M. Newcomb, and E. L. Hartley (Eds.), *Readings in social psychology* (3d ed.). New York: Holt, Rinehart and Winston. Pp. 359–370.

Whorf, B. L. (1956). *Language, thought, and reality.* Cambridge, Mass.: Technology Press.

Whyte, W. H., Jr. (1956). *The organization man.* Garden City, N.Y.: Doubleday.

Wikler, A. (1957). *The relation of psychiatry to pharmacology.* Baltimore: Williams & Wilkins.

Wilkins, L., and Richter, C. P. (1940). A great craving for salt by a child with cortico-adrenal insufficiency. *J. Amer. med. Ass.,* 114, 866–868.

Williams, A. C., Jr., Adelson, M., and Ritchie, M. (1956). A program of human engineering research on the design of aircraft instrument displays and controls. Wright Air Development Center. *WADC Tech. Rep.* 516–526.

Wilson, W. A., and Mishkin, M. (1959). Comparison of the effects of inferotemporal and lateral occipital lesions on visually guided behavior in monkeys. *J. comp. physiol. Psychol.,* 52, 10–17.

Winterbottom, M. R. (1958). The relation of need for achievement to learning experience in independence and mastery. In J. W. Atkinson (Ed.), *Motives in fantasy, action and society.* Princeton, N.J.: Van Nostrand. Pp. 453–478.

Witmer, L. R. (1935). The association value of three-place consonant syllables. *J. genet. Psychol.,* 47, 337–360.

Wittenborn, J. R. (1965). Depression. In B. B. Wolman (Ed.), *Handbook of clinical psychology.* New York: McGraw-Hill. Pp. 1030–1057.

Wolf, M., Mees, H., and Risley, T. (1964). Application of operant conditioning procedures to the behavior problems of an autistic child. *Behav. Res. Ther.,* 1, 305–312.

Wolf, S., and Wolff, H. G. (1947). *Human gastric function.* New York: Oxford Univer. Press.

Wolfe, J. B. (1936). Effectiveness of token rewards for chimpanzees. *Comp. Psychol. Monogr.,* 12 (Whole No. 60).

Wolff, H. G., and Wolf, S. (1948). *Pain.* Springfield, Ill.: Charles C Thomas

Wolman, B. B. (Ed.) (1965). *Handbook of Clinical psychology.* New York: McGraw-Hill.

Wolpe, J. (1958). *Psychotherapy by reciprocal inhibition.* Stanford, Calif.: Stanford Univer. Press.

Woodrow, G. (1946). The ability to learn. *Psychol. Rev.,* 53, 147–158.

Woodson, W. E. (1954). *Human engineering guide for equipment designers.* Berkeley, Calif.: Univer. Calif. Press.

Woodson, W. E., and Conover, D. W. (1964). *Human engineering guide for equipment designers.* (2d ed.). Berkeley, Calif.: Univer. Calif. Press.

Woodworth, R. S., and Schlosberg, H. (1954). *Experimental psychology* (rev. ed.). New York: Holt, Rinehart and Winston.

Woodworth, R. S., and Sheehan, M. R. (1964). *Contemporary schools of psychology.* (3d ed.). New York: Ronald.

Wooldridge, D. E. (1963). *The machinery of the brain.* New York: McGraw-Hill.

Wright, R. H. (1964). *The science of smell.* New York: Basic Books.

Wulf, F. (1922). Über die Veränderung von Vorstellungen (Gedächtnis und Gestalt). *Psychol. Forsch.,* 1, 333–373.

Wyburn, G. M., Pickford, R. W., and Hirst, R. J. (1964). *Human senses and perception.* Edinburgh: Oliver & Boyd.

Yates, A. J. (Ed.) (1965). *Frustration and conflict.* Princeton, N.J.: Van Nostrand.

Yerkes, R. M. (1943). *Chimpanzees*. New Haven, Conn.: Yale Univer. Press.

Young, F. M. (1941). An analysis of certain variables in a developmental study of language. *Genet. Psychol. Monogr.*, 23, 3–141.

Young, P. T. (1944). Studies of food preference, appetite and dietary habit. I. Running activity and dietary habit of the rat in relation to food preference. *J. comp. Psychol.*, 37, 327–370.

Young, P. T. (1961). *Motivation and emotion: A survey of the determinants of human and animal activity.* New York: Wiley.

Zeller, A. F. (1950). An experimental analogue of repression. II. The effect of individual failure and success on memory measured by relearning. *J. exp. Psychol.*, 40, 411–422.

Zeigarnik, B. (1927). Das Behalten erledigter und unerledigter Handlungen. *Psychol. Forsch.*, 9, 1–85.

Zener, K., and Gaffron, M. (1962). Perceptual experience: An analysis of the relations to the external world through internal processing. In S. Koch (Ed.), *Psychology: A study of a science.* Vol. 4. New York: McGraw-Hill. Pp. 515–618.

Zilboorg, G., and Henry, G. W. (1941). *A history of medical psychology.* New York: Norton.

Zotterman, Y. (1959). Thermal sensations. In J. Field, H. W. Magoun, and V. E. Hall (Eds.), *Handbook of Physiology: Neurophysiology.* Vol. 1. Washington: American Physiological Society. Pp. 431–458.

GLOSSARY

THIS GLOSSARY DEFINES most of the important terms and phrases used in the book—and a few which are not. It includes both technical terms and common words used in a special or restricted sense in psychology. In each case, the meaning given is that used in the book. For other meanings, more complete definitions, and terms not used in the book, see H. B. English and A. C. English. *A comprehensive dictionary of psychological and psychoanalytical terms.* New York: Longmans, Green, 1958.

ABILITY A general term referring to the potential for the acquisition of a skill or to an already acquired skill. Cf. *aptitude and achievement.*

ABSCISSA The horizontal axis of a graph; measures of the independent variable (*q.v.*) are usually plotted on this axis.

ABSOLUTE REFRACTORY PERIOD A brief period during the discharge of a nerve impulse when the neuron cannot be fired again.

ABSOLUTE THRESHOLD The smallest amount of a stimulus that can be perceived. *Cs. differential threshold.*

ABSTRACTION A learning process in which an individual learns to disregard some properties of objects and to respond only to certain properties that the objects have in common. It is the process through which concepts (*q.v.*) are formed.

ACCOMMODATION A change in the shape of the lens of the eye that focuses the image of an object on the retina. It compensates for the distance of the object from the observer.

ACHIEVEMENT Accomplishment on a test of knowledge or skill; also a personal motive.

ACHIEVEMENT MOTIVE A need to succeed and to strive against standards of excellence; it serves to motivate an individual to do well.

ACHIEVEMENT TEST Any test used to measure present knowledge or skills—especially knowledge or skills developed through specific training.

ACHROMATISM Total color blindness (*q.v.*); extremely rare.

ACQUIRED FEAR A learned fear.

ACQUIRED NEED A learned motive.

ACQUISITION The gradual strengthening of a learned response.

ACQUISITION CURVE The graphic representation of the acquisition process in which the strength of the response is measured on the vertical axis and the number of learning trials on the horizontal.

ACTION POTENTIAL Alterations in electrical potential along a nerve fiber which accompany the conduction of an impulse.

ACTIVATOR A drug used to increase the activity level of a person otherwise depressed or withdrawn.

ACTIVITY A general term covering restlessness, exploration, and miscellaneous responses to environmental stimuli; considered to be a general drive (*q.v.*).

ACUTE EXPERIMENT In biological psychology, an experiment usually done on anesthetized, nonbehaving animals, often done over a relatively short time. *Cf. chronic experiment.*

ADAPTATION A change in the sensitivity of a sense organ due to stimulation or lack of stimulation. In general, all senses become less sensitive as they are stimulated and more sensitive in the absence of stimulation. *See also dark adaptation.*

ADAPTATION LEVEL A theory of context effects which holds that background acts to set a standard against which events or objects are perceived.

ADDICTION Overdependence upon drugs or alcohol.

ADEQUATE STIMULUS Stimulation of the type that typically excites a sensory channel. E.g., light is the adequate stimulus for vision.

ADJUSTMENT The relationship that exists between an individual and his environment, especially his social environment, in the satisfaction of his motives. *See also method of adjustment.*

ADRENAL GLANDS A pair of endocrine glands located on the top of the kidneys. They secrete the hormones epinephrine (*q.v.*), nonepinephrine (*q.v.*) and cortin (*q.v.*).

ADRENALINE *See epinephrine.*

AFFECTIONAL DRIVE A general drive (*q.v.*) to have contact with and be close to another organism.

AFFECTIVE REACTIONS Psychotic reactions marked by extremes of mood, e.g., depression or manic elation.

AFFERENT FIBERS Nerve fibers which receive and carry impulses produced by internal and external stimuli to the central nervous system.

AFFILIATIVE NEEDS Needs to associate with or belong with other people.

AGGRESSION A general term applying to feelings of anger or hostility. Aggression functions as a motive which is often the result of frustration.

AGNOSIA Inability to recognize objects and their meaning, usually owing to damage to the brain. *See also aphasia, apraxia.*

ALARM REACTION The first stage of the general-adaptation syndrome (*q.v.*), in which a person reacts vigorously to a stressful situation.

ALL-OR-NONE LAW The principle that a nerve impulse is either evoked at full strength or not evoked at all.

ALTERNATION An experimental method in which the subject is required to alternate responses in a pattern such as left-right-left-right or left-left-right-right. The method has been used in the study of thinking in animals and children. *See also delayed alternation, delayed reaction.*

AMBIVALENCE Having both positive and negative feelings toward some object or individual at the same time.

AMNESIA Generally any loss of memory; specifically, a neurotic reaction in which a person forgets his own identity and is unable to recognize familiar people and situations. *See also dissociative reaction.*

AMPLITUDE The intensity at any

given instant of energy, e.g., acoustic or electric energy.

AMYGDALA A structure of the fore-brain connected with the hypo-thalamus and concerned in emotion.

ANAL STAGE The stage, according to psychoanalytic theory, during which the child's interest centers on anal activities.

ANIMISTIC REASONING Reasoning based on coincidences of nature. For example, if there is a thunderstorm on the day a boy plays hooky from school, then according to animistic reasoning, the boy's truancy caused the thunderstorm.

ANOMALOUS COLOR DEFECT Color weakness in which a person is able to discriminate colors when they are vivid but is colorblind when they are poorly saturated.

ANTISOCIAL REACTION Little or no concern for other people and little feeling of right and wrong.

ANXIETY A vague, or objectless, fear.

ANXIETY REACTION One of the major classes of psychoneurosis, characterized by anxiety.

APERIODIC SOUND A complex sound consisting of waves of various heights and widths appearing in random order. See also random noise; cf. periodic sound.

APHASIA A language defect ordinarily due to damage or disease of the brain. It may be a sensory disorder consisting of some impairment in reading or understanding of speech, or it may be a motor disorder consisting of an impairment in the writing or speaking of language. See also agnosia, apraxia.

APPARENT MOTION Perceived motion in which no actual movement of the stimulus pattern over the receptor occurs.

APPROACH-APPROACH CONFLICT Conflict in which a person is motivated to approach two different goals that are incompatible.

APPROACH-AVOIDANCE CONFLICT Conflict in which a person is both attracted and repelled by the same goal.

APRAXIA A disorder due to brain injury, characterized by inability to remember how to perform skilled movements such as driving a car, dressing oneself, or playing baseball. See also agnosia, aphasia.

APTITUDE Ability to profit by training. See also scholastic aptitude, vocational aptitude.

AREA AND BLOCK SAMPLING A sampling procedure, used in surveys and public-opinion polls, in which the interviewer is sent to specific addresses previously selected from a detailed map. See also sampling, survey methods.

ARITHMETIC MEAN One measure of central tendency, commonly called the average, computed by summing all the scores in a frequency distribution, then dividing by the number of scores. Cf. median.

ASSOCIATION A general term referring to any connection formed through learning.

"ASSOCIATION" CORTEX A general term for areas of the cortex outside the primary sensory and motor areas.

ASSOCIATION NEURON A neuron, usually within the central nervous system, which occupies a position between sensory and motor neurons.

ASSOCIATIVE PROCESS A process within the organism that is some part or fraction of an original, either unlearned or previously learned, process.

ASTIGMATISM Irregularities in the shape of the cornea or other structures of the eye transmitting light to the retina; these cause parts of an image projected on the retina to be out of focus.

ATTENTION Focusing on certain aspects of current experience and neglecting others. Attention has a focus in which events are clearly perceived and a margin in which they are less clearly perceived.

ATTITUDE A tendency to respond either positively or negatively to certain persons, objects, or situations. See also set.

ATTITUDE SCALE A method of measuring attitudes which typically consists of a set of items, each having a preestablished scale value, to be checked with favor or disfavor by the examinee. See also Thurstone scale and Likert scale.

ATTRIBUTE The perceived quality or aspect of a stimulus; a psychological dimension of sensory experience.

AUDIENCE MEASUREMENT Measurement of the characteristics of the people who read a periodical or listen to radio and television programs, designed to assist advertisers in determining what and how to advertise in a particular medium.

AUDIOGRAM A graph representing the absolute threshold of hearing at different frequencies.

AUDIOMETER A device for obtaining an audiogram, used to detect deafness.

AUDITORY CANAL The canal leading from the outside of the head to the eardrum; also called the external auditory meatus.

AUDITORY NERVE The nerve leading from the cochlea and conducting impulses to the brain.

AUTHORITARIAN PERSONALITY The traits that characterize an individual who seeks security in authority and wants a social hierarchy in which everybody has and knows his place. See also ethnocentric personality.

AUTISTIC Thoughts which do not correspond to perceptual reality and are strongly determined by a person's needs.

AUTONOMIC CHANGES Changes in heart rate, blood pressure, and so forth, controlled by impulses in the autonomic system.

AUTONOMIC SYSTEM A division of the nervous system serving the endocrine glands and the smooth muscles. It controls internal changes in the body during emotion as well as other functions that are essential to homeostasis. See also parasympathetic and sympathetic systems.

AVOIDANCE-AVOIDANCE CONFLICT Conflict in which a person is caught between two negative goals. As he tries to avoid one goal, he is brought closer to the other, and vice versa.

AVOIDANCE LEARNING Learning to avoid a noxious stimulus, e.g., shock, by responding appropriately to a warning signal.

AXON A nerve fiber transmitting impulses from the cell body to an adjacent neuron or to an effector.

BACKWARD CONDITIONING Presenting the CS after the US in classical conditioning; little or no conditioning results from such pairing of stimuli.

BASIC ANXIETY A concept in Karen Horney's theory of personality; anxiety learned as a reaction to a variety of tension-laden situations giving rise to neurotic needs.

BASIC MOTIVES A set of motives that can be used generally to describe and compare the motives of different people.

BASILAR MEMBRANE The membrane in the cochlea on which the organ of Corti is located. Its motion is important in hearing.

BASKET NERVE ENDING A specialized structure at the root of hairs on the body. It is regarded as a sense organ for pressure or touch.

BEGINNING SPURT The tendency for the work curve to be elevated briefly at the beginning of a period of work. Cf. warming up.

BEHAVIOR Any observable action of a person or animal.

BEHAVIOR DISORDER A general term referring to psychoneurotic reactions (q.v.), psychotic reactions (q.v.), personality disorders (q.v.), and chronic brain syndromes (q.v.). Means about the same thing as "mental disorder" or "mental illness."

BEHAVIOR THERAPY A form of psychotherapy which focuses on changing the problem behavior by using techniques of classical conditioning and instrumental learning. See also desensitization.

BEHAVIORAL SCIENCES The sciences most concerned with human and animal behavior. The principal behavioral sciences are psychology, sociology, and social anthropology, but they also include certain aspects of history, economics, political science, and zoology.

BEHAVIORISM A viewpoint held early in the twentieth century by some experimental psychologists who were opposed to the method of introspection and proposed that psychology be limited to the study of observable behavior.

BELIEF The acceptance of a statement or proposition. It does not necessarily involve an attitude (q.v.), although it may.

BINAURAL Pertaining to the simultaneous use of the two ears.

BINOCULAR Pertaining to the simultaneous use of the two eyes.

BIPOLAR CELL A neuron (q.v.) with a single axon and a single dendrite; in the eye, a cell connecting the rods and cones (q.v.), with ganglion cells (q.v.).

BISECTION A method of constructing a sensory scale (q.v.) in which the observer sets a stimulus so that it is perceived to be half-way between two other stimuli.

BLIND SPOT The region of the retina where fibers leave the eyeball to form the optic nerve. There are no photosensitive receptors at this point.

BRAIN The part of the nervous system cased in the skull. It is the site of centers for sensory experience, motivation, learning, and thinking.

BRAIN WAVES Electrical fluctuations of the brain normally recorded from the skull. See also electroencephalogram.

BRAIN WASHING Systematic attempts to change attitudes, especially political attitudes.

BRIGHTNESS A dimension of color that refers to the relative degree of whiteness, grayness, or blackness of the color, as distinguished from hue and saturation (q.v.). The term is also used to refer to the perceived intensity of a light.

BRIGHTNESS CONSTANCY A phenomenon of perception in which a person perceives an object as having the same brightness despite marked differences in the physical energy stimulating the eye.

BRIL A subjective unit of visual brightness.

CA See chronological age.

CASTRATION Operative removal of the male gonads, used experimentally to study the effects of reducing sex hormones. Cf. ovariectomy.

CATATONIA A state of muscular rigidity, seen in certain cases of schizophrenia. In the catatonic state, a person may remain fixed in a position for minutes or hours.

CELL ASSEMBLY A functionally organized group of neurons; thought, in one theory, to be the neural basis for simple perceptual experiences.

CENTILE SCORE The percentage of the scores in a distribution that are equal to or less than the obtained score; sometimes called percentile score.

CENTRAL NERVOUS SYSTEM The part of the nervous system enclosed in the bony case of the skull and backbone. Cf. peripheral nervous system.

CENTRAL STIMULATION Electrical or chemical stimulation of some region of the brain, usually in the waking animal, by means of a permanently implanted electrode or pipette.

CENTRAL FISSURE A grove in the cerebral cortex dividing the frontal lobe from the parietal lobe.

CER See conditioned emotional response.

CEREBRAL CORTEX The gray matter covering the cerebrum.

CEREBELLUM A structure in the hindbrain concerned with the coordination of movements and balance.

CEREBRAL HEMISPHERES The two symmetrical halves of the cerebrum (q.v.).

CEREBRUM The largest structure of the forebrain consisting of white matter (fiber tracts), deeper structures, and covered by the cerebral cortex (*q.v.*), or gray matter.

CHAINING Learning of a series of responses in which the stimulus arising from one response is associated with the next response in the series.

CHEMICAL SENSES The senses of taste and smell.

CHEMOTHERAPY The treatment of a psychoneurotic or a psychotic reaction with a drug or chemical substance, e.g., with a tranquilizer (*q.v.*).

CHOROID LAYER The middle layer of the wall of the eyeball, dark in color and opaque.

CHROMOSOMES Long chain-like structures in the nuclei of body and germ cells containing genes.

CHRONIC BRAIN SYNDROME Behavior disorders produced by long-lasting disturbances in brain function.

CHRONIC EXPERIMENT In biological psychology, experiments usually done on awake, behaving animals, and often carried out over a long period of time. *Cf. acute experiment.*

CHRONOLOGICAL AGE (CA). Age in years. *Cf. mental age.*

CILIARY MUSCLE A muscle attached to the lens of the eye which thickens the lens when it contracts, and flattens the lens when it relaxes. It controls accommodation.

CINGULATE GYRUS A cortical portion of the limbic system (*q.v.*) which lies in the longitudinal fissure (*q.v.*). above the corpus callosum (*q.v.*).

CLASS *See social class.*

CLASSICAL CONDITIONING Learning that takes place when a conditioned stimulus is paired with an unconditioned stimulus.

CLIENT-CENTERED THERAPY A non-directive therapy (*q.v.*) developed by Carl Rogers which typically is not so intensive or prolonged as psychoanalysis.

CLINICAL METHODS Methods of collecting data in which information is obtained about people who come to physicians and psychologists for assistance.

CLINICAL PSYCHOLOGY A branch of psychology concerned with psychological methods of recognizing and treating behavior disorders, and research into their causes.

CLOSURE The tendency for gaps to be perceived as filled in.

COCHLEA A bony cavity, coiled like a snail shell, containing receptor organs for hearing. It contains three canals: vestibular, tympanic, and cochlear.

COCHLEAR DUCT One of the canals in the cochlea.

COEFFICIENT OF CONTINGENCY A measure of correlation that may be computed from nominal measurements, i.e., when individuals have been classified in categories. Symbol: *C. See also coefficient or correlation, rank-difference correlation, and product-moment correlation.*

COEFFICIENT OF CORRELATION A number between +1.00 and −1.00 expressing the degree of relationship between two sets of measurements arranged in pairs. A coefficient of +1.00 (or −1.00) represents perfect correlation, and a coefficient of .00 represents no correlation at all. *See also rank-difference correlation, product-moment correlation.*

COGNITION A thought or idea.

COGNITIVE DISSONANCE A motivational state produced by inconsistencies between simultaneously held cognitions (*q.v.*), or between a cognition and behavior.

COGNITIVE MAP Tolman's term for the learned representation of a subject's environment.

COLOR BLINDNESS A defect that makes a person unable to tell the difference between two or more colors that most other people can easily distinguish.

COLOR CIRCLE An arrangement of colors in which hues are spokes of a wheel and saturation is represented by radial distance on the spokes.

COLOR SOLID A three-dimensional diagram representing the relationships of hue, saturation, and brightness in the perception of color.

COMMUNICATION STRUCTURE The pattern of closed and open channels of communication within a group of individuals.

COMPENSATION A defense mechanism in which an individual substitutes one activity for another in an attempt to satisfy frustrated motives. It usually implies failure or loss of self-esteem in one activity and the compensation of this loss by efforts in some other realm of endeavor.

COMPETENCE MOTIVATION The motive to develop skills which make possible effective interaction with the environment.

COMPLEMENTARY COLORS Pairs of hues that, when mixed in proper proportions, are seen as gray.

COMPULSION An irrational act that constantly intrudes into a person's behavior.

COMPULSIVE PERSONALITY Personality pattern disturbance characterized by rigidity of habits and excessive conscientiousness.

COMPULSIVE REACTION Behavior disorder in which a person finds ambiguity and uncertainty extremely uncomfortable. Extreme emphasis is put on "doing things the right way."

CONCEPT An internal process representing a common property of objects or events, usually represented by a word or name.

CONCRETE OPERATIONS The fourth stage in Piaget's characterization of mental development in which the child became able to use rules based on concrete instances, but is still unable to deal with abstract qualities.

CONDITIONED EMOTIONAL RESPONSE (CER) Fear conditioned to stimuli associated with noxious events; often investigated by using a baseline technique in a Skinner box (*q.v.*).

CONDITIONED REINFORCEMENT *Cf. secondary reinforcement.*

CONDITIONED RESPONSE A response produced by a conditioned stimulus after learning.

CONDITIONED STIMULUS The stimulus that is originally ineffective but that, after pairing with an unconditioned stimulus, evokes the conditioned response. *See also classical conditioning.*

CONDITIONING A general term referring to the learning of some particular response. *See also classical conditioning.*

CONDUCTION DEAFNESS Deafness due to an impairment of the conduction of energy to the cochlea. *Cf. nerve deftness.*

CONE A photosensitive receptor in the retina and most sensitive under daytime conditions of seeing. Cones are closely packed in the fovea and are the receptors in color vision.

CONFLICT *See approach-avoidance, approach-approach, avoidance-avoidance, motivational conflict.*

CONFLICT OF MOTIVES *See motivational conflict.*

CONFORMITY The tendency to be influenced by group pressure and to acquiesce to group norms (*q.v.*).

CONNOTATIVE MEANING The emotional and evaluative meaning of a concept.

CONSCIENCE *See superego.*

CONSERVATION Piaget's term for the ability of the child to ignore irrelevant transformations.

CONSTANCY *See perceptual constancy.*

CONSTANT STIMULI A method of obtaining sensory thresholds in which preselected intensities, or values of a stimulus, are presented to an observer for comparison with a standard stimulus.

CONTIGUITY, LAW OF The principle that two events must occur close together in time and space to be associated in learning.

CONTINGENCY *See coefficient of contingency.*

CONTINUATION The tendency to perceive objects as forming a line, curve, or other continuous pattern. *See also grouping.*

CONTINUITY THEORY A theory which holds that learning occurs by a gradual strengthening of S-R bonds.

CONTINUOUS REINFORCEMENT Reinforcement of all correct responses.

CONTOUR The line of demarcation perceived by an observer whenever there is a marked difference between the brightness or color in one place and that in an adjoining region.

CONTRAST A marked difference in stimulation, as between light and dark, silence and noise, and hot and cold; also, more specifically, the difference in brightness between an object and its immediate surround.

CONTRAST THRESHOLD *See differential threshold.*

CONTROL Used in two senses: (1) The group or condition in an experiment that is similar in all respects to the experimental group or condition except that it does not include the independent variable. (2) Any stick, switch, wheel, or other device used by an individual to operate a device or machine.

CONTROLLED SAMPLING Sampling (*q.v.*) according to some plan that provides for certain numbers of people in each category according to their incidence in the population sampled.

CONVERGENCE Turning the eyes inward toward the nose as objects are brought closer to the eyes.

CONVERSION REACTION A psychoneurotic reaction in which motivational conflict has been converted into physical symptoms, so that the person appears to have various ailments that have no physical basis.

CORNEA The outermost, transparent layer of the front of the eye.

CORPUS CALLOSUM A band of fibers connecting the two cerebral hemispheres (*q.v.*).

CORRELATION COEFFICIENT *See coefficient of correlation.*

CORTEX A rind or covering. *See also cerebral cortex.*

CORTICAL Pertaining to a cortex; usually refers to the cerebral cortex, but can also refer to the cortex of other structures, e.g., the adrenal gland.

CORTIN A general term for the hormones secreted by the cortical part of the adrenal glands. It governs, among other things, levels of sodium and water in the internal environment.

COSTS In social psychology (*q.v.*) anything that would deter or inhibit behavior.

COUNSELING The giving of advice and assistance to individuals with vocational or personal problems.

CRANIAL NERVES The nerves serving the brain. There are 12 cranial nerves, some sensory, some motor, and some of mixed function.

CR *See conditioned response.*

CRETINISM A physical disorder caused by insufficient thyroxin in infancy and childhood. It results in dwarfism and mental retardation, but it can be alleviated or cured by administration of thyroxin.

CRITERION In the evaluation of tests, the job or performance that a test is supposed to predict; in learning, the level of performance considered to represent relatively complete learning.

CRITICAL INCIDENTS A technique of making a job analysis by compiling instances that are critical for doing the job satisfactorily, as distinguished from those representing work that can be done by almost anybody and are not important in determining whether a job is done satisfactorily.

CRITICAL PERIOD A period of time in which an organism is most ready for the acquisition of certain responses.

CROSS-CULTURAL METHOD The approach which studies cultural patterns in a wide sample of societies.

CUE-PRODUCING RESPONSE A response which serves as a kinesthetic stimulus for another response. It may be either an observable response or an implicit response.

CULTURE The customs, habits, traditions, and artifacts that characterize a people or a social group. It includes the attitudes and beliefs that the group has about important aspects of its life.

CULTURE PATTERN Widely shared ways of behaving in a society together with the beliefs that accompany them.

CURIOSITY A tendency to prefer or to respond to novel stimulation; considered to be a general drive. *See also exploratory drive, manipulative drive.*

DALTONISM Color blindness (*q.v.*).

DARK ADAPTATION The increase in sensitivity of the eye that takes place when the eye is allowed to remain in the dark.

DEAF-MUTE A person who is completely deaf and consequently unable to talk. Such a person, however, ordinarily can be taught how to talk.

DECIBEL The unit of measurement used to express the intensity of a sound. It is essentially the logarithm of a ratio of pressures or energies; usually expressed by the formula

$$\text{db} = 20 \log \frac{P_1}{P_2}$$

A reference must be given. In hearing, the reference level is a pressure of 0.0002 dyne per square centimeter.

DECORTICATE Lacking the cerebral cortex.

DEDUCTION A logical process for deriving conclusions from *a priori* assumptions.

DEEP SENSES The kinesthetic sense, vestibular sense, and organic sense.

DEFENSE MECHANISM A reaction to frustration that defends the person against anxiety and serves to disguise his motives, so that he deceives himself about his real motives and goals. For examples, *see displacement, reaction formation, repression.*

DEGENERATION A neuroanatomical means for studying the course of fiber pathways.

DELAY CONDITIONING A classical-conditioning situation in which the CS persists at least until the beginning of the US.

DELAYED ALTERNATION A variation on the alternation method in which a subject is required to wait for an interval between each response in a series of alternations. *See also alternation, delayed reaction.*

DELAYED REACTION A type of experiment in which a subject is shown the correct stimulus, usually along with incorrect stimuli, but must wait for an interval before having an opportunity to make the correct choice.

DELAYED-RESPONSE TEST One of several behavioral situations in which there is a delay between the presentation of a stimulus and the opportunity to respond. *See delayed reaction.*

DELUSION A groundless, irrational belief or thought, usually of grandeur or of persecution. It is characteristic of paranoid reactions.

DENDRITE A nerve fiber that normally is stimulated by an external physical stimulus or by the impulse brought to it by an axon (*q.v.*).

DENOTATIVE MEANING The socially accepted definition of a concept.

DEOXYRIBONUCLEIC ACID (DNA) Large molecules found in the nuclei of cells, thought to be the chemical basis of reproduction.

DEPENDENCY NEED The need to depend on other people for advice, counsel, and moral support.

DEPENDENT VARIABLE The variable that changes as a result of changes in the independent variable (*q.v.*).

DEPOLARIZATION A decrease in the internal negativity of a nerve cell, especially when stimulated. If depolarization goes to threshold (*q.v.*), the cell will fire.

DEPRESSIVE DISORDER A mental disorder characterized by anxiety, guilt feelings, self-depreciation, or suicidal tendencies.

DEPRESSIVE REACTION Psychoneurotic reaction characterized by severe depression; often a reaction to a severe loss.

DEPTH PERCEPTION Perception of the relative distance of objects from the observer.

DESCRIPTIVE STATISTICS Statistical measures that summarize the characteristics of a frequency distribution, or the relationship between two or more distributions. *Cf. inferential statistics.*

DESENSITIZATION Generally, a weakening of a response, usually an emotional response, with repeated exposure to a situation; more specifically, a method used in psychotherapy to enable a person to be comfortable in situations in which he was previously highly anxious.

DEVIATION IQ An intelligence quotient (*q.v.*) based on standard scores (*q.v.*), so that IQs more nearly compare in meaning from one age to another.

DEVIATION SCORE The difference between the score obtained and the mean of the distribution that includes the obtained score. Symbol: *x*.

DICHROMATISM Partial color blindness (*q.v.*) consisting of two-color vision. All colors are seen as shades of two hues.

DIFFERENTIAL REINFORCEMENT Reinforcement of the response to one stimulus but not to another. Such reinforcement is used experimentally to establish a discrimination. *Cf. discrimination.*

DIFFERENTIAL THRESHOLD The smallest difference in a stimulus that can be perceived. *See also absolute threshold.*

DIRECTIVE THERAPY Therapy in which the therapist prescribes remedies and courses of action much as a physician prescribes medicine. It was used extensively in the early history of psychotherapy. *Cf. nondirective therapy.*

DISCRIMINATION The process of learning to respond differentially to different stimuli.

DISJUNCTIVE CONCEPT A class of concepts in which the members of the class contain at least one element from a larger group of elements, e.g., a strike in baseball.

DISPLACEMENT The disguising of the goal of a motive by substituting another in place of it.

DISPLAY Any means of presenting information to a person.

DISSOCIATIVE REACTION A neurotic reaction involving repression in which certain aspects of personality and memory are compartmentalized and function more or less independently, e.g., amnesia and multiple personality (*q.v.*).

DISTRIBUTED PRACTICE Periods of practice interspersed with periods of rest, often permitting more efficient learning than continuous practice.

DISTRIBUTION *See frequency distribution.*

DOL A subjective unit of pain.

DOMINANT GENE A gene whose hereditary characteristics are always expressed. *Cf. recessive gene.*

DOUBLE-BIND THEORY States that the psychological stress involved in schizophrenia is due to the inconsistencies in verbal and behavioral communication between parent and child.

DOUBLE-BLIND TECHNIQUE A method used in the study of drug effects in which neither subject nor observer knows what drug is being administered.

DREAM ANALYSIS The analysis of the dream content to obtain information about the source of a person's emotional problems; sometimes used in psychoanalysis.

DRIVE A term implying an impetus to behavior or active striving; often used synonomously with motive or need (*q.v.*). *See also general drive.*

DRIVE-REDUCTION THEORY The theory that the satisfaction or alleviation of a drive is necessary for a response to be learned.

DRIVE-STIMULUS REDUCTION THEORY A theory of reinforcement which says that reinforcement is due to the reduction of the intensity of unpleasant or uncomfortable stimuli. *Cf. drive-reduction theory.*

DYAD A two-person group.

DYSSOCIAL REACTION Deviant criminal behavior pattern which exists because the individual was socialized (*q.v.*) in an environment in which such behavior was the "normal" pattern.

EAR DRUM A thin membrane which separates the outer ear from the middle ear and which vibrates when sound waves reach it.

EDUCATIONAL PSYCHOLOGY A field of specialization concerned with psychological aspects of teaching and the formal learning processes in school.

EEG *See electroencephalogram.*

EFFECTORS Organs of response; muscles and glands.

EFFERENT FIBERS Nerve fibers which carry impulses from the central nervous system to the organs of response.

EGO In psychoanalysis, a term referring to the self and to ways of behaving and thinking realistically. The ego delays the satisfaction of motives when necessary; it directs motives into socially acceptable channels. *See also id, superego.*

EIDETIC IMAGERY Extremely detailed imagery; a sort of projection of an image on a mental screen.

ELECTROCONVULSIVE SHOCK THERAPY (EST) A form of therapy used primarily with depressed patients; consists of administering electrical shocks to the brain sufficient to produce convulsions and to render the patient unconscious.

ELECTROENCEPHALOGRAM (EEG) A record of electrical fluctuations in the brain (brain waves), usually obtained by placing electrodes on the skull.

ELECTROLYTIC LESION A lesion, usually in the nervous system, made by passing an electrical current through an area.

ELECTROMAGNETIC RADIATION A general term referring to a variety of physical changes in the environment, including light, radio waves, X rays, and cosmic rays. It travels at approximately 186,000 miles per second and can be specified in terms of either wavelength or frequency of vibrations.

ELECTRORETINOGRAM (ERG) A record of electrical activity obtained from the eye when it is exposed to light.

EMBRYO A young organism in the early stages of development. In man, it refers to the period from shortly after conception until 2 months later. *Cf. fetus.*

EMOTION Affective states which can be experienced and have arousing and motivational properties.

EMPIRICAL Founded on experiments, surveys, and proven facts, as distinguished from that which is asserted by argument, reasoning, or opinion.

EMPIRICAL LAW OF EFFECT A statement of the fact that responses that produce certain changes in the environment increase in their probability of occurrence.

EMPIRICAL VALIDITY Validity based on observations. *Cf. face validity.*

END SPURT A tendency to give a final spurt of effort at the end of a period of work. It is a factor in the shape of the work curve.

ENDOCRINE GLANDS Glands that secrete substances called hormones directly into the blood. The thyroid gland is an example. *Cf. exocrine glands.*

ENGINEERING PSYCHOLOGY An applied field of psychology concerned with psychological factors in the design and use of equipment.

ENGRAM The hypothetical memory trace.

ENZYME An organic catalyst regulating particular chemical steps in metabolism.

EPSP *See excitatory postsynaptic potential.*

EPINEPHRINE A chemical substance produced by the adrenal medulla that stimulates the sympathetic nervous system. Probably a transmitter (*q.v.*) at certain synapses of the sympathetic nervous system. (Preferred over adrenaline.) *See norepinephrine.*

ERG *See electroretinogram.*

ESCAPE LEARNING Learning to escape from a noxious or unpleasant situation by making an appropriate response.

ESP *See extrasensory perception.*

ETHNOCENTRIC PERSONALITY The traits that characterize an individual who is generally hostile or prejudiced toward most groups to which he does not belong. *See also authoritarian personality.*

EVOKED POTENTIAL The electrical activity recorded from the nervous system that is produced by a stimulus.

EXCITATORY POSTSYNAPTIC POTENTIAL (EPSP) An electric potential of nerve cells due to depolarization (*q.v.*); a decrease in the internal negativity of a nerve cell due to impulses arriving over excitatory fibers. If depolarization goes far enough, the cell fires.

EXHAUSTION The third stage of the general-adaptation syndrome (*q.v.*), in which a person is no longer able to endure stress.

EXOCRINE GLANDS Glands that secrete through ducts into cavities of the body, e.g., salivary glands. *Cf. endocrine glands.*

EXORCISM The attempt to cast out demons or evil spirits by such acts as prayer, religious rites, medicines, or whipping.

EXPERIMENTAL METHOD A scientific method in which conditions that are likely to affect a result are controlled by the experimenter. It involves dependent and independent variables. *Cf. method of systematic observation.*

EXPERIMENTAL PSYCHOLOGY A subfield of psychology which seeks to learn more about the fundamental causes of behavior by investigating problems in the areas of sensation and perception, learning and memory, motivation, and the physiological basis of behavior. *Cf. clinical psychology.*

EXPLORATORY DRIVE A tendency to explore a novel environment; is considered a general drive not clearly distinguishable from curiosity or manipulative drive.

EXTENSION REFLEX A reflex in which a limb is straightened. *Cf flexion reflex.*

EXTENSIONAL MEANING Meaning that can be established by pointing to objects or events. *Cf. intentional meaning.*

EXTERNAL AUDITORY MEATUS *See auditory canal.*

EXTINCTION The procedure of presenting the conditioned stimulus without reinforcement to an organism previously conditioned; also the diminution of a conditioned response resulting from this procedure.

EXTINCTION CURVE A graph of the diminution of previously learned responses during the course of extinction (*q.v.*).

EXTIRPATION The removal of a part, usually of the nervous system.

EXTRAOCULAR MUSCLES Muscles attached to the sclera layer that turn the eyeball.

EXTRASENSORY PERCEPTION (ESP) Perception that purportedly takes place outside of sensory channels.

FACE VALIDITY The appearance of validity (*q.v.*) in a test because of the similarity of the test to the job to be performed. Face validity is not, however, necessarily true validity. Tests should always be examined with validating procedures to determine whether they are, in fact, valid.

FACTOR ANALYSIS A general statistical method, involving coefficients of correlation, that isolates a few common factors in a large number of tests, ratings, or other measurements.

FANTASY Daydreaming and imagining a world of one's own, often used as a defense mechanism.

FATHER FIGURE An instance of transference (*q.v.*) in which a person is regarded as though he were a father.

FATIGUE A general term referring to the effects of prolonged work or lack of sleep, probably best defined as a feeling of being tired.

FEEBLE-MINDEDNESS A term no longer in professional use. *See mental retardation.*

FEEDBACK The situation in which some aspect of the output regulates the state of the system.

FETUS A young organism in the later stages of prenatal development. In man, it refers to the period from 2 months after conception until birth. *Cf. embryo.*

FIELD THEORY A type of psychological theory that stresses the importance of interactions between events in the person's environment.

FIGURAL AFTER-EFFECT A perceptual phenomenon used by gestalt psychologists to demonstrate that events in one part of the perceptual field may affect perception in another part.

FIGURE-GROUND PERCEPTION Perception of objects or events as standing out clearly from a background.

FISSURE A relatively deep crevice in the cerebral cortex. *Cf. sulcus. See also central fissure, lateral fissure, longitudinal fissure.*

FIXATION A rigid habit developed by repeated reinforcement or as a consequence of frustration.

FIXED-INTERVAL SCHEDULE A schedule of partial reinforcement (*q.v.*) in which a response made after a certain interval of time is reinforced.

FIXED-RATIO SCHEDULE A schedule of partial reinforcement (*q.v.*) in which every *n*th response is reinforced.

FLEXION REFLEX A reflex in which a limb is bent. *Cf. extension reflex.*

FOLKWAYS Conventions and habitual behavior that serve to perpetuate social values.

FORCED CHOICE A method for evaluating the effectiveness of a worker by forcing an informed judge to choose between phrases that describe workers.

FOREBRAIN The most forward of three divisions of the brain. It includes the cerebrum, thalamus, and hypothalamus. *See also hindbrain, midbrain.*

FORGETTING A partial or total loss of retention of material previously learned.

FORMAL-DISCIPLINE THEORY *See mental-faculty theory.*

FORMAL GROUP A social group that has a relatively permanent structure of positions, jobs, and roles.

FORMAL OPERATIONS The fifth stage in Piaget's characterization of mental development which is marked by the ability to use abstract rules. The stage of adult thought.

FOURIER ANALYSIS The analysis of a complex tone into sine-wave components, each specified in terms of frequency and intensity.

FOVEA A central region of the retina where cones are closely packed together and visual acuity is at its best.

FRACTIONATION A method of constructing sensory scales (*q.v.*) in which an observer judges the value of a stimulus that is some fraction, e.g., half, of another stimulus.

FRATERNAL TWINS Twins who develop from two different fertilized eggs (ova), and who consequently may be as different in hereditary characteristics as ordinary brothers and sisters. *Cf. identical twins.*

FREE ASSOCIATION The technique of requiring a patient in psychotherapy to say whatever comes to his mind, regardless of how irrelevant or objectionable it may seem.

FREE NERVE ENDINGS Nerve endings that are not associated with any special receptive structures. They are found in the skin, blood vessels, and many parts of the body. They are regarded as sense organs for pain and probably also for touch and temperature.

FREE-RESPONSE METHOD A method of measuring the meaning of concepts in which a person is asked to describe or define a concept.

FREQUENCY One of the dimensions of vibrational stimuli, such as light or sound. It is most often used with sound and is stated in number of cycles per second, which is the number of alternations in air pressure per second.

FREQUENCY COMPOSITION The composition of complex tones as specified by Fourier analysis (*q.v.*).

FREQUENCY DISTRIBUTION A set of measurements arranged from lowest to highest (or highest to lowest) and accompanied by a count (frequency) of the number of times each measurement or class of measurements occurs.

FREQUENCY POLYGON A frequency distribution represented by plotting a point on a graph for each frequency of each score, or class of scores, and connecting the points with straight lines.

FRONTAL ASSOCIATION AREA The nonmotor areas of the frontal lobes said to be envolved in certain complex behavioral functions. *See prefrontal lobotomy.*

FRUSTRATION The thwarting of motivated behavior directed at a goal.

FRUSTRATION TOLERANCE Ability to tolerate frustration and its accompanying anxiety. It is characteristic of well-adjusted people and is something to be learned in achieving mental health.

FUNCTIONAL AUTONOMY The ability of certain motives to continue functioning without further reinforcement of the conditions under which they were learned. *See also learned goal.*

FUNCTIONAL FIXEDNESS A special type of set in which individuals cannot use objects in novel ways. It may hinder problem solving.

FUNCTIONALISM A viewpoint taking the middle course among introspectionism, behaviorism, and gestalt psychology. Functionalists proposed that all activities serving some adaptive function, including both behavior and experience, be studied by psychologists.

FUNDAMENTAL In hearing, the lowest frequency in a complex tone.

GALVANIC SKIN RESPONSE (GSR) A change in the electrical resistance of the skin, occurring in emotion and in certain other conditions.

GANGLION A collection of the cell bodies of neurons.

GANGLION CELL In the eye, the cells of the third cell layer of the retina. Fibers of the retinal ganglion cells make up the optic nerve.

GENERAL ADAPTATION SYNDROME (GAS) A sequence of physiological reactions to prolonged physical or emotional stress; consists of three stages: the alarm reaction, resistance to stress, and exhaustion (*q.v.*).

GENERAL DRIVE A drive that is unlearned but is not aroused by a specific physiological need.

GENERALIZATION The phenomenon of an organism's responding to all situations similar to one in which it has been conditioned. *See also stimulus generalization.*

GENERATOR POTENTIAL The voltage change that occurs in receptor cells when acted upon by physical energy. Generator potentials trigger nerve impulses from the receptor organ.

GENES The essential elements in the transmission of hereditary characteristics, carried in chromosomes. *See also dominant gene, recessive gene.*

GENITAL STAGE A stage in development, according to psychoanalytic theory, during which the adolescent displays heterosexual interests.

GENOTYPE The genetic constitution of an organism made up of dominant and recessive genes. *Cf. phenotype.*

GERM CELL An egg or sperm cell.

GESTALT PSYCHOLOGY A viewpoint, developed by German psychologists, that considered introspectionism and behaviorism too atomistic and emphasized the importance of configuration in preception and insight in learning.

GLAND An organ that secretes. There are two general types, endocrine glands and exocrine glands (*q.v.*).

GOAL The place, condition, or object that satisfies a motive.

GOAL GRADIENT In the study of motivational conflict, the increasing strength of a goal, the nearer one is to the goal. Other things being equal, the avoidance gradient for negative goals is steeper than the approach gradient for positive goals.

GOLGI TENDON ORGANS Receptors located in tendons that are activated when the muscle to which the tendon is attached contracts putting tension on the tendon.

GONADS The sex glands, which are the testicles in the male and the ovaries in the female. They determine secondary sex characteristics such as growth of the breasts, beginning of menstruation, growth of the beard, and change of the voice and also influence sexual motivation.

GRADIENT A state of affairs in which a condition varies continuously and evenly in amount.

GRADIENT OF REINFORCEMENT The concept that the closer a response is in time and space to a reinforcement, the more the response is strengthened.

GRADIENT OF TEXTURE One of the principal monocular cues for depth perception. Consists of a gradation in the fineness of detail which can be seen at increasing distances from a person.

GRAY MATTER Collections of cell bodies in the nervous system. *Cf. white matter.*

GROUP *See social group.*

GROUP NORM A widely shared expectation or standard of behavior among most members of a group, class, or culture.

GROUP TEST A test that may be administered to a group of people at one time.

GROUP THERAPY A specialized technique of psychotherapy, consisting of a group of patients discussing their personal problems under the guidance of a therapist.

GROUPING The tendency to perceive objects in groups rather than as isolated elements. Grouping is determined by such factors as nearness, similarity, symmetry, and continuation of objects.

GROWTH HORMONE A hormone secreted by the pituitary gland and controlling the general rate of growth of the body.

GSR *See galvanic skin response.*

GUST A subjective unit of taste.

GYRUS A ridge in the cerebral cortex of the brain. *Cf. sulcus.*

HABIT A learned response.

HABITUATION The tendency of a response to weaken with repeated presentation of a stimulus; similar to desensitization (*q.v.*).

HAIR CELL Pressure sensitive cells located in the organ of Corti which convert pressure waves to nerve impulses.

HARMONICS Components of complex tones that are multiples of the fundamental frequency.

HALLUCINATION Sensory experience in the absence of stimulation of receptors. Hallucinations are present in certain behavior disorders such as schizophrenia.

HEBEPHRENIC TYPE A variety of schizophrenia characterized by childishness and regressive behavior.

HERING THEORY *See opponent process theory.*

HIGHER-ORDER CONDITIONING Conditioning of a response to a stimulus by pairing the stimulus with another stimulus to which the response has previously been conditioned.

HINDBRAIN The third of three divisions of the brain. It includes the medulla, cerebellum, and pons. *See also forebrain, midbrain.*

HISTOGRAM A frequency distribution represented by bars whose heights vary with the frequencies of the scores or classes of scores.

HOMEOSTASIS The tendency of the body to maintain a balance among internal physiological conditions, such as temperature, sugar, air, and salt.

HORMONES Secretions of endocrine glands that help or inhibit certain chemical steps in the body.

HOSTILITY *See aggression.*

HUE The aspect of a color that is largely determined by wavelength and that enables us to discriminate blue from red, red from yellow, and so on, as distinguished from brightness and saturation (*q.v.*).

HUMAN ENGINEERING In psychological usage, the field of specialization concerned with the design of equipment and of tasks performed in the operation of equipment; sometimes called engineering psychology.

HUNGER A drive stemming from a physiological need for food.

HYPERPHAGIA Eating abnormally large quantities of food; associated with injuries in certain regions of the hypothalamus.

HYPERPOLARIZATION An increase in the internal negativity of a nerve cell, especially when stimulated. *See inhibitory postsynaptic potential.*

HYPNOSIS A state in which a person is extremely susceptible to the suggestion of the hypnotist.

HYPOCHONDRIASIS A neurotic reaction in which a person is excessively concerned with his physical welfare or constantly complaining of minor ailments; seen in anxiety reactions.

HYPOTHALAMUS A region of the forebrain which contains centers for the regulation of sleep, temperature, thirst, sex, hunger, and emotion.

HYSTERIA *Cf. conversion reactions.*

ID In psychoanalytic theory, the aspect of personality concerned with instinctual reactions for satisfying motives. The id seeks immediate gratification of motives with little regard for the consequences or for the realities of life. *See also ego, superego.*

IDENTICAL TWINS Twins who develop from the same fertilized egg (ovum). They have exactly the same kinds of chromosomes and genes and hence the same hereditary characteristics. *Cf. fraternal twins.*

IDENTIFICATION The tendency of children to model their behavior after that of appropriate adults; a defense mechanism in which one thinks himself to be like someone else.

IDIOGRAPHIC Emphasis on the study of an individual's characteristics. *Cf. nomothetic.*

IDIOT A term no longer in professional use. *See profound retardation.*

ILLUSION A perception that does not agree with other, more trustworthy perceptions.

IMAGE A representation in the brain of sensory experience. Images maybe involved in some thinking (*q.v.*).

IMAGELESS THOUGHT Thought occuring without the presence of images. The phrase refers particularly to a theory of the nature of thinking entertained by a group of German psychologists about 1900.

IMBECILE   A term no longer in professional use. *See severe retardation.*

IMITATION   Copying the behavior of another.

IMPLICIT RESPONSE   A minute muscle movement ordinarily detectable only by special electrical or mechanical recording methods. Implicit responses, miniatures of large, observable movements, are acquired in previous learning and may be involved in thinking.

IMPRINTING   The very rapid development of response to a stimulus at some critical period of development (*q.v.*). Particularly characteristic of some species of birds.

IMPULSE   (1) Sometimes used in psychoanalysis to refer to motive (*q.v.*). (2) The spike potential—the nerve impulse.

INCENTIVE   A term approximately synonymous with goal, but implying the manipulation of a goal to motivate the individual. Money, for example, is used as an incentive to motivate people to work.

INCIDENTAL LEARNING   Learning without an incentive and without reinforcement. *See also latent learning.*

INCUBATION   A stage in creative thinking during which the problem is put aside and unconscious factors are permitted to work.

INDEPENDENT VARIABLE   The variable that may be selected or changed by the experimenter and is responsible for changes in the dependent variable (*q.v.*).

INDIVIDUAL PSYCHOGRAPH   A profile of an individual's traits and abilities. It may be compared with a job psychograph (*q.v.*) to determine whether the individual is fitted for a particular job.

INDIVIDUAL TEST   A test that can be given to only one individual at a time, e.g., the Stanford-Binet intelligence test.

INDUCTION   The logical process by which principles or rules are derived from observed facts.

INDUSTRIAL PSYCHOLOGY   A field of specialization concerned with methods of selecting, training, counseling, and supervising personnel in business and industry. It sometimes includes problems of increasing efficency in work and of redesigning machines to suit better the capacities of the worker. *See also human engineering.*

INFERENTIAL STATISTICS   The statistical methods for inferring population values from obtained sample values.

INFERIORITY COMPLEX   A concept put forth by Alfred Adler; an attitude developed out of frustration in striving for superiority.

INFORMAL GROUP   A social group having no formal or permanent structure and consisting of people who happen to be assembled together at a particular time. Sometimes, however, the members of a formal group (e.g., the emloyees of a company) may constitute an informal group that is different from the one prescribed by the formal structure of the organization.

INHIBITION   (1) A decreasing tendency to respond with repetition of a response. 2) Hyperpolarization (*q.v.*) of a nerve cell making it less responsive to stimulation.

INHIBITORY POSTSYNAPTIC POTENTIAL (IPSP)   An electrical potential of the nerve cell due to hyperpolarization (*q.v.*); an increase in the internal negativity of a nerve cell, due to impulses arriving over inhibitory fibers makes the cell less excitable.

INNER EAR   *See cochlea, vestibular sense.*

INSIGHT   (1) In learning and problem solving, the relatively sudden solution of a problem. (2) In psychotherapy, the understanding of one's own motives and their origins.

INSIGHT THERAPY   Treatment of a personality disorder by attempting to uncover the deep causes of the patient's difficulty and to help him rid himself of his defense mechanisms. It represents an attempt to guide the patient in self-understanding of his motives and his resources for satisfying them. Sometimes it is called uncovering therapy. *Cf. supportive therapy.*

INSTINCTIVE BEHAVIOR   A complex, unlearned, pattern of behavior which persists beyond the duration of the stimulus instigating it.

INSTITUTIONAL WAYS   The laws of a society used to enforce social values considered essential to the society's way of life.

INSTRUMENTAL LEARNING   Learning situations in which the responses of the subject are instrumental in producing reinforcement. Sometimes known as instrumental conditioning. *See also operant behavior.*

INSTRUMENTAL BEHAVIOR   Behavior that typically accomplishes a purpose, usually the satisfaction of a need, e.g., working for a living.

INSULIN   A hormone secreted by the pancreas and concerned in controlling the amount of sugar in the blood; used in insulin-shock therapy.

INSULIN SHOCK   A method, infrequently used today, for treating severe psychotic reaction; causes convulsions and coma.

INTELLIGENCE   A general term covering a person's abilities on a wide range of tasks involving vocabulary, numbers, problem solving, concepts, and so on. As measured by a standardized intelligence test, it generally involves several specific abilities, with special emphasis on verbal abilities.

INTELLIGENCE QUOTIENT (IQ)   A number obtained by dividing chronological age into mental age and multiplying by 100. This rule applies only to children; other methods are used to compute the intelligence quotient for teenagers and adults.

INTENSITY   A general term referring to the amount of physical energy stimulating a sense organ. It is expressed in physical units appropriate to the kind of energy involved.

INTENTIONAL MEANING   Meaning of a word derived by using other words, e.g., its dictionary meaning.

INTERFERENCE   A factor in learning and forgetting; the incompatibility of two learned associations.

INTERFERENCE THEORY   A theory of extinction which holds that non-reinforced responses decline in strength because other incompatible responses are learned during the extinction period.

INTERNAL ENVIRONMENT   The environment of the bodily organs, including the temperature of the body, oxygen, food supplies, minerals, hormones, and related substances.

INTERSTIMULUS INTERVAL   In a classical conditioning situation, the time between the onset of the CS and the onset of the US.

INTERVAL SCALE   A scale in which differences between numbers may be regarded as equal, e.g., $3 - 1 = 4 - 2$. Cf. nominal scale, ordinal scale, ratio scale.

INTOXICATION PSYCHOSIS (ALCOHOL)   A psychosis developing as a result of prolonged alcoholism. It is characterized by defects of memory, disorientation, delusions, and other symptoms similar to those seen in senile psychosis (q.v.).

INTROSPECTION   A method of psychological experimentation in which a subject is presented with some stimulus, such as a colored light, and asked to give a detailed report of his sensations; seldom used at the present time.

INTROSPECTIONISM   A viewpoint held early in the twentieth century by one group of experimental psychologists who employed the method of introspection. It regarded sensation as the important psychological element in consciousness and attempted to analyze mental content.

INTUITIVE THOUGHT   The third stage in Piaget's characterization of mental development in which the child begins to group objects according to their outstanding perceptual qualities.

INVENTORY   A detailed questionnaire that provides specific information about a person's likes, dislikes, habits, preferences, and so on. It usually refers to a personality or interest test.

INVOLUTIONAL REACTION   Agitated depression or paranoid reactions (q.v.) in women at menopause and in men at slightly older ages. Perhaps a physical brain disorder is responsible, but the most prevalent idea of causation emphasizes the psychological stress of approaching old age.

IODOPSIN   A photosensitive substance found in the cones of the retina of some animals.

IPSP   See inhibitory postsynaptic potential.

IQ   See intelligence quotient.

IRIS   The set of muscles, controlled by the autonomic system, that varies the amount of light admitted to the eye by narrowing or enlarging the pupil. It gives the eye its distinctive color, such as blue or brown.

ITEM ANALYSIS   Techniques for discriminating between good and bad items on a psychometric scale.

JND   See just noticeable difference.

JOB   A set of activities performed by an individual worker.

JOB ANALYSIS   The process of finding out what constitutes a particular job. It is carried out with a variety of different methods, according to the type of job being analyzed.

JOB DESCRIPTION   A statement of the significant characteristics of a job and of the worker characteristics (q.v.) necessary to perform the job satisfactorily.

JOB EVALUATION   The assessment of the remuneration to be offered or paid for a particular job.

JOB PSYCHOGRAPH   A profile of the traits and abilities required in a job or a family of jobs. Cf. individual psychograph.

JUST NOTICEABLE DIFFERENCE (JND)   See differential threshold.

KINESTHETIC RECEPTORS   Sense organs located in the muscles, tendons, and joints that provide information about the position of the limbs and body in space.

KNOWLEDGE OF RESULTS   A person's knowledge of how he is progressing in training or in the performance of his job. It is usually necessary for the most rapid learning and for the best performance of the job.

KYMOGRAPH   A device which records the amplitude of a response through time.

LANDOLT RING   A test object used in measurements of visual acuity; consists of an incompleted circle.

LATENT LEARNING   Learning that becomes evident only when the occasion arises for using it. See also incidental learning.

LATERAL FISSURE   A deep cleft in the cerebral cortex dividing the temporal lobe from the frontal and parietal lobes. Cf. central fissure.

LEARNED GOAL   A goal that has been acquired through learning, as distinguished from a physiological goal.

LEARNING   A general term referring to a relatively permanent change in behavior that is the result of past experience or practice. It includes conditioning, instrumental learning, and perceptual learning.

LEARNING CURVE   Any graphical representation of progress in learning. Usually a curve in which performance is plotted on the ordinate (q.v.) and trials or time are plotted on the abscissa (q.v.).

LEARNING SET   A kind of transfer of training (q.v.) in which a subject becomes increasingly adept at learning problems of the same general type.

LESION   Any damage or change in a tissue due to injury or disease.

LEVEL OF ASPIRATION   The level at which a person sets certain goals.

LEVEL OF PERFORMANCE   The achievement of a person, as distinguished from his level of aspiration.

LIBIDO   Freud's term for the instinctive drives, or energies, that motivate behavior. *See also id.*

LIE DETECTOR A popular name for a device designed to detect emotional responses when a person lies. It usually involves measures of breathing, heart rate, blood pressure, and galvanic skin response.

LIGHT The visible spectrum (*q.v.*) of electromagnetic radiation. It may be specified by wavelength and intensity.

LIKERT SCALE A method for constructing attitude scales based on the intercorrelation of items.

LIMBIC SYSTEM A series of related structures in the core of the brain concerned with emotion and motivation. The septal area (*q.v.*) hypothalamus (*q.v.*) amygdala (*q.v.*) and cingulate gyrus (*q.v.*) are important limbic system structures.

LINEAR PERSPECTIVE The perception of faraway objects as close together and of nearby objects as far apart. It is an important factor in depth perception.

LOADED WORDS Words having an emotional tone, used by propagandists and advertisers for creating and maintaining attitudes.

LOGICAL THINKING Reasoning carried out according to the formal rules of logic; not very common in human thinking.

LONGITUDINAL FISSURE The midline crevice which divides the cerebrum (*q.v.*) into two symmetrical halves.

LOUDNESS A psychological attribute of tones, related to intensity but not directly proportional to it. *See also psychophysics.*

LUMINOSITY The perceived brightness of a visual stimulus. *See also luminosity curve.*

LUMINOSITY CURVE A curve depicting the visual threshold at different wavelengths. The luminosity curve for daylight vision has its greatest sensitivity at about 555 millimicrons; the comparable curve for night vision has its greatest sensitivity at about 505 millimicrons. *See also cone, rod.*

MA *See mental age.*

MAGNITUDE ESTIMATION A method of making sensory measurements in which the observer estimates the magnitude, or some other characteristic, of a single stimulus.

MALADJUSTMENT A broad term covering not only the psychoneurotic and psychotic but also mild disturbances in which a person is anxious or behaves peculiarly.

MANIC DEPRESSIVE PSYCHOSIS *See affective reactions.*

MANIPULATIVE DRIVE A tendency to explore and manipulate objects; considered to be a general drive not clearly distinguishable from curiosity or exploratory drive.

MAN-TO-MAN RATING A method of evaluating workers by having informed judges compare individuals two at a time and rate one as better than the other. It is a specific case of the method of paired comparisons (*q.v.*).

MARKET RESEARCH Research consisting of surveys conducted in much the same manner as public-opinion polls but with the purpose of measuring attitudes concerning specific products, the effectiveness of advertising, and the relative preferences of consumers for different brands.

MASKING The deleterious effect of one sound on a person's ability to hear other sounds simultaneously.

MATERNAL BEHAVIOR Behavior concerned with giving birth to young, nursing them, and caring for them. Maternal behavior in animals presents many characteristics of truly instinctive behavior.

MATURATION The completion of developmental processes in the body. Maturation is governed both by heredity and by environmental conditions.

MAZE A device used in animal and human learning experiments that has blind alleys and a correct path. It presents the subject with the task of taking a path through it without entering any blind alleys.

MEAN *See arithmetic mean.*

MEASUREMENT The assignment of numerals or numbers to objects or events according to rules.

MECHANICAL-ABILITY TEST A vocational-aptitude test for predicting success in jobs requiring mechanical ability.

MEDIAN The middle score in a frequency distribution when all scores are ranked from highest to lowest (or lowest to highest). It is one measure of central tendency. *Cf. arithmetic mean.*

MEDIATING PROCESS An associative process connecting previously learned processes and responses.

MEDICAL THERAPY The treatment of an illness by using medicines, drugs, or surgery. *Cf. psychotherapy.*

MEDULLA The lowest division of the brain stem; contains several kinds of nuclei, especially those concerned with the vital functions of breathing and cardiovascular regulation.

MEISSNER CORPUSCLE A specialized structure in the skin regarded as a sense organ for pressure or touch.

MEL A subjective unit of pitch.

MEMORY *See retention.*

MEMORY DRUM Apparatus used to present verbal material in studies of verbal learning.

MENTAL AGE (MA) A type of norm. Gives the relative degree of mental development of a child by stating the age level at which the child is performing. For example, if a five-year-old child does as well on an intelligence test as the average child of seven, his mental age is 7. *See also intelligence quotient.*

MENTAL DEFICIENCY *See mental retardation.*

MENTAL DISORDER *See behavior disorder.*

MENTAL-FACULTY THEORY The theory that formal education generally develops mental faculties so that a person is better able to solve all sorts of problems. The theory is sometimes called formal-discipline theory, or the doctrine of formal discipline.

MENTAL HEALTH A general term referring to personal adjustments relatively free of psychoneurotic and psychotic symptoms.

MENTAL HYGIENE A general term, similar in meaning to mental health, which refers to the maintenance of satisfying personal adjustments.

MENTAL ILLNESS *See behavior disorder.*

MENTAL RETARDATION A condition marked by a deficiency in general intellectual ability. Usually an IQ below 70. *See also intelligence quotient.*

METABOLISM A general term referring to chemical processes in the cells of the body. It includes the assimilation of food, the storing of energy, the utilization of energy, the repairing of tissues, and the disposition of cellular wastes.

METER A unit of length in the metric system; 39.37 inches.

METHOD OF ADJUSTMENT A method of obtaining sensory thresholds in which the observer adjusts the intensity of a stimulus until he just barely senses it or distinguishes the difference between it and a standard stimulus.

METHOD OF CONSTANT STIMULI Presenting a stimulus of a given intensity to an observer and asking him to indicate whether or not he detects it; numerous trials with several intensities of stimuli are used in determining absolute threshold (*q.v.*).

METHOD OF LIMITS A method for determining sensory thresholds in which series of stimuli of ascending and descending order are presented.

METHOD OF RATING A method that requires a person to assign comparative adjectives or numbers on a scale to indicate preferences, judgments, or opinions. *See also rating.*

METHOD OF SYSTEMATIC OBSERVATION Scientific study of a natural situation or problem, under controlled conditions, without any experimental manipulation of the variables involved. *Cf. experimental method.*

METRAZOL A drug which causes convulsions, infrequently used to-

day in the treatment of psychotic reaction.

MICROELECTRODE An electrode so small that it can provide a record of electrical activity in a single neuron or sensory cell.

MIDBRAIN The middle of three divisions of the brain. It contains reflex centers for hearing and vision, pathways to and from the forebrain, and several other centers. *See also forebrain, hindbrain.*

MIDDLE EAR A bony cavity containing ossicles which link the eardrum to the cochlea.

MILD RETARDATION A degree of mental retardation characterized by an IQ of from 69 to 53.

MILLIMICRON A unit of measurement used with light and other electromagnetic radiations. It is usually abbreviated mμ. "Milli" means one-thousandth, and "micron" means one-millionth of a meter.

MINNESOTA MULTIPHASIC PERSONALITY INVENTORY (MMPI) A widely used pencil-and-paper personality questionnaire. An important feature is its empirical validity (*q.v.*).

MMPI *See Minnesota Multiphasic Personality Inventory.*

MODE The most frequent score or category in a distribution of measurements.

MODE OF ADJUSTMENT The characteristic way in which an individual attempts to satisfy his motives.

MODERATE RETARDATION A degree of mental retardation characterized by an IQ of from 52 to 36.

MONGOLISM A mild to moderate form of mental retardation in which the facial features resemble somewhat those of Mongoloid people.

MONGOLOID *See Mongolism.*

MONOCULAR Pertaining to the use of only one eye. *Cf. binocular.*

MORES Customs that enforce social values having ethical or moral significance. Violation brings strong social disapproval.

MORON A term no longer in pro-

fessional use. *See mild retardation.*

MOTIVATED FORGETTING Forgetting due to active forces relating to a person's needs. Repression (*q.v.*) and forgetting due to weakening of tension systems are two examples. *See Zeigarnik effect.*

MOTIVATION A general term referring to behavior instigated by needs and directed toward goals.

MOTIVATIONAL CONFLICT A conflict between two or more motives resulting in the frustration of a motive. Most motivational conflict involves acquired motives. *See approach-approach conflict, avoidance-avoidance conflict, and approach-avoidance conflict.*

MOTIVE A term implying a need and the direction of behavior toward a goal; often used synonymously with need or drive (*q.v.*).

MOTOR AREA An area of the cerebral cortex lying around the central fissure. Movements can be elicited by stimulation of this region. The threshold for movement is least for the portion just in front of the central fissure.

MOTOR NEURON A neuron conveying impulses away from the central nervous system toward a muscle. *See efferent fibers.*

MULTIPLE PERSONALITY A dissociative reaction (*q.v.*) in which a person displays two or more relatively distinct personalities, each with its own set of memories. *See also amnesia, dissociative reaction.*

MUTATION A change in a gene and hence in the characteristic it determines.

MYELIN SHEATH A white covering around some fibers of the nervous system.

NARCOANALYSIS Analysis of a person's memories, usually those involving a traumatic experience, and of his emotional problems under the influence of a sleep-inducing drug, e.g., sodium amytal.

NARCOSIS Sleep or sleepness caused by drugs, e.g., sodium amytal.

NATIONALISM A set of attitudes, held by numbers of people; the attitudes are prejudicial to foreigners and other countries. It includes a feeling that one's own country is superior in manners, and way of life.

NATURAL OBSERVATION The observation of events as they occur in nature or in the course of human affairs without exercising experimental controls and without using methods of systematic sampling. *Cf. method of systematic observation.*

NEED Any lack or deficit within the individual, either acquired or physiological (*q.v.*); often used synonymously with drive or motive (*q.v.*). *See also social needs.*

NEGATIVE ACCELERATION The characteristic of a curve that is steep at its beginning but becomes increasingly flat as it approaches its end. Learning curves are typically of this shape.

NEGATIVE TRANSFER The harmful effect on learning in one situation because of previous learning in another situation. It is due to incompatible responses being required in the two situations. *Cf. positive transfer.*

NEOCORTEX The six-layered covering of the cerebrum. *See gray matter, cerebral cortex.*

NERVE A bundle of nerve fibers.

NERVE DEAFNESS Deafness due to an impairment of the sense organs or of the nerves concerned in hearing. It is also called perception deafness or perceptual deafness. *Cf. conduction deftness.*

NERVE FIBER An axon or a dendrite of a neuron. It conducts nerve impulses.

NERVE IMPULSE An electrical change in the membrane of a nerve fiber, propagated along the length of the fiber. It is the basic message unit of the nervous system and obeys an all-or-none law (*q.v.*).

NERVOUS SYSTEM The brain, spinal cord, and nerves serving the various sense organs, endocrine glands, and muscles of the body.

NEURASTHENIA Type of anxiety reaction (*q.v.*) in which the person complains of general nervousness, fatigue, and insomnia; often accompanied by depression, feelings of inadequacy, and inability to work.

NEURON The cell that is the basic unit of the nervous system. It conducts nerve impulses and consists of dendrite(s) (*q.v.*), cell body, and axon (*q.v.*).

NEUROSIS *See psychoneurotic reaction.*

NEUROTIC NEED According to Horney, a learned need for something connected with the alleviation of basic anxiety.

NOMINAL SCALE A scale in which numbers are assigned to objects or persons only to distinguish those that are alike from those that are different, e.g., postal ZIP numbers. The numbers of a nominal scale may not be used additively.

NOMOTHETIC Emphasis on the development of general laws of behavior. *Cf. idiographic.*

NONCONTINUITY THEORY A theory which holds that learning occurs by sudden "all-or-none" associations.

NONDIRECTIVE THERAPY Psychotherapy in which the patient is dominant and given the greatest possible opportunity to express himself. The method is based on the principle that the patient must learn how to solve his own problems and cannot have them solved for him by the therapist. *Cf. directive therapy.*

NONSENSE FIGURE A set of lines, marks, or contours having little or no meaning. *See nonsense syllable.*

NONSENSE SYLLABLE A syllable, usually of three letters, constructed so as to resemble meaningful English as little as possible. Nonsense syllables are used in learning experiments as new or unfamiliar material.

NOREPINEPHRINE A chemical substance which is believed to be the transmitter (*q.v.*) in some sympathetic synapses (*q.v.*). (Preferred over noradrenaline.) *See epinephrine.*

NORMAL CURVE A bell-shaped frequency distribution, also called the normal-probability curve, which is an ideal approximated by many distributions obtained in psychology and biological sciences. It can be derived mathematically from the laws of chance.

NORMS An average or standard, or a distribution of measurements, obtained from a large number of people. It permits the comparison of an individual score with the scores of comparable individuals.

NUCLEUS A collection of cell bodies of neurons within the central nervous system; also a structure within cells containing chromosomes. Plural: nuclei.

OBSESSION A seemingly groundless idea that constantly intrudes into a person's thoughts; seen in obsessive-compulsive reactions. *Cf. compulsion.*

OBSESSIVE-COMPULSIVE REACTION A psychoneurotic reaction characterized by obsessions and/or compulsions (*q.v.*).

OBSTRUCTION METHOD A method for measuring the strength of a motive by seeing how much noxious stimulation an organism will tolerate in order to satisfy the motive.

OCCIPITAL LOBE The part of the cerebral cortex lying at the back of the head. It contains the primary sensory areas for vision.

ODDITY METHOD A method used for various purposes in which three or more stimuli are presented and the subject is asked to indicate which stimulus is different.

OEDIPUS COMPLEX A syndrome (*q.v.*) postulated by Freudian personality theory in which the child directs affectional response toward the parent of the opposite sex. *See phallic stage.*

OLDSIGHTEDNESS Farsightedness characteristic of old age and typically increasing beyond the age of forty.

OPEN-END QUESTION The type of question that allows a respondent to answer in his own words.

OPERATIONAL DEFINITION A method

of defining terms and concepts in terms of the operations performed to measure them.

OPERANT BEHAVIOR Behavior, usually occurring without a known stimulus, that has some consequence, i.e., operates on the environment; e.g., bar-pressing that supplies food or turns off a light. *See instrumental learning.*

OPINION Acceptance of a statement accompanied by an attitude of pro or con; in practice, difficult to distinguish from an attitude or belief (*q.v.*).

OPPONENT PROCESS THEORY The theory that human color vision depends on three pairs of opposing processes: white-black, yellow-blue, and red-green.

OPSIN A breakdown product of rhodospin in rod vision.

OPTIC NERVE The nerve formed by axons of the ganglion cells of the retina. It leaves the eye at the blind spot and ends in relay centers of the thalamus.

ORAL STAGE The stage, postulated in psychoanalytic theory, during which an infant's satisfactions center around his mouth and sucking.

ORDINAL SCALE A scale in which numbers are assigned to objects or persons so as to rank them in order according to some quality or magnitude, e.g., ranking students 1, 2, 3, etc., according to their grades.

ORDINATE The vertical axis of a graph; values of the dependent variable (*q.v.*) are usually plotted on this axis.

ORGAN OF CORTI The organ containing receptors for hearing, located on the basilar membrane which separates the vestibular canal and tympanic ducts of the cochlea.

ORGANIC SENSES Sense organs located in the internal organs of the body, such as receptors for cold and warmth in the stomach.

OSCILLOSCOPE An electronic voltage recording device. In psychology, used especially in studies of audition and neural activity. It typically records changes of voltage over time.

OSMORECEPTOR A type of cell in the hypothalamus which is thought to be sensitive to changes in the osmotic pressure of the blood plasma.

OSSICLES Three bones in the middle ear through which sound is conducted from the eardrum to the oval window of the cochlea.

OTOLITH ORGANS Sense organs found in chambers near the cochlea. They are sensitive to gravity and to the position of the head; they are part of the vestibular sense.

OVAL WINDOW The entrance to the cochlea through which sound vibrations pass from the ossicles of the middle ear to the canals of the cochlea.

OVARIECTOMY Operative removal of the female ovaries, used experimentally to study the effect on behavior of a reduction in sex hormones. *Cf. castration.*

OVERCOMPENSATION According to Adler, an overreaction to feelings of inferiority so that a person becomes superior in things in which he otherwise would not be. *See also compensation.*

OVUM The cell formed in the ovary of the female which, when fertilized by the sperm of the male, may develop into a new individual. Plural: ova.

PACINIAN CORPUSCLE A specialized structure serving as a receptor for pressure, located below the skin, in joints, and other deep parts of the body.

PAIRED-ASSOCIATE LEARNING Learning in which the subject must respond with one word or syllable when presented with another word or syllable.

PAIRED COMPARISONS A method of measurement in which things or people are taken two at a time and a judgment is made as to which is greater than the other, better than the other, etc.

PANCREAS An endocrine gland, located along the lower wall of the stomach, which secretes the hormone insulin. This hormone controls blood-sugar level.

PAPILLAE Bumps on the tongue that are heavily populated with taste buds.

PARALLEL BARS A test object used in measurements of visual acuity in place of the letters of the familiar eye chart.

PARANOID REACTION Behavior disorder marked by extreme suspiciousness of the motives of others, often taking the form of elaborate beliefs that they are plotting against the person. In the paranoid reactions the delusions (*q.v.*) of persecution are usually systematized. *See also projection.*

PARASYMPATHETIC SYSTEM A subdivision of the autonomic system arising in the cranial and sacral portions of the central nervous system. Tends to be active during quiescent states of organism. *Cf. sympathetic system.*

PARATHORMONE The hormone secreted by the parathyroid glands.

PARATHYROID GLANDS Two pairs of endocrine glands located on the thyroid glands of the neck. They secrete hormones concerned in the regulation of calcium and phosphorus levels in the body.

PARIETAL LOBE The part of the cerebral cortex lying immediately behind the central fissure. It contains areas involved in somesthesis and somesthetic discrimination learning.

PART LEARNING Learning, usually in the sense of memorizing, in which the task is divided into smaller units and each unit is separately learned. *Cf. whole learning.*

PARTIAL REINFORCEMENT Reinforcement of some proportion of unconditioned responses (in classical conditioning), or of some proportion of instrumental responses (in instrumental learning). *See schedule of reinforcement.*

PASSIVE-AGGRESSIVE PERSONALITY A person who expresses hostility by excessive aggression, stubborn pouting, or extreme dependence.

PEER An equal in a given respect;

an associate at roughly the same level.

PERCEPTION A general term referring to the awareness of objects, qualities, or events stimulating the sense organs; also refers to a person's experience of the world.

PERCEPTION DEAFNESS See nerve deafness.

PERCEPTUAL CONSTANCY A general term referring to the tendency of objects to be perceived in the same way despite wide variations in the energies impinging upon the receptors. See also brightness constancy, shape constancy, size constancy.

PERCEPTUAL LEARNING Used in two senses. (1) the influence of learning on perceptual organization; (2) learning to associate stimulus events with each other.

PERFORMANCE (1) Observed behavior; as distinct from hypothetical internal states of an organism. See latent learning. (2) nonlinguistic ability; performance tests are so constructed that they do not handicap a person who speaks no English or who has verbal deficiencies.

PERFORMANCE TEST Tests which measure nonverbal activity or performance.

PERIODIC SOUND A complex sound consisting of repetitive patterns of waves. Cf. aperiodic sound, random noise.

PERIPHERAL NERVOUS SYSTEM The part of the nervous system lying outside the skull and the backbone. Cf. central nervous system.

PERSONALITY The traits, modes of adjustment, defense mechanisms, and ways of behaving that characterize the individual and his relation to others in his environment.

PERSONALITY DISORDERS Characterized by developmental defects or pathological trends in the personality structure, with minimal accompanying anxiety.

PERSONALITY STRUCTURE In general, the unique organization of traits, motives, and ways of behaving that characterizes a particular person; in psychoanalysis, the conception of the personality in terms of id, ego, and superego.

PHALLIC STAGE The third stage in development, according to psychoanalytic theory, during which the child becomes interested in his sexual organs and forms a romantic attachment to the parent of the opposite sex. See Oedipus complex.

PHASE DIFFERENCE The difference in intensity (negative or positive) between two energies at any particular instant.

PHASE SEQUENCE A combination of cell assemblies (q.v.).

PHENOMENOLOGY The study of the phenomena of human experience and behavior without elaboration or analysis into elements.

PHENOTYPE The observable characteristics of an organism. Cf. genotype.

PHENYLKETONURIA (PKU) A form of mental retardation due to an inherited metabolism disorder.

PHENYLPYRUVIC OLIGOPHRENIA A type of mental retardation that is inherited and that is caused by a lack of an enzyme for utilizing phenylpyruvic acid, a product of brain metabolism. It is recognized by the presence of phenylpyruvic acid in the urine. See phenylketonuria.

PHI PHENOMENON Perceived movement between two successive presentations of separate points of light. "Pure" movement. Cf. stroboscopic movement.

PHILOLOGY The study of the history and development of languages.

PHOBIC REACTION A psychoneurotic reaction characterized by intense irrational fear.

PHONEME A speech sound which must be distinguished in the everyday use of language.

PHONETICS The study of the sounds made in speech.

PHOTOCHROMATIC INTERVAL The interval of intensities, representing the difference between rod and cone sensitivities, in which light but not color is perceived.

PHOTOSENSITIVE SUBSTANCES Chemical substances in the rods and cones of the retina that are de-composed by light and initiate the visual process.

PHYSIOLOGICAL NEEDS Needs arising from some lack or deficit in the body, as distinguished from acquired needs (q.v.).

PICTORIAL DISPLAY A display that reproduces with some realism the situation it represents. Cf. symbolic display.

PINNA The part of the external ear that protrudes from the head; the structure which in common parlance is called simply the ear.

PITCH A psychological attribute of tones, related to frequency but not directly proportional to it. See psychophysics.

PITCH SCALE A curve depicting the relationship between physical frequency and perceived pitch.

PITUITARY GLAND A gland located beneath the hypothalamus that secretes a number of hormones which stimulate or inhibit other glands of the body. It also secretes a growth hormone that controls general rate of growth of the body.

PKU See phenylketonuria.

PLACE THEORY A theory of pitch, widely accepted, that assumes different places on the basilar membrane (q.v.) are activated by different frequencies of a sound stimulus.

PLAY THERAPY A technique for the study of personality and for the treatment of personality problems in children. It permits the child to express his conflicts in play. See also release therapy.

PLEASURE PRINCIPLE In psychoanalytic theory, the tendency to satisfy id impulses. Cf. reality principle.

POINT-TO-POINT PROJECTION See topographical arrangement.

POLARIZED MEMBRANE The inside of a nerve cell is negatively charged with respect to the outside. See depolarization, hyperpolarization.

POLL QUESTION The type of question, used in public-opinion polls, that gives the respondent a fixed number of alternatives.

POLYDIPSIA Drinking abnormally large quantities of water.

PONS   A region of the brain stem above the medulla (*q.v.*) which contains ascending and descending pathways, fibers connecting the lobes of the cerebellum (*q.v.*), and many nuclei.

POSITIVE TRANSFER   More rapid learning in one situation because of previous learning in another situation. It is due to a similarity of the stimuli and/or responses required in the two situations. *Cf. negative transfer.*

POSTHYPNOTIC SUGGESTION   Suggestion made by the hypnotist while a person is in a hypnotic state but carried out after the hypnosis has been terminated.

POSTSYNAPTIC MEMBRANE   The membrane in the synaptic region (*q.v.*) of the neuron to which information is being transmitted.

POWER   In psychological usage, the ability to control or influence the behavior of others; a social need.

POWER TEST   A test not limited in time, or a test having a nominal time limit, designed to measure ability, irrespective of speed of taking the test. *Cf. speed test.*

PRECONCEPTUAL THOUGHT   The second stage in Piaget's characterization of mental development in which representational thought begins.

PREDISPOSITION   In the study of personal adjustment, a tendency that is inherited and gives a biological basis for the development of certain temperamental (*q.v.*) and personality characteristics.

PREFRONTAL AREAS   *See frontal association area.*

PREFRONTAL LOBOTOMY   The surgical interruption of pathways from the frontal association areas, sometimes performed in extreme cases of behavior disorder after other forms of therapy have failed.

PREHENSION   The grasping of objects with the hands, the fingers, or (in the case of some monkeys) the tail.

PREJUDICE   Literally, a prejudgment; more generally, an emotionally toned attitude for or against an object, person, or group of persons. Typically, it is a hostile attitude that places a person or group at a disadvantage.

PRENATAL   Before birth.

PRESTIGE   The feeling of being better than other persons with whom one compares oneself. The prestige need is a social need to achieve prestige. The need is frequently exploited with propaganda and social techniques.

PRESYNAPTIC MEMBRANE   The membrane in the synaptic region along which the nerve impulse comes to the synapse (*q.v.*); contains transmitter (*q.v.*) substances.

PRIMARY GOAL   The unlearned goal of a physiological or general drive, e.g., food or water.

PRIMARY GROUP   A small group with which a person has frequent informal contacts, such as family, friends, associates.

PRIMARY MENTAL RETARDATION   Mental retardation in which there is no obvious organic defect or evidence of disease. Also called familial retardation.

PRIMARY REINFORCEMENT   In conditioning, the presentation of the unconditioned stimulus immediately following the conditioned stimulus; in instrumental learning, the presentation of an incentive immediately following the instrumental response.

PRIMARY SENSORY AREA   An area of the cerebral cortex to which fibers transmit impulses from the receptors of a particular sense. There are primary sensory areas for each of the senses except pain, the vestibular sense, and smell.

PROACTIVE INHIBITION   *See negative transfer.*

PRODUCT-MOMENT CORRELATION   A widely used coefficient of correlation (*q.v.*) devised by the British mathematician Karl Pearson. Used for interval and ratio measurements. Symbol: *r*.

PROBABILITY   The relative frequency of occurence of an event expected over the long run.

PROFOUND RETARDATION   A degree of mental retardation characterized by an IQ of 20 or below.

PROGRAMMED LEARNING   Self-instruction by means of carefully designed questions or items which, through immediate reinforcement, motivate and enhance the learning process. *See also teaching machine.*

PROJECTION   The disguising of a source of conflict by ascribing one's own motives to someone else; prominent in paranoid reactions.

PROJECTIVE METHODS   Methods used in the study of personality, in which a subject is presented with a relatively ambiguous stimulus and asked to describe it in a meaningful way or to tell a story about it. *See Thematic Apperception Test, Rorschach test.*

PROLACTIN   A hormone secreted by the pituitary gland. It stimulates the development of the breasts and is concerned in maternal behavior.

PROPAGANDA   The deliberate attempt to influence attitudes and beliefs.

PROPRIOCEPTIVE SENSE   The sensory input arising from the kinesthetic and vestibular receptors within the body.

PSEUDO CONDITIONING   The strengthening of a response by prior presentation of some alerting stimulus, e.g., a siren; not true conditioning. *See also sensitization.*

PSEUDO-ISOCHROMATIC PLATES   Plates consisting of colored dots so arranged that the colorblind person sees either no pattern at all or a different pattern of dots from the normal person. They are used as a test for color blindness.

PSEUDO WORDS   Words constructed by choosing letters at random according to the frequency with which these letters are used in language, and according to the probability of one particular letter following another.

PSEUDOPHONE   A device used in experiments on perception to reverse the reception of sound by the two ears. It carries sound normally reaching the right ear to the left ear, and vice versa.

PSYCHIATRY   A branch of medicine

specializing in the diagnosis and treatment of behavior disorders.

PSYCHOANALYSIS   Primarily a method of psychotherapy developed by Sigmund Freud, but also a theory of the development and structure of personality. As a psychotherapy, it emphasizes the techniques of free association (*q.v.*) and the phenomenon of transference (*q.v.*).

PSYCHODRAMA   A specialized technique of psychotherapy in which patients act out the roles, situations, and fantasies relevant to their personal problems. Psychodrama is usually conducted in front of a small audience of patients.

PSYCHOGRAPH   A profile of traits and abilities involved in the performance of a job. *See also individual psychograph, job psychograph.*

PSYCHOLOGY   The science that studies the behavior of animals and human beings.

PSYCHOMOTOR TEST   A test involving movement and coordination; usually a vocational-aptitude test.

PSYCHONEUROSIS   *See psychoneurotic reaction.*

PSYCHONEUROTIC REACTION   A behavior disorder, less severe than a psychotic reaction (*q.v.*), in which a person is unusually anxious, miserable, troubled, or incapacitated in his work and his relations with other people. He often attempts to ward off anxiety by using exaggerated defense mechanisms. Also called a neurosis or psychoneurosis.

PSYCHOPATHIC DEVIATE   An individual with a personality disorder characterized by antisocial, amoral conduct.

PSYCHOPHARMACOLOGY   The study of the effects of drugs on behavior and psychological functions.

PSYCHOPHYSICS   The study of the relationship between physical energy and reported experience.

PSYCHOTIC REACTION   A behavior disorder more severe than a psychoneurotic reaction (*q.v.*) and often requiring custodial care. *See affective reactions, par-* *anoid reactions, schizophrenic reactions, involutional reactions.*

PSYCHOSOMATIC ILLNESS   A bodily disorder precipitated or aggravated by emotional disturbance.

PSYCHOSURGERY   *See prefrontal lobotomy.*

PSYCHOTHERAPEUTIC DRUG   A drug having beneficial effects in treating behavior disorders. *See tranquilizer.*

PSYCHOTHERAPY   The treatment of behavior disorders and mild adjustment problems by means of psychological techniques. *Cf. medical therapy.*

PSYCHOTOMIMETIC DRUG   A drug that induces some of the symptoms of certain psychotic reactions.

PUBLIC-OPINION POLL   A method of surveying opinions on certain issues by selecting a sample of the population and interviewing each member of the sample.

PUNCTATE SENSITIVITY   In the study of the skin senses, greater sensitivity in certain spots of the skin than in others. It is a phenomenon that allows us to distinguish four primary senses among the skin senses.

PUNISHMENT   The application of an unpleasant stimulus for the purpose of eliminating undesirable behavior.

PUPIL   The aperture through which light is admitted to the eye; altered in size by the action of the iris muscles.

PURE TONE   One resulting from simple sine-wave (*q.v.*) energy.

PURKINJE EFFECT   A change in the perception of color as the eye shifts from daylight to twilight, or from cone to rod levels of adaptation.

QUOTA SAMPLING   A method of sampling (*q.v.*) in which the polling agency sets quotas for certain categories, such as age, sex, and socioeconomic status, and then permits the interviewer to select the particular individuals who satisfy the quota requirements.

RACE   A group of human beings having common and distinctive innate physical characteristics.

RANDOM NOISE   A noise consisting of a random mixture of many different frequencies that are not multiples or harmonics of each other. *Cf. periodic soundness.*

RANDOM SAMPLING   Selecting samples of individuals, objects, or measurements solely by chance. *See also sampling.*

RANGE   The difference between the highest score and the lowest score in a frequency distribution. It is a crude measure of the variability of a distribution.

RANK-DIFFERENCE CORRELATION   A method of computing correlation when individuals have been separately ranked on two different variables. Symbol: ρ

RAS   *See reticular activating system.*

RATING   A general term for the method in which a judge or observer rates the amount of aptitude, interest, ability, or other characteristic that an individual is considered to have.

RATIO SCALE   A scale in which equal ratios may be regarded as equal, e.g., $4:2 = 10:5$.

RATIONALIZATION   The interpretation of one's own behavior so as to conceal the motive it expresses and to assign the behavior to some other motive.

REACTION FORMATION   The disguising of a motive so completely that it is expressed in a form that is directly opposite to its original intent.

REACTION TIME   The time from the onset of a stimulus until the organism responds.

REALITY PRINCIPLE   In personal adjustment, the behavior which consists of setting attainable goals and of finding practicable ways of eliminating motivational conflicts and hence of satisfying motives; in psychoanalysis, a function served by the ego. *Cf. pleasure principle.*

REASONING   Thinking in which one attempts to solve a problem by combining two or more elements from past experience.

RECALL A method of measuring retention in which the subject must reproduce with a minimum of cues something that he has previously learned.

RECEPTIVE FIELD The area of a receptor which influences the activity of a neuron.

RECESSIVE GENE A gene whose hereditary characteristics are not expressed when it is paired with a dominant gene (*q.v.*).

RECIPROCAL INHIBITION The relaxation of a muscle simultaneously with the contraction of its antagonist.

RECOGNITION A method of measuring retention in which the subject is required only to recognize the correct answer when it is presented to him along with incorrect answers, e.g., in a true-false or multiple-choice examination.

RECOLLECTION A general term meaning about the same thing as recall, i.e., remembering past events and their related circumstances.

REFRACTORY PERIOD *See absolute refractory period, relative refractory period.*

REGRESSION A retreat to earlier or more primitive forms of behavior, frequently encountered in children and adults faced with frustration.

REGULATORY BEHAVIOR Behavior that aids in maintaining a homeostatic balance by leading to the satisfaction of physiological needs.

REFLEX A relatively rapid and consistent unlearned response to a stimulus. It is ordinarily not conscious or subject to voluntary control. It lasts only so long as the stimulus is present. *Cf. instinctive behavior.*

REINFORCEMENT *See primary reinforcement, secondary reinforcement.*

RELATIONAL CONCEPT The relationships between elements in a situation form the basis of classification into a concept class.

RELATIVE REFRACTORY PERIOD A brief period after the discharge of a nerve impulse when the neuron can only be fired by a stimulus that is much stronger than normal. *Cf. absolute refractory.*

RELEASE THERAPY Similar to play therapy (*q.v.*); useful with older children and adults. It may consist of finger painting, games, or other unstructured activities. Its general purpose is to permit the expression of deep-seated motivational conflicts.

RELEASERS Stimulus situations that trigger instinctive (*q.v.*) movements.

RELIABILITY The self-consistency of a method of measurement, or the degree to which separate, independent measurements of the same thing agree with each other. Reliability is usually expressed by a coefficient of correlation (*q.v.*) representing the relationship between two sets of measurements of the same thing. *See also validity.*

REPLACEMENT THERAPY Compensation for the effects of gland removal or deficiency by administration of the gland's hormone.

REPRESENTATIVE SAMPLING Sampling (*q.v.*) so as to obtain a fair cross section of a population without introducing biases that make the sample unrepresentative.

REPRESSION A psychological process in which memories and motives are not permitted to enter consciousness but are operative at an unconscious level. Repression is one of several reactions to frustration and anxiety. It serves as a means of altering conscious motives and goals.

RESISTANCE A phenomenon observed in psychotherapy, exhibited as an inability to remember important events in one's past or to talk about certain anxiety-charged subjects. Resistance may be indicated by a blocking of free associations or by a person's steering away from certain subjects during free association (*q.v.*).

RESISTANCE TO STRESS The second stage of the general-adaptation syndrome in which a person endures stress without showing any observable impairment.

RESPONDENT CONDITIONING *See classical conditioning.*

RESPONSE-PRODUCED STIMULI Stimuli produced by stimulation of receptors in muscles and joints. *See chaining.*

RESTING POTENTIAL A voltage difference, found in the inactive nerve fiber between the outside and the inside of the polarized membrane (*q.v.*). The inside is negative with respect to the outside.

RETENTION The amount correctly remembered. The principal methods of measuring retention are savings, recognition, and recall.

RETICULAR ACTIVATING SYSTEM (RAS) A network of cell bodies and fibers extending through the medulla, midbrain, hypothalamus, and thalamus forming an indirect sensory pathway to the cerebral cortex.

RETINA The photosensitive layer of the eye on which images of objects are projected. It contains receptors, known as rods and cones, and nerve cells that convey impulses to the brain.

RETINAL DISPARITY A slight difference in the images of an object projected on the retinas of the two eyes. It arises from the fact that the two eyes view the object from slightly different angles.

RETINENE A breakdown product of the photosensitive substances involved in vision.

RETROACTIVE INHIBITION The harmful effect of learning or activity on the retention of previous learning.

REVERBERATING CIRCUIT An endless loop made by the fibers of neurons, permitting nerve impulses to circle back to the point from which they originated.

REWARD (1) Loosely equivalent to reinforcement (*q.v.*). (2) In social psychology, pleasures or satisfactions occurring as a result of behaviors chosen.

RHODOPSIN A photosensitive substance found in the rods of man and many animals.

RIBONUCLEIC ACID (RNA) Complex molecules found within cells. Essential in the production of proteins and thought by some to play a role in memory storage.

RNA *See ribonucleic acid.*

ROD A photosensitive receptor in the retina, long and cylindrical like a rod, and most sensitive in nighttime conditions of seeing.

ROLE A pattern of behavior that a person in a particular social status (*q.v.*) is expected to exhibit.

ROLE-PLAYING METHOD A technique used in simulation of real situations, designed to promote understanding of the problems involved. Can be used in management training, for example, or as a psychotherapeutic technique.

RORSCHACH TEST A projective method (*q.v.*) using ink-blots as stimuli.

ROTARY PURSUITMETER A device used in human learning experiments that requires the subject to keep a stylus on a moving spot while the spot rotates on a circular platform.

ROTATION NYSTAGMUS Movement of the eyes, slowly in one direction and quickly in the other, caused by rotation of the head.

SAFETY NEEDS According to Maslow, needs for security, stability, and order that are less important than physiological needs but take precedence over needs for belonging, esteem, and self-actualization.

SAMPLING The process of selecting a set of individuals or measurements from a large population of possible individuals or measurements. Almost all frequency distributions in psychology are samples. *See also controlled sampling, quota sampling, random sampling, representative sampling.*

SAMPLING ERROR The error due to chance differences in selecting a sample from a population.

SATURATION A dimension of color that refers to the amount or richness of a hue, as distinguished from brightness or hue (*q.v.*); e.g., a red that is barely distinguishable from a gray is low in saturation.

SAVINGS A method of measuring retention in which the subject learns again what he previously learned. Savings are measured by the difference between the number of trials or errors originally required to learn and the number required in relearning.

SCALE OF MEASUREMENT In general, a set of numbers assigned to some aspect of objects or events according to some rule. The term is also used in a more limited sense to refer to a well-standardized test, such as the Wechsler Intelligence Scale for Children.

SCALE VALUE In the measurement of attitudes, a number assigned to a statement that indicates the degree to which the statement represents an attitude that is favorable or unfavorable to an object or issue. *See Thurstone scale.*

SCAPEGOATING The displacement of aggression to a convenient group or class.

SCATTER DIAGRAM A plot of the scores made by the same individuals on two different variables providing a visual picture of the degree of correlation between the variables.

SCHEDULE OF REINFORCEMENT Some specified sequence of partial reinforcement (*q.v.*) such as a ratio schedule or an interval schedule. *See also partial reinforcement, fixed-internal schedule, fixed-ratio schedule, variable-internal schedule, variable-ratio schedule.*

SCHIZOID PERSONALITY A personality disorder characterized by withdrawal from other people and eccentric thinking; not psychotic. *Cf. schizophrenic reactions.*

SCHIZOPHRENIC REACTIONS One of the psychotic reactions, characterized by fantasy, regression, hallucinations, delusions, and general withdrawal from contact with the person's environment. Also called schizophrenia.

SCHIZOPHRENOGENIC MOTHER The kind of mother who intensifies psychological stress for an individual, possibly playing a role in fostering schizophrenia in her offspring.

SCHOLASTIC APTITUDE Ability to succeed in some specified type of formal schooling. For example, college aptitude refers to aptitude for doing college work.

SCLERA LAYER The white outermost coat of the eyeball. In the front of the eye, it becomes the transparent cornea.

SECONDARY GOAL A goal learned through association with a primary goal. *Cf. secondary reinforcement.*

SECONDARY MENTAL RETARDATION Low intelligence caused by biochemical abnormality, physical damage, or disease of the brain.

SECONDARY REINFORCEMENT The reinforcing effect of a stimulus that has been paired with a primary reinforcement (*q.v.*). *See conditioned reinforcement.*

SECURITY The feeling of being safe against loss of status, friends, loved ones, income, etc. The need to feel secure is an important social need.

SELF-ACTUALIZATION According to Maslow, the highest need in man's hierarchy of needs; the name for Maslow's motivational theory of personality.

SELF-STIMULATION Central stimulation, usually electrical, of the brain which is administered by the animal's pressing a bar or switch.

SEMANTIC DIFFERENTIAL A method of measuring the connotative meaning of a concept in which the person rates the concept on several bipolar scales.

SEMANTICS The study of the meaning of words and sounds.

SEMICIRCULAR CANALS Three canals found near the cochlea in each ear. They are sensitive to rotation and to changes in the position of the head. *See vestibular.*

SENILE PSYCHOSIS A psychotic reaction that tends to appear in some individuals with advancing age; characterized by defects of memory, general disorientation, and delusions. *See also intoxication psychosis (alcohol).*

SENSITIZATION A phenomenon in in which a response is facilitated by an intense or unpleasant stimulus. For example, an animal that has become habituated to a loud sound may again show fright to the sound if the sound is preceded by an electric shock.

SENSORIMOTOR OPERATIONS The first stage in Piaget's characterization of mental development in which the child learns to deal with objects.

SENSORY AREA An area of the brain concerned in sensory functions. It is usually an area of the cerebral cortex. *See also primary sensory area.*

SENSORY DEPRIVATION Experimental restriction of sensory input; used in the study of perceptual organization.

SENSORY NEURON A neuron that conveys nerve impulses away from sense organs into the central nervous system. *See also afferent fibers.*

SENSORY SCALE A curve or function showing the relationship of perceived magnitude to physical units of stimulation. *See psychophysics.*

SEPTAL AREA One of the structures in the limbic system (*q.v.*) of the forebrain containing complex connections with other parts of the brain; seems involved in emotional expression.

SERIAL ANTICIPATION A learning method in which items are arranged in a series and the subject must anticipate the next item in the series. *Cf. paired-associate learning.*

SERIAL LEARNING Learning to make a series of responses in exact order.

SERIAL-POSITION EFFECT The effect of the position of an item in a series on the rate of learning the item. The middle items in a series are usually the most difficult.

SET A readiness to react in a certain way when confronted with a problem or stimulus situation.

SEVERE RETARDATION A degree of mental retardation characterized by an IQ of from 35 to 20.

SEX DIFFERENCES Differences between men and women in interests, abilities, etc.

SEX HORMONES Hormones secreted by the gonads and responsible for the development of secondary sex characteristics such as the male's beard and the female's breasts. They are involved in sexual motivation.

SEX-LINKED CHARACTERISTIC A hereditary characteristic controlled by a gene carried on the chromosomes that determine sex; for example, color blindness (*q.v.*).

SEXUAL DEVIATION Sexual excitement and satisfaction from unusual objects and behavior.

SHAPE CONSTANCY The tendency to perceive the "true" shape of an object even when the image on the retina is distorted. For example, a circle is seen as a circle even when viewed at an angle.

SHAPING Teaching a desired response through a series of successive steps which lead the learner to the final response. Each small step leading to the final response is reinforced. *See also successive approximations.*

SHOCK THERAPY The treatment of behavior disorders by some agent causing convulsion and/or coma. Such agents include insulin, metrazol, and electric shock to the brain.

SIGNIFICANCE A probability statement of the likelihood of obtaining a given difference or correlation between two sets of measurements by chance. Often stated by giving P values, e.g., $P < .001$.

SIBLING A brother or sister.

SIGN Any stimulus that stands for something else. *See also symbol.*

SIGNAL A stimulus used to indicate that the time and place for something to happen is at hand.

SIMULTANEOUS DISCRIMINATION LEARNING Presentation of the positive (S^D) and negative (S^Δ) stimuli at the same time, rather than one after the other. *Cf. succesive discrimination learning.*

SINE WAVE A particular type of energy wave. In audition, the simplest kind of sound wave, generated by a vibrating object mov-

ing back and forth freely like a pendulum. *See also Fourier analysis.*

SITUATION TEST A test in which a person is observed in some real-life situation, e.g., in managing a group of men in the building of a small bridge.

SITUATIONAL THERAPY The treatment of a personality problem by changing the person's situation—his work, his way of life, or his relationships with family and associates.

SIZE CONSTANCY The tendency to perceive the size of familiar objects as relatively constant even when viewed at a distance that makes the image of them on the retina very small.

SKEWNESS The degree to which a frequency distribution departs from a symmetrical shape. The curve of a distribution that has its longer tail toward the high scores is said to be positively skewed; with the longer tail towards the low scores, it is said to be negatively skewed.

SKIN SENSES The senses of pain, warmth, cold, and pressure located in the skin.

SKINNER BOX A simple box with a device at one end, which, if operated, will produce reinforcement; used to study instrumental learning and operant behavior.

SMELL PRISM A three-dimensional diagram representing six primary odors and their mixture.

SLEEP CENTER A center in the hypothalamus whose destruction is said to result in chronic insomnia. *Cf. waking center.*

SMOOTH MUSCLE Muscle that under the microscope exhibits no stripes. It is found in blood vessels, intestines, and certain other organs. *Cf. striped muscle.*

SOCIAL ANTHROPOLOGY The social or behavioral science that studies cultural customs, habits, and beliefs, chiefly of primitive societies, but also of modern societies and communities.

SOCIAL APPROVAL A common, strong motive in most human beings.

SOCIAL ATTITUDE An attitude held in common with a number of other persons, as distinguished from personal attitudes which may be unique to a single individual.

SOCIAL CLASS A grouping of people on a scale of prestige in a society according to their social status. It is determined by many factors, such as nature of occupation, kind of income, moral standing, family genealogy, social relationships and organizations, and area of residence.

SOCIAL FACILITATION Increased motivation and effort arising from the stimulus provided by other people.

SOCIAL GROUP Any group of people, formal or informal, assembled or dispersed, who are related to each other by some common interest or attachment. When a social group is defined in a more limited sense as people in a face-to-face relationship, other dispersed groups such as unions are defined as social organizations or institutions.

SOCIAL INSTITUTION A collection of objects, customary methods of behavior, and techniques of enforcing such behavior on individuals, e.g., a union, an army, or a political party.

SOCIAL MATURITY The degree of development of social and vocational abilities. It may be measured by the Vineland Social Maturity Scale, from which a social-maturity quotient can be computed in much the same way as an intelligence quotient is obtained.

SOCIAL NEEDS Needs, usually learned, that require the presence or reaction of other people for their satisfaction. *See also affiliative needs, status needs.*

SOCIAL PREJUDICE A hostile attitude toward some social group. *See prejudice.*

SOCIAL PSYCHOLOGY A field of specialization concerned with the effects of group membership upon the behavior, attitudes, and beliefs of an individual.

SOCIAL STRUCTURE A general term referring to the fact that each society typically assigns ranks to

its members, expects them to do certain kinds of work and to have certain attitudes and beliefs.

SOCIAL TECHNIQUE Behavior that makes use of other people to achieve satisfaction of a need.

SOCIAL VALUE A learned goal involving one's relationship to society and other people.

SOCIAL WORKER A person with advanced training in sociology who investigates the family and social background of persons with personality problems and who assists the psychotherapist by maintaining contact with a patient and his family. The social worker is often a member of a psychiatric team consisting also of psychiatrists and clinical psychologists.

SOCIALIZATION Learning to behave in a manner prescribed by one's family and culture and to adjust in relationships with other people.

SOCIETY A group of individuals, as large as several countries or as small as a portion of a community, that have a distinguishable culture.

SOCIOGRAM A diagram showing preferences and aversions among members of a group; a way of depicting the structure of an informal group.

SOCIOPATHIC PERSONALITY A type of behavior disorder characterized by little anxiety. May take several forms: antisocial reaction (*q.v.*), dyssocial reaction (*q.v.*), sexual deviation (*q.v.*), or an addiction (*q.v.*).

SODIUM AMYTAL A drug that, given in light doses, tends to make a person talk more freely. It is sometimes used in psychotherapy as a way of uncovering repressed memories.

SOMATIC SYSTEM The part of the nervous system serving the sense organs and the skeletal muscles.

SOMESTHESIS The senses of the skin and of kinesthesis—the body sense.

SOMNOLENCE A tendency to sleep all the time.

SONE A subjective unit of loudness.

SOUND-PRESSURE LEVEL (SPL) The

intensity of a tone expressed in decibels (*q.v.*) above a standard reference level—0.0002 dyne per square centimeter.

SOUND WAVE Alternating increases and decreases in pressure propagated through a medium, usually air. It may be regarded as a vibration having a certain frequency (or wavelength) and a certain intensity.

SPAYING *See ovariectomy.*

SPECIFIC HUNGER A hunger for a specific kind of food.

SPECTRAL-ABSORPTION CURVE A curve representing the absorption, and hence the sensitivity, of a photochemical substance at different wavelengths; often refers to visual photochemical substances of the rods and cones.

SPECTRAL SENSITIVITY Sensitivity of the eye, often measured by the absolute threshold (*q.v.*), at different wavelengths of the spectrum.

SPEED TEST A test limited in time and favoring the person who can do tasks quickly. *Cf. power test.*

SPERM Male germ cell.

SPHINCTER Smooth muscle whose action controls elimination from such organs as the stomach, bladder, and bowels.

SPINAL CORD The part of the nervous system encased in the backbone. It is a reflex center and a pathway for impulses to and from the brain.

SPL *See sound-pressure level.*

SPONTANEOUS DISCRIMINATION A discrimination learned without any specific learning procedure and without any identifiable reinforcement. *See perceptual learning.*

SPONTANEOUS RECOVERY An increase in the strength of an extinguished (*q.v.*) conditioned response after the passage of an interval of time.

S-R ASSOCIATION Stimulus-response association; a learned connection between a stimulus and a response.

S-S ASSOCIATION Stimulus-stimulus, or sensory-sensory, association; a learned association between two stimuli.

STANDARD DEVIATION A precise measure of the variability of a frequency distribution (*q.v.*), computed by squaring the deviation of each score from the arithmetic mean (*q.v.*), summing the resulting squares, dividing by the number of scores, and finally taking the square root of the resulting quantity. In other words, it is the root-mean-square of the deviations from the mean. Symbol: SD.

STANDARD SCORE In the strict sense, the *z* score (*q.v.*), but often a score obtained by multiplying a *z* score by an arbitrary constant (e.g., 10 or 20) and adding the result to an arbitrary mean (e.g., 50 or 100). It permits a direct comparison with scores made by a standardization group.

STANDARDIZATION The establishment of uniform conditions for administering a test and interpreting test results. A large number of individuals are tested in the same way to provide norms (*q.v.*) with which to compare any particular test score.

STANDARDIZATION GROUP The group of people on which a test is standardized. To interpret individual scores on a test, one should know the characteristics of the standardization group.

STAPES One of the bones in the middle ear. *See ossicles.*

STARTLE PATTERN An extremely rapid reaction to a sudden, unexpected stimulus (e.g., a gunshot), relatively consistent from person to person. It consists in part of a closing of the eyes, a widening of the mouth, and a thrusting forward of the head and neck.

STATIC SENSES The part of the vestibular senses responding to gravity and to position of the head. *See otolith organs.*

STATISTICS A collection of techniques used in the quantitative analysis of data, and used to facilitate evaluation of the data. Also, numbers used to describe distributions and to estimate errors of measurement.

STATUS In motivation, a social motive; in a social structure, a position representing differences that are important in the exchange of goods and services and in the satisfaction of needs in a society. *Cf. role.*

STATUS NEEDS Needs to achieve a status with respect to other people in a group. They include more specific needs, such as needs for prestige, power, and security.

STEREOTAXIC INSTRUMENT Apparatus which permits precise placement of electrodes in the brain.

STEREOTYPE A fixed set of greatly oversimplified beliefs that are held generally by members of a group.

STIMULUS Any object, energy, or energy change in the physical environment that excites a sense organ.

STIMULUS GENERALIZATION The tendency to react to stimuli that are different from, but somewhat similar to, the stimulus used as a conditioned stimulus.

STRIPED MUSCLE Muscle that, under the microscope, appears to be striped. It is found in the muscles of the skeleton, such as those that move the trunk and limbs. *Cf. smooth muscle.*

STROBOSCOPIC MOVEMENT Apparent motion (*q.v.*) due to successive presentation of visual stimuli. *See phi phenomenon.*

STRUCTURALISM An early school of psychological thought which held that all mental contents could be analyzed into mental elements through the experimental method of introspection (*q.v.*). *Cf. functionalism, gestalt psychology, behaviorism.*

SUBCORTICAL CENTERS Centers of the brain below the cerebral cortex.

SUBLIMATION The use of a substitute activity to gratify a frustrated motive. Freud believed, for example, that a frustrated sex drive could be partially gratified by channeling it into some aesthetic activity.

SUBLIMINAL PERCEPTION Perception of a stimulus or some feature of a stimulus, as measured by a re-

sponse, without conscious awareness of the perception.

SUBVOCAL SPEECH Talking that is inaudible to others, but sufficiently stimulating (kinesthetically) to oneself to permit an internal conversation. It may be one kind of implicit response involved in thinking.

SUCCESSIVE APPROXIMATIONS Reinforcing components of the final complex response in an effort to lead the learner to this final response. *See also shaping.*

SUCCESSIVE DISCRIMINATION LEARNING Presentation of the positive (S^D) and negative (S^Δ) stimuli one after the other, rather than at the same time. *Cf. simultaneous discrmination learning.*

SUGGESTION The uncritical acceptance of an idea. Sugestion is used in psychotherapy to effect temporary relief of neurotic symptoms, particularly hysterical symptoms. It is also used by propagandists and advertisers to change or maintain attitudes and beliefs.

SULCUS A relatively shallow crevice in the cerebral cortex. *Cf. fissure.*

SUPEREGO In psychoanalytic theory, that which restrains the activity of the ego and the id (*q.v.*). The superego corresponds closely to what is commonly called conscience; it keeps a person working toward ideals acquired in childhood.

SUPERIORITY According to Adler, a major striving of the person. Failure to achieve superiority may generate an inferiority complex.

SUPERSTITION A belief concerning natural phenomena that is widely held but is demonstrably false.

SUPPORTIVE THERAPY Treatment of a personality problem by listening to a person's problems, suggesting courses of action, and reassuring him about what he has done or proposes to do. Such therapy may be effective in mild or temporary disturbances. *Cf. insight therapy.*

SURVEY METHODS Methods of collecting data by sampling a cross section of people, e.g., questioning a large number of married couples about factors in marital happiness, or conducting a public-opinion poll. Sometimes used as a rough synonym for the method of systematic observation (*q.v.*).

SURVEY Q3R A method of study in which the sequence is survey, question, read, recite, and review.

SYMBOL A stimulus that represents something else by reason of relationship, association, convention, etc. A symbol may be an external stimulus, e.g., a spoken word, or an internal process, e.g., an image involved in thinking. The latter may also be called a symbolic process (*q.v.*).

SYMBOLIC DISPLAY Any means of presenting information indirectly, as by a dial, pointer, or light. *Cf. pictorial display.*

SYMBOLIC PROCESS A representative process standing for previous experience; essential in thinking.

SYMPATHETIC SYSTEM A subdivision of the autonomic system (*q.v.*) arising in the thoracic and lumbar portions of the spinal cord. Most active in aroused states of the organism. *Cf. parasympathetic system.*

SYNAPSE The gap between two neurons.

SYNAPTIC REGION The area at the functional connection of two neurons. Includes the synapse (*q.v.*), the presynaptic membrane (*q.v.*), and the postsynaptic membrane (*q.v.*).

SYNDROME Generally, a collection of symptoms. In psychology, a pattern of personality characteristics and their underlying causes in the life history of the person.

T SCORE A particular standard score, obtained by multiplying the *z* score (*q.v.*) by 10 and adding 50 to the result. *See also standard score.*

TABES DORSALIS The result of one type of syphilitic infection of the central nervous system, principally of the spinal cord, in which

pathways of the kinesthetic senses degenerate.

TABOOS The do's and don't's of a particular society, strongly inculcated into most members of that society.

TACHISTOSCOPE An apparatus for presenting perceptual materials for a very brief time.

TAT *See Thematic Apperception Test.*

TEACHING MACHINE A mechanical or electronic device which presents programmed material. *See also programmed learning.*

TELEPHONE THEORY A theory of pitch perception that assumes that frequencies of impulses in the auditory nerve represent frequencies of the sound stimulus.

TEMPERAMENT The aspects of personality pertaining to mood, activity, general level of energy, and tempo.

TEMPORAL LOBE The part of the cerebral cortex lying on the side of the head beneath the lateral fissure.

TEMPORAL MAZE A maze so constructed that the subject keeps returning to the same choice point, but must turn left or right each time according to some sequence established by the experimenter. Such a maze has been used in conjunction with the alternation method, in which a sequence of simple or double alternations (*q.v.*) is required.

TEST A standardized sample of the performance of a person on a task or set of tasks.

THALAMUS An area in the forebrain concerned with relaying nerve impulses to the cerebral cortex.

THEMATIC APPERCEPTION TEST (TAT) A frequently used projective method (*q.v.*) consisting of pictures about which a person tells stories.

THEORETICAL LAW OF EFFECT Several theories which discuss the hypothetical mechanism through which reinforcement may act.

THEORY In science, a principle or set of principles that explains a number of facts and predicts fu-

ture events and outcomes of experiments.

THERAPY The treatment of an illness. *See also medical therapy, psychotherapy.*

THINKING Processes that are representative of previous experience; consisting of images, minute muscle movements, and other activities in the central nervous system. *See also image, implicit response.*

THIRST A drive stemming from a physiological need for water.

THOUGHT EXPERIMENT A type of experiment employed by early experimental psychologists in an attempt to discover the nature of thought. *See also imageless thought.*

THRESHOLD Generally, the level of stimulus energy which must be exceeded before a response occurs. In neuron (*q.v.*) physiology, the amount by which a cell must be depolarized before it fires. In psychophysics (*q.v.*), the amount of energy necessary for detection of a stimulus, or the difference between two stimuli. *See absolute threshold, differential threshold.*

THURSTONE SCALE One method of scaling attitudes; it involves the ranking of items by judges.

THYROID GLAND An endocrine gland in the neck which produces the hormone thyroxin.

THYROXIN The hormone secreted by the thyroid gland. It controls the general rate at which energy is produced in the body; it is a regulator of metabolism.

TIMBRE The tonal quality that enables us to distinguish different musical instruments and voices having the same fundamental frequency. It is determined by the pattern of frequencies comprising a sound, especially the harmonics.

TONOTOPIC ORGANIZATION A topographical arrangement of auditory areas of the brain corresponding to different parts of the cochlea, and consequently to different frequencies of stimulation.

TOPOGRAPHICAL ARRANGEMENT The orderly correspondence between receptor surfaces and their projections to the central nervous system. Also refers to the correspondence between parts of the nervous system and the muscles controlled.

TRACE CONDITIONING An arrangement of the interstimulus interval (*q.v.*) in classical conditioning (*q.v.*) in which the CS terminates before the onset of the US.

TRACE PROCESS A memory lasting for a brief period and serving as a stimulus-cue.

TRACE THEORY A physiological theory of forgetting which states that the memory trace in the brain gradually fades away with time.

TRADE TEST An achievement test that measures a person's knowledge of important elements in his trade.

TRAIT An aspect of personality that is reasonably characteristic of a person and distinguishes him in some way from many other people.

TRANSDUCTION The process of converting one kind of energy into another kind. In sensory perception, the conversion of physical energy into nerve impulses. *See generator potential.*

TRANSFER SURFACE A schematic representation of the amount and direction of transfer as related to the similarity of stimuli and responses in the learning and transfer tasks. Also called the Osgood transfer surface.

TRANSFER OF TRAINING More rapid learning in one situation because of previous learning in another situation (positive transfer, *q.v.*); or slower learning in one situation because of previous learning in another situation (negative transfer, *q.v.*). *See also stimulus generalization.*

TRANSFERENCE In psychotherapy and especially psychoanalysis, the reenactment of previous relationships with people and principally of the parent-child relationship. In psychoanalysis, the therapist becomes the object of transference; the transference

aids in the analysis because it permits the patient to express toward the therapist attitudes and feelings he has held toward other people.

TRANSMITTER A substance released from the presynaptic element (*q.v.*) which depolarizes (*q.v.*) or hyperpolarizes (*q.v.*) the postsynaptic element (*q.v.*).

TRANQUILIZER Any one of several drugs used to reduce anxiety.

TRIAD A three-person group.

TRIAL AND ERROR A phrase describing attempts to learn, or to solve a problem, by trying alternative possibilities and eliminating those that prove to be incorrect. Such behavior is characteristic of instrumental learning and is involved in some thinking.

TYMPANIC MEMBRANE Another name for eardrum (*q.v.*).

TYPE A class of individuals alleged to have a particular trait; but a concept not accepted as valid by psychologists because individuals cannot be grouped together into a few discrete classes.

TYPE-TOKEN RATIO The ratio of the number of different words a person uses to the total number of words in a sample of his speech or writing. It is one index of verbal diversification.

TWO-FACTOR THEORY A theory which postulates that both classical and instrumental conditioning are involved in avoidance learning (*q.v.*).

UNCONDITIONED RESPONSE (UR) The response elicited by the unconditioned stimulus (US).

UNCONDITIONED STIMULUS (US) A stimulus which consistently elicits a response. *See also classical conditioning.*

UNCONSCIOUS MOTIVATION Motivation that can be inferred from person's behavior but the person does not realize the presence of the motive.

UNCONSCIOUS PROCESSES Psychological processes or events of which a person is unaware.

UNIQUE COLOR A pure color judged

not to be tinged with any other hue.

UR *See unconditioned response.*

US *See unconditioned stimulus.*

VALENCE A term proposed by Lewin to refer to the attraction or repulsion of a goal. It is indicated by a plus or minus sign. Goals with negative valences are those a person fears or tries to avoid; those with positive valences are those he seeks to attain.

VALIDITY The extent to which a method of measurement measures what it is supposed to measure. Validity is expressed in terms of a coefficient of correlation (*q.v.*) representing the relationship of a set of measurements to some criterion.

VALUE A learned goal.

VARIABILITY The spread of scores in a frequency distribution. *See also standard deviation.*

VARIABLE One of the conditions measured or controlled in an experiment. *See also dependent variable, independent variable.*

VARIABLE-INTERVAL SCHEDULE A program used in instrumental learning experiments in which subjects are reinforced after an interval of time which varies around a specified average.

VARIABLE-RATIO SCHEDULE A program used in instrumental learning experiments in which subjects are reinforced after a number of responses which varies around a specified average.

VECTOR A term proposed by Lewin to mean the resultant of motivational forces when a person is attracted and/or repelled by different goals; in psychology, analogous to "vector" as used in physics.

VEG A subjective unit of weightiness.

VERB-ADJECTIVE RATIO The ratio of the number of verbs used to the number of adjectives used in a sample of speech or writing. It varies with conditions of measurement and with personality characteristics. It is one index of verbal diversification.

VERBAL DIVERSIFICATION   The degree to which different words and different constructions of words are employed in a person's language.

VESTIBULAR SENSE   The sense of balance and movement, consisting of two groups of sense organs: the semicircular canals and the otolith organs (*q.v.*).

VICARIOUS TRIAL AND ERROR (VTE)   Behavior in which the organism substitutes partial responses, correct or incorrect, for completed, reinforced responses.

VISIBLE SPECTRUM   Those electromagnetic radiations that are visible, extending from about 380 to 760 millimicrons (mμ) (*q.v.*).

VISUAL ACUITY   Ability to discriminate fine differences in visual detail. It may be measured with the physician's eye chart or by more precise tests, such as the Landolt ring (*q.v.*) or parallel bars.

VISUAL CYCLE   The cycle of decomposition and regeneration of photosensitive substances in rod and cone vision.

VISUAL PURPLE   *See rhodopsin.*

VITAMIN   A substance essential to metabolism but not manufactured in the body. Thus, it must be obtained in food.

VOCABULARY   A general and somewhat vague term referring to the words a person knows. However, the words he can recognize are more numerous than those he uses; and those he uses in writing are more numerous than those he uses in everyday speech. Hence, size of vocabulary varies greatly with the circumstances under which it is measured.

VOCATIONAL APTITUDE   Aptitude for learning a specific vocation. For example, clerical aptitude is the ability to learn a clerical vocation.

VTE   *See vicarious trial and error.*

WAIS   *See Wechsler Adult Intelligence Scale.*

WAKING CENTER   A center in the hypothalamus whose destruction results in somnolence. *Cf. sleep center.*

WARMING UP   The tendency for the work curve to rise at the beginning of a period of work; opposite in effect to the beginning spurt (*q.v.*). It is a factor in the shape of the work curve.

WECHSLER ADULT INTELLIGENCE SCALE   An individual intelligence test for adults with eleven subtests.

WECHSLER INTELLIGENCE SCALE FOR CHILDREN (WISC)   An individual intelligence test for children, with several subtests.

WHITE MATTER   Nerve fibers covered with a white myelin sheath. The peripheral part of the spinal cord is white matter; so are several different regions of the brain. Its presence indicates tracts of nerve fibers, as distinguished from cell bodies. *Cf. gray matter.*

WHOLE LEARNING   Learning, usually in the sense of memorizing, in which the entire learning material is studied before going through it again. *Cf. part learning.*

WISC   *See Wechsler Intelligence Scale for Children.*

WORD ASSOCIATION   A method of testing or measuring in which a person is given a stimulus word and asked to respond with a word he associates with it.

WORK CURVE   A graph representing some measure of work for some given period of time.

WORKER CHARACTERISTICS   The physical and psychological characteristics required of a person in a particular job.

WORK-SAMPLE PERFORMANCE TEST   A test consisting of a sample of the work for which a person is being evaluated.

X CHROMOSOME   Carrier of genes. Females have two X chromosomes; males have an X and a Y chromosome (*q.v.*).

Y CHROMOSOME   Carrier of genes which determine that the individual will be male. Females have two X chromosomes (*q.v.*); males have an X and a Y chromosome.

YOUNG-HELMHOLTZ THEORY   The theory that human color vision depends on three receptors, a "blue" receptor, a "green" receptor, and a "red" receptor.

z SCORE   A score obtained by dividing the standard deviation (*q.v.*) into the deviation of an obtained score from the arithmetic mean (*q.v.*) of the frequency distribution (*q.v.*). It is convenient for the comparison of scores without regard to the unts of measurement employed.

ZEIGARNIK EFFECT   Completed tasks are forgotten more rapidly than incompleted ones. One type of motivated forgetting (*q.v.*).

ZYGOTE   The product of the union of a sperm cell from the father and an egg cell from the mother.

In addition to the acknowledgments in the text itself, we wish to give special credits to the following:

Page 41. Quotations from: Scott, J. P., *Animal Behavior*. Copyright © 1958 by The University of Chicago.

Pages 87–88. Quotation modified from: Dashiell, J. F., *Fundamentals of General Psychology* (3d ed.). Copyright © 1949 by John Frederick Dashiell. Reprinted by permission of Houghton Mifflin Company.

Figure 3.13. Modified from: Wolf, M., Mees, M., and Risley, P., Application of operant conditioning procedures to the behavior problems of an autistic child. *Behav. Res. Ther.* Copyright © 1964 by Pergamon Press.

Figures 3.16 and 3.17. Adapted from: *Schedules of Reinforcement* by C. B. Ferster and B. F. Skinner. Copyright © 1957 by Appleton-Century-Crofts, Inc.

Page 107. Quotation from: *Brain Mechanisms and Intelligence* by K. S. Lashley. Copyright © 1929 by The University of Chicago.

Figure 4.16. Modified from: Robinson, E. S., *The "Similarity" Factor in Retroaction*. Copyright © 1927 by The American Journal of Psychology.

Page 184. Quotation reprinted by permission of Dodd, Mead and Company from: *Directed Thinking* by George Humphrey. Copyright © 1948 by George Humphrey.

Pages 184–185. Quotation from: Housman, A. E., *The Name and Nature of Poetry*. Reprinted here by permission of the Cambridge University Press.

Page 185. Quotation from: *The Road to Xanadu: A Study in the Ways of the Imagination* (enlarged ed.) by John Livingston Lowes. Copyright © 1927 by John Livingston Lowes. Reprinted here by permission.

Page 235. Quotation from: Atkinson, J. W. (Ed.), *Motives in Fantasy, Action, and Society*. Copyright © 1958 by D. VanNostrand Co., Inc.

Table 8.1. Modified from: *New Directions in Psychology*, Vol. I. Copyright © 1962 by Holt, Rinehart and Winston, Inc. All rights reserved.

Figure 8.6. From: *New Directions in Psychology*, Vol. I. Copyright © 1962 by Holt, Rinehart and Winston, Inc. All rights reserved.

Figure 8.7. From: *Sensory Communication* by Walter Rosenblith. Copyright © 1961 by The Massachusetts Institute of Technology.

Figure 8.14. Modified from: *Psychology and Life* by F. L. Ruch. Copyright © 1958 by Scott, Foresman and Co.

Page 300. Quotation from: *Sensation and Perception in the History of Experimental Psychology* by Edwin G. Boring. Copyright © 1942 by D. Appleton-Century Co., Inc. Reprinted by permission of Appleton-Century-Crofts.

Figure 9.15. From: Erickson, R. P., Sensory Neural Patterns and Gustation. In Y. Zotterman (Ed.), *Olfaction and Taste*. Copyright © 1963 by Pergamon Press Ltd.

Page 368. Quotation from: Heron, W., Doane, B. K., and Scott, T. H., Visual disturbance after prolonged perceptual isolation. *Canad. J. Psychol.*, 1956. Published by the University of Toronto Press.

Pages 414–415. Quotation from: *Psychological Testing* (2d ed.) by Anne Anastasi. Copyright © 1961 by The Macmillan Company.

Figure 12.2. Modified from: Terman, L. M., and Merrill, M. A., *Stanford-Binet Intelligence Scale: Manual for the Third Revision of Form L-M*. Copyright © 1960 by Houghton Mifflin Company.

Tables 12.2 and 12.3. Reproduced by permission. Copyright © 1955 by The Psychological Corporation, New York, N. Y. All rights reserved.

Figure 12.3. Modified from: *Psychological Testing* (2d ed.) by Anne Anastasi. Copyright © 1961 by the Macmillan Company.

Figure 12.12. Reproduced by permission. Copyright © 1947, 1961, 1962, by The Psychological Corporation, New York, N. Y. All rights reserved.

Figure 12.13. Reproduced by permission. Copyright © 1951 by The Psychological Corporation, New York, N. Y. All rights reserved.

Page 492. Quotation from: *The Basic Writings of Sigmund Freud* (transl. A. A. Brill). Copyright © 1938 by Random House, Inc.

Page 507. Quotation from: *Principles of Dynamic Psychiatry* (3d ed.) by J. H. Masserman. Copyright © 1961 by W. B. Saunders Co.

Page 530. Epigraph from: Lomax, J. A., and Lomax, A., *111 Best American Ballads. Folksong U.S.A.* Copyright © 1947 by John A. and Alan Lomax under the title: *Folksong U.S.A.*

Page 566. Quotation from: *Principles of Psychology* by Fred F. Keller and William N. Schoenfeld. Copyright © 1950 by Appleton-Century-Crofts, Inc. Reprinted by permission.

Page 572. Quotation from: *The Cultural Background* of *Personality* by Ralph Linton. Copyright © 1945 by D. Appleton-Century Co., Inc. Reprinted by permission of Appleton-Century-Crofts, Inc.

Page 574. Quotation from: Davis, A., and Havighurst, R. J., Social class and color differences in child-rearing. *Amer. Sociol. Rev.*, 1946. Reprinted by permission of the American Sociological Association.

Figure 16.4. Modified from: Bales, R. F., A set of categories for the analysis of small group interaction. *Amer. Sociol. Rev.*, 1950. Reprinted by permission of the American Sociological Association.

Figure 17.3. From: *Social Psychology* by T. M. Newcomb, R. H. Turner, and P. E. Converse. Copyright © 1965 by Holt, Rinehart and Winston.